2 0 0 5

SECURITIES

REGULATION

SELECTED STATUTES, RULES, AND FORMS

2 0 0 5
SECURITIES
REGULATION

SELECTED STATUTES, RULES, AND FORMS

James D. Cox
Brainerd Currie Professor of Law
Duke University

Robert W. Hillman
Fair Business Practices Professor of Law
University of California, Davis

Donald C. Langevoort
Thomas Aquinas Reynolds Professor of Law
Georgetown University

PUBLISHERS

1185 Avenue of the Americas, New York, NY 10036
www.aspenpublishers.com

Printed in the United States of America.

1 2 3 4 5 6 7 8 9 0

0-7355-3987-1

About Aspen Publishers

Aspen Publishers, headquartered in New York City, is a leading information provider for attorneys, business professionals, and law students. Written by preeminent authorities, our products consist of analytical and practical information covering both U.S. and international topics. We publish in the full range of formats, including updated manuals, books, periodicals, CDs, and online products.

Our proprietary content is complemented by 2,500 legal databases, containing over 11 million documents, available through our Loislaw division. Aspen Publishers also offers a wide range of topical legal and business databases linked to Loislaw's primary material. Our mission is to provide accurate, timely, and authoritative content in easily accessible formats, supported by unmatched customer care.

To order any Aspen Publishers title, go to *www.aspenpublishers.com* or call 1-800-638-8437.

To reinstate your manual update service, call 1-800-638-8437.

For more information on Loislaw products, go to *www.loislaw.com* or call 1-800-364-2512.

For Customer Care issues, e-mail CustomerCare@aspenpublishers.com; call 1-800-234-1660; or fax 1-800-901-9075.

Aspen Publishers
A Wolters Kluwer Company

Summary of Contents

2 0 0 5

SECURITIES

REGULATION

SELECTED STATUTES, RULES, AND FORMS

SECURITIES ACT OF 1933
15 U.S.C. §§ 77a et seq.

Sec. 1. SHORT TITLE

This title may be cited as the "Securities Act of 1933."

Sec. 2. DEFINITIONS

(a) When used in this title, unless the context otherwise requires—

(1) [Security]

The term "security" means any note, stock, treasury stock, security future, bond, debenture, evidence of indebtedness, certificate of interest or participation in any profit-sharing agreement, collateral-trust certificate, preorganization certificate or subscription, transferable share, investment contract, voting-trust certificate, certificate of deposit for a security, fractional undivided interest in oil, gas, or other mineral rights, any put, call, straddle, option, or privilege on any security, certificate of deposit, or group or index of securities (including any interest therein or based on the value thereof), or any put, call, straddle, option, or privilege entered into on a national securities exchange relating to foreign currency, or, in general, any interest or instrument commonly known as a "security," or any certificate of interest or participation in, temporary or interim certificate for, receipt for, guarantee of, or warrant or right to subscribe to or purchase, any of the foregoing.

(2) [Person]

The term "person" means an individual, a corporation, a partnership, an association, a joint-stock company, a trust, any unincorporated organization, or a government or political subdivision thereof. As used in this paragraph the term "trust" shall include only a trust where the interest or interests of the beneficiary or beneficiaries are evidenced by a security.

(3) [Sale, Sell, Offer to Sell, Offer for Sale]

The term "sale" or "sell" shall include every contract of sale or disposition of a security or interest in a security, for value. The term "offer to sell", "offer for sale", or "offer" shall include every attempt or offer to dispose of, or solicitation of an offer to buy, a security or interest in a security, for value. The terms defined in this paragraph and the term "offer to buy" as used in subsection (c) of section 5 shall not include preliminary negotiations or agreements between an issuer (or any person directly or indirectly controlling or controlled by an issuer, or under direct or indirect common control with an issuer) and any underwriter or among underwriters who are or are to be in privity of contract with an issuer (or any person directly or indirectly controlling or controlled by an issuer, or under direct or indirect common control with an issuer). Any security given or delivered with, or as a bonus on account of, any purchase of securities or any other thing, shall be conclusively presumed to constitute a part of the subject of such purchase and to have been offered and sold for value. The issue or transfer of a right or privilege, when originally issued or transferred with a security, giving the holder of such security the right to convert such security into another security of the same issuer or of another person, or giving a right to subscribe to another security of the same issuer or of another person, which right cannot be exercised until some future date, shall not be deemed to be an offer or sale of such other security; but the issue or transfer of such other security upon the exercise of such right of conversion or subscription shall be deemed a sale of such other security. Any offer or sale of a security futures product by or on behalf of the issuer of the securities underlying the security futures product, an affiliate of the issuer, or an un derwriter, shall constitute a contract for sale of, sale of, offer for sale, or offer to sell the underlying securities.

(4) [Issuer]

The term "issuer" means every person who issues or proposes to issue any security; except that with respect to certificates of deposit, voting-trust certificates, or collateral-trust certificates, or with respect to certificates of interest or shares in an unincorported investment trust not having a board of directors (or persons performing similar functions) or of the fixed, restricted management, or unit type, the term "issuer" means the person or persons performing the acts and assuming the duties of depositor or manager pursuant to the provision of the trust or other agreement or instrument under which such securities are issued; except that in the case of an unincorporated association which provides by its articles for limited liability of any or all of its members, or in the case of a trust, committee, or other legal entity, the trustees or members thereof shall not be individually liable as issuers of any security issued by the association, trust, committee, or other legal entity; except that with respect to equipment-trust certificates or like securities, the term "issuer" means the person by whom the equipment or property is or is to be used; and except that with respect to fractional undivided interest in oil, gas, or other mineral rights, the term "issuer" means the owner of any such right or of any interest in such right (whether whole or fractional) who creates fractional interests therein for the purpose of public offering.

(5) [Commission]

The term "Commission" means the Securities and Exchange Commission.

(6) [Territory]

The term "Territory" means Puerto Rico, the Virgin Islands, and the insular possessions of the United States.

(7) [Interstate Commerce]

The term "interstate commerce" means trade or commerce in securities or any transportation or communication relating thereto among the several States or between the District of Columbia or any Territory of the United States and any State or other Territory, or between any foreign country and any State, Territory, or the District of Columbia, or within the District of Columbia.

(8) [Registration Statement]

The term "registration statement" means the statement provided for in section 6, and includes any amendment thereto and any report, document, or memorandum filed as part of such statement or incorporated therein by reference.

(9) [Write, Written]

The term "write" or "written" shall include printed, lithographed, or any means of graphic communication.

(10) [Prospectus]

The term "prospectus" means any prospectus, notice, circular, advertisement, letter, or communication, written or by radio or television, which offers any security for sale or confirms the sale of any security; except that (a) a communication sent or given after the effective date of the registration statement (other than a prospectus permitted under subsection (b) of section 10) shall not be deemed a prospectus if it is proved that prior to or at the same time with such communication a written prospectus meeting the requirements of subsection (a) of section 10 at the time of such communication was sent or given to the person to whom the communication was made, and (b) a notice, circular, advertisement, letter, or communication in respect of a security shall not be deemed to be a prospectus if it states from whom a written prospectus meeting the requirements of section 10 may be obtained and, in addition, does no more than identify the security, state the price thereof, state by whom orders will be executed, and contain such other information as the Commission, by rules or regulations deemed necesssary or appropriate in the public interest and for the protection of investors, and subject to such terms and conditions as may be prescribed therein, may permit.

(11) [Underwriter]

The term "underwriter" means any person who has purchased from an issuer with a view to, or offers or sells for an issuer in connection with, the distribution of any security, or participates or has a direct or indirect participation in any such undertaking, or participates or has a participation in the direct or indirect underwriting of any such undertaking; but such term shall not include a person whose interest is limited to a commission from an underwriter or dealer not in excess of the usual and customary distributors' or sellers' commission. As used in this paragraph the term "issuer" shall include, in addition to an issuer, any person directly or indirectly controlling or controlled by the issuer, or any person under direct or indirect common control with the issuer.

(12) [Dealer]

The term "dealer" means any person who engages either for all or part of his time, directly or indirectly, as agent, broker, or principal, in the business of offering, buying, selling, or otherwise dealing or trading in securities issued by another person.

(13) [Insurance Company]

The term "insurance company" means a company which is organized as an insurance company whose primary and predominant business activity is the writing of insurance or the reinsuring of risks underwritten by insurance companies, and which is subject to supervision by the insurance commissioner, or a similar official or agency, of a State or territory or the District of Columbia; or any receiver or similar official or any liquidating agent for such company, in his capacity as such.

(14) [Separate Account]

The term "separate account" means an account established and maintained by an insurance company pursuant to the laws of any State or territory of the United States, the District of

Columbia, or of Canada or any province thereof, under which income, gains and losses, whether or not realized, from assets allocated to such account are, in accordance with the applicable contract, credited to or charged against such account without regard to other income, gains, or losses of the insurance company.

(15) [Accredited Investor]

The term "accredited investor" shall mean—

(i) a bank as defined in section 3(a)(2) whether acting in its individual or fiduciary capacity; and insurance company as defined in paragraph (13) of this subsection; an investment company registered under the Investment Company Act of 1940 or a business development company as defined in section 2(a)(48) of that Act; a Small Business Investment Company licensed by the Small Business Administration; or an employee benefit plan, including an individual retirement account, which is subject to the provisions of the Employee Retirement Income Security Act of 1974, if the investment decision is made by a plan fiduciary, as defined in section 3(21) of such Act, which is either a bank, insurance company, or registered investment adviser; or

(ii) any person who, on the basis of such factors as financial sophistication, net worth, knowledge, and experience in financial matters, or amount of assets under management qualifies as an accredited investor under rules and regulations which the Commission shall prescribe.

(16) [Security Future; Narrow-Based Security Index; Security Futures Product]

The terms 'security future', 'narrowbased security index', and 'security futures product' have the same meanings as provided in section 3(a)(55) of the Securities Exchange Act of 1934.

(b) [Efficiency, Competition and Capital Formation]

CONSIDERATION OF PROMOTION OF EFFICIENCY, COMPETITION, AND CAPITAL FORMATION. Whenever pursuant to this title the Commission is engaged in rulemaking and is required to consider or determine whether an action is necessary or appropriate in the public interest, the Commission shall also consider, in addition to the protection of investors, whether the action will promote efficiency, competition, and capital formation.

Sec. 2A. SWAP AGREEMENTS

(a) NON-SECURITY-BASED SWAP AGREEMENTS.—The definition of 'security' in section 2(a)(1) of this title does not include any non-security-based swap agreement (as defined in section 206C of the Gramm-Leach-Bliley Act).

(b) SECURITY-BASED SWAP AGREEMENTS.—

(1) The definition of 'security' in section 2(a)(1) of this title does not include any security-based swap agreement (as defined in section 206B of the Gramm-Leach-Bliley Act).

(2) The Commission is prohibited from registering, or requiring, recommending, or suggesting, the registration under this title of any security-based swap agreement (as defined in section 206B of the Gramm-Leach-Bliley Act). If the Commission becomes aware that a registrant has filed a registration statement with respect to such a swap agreement, the Commission shall promptly so notify the registrant. Any such registration statement with respect to such a swap agreement shall be void and of no force or effect.

(3) The Commission is prohibited from—

(A) promulgating, interpreting, or enforcing rules; or

(B) issuing orders of general applicability; under this title in a manner that imposes or specifies reporting or recordkeeping requirements, procedures, or standards as prophylactic measures against fraud, manipulation, or insider trading with respect to any security-based swap agreement (as defined in section 206B of the Gramm-Leach-Bliley Act).

(4) References in this title to the 'purchase' or 'sale' of a security-based swap agreement shall be deemed to mean the execution, termination (prior to its scheduled maturity date), assignment, exchange, or similar transfer or conveyance of, or extinguishing of rights or obligations under, a

security-based swap agreement (as defined in section 206B of the Gramm-Leach-Bliley Act), as the context may require.

Sec. 3. EXEMPTED SECURITIES

(a) Except as hereinafter expressly provided the provisions of this title shall not apply to any of the following classes of securities:

(1) Reserved.

(2) Any security issued or guaranteed by the United States or any territory thereof, or by the District of Columbia, or by any State of the United States, or by any political subdivision of a State or Territory, or by any public instrumentality of one or more States or Territories, or by any person controlled or supervised by and acting as an instrumentality of the Government of the United States pursuant to authority granted by the Congress of the United States; or any certificate of deposit for any of the foregoing; or any security issued or guaranteed by any bank; or any security issued by or representing an interest in or a direct obligation of a Federal Reserve bank; or any interest or participation in any common trust fund or similar fund that is excluded from the definition of the term 'investment company' under section 3(c)(3) of the Investment Company Act of 1940; or any security which is an industrial development bond (as defined in section 103(c)(2) of the Internal Revenue Code of 1954) the interest on which is excludable from gross income under section 103(a)(1) of such Code if, by reason of the application of paragraph (4) or (6) of section 103(c) of such Code (determined as if paragraphs (4)(A), (5), and (7) were not included in such section 103(c)), paragraph (1) of such section 103(c) does not apply to such security; or any interest or participation in a single trust fund, or in a collective trust fund maintained by a bank, or any security arising out of a contract issued by an insurance company, which interest, participation, or security is issued in connection with (A) a stock bonus, pension, or profit-sharing plan which meets the requirements for qualification under section 401 of the Internal Revenue Code of 1954, (B) an annuity plan which meets the requirements for the deduction of the employer's contributions under section 404(a)(2) of such Code, or (C) a governmental plan as defined in section 414(d) of such Code which has been e stablished by an employer for the exclusive benefit of its employees or their beneficiaries for the purpose of distributing to such employees or their beneficiaries the corpus and income of the funds accumulated under such plan, if under such plan it is impossible, prior to the satisfaction of all liabilities with respect to such employees and their beneficiaries, for any part of the corpus or income to be used for, or diverted to, purposes other than the exclusive benefit of such employees or their beneficiaries, other than any plan described in clause (A), (B), or (C) of this paragraph (i) the contributions under which are held in a single trust fund or in a separate account maintained by an insurance company for a single employer and under which an amount in excess of the employer's contribution is allocated to the purchase of securities (other than interests or participations in the trust or separate account itself) issued by the employer or any company directly or indirectly controlling, controlled by, or under common control with the employer, (ii) which covers employees some or all of whom are employees within the meaning of section 401(c)(1) of such Code, or (iii) which is a plan funded by an annuity contract described in section 403(b) of such Code. The Commission, by rules and regulations or order, shall exempt from the provisions of section 5 of this title any interest or participation issued in connection with a stock bonus, pension, profit-sharing, or annuity plan which covers employees some or all of whom are employees within the meaning of section 401(c)(1) of the Internal Revenue Code of 1954, if and to the extent that the Commission determines this to be necessary or appropriate in the public interest and consistent with the protection of investors and the purposes fairly intended by the policy and provisions of this title. For the purposes of this paragraph, a security issued or guaranteed by a bank shall not include any interest or participation i n any collective trust fund maintained by a bank; and the term "bank" means any national bank, or any banking institution organized under the laws of any State, Territory, or the District of Columbia, the business of which is substantially confined to banking and is supervised by the State or territorial banking commission or similar official; except that in the case of a common trust fund or similar fund, or a

collective trust fund, the term "bank" has the same meaning as in the Investment Company Act of 1940;

(3) Any note, draft, bill of exchange, or banker's acceptance which arises out of a current transaction or the proceeds of which have been or are to be used for current transactions, and which has a maturity at the time of issuance of not exceeding nine months, exclusive of days of grace, or any renewal thereof the maturity of which is likewise limited;

(4) Any security issued by a person organized and operated exclusively for religious, educational, benevolent, fraternal, charitable, or reformatory purposes and not for pecuniary profit, and no part of the net earnings of which inures to the benefit of any person, private stockholder, or individual; or any security of a fund that is excluded from the definition of an investment company under section 3(c)(10)(B) of the Investment Company Act of 1940;

(5) Any security issued (A) by a savings and loan association, building and loan association, cooperative bank, homestead association, or similar institution, which is supervised and examined by State or Federal authority having supervision over any such institution; or (B) by (i) a farmer's cooperative organization exempt from tax under section 521 of the Internal Revenue Code of 1954, (ii) a corporation described in section 501(c)(16) of such Code and exempt from tax under section 501(a) of such Code, or (iii) a corporation described in section 501(c)(2) of such Code which is exempt from tax under section 501(a) of such Code and is organized for the exclusive purpose of holding title to property, collecting income therefrom, and turning over the entire amount thereof, less expenses, to an organization or corporation described in clause (i) or (ii);

(6) Any interest in a railroad equipment trust. For purposes of this paragraph "interest in a railroad equipment trust" means any interest in an equipment trust, lease, conditional sales contract or other similar arrangement entered into, issued, assumed, guaranteed by, or for the benefit of a common carrier to finance the acquisition of rolling stock including motive power;

(7) Certificates issued by a receiver or by a trustee or debtor in possession in a case under title 11 of the United States Code, with the approval of the court;

(8) Any insurance or endowment policy or annuity contract or optional annuity contract, issued by a corporation subject to the supervision of the insurance commissioner, bank commissioner, or any agency or officer performing like functions, of any State or Territory of the United States or the District of Columbia;

(9) Except with respect to a security exchanged in a case under title 11 of the United States Code, any security exchanged by the issuer with its existing security holders exlusively where no commission or other remuneration is paid or given directly or indirectly for soliciting such exchange;

(10) Except with respect to a security exchanged in a case under title 11 of the United States Code, any security which is issued in exchange for one or more bona fide outstanding securities, claims or property interests, or partly in such exchange and partly for cash, where the terms and conditions of such issuance and exchange are approved, after a hearing upon the fairness of such terms and conditions at which all persons to whom it is proposed to issue securities in such exchange shall have the right to appear, by any court, or by any official or agency of the United States, or by any State or Territorial banking or insurance commission or other governmental authority expressly authorized by law to grant such approval;

(11) Any security which is a part of an issue offered and sold only to persons resident within a single State or Territory, where the issuer of such security is a person resident and doing business within, or, if a corporation, incorporated by and doing business within, such State or Territory.

(12) Any equity security issued in connection with the acquisition by a holding company of a bank under section 3(a) of the Bank Holding Company Act of 1956 or a savings association under section 10(e) of the Home Owners' Loan Act, if—

(A) the acquisition occurs solely as part of a reorganization in which security holders exchange their shares of a bank or savings association for shares of a newly formed holding company with no significant assets other than securities of the bank or savings association and the existing subsidiaries of the bank or savings association;

(B) the security holders receive, after that reorganization, substantially the same proportional share interests in the holding company as they held in the bank or savings association, except for nominal changes in shareholders' interests resulting from lawful elimination of fractional interests and the exercise of dissenting shareholders' rights under State or Federal law;

(C) the rights and interests of security holders in the holding company are substantially the same as those in the bank or savings association prior to the transaction, other than as may be required by law; and

(D) the holding company has substantially the same assets and liabilities, on a consolidated basis, as the bank or savings association had prior to the transaction.

For purposes of this paragraph, the term "savings association" means a savings association (as defined in section 3(b) of the Federal Deposit Insurance Act) the deposits of which are insured by the Federal Deposit Insurance Corporation.

(13) Any security issued by or any interest or participation in any church plan, company or account that is excluded from the definition of an investment company under section 3(c)(14) of the Investment Company Act of 1940.

(14) Any security futures product that is—

(A) cleared by a clearing agency registered under section 17A of the Securities Exchange Act of 1934 or exempt from registration under subsection (b)(7) of such section 17A; and

(B) traded on a national securities exchange or a national securities association registered pursuant to section 15A(a) of the Securities Exchange Act of 1934.

(b) The Commission may from time to time by its rules and regulations and subject to such terms and conditions as may be prescribed therein, add any class of securities to the securities exempted as provided in this section, if it finds that the enforcement of this title with respect to such securities is not necessary in the public interest and for the protection of investors by reason of the small amount involved or the limited character of the public offering; but no issue of securities shall be exempted under this subsection where the aggregate amount at which such issue is offered to the public exceeds $5,000,000.

(c) The Commission may from time to time by its rules and regulations and subject to such terms and conditions as may be prescribed therein, add to the securities exempted as provided in this section any class of securities issued by a small business investment company under the Small Business Investment Act of 1958 if it finds, having regard to the purposes of that Act, that the enforcement of this Act with respect to such securities is not necessary in the public interest and for the protection of investors.

Sec. 4. EXEMPTED TRANSACTIONS

The provisions of section 5 shall not apply to—

(1) transactions by any person other than an issuer, underwriter, or dealer.

(2) transactions by an issuer not involving any public offering.

(3) transactions by a dealer (including an underwriter no longer acting as an underwriter in respect of the security involved in such transaction), except—

(A) transactions taking place prior to the expiration of forty days after the first date upon which the security was bona fide offered to the public by the issuer or by or through an underwriter,

(B) transactions in a security as to which a registration statement has been filed taking place prior to the expiration of forty days after the effective date of such registration statement or prior to the expiration of forty days after the first date upon which the security was bona fide offered to the public by the issuer or by or through an underwriter after such effective date, whichever is later (excluding in the computation of such forty days any time during which a stop order issued under section 8 is in effect as to the security), or such shorter period as the Commission may specify by rules and regulations or order, and

(C) transactions as to securities constituting the whole or a part of an unsold allotment to or subscription by such dealer as a participant in the distribution of such securities by the issuer or by or through an underwriter.

With respect to transactions referred to in clause (B), if securities of the issuer have not previously been sold pursuant to an earlier effective registration statement the applicable period, instead of forty days, shall be ninety days, or such shorter period as the Commission may specify by rules and regulations or order.

(4) brokers' transactions, executed upon customers' orders on any exchange or in the over-the-counter market but not the solicitation of such orders.

(5) (A) Transactions involving offers or sales of one or more promissory notes directly secured by a first lien on a single parcel of real estate upon which is located a dwelling or other residential or commercial structure, and participation interests in such notes—

(i) where such securities are originated by a savings and loan association, savings bank, commercial bank, or similar banking institution which is supervised and examined by a Federal or State authority, and are offered and sold subject to the following conditions:

(a) the miminum aggregate sales price per purchaser shall not be less than $250,000;

(b) the purchaser shall pay cash either at the time of the sale or within sixty days thereof; and

(c) each purchaser shall buy for his own account only; or

(ii) where such securities are originated by a mortgagee approved by the Secretary of Housing and Urban Development pursuant to sections 203 and 211 of the National Housing Act and are offered or sold subject to the three conditions specified in subparagraph (A) (i) to any institution described in such subparagraph or to any insurance company subject to the supervision of the insurance commissioner, or any agency or officer performing like function, of any State or territory of the United States or the District of Columbia, or the Federal Home Loan Mortgage Corporation, the Federal National Mortgage Association, or the Government National Mortgage Association.

(B) Transactions between any of the entities described in subparagraph (A) (i) or (A) (ii) hereof involving non-assignable contracts to buy or sell the foregoing securities which are to be completed within two years, where the seller of the foregoing securities pursuant to any such contract is one of the parties described in subparagraph (A) (i) or (A) (ii) who may originate such securities and the purchaser of such securities pursuant to any such contract in any institution described in subparagraph (A) (i) or any insurance company described in subparagraph (A) (ii), the Federal Home Loan Mortgage Corporation, Federal National Mortgage Association, or the Government National Mortgage Association and where the foregoing securities are subject to the three conditions for sale set forth in subparagraphs (A) (i) (a) through (c).

(C) The exemption provided by subparagraphs (A) and (B) hereof shall not apply to resales of the securities acquired pursuant thereto, unless each of the conditions for sale contained in subparagraphs (A) (i) (a) through (c) are satisfied.

(6) transactions involving offers or sales by an issuer solely to one or more accredited investors, if the aggregate offering price of an issue of securities offered in reliance on this paragraph does not exceed the amount allowed under section 3(b) of this title, if there is no advertising or public solicitation in connection with the transaction by the issuer or anyone acting on the issuer's behalf, and if the issuer files such notice with the Commission as the Commission shall prescribe.

Sec. 5. PROHIBITIONS RELATING TO INTERSTATE COMMERCE AND THE MAILS

(a) Unless a registration statement is in effect as to a security, it shall be unlawful for any person, directly or indirectly—

(1) to make use of any means or instruments of transportation or communication in interstate commerce or of the mails to sell such security through the use or medium of any prospectus or otherwise; or

(2) to carry or cause to be carried through the mails or in interstate commerce, by any means or instruments of transportation, any such security for the purpose of sale or for delivery after sale.

(b) It shall be unlawful for any person, directly or indirectly—

(1) to make use of any means or instruments of transportation or communication in interstate commerce or of the mails to carry or transmit any prospectus relating to any security with respect to which a registration statement has been filed under this title, unless such prospectus meets the requirements of section 10, or

(2) to carry or to cause to be carried through the mails or in interstate commerce any such security for the purpose of sale or for delivery after sale, unless accompanied or preceded by a prospectus that meets the requirements of subsection (a) of section 10.

(c) It shall be unlawful for any person, directly or indirectly, to make use of any means or instruments of transportation or communication in interstate commerce or of the mails to offer to sell or offer to buy through the use or medium of any prospectus or otherwise any security, unless a registration statement has been filed as to such security, or while the registration statement is the subject of a refusal order or stop order or (prior to the effective date of the registration statement) any public proceeding of examination under section 8.

Sec. 6. REGISTRATION OF SECURITIES AND SIGNING OF REGISTRATION STATEMENT

(a) Any security may be registered with the Commission under the terms and conditions hereinafter provided, by filing a registration statement in triplicate, at least one of which shall be signed by each issuer, its principal executive officer or officers, its principal financial officer, its comptroller or principal accounting officer, and the majority of its board of directors or persons performing similar functions (or, if there is no board of directors or persons performing similar functions, by the majority of the persons or board having the power of management of the issuer), and in case the issuer is a foreign or Territorial person by its duly authorized representative in the United States; except that when such registration statement relates to a security issued by a foreign government, or political subdivision thereof, it need be signed only by the underwriter of such security. Signatures of all such persons when written on the said registration statements shall be presumed to have been so written by authority of the person whose signature is so affixed and the burden of proof, in the event such authority shall be denied, shall be upon the party denying the same. The affixing of any signature without the authority of the purported signer shall constitute a violation of this title. A registration statement shall be deemed effective only as to the securities specified therein as proposed to be offered.

(b) Registration Fee.—

(1) Recovery of cost of services.—The Commission shall, in accordance with this subsection, collect registration fees that are designed to recover the costs to the government of the securities registration process, and costs related to such process, including enforcement activities, policy and rulemaking activities, administration, legal services, and international regulatory activities.

(2) Fee Payment Required.—At the time of filing a registration statement, the applicant shall pay to the Commission a fee at a rate that shall be equal to $92 per $1,000,000 of the maximum aggregate price at which such securities are proposed to be offered, except that during fiscal year 2003 and any succeeding fiscal year such fee shall be adjusted pursuant to paragraph (5) or (6).

(3) Offsetting Collections.—Fees collected pursuant to this subsection for any fiscal year—

(A) shall be deposited and credited as offsetting collections to the account providing appropriations to the Commission; and

(B) except as provided in paragraph (9), shall not be collected for any fiscal year except to the extent provided in advance in appropriation Acts.

(4) General Revenues Prohibited.—No fees collected pursuant to this subsection for fiscal year 2002 or any succeeding fiscal year shall be deposited and credited as general revenue of the Treasury.

(5) Annual Adjustment.—For each of the fiscal years 2003 through 2011, the Commission shall by order adjust the rate required by paragraph (2) for such fiscal year to a rate that, when applied to the baseline estimate of the aggregate maximum offering prices for such fiscal year, is reasonably likely to produce aggregate fee collections under this subsection that are equal to the target offsetting collection amount for such fiscal year.

(6) Final Rate Adjustment.—For fiscal year 2012 and all of the succeeding fiscal years, the Commission shall by order adjust the rate required by paragraph (2) for all of such fiscal years to a rate that, when applied to the baseline estimate of the aggregate maximum offering prices for fiscal year 2012, is reasonably likely to produce aggregate fee collections under this subsection in fiscal year 2012 equal to the target offsetting collection amount for fiscal year 2011.

(7) Pro Rata Application.—The rates per $1,000,000 required by this subsection shall be applied pro rata to amounts and balances of less than $1,000,000.

(8) Review And Effective Date.—In exercising its authority under this subsection, the Commission shall not be required to comply with the provisions of section 553 of title 5, United States Code. An adjusted rate prescribed under paragraph (5) or (6) and published under paragraph (10) shall not be subject to judicial review. Subject to paragraphs (3)(B) and (9)—

(A) an adjusted rate prescribed under paragraph (5) shall take effect on the later of—

(i) the first day of the fiscal year to which such rate applies; or (ii) five days after the date on which a regular appropriation to the Commission for such fiscal year is enacted; and

(B) an adjusted rate prescribed under paragraph (6) shall take effect on the later of—

(i) the first day of fiscal year 2012; or

(ii) five days after the date on which a regular appropriation to the Commission for fiscal year 2012 is enacted.

(9) Lapse of Appropriation.—If on the first day of a fiscal year a regular appropriation to the Commission has not been enacted, the Commission shall continue to collect fees (as offsetting collections) under this subsection at the rate in effect during the preceding fiscal year, until 5 days after the date such a regular appropriation is enacted.

(10) Publication.—The Commission shall publish in the Federal Register notices of the rate applicable under this subsection and under sections 13(e) and 14(g) for each fiscal year not later than April 30 of the fiscal year preceding the fiscal year to which such rate applies, together with any estimates or projections on which such rate is based.

(11) Definitions.—For purposes of this subsection:

(A) Target Offsetting Collection Amount.—The target offsetting collection amount for each of the fiscal years 2002 through 2011 is determined according to the following table:

Fiscal year:	Target offsetting collection amount	Fiscal year:	Target offsetting collection amount
2002	$ 337,000,000	2007	$ 214,000,000
2003	$ 435,000,000	2008	$ 234,000,000
2004	$ 467,000,000	2009	$ 284,000,000
2005	$ 570,000,000	2010	$ 334,000,000
2006	$ 689,000,000	2011	$ 394,000,000

(B) Baseline Estimate Of The Aggregate Maximum Offering Prices.—The baseline estimate of the aggregate maximum offering prices for any fiscal year is the baseline estimate of the aggregate maximum offering price at which securities are proposed to be offered pursuant to registration statements filed with the Commission during such fiscal year as determined by the Commission, after consultation with the Congressional Budget Office and the Office of Management and Budget, using the methodology required for projections pursuant to section 257 of the Balanced Budget and Emergency Deficit Control Act of 1985.

(c) The filing with the Commission of a registration statement, or of an amendment to a registration statement, shall be deemed to have taken place upon the receipt thereof, but the filing of a registration statement shall not be deemed to have taken place unless it is accompanied by a United States postal money order or a certified bank check or cash for the amount of the fee required under subsection (b).

(d) The information contained in or filed with any registration statement shall be made available to the public under such regulations as the Commission may prescribe, and copies thereof, photostatic or otherwise, shall be furnished to every applicant at such reasonable charge as the Commission may prescribe.

Sec. 7. INFORMATION REQUIRED IN REGISTRATION STATEMENT

(a) The registration statement, when relating to a security other than a security issued by a foreign government, or political subdivision therof, shall contain the information, and be accompanied by the documents, specified in Schedule A, and when relating to a security issued by a foreign government, or political subdivision thereof, shall contain the information, and be accompanied by the documents, specified in Schedule B; except that the Commission may by rules or regulations provide that any such information or document need not be included in respect of any class of issuers or securities if it finds that the requirement of such information or document is inapplicable to such class and that disclosure fully adequate for the protection of investors is otherwise required to be included within the registration statement. If any accountant, engineer, or appraiser, or any person whose profession gives authority to a statement made by him, is named as having prepared or certified any part of the registration statement, or is named as having prepared or certified a report or valuation for use in connection with the registration statement, the written consent of such person shall be filed with the registration statement. If any such person is named as having prepared or certified a report or valuation (other than a public official document or statement) which is used in connection with the registration statement, but is not named as having prepared or certified such report or valuation for use in connection with the registration statement, the written consent of such person shall be filed with the registration statement unless the Commission dispenses with such filing as impracticable or as involving undue hardship on the person filing the registration statement. Any such registration statement shall contain such other information, and be accompanied by such other documents, as the Commission may by rules or regulations require as being necessary or appropriate in t he public interest or for the protection of investors.

(b) (1) The Commission shall prescribe special rules with respect to registration statements filed by any issuer that is a blank check company. Such rules may, as the Commission determines necessary or appropriate in the public interest or for the protection of investors—

(A) require such issuers to provide timely disclosure, prior to or after such statement becomes effective under section 8, of (i) information regarding the company to be acquired and the specific application of the proceeds of the offering, or (ii) additional information necessary to prevent such statement from being misleading;

(B) place limitations on the use of such proceeds and the distribution of securities by such issuer until the disclosures required under subparagraph (A) have been made; and

(C) provide a right of rescission to shareholders of such securities.

(2) The Commission may, as it determines consistent with the public interest and the protection of investors, by rule or order exempt any issuer or class of issuers from the rules prescribed under paragraph (1).

(3) For purposes of paragraph (1) of this subsection, the term "blank check company" means any development stage company that is issuing a penny stock (within the meaning of section 3(a)(51) of the Securities Exchange Act of 1934) and that—

(A) has no specific business plan or purpose; or

(B) has indicated that its business plan is to merge with an unidentified company or companies.

Sec. 8. TAKING EFFECT OF REGISTRATION STATEMENTS AND AMENDMENTS THERETO

(a) Except as hereinafter provided, the effective date of a registration statement shall be the twentieth day after the filing thereof or such earlier date as the Commission may determine, having due regard to the adequacy of the information respecting the issuer theretofore available to the public, to the facility with which the nature of the securities to be registered, their relationship to the capital structure of the issuer and the rights of holders thereof can be understood, and to the public interest and the protection of investors. If any amendment to any such statement is filed prior to the effective date of such statement, the registration statement shall be deemed to have been filed when such amendment was filed; except that an amendment filed with the consent of the Commission, prior to the effective date of the registration statement, or filed pursuant to an order of the Commission, shall be treated as a part of the registration statement.

(b) If it appears to the Commission that a registration statement is on its face incomplete or inaccurate in any material respect, the Commission may, after notice by personal service or the sending of confirmed telegraphic notice not later than ten days after the filing of the registration statement, and opportunity for hearing (at a time fixed by the Commission) within ten days after such notice by personal service or the sending of such telegraphic notice, issue an order prior to the effective date of registration refusing to permit such statement to become effective until it has been amended in accordance with such order. When such statement has been amended in accordance with such order the Commission shall so declare and the registration shall become effective at the time provided in subsection (a) or upon the date of such declaration, whichever date is the later.

(c) An amendment filed after the effective date of the registration statement, if such amendment, upon its face, appears to the Commission not to be incomplete or inaccurate in any material respect, shall become effective on such date as the Commission may determine, having due regard to the public interest and the protection of investors.

(d) If it appears to the Commission at any time that the registration statement includes any untrue statement of a material fact or omits to state any material fact required to be stated therein or necessary to make the statements therein not misleading, the Commission may, after notice by personal service or the sending of confirmed telegraphic notice, and after opportunity for hearing (at a time fixed by the Commission) within fifteen days after such notice by personal service or the sending of such telegraphic notice, issue a stop order suspending the effectiveness of the registration statement. When such statement has been amended in accordance with such stop order the Commission shall so declare and thereupon the stop order shall cease to be effective.

(e) The Commission is hereby empowered to make an examination in any case in order to determine whether a stop order should issue under subsection (d). In making such examination the Commission or any officer or officers designated by it shall have access to and may demand the production of any books and papers of, and may administer oaths and affirmations to and examine, the issuer, underwriter, or any other person, in respect of any matter relevant to the examination, and may, in its discretion, require the production of a balance sheet exhibiting the assets and liabilities of the issuer, or its income statement, or both, to be certified to by a public or certified accountant approved by the Commission. If the issuer or underwriter shall fail to cooperate, or shall obstruct or refuse to permit the making of an examination, such conduct shall be proper ground for the issuance of a stop order.

(f) Any notice required under this section shall be sent to or served on the issuer, or, in case of a foreign government political subdivision thereof, to or on the underwriter, or, in the case of a foreign or Territorial person, to or on its duly authorized representative in the United States named in the registration statement, properly directed in each case of telegraphic notice to the address given in such statement.

Sec. 8A. CEASE-AND-DESIST PROCEEDINGS

(a) AUTHORITY OF THE COMMISSION.—If the Commission finds, after notice and opportunity for hearing, that any person is violating, has violated, or is about to violate any provision of this title, or any rule or regulation thereunder, the Commission may publish its findings and enter an order requiring such person, and any other person that is, was, or would be a cause of the violation, due to an act or omission the person knew or should have known would contribute to such violation, to cease and desist from committing or causing such violation and any future violation of the same provision, rule or regulation. Such order may, in addition to requiring a person to cease and desist from committing or causing a violation, require such person to comply, or to take steps to effect compliance, with such provision, rule, or regulation, upon such terms and conditions and within such time as the Commission may specify in such order. Any such order may, as the Commission deems appropriate, require future compliance or steps to effect future compliance, either permanently or for such period of time as the Commission may specify, with such provision, rule, or regulation with respect to any security, any issuer, or any other person.

(b) HEARING.—The notice instituting proceedings pursuant to subsection (a) shall fix a hearing date not earlier than 30 days nor later than 60 days after service of the notice unless an earlier or a later date is set by the Commission with the consent of any respondent so served.

(c) TEMPORARY ORDER.—

(1) IN GENERAL.—Whenever the Commission determines that the alleged violation or threatened violation specified in the notice instituting proceedings pursuant to subsection (a), or the continuation thereof, is likely to result in significant dissipation or conversion of assets, significant harm to investors, or substantial harm to the public interest, including, but not limited to, losses to the Securities Investor Protection Corporation, prior to the completion of the proceedings, the Commission may enter a temporary order requiring the respondent to cease and desist from the violation or threatened violation and to take such action to prevent the violation or threatened violation and to prevent dissipation or conversion of assets, significant harm to investors, or substantial harm to the public interest as the Commission deems appropriate pending completion of such proceeding. Such an order shall be entered only after notice and opportunity for a hearing, unless the Commission determines that notice and hearing prior to entry would be impracticable or contrary to the public interest. A temporary order shall become effective upon service upon the respondent and, unless set aside, limited, or suspended by the Commission or a court of competent jurisdiction, shall remain effective and enforceable pending the completion of the proceedings.

(2) APPLICABILITY.—This subsection shall apply only to a respondent that acts, or, at the time of the alleged misconduct acted, as a broker, dealer, investment adviser, investment company, municipal securities dealer, government securities broker, government securities dealer, or transfer agent, or is, or was at the time of the alleged misconduct, an associated person of, or a person seeking to become associated with, any of the foregoing.

(d) REVIEW OF TEMPORARY ORDERS.—

(1) COMMISSION REVIEW.—At any time after the respondent has been served with a temporary cease-and-desist order pursuant to subsection (c), the respondent may apply to the Commission to have the order set aside, limited, or suspended. If the respondent has been served with a temporary cease-and-desist order entered without a prior Commission hearing, the respondent may, within 10 days after the date on which the order was served, request a hearing on such application and the Commission shall hold a hearing and render a decision on such application at the earliest possible time.

(2) JUDICIAL REVIEW.—Within—

(A) 10 days after the date the respondent was served with a temporary cease-and-desist order entered with a prior Commission hearing, or

(B) 10 days after the Commission renders a decision on an application and hearing under paragraph (1), with respect to any temporary cease-and-desist order entered without a prior Commission hearing,

the respondent may apply to the United States district court for the district in which the respondent resides or has its principal place of business, or for the District of Columbia, for an order setting aside, limiting, or suspending the effectiveness or enforcement of the order, and the court shall have jurisdiction to enter such an order. A respondent served with a temporary cease-

and-desist order entered without a prior Commission hearing may not apply to the court except after hearing and decision by the Commission on the respondent's application under paragraph (1) of this subsection.

(3) No AUTOMATIC STAY OF TEMPORARY ORDER.—The commencement of proceedings under paragraph (2) of this subsection shall not, unless specifically ordered by the court, operate as a stay of the Commission's order.

(4) EXCLUSIVE REVIEW.—Section 9(a) of this title shall not apply to a temporary order entered pursuant to this section.

(e) AUTHORITY TO ENTER AN ORDER REQUIRING AN ACCOUNTING and DISGORGEMENT.—In any cease-and-desist proceeding under subsection (a), the Commission may enter an order requiring accounting and disgorgement, including reasonable interest. The Commission is authorized to adopt rules, regulations, and orders concerning payments to investors, rates of interest, periods of accrual, and such other matters as it deems appropriate to implement this subsection.

(f) AUTHORITY OF THE COMMISSION TO PROHIBIT PERSONS FROM SERVING AS OFFICERS OR DIRECTORS.—In any cease-and-desist proceeding under subsection (a), the Commission may issue an order to prohibit, conditionally or unconditionally, and permanently or for such period of time as it shall determine, any person who has violated section 17(a)(1) or the rules or regulations thereunder, from acting as an officer or director of any issuer that has a class of securities registered pursuant to section 12 of the Securities Exchange Act of 1934, or that is required to file reports pursuant to section 15(d) of that Act, if the conduct of that person demonstrates unfitness to serve as an officer or director of any such issuer.

Sec. 9. COURT REVIEW OF ORDERS

(a) Any person aggrieved by an order to the Commission may obtain a review of such order in the court of appeals of the United States, within any circuit wherein such person resides or has his principal place of business, or in the United States Court of Appeals for the District of Columbia, by filing in such Court, within sixty days after the entry of such order, a written petition praying that the order of the Commission be modified or be set aside in whole or in part. A copy of such petition shall be forthwith transmitted by the clerk of the court to the Commission, and thereupon the Commission shall file in the court the record upon which the order complained of was entered, as provided in section 2112 of title 28, United States Code. No objection to the order of the Commission shall be considered by the courts unless such objection shall have been urged before the Commission. The finding of the Commission as to the facts, if supported by evidence, shall be conclusive. If either party shall apply to the court for leave to adduce additional evidence, and shall show to the satisfaction of the court that such additional evidence is material and that there were reasonable grounds for failure to adduce such evidence in the hearing before the Commission, the court may order such additional evidence to be taken before the Commission and to be adduced upon the hearing in such manner and upon such terms and conditions as to the court may seem proper. The Commission may modify its findings as to the facts, by reason of the additional evidence so taken, and it shall file such modified or new findings, which, if supported by evidence, shall be conclusive, and its recommendation, if any, for the modification or setting aside of the original order. The jurisdiction of the court shall be exclusive and its judgement and decree, affirming, modifying, or setting aside, in whole or in part, any order of the Commission, shall be final, subject to review by the Supreme Court of the United States upon certiorari or certification as provided in section 1254 of Title 28, United States Code.

(b) The commencement of proceedings under subsection (a) shall not, unless specifically ordered by the court, operate as a stay of the Commission's order.

Sec. 10. INFORMATION REQUIRED IN PROSPECTUS

(a) Except to the extent otherwise permitted or required pursuant to this subsection or subsections (c), (d), or (e)—

(1) a prospectus relating to a security other than a security issued by a foreign government or political subdivision thereof, shall contain the information contained in the registration statement, but it need not include the documents referred to in paragraphs (28) to (32), inclusive, of Schedule A;

(2) a prospectus relating to a security issued by a foreign government or political subdivision thereof shall contain the information contained in the registration statement, but it need not include the documents referred to in paragraphs (13) and (14) of Schedule B;

(3) notwithstanding the provisions of paragraphs (1) and (2) of this subsection (a) when a prospectus is used more than nine months after the effective date of the registration statement, the information contained therein shall be as of a date not more than sixteen months prior to such use so far as such information is known to the user of such prospectus or can be furnished by such user without unreasonable effort or expense;

(4) there may be omitted from any prospectus any of the statements required under such subsection (a) which the Commission may by rules or regulations designate as not being necessary or appropriate in the public interest or for the protection of investors.

(b) In addition to the prospectus permitted or required in subsection (a), the Commission shall by rules or regulations deemed necessary or appropriate in the public interest or for the protection of investors permit the use of a prospectus for the purposes of subsection (b)(1) of section 5 which omits in part or summarizes information in the prospectus specified in subsection (a). A prospectus permitted under this subsection shall, except to the extent the Commission by rules or regulations deemed necessary or appropriate in the public interest or for the protection of investors otherwise provides, be filed as part of the registration statement but shall not be deemed a part of such registration statement for the purposes of section 11. The Commission may at any time issue an order preventing or suspending the use of a prospectus permitted under this subsection (b), if it has reason to believe that such prospectus has not been filed (if required to be filed as part of the registration statement) or includes any untrue statement of a material fact or omits to state any material fact required to be stated therein or necessary to make the statements therein, in the light of the circumstances under which such prospectus is or is to be used, not misleading. Upon issuance of an order under this subsection, the Commission shall give notice of the issuance of such order and opportunity for hearing by personal service or the sending of confirmed telegraphic notice. The Commission shall vacate or modify the order at any time for good cause or if such prospectus has been filed or amended in accordance with such order.

(c) Any prospectus shall contain such other information as the Commission may by rules or regulations require as being necessary or appropriate in the public interest or for the protection of investors.

(d) In the exercise of its powers under subsections (a), (b), or (c), the Commission shall have authority to classify prospectuses according to the nature and circumstances of their use or the nature of the security, issue, issuer, or otherwise, and, by rules and regulations and subject to such terms and conditions as it shall specify therein, to prescribe as to each class the form and contents which it may find appropriate and consistent with the public interest and the protection of investors.

(e) The statements or information required to be included in a prospectus by or under authority of subsections (a), (b), (c), or (d), when written, shall be placed in a conspicuous part of the prospectus and, except as otherwise permitted by rules or regulations, in type as large as that used generally in the body of the prospectus.

(f) In any case where a prospectus consists of a radio or television broadcast, copies thereof shall be filed with the Commission under such rules and regulations as it shall prescribe. The Commission may by rules and regulations require the filing with it of forms of prospectuses used in connection with the sale of securities registered under this title.

Sec. 11. CIVIL LIABILITIES ON ACCOUNT OF FALSE REGISTRATION STATEMENT

(a) In case any part of the registration statement, when such part became effective, contained an untrue statement of a material fact or omitted to state a material fact required to be stated therein or necessary to make the statements therein not misleading, any person acquiring such security (unless it is proved that at the time of such acquisition he knew of such untruth or omission) may, either at law or in equity, in any court of competent jurisdiction, sue—

(1) every person who signed the registration statement;

(2) every person who was a director of (or person performing similar functions), or partner in, the issuer at the time of the filing of the part of the registration statement with respect to which his liability is asserted;

(3) every person who, with his consent, is named in the registration statement as being or about to become a director, person performing similar functions, or partner;

(4) every accountant engineer, or appraiser, or any person whose profession gives authority to a statement made by him, who has with his consent been named as having prepared or certified any part of the registration statement, or as having prepared or certified any report or valuation which is used in connection with the registration statement, with respect to the statement in such registration statement, report, or valuation, which purports to have been prepared or certified by him;

(5) every underwriter with respect to such security.

If such person acquired the security after the issuer has made generally available to its security holders an earning statement covering a period of at least twelve months beginning after the effective date of the registration statement, then the right of recovery under this subsection shall be conditioned on proof that such person acquired the securities relying on such untrue statement in the registration statement or relying upon the registration statement and not knowing of such omission, but such reliance may be established without proof of the reading of the registration statement by such person.

(b) Notwithstanding the provisions of subsection (a) no person, other than the issuer, shall be liable as provided therein who shall sustain the burden of proof—

(1) that before the effective date of the part of the registration statement with respect to which his liability is asserted (A) he had resigned from or had taken such steps as are permitted by law to resign from, or ceased or refused to act in, every office, capacity, or relationship in which he was described in the registration statement as acting or agreeing to act, and (B) he had advised the Commission and the issuer in writing, that he had taken such action and that he would not be responsible for such part of the registration statement; or

(2) that if such part of the registration statement became effective without his knowledge, upon becoming aware of such fact he forthwith acted and advised the Commission, in accordance with paragraph (1), and, in addition, gave reasonable public notice that such part of the registration statement had become effective without his knowledge; or

(3) that (A) as regards any part of the registration statement not purporting to be made on the authority of an expert, and not purporting to be a copy of or extract from a report or valuation of an expert and not purporting to be made on the authority of a public official document or statement, he had, after reasonable investigation, reasonable ground to believe and did believe, at the time such part of the registration statement became effective, that the statements therein were true and that there was no omission to state a material fact required to be stated therein or necessary to make the statements therein not misleading; and

(B) as regards any part of the registration statement purporting to be made upon his authority as an expert or purporting to be a copy of or extract from a report or valuation of himself as an expert, (i) he had, after reasonable investigation, reasonable ground to believe and did believe, at the time such part of the registration statement became effective, that the statements therein were true and that there was no omission to state a material fact required to be stated therein or necessary to make the statements therein not misleading, or (ii) such part of the registration statement did not fairly represent his statement as an expert or was not a fair copy of or extract from his report or valuation as an expert; and

(C) as regards any part of the registration statement purporting to be made on the authority of an expert (other than himself) or purporting to be a copy of or extract from a report or valuation of an expert (other than himself), he had no reasonable ground to believe and did not believe, at the time such part of the registration statement became effective, that the statements therein were untrue or that there was an omission to state a material fact required to be stated therein or necessary to make the statements therein not misleading, or that such part of the registration statement did not fairly represent the statement of the expert or was not a fair copy of or extract from the report or valuation of the expert; and

(D) as regards any part of the registration statement purporting to be a statement made by an official person or purporting to be a copy of or extract from a public official document, he had no reasonable ground to believe and did not believe, at the time such part of the registration statement became effective, that the statements therein were untrue, or that there was an omission to state a material fact required to be stated therein or necessary to make the statements therein not misleading, or that such part of the registration statement did not fairly represent the statement made by the official person or was not a fair copy of or extract from the public official document.

(c) In determining, for the purpose of paragraph (3) of subsection (b) of this section, what constitutes reasonable investigation and reasonable ground for belief, the standard of reasonableness shall be that required of a prudent man in the management of his own property.

(d) If any person becomes an underwriter with respect to the security after the part of the registration statement with respect to which his liability is asserted has become effective, then for the purposes of paragraph (3) of subsection (b) of this section such part of the registration statement shall be considered as having become effective with respect to such person as of the time when he became an underwriter.

(e) The suit authorized under subsection (a) may be to recover such damages as shall represent the difference between the amount paid for the security (not exceeding the price at which the security was offered to the public) and (1) the value thereof as of the time such suit was brought, or (2) the price at which such security shall have been disposed of in the market before suit, or (3) the price at which such security shall have been disposed of after suit but before judgment if such damages shall be less than the damages representing the difference between the amount paid for the security (not exceeding the price at which the security was offered to the public) and the value thereof as of the time such suit was brought: Provided, That if the defendant proves that any portion or all of such damages represents other than the depreciation in value of such security resulting from such part of the registration statement, with respect to which his liability is asserted, not being true or omitting to state a material fact required to be stated therein or necessary to make the statements therein not misleading, such portion of or all such damages shall not be recoverable. In no event shall any underwriter (unless such underwriter shall have knowingly received from the issuer for acting as an underwriter some benefit, directly or indirectly in which all other underwriters similarly situated did not share in proportion to their respective interests in the underwriting) be liable in any suit or as a consequence of suits authorized under subsection (a) for damages in excess of the total price at which the securities underwritten by him and distributed to the public were offered to the public. In any suit under this or any other section of this title the court may, in its discretion, require an undertaking for the payment of the costs of such suit, including reasonable attorney's fees, and if judgment shall be rendered against a party litigant, upon the motion of the other party litigant, such costs may be assessed in favor of such party litigant (whether or not such undertaking has been required) if the court believes the suit or the defense to have been without merit, in an amount sufficient to reimburse him for the reasonable expenses incurred by him, in connection with such suit, such costs to be taxed in the manner usually provided for taxing of costs in the court in which the suit was heard.

(f)(1) Except as provided in paragraph (2), all or any one or more of the persons specified in subsection (a) shall be jointly and severally liable, and every person who becomes liable to make any payment under this section may recover contribution as in cases of contract from any person who, if sued separately, would have been liable to make the same payment, unless the person who has become liable was, and the other was not, guilty of fraudulent misrepresentation.

(2)(A) The liability of an outside director under subsection (e) shall be determined in accordance with section 21D(f) of the Securities Exchange Act of 1934.

(B) For purposes of this paragraph, the term "outside director" shall have the meaning given such term by rule or regulation of the Commission.

(g) In no case shall the amount recoverable under this section exceed the price at which the security was offered to the public.

Sec. 12. CIVIL LIABILITIES ARISING IN CONNECTION WITH PROSPECTUSES AND COMMUNICATIONS

(a) IN GENERAL.—Any person who—

(1) offers or sells a security in violation of section 5, or

(2) offers or sells a security (whether or not exempted by the provisions of section 3, other than paragraphs (2) and (14) of subsection (a) thereof), by the use of any means or instruments of transportation or communication in interstate commerce or of the mails, by means of a prospectus or oral communication, which includes an untrue statement of a material fact or omits to state a material fact necessary in order to make the statements, in the light of the circumstances under which they were made, not misleading (the purchaser not knowing of such untruth or omission), and who shall not sustain the burden of proof that he did not know, and in the exercise of reasonable care could not have known, of such untruth or omission, shall be liable, subject to subsection (b), to the person purchasing such security from him, who may sue either at law or in equity in any court of competent jurisdiction, to recover the consideration paid for such security with interest thereon, less the amount of any income received thereon, upon the tender of such security, or for damages if he no longer owns the security.

(b) LOSS CAUSATION.—In an action described in subsection (a)(2), if the person who offered or sold such security proves that any portion or all of the amount recoverable under subsection (a)(2) represents other than the depreciation in value of the subject security resulting from such part of the prospectus or oral communication, with respect to which the liability of that person is asserted, not being true or omitting to state a material fact required to be stated therein or necessary to make the statement not misleading, then such portion or amount, as the case may be, shall not be recoverable.

Sec. 13. LIMITATION OF ACTIONS

No action shall be maintained to enforce any liability created under section 11 or section 12(a)(2) unless brought within one year after the discovery of the untrue statement or the omission, or after such discovery should have been made by the exercise of reasonable diligence, or, if the action is to enforce a liability created under section 12(a)(1), unless brought within one year after the violation upon which it is based. In no event shall any such action be brought to enforce a liability created under section 11 or section 12(a)(1) more than three years after the security was bona fide offered to the public, or under section 12(a)(2) more than three years after the sale.

Sec. 14. CONTRARY STIPULATIONS VOID

Any condition, stipulation, or provision binding any person acquiring any security to waive compliance with any provision of this title or of the rules and regulations of the Commission shall be void.

Sec. 15. LIABILITY OF CONTROLLING PERSONS

Every person who, by or through stock ownership, agency, or otherwise, or who, pursuant to or in connection with an agreement or understanding with one or more other persons by or through stock ownership, agency, or otherwise, controls any person liable under section 11, or 12, shall also be liable jointly and severally with and to the same extent as such controlled person to any person to whom such controlled person is liable, unless the controlling person had no knowledge of or reasonable ground to believe in the existence of the facts by reason of which the liability of the controlled person is alleged to exist.

Sec. 16. ADDITIONAL REMEDIES; LIMITATIONS ON REMEDIES

(a) Remedies Additional.—Except as provided in subsection (b), the rights and remedies provided by this title shall be in addition to any and all other rights and remedies that may exist at law or in equity.

(b) Class Action Limitations.—No covered class action based upon the statutory or common law of any State or subdivision thereof may be maintained in any State or Federal court by any private party alleging—

(1) an untrue statement or omission of a material fact in connection with the purchase or sale of a covered security; or

(2) that the defendant used or employed any manipulative or deceptive device or contrivance in connection with the purchase or sale of a covered security.

(c) Removal of Covered Class Actions.—Any covered class action brought in any State court involving a covered security, as set forth in subsection (b), shall be removable to the Federal district court for the district in which the action is pending, and shall be subject to subsection (b).

(d) Preservation of Certain Actions.—

(1) Actions under state law of state of incorporation.—

(A) Actions preserved.—Notwithstanding subsection (b) or (c), a covered class action described in subparagraph (B) of this paragraph that is based upon the statutory or common law of the State in which the issuer is incorporated (in the case of a corporation) or organized (in the case of any other entity) may be maintained in a State or Federal court by a private party.

(B) Permissible actions.—A covered class action is described in this subparagraph if it involves—

(i) the purchase or sale of securities by the issuer or an affiliate of the issuer exclusively from or to holders of equity securities of the issuer; or

(ii) any recommendation, position, or other communication with respect to the sale of securities of the issuer that—

(I) is made by or on behalf of the issuer or an affiliate of the issuer to holders of equity securities of the issuer; and

(II) concerns decisions of those equity holders with respect to voting their securities, acting in response to a tender or exchange offer, or exercising dissenters' or appraisal rights.

(2) State actions.—

(A) In general.—Notwithstanding any other provision of this section, nothing in this section may be construed to preclude a State or political subdivision thereof or a State pension plan from bringing an action involving a covered security on its own behalf, or as a member of a class comprised solely of other States, political subdivisions, or State pension plans that are named plaintiffs, and that have authorized participation, in such action.

(B) State pension plan defined.—For purposes of this paragraph, the term 'State pension plan' means a pension plan established and maintained for its employees by the government of the State or political subdivision thereof, or by any agency or instrumentality thereof.

(3) Actions under contractual agreements between issuers and indenture trustees.—Notwithstanding subsection (b) or (c), a covered class action that seeks to enforce a contractual agreement between an issuer and an indenture trustee may be maintained in a State or Federal court by a party to the agreement or a successor to such party.

(4) Remand of removed actions.—In an action that has been removed from a State court pursuant to subsection (c), if the Federal court determines that the action may be maintained in State court pursuant to this subsection, the Federal court shall remand such action to such State court.

(e) Preservation of State Jurisdiction.—The securities commission (or any agency or office performing like functions) of any State shall retain jurisdiction under the laws of such State to investigate and bring enforcement actions.

(f) Definitions.—For purposes of this section, the following definitions shall apply:

(1) Affiliate of the issuer.—The term 'affiliate of the issuer' means a person that directly or indirectly, through one or more intermediaries, controls or is controlled by or is under common control with, the issuer.

(2) Covered class action.—

(A) In general.—The term 'covered class action' means—

(i) any single lawsuit in which—

(I) damages are sought on behalf of more than 50 persons or prospective class members, and questions of law or fact common to those persons or members of the prospective class, without reference to issues of individualized reliance on an alleged misstatement or omission, predominate over any questions affecting only individual persons or members; or

(II) one or more named parties seek to recover damages on a representative basis on behalf of themselves and other unnamed parties similarly situated, and questions of law or fact common to those persons or members of the prospective class predominate over any questions affecting only individual persons or members; or

(ii) any group of lawsuits filed in or pending in the same court and involving common questions of law or fact, in which—

(I) damages are sought on behalf of more than 50 persons; and

(II) the lawsuits are joined, consolidated, or otherwise proceed as a single action for any purpose.

(B) Exception for derivative actions.—Notwithstanding subparagraph (A), the term 'covered class action' does not include an exclusively derivative action brought by one or more shareholders on behalf of a corporation.

(C) Counting of certain class members.—For purposes of this paragraph, a corporation, investment company, pension plan, partnership, or other entity, shall be treated as one person or prospective class member, but only if the entity is not established for the purpose of participating in the action.

(D) Rule of construction.—Nothing in this paragraph shall be construed to affect the discretion of a State court in determining whether actions filed in such court should be joined, consolidated, or otherwise allowed to proceed as a single action.

(3) Covered security.—The term 'covered security' means a security that satisfies the standards for a covered security specified in paragraph (1) or (2) of section 18(b) at the time during which it is alleged that the misrepresentation, omission, or manipulative or deceptive conduct occurred, except that such term shall not include any debt security that is exempt from registration under this title pursuant to rules issued by the Commission under section 4(2).

Sec. 17. FRAUDULENT INTERSTATE TRANSACTIONS

(a) It shall be unlawful for any person in the offer or sale of any securities or any security-based swap agreement (as defined in section 206B of the Gramm-Leach-Bliley Act) by the use of any means or instruments of transportation or communication in interstate commerce or by use of the mails, directly or indirectly—

(1) to employ any device, scheme, or artifice to defraud, or

(2) to obtain money or property by means of any untrue statement of a material fact or any omission to state a material fact necessary in order to make the statements made, in light of the circumstances under which they were made, not misleading; or

(3) to engage in any transaction, practice, or course of business which operates or would operate as a fraud or deceit upon the purchaser.

(b) It shall be unlawful for any person, by the use of any means or instruments of transportation or communication in interstate commerce or by the use of the mails, to publish, give publicity to, or circulate any notice, circular, advertisement, newspaper, article, letter, investment service, or communication which, though not purporting to offer a security for sale, describes such security for a consideration received or to be received, directly or indirectly, from an issuer, underwriter, or dealer, without fully disclosing the receipt, whether past or prospective, of such consideration and the amount thereof.

(c) The exemptions provided in section 3 shall not apply to the provisions of this section.

(d) The authority of the Commission under this section with respect to security-based swap agreements (as defined in section 206B of the Gramm-Leach-Bliley Act) shall be subject to the restrictions and limitations of section 2A(b) of this title.

Sec. 18. EXEMPTION FROM STATE REGULATION OF SECURITIES OFFERINGS

(a) Scope of Exemption.—Except as otherwise provided in this section, no law, rule, regulation, or order, or other administrative action of any State or any political subdivision thereof—

(1) requiring, or with respect to, registration or qualification of securities, or registration or qualification of securities transactions, shall directly or indirectly apply to a security that—

(A) is a covered security; or

(B) will be a covered security upon completion of the transaction;

(2) shall directly or indirectly prohibit, limit, or impose any conditions upon the use of—

(A) with respect to a covered security described in subsection (b), any offering document that is prepared by or on behalf of the issuer; or

(B) any proxy statement, report to shareholders, or other disclosure document relating to a covered security or the issuer thereof that is required to be and is filed with the Commission or any national securities organization registered under section 15A of the Securities Exchange Act of 1934, except that this subparagraph does not apply to the laws, rules, regulations, or orders, or other administrative actions of the State of incorporation of the issuer; or

(3) shall directly or indirectly prohibit, limit, or impose conditions, based on the merits of such offering or issuer, upon the offer or sale of any security described in paragraph (1).

(b) Covered Securities—For purposes of this section, the following are covered securities:

(1) Exclusive federal registration of nationally traded securities.—A security is a covered security if such security is—

(A) listed, or authorized for listing, on the New York Stock Exchange or the American Stock Exchange, or listed, or authorized for listing, on the National Market System of the Nasdaq Stock Market (or any successor to such entities);

(B) listed, or authorized for listing, on a national securities exchange (or tier or segment thereof) that has listing standards that the Commission determines by rule (on its own initiative or on the basis of a petition) are substantially similar to the listing standards applicable to securities described in subparagraph (A); or

(C) is a security of the same issuer that is equal in seniority or that is a senior security to a security described in subparagraph (A) or (B).

(2) Exclusive federal registration of investment companies.—A security is a covered security if such security is a security issued by an investment company that is registered, or that has filed a registration statement, under the Investment Company Act of 1940.

(3) Sales to qualified purchasers.—A security is a covered security with respect to the offer or sale of the security to qualified purchasers, as defined by the Commission by rule. In prescribing such rule, the Commission may define the term 'qualified purchaser' differently with respect to different categories of securities, consistent with the public interest and the protection of investors.

(4) Exemption in connection with certain exempt offerings.—A security is a covered security with respect to a transaction that is exempt from registration under this title pursuant to—

(A) paragraph (1) or (3) of section 4, and the issuer of such security files reports with the Commission pursuant to section 13 or 15(d) of the Securities Exchange Act of 1934;

(B) section 4(4);

(C) section 3(a), other than the offer or sale of a security that is exempt from such registration pursuant to paragraph (4), (10), or (11) of such section, except that a municipal security that is exempt from such registration pursuant to paragraph (2) of such section is not a covered security with respect to the offer or sale of such security in the State in which the issuer of such security is located; or

(D) Commission rules or regulations issued under section 4(2), except that this subparagraph does not prohibit a State from imposing notice filing requirements that are substantially similar to those required by rule or regulation under section 4(2) that are in effect on September 1, 1996.

(c) PRESERVATION OF AUTHORITY.—

(1) Fraud authority.—Consistent with this section, the securities commission (or any agency or office performing like functions) of any State shall retain jurisdiction under the laws of such State to investigate and bring enforcement actions with respect to fraud or deceit, or unlawful conduct by a broker or dealer, in connection with securities or securities transactions.

(2) Preservation of filing requirements.—

(A) Notice filings permitted.—Nothing in this section prohibits the securities commission (or any agency or office performing like functions) of any State from requiring the filing of any document filed with the Commission pursuant to this title, together with annual or periodic reports of the value of securities sold or offered to be sold to persons located in the State (if such sales data is not included in documents filed with the Commission), solely for notice purposes and the assessment of any fee, together with a consent to service of process and any required fee.

(B) Preservation of fees.—

(i) In general.—Until otherwise provided by law, rule, regulation, or order, or other administrative action of any State, or any political subdivision thereof, adopted after the date of enactment of the National Securities Markets Improvement Act of 1996, filing or registration fees with respect to securities or securities transactions shall continue to be collected in amounts determined pursuant to State law as in effect on the day before such date.

(ii) Schedule.—The fees required by this subparagraph shall be paid, and all necessary supporting data on sales or offers for sales required under subparagraph (A), shall be reported on the same schedule as would have been applicable had the issuer not relied on the exemption provided in subsection (a).

(C) Availability of preemption contingent on payment of fees.—

(i) In general.—During the period beginning on the date of enactment of the National Securities Markets Improvement Act of 1996 and ending 3 years after that date of enactment, the securities commission (or any agency or office performing like functions) of any State may require the registration of securities issued by any issuer who refuses to pay the fees required by subparagraph (B).

(ii) Delays.—For purposes of this subparagraph, delays in payment of fees or underpayments of fees that are promptly remedied shall not constitute a refusal to pay fees.

(D) Fees not permitted on listed securities.—Notwithstanding subparagraphs (A), (B), and (C), no filing or fee may be required with respect to any security that is a covered security pursuant to subsection (b)(1), or will be such a covered security upon completion of the transaction, or is a security of the same issuer that is equal in seniority or that is a senior security to a security that is a covered security pursuant to subsection (b)(1).

(3) Enforcement of requirements.—Nothing in this section shall prohibit the securities commission (or any agency or office performing like functions) of any State from suspending the offer or sale of securities within such State as a result of the failure to submit any filing or fee required under law and permitted under this section.

(d) DEFINITIONS.—For purposes of this section, the following definitions shall apply:

(1) Offering document.—The term 'offering document'—

(A) has the meaning given the term 'prospectus' in section 2(a)(10), but without regard to the provisions of subparagraphs (a) and (b) of that section; and

(B) includes a communication that is not deemed to offer a security pursuant to a rule of the Commission.

(2) Prepared by or on behalf of the issuer.—Not later than 6 months after the date of enactment of the National Securities Markets Improvement Act of 1996, the Commission shall, by rule, define the term 'prepared by or on behalf of the issuer' for purposes of this section.

(3) State.—The term 'State' has the same meaning as in section 3 of the Securities Exchange Act of 1934.

(4) Senior security.—The term 'senior security' means any bond, debenture, note, or similar obligation or instrument constituting a security and evidencing indebtedness, and any stock of a class having priority over any other class as to distribution of assets or payment of dividends.

Sec. 19. SPECIAL POWERS OF COMMISSION

(a) The Commission shall have authority from time to time to make, amend, and rescind such rules and regulations as may be necessary to carry out the provisions of this title, including rules and regulations governing registration statements and prospectuses for various classes of securities and issuers, and defining accounting, technical and trade terms used in this title. Among other things, the Commission shall have authority, for the purposes of this title, to prescribe the form or forms in which required information shall be set forth, the items or details to be shown in the balance sheet and earning statement, and the methods to be followed in the preparation of accounts, in the appraisal or valuation of assets and liabilities, in the determination of depreciation and depletion, in the differentiation of recurring and nonrecurring income, in the differentiation of investment and operating income, and in the preparation, where the Commission deems it necessary or desirable, of consolidated balance sheets or income accounts of any person directly or indirectly controlling or controlled by the issuer, or any person under direct or indirect common control with the issuer. The rules and regulations of the Commission shall be effective upon publication in the manner which the Commission shall prescribe. No provision of this title imposing any liability shall apply to any act done or omitted in good faith in conformity with any rule or regulation of the Commission, notwithstanding that such rule or regulation may, after such act or omission be amended or rescinded or be determined by judicial or other authority to be invalid for any reason.

(b) RECOGNITION OF ACCOUNTING STANDARDS.—

(1) IN GENERAL.—In carrying out its authority under subsection (a) and under section 13(b) of the Securities Exchange Act of 1934, the Commission may recognize, as for purposes of the securities laws, any accounting principles established by a standard setting body—

(A) that—

(i) is organized as a private entity;

(ii) has, for administrative and operational purposes, a board of trustees (or equivalent body) serving in the public interest, the majority of whom are not, concurrent with their service on such board, and have not been during the 2-year period preceding such service, associated persons of any registered public accounting firm;

(iii) is funded as provided in section 109 of the Sarbanes-Oxley Act of 2002;

(iv) has adopted procedures to ensure prompt consideration, by majority vote of its members, of changes to accounting principles necessary to reflect emerging accounting issues and changing business practices; and

(v) considers, in adopting accounting principles, the need to keep standards current in order to reflect changes in the business environment, the extent to which international convergence on high quality accounting standards is necessary or appropriate in the public interest and for the protection of investors; and

(B) that the Commission determines has the capacity to assist the Commission in fulfilling the requirements of subsection (a) and section 13(b) of the Securities Exchange Act of 1934, because, at a minimum, the standard setting body is capable of improving the accuracy and effectiveness of financial reporting and the protection of investors under the securities laws.

(2) ANNUAL REPORT.—A standard setting body described in paragraph (1) shall submit an annual report to the Commission and the public, containing audited financial statements of that standard setting body.

(c) For the purpose of all investigations which, in the opinion of the Commission, are necessary and proper for the enforcement of this title, any member of the Commission or any officer or officers designated by it are empowered to administer oaths and affirmations, subpena witnesses, take evidence, and require the production of any books, papers, or other documents which the Commission deems relevant or material to the inquiry. Such attendance of witnesses and the production of such documentary evidence may be required from any place in the United States or any Territory at any designated place of hearing.

(d)(1) The Commission is authorized to cooperate with any association composed of duly constituted representatives of State governments whose primary assignment is the regulation of the securities business within those States, and which, in the judgment of the Commission, could assist in effectuating greater uniformity in Federal-State securities matters. The Commission shall, at its discretion, cooperate, coordinate, and share information with such an association for the purposes of carrying out the policies and projects set forth in paragraphs (2) and (3).

(2) It is the declared policy of this subsection that there should be greater Federal and State cooperation in securities matters, including—

(A) maximum effectiveness of regulation,

(B) maximum uniformity in Federal and State regulatory standards,

(C) minimum interference with the business of capital formation, and

(D) a substantial reduction in costs and paperwork to diminish the burdens of raising investment capital (particularly by small business) and to diminish the costs of the administration of the Government programs involved.

(3) The purpose of this subsection is to engender cooperation between the Commission, any such association of State securities officials, and other duly constituted securities associations in the following areas:

(A) the sharing of information regarding the registration or exemption of securities issues applied for in the various States;

(B) the development and maintenance of uniform securities forms and procedures; and

(C) the development of a uniform exemption from registration for small issuers which can be agreed upon among several States or between the States and the Federal Government. The Commission shall have the authority to adopt such an exemption as agreed upon for Federal purposes. Nothing in this Act shall be construed as authorizing preemption of State law.

(4) In order to carry out these policies and purposes, the Commission shall conduct an annual conference as well as such other meetings as are deemed necessary, to which representatives from such securities associations, securities self-regulatory organizations, agencies, and private organizations involved in capital formation shall be invited to participate.

(5) For fiscal year 1982, and for each of the three succeeding fiscal years, there are authorized to be appropriated such amounts as may be necessary and appropriate to carry out the policies, provisions, and purposes of this subsection. Any sums so appropriated shall remain available until expended.

(6) Notwithstanding any other provision of law, neither the Commission nor any other person shall be required to establish any procedures not specifically required by the securities laws, as that term is defined in section 3(a)(47) of the Securities Exchange Act of 1934, or by chapter 5 of title 5, United States Code, in connection with cooperation, coordination, or consultation with—

(A) any association referred to in paragraph (1) or (3) or any conference or meeting referred to in paragraph (4), while such association, conference, or meeting is carrying out activities in furtherance of the provisions of this subsection; or

(B) any forum, agency, or organization, or group referred to in section 503 of the Small Business Investment Incentive Act of 1980, while such forum, agency, organization, or group is carrying out activities in furtherance of the provisions of such section 503.

As used in this paragraph, the terms "association", "conference", "meeting", "forum", "agency", "organization", and "group" include any committee, subgroup, or representative of such entities.

Sec. 20. INJUNCTIONS AND PROSECUTION OF OFFENSES

(a) Whenever it shall appear to the Commission, either upon complaint or otherwise, that the provisions of this title, or of any rule or regulation prescribed under authority thereof, have been or are about to be violated, it may, in its discretion, either require or permit such person to file with it a statement in writing, under oath, or otherwise, as to all the facts and circumstances concerning the subject matter which it believes to be in the public interest to investigate, and may investigate such facts.

(b) Whenever it shall appear to the Commission that any person is engaged or about to engage in any acts or practices which constitute or will constitute a violation of the provisions of this title, or of any rule or regulation prescribed under authority thereof, the Commission may, in its discretion, bring an action in any district court of the United States, or United States court of any Territory, to enjoin such acts or practices, and upon a proper showing, a permanent or temporary injunction or restraining order shall be granted without bond. The Commission may transmit such evidence as may be available concerning such acts or practices to the Attorney General who may, in his discretion, institute the necessary criminal proceedings under this title. Any such criminal proceeding may be brought either in the district wherein the transmittal of the prospectus or security complained of begins, or in the district wherein such prospectus or security is received.

(c) Upon application of the Commission, the district courts of the United States and the United States courts of any Territory shall have jurisdiction to issue writs of mandamus commanding any person to comply with the provisions of this title or any order of the Commission made in pursuance thereof.

(d) MONEY PENALTIES IN CIVIL ACTIONS.—

(1) AUTHORITY OF COMMISSION.— Whenever it shall appear to the Commission that any person has violated any provision of this title, the rules or regulations thereunder, or a cease-and-desist order entered by the Commission pursuant to section 8A of this title, other than by committing a violation subject to a penalty pursuant to section 21A of the Securities Exchange Act of 1934, the Commission may bring an action in a United States district court to seek, and the court shall have jurisdiction to impose, upon a proper showing, a civil penalty to be paid by the person who committed such violation.

(2) AMOUNT OF PENALTY.—

(A) FIRST TIER.—The amount of the penalty shall be determined by the court in light of the facts and circumstances. For each violation, the amount of the penalty shall not exceed the greater of (i) $5,000 for a natural person or $50,000 for any other person, or (ii) the gross amount of pecuniary gain to such defendant as a result of the violation.

(B) SECOND TIER.—Notwithstanding subparagraph (A), the amount of penalty for each such violation shall not exceed the greater of (i) $50,000 for a natural person or $250,000 for any other person, or (ii) the gross amount of pecuniary gain to such defendant as a result of the violation, if the violation described in paragraph (1) involved fraud, deceit, manipulation, or deliberate or reckless disregard of a regulatory requirement.

(C) THIRD TIER.—Notwithstanding subparagraphs (A) and (B), the amount of penalty for each such violation shall not exceed the greater of (i) $100,000 for a natural person or $500,000 for any other person, or (ii) the gross amount of pecuniary gain to such defendant as a result of the violation, if—

(I) the violation described in paragraph (1) involved fraud, deceit, manipulation, or deliberate or reckless disregard of a regulatory requirement; and

(II) such violation directly or indirectly resulted in substantial losses or created a significant risk of substantial losses to other persons.

(3) PROCEDURES FOR COLLECTION.—

(A) PAYMENT OF PENALTY TO TREASURY.—A penalty imposed under this section shall be payable into the Treasury of the United States, except as otherwise provided in section 308 of the Sarbanes-Oxley Act of 2002.

(B) COLLECTION OF PENALTIES.—If a person upon whom such a penalty is imposed shall fail to pay such penalty within the time prescribed in the court's order, the Commission may refer the matter to the Attorney General who shall recover such penalty by action in the appropriate United States district court.

(C) REMEDY NOT EXCLUSIVE.—The actions authorized by this subsection may be brought in addition to any other action that the Commission or the Attorney General is entitled to bring.

(D) JURISDICTION AND VENUE.—For purposes of section 22 of this title, actions under this section shall be actions to enforce a liability or a duty created by this title.

(4) SPECIAL PROVISIONS RELATING TO A VIOLATION OF A CEASE-AND-DESIST ORDER.—In an action to enforce a cease-and-desist order entered by the Commission pursuant to section 8A, each separate violation of such order shall be a separate offense, except that in the case of a violation through a continuing failure to comply with such an order, each day of the failure to comply with the order shall be deemed a separate offense.

(e) AUTHORITY OF A COURT TO PROHIBIT PERSONS FROM SERVING AS OFFICERS AND DIRECTORS.—In any proceeding under subsection (b), the court may prohibit, conditionally or unconditionally, and permanently or for such period of time as it shall determine, any person who violated section 17(a)(1) of this title from acting as an officer or director of any issuer that has a class of securities registered pursuant to section 12 of the Securities Exchange Act of 1934 or that is required to file reports pursuant to section 15(d) of such Act if the person's conduct demonstrates unfitness to serve as an officer or director of any such issuer.

(f) PROHIBITION OF ATTORNEYS' FEES PAID FROM COMMISSION DISGORGEMENT FUNDS.—Except as otherwise ordered by the court upon motion by the Commission, or, in the case of an administrative action, as otherwise ordered by the Commission, funds disgorged as the result of an action brought by the Commission in Federal court, or as a result of any Commission administrative action, shall not be distributed as payment for attorneys' fees or expenses incurred by private parties seeking distribution of the disgorged funds.

(g) AUTHORITY OF A COURT TO PROHIBIT PERSONS FROM PARTICIPATING IN AN OFFERING OF PENNY STOCK.—

(1) IN GENERAL.—In any proceeding under subsection (a) against any person participating in, or, at the time of the alleged misconduct, who was participating in, an offering of penny stock, the court may prohibit that person from participating in an offering of penny stock, conditionally or unconditionally, and permanently or for such period of time as the court shall determine.

(2) DEFINITION.—For purposes of this subsection, the term "person participating in an offering of penny stock" includes any person engaging in activities with a broker, dealer, or issuer for purposes of issuing, trading, or inducing or attempting to induce the purchase or sale of, any penny stock. The Commission may, by rule or regulation, define such term to include other activities, and may, by rule, regulation, or order, exempt any person or class of persons, in whole or in part, conditionally or unconditionally, from inclusion in such term.

Sec. 21. HEARINGS BY COMMISSION

All hearings shall be public and may be held before the Commission or an officer or officers of the Commission designated by it, and appropriate records thereof shall be kept.

Sec. 22. JURISDICTION OF OFFENSES AND SUITS

(a) The district courts of the United States and United States courts of any Territory shall have jurisdiction of offenses and violations under this title and under the rules and regulations promulgated by the Commission in respect thereto, and, concurrent with State and Territorial courts, except as provided in section 16 with respect to covered class actions, of all suits in equity and actions at law brought to enforce any liability or duty created by this title. Any such suit or action may be brought in the district wherein the defendant is found or is an inhabitant or transacts business, or in the district where the offer or sale took place, if the defendant participated therein, and process in such cases may be served in any other district of which the defendant is an inhabitant or wherever the defendant may be found. Judgments and decrees so rendered shall be subject to review as provided in sections 1254, 1291, 1292, and 1294 of title 28, United States Code. Except as provided in section 16(c), no case arising under this title and brought in any State court of competent jurisdiction shall be removed to any court of the United States. No costs shall be assessed for or against the Commission in any proceeding under this title brought by or against it in the Supreme Court or such other courts.

(b) In case of contumacy or refusal to obey a subpena issued to any person, any of the said United States courts within the jurisdiction of which said person guilty of contumacy or refusal to obey is found or resides, upon application by the Commission may issue to such person an order requiring such person to appear before the Commission, or one of its examiners designated by it, there to produce documentary evidence if so ordered, or there to give evidence touching the matter in question; and any failure to obey such order of the court may be punished by said court as a contempt thereof.

Sec. 23. UNLAWFUL REPRESENTATIONS

Neither the fact that the registration statement for a security has been filed or is in effect nor the fact that a stop order is not in effect with respect thereto shall be deemed a finding by the Commission that the registration statement is true and accurate on its face or that it does not contain an untrue statement of fact or omit to state a material fact, or be held to mean that the Commission has in any way passed upon the merits of, or given approval to, such security. It shall be unlawful to make, or cause to be made, to any prospective purchaser any representation contrary to the foregoing provisions of this section.

Sec. 24. PENALTIES

Any person who willfully violates any of the provisions of this title, or the rules and regulations promulgated by the Commission under authority thereof, or any person who willfully, in a registration statement filed under this title, makes any untrue statement of a material fact or omits to state any material fact required to be stated therein or necessary to make the statements therein not misleading, shall upon conviction be fined not more than $10,000 or imprisoned not more than five years, or both.

Sec. 25. JURISDICTION OF OTHER GOVERNMENT AGENCIES OVER SECURITIES

Nothing in this title shall relieve any person from submitting to the respective supervisory units of the Government of the United States information, reports, or other documents that are now or may hereafter be required by any provision of law.

Sec. 26. SEPARABILITY OF PROVISIONS

If any provision of this Act, or the application of such provision to any person or circumstance, shall be held invalid, the remainder of this Act, or the application of such provision to persons or circumstances other than those as to which it is held invalid, shall not be affected thereby.

Sec. 27. PRIVATE SECURITIES LITIGATION

(a) PRIVATE CLASS ACTIONS.—

(1) IN GENERAL.—The provisions of this subsection shall apply to each private action arising under this title that is brought as a plaintiff class action pursuant to the Federal Rules of Civil Procedure.

(2) CERTIFICATION FILED WITH COMPLAINT.—

(A) IN GENERAL.—Each plaintiff seeking to serve as a representative party on behalf of a class shall provide a sworn certification, which shall be personally signed by such plaintiff and filed with the complaint, that—

(i) states that the plaintiff has reviewed the complaint and authorized its filing;

(ii) states that the plaintiff did not purchase the security that is the subject of the complaint at the direction of plaintiff's counsel or in order to participate in any private action arising under this title;

(iii) states that the plaintiff is willing to serve as a representative party on behalf of a class, including providing testimony at deposition and trial, if necessary;

(iv) sets forth all of the transactions of the plaintiff in the security that is the subject of the complaint during the class period specified in the complaint;

(v) identifies any other action under this title, filed during the 3-year period preceding the date on which the certification is signed by the plaintiff, in which the plaintiff has sought to serve, or served, as a representative party on behalf of a class; and

(vi) states that the plaintiff will not accept any payment for serving as a representative party on behalf of a class beyond the plaintiff's pro rata share of any recovery, except as ordered or approved by the court in accordance with paragraph (4).

(B) NONWAIVER OF ATTORNEY-CLIENT PRIVILEGE.—The certification filed pursuant to subparagraph (A) shall not be construed to be a waiver of the attorney-client privilege.

(3) APPOINTMENT OF LEAD PLAINTIFF.—

(A) EARLY NOTICE TO CLASS MEMBERS.—

(i) IN GENERAL.—Not later than 20 days after the date on which the complaint is filed, the plaintiff or plaintiffs shall cause to be published, in a widely circulated national business-oriented publication or wire service, a notice advising members of the purported plaintiff class—

(I) of the pendency of the action, the claims asserted therein, and the purported class period; and

(II) that, not later than 60 days after the date on which the notice is published, any member of the purported class may move the court to serve as lead plaintiff of the purported class.

(ii) MULTIPLE ACTIONS.—If more than one action on behalf of a class asserting substantially the same claim or claims arising under this title is filed, only the plaintiff or plaintiffs in the first filed action shall be required to cause notice to be published in accordance with clause (i).

(iii) ADDITIONAL NOTICES MAY BE REQUIRED UNDER FEDERAL RULES.—Notice required under clause (i) shall be in addition to any notice required pursuant to the Federal Rules of Civil Procedure.

(B) APPOINTMENT OF LEAD PLAINTIFF.—

(i) IN GENERAL.—Not later than 90 days after the date on which a notice is published under subparagraph (A)(i), the court shall consider any motion made by a purported class member in response to the notice, including any motion by a class member who is not individually named as a plaintiff in the complaint or complaints, and shall appoint as lead plaintiff the member or members of the purported plaintiff class that the court determines to be most capable of adequately representing the interests of class members (hereafter in this paragraph referred to as the "most adequate plaintiff") in accordance with this subparagraph.

(ii) CONSOLIDATED ACTIONS.—If more than one action on behalf of a class asserting substantially the same claim or claims arising under this title has been filed, and any party has sought to consolidate those actions for pretrial purposes or for trial, the court shall not make the determination required by clause (i) until after the decision on the motion to consolidate is rendered. As soon as practicable after such decision is rendered, the court shall appoint the most adequate plaintiff as lead plaintiff for the consolidated actions in accordance with this subparagraph.

(iii) REBUTTABLE PRESUMPTION.—

(I) IN GENERAL.—Subject to subclause (II), for purposes of clause (i), the court shall adopt a presumption that the most adequate plaintiff in any private action arising under this title is the person or group of persons that—

(aa) has either filed the complaint or made a motion in response to a notice under subparagraph (A)(i);

(bb) in the determination of the court, has the largest financial interest in the relief sought by the class; and

(cc) otherwise satisfies the requirements of Rule 23 of the Federal Rules of Civil Procedure.

(II) REBUTTAL EVIDENCE.—The presumption described in subclause (I) may be rebutted only upon proof by a member of the purported plaintiff class that the presumptively most adequate plaintiff—

(aa) will not fairly and adequately protect the interests of the class; or

(bb) is subject to unique defenses that render such plaintiff incapable of adequately representing the class.

(iv) DISCOVERY.—For purposes of this subparagraph, discovery relating to whether a member or members of the purported plaintiff class is the most adequate plaintiff may be conducted by a plaintiff only if the plaintiff first demonstrates a reasonable basis for a finding that the presumptively most adequate plaintiff is incapable of adequately representing the class.

(v) SELECTION OF LEAD COUNSEL.—The most adequate plaintiff shall, subject to the approval of the court, select and retain counsel to represent the class.

(vi) RESTRICTIONS ON PROFESSIONAL PLAINTIFFS.—Except as the court may otherwise permit, consistent with the purposes of this section, a person may be a lead plaintiff, or an officer, director, or fiduciary of a lead plaintiff, in no more than 5 securities class actions brought as plaintiff class actions pursuant to the Federal Rules of Civil Procedure during any 3-year period.

(4) RECOVERY BY PLAINTIFFS.—The share of any final judgment or of any settlement that is awarded to a representative party serving on behalf of a class shall be equal, on a per share basis, to the portion of the final judgment or settlement awarded to all other members of the class. Nothing in this paragraph shall be construed to limit the award of reasonable costs and expenses (including lost wages) directly relating to the representation of the class to any representative party serving on behalf of the class.

(5) RESTRICTIONS ON SETTLEMENTS UNDER SEAL.—The terms and provisions of any settlement agreement of a class action shall not be filed under seal, except that on motion of any party to the settlement, the court may order filing under seal for those portions of a settlement agreement as to which good cause is shown for such filing under seal. For purposes of this paragraph, good cause shall exist only if publication of a term or provision of a settlement agreement would cause direct and substantial harm to any party.

(6) RESTRICTIONS ON PAYMENT OF ATTORNEYS' FEES AND EXPENSES.—Total attorneys' fees and expenses awarded by the court to counsel for the plaintiff class shall not exceed a reasonable percentage of the amount of any damages and prejudgment interest actually paid to the class.

(7) DISCLOSURE OF SETTLEMENT TERMS TO CLASS MEMBERS.—Any proposed or final settlement agreement that is published or otherwise disseminated to the class shall include each of the following statements, along with a cover page summarizing the information contained in such statements:

(A) STATEMENT OF PLAINTIFF RECOVERY.—The amount of the settlement proposed to be distributed to the parties to the action, determined in the aggregate and on an average per share basis.

(B) STATEMENT OF POTENTIAL OUTCOME OF CASE.—

(i) AGREEMENT ON AMOUNT OF DAMAGES.—If the settling parties agree on the average amount of damages per share that would be recoverable if the plaintiff prevailed on each claim alleged under this title, a statement concerning the average amount of such potential damages per share.

(ii) DISAGREEMENT ON AMOUNT OF DAMAGES.—If the parties do not agree on the average amount of damages per share that would be recoverable if the plaintiff prevailed on each claim alleged under this title, a statement from each settling party concerning the issue or issues on which the parties disagree.

(iii) INADMISSIBILITY FOR CERTAIN PURPOSES.—A statement made in accordance with clause (i) or (ii) concerning the amount of damages shall not be admissible in any Federal or State judicial action or administrative proceeding, other than an action or proceeding arising out of such statement.

(C) STATEMENT OF ATTORNEYS' FEES OR COSTS SOUGHT.—If any of the settling parties or their counsel intend to apply to the court for an award of attorneys' fees or costs from any fund established as part of the settlement, a statement indicating which parties or counsel intend to make such an application, the amount of fees and costs that will be sought (including the amount of such fees and costs determined on an average per share basis), and a brief explanation supporting the fees and costs sought.

(D) IDENTIFICATION OF LAWYERS' REPRESENTATIVES.—The name, telephone number, and address of one or more representatives of counsel for the plaintiff class who will be reasonably available to answer questions from class members concerning any matter contained in any notice of settlement published or otherwise disseminated to the class.

(E) REASONS FOR SETTLEMENT.—A brief statement explaining the reasons why the parties are proposing the settlement.

(F) OTHER INFORMATION.—Such other information as may be required by the court.

(8) ATTORNEY CONFLICT OF INTEREST.—If a plaintiff class is represented by an attorney who directly owns or otherwise has a beneficial interest in the securities that are the subject of the litigation, the court shall make a determination of whether such ownership or other interest constitutes a conflict of interest sufficient to disqualify the attorney from representing the plaintiff class.

(b) STAY OF DISCOVERY; PRESERVATION OF EVIDENCE.—

(1) IN GENERAL.—In any private action arising under this title, all discovery and other proceedings shall be stayed during the pendency of any motion to dismiss, unless the court finds, upon the motion of any party, that particularized discovery is necessary to preserve evidence or to prevent undue prejudice to that party.

(2) PRESERVATION OF EVIDENCE.—During the pendency of any stay of discovery pursuant to this subsection, unless otherwise ordered by the court, any party to the action with actual notice of the allegations contained in the complaint shall treat all documents, data compilations (including electronically recorded or stored data), and tangible objects that are in the custody or control of such person and that are relevant to the allegations, as if they were the subject of a continuing request for production of documents from an opposing party under the Federal Rules of Civil Procedure.

(3) SANCTION FOR WILLFUL VIOLATION.—A party aggrieved by the willful failure of an opposing party to comply with paragraph (2) may apply to the court for an order awarding appropriate sanctions.

(4) CIRCUMVENTION OF STAY OF DISCOVERY.—Upon a proper showing, a court may stay discovery proceedings in any private action in a State court as necessary in aid of its jurisdiction, or to protect or effectuate its judgments, in an action subject to a stay of discovery pursuant to this subsection.

(c) SANCTIONS FOR ABUSIVE LITIGATION.—

(1) MANDATORY REVIEW BY COURT.—In any private action arising under this title, upon final adjudication of the action, the court shall include in the record specific findings regarding compliance by each party and each attorney representing any party with each requirement of Rule 11(b) of the Federal Rules of Civil Procedure as to any complaint, responsive pleading, or dispositive motion.

(2) MANDATORY SANCTIONS.—If the court makes a finding under paragraph (1) that a party or attorney violated any requirement of Rule 11(b) of the Federal Rules of Civil Procedure as to any complaint, responsive pleading, or dispositive motion, the court shall impose sanctions on such party or attorney in accordance with Rule 11 of the Federal Rules of Civil Procedure. Prior to making a finding that any party or attorney has violated Rule 11 of the Federal Rules of Civil Procedure, the court shall give such party or attorney notice and an opportunity to respond.

(3) PRESUMPTION IN FAVOR OF ATTORNEYS' FEES AND COSTS.—

(A) IN GENERAL.—Subject to subparagraphs (B) and (C), for purposes of paragraph (2), the court shall adopt a presumption that the appropriate sanction—

(i) for failure of any responsive pleading or dispositive motion to comply with any requirement of Rule 11(b) of the Federal Rules of Civil Procedure is an award to the opposing party of the reasonable attorneys' fees and other expenses incurred as a direct result of the violation; and

(ii) for substantial failure of any complaint to comply with any requirement of Rule 11(b) of the Federal Rules of Civil Procedure is an award to the opposing party of the reasonable attorneys' fees and other expenses incurred in the action.

(B) REBUTTAL EVIDENCE.—The presumption described in subparagraph (A) may be rebutted only upon proof by the party or attorney against whom sanctions are to be imposed that—

(i) the award of attorneys' fees and other expenses will impose an unreasonable burden on that party or attorney and would be unjust, and the failure to make such an award would not impose a greater burden on the party in whose favor sanctions are to be imposed; or

(ii) the violation of Rule 11(b) of the Federal Rules of Civil Procedure was de minimis.

(C) SANCTIONS.—If the party or attorney against whom sanctions are to be imposed meets its burden under subparagraph (B), the court shall award the sanctions that the court deems appropriate pursuant to Rule 11 of the Federal Rules of Civil Procedure.

(d) DEFENDANT'S RIGHT TO WRITTEN INTERROGATORIES.—In any private action arising under this title in which the plaintiff may recover money damages only on proof that a defendant acted with a particular state of mind, the court shall, when requested by a defendant, submit to the jury a written interrogatory on the issue of each such defendant's state of mind at the time the alleged violation occurred.

Sec. 27A. APPLICATION OF SAFE HARBOR FOR FORWARD-LOOKING STATEMENTS

(a) APPLICABILITY.—This section shall apply only to a forward-looking statement made by—

(1) an issuer that, at the time that the statement is made, is subject to the reporting requirements of section 13(a) or section 15(d) of the Securities Exchange Act of 1934;

(2) a person acting on behalf of such issuer;

(3) an outside reviewer retained by such issuer making a statement on behalf of such issuer; or

(4) an underwriter, with respect to information provided by such issuer or information derived from information provided by the issuer.

(b) EXCLUSIONS.—Except to the extent otherwise specifically provided by rule, regulation, or order of the Commission, this section shall not apply to a forward-looking statement—

(1) that is made with respect to the business or operations of the issuer, if the issuer—

(A) during the 3-year period preceding the date on which the statement was first made—

(i) was convicted of any felony or misdemeanor described in clauses (i) through (iv) of section 15(b)(4)(B) of the Securities Exchange Act of 1934; or

(ii) has been made the subject of a judicial or administrative decree or order arising out of a governmental action that—

(I) prohibits future violations of the antifraud provisions of the securities laws;

(II) requires that the issuer cease and desist from violating the antifraud provisions of the securities laws; or

(III) determines that the issuer violated the antifraud provisions of the securities laws;

(B) makes the forward-looking statement in connection with an offering of securities by a blank check company;

(C) issues penny stock;

(D) makes the forward-looking statement in connection with a rollup transaction; or

(E) makes the forward-looking statement in connection with a going private transaction; or

(2) that is—

(A) included in a financial statement prepared in accordance with generally accepted accounting principles;

(B) contained in a registration statement of, or otherwise issued by, an investment company;

(C) made in connection with a tender offer;

(D) made in connection with an initial public offering;

(E) made in connection with an offering by, or relating to the operations of, a partnership, limited liability company, or a direct participation investment program; or

(F) made in a disclosure of beneficial ownership in a report required to be filed with the Commission pursuant to section 13(d) of the Securities Exchange Act of 1934.

(c) SAFE HARBOR.—

(1) IN GENERAL.—Except as provided in subsection (b), in any private action arising under this title that is based on an untrue statement of a material fact or omission of a material fact necessary to make the statement not misleading, a person referred to in subsection (a) shall not be liable with respect to any forward-looking statement, whether written or oral, if and to the extent that—

(A) the forward-looking statement is—

(i) identified as a forward-looking statement, and is accompanied by meaningful cautionary statements identifying important factors that could cause actual results to differ materially from those in the forward-looking statement; or

(ii) immaterial; or

(B) the plaintiff fails to prove that the forward-looking statement—

(i) if made by a natural person, was made with actual knowledge by that person that the statement was false or misleading; or

(ii) if made by a business entity; was—

(I) made by or with the approval of an executive officer of that entity, and

(II) made or approved by such officer with actual knowledge by that officer that the statement was false or misleading.

(2) ORAL FORWARD-LOOKING STATEMENTS.—In the case of an oral forward-looking statement made by an issuer that is subject to the reporting requirements of section 13(a) or section 15(d) of the Securities Exchange Act of 1934, or by a person acting on behalf of such issuer, the requirement set forth in paragraph (1)(A) shall be deemed to be satisfied—

(A) if the oral forward-looking statement is accompanied by a cautionary statement—

(i) that the particular oral statement is a forward-looking statement; and

(ii) that the actual results could differ materially from those projected in the forward-looking statement; and

(B) if—

(i) the oral forward-looking statement is accompanied by an oral statement that additional information concerning factors that could cause actual results to differ materially from those in the forward-looking statement is contained in a readily available written document, or portion thereof;

(ii) the accompanying oral statement referred to in clause (i) identifies the document, or portion thereof, that contains the additional information about those factors relating to the forward-looking statement; and

(iii) the information contained in that written document is a cautionary statement that satisfies the standard established in paragraph (1)(A).

(3) AVAILABILITY.—Any document filed with the Commission or generally disseminated shall be deemed to be readily available for purposes of paragraph (2).

(4) EFFECT ON OTHER SAFE HARBORS.—The exemption provided for in paragraph (1) shall be in addition to any exemption that the Commission may establish by rule or regulation under subsection (g).

(d) DUTY TO UPDATE.—Nothing in this section shall impose upon any person a duty to update a forward-looking statement.

(e) DISPOSITIVE MOTION.—On any motion to dismiss based upon subsection (c)(1), the court shall consider any statement cited in the complaint and cautionary statement accompanying the forward-looking statement, which are not subject to material dispute, cited by the defendant.

(f) STAY PENDING DECISION ON MOTION.—In any private action arising under this title, the court shall stay discovery (other than discovery that is specifically directed to the applicability of the exemption provided for in this section) during the pendency of any motion by a defendant for summary judgment that is based on the grounds that—

(1) the statement or omission upon which the complaint is based is a forward-looking statement within the meaning of this section; and

(2) the exemption provided for in this section precludes a claim for relief.

(g) EXEMPTION AUTHORITY.—In addition to the exemptions provided for in this section, the Commission may, by rule or regulation, provide exemptions from or under any provision of this title, including with respect to liability that is based on a statement or that is based on projections or other forward-looking information, if and to the extent that any such exemption is consistent with the public interest and the protection of investors, as determined by the Commission.

(h) EFFECT ON OTHER AUTHORITY OF COMMISSION.—Nothing in this section limits, either expressly or by implication, the authority of the Commission to exercise similar authority or to adopt similar rules and regulations with respect to forward-looking statements under any other statute under which the Commission exercises rulemaking authority.

(i) DEFINITIONS.—For purposes of this section, the following definitions shall apply:

(1) FORWARD-LOOKING STATEMENT.—The term "forward-looking statement" means—

(A) a statement containing a projection of revenues, income (including income loss), earnings (including earnings loss) per share, capital expenditures, dividends, capital structure, or other financial items;

(B) a statement of the plans and objectives of management for future operations, including plans or objectives relating to the products or services of the issuer;

(C) a statement of future economic performance, including any such statement contained in a discussion and analysis of financial condition by the management or in the results of operations included pursuant to the rules and regulations of the Commission;

(D) any statement of the assumptions underlying or relating to any statement described in subparagraph (A), (B), or (C);

(E) any report issued by an outside reviewer retained by an issuer, to the extent that the report assesses a forward-looking statement made by the issuer; or

(F) a statement containing a projection or estimate of such other items as may be specified by rule or regulation of the Commission.

(2) INVESTMENT COMPANY.—The term "investment company" has the same meaning as in section 3(a) of the Investment Company Act of 1940.

(3) PENNY STOCK.—The term "penny stock" has the same meaning as in section 3(a)(51) of the Securities Exchange Act of 1934, and the rules and regulations, or orders issued pursuant to that section.

(4) GOING PRIVATE TRANSACTION.—The term "going private transaction" has the meaning given that term under the rules or regulations of the Commission issued pursuant to section 13(e) of the Securities Exchange Act of 1934.

(5) SECURITIES LAWS.—The term "securities laws" has the same meaning as in section 3 of the Securities Exchange Act of 1934.

(6) PERSON ACTING ON BEHALF OF AN ISSUER.—The term "person acting on behalf of an issuer" means an officer, director, or employee of the issuer.

(7) OTHER TERMS.—The terms "blank check company", "rollup transaction", "partnership", "limited liability company", "executive officer of an entity" and "direct participation investment program", have the meanings given those terms by rule or regulation of the Commission.

Sec. 28. GENERAL EXEMPTIVE AUTHORITY

GENERAL EXEMPTIVE AUTHORITY

The Commission, by rule or regulation, may conditionally or unconditionally exempt any person, security, or transaction, or any class or classes of persons, securities, or transactions, from any provision or provisions of this title or of any rule or regulation issued under this title, to the extent that such exemption is necessary or appropriate in the public interest, and is consistent with the protection of investors.

SCHEDULE A

(1) The name under which the issuer is doing or intends to do business;

(2) the name of the State or other sovereign power under which the issuer is organized;

(3) the location of the issuer's principal business office, and if the issuer is a foreign or territorial person, the name and address of its agent in the United States authorized to receive notice;

(4) the names and addresses of the directors or persons performing similar functions, and the chief executive, financial and accounting officers, chosen or to be chosen if the issuer be a corporation, association, trust or other entity; of all partners, if the issuer be a partnership; and of the issuer, if the issuer be an individual; and of the promoters in the case of a business to be formed, or formed within two years prior to the filing of the registration statement;

(5) the names and addresses of the underwriters;

(6) the names and addresses of all persons, if any, owning of record or beneficially, if known, more than 10 per centum of any class of stock of the issuer, or more than 10 per centum in the aggregate of the outstanding stock of the issuer as of a date within 20 days prior to the filing of the registration statement;

(7) the amount of securities of the issuer held by any person specified in paragraphs (4), (5), and (6) of this schedule, as of a date within 20 days prior to the filing of the registration statement, and, if possible, as of one year prior thereto, and the amount of the securities, for which the registration statement is filed, to which such persons have indicated their intention to subscribe;

(8) the general character of the business actually transacted or to be transacted by the issuer;

(9) a statement of the capitalization of the issuer, including the authorized and outstanding amounts of its capital stock and the proportion thereof paid up, the number and classes of shares in which such capital stock is divided, par value thereof, or if it has no par value, the stated or assigned value thereof, a description of the respective voting rights, preferences, conversion and exchange rights, rights to dividends, profits, or capital of each class, with respect to each other class, including the retirement and liquidation rights or values thereof;

(10) a statement of the securities, if any, covered by options outstanding or to be created in connection with the security to be offered, together with the names and addresses of all persons, if any, to be allotted more than 10 per centum in the aggregate of such options;

(11) the amount of capital stock of each class issued or included in the shares of stock to be offered;

(12) the amount of the funded debt outstanding and to be created by the security to be offered, with a brief description of the date, maturity, and character of such debt, rate of interest,

character of amortization provisions, and the security, if any, therefor. If substitution of any security is permissible, a summarized statement of the conditions under which such substitution is permitted. If substitution is permissible without notice, a specific statement to that effect;

(13) the specific purposes in detail and the approximate amounts to be devoted to such purposes, so far as determinable, for which the security to be offered is to supply funds, and if the funds are to be raised in part from other sources, the amounts thereof and the sources thereof, shall be stated;

(14) the remuneration, paid or estimated to be paid, by the issuer or its predecessor, directly or indirectly, during the past year and ensuing year to (a) the directors or persons performing similar functions, and (b) its officers and other persons, naming them wherever such remuneration exceeded $25,000 during any such year;

(15) the estimated net proceeds to be derived from the security to be offered;

(16) the price at which it is proposed that the security shall be offered to the public or the method by which such price is computed and any variation therefrom at which any portion of such security is proposed to be offered to any persons or classes of persons, other than the underwriters, naming them or specifying the class. A variation in price may be proposed prior to the date of the public offering of the security, but the Commission shall immediately be notified of such variation;

(17) all commissions or discounts paid or to be paid, directly or indirectly, by the issuer to the underwriters in respect of the sale of the security to be offered. Commissions shall include all cash, securities, contracts, or anything else of value, paid, to be set aside, disposed of, or understandings with or for the benefit of any other persons in which any underwriter is interested, made, in connection with the sale of such security. A commission paid or to be paid in connection with the sale of such security by a person in which the issuer has an interest or which is controlled or directed by, or under common control with, the issuer shall be deemed to have been paid by the issuer. Where any such commission is paid, the amount of such commission paid to each underwriter shall be stated;

(18) the amount or estimated amounts, itemized in reasonable detail, of expenses, other than commissions specified in paragraph (17) of this schedule, incurred or borne by or for the account of the issuer in connection with the sale or the security to be offered or properly chargeable thereto, including legal, engineering, certification, authentication, and other charges;

(19) the net proceeds derived from any security sold by the issuer during the two years preceding the filing of the registration statement, the price at which such security was offered to the public, and the names of the principal underwriters of such security;

(20) any amount paid within two years preceding the filing of the registration statement or intended to be paid to any promoter and the consideration for any such payment;

(21) the names and addresses of the vendors and the purchase price of any property, or good will, acquired or to be acquired, not in the ordinary course of business, which is to be defrayed in whole or in part from the proceeds of the security to be offered, the amount of any commission payable to any person in connection with such acquisition, and the name or names of such person or persons, together with any expense incurred or to be incurred in connection with such acquisition, including the cost of borrowing money to finance such acquisition;

(22) full particulars of the nature and extent of the interest, if any, of every director, principal executive officer, and of every stockholder holding more than 10 per centum of any class of stock or more than 10 per centum in the aggregate of the stock of the issuer, in any property acquired, not in the ordinary course of business of the issuer, within two years preceding the filing of the registration statement or proposed to be acquired at such date;

(23) the names and addresses of counsel who have passed on the legality of the issue;

(24) dates of and parties to, and the general effect concisely stated of every material contract made, not in the ordinary course of business, which contract is to be executed in whole or in part at or after the filing of the registration statement or which contract has been made not more than two years before such filing. Any management contract or contract providing for special bonuses or profit-sharing arrangements, and every material patent or contract for a material patent right,

and every contract by or with a public utility company or an affiliate thereof, providing for the giving or receiving of technical of financial advice or service (if such contract may involve a charge to any party thereto at a rate in excess of $2,500 per year in cash or securities or anything else of value), shall be deemed a material contract;

(25) a balance sheet as of a date not more than ninety days prior to the date of the filing of the registration statement showing all of the assets of the issuer, the nature and cost thereof, whenever determinable, in such detail and in such form as the Commission shall prescribe (with intangible items segregated), including any loan in excess of $20,000 to any officer, director, stockholder or person directly or indirectly controlling or controlled by the issuer, or person under direct or indirect common control with the issuer. All the liabilities of the issuer in such detail and such form as the Commission shall prescribe, including surplus of the issuer showing how and from what sources such surplus was created, all as of a date not more than ninety days prior to the filing of the registration statement. If such statement be not certified by an independent public or certified accountant, in addition to the balance sheet required to be submitted under this schedule, a similar detailed balance sheet of the assets and liabilities of the issuer, certified by an independent public or certified accountant, of a date not more than one year prior to the filing of the registration statement, shall be submitted;

(26) a profit and loss statement of the issuer showing earnings and income, the nature and source thereof, and the expenses and fixed charges in such detail and such form as the Commission shall prescribe for the latest fiscal year for which such statement is available and for the two preceding fiscal years, year by year, or, if such issuer has been in actual business for less than three years, then for such time as the issuer has been in actual business, year by year. If the date of the filing of the registration statement is more than six months after the close of the last fiscal year, a statement from such closing date to the latest practicable date. Such statement shall show what the practice of the issuer has been during the three years or lesser period as to the character of the charges, dividends or other distributions made against its various surplus accounts, and as to depreciation, depletion, and maintenance charges, in such detail and form as the Commission shall prescribe, and if stock dividends or avails from the sale of rights have been credited to income, they shall be shown separately with a statement of the basis upon which the credit is computed. Such statement shall also differentiate between any recurring and non-recurring income and between any investment and operating income. Such statement shall be certified by an independent public or certified accountant;

(27) if the proceeds, or any part of the proceeds, of the security to be issued is to be applied directly or indirectly to the purchase of any business, a profit and loss statement of such business certified by an independent public or certified accountant, meeting the requirements of paragraph (26) of this schedule, for the three preceding fiscal years, together with a balance sheet, similarly certified, of such business, meeting the requirements of paragraph (25) of this schedule of a date not more than ninety days prior to the filing of the registration statement or at the date such business was acquired by the issuer if the business was acquired by the issuer more than ninety days prior to the filing of the registration statement;

(28) a copy of any agreement or agreements (or, if identical agreements are used, the forms thereof) made with any underwriter, including all contracts and agreements referred to in paragraph (17) of this schedule;

(29) a copy of the opinion or opinions of counsel in respect to the legality of the issue, with a translation of such opinion, when necessary, into the English language;

(30) a copy of all material contracts referred to in paragraph (24) of this schedule, but no disclosure shall be required of any portion of any such contract if the Commission determines that disclosure of such portion would impair the value of the contract and would not be necessary for the protection of investors;

(31) unless previously filed and registered under the provisions of this title, and brought up to date, (a) a copy of its articles of incorporation, with all amendments thereof and of its existing by-laws or instruments corresponding thereto, whatever the name, if the issuer be a corporation; (b) copy of all instruments by which the trust is created or declared, if the issuer is a trust; (c) a copy of its articles of partnership or association and all other papers pertaining to its organization, if the

issuer is a partnership, unincorporated association, joint-stock company, or any other form of organization; and

(32) a copy of the underlying agreements or indentures affecting any stock, bonds, or debentures offered or to be offered.

In case of certificates of deposit, voting trust certificates, collateral trust certificates, certificates of interest or shares in unincorporated investment trusts, equipment trust certificates, interim or other receipts for certificates, and like securities, the Commission shall establish rules and regulations requiring the submission of information of a like character applicable to such cases, together with such other information as it may deem appropriate and necessary regarding the character, financial or otherwise, of the actual issuer of the securities and/or the person performing the acts and assuming the duties of depositor or manager.

SCHEDULE B

(1) Name of borrowing government or subdivision thereof;

(2) specific purposes in detail and the approximate amounts to be devoted to such purposes, so far as determinable, for which the security to be offered is to supply funds, and if the funds are to be raised in part from other sources, the amounts thereof and the sources thereof, shall be stated;

(3) the amount of the funded debt and the estimated amount of the floating debt outstanding and to be created by the security to be offered, excluding intergovernmental debt, and a brief description of the date, maturity, character of such debt, rate of interest, character of amortization provisions, and the security, if any, therefor. If substitution or any security is permissible, a statement of the conditions under which such substitution is permitted. If substitution is permissible without notice, a specific statement to that effect;

(4) whether or not the issuer or its predecessor has, within a period of twenty years prior to the filing of the registration statement, defaulted on the principal or interest of any external security, excluding intergovernmental debt, and, if so, the date, amount, and circumstances of such default, and the terms of the succeeding arrangement, if any;

(5) the receipts, classified by source, and the expenditures, classified by purpose, in such detail and form as the Commission shall prescribe for the latest fiscal year for which such information is available and the two preceding fiscal years, year by year;

(6) the names and addresses of the underwriters;

(7) the names and address of its authorized agent, if any, in the United States;

(8) the estimated net proceeds to be derived from the sale in the United States of the security to be offered;

(9) the price at which it is proposed that the security shall be offered in the United States to the public or the method by which such price is computed. A variation in price may be proposed prior to the date of the public offering of the security, but the Commission shall immediately be notified of such variation;

(10) all commissions paid or to be paid, directly or indirectly, by the issuer to the underwriters in respect of the sale of the security to be offered. Commissions shall include all cash, securities, contracts, or anything else of value, paid, to be set aside, disposed of, or understandings with or for the benefit of any other persons in which the underwriter is interested, made, in connection with the sale of such security. Where any such commission is paid, the amount of such commission paid to each underwriter shall be stated;

(11) the amount of estimated amounts, itemized in reasonable detail, of expenses, other than the commissions specified in paragraph (10) of this schedule, incurred or borne by or for the account of the issuer in connection with the sale of the security to be offered or properly chargeable thereto, including legal, engineering, certification, and other charges;

(12) the names and addresses of counsel who have passed upon the legality of the issue;

(13) a copy of any agreement or agreements made with any underwriter governing the sale of the security within the United States; and

(14) an agreement of the issuer to furnish a copy of the opinion or opinions of counsel in respect to the legality of the issue, with a translation, where necessary, into the English language. Such opinion shall set out in full all laws, decrees, ordinances, or other acts of Government under which the issue of such security has been authorized.

SECURITIES ACT RULES

17 C.F.R. §§ 230.100-230.905

Regulation A—Conditional Small Issues Exemption

GENERAL

Rule 100. Definitions of Terms Used in the Rules and Regulations

(a) As used in the rules and regulations prescribed by the Securities and Exchange Commission pursuant to the Securities Act of 1933, unless the context otherwise requires:

(1) The term "Commission" means the Securities and Exchange Commission.

(2) The term "Act" means the Securities Act of 1933.

(3) The term "rules and regulations" refers to all rules and regulations adopted by the Commission pursuant to the Act, including the forms for registration and accompanying instructions thereto.

(4) The term "registrant" means the issuer of securities for which a registration statement is filed.

(5) The term "agent for service" means the person authorized in the registration statement to receive notices and communications from the Commission.

(6) The term "electronic filer" means a person or an entity that submits filings electronically pursuant to Rules 101, 901, 902 or 903 of Regulation S-T (§§ 232.101, 232.901, 232.902 or 232.903 of this chapter, respectively).

(7) The term "electronic filing" means a document under the federal securities laws that is transmitted or delivered to the Commission in electronic format.

(b) Unless otherwise specifically provided, the terms used in the rules and regulations shall have the meanings defined in the Act.

(c) A rule in the General Rules and Regulations which defines a term without express reference to the Act or to the rules and regulations or to a portion thereof defines such term for all purposes as used both in the Act and in the rules and regulations, unless the context otherwise requires.

Rule 110. Business Hours of the Commission

The principal office of the Commission, at 450 Fifth Street, N.W., Washington, D.C. 20549, is open each day, except Saturdays, Sundays and Federal holidays, from 9:00 a.m. to 5:30 p.m., Eastern Standard Time or Eastern Daylight Saving Time, whichever is currently in effect, *provided that* hours for the filing of documents pursuant to the Act or the rules and regulations thereunder are as set forth in paragraphs (b), (c) and (d) of this section.

(b) *Submissions made in paper.* Paper documents filed with or otherwise furnished to the Commission may be submitted each day, except Saturdays, Sundays and federal holidays, from 8 a.m. to 5:30 p.m., Eastern Standard Time or Eastern Daylight Saving Time, whichever is currently in effect.

(c) *Filings by direct transmission.* Filings made by direct transmission may be submitted to the Commission each day, except Saturdays, Sundays and federal holidays, from 8:00 a.m. to 10:00 p.m., Eastern Standard Time or Eastern Daylight Saving Time, whichever is currently in effect.

(d) *Filings by facsimile.* Registration statements and post-effective amendments thereto filed by facsimile transmission pursuant to Rule 462(b) (§ 230.462(b)) and Rule 455 (§ 230.455) may be filed with the Commission each day, except Saturdays, Sundays and federal holidays, from 5:30 p.m. to 10:00 p.m., Eastern Standard Time or Eastern Daylight Savings Time, whichever is currently in effect.

Rule 111. Payment of Fees

(a) All payments of fees for registration statements under the Act shall be made in cash or by United States postal money order, certified check, bank cashier's check or bank money order payable to the Securities and Exchange Commission, omitting the name or title of any official of the Commission. In addition, all other filing fees may be paid by personal check. There will be no refunds.

45

(b) Notwithstanding paragraph (a) of this section, for registration statements filed pursuant to Rule 462(b) (§ 230.462(b)) and Rule 110(d) (§ 230.110(d)), payment of filing fees for the purposes of this section may be made by:

(1) The registrant or its agent instructing its bank or a wire transfer service to transmit to the Commission the applicable filing fee by a wire transfer of such amount from the issuer's account or its agent's account to the Commission's account at Mellon Bank as soon as practicable but no later than the close of the next business day following the filing of the registration statement; and

(2) The registrant submitting with the registration statement at the time of filing a certification that:

(i) The registrant or its agent has so instructed its bank or a wire transfer service;

(ii) The registrant or its agent will not revoke such instructions; and

(iii) The registrant or its agent has sufficient funds in such account to cover the amount of such filing fee.

Note to paragraph (b): Such instructions may be sent on the date of filing the registration statement after the close of business of such bank or wire transfer service, provided that the registrant undertakes in the certification sent to the Commission with the registration statement that it will confirm receipt of such instructions by the bank or wire transfer service during regular business hours on the following business day.

Rule 120. Inspection of Registration Statements

Except for material contracts or portions thereof accorded confidential treatment pursuant to § 230.406, all registration statements are available for public inspection, during business hours, at the principal office of the Commission in Washington, D.C. Electronic registration statements made through the Electronic Data Gathering, Analysis, and Retrieval system are publicly available through the Commission's Web site (http://www.sec.gov).

Rule 122. Non-disclosure of Information Obtained in the Course of Examinations and Investigations

Information or documents obtained by officers or employees of the Commission in the course of any examination or investigation pursuant to Section 8(e) or 20(a) shall, unless made a matter of public record, be deemed confidential. Except as provided by 17 CFR 203.2, officers and employees are hereby prohibited from making such confidential information or documents or any other non-public records of the Commission available to anyone other than a member, officer or employee of the Commission, unless the Commission or the General Counsel, pursuant to delegated authority, authorizes the disclosure of such information or the production of such documents as not being contrary to the public interest. Any officer or employee who is served with a subpoena requiring the disclosure of such information or the production of such documents shall appear in court and, unless the authorization described in the preceding sentence shall have been given, shall respectfully decline to disclose the information or produce the documents called for, basing his refusal upon this rule. Any officer or employee who is served with such a subpoena shall promptly advise the General Counsel of the service of such subpoena, the nature of the information or documents sought, and any circumstances which may bear on the desirability of making available such information or documents.

Rule 130. Definition of "Rules and Regulations" as Used in Certain Sections of the Act

The term "rules and regulations" as used in Sections 7, 10(a), (c) and (d) and 19(a) of the Act, shall include the forms for registration of securities under the Act and the related instructions thereto.

Rule 131. Definition of Security Issued Under Governmental Obligations

(a) Any part of an obligation evidenced by any bond, note, debenture, or other evidence of indebtedness issued by any governmental unit specified in Section 3(a)(2) of the Act which is payable from payments to be made in respect of property or money which is or will be used, under a lease, sale, or loan arrangement, by or for industrial or commercial enterprise, shall be deemed to be a separate "security" within the meaning of Section 2(1) of the Act, issued by the lessee or obligor under the lease, sale or loan arrangement.

(b) An obligation shall not be deemed a separate "security" as defined in paragraph (a) hereof if, (1) the obligation is payable from the general revenues of a governmental unit, specified in Section 3(a)(2) of the Act, having other resources which may be used for payment of the obligation, or (2) the obligation relates to a public project or facility owned and operated by or on behalf of and under the control of a governmental unit specified in such section, or (3) the obligation relates to a facility which is leased to and under the control of an industrial or commercial enterprise but is a part of a public project which, as a whole, is owned by and under the general control of a governmental unit specified in such section, or an instrumentality thereof.

(c) This rule shall apply to transactions of the character described in paragraph (a) only with respect to bonds, notes, debentures or other evidences of indebtedness sold after December 31, 1968.

Rule 132. Definition of "Common Trust Fund" as Used in Section 3(a)(2) of the Act

The term "common trust fund" as used in section 3(a)(2) of the Act [15 U.S.C. 77c(a)(2)] shall include a common trust fund which is maintained by a bank which is a member of an affiliated group, as defined in section 1504(a) of the Internal Revenue Code of 1954 [26 U.S.C. 1504(a)], and which is maintained exclusively for the collective investment and reinvestment of monies contributed thereto by one or more bank members of such affiliated group in the capacity of trustee, executor, administrator, or guardian, provided that:

(a) the common trust fund is operated in compliance with the same state and federal regulatory requirements as would apply if the bank maintaining such fund and any other contributing banks were the same entity; and

(b) the rights of persons for whose benefit a contributing bank acts as trustee, executor, administrator, or guardian would not be diminished by reason of the maintenance of such common trust fund by another bank member of the affiliated group. (15 U.S.C. 77s(a)).

Rule 134. Communications Not Deemed a Prospectus

The term "prospectus" as defined in Section 2(10) of the Act shall not include a notice, circular, advertisement, letter, or other communication published or transmitted to any person after a registration statement has been filed if it contains only the statements required or permitted to be included therein by the following provisions of this rule:

(a) Such communication may include any one or more of the following items of information, which need not follow the numerical sequence of this paragraph:

(1) the name of the issuer of the security;

(2) the full title of the security and the amount being offered;

(3) a brief indication of the general type of business of the issuer, limited to the following:

(i) in the case of a manufacturing company, the general type of manufacturing and the principal products or classes of products manufactured;

(ii) in the case of a public utility company, the general type of services rendered and a brief indication of the area served;

(iii) in the case of any other type of company, a corresponding statement;

(4) the price of the security, or if the price is not known, the method of its determination or the probable price range as specified by the issuer or the managing underwriter;

(5) in the case of a debt security with a fixed (non-contingent) interest provision, the yield or, if the yield is not known, the probable yield range, as specified by the issuer or the managing underwriter;

(6) the name and address of the sender of the communication and the fact that he is participating, or expects to participate, in the distribution of the security;

(7) the names of the managing underwriters;

(8) the approximate date upon which it is anticipated the proposed sale to the public will commence;

(9) whether, in the opinion of counsel, the security is a legal investment for savings banks, fiduciaries, insurance companies, or similar investors under the laws of any State or Territory or the District of Columbia;

(10) whether, in the opinion of counsel, the security is exempt from specified taxes, or the extent to which the issuer has agreed to pay any tax with respect to the security or measured by the income therefrom;

(11) whether the security is being offered through rights issued to security holders, and, if so, the class of securities the holders of which will be entitled to subscribe, the subscription ratio, the actual or proposed record date, the date upon which the rights were issued or are expected to be issued, the actual or anticipated date upon which they will expire, and the approximate subscription price, or any of the foregoing;

(12) any statement or legend required by any state law or administrative authority.

(13) (i) With respect to any class of debt securities, any class of convertible debt securities or any class of preferred stock, the security rating or ratings assigned to the class of securities by any nationally recognized statistical rating organization and the name or names of the nationally recognized statistical rating organization(s) which assigned such rating(s), and with respect to any class of debt securities, any class of convertible debt securities or any class of preferred stock registered on Form F-9 (§ 239.39 of this chapter), the security rating or ratings assigned to the class of securities by any other rating organization specified in the Instruction to paragraph (a)(2) of General Instruction I of Form F-9 and the name or names of the rating organization or organizations which assigned such rating(s).

(ii) For the purpose of paragraph (a)(13)(i) of this section, the term "nationally recognized statistical rating organization" shall have the same meaning as used in Rule 15c3-1(c)(2)(vi)(F) under Securities Exchange Act of 1934 (17 CFR 240.15c3-1(c)(2)(vi)(F)).

(b) Except as provided in paragraph (c), every communication used pursuant to this rule shall contain the following:

(1) if the registration statement has not yet become effective, the following statement:

"A registration statement relating to these securities has been filed with the Securities and Exchange Commission but has not yet become effective. These securities may not be sold nor may offers to buy be accepted prior to the time the registration statement becomes effective. This (communication) shall not constitute an offer to sell or the solicitation of an offer to buy nor shall there be any sale of these securities in any State in which such offer, solicitation or sale would be unlawful prior to registration or qualification under the securities laws of any such State."

(2) a statement whether the security is being offered in connection with a distribution by the issuer or by a security holder, or both, and whether the issue represents new financing or refunding or both; and

(3) the name and address of a person or persons from whom a written prospectus meeting the requirements of Section 10 of the Act may be obtained.

(c) Any of the statements or information specified in paragraph (b) may, but need not, be contained in a communication: (i) which does no more than state from whom a written prospectus meeting the requirements of Section 10 of the Act may be obtained, identify the security, state the price thereof and state by whom orders will be executed; or (ii) which is accompanied or preceded by a prospectus or a summary prospectus which meets the requirements of Section 10 of the Act at the date of such preliminary communication.

(d) A communication sent or delivered to any person pursuant to this rule which is accompanied or preceded by a prospectus which meets the requirements of Section 10 of the Act at the date of such communication, may solicit from the recipient of the communication an offer to buy the security or request the recipient to indicate, upon an enclosed or attached coupon or card, or in some other manner, whether he might be interested in the security, if the communication contains substantially the following statement:

"No offer to buy the securities can be accepted and no part of the purchase price can be received until the registration statement has become effective, and any such offer may be withdrawn or revoked, without obligation or commitment of any kind, at any time prior to notice of its acceptance given after the effective date. An indication of interest in response to this advertisement will involve no obligation or commitment of any kind."

Provided, that such statement need not be included in such a communication to a dealer if the communication refers to a prior communication to the dealer, with respect to the same security, in which the statement was included.

(e) This § 230.134 does not apply to a notice, circular, advertisement, letter, or other communication relating to an investment company registered under the Investment Company Act of 1940 (15 U.S.C. 80a-1 *et seq.*) or a business development company as defined in section 2(a)(48) of the Investment Company Act (15 U.S.C. 80a-2(a)(48)).

Rule 134a. Options Material Not Deemed a Prospectus

Written materials, including advertisements, relating to standardized options, as that term is defined in Rule 9b-1 under the Securities Exchange Act of 1934, shall not be deemed to be a prospectus for the purposes of Section 2(10) of the Securities Act of 1933: *Provided,* That such materials are limited to explanatory information describing the general nature of the standardized options markets or one or more strategies: *And, Provided Further,* That:

(a) The potential risks related to options trading generally and to each strategy addressed are explained;

(b) No past or projected performance figures, including annualized rates of return are used;

(c) No recommendation to purchase or sell any option contract is made;

(d) No specific security is identified, other than

(i) An option or other security exempt from registration under the Act, or

(ii) An index option, including the component securities of the index; and

(e) If there is a definitive options disclosure document, as defined in Rule 9b-1 under the Securities Exchange Act of 1934, the materials shall contain the name and address of a person or persons from whom a copy of such document may be obtained.

Rule 134b. Statement of Additional Information

For the purpose only of Section 5(b) of the Act (15 U.S.C. 77e(b)), the term "prospectus" as defined in Section 2(a)(10) of the Act (15 U.S.C. 77b(a)(10)) does not include a Statement of Additional Information filed as part of a registration statement on Form N-1A (§ 239.15A and § 274.11A of this chapter), Form N-2 (§ 239.14 and § 274.11a-1 of this chapter), Form N-3 (§ 239.17a and § 274.11b of this chapter), Form N-4 (§ 239.17b and § 274.11c of this chapter), or Form N-6 (§ 239.17c and § 274.11d of this chapter) transmitted prior to the effective date of the registration statement if it is accompanied or preceded by a preliminary prospectus meeting the requirements of § 230.430.

Rule 135. Notice of Proposed Registered Offerings

(a) For purposes of Section 5 of the Act (15 U.S.C. 77e) only, an issuer or a selling security holder (and any person acting on behalf of either of them) that publishes through any medium a notice of a proposed offering to be registered under the Act will not be deemed to offer its securities for sale through that notice if:

(1) *Legend.* The notice includes a statement to the effect that it does not constitute an offer of any securities for sale; and

(2) *Limited notice content.* The notice otherwise includes no more than the following information:

(i) The name of the issuer;

(ii) The title, amount and basic terms of the securities offered;

(iii) The amount of the offering, if any, to be made by selling security holders;

(iv) The anticipated timing of the offering;

(v) A brief statement of the manner and the purpose of the offering, without naming the underwriters;

(vi) Whether the issuer is directing its offering to only a particular class of purchasers;

(vii) Any statements or legends required by the laws of any state or foreign country or administrative authority; and

(viii) In the following offerings, the notice may contain additional information, as follows:

(A) *Rights offering.* In a rights offering to existing security holders:

(*1*) The class of security holders eligible to subscribe;

(*2*) The subscription ratio and expected subscription price;

(*3*) The proposed record date;

(*4*) The anticipated issuance date of the rights; and

(*5*) The subscription period or expiration date of the rights offering.

(B) *Offering to employees.* In an offering to employees of the issuer or an affiliated company:

(*1*) The name of the employer;

(*2*) The class of employees being offered the securities;

(*3*) The offering price; and

(*4*) The duration of the offering period.

(C) *Exchange offer.* In an exchange offer:

(*1*) The basic terms of the exchange offer;

(*2*) The name of the subject company;

(*3*) The subject class of securities sought in the exchange offer.

(D) *Rule 145(a) offering.* In a § 230.145(a) offering:

(*1*) The name of the person whose assets are to be sold in exchange for the securities to be offered;

(*2*) The names of any other parties to the transaction;

(*3*) A brief description of the business of the parties to the transaction;

(*4*) The date, time and place of the meeting of security holders to vote on or consent to the transaction; and

(*5*) A brief description of the transaction and the basic terms of the transaction.

(b) *Corrections of misstatements about the offering.* A person that publishes a notice in reliance on this section may issue a notice that contains no more information than is necessary to correct inaccuracies published about the proposed offering.

Note to § 230.135: Communications under this section relating to business combination transactions must be filed as required by § 230.425(b).

Rule 135a. Generic Advertising

For the purposes only of Section 5 of the Act, a notice, circular, advertisement, letter, sign or other communication, published or transmitted to any person which does not specifically refer by name to the securities of a particular investment company, to the investment company itself, or to any other securities not exempt under Section 3(a) of the Act, will not be deemed to offer any security for sale, provided:

(a) such communication is limited to any one or more of the following:

1. Explanatory information relating to securities of investment companies generally or to the nature of investment companies, or to services offered in connection with the ownership of such securities.

2. The mention or explanation of investment companies of different generic types or having various investment objectives, such as "balanced funds", "growth funds", "income funds", "leveraged funds", "specialty funds", "variable annuities", "bond funds", and "no-load funds",

3. Offers, descriptions and explanation of various products and services not constituting a security subject to registration under the Act, provided that such offers, descriptions and explana-

tions do not relate directly to the desirability of owning or purchasing a security issued by a registered investment company,

4. Invitation to inquire for further information and

(b) such communication contains the name and address of a registered broker or dealer or other person sponsoring the communication.

If such communication contains a solicitation of inquiries and prospectuses for investment company securities are to be sent or delivered in response to such inquiries, the number of such investment companies and, if applicable, the fact that the sponsor of the communication is the principal underwriter or investment adviser in respect to such investment companies shall be stated.

(c) With respect to any communication describing any type of security, service or product, the broker, dealer or other person sponsoring such communication must offer for sale a security, service or product of the type described in such communication.

Rule 135b. Materials Not Deemed an Offer to Sell or Offer to Buy Nor a Prospectus

Materials meeting the requirements of § 240.9b-1 of this chapter shall not be deemed an offer to sell or offer to buy a security for purposes solely of Section 5 (15 U.S.C. 77e) of the Act, nor shall such materials be deemed a prospectus for purposes of Sections 2(a)(10) and 12(a)(2) (15 U.S.C. 77b(a)(10) and 77l(a)(2)) of the Act, even if such materials are referred to in, deemed to be incorporated by reference into, or otherwise in any manner deemed to be a part of a Form S-20 prospectus.

Rule 135c. Notice of Certain Proposed Unregistered Offerings

(a) For the purposes only of Section 5 of the Act, a notice given by an issuer required to file reports pursuant to Section 13 or 15(d) of the Securities Exchange Act of 1934 or a foreign issuer that is exempt from registration under the Securities Exchange Act of 1934 pursuant to § 240.12g3-2(b) of this chapter that it proposes to make, is making or has made an offering of securities not registered or required to be registered under the Act shall not be deemed to offer any securities for sale if:

(1) Such notice is not used for the purpose of conditioning the market in the United States for any of the securities offered;

(2) Such notice states that the securities offered will not be or have not been registered under the Act and may not be offered or sold in the United States absent registration or an applicable exemption from registration requirements; and

(3) Such notice contains no more than the following additional information:

(i) The name of the issuer;

(ii) The title, amount and basic terms of the securities offered, the amount of the offering, if any, made by selling security holders, the time of the offering and a brief statement of the manner and purpose of the offering without naming the underwriters;

(iii) In the case of a rights offering to security holders of the issuer, the class of securities the holder of which will be or were entitled to subscribe to the securities offered, the subscription ratio, the record date, the date upon which the rights are proposed to be or were issued, the term or expiration date of the rights and the subscription price, or any of the foregoing;

(iv) In the case of an offering of securities in exchange for other securities of the issuer or of another issuer, the name of the issuer and the title of the securities to be surrendered in exchange for the securities offered, the basis upon which the exchange may be made, or any of the foregoing;

(v) In the case of an offering to employees of the issuer or to employees of any affiliate of the issuer, the name of the employer and class or classes of employees to whom the securities are offered, the offering price or basis of the offering and the period during which the offering is to be or was made or any of the foregoing; and

(vi) Any statement or legend required by State or foreign law or administrative authority.

(b) Any notice contemplated by this section may take the form of a news release or a written communication directed to security holders or employees, as the case may be, or other published statements.

(c) Notwithstanding the provisions of paragraphs (a) and (b) of this section, in the case of a rights offering of a security listed or subject to unlisted trading privileges on a national securities exchange or quoted on the NASDAQ inter-dealer quotation system information with respect to the interest rate, conversion ratio and subscription price may be disseminated through the facilities of the exchange, the consolidated transaction reporting system, the NASDAQ system or the Dow Jones broad tape, provided such information is already disclosed in a Form 8-K (§ 249.308 of this chapter) on file with the Commission, in a Form 6-K (§ 249.306 of this chapter) furnished to the Commission or, in the case of an issuer relying on § 240.12g3-2(b) of this chapter, in a submission made pursuant to that Section to the Commission.

(d) The issuer shall file any notice contemplated by this section with the Commission under cover of Form 8-K (§ 249.308 of this chapter) or furnish such notice under Form 6-K (§ 249.306 of this chapter), as applicable, and, if relying on § 240.12g3-2(b) of this chapter, shall furnish such notice to the Commission in accordance with the provisions of that exemptive Section.

Rule 135e. Offshore Press Conferences, Meetings with Issuer Representatives Conducted Offshore, and Press-Related Materials Released Offshore

(a) For the purposes only of Section 5 of the Act [15 U.S.C. 77e], an issuer that is a foreign private issuer (as defined in § 230.405) or a foreign government issuer, a selling security holder of the securities of such issuers, or their representatives will not be deemed to offer any security for sale by virtue of providing any journalist with access to its press conferences held outside of the United States, to meetings with issuer or selling security holder representatives conducted outside of the United States, or to written press-related materials released outside the United States, at or in which a present or proposed offering of securities is discussed, if:

(1) The present or proposed offering is not being, or to be, conducted solely in the United States;

Note to Paragraph (a)(1): An offering will be considered not to be made solely in the United States under this paragraph (a)(1) only if there is an intent to make a bona fide offering offshore.

(2) Access is provided to both U.S. and foreign journalists; and

(3) Any written press-related materials pertaining to transactions in which any of the securities will be or are being offered in the United States satisfy the requirements of paragraph (b) of this section.

(b) Any written press-related materials specified in paragraph (a)(3) of this section must:

(1) State that the written press-related materials are not an offer of securities for sale in the United States, that securities may not be offered or sold in the United States absent registration or an exemption from registration, that any public offering of securities to be made in the United States will be made by means of a prospectus that may be obtained from the issuer or the selling security holder and that will contain detailed information about the company and management, as well as financial statements;

(2) If the issuer or selling security holder intends to register any part of the present or proposed offering in the United States, include a statement regarding this intention; and

(3) Not include any purchase order, or coupon that could be returned indicating interest in the offering, as part of, or attached to, the written press-related materials.

(c) For the purposes of this section, "United States" means the United States of America, its territories and possessions, any State of the United States, and the District of Columbia.

Rule 136. Definition of Certain Terms in Relation to Assessable Stock

(a) An "offer," "offer to sell" or "offer for sale" of securities shall be deemed to be made to the holders of assessable stock of a corporation when such corporation shall give notice of an assessment to the holders of such assessable stock. A "sale" shall be deemed to occur when a stockholder shall pay or agree to pay all or any part of such an assessment.

(b) The term "transactions by any person other than an issuer, underwriter or dealer" in section 4(1) of the Act shall not be deemed to include the offering or sale of assessable stock, at public auction or otherwise, upon the failure of the holder of such stock to pay an assessment levied thereon by the issuer, where the offer or sale is made for the purpose of realizing the amount of the assessment and any of the proceeds of such sale are to be received by the issuer. However, any person whose functions are limited to acting as auctioneer at such an auction sale shall not be deemed to be an underwriter of the securities offered or sold at the auction sale. Any person who acquires assessable stock at any such public auction or other sale with a view to the distribution thereof shall be deemed to be an underwriter of such assessable stock.

(c) The term "assessable stock" means stock which is subject to resale by the issuer pursuant to statute or otherwise in the event of a failure of the holder of such stock to pay any assessment levied thereon.

Rule 137. Definition of "Offers", "Participates", or "Participation" in Section 2(11) in Relation to Certain Publications by Persons Independent of Participants in a Distribution

The terms "offers", "participates", or "participation" in section 2(11) of the Act shall not be deemed to apply to the publication or distribution of information, opinions or recommendations with respect to the securities of a registrant which is required to file reports pursuant to section 13 or 15(d) of the Securities Exchange Act of 1934 and proposes to file, has filed or has an effective registration statement under the Securities Act of 1933 if—

(a) Such information, opinions, and recommendations are published and distributed in the regular course of its business by a broker or dealer which is not and does not propose to be a participant in the distribution of the security to which the registration statement relates; and

(b) Such broker or dealer receives no consideration, directly or indirectly, in connection with the publication and distribution of such information, opinions or recommendations from the registrant, a selling security holder or any participant in the distribution or any other person interested in the securities to which the registration statement relates, and such information, opinions or recommendations are not published or distributed pursuant to any arrangement or understanding, direct or indirect, with such registrant, underwriter, dealer, or selling security holder; *Provided, however,* That nothing herein shall forbid payment of the regular subscription or purchase price of the document or other written communication in which such information, opinions or recommendations appear.

Rule 138. Definition of "Offer for Sale" and "Offer to Sell" in Sections 2(10) and 5(c) in Relation to Certain Publications

(a) Where a registrant which meets the requirements of paragraph (c)(1), (c)(2) or (c)(3) of this section proposes to file, has filed or has an effective registration statement under the Act relating solely to a nonconvertible debt security or to a nonconvertible, nonparticipating preferred stock, publication or distribution in the regular course of its business by a broker or dealer of information, opinions or recommendations relating solely to common stock or to debt or preferred stock convertible into common stock of such registrant shall not be deemed to constitute an offer for sale or offer to sell the security to which such registration statement relates for purposes of sections 2(10) and 5(c) of the Act (15 U.S.C. § 77a *et seq.*) even though such broker or dealer is or will be a participant in the distribution of the security to which such registration statement relates.

(b) Where a registrant which meets the requirements of paragraph (c)(1), (c)(2) or (c)(3) of this section proposes to file, has filed or has an effective registration statement under the Act relating solely to common stock, or to debt or preferred stock convertible into common stock, the publication or distribution in the regular course of its business by a broker or dealer of information, opinions or recommendations relating solely to a nonconvertible debt security, or to a nonconvertible nonparticipating preferred stock shall not be deemed to constitute an offer for sale or offer to sell the security to which such registration statement relates for purposes of sections 2(10) and 5(c) of the Act (15 U.S.C. § 77a *et seq.*), even though such broker or dealer is or will be a participant in the distribution of the security to which such registration statement relates.

(c) (1) The registrant meets all of the conditions for the use of Form S-2 [§ 239.12 of this chapter] or Form F-2 [§ 239.32 of this chapter];

(2) The registrant meets the registrant requirements of Form S-3 [§ 239.13 of this chapter] or Form F-3 [§ 239.33 of this chapter]; or

(3) The registrant is a foreign private issuer which meets all the registrant requirements of Form F-3 [§ 239.33 of this chapter], other than the reporting history provisions of paragraph A.1. and A.2. (a) of General Instruction I of such form, and meets the minimum float or investment grade securities provisions of either paragraph B.1. or B.2. of General Instruction I. of such form and the registrant's securities have been traded for a period of at least 12 months on a designated offshore securities market, as defined in § 230.902(a).

Instruction to Rule 138

When a registration statement relates to securities which are being registered for an offering to be made on a continuous or delayed basis pursuant to Rule 415(a)(1)(x) under the Act (§ 230.415(a)(1)(x)) and the securities which are being registered include classes of securities which are specified in both paragraph (a) and (b) of this section on either an allocated or unallocated basis, a broker or dealer may nonetheless rely on:

(1) paragraph (a) of this section when the offering in which such broker or dealer is or will be a participant relates solely to classes of securities specified in paragraph (a) of this section, and

(2) paragraph (b) of this section when the offering in which such broker or dealer is or will be a participant relates solely to classes of securities specified in paragraph (b) of this section.

Rule 139. Definition of "Offer for Sale" and "Offer to Sell" in Sections 2(10) and 5(c) in Relation to Certain Publications

Where a registrant which is required to file reports pursuant to section 13 or 15(d) of the Securities Exchange Act of 1934 (15 U.S.C. § 78a *et seq.*) or which is a foreign private issuer meeting the conditions of paragraph (a)(2) of this section proposes to file, has filed or has an effective registration statement under the Securities Act of 1933 (15 U.S.C. § 77a *et seq.*) relating to its securities, the publication or distribution by a broker or dealer of information, an opinion or a recommendation with respect to the registrant or any class of its securities shall not be deemed to constitute an offer for sale or offer to sell the securities registered or proposed to be registered for purposes of sections 2(10) and 5(c) of the Act (15 U.S.C. § 77a *et seq.*), even though such broker or dealer is or will be a participant in the distribution of such securities, if the conditions of paragraph (a) or (b) of this section have been met:

(a) (1) The registrant meets the registrant requirements of Form S-3 (§ 239.13 of this chapter) or Form F-3 (§ 239.33 of this chapter) and the minimum float or investment grade securities provisions of either paragraph (B)(1) or (2) of General Instruction I of the respective form and such information, opinion or recommendation is contained in a publication which is distributed with reasonable regularity in the normal course of business; or

(a) (2) The registrant is a foreign private issuer that meets all the registrant requirements of Form F-3 (§ 239.33 of this chapter), other than the reporting history provisions of paragraphs A.1. and A.2. (a) of General Instruction I of such form, and meets the minimum float or investment grade securities provisions of either paragraph B.1. or B.2. of General Instruction I of such form, and the registrant's securities have been traded for a period of at least 12 months on a designated offshore securities market, as defined in § 230.902(a), and such information, opinion or recommendation is contained in a publication which is distributed with reasonable regularity in the normal course of business.

(b) (1) Such information, opinion or recommendation is contained in a publication which:

(i) Is distributed with reasonable regularity in the normal course of business and

(ii) Includes similar information, opinions or recommendations with respect to a substantial number of companies in the registrant's industry or sub-industry, or contains a comprehensive list of securities currently recommended by such broker or dealer;

(2) Such information, opinion or recommendation is given no materially greater space or prominence in such publication than that given to other securities or registrants; and

(3) An opinion or recommendation as favorable or more favorable as to the registrant or any class of its securities was published by the broker or dealer in the last publication of such broker or dealer addressing the registrant or its securities prior to the commencement of participation in the distribution.

Instructions to Rule 139.

1. For purposes of paragraph (a), a research report has not been distributed with "reasonable regularity" if it contains information, an opinion, or a recommendation concerning a company with respect to which a broker or dealer currently is not publishing research.

2. Where projections of a registrant's sales or earnings are included, the publication must comply with the following in order to meet paragraphs (b)(1) and (b)(3).

A. The projections must have been published previously on a regular basis in order for the publication to meet paragraph (b)(1)(i);

B. The projections must be included with respect to either a substantial number of companies in the registrant's industry or sub-industry or all companies in a comprehensive list which is contained in the publication, and must cover the same periods with respect to such companies as with respect to the registrant, in order to meet the requirements of paragraph (b)(1)(ii); and

C. Because projections constitute opinions within the meaning of the Rule, they must come within paragraph (b)(3).

Rule 140. Definition of "Distribution" in Section 2(11) for Certain Transactions

A person, the chief part of whose business consists of the purchase of the securities of one issuer, or of two or more affiliated issuers, and the sale of its own securities, including the levying of assessments on its assessable stock and the resale of such stock upon the failure of the holder thereof to pay any assessment levied thereon, to furnish the proceeds with which to acquire the securities of such issuer or affiliated issuers, is to be regarded as engaged in the distribution of the securities of such issuer or affiliated issuers within the meaning of Section 2(11) of the Act.

Rule 141. Definition of "Commission from an Underwriter or Dealer Not in Excess of the Usual and Customary Distributors' or Sellers' Commissions" in Section 2(11), for Certain Transactions

(a) The term "commission" in Section 2(11) shall include such remuneration, commonly known as a spread, as may be received by a distributor or dealer as a consequence of reselling securities bought from an underwriter or dealer at a price below the offering price of such securities, where such resales afford the distributor or dealer a margin of profit not in excess of what is usual and customary in such transactions.

(b) The term "commission from an underwriter or dealer" in Section 2(11) shall include commissions paid by an underwriter or dealer directly or indirectly controlling or controlled by, or under direct or indirect common control with the issuer.

(c) The term "usual and customary distributors' or sellers' commission" in Section 2(11) shall mean a commission or remuneration, commonly known as a spread, paid to or received by any person selling securities either for his own account or for the account of others, which is not in excess of the amount usual and customary in the distribution and sale of issues of similar type and size, and not in excess of the amount allowed to other persons, if any, for comparable service in the distribution of the particular issue; but such term shall not include amounts paid to any person whose function is the management of the distribution of all or a substantial part of the particular issue, or who performs the functions normally performed by an underwriter or underwriting syndicate.

Rule 142. Definition of "Participates" and "Participation", as Used in Section 2(11), in Relation to Certain Transactions

(a) The terms "participates" and "participations" in section 2(11) shall not include the interest of a person (1) who is not in privity of contract with the issuer nor directly or indirectly controlling, controlled by, or under common control with, the issuer, and (2) who has no association with any principal underwriter of the securities being distributed, and (3) whose function in the distribution is confined to an undertaking to purchase all or some specified proportion of the securities remaining unsold after the lapse of some specified period of time, and (4) who purchase such securities for investment and not with a view to distribution.

(b) As used in this rule—

(1) The term "issuer" shall have the meaning defined in section 2(4) and in the last sentence of section 2(11).

(2) The term "association" shall include a relationship between two persons under which one—

(i) Is directly or indirectly controlling, controlled by, or under common control with, the other, or

(ii) Has, in common with the other, one or more partners, officers, directors, trustees, branch managers, or other persons occupying a similar status or performing similar functions, or

(iii) Has a participation, direct or indirect, in the profits of the other, or has a financial stake, by debtor-creditor relationship, stock ownership, contract or otherwise, in the income or business of the other.

(3) The term "principal underwriter" shall have the meaning defined in Reg. § 230.405.

Rule 143. Definition of "Has Purchased", "Sells For", "Participates", and "Participation", as Used in Section 2(11), in Relation to Certain Transactions of Foreign Governments for War Purposes

The terms "has purchased", "sells for", "participates", and "participation", in section 2(11), shall not be deemed to apply to any action of a foreign government in acquiring, for war purposes and by or in anticipation of the exercise of war powers, from any person subject to its jurisdiction securities of a person organized under the laws of the United States or any State or Territory, or in disposing of such securities with a view to their distribution by underwriters in the United States, notwithstanding the fact that the price to be paid to such foreign government upon the disposition of such securities by it may be measured by or may be in direct or indirect relation to such price as may be realized by the underwriters.

Rule 144. Persons Deemed Not to Be Engaged in a Distribution and Therefore Not Underwriters

Preliminary Note to Rule 144

Rule 144 is designed to implement the fundamental purposes of the Act, as expressed in its preamble, "To provide full and fair disclosure of the character of the securities sold in interstate commerce and through the mails, and to prevent fraud in the sale thereof . . ." The rule is designed to prohibit the creation of public markets in securities of issuers concerning which adequate current information is not available to the public. At the same time, where adequate current information concerning the issuer is available to the public, the rule permits the public sale in ordinary trading transactions of limited amounts of securities owned by persons controlling, controlled by or under common control with the issuer and by persons who have acquired restricted securities of the issuer.

Certain basic principles are essential to an understanding of the requirement of registration in the Act:

1. If any person utilizes the jurisdictional means to sell any non-exempt security to any other person, the security must be registered unless a statutory exemption can be found for the transaction.

2. In addition to the exemptions found in Section 3, four exemptions applicable to transactions in securities are contained in Section 4. Three of these Section 4 exemptions are clearly not available to anyone acting as an "underwriter" of securities. (The fourth, found in Section 4(4), is available only to those who act as brokers under certain limited circumstances.) An understanding of the term "underwriter" is therefore important to anyone who wishes to determine whether or not an exemption from registration is available for his sale of securities.

The term underwriter is broadly defined in Section 2(11) of the Act to mean any person who has purchased from an issuer with a view to, or offers or sells for an issuer in connection with, the distribution of any security, or participates or has a direct or indirect participation in any such undertaking, or participates or has a participation in the direct or indirect underwriting of any such undertaking. The interpretation of this definition has traditionally focused on the words "with the view to" in the phrase "purchased from an issuer with a view to . . . distribution." Thus, an investment banking firm which arranges with an issuer for the public sale of its securities is clearly an "underwriter" under that Section. Individual investors who are not professionals in the securities business may also be "underwriters" within the meaning of that term as used in the Act if they act as links in a chain of transactions through which securities move from an issuer to the public. Since it is difficult to ascertain the mental state of the purchaser at the time of his acquisition, subsequent acts and circumstances have been considered to determine whether such person took with a view to distribution at the time of his acquisition. Emphasis has been placed on factors such as the length of time the person has held the securities and whether there has been an unforeseeable change in circumstances of the holder. Experience has shown, however, that reliance upon such factors as the above has not assured adequate protection of investors through the maintenance of informed trading markets and has led to uncertainty in the application of the registration provisions of the Act.

It should be noted that the statutory language of Section 2(11) is in the disjunctive. Thus, it is insufficient to conclude that a person is not an underwriter solely because he did not purchase securities from an issuer with a view to their distribution. It must also be established that the person is not offering or selling for an issuer in connection with the distribution of the securities, does not participate or have a direct or indirect participation in any such undertaking, and does not participate or have a participation in the direct or indirect underwriting of such an undertaking.

In determining when a person is deemed not to be engaged in a distribution several factors must be considered.

First, the purpose and underlying policy of the Act to protect investors requires that there be adequate current information concerning the issuer, whether the resales of securities by persons result in a distribution or are effected in trading transactions. Accordingly, the availability of the rule is conditioned on the existence of adequate current public information.

Secondly, a holding period prior to resale is essential, among other reasons, to assure that those persons who buy under a claim of a Section 4(2) exemption have assumed the economic risks of investment, and therefore are not acting as conduits for sale to the public of unregistered securities, directly or indirectly, on behalf of an issuer. It should be noted that there is nothing in Section 2(11) which places a time limit on a person's status as an underwriter. The public has the same need for protection afforded by registration whether the securities are distributed shortly after their purchase or after a considerable length of time.

A third factor, which must be considered in determining what is deemed not to constitute a "distribution," is the impact of the particular transaction or transactions on the trading markets. Section 4(1) was intended to exempt only routine trading transactions between individual investors with respect to securities already issued and not to exempt distributions by issuers or acts of other individuals who engage in steps necessary to such distributions. Therefore, a person reselling securities under Section 4(1) of the Act must sell the securities in such limited quantities and in such a manner as not to disrupt the trading markets. The larger the amount of securities involved, the more likely it is that such resales may involve methods of offering and amounts of compensation usually associated with a distribution rather than routine trading transactions. Thus, solicitation of buy orders or the payment of extra compensation are not permitted by the rule.

In summary, if the sale in question is made in accordance with *all* of the provisions of the rule, as set forth below, any person who sells restricted securities shall be deemed not to be engaged in a distribution of such securities and therefore not an underwriter thereof. The rule also provides that any person who sells restricted or other securities on behalf of a person in a control relationship with the issuer shall be deemed not to be engaged in a distribution of such securities and therefore not to be an underwriter thereof, if the sale is made in accordance with *all* the conditions of the rule.

Rule 144. (a) *Definitions.* The following definitions shall apply for the purposes of this rule.

(1) An "affiliate" of an issuer is a person that directly, or indirectly through one or more intermediaries, controls, or is controlled by, or is under common control with, such issuer.

(2) The term "person" when used with reference to a person for whose account securities are to be sold in reliance upon this rule includes, in addition to such person, all of the following persons:

(i) Any relative or spouse of such person, or any relative of such spouse, any one of whom has the same home as such person;

(ii) Any trust or estate in which such person or any of the persons specified in paragraph (a)(2)(i) of this section collectively own ten percent or more of the total beneficial interest or of which any of such persons serve as trustee, executor or in any similar capacity; and

(iii) Any corporation or other organization (other than the issuer) in which such person or any of the persons specified in paragraph (a)(2)(i) of this section are the beneficial owners collectively of ten percent or more of any class of equity securities or ten percent or more of the equity interest.

(3) The term *restricted securities* means:

(i) Securities acquired directly or indirectly from the issuer, or from an affiliate of the issuer, in a transaction or chain of transactions not involving any public offering;

(ii) Securities acquired from the issuer that are subject to the resale limitations of § 230.502(d) under Regulation D or § 230.701(c);

(iii) Securities acquired in a transaction or chain of transactions meeting the requirements of § 230.144A;

(iv) Securities acquired from the issuer in a transaction subject to the conditions of Regulation CE (§ 230.1001);

(v) Equity securities of domestic issuers acquired in a transaction or chain of transactions subject to the conditions of § 230.901 or § 230.903 under Regulation S (§ 230.901 through § 230.905, and Preliminary Notes);

(vi) Securities acquired in a transaction made under § 230.801 to the same extent and proportion that the securities held by the security holder of the class with respect to which the rights offering was made were as of the record date for the rights offering "restricted securities" within the meaning of this paragraph (a)(3); and

(vii) Securities acquired in a transaction made under § 230.802 to the same extent and proportion that the securities that were tendered or exchanged in the exchange offer or business combination were "restricted securities" within the meaning of this paragraph (a)(3).

(b) *Conditions to be Met.* Any affiliate or other person who sells restricted securities of an issuer for his own account, or any person who sells restricted or any other securities for the account of an affiliate of the issuer of such securities, shall be deemed not to be engaged in a distribution of such securities and therefore not to be an underwriter thereof within the meaning of Section 2(11) of the Act if all of the conditions of this rule are met.

(c) *Current Public Information.* There shall be available adequate current public information with respect to the issuer of the securities. Such information shall be deemed to be available only if either of the following conditions is met:

(1) *Filing of reports.* The issuer has securities registered pursuant to section 12 of the Securities Exchange Act of 1934, has been subject to the reporting requirements of section 13 of that Act for a period of at least 90 days immediately preceding the sale of the securities and has filed all the reports required to be filed thereunder during the 12 months preceding such sale (or for such shorter period that the issuer was required to file such reports), other than Form 8-K reports (§ 249.308 of this chapter); or has securities registered pursuant to the Securities Act of 1933, has been subject to the reporting requirements of section 15(d) of the Securities Exchange Act of 1934 for a period of at least 90 days immediately preceding the sale of the securities and has filed all the reports required to be filed thereunder during the 12 months preceding such sale (or

for such shorter period that the issuer was required to file such reports), other than Form 8-K reports (§ 249.308 of this chapter). The person for whose account the securities are to be sold shall be entitled to rely upon a statement in whichever is the most recent report, quarterly or annual, required to be filed and filed by the issuer that such issuer has filed all reports required to be filed by section 13 or 15(d) of the Securities Exchange Act of 1934 during the preceding 12 months (or for such shorter period that the issuer was required to file such reports), other than Form 8-K reports (§ 249.308 of this chapter), and has been subject to such filing requirements for the past 90 days, unless he knows or has reason to believe that the issuer has not complied with such requirements. Such person shall also be entitled to rely upon a written statement from the issuer that it has complied with such reporting requirements unless he knows or has reasons to believe that the issuer has not complied with such requirements.

(2) *Other Public Information.* If the issuer is not subject to Section 13 or 15(d) of the Securities Exchange Act of 1934, there is publicly available the information concerning the issuer specified in paragraph (a)(5)(i) to (xiv), inclusive, and paragraph (a)(5)(xvi) of Rule 15c2-11 (§ 240.15c2-11 of this chapter) under that Act or, if the issuer is an insurance company, the information specified in Section 12(g)(2)(G)(i) of that Act.

(d) *Holding Period for Restricted Securities.* If the securities sold are restricted securities, the following provisions apply:

(1) *General Rule.* A minimum of one year must elapse between the later of the date of the acquisition of the securities from the issuer or from an affiliate of the issuer, and any resale of such securities in reliance on this section for the account of either the acquiror or any subsequent holder of those securities. If the acquiror takes the securities by purchase, the one-year period shall not begin until the full purchase price or other consideration is paid or given by the person acquiring the securities from the issuer or from an affiliate of the issuer.

(2) *Promissory Notes, Other Obligations or Installment Contracts.* Giving the issuer or affiliate of the issuer from whom the securities were purchased a promissory note or other obligation to pay the purchase price, or entering into an installment purchase contract with such seller, shall not be deemed full payment of the purchase price unless the promissory note, obligation or contract:

(i) provides for full recourse against the purchaser of the securities;

(ii) is secured by collateral, other than the securities purchased, having a fair market value at least equal to the purchase price of the securities purchased; and

(iii) shall have been discharged by payment in full prior to the sale of the securities.

(3) *Determination of Holding Period.* The following provisions shall apply for the purpose of determining the period securities have been held:

(i) *Stock Dividends, Splits and Recapitalizations.* Securities acquired from the issuer as a dividend or pursuant to a stock split, reverse split or recapitalization shall be deemed to have been acquired at the same time as the securities on which the dividend or, if more than one, the initial dividend was paid, the securities involved in the split or reverse split, or the securities surrendered in connection with the recapitalization;

(ii) *Conversions.* If the securities sold were acquired from the issuer for a consideration consisting solely of other securities of the same issuer surrendered for conversion, the securities so acquired shall be deemed to have been acquired at the same time as the securities surrendered for conversion;

(iii) *Contingent Issuance of Securities.* Securities acquired as a contingent payment of the purchase price of an equity interest in a business, or the assets of a business, sold to the issuer or an affiliate of the issuer shall be deemed to have been acquired at the time of such sale if the issuer or affiliate was then committed to issue the securities subject only to conditions other than the payment of further consideration for such securities. An agreement entered into in connection with any such purchase to remain in the employment of, or not to compete with, the issuer or affiliate or the rendering of services pursuant to such agreement shall not be deemed to be the payment of further consideration for such securities.

(iv) *Pledged Securities.* Securities which are bonafide pledged by an affiliate of the issuer when sold by the pledgee, or by a purchaser, after a default in the obligation secured by the pledge, shall be deemed to have been acquired when they were acquired by the pledgor, except that if the securities were pledged without recourse they shall be deemed to have been acquired by the pledgee at the time of the pledge or by the purchaser at the time of purchase.

(v) *Gifts of Securities.* Securities acquired from an affiliate of the issuer by gift shall be deemed to have been acquired by the donee when they were acquired by the donor.

(vi) *Trusts.* Where a trust settlor is an affiliate of the issuer, securities acquired from the settlor by the trust, or acquired from the trust by the beneficiaries thereof, shall be deemed to have been acquired when such securities were acquired by the settlor.

(vii) *Estates.* Where a deceased person was an affiliate of the issuer, securities held by the estate of such person or acquired from such estate by the beneficiaries thereof shall be deemed to have been acquired when they were acquired by the deceased person, except that no holding period is required if the estate is not an affiliate of the issuer or if the securities are sold by a beneficiary of the estate who is not such an affiliate.

> *NOTE.* While there is no holding period or amount limitation for estates and beneficiaries thereof which are not affiliates of the issuer, paragraphs (c), (h) and (i) of the rule apply to securities sold by such persons in reliance upon the rule.

(viii) *Rule 145(a) transactions.* The holding period for securities acquired in a transaction specified in Rule 145(a) shall be deemed to commence on the date the securities were acquired by the purchaser in such transaction. This provision shall not apply, however, to a transaction effected solely for the purpose of forming a holding company.

(e) *Limitation on Amount of Securities Sold.* Except as hereinafter provided, the amount of securities which may be sold in reliance upon this rule shall be determined as follows:

(1) *Sales by affiliates.* If restricted or other securities are sold for the account of an affiliate of the issuer, the amount of securities sold, together with all sales of restricted and other securities of the same class for the account of such person within the preceding three months, shall not exceed the greater of (i) one percent of the shares or other units of the class outstanding as shown by the most recent report or statement published by the issuer, or (ii) the average weekly reported volume of trading in such securities on all national securities exchanges and/or reported through the automated quotation system of a registered securities association during the four calendar weeks preceding the filing of notice required by paragraph (h), or if no such notice is required the date of receipt of the order to execute the transaction by the broker or the date of execution of the transaction directly with a market maker, or (iii) the average weekly volume of trading in such securities reported through the consolidated transaction reporting system, contemplated by Rule 11Aa3-1 under the Securities Exchange Act of 1934 (§ 240.11Aa3-1) during the four-week period specified in subdivision (ii) of this paragraph.

(2) *Sales by persons other than affiliates.* The amount of restricted securities sold for the account of any person other than an affiliate of the issuer, together with all other sales of restricted securities of the same class for the account of such person within the preceding three months, shall not exceed the amount specified in paragraphs (e)(1)(i), (1)(ii) or (1)(iii) of this section, whichever is applicable, unless the conditions in paragraph (k) of this rule are satisfied.

(3) *Determination of Amount.* For the purpose of determining the amount of securities specified in paragraphs (e)(1) and (2) of this rule, the following provisions shall apply:

(i) Where both convertible securities and securities of the class into which they are convertible are sold, the amount of convertible securities sold shall be deemed to be the amount of securities of the class into which they are convertible for the purpose of determining the aggregate amount of securities of both classes sold;

(ii) The amount of securities sold for the account of a pledgee thereof, or for the account of a purchaser of the pledged securities, during any period of three months within one year after a default in the obligation secured by the pledge, and the amount of securities sold during the same three-month period for the account of the pledgor shall not exceed, in the aggregate, the amount specified in paragraph (e)(1) or (2) of this section, whichever is applicable;

(iii) The amount of securities sold for the account of a donee thereof during any period of three months within one year after the donation, and the amount of securities sold during the same three-month period for the account of the donor, shall not exceed, in the aggregate, the amount specified in paragraph (e)(1) or (2) of this section, whichever is applicable;

(iv) Where securities were acquired by a trust from the settlor of the trust, the amount of such securities sold for the account of the trust during any period of three months within one year after the acquisition of the securities by the trust, and the amount of securities sold during the same three-month period for the account of the settlor, shall not exceed, in the aggregate, the amount specified in paragraph (e)(1) or (2) of this section, whichever is applicable;

(v) The amount of securities sold for the account of the estate of a deceased person, or for the account of a beneficiary of such estate, during any period of three months and the amount of securities sold during the same period for the account of the deceased person prior to his death shall not exceed, in the aggregate, the amount specified in subparagraph (1) or (2) of this paragraph, whichever is applicable; *Provided,* That no limitation on amount shall apply if the estate or beneficiary thereof is not an affiliate of the issuer;

(vi) When two or more affiliates or other persons agree to act in concert for the purpose of selling securities of an issuer, all securities of the same class sold for the account of all such persons during any period of three months shall be aggregated for the purpose of determining the limitation on the amount of securities sold;

(vii) The following sales of securities need not be included in determining the amount of securities sold in reliance upon this section: securities sold pursuant to an effective registration statement under the Act; securities sold pursuant to an exemption provided by Regulation A (§ 230.251 through § 230.263) under the Act; securities sold in a transaction exempt pursuant to Section 4 of the Act (15 U.S.C. 77d) and not involving any public offering; and securities sold offshore pursuant to Regulation S (§ 230.901 through § 230.905, and Preliminary Notes) under the Act.

(f) *Manner of sale.* The securities shall be sold in "brokers' transactions" within the meaning of section 4(4) of the Act or in transactions directly with a "market maker," as that term is defined in section 3(a)(38) of the Securities Exchange Act of 1934, and the person selling the securities shall not (1) solicit or arrange for the solicitation of orders to buy the securities in anticipation of or in connection with such transaction, or (2) make any payment in connection with the offer or sale of the securities to any person other than the broker who executes the order to sell the securities. The requirements of this paragraph, however, shall not apply to securities sold for the account of the estate of a deceased person or for the account of a beneficiary of such estate provided the estate or beneficiary thereof is not an affiliate of the issuer; nor shall they apply to securities sold for the account of any person other than an affiliate of the issuer, provided the conditions of paragraph (k) of this rule are satisfied.

(g) *Brokers' Transactions.* The term "brokers' transactions" in Section 4(4) of the Act shall for the purposes of this rule be deemed to include transactions by a broker in which such broker—

(1) does no more than execute the order or orders to sell the securities as agent for the person for whose account the securities are sold; and receives no more than the usual and customary broker's commission;

(2) neither solicits nor arranges for the solicitation of customers' orders to buy the securities in anticipation of or in connection with the transaction; provided, that the foregoing shall not preclude (*i*) inquiries by the broker of other brokers or dealers who have indicated an interest in the securities within the preceding 60 days, (*ii*) inquiries by the broker of his customers who have indicated an unsolicited bona fide interest in the securities within the preceding 10 business days; or (*iii*) the publication by the broker of bid and ask quotations for the security in an inter-dealer quotation system provided that such quotations are incident to the maintenance of a bona fide inter-dealer market for the security for the broker's own account and that the broker has published bona fide bid and ask quotations for the security in an inter-dealer quotation system on each of at least twelve days within the preceding thirty calendar days with no more than four business days in succession without such two-way quotations;

Note to Paragraph g(2)(ii): The broker should obtain and retain in his files written evidence of indications of bona fide unsolicited interest by his customers in the securities at the time such indications are received.

(3) after reasonable inquiry is not aware of circumstances indicating that the person for whose account the securities are sold is an underwriter with respect to the securities or that the transaction is a part of a distribution of securities of the issuer. Without limiting the foregoing, the broker shall be deemed to be aware of any facts or statements contained in the notice required by paragraph (h) below.

Notes. (i) The broker, for his own protection, should obtain and retain in his files a copy of the notice required by paragraph (h).

(ii) The reasonable inquiry required by paragraph (g)(3) of this section should include, but not necessarily be limited to, inquiry as to the following matters:

a. The length of time the securities have been held by the person for whose account they are to be sold. If practicable, the inquiry should include physical inspection of the securities;

b. The nature of the transaction in which the securities were acquired by such person;

c. The amount of securities of the same class sold during the past three months by all persons whose sales are required to be taken into consideration pursuant to paragraph (e) of this section;

d. Whether such person intends to sell additional securities of the same class through any other means;

e. Whether such person has solicited or made any arrangement for the solicitation of buy orders in connection with the proposed sale of securities;

f. Whether such person has made any payment to any other person in connection with the proposed sale of the securities; and

g. The number of shares or other units of the class outstanding, or the relevant trading volume.

(h) *Notice of proposed sale.* If the amount of securities to be sold in reliance upon the rule during any period of three months exceeds 500 shares or other units or has an aggregate sale price in excess of $10,000, three copies of a notice on Form 144 shall be filed with the Commission at its principal office in Washington, D.C.; and if such securities are admitted to trading on any national securities exchange, one copy of such notice shall also be transmitted to the principal exchange on which such securities are so admitted. The Form 144 shall be signed by the person for whose account the securities are to be sold and shall be transmitted for filing concurrently with either the placing with a broker of an order to execute a sale of securities in reliance upon this rule or the execution directly with a market maker of such a sale. Neither the filing of such notice nor the failure of the Commission to comment thereon shall be deemed to preclude the Commission from taking any action it deems necessary or appropriate with respect to the sale of the securities referred to in such notice. The requirements of this paragraph, however, shall not apply to securities sold for the account of any person other than an affiliate of the issuer, provided the conditions of paragraph (k) of this rule are satisfied.

(i) *Bona Fide Intention to Sell.* The person filing the notice required by paragraph (h) shall have a bona fide intention to sell the securities referred to therein within a reasonable time after the filing of such notice.

(j) *Non-exclusive rule.* Although this rule provides a means for reselling restricted securities and securities held by affiliates without registration, it is not the exclusive means for reselling such securities in that manner. Therefore, it does not eliminate or otherwise affect the availability of any exemption for resales under the Securities Act that a person or entity may be able to rely upon.

(k) *Termination of certain restrictions on sales of restricted securities by persons other than affiliates.* The requirements of paragraphs (c), (e), (f) and (h) of this section shall not apply to restricted securities sold for the account of a person who is not an affiliate of the issuer at the time of the sale and has not been an affiliate during the preceding three months, provided a period of at least two years has elapsed since the later of the date the securities were acquired from the issuer or from an affiliate of the issuer. The two-year period shall be calculated as described in paragraph (d) of this section.

Rule 144A. Private Resales of Securities to Institutions
Preliminary Notes to Rule 144A

1. This section relates solely to the application of Section 5 of the Act and not to antifraud or other provisions of the federal securities laws.

2. Attempted compliance with this section does not act as an exclusive election; any seller hereunder may also claim the availability of any other applicable exemption from the registration requirements of the Act.

3. In view of the objective of this section and the policies underlying the Act, this section is not available with respect to any transaction or series of transactions that, although in technical compliance with this section, is part of a plan or scheme to evade the registration provisions of the Act. In such cases, registration under the Act is required.

4. Nothing in this section obviates the need for any issuer or any other person to comply with the securities registration or broker-dealer registration requirements of the Securities Exchange Act of 1934 (the "Exchange Act"), whenever such requirements are applicable.

5. Nothing in this section obviates the need for any person to comply with any applicable state law relating to the offer or sale of securities.

6. Securities acquired in a transaction made pursuant to the provisions of this section are deemed to be "restricted securities" within the meaning of § 230.144 (a) (3) of this chapter.

7. The fact that purchasers of securities from the issuer thereof may purchase such securities with a view to reselling such securities pursuant to this section will not affect the availability to such issuer of an exemption under Section 4(2) of the Act, or Regulation D under the Act, from the registration requirements of the Act.

Rule 144A.

(a) *Definitions*

(1) For purposes of this section, "qualified institutional buyer" shall mean:

(i) Any of the following entities, acting for its own account or the accounts of other qualified institutional buyers, that in the aggregate owns and invests on a discretionary basis at least $100 million in securities of issuers that are not affiliated with the entity:

(A) Any *insurance company* as defined in Section 2(13) of the Act;

NOTE: A purchase by an insurance company for one or more of its separate accounts, as defined by section 2(a)(37) of the Investment Company Act of 1940 (the "Investment Company Act"), which are neither registered under section 8 of the Investment Company Act nor required to be so registered, shall be deemed to be a purchase for the account of such insurance company.

(B) Any *investment company* registered under the Investment Company Act or any *business development company* as defined in Section 2(a)(48) of that Act;

(C) Any *Small Business Investment Company* licensed by the U.S. Small Business Administration under Section 301(c) or (d) of the Small Business Investment Act of 1958;

(D) Any *Plan* established and maintained by a state, its political subdivisions, or any agency or instrumentality of state or its political subdivisions, for the benefit of its employees;

(E) Any *employee benefit plan* within the meaning of Title I of the Employee Retirement Income Security Act of 1974;

(F) Any *trust fund* whose trustee is a bank or trust company and whose participants are exclusively plans of the types identified in paragraph (a)(1)(i)(D) or (E) of this section, except trust funds that include as participants individual retirement accounts or H.R. 10 plans.

(G) Any *business development company* as defined in Section 202(a)(22) of the Investment Advisers Act of 1940;

(H) Any *organization described in Section 501(c)(3)* of the Internal Revenue Code, *corporation (other than a bank as defined in Section 3(a)(2) of the Act or a savings and loan association or other institution referenced in Section 3(a)(5)(A) of the Act or a foreign bank or savings and loan association or equivalent institution), partnership, or Massachusetts or similar business trust;* and

(I) Any *investment adviser* registered under the Investment Advisers Act.

(ii) Any *dealer* registered pursuant to Section 15 of the Exchange Act, acting for its own account or the accounts of other qualified institutional buyers, that in the aggregate owns and invests on a discretionary basis at least $10 million of securities of issuers that are not affiliated with the dealer, *provided that* securities constituting the whole or a part of an unsold allotment to or subscription by a dealer as a participant in a public offering shall not be deemed to be owned by such dealer;

(iii) Any *dealer* registered pursuant to Section 15 of the Exchange Act acting in a riskless principal transaction on behalf of a qualified institutional buyer;

NOTE: A registered dealer may act as agent, on a non-discretionary basis, in a transaction with a qualified institutional buyer without itself having to be a qualified institutional buyer.

(iv) Any investment company registered under the Investment Company Act, acting for its own account or for the accounts of other qualified institutional buyers, that is part of a *family of investment companies* which own in the aggregate at least $100 million in securities of issuers other than issuers that are affiliated with the investment company or are part of such family of investment companies. "Family of investment companies" means any two or more investment companies registered under the Investment Company Act, except for a unit investment trust whose assets consist solely of shares of one or more registered investment companies, that have the same investment adviser (or, in the case of unit investment trusts, the same depositor), *provided that,* for purposes of this section:

(A) each series of a series company (as defined in Rule 18f-2 under the Investment Company Act [17 CFR 270.18f-2]) shall be deemed to be a separate investment company; and

(B) investment companies shall be deemed to have the same adviser (or depositor) if their advisers (or depositors) are majority-owned subsidiaries of the same parent, or if one investment company's adviser (or depositor) is a majority-owned subsidiary of the other investment company's adviser (or depositor);

(v) Any entity, all of the equity owners of which are qualified institutional buyers, acting for its own account or the accounts of other qualified institutional buyers; and

(vi) Any *bank* as defined in Section 3(a)(2) of the Act, any *savings and loan association* or other institution as referenced in Section 3(a)(5)(A) of the Act, *or any foreign bank or savings and loan association or equivalent institution,* acting for its own account or the accounts of other qualified institutional buyers, that in the aggregate owns and invests on a discretionary basis at least $100 million in securities of issuers that are not affiliated with it and that has an audited net worth of at least $25 million as demonstrated in its latest annual financial statements, as of a date not more than 16 months preceding the date of sale under the Rule in the case of a U.S. bank or savings and loan association, and not more than 18 months preceding such date of sale for a foreign bank or savings and loan association or equivalent institution.

(2) In determining the aggregate amount of securities owned and invested on a discretionary basis by an entity, the following instruments and interests shall be excluded: bank deposit notes and certificates of deposit; loan participations; repurchase agreements; securities owned but subject to a repurchase agreement; and currency, interest rate and commodity swaps.

(3) The aggregate value of securities owned and invested on a discretionary basis by an entity shall be the cost of such securities, except where the entity reports its securities holdings in its financial statements on the basis of their market value, and no current information with respect to the cost of those securities has been published. In the latter event, the securities may be valued at market for purposes of this section.

(4) In determining the aggregate amount of securities owned by an entity and invested on a discretionary basis, securities owned by subsidiaries of the entity that are consolidated with the entity in its financial statements prepared in accordance with generally accepted accounting principles may be included if the investments of such subsidiaries are managed under the direction of the entity, except that, unless the entity is a reporting company under Section 13 or

15(d) of the Exchange Act, securities owned by such subsidiaries may not be included if the entity itself is a majority-owned subsidiary that would be included in the consolidated financial statements of another enterprise.

(5) For purposes of this section, "riskless principal transaction" means a transaction in which a dealer buys a security from any person and makes a simultaneous offsetting sale of such security to a qualified institutional buyer, including another dealer acting as riskless principal for a qualified institutional buyer.

(6) For purposes of this section, "effective conversion premium" means the amount, expressed as a percentage of the security's conversion value, by which the price at issuance of a convertible security exceeds its conversion value.

(7) For purposes of this section, "effective exercise premium" means the amount, expressed as a percentage of the warrant's exercise value, by which the sum of the price at issuance and the exercise price of a warrant exceeds its exercise value.

(b) *Sales by Persons other than Issuers or Dealers.* Any person, other than the issuer or a dealer, who offers or sells securities in compliance with the conditions set forth in paragraph (d) of this section shall be deemed not to be engaged in a distribution of such securities and therefore not to be an underwriter of such securities within the meaning of Sections 2(11) and 4(1) of the Act.

(c) *Sales by Dealers.* Any dealer who offers or sells securities in compliance with the conditions set forth in paragraph (d) of this section shall be deemed not to be a participant in a distribution of such securities within the meaning of Section 4(3)(C) of the Act and not to be an underwriter of such securities within the meaning of Section 2(11) of the Act, and such securities shall be deemed not to have been offered to the public within the meaning of Section 4(3)(A) of the Act.

(d) *Conditions to be Met.* To qualify for exemption under this section, an offer or sale must meet the following conditions:

(1) The securities are offered or sold only to a qualified institutional buyer or to an offeree or purchaser that the seller and any person acting on behalf of the seller reasonably believe is a qualified institutional buyer. In determining whether a prospective purchaser is a qualified institutional buyer, the seller and any person acting on its behalf shall be entitled to rely upon the following non-exclusive methods of establishing the prospective purchaser's ownership and discretionary investments of securities:

(i) The prospective purchaser's most recent publicly available financial statements, *provided that* such statements present the information as of a date within 16 months preceding the date of sale of securities under this section in the case of a U.S. purchaser and within 18 months preceding such date of sale for a foreign purchaser;

(ii) The most recent publicly available information appearing in documents filed by the prospective purchaser with the Commission or another United States federal, state, or local governmental agency or self-regulatory organization, or with a foreign governmental agency or self-regulatory organization, *provided that* any such information is as of a date within 16 months preceding the date of sale of securities under this section in the case of a U.S. purchaser and within 18 months preceding such date of sale for a foreign purchaser;

(iii) The most recent publicly available information appearing in a recognized securities manual, *provided that* such information is as of a date within 16 months preceding the date of sale of securities under this section in the case of a U.S. purchaser and within 18 months preceding such date of sale for a foreign purchaser; or

(iv) A certification by the chief financial officer, a person fulfilling an equivalent function, or other executive officer of the purchaser, specifying the amount of securities owned and invested on a discretionary basis by the purchaser as of a specific date on or since the close of the purchaser's most recent fiscal year, or, in the case of a purchaser that is a member of a family of investment companies, a certification by an executive officer of the investment adviser specifying the amount of securities owned by the family of investment companies as of a specific date on or since the close of the purchaser's most recent fiscal year;

(2) The seller and any person acting on its behalf takes reasonable steps to ensure that the purchaser is aware that the seller may rely on the exemption from the provisions of Section 5 of the Act provided by this section;

(3) The securities offered or sold:

(i) Were not, when issued, of the same class as securities listed on a national securities exchange registered under Section 6 of the Exchange Act or quoted in a U.S. automated inter-dealer quotation system; *Provided,* that securities that are convertible or exchangeable into securities so listed or quoted at the time of issuance and that had an effective conversion premium of less than 10 percent, shall be treated as securities of the class into which they are convertible or exchangeable; and that warrants that may be exercised for securities so listed or quoted at the time of issuance, for a period of less than 3 years from the date of issuance, or that had an effective exercise premium of less than 10 percent, shall be treated as securities of the class to be issued upon exercise; and *provided further* that the Commission may from time to time, taking into account then-existing market practices, designate additional securities and classes of securities that will not be deemed of the same class as securities listed on a national securities exchange or quoted in a U.S. automated inter-dealer quotation system; and

(ii) Are not securities of an open-end investment company, unit investment trust or face-amount certificate company that is or is required to be registered under Section 8 of the Investment Company Act; and

(4) (i) In the case of securities of an issuer that is neither subject to Section 13 or 15(d) of the Exchange Act, nor exempt from reporting pursuant to Rule 12g3-2(b) (§ 240.12g3-2(b) of this chapter) under the Exchange Act, nor a foreign government as defined in Rule 405 (§ 230.405 of this chapter) eligible to register securities under Schedule B of the Act, the holder and a prospective purchaser designated by the holder have the right to obtain from the issuer, upon request of the holder, and the prospective purchaser has received from the issuer, the seller, or a person acting on either of their behalf, at or prior to the time of sale, upon such prospective purchaser's request to the holder or the issuer, the following information (which shall be reasonably current in relation to the date of resale under this section): a very brief statement of the nature of the business of the issuer and the products and services it offers; and the issuer's most recent balance sheet and profit and loss and retained earnings statements, and similar financial statements for such part of the two preceding fiscal years as the issuer has been in operation (the financial statements should be audited to the extent reasonably available).

(ii) The requirement that the information be "reasonably current" will be presumed to be satisfied if:

(A) the balance sheet is as of a date less than 16 months before the date of resale, the statements of profit and loss and retained earnings are for the 12 months preceding the date of such balance sheet, and if such balance sheet is not as of a date less than 6 months before the date of resale, it shall be accompanied by additional statements of profit and loss and retained earnings for the period from the date of such balance sheet to a date less than 6 months before the date of resale; and

(B) the statement of the nature of the issuer's business and its products and services offered is as of a date within 12 months prior to the date of resale; or

(C) with regard to foreign private issuers, the required information meets the timing requirements of the issuer's home country or principal trading markets.

(e) Offers and sales of securities pursuant to this section shall be deemed not to affect the availability of any exemption or safe harbor relating to any previous or subsequent offer or sale of such securities by the issuer or any prior or subsequent holder thereof.

Rule 145. Reclassifications of Securities, Mergers, Consolidations and Acquisitions of Assets

Preliminary Note

Rule 145 (§ 230.145 of this chapter) is designed to make available the protection provided by registration under the Securities Act of 1933, as amended (Act), to persons who are offered securities in a business combination of the type described in paragraphs (a)(1), (2) and (3) of the rule. The thrust of the rule is that an *offer, offer to sell, offer for sale,* or *sale* occurs when there is submitted to security holders a plan or agreement pursuant to which such holders are required to elect, on the basis of what is in substance a new investment decision, whether to accept a new or different security in exchange for their existing security. Rule 145 embodies the Commission's determination that such transactions are subject to the registration requirements of the Act, and that the previously existing *no-sale* theory of Rule 133 is no longer consistent with the statutory purposes of the Act. *See* Release No. 33-5316 (October 6, 1972) [37 FR 23631]. Securities issued in transactions described in paragraph (a) of Rule 145 may be registered on Form S-4 or F-4 (§ 239.25 or § 239.34 of this chapter) or Form N-14 (§ 239.23 of this chapter) under the Act.

Transactions for which statutory exemptions under the Act, including those contained in sections 3(a)(9), (10), (11) and 4(2), are otherwise available are not affected by Rule 145.

NOTE 1: Reference is made to Rule 153a (§ 230.153a of this chapter) describing the prospectus delivery required in a transaction of the type referred to in Rule 145.

NOTE 2: A reclassification of securities covered by Rule 145 would be exempt from registration pursuant to section 3(a)(9) or (11) of the Act if the conditions of either of these sections are satisfied.

[Text of Rule]

(a) *Transactions within this section.* An *offer, offer to sell, offer for sale* or *sale* shall be deemed to be involved, within the meaning of section 2(3) of the Act, so far as the security holders of a corporation or other person are concerned where, pursuant to statutory provisions of the jurisdiction under which such corporation or other person is organized, or pursuant to provisions contained in its certificate of incorporation or similar controlling instruments, or otherwise, there is submitted for the vote or consent of such security holders a plan or agreement for:

(1) *Reclassifications.* A reclassification of securities of such corporation or other person, other than a stock split, reverse stock split, or change in par value, which involves the substitution of a security for another security;

(2) *Mergers or Consolidations.* A statutory merger or consolidation or similar plan or acquisition in which securities of such corporation or other person held by such security holders will become or be exchanged for securities of any person, unless the sole purpose of the transaction is to change an issuer's domicile solely within the United States; or

(3) *Transfers of assets.* A transfer of assets of such corporation or other person, to another person in consideration of the issuance of securities of such other person or any of its affiliates, if:

(i) Such plan or agreement provides for dissolution of the corporation or other person whose security holders are voting or consenting; or

(ii) Such plan or agreement provides for a pro rata or similar distribution of such securities to the security holders voting or consenting; or

(iii) The board of directors or similar representatives of such corporation or other person, adopts resolutions relative to paragraph (a)(3)(i) or (ii) of this section within 1 year after the taking of such vote or consent; or

(iv) The transfer of assets is a part of a pre-existing plan for distribution of such securities, notwithstanding paragraph (a)(3)(i), (ii), or (iii) of this section.

(b) *Communications before a Registration Statement is filed.* Communications made in connection with or relating to a transaction described in paragraph (a) of this section that will be registered under the Act may be made under § 230.135, § 230.165 or § 230.166.

(c) *Persons and parties deemed to be underwriters.* For purposes of this section, any party to any transaction specified in paragraph (a) of this section, other than the issuer, or any person who is an affiliate of such party at the time any such transaction is submitted for vote or consent, who publicly offers or sells securities of the issuer acquired in connection with any such transaction, shall be deemed to be engaged in a distribution and therefore to be an underwriter thereof within the meaning of section 2(11) of the Act. The term *party* as used in this paragraph (c) shall mean the corporations, business entities, or other persons, other than the issuer, whose assets or capital structure are affected by the transactions specified in paragraph (a) of this section.

(d) *Resale provisions for persons and parties deemed underwriters.* Notwithstanding the provisions of paragraph (c), a person or party specified therein shall not be deemed to be engaged in a distribution and therefore not to be an underwriter of registered securities acquired in a transaction specified in paragraph (a) of this section if:

(1) Such securities are sold by such person or party in accordance with the provisions of paragraphs (c), (e), (f) and (g) of §230.144;

(2) Such person or party is not an affiliate of the issuer, and a period of at least one year, as determined in accordance with paragraph (d) of §230.144, has elapsed since the date the securities were acquired from the issuer in such transaction, and the issuer meets the requirements of paragraph (c) of §230.144; or

(3) Such person or party is not, and has not been for at least three months, an affiliate of the issuer, and a period of at least two years, as determined in accordance with paragraph (d) of §230.144, has elapsed since the date the securities were acquired from the issuer in such transaction.

(e) *Definition of Person.* The term *person* as used in paragraphs (c) and (d) of this section, when used with reference to a person for whose account securities are to be sold, shall have the same meaning as the definition of that term in paragraph (a)(2) of §230.144.

Rule 146. Rules Under Section 18 of the Act

(a) *Prepared by or on behalf of the issuer.* An offering document (as defined in Section 18(d)(1) of the Act [15 U.S.C. 77r(d)(1)]) is "prepared by or on behalf of the issuer" for purposes of Section 18 of the Act, if the issuer or an agent or representative:

(1) Authorizes the document's production, and (a)(2) Approves the document before its use.

(b) *Covered securities for purposes of Section 18.*

(1) For purposes of Section 18(b) of the Act (15 U.S.C. 77r), the Commission finds that the following national securities exchanges, or segments or tiers thereof, have listing standards that are substantially similar to those of the New York Stock Exchange ("NYSE"), the American Stock Exchange ("Amex"), or the National Market System of the Nasdaq Stock Market ("Nasdaq/ NMS"), and that securities listed on such exchanges shall be deemed covered securities:

(i) Tier I of the Pacific Exchange, Incorporated;

(ii) Tier I of the Philadelphia Stock Exchange, Incorporated;

(iii) The Chicago Board Options Exchange, Incorporated; and

(iv) Options listed on the International Securities Exchange, Incorporated.

(2) The designation of securities in paragraphs (b)(1)(i) through (iv) of this section as covered securities is conditioned on such exchanges' listing standards (or segments or tiers thereof) continuing to be substantially similar to those of the NYSE, Amex, or Nasdaq/NMS.

Rule 147. "Part of an Issue," "Person Resident," and "Doing Business Within" for Purposes of Section 3(a)(11)

Preliminary Notes

1. This rule shall not raise any presumption that the exemption provided by Section 3(a)(11) of the Act is not available for transactions by an issuer which do not satisfy all of the provisions of the rule.

2. Nothing in this rule obviates the need for compliance with any state law relating to the offer and sale of the securities.

3. Section 5 of the Act requires that all securities offered by the use of the mails or by any means or instruments of transportation or communication in interstate commerce be registered with the Commission. Congress, however, provided certain exemptions in the Act from such registration provisions where there was no practical need for registration or where the benefits of registration were too remote. Among those exemptions is that provided by Section 3(a)(11) of the Act for transactions in "any security which is a part of an issue offered and sold only to persons resident within a single State or Territory, where the issuer of such security is a person resident and doing business within ... such State or Territory." The legislative history of that Section

suggests that the exemption was intended to apply only to issues genuinely local in character, which in reality represent local financing by local industries, carried out through local investment. Rule 147 is intended to provide more objective standards upon which responsible local business-men intending to raise capital from local sources may rely in claiming the Section 3(a)(11) exemption.

All of the terms and conditions of the rule must be satisfied in order for the rule to be available. These are: (i) that the issuer be a resident of and doing business within the state or territory in which all offers and sales are made; and (ii) that no part of the issue be offered or sold to nonresidents within the period of time specified in the rule. For purposes of the rule the definition of "issuer" in Section 2(4) of the Act shall apply.

All offers, offers to sell, offers for sale, and sales which are part of the same issue must meet all of the conditions of Rule 147 for the rule to be available. The determination whether offers, offers to sell, offers for sale and sales of securities are part of the same issue (i.e., are deemed to be "integrated") will continue to be a question of fact and will depend on the particular circumstances. See Securities Act of 1933 Release No. 4434 (December 6, 1961). Release 33-4434 indicates that in determining whether offers and sales should be regarded as part of the same issue and thus should be integrated any one or more of the following factors may be determinative:

　(i)　Are the offerings part of a single plan of financing;

　(ii)　Do the offerings involve issuance of the same class of securities;

　(iii)　Are the offerings made at or about the same time;

　(iv)　Is the same type of consideration to be received; and

　(v)　Are the offerings made for the same general purpose.

Subparagraph (b)(2) of the rule, however, is designed to provide certainty to the extent feasible by identifying certain types of offers and sales of securities which will be deemed not part of an issue, for purposes of the rule *only*.

Persons claiming the availability of the rule have the burden of proving that they have satisfied all of its provisions. However, the rule does not establish exclusive standards for complying with the Section 3(a)(11) exemption. The exemption would also be available if the issuer satisfied the standards set forth in relevant administrative and judicial interpretations at the time of the offering but the issuer would have the burden of proving the availability of the exemption. Rule 147 relates to transactions exempted from the registration requirements of Section 5 of the Act by Section 3(a)(11). Neither the rule nor Section 3(a)(11) provides an exemption from the registration requirements of Section 12(g) of the Securities Exchange Act of 1934, the anti-fraud provisions of the federal securities laws, the civil liability provisions of Section 12(2) of the Act or other provisions of the federal securities laws.

Finally, in view of the objectives of the rule and the purposes and policies underlying the Act, the rule shall not be available to any person with respect to any offering which, although in technical compliance with the rule, is part of a plan or scheme by such person to make interstate offers or sales of securities. In such cases registration pursuant to the Act is required.

4. The rule provides an exemption for offers and sales by the issuer *only*. It is not available for offers or sales of securities by other persons. Section 3(a)(11) of the Act has been interpreted to permit offers and sales by persons controlling the issuer, if the exemption provided by that Section would have been available to the issuer at the time of the offering. See Securities Act Release No. 4434 (December 6, 1961). Controlling persons who want to offer or sell securities pursuant to Section 3(a)(11) may continue to do so in accordance with applicable judicial and administrative interpretations.

　(a) *Transactions Covered.*

Offers, offers to sell, offers for sale and sales by an issuer of its securities made in accordance with all of the terms and conditions of this rule shall be deemed to be part of an issue offered and sold only to persons resident and doing business within such state or territory, within the meaning of Section 3(a)(11) of the Act.

(b) *Part of an Issue.*

(1) For purposes of this rule, all securities of the issuer which are part of an issue shall be offered, offered for sale or sold in accordance with all of the terms and conditions of this rule.

(2) For purposes of this rule only, an issue shall be deemed not to include offers, offers to sell, offers for sale or sales of securities of the issuer pursuant to the exemptions provided by Section 3 or Section 4(2) of the Act or pursuant to a registration statement filed under the Act, that take place prior to the six month period immediately preceding or after the six month period immediately following any offers, offers for sale or sales pursuant to this rule, *provided that,* there are during either of said six month periods no offers, offers for sale or sales of securities by or for the issuer of the same or similar class as those offered, offered for sale or sold pursuant to the rule.

> NOTE: In the event that securities of the same or similar class as those offered pursuant to the rule are offered, offered for sale or sold less than six months prior to or subsequent to any offer, offer for sale or sale pursuant to this rule, see Preliminary Note 3 hereof, as to which offers, offers to sell, offers for sale, or sales are part of an issue.

(c) *Nature of the Issuer.*

The issuer of the securities shall at the time of any offers and the sales be a person resident and doing business within the state or territory in which all of the offers, offers to sell, offers for sale and sales are made.

(1) The issuer shall be deemed to be a resident of the state or territory in which:

(i) it is incorporated or organized, if a corporation, limited partnership, trust or other form of business organization that is organized under state or territorial law;

(ii) its principal office is located, if a general partnership or other form of business organization that is not organized under any state or territorial law;

(iii) his principal residence is located, if an individual.

(2) The issuer shall be deemed to be doing business within a state or territory if:

(i) the issuer derived at least 80% of its gross revenues and those of its subsidiaries on a consolidated basis;

(A) for its most recent fiscal year, if the first offer of any part of the issue is made during the first six months of the issuer's current fiscal year; or

(B) for the first six months of its current fiscal year or during the twelve month fiscal period ending with such six month period, if the first offer of any part of the issue is made during the last six months of the issuer's current fiscal year from the operation of a business or of real property located in or from the rendering of services within such state or territory; provided, however, that this provision does not apply to any issuer which has not had gross revenues in excess of $5,000 from the sale of products or services or other conduct of its business for its most recent twelve month fiscal period;

(ii) the issuer had at the end of its most recent semi-annual fiscal period prior to the first offer of any part of the issue, at least 80 percent of its assets and those of its subsidiaries on a consolidated basis located within such state or territory;

(iii) the issuer intends to use and uses at least 80% of the net proceeds to the issuer from sales made pursuant to this rule in connection with the operation of a business or of real property, the purchase of real property located in, or the rendering of services within such state or territory; and

(iv) the principal office of the issuer is located within such state or territory.

(d) *Offerees and Purchasers: Person Resident.*

Offers, offers to sell, offers for sale and sales of securities that are part of an issue shall be made only to persons resident within the state or territory of which the issuer is a resident. For purposes of determining the residence of offerees and purchasers:

(1) A corporation, partnership, trust or other form of business organization shall be deemed to be a resident of a state or territory if, at the time of the offer and sale to it, it has its principal office within such state or territory.

(2) An individual shall be deemed to be a resident of a state or territory if such individual has, at the time of the offer and sale to him, his principal residence in the state or territory.

(3) A corporation, partnership, trust or other form of business organization which is organized for the specific purpose of acquiring part of an issue offered pursuant to this rule shall be deemed not to be a resident of a state or territory unless all of the beneficial owners of such organization are residents of such state or territory.

(e) *Limitation of Resales.*

During the period in which securities that are part of an issue are being offered and sold by the issuer, and for a period of nine months from the date of the last sale by the issuer of such securities, all resales of any part of the issue, by any person, shall be made only to persons resident within such state or territory.

NOTES: 1. In the case of convertible securities resales of either the convertible security, or if it is converted, the underlying security, could be made during the period described in paragraph (e) only to persons resident within such state or territory. For purposes of this rule a conversion in reliance on Section 3(a)(9) of the Act does not begin a new period.

2. Dealers must satisfy the requirements of Rule 15c2-11 under the Securities Exchange Act of 1934 prior to publishing any quotation for a security, or submitting any quotation for publication, in any quotation medium.

(f) *Precautions Against Interstate Offers and Sales.*

(1) The issuer shall, in connection with any securities sold by it pursuant to this rule:

(i) Place a legend on the certificate or other document evidencing the security stating that the securities have not been registered under the Act and setting forth the limitations on resale contained in paragraph (e);

(ii) Issue stop transfer instructions to the issuer's transfer agent, if any, with respect to the securities, or, if the issuer transfers its own securities, make a notation in the appropriate records of the issuer; and

(iii) Obtain a written representation from each purchaser as to his residence.

(2) The issuer shall, in connection with the issuance of new certificates for any of the securities that are part of the same issue that are presented for transfer during the time period specified in paragraph (e), take the steps required by subsections (f)(1)(i) and (ii).

(3) The issuer shall, in connection with any offers, offers to sell, offers for sale or sales by it pursuant to this rule, disclose, in writing, the limitations on resale contained in paragraph (e) and the provisions of subsections (f)(1)(i) and (ii) and subparagraph (f)(2).

Rule 148. Persons Not Deemed to be Underwriters of Securities Issued or Sold in Connection with Bankruptcy Proceedings

[Removed and reserved in Release No. 33-7300, May 31, 1996, effective July 15, 1996, 61 F.R. 30397.]

Rule 149. Definition of "Exchanged" in Section 3(a)(9), for Certain Transactions

The term "exchanged" in section 3(a)(9) shall be deemed to include the issuance of a security in consideration of the surrender by the existing security holders of the issuer, of outstanding securities of the issuer, notwithstanding the fact that the surrender of the outstanding securities may be required by the terms of the plan of exchange to be accompanied by such payment in cash by the security holder as may be necessary to effect an equitable adjustment, in respect of dividends or interest paid or payable on the securities involved in the exchange, as between such security holder and other security holders of the same class accepting the offer of exchange.

Rule 150. Definition of "Commission or Other Remuneration" in Section 3(a)(9), for Certain Transactions

The term "commission or other remuneration" in Section 3(a)(9) shall not include payments made by the issuer, directly or indirectly, to its security holders in connection with an exchange of securities for outstanding securities, when such payments are part of the terms of the offer of exchange.

Rule 151. Safe Harbor Definition of Certain "Annuity Contracts or Optional Annuity Contracts" Within the Meaning of Section 3(a)(8)

(a) Any annuity contract or optional annuity contract (a "contract") shall be deemed to be within the provisions of section 3(a)(8) of the Securities Act of 1933 [15 U.S.C. 77c(a)(8)], *Provided,* That

(1) The annuity or optional annuity contract is issued by a corporation (the "insurer") subject to the supervision of the insurance commissioner, bank commissioner, or any agency or officer performing like functions, of any –State or Territory of the United States or the District of Columbia;

(2) The insurer assumes the investment risk under the contract as prescribed in paragraph (b) of this rule; and

(3) The contract is not marketed primarily as an investment.

(b) The insurer shall be deemed to assume the investment risk under the contract if:

(1) The value of the contract does not vary according to the investment experience of a separate account;

(2) The insurer for the life of the contract

(i) Guarantees the principal amount of purchase payments and interest credited thereto, less any deduction (without regard to its timing) for sales, administrative or other expenses or charges; and

(ii) Credits a specified rate of interest (as defined in paragraph (c) of this rule) to net purchase payments and interest credited thereto; and

(3) The insurer guarantees that the rate of any interest to be credited in excess of that described in paragraph (b)(2)(ii) will not be modified more frequently than once per year.

(c) The term "specified rate of interest," as used in paragraph (b)(2)(ii) of this rule, means a rate of interest under the contract that is at least equal to the minimum rate required to be credited by the relevant nonforfeiture law in the jurisdiction in which the contract is issued. If that jurisdiction does not have an applicable nonforfeiture law at the time the contract is issued (or if the minimum rate applicable to an existing contract is no longer mandated in that jurisdiction), the specified rate under the contract must at least be equal to the minimum rate then required for individual annuity contracts by the NAIC Standard Nonforfeiture Law.

Rule 152. Definition of "Transactions by an Issuer Not Involving Any Public Offering" in Section 4(2), for Certain Transactions

The phrase "transactions by an issuer not involving any public offering" in Section 4(2) shall be deemed to apply to transactions not involving any public offering at the time of said transactions although subsequently thereto the issuer decides to make a public offering and/or files a registration statement.

Rule 152a. Offer or Sale of Certain Fractional Interests

Any offer or sale of a security, evidenced by a scrip certificate, order form or similar document which represents a fractional interest in a share of stock or similar security shall be deemed a transaction by a person other than an issuer, underwriter or dealer, within the meaning of Section 4(1) of the Act, if the fractional interest (a) resulted from a stock dividend, stock split, reverse stock split, conversion, merger or similar transaction, and (b) is offered or sold pursuant to arrangements for the purchase and sale of fractional interests among the persons entitled to such fractional interests for the purpose of combining such interests into whole shares, and for the sale of such number of whole shares as may be necessary to compensate security holders for any remaining fractional interests not so combined, notwithstanding that the issuer or an affiliate of the issuer may act on behalf of or as agent for the security holders in effecting such transactions.

Rule 153. Definition of "Preceded by a Prospectus," as Used in Section 5(b)(2), in Relation to Certain Transactions

(a) The term "preceded by a prospectus," as used in Section 5(b)(2) of the Securities Act of 1933, as amended, in respect of any requirement of delivery of a prospectus to a member of a national securities exchange, on account of a transaction in a security effected on such exchange, shall mean delivery, prior to such transaction, of copies of a prospectus descriptive of such security and meeting the requirements of Section 10(a), to such exchange by the issuer or any underwriter, for the purpose of redelivery to members of such exchange upon their request, *Provided,* That as to any transaction occurring prior to the expiration of forty days after the effective date of the registration statement or the expiration of forty days after the first date upon which the security was *bona fide* offered to the public by the issuer or by or through an underwriter after such effective date, whichever is later (exclusive of the time during which a stop order issued under Section 8 is in effect as to such security):

(1) Such exchange shall theretofore have requested of the issuer or, if such request shall not have been complied with, of a "principal underwriter" (as that term is defined in § 230.405), from time to time, such number of copies of such prospectus as may have appeared reasonably necessary to comply with the requests of its members, and shall have delivered from its supply on hand a copy to any member theretofore making a written request therefor: and

(2) The issuer or any underwriter shall theretofore have furnished such exchange with such reasonable number of copies of such prospectus as may have been requested by the exchange for the purpose stated above.

["National Securities Exchange" Defined]

(b) The term "national securities exchange," as used herein, shall mean a securities exchange registered as a national securities exchange under the Securities Exchange Act of 1934, as amended.

Rule 153a. Definition of "Preceded by a Prospectus" as Used in Section 5(b)(2) in Relation to Certain Transactions Requiring Approval of Security Holders

The term "preceded by a prospectus", as used in Section 5(b)(2) of the Act with respect to any requirement for the delivery of a prospectus to security holders of a corporation or other person, in connection with transactions of the character specified in paragraph (a) of Rule 145 under the Act, shall mean the delivery of a prospectus:

(i) prior to the vote of security holders on such transaction; or,

(ii) with respect to actions taken by consent, prior to the earliest date on which the corporate action may be taken;

to all security holders of record of such corporation or other person, entitled to vote on or consent to the proposed transaction, at their address of record on the transfer records of the corporation or other person:

Rule 153b. Definition of "Preceded by a Prospectus," as Used in Section 5(b)(2), in Connection with Certain Transactions in Standardized Options

The term "preceded by a prospectus", as used in Section 5(b)(2) of the Act with respect to any requirement for the delivery of a prospectus relating to standardized options registered on Form S-20, shall mean the delivery, prior to any transactions, of copies of such prospectus to each options market upon which the options are traded, for the purpose of redelivery to options customers upon their request, *Provided* That:

(a) Such options market shall thereto have requested of the issuer, from time to time, such number of copies of such prospectus as may have appeared reasonably necessary to comply with the requests of options customers, and shall have delivered promptly from its supply on hand a copy to any options customer making a request thereof; and

(b) The issuer shall have furnished such options market with such reasonable number of copies of such prospectus as may have been requested by the options market for the purpose stated above.

Rule 154. Delivery of Prospectuses to Investors at the Same Address

(a) *Delivery of a single prospectus.* If you must deliver a prospectus under the federal securities laws, for purposes of sections 5(b) and 2(a)(10) of the Act (15 U.S.C. 77e(b) and 77b(a)(10)) or § 240.15c2-8(b) of this chapter, you will be considered to have delivered a prospectus to investors who share an address if:

(1) You deliver a prospectus to the shared address;

(2) You address the prospectus to the investors as a group (for example, "ABC Fund [or Corporation] Shareholders," "Jane Doe and Household," "The Smith Family") or to each of the investors individually (for example, "John Doe and Richard Jones"); and

(3) The investors consent in writing to delivery of one prospectus.

(b) *Implied consent.* You do not need to obtain written consent from an investor under paragraph (a)(3) of this section if all of the following conditions are met:

(1) The investor has the same last name as the other investors, or you reasonably believe that the investors are members of the same family;

(2) You have sent the investor a notice at least 60 days before you begin to rely on this section concerning delivery of prospectuses to that investor. The notice must be a separate written statement and:

(i) State that only one prospectus will be delivered to the shared address unless you receive contrary instructions;

(ii) Include a toll-free telephone number or be accompanied by a reply form that is pre-addressed with postage provided, that the investor can use to notify you that he or she wishes to receive a separate prospectus;

(iii) State the duration of the consent;

(iv) Explain how an investor can revoke consent;

(v) State that you will begin sending individual copies to an investor within 30 days after you receive revocation of the investor's consent; and

(vi) Contain the following prominent statement, or similar clear and understandable statement, in bold-face type: "Important Notice Regarding Delivery of Shareholder Documents." This statement also must appear on the envelope in which the notice is delivered. Alternatively, if the notice is delivered separately from other communications to investors, this statement may appear either on the notice or on the envelope in which the notice is delivered;

NOTE to Sec. 230.154(b)(2): The notice should be written in plain English. See § 230.421(d)(2) of this chapter for a discussion of plain English principles.

(3) You have not received the reply form or other notification indicating that the investor wishes to continue to receive an individual copy of the prospectus, within 60 days after you sent the notice; and

(4) You deliver the prospectus to a post office box or to a residential street address. You can assume a street address is a residence unless you have information that indicates it is a business.

(c) *Revocation of consent.* If an investor, orally or in writing, revokes consent to delivery of one prospectus to a shared address (provided under paragraphs (a)(3) or (b) of this section), you must begin sending individual copies to that investor within 30 days after you receive the revocation. If the individual's consent concerns delivery of the prospectus of a registered open-end management investment company, at least once a year you must explain to investors who have consented how they can revoke their consent. The explanation must be reasonably designed to reach these investors.

(d) *Definition of address.* For purposes of this section, *address* means a street address, a post office box number, an electronic mail address, a facsimile telephone number, or other similar destination to which paper or electronic documents are delivered, unless otherwise provided in this section. If you have reason to believe that an address is the street address of a multi-unit building, the address must include the unit number.

Rule 155. Integration of Abandoned Offerings
Preliminary Note

Compliance with paragraph (b) or (c) of this section provides a non-exclusive safe harbor from integration of private and registered offerings. Because of the objectives of Rule 155 and the policies underlying the Act, Rule 155 is not available to any issuer for any transaction or series of transactions that, although in technical compliance with the rule, is part of a plan or scheme to evade the registration requirements of the Act.

(a) *Definition of terms.* For the purposes of this section only, a *private offering* means an unregistered offering of securities that is exempt from registration under Section 4(2) or 4(6) of the Act (15 U.S.C. §§ 77d(2) and 77d(6)) or § 230.506 of Regulation D.

(b) *Abandoned private offering followed by a registered offering.* A private offering of securities will not be considered part of an offering for which the issuer later files a registration statement if:

(1) No securities were sold in the private offering;

(2) The issuer and any person(s) acting on its behalf terminate all offering activity in the private offering before the issuer files the registration statement;

(3) The Section 10(a) final prospectus and any Section 10 preliminary prospectus used in the registered offering disclose information about the abandoned private offering, including:

(i) The size and nature of the private offering;

(ii) The date on which the issuer abandoned the private offering;

(iii) That any offers to buy or indications of interest given in the private offering were rejected or otherwise not accepted; and

(iv) That the prospectus delivered in the registered offering supersedes any offering materials used in the private offering; and

(4) The issuer does not file the registration statement until at least 30 calendar days after termination of all offering activity in the private offering, unless the issuer and any person acting on its behalf offered securities in the private offering only to persons who were (or who the issuer reasonably believes were):

(i) Accredited investors (as that term is defined in § 230.501(a)); or

(ii) Persons who satisfy the knowledge and experience standard of § 230.506(b)(2)(ii).

(c) *Abandoned registered offering followed by a private offering.* An offering for which the issuer filed a registration statement will not be considered part of a later commenced private offering if:

(1) No securities were sold in the registered offering;

(2) The issuer withdraws the registration statement under § 230.477;

(3) Neither the issuer nor any person acting on the issuer's behalf commences the private offering earlier than 30 calendar days after the effective date of withdrawal of the registration statement under § 230.477;

(4) The issuer notifies each offeree in the private offering that:

(i) The offering is not registered under the Act;

(ii) The securities will be "restricted securities" (as that term is defined in § 230.144(a)(3)) and may not be resold unless they are registered under the Act or an exemption from registration is available;

(iii) Purchasers in the private offering do not have the protection of Section 11 of the Act (15 U.S.C. 77k); and

(iv) A registration statement for the abandoned offering was filed and withdrawn, specifying the effective date of the withdrawal; and

(5) Any disclosure document used in the private offering discloses any changes in the issuer's business or financial condition that occurred after the issuer filed the registration statement that are material to the investment decision in the private offering.

Rule 156. Investment Company Sales Literature

(a) Under the federal securities laws, including section 17(a) of the Securities Act of 1933 [15 U.S.C. 77q(a)] and section 10(b) of the Securities Exchange Act of 1934 [15 U.S.C. 78j(b)] and

Rule 10b-5 thereunder [17 CFR Part 240], it is unlawful for any person, directly or indirectly, by the use of any means or instrumentality of interstate commerce or of the mails, to use sales literature which is materially misleading in connection with the offer or sale of securities issued by an investment company. Under these provisions, sales literature is materially misleading if it: (1) contains an untrue statement of a material fact or (2) omits to state a material fact necessary in order to make a statement made, in the light of the circumstances of its use, not misleading.

(b) Whether or not a particular description, representation, illustration, or other statement involving a material fact is misleading depends on evaluation of the context in which it is made. In considering whether a particular statement involving a material fact is or might be misleading, weight should be given to all pertinent factors, including, but not limited to, those listed below:

(1) A statement could be misleading because of:

(i) Other statements being made in connection with the offer of sale or sale of the securities in question;

(ii) The absence of explanations, qualifications, limitations or other statements necessary or appropriate to make such statement not misleading; or

(iii) General economic or financial conditions or circumstances.

(2) Representations about past or future investment performance could be misleading because of statements or omissions made involving a material fact, including situations where:

(i) Portrayals of past income, gain, or growth of assets convey an impression of the net investment results achieved by an actual or hypothetical investment which would not be justified under the circumstances, including portrayals that omit explanations, qualifications, limitations, or other statements necessary or appropriate to make the portrayals not misleading; and

(ii) Representations, whether express or implied, about future investment performance, including: (A) Representations, as to security of capital, possible future gains or income, or expenses associated with an investment; (B) Representations implying that future gain or income may be inferred from or predicted based on past investment performance; or (C) Portrayals of past performance, made in a manner which would imply that gains or income realized in the past would be repeated in the future.

(3) A statement involving a material fact about the characteristics or attributes of an investment company could be misleading because of:

(i) Statements about possible benefits connected with or resulting from services to be provided or methods of operation which do not give equal prominence to discussion of any risks or limitations associated therewith;

(ii) Exaggerated or unsubstantiated claims about management skill or techniques, characteristics of the investment company or an investment in securities issued by such company, services, security of investment or funds, effects of government supervision, or other attributes; and

(iii) Unwarranted or incompletely explained comparisons to other investment vehicles or to indexes.

(c) For purposes of this section, the term *sales literature* shall be deemed to include any communication (whether in writing, by radio, or by television) used by any person to offer to sell or induce the sale of securities of any investment company. Communications between issuers, underwriters and dealers are included in this definition of sales literature if such communications, or the information contained therein, can be reasonably expected to be communicated to prospective investors in the offer or sale of securities or are designed to be employed in either written or oral form in the sale of securities.

Rule 157. Small Entities Under the Securities Act for Purposes of the Regulatory Flexibility Act

For purposes of Commission rulemaking in accordance with the provisions of Chapter Six of the Administrative Procedure Act [5 U.S.C. § 601 *et seq.*], and unless otherwise defined for purposes of a particular rulemaking proceeding, the term "small business" or "small organization" shall—

(a) When used with reference to an issuer, other than an investment company, for purposes of the Securities Act of 1933, mean an issuer whose total assets on the last day of its most recent fiscal year were $5,000,000 or less and that is engaged or proposing to engage in small business financing. An issuer is considered to be engaged or proposing to engage in small business financing under this section if it is conducting or proposes to conduct an offering of securities which does not exceed the dollar limitation prescribed by section 3(b) of the Securities Act.

(b) When used with reference to an investment company that is an issuer for purposes of the Act, have the meaning ascribed to those terms by § 270.0-10 of this chapter.

Rule 158. Definitions of Certain Terms in the Last Paragraph of Section 11(a)

(a) An "earning statement" made generally available to security holders of the registrant pursuant to the last paragraph of section 11(a) of the Act shall be sufficient for the purposes of such paragraph if:

(1) there is included the information required for statements of income contained either:

(i) in Item 8 of Form 10-K and Form 10-KSB (§ 249.310 and 249.310b of this chapter), Part I, Item 1 of Form 10-Q and Form 10-QSB (§ 249.308a and § 249.308b of this chapter), or Rule 14a-3(b) (Section 240.14a-3(b) of this chapter) under the Securities Exchange Act of 1934;

(ii) in Item 17 of Form 20-F (Section 249.220f of this chapter), if appropriate; or

(iii) In Form 40-F (§ 249.240f of this chapter); and

(2) The information specified in the last paragraph of Section 11(a) is contained in one report or any combination of reports either:

(i) On Form 10-K and Form 10-KSB, Form 10-Q and Form 10-QSB, Form 8-K (§ 249.308 of this chapter), or in the annual report to securityholders pursuant to Rule 14a-3 under the Securities Exchange Act of 1934; or

(ii) On Form 20-F, Form 40-F or Form 6-K (§ 249.306 of this chapter).

A subsidiary issuing debt securities guaranteed by its parent will be deemed to have met the requirements of this paragraph if the parent's income statements satisfy the criteria of this paragraph and information respecting the subsidiary is included to the same extent as was presented in the registration statement. An "earning statement" not meeting the requirements of this paragraph may otherwise be sufficient for purposes of the last paragraph of Section 11(a).

(b) For purposes of the last paragraph of Section 11(a) only, the "earning statement" contemplated by paragraph (a) of this section shall be deemed to be "made generally available to its security holders" if the registrant:

(1) is required to file reports pursuant to Section 13 or 15(d) of the Securities Exchange Act of 1934 and

(2) has filed its report or reports on Form 10-K and Form 10-KSB, Form 10-Q and Form 10-QSB, Form 8-K, Form 20-F, Form 40-F, or Form 6-K, or has supplied to the Commission copies of the annual report sent to securityholders pursuant to Rule 14a-3(c), containing such information.

A registrant may use other methods to make an earning statement "generally available to its securityholders" for purposes of the last paragraph of section 11(a).

(c) For purposes of the last paragraph of section 11(a) only, the "effective date of the registration statement" is deemed to be the date of the latest to occur of (1) the effective date of the registration statement; (2) the effective date of the last post-effective amendment to the registration statement, next preceding a particular sale by the registrant of registered securities to the public filed for purposes of (i) including any prospectus required by section 10(a)(3) of the Act, (ii) reflecting in the prospectus any facts or events arising after the effective date of the registration statement (or the most recent post-effective amendment thereof) which, individually or in the aggregate, represent a fundamental change in the information set forth in the registration statement, or (iii) including any material information with respect to the plan of distribution not previously disclosed in this registration statement or any material change to such information in the registration statement, or (3) the date of filing of the last report of the registrant incorporated by reference into the prospectus, and relied upon in lieu of filing a post-effective amendment for purposes of paragraphs (c)(2)(i) and (ii) of this rule, next preceding a particular sale by the registrant of registered securities to the public.

(d) If an earnings statement was made available by "other methods" than those specified in paragraphs (a) and (b) of this section, the earnings statement must be filed as exhibit 99 to the next periodic report required by section 13 or 15(d) of the Exchange Act covering the period in which the earnings statement was released.

Rule 161. Amendments to Rules and Regulations Governing Exemptions

The rules and regulations governing the exemption of securities under Section 3(b) of the Act, as in effect at the time the securities are first bona fide offered to the public in conformity therewith, shall continue to govern the exemption of such securities notwithstanding the subsequent amendment of such rules and regulations. This rule shall not apply, however, to any new offering of such securities by an issuer or underwriter after the effective date of any such amendment, nor shall it apply to any offering after January 1, 1959, of securities by an issuer or underwriter pursuant to Regulation D or pursuant to Regulation A as in effect at any time prior to July 23, 1956.

Rule 162. Submission of Tenders in Registered Exchange Offers

(a) Notwithstanding Section 5(a) of the Act (15 U.S.C. 77e(a)), offerors may solicit tenders of securities in an exchange offer subject to § 240.13e-4(e) or § 240.14d-4(b) of this chapter before a registration statement is effective as to the security offered, so long as no securities are purchased until the registration statement is effective and the tender offer has expired in accordance with the tender offer rules.

(b) Notwithstanding Section 5(b)(2) of the Act (15 U.S.C. 77e(b)(2)), a prospectus that meets the requirements of Section 10(a) of the Act (15 U.S.C. 77j(a)) need not be delivered to security holders in an exchange offer subject to § 240.13e-4(e) or § 240.14d-4(b) of this chapter, so long as a preliminary prospectus, prospectus supplements and revised prospectuses are delivered to security holders in accordance with § 240.13e-4(e)(2) or § 240.14d-4(b) of this chapter, as applicable.

Rule 165. Offers Made in Connection with a Business Combination Transaction
Preliminary Note

This section is available only to communications relating to business combinations. The exemption does not apply to communications that may be in technical compliance with this section, but have the primary purpose or effect of conditioning the market for another transaction, such as a capital-raising or resale transaction.

(a) *Communications before a registration statement is filed.* Notwithstanding Section 5(c) of the Act (15 U.S.C. 77e(c)), the offeror of securities in a business combination transaction to be registered under the Act may make an offer to sell or solicit an offer to buy those securities from and including the first public announcement until the filing of a registration statement related to the transaction, so long as any written communication (other than non-public communications among participants) made in connection with or relating to the transaction (*i.e.*, prospectus) is filed in accordance with § 230.425 and the conditions in paragraph (c) of this section are satisfied.

(b) *Communications after a registration statement is filed.* Notwithstanding Section 5(b)(1) of the Act (15 U.S.C. 77e(b)(1)), any written communication (other than non-public communications among participants) made in connection with or relating to a business combination transaction (*i.e.*, prospectus) after the filing of a registration statement related to the transaction need not satisfy the requirements of Section 10 (15 U.S.C. 77j) of the Act, so long as the prospectus is filed in accordance with § 230.424 or § 230.425 and the conditions in paragraph (c) of this section are satisfied.

(c) *Conditions.* To rely on paragraphs (a) and (b) of this section:

(1) Each prospectus must contain a prominent legend that urges investors to read the relevant documents filed or to be filed with the Commission because they contain important

information. The legend also must explain to investors that they can get the documents for free at the Commission's web site and describe which documents are available free from the offeror; and

(2) In an exchange offer, the offer must be made in accordance with the applicable tender offer rules (§ § 240.14d-1 through 240.14e-8 of this chapter); and, in a transaction involving the vote of security holders, the offer must be made in accordance with the applicable proxy or information statement rules (§ § 240.14a-1 through 240.14a-101 and § § 240.14c-1 through 240.14c-101 of this chapter).

(d) This section is applicable not only to the offeror of securities in a business combination transaction, but also to any other participant that may need to rely on and complies with this section in communicating about the transaction.

(e) An immaterial or unintentional failure to file or delay in filing a prospectus described in this section will not result in a violation of Section 5(b)(1) or (c) of the Act (15 U.S.C. 77e(b)(1) and (c)), so long as:

(1) A good faith and reasonable effort was made to comply with the filing requirement; and

(2) The prospectus is filed as soon as practicable after discovery of the failure to file.

(f) *Definitions.*

(1) A *business combination transaction* means any transaction specified in § 230.145(a) or exchange offer;

(2) A *participant* is any person or entity that is a party to the business combination transaction and any persons authorized to act on their behalf; and

(3) *Public announcement* is any oral or written communication by a participant that is reasonably designed to, or has the effect of, informing the public or security holders in general about the business combination transaction.

Rule 166. Exemption from Section 5(c) for Certain Communications in Connection with Business Combination Transactions
Preliminary Note

This section is available only to communications relating to business combinations. The exemption does not apply to communications that may be in technical compliance with this section, but have the primary purpose or effect of conditioning the market for another transaction, such as a capital-raising or resale transaction.

(a) In a registered offering involving a business combination transaction, any communication made in connection with or relating to the transaction before the first public announcement of the offering will not constitute an offer to sell or a solicitation of an offer to buy the securities offered for purposes of Section 5(c) of the Act (15 U.S.C. 77e(c)), so long as the participants take all reasonable steps within their control to prevent further distribution or publication of the communication until either the first public announcement is made or the registration statement related to the transaction is filed.

(b) *Definitions.* The terms business combination transaction, participant and public announcement have the same meaning as set forth in § 230.165(f) of this chapter.

Rule 170. Prohibition of Use of Certain Financial Statements

Financial statements which purport to give effect to the receipt and application of any part of the proceeds from the sale of securities for cash shall not be used unless such securities are to be offered through underwriters and the underwriting arrangements are such that the underwriters are or will be committed to take and pay for all of the securities, if any are taken, prior to or within a reasonable time after the commencement of the public offering, or if the securities are not so taken to refund to all subscribers the full amount of all subscription payments made for the securities. The caption of any such financial statement shall clearly set forth the assumptions upon which such statement is based. The caption shall be in type at least as large as that used generally in the body of the statement.

Rule 171. Disclosure Detrimental to the National Security

(a) Any requirement to the contrary notwithstanding, no registration statement, prospectus, or other document filed with the Commission or used in connection with the offering or sale of any securities shall contain any document or information which, pursuant to Executive order, has been classified by an appropriate department or agency of the United States for protection in the interest of national defense or foreign policy.

(b) Where a document or information is omitted pursuant to paragraph (a) of this section, there shall be filed, in lieu of such document or information, a statement from an appropriate department or agency of the United States to the effect that such document or information has been classified or that the status thereof is awaiting determination. Where a document is omitted pursuant to paragraph (a) of this section, but information relating to the subject-matter of such document is nevertheless included in material filed with the Commission pursuant to a determination of an appropriate department or agency of the United States that disclosure of such information would not be contrary to the interests of national defense or foreign policy, a statement from such department or agency to that effect shall be submitted for the information of the Commission. A registrant may rely upon any such statement in filing or omitting any document or information to which the statement relates.

(c) The Commission may protect any information in its possession which may require classification in the interests of national defense or foreign policy pending determination by an appropriate department or agency as to whether such information should be classified.

(d) It shall be the duty of the registrant to submit the documents or information referred to in paragraph (a) of this section to the appropriate department or agency of the United States prior to filing them with the Commission and to obtain and submit to the Commission, at the time of filing such documents or information, or in lieu thereof, as the case may be, the statements from such department or agency required by paragraph (b) of this section. All such statements shall be in writing.

Rule 174. Delivery of Prospectus by Dealers; Exemptions under Section 4(3) of the Act

The obligations of a dealer (including an underwriter no longer acting as an underwriter in respect of the security involved in such transactions) to deliver a prospectus in transactions in a security as to which a registration statement has been filed taking place prior to the expiration of the 40 or 90 day period specified in Section 4(3) of the Act after the effective date of such registration statement or prior to the expiration of such period after the first date upon which the security was bona fide offered to the public by the issuer or by or through an underwriter after such effective date, whichever is later, shall be subject to the following provisions:

(a) No prospectus need be delivered if the registration statement is on Form F-6 (§ 239.36 of this chapter).

(b) No prospectus need be delivered if the issuer is subject, immediately prior to the time of filing the registration statement, to the reporting requirements of Section 13 or 15(d) of the Securities Exchange Act of 1934.

(c) Where a registration statement relates to offerings to be made from time to time no prospectus need be delivered after the expiration of the initial prospectus delivery period specified in Section 4(3) of the Act following the first bona fide offering of securities under such registration statement.

(d) If (1) the registration statement relates to the security of an issuer that is not subject, immediately prior to the time of filing the registration statement, to the reporting requirements of Section 13 or 15(d) of the Securities Exchange Act of 1934, and (2) as of the offering date, the security is listed on a registered national securities exchange or authorized for inclusion in an electronic inter-dealer quotation system sponsored and governed by the rules of a registered securities association, no prospectus need be delivered after the expiration of twenty-five calendar days after the offering date. For purposes of this provision, the term "offering date" refers to the later of the effective date of the registration statement or the first date on which the security was bona fide offered to the public.

(e) Notwithstanding the foregoing, the period during which a prospectus must be delivered by a dealer shall be:

(1) As specified in Section 4(3) of the Act if the registration statement was the subject of a stop order issued under Section 8 of the Act; or

(2) As the Commission may provide upon application or on its own motion in a particular case.

(f) Nothing in this section shall affect the obligation to deliver a prospectus pursuant to the provisions of Section 5 of the Act by a dealer who is acting as an underwriter with respect to the securities involved or who is engaged in a transaction as to securities constituting the whole or a part of an unsold allotment to or subscription by such dealer as a participant in the distribution of such securities by the issuer or by or through an underwriter.

(g) If the registration statement relates to an offering of securities of a "blank check company," as defined in Rule 419 under the Act [17 CFR 230.419], the statutory period for prospectus delivery specified in Section 4(3) of the Act shall not terminate until 90 days after the date funds and securities are released from the escrow or trust account pursuant to Rule 419 under the Act.

Rule 175. Liability for Certain Statements by Issuers

(a) A statement within the coverage of paragraph (b) of this section which is made by or on behalf of an issuer or by an outside reviewer retained by the issuer shall be deemed not to be a fraudulent statement (as defined in paragraph (d) of this section), unless it is shown that such statement was made or reaffirmed without a reasonable basis or was disclosed other than in good faith.

(b) This rule applies to the following statements:

(1) A forward looking statement (as defined in paragraph (c) of this section) made in a document filed with the Commission, in Part I of a quarterly report on Form 10-Q, 17 CFR 249.308a, and Form 10-QSB, 17 CFR 249.308b, or in an annual report to shareholders meeting the requirements of Rules 14a-3(b) and (c) or 14c-3(a) and (b) under the Securities Exchange Act of 1934, a statement reaffirming such forward looking statement subsequent to the date the document was filed or the annual report was made publicly available, or a forward looking statement made prior to the date the document was filed or the date the annual report was made publicly available if such statement is reaffirmed in a filed document or annual report made publicly available within a reasonable time after the making of such forward looking statement; *Provided,* That

(i) At the time such statements are made or reaffirmed, either the issuer is subject to the reporting requirements of section 13(a) or 15(d) of the Securities Exchange Act of 1934 and has complied with the requirements of Rule 13a-1 or 15d-1 thereunder, if applicable, to file its most recent annual report on Form 10-K and Form 10-KSB, Form 20-F or Form 40-F; or if the issuer is not subject to the reporting requirements of section 13(a) or 15(d) of the Securities Exchange Act of 1934, the statements are made in a registration statement filed under the Securities Act of 1933, offering statement or solicitation of interest written document or broadcast script under Regulation A or pursuant to Section 12(b) or (g) of the Securities Exchange Act of 1934, and

(ii) The statements are not made by or on behalf of an issuer that is an investment company registered under the Investment Company Act of 1940;

(2) Information which is disclosed in a document filed with the Commission, in Part I of a quarterly report on Form 10-Q (§ 249.308a of this chapter) and Form 10-QSB (§ 249.308b of this chapter) or in an annual report to shareholders meeting the requirements of Rules 14a-3(b) and (c) or 14c-3(a) and (b) under the Securities Exchange Act of 1934 (§ 240.14a-3(b) and (c) or 240.14c-3(a) and (b) of this chapter) and which relates to

(i) the effects of changing prices on the business enterprise, presented voluntarily or pursuant to Item 303 of Regulation S-K (§ 229.303 of this chapter) or Regulation S- B (§ 228.303 of this chapter) or "Management's Discussion and Analysis of Financial Condition and Results of Operations, or Item 5 of Form 20-F, Operating and Financial Review and Prospects, (§ 249.220f of this chapter)" or Item 302 of Regulation S-K (§ 229.302 of this chapter), "Supplementary financial information," or Rule 3-20(c) of Regulation S-X (§ 210.3-20(c) of this chapter), or

(ii) the value of proved oil and gas reserves (such as a standardized measure of discounted future net cash flows relating to proved oil and gas reserves as set forth in paragraphs 30-34 of Statement of Financial Accounting Standards No. 69) presented voluntarily or pursuant to Item 302 of Regulation S-K (§ 229.302 of this chapter).

(c) For the purpose of this rule the term "forward looking statement" shall mean and shall be limited to:

(1) A statement containing a projection of revenues, income (loss), earnings (loss) per share, capital expenditures, dividends, capital structure or other financial items;

(2) A statement of management's plans and objectives for future operations;

(3) A statement of future economic performance contained in management's discussion and analysis of financial condition and results of operations included pursuant to Item 303 of Regulation S-K (§ 229.303 of this chapter) or Item 5 of Form 20-F; or

(4) Disclosed statements of the assumptions underlying or relating to any of the statements described in (1), (2), or (3) above.

(d) For the purpose of this rule the term "fraudulent statement" shall mean a statement which is an untrue statement of a material fact, a statement false or misleading with respect to any material fact, an omission to state a material fact necessary to make a statement not misleading, or which constitutes the employment of a manipulative, deceptive, or fraudulent device, contrivance, scheme, transaction, act, practice, course of business, or an artifice to defraud, as those terms are used in the Securities Act of 1933 or the rules or regulations promulgated thereunder.

Rule 176. Circumstances Affecting the Determination of What Constitutes Reasonable Investigation and Reasonable Grounds for Belief Under Section 11 of the Securities Act

In determining whether or not the conduct of a person constitutes a reasonable investigation or a reasonable ground for belief meeting the standard set forth in section 11(c), relevant circumstances include, with respect to a person other than the issuer.

(a) The type of issuer;

(b) The type of security;

(c) The type of person;

(d) The office held when the person is an officer;

(e) The presence or absence of another relationship to the issuer when the person is a director or proposed director;

(f) Reasonable reliance on officers, employees, and others whose duties should have given them knowledge of the particular facts (in the light of the functions and responsibilities of the particular person with respect to the issuer and the filing);

(g) When the person is an underwriter, the type of underwriting arrangement, the role of the particular person as an underwriter and the availability of information with respect to the registration; and

(h) Whether, with respect to a fact or document incorporated by reference, the particular person had any responsibility for the fact or document at the time of the filing from which it was incorporated.

Rule 215. Accredited Investor

The term "accredited investor" as used in section 2(15)(ii) of the Securities Act of 1933 [15 U.S.C. 77b(15)(ii)] shall include the following persons:

(a) Any savings and loan association or other institution specified in section 3(a)(5)(A) of the Act whether acting in its individual or fiduciary capacity; any broker or dealer registered pursuant to section 15 of the Securities Exchange Act of 1934; any plan established and maintained by a state, its political subdivisions, or any agency or instrumentality of a state or its political subdivisions, for the benefit of its employees, if such plan has total assets in excess of $5,000,000; any employee benefit plan within the meaning of Title I of the Employee Retirement Income Security Act of 1974, if the investment decision is made by a plan fiduciary, as defined in section 3(21) of such Act, which is a savings and loan association, or if the employee benefit plan has total assets in excess of $5,000,000 or, if a self-directed plan, with investment decisions made solely by persons that are accredited investors;

(b) Any private business development company as defined in section 202(a)(22) of the Investment Advisers Act of 1940;

(c) Any organization described in section 501(c)(3) of the Internal Revenue Code, corporation, Massachusetts or similar business trust, or partnership, not formed for the specific purpose of acquiring the securities offered, with total assets in excess of $5,000,000;

(d) Any director, executive officer, or general partner of the issuer of the securities being offered or sold, or any director, executive officer, or general partner of a general partner of that issuer;

(e) Any natural person whose individual net worth, or joint net worth with that person's spouse, at the time of his purchase exceeds $1,000,000;

(f) Any natural person who had an individual income in excess of $200,000 in each of the two most recent years or joint income with that person's spouse in excess of $300,000 in each of those years and has a reasonable expectation of reaching the same income level in the current year;

(g) Any trust, with total assets in excess of $5,000,000, not formed for the specific purpose of acquiring the securities offered, whose purchase is directed by a sophisticated person as described in § 230.506(b)(2)(ii); and

(h) Any entity in which all of the equity owners are accredited investors.

SPECIAL EXEMPTIONS

Rule 236. Exemption of Shares Offered in Connection with Certain Transactions

Shares of stock or similar security offered to provide funds to be distributed to shareholders of the issuer of such securities in lieu of issuing fractional shares, scrip certificates or order forms, in connection with a stock dividend, stock split, reverse stock split, conversion, merger or similar transaction, shall be exempt from registration under the Act if the following conditions are met:

(a) The issuer of such shares is required to file and has filed reports with the Commission pursuant to Section 13 or 15(d) of the Securities Exchange Act of 1934.

(b) The aggregate gross proceeds from the sale of all shares offered in connection with the transaction for the purpose of providing such funds does not exceed $300,000.

(c) At least ten days prior to the offering of the shares, the issuer shall furnish to the Commission in writing the following information: (1) that it proposes to offer shares in reliance upon the exemption provided by this rule; (2) the estimated number of shares to be so offered; (3) the aggregate market value of such shares as of the latest practicable date; and (4) a brief description of the transaction in connection with which the shares are to be offered.

Rule 238. Exemption for Standarized Options

(a) *Exemption.* Except as expressly provided in paragraphs (b) and (c) of this section, the Act does not apply to any standardized option, as that term is defined by section 240.9b-1(a)(4) of this chapter, that is:

(1) Issued by a clearing agency registered under section 17A of the Securities Exchange Act of 1934 (15 U.S.C. 78q-1); and

(2) Traded on a national securities exchange registered pursuant to section 6(a) of the Securities Exchange Act of 1934 (15 U.S.C. 78f(a)) or on a national securities association registered pursuant to section 15A(a) of the Securities Exchange Act of 1934 (15 U.S.C. 78o-3(a)).

(b) *Limitation.* The exemption provided in paragraph (a) of this section does not apply to the provisions of section 17 of the Act (15 U.S.C. 77q).

(c) *Offers and sales.* Any offer or sale of a standardized option by or on behalf of the issuer of the securities underlying the standardized option, an affiliate of the issuer, or an underwriter, will constitute a contract for sale of, sale of, offer for sale, or offer to sell the underlying securities as defined in section 2(a)(3) of the Act (15 U.S.C. 77b(a)(3)).

REGULATION A—GENERAL EXEMPTIONS
REGULATION A—CONDITIONAL SMALL ISSUES EXEMPTION

Rule 251. Scope of Exemption

A public offer or sale of securities that meets the following terms and conditions shall be exempt under section 3(b) from the registration requirements of the Securities Act of 1933 (the "Securities Act"):

(a) *Issuer.* The issuer of the securities:

(1) is an entity organized under the laws of the United States or Canada, or any State, Province, Territory or possession thereof, or the District of Columbia, with its principal place of business in the United States or Canada;

(2) is not subject to section 13 or 15(d) of the Securities Exchange Act of 1934 (the "Exchange Act") (15 U.S.C. 78a *et seq.*) immediately before the offering;

(3) is not a development stage company that either has no specific business plan or purpose, or has indicated that its business plan is to merge with an unidentified company or companies;

(4) is not an investment company registered or required to be registered under the Investment Company Act of 1940 [15 U.S.C. 80a-1 *et seq.*];

(5) is not issuing fractional undivided interests in oil or gas rights as defined in § 230.300, or a similar interest in other mineral rights; and

(6) is not disqualified because of § 230.262.

(b) *Aggregate Offering Price.* The sum of all cash and other consideration to be received for the securities ("aggregate offering price") shall not exceed $5,000,000, including no more than $1,500,000 offered by all selling security holders, less the aggregate offering price for all securities sold within the twelve months before the start of and during the offering of securities in reliance upon Regulation A. No affiliate resales are permitted if the issuer has not had net income from continuing operations in at least one of its last two fiscal years.

NOTE: Where a mixture of cash and non-cash consideration is to be received, the aggregate offering price shall be based on the price at which the securities are offered for cash. Any portion of the aggregate offering price attributable to cash received in a foreign currency shall be translated into United States currency at a currency exchange rate in effect on or at a reasonable time prior to the date of the sale of the securities. If securities are not offered for cash, the aggregate offering price shall be based on the value of the consideration as established by bona fide sales of that consideration made within a reasonable time, or, in the absence of sales, on the fair value as determined by an accepted standard. Valuations of non-cash consideration must be reasonable at the time made.

(c) *Integration with Other Offerings.* Offers and sales made in reliance on this Regulation A will not be integrated with:

(1) prior offers or sales of securities; or

(2) subsequent offers or sales of securities that are:

(i) registered under the Securities Act, except as provided in § 230.254(d);

(ii) made in reliance on § 230.701;

(iii) made pursuant to an employee benefit plan;

(iv) made in reliance on Regulation S [§ 230.901-904]; or

(v) made more than six months after the completion of the Regulation A offering.

NOTE: If the issuer offers or sells securities for which the safe harbor rules are unavailable, such offers and sales still may not be integrated with the Regulation A offering, depending on the particular facts and circumstances. *See* Securities Act Release No. 4552 (November 6, 1962) [27 FR 11316].

(d) *Offering Conditions.*

(1) *Offers.*

(i) Except as allowed by § 230.254, no offer of securities shall be made unless a Form 1-A offering statement has been filed with the Commission.

(ii) After the Form 1-A offering statement has been filed:

(A) oral offers may be made;

(B) written offers under § 230.255 may be made;

(C) printed advertisements may be published or radio or television broadcasts made, if they state from whom a Preliminary Offering Circular or Final Offering Circular may be obtained, and contain no more than the following information:

(*1*) the name of the issuer of the security;

(*2*) the title of the security, the amount being offered and the per unit offering price to the public;

(*3*) the general type of the issuer's business; and

(*4*) a brief statement as to the general character and location of its property.

(iii) after the Form 1-A offering statement has been qualified, other written offers may be made, but only if accompanied with or preceded by a Final Offering Circular.

(2) *Sales.*

(i) No sale of securities shall be made until:

(A) the Form 1-A offering statement has been qualified;

(B) a Preliminary Offering Circular or Final Offering Circular is furnished to the prospective purchaser at least 48 hours prior to the mailing of the confirmation of sale to that person; and

(C) a Final Offering Circular is delivered to the purchaser with the confirmation of sale, unless it has been delivered to that person at an earlier time.

(ii) Sales by a dealer (including an underwriter no longer acting in that capacity for the security involved in such transaction) that take place within 90 days after the qualification of the Regulation A offering statement may be made only if the dealer delivers a copy of the current offering circular to the purchaser before or with the confirmation of sale. The issuer or under-writer of the offering shall provide requesting dealers with reasonable quantities of the offering circular for this purpose.

(3) *Continuous or delayed offerings.* Continuous or delayed offerings may be made under this Regulation A if permitted by § 230.415.

Rule 252. Offering Statement

(a) *Documents to be Included.* The offering statement consists of the facing sheet of Form 1-A [§ 239.90 of this chapter], the contents required by the form and any other material information necessary to make the required statements, in the light of the circumstances under which they are made, not misleading.

(b) *Paper, printing, language and pagination.* The requirements for offering statements are the same as those specified in § 230.403 for registration statements under the Act.

(c) *Confidential treatment.* A request for confidential treatment may be made under § 230.406 for information required to be filed, and § 200.83 of this chapter for information not required to be filed.

(d) *Signatures.* The issuer, its Chief Executive Officer, Chief Financial Officer, a majority of the members of its board of directors or other governing body, and each selling security holder shall sign the offering statement. If a signature is by a person on behalf of any other person, evidence of authority to sign shall be filed, except where an executive officer signs for the issuer. If the issuer is Canadian, its authorized representative in the United States shall sign. If the issuer is a limited partnership, a majority of the board of directors of any corporate general partner also shall sign.

(e) *Number of copies and where to file.* Seven copies of the offering statement, at least one of which is manually signed, shall be filed with the Commission's main office in Washington, D.C.

(f) [Removed and reserved in Release No. 33-7331, September 17, 1996, effective October 7, 1996, 61 F.R. 49957.].

(g) *Qualification.* (1) If there is no delaying notation as permitted by paragraph (g)(2) of this section or suspension proceeding under §230.258, an offering statement is qualified without Commission action on the 20th calendar day after its filing.

(2) An offering statement containing the following notation can be qualified only by order of the Commission, unless such notation is removed prior to Commission action as described in paragraph (g)(3) of this section:

> This offering statement shall only be qualified upon order of the Commission, unless a subsequent amendment is filed indicating the intention to become qualified by operation of the terms of Regulation A.

(3) The delaying notation specified in paragraph (g)(2) of this section can be removed only by an amendment to the offering statement that contains the following language:

> This offering statement shall become qualified on the 20th calendar day following the filing of this amendment.

(h) *Amendments.*

(1) If any information in the offering statement is amended, an amendment, signed in the same manner as the initial filing, shall be filed. Seven copies of every amendment shall be filed with the Commission's main office in Washington, D.C.

(2) An amendment to include a delaying notation pursuant to paragraph (g)(2) or to remove one pursuant to paragraph (g)(3) of this section after the initial filing of an offering statement may be made by telegram, letter or facsimile transmission. Each such telegraphic amendment shall be confirmed in writing within a reasonable time by filing a signed copy. Such confirmation shall not be deemed an amendment.

Rule 253. Offering Circular

(a) *Contents.* An offering circular shall include the narrative and financial information required by Form 1-A.

(b) *Presentation of Information.* (1) Information in the offering circular shall be presented in a clear, concise and understandable manner and in a type size that is easily readable. Repetition of information should be avoided; cross-referencing of information within the document is permitted.

(2) Where an offering circular is distributed through an electronic medium, issuers may satisfy legibility requirements applicable to printed documents by presenting all required information in a format readily communicated to investors.

(c) *Date.* An offering circular shall be dated approximately as of the date of the qualification of the offering statement of which it is a part.

(d) *Cover page legend.* The cover page of every offering circular shall display the following statement in capital letters printed in boldfaced type at least as large as that used generally in the body of such offering circular:

> THE UNITED STATES SECURITIES AND EXCHANGE COMMISSION DOES NOT PASS UPON THE MERITS OF OR GIVE ITS APPROVAL TO ANY SECURITIES OFFERED OR THE TERMS OF THE OFFERING, NOR DOES IT PASS UPON THE ACCURACY OR COMPLETENESS OF ANY OFFERING CIRCULAR OR OFFERED SELLING LITERATURE. THESE SECURITIES ARE OFFERED PURSUANT TO AN EXEMPTION FROM REGISTRATION WITH THE COMMISSION; HOWEVER, THE COMMISSION HAS NOT MADE AN INDEPENDENT DETERMINATION THAT THE SECURITIES OFFERED HEREUNDER ARE EXEMPT FROM REGISTRATION.

(e) *Revisions.* (1) An offering circular shall be revised during the course of an offering whenever the information it contains has become false or misleading in light of existing circumstances, material developments have occurred, or there has been a fundamental change in the information initially presented.

(2) An offering circular for a continuous offering shall be updated to include, among other things, updated financial statements, 12 months after the date the offering statement was qualified.

(3) Every revised or updated offering circular shall be filed as an amendment to the offering statement and requalified in accordance with § 230.252.

Rule 254. Solicitation of Interest Document for Use Prior to an Offering Statement

(a) An issuer may publish or deliver to prospective purchasers a written document or make scripted radio or television broadcasts to determine whether there is any interest in a contemplated securities offering. Following submission of the written document or script of the broadcast to the Commission, as required by paragraph (b) of this section, oral communications with prospective investors and other broadcasts are permitted. The written documents, broadcasts and oral communications are each subject to the antifraud provisions of the federal securities laws. No solicitation or acceptance of money or other consideration, nor of any commitment, binding or otherwise, from any prospective investor is permitted. No sale may be made until qualification of the offering statement.

(b) While not a condition to any exemption pursuant to this section:

(1) On or before the date of its first use, the issuer shall submit a copy of any written document or the script of any broadcast with the Commission's main office in Washington, D.C. (*Attention*: Office of Small Business Review). The document or broadcast script shall either contain or be accompanied by the name and telephone number of a person able to answer questions about the document or the broadcast.

NOTE: Only solicitation of interest material that contains substantive changes from or additions to previously submitted material needs to be submitted.

(2) The written document or script of the broadcast shall:

(i) state that no money or other consideration is being solicited, and if sent in response, will not be accepted;

(ii) state that no sales of the securities will be made or commitment to purchase accepted until delivery of an offering circular that includes complete information about the issuer and the offering;

(iii) state that an indication of interest made by a prospective investor involves no obligation or commitment of any kind; and

(iv) identify the chief executive officer of the issuer and briefly and in general its business and products.

(3) Solicitations of interest pursuant to this provision may not be made after the filing of an offering statement.

(4) Sales may not be made until 20 calendar days after the last publication or delivery of the document or radio or television broadcast.

(c) Any written document under this section may include a coupon, returnable to the issuer indicating interest in a potential offering, revealing the name, address and telephone number of the prospective investor.

(d) Where an issuer has a bona fide change of intention and decides to register an offering after using the process permitted by this section without having filed the offering statement prescribed by § 230.252, the Regulation A exemption for offers made in reliance upon this section will not be subject to integration with the registered offering, if at least 30 calendar days have elapsed between the last solicitation of interest and the filing of the registration statement with the Commission, and all solicitation of interest documents have been submitted to the Commission. With respect to integration with other offerings, see § 230.251(c).

(e) Written solicitation of interest materials submitted to the Commission and otherwise in compliance with this section shall not be deemed to be a prospectus as defined in Section 2(10) of the Securities Act [15 U.S.C. 77b(10)].

Rule 255. Preliminary Offering Circulars

(a) Prior to qualification of the required offering statement, but after its filing, a written offer of securities may be made if it meets the following requirements:

(1) The outside front cover page of the material bears the caption "Preliminary Offering Circular," the date of issuance, and the following statement, which shall run along the left hand margin of the page and be printed perpendicular to the text, in boldfaced type at least as large as that used generally in the body of such offering circular:

An offering statement pursuant to Regulation A relating to these securities has been filed with the Securities and Exchange Commission.

Information contained in this Preliminary Offering Circular is subject to completion or amendment. These securities may not be sold nor may offers to buy be accepted prior to the time an offering circular which is not designated as a Preliminary Offering Circular is delivered and the offering statement filed with the Commission becomes qualified. This Preliminary Offering Circular shall not constitute an offer to sell or the solicitation of an offer to buy nor shall there be any sales of these securities in any state in which such offer, solicitation or sale would be unlawful prior to registration or qualification under the laws of any such state.

(2) The Preliminary Offering Circular contains substantially the information required in an offering circular by Form 1-A (§ 239.90 of this chapter), except that information with respect to offering price, underwriting discounts or commissions, discounts or commissions to dealers, amount of proceeds, conversions rates, call prices, or other matters dependent upon the offering price may be omitted. The outside front cover page of the Preliminary Offering Circular shall include a bona fide estimate of the range of the maximum offering price and maximum number of shares or other units of securities to be offered or a bona fide estimate of the principal amount of debt securities to be offered.

(3) The material is filed as a part of the offering statement.

(b) If a Preliminary Offering Circular is inaccurate or inadequate in any material respect, a revised Preliminary Offering Circular or a complete Offering Circular shall be furnished to all persons to whom securities are to be sold at least 48 hours prior to the mailing of any confirmation of sale to such persons, or shall be sent to such persons under such circumstances that it would normally be received by them 48 hours prior to receipt of confirmation of the sale.

Rule 256. Filing of Sales Material

While not a condition to an exemption pursuant to this provision, seven copies of any advertisement or written communication, or the script of any radio or television broadcast, shall be filed with the main office of the Commission in Washington, D.C.

NOTE: Only sales material that contains substantive changes from or additions from previously filed material Deeds to be filed.

Rule 257. Reports of Sales and Use of Proceeds

While not a condition to an exemption pursuant to this provision, the issuer and/or each selling security holder shall file seven copies of a report concerning sales and use of proceeds on Form 2-A [§ 239.91 of this chapter], or other prescribed form with the main office of the Commission in Washington, D.C. This report shall be filed at the following times:

(a) every six months after the qualification of the offering statement or any amendment until substantially all the proceeds have been applied; and

(b) within 30 calendar days after the termination, completion or final sale of securities in the offering, or the application of the proceeds from the offering, whichever is the latest event. This report should be labelled the final report. For purposes of this section, the temporary investment of proceeds pending final application shall not constitute application of the proceeds.

Rule 258. Suspension of the Exemption

(a) The Commission may at any time enter an order temporarily suspending a Regulation A exemption if it has reason to believe that:

(1) no exemption is available or any of the terms, conditions or requirements of the Regulation have not been complied with, including failures to provide the Commission a copy of the document or broadcast script under § 230.254, to file any sales material as required by § 230.256 or report as required by § 230.257;

(2) the offering statement, any sales or solicitation of interest material contains any untrue statement of a material fact or omits to state a material fact necessary in order to make the statements made, in light of the circumstances under which they are made, not misleading;

(3) the offering is being made or would be made in violation of section 17 of the Securities Act;

(4) an event has occurred after the filing of the offering statement which would have rendered the exemption hereunder unavailable if it had occurred prior to such filing;

(5) any person specified in paragraph (a) of § 230.262 has been indicted for any crime or offense of the character specified in paragraph (a)(3) of § 230.262, or any proceeding has been initiated for the purpose of enjoining any such person from engaging in or continuing any conduct or practice of the character specified in paragraph (a)(4) of § 230.262;

(6) any person specified in paragraph (b) of § 230.262 has been indicted for any crime or offense of the character specified in paragraph (b)(1) of § 230.262, or any proceeding has been initiated for the purpose of enjoining any such person from engaging in or continuing any conduct or practice of the character specified in paragraph (b)(2) of § 230.262; or

(7) the issuer or any promoter, officer, director or underwriter has failed to cooperate, or has obstructed or refused to permit the making of an investigation by the Commission in connection with any offering made or proposed to be made in reliance on Regulation A.

(b) Upon the entry of an order under paragraph (a) of this section, the Commission will promptly give notice to the issuer, any underwriter and any selling security holder:

(1) that such order has been entered, together with a brief statement of the reasons for the entry of the order; and

(2) that the Commission upon receipt of a written request within 30 calendar days after the entry of the order, will within 20 calendar days after receiving the request, order a hearing at a place to be designated by the Commission.

(c) If no hearing is requested and none is ordered by the Commission, an order entered under paragraph (a) of this section shall become permanent on the 30th calendar day after its entry and shall remain in effect unless or until it is modified or vacated by the Commission. Where a hearing is requested or is ordered by the Commission, the Commission will, after notice of and opportunity for such hearing, either vacate the order or enter an order permanently suspending the exemption.

(d) The Commission may, at any time after notice of and opportunity for hearing, enter an order permanently suspending the exemption for any reason upon which it could have entered a temporary suspension order under paragraph (a) of this section. Any such order shall remain in effect until vacated by the Commission.

(e) All notices required by this section shall be given by personal service, registered or certified mail to the addresses given by the issuer, any underwriter and any selling security holder in the offering statement.

Rule 259. Withdrawal or Abandonment of Offering Statements

(a) If none of the securities which are the subject of an offering statement have been sold and such offering statement is not the subject of a proceeding under § 230.258, the offering statement may be withdrawn with the Commission's consent. The application for withdrawal shall state the reason the offering statement is to be withdrawn, shall be signed by an authorized representative of the issuer and shall be provided to the main office of the Commission in Washington, D.C.

(b) When an offering statement has been on file with the Commission for nine months without amendment and has not become qualified, the Commission may, in its discretion, proceed in the following manner to determine whether such offering statement has been abandoned by the issuer. If the offering statement has been amended, the 9-month period shall be computed from the date of the latest amendment.

(1) Notice will be sent to the issuer, and to any counsel for the issuer named in the offering statement, by registered or certified mail, return receipt requested, addressed to the most recent addresses for the issuer and issuer's counsel as reflected in the offering statement. Such notice will inform the issuer and issuer's counsel that the offering statement or amendments thereto is out of date and must be either amended to comply with applicable requirements of Regulation A or be withdrawn within 30 calendar days after the notice.

(2) If the issuer or issuer's counsel fail to respond to such notice by filing a substantive amendment or withdrawing the offering statement or does not furnish a satisfactory explanation as to why the issuer has not done so within 30 calendar days, the Commission may declare the offering statement abandoned.

Rule 260. Insignificant Deviations from a Term, Condition or Requirement of Regulation A

(a) A failure to comply with a term, condition or requirement of Regulation A will not result in the loss of the exemption from the requirements of section 5 of the Securities Act for any offer or sale to a particular individual or entity, if the person relying on the exemption establishes:

(1) the failure to comply did not pertain to a term, condition or requirement directly intended to protect that particular individual or entity;

(2) the failure to comply was insignificant with respect to the offering as a whole, provided that any failure to comply with paragraphs (a), (b), (d)(1) and (3) of § 230.251 shall be deemed to be significant to the offering as a whole; and

(3) a good faith and reasonable attempt was made to comply with all applicable terms, conditions and requirements of Regulation A

(b) A transaction made in reliance upon Regulation A shall comply with all applicable terms, conditions and requirements of the regulation. where an exemption is established only through reliance upon paragraph (a) of this section, the failure to comply shall nonetheless be actionable by the Commission under section 20 of the Act.

(c) This provision provides no relief or protection from a proceeding under § 230.258.

Rule 261. Definitions

As used in this Regulation A, all terms have the same meanings as in § 230.405, except that all references to "registrant" in those definitions shall refer to the issuer of the securities to be offered and sold under Regulation A. In addition, these terms have the following meanings:

(a) *Final Offering Circular*—The current offering circular contained in a qualified offering statement;

(b) *Preliminary Offering Circular*—The offering circular described in § 230.255(a).

Rule 262. Disqualification Provisions

Unless, upon a showing of good cause and without prejudice to any other action by the Commission, the Commission determines that it is not necessary under the circumstances that the exemption provided by this Regulation A be denied, the exemption shall not be available for the offer or sale of securities, if:

(a) the issuer, any of its predecessors or any affiliated issuer:

(1) has filed a registration statement which is the subject of any pending proceeding or examination under section 8 of the Act, or has been the subject of any refusal order or stop order thereunder within 5 years prior to the filing of the offering statement required by § 230.252;

(2) is subject to any pending proceeding under § 230.258 or any similar section adopted under section 3(b) of the Securities Act, or to an order entered thereunder within 5 years prior to the filing of such offering statement;

(3) has been convicted within 5 years prior to the filing of such offering statement of any felony or misdemeanor in connection with the purchase or sale of any security or involving the making of any false filing with the Commission;

(4) is subject to any order, judgment, or decree of any court of competent jurisdiction temporarily or preliminarily restraining or enjoining, or is subject to any order, judgment or decree of any court of competent jurisdiction, entered within 5 years prior to the filing of such offering statement, permanently restraining or enjoining, such person from engaging in or continuing any conduct or practice in connection with the purchase or sale of any security or involving the making of any false filing with the Commission; or

(5) is subject to a United States Postal Service false representation order entered under 39 U.S.C. § 3005 within 5 years prior to the filing of the offering statement, or is subject to a temporary restraining order or preliminary injunction entered under 39 U.S.C. § 3007 with respect to conduct alleged to have violated 39 U.S.C. § 3005. The entry of an order, judgment or decree against any affiliated entity before the affiliation with the issuer arose, if the affiliated entity is not in control of the issuer and if the affiliated entity and the issuer are not under the common control of a third party who was in control of the affiliated entity at the time of such entry does not come within the purview of this paragraph (a) of this section.

(b) any director, officer or general partner of the issuer, beneficial owner of 10 percent or more of any class of its equity securities, any promoter of the issuer presently connected with it in any capacity, any underwriter of the securities to be offered, or any partner, director or officer of any such underwriter:

(1) has been convicted within 10 years prior to the filing of the offering statement required by § 230.252 of any felony or misdemeanor in connection with the purchase or sale of any security, involving the making of a false filing with the Commission, or arising out of the conduct of the business of an underwriter, broker, dealer, municipal securities dealer, or investment adviser;

(2) is subject to any order, judgment, or decree of any court of competent jurisdiction temporarily or preliminarily enjoining or restraining, or is subject to any order, judgment, or decree of any court of competent jurisdiction, entered within 5 years prior to the filing of such offering statement, permanently enjoining or restraining such person from engaging in or continuing any conduct or practice in connection with the purchase or sale of any security, involving the making of a false filing with the Commission, or arising out of the conduct of the business of an underwriter, broker, dealer, municipal securities dealer, or investment adviser;

(3) is subject to an order of the Commission entered pursuant to section 15(b), 15B(a), or 15B(c) of the Exchange Act, or section 203(e) or (f) of the Investment Advisers Act of 1940 [15 U.S.C. 80b-1 *et seq.*];

(4) is suspended or expelled from membership in, or suspended or barred from association with a member of, a national securities exchange registered under section 6 of the Exchange Act or a national securities association registered under section 15A of the Exchange Act for any act or omission to act constituting conduct inconsistent with just and equitable principles of trade; or

(5) is subject to a United States Postal Service false representation order entered under 39 U.S.C. § 3005 within 5 years prior to the filing of the offering statement required by § 230.252, or is subject to a restraining order or preliminary injunction entered under 39 U.S.C. § 3007 with respect to conduct alleged to have violated 39 U.S.C. § 3005.

(c) any underwriter of such securities was an underwriter or was named as an underwriter of any securities:

(1) covered by any registration statement which is the subject of any pending proceeding or examination under section 8 of the Act, or is the subject of any refusal order or stop order entered thereunder within 5 years prior to the filing of the offering statement required by § 230.252; or

91

(2) covered by any filing which is subject to any pending proceeding under § 230.258 or any similar rule adopted under section 3(b) of the Securities Act, or to an order entered thereunder within 5 years prior to the filing of such offering statement.

Rule 263. Consent to Service of Process

(a) If the issuer is not organized under the laws of any of the states of or the United States of America, it shall at the time of filing the offering statement required by § 230.252, furnish to the Commission a written irrevocable consent and power of attorney on Form F-X [§ 239.42 of this chapter].

(b) Any change to the name or address of the agent for service of the issuer shall be communicated promptly to the Commission through amendment of the requisite form and referencing the file number of the relevant offering statement.

REGULATION C—REGISTRATION

Rule 400. Application of § 230.400 to § 230.494, Inclusive

Sections 230.400 to 230.494 shall govern every registration of securities under the Act, except that any provision in a form, or an item of Regulation S-K (17 CFR 229.001 *et seq.*) referred to in such form, covering the same subject matter as any such rule shall be controlling unless otherwise specifically provided in § § 230.400 to 230.494.

Rule 402. Number of Copies—Binding—Signatures

(a) Three copies of the complete registration statement, including exhibits and all other papers and documents filed as a part of the statement, shall be filed with the Commission. Each copy shall be bound, in one or more parts, without stiff covers. The binding shall be made on the side or stitching margin in such manner as to leave the reading matter legible. At least one such copy of every registration shall be signed by the persons specified in section 6(a) of the Act. Unsigned copies shall be conformed.

(b) Ten additional copies of the registration statement, similarly bound, shall be furnished for use in the examination of the registration statement, public inspection, copying and other purposes. Where a registration statement incorporates into the prospectus documents which are required to be delivered with the prospectus in lieu of prospectus presentation, the ten additional copies of the registration statement shall be accompanied by ten copies of such documents. No other exhibits are required to accompany such additional copies.

(c) Notwithstanding any other provision of this section, if a registration statement is filed on Form S-8 (§ 239.16b of this chapter), three copies of the complete registration statement, including exhibits and all other papers and documents filed as a part of the statement, shall be filed with the Commission. Each copy shall be bound, in one or more parts, without stiff covers. The binding shall be made on the side or stitching margin in such manner as to leave the reading matter legible. At least one such copy shall be signed by the persons specified in Section 6(a) of the Act. Unsigned copies shall be conformed. Three additional copies of the registration statement, similarly bound, also shall be furnished to the Commission for use in the examination of the registration statement, public inspection, copying and other purposes. No exhibits are required to accompany the additional copies of registration statements filed on Form S-8.

(d) Notwithstanding any other provision of this section, if a registration statement is filed pursuant to Rule 462(b) (§ 230.462(b)) and Rule 110(d) (§ 230.110(d)), one copy of the complete registration statement, including exhibits and all other papers and documents filed as a part thereof shall be filed with the Commission. Such copy should not be bound and may contain facsimile versions of manual signatures in accordance with paragraph (e) of this section.

(e) *Signatures.* Where the Act or the rules thereunder, including paragraphs (a) and (c) of this section, require a document filed with or furnished to the Commission to be signed, such document shall be manually signed, or signed using either typed signatures or duplicated or facsimile versions of manual signatures. Where typed, duplicated or facsimile signatures are used, each signatory to the filing shall manually sign a signature page or other document authenticating, acknowledging or otherwise adopting his or her signature that appears in the filing. Such document shall be executed before or at the time the filing is made and shall be retained by the registrant for a period of five years. Upon request, the registrant shall furnish to the Commission or its staff a copy of any or all documents retained pursuant to this section.

Rule 404. Preparation of Registration Statement

(a) A registration statement shall consist of the facing sheet of the applicable form a prospectus containing the information called for by Part 1 of such form; the information, list of exhibits, undertakings and signatures required to be set forth in Part II of such form; financial statements and schedules; exhibits; any other information or documents filed as part of the registration statement; and all documents or information incorporated by reference in the foregoing (whether or not required to be filed).

(b) All general instructions, instructions to items of the form, and instructions as to financial statements, exhibits, or prospectuses are to be omitted from the registration statement in all cases.

(c) The prospectus shall contain the information called for by all of the items of Part I of the applicable form, except that unless otherwise specified, no reference need be made to inapplicable items, and negative answers to any item in Part I may be omitted. A copy of the prospectus may be filed as a part of the registration statement in lieu of furnishing the information in item-and-answer form. Wherever a copy of the prospectus is filed in lieu of information in item-and-answer form, the text of the items of the form is to be omitted from the registration statement, as well as from the prospectus, except to the extent provided in paragraph (d) of this rule.

(d) Where any items of a form called for information not required to be included in the prospectus, generally Part II of such form, the text of such items, including the numbers and captions thereof, together with the answers thereto shall be filed with the prospectus under cover of the facing sheet of the form as a part of the registration statement. However, the text of such items may be omitted provided the answers are so prepared as to indicate the coverage of the item without the necessity of reference to the text of the item. If any such item is inapplicable, or the answer thereto is in the negative, a statement to that effect shall be made. Any financial statements not required to be included in the prospectus shall also be filed as a part of the registration statement proper, unless incorporated by reference pursuant to Rule 411 (§ 230.411).

Rule 405. Definitions of Terms

Unless the context otherwise requires, all terms used in § § 230.400 to 230.494, inclusive, or in the forms for registration have the same meanings as in the Act and in the general rules and regulations. In addition, the following definitions apply, unless the context otherwise requires:

Affiliate. An "affiliate" of, or person "affiliated" with, a specified person, is a person that directly, or indirectly through one or more intermediaries, controls or is controlled by, or is under common control with, the person specified.

Amount. The term "amount," when used in regard to securities, means the principal amount if relating to evidences of indebtedness, the number of shares if relating to shares, and the number of units if relating to any other kind of security.

Associate. The term "associate," when used to indicate a relationship with any person, means (1) a corporation or organization (other than the registrant or a majority-owned subsidiary of the registrant) of which such person is an officer or partner or is, directly or indirectly, the beneficial owner of 10 percent or more of any class of equity securities, (2) any trust or other estate in which such person has a substantial beneficial interest or as to which such person serves as trustee or in a similar capacity, and (3) any relative or spouse of such person, or any relative of such spouse, who has the same home as such person or who is a director or officer of the registrant or any of its parents or subsidiaries.

Business development. The term "business development company" refers to a company which has elected to be regulated as a business development under sections 55 through 65 of the Investment Company Act of 1940.

Certified. The term "certified," when used in regard to financial statements, means examined and reported upon with an opinion expressed by an independent public or certified public accountant.

Charter. The term "charter" includes articles of incorporation, declarations of trust, articles of association or partnership, or any similar instrument, as amended, affecting (either with or without filing with any governmental agency) the organization or creation of an incorporated or unincorporated person.

Common equity. The term "common equity" means any class of common stock, or an equivalent interest, including but not limited to a unit of beneficial interest in a trust or a limited partnership interest.

Commission. The term "Commission" means the Securities and Exchange Commission.

Control. The term "control" (including the terms "controlling," "controlled by" and "under common control with") means the possession, direct or indirect, of the power to direct or cause the direction of the management and policies of a person, whether through the ownership of voting securities, by contract, or otherwise.

Depositary share. The term "depositary share" means a security, evidenced by an American Depositary Receipt, that represents a foreign security or a multiple of or fraction thereof deposited with a depositary.

Director. The term "director" means any director of a corporation or any person performing similar functions with respect to any organization whether incorporated or unincorporated.

Dividend or interest reinvestment plan. The term "dividend or interest reinvestment plan" means a plan which is offered solely to the existing security holders of the registrant, which allows such persons to reinvest dividends or interest paid to them on securities issued by the registrant, and also may allow additional cash amounts to be contributed by the participants in the plan, provided the securities to be registered are newly issued, or are purchased for the account of plan participants, at prices not in excess of current market prices at the time of purchase, or at prices not in excess of an amount determined in accordance with a pricing formula specified in the plan and based upon average or current market prices at the time of purchase.

Electronic filer. The term "electronic filer" means a person or an entity that submits filings electronically pursuant to Rules 100 and 101 of Regulation S-T (§ 232.100 and § 232.101 of this chapter, respectively). respectively).

Electronic filing. The term "electronic filing" means a document under the federal securities laws that is transmitted or delivered to the Commission in electronic format.

Employee. The term "employee" does not include a director, trustee, or officer.

Employee benefit plan. The term employee benefit plan means any written purchase, savings, option, bonus, appreciation, profit sharing, thrift, incentive, pension or similar plan or written compensation contract solely for employees, directors, general partners, trustees (where the registrant is a business trust), officers, or consultants or advisors. However, consultants or advisors may participate in an employee benefit plan only if:

(1) They are natural persons;

(2) They provide bona fide services to the registrant; and

(3) The services are not in connection with the offer or sale of securities in a capital-raising transaction, and do not directly or indirectly promote or maintain a market for the registrant's securities.

Equity security. The term *equity security* means any stock or similar security, certificate of interest or participation in any profit sharing agreement, preorganization certificate or subscription, transferable share, voting trust certificate or certificate of deposit for an equity security, limited partnership interest, interest in a joint venture, or certificate of interest in a business trust; any security future on any such security; or any security convertible, with or without consideration into such a security, or carrying any warrant or right to subscribe to or purchase such a security;

or any such warrant or right; or any put, call, straddle, or other option or privilege of buying such a security from or selling such a security to another without being bound to do so.

Executive officer. The term "executive officer," when used with reference to a registrant, means its president, any vice president of the registrant in charge of a principal business unit, division or function (such as sales, administration or finance), any other officer who performs a policy making function or any other person who performs similar policy making functions for the registrant. Executive officers of subsidiaries may be deemed executive officers of the registrant if they perform such policy making functions for the registrant.

Fiscal year. The term "fiscal year" means the annual accounting period or, if no closing date has been adopted, the calendar year ending on December 31.

Foreign government. The term "foreign government" means the government of any foreign country or of any political subdivision of a foreign country.

Foreign issuer. The term "foreign issuer" means any issuer which is a foreign government, a national of any foreign country or a corporation or other organization incorporated or organized under the laws of any foreign country.

Foreign private issuer. The term foreign private issuer means any foreign issuer other than a foreign government except an issuer meeting the following conditions:

(1) More than 50 percent of the outstanding voting securities of such issuer are directly or indirectly owned of record by residents of the United States; and

(2) Any of the following:

(i) The majority of the executive officers or directors are United States citizens or residents;

(ii) More than 50 percent of the assets of the issuer are located in the United States; or

(iii) The business of the issuer is administered principally in the United States.

Instructions to paragraph (1) of this definition: To determine the percentage of outstanding voting securities held by U.S. residents:

A. Use the method of calculating record ownership in Rule 12g3-2(a) under the Exchange Act (§ 240.12g3-2(a) of this chapter), except that your inquiry as to the amount of shares represented by accounts of customers resident in the United States may be limited to brokers, dealers, banks and other nominees located in (1) the United States, (2) your jurisdiction of incorporation, and (3) the jurisdiction that is the primary trading market for your voting securities, if different than your jurisdiction of incorporation.

B. If, after reasonable inquiry, you are unable to obtain information about the amount of shares represented by accounts of customers resident in the United States, you may assume, for purposes of this definition, that the customers are residents of the jurisdiction in which the nominee has its principal place of business.

C. Count shares of voting securities beneficially owned by residents of the United States as reported on reports of beneficial ownership that are provided to you or publicly filed and based on information otherwise provided to you.

Graphic communication. The term "graphic communication," which appears in the definition of "write, written" in Section 2(9) of the Securities Act, shall include magnetic impulses or other forms of computer data compilation.

Majority-owned subsidiary. The term "majority-owned subsidiary" means a subsidiary more than 50 percent of whose outstanding securities representing the right, other than as affected by events of default, to vote for the election of directors, is owned by the subsidiary's parent and/or one or more of the parent's other majority-owned subsidiaries.

Material. The term "material," when used to qualify a requirement for the furnishing of information as to any subject, limits the information required to those matters to which there is a substantial likelihood that a reasonable investor would attach importance in determining whether to purchase the security registered.

Officer. The term "officer" means a president, vice president, secretary, treasurer or principal financial officer, comptroller or principal accounting officer, and any person routinely performing corresponding functions with respect to any organization whether incorporated or unincorporated.

Parent. A "parent" of a specified person is an affiliate controlling such person directly, or indirectly through one or more intermediaries.

Predecessor. The term "predecessor" means a person the major portion of the business and assets of which another person acquired in a single succession, or in a series of related successions in each of which the acquiring person acquired the major portion of the business and assets of the acquired person.

Principal underwriter. The term "principal underwriter" means an underwriter in privity of contract with the issuer of the securities as to which he is underwriter, the term "issuer" having the meaning given in sections 2(4) and 2(11) of the Act.

Promoter. (1) The term "promoter" includes—

(i) Any person who, acting alone or in conjunction with one or more other persons, directly or indirectly takes initiative in founding and organizing the business or enterprise of an issuer; or

(ii) Any person who, in connection with the founding and organizing of the business or enterprise of an issuer, directly or indirectly receives in consideration of services or property, or both services and property, 10 percent or more of any class of securities of the issuer or 10 percent or more of the proceeds from the sale of any class of such securities. However, a person who receives such securities or proceeds either solely as underwriting commissions or solely in consideration of property shall not be deemed a promoter within the meaning of this paragraph if such person does not otherwise take part in founding and organizing the enterprise.

(2) All persons coming within the definition of "promoter" in paragraph (1) of this section may be referred to as "founders" or "organizers" or by another term provided that such term is reasonably descriptive of those persons' activities with respect to the issuer.

Prospectus. Unless otherwise specified or the context otherwise requires, the term "prospectus" means a prospectus meeting the requirements of section 10(a) of the Act.

Registrant. The term "registrant" means the issuer of the securities for which the registration statement is filed.

Share. The term "share" means a share of stock in a corporation or unit of interest in an unincorporated person.

Significant Subsidiary. The term "significant subsidiary" means a subsidiary, including its subsidiaries, which meets any of the following conditions.

(1) The registrant's and its other subsidiaries' investments in and advances to the subsidiary exceed 10 percent of the total assets of the registrant and its subsidiaries consolidated as of the end of the most recently completed fiscal year (for a proposed business combination to be accounted for as a pooling of interests, this condition is also met when the number of common shares exchanged or to be exchanged by the registrant exceeds 10 percent of its total common shares outstanding at the date the combination is initiated) or

(2) The registrant's and its other subsidiaries' proportionate share of the total assets (after intercompany eliminations) of the subsidiary exceeds 10 percent of the total assets of the registrants and its subsidiaries consolidated as of the end of the most recently completed fiscal year; or

(3) The registrant's and its other equity in the income from continuing operations before income taxes, extraordinary items and cumulative effect of a change in accounting principle of the subsidiary exceeds 10 percent of such income of the registrant and its subsidiaries consolidated for the most recently completed year.

Computational note: For purposes of making the prescribed income test the following guidance should be applied:

1. When a loss has been incurred by either the parent and its subsidiaries consolidated or the tested subsidiary, but not both, the equity in the income or loss of the tested subsidiary should be excluded from the income of the registrant and its subsidiaries consolidated for purposes of the computation.

2. If income of the registrant and its subsidiaries consolidated for the most recent fiscal year is at least 10 percent lower than the average of the income for the last five fiscal years, such

average income should be substituted for purposes of the computation. Any loss years should be omitted for purposes of computing average income.

Small Business Issuer. The term "small business issuer" means an entity that meets the following criteria:

(1) has revenues of less than $25,000,000;

(2) is a U.S. or Canadian issuer;

(3) is not an investment company; and

(4) if a majority owned subsidiary, the parent corporation is also a small business issuer.

Provided however, that an entity is not a small business issuer if it has a public float (the aggregate market value of the outstanding voting and non-voting common equity held by non-affiliates) of $25,000,000 or more.

NOTE: The public float of a reporting company shall be computed by use of the price at which the stock was last sold, or the average of the bid and asked prices of such stock, on a date within 60 days prior to the end of its most recent fiscal year. The public float of a company filing an initial registration statement under the Exchange Act shall be determined as of a date within 60 days of the date the registration statement is filed. In the case of an initial public offering of securities, public float shall be computed on the basis of the number of shares outstanding prior to the offering and the estimated public offering price of the securities.

Subsidiary. A "subsidiary" of a specified person is an affiliate controlled by such person directly, or indirectly through one or more intermediaries. (See also "majority owned subsidiary," "significant subsidiary," "totally held subsidiary" and "wholly owned subsidiary.")

Succession. The term "succession" means the direct acquisition of the assets comprising a going business, whether by merger, consolidation, purchase, or other direct transfer. The term does not include the acquisition of control of a business unless followed by the direct acquisition of its assets. The terms "succeed" and "successor" have meanings correlative to the foregoing.

Totally held subsidiary. The term "totally held subsidiary" means a subsidiary (1) substantially all of whose outstanding securities are owned by its parent and/or the parent's other totally held subsidiaries, and (2) which is not indebted to any person other than its parent and/or the parent's other totally held subsidiaries in an amount which is material in relation to the particular subsidiary, excepting indebtedness incurred in the ordinary course of business which is not overdue and which matures within one year from the date of its creation, whether evidenced by securities or not.

Voting securities. The term "voting securities" means securities the holders of which are presently entitled to vote for the election of directors.

Wholly owned subsidiary. The term "wholly owned subsidiary" means a subsidiary substantially all of whose outstanding voting securities are owned by its parent and/or the parent's other wholly owned subsidiaries.

Rule 406. Confidential Treatment of Information Filed with the Commission
Preliminary Notes

(1) Confidential treatment of supplemental information or other information not required to be filed under the Act should be requested under 17 CFR § 200.83 and not under this rule.

(2) All confidential treatment requests shall be submitted in paper format only, whether or not the filer is an electronic filer. *See* Rule 101(c)(1)(i) of Regulation S-T (§ 232.101(c)(1)(i) of this chapter.

(a) Any person submitting any information in a document required to be filed under the Act may make written objection to its public disclosure by following the procedure in paragraph (b) of this section, which shall be the exclusive means of requesting confidential treatment of information included in any document (hereinafter referred to as the "material filed") required to be filed under the Act, *except* that if the material filed is a registration statement on Form S-8 (§ 239.16b of this chapter) or on Form S-3, F-2, F-3 (§ 239.13, 32 or 33 of this chapter) relating to a dividend or interest reinvestment plan, or on Form S-4 (§ 239.25 of this chapter) complying with General Instruction G of that Form, or if the material filed is a registration statement that does not contain a delaying amendment pursuant to Rule 473 (§ 230.473 of this chapter), the person shall comply with the procedure in paragraph (b) *prior* to the filing of a registration statement.

(b) The person shall omit from the material filed the portion thereof which it desires to keep undisclosed (hereinafter called the "confidential portion"). In lieu thereof, the person shall indicate at the appropriate place in the material filed that the confidential portion has been so omitted and filed separately with the Commission. The person shall file with the material filed:

(1) One copy of the confidential portion, marked "Confidential Treatment", of the material filed with the Commission. The copy shall contain an appropriate identification of the item or other requirement involved and, notwithstanding that the confidential portion does not constitute the whole of the answer or required disclosure, the entire answer or required disclosure, except that in the case where the confidential portion is part of a financial statement or schedule, only the particular financial statement or schedule need be included. The copy of the confidential portion shall be in the same form as the remainder of the material filed;

(2) An application making objection to the disclosure of the confidential portion. Such application shall be on a sheet or sheets separate from the confidential portion, and shall contain (i) an identification of the portion; (ii) a statement of the grounds of the objection referring to and analyzing the applicable exemption(s) from disclosure under § 200.80 of this chapter, the Commission's rule adopted under the Freedom of Information Act (5 U.S.C. 552), and a justification of the period of time for which confidential treatment is sought; (iii) a detailed explanation of why, based on the facts and circumstances of the particular case, disclosure of the information is unnecessary for the protection of investors; (iv) a written consent to the furnishing of the confidential portion to other government agencies, offices or bodies and to the Congress; and (v) the name, address and telephone number of the person to whom all notices and orders issued under this rule at any time should be directed.

(3) The copy of the confidential portion and the application filed in accordance with this paragraph (b) shall be enclosed in a separate envelope marked "Confidential Treatment" and addressed to the Secretary, Securities and Exchange Commission, Washington, D.C. 20549.

(c) Pending a determination as to the objection, the material for which confidential treatment has been applied will not be made available to the public.

(d) If it is determined by the Division, acting pursuant to delegated authority, that the application should be granted, an order to that effect will be entered, and a notation to that effect will be made at the appropriate place in the material filed. Such a determination will not preclude reconsideration whenever appropriate, such as upon receipt of any subsequent request under the Freedom of Information Act and, if appropriate, revocation of the confidential status of all or a portion of the information in question.

(e) If the Commission denies the application, or the Division, acting pursuant to delegated authority, denies the application and Commission review is not sought pursuant to § 201.431 of this chapter, confirmed telegraphic notice of the order of denial will be sent to the person named in the application pursuant to paragraph (b)(2)(v) of this section. In such case, if the material filed may be withdrawn pursuant to an applicable statute, rule, or regulation, the registrant shall have the right to withdraw the material filed in accordance with the terms of the applicable statute, rule, or regulation, but without the necessity of stating any grounds for the withdrawal or of obtaining the further assent of the Commission. In the event of such withdrawal, the confidential portion will be returned to the registrant. If the material filed may not be so withdrawn, the confidential portion will be made available for public inspection in the same manner as if confidential treatment had been revoked under paragraph (h) of this section.

(f) If a right of withdrawal pursuant to paragraph (e) of this section is not exercised, the confidential portion will be made available for public inspection as part of the material filed, and the registrant shall amend the material filed to include all information required to be set forth in regard to such confidential portion.

(g) In any case where a prior grant of confidential treatment has been revoked, the person named in the application pursuant to paragraph (b)(2)(v) of this section will be so informed by registered or certified mail. Pursuant to § 201.26 of this chapter, persons making objections to disclosure may petition the Commission for review of a determination by the Division revoking confidential treatment.

(h) Upon revocation of confidential treatment, the confidential portion shall be made available to the public at the time and according to the conditions specified in paragraphs (h) (1)—(2):

(1) Upon the lapse of five days after the dispatch of notice by registered or certified mail of a determination disallowing an objection, if prior to the lapse of such five days the person shall not have communicated to the Secretary of the Commission his intention to seek review by the Commission under § 201.431 of this chapter of the determination made by the Division; or

(2) If such a petition for review shall have been filed under § 201.431 of this chapter, upon final disposition adverse to the petitioner.

(i) If the confidential portion is made available to the public, one copy thereof shall be attached to each copy of the material filed with the Commission.

Rule 408. Additional Information

In addition to the information expressly required to be included in a registration statement, there shall be added such further material information, if any, as may be necessary to make the required statements, in the light of the circumstances under which they are made, not misleading.

Rule 409. Information Unknown or Not Reasonably Available

Information required need be given only insofar as it is known or reasonably available to the registrant. If any required information is unknown and not reasonably available to the registrant, either because the obtaining thereof would involve unreasonable effort or expense, or because it rests peculiarly within the knowledge of another person not affiliated with the registrant, the information may be omitted, subject to the following conditions:

(a) The registrant shall give such information on the subject as it possesses or can acquire without unreasonable effort or expense, together with the sources thereof.

(b) The registrant shall include a statement either showing that unreasonable effort or expense would be involved or indicating the absence of any affiliation with the person within whose knowledge the information rests and stating the result of a request made to such person for the information.

Rule 410. Disclaimer of Control

If the existence of control is open to reasonable doubt in any instance, the registrant may disclaim the existence of control and any admission thereof; in such case, however, the registrant shall state the material facts pertinent to the possible existence of control.

Rule 411. Incorporation by Reference

(a) *Prospectus.* Except as provided by this section or unless otherwise provided in the appropriate form, information shall not be incorporated by reference in a prospectus. Where a summary or outline of the provisions of any document is required in the prospectus, the summary or outline may incorporate by reference particular items, sections or paragraphs of any exhibit and may be qualified in its entirety by such reference.

(b) *Information not required in a prospectus.* Except for exhibits covered by paragraph (c) of this section, information may be incorporated by reference in answer, or partial answer, to any item that calls for information not required to be included in a prospectus subject to the following provisions:

(1) Non-financial information may be incorporated by reference to any document;

(2) Financial information may be incorporated by reference to any document, provided any financial statement so incorporated meets the requirements of the forms on which the statement is filed. Financial statements or other financial data required to be given in comparative form for two or more fiscal years or periods shall not be incorporated by reference unless the information incorporated by reference includes the entire period for which the comparative data is given;

(3) Information contained in any part of the registration statement, including the prospectus, may be incorporated by reference in answer, or partial answer, to any item that calls for information not required to be included in the prospectus; and

(4) Unless the information is incorporated by reference to a document which complies with the time limitations of § 228.10(f) and § 229.10(d) of this chapter, then the document, or part thereof, containing the incorporated information is required to be filed as an exhibit.

(c) *Exhibits.* Any document or part thereof filed with the Commission pursuant to any Act administered by the Commission may, subject to the limitations of § 228.10(f) and § 229.10(d) of this chapter, be incorporated by reference as an exhibit to any registration statement. If any modification has occurred in the text of any document incorporated by reference since the filing thereof, the registrant shall file with the reference a statement containing the text of such modification and the date thereof.

(d) *General.* Any incorporation by reference of information pursuant to this section shall be subject to the provisions of Rule 24 of the Commission's Rules of Practice restricting incorporation by reference of documents which incorporate by reference other information. Information incorporated by reference shall be clearly identified in the reference by page, paragraph, caption or otherwise. If the information is incorporated by reference to a previously filed document, the file number of such document shall be included. Where only certain pages of a document are incorporated by reference and filed with the statement, the document from which the information is taken shall be clearly identified in the reference. An express statement that the specified matter is incorporated by reference shall be made at the particular place in the registration statement where the information is required. Information shall not be incorporated by reference in any case where such incorporation would render the statement incomplete, unclear or confusing.

Rule 412. Modified or Superseded Documents

(a) Any statement contained in a document incorporated or deemed to be incorporated by reference shall be deemed to be modified or superseded for purposes of the registration statement or the prospectus to the extent that a statement contained in the prospectus or in any other subsequently filed document which also is or is deemed to be incorporated by reference modifies or replaces such statement.

(b) The modifying or superseding statement may, but need not, state that it has modified or superseded a prior statement or include any other information set forth in the document which is not so modified or superseded. The making of a modifying or superseding statement shall not be deemed an admission that the modified or superseded statement, when made, constituted an untrue statement of a material fact, an omission to state a material fact necessary to make a statement not misleading, or the employment of a manipulative, deceptive, or fraudulent device, contrivance, scheme, transaction, act, practice, course of business or artifice to defraud, as those terms are used in the Act, the Securities Exchange Act of 1934, the Public Utility Holding Company Act of 1935, the Investment Company Act of 1940, or the rules and regulations thereunder.

(c) Any statement so modified shall not be deemed in its unmodified form to constitute part of the registration statement or prospectus for purpose of the Act. Any statement so superseded shall not be deemed to constitute a part of the registration statement or the prospectus for purpose of the Act.

Rule 413. Registration of Additional Securities

Except as provided in sections 24(e)(1) and 24(f) of the Investment Company Act of 1940, the registration of additional securities of the same class as other securities for which a registration statement is already in effect shall be effected through a separate registration statement relating to the additional securities.

Rule 415. Delayed or Continuous Offering and Sale of Securities

(a) Securities may be registered for an offering to be made on a continuous or delayed basis in the future. *Provided,* That—

(1) The registration statement pertains only to:

(i) Securities which are to be offered or sold solely by or on behalf of a person or persons other than the registrant, a subsidiary of the registrant or a person of which the registrant is a subsidiary;

(ii) Securities which are to be offered and sold pursuant to a dividend or interest reinvestment plan or an employee benefit plan of the registrant;

(iii) Securities which are to be issued upon the exercise of outstanding options, warrants or rights;

(iv) Securities which are to be issued upon conversion of other outstanding securities;

(v) Securities which are pledged as collateral;

(vi) Securities which are registered on Form F-6 (§ 239.36 of this chapter);

(vii) Mortgage related securities, including such securities as mortgage backed debt and mortgage participation or pass through certificates;

(viii) Securities which are to be issued in connection with business combination transactions;

(ix) Securities the offering of which will be commenced promptly, will be made on a continuous basis and may continue for a period in excess of 30 days from the date of initial effectiveness; or

(x) Securities registered (or qualified to be registered) on Form S-3 or Form F-3 (§ 239.13 or 239.33 of this chapter) which are to be offered and sold on a continuous or delayed basis by or on behalf of the registrant, a subsidiary of the registrant or a person of which the registrant is a subsidiary.

(xi) Shares of common stock which are to be offered and sold on a delayed or continuous basis by or on behalf of a registered closed-end management investment company or business development company that makes periodic repurchase offers pursuant to § 270.23c-3 of this chapter.

(2) Securities in paragraphs (a)(1)(viii) through (x) may only be registered in an amount which, at the time the registration statement becomes effective, is reasonably expected to be offered and sold within two years from the initial effective date of the registration.

(3) The registrant furnishes the undertakings required by Item 512(a) of Regulation S-K (§ 229.512 of this chapter).

(4) In the case of a registration statement pertaining to an at the market offering of equity securities by or on behalf of the registrant:

(i) The offering comes within paragraph (a)(1)(x); (ii) where voting stock is registered, the amount of securities registered for such purposes must not exceed 10% of the aggregate market value of the registrant's outstanding voting stock held by non-affiliates of the registrant (calculated as of a date within 60 days prior to the date of filing); (iii) the securities must be sold through an underwriter or underwriters, acting as principal(s) or as agent(s) for the registrant; and (iv) the underwriter or underwriters must be named in the prospectus which is part of the registration statement. As used in this paragraph, the term "at the market offering" means an offering of securities into an existing trading market for outstanding shares of the same class at other than a fixed price on or through the facilities of a national securities exchange or to or through a market maker otherwise than on an exchange.

(b) This section shall not apply to any registration statement pertaining to securities issued by a face-amount certificate company or redeemable securities issued by an open-end management company or unit investment trust under the Investment Company Act of 1940 or any registration statement filed by any foreign government or political subdivision thereof.

Rule 418. Supplemental Information

(a) The Commission or its staff may, where it is deemed appropriate, request supplemental information concerning the registrant, the registration statement, the distribution of the securities, market activities and underwriters' activities. Such information includes, but is not limited to, the following items which the registrant should be prepared to furnish promptly upon request:

(1) (i) Any reports or memoranda which have been prepared for external use by the registrant or a principal underwriter, as defined in Rule 405 (§ 230.405), in connection with the proposed offering;

(ii) A statement as to the actual or proposed use and distribution of the reports or memoranda specified in paragraph (a)(1)(i) of this section, identifying each class of persons who have received or will receive such reports or memoranda and the number of copies distributed to each such class;

(2) In the case of a registration statement relating to a business combination as defined in Rule 145(a) (17 CFR 230.145(a)), exchange offer, tender offer or similar transaction, any feasibility studies, management analyses, fairness opinions or similar reports prepared by or for any of the parties to the subject transaction in connection with such transaction;

(3) Except in the case of a registrant eligible to use Form S-2 or Form S-3 (§§ 239.12 or 239.13 of this chapter), any engineering, management or similar reports or memoranda relating to broad aspects of the business, operations or products of the registrant, which have been prepared within the past twelve months for or by the registrant, any affiliate of the registrant or any principal underwriter, as defined in Rule 405 (§ 230.405), of the securities being registered except for:

(i) Reports solely comprised of recommendations to buy, sell or hold the securities of the registrant, unless such recommendations have changed within the past six months; and

(ii) Any information contained in documents already filed with the Commission.

(4) Where there is a registration of an at-the-market offering, as defined in § 242.100 of this chapter, of more than 10 percent of the securities outstanding, where the offering includes securities owned by officers, directors or affiliates of the registrant and where there is no underwriting agreement, information (i) concerning contractual arrangements between selling security holders of a limited group or of several groups of related shareholders to comply with the anti-manipulation rules until the offering by all members of the group is completed and to inform the exchange, brokers and selling security holders when the distribution by the members of the group is over, or (ii) concerning the registrant's efforts to notify members of a large group of unrelated sellers of the applicable Commission rules and regulations;

(5) Where the registrant recently has introduced a new product or has begun to do business in a new industry segment or has made public its intentions to introduce a new product or to do business in a new industry segment, and this action requires the investment of a material amount of the assets of the registrant or otherwise is material, copies of any studies prepared for the registrant by outside persons or any internal studies, documents, reports or memoranda the contents of which were material to the decision to develop the product or to do business in the new segment including, but not limited to, documents relating to financial requirements and engineering, competitive, environmental and other considerations, but excluding technical documents;

(6) Where reserve estimates are referred to in a document, a copy of the full report of the engineer or other expert who estimated the reserves; and

(7) With respect to the extent of the distribution of a preliminary prospectus, information concerning:

(i) The date of the preliminary prospectus distributed;

(ii) The dates of approximate dates of distribution;

(iii) The number of prospective underwriters and dealers to whom the preliminary prospectus was furnished;

(iv) The number of prospectuses so distributed;

(v) The number of prospectuses distributed to others, identifying them in general terms; and

(vi) The steps taken by such underwriters and dealers to comply with the provisions of Rule 15c2-8 under the Securities Exchange Act of 1934 (§ 240.15c2-8 of this chapter).

(b) Supplemental information described in paragraph (a) of this section shall not be required to be filed with or deemed part of the registration statement. The information shall be returned to the registrant upon request, provided that:

(1) Such request is made at the time such information is furnished to the staff;

(2) The return of such information is consistent with the protection of investors;

(3) The return of such information is consistent with the provisions of the Freedom of Information Act [5 U.S.C. 552];

(4) The information was not filed in electronic format.

Rule 419. Offerings by Blank Check Companies

(a) *Scope of the Rule and Definitions.*

(1) The provisions of this section shall apply to every registration statement filed under the Act relating to an offering by a blank check company.

(2) For purposes of this Section, the term "blank check company" shall mean a company that:

(i) is a development stage company that has no specific business plan or purpose or has indicated that its business plan is to engage in a merger or acquisition with an unidentified company or companies, or other entity or person; and

(ii) is issuing "penny stock," as defined in Rule 3a51-1 [17 CFR 240.3a51-1] under the Securities Exchange Act of 1934 ("Exchange Act").

(3) For purposes of this section, the term "purchaser" shall mean any person acquiring securities directly or indirectly in the offering, for cash or otherwise, including promoters or others receiving securities as compensation in connection with the offering.

(b) *Deposit of Securities and Proceeds in Escrow or Trust Account.*

(1) *General.*

(i) Except as otherwise provided in this section or prohibited by other applicable law, all securities issued in connection with an offering by a blank check company and the gross proceeds from the offering shall be deposited promptly into:

(A) an escrow account maintained by an "insured depository institution," as that term is defined in Section 3(c)(2) of the Federal Deposit Insurance Act [12 U.S.C. 1813(c)(2) (1991)]; or

(B) a separate bank account established by a broker or dealer registered under the Exchange Act maintaining net capital equal to or exceeding $25,000 (as calculated pursuant to Exchange Act Rule 15c3-1 [17 CFR 240.15c3-1]), in which the broker or dealer acts as trustee for persons having the beneficial interests in the account.

(ii) If funds and securities are deposited into an escrow account maintained by an insured depository institution, the deposit account records of the insured depository institution must provide that funds in the escrow account are held for the benefit of the purchasers named and identified in accordance with section 330.1 of the regulations of the Federal Deposit Insurance Corporation [12 CFR 330.1], and the records of the escrow agent, maintained in good faith and in the regular course of business, must show the name and interest of each party to the account. If funds and securities are deposited in a separate bank account established by a broker or dealer acting as a trustee, the books and records of the broker-dealer must indicate the name, address, and interest of each person for whom the account is held.

(2) *Deposit and Investment of Proceeds.*

(i) All offering proceeds, after deduction of cash paid for underwriting commissions, underwriting expenses and dealer allowances, and amounts permitted to be released to the registrant pursuant to (b)(2)(vi) of this section, shall be deposited promptly into the escrow or trust account; *provided, however,* that no deduction may be made for underwriting commissions, underwriting expenses or dealer allowances payable to an affiliate of the registrant.

(ii) Deposited proceeds shall be in the form of checks, drafts, or money orders payable to the order of the escrow agent or trustee.

(iii) Deposited proceeds and interest or dividends thereon, if any, shall be held for the sole benefit of the purchasers of the securities.

(iv) Deposited proceeds shall be invested in one of the following:

(A) an obligation that constitutes a "deposit," as that term is defined in section 3(*l*) of the Federal Deposit Insurance Act [12 U.S.C. 1813(*l*) (1991)];

(B) securities of any open-end investment company registered under the Investment Company Act of 1940 [15 U.S.C. 80a-1 *et. seq.*] that holds itself out as a money market fund meeting the conditions of paragraphs (c)(2), (c)(3), and (c)(4) of Rule 2a-7 [17 CFR 270.2a-7] under the Investment Company Act; or

(C) securities that are direct obligations of, or obligations guaranteed as to principal or interest by, the United States.

Note to Rule 419(b)(2)(iv): Issuers are cautioned that investments in government securities are inappropriate unless such securities can be readily sold or otherwise disposed of for cash at the time required without any dissipation of offering proceeds invested.

(v) Interest or dividends earned on the funds, if any, shall be held in the escrow or trust account until the funds are released in accordance with the provisions of this section. If funds held in the escrow or trust account are released to a purchaser of the securities, the purchasers shall receive interest or dividends earned, if any, on such funds up to the date of release. If funds held in the escrow or trust account are released to the registrant, interest or dividends earned on such funds up to the date of release may be released to the registrant.

(vi) The registrant may receive up to 10 percent of the proceeds remaining after payment of underwriting commissions, underwriting expenses and dealer allowances permitted by paragraph (b)(2)(i) of this section, exclusive of interest or dividends, as those proceeds are deposited into the escrow or trust account.

(3) *Deposit of Securities.*

(i) All securities issued in connection with the offering, whether or not for cash consideration, and any other securities issued with respect to such securities, including securities issued with respect to stock splits, stock dividends, or similar rights, shall be deposited directly into the escrow or trust account promptly upon issuance. The identity of the purchaser of the securities shall be included on the stock certificates or other documents evidencing such securities. *See also* 17 CFR 240.15g-8 regarding restrictions on sales of, or offers to sell, securities deposited in the escrow or trust account.

(ii) Securities held in the escrow or trust account are to remain as issued and deposited and shall be held for the sole benefit of the purchasers, who shall have voting rights, if any, with respect to securities held in their names, as provided by applicable state law. No transfer or other disposition of securities held in the escrow or trust account or any interest related to such securities shall be permitted other than by will or the laws of descent and distribution, or pursuant to a qualified domestic relations order as defined by the Internal Revenue Code of 1986 as amended [26 U.S.C. 1 *et seq.*], or Title 1 of the Employee Retirement Income Security Act [29 U.S.C. 1001 *et seq.*], or the rules thereunder.

(iii) Warrants, convertible securities or other derivative securities relating to securities held in the escrow or trust account may be exercised or converted in accordance with their terms; *provided, however,* that securities received upon exercise or conversion, together with any cash or other consideration paid in connection with the exercise or conversion, are promptly deposited into the escrow or trust account.

(4) *Escrow or Trust Agreement.* A copy of the executed escrow or trust agreement shall be filed as an exhibit to the registration statement and shall contain the provisions of paragraphs (b)(2), and (e)(3) of this section.

(5) *Request for Supplemental Information.* Upon request by the Commission or the staff, the registrant shall furnish as supplemental information the names and addresses of persons for whom securities are held in the escrow or trust account.

Note to Rule 419(b): With respect to a blank check offering subject to both Rule 419 and Exchange Act Rule 15c2-4 17 CFR 240.15c2-4], the requirements of Rule 15c2-4 are applicable only until the conditions of the offering governed by tha Rule are met (*e.g.*, reaching the minimum in a "part-or-none" offering). When those conditions are satisfied, Rule 419 continues to govern the use of offering proceeds.

(c) *Disclosure of Offering Terms.*

The initial registration statement shall disclose the specific terms of the offering, including, but not limited to:

(1) the terms and provisions of the escrow or trust agreement and the effect thereof upon the registrant's right to receive funds and the effect of the escrow or trust agreement upon the purchaser's funds and securities required to be deposited into the escrow or trust account, including, if applicable, any material risk of non-insurance of purchasers' funds resulting from deposits in excess of the insured amounts; and

(2) the obligation of the registrant to provide, and the right of the purchaser to receive, information regarding an acquisition, including the requirement that pursuant to this section, purchasers confirm in writing their investment in the registrant's securities as specified in paragraph (e) of this section.

(d) *Probable Acquisition Post-Effective Amendment Requirement.*

If, during any period in which offers or sales are being made, a significant acquisition becomes probable, the registrant shall file promptly a post-effective amendment disclosing the information specified by the applicable registration statement form and Industry Guides, including financial statements of the registrant and the company to be acquired a well as pro forma financial information required by the form and applicable rules and regulations. Where warrants, rights or other derivative securities issued in the initial offering are exercisable, there is a continuous offering of the underlying security.

(e) *Release of Deposited and Funds Securities.*

(1) *Post-Effective Amendment for Acquisition Agreement.* Upon execution of an agrement(s) for the acquisition(s) of a business(es) or assets that will constitute the business (or a line of business) of the registrant and for which the fair value of the business(es) or net assets to be acquired represents at least 80 percent of the maximum offering proceeds, including proceeds received or to be received upon the exercise or conversion of any securities offered, but excluding amounts payable to non-affiliates for underwriting commissions, underwriting expenses, and dealer allowances, the registrant shall file a post-effective amendment that:

(i) discloses the information specified by the applicable registration statement form and Industry Guides, including financial statements of the registrant and the company acquired or to be acquired and pro forma financial information required by the form and applicable rules and regulations;

(ii) discloses the results of the initial offering, including but not limited to:

(A) the gross offering proceeds received to date, specifying the amounts paid for underwriter commissions, underwriting expenses and dealer allowances, amounts disbursed to the registrant, and amounts remaining in the escrow or trust account; and

(B) the specific amount, use and application of funds disbursed to the registrant to date, including, but not limited to, the amounts paid to officers, directors, promoters, controlling shareholders or affiliates, either directly or indirectly, specifying the amounts and purposes of such payments; and

(iii) discloses the terms of the offering as described pursuant to paragraph (e)(2) of this section.

(2) *Terms of the Offering.* The terms of the offering must provide, and the registrant must satisfy, the following conditions:

(i) within five business days after the effective date of the post-effective amendment(s), the registrant shall send by first class mail or other equally prompt means, to each purchaser of securities held in escrow or trust, a copy of the prospectus contained in the post-effective amendment and any amendment or supplement thereto;

(ii) each purchaser shall have no fewer than 20 business days and no more than 45 business days from the effective date of the post-effective amendment to notify the registrant in writing that

105

the purchaser elects to remain an investor. If the registrant has not received such written notification by the 45th business day following the effective date of the post-effective amendment, funds and interest or dividends, if any, held in the escrow or trust account shall be sent by first class mail or other equally prompt means to the purchaser within five business days;

(iii) the acquisition(s) meeting the criteria set forth in paragraph (e)(1) of this section will be consummated if a sufficient number of purchasers confirm their investments; and

(iv) if a consummated acquisition(s) meeting the requirements of this section has not occurred by a date 18 months after the effective date of the initial registration statement, funds held in the escrow or trust account shall be returned by first class mail or equally prompt means to the purchaser within five business days following that date.

(3) *Conditions for Release of Deposited Securities and Funds.* Funds held in the escrow or trust account may be released to the registrant and securities may be delivered to the purchaser or other registered holder identified on the deposited securities only at the same time as or after:

(i) the escrow agent or trustee has received a signed representation from the registrant, together with other evidence acceptable to the escrow agent or trustee, that the requirements of paragraphs (e)(1) and (e)(2) of this section have been met; and

(ii) consummation of an acquisition(s) meeting the requirements of paragraph (e)(2)(iii) of this section.

(4) *Prospectus Supplement.* If funds and securities are released from the escrow or trust account to the registrant pursuant to this paragraph, the prospectus shall be supplemented to indicate the amount of funds and securities released and the date of release.

Notes to Rule 419(e)

Note 1. With respect to a blank check offering subject to both Rule 419 and Exchange Act Rule 10b-9 [17 CFR 240.10b-9], the requirements of Rule 10b-9 are applicable only until the conditions of the offering governed by that Rule are met (*e.g.,* reaching the minimum in a "part-or-none" offering). When those conditions are satisfied, Rule 419 continues to govern the use of offering proceeds.

Note 2. If the business(es) or assets are acquired for cash, the fair value shall be presumed to be equal to the cash paid. If all or part of the consideration paid consists of securities or other non-cash consideration, the fair value shall be determined by an accepted standard, such as bona fide sales of the assets or similar assets made within a reasonable time, forecasts of expected cash flows, independent appraisals, etc. Such valuation must be reasonable at the time made.

(f) *Financial Statements.*

The registrant shall:

(1) Furnish to security holders audited financial statements for the first full fiscal year of operations following consummation of an acquisition pursuant to paragraph (e) of this section, together with the information required by Item 303(a) of Regulation S-K [17 CFR 229.303(a)], no later than 90 days after the end of such fiscal year; and

(2) File the financial statements and additional information with the Commission under cover of Form 8-K [17 CFR 249.308]; *provided, however,* that such financial statements and related information need not be filed separately if the registrant is filing reports pursuant to Section 13(a) or 15(d) of the Exchange Act.

Rule 420. Legibility of Prospectus

(a) The body of all printed prospectuses and all notes to financial statements and other tabular data included therein shall be in roman type at least as large and as legible as 10-point modern type. However, (1) to the extent necessary for convenient presentation, financial statements and other tabular data, including tabular data in notes, and (2) prospectuses deemed to be omitting prospectuses under rule 482 [17 CFR 230.482] may be in roman type at least and as legible as 8-point modern type. All such type shall be leaded at least 2-points.

(b) Where a prospectus is distributed through an electronic medium, issuers may satisfy legibility requirements applicable to printed documents, such as paper size, type size and font, bold-face type, italics and red ink, by presenting all required information in a format readily communicated to investors, and where indicated, in a manner reasonably calculated to draw investor attention to specific information.

Rule 421. Presentation of Information in Prospectuses

(a) The information required in a prospectus need not follow the order of the items or other requirements in the form. Such information shall not, however, be set forth in such fashion as to obscure any of the required information or any information necessary to keep the required information from being incomplete or misleading. Where an item requires information to be given in a prospectus in tabular form it shall be given in substantially the tabular form specified in the item.

(b) You must present the information in a prospectus in a clear, concise and understandable manner. You must prepare the prospectus using the following standards:

(1) Present information in clear, concise sections, paragraphs, and sentences. Whenever possible, use short, explanatory sentences and bullet lists;

(2) Use descriptive headings and subheadings;

(3) Avoid frequent reliance on glossaries or defined terms as the primary means of explaining information in the prospectus. Define terms in a glossary or other section of the document only if the meaning is unclear from the context. Use a glossary only if it facilitates understanding of the disclosure; and

(4) Avoid legal and highly technical business terminology.

Note to § 230.421(b):

In drafting the disclosure to comply with this section, you should avoid the following:

1. Legalistic or overly complex presentations that make the substance of the disclosure difficult to understand;

2. Vague "boilerplate" explanations that are imprecise and readily subject to different interpretations;

3. Complex information copied directly from legal documents without any clear and concise explanation of the provision(s); and

4. Disclosure repeated in different sections of the document that increases the size of the document but does not enhance the quality of the information.

(c) All information required to be included in a prospectus shall be clearly understandable without the necessity of referring to the particular form or to the general rules and regulations. Except as to financial statements and information required in a tabular form, the information set forth in a prospectus may be expressed in condensed or summarized form. In lieu of repeating information in the form of notes to financial statements, references may be made to other parts of the prospectus where such information is set forth.

(d)(1) To enhance the readability of the prospectus, you must use plain English principles in the organization, language, and design of the front and back cover pages, the summary, and the risk factors section.

(2) You must draft the language in these sections so that at a minimum it substantially complies with each of the following plain English writing principles:

(i) Short sentences;

(ii) Definite, concrete, everyday words;

(iii) Active voice;

(iv) Tabular presentation or bullet lists for complex material, whenever possible;

(v) No legal jargon or highly technical business terms; and

(vi) No multiple negatives.

(3) In designing these sections or other sections of the prospectus, you may include pictures, logos, charts, graphs, or other design elements so long as the design is not misleading and the required information is clear. You are encouraged to use tables, schedules, charts and graphic illustrations of the results of operations, balance sheet, or other financial data that present the data in an understandable manner. Any presentation must be consistent with the financial statements

and non-financial information in the prospectus. You must draw the graphs and charts to scale. Any information you provide must not be misleading.

Instruction to § 230.421

You should read Securities Act Release No. 33-7497 (January 28, 1998) for information on plain English principles.

Rule 423. Date of Prospectuses

Except for a form of prospectus used after the effective date of the registration statement and before the determination of the offering price as permitted by Rule 430A(c) under the Securities Act (§ 230.430A(c) of this chapter) or before the opening of bids as permitted by Rule 445(c) under the Securities Act (§ 230.445(c) of this chapter), each prospectus used after the effective date of the registration statement shall be dated approximately as of such effective date; provided, however, that a revised or amended prospectus used thereafter need only bear the approximate date of its issuance. Each supplement to a prospectus shall be dated separately the approximate date of its issuance.

Rule 424. Filing of Prospectuses, Number of Copies

(a) Except as provided in paragraph (f) of this section, five copies of every form of prospectus sent or given to any person prior to the effective date of the registration statement which varies from the form or forms of prospectus included in the registrant statement as filed pursuant to § 230.402(a) of this chapter shall be filed as a part of the registration statement not later than the date such form of prospectus is first sent or given to any person: *Provided, however,* That only a form of prospectus that contains substantive changes from or additions to a prospectus previously filed with the Commission as part of a registration statement need be filed pursuant to this paragraph (a).

(b) Ten copies of each form of prospectus purporting to comply with section 10 of the Securities Act [15 U.S.C. 77j] except for documents constituting a prospectus pursuant to Rule 428(a) (§ 230.428(a) of this chapter), shall be filed with the Commission in the form in which it is used after the effectiveness of the registration statement and identified as required by paragraph (e); *Provided, however,* that only a form of prospectus that contains substantive changes from or additions to a previously filed prospectus is required to be filed; *Provided, further,* that this paragraph (b) shall not apply in respect of a form of prospectus contained in a registration statement and relating solely to securities offered at competitive bidding, which prospectus is intended for use prior to the opening of bids. The ten copies shall be filed or transmitted for filing as follows:

(1) A form of prospectus that discloses information previously omitted from the prospectus filed as part of an effective registration statement in reliance upon Rule 430A under the Securities Act [§ 230.430A of this chapter] shall be filed with the Commission no later than the second business day following the earlier of the date of determination of the offering price or the date it is first used after effectiveness in connection with a public offering or sales, or transmitted by a means reasonably calculated to result in filing with the Commission by that date.

(2) A form of prospectus used in connection with a primary offering of securities on a delayed basis pursuant to Rule 415(a)(1)(vii), (viii) or (x) under the Securities Act [§ 230.415(a)(1)(vii), (viii) or (x) of this chapter] that discloses the public offering price, description of securities, specific method of distribution or similar matters shall be filed with the Commission no later than the second business day following the earlier of the date of the determination of the offering price or the date it is first used after effectiveness in connection with a public offering or sales, or transmitted by a means reasonably calculated to result in filing with the Commission by that date.

(3) A form of prospectus that reflects facts or events other than those covered in paragraphs (b)(1), (2) and (6) of this section that constitute a substantive change from or addition to the information set forth in the last form of prospectus filed with the Commission under this section or as part of a registration statement under the Securities Act shall be filed with the Commission no later than the fifth business day after the date it is first used after effectiveness in connection with

a public offering or sales, or transmitted by a means reasonably calculated to result in filing with the Commission by that date.

(4) A form of prospectus that discloses information, facts or events covered in both paragraphs (b)(1) and (3) shall be filed with the Commission no later than the second business day following the earlier of the date of the determination of the offering price or the date it is first used after effectiveness in connection with a public offering or sales, or transmitted by a means reasonably calculated to result in filing with the Commission by that date.

(5) A form of prospectus that discloses information, facts or events covered in both paragraphs (b)(2) and (3) shall be filed with the Commission no later than the second business day following the earlier of the date of the determination of the offering price or the date it is first used after effectiveness in connection with a public offering or sales, or transmitted by a means reasonably calculated to result in filing with the Commission by that date.

(6) A form of prospectus used in connection with an offering of securities under Canada's National Policy Statement No. 45 pursuant to Rule 415 under the Securities Act (§ 230.415 of this chapter) that is not made in the United States shall be filed with the Commission no later than the date it is first used in Canada, or transmitted by a means reasonably calculated to result in filing with the Commission by that date.

(7) Ten copies of a term sheet or abbreviated term sheet sent or given in reliance upon Rule 434 under the Act (§ 230.434) shall be filed with the Commission pursuant to this paragraph no later than the second business day following the earlier of the date of determination of the offering price, or the date it is first used after effectiveness in connection with a public offering or sales, or transmitted by a means reasonably calculated to result in filing with the Commission by that date. In addition to the information required by paragraph (e) of this section, each copy of such term sheet or abbreviated term sheet shall include the information required by Rule 434(e) (§ 230.434(e)).

Instruction 1. Notwithstanding § 230.424(b)(2) and (b)(5) above, a form of prospectus or prospectus supplement relating to an offering of mortgage-related securities on a delayed basis under § 230.415(a)(1)(vii) or asset-backed securities on a delayed basis under § 230.415(a)(1)(x) that is required to be filed pursuant to paragraph (b) of this section shall be filed with the Commission no later than the second business day following the date it is first used after effectiveness in connection with a public offering or sales, or transmitted by a means reasonably calculated to result in filing with the Commission by that date.

Instruction 2: Notwithstanding paragraphs (b)(1), (b)(2), (b)(4) and (b)(5) of this section, a form of prospectus sent or given in reliance on Rule 434(c) (§ 230.434(c)) with respect to securities registered on Form S-3 or Form F-3 (§ 239.13 or § 239.33 of this chapter), other than an abbreviated term sheet filed pursuant to paragraph (b)(7) of this section, shall be filed with the Commission on or prior to the date on which a confirmation is sent or given.

(c) If a form of prospectus, other than one filed pursuant to paragraph (b)(1) or (b)(4) of this Rule, consists of a prospectus supplement attached to a form of prospectus that (1) previously has been filed or (2) was not required to be filed pursuant to paragraph (b) because it did not contain substantive changes from a prospectus that previously was filed, only the prospectus supplement need be filed under paragraph (b) of this rule, provided that the first page of each prospectus supplement includes a cross reference to the date(s) of the related prospectus and any prospectus supplements thereto that together constitute the prospectus required to be delivered by Section 5(b) of the Securities Act [15 U.S.C. 77e(b)] with respect to the securities currently being offered or sold. The cross reference may be set forth in longhand, provided it is legible.

NOTE: Any prospectus supplement being filed separately that is smaller than a prospectus page should be attached to an 8½" × 11" sheet of paper.

(d) Every prospectus consisting of a radio or television broadcast shall be reduced to writing. Five copies of every such prospectus shall be filed with the Commission in accordance with the requirements of this section.

(e) Each copy of a form of prospectus filed under this rule shall contain in the upper right corner of the cover page the paragraph of this rule, including the subparagraph if applicable, under which the filing is made, and the file number of the registration statement to which the prospectus relates. The information required by this paragraph may be set forth in longhand, provided it is legible.

(f) This rule shall not apply with respect to prospectuses of an investment company registered under the Investment Company Act of 1940 or a business development company.

Rule 425. Filing of Certain Prospectuses and Communications under §230.135 in Connection with Business Combination Transactions

(a) All written communications made in reliance on §230.165 are prospectuses that must be filed with the Commission under this section on the date of first use.

(b) All written communications that contain no more information than that specified in §230.135 must be filed with the Commission on or before the date of first use except as provided in paragraph (d)(1) of this section. A communication limited to the information specified in §230.135 will not be deemed an offer in accordance with §230.135 even though it is filed under this section.

(c) Each prospectus or §230.135 communication filed under this section must identify the filer, the company that is the subject of the offering and the Commission file number for the related registration statement or, if that file number is unknown, the subject company's Exchange Act or Investment Company Act file number, in the upper right corner of the cover page.

(d) Notwithstanding paragraph (a), the following need not be filed under this section:

(1) Any written communication that is limited to the information specified in §230.135 and does not contain new or different information from that which was previously publicly disclosed and filed under this section.

(2) Any research report used in reliance on §230.137, §230.138 and §230.139;

(3) Any confirmation described in §240.10b-10 of this chapter; and

(4) Any prospectus filed under §230.424.

Notes to §230.425: 1. File five copies of the prospectus or §230.135 communication if paper filing is permitted.

2. No filing is required under §240.13e-4(c), §240.14a-12(b), §240.14d-2(b), or §240.14d-9(a), if the communication is filed under this section. Communications filed under this section also are deemed filed under the other applicable sections.

Rule 427. Contents of Prospectus Used After Nine Months

There may be omitted from any prospectus used more than 9 months after the effective date of the registration statement any information previously required to be contained in the prospectus insofar as later information covering the same subjects, including the latest available certified financial statement, as of a date not more than 16 months prior to the use of the prospectus is contained therein.

Rule 428. Documents Constituting a Section 10(a) prospectus for Form S-8 Registration Statement; Requirements Relating to Offerings of Securities Registered on Form S-8

(a) (1) Where securities are to be offered pursuant to a registration statement on Form S-8 (§239.16b of this chapter), the following, taken together, shall constitute a prospectus that meets the requirements of Section 10(a) of the Act: (i) the document(s), or portions thereof as permitted by paragraph (b)(1)(ii) of this section, containing the employee benefit plan information required by Item 1 of the Form; (ii) the statement of availability of registrant information, employee benefit plan annual reports and other information required by Item 2; and (iii) the documents containing registrant information and employee benefit plan annual reports that are incorporated by reference in the registration statement pursuant to Item 3.

(2) The registrant shall maintain a file of the documents that, pursuant to paragraph (a) of this section, at any time are part of the Section 10(a) prospectus, except for documents required to be incorporated by reference in the registration statement pursuant to Item 3 of Form S-8. Each such document shall be included in the file until five years after it is last used as part of the Section 10(a) prospectus to offer or sell securities pursuant to the plan. With respect to documents

containing specifically designated portions that constitute part of the Section 10(a) prospectus pursuant to paragraph (b)(1)(ii) of this section, the entire document shall be maintained in the file. Upon request, the registrant shall furnish to the Commission or its staff a copy of any or all of the documents included in the file.

(b) Where securities are offered pursuant to a registration statement on Form S-8:

(1)(i) The registrant shall deliver or cause to be delivered, to each employee who is eligible to participate (or selected by the registrant to participate, in the case of a stock option or other plan with selective participation) in an employee benefit plan to which the registration statement relates, the information required by Part I of Form S-8. The information shall be in written form and shall be updated in writing in a timely manner to reflect any material changes during any period in which offers or sales are being made. When updating information is furnished, documents previously furnished need not be re-delivered, but the registrant shall furnish promptly without charge to each employee, upon written or oral request, a copy of all documents containing the plan information required by Part I that then constitute part of the Section 10(a) prospectus.

(ii) The registrant may designate an entire document or only portions of a document as constituting part of the Section 10(a) prospectus. If the registrant designates only portions of a document as constituting part of the prospectus, rather than the entire document, a statement clearly identifying such portions, for example, by reference to section headings, section numbers, paragraphs or page numbers within the document must be included in a conspicuous place in the forepart of the document, or such portions must be specifically designated throughout the text of the document. Registrants shall not designate only words or sentences within a paragraph as part of a prospectus. Unless the portions of a document constituting part of the Section 10(a) prospectus are clearly identified, the entire document shall constitute part of the prospectus.

(iii) The registrant shall date any document constituting part of the Section 10(a) prospectus or containing portions constituting part of the prospectus and shall include the following printed, stamped or typed legend in a conspicuous place in the forepart of the document, substituting the bracketed language as appropriate: "This document [Specifically designated portions of this document] constitutes [constitute] part of a prospectus covering securities that have been registered under the Securities Act of 1933."

(iv) The registrant shall revise the document(s) containing the plan information sent or given to newly eligible participants pursuant to paragraph (b)(1)(i) of this section, if documents containing updating information would obscure the readability of the plan information.

(2) The registrant shall deliver or cause to be delivered with the document(s) containing the information required by Part I of Form S-8, to each employee to whom such information is sent or given, a copy of any one of the following:

(i) the registrant's annual report to security holders containing the information required by Rule 14a-3(b) (§ 240.14a-3(b) of this chapter) under the Securities Exchange Act of 1934 (*Exchange Act*) for its latest fiscal year;

(ii) the registrant's annual report on Form 10-K (§ 249.310 of this chapter) and Form 10-KSB (§ 249.310b of this chapter), U5S (§ 259.5s of this chapter), 20-F (§ 249.220f of this chapter) or, in the case of registrants described in General Instruction A.(2) of Form 40-F, 40-F (§ 249.240f of this chapter) for its latest fiscal year;

(iii) the latest prospectus filed pursuant to Rule 424(b) (§ 230.424(b) of this chapter) under the Act that contains audited financial statements for the registrant's latest fiscal year, *provided that* the financial statements are not incorporated by reference from another filing, and *provided further* that such prospectus contains substantially the information required by Rule 14a-3(b) or the registration statement was on Form SB-2 (§ 239.10 of this chapter) or F-1 (§ 239.31 of this chapter); or

(iv) the registrant's effective Exchange Act registration statement on Form 10 (§ 249.210 of this chapter) and Form 10-SB (§ 249.210b of this chapter), 20-F or, in the case of registrants described in General Instruction A.(2) of Form 40-F, 40-F containing audited financial statements for the registrant's latest fiscal year.

Instructions.

1. If a registrant has previously sent or given an employee a copy of any document specified in clauses (i)-(iv) of paragraph (b)(2) for the latest fiscal year, it need not be re-delivered, but the registrant shall furnish promptly, without charge, a copy of such document upon written or oral request of the employee.

2. If the latest fiscal year of the registrant has ended within 120 days (or 190 days with respect to foreign private issuers) prior to the delivery of the documents containing the information specified by Part I of Form S-8, the registrant may deliver a document containing financial statements for the fiscal year preceding the latest fiscal year, *provided that* within the 120 or 190 day period a document containing financial statements for the latest fiscal year is furnished to each employee.

(3) The registrant shall deliver or cause to be delivered promptly, without charge, to each employee to whom information is required to be delivered, upon written or oral request, a copy of the information that has been incorporated by reference pursuant to Item 3 of Form S-8 (not including exhibits to the information that is incorporated by reference unless such exhibits are specifically incorporated by reference into the information that the registration statement incorporates).

(4) Where interests in a plan are registered, the registrant shall deliver or cause to be delivered promptly, without charge, to each employee to whom information is required to be delivered, upon written or oral request, a copy of the then latest annual report of the plan filed pursuant to Section 15(d) of the Exchange Act, whether on form 11-K (§ 249.311 of this chapter) or included as part of the registrant's annual report on Form 10-K and Form 10-KSB.

(5) The registrant shall deliver or cause to be delivered to all employees participating in a stock option plan or plan fund that invests in registrant securities (and other plan participants who request such information orally or in writing) who do not otherwise receive such material, copies of all reports, proxy statements and other communications distributed to its security holders generally, provided that such material is sent or delivered no later than the time it is sent to security holders.

(c) As used in this Rule, the term "employee benefit plan" is defined in Rule 405 of Regulation C (§ 230.405 of this chapter) and the term "employee" is defined in General Instruction A.1 of Form S-8.

Rule 430. Prospectus For Use Prior to Effective Date

(a) A form of prospectus filed as a part of the registration statement shall be deemed to meet the requirements of section 10 of the Act for the purpose of section 5(b)(1) thereof prior to the effective date of the registration statement, provided such form of prospectus contains substantially the information required by the Act and the rules and regulations thereunder to be included in a prospectus meeting the requirements of section 10(a) of the Act for the securities being registered, or contains substantially that information except for the omission of information with respect to the offering price, underwriting discounts or commissions, discounts or commissions to dealers, amount of proceeds, conversion rates, call prices, or other matters dependent upon the offering price. Every such form of prospectus shall be deemed to have been filed as a part of the registration statement for the purpose of section 7 of the Act.

(b) A form of prospectus filed as part of a registration statement on Form N-1A (§ 239.15A and § 274.11A of this chapter), Form N-2 (§ 239.14 and § 274.11a-1 of this chapter), Form N-3 (§ 239.17a and § 274.11b of this chapter), Form N-4 (§ 239.17b and § 274.11c of this chapter), or Form N-6 (§ 239.17c and § 274.11d of this chapter) shall be deemed to meet the requirements of Section 10 of the Act (15 U.S.C. 77j) for the purpose of Section 5(b)(1) thereof (15 U.S.C. 77e(b)(1)) prior to the effective date of the registration statement, provided that:

(1) Such form of prospectus meets the requirements of paragraph (a) of this section; and

(2) Such registration statement contains a form of Statement of Additional Information that is made available to persons receiving such prospectus upon written or oral request, and without charge, unless the form of prospectus contains the information otherwise required to be disclosed in the form of Statement of Additional Information. Every such form of prospectus shall be

deemed to have been filed as part of the registration statement for the purpose of section 7 of the Act.

Rule 430A. Prospectus in a Registration Statement at the Time of Effectiveness

(a) The form of prospectus filed as part of a registration statement that is declared effective may omit information with respect to the public offering price, underwriting syndicate (including any material relationships between the registrant and underwriters not named therein), underwriting discounts or commissions, discounts or commissions to dealers, amount of proceeds, conversion rates, call prices and other items dependent upon the offering price, delivery dates, and terms of the securities dependent upon the offering date; and such form of prospectus need not contain such information in order for the registration statement to meet the requirements of Section 7 of the Securities Act [15 U.S.C. 77g] for the purposes of Section 5 thereof [15 U.S.C. 77e], *Provided that:*

(1) the securities to be registered are offered for cash;

(2) the registrant furnishes the undertakings required by Item 512(i) of Regulation S-K (§ 229.512(i) of this chapter); and

(3) the information omitted in reliance upon paragraph (a) from the form of prospectus filed as part of a registration statement that is declared effective is contained in a form of prospectus filed with the Commission pursuant to Rule 424(b) or Rule 497(h) under the Securities Act [§§ 230.424(b) or 230.497(h) of this chapter]; except that if such form of prospectus is not so filed by the later of fifteen business days after the effective date of the registration statement or fifteen business days after the effectiveness of a post-effective amendment thereto that contains a form of prospectus, or transmitted by a means reasonably calculated to result in filing with the Commission by that date, the information omitted in reliance upon paragraph (a) must be contained in an effective post-effective amendment to the registration statement.

Instruction to paragraph (a): A decrease in the volume of securities offered or changed in the bona fide estimate of the maximum offering price range from that indicated in the form of prospectus filed as part of a registration statement that is declared effective may be disclosed in the form of prospectus filed with the Commission pursuant to § 230.424(b) or § 230.497(h) under the Securities Act so long as the decrease in the volume or change in the price range would not materially change the disclosure contained in the registration statement at effectiveness. Notwithstanding the foregoing, any increase or decrease in volume (if the total dollar value of securities offered would not exceed that which was registered) and any deviation from the low or high end of the range may be reflected in the form of prospectus filed with the Commission pursuant to Rule 424(b)(1) (§ 230.424(b)(1)) or Rule 497(h) (§ 230.497(h)) if, in the aggregate, the changes in volume and price represent no more than a 20% change in the maximum aggregate offering price set forth in the "Calculation of Registration Fee" table in the effective registration statement.

(b) The information omitted in reliance upon paragraph (a) from the form of prospectus filed as part of an effective registration statement, and contained in the form of prospectus filed with the Commission pursuant to Rule 424(b) or Rule 497(h) under the Securities Act [§§ 230.424(b) or 230.497(h) of this chapter], shall be deemed to be a part of the registration statement as of the time it was declared effective.

(c) When used prior to determination of the offering price of the securities, a form of prospectus relating to the securities offered pursuant to a registration statement that is declared effective with information omitted from the form of prospectus filed as part of such effective registration statement in reliance upon this Rule 430A need not contain information omitted pursuant to paragraph (a), in order to meet the requirements of Section 10 of the Securities Act [15 U.S.C. 77j] for the purpose of Section 5(b)(1) [15 U.S.C. 77e(b)(1)] thereof. This provision shall not limit the information required to be contained in a form of prospectus meeting the requirements of Section 10(a) of the Act for the purposes of Section 5(b)(2) thereof or exception (a) of Section 2(10) [15 U.S.C. 77b(10)] thereof.

(d) This rule shall not apply to registration statements for securities to be offered by competitive bidding.

(e) In the case of a registration statement filed on Form N-1A (§ 239.15A and § 274.11A of this chapter), Form N-2 (§ 239.14 and § 274.11a-1 of this chapter), Form N-3 (§ 239.17a and § 274.11b of this chapter), Form N-4 (§ 239.17b and § 274.11c of this chapter), or Form N-6 (§ 239.17c and § 274.11d of this chapter), the references to "form of prospectus" in paragraphs (a) and (b) of this section and the accompanying Note shall be deemed also to refer to the form of Statement of Additional Information filed as part of such a registration statement.

NOTE: If information is omitted in reliance upon paragraph (a) from the form of prospectus filed as part of an effective registration statement, or effective post-effective amendment thereto, the registrant must ascertain promptly whether a form of prospectus transmitted for filing under Rule 424(b) or Rule 497(h) under the Securities Act actually was received for filing by the Commission and, in the event that it was not, promptly file such prospectus.

Rule 431. Summary Prospectuses

(a) A summary prospectus prepared and filed (except a summary prospectus filed by an open-end management investment company registered under the Investment Company Act of 1940) as part of a registration statement in accordance with this section shall be deemed to be a prospectus permitted under section 10(b) of the Act (15 U.S.C. 77j(b)) for the purposes of section 5(b)(1) of the Act (15 U.S.C. 77e(b)(1)) if the form used for registration of the securities to be offered provides for the use of a summary prospectus and the following conditions are met:

(1)(i) The registrant is organized under the laws of the United States or any State or Territory or the District of Columbia and has its principal business operations in the United States or its territories; or

(ii) The registrant is a foreign private issuer eligible to use Form F-2 (§ 239.32 of this chapter);

(2) The registrant has a class of securities registered pursuant to section 12(b) of the Securities Exchange Act of 1934 or has a class of equity securities registered pursuant to section 12(g) of that Act or is required to file reports pursuant to section 15(d) of that Act;

(3) The registrant: (i) has been subject to the requirements of section 12 or 15(d) of the Securities Exchange Act of 1934 and has filed all the material required to be filed pursuant to sections 13, 14 or 15(d) of that Act for a period of at least thirty-six calendar months immediately preceding the filing of the registration statement; and (ii) has filed in a timely manner all reports required to be filed during the twelve calendar months and any portion of a month immediately preceding the filing of the registration statement and, if the registrant has used (during the twelve calendar months and any portion of a month immediately preceding the filing of the registration statement) Rule 12b-25(b) under the Securities Exchange Act of 1934 (§ 240.12b-25 of this chapter) with respect to a report or portion of a report, that report or portion thereof has actually been filed within the time period prescribed by that Rule; and

(4) Neither the registrant nor any of its consolidated or unconsolidated subsidiaries has, since the end of its last fiscal year for which certified financial statements of the registrant and its consolidated subsidiaries were included in a report filed pursuant to section 13(a) or 15(d) of the Securities Exchange Act of 1934; (i) failed to pay any dividend or sinking fund installment on preferred stock; or (ii) defaulted on any installment or installments on indebtedness for borrowed money, or on any rental on one or more long term leases, which defaults in the aggregate are material to the financial position of the registrant and its consolidated and unconsolidated subsidiaries, taken as a whole.

(b) A summary prospectus shall contain the information specified in the instructions as to summary prospectuses in the form used for registration of the securities to be offered. Such prospectus may include any other information the substance of which is contained in the registration statement except as otherwise specifically provided in the instructions as to summary prospectuses in the form used for registration. It shall not include any information the substance of which is not contained in the registration statement except that a summary prospectus may contain any information specified in Rule 134(a) (§ 230.134(a)). No reference need be made to inapplicable terms and negative answers to any item of the form may be omitted.

(c) All information included in a summary prospectus, other than the statement required by paragraph (e) of this section, may be expressed in such condensed or summarized form as may be appropriate in the light of the circumstances under which the prospectus is to be used. The information need not follow the numerical sequence of the items of the form used for registration. Every summary prospectus shall be dated approximately as of the date of its first use.

(d) When used prior to the effective date of the registration statement, a summary prospectus shall be captioned a "Preliminary Summary Prospectus" and shall comply with the applicable requirements relating to a preliminary prospectus.

(e) A statement to the following effect shall be prominently set forth in conspicuous print at the beginning or at the end of every summary prospectus:

"Copies of a more complete prospectus may be obtained from" (insert name(s), address(es) and telephone number(s)). Copies of a summary prospectus filed with the Commission pursuant to paragraph (g) of this section may omit the names of persons from whom the complete prospectus may be obtained.

(f) Any summary prospectus published in a newspaper, magazine or other periodical need only be set in type at least as large as 7 point modern type. Nothing in this rule shall prevent the use of reprints of a summary prospectus published in a newspaper, magazine, or other periodical, if such reprints are clearly legible.

(g) Eight copies of every proposed summary prospectus shall be filed as a part of the registration statement, or as an amendment thereto, at least 5 days (exclusive of Saturdays, Sundays and holidays) prior to the use thereof, or prior to the release for publication by any newspaper, magazine or other person, whichever is earlier. The Commission may, however, in its discretion, authorize such use or publication prior to the expiration of the 5-day period upon a written request for such authorization. Within 7 days after the first use or publication thereof, 5 additional copies shall be filed in the exact form in which it was used or published.

Rule 432. Additional Information Required to be Included in Prospectuses Relating to Tender Offers

Notwithstanding the provisions of any form for the registration of securities under the Act, any prospectus relating to securities to be offered in connection with a tender offer for, or a request or invitation for tenders of, securities subject to either § 240.13e-4 or section 14(d) of the Securities Exchange Act of 1934 (15 U.S.C. 78n(d)) must include the information required by § 240.13e-4(d) (1) or § 240.14d-6(d)(1) of this chapter, as applicable, in all tender offers, requests or invitations that are published, sent or given to security holders.

Rule 434. Prospects Delivery Requirements in Firm Commitment Underwritten Offerings of Securities for Cash

(a) Where securities are offered for cash in a firm commitment underwritten offering or investment grade debt securities are offered for cash on an agency basis under a medium term note program, and such securities are neither asset-backed securities nor structured securities, and the conditions described in paragraph (b) or paragraph (c) of this section are satisfied, then:

(1) The prospectus subject to completion and the term sheet described in paragraph (b) of this section, taken together, and the prospectus subject to completion and the abbreviated term sheet described in paragraph (c) of this section, taken together, shall constitute prospectuses that meet the requirements of Section 10(a) of the Act (15 U.S.C. § 77j(a)) for purposes of Section 5(b)(2) of the Act (15 U.S.C. § 77e(b)(2)) and Section 2(10)(a) of the Act (15 U.S.C. § 77b(10)(a)); and

(2) The Section 10(a) prospectus described in paragraph (a)(1) of this section shall have:

(i) Been sent or given prior to or at the same time that a confirmation is sent or given for purposes of Section 2(10)(a) of the Act; and

(ii) Accompanied or preceded the transmission of the securities for purposes of sale or for delivery after sale for purposes of Section 5(b)(2) of the Act.

(b) With respect to offerings of securities that are registered on a form other than Form S-3 or Form F-3 (§ 239.13 or § 239.33 of this chapter), and with respect to offerings of securities by only those investment companies registered under the Investment Company Act of 1940 (15 U.S.C. § 80a-1 *et seq.*) that register their securities on Form N-2 (§ 274.11a-1 of this chapter) or Form S-6 (§ 239.16 of this chapter), the following conditions are satisfied:

(1) A prospectus subject to completion and any term sheet described in paragraph (b)(3) of this section, together or separately, are sent or given prior to or at the same time with the confirmation;

(2) Such prospectus subject to completion and term sheet, together, are not materially different from the prospectus in the registration statement at the time of its effectiveness or an effective post-effective amendment thereto (including, in both, instances, information deemed to be a part of the registration statement at the time of effectiveness pursuant to Rule 430A(b) (§ 230.430A(b)); and

(3) A term sheet under this paragraph (b) shall set forth all information material to investors with respect to the offering that is not disclosed in the prospectus subject to completion or the confirmation.

(c) With respect to offerings of securities registered on Form S-3 or Form F-3 (§ 239.13 or § 239.33 of this chapter), the following conditions are satisfied:

(1) A prospectus subject to completion and the abbreviated term sheet described in paragraph (c)(3) of this section, together or separately, are sent or given prior to or at the same time with the confirmation;

(2) A form of prospectus that:

(i) Discloses information previously omitted from the prospectus filed as part of an effective registration statement in reliance upon Rule 430A (§ 230.430A), to the extent not set forth in the abbreviated term sheet (as described in paragraph (c)(3) of this section), shall be filed pursuant to Rule 424(b) (§ 230.424(b)) on or prior to the date on which a confirmation is sent or given; or

(ii) Discloses the public offering price, description of securities, to the extent not set forth in the abbreviated term sheet (as described in paragraph (c)(3) of this section), and specific method of distribution or similar matters shall be filed pursuant to Rule 424(b) (§ 230.424(b)) on or prior to the date on which a confirmation is sent or given; and

(3) The abbreviated term sheet under this paragraph (c) shall set forth, if not previously disclosed in the prospectus subject to completion or the registrant's Exchange Act filings incorporated by reference into the prospectus:

(i) The description of securities required by Item 202 of Regulations S-K (§ 229.202 of this chapter) or by Items 9, 10 and 12 of Form 20-F (§ 249.220f of this chapter) as applicable, or a fair and accurate summary thereof; and

(ii) All material changes to the registrant's affairs required to be disclosed pursuant to Item 11 of Form S-3 or Item 5 of Form F-3 (§ 239.13 or § 239.33 of this chapter), as applicable.

(d) Except in the case of offerings pursuant to Rule 415(a)(1)(x), (§ 230.415(a)(1)(x), the information contained in any term sheet or abbreviated term sheet described under this section shall be deemed to be a part of the registration statement as of the time such registration statement was declared effective. In the case of offerings pursuant to Rule 415(a)(1)(x) (§ 230.415(a)(1)(x)), the information contained in any term sheet or abbreviated term sheet described under this section shall be deemed to be a part of the registration statement as of the time such information is filed with the Commission.

Instruction: With respect to the obligation to file any form of prospectus, term sheet, or abbreviated term sheet used in reliance on this section, see Rule 424(b) (§ 230.424(b)) or Rule 497(h) (§ 230.497(h)).

(e) Any term sheet or abbreviated term sheet described under this section shall, in the top center of the cover page thereof, state that such document is a supplement to a prospectus and identify that prospectus by issuer name and date; clearly identify that such document is a term sheet or abbreviated term sheet used in reliance on Rule 434; set forth the approximate date of first use of such document; and clearly identify the documents that, when taken together, constitute the Section 10(a) prospectus.

(f) For purposes of this section, *asset-backed securities* shall mean asset-backed securities as defined in General Instruction I.B.5. of Form S-3 (§ 239.13 of this chapter).

(g) For purposes of this section, *prospectus subject to completion* shall mean any prospectus that is either a preliminary prospectus used in reliance on Rule 430 (§ 230.430), a prospectus omitting information in reliance upon Rule 430A (§ 230.430A), or a prospectus omitting information that is not yet known concerning a delayed offering pursuant to Rule 415(a)(i)(x) (§ 230.415(a)(1)(x)) that is contained in a registration statement at the time of effectiveness or as subsequently revised.

(h) For purposes of this section, *structured securities* shall mean securities whose cash flow characteristics depend upon one or more indices or that have imbedded forwards or options or securities where an investor's investment return and the issuer's payment obligations are contingent on, or highly sensitive to, changes in the value of underlying assets, indices, interest rates or cash flows.

(i) For purposes of this section, *investment grade securities* shall mean investment grade securities as defined in General Instruction I.B.2. of Form S-3 or Form F-3 (§ 239.13 or § 239.33 of this chapter).

(j) For the purposes of this section, a firm commitment underwritten offering shall include a firm commitment underwritten offering of securities by a closed-end company or by a unit investment trust registered under the Investment Company Act of 1940.

Rule 436. Consents Required in Special Cases

(a) If any portion of the report or opinion of an expert or counsel is quoted or summarized as such in the registration statement or in a prospectus, the written consent of the expert or counsel shall be filed as an exhibit to the registration statement and shall expressly state that the expert or counsel consents to such quotation or summarization.

(b) If it is stated that any information contained in the registration statement has been reviewed or passed upon by any persons and that such information is set forth in the registration statement upon the authority of or in reliance upon such persons as experts, the written consents of such persons shall be filed as exhibits to the registration statement.

(c) Notwithstanding the provisions of paragraph (b) of this section, a report on unaudited interim financial information (as defined in paragraph (d) of this section) by an independent accountant who has conducted a review of such interim financial information shall not be considered a part of a registration statement prepared or certified by an accountant or a report prepared or certified by an accountant within the meaning of sections 7 and 11 of the Act.

(d) The term "report on unaudited interim financial information" shall mean a report which consists of the following: (1) a statement that the review of interim financial information was made in accordance with established professional standards for such reviews; (2) an identification of the interim financial information reviewed; (3) a description of the procedures for a review of interim financial information; (4) a statement that a review of interim financial information is substantially less in scope that an examination in accordance with generally accepted auditing standards, the objective of which is an expression of opinion regarding the financial statements taken as a whole, and, accordingly, no such opinion is expressed; and (5) a statement about whether the accountant is aware of any material modifications that should be made to the accompanying financial information so that it conforms with generally accepted accounting principles.

(e) Where a counsel is named as having acted for the underwriters or selling security holders, no consent will be required by reason of his being named as having acted in such capacity.

(f) Where the opinion of one counsel relies upon the opinion of another counsel, the consent of the counsel whose prepared opinion is relied upon need not be furnished.

(g)(1) Notwithstanding the provisions of paragraphs (a) and (b) of this section, the security rating assigned to a class of debt securities, a class of convertible debt securities, or a class of preferred stock by a nationally recognized statistical rating organization, or with respect to registration statements on Form F-9 (§ 239.39 of this chapter) by any other rating organization specified in the Instruction to paragraph (a)(2) of General Instruction I of Form F-9, shall not be considered a part of the registration statement prepared or certified by a person within the meaning of sections 7 and 11 of the Act.

(2) For the purpose of paragraph (g)(1) of this section, the term "nationally recognized statistical rating organization" shall have the same meaning as used in Rule 15c3-1(c)(2)(vi)(F) [17 CFR 240.15c3-1(c)(2)(vi)(F)].

Rule 455. Place of Filing

All registration statements and other papers filed with the Commission shall be filed at its principal office, except for statements of Form SB-1 (§ 239.9 of this chapter) and Form SB-2 (§ 239.10 of this chapter). Registration statements on Form SB-1 or SB-2 may be filed with the Commission either at its principal office or at the Commission's regional or district offices as specified in General Instruction A to each of those forms, except that registration statements and post-effective amendments thereto on such forms that are filed pursuant to Rule 462(b) (§ 230.462(b)) and Rule 110(d) (§ 230.110(d)) shall be filed at the Commission's principal office. Such material may be filed by delivery to the Commission through the mails or otherwise; provided, however, that only registration statements and post-effective amendments thereto filed pursuant to Rule 462(b) (§ 230-462(b)) and Rule 110(d) (§ 230.110(d)) may be filed by means of facsimile transmission.

Rule 456. Date of Filing

The date on which any papers are actually received by the Commission shall be the date of filing thereof, if all requirements of the Act and the rules with respect to such filing have been complied with and the required fee paid. The failure to pay an insignificant amount of the required fee at the time of filing, as the result of a bona fide error, shall not be deemed to affect the date of filing.

Rule 460. Distribution of Preliminary Prospectus

(a) Pursuant to the statutory requirement that the Commission in ruling upon requests for acceleration of the effective date of a registration statement shall have due regard to the adequacy of the information respecting the issuer theretofore available to the public, the Commission may consider whether the persons making the offering have taken reasonable steps to make the information contained in the registration statement conveniently available to underwriters and dealers who it is reasonably anticipated will be invited to participate in the distribution of the security to be offered or sold.

(b)(1) As a minimum, reasonable steps to make the information conveniently available would involve the distribution, to each underwriter and dealer who it is reasonably anticipated will be invited to participate in the distribution of the security, a reasonable time in advance of the anticipated effective date of the registration statement, of as many copies of the proposed form of preliminary prospectus permitted by Rule 430 (§ 230.430) as appears to be reasonable to secure adequate distribution of the preliminary prospectus.

(2) In the case of a registration statement filed by a closed-end investment company on Form N-2 (§ 239.14 and § 274.11a-1 of this chapter), reasonable steps to make information conveniently available would involve distribution of a sufficient number of copies of the Statement of Additional Information required by § 230.430(b) as it appears to be reasonable to secure their adequate distribution either to each underwriter or dealer who it is reasonably anticipated will be invited to participate in the distribution of the security, or to the underwriter, dealer or other source named on the cover page of the preliminary prospectus as being the person investors should contract in order to obtain in the Statement of Additional Information.

(c) The granting of acceleration will not be conditioned upon

(1) The distribution of a preliminary prospectus in any state where such distribution would be illegal; or

(2) The distribution of a preliminary prospectus (i) in the case of a registration statement relating solely to securities to be offered at competitive bidding, provided the undertaking in Item 512(d)(1) of Regulation S-K (§ 229.512(d)(2) of this chapter) is included in the registration statement and distribution of prospectuses pursuant to such undertaking is made prior to the publication or distribution of the invitation for bids, or (ii) in the case of a registration statement relating to a security issued by a face-amount certificate company or a redeemable security issued by an open-end management company or unit investment trust if any other security of the same class is currently being offered or sold, pursuant to an effective registration statement by the issuer or by or through an underwriter, or (iii) in the case of an offering of subscription rights unless it is contemplated that the distribution will be made through dealers and the underwriters intend to make the offering during the stockholders' subscription period, in which case copies of the preliminary prospectus must be distributed to dealers prior to the effective date of the registration statement in the same fashion as is required in the case of other offerings through underwriters, or (iv) in the case of a registration statement pertaining to a security to be offered pursuant to an exchange offer or transaction described in Rule 145 (§ 230.145).

Rule 461. Acceleration of Effective Date

(a) Requests for acceleration of the effective date of a registration statement shall be made by the registrant and the managing underwriters of the proposed issue, or, if there are no managing underwriters, by the principal underwriters of the proposed issue, and shall state the date upon which it is desired that the registration statement shall become effective. Such requests may be made in writing or orally, provided that, if an oral request is to be made, a letter indicating that fact and stating that the registrant and the managing or principal underwriters are aware of their obligations under the Act must accompany the registration statement (or a pre-effective amendment thereto) at the time of filing with the Commission. Written requests may be sent to the Commission by facsimile transmission. If by reason of the expected arrangement in connection with the offering, it is to be requested that the registration statement shall become effective at a particular hour of the day, the Commission must be advised to that effect not later than the second business day before the day which it is desired that the registration statement shall become effective. A person's request for acceleration will be considered confirmation of such person's awareness of the person's obligations under the Act. Not later than the time of filing the last amendment prior to the effective date of the registration statement, the registrant shall inform the Commission as to whether or not the amount of compensation to be allowed or paid to the underwriters and any other arrangements among the registrant, the underwriters and other broker dealers participating in the distribution, as described in the registration statement, have been reviewed to the extent required by the National Association of Securities Dealers, Inc. and such Association has issued a statement expressing no objections to the compensation and other arrangements.

(b) Having due regard to the adequacy of information respecting the registrant theretofore available to the public, to the facility with which the nature of the securities to be registered, their relationship to the capital structure of the registrant issuer and the rights of holders thereof can be understood, and to the public interest and the protection of investors, as provided in section 8(a) of the Act, it is the general policy of the Commission, upon request, as provided in paragraph (a) of this section, to permit acceleration of the effective date of the registration statement as soon as possible after the filing of appropriate amendments, if any. In determining the date on which a registration statement shall become effective, the following are included in the situations in which the Commission considers that the statutory standards of section 8(a) may not be met and may refuse to accelerate the effective date:

(1) Where there has not been a bona fide effort to make the prospectus reasonably concise, readable, and in compliance with the plain English requirements of Rule 421(d) of Regulation C (17 CFR 230.421(d)) in order to facilitate an understanding of the information in the prospectus.

(2) Where the form of preliminary prospectus, which has been distributed by the issuer or underwriter, is found to be inaccurate or inadequate in any material respect, until the Commission has received satisfactory assurance that appropriate correcting material has been sent to all underwriters and dealers who received such preliminary prospectus or prospectuses in quantity sufficient for their information and the information of others to whom the inaccurate or inadequate material was sent.

(3) Where the Commission is currently making an investigation of the issuer, a person controlling the issuer, or one of the underwriters, if any, of the securities to be offered, pursuant to any of the Acts administered by the Commission.

(4) Where one or more of the underwriters, although firmly committed to purchase securities covered by the registration statement, is subject to and does not meet the financial responsibility requirements of Rule 15c3-1 under the Securities Exchange Act of 1934 (§ 240.15c3-1 of this chapter). For the purposes of this paragraph underwriters will be deemed to be firmly committed even though the obligation to purchase is subject to the usual conditions as to receipt of opinions of counsel, accountants, etc., the accuracy of warranties or representations, the happening of calamities or the occurrence of other events the determination of which is not expressed to be in the sole or absolute discretion of the underwriters.

(5) Where there have been transactions in securities of the registrant by persons connected with or proposed to be connected with the offering which may have artificially affected or may artificially affect the market price of the security being offered.

(6) Where the amount of compensation to be allowed or paid to the underwriters and any other arrangements among the registrant, the underwriters and other broker dealers participating in the distribution, as described in the registration statement, if required to be reviewed by the National Association of Securities Dealers, Inc. (NASD), have been reviewed by the NASD and the NASD has not issued a statement expressing no objections to the compensation and other arrangements.

(7) Where, in the case of a significant secondary offering at the market, the registrant, selling security holders and underwriters have not taken sufficient measures to insure compliance with Regulation M (§ § 242.100 through 242.105 of this chapter).

(c) Insurance against liabilities arising under the Act, whether the cost of insurance is borne by the registrant, the insured or some other person, will not be considered a bar to acceleration, unless the registrant is a registered investment company or a business development company and the cost of such insurance is borne by other than an insured officer or director of the registrant. In the case of such a registrant, the Commission may refuse to accelerate the effective date of the registration statement when the registrant is organized or administered pursuant to any instrument (including a contract for insurance against liabilities arising under the Act) that protects or purports to protect any director or officer of the company against any liability to the company or its security holders to which he or she would otherwise be subject by reason of willful misfeasance, bad faith, gross negligence or reckless disregard of the duties involved in the conduct of his or her office.

Rule 462. Immediate Effectiveness of Certain Registration Statements and Post-Effective Amendments

(a) A registration statement on Form S-8 (§ 239.16b of this chapter) and a registration statement on Form S-3 (§ 239.13 of this chapter) or on Form F-3 (§ 239.33 of this chapter) for a dividend or interest reinvestment plan shall become effective upon filing with the Commission.

(b) A registration statement and any post-effective amendment thereto shall become effective upon filing with the Commission if:

(1) The registration statement is for registering additional securities of the same class(es) as were included in an earlier registration statement for the same offering and declared effective by the Commission;

(2) The new registration statement is filed prior to the time confirmations are sent or given; and

(3) The new registration statement registers additional securities in an amount and at a price that together represent no more than 20% of the maximum aggregate offering price set forth for each class of securities in the "Calculation of Registration Fee" table contained in such earlier registration statement.

(c) If the prospectus contained in a post-effective amendment filed prior to the time confirmations are sent or given contains no substantive changes from or additions to the prospectus previously filed as part of the effective registration statement, other than price-related information omitted from the registration statement in reliance on Rule 430A of the Act (§ 230.430A), such post-effective amendment shall become effective upon filing with the Commission.

(d) A post-effective amendment filed solely to add exhibits to a registration statement shall become effective upon filing with the Commission.

Rule 463. Report of Offering of Securities and Use of Proceeds Therefrom

(a) Except as provided in this section, following the effective date of the first registration statement filed under the Act by an issuer, the issuer or successor issuer shall report the use of proceeds pursuant to Item 701 of Regulation S-B or S-K or Item 14(e) of Form 20-F, as applicable, on its first periodic report filed pursuant to Sections 13(a) and 15(d) (15 U.S.C. 78m(a) and 78o(d)) of the Securities Exchange Act of 1934 after effectiveness, and thereafter on each of its subsequent periodic reports filed pursuant to Sections 13(a) and 15(d) of the Securities Exchange Act of 1934 through the later of disclosure of the application of all the offering proceeds or disclosure of the termination of the offering.

(b) A successor issuer shall comply with paragraph (a) of this section only if a report of the use of proceeds is required with respect to the first effective registration statement of the predecessor issuer.

(c) For purposes of this section:

(1) The term "offering proceeds" shall not include any amount(s) received for the account(s) of any selling security holder(s).

(2) The term "application" shall not include the temporary investment of proceeds by the issuer pending final application.

(d) This section shall not apply to any effective registration statement for securities to be issued:

(1) In a business combination described in Rule 145(a) (§ 230.145(a));

(2) By an issuer which pursuant to a business combination described in Rule 145(a) has succeeded to another issuer that prior to such business combination had a registration statement become effective under the Act and on the date such business combination was not subject to paragraph (a) of this section;

(3) Pursuant to an employee benefit plan;

(4) Pursuant to a dividend or interest reinvestment plan;

(5) As American depository receipts for foreign securities;

(6) By any investment company registered under the Investment Company Act of 1940 and any issuer that has elected to be regulated as a business development company under sections 54 through 65 of the Investment Company Act of 1940 (15 U.S.C. 80a-53 through 80a-64);

(7) By any public utility company or public utility holding company required to file reports with any State or Federal authority;

(8) In a merger in which a vote or consent of the security holders of the company being acquired is not required pursuant to applicable state law; or

(9) In an exchange offer for the securities of the issuer or another entity.

Rule 464. Effective Date of Post-Effective Amendments to Registration Statements Filed on Form S-8 and on Certain Forms S-3, S-4, F-2 and F-3

Provided. That, at the time of filing of each post-effective amendment with the Commission, the issuer continues to meet the requirements of filing on Form S-8 (§ 239.16b of this chapter); or on

Form S-3, F-2 or F-3 (§ 239.13, 32 or 33 of this chapter) for a registration statement relating to a dividend or interest reinvestment plan; or in the case of a registration statement on Form S-4 (§ 239.25 of this chapter) that there is continued compliance with General Instruction G of that Form:

(a) The post-effective amendment shall become effective upon filing with the Commission; and

(b) With respect to securities sold on or after the filing date pursuant to a prospectus which forms a part of a Form S-8 registration statement; or a Form S-3, F-2, or F-3 registration statement relating to a dividend or interest reinvestment plan; or a Form S-4 registration statement complying with General Instruction G of that Form and which has been amended to include or incorporate new full year financial statements or to comply with the provisions of section 10(a)(3) of the Act, the effective date of the registration statement shall be deemed to be the filing date of the post-effective amendment.

Rule 473. Delaying Amendments

(a) An amendment in the following form filed with a registration statement, or as an amendment to a registration statement which has not become effective, shall be deemed, for the purpose of section 8(a) of the Act, to be filed on such date or dates as may be necessary to delay the effective date of such registration statement (1) until the registrant shall file a further amendment which specifically states as provided in paragraph (b) of this section that such registration statement shall thereafter become effective in accordance with section 8(a) of the Act, or (2) until the registration statement shall become effective on such date as the Commission, acting pursuant to section 8(a), may determine:

The registrant hereby amends this registration statement on such date or dates as may be necessary to delay its effective date until the registrant shall file a further amendment which specifically states that this registration statement shall thereafter become effective in accordance with section 8(a) of the Securities Act of 1933 or until the registration statement shall become effective on such date as the Commission acting pursuant to said section 8(a), may determine.

(b) An amendment which for the purpose of paragraph (a)(1) of this section specifically states that a registration statement shall thereafter become effective in accordance with section 8(a) of the Act, shall be in the following form:

This registration statement shall hereafter become effective in accordance with the provisions of section 8(a) of the Securities Act of 1933.

(c) An amendment pursuant to paragraph (a) of this section which is filed with a registration statement shall be set forth on the facing page thereof following the calculation of the registration fee. Any such amendment filed after the filing of the registration statement, any amendment altering the proposed date of public sale of the securities being registered, or any amendment filed pursuant to paragraph (b) of this section may be made by telegram, letter or facsimile transmission. Each such telegraphic amendment shall be confirmed in writing within a reasonable time by the filing of a signed copy of the amendment. Such confirmation shall not be deemed an amendment.

(d) No amendments pursuant to paragraph (a) of this section may be filed with a registration statement on Form F-7, F-8 or F-80 (§ 239.37, § 239.38 or § 239.41 of this chapter); on Form F-9 or F-10 (§ 239.39 or § 239.40 of this chapter) relating to an offering being made contemporaneously in the United States and the registrant's home jurisdiction; on Form S-8 (§ 239.16b of this chapter); on Form S-3, F-2 or F-3 (§ 239.13, § 239.32 or § 239.33 of this chapter) relating to a dividend or interest reinvestment plan; or on Form S-4 (§ 239.25 of this chapter) complying with General Instruction G of that Form.

Rule 474. Date of Filing of Amendments

The date on which amendments are actually received by the Commission shall be the date of filing thereof, if all of the requirements of the Act and the rules with respect to such filing have been complied with.

Rule 477. Withdrawal of Registration Statement or Amendment

(a) Except as provided in paragraph (b) of this section, any registration statement or any amendment or exhibit thereto may be withdrawn upon application if the Commission, finding such withdrawal consistent with the public interest and the protection of investors, consents thereto.

(b) Any application for withdrawal of a registration statement filed on Form F-2 (§ 239.32 of this chapter) relating to a dividend or interest reinvestment plan, or on Form S-4 (§ 239.25 of this chapter) complying with General Instruction G of that Form, and/or any pre-effective amendment thereto, will be deemed granted upon filing if such filing is made prior to the effective date. Any other application for withdrawal of an entire registration statement made before the effective date of the registration statement will be deemed granted at the time the application is filed with the Commission unless, within 15 calendar days after the registrant files the application, the Commission notifies the registrant that the application for withdrawal will not be granted.

(c) The registrant must sign any application for withdrawal and must state fully in it the grounds on which the registrant makes the application. The fee paid upon the filing of the registration statement will not be refunded to the registrant. The registrant must state in the application that no securities were sold in connection with the offering. If the registrant applies for withdrawal in anticipation of reliance on § 230.155(c), the registrant must, without discussing any terms of the private offering, state in the application that the registrant may undertake a subsequent private offering in reliance on § 230.155(c).

(d) Any withdrawn document will remain in the Commission's public files, as well as the related request for withdrawal.

Rule 478. Powers to Amend or Withdraw Registration Statement

All persons signing a registration statement shall be deemed, in the absence of a statement to the contrary, to confer upon the registrant, and upon the agent for service named in the registration statement, the following powers:

(a) A power to amend the registration statement (1) by filing an amendment as provided in § 230.473; (2) by filing any written consent; (3) by correcting typographical errors; (4) by reducing the amount of securities registered, pursuant to an undertaking contained in the registration statement.

(b) A power to make application pursuant to § 230.475 for the Commission's consent to the filing of an amendment.

(c) A power to withdraw the registration statement or any amendment or exhibit thereto.

(d) A power to consent to the entry of an order under Section 8(b) of the Act, waiving notice and hearing, such order being entered without prejudice to the right of the registrant thereafter to have the order vacated upon a showing to the Commission that the registration statement as amended is no longer incomplete or inaccurate on its face in any material respect.

Investment Companies; Business Development Companies

Note: The rules in this section of Regulation C (§ § 230.480 to 230.488 and § § 230.495 to 230.498) apply only to investment companies and business development companies. Section 230.489 applies to certain entities excepted from the definition of investment company by rules under the Investment Company Act of 1940. The rules in the rest of Regulation C (§ § 230.400 to 230.479 and § § 230.490 to 230.494), unless the context specifically indicates otherwise, also apply to investment companies and business development companies. See § 230.400.

Rule 482. Advertising by an Investment Company as Satisfying Requirements of Section 10

(a) *Scope of rule.* This section applies to an advertisement or other sales material (*advertisement*) with respect to securities of an investment company registered under the Investment Company Act of 1940 (15 U.S.C. 80a-1 *et seq.*) (*1940 Act*), or a business development company, that is selling or proposing to sell its securities pursuant to a registration statement that has been filed under the Act. This section does not apply to an advertisement that is excepted from the definition of prospectus by section 2(a)(10) of the Act (15 U.S.C. 77b(a)(10)), or a Profile under § 230.498. An advertisement that complies with this section, which may include information the substance of which is not included in the prospectus specified in section 10(a) of the Act (15 U.S.C 77j(a)), will be deemed to be a prospectus under section 10(b) of the Act (15 U.S.C. 77j(b)) for the purpose of section 5(b)(1) of the Act (15 U.S.C. 77e(b)(1)).

Note to paragraph (a): The fact that an advertisement complies with this section does not relieve the investment company, underwriter, or dealer of any obligations with respect to the advertisement under the antifraud provisions of the federal securities laws. For guidance about factors to be weighed in determining whether statements, representations, illustrations, and descriptions contained in investment company advertisements are misleading, *see* § 230.156. In addition, an advertisement that complies with this section is subject to the legibility requirements of § 230.420.

(b) *Required disclosure.* This paragraph describes information that is required to be included in an advertisement in order to comply with this section.

(1) *Availability of additional information.* An advertisement must include a statement that:

(i) Advises an investor to consider the investment objectives, risks, and charges and expenses of the investment company carefully before investing; explains that the prospectus contains this and other information about the investment company; identifies a source from which an investor may obtain a prospectus; and states that the prospectus should be read carefully before investing; or

(ii) If used with a Profile, advises an investor to consider the investment objectives, risks, and charges and expenses of the investment company carefully before investing; explains that the accompanying Profile contains this and other information about the investment company; describes the procedures for investing in the investment company; and indicates the availability of the investment company's prospectus.

(2) *Advertisements used prior to effectiveness of registration statement.* An advertisement that is used prior to effectiveness of the investment company's registration statement or the determination of the public offering price (in the case of a registration statement that becomes effective omitting information from the prospectus contained in the registration statement in reliance upon § 230.430A) must include the "Subject to Completion" legend required by § 230.481(b)(2).

(3) *Advertisements including performance data.* An advertisement that includes performance data of an open-end management investment company or a separate account registered under the 1940 Act as a unit investment trust offering variable annuity contracts (*trust account*) must include the following:

(i) A legend disclosing that the performance data quoted represents past performance; that past performance does not guarantee future results; that the investment return and principal value of an investment will fluctuate so that an investor's shares, when redeemed, may be worth more or less than their original cost; and that current performance may be lower or higher than the performance data quoted. The legend should also identify either a toll-free (or collect) telephone number or a website where an investor may obtain performance data current to the most recent month-end unless the advertisement includes total return quotations current to the most recent month ended seven business days prior to the date of use. An advertisement for a money market fund may omit the disclosure about principal value fluctuation; and

Note to paragraph (b)(3)(i): The date of use refers to the date or dates when an advertisement is used by investors, not the date on which an advertisement is published or submitted for publication. The date of use refers to the entire period of use by investors and not simply the first date on which an advertisement is used.

(ii) If a sales load or any other nonrecurring fee is charged, the maximum amount of the load or fee, and if the sales load or fee is not reflected, a statement that the performance data does not reflect the deduction of the sales load or fee, and that, if reflected, the load or fee would reduce the performance quoted.

(4) *Money market funds.* An advertisement for an investment company that holds itself out to be a money market fund must include the following statement:

An investment in the Fund is not insured or guaranteed by the Federal Deposit Insurance Corporation or any other government agency. Although the Fund seeks to preserve the value of your investment at $1.00 per share, it is possible to lose money by investing in the Fund.

A money market fund that does not hold itself out as maintaining a stable net asset value may omit the second sentence of this statement.

(5) *Presentation.* In a print advertisement, the statements required by paragraphs (b)(1) through (b)(4) of this section must be presented in a type size at least as large as and of a style different from, but at least as prominent as, that used in the major portion of the advertisement, provided that when performance data is presented in a type size smaller than that of the major portion of the advertisement, the statements required by paragraph (b)(3) of this section may appear in a type size no smaller than that of the performance data. If an advertisement is delivered through an electronic medium, the legibility requirements for the statements required by paragraphs (b)(1) through (b)(4) of this section relating to type size and style may be satisfied by presenting the statements in any manner reasonably calculated to draw investor attention to them. In a radio or television advertisement, the statements required by paragraphs (b)(1) through (b)(4) of this section must be given emphasis equal to that used in the major portion of the advertisement. The statements required by paragraph (b)(3) of this section must be presented in close proximity to the performance data, and, in a print advertisement, must be presented in the body of the advertisement and not in a footnote.

(6) *Commission legend.* An advertisement that complies with this section need not contain the Commission legend required by § 230.481(b)(1).

(c) *Use of applications.* An advertisement that complies with this section may not contain or be accompanied by any application by which a prospective investor may invest in the investment company, except that:

(1) *Variable annuity and variable life insurance contracts.* A prospectus meeting the requirements of section 10(a) of the Act (15 U.S.C. 77j(a)) by which a unit investment trust offers variable annuity or variable life insurance contracts may contain a contract application although the prospectus includes, or is accompanied by, information about an investment company in which the unit investment trust invests that, pursuant to this section, is deemed a prospectus under section 10(b) of the Act (15 U.S.C. 77j(b)); and

(2) *Profile.* An advertisement that complies with this section may be used with a Profile that includes, or is accompanied by, an application to purchase shares of the investment company as permitted under § 230.498.

(d) *Performance data for non-money market funds.* In the case of an open-end management investment company or a trust account (other than a money market fund referred to in paragraph (e) of this section), any quotation of the company's performance contained in an advertisement shall be limited to quotations of:

(1) *Current yield.* A current yield that:

(i) Is based on the methods of computation prescribed in Form N-1A (§§ 239.15A and 274.11A of this chapter), N-3 (§§ 239.17a and 274.11b of this chapter), or N-4 (§§ 239.17b and 274.11c of this chapter);

(ii) Is accompanied by quotations of total return as provided for in paragraph (d)(3) of this section;

(iii) Is set out in no greater prominence than the required quotations of total return; and

(iv) Adjacent to the quotation and with no less prominence than the quotation, identifies the length of and the date of the last day in the base period used in computing the quotation.

(2) *Tax-equivalent yield.* A tax-equivalent yield that:

(i) Is based on the methods of computation prescribed in Form N-1A (§§ 239.15A and 274.11A of this chapter), N-3 (§§ 239.17a and 274.11b of this chapter), or N-4 (§§ 239.17b and 274.11c of this chapter);

(ii) Is accompanied by quotations of yield as provided for in paragraph (d)(1) of this section and total return as provided for in paragraph (d)(3) of this section;

(iii) Is set out in no greater prominence than the required quotations of yield and total return;

(iv) Relates to the same base period as the required quotation of yield; and

(v) Adjacent to the quotation and with no less prominence than the quotation, identifies the length of and the date of the last day in the base period used in computing the quotation.

(3) *Average annual total return.* Average annual total return for one, five, and ten year periods, except that if the company's registration statement under the Act (15 U.S.C. 77a *et seq.*) has been in effect for less than one, five, or ten years, the time period during which the registration statement was in effect is substituted for the period(s) otherwise prescribed. The quotations must:

(i) Be based on the methods of computation prescribed in Form N-1A (§§ 239.15A and 274.11A of this chapter), N-3 (§§ 239.17a and 274.11b of this chapter), or N-4 (§§ 239.17b and 274.11c of this chapter);

(ii) Be current to the most recent calendar quarter ended prior to the submission of the advertisement for publication;

(iii) Be set out with equal prominence; and

(iv) Adjacent to the quotation and with no less prominence than the quotation, identify the length of and the last day of the one, five, and ten year periods.

(4) *After-tax return.* For an open-end management investment company, average annual total return (after taxes on distributions) and average annual total return (after taxes on distributions and redemption) for one, five, and ten year periods, except that if the company's registration statement under the Act (15 U.S.C. 77a *et seq.*) has been in effect for less than one, five, or ten years, the time period during which the registration statement was in effect is substituted for the period(s) otherwise prescribed. The quotations must:

(i) Be based on the methods of computation prescribed in Form N-1A (§§ 239.15A and 274.11A of this chapter);

(ii) Be current to the most recent calendar quarter ended prior to the submission of the advertisement for publication;

(iii) Be accompanied by quotations of total return as provided for in paragraph (d)(3) of this section;

(iv) Include both average annual total return (after taxes on distributions) and average annual total return (after taxes on distributions and redemption);

(v) Be set out with equal prominence and be set out in no greater prominence than the required quotations of total return; and

(vi) Adjacent to the quotations and with no less prominence than the quotations, identify the length of and the last day of the one, five, and ten year periods.

(5) *Other performance measures.* Any other historical measure of company performance (not subject to any prescribed method of computation) if such measurement:

(i) Reflects all elements of return;

(ii) Is accompanied by quotations of total return as provided for in paragraph (d)(3) of this section;

(iii) In the case of any measure of performance adjusted to reflect the effect of taxes, is accompanied by quotations of total return as provided for in paragraph (d)(4) of this section;

(iv) Is set out in no greater prominence than the required quotations of total return; and

(v) Adjacent to the measurement and with no less prominence than the measurement, identifies the length of and the last day of the period for which performance is measured.

(e) *Performance data for money market funds.* In the case of a money market fund:

(1) *Yield.* Any quotation of the money market fund's yield in an advertisement shall be based on the methods of computation prescribed in Form N-1A (§§ 239.15A and 274.11A of this chapter), N-3 (§§ 239.17a and 274.11b of this chapter), or N-4 (§§ 239.17b and 274.11c of this chapter) and may include:

(i) A quotation of current yield that, adjacent to the quotation and with no less prominence than the quotation, identifies the length of and the date of the last day in the base period used in computing that quotation;

(ii) A quotation of effective yield if it appears in the same advertisement as a quotation of current yield and each quotation relates to an identical base period and is presented with equal prominence; or

(iii) A quotation or quotations of tax-equivalent yield or tax-equivalent effective yield if it appears in the same advertisement as a quotation of current yield and each quotation relates to the same base period as the quotation of current yield, is presented with equal prominence, and states the income tax rate used in the calculation.

(2) *Total return.* Accompany any quotation of the money market fund's total return in an advertisement with a quotation of the money market fund's current yield under paragraph (e)(1)(i) of this section. Place the quotations of total return and current yield next to each other, in the same size print, and if there is a material difference between the quoted total return and the quoted current yield, include a statement that the yield quotation more closely reflects the current earnings of the money market fund than the total return quotation.

(f) *Advertisements that make tax representations.* An advertisement for an open-end management investment company (other than a company that is permitted under § 270.35d-1(a)(4) of this chapter to use a name suggesting that the company's distributions are exempt from federal income tax or from both federal and state income tax) that represents or implies that the company is managed to limit or control the effect of taxes on company performance must accompany any quotation of the company's performance permitted by paragraph (d) of this section with quotations of total return as provided for in paragraph (d)(4) of this section.

(g) *Timeliness of performance data.* All performance data contained in any advertisement must be as of the most recent practicable date considering the type of investment company and the media through which the data will be conveyed, except that any advertisement containing total return quotations will be considered to have complied with this paragraph provided that:

(1) (i) The total return quotations are current to the most recent calendar quarter ended prior to the submission of the advertisement for publication; and

(ii) Total return quotations current to the most recent month ended seven business days prior to the date of use are provided at the toll-free (or collect) telephone number or website identified pursuant to paragraph (b)(3)(i) of this section; or

(2) The total return quotations are current to the most recent month ended seven business days prior to the date of use of the advertisement.

Note to paragraph (g): The date of use refers to the date or dates when an advertisement is used by investors, not the date on which an advertisement is published or submitted for publication. The date of use refers to the entire period of use by investors and not simply the first date on which an advertisement is used.

(h) *Filing.* An advertisement that complies with this section need not be filed as part of the registration statement filed under the Act.

Note to paragraph (h): These advertisements, unless filed with NASD Regulation, Inc., are required to be filed in accordance with the requirements of § 230.497.

REGULATION D—RULES GOVERNING THE LIMITED OFFER AND SALE OF SECURITIES WITHOUT REGISTRATION UNDER THE SECURITIES ACT OF 1933

Preliminary Notes

1. The following rules relate to transactions exempted from the registration requirements of section 5 of the Securities Act of 1933 (the "Act") [15 U.S.C. 77a et seq., as amended]. Such transactions are not exempt from the antifraud, civil liability, or other provisions of the federal securities laws. Issuers are reminded of their obligation to provide such further material information, if any, as may be necessary to make the information required under this regulation, in light of the circumstances under which it is furnished, not misleading.

2. Nothing in these rules obviates the need to comply with any applicable state law relating to the offer and sale of securities. Regulation D is intended to be a basic element in a uniform system of federal-state limited offering exemptions consistent with the provisions of sections 18 and 19(c) of the Act. In those states that have adopted Regulation D, or any version of Regulation D, special attention should be directed to the applicable state laws and regulations, including those relating to registration of persons who receive remuneration in connection with the offer and sale of securities, to disqualification of issuers and other persons associated with offerings based on state administrative orders or judgments, and to requirements for filings of notices of sales.

3. Attempted compliance with any rule in Regulation D does not act as an exclusive election; the issuer can also claim the availability of any other applicable exemption. For instance, an issuer's failure to satisfy all the terms and conditions of Rule 506 shall not raise any presumption that the exemption provided by section 4(2) of the Act is not available.

4. These rules are available only to the issuer of the securities and not to any affiliate of that issuer or to any other person for resales of the issuer's securities. The rules provide an exemption only for the transactions in which the securities are offered or sold by the issuer, not for the securities themselves.

5. These rules may be used for business combinations that involve sales by virtue of Rule 145(a) (17 CFR 230.145(a)) or otherwise.

6. In view of the objectives of these rules and the policies underlying the Act, Regulation D is not available to any issuer for any transaction or chain of transactions that, although in technical compliance with these rules, is part of a plan or scheme to evade the registration provisions of the Act. In such cases, registration under the Act is required.

7. Securities offered and sold outside the United States in accordance with Regulation S need not be registered under the Act. See Release No. 33-6863. Regulation S may be relied upon for such offers and sales even if coincident offers and sales are made in accordance with Regulation D inside the United States. Thus, for example, persons who are offered and sold securities in accordance with Regulation S would not be counted in the calculation of the number of purchasers under Regulation D. Similarly, proceeds from such sales would not be included in the aggregate offering price. The provisions of this note, however, do not apply if the issuer elects to rely solely on Regulation D for offers or sales to persons made outside the United States.

Rule 501. Definitions and Terms Used in Regulation D

As used in Regulation D [§§ 230.501-230.508], the following terms shall have the meaning indicated:

(a) *Accredited investor.* "Accredited investor" shall mean any person who comes within any of the following categories, or who the issuer reasonably believes comes within any of the following categories, at the time of the sale of the securities to that person:

(1) Any bank as defined in section 3(a)(2) of the Act, or any savings and loan association or other institution as defined in section 3(a)(5)(A) of the Act whether acting in its individual or fiduciary capacity; any broker or dealer registered pursuant to section 15 of the Securities Exchange Act of 1934; any insurance company as defined in section 2(13) of the Act; any investment company registered under the Investment Company Act of 1940 or a business development company as defined in section 2(a)(48) of that Act; any Small Business Investment Company licensed by the U.S. Small Business Administration under section 301(c) or (d) of the Small Business Investment Act of 1958; any plan established and maintained by a state, its political subdivisions, or any agency or instrumentality of a state or its political subdivisions, for the benefit of its employees, if such plan has total assets in excess of $5,000,000; any employee benefit plan within the meaning of the Employee Retirement Income Security Act of 1974 if the investment decision is made by a plan fiduciary, as defined in section 3(21) of such Act, which is either a bank, savings and loan association, insurance company, or registered investment adviser, or if the employee benefit plan has total assets in excess of $5,000,000 or, if a self-directed plan, with investment decisions made solely by persons that are accredited investors;

(2) Any private business development company as defined in section 202(a)(22) of the Investment Advisers Act of 1940;

(3) Any organization described in section 501(c)(3) of the Internal Revenue Code, corporation, Massachusetts or similar business trust, or partnership, not formed for the specific purpose of acquiring the securities offered, with total assets in excess of $5,000,000;

(4) Any director, executive officer, or general partner of the issuer of the securities being offered or sold, or any director, executive officer, or general partner of a general partner of that issuer;

(5) Any natural person whose individual net worth, or joint net worth with that person's spouse, at the time of his purchase exceeds $1,000,000;

(6) Any natural person who had an individual income in excess of $200,000 in each of the two most recent years or joint income with that person's spouse in excess of $300,000 in each of those years and has a reasonable expectation of reaching the same income level in the current year;

(7) Any trust, with total assets in excess of $5,000,000, not formed for the specific purpose of acquiring the securities offered, whose purchase is directed by a sophisticated person as described in § 230.506(b)(2)(ii); and

(8) Any entity in which all of the equity owners are accredited investors.

(b) *Affiliate.* An "affiliate" of, or person "affiliated" with, a specified person shall mean a person that directly, or indirectly through one or more intermediaries, controls or is controlled by, or is under common control with, the person specified.

(c) *Aggregate offering price.* "Aggregate offering price" shall mean the sum of all cash, services, property, notes, cancellation of debt, or other consideration to be received by an issuer for issuance of its securities. Where securities are being offered for both cash and non-cash consideration, the aggregate offering price shall be based on the price at which the securities are offered for cash. Any portion of the aggregate offering price attributable to cash received in a foreign currency shall be translated into United States currency at the currency exchange rate in effect at a reasonable time prior to or on the date of the sale of the securities. If securities are not offered for cash, the aggregate offering price shall be based on the value of the consideration as established by bona fide sales of that consideration made within a reasonable time, or, in the absence of sales, on the fair value as determined by an accepted standard. Such valuations of non-cash consideration must be reasonable at the time made.

(d) *Business combination.* "Business combination" shall mean any transaction of the type specified in paragraph (a) of Rule 145 under the Act (17 CFR 230.145) and any transaction involving the acquisition by one issuer, in exchange for all or a part of its own or its parent's stock, of stock of another issuer if, immediately after the acquisition, the acquiring issuer has control of the other issuer (whether or not it had control before the acquisition).

(e) *Calculation of number of purchasers.* For purposes of calculating the number of purchasers under §§ 230.505(b) and 230.506(b) only, the following shall apply:

(1) The following purchasers shall be excluded:

(i) Any relative, spouse or relative of the spouse of a purchaser who has the same principal residence as the purchaser;

(ii) Any trust or estate in which a purchaser and any of the persons related to him as specified in paragraph (e)(1)(i) or (e)(1)(iii) of this § 230.501 collectively have more than 50 percent of the beneficial interest (excluding contingent interests);

(iii) Any corporation or other organization of which a purchaser and any of the persons related to him as specified in paragraph (e)(1)(i) or (e)(1)(ii) of this § 230.501 collectively are beneficial owners of more than 50 percent of the equity securities (excluding directors' qualifying shares) or equity interests; and

(iv) Any accredited investor.

(2) A corporation, partnership or other entity shall be counted as one purchaser. If, however, that entity is organized for the specific purpose of acquiring the securities offered and is not an accredited investor under paragraph (a)(8) of this section, then each beneficial owner of equity securities or equity interests in the entity shall count as a separate purchaser for all provisions of

Regulation D (§§ 230.501-230.508), except to the extent provided in paragraph (e)(1) of this section.

(3) A non-contributory employee benefit plan within the meaning of Title I of the Employee Retirement Income Security Act of 1974 shall be counted as one purchaser where the trustee makes all investment decisions for the plan.

Note: The issuer must satisfy all the other provisions of Regulation D for all purchasers whether or not they are included in calculating the number of purchasers. Clients of an investment adviser or customers of a broker or dealer shall be considered the "purchasers" under Regulation D regardless of the amount of discretion given to the investment adviser or broker or dealer to act on behalf of the client or customer.

(f) *Executive officer.* "Executive officer" shall mean the president, any vice president in charge of a principal business unit, division or function (such as sales, administration or finance), any other officer who performs a policy making function, or any other person who performs similar policy making functions for the issuer. Executive officers of subsidiaries may be deemed executive officers of the issuer if they perform such policy making functions for the issuer.

(g) *Issuer.* The definition of the term "issuer" in section 2(4) of the Act shall apply, except that in the case of a proceeding under the Federal Bankruptcy Code [11 U.S.C. 101 et seq.], the trustee or debtor in possession shall be considered the issuer in an offering under a plan or reorganization, if the securities are to be issued under the plan.

(h) *Purchaser representative.* "Purchaser representative" shall mean any person who satisfies all of the following conditions or who the issuer reasonably believes satisfies all of the following conditions:

(1) Is not an affiliate, director, officer or other employee of the issuer, or beneficial owner of 10 percent or more of any class of the equity securities or 10 percent or more of the equity interest in the issuer, except where the purchaser is:

(i) A relative of the purchaser representative by blood, marriage or adoption and not more remote than a first cousin;

(ii) A trust or estate in which the purchaser representative and any persons related to him as specified in paragraph (h)(1)(i) or (h)(1)(iii) of this § 230.501 collectively have more than 50 percent of the beneficial interest (excluding contingent interest) or of which the purchaser representative serves as trustee, executor, or in any similar capacity; or

(iii) A corporation or other organization of which the purchaser representative and any persons related to him as specified in paragraph (h)(1)(i) or (h)(1)(ii) of this § 230.501 collectively are the beneficial owners of more than 50 percent of the equity securities (excluding directors' qualifying shares) or equity interests;

(2) Has such knowledge and experience in financial and business matters that he is capable of evaluating, alone, or together with other purchaser representatives of the purchaser, or together with the purchaser, the merits and risks of the prospective investment;

(3) Is acknowledged by the purchaser in writing, during the course of the transaction, to be his purchaser representative in connection with evaluating the merits and risks of the prospective investment; and

(4) Discloses to the purchaser in writing a reasonable time prior to the sale of securities to that purchaser any material relationship between himself or his affiliates and the issuer or its affiliates that then exists, that is mutually understood to be contemplated, or that has existed at any time during the previous two years, and any compensation received or to be received as a result of such relationship.

Note 1: A person acting as a purchaser representative should consider the applicability of the registration and antifraud provisions relating to brokers and dealers under the Securities Exchange Act of 1934 ("Exchange Act") [15 U.S.C. 78a et seq., as amended] and relating to investment advisers under the Investment Advisers Act of 1940.

Note 2: The acknowledgement required by paragraph (h)(3) and the disclosure required by paragraph (h)(4) of this § 230.501 must be made with specific reference to each prospective investment. Advance blanket acknowledgment, such as for "all securities transactions" or "all private placements," is not sufficient.

Note 3: Disclosure of any material relationships between the purchaser representative or his affiliates and the issuer or its affiliates does not relieve the purchaser representative of his obligation to act in the interest of the purchaser.

Rule 502. General Conditions to be Met

The following conditions shall be applicable to offers and sales made under Regulation D (§§ 230.501-230.508):

(a) *Integration.* All sales that are part of the same Regulation D offering must meet all of the terms and conditions of Regulation D. Offers and sales that are made more than six months before the start of a Regulation D offering or are made more than six months after completion of a Regulation D offering will not be considered part of that Regulation D offering, so long as during those six month periods there are no offers or sales of securities by or for the issuer that are of the same or a similar class as those offered or sold under Regulation D, other than those offers or sales of securities under an employee benefit plan as defined in Rule 405 under the Act [17 CFR 230.405].

Note: The term "offering" is not defined in the Act or in Regulation D. If the issuer offers or sells securities for which the safe harbor rule in paragraph (a) of this § 230.502 is unavailable, the determination as to whether separate sales of securities are part of the same offering (i.e. are considered "integrated") depends on the particular facts and circumstances. Generally, transactions otherwise meeting the requirements of an exemption will not be integrated with simultaneous offerings being made outside the United States in compliance with Regulation S. See Release No. 33-6863.

The following factors should be considered in determining whether offers and sales should be integrated for purposes of the exemptions under Regulation D:

(a) whether the sales are part of a single plan of financing;

(b) whether the sales involve issuance of the same class of securities;

(c) whether the sales have been made at or about the same time;

(d) whether the same type of consideration is being received; and

(e) whether the sales are made for the same general purpose.

See Release No. 33-4552 (November 6, 1962) [27 FR 11316].

(b) *Information requirements.*

(1) *When information must be furnished.*

If the issuer sells securities under § 230.505 or § 230.506 to any purchaser that is not an accredited investor, the issuer shall furnish the information specified in paragraph (b)(2) of this section to such purchaser a reasonable time prior to sale. The issuer is not required to furnish the specified information to purchasers when it sells securities under § 230.504, or to any accredited investor.

Note: When an issuer provides information to investors pursuant to paragraph (b)(1), it should consider providing such information to accredited investors as well, in view of the anti-fraud provisions of the federal securities laws.

(2) *Type of information to be furnished.*

(i) If the issuer is not subject to the reporting requirements of section 13 or 15(d) of the Exchange Act, at a reasonable time prior to the sale of securities the issuer shall furnish to the purchaser, to the extent material to an understanding of the issuer, its business and the securities being offered:

(A) *Non-financial statement information.* If the issuer is eligible to use Regulation A (§ 230.251-263), the same kind of information as would be required in Part II of Form 1-A (§ 239.90 of this chapter). If the issuer is not eligible to use Regulation A, the same kind of information as required in Part I of a registration statement filed under the Securities Act on the form that the issuer would be entitled to use.

(B) *Financial statement information.* (*1*) *Offering up to $2,000,000.* The information required in Item 310 of Regulation S-B (§ 228.310 of this chapter), except that only the issuer's balance sheet, which shall be dated within 120 days of the start of the offering, must be audited.

(*2*) *Offerings up to $7,500,000.* The financial statement information required in Form SB-2 (§ 239.10 of this chapter). If an issuer, other than a limited partnership, cannot obtain audited financial statements without unreasonable effort or expense, then only the issuer's balance sheet, which shall be dated within 120 days of the start of the offering, must be audited. If the issuer is a limited partnership and cannot obtain the required financial statements without unreasonable effort or expense, it may furnish financial statements that have been prepared on the basis of Federal income tax requirements and examined and reported on in accordance with generally accepted auditing standards by an independent public or certified accountant.

(*3*) *Offerings over $7,500,000.* The financial statement as would be required in a registration statement filed under the Act on the form that the issuer would be entitled to use. If an issuer, other than a limited partnership, cannot obtain audited financial statements without unreasonable effort or expense, then only the issuer's balance sheet, which shall be dated within 120 days of the start of the offering, must be audited. If the issuer is a limited partnership and cannot obtain the required financial statements without unreasonable effort or expense, it may furnish financial statements that have been prepared on the basis of Federal income tax requirements and examined and reported on in accordance with generally accepted auditing standards by an independent public or certified accountant.

(C) If the issuer is a foreign private issuer eligible to use Form 20-F (§ 249.220f of this chapter), the issuer shall disclose the same kind of information required to be included in a registrtion statement filed under the Act on the form that the issuer would be entitled to use. The financial statements need be certified only to the extent required by paragraph (b)(2)(i)(B)(*1*), (*2*) or (*3*) of this section, as appropriate.

(ii) If the issuer is subject to the reporting requirements of section 13 or 15(d) of the Exchange Act, at a reasonable time prior to the sale of securities, the issuer shall furnish to the purchaser the information specified in paragraph (b)(2)(ii)(A) or (B) of this section, and in either event the information specified in paragraph (b)(2)(ii)(C) of this section:

(A) The issuer's annual report to shareholders for the most recent fiscal year, if such annual report meets the requirements of § 240.14a-3 or 240.14c-3 under the Exchange Act, the definitive proxy statement filed in connection with that annual report, and, if requested by the purchaser in writing, a copy of the issuer's most recent Form 10-K and Form 10-KSB [17 CFR 249.310 and 249.310b] under the Exchange Act.

(B) The information contained in an annual report on Form 10-K (§ 249.310 of this chapter) or 10-KSB (§ 249.310b of this chapter) under the Exchange Act or in a registration statement on Form S-1 (§ 239.11 of this chapter), SB-1 (§ 239.9 of this chapter), SB-2 (§ 239.10 of this chapter) or S-11 (§ 239.18 of this chapter) under the Act or on Form 10 (§ 249.210 of this chapter) or Form 10-SB (§ 249.210b of this chapter) under the Exchange Act, whichever filing is the most recent required to be filed.

(C) The information contained in any reports or documents required to be filed by the issuer under sections 13(a), 14(a), 14(c), and 15(d) of the Exchange Act since the distribution or filing of the report or registration statement specified in paragraph (A) or (B), and a brief description of the securities being offered, the use of the proceeds from the offering, and any material changes in the issuer's affairs that are not disclosed in the documents furnished.

(D) If the issuer is a foreign private issuer, the issuer may provide in lieu of the information specified in paragraph (b)(2)(ii)(A) or (B) of this section, the information contained in its most recent filing on Form 20-F or Form F-1 (§ 239.31 of the chapter).

(iii) Exhibits required to be filed with the Commission as part of a registration statement or report, other than an annual report to shareholders or parts of that report incorporated by reference in a Form 10-K and Form 10-KSB report, need not be furnished to each purchaser that is not an accredited investor if the contents of material exhibits are identified and such exhibits are made available to a purchaser, upon his written request, a reasonable time prior to his purchase.

(iv) At a reasonable time prior to the sale of securities to any purchaser that is not an accredited investor in a transaction under § 230.505 or § 230.506, the issuer shall furnish to the purchaser a brief description in writing of any material written information concerning the offering that has been provided by the issuer to any accredited investor but not previously delivered to such unaccredited purchaser. The issuer shall furnish any portion or all of this information to the purchaser, upon his written request a reasonable time prior to his purchase.

(v) The issuer shall also make available to each purchaser at a reasonable time prior to his purchase of securities in a transaction under § 230.505 or 230.506 the opportunity to ask questions and receive answers concerning the terms and conditions of the offering and to obtain any additional information which the issuer possesses or can acquire without unreasonable effort or expense that is necessary to verify the accuracy of information furnished under paragraph (b)(2)(i) or (ii) of this § 230.502.

(vi) For business combinations or exchange offers, in addition to information required by Form S-4 [17 CFR 239.25], the issuer shall provide to each purchaser at the time the plan is submitted to security holders, or, with an exchange, during the course of the transaction and prior to sale, written information about any terms or arrangements of the proposed transactions that are materially different from those for all other security holders. For purposes of this subsection, an issuer which is not subject to the reporting requirements of section 13 or 15(d) of the Exchange Act may satisfy the requirements of Part I.B. or C. of Form S-4 by compliance with paragraph (b)(2)(i) of this § 230.502.

(vii) At a reasonable time prior to the sale of securities to any purchaser that is not an accredited investor in a transaction under § 230.505 or § 230.506, the issuer shall advise the purchaser of the limitations on resale in the manner contained in paragraph (d)(2) of this section. Such disclosure may be contained in other materials required to be provided by this paragraph.

(c) *Limitation on manner of offering.* Except as provided in § 230.504(b)(1), neither the issuer nor any person acting on its behalf shall offer or sell the securities by any form of general solicitation or general advertising, including, but not limited to, the following:

(1) Any advertisement, article, notice or other communication published in any newspaper, magazine, or similar media or broadcast over television or radio; and

(2) Any seminar or meeting whose attendees have been invited by any general solicitation or general advertising,

Provided, however, that publication by an issuer of a notice in accordance with § 230.135c shall not be deemed to constitute general solicitation or general advertising for purposes of this section; *Provided further,* that, if the requirements of § 230.135e are satisfied, providing any journalist with access to press conferences held outside of the United States, to meeting with issuer or selling security holder representatives conducted outside of the United States, or to written press-related materials released outside the United States, at or in which a present or proposed offering of securities is discussed, will not be deemed to constitute general solicitation or general advertising for purposes of this section.

(d) *Limitations on resale.* Except as provided in § 230.504(b)(1), securities acquired in a transaction under Regulation D shall have the status of securities acquired in a transaction under section 4(2) of the Act and cannot be resold without registration under the Act or an exemption therefrom. The issuer shall exercise reasonable care to assure that the purchasers of the securities are not underwriters within the meaning of section 2(11) of the Act, which reasonable care may be demonstrated by the following;

Provided, however, that publication by an issuer of a notice in accordance with § 230.135c shall not be deemed to constitute general solicitation or general advertising for purposes of this section.

(1) Reasonable inquiry to determine if the purchaser is acquiring the securities for himself or for other persons;

(2) Written disclosure to each purchaser prior to sale that the securities have not been registered under the Act and, therefore, cannot be resold unless they are registered under the Act or unless an exemption from registration is available; and

(3) Placement of a legend on the certificate or other document that evidences the securities stating that the securities have not been registered under the Act and setting forth or referring to the restrictions on transferability and sale of the securities.

While taking these actions will establish the requisite reasonable care, it is not the exclusive method to demonstrate such care. Other actions by the issuer may satisfy this provision. In addition, § 230.502(b)(2)(vii) requires the delivery of written disclosure of the limitations on resale to investors in certain instances.

Rule 503. Filing of Notice of Sales

(a) An issuer offering or selling securities in reliance on § 230.504, § 230.505 or § 230.506 shall file with the Commission five copies of a notice on Form D (17 CFR 239.500) no later than 15 days after the first sale of securities.

(b) One copy of every notice on Form D shall be manually signed by a person duly authorized by the issuer.

(c) If sales are made under § 230.505, the notice shall contain an undertaking by the issuer to furnish to the Commission, upon the writen request of its staff, the information furnished by the issuer under § 230.502(b)(2) to any purchaser that is not an accredited investor.

(d) Amendments to notices filed under paragraph (a) of this § 230.503 need only report the issuer's name and the information required by Part C and any material change in the facts from those set forth in Parts A and B.

(e) A notice on Form D shall be considered filed with the Commission under paragraph (a) of this § 230.503:

(1) As of the date on which it is received at the Commission's principal office in Washington, D.C.; or

(2) As of the date on which the notice is mailed by means of United States registered or certified mail to the Commission's principal office in Washington, D.C., if the notice is delivered to such office after the date on which it is required to be filed.

Rule 504. Exemption for Limited Offerings and Sales of Securities Not Exceeding $1,000,000

(a) *Exemption.* Offers and sales of securities that satisfy the conditions in paragraph (b) of this § 230.504 by an issuer that is not:

(1) subject to the reporting requirements of section 13 or 15(d) of the Exchange Act;

(2) an investment company; or

(3) a development stage company that either has no specific business plan or purpose or has indicated that its business plan is to engage in a merger or acquisition with an unidentified company or companies, or other entity or person, shall be exempt from the provision of section 5 of the Act under section 3(b) of the Act.

(b) *Conditions to be met.*

(1) *General conditions.* To qualify for exemption under this 230.504, offers and sales must satisfy the terms and conditions of 230.501 and 230.502(a), (c) and (d), except that the provisions of 230.502(c) and (d) will not apply to offers and sales of securities under this 230.504 that are made:

(i) Exclusively in one or more states that provide for the registration of the securities, and require the public filing and delivery to investors of a substantive disclosure document before sale, and are made in accordance with those state provisions;

(ii) In one or more states that have no provision for the registration of the securities or the public filing or delivery of a disclosure document before sale, if the securities have been registered in at least one state that provides for such registration, public filing and delivery before sale, offers and sales are made in that state in accordance with such provisions, and the disclosure document is delivered before sale to all purchasers (including those in the states that have no such procedure); or

(iii) Exclusively according to state law exemptions from registration that permit general solicitation and general advertising so long as sales are made only to "accredited investors" as defined in 230.501(a).

(2) The aggregate offering price for an offering of securities under this § 230.504, as defined in § 230.501(c), shall not exceed $1,000,000, less the aggregate offering price for all securities sold within the twelve months before the start of and during the offering of securities under this § 230.504, in reliance on any exemption under Section 3(b), or in violation of section 5(a) of the Securities Act.

NOTE 1: The calculation of the aggregate offering price is illustrated as follows:

If an issuer sold $900,000 on June 1, 1987 under this § 230.504 and an additional $4,100,000 on December 1, 1987 under § 230.505, the issuer could not sell any of its securities under this § 230.504 until December 1, 1988. Until then the issuer must count the December 1, 1987 sale towards the $1,000,000 limit within the preceding twelve months.

NOTE 2: If a transaction under § 230.504 fails to meet the limitation on the aggregate offering price, it does not affect the availability of this § 230.504 for the other transactions considered in applying such limitation. For example, if an issuer sold $1,000,000 worth of its securities on January 1, 1988 under this § 230.504 and an additional $500,000 worth on July 1, 1988, this § 230.504 would not be available for the later sale, but would still be applicable to the January 1, 1988 sale.

Rule 505. Exemption for Limited Offers and Sales of Securities Not Exceeding $5,000,000

(a) *Exemption.* Offers and sales of securities that satisfy the conditions in paragraph (b) of this § 230.505 by an issuer that is not an investment company shall be exempt from the provisions of section 5 of the Act under section 3(b) of the Act.

(b) *Conditions to be met.*

(1) *General conditions.* To qualify for exemption under this section, offers and sales must satisfy the terms and conditions of § § 230.501 and 230.502.

(2) *Specific conditions.*

(i) *Limitation on aggregate offering price.* The aggregate offering price for an offering of securities under this § 230.505, as defined in § 230.501(c), shall not exceed $5,000,000, less the aggregate offering price for all securities sold within the twelve months before the start of and during the offering of securities under this § 230.505 in reliance on any exemption under section 3(b) of the Act or in violation of section 5(a) of the Act.

Note: The calculation of the aggregate offering price is illustrated as follows:

Example 1. If an issuer sold $2,000,000 of its securities on June 1, 1982 under this § 230.505 and an additional $1,000,000 on September 1, 1982, the issuer would be permitted to sell only $2,000,000 more under this § 230.505 until June 1, 1983. Until that date the issuer must count both prior sales towards the $5,000,000 limit. However, if the issuer made its third sale on June 1, 1983, the issuer could then sell $4,000,000 of its securities because the June 1, 1982 sale would not be within the preceding twelve months.

Example 2. If an issuer sold $500,000 of its securities on June 1, 1982 under § 230.504 and an additional $4,500,000 on December 1, 1982 under this § 230.505, then the issuer could not sell any of its securities under this § 230.505 until June 1, 1983. At that time it could sell an additional $500,000 of its securities.

(ii) *Limitation on number of purchasers.* There are no more than or the issuer reasonably believes that there are no more than 35 purchasers of securities from the issuer in any offering under this § 230.505.

Note: See § 230.501(e) for the calculation of the number of purchasers and § 230.502(a) for what may or may not constitute an offering under this section.

(iii) *Disqualifications.* No exemption under this section shall be available for the securities of any issuer described in § 230.262 of Regulation A, except that for purposes of this section only:

(A) The term "filing of the offering statement required by § 230.252" as used in § 230.262(a), (b) and (c) shall mean the first sale of securities under this section;

(B) The term "underwriter" as used in § 230.262(b) and (c) shall mean a person that has been or will be paid directly or indirectly remuneration for solicitation of purchasers in connection with sales of securities under this section; and

(C) Paragraph (b)(2)(iii) of this § 230.505 shall not apply to any issuer if the Commission determines, upon a showing of good cause, that it is not necessary under the circumstances that the exemption be denied. Any such determination shall be without prejudice to any other action by the Commission in any other proceeding or matter with respect to the issuer or any other person.

Rule 506. Exemption for Limited Offers and Sales Without Regard to Dollar Amount of Offering

(a) *Exemption.* Offers and sales of securities by an issuer that satisfy the conditions in paragraph (b) of this § 230.506 shall be deemed to be transactions not involving any public offering within the meaning of section 4(2) of the Act.

(b) *Conditions to be met.*

(1) *General conditions.* To qualify for exemption under this section, offers and sales must satisfy all the terms and conditions of §§ 230.501 and 230.502.

(2) *Specific conditions.*

(i) *Limitation on number of purchasers.* There are no more than or the issuer reasonably believes that there are no more than 35 purchasers of securities from the issuer in any offering under this § 230.506.

Note: See § 230.501(e) for the calculation of the number of purchasers and § 230.502(a) for what may or may not constitute an offering under this section 230.506.

(ii) *Nature of purchasers.* Each purchaser who is not an accredited investor either alone or with his purchaser representative(s) has such knowledge and experience in financial and business matters that he is capable of evaluating the merits and risks of the prospective investment, or the issuer reasonably believes immediately prior to making any sale that such purchaser comes within this description.

Rule 507. Disqualifying Provision Relating to Exemptions Under §§ 230.504, 230.505 and 230.506

(a) No exemption under § 230.504, § 230.505 or § 230.506 shall be available for an issuer if such issuer, any of its predecessors or affiliates have been subject to any order, judgment, or decree of any court of competent jurisdiction temporarily, preliminarily or permanently enjoining such person for failure to comply with § 230.503.

(b) Paragraph (a) of this section shall not apply if the Commission determines, upon a showing of good cause, that it is not necessary under the circumstances that exemption be denied.

Rule 508. Insignificant Deviations From a Term, Condition or Requirement of Regulation D

(a) A failure to comply with a term, condition or requirement of § 230.504, § 230.505 or § 230.506 will not result in the loss of the exemption from the requirements of section 5 of the Act for any offer or sale to a particular individual or entity, if the person relying on the exemption shows:

(1) the failure to comply did not pertain to a term, condition or requirement directly intended to protect that particular individual or entity; and

(2) the failure to comply was insignificant with respect to the offering as a whole, provided that any failure to comply with paragraph (c) of § 230.502, paragraph (b)(2) of § 230.504, paragraphs (b)(2)(i) and (ii) of § 230.505 and paragraph (b)(2)(i) of § 230.506 shall be deemed to be significant to the offering as a whole; and

(3) a good faith and reasonable attempt was made to comply with all applicable terms, conditions and requirements of § 230.504, § 230.505 or § 230.506.

(b) A transaction made in reliance on § 230.504, § 230.505 or § 230.506 shall comply with all applicable terms, conditions and requirements of Regulation D. Where an exemption is established only through reliance upon paragraph (a) of this section, the failure to comply shall nonetheless be actionable by the Commission under section 20 of the Act.

Rule 701. Exemption For Offers and Sales of Securities Pursuant to Certain Compensatory Benefit Plans and Contracts Relating to Compensation
Preliminary Notes

1. This section relates to transactions exempted from the registration requirements of section 5 of the Act (15 U.S.C. 77e). These transactions are not exempt from the antifraud, civil liability, or other provisions of the federal securities laws. Issuers and persons acting on their behalf have an obligation to provide investors with disclosure adequate to satisfy the antifraud provisions of the federal securities laws.

2. In addition to complying with this section, the issuer also must comply with any applicable state law relating to the offer and sale of securities.

3. An issuer that attempts to comply with this section, but fails to do so, may claim any other exemption that is available.

4. This section is available only to the issuer of the securities. Affiliates of the issuer may not use this section to offer or sell securities. This section also does not cover resales of securities by any person. This section provides an exemption only for the transactions in which the securities are offered or sold by the issuer, not for the securities themselves.

5. The purpose of this section is to provide an exemption from the registration requirements of the Act for securities issued in compensatory circumstances. This section is not available for plans or schemes to circumvent this purpose, such as to raise capital. This section also is not available to exempt any transaction that is in technical compliance with this section but is part of a plan or scheme to evade the registration provisions of the Act. In any of these cases, registration under the Act is required unless another exemption is available.

Rule 701. (a) *Exemption.* Offers and sales made in compliance with all of the conditions of this section are exempt from section 5 of the Act (15 U.S.C. 77e).

(b) *Issuers eligible to use this section.*

(1) *General.* This section is available to any issuer that is not subject to the reporting requirements of section 13 or 15(d) of the Securities Exchange Act of 1934 (the "Exchange Act") (15 U.S.C. 78m or 78o(d)) and is not an investment company registered or required to be registered under the Investment Company Act of 1940 (15 U.S.C. 80a-1 *et seq.*).

(2) *Issuers that become subject to reporting.* If an issuer becomes subject to the reporting requirements of section 13 or 15(d) of the Exchange Act (15 U.S.C. 78m or 78o(d)) after it has made offers complying with this section, the issuer may nevertheless rely on this section to sell the securities previously offered to the persons to whom those offers were made.

(3) *Guarantees by reporting companies.* An issuer subject to the reporting requirements of section 13 or 15(d) of the Exchange Act (15 U.S.C. 78m, 78o(d)) may rely on this section if it is merely guaranteeing the payment of a subsidiary's securities that are sold under this section.

(c) *Transactions exempted by this section.* This section exempts offers and sales of securities (including plan interests and guarantees pursuant to paragraph (d)(2)(ii) of this section) under a written compensatory benefit plan (or written compensation contract) established by the issuer, its parents, its majority-owned subsidiaries or majority-owned subsidiaries of the issuer's parent, for the participation of their employees, directors, general partners, trustees (where the issuer is a business trust), officers, or consultants and advisors, and their family members who acquire such securities from such persons through gifts or domestic relations orders. This section exempts offers and sales to former employees, directors, general partners, trustees, officers, consultants and advisors only if such persons were employed by or providing services to the issuer at the time the securities were offered. In addition, the term "employee" includes insurance agents who are exclusive agents of the issuer, its subsidiaries or parents, or derive more than 50% of their annual income from those entities.

(1) **Special requirements for consultants and advisors.** This section is available to consultants and advisors only if:

(i) They are natural persons;

(ii) They provide *bona fide* services to the issuer, its parents, its majority-owned subsidiaries or majority-owned subsidiaries of the issuer's parent; and

(iii) The services are not in connection with the offer or sale of securities in a capital-raising transaction, and do not directly or indirectly promote or maintain a market for the issuer's securities.

(2) **Definition of "Compensatory Benefit Plan."** For purposes of this section, a *compensatory benefit plan* is any purchase, savings, option, bonus, stock appreciation, profit sharing, thrift, incentive, deferred compensation, pension or similar plan.

(3) **Definition of "Family Member."** For purposes of this section, *family member* includes any child, stepchild, grandchild, parent, stepparent, grandparent, spouse, former spouse, sibling, niece, nephew, mother-in-law, father-in-law, son-in-law, daughter-in-law, brother-in-law, or sister-in-law, including adoptive relationships, any person sharing the employee's household (other than a tenant or employee), a trust in which these persons have more than fifty percent of the beneficial interest, a foundation in which these persons (or the employee) control the management of assets, and any other entity in which these persons (or the employee) own more than fifty percent of the voting interests.

(d) **Amounts that may be sold.**

(1) **Offers.** Any amount of securities may be offered in reliance on this section. However, for purposes of this section, sales of securities underlying options must be counted as sales on the date of the option grant.

(2) **Sales.** The aggregate sales price or amount of securities sold in reliance on this section during any consecutive 12-month period must not exceed the greatest of the following:

(i) $1,000,000;

(ii) 15% of the total assets of the issuer (or of the issuer's parent if the issuer is a wholly-owned subsidiary and the securities represent obligations that the parent fully and unconditionally guarantees), measured at the issuer's most recent balance sheet date (if no older than its last fiscal year end); or

(iii) 15% of the outstanding amount of the class of securities being offered and sold in reliance on this section, measured at the issuer's most recent balance sheet date (if no older than its last fiscal year end).

(3) **Rules for calculating prices and amounts.**

(i) **Aggregate sales price.** The term *aggregate sales price* means the sum of all cash, property, notes, cancellation of debt or other consideration received or to be received by the issuer for the sale of the securities. Non-cash consideration must be valued by reference to *bona fide* sales of that consideration made within a reasonable time or, in the absence of such sales, on the fair value as determined by an accepted standard. The value of services exchanged for securities issued must be measured by reference to the value of the securities issued. Options must be valued based on the exercise price of the option.

(ii) **Time of the calculation.** With respect to options to purchase securities, the aggregate sales price is determined when an option grant is made (without regard to when the option becomes exercisable). With respect to other securities, the calculation is made on the date of sale. With respect to deferred compensation or similar plans, the calculation is made when the irrevocable election to defer is made.

(iii) **Derivative securities.** In calculating outstanding securities for purposes of paragraph (d)(2)(iii) of this section, treat the securities underlying all currently exercisable or convertible options, warrants, rights or other securities, other than those issued under this exemption, as outstanding. In calculating the amount of securities sold for other purposes of paragraph (d)(2) of this section, count the amount of securities that would be acquired upon exercise or conversion in connection with sales of options, warrants, rights or other exercisable or convertible securities, including those to be issued under this exemption.

(iv) *Other exemptions.* Amounts of securities sold in reliance on this section do not affect "aggregate offering prices" in other exemptions, and amounts of securities sold in reliance on other exemptions do not affect the amount that may be sold in reliance on this section.

(e) *Disclosure that must be provided.* The issuer must deliver to investors a copy of the compensatory benefit plan or the contract, as applicable. In addition, if the aggregate sales price or amount of securities sold during any consecutive 12-month period exceeds $5 million, the issuer must deliver the following disclosure to investors a reasonable period of time before the date of sale:

(1) If the plan is subject to the Employee Retirement Income Security Act of 1974 ("ERISA") (29 U.S.C. 1104 - 1107), a copy of the summary plan description required by ERISA;

(2) If the plan is not subject to ERISA, a summary of the material terms of the plan;

(3) Information about the risks associated with investment in the securities sold pursuant to the compensatory benefit plan or compensation contract; and

(4) Financial statements required to be furnished by Part F/S of Form 1-A (Regulation A Offering Statement) (§ 239.90 of this chapter) under Regulation A (§ § 230.251 - 230.263). Foreign private issuers as defined in § 230.405 must provide a reconciliation to generally accepted accounting principles in the United States (U.S. GAAP) if their financial statements are not prepared in accordance with U.S. GAAP (Item 17, of Form 20-F (§ 249.220f of this chapter)). The financial statements required by this section must be as of a date no more than 180 days before the sale of securities in reliance on this exemption.

(5) If the issuer is relying on paragraph (d)(2)(ii) of this section to use its parent's total assets to determine the amount of securities that may be sold, the parent's financial statements must be delivered. If the parent is subject to the reporting requirements of section 13 or 15(d) of the Exchange Act (15 U.S.C. 78m or 78o(d)), the financial statements of the parent required by Rule 10-01 of Regulation S-X (§ 210.10-01 of this chapter) and Item 310 of Regulation S-B (§ 228.310 of this chapter), as applicable, must be delivered.

(6) If the sale involves a stock option or other derivative security, the issuer must deliver disclosure a reasonable period of time before the date of exercise or conversion. For deferred compensation or similar plans, the issuer must deliver disclosure to investors a reasonable period of time before the date the irrevocable election to defer is made.

(f) *No integration with other offerings.* Offers and sales exempt under this section are deemed to be a part of a single, discrete offering and are not subject to integration with any other offers or sales, whether registered under the Act or otherwise exempt from the registration requirements of the Act.

(g) *Resale limitations.*

(1) Securities issued under this section are deemed to be "restricted securities" as defined in § 230.144.

(2) Resales of securities issued pursuant to this section must be in compliance with the registration requirements of the Act or an exemption from those requirements.

(3) Ninety days after the issuer becomes subject to the reporting requirements of section 13 or 15(d) of the Exchange Act (15 U.S.C. 78m or 78o(d)), securities issued under this section may be resold by persons who are not affiliates (as defined in § 230.144) in reliance on § 230.144 without compliance with paragraphs (c), (d), (e) and (h) of § 230.144, and by affiliates without compliance with paragraph (d) of § 230.144.

REGULATION S—RULES GOVERNING OFFERS AND SALES MADE OUTSIDE THE UNITED STATES WITHOUT REGISTRATION UNDER THE SECURITIES ACT OF 1933

Preliminary Notes

1. The following rules relate solely to the application of Section 5 of the Securities Act of 1933 (the "Act") [15 U.S.C. § 77e] and not to antifraud or other provisions of the federal securities laws.

2. In view of the objective of these rules and the policies underlying the Act, Regulation S is not available with respect to any transaction or series of transactions that, although in technical compliance with these rules, is part of a plan or scheme to evade the registration provisions of the Act. In such cases, registration under the Act is required.

3. Nothing in these rules obviates the need for any issuer or any other person to comply with the securities registration or broker-dealer registration requirements of the Securities Exchange Act (the "Exchange Act"), whenever such requirements are applicable.

4. Nothing in these rules obviates the need to comply with any applicable state law relating to the offer and sale of securities.

5. Attempted compliance with any rule in Regulation S does not act as an exclusive election; a person making an offer or sale of securities may also claim the availability of any other applicable exemption from the registration requirements of the Act. The availability of the Regulation S safe harbor to offers and sales that occur outside of the United States will not be affected by the subsequent offer and sale of these securities into the United States or to U.S. persons during the distribution compliance period, as long as the subsequent offer and sale are made pursuant to registration or an exemption therefrom under the Act.

6. Regulation S is available only for offers and sales of securities outside the United States. Securities acquired overseas, whether or not pursuant to Regulation S, may be resold in the United States only if they are registered under the Act or an exemption from registration is available.

7. Nothing in these rules precludes access by journalists for publications with a general circulation in the United States to offshore press conferences, press releases and meetings with company press spokespersons in which an offshore offering or tender offer is discussed, provided that the information is made available to the foreign and United States press generally and is not intended to induce purchases of securities by persons in the United States or tenders of securities by United States holders in the case of exchange offers. Where applicable, issuers and bidders may also look to § 230.135e and § 240.14d-1(c) of this chapter.

8. The provisions of this Regulation S shall not apply to offers and sales of securities issued by open-end investment companies or unit investment trusts registered or required to be registered or closed-end investment companies required to be registered, but not registered, under the Investment Company Act of 1940 [15 U.S.C. § 80a-1 *et seq.*] (the "1940 Act").

Rule 901. General Statement

For the purposes only of section 5 of the Act (15 U.S.C. § 77e), the terms "offer," "offer to sell," "offer for sell," "sell," "sale," and "offer to buy" shall be deemed to include offers and sales that occur within the United States and shall be deemed not to include offers and sales that occur outside the United States.

Rule 902. Definitions

As used in Regulation S, the following terms shall have the meanings indicated.

(a) *Debt securities.* "Debt securities" of an issuer is defined to mean any security other than an equity security as defined in § 230.405, as well as the following:

(1) Non-participatory preferred stock, which is defined as non-convertible capital stock, the holders of which are entitled to a preference in payment of dividends and in distribution of assets on liquidation, dissolution, or winding up of the issuer, but are not entitled to participate in residual earnings or assets of the issuer; and

(2) Asset-backed securities, which are securities of a type that either:

(i) Represent an ownership interest in a pool of discrete assets, or certificates of interest or participation in such assets (including any rights designed to assure servicing, or the receipt or timeliness of receipt by holders of such assets, or certificates of interest or participation in such assets, of amounts payable thereunder), provided that the assets are not generated or originated between the issuer of the security and its affiliates; or

(ii) Are secured by one or more assets or certificates of interest or participation in such assets, and the securities, by their terms, provide for payments of principal and interest (if any) in relation to payments or reasonable projections of payments on assets meeting the requirements of paragraph (a)(2)(i) of this section, or certificates of interest or participations in assets meeting such requirements.

(iii) For purposes of paragraph (a)(2) of this section, the term "assets" means securities, installment sales, accounts receivable, notes, leases or other contracts, or other assets that by their terms convert into cash over a finite period of time.

(b) *Designated offshore securities market.* "Designated offshore securities market" means:

(1) The Eurobond market, as regulated by the International Securities Market Association; the Alberta Stock Exchange; the Amsterdam Stock Exchange; the Australian Stock Exchange Limited; the Bermuda Stock Exchange; the Bourse de Bruxelles; the Copenhagen Stock Exchange; the European Association of Securities Dealers Automated Quotation; the Frankfurt Stock Exchange; the Helsinki Stock Exchange; The Stock Exchange of Hong Kong Limited; the Irish Stock Exchange; the Istanbul Stock Exchange; the Johannesburg Stock Exchange; the London Stock Exchange; the Bourse de Luxembourg; the Mexico Stock Exchange; the Borsa Valori di Milan; the Montreal Stock Exchange; the Oslo Stock Exchange; the Bourse de Paris; the Stock Exchange of Singapore Ltd.; the Stockholm Stock Exchange; the Tokyo Stock Exchange; the Toronto Stock Exchange; the Vancouver Stock Exchange; the Warsaw Stock Exchange and the Zurich Stock Exchange; and

(2) Any foreign securities exchange or non-exchange market designated by the Commission. Attributes to be considered in determining whether to designate an offshore securities market, among others, include:

(i) Organization under foreign law;

(ii) Association with a generally recognized community of brokers, dealers, banks, or other professional intermediaries with an established operating history;

(iii) Oversight by a governmental or self-regulatory body;

(iv) Oversight standards set by an existing body of law;

(v) Reporting of securities transactions on a regular basis to a governmental or self-regulatory body;

(vi) A system for exchange of price quotations through common communications media; and

(vii) An organized clearance and settlement system.

(c) *Directed selling efforts.*

(1) "Directed selling efforts" means any activity undertaken for the purpose of, or that could reasonably be expected to have the effect of, conditioning the market in the United States for any of the securities being offered in reliance on this Regulation S (§ 230.901 through § 230.905, and Preliminary Notes). Such activity includes placing an advertisement in a publication "with a general circulation in the United States" that refers to the offering of securities being made in reliance upon this Regulation S.

(2) Publication "with a general circulation in the United States":

(i) Is defined as any publication that is printed primarily for distribution in the United States, or has had, during the preceding twelve months, an average circulation in the United States of 15,000 or more copies per issue; and

(ii) Will encompass only the U.S. edition of any publication printing a separate U.S. edition if the publication, without considering its U.S. edition, would not constitute a publication with a general circulation in the United States.

(3) The following are not "directed selling efforts":

(i) Placing an advertisement required to be published under U.S. or foreign law, or under rules or regulations of a U.S. or foreign regulatory or self-regulatory authority, provided the advertisement contains no more information than legally required and includes a statement to the effect that the securities have not been registered under the Act and may not be offered or sold in the United States (or to a U.S. person, if the advertisement relates to an offering under Category 2

141

or 3 (paragraph (b)(2) or (b)(3)) in § 230.903) absent registration or an applicable exemption from the registration requirements;

(ii) Contact with persons excluded from the definition of "U.S. person" pursuant to paragraph (k)(2)(vi) of this section or persons holding accounts excluded from the definition of "U.S. person" pursuant to paragraph (k)(2)(i) of this section, solely in their capacities as holders of such accounts;

(iii) A tombstone advertisement in any publication with a general circulation in the United States, provided:

(A) The publication has less than 20% of its circulation, calculated by aggregating the circulation of its U.S. and comparable non-U.S. editions, in the United States;

(B) Such advertisement contains a legend to the effect that the securities have not been registered under the Act and may not be offered or sold in the United States (or to a U.S. person, if the advertisement relates to an offering under Category 2 or 3 (paragraph (b)(2) or (b)(3)) in § 230.903) absent registration or an applicable exemption from the registration requirements; and

(C) Such advertisement contains no more information than:

(1) The issuer's name;

(2) The amount and title of the securities being sold;

(3) A brief indication of the issuer's general type of business;

(4) The price of the securities;

(5) The yield of the securities, if debt securities with a fixed (non-contingent) interest provision;

(6) The name and address of the person placing the advertisement, and whether such person is participating in the distribution;

(7) The names of the managing underwriters;

(8) The dates, if any, upon which the sales commenced and concluded;

(9) Whether the securities are offered or were offered by rights issued to security holders and, if so, the class of securities that are entitled or were entitled to subscribe, the subscription ratio, the record date, the dates (if any) upon which the rights were issued and expired, and the subscription price; and

(10) Any legend required by law or any foreign or U.S. regulatory or self-regulatory authority;

(iv) Bona fide visits to real estate, plants or other facilities located in the United States and tours thereof conducted for a prospective investor by an issuer, a distributor, any of their respective affiliates or a person acting on behalf of any of the foregoing;

(v) Distribution in the United States of a foreign broker-dealer's quotations by a third-party system that distributes such quotations primarily in foreign countries if:

(A) Securities transactions cannot be executed between foreign broker-dealers and persons in the United States through the system; and

(B) The issuer, distributors, their respective affiliates, persons acting on behalf of any of the foregoing, foreign broker-dealers and other participants in the system do not initiate contacts with U.S. persons or persons within the United States, beyond those contacts exempted under § 240.15a-6 of this chapter; and

(vi) Publication by an issuer of a notice in accordance with § 230.135 or § 230.135c.

(vii) Providing any journalist with access to press conferences held outside of the United States, to meetings with the issuer or selling security holder representatives conducted outside the United States, or to written press-related materials released outside the United States, at or in which a present or proposed offering of securities is discussed, if the requirements of § 230.135e are satisfied.

(d) *Distributor.* "Distributor" means any underwriter, dealer, or other person who participates, pursuant to a contractual arrangement, in the distribution of the securities offered or sold in reliance on this Regulation S (§ 230.901 through § 230.905, and Preliminary Notes).

(e) *Domestic issuer/Foreign issuer.* "Domestic issuer" means any issuer other than a "foreign government" or "foreign private issuer" (both as defined in § 230.405). "Foreign issuer" means any issuer other than a "domestic issuer."

(f) *Distribution compliance period.* "Distribution compliance period" means a period that begins when the securities were first offered to persons other than distributors in reliance upon this Regulation S (§ 230.901 through § 230.905, and Preliminary Notes) or the date of closing of the offering, whichever is later, and continues until the end of the period of time specified in the relevant provision of § 230.903, except that:

(1) All offers and sales by a distributor of an unsold allotment or subscription shall be deemed to be made during the distribution compliance period;

(2) In a continuous offering, the distribution compliance period shall commence upon completion of the distribution, as determined and certified by the managing underwriter or person performing similar functions;

(3) In a continuous offering of non-convertible debt securities offered and sold in identifiable tranches, the distribution compliance period for securities in a tranche shall commence upon completion of the distribution of such tranche, as determined and certified by the managing underwriter or person performing similar functions; and

(4) That in a continuous offering of securities to be acquired upon the exercise of warrants, the distribution compliance period shall commence upon completion of the distribution of the warrants, as determined and certified by the managing underwriter or person performing similar functions, if requirements of § 230.903(b)(5) are satisfied.

(g) *Offering restrictions.* "Offering restrictions" means:

(1) Each distributor agrees in writing:

(i) That all offers and sales of the securities prior to the expiration of the distribution compliance period specified in Category 2 or 3 (paragraph (b)(2) or (b)(3)) in § 230.903, as applicable, shall be made only in accordance with the provisions of § 230.903 or § 230.904; pursuant to registration of the securities under the Act; or pursuant to an available exemption from the registration requirements of the Act; and

(ii) For offers and sales of equity securities of domestic issuers, not to engage in hedging transactions with regard to such securities prior to the expiration of the distribution compliance period specified in Category 2 or 3 (paragraph (b)(2) or (b)(3)) in § 230.903, as applicable, unless in compliance with the Act; and

(2) All offering materials and documents (other than press releases) used in connection with offers and sales of the securities prior to the expiration of the distribution compliance period specified in Category 2 or 3 (paragraph (b)(2) or (b)(3)) in § 230.903, as applicable, shall include statements to the effect that the securities have not been registered under the Act and may not be offered or sold in the United States or to U.S. persons (other than distributors) unless the securities are registered under the Act, or an exemption from the registration requirements of the Act is available. For offers and sales of equity securities of domestic issuers, such offering materials and documents also must state that hedging transactions involving those securities may not be conducted unless in compliance with the Act. Such statements shall appear:

(i) On the cover or inside cover page of any prospectus or offering circular used in connection with the offer or sale of the securities;

(ii) In the underwriting section of any prospectus or offering circular used in connection with the offer or sale of the securities; and

(iii) In any advertisement made or issued by the issuer, any distributor, any of their respective affiliates, or any person acting on behalf of any of the foregoing. Such statements may appear in summary form on prospectus cover pages and in advertisements.

(h) *Offshore transaction.*

(1) An offer or sale of securities is made in an "offshore transaction" if:

(i) The offer is not made to a person in the United States; and

(ii) Either:

(A) At the time the buy order is originated, the buyer is outside the United States, or the seller and any person acting on its behalf reasonably believe that the buyer is outside the United States; or

(B) For purposes of:

(*1*) §230.903, the transaction is executed in, on or through a physical trading floor of an established foreign securities exchange that is located outside the United States; or

(*2*) §230.904, the transaction is executed in, on or through the facilities of a designated offshore securities market described in paragraph (b) of this section, and neither the seller nor any person acting on its behalf knows that the transaction has been pre-arranged with a buyer in the United States.

(2) Notwithstanding paragraph (h)(1) of this section, offers and sales of securities specifically targeted at identifiable groups of U.S. citizens abroad, such as members of the U.S. armed forces serving overseas, shall not be deemed to be made in "offshore transactions."

(3) Notwithstanding paragraph (h)(1) of this section, offers and sales of securities to persons excluded from the definition of "U.S. person" pursuant to paragraph (k)(2)(vi) of this section or persons holding accounts excluded from the definition of "U.S. person" pursuant to paragraph (k)(2)(i) of this section, solely in their capacities as holders of such accounts, shall be deemed to be made in "offshore transactions."

(i) *Reporting issuer.* "Reporting issuer" means an issuer other than an investment company registered or required to register under the 1940 Act that:

(1) Has a class of securities registered pursuant to Section 12(b) or 12(g) of the Exchange Act (15 U.S.C. §§78*l* (b) or 78*l* (g)) or is required to file reports pursuant to Section 15(d) of the Exchange Act (15 U.S.C. §78*o* (d)); and

(2) Has filed all the material required to be filed pursuant to Section 13(a) or 15(d) of the Exchange Act (15 U.S.C. §§78m(a) or 78*o* (d)) for a period of at least twelve months immediately preceding the offer or sale of securities made in reliance upon this Regulation S (§230.901 through §230.905, and Preliminary Notes) (or for such shorter period that the issuer was required to file such material).

(j) *Substantial U.S. market interest.*

(1) "Substantial U.S. market interest" with respect to a class of an issuer's equity securities means:

(i) The securities exchanges and inter-dealer quotation systems in the United States in the aggregate constituted the single largest market for such class of securities in the shorter of the issuer's prior fiscal year or the period since the issuer's incorporation; or

(ii) 20 percent or more of all trading in such class of securities took place in, on or through the facilities of securities exchanges and inter-dealer quotation systems in the United States and less than 55 percent of such trading took place in, on or through the facilities of securities markets of a single foreign country in the shorter of the issuer's prior fiscal year or the period since the issuer's incorporation.

(2) "Substantial U.S. market interest" with respect to an issuer's debt securities means:

(i) Its debt securities, in the aggregate, are held of record (as that term is defined in §240.12g5-1 of this chapter and used for purposes of paragraph (j)(2) of this section) by 300 or more U.S. persons;

(ii) $1 billion or more of: the principal amount outstanding of its debt securities, the greater of liquidation preference or par value of its securities described in §230.902(a)(1), and the principal amount or principal balance of its securities described in §230.902(a)(2), in the aggregate, is held of record by U.S. persons; and

(iii) 20 percent or more of: the principal amount outstanding of its debt securities, the greater of liquidation preference or par value of its securities described in §230.902(a)(1), and the principal amount or principal balance of its securities described in §230.902(a)(2), in the aggregate, is held of record by U.S. persons.

(3) Notwithstanding paragraph (j)(2) of this section, substantial U.S. market interest with respect to an issuer's debt securities is calculated without reference to securities that qualify for the exemption provided by Section 3(a)(3) of the Act (15 U.S.C. §77c(a)(3)).

(k) *U.S. person.*

(1) "U.S. person" means:

(i) Any natural person resident in the United States;

(ii) Any partnership or corporation organized or incorporated under the laws of the United States;

(iii) Any estate of which any executor or administrator is a U.S. person;

(iv) Any trust of which any trustee is a U.S. person;

(v) Any agency or branch of a foreign entity located in the United States;

(vi) Any non-discretionary account or similar account (other than an estate or trust) held by a dealer or other fiduciary for the benefit or account of a U.S. person;

(vii) Any discretionary account or similar account (other than an estate or trust) held by a dealer or other fiduciary organized, incorporated, or (if an individual) resident in the United States; and

(viii) Any partnership or corporation if:

(A) Organized or incorporated under the laws of any foreign jurisdiction; and

(B) Formed by a U.S. person principally for the purpose of investing in securities not registered under the Act, unless it is organized or incorporated, and owned, by accredited investors (as defined in §230.501(a)) who are not natural persons, estates or trusts.

(2) The following are not "U.S. persons":

(i) Any discretionary account or similar account (other than an estate or trust) held for the benefit or account of a non-U.S. person by a dealer or other professional fiduciary organized, incorporated, or (if an individual) resident in the United States;

(ii) Any estate of which any professional fiduciary acting as executor or administrator is a U.S. person if:

(A) An executor or administrator of the estate who is not a U.S. person has sole or shared investment discretion with respect to the assets of the estate; and

(B) The estate is governed by foreign law;

(iii) Any trust of which any professional fiduciary acting as trustee is a U.S. person, if a trustee who is not a U.S. person has sole or shared investment discretion with respect to the trust assets, and no beneficiary of the trust (and no settlor if the trust is revocable) is a U.S. person;

(iv) An employee benefit plan established and administered in accordance with the law of a country other than the United States and customary practices and documentation of such country;

(v) Any agency or branch of a U.S. person located outside the United States if:

(A) The agency or branch operates for valid business reasons; and

(B) The agency or branch is engaged in the business of insurance or banking and is subject to substantive insurance or banking regulation, respectively, in the jurisdiction where located; and

(vi) The International Monetary Fund, the International Bank for Reconstruction and Development, the Inter-American Development Bank, the Asian Development Bank, the African Development Bank, the United Nations, and their agencies, affiliates and pension plans, and any other similar international organizations, their agencies, affiliates and pension plans.

(l) *United States.* "United States" means the United States of America, its territories and possessions, any State of the United States, and the District of Columbia.

Rule 903. Offers or Sales of Securities by the Issuer, a Distributor, Any of Their Respective Affiliates, or Any Person Acting on Behalf of Any of the Foregoing; Conditions Relating to Specific Securities

An offer or sale of securities by the issuer, a distributor, any of their respective affiliates, or any person acting on behalf of any of the foregoing, shall be deemed to occur outside the United States within the meaning of §230.901 if:

(1) The offer or sale is made in an offshore transaction;

(2) No directed selling efforts are made in the United States by the issuer, a distributor, any of their respective affiliates, or any person acting on behalf of any of the foregoing; and

(3) The conditions of paragraph (b) of this section, as applicable, are satisfied.

(b) *Additional Conditions.*

(1) *Category 1.* No conditions other than those set forth in § 230.903(a) apply to securities in this category. Securities are eligible for this category if:

(i) The securities are issued by a foreign issuer that reasonably believes at the commencement of the offering that:

(A) There is no substantial U.S. market interest in the class of securities to be offered or sold (if equity securities are offered or sold);

(B) There is no substantial U.S. market interest in its debt securities (if debt securities are offered or sold);

(C) There is no substantial U.S. market interest in the securities to be purchased upon exercise (if warrants are offered or sold); and

(D) There is no substantial U.S. market interest in either the convertible securities or the underlying securities (if convertible securities are offered or sold);

(ii) The securities are offered and sold in an overseas directed offering, which means:

(A) An offering of securities of a foreign issuer that is directed into a single country other than the United States to the residents thereof and that is made in accordance with the local laws and customary practices and documentation of such country; or

(B) An offering of non-convertible debt securities of a domestic issuer that is directed into a single country other than the United States to the residents thereof and that is made in accordance with the local laws and customary practices and documentation of such country, provided that the principal and interest of the securities (or par value, as applicable) are denominated in a currency other than U.S. dollars and such securities are neither convertible into U.S. dollar-denominated securities nor linked to U.S. dollars (other than through related currency or interest rate swap transactions that are commercial in nature) in a manner that in effect converts the securities to U.S. dollar-denominated securities.

(iii) The securities are backed by the full faith and credit of a foreign government; or

(iv) The securities are offered and sold to employees of the issuer or its affiliates pursuant to an employee benefit plan established and administered in accordance with the law of a country other than the United States, and customary practices and documentation of such country, provided that:

(A) The securities are issued in compensatory circumstances for bona fide services rendered to the issuer or its affiliates in connection with their businesses and such services are not rendered in connection with the offer or sale of securities in a capital-raising transaction;

(B) Any interests in the plan are not transferable other than by will or the laws of descent or distribution;

(C) The issuer takes reasonable steps to preclude the offer and sale of interests in the plan or securities under the plan to U.S. residents other than employees on temporary assignment in the United States; and

(D) Documentation used in connection with any offer pursuant to the plan contains a statement that the securities have not been registered under the Act and may not be offered or sold in the United States unless registered or an exemption from registration is available.

(2) *Category 2.* The following conditions apply to securities that are not eligible for Category 1 (paragraph (b)(1)) of this section and that are equity securities of a reporting foreign issuer, or debt securities of a reporting issuer or of a non-reporting foreign issuer.

(i) Offering restrictions are implemented;

(ii) The offer or sale, if made prior to the expiration of a 40-day distribution compliance period, is not made to a U.S. person or for the account or benefit of a U.S. person (other than a distributor); and

(iii) Each distributor selling securities to a distributor, a dealer, as defined in section 2(a)(12) of the Act (15 U.S.C. § 77b(a)(12)), or a person receiving a selling concession, fee or other remuneration in respect of the securities sold, prior to the expiration of a 40-day distribution compliance period, sends a confirmation or other notice to the purchaser stating that the purchaser is subject to the same restrictions on offers and sales that apply to a distributor.

(3) *Category 3.* The following conditions apply to securities that are not eligible for Category 1 or 2 (paragraph (b)(1) or (b)(2)) of this section:

(i) Offering restrictions are implemented;

(ii) In the case of debt securities:

(A) The offer or sale, if made prior to the expiration of a 40-day distribution compliance period, is not made to a U.S. person or for the account or benefit of a U.S. person (other than a distributor); and

(B) The securities are represented upon issuance by a temporary global security which is not exchangeable for definitive securities until the expiration of the 40-day distribution compliance period and, for persons other than distributors, until certification of beneficial ownership of the securities by a non-U.S. person or a U.S. person who purchased securities in a transaction that did not require registration under the Act;

(iii) In the case of equity securities:

(A) The offer or sale, if made prior to the expiration of a one-year distribution compliance period, is not made to a U.S. person or for the account or benefit of a U.S. person (other than a distributor); and

(B) The offer or sale, if made prior to the expiration of a one-year distribution compliance period, is made pursuant to the following conditions:

(*1*) The purchaser of the securities (other than a distributor) certifies that it is not a U.S. person and is not acquiring the securities for the account or benefit of any U.S. person or is a U.S. person who purchased securities in a transaction that did not require registration under the Act;

(*2*) The purchaser of the securities agrees to resell such securities only in accordance with the provisions of this Regulation S (§ 230.901 through § 230.905, and Preliminary Notes), pursuant to registration under the Act, or pursuant to an available exemption from registration; and agrees not to engage in hedging transactions with regard to such securities unless in compliance with the Act;

(*3*) The securities of a domestic issuer contain a legend to the effect that transfer is prohibited except in accordance with the provisions of this Regulation S (§ 230.901 through § 230.905, and Preliminary Notes), pursuant to registration under the Act, or pursuant to an available exemption from registration; and that hedging transactions involving those securities may not be conducted unless in compliance with the Act;

(*4*) The issuer is required, either by contract or a provision in its bylaws, articles, charter or comparable document, to refuse to register any transfer of the securities not made in accordance with the provisions of this Regulation S (§ 230.901 through § 230.905, and Preliminary Notes), pursuant to registration under the Act, or pursuant to an available exemption from registration; *provided, however,* that if the securities are in bearer form or foreign law prevents the issuer of the securities from refusing to register securities transfers, other reasonable procedures (such as a legend described in paragraph (b)(3)(iii)(B)(*3*) of this section) are implemented to prevent any transfer of the securities not made in accordance with the provisions of this Regulation S; and

(iv) Each distributor selling securities to a distributor, a dealer (as defined in section 2(a)(12) of the Act (15 U.S.C. § 77b(a)(12)), or a person receiving a selling concession, fee or other remuneration, prior to the expiration of a 40-day distribution compliance period in the case of debt securities, or a one-year distribution compliance period in the case of equity securities, sends a confirmation or other notice to the purchaser stating that the purchaser is subject to the same restrictions on offers and sales that apply to a distributor.

(4) *Guaranteed securities.* Notwithstanding paragraphs (b)(1) through (b)(3) of this section, in offerings of debt securities fully and unconditionally guaranteed as to principal and interest by the parent of the issuer of the debt securities, only the requirements of paragraph (b) of this

section that are applicable to the offer and sale of the guarantee must be satisfied with respect to the offer and sale of the guaranteed debt securities.

(5) *Warrants.* An offer or sale of warrants under Category 2 or 3 (paragraph (b)(2) or (b)(3)) of this section also must comply with the following requirements:

(i) Each warrant must bear a legend stating that the warrant and the securities to be issued upon its exercise have not been registered under the Act and that the warrant may not be exercised by or on behalf of any U.S. person unless registered under the Act or an exemption from such registration is available;

(ii) Each person exercising a warrant is required to give:

(A) Written certification that it is not a U.S. person and the warrant is not being exercised on behalf of a U.S. person; or

(B) A written opinion of counsel to the effect that the warrant and the securities delivered upon exercise thereof have been registered under the Act or are exempt from registration thereunder; and

(iii) Procedures are implemented to ensure that the warrant may not be exercised within the United States, and that the securities may not be delivered within the United States upon exercise, other than in offerings deemed to meet the definition of "offshore transaction" pursuant to § 230.902(h), unless registered under the Act or an exemption from such registration is available.

Rule 904. Offshore Resales

(a) An offer or sale of securities by any person other than the issuer, a distributor, any of their respective affiliates (except any officer or director who is an affiliate solely by virtue of holding such position), or any person acting on behalf of any of the foregoing, shall be deemed to occur outside the United States within the meaning of § 230.901 if:

(1) The offer or sale are made in an offshore transaction;

(2) No directed selling efforts are made in the United States by the seller, an affiliate, or any person acting on their behalf; and

(3) The conditions of paragraph (b) of this section, if applicable, are satisfied.

(b) *Additional conditions.*

(1) *Resales by dealers and persons receiving selling concessions.* In the case of an offer or sale of securities prior to the expiration of the distribution compliance period specified in Category 2 or 3 (paragraph (b)(2) or (b)(3)) of § 230.903, as applicable, by a dealer, as defined in Section 2(a)(12) of the Act (15 U.S.C. § 77b(a)(12)), or a person receiving a selling concession, fee or other remuneration in respect of the securities offered or sold:

(i) Neither the seller nor any person acting on its behalf knows that the offeree or buyer of the securities is a U.S. person; and

(ii) If the seller or any person acting on the seller's behalf knows that the purchaser is a dealer, as defined in Section 2(a)(12) of the Act (15 U.S.C. § 77b(a)(12)), or is a person receiving a selling concession, fee or other remuneration in respect of the securities sold, the seller or a person acting on the seller's behalf sends to the purchaser a confirmation or other notice stating that the securities may be offered and sold during the distribution compliance period only in accordance with the provisions of this Regulation S (§ 230.901 through § 230.905, and Preliminary Notes); pursuant to registration of the securities under the Act; or pursuant to an available exemption from the registration requirements of the Act.

(2) *Resales by certain affiliates.* In the case of an offer or sale of securities by an officer or director of the issuer or a distributor, who is an affiliate of the issuer or distributor solely by virtue of holding such position, no selling concession, fee or other remuneration is paid in connection with such offer or sale other than the usual and customary broker's commission that would be received by a person executing such transaction as agent.

Rule 905. Resale Limitations

Equity securities of domestic issuers acquired from the issuer, a distributor, or any of their respective affiliates in a transaction subject to the conditions of § 230.901 or § 230.903 are deemed to be "restricted securities" as defined in § 230.144. Resales of any of such restricted securities by the offshore purchaser must be made in accordance with this Regulation S (§ 230.901 through § 230.905, and Preliminary Notes), the registration requirements of the Act or an exemption therefrom. Any "restricted securities," as defined in § 230.144, that are equity securities of a domestic issuer will continue to be deemed to be restricted securities, notwithstanding that they were acquired in a resale transaction made pursuant to § 230.901 or § 230.904.

REGULATION CE—COORDINATED EXEMPTIONS FOR CERTAIN ISSUES OF SECURITIES EXEMPT UNDER STATE LAW

Preliminary Notes

(1) Nothing in this section is intended to be or should be construed as in any way relieving issuers or persons acting on behalf of issuers from providing disclosure to prospective investors necessary to satisfy the antifraud provisions of the federal securities laws. This section only provides an exemption from the registration requirements of the Securities Act of 1933 ("the Act") [15 U.S.C. 77a et seq.].

(2) Nothing in this section obviates the need to comply with any applicable state law relating to the offer and sales of securities.

(3) Attempted compliance with this section does not act as an exclusive election; the issuer also can claim the availability of any other applicable exemption.

(4) This exemption is not available to any issuer for any transaction which, while in technical compliance with the provision of this section, is part of a plan or scheme to evade the registration provisions of the Act. In such cases, registration under the Act is required.

Rule 1001. Exemption for Transactions Exempt From Qualification Under Sec. 25102(n) of the California Corporations Code

(a) Exemption. Offers and sales of securities that satisfy the conditions of paragraph (n) of Sec. 25102 of the California Corporations Code, and paragraph (b) of this section, shall be exempt from the provisions of Section 5 of the Securities Act of 1933 by virtue of Section 3(b) of that Act.

(b) Limitation on and computation of offering price. The sum of all cash and other consideration to be received for the securities shall not exceed $5,000,000, less the aggregate offering price for all other securities sold in the same offering of securities, whether pursuant to this or another exemption.

(c) Resale limitations. Securities issued pursuant to this Sec. 230.1001 are deemed to be "restricted securities" as defined in Securities Act Rule 144 [Sec. 230.144]. Resales of such securities must be made in compliance with the registration requirements of the Act or an exemption therefrom.

NASAA UNIFORM LIMITED OFFERING EXEMPTION (ULOE)
Adopted September 21, 1983
North American Securities Administrators Association, Inc.

Preliminary Notes

1. Nothing in this exemption is intended to or should be construed as in any way relieving issuers or persons acting on behalf of issuers from providing disclosure to prospective investors adequate to satisfy the anti-fraud provisions of this state's securities law.

2. In view of the objective of this rule and the purposes and policies underlying this act, the exemption is not available to any issuer with respect to any transaction which, although in technical compliance with this rule, is part of a plan or scheme to evade registration or the conditions or limitations explicitly stated in this rule.

3. Nothing in this rule is intended to relieve registered broker/dealers or agents from the due diligence, suitability, or know your customer standards or any other requirements of law otherwise applicable to such registered persons.

RULE

By authority delegated the administrator in Section —— of this act to promulgate rules, the following transaction is determined to be exempt from the registration provisions of this act:

1. Any offer or sale of securities offered or sold in compliance with Securities Act of 1933, Regulation D, Rules 230.505 and/or 230.506[1], including any offer or sale made exempt by application of Rule 508(a), as made effective in Release No. 33-6389 and as amended in Release Nos. 33-6437, 33-6663, 33-6758, and 33-6825, and which satisfies the following further conditions and limitations:

   A. No commission, fee or other remuneration shall be paid or given, directly or indirectly, to any person for soliciting any prospective purchaser in this state unless such person is appropriately registered in this state.[2 &3]

---

[1] In those states where facts and circumstances permit, it would not be inconsistent with the regulatory objectives of this exemption for a state to elect to accept Rule 506 offerings within the ambit of this exemption. In doing so, however, the state disqualification provisions of this rule and the federal disqualification provisions of Rule 505 should be made applicable.

With inclusion of Rule 506, the major objective of the exemption is not limited to facilitating the capital-raising ability of small business. The removal of the dollar limit makes the exemption available to private placements of all sizes. In large private offerings, the problems associated with determining that all the investors are experienced enough to fully understand the risks of the offering and controlling the manner and scope of the offering so that it does not become a public offering are magnified. Also, and largely because of the removal of the dollar limit, the exemption becomes more attractive to tax shelter investments.

Tax shelter offerings that would be permitted by Rule 506, particularly those with abusively high write-off ratios, involve special facts and circumstances, and enforcement experience shows that they have a greater potential for regulatory concerns and many lack economic substance and fail to contribute to job creation. In recognition of these concerns, Rule 506 is not adopted as part of the basic ULOE.

In those states where facts and circumstances permit, it would not be inconsistent with the regulatory objec-

tives of this exemption to further condition the exemption with the following provision:

"In the case of offerings of direct participation programs as defined in Section 34 or Article III of the National Association of Securities Dealers, Inc., Rules of Fair Practice, delivery of a disclosure document containing the information required by Rule 502(b) of Regulation D to individuals covered by subsections (5) and (6) of Rule 501(a) of Regulation D is required."

[2] In those states where facts and circumstances permit, it would not be inconsistent with the regulatory objectives of this exemption for a state to substitute the following for section 1.A.

a. All persons who offer or sell securities in this state to nonaccredited and/or accredited investors as defined in Securities Act of 1933, Regulation D, Rule 230.501(a)(5)—(6) shall be appropriately registered in accordance with this state's securities law.

It is a defense to a violation of this subsection if the issuer sustains the burden of proof to establish that he or she did not know and in the exercise of reasonable care could not have known that the person who received a commission fee or other remuneration was not appropriately registered in this state.

[3] In those states where facts and circumstances permit, it would not be inconsistent with the regulatory objectives of this exemption for a state to provide for a system or process to simplify and facilitate the registration of broker/dealers and agents which would not

It is a defense to a violation of this subsection if the issuer sustains the burden of proof to establish that he or she did not know and in the exercise of reasonable care could not have known that the person who received a commission, fee or other remuneration was not appropriately registered in this state.

B. No exemption under this rule shall be available for the securities of any issuer if any of the parties described in Securities Act of 1933, Regulation A, Rule 230.252 sections (c), (d), (e) or (f):

1. Has filed a registration statement which is subject of a currently effective registration stop order entered pursuant to any state's securities law within five years prior to the filing of the notice required under this exemption.

2. Has been convicted within five years prior to the filing of the notice required under this exemption of any felony or misdemeanor in connection with the offer, purchase or sale of any security or any felony involving fraud or deceit, including but not limited to forgery, embezzlement, obtaining money under false pretenses, larceny or conspiracy to defraud.

3. Is currently subject to any state administrative enforcement order or judgment entered by that state's securities administrator within five years prior to the filing of the notice required under this exemption or is subject to any state's administrative enforcement order or judgment in which fraud or deceit, including but not limited to making untrue statements of material facts and omitting to state material facts, was found and the order or judgment was entered within five years prior to the filing of the notice required under this exemption.

4. Is subject to any state's administrative enforcement order or judgment which prohibits, denies or revokes the use of any exemption from registration in connection with the offer, purchase or sale of securities.

5. Is currently subject to any order, judgment, or decree of any court of competent jurisdiction temporarily or preliminarily restraining or enjoining, or is subject to any order, judgment or decree of any court of competent jurisdiction, permanently restraining or enjoining, such party from engaging in or continuing any conduct or practice in connection with the purchase or sale of any security or involving the making of any false filing with the state entered within five years prior to the filing of the notice required under this exemption.

6. The prohibitions of paragraphs 1-3 and 5 above shall not apply if the person subject to the disqualification is duly licensed or registered to conduct securities related business in the state in which the administrative order or judgment was entered against such person or if the broker/dealer employing such party is licensed or registered in this state and the Form B-D filed with this state discloses the order, conviction, judgment or decree relating to such person. No person disqualified under this subsection may act in a capacity other than that for which the person is licensed or registered.

7. Any disqualification caused by this section is automatically waived if the state securities administrator or agency of the state which created the basis for disqualification determines upon a showing of good cause that it is not necessary under the circumstances that the exemption be denied.

It is a defense to a violation of this subsection if issuer sustains the burden of proof to establish that he or she did not know and in the exercise of reasonable care could not have known that a disqualification under this subsection existed.

C. The issuer shall file with the state administrator a notice on Form D (17CFR239.500):

> 1. No later than (10 days prior)[4] to the receipt of consideration or the delivery of a subscription agreement by an investor in this state which results from an offer being made in reliance upon this exemption and at such other times and in the form required

---

(Footnote Continued)

otherwise be required to be registered except for this exemption. Such a system or process should as a minimum, grant jurisdiction as well as the ability to effectively limit and control persons offering and selling securities within the state.

[4] In those states where facts and circumstances permit, it would not be inconsistent with the Regulatory objectives of this exemption for a state to consider a post-sale notice patterned after the notice provisions of Regulation D (Rule 230.503).

under Regulation D, Rule 230.503 to be filed with the Securities and Exchange Commission.

2. The notice shall contain an undertaking by the issuer to furnish to the state securities administrator, upon written request, the information furnished by the issuer to offerees, except where the state administrator pursuant to regulation requires that the information be filed at the same time with the filing of the notice.[5]

3. Unless otherwise available, included with or in the initial notice shall be a consent to service of process.

4. Every person filing the initial notice provided for in 1 above shall pay a filing fee of . . .

D. In all sales to nonaccredited investors in this state one of the following conditions must be satisfied or the issuer and any person acting on its behalf shall have reasonable grounds to believe and after making reasonable inquiry shall believe that one of the following conditions is satisfied:

1. The investment is suitable for the purchaser upon the basis of the facts, if any, disclosed by the purchaser as to the purchaser's other security holdings, financial situation and needs. For the purpose of this condition only, it may be presumed that if the investment does not exceed 10% of the investor's net worth, it is suitable.

2. The purchaser either alone or with his/her purchaser representative(s) has such knowledge and experience in financial and business matters that he/she is or they are capable of evaluating the merits and risks of the prospective investment.

2. A failure to comply with a term, condition or requirement of Sections 1.A, [C[6]], and D of this rule will not result in loss of the exemption from the requirements of section [301] of this act for any offer or sale to a particular individual or entity if the person relying on the exemption shows:

A. the failure to comply did not pertain to a term, condition or requirement directly intended to protect that particular individual or entity; and

B. the failure to comply was insignificant with respect to the offering as a whole; and

C. a good faith and reasonable attempt was made to comply with all applicable terms, conditions and requirements of Sections 1.A [C[6]], and D.

3. Where an exemption is established only through reliance upon section 2 of this rule, the failure to comply shall nonetheless be actionable by the [administrator] under section [408] of the Act.[7]

4. Transactions which are exempt under this rule may not be combined with offers and sales exempt under any other rule or section of this act; however, nothing in this limitation shall act as an election. Should for any reason the offer and sale fail to comply with all of the conditions for this exemption, the issuer may claim the availability of any other applicable exemption.

5. The administrator may, by rule or order, increase the number of purchasers or waive any other conditions of this exemption.

6. The exemption authorized by this rule shall be known and may be cited as the "Uniform Limited Offering Exemption."

---

[5] This latter filing requirement is not intended to provide the basis for a fairness type of review of the offering.

[6] In those states which have adopted a post-sale notice patterned after the notice provisions of Regulation D (Rule 230.503) it would not be inconsistent with the regulatory objectives of this exemption to include the notice filing requirements of section 1.C within the substantial compliance provisions of section 2 or to eliminate the filing as a condition and adopt a rule similar to Rule 230.507.

[7] The cited reference is to the section of the Uniform Securities Act which authorizes the state administrator to bring a civil action to enjoin rule violations. Those states which have authority to bring an administrative enforcement action for rule violations may wish to include a reference to that statutory authority. If the administrator lacks authority to bring enforcement actions based solely on rule violations, he/she may wish to consider a statutory amendment.

SECURITIES ACT—SELECTED FORMS

Selected Forms Under the Securities Act of 1933

Form	Subject
	Registration Statements
F-6	For registration under the Securities Act of 1933 of depositary shares represented by American depositary receipts
S-1	General form of registration statement
S-2	For registration under the Securities Act of 1933 of securities of certain issuers
S-3	For registration under the Securities Act of 1933 of securities of certain issuers offered pursuant to certain types of transactions
S-8	For securities to be offered to employees pursuant to certain plans
SB-1	Optional form for the registration of securities to be sold to the public by certain small business issuers
SB-2	Optional form for the registration of securities to be sold to the public by small business issuers
	Regulation A Notification and Consents
1-A	Offering statement under Regulation A
2-A	Report pursuant to Rule 257 of Regulation A
	Regulation D or Section 4(6) Notification
D	Notice of sales of securities pursuant to Regulation D or Section 4(6)
	Rule 144 Notification
144	Notice of proposed sale of securities pursuant to Rule 144

FORM F-6

SECURITIES AND EXCHANGE COMMISSION

FORM F-6
REGISTRATION STATEMENT UNDER THE SECURITIES ACT OF 1933 FOR DEPOSITARY SHARES EVIDENCED BY AMERICAN DEPOSITARY RECEIPTS

. . . .

(Exact name of issuer of deposited securities as specified in its charter)

. . . .

(Translation of issuer's name into English)

. . . .

(Jurisdiction of incorporation or organization of issuer)

. . . .

(Exact name of depositary as specified in its charter)

. . . .

(Address, including zip code, and telephone number, including area code, of depositary's principal executive offices)

. . . .

(Address, including zip code, and telephone number, including area code, of agent for service)

It is proposed that this filing become effective under Rule 466

(check appropriate box)

[ ] immediately upon filing

[ ] on (Date) at (Time).

If a separate registration statement has been filed to register the deposited shares, check the following box. [ ]

Calculation of Registration Fee

Title of each class of securities to be registered	Amount to be registered	Proposed maximum aggregate price per unit	Proposed maximum aggregate offering price	Amount of registration fee

GENERAL INSTRUCTIONS

I. Eligibility Requirements for Use of Form F-6

A. General. Form F-6 may be used for the registration under the Securities Act of 1933 (the "Securities Act") of Depositary Shares evidenced by American Depositary Receipts ("ADRs") issued by a depositary against the deposit of the securities of a foreign issuer (regardless of the physical location of the certificates) if the following conditions are met:

(1) The holder of the ADRs is entitled to withdraw the deposited securities at any time subject only to (i) temporary delays caused by closing transfer books of the depositary or the issuer of the deposited securities or the deposit of shares in connection with voting at a shareholders' meeting, or the payment of dividends, (ii) the payment of fees, taxes, and similar charges, and (iii) compliance with any laws or governmental regulations relating to ADRs or to the withdrawal of deposited securities;

154

(2) The deposited securities are offered or sold in transactions registered under the Securities Act or in transactions that would be exempt therefrom if made in the United States; and

(3) As of the filing date of this registration statement, the issuer of the deposited securities is reporting pursuant to the periodic reporting requirements of section 13(a) or 15(d) of the Securities Exchange Act of 1934 or the deposited securities are exempt therefrom by Rule 12g3-2(b) (§ 240.12g3-2(b) of this chapter) unless the issuer of the deposited securities concurrently files a registration statement on another form for the deposited securities.

B. Registration of Deposited Securities. Form F-6 is available for registration of the Depositary Shares only. The registration of the deposited securities, if necessary, shall be on any other form the registrant is eligible to use. Alternatively, Depositary Shares may also be registered on any form used to register the deposited securities if such registration statement also conforms to the requirements of Parts I and II of Form F-6 and either the depositary or the legal entity created by the agreement for the issuance of ADRs signs the registration statement with respect to the disclosure and undertakings made in response to such requirements. The amount of fees charged need not be disclosed in the prospectus if the depositary makes and follows the undertakings in Item 4(c) and if the prospectus lists the various services for which fees may be charged, states that such fees may differ from those other depositaries charge, states that the fee schedule is available without charge from the depositary, and states that each registered holder of an ADR will receive thirty days notice of a change in the fee schedule.

II. Amount of Securities; Filing Fee

An ADR evidences one or more Depositary Shares, as defined in Rule 405 (§ 230.405 of this chapter). The registration statement relates to Depositary Shares, not the number of physical certificates issued. For example, if an ADR is issued against a Depositary Share, which equals two common shares in a foreign issuer, the registration of 100,000 Depositary Shares represents 200,000 common shares. If the depositary issues a certificate for 10,000 Depositary Shares and another for 15,000 Depositary Shares, then 75,000 (100,000 minus 25,000) Depositary Shares (not 99,998) remain available for distribution under the registration statement.

Rule 457(k) (§ 230.457(k) of this chapter) describes the method of computing the filing fee.

III. Application of General Rules and Regulations

A. Attention is directed to the General Rules and Regulations under the Securities Act, particularly Regulation C (§ 230.400 et seq. of this chapter). That Regulation contains general requirements regarding the preparation and filing of registration statements.

B. The prospectus may consist of the ADR certificate if it includes the information required in Part I of this Form. Such prospectus need not conform to the requirements of Rule 420 (§ 240.420 of this chapter) except that the type shall be roman type at least as large as 5½-point modern type.

C. You must file the Form F-6 registration statement in electronic format via the Commission's Electronic Data Gathering, Analysis, and Retrieval (EDGAR) system in accordance with the EDGAR rules set forth in Regulation S-T (17 CFR Part 232). For assistance with technical questions about EDGAR or to request an access code, call the EDGAR Filer Support Office at (202) 942-8900. For assistance with the EDGAR rules, call the Office of EDGAR and Information Analysis at (202) 942-2940.

If filing the registration statement in paper under a hardship exemption in Rule 201 or 202 of Regulation S-T (17 CFR 232.201 or 232.202), or as otherwise permitted, you must file the number of copies of the registration statement and of each amendment required by Securities Act Rules 402 and 472 (17 CFR 230.402 and 230.472), except that you need only file three additional copies instead of the ten referred to in Rule 402(b) (17 CFR 230.402(b)). You may also file only three additional copies instead of the eight referred to in Securities Act Rule 472(a) (17 CFR 230.472(a)).

PART I—INFORMATION REQUIRED IN PROSPECTUS

Item 1. Description of Securities to be Registered

Furnish the information required by Item 12.E. of Form 20-F (§ 249.220f of this chapter).

Item 2. Available Information

State the information in either (a) or (b) below, whichever is applicable, and that the documents described therein can be inspected by holders of ADRs and copied at public reference facilities maintained by the Commission in Washington, D.C.

(a) The foreign issuer furnishes the Commission with certain public reports and documents required by foreign law or otherwise under Rule 12g3-2(b) under the Securities Exchange Act of 1934.

(b) The foreign issuer is subject to the periodic reporting requirements of the Securities Exchange Act of 1934 and, accordingly, files certain reports with the Commission.

PART II—INFORMATION NOT REQUIRED IN PROSPECTUS

Item 3. Exhibits

Subject to the rules as to incorporation by reference, the exhibits specified below shall be filed as a part of the registration statement. Exhibits shall be appropriately lettered or numbered for convenient reference. Exhibits incorporated by reference may bear the designation given in the previous filing. Instruction 1 to Item 601 of Regulation S-K applies to this paragraph.

(a) A copy of the Deposit Agreement or Deposit Agreements under which the securities registered hereunder are issued. If the Deposit Agreement is amended during the offering of the Depositary Shares, such amendments shall be filed as amendments to the registration statement.

(b) Any other agreement, to which the depositary is a party relating to the issuance of the Depositary Shares registered hereby or the custody of the deposited securities represented thereby.

(c) Every material contract relating to the deposited securities between the depositary and the issuer of the deposited securities in effect at any time within the last three years.

(d) An opinion of counsel as to the legality of the securities being registered, indicating whether they will when sold be legally issued, and entitle the holders thereof to the rights specified therein.

(e) If the procedure in Rule 466 is being used, a certification in the following form:

Certification under Rule 466

The depositary, ..., represents and certifies the following:

(1) That it previously had filed a registration statement on Form F-6 (Name and File No.), which the Commission declared effective, with terms of deposit identical to the terms of deposit of this registration statement except for the number of foreign securities a Depositary Share represents.

(2) That is ability to designate the date and time of effectiveness under Rule 466 has not been suspended.

[Depositary] ....

By [Signature and Title] ....

Item 4. Undertakings

Notwithstanding the provisions of Rule 415(a)(2) (§ 230.415(a)(2) of this chapter), the undertakings in Item 512(a) of Regulation S-K are not required. Furnish the following undertakings:

(a) The depositary hereby undertakes to make available at the principal office of the depositary in the United States, for inspection by holders of the ADRs, any reports and communications received from the issuer of the deposited securities which are both (1) received by the depositary as the holder of the deposited securities; and (2) made generally available to the holders of the underlying securities by the issuer.

(b) If the amounts of fees charged are not disclosed in the prospectus, the depositary undertakes to prepare a separate document stating the amount of any fee charged and describing the service for which it is charged and to deliver promptly a copy of such fee schedule without charge to anyone upon request. The depositary undertakes to notify each registered holder of an ADR thirty days before any change in the fee schedule.

SIGNATURES

Pursuant to the requirements of the Securities Act of 1933, the registrant certifies that it has reasonable grounds to believe that all the requirements for filing on Form F-6 are met and has duly caused this registration statement to be signed on its behalf by the undersigned, thereunto duly authorized, in the City of ...., State of ...., on ...., 19.....
. . .

[Legal entity created by the agreement

for the issuance of American Depositary

Receipts for shares of ....
..............]...

By [Signature and Title] ....

[Registrant] ....

By [Signature and Title] ....

Pursuant to the requirements of the Securities Act of 1933, this registration statement has been signed by the following persons in the capacities and on the dates indicated.

[Signature] ....

[Title] ....

[Date] ....

Instructions 1. The legal entity created by the agreement for the issuance of ADRs shall sign the registration statement as registrant. The depositary may sign on behalf of such entity, but the depositary for the issuance of ADRs itself shall not be deemed to be an issuer, a person signing the registration statement, or a person controlling such issuer. If the issuer of the deposited securities sponsors the ADR arrangement, the registration statement shall also be signed by the issuer and its principal executive officer or officers, its principal financial officer, its controller or principal accounting officer, at least a majority of the board of directors or persons performing similar functions, and its authorized representative in the United States.

2. The name of each person who signs the registration statement shall be typed or printed beneath his signature. Any person who occupies more than one of the specified positions shall indicate each capacity in which he signs the registration statement. Attention is directed to Rule 402 concerning manual signatures and Item 601 of Regulation S-K concerning signatures pursuant to powers of attorney.

FORM S-1

UNITED STATES SECURITIES AND EXCHANGE COMMISSION
Washington, D.C. 20549
FORM S-1

REGISTRATION STATEMENT UNDER THE SECURITIES ACT OF 1933

. . . .
(Exact name of registrant as specified in its charter)

. . . .
(State or other jurisdiction of incorporation or organization)

. . . .
(Primary Standard Industrial Classification Code Number)

. . . .
(I.R.S. Employer Identification Number)

. . . .
(Address, including zip code, and telephone number, including area code, of registrant's principal executive offices)

. . . .
(Name, address, including zip code, and telephone number, including area code, of agent for service)

. . . .
(Approximate date of commencement of proposed sale to the public)

If any of the securities being registered on this Form are to be offered on a delayed or continuous basis pursuant to Rule 415 under the Securities Act, check the following box: ☐

If this Form is filed to register additional securities for an offering pursuant to Rule 462(b) under the Securities Act, please check the following box and list the Securities Act registration statement number of the earlier effective registration statement for the same offering. ☐

If this Form is a post-effective amendment filed pursuant to Rule 462(c) under the Securities Act, check the following box and list the Securities Act registration statement number of the earlier effective registration statement for the same offering. ☐

If this Form is a post-effective amendment filed pursuant to Rule 462(d) under the Securities Act, check the following box and list the Securities Act registration statement number of the earlier effective registration statement for the same offering. ☐

If delivery of the prospectus is expected to be made pursuant to Rule 434, check the following box. ☐

Calculation of Registration Fee

Title of each class of securities to be registered	Amount to be registered	Proposed maximum offering price per unit	Proposed maximum aggregate offering price	Amount of registration fee

Note: Specific details relating to the fee calculation shall be furnished in notes to the table, including references to provisions of *Rule 457* (§ 230.457 of this chapter) relied upon, if the basis of the calculation is not otherwise evident from the information presented in the table. If the filing fee is calculated pursuant to Rule 457(o) under the Securities Act, only the title of the class of securities to be registered, the proposed maximum aggregate offering price for that class of securities and the amount of registration fee need to appear in the Calculation of Registration Fee table. Any difference between the dollar amount of securities registered for such offerings and the dollar amount of securities sold may be carried forward on a future registration statement pursuant to *Rule 429* under the Securities Act.

GENERAL INSTRUCTIONS

I. Eligibility Requirements for Use of Form S-1

This Form shall be used for the registration under the Securities Act of 1933 ("Securities Act") of securities of all registrants for which no other form is authorized or prescribed, except that this Form shall not be used for securities of foreign governments or political subdivisions thereof.

II. Application of General Rules and Regulations

A. Attention is directed to the General Rules and Regulations under the Securities Act, particularly those comprising *Regulation C* (17 CFR 230.400 to 230.494) thereunder. That Regulation contains general requirements regarding the preparation and filing of the registration statement.

B. Attention is directed to *Regulation S-K* (17 CFR Part 229) for the requirements applicable to the content of the non-financial statement portions of registration statements under the Securities Act. Where this Form directs the registrant to furnish information required by Regulation S-K and the item of Regulation S-K so provides, information need only be furnished to the extent appropriate.

III. Exchange Offers

If any of the securities being registered are to be offered in exchange for securities of any other issuer, the prospectus shall also include the information which would be required by item 11 if the securities of such other issuer were registered on this Form. There shall also be included the information concerning such securities of such other issuer which would be called for by Item 9 if such securities were being registered. In connection with this instruction, reference is made to *Rule 409*.

IV. Roll-up Transactions

If the securities to be registered on this Form will be is[s]ued in a roll-up trans[a]ction as defined in *Item 901(c)* of Regulation S-K (17 CFR 229.901(c)), attention is directed to the requirements of Form S-4 applicable to roll-up transactions, including, but not limited to, General Instruction I.

V. Registration of Additional Securities

With respect to the registration of additional securities for an offering pursuant to *Rule 462(b)* under the Securities Act, the registrant may file a registration statement consisting only of the following: the facing page; a statement that the contents of the earlier registration statement, identified by file number, are incorporated by reference; required opinions and consents; the signature page; and any price-related information omitted from the earlier registration statement in reliance on *Rule 430A* that the registrant chooses to include in the new registration statement. The information contained in such a Rule 462(b) registration statement shall be deemed to be a part of the earlier registration statement as of the date of effectiveness of the Rule 462(b) registration statement. Any opinion or consent required in the Rule 462(b) registration statement may be incorporated by reference from the earlier registration statement with respect to the offering, if: (i) such opinion or consent expressly provides for such incorporation; and (ii) such opinion relates to the securities registered pursuant to Rule 462(b). *See Rule 411(c)* and *Rule 439(b)* under the Securities Act.

PART I—INFORMATION REQUIRED IN PROSPECTUS

Item 1. Forepart of the Registration Statement and Outside Front Cover Page of Prospectus

Set forth in the forepart of the registration statement and on the outside front cover page of the prospectus the information required by *Item 501* of Regulation S-K (§ 229.501 of this chapter).

Item 2. Inside Front and Outside Back Cover Pages of Prospectus

Set forth on the inside front cover page of the prospectus or, where permitted, on the outside back cover page, the information required by *Item 502* of Regulation S-K (§ 229.502 of this chapter).

Item 3. Summary Information, Risk Factors and Ratio of Earnings to Fixed Charges

Furnish the information required by *Item 503* of Regulation S-K (§ 229.503 of this chapter).

Item 4. Use of Proceeds

Furnish the information required by *Item 504* of Regulation S-K (§ 229.504 of this chapter).

Item 5. Determination of Offering Price

Furnish the information required by *Item 505* of Regulation S-K (§ 229.505 of this chapter).

Item 6. Dilution

Furnish the information required by *Item 506* of Regulation S-K (§ 229.506 of this chapter).

Item 7. Selling Security Holders

Furnish the information required by *Item 507* of Regulation S-K (§ 229.507 of this chapter).

Item 8. Plan of Distribution

Furnish the information required by *Item 508* of Regulation S-K (§ 229.508 of this chapter).

Item 9. Description of Securities to be Registered

Furnish the information required by *Item 202* of Regulation S-K (§ 229.202 of this chapter).

Item 10. Interests of Named Experts and Counsel

Furnish the information required by *Item 509* of Regulation S-K (§ 229.509 of this chapter).

Item 11. Information with Respect to the Registrant

Furnish the following information with respect to the registrant:

(a) Information required by *Item 101* of Regulation S-K (§ 229.101 of this chapter), description of business;

(b) Information required by *Item 102* of Regulation S-K (§ 229.102 of this chapter), description of property;

(c) Information required by *Item 103* of Regulation S-K (§ 229.103 of this chapter), legal proceedings;

(d) Where common equity securities are being offered, information required by *Item 201* of Regulation S-K (§ 229.201 of this chapter), market price of and dividends on the registrant's common equity and related stockholder matters;

(e) Financial statements meeting the requirements of *Regulation S-X* (17 CFR Part 210) (Schedules required under Regulation S-X shall be filed as "Financial Statement Schedules" pursuant to Item 15, Exhibits and Financial Statement Schedules, of this Form), as well as any financial information required by *Rule 3-05* and *Article 11 of Regulation S-X*;

(f) Information required by *Item 301* of Regulation S-K (§ 229.301 of this chapter), selected financial data;

(g) Information required by *Item 302* of Regulation S-K (§ 229.302 of this chapter), supplementary financial in formation;

(h) Information required by *Item 303* of Regulation S-K (§ 229.303 of this chapter), management's discussion and analysis of financial condition and results of operations;

(i) Information required by *Item 304* of Regulation S-K (§ 229.304 of this chapter), changes in and disagreements with accountants on accounting and financial disclosure;

(j) Information required by *Item 305* of Regulation S-K (§ 229.305 of this chapter), quantitative and qualitative disclosures about market risk.

(k) Information required by *Item 401* of Regulation S-K (§ 229.401 of this chapter), directors and executive officers;

(l) Information required by *Item 402* of Regulation S-K (§ 229.402 of this chapter), executive compensation;

(m) Information required by *Item 403* of Regulation S-K (§ 229.403 of this chapter), security ownership of certain beneficial owners and management; and

(n) Information required by *Item 404* of Regulation S-K (§ 229.404 of this chapter), certain relationships and related transactions.

Item 12. Disclosure of Commission Position on Indemnification for Securities Act Liabilities

Furnish the information required by *Item 510* of Regulation S-K (§ 229.510 of this chapter).

PART II—INFORMATION NOT REQUIRED IN PROSPECTUS

Item 13. Other Expenses of Issuance and Distribution

Furnish the information required by *Item 511* of Regulation S-K (§ 229.511 of this chapter).

Item 14. Indemnification of Directors and Officers

Furnish the information required by *Item 702* of Regulation S-K (§ 229.702 of this chapter).

Item 15. Recent Sales of Unregistered Securities

Furnish the information required by *Item 701* of Regulation S-K (§ 229.701 of this chapter).

Item 16. Exhibits and Financial Statement Schedules

(a) Subject to the rules regarding incorporation by reference, furnish the exhibits as required by *Item 601* of Regulation S-K (§ 229.601 of this chapter).

(b) Furnish the financial statement schedules required by *Regulation S-X* (17 CFR Part 210) and Item 11(e) of this Form. These schedules shall be lettered or numbered in the manner described for exhibits in paragraph (a).

Item 17. Undertakings

Furnish the undertakings required by *Item 512* of Regulation S-K (§ 229.512 of this chapter).

SIGNATURES

Pursuant to the requirements of the Securities Act of 1933, the registrant has duly caused this registration statement to be signed on its behalf by the undersigned, thereunto duly authorized in the   City   of

_____ ,

State   of

_____ ,

———————————————————, 19———.

_____

(Registrant)

By (Signature and Title)

Pursuant to the requirements of the Securities Act of 1933, this registration statement has been signed by the following persons in the capacities and on the dates indicated.

(Signature)

(Title)

(Date)

Instructions.

1. The registration statement shall be signed by the registrant, its principal executive officer or officers, its principal financial officer, its controller or principal accounting officer and by at least a majority of the board of directors or persons performing similar functions. If the registrant is a foreign person, the registration statement shall also be signed by its authorized representative in the United States. Where the registrant is a limited partnership, the registration statement shall be signed by a majority of the board of directors of any corporate general partner signing the registration statement.

2. The name of each person who signs the registration statement shall be typed or printed beneath his signature. Any person who occupies more than one of the specified positions shall indicate each capacity in which he signs the registration statement. Attention is directed to *Rule 402* concerning manual signatures and to *Item 601* of Regulation S-K concerning signatures pursuant to powers of attorney.

INSTRUCTIONS AS TO SUMMARY PROSPECTUSES

1. A summary prospectus used pursuant to *Rule 431* (§ 230.431 of this chapter), shall at the time of its use contain much of the information specified below as is then included in the registration statement. All other information and documents contained in the registration statement may be omitted.

(a) As to Item 1, the aggregate offering price to the public, the aggregate underwriting discounts and commissions and the offering price per unit to the public;

(b) As to Item 4, a brief statement of the principal purposes for which the proceeds are to be used;

(c) As to Item 7, a statement as to the amount of the offering, if any, to be made for the account of security holders;

(d) As to Item 8, the name of the managing underwriter or underwriters and a brief statement as to the nature of the underwriter's obligation to take the securities; if any securities to be registered are to be offered otherwise than through underwriters, a brief statement as to the manner of distribution; and, if securities are to be offered otherwise than for cash. a brief statement as to the general purposes of the distribution, the basis upon which the securities are to be offered, the amount of compensation and other expenses of distribution, and by whom they are to be borne;

(e) As to Item 9, a brief statement as to dividend rights, voting rights, conversion rights, interest, maturity;

(f) As to Item 11, a brief statement of the general character of the business done and intended to be done, the selected financial data (*Item 301* of Regulation S-K (§ 229.301 of this chapter)) and a brief statement of the nature and present status of any material pending legal proceedings; and

(g) A tabular presentation of notes payable, long term debt, deferred credits, minority interests, if material, and the equity section of the latest balance sheet filed, as may be appropriate.

2. The summary prospectus shall not contain a summary or condensation of any other required financial information except as provided above.

3. Where securities being registered are to be offered in exchange for securities of any other issuer, the summary prospectus also shall contain that information as to Items 9 and 11 specified in paragraphs (e) and (f) above which would be required if the securities of such other issuer were registered on this Form.

4. The Commission may, upon the request of the registrant, and where consistent with the protection of investors, permit the omission of any of the information herein required or the furnishing in substitution therefor of appropriate information of comparable character. The Commission may also require the inclusion of other information in addition to, or in substitution for, the information herein required in any case where such information is necessary or appropriate for the protection of investors.

FORM S-2

UNITED STATES SECURITIES AND EXCHANGE COMMISSION

Washington D.C. 20549

FORM S-2
REGISTRATION STATEMENT UNDER THE SECURITIES ACT OF 1933

. . . .

(Exact name of registrant as specified in its charter)

. . . .

(State or other jurisdiction of incorporation or organization)

. . . .

(I.R.S. Employer Identification No.)

. . . .

(Address, including zip code, and telephone number, including area code, of
registrant's principal executive offices)

. . . .

(Name, address, including zip code, and telephone number, including area code,
of agent for service)

Approximate date of commencement of proposed sale to the public . . . .

If any of the securities being registered on this Form are to be offered on a delayed or continuous
basis pursuant to Rule 415 under the Securities Act, check the following box.   ☐

If the registrant elects to deliver its latest annual report to security holders, or a complete and legal
facsimile thereof, pursuant to Item 11(a)(1) of this Form, check the following box.   ☐

If this Form is filed to register additional securities for an offering pursuant to Rule 462(b) under the Securities Act, check the following box and list the Securities Act registration statement number of
the earlier effective registration statement for the same offering.   ☐ . . . .

If this Form is a post-effective amendment filed pursuant to Rule 462(c) under the Securities Act, check the following box and list the Securities Act registration statement number of the earlier effective
registration statement for the same offering.   ☐ . . . .

If this Form is a post-effective amendment filed pursuant to Rule 462(d) under the Securities Act, check the following box and list the Securities Act registration statement number of the earlier effective
registration statement for the same offering.   ☐ . . . .

If delivery of the prospectus is expected to be made pursuant to Rule 434, check the following
box.   ☐

Calculation of Registration Fee

Title of each class of securities to be registered	Amount to be registered	Proposed maximum offering price per unit	Proposed maximum aggregate offering price	Amount of registration fee

Note: Specific details relating to the fee calculation shall be furnished in notes to the table, including references to provisions of Rule 457 (§ 230.457 of this chapter) relied upon, if the basis of the calculation is not otherwise evident from the information presented in the table. If the filing fee is calculated pursuant to Rule 457(o) under the Securities Act, only the title of the class of securities to be registered, the proposed maximum aggregate offering price for that class of securities and the amount of registration fee need to appear in the Calculation of Registration Fee table. Any difference between the dollar amount of securities registered for such offering and the dollar amount of securities sold may be carried forward on a future registration statement pursuant to Rule 429 under the Securities Act.

GENERAL INSTRUCTIONS

I. Eligibility Requirements for Use of Form S-2

Any registrant which meets the following conditions may use this Form for registration of securities under the Securities Act of 1933 ("Securities Act") which are offered or to be offered in any transaction other than an exchange offer for securities of another person:

A. The registrant is organized under the laws of the United States or any State or Territory or the District of Columbia and has its principal business operations in the United States or its territories.

B. The registrant has a class of securities registered pursuant to Section 12(b) of the Securities Exchange Act of 1934 ("Exchange Act") or has a class of equity securities registered pursuant to Section 12(g) of the Exchange Act or is required to file reports pursuant to Section 15(d) of the Exchange Act.

C. The registrant:

(1) has been subject to the requirements of Section 12 or 15(d) of the Exchange Act and has filed all the material required to be filed pursuant to Section 13, 14 or 15(d) for a period of at least thirty-six calendar months immediately preceding the filing of the registration statement on this Form; and

(2) has filed in a timely manner all reports required to be filed during the twelve calendar months and any portion of a month immediately preceding the filing of the registration statement, other than a report that is required solely pursuant to Item 1.01, 1.02, 2.03, 2.04, 2.05, 2.06 or 4.02(a) of Form 8-K (§ 249.308 of this chapter). If the registrant has used (during the twelve calendar months and any portion of a month immediately preceding the filing of the registration statement) Rule 12b-25(b) (§ 240.12b-25(b) of this chapter) under the Exchange Act with respect to a report or a portion of a report, that report or portion thereof has actually been filed within the time period prescribed by that rule.

D. Neither the registrant nor any of its consolidated or unconsolidated subsidiaries have, since the end of their last fiscal year for which certified financial statements of the registrant and its consolidated subsidiaries were included in a report filed pursuant to Section 13(a) or 15(d) of the Exchange Act: (a) failed to pay any dividend or sinking fund installment on preferred stock; or (b) defaulted (i) on any installment or installments on indebtedness for borrowed money, or (ii) on any rental on one or more long term leases, which defaults in the aggregate are material to the financial position of the registrant and its consolidated and unconsolidated subsidiaries, taken as a whole.

E. A foreign issuer, other than a foreign government, which satisfies all of the above provisions of these registrant eligibility requirements except the provisions in I.A. relating to organization and principal business shall be deemed to have met these registrant eligibility requirements provided that such foreign issuer files the same reports with the Commission under section 13(a) or 15(d) of the Exchange Act as a domestic registrant pursuant to I.C. above.

F. If a registrant is a successor registrant it shall be deemed to have met conditions A., B., C., and D. above if: (1) its predecessor and it, taken together, do so, provided that the succession was primarily for the purpose of changing the state of incorporation of the predecessor or forming a holding company and that the assets and liabilities of the successor at the time of succession were substantially the same as those of the predecessor, or (2) all predecessors met the conditions at the time of succession and the registrant has continued to do so since the succession.

G. If a registrant is a majority-owned subsidiary which does not itself meet the conditions of these eligibility requirements, it shall nevertheless be deemed to have met such conditions if its parent meets the conditions and if the parent fully guarantees the securities being registered as to principal and interest. Note: In such an instance the parent-guarantor is the issuer of a separate security consisting of the guarantee which must be concurrently registered but may be registered on the same registration statement as are the guaranteed securities.

H. *Electronic filings.* In addition to satisfying the foregoing conditions, a registrant subject to the electronic filing requirements of Rule 101 of Regulation S-T (232.101 of this chapter) shall have filed with the Commission all required electronic filings, including confirming electronic copies of documents submitted in paper pursuant to a hardship exemption as provided by Rule 201 or Rule 202(d) of Regulation S-T (§ 232.201 or § 232.202(d) of this chapter).

II. Application of General Rules and Regulations

A. Attention is directed to the General Rules and Regulations under the Securities Act, particularly those comprising Regulation C thereunder (17 CFR 230.400 to 230.494). That Regulation contains general requirements regarding the preparation and filing of registration statements.

B. Attention is directed to Regulation S-K (17 CFR Part 229) for the requirements applicable to the content of the non-financial statement portions of registration statements under the Securities Act. Where this Form directs the registrant to furnish information required by Regulation S-K and the item of Regulation S-K so provides, information need only be furnished to the extent appropriate.

C. A "small business issuer," defined in Rule 405 (17 CFR 230.405), that is eligible to use Form S-2, shall refer to the disclosure items in Regulation S-B (17 CFR 228.10 *et seq.*) and not Regulation S-K. For example, while Item 1 of Form S-2 requires the information required by Item 501 of Regulation S-K, a small business issuer shall provide the information in Item 501 of Regulation S-B. Where Regulation S-B does not contain a comparable Item, for example there is no Item "301" in Regulation S-B, then a small business issuer may omit the Item. A small business issuer shall provide the financial information in Item 310 of Regulation S-B in lieu of the financial information called for by Item 11 of Form S-2.

D. A "small business issuer," as defined in Rule 405 (17 CFR 230.405), that provided the "Information Required in Annual Report of Transitional Small Business Issuers" in its most recent annual report on Form 10-KSB is not eligible for use of this Form S-2.

III. Registration of Additional Securities

With respect to the registration of additional securities for an offering pursuant to Rule 462(b) under the Securities Act, the registrant may file a registration statement consisting only of the following: the facing page; a statement that the contents of the earlier registration statement, identified by file number, are incorporated by reference; required opinions and consents; the signature page; and any price-related information omitted from the earlier registration statement in reliance on Rule 430A that the registrant chooses to include in the new registration statement. The information contained in such a Rule 462(b) registration statement shall be deemed to be a part of the earlier registration statement as of the date of effectiveness of the Rule 462(b) registration statement. Any opinion or consent required in the Rule 462(b) registration statement may be incorporated by reference from the earlier registration statement with respect to the offering, if: (i) such opinion or consent expressly provides for such incorporation; and (ii) such opinion relates to the securities registered pursuant to Rule 462(b). *See* Rule 411(c) and Rule 439(b) under the Securities Act.

PART I
INFORMATION REQUIRED IN PROSPECTUS

Item 1. Forepart of the Registration Statement and Outside Front Cover Page of Prospectus

Set forth in the forepart of the registration statement and on the outside front cover page of the prospectus the information required by Item 501 of Regulation S-K (§ 229.501 of this chapter).

Item 2. Inside Front and Outside Back Cover Pages of Prospectus

Set forth on the inside front cover page of the prospectus or, where permitted, on the outside back cover page, the information required by Item 502 of Regulation S-K (§ 229.502 of this chapter).

Item 3. Summary Information, Risk Factors and Ratio of Earnings to Fixed Charges

Furnish the information required by Item 503 of Regulation S-K (§ 229.503 of this chapter).

Item 4. Use of Proceeds

Furnish the information required by Item 504 of Regulation S-K (§ 229.504 of this chapter).

Item 5. Determination of Offering Price

Furnish the information required by Item 505 of Regulation S-K (§ 229.505 of this chapter).

Item 6. Dilution

Furnish the information required by Item 506 of Regulation S-K (§ 229.506 of this chapter).

Item 7. Selling Security Holders

Furnish the information required by Item 507 of Regulation S-K (§ 229.507 of this chapter).

Item 8. Plan of Distribution

Furnish the information required by Item 508 of Regulation S-K (§ 229.508 of this chapter).

Item 9. Description of Securities to be Registered

Furnish the information required by Item 202 of Regulation S-K (§ 229.202 of this chapter).

Item 10. Interests of Named Experts and Counsel

Furnish the information required by Item 509 of Regulation S-K (§ 229.509 of this chapter).

Item 11. Information with Respect to the Registrant

Furnish the information required by either paragraph (a) or paragraph (b) of this Item. The information required by paragraph (b) shall be furnished if the registrant satisfies the conditions of paragraph (c) of this Item.

(a) If the registrant elects to deliver this prospectus together with a copy of either its latest Form 10-K or Form 10-KSB filed pursuant to Sections 13(a) or 15(d) of the Exchange Act or its latest annual report to security holders, which at the time of original preparation met the requirements of either Rule 14a-3 or Rule 14c-3:

(1) Indicate that the prospectus is accompanied by either a copy of the registrant's latest Form 10-K or Form 10-KSB or a copy of its latest annual report to security holders, whichever the registrant elects to deliver pursuant to paragraph (a) of this Item.

(2) Provide financial and other information with respect to the registrant in the form required by Part I of Form 10-Q or Form 10-QSB as of the end of the most recent fiscal quarter which ended after the end of the latest fiscal year for which certified financial statements were included in the latest Form 10-K or Form 10-KSB or the latest report to security holders (whichever the registrant elects to deliver pursuant to paragraph (a) of this Item), and more than forty-five days

167

prior to the effective date of this registration statement (or as of a more recent date) by one of the following means:

(i) Including such information in the prospectus; or

(ii) Providing without charge to each person to whom a prospectus is delivered a copy of the registrant's latest Form 10-Q or Form 10-QSB; or

(iii) Providing without charge to each person to whom a prospectus is delivered a copy of the registrant's latest quarterly report which was delivered to its shareholders and which included the required financial information.

(3) If not reflected in the registrant's latest Form 10-K or Form 10-KSB or its latest annual report to security holders (whichever the registrant elects to deliver pursuant to paragraph (a) of this Item), provide information required by Rule 3-05 (§ 210.3-05 of this chapter) and Article 11 (§ 210.11-01 through § 210.11.03 of this chapter) of Regulation S-X.

(4) Describe any and all material changes in the registrant's affairs which have occurred since the end of the latest fiscal year for which certified financial statements were included in the latest Form 10-K or Form 10-KSB or the latest annual report to security holders (whichever the registrant elects to deliver pursuant to paragraph (a) of this Item) and which were not described in a Form 10-Q, Form 10-QSB or quarterly report delivered with the prospectus in accordance with paragraph (a) (2) (ii) or (iii) of this Item.

Instruction. Where the registrant elects to deliver the documents identified in paragraph (a) with a preliminary prospectus, such documents need not be redelivered with the final prospectus.

(b) If the registrant does not elect to deliver its latest Form 10-K or 10-KSB or its latest annual report to security holders:

(1) Furnish a brief description of the business done by the registrant and its subsidiaries during the most recent fiscal year as required by Rule 14a-3 to be included in annual reports to security holders. The description also should take into account changes in its business which have occurred between the end of the last fiscal year and the effective date of the registration statement.

(2) Include financial statements and information as required by Rule 14a-3(b) (1) to be included in annual reports to security holders as well as: (i) the interim financial information required by Rule 10-01 of Regulation S-X for a filing on Form 10-Q and Form 10-QSB; (ii) any financial information required by Rule 3-05 and Article 11 of Regulation S-X; and (iii) any financial information required because of a material disposition of assets outside the normal course of business. The financial statements shall be restated if there has been a change in accounting principles or a correction of an error where such change or correction requires a material retroactive restatement of financial statements, or where one or more business combinations accounted for by the pooling of interest method of accounting have been consummated subsequent to the most recent fiscal year and the acquired businesses, considered in the aggregate, are significant pursuant to Rule 11-01(b).

(3) Furnish information relating to industry segments, classes or similar products or services, foreign and domestic operations, and export sales required by paragraphs (b), (c) (1) (i) and (d) of Item 101 of Regulation S-K (§ 229.101 of this chapter).

(4) Where common equity securities are being offered, furnish information required by Item 201 of Regulation S-K (§ 229.201 of this chapter), market price and dividends on the registrant's common stock and related stockholder matters.

(5) Furnish selected financial data required by Item 301 of Regulation S-K (§ 229.301 of this chapter).

(6) Furnish supplementary financial information required by Item 302 of Regulation S-K (§ 229.302 of this chapter).

(7) Furnish management's discussion and analysis of the registrant's financial condition and results of operations required by Item 303 of Regulation S-K (§ 229.303 of this chapter).

(8) Furnish information concerning changes in and disagreements with accountants on accounting and financial disclosure required by Item 304 of Regulation S-K (§ 229.304) of this chapter.

(9) Furnish quantitative and qualitative disclosures about market risk required by Item 305 of Regulation S-K (§ 229.305 of this chapter).

(c) The registrant shall furnish the information required by paragraph (b) of this Item if:

(1) the registrant was required to make a material retroactive restatement of financial statements because of:

(i) a change in accounting principles; or

(ii) a correction of an error; or

(iii) a consummation of one or more business combinations accounted for by the pooling of interest method of accounting was effected subsequent to the most recent fiscal year and the acquired businesses considered in the aggregate meet the test of a significant subsidiary;

OR

(2) the registrant engaged in a material disposition of assets outside the normal course of business; AND

(3) such restatement of financial statements or disposition of assets was not reflected in the registrant's latest annual report to security holders and/or its latest Form 10-K or Form 10-KSB filed pursuant to Sections 13(a) or 15(d) of the Exchange Act.

Item 12. Incorporation of Certain Information by Reference

(a) The documents listed in (1), (2), and, if applicable, the portions of the documents listed in (3) and (4) below, shall be specifically incorporated by reference into the prospectus, by means of a statement to that effect in the prospectus listing all such documents. In lieu of incorporating portions of the documents listed in (3) and (4) below, the registrant may incorporate by reference its entire annual or quarterly report to security holders.

(1) The registrant's latest Form 10-K and Form 10-KSB (§ 249.310 and § 249.310b of this chapter) filed pursuant to Section 13(a) or 15(d) of the Exchange Act which contains certified financial statements for the registrant's latest fiscal year for which a Form 10-K and Form 10-KSB was required to have been filed.

(2) All other reports filed pursuant to Section 13(a) or 15(d) of the Exchange Act since the end of the fiscal year covered by the annual report referred to in (1) above.

(3) If the registrant elects to deliver its latest annual report to security holders, pursuant to Item 11(a)(1) of this Form:

(i) description of business furnished in accordance with the provisions of Rule 14a-3(b)(6) under the Exchange Act (§ 240.14a-3(b)(6) of this chapter);

(ii) financial statements and information furnished in accordance with the provisions of Rule 14a-3(b)(1);

(iii) information relating to industry segments, classes of similar products or services, foreign and domestic operations, and export sales furnished as required by paragraphs (b), (c)(1)(i) and (d) of Item 101 of Regulation S-K (§ 229.101 of this chapter);

(iv) where common equity securities are being offered, market price and dividends on the registrant's common equity and related stockholder matters furnished as required by Item 201 of Regulation S-K (§ 229.201 of this chapter);

(v) selected financial data furnished as required by Item 301 of Regulation S-K (§ 229.301 of this chapter);

(vi) supplementary financial information furnished as required by Item 302 of Regulation S-K (§ 229.302 of this chapter);

(vii) management's discussion and analysis of financial condition and results of operations furnished as required by Item 303 of Regulation S-K (§ 229.303 of this chapter);

(viii) information concerning disagreements with accountants on accounting and financial disclosure furnished as required by Item 304 of Regulation S-K (§ 229.304 of this chapter); and

(ix) quantitative and qualitative disclosures about market risk as required by Item 305 of Regulation S-K (§ 229.305 of this chapter).

(4) If the registrant elects, pursuant to Item 11(a)(2)(iii) of this Form, to provide a copy of its latest quarterly report which was delivered to shareholders, the financial information equivalent to that required to be presented in Part I of Form 10-Q.

Instruction. Attention is directed to Rule 439 (§ 230.439 of this chapter) regarding consent to use of material incorporated by reference.

(b) The registrant may also state, if it so chooses, that specifically described portions of its annual or quarterly report to security holders, other than those portions required to be incorporated by reference pursuant to paragraphs (a)(3) and (4) above, are not part of the registration statement. In such case, the description of portions which are not incorporated by reference or which are excluded shall be made with clarity and in reasonable detail.

(c) *Electronic filings.* Electronic filers electing to deliver and incorporate by reference all, or any portion, of the quarterly or annual report to security holders pursuant to this Item shall file as an exhibit such quarterly or annual report to security holders, or such portion thereof that is incorporated by reference, in electronic format.

(d)(1) You must state (i) that you will provide to each person, including any beneficial owner, to whom a prospectus is delivered, a copy of any or all of the information that has been incorporated by reference in the prospectus but not delivered with the prospectus;

(ii) that you will provide this information upon written or oral request;

(iii) that you will provide this information at no cost to the requester; and

(iv) the name, address, and telephone number to which the request for this information must be made.

Note to Item 12(d)(1)

If you send any of the information that is incorporated by reference in the prospectus to security holders, you also must send any exhibits that are specifically incorporated by reference in that information.

(2) You must (i) identify the reports and other information that you file with the SEC; and

(ii) state that the public may read and copy any materials you file with the SEC at the SEC's Public Reference Room at 450 Fifth Street, N.W., Washington, D.C. 20549. State that the public may obtain information on the operation of the Public Reference Room by calling the SEC at 1-800-SEC-0330. If you are an electronic filer, state that the SEC maintains an Internet site that contains reports, proxy and information statements, and other information regarding issuers that file electronically with the SEC and state the address of that site (http://www.sec.gov). You are encouraged to give your Internet address, if available.

Item 13. Disclosure of Commission Position on Indemnification for Securities Act Liabilities

Furnish the information required by Item 510 of Regulation S-K (§ 229.510 of this chapter).

PART II
INFORMATION NOT REQUIRED IN PROSPECTUS

Item 14. Other Expenses of Issuance and Distribution

Furnish the information required by Item 511 of Regulation S-K (§ 229.511 of this chapter).

Item 15. Indemnification of Directors and Officers

Furnish the information required by Item 702 of Regulation S-K (§ 229.702 of this chapter).

Item 16. Exhibits

Subject to the rules regarding incorporation by reference, furnish the exhibits required by Item 601 of Regulation S-K (§ 229.601 of this chapter).

Item 17. Undertakings

Furnish the undertakings required by Item 512 of Regulation S-K (§ 229.512 of this chapter).

SIGNATURES

Pursuant to the requirements of the Securities Act of 1933, the registrant certifies that it has reasonable grounds to believe that it meets all of the requirements for filing on Form S-2 and has duly caused this registration statement to be signed on its behalf by the undersigned, thereunto duly authorized, in the City of . . . . , State of . . . . , on . . . ., 19 . . . .

(Registrant) . . . .

By (Signature and Title) . . . .

Pursuant to the requirements of the Securities Act of 1933, this registration statement has been signed by the following persons in the capacities and on the dates indicated.

(Signature) . . . .

(Title) . . . .

(Date) . . . .

Instructions. 1. The registration statement shall be signed by the registrant, its principal executive officer, or officers, its principal financial officer, its controller or principal accounting officer, and by at least a majority of the board of directors or persons performing similar functions. If the registrant is a foreign person, the registration statement shall also be signed by its authorized representative in the United States. Where the registrant is a limited partnership, the registration statement shall be signed by a majority of the board of directors of any corporate general partner signing the registration statement.

2. The name of each person who signs the registration statement shall be typed or printed beneath his signature. Any person who occupies more than one of the specified positions shall indicate each capacity in which he signs the registration statement. Attention is directed to Rule 402 concerning manual signatures and to Item 601 of Regulation S-K concerning signatures pursuant to powers of attorney.

INSTRUCTIONS AS TO SUMMARY PROSPECTUSES

1. A summary prospectus used pursuant to Rule 431 (17 CFR § 230.431 of this chapter) shall at the time of its use contain such of the information specified below as is then included in the registration statement. All other information and documents contained in the registration statement may be omitted.

(a) As to Item 1, the aggregate offering price to the public, the aggregate underwriting discounts and commissions and the offering price per unit to the public;

(b) As to Item 4, a brief statement of the principal purposes for which the proceeds are to be used;

(c) As to Item 7, a statement as to the amount of the offering, if any, to be made for the account of security holders;

(d) As to Item 8, the name of the managing underwriter or underwriters and a brief statement as to the nature of the underwriter's obligation to take the securities, if any securities to be registered are to be offered otherwise than through underwriters, a brief statement as to the manner of distribution;

(e) As to Item 9 (a brief statement as to dividend rights, voting rights, conversion rights, interest, maturity;

(f) As to Item 11, a brief statement of the general character of the business done and intended to be done and the selected financial data Item 301 of Regulation S-K (§ 229.301 of this chapter); and

(g) A tabular presentation of notes payable, long term debt, deferred credits, minority interests, if material, and the equity section of the latest balance sheet filed, as may be appropriate.

2. The summary prospectus shall not contain a summary or condensation of any other required financial information except as provided above.

3. The Commission may, upon the request of the registrant, and where consistent with the protection of investors, permit the omission of any of the information herein required or the furnishing in substitution therefor of appropriate information of comparable character. The Commission may also require the inclusion of other information in addition to, or in substitution for, the information herein required in any case where such information is necessary or appropriate for the protection of investors.

FORM S-3

UNITED STATES SECURITIES AND EXCHANGE COMMISSION

Washington, D.C. 20549

FORM S-3
REGISTRATION STATEMENT UNDER THE SECURITIES ACT OF 1933

....

(Exact name of registrant as specified in its charter)

....

(State or other jurisdiction of incorporation or organization)

....

(I.R.S. Employer Identification No.)

....

(Address, including zip code, and telephone number, including area code, of
registrant's principal executive offices)

....

(Name, address, including zip code, and telephone number, including area code,
of agent for service)

Approximate date of commencement of proposed sale to the public ....

If the only securities being registered on this Form are being offered pursuant to dividend or interest reinvestment plans, please check the following box. ☐

If any of the securities being registered on this Form are to be offered on a delayed or continuous basis pursuant to Rule 415 under the Securities Act of 1933, other than securities offered only in
connection with dividend or interest reinvestment plans, check the following box. ☐

If this Form is filed to register additional securities for an offering pursuant to Rule 462(b) under the Securities Act, please check the following box and list the Securities Act registration statement
number of the earlier effective registration statement for the same offering. ☐ .

If this Form is a post-effective amendment filed pursuant to Rule 462(c) under the Securities Act, check the following box and list the Securities Act registration statement number of the earlier effective
registration statement for the same offering. ☐ .

If delivery of the prospectus is expected to be made pursuant to Rule 434, please check the following box. ☐

Calculation of Registration Fee

Title of each class of securities to be registered	Amount to be registered	Proposed maximum offering price per unit	Proposed maximum aggregate offering price	Amount of registration fee

Note: Specific details relating to the fee calculation shall be furnished in notes to the table, including references to provisions of Rule 457 (§ § 230.457 of this chapter) relied upon, if the basis of the calculation is not otherwise evident from the information presented in the table. If the filing fee is calculated pursuant to Rule 457(o) under the Securities Act, only the title of the class of securities to be registered, the proposed maximum aggregate offering price for that class of securities and the amount of registration fee need to appear in the "Calculation of Registration Fee" Table ("Fee Table"). Where two or more classes of securities are being registered pursuant to General Instruction II.D, however, the Fee Table need only specify the maximum aggregate offering price for all classes; the Fee Table need not specify by each class the proposed maximum aggregate offering price (See General Instruction II.D). Any difference between the dollar amount of securities registered for such offerings and the dollar amount of securities sold may be carried forward on a future registration statement pursuant to Rule 429 under the Securities Act.

GENERAL INSTRUCTIONS

I. Eligibility Requirements for Use of Form S-3

This instruction sets forth registrant requirements and transaction requirements for the use of Form S-3. Any registrant which meets the requirements of I.A. below ("Registrant Requirements") may use this Form for the registration of securities under the Securities Act of 1933 ("Securities Act") which are offered in any transaction specified in I.B. below ("Transaction Requirement") provided that the requirements applicable to the specified transaction are met. With respect to majority-owned subsidiaries, see Instruction I.C. below.

A. *Registrant Requirements.* Registrants must meet the following conditions in order to use this Form for registration under the Securities Act of securities offered in the transactions specified in I.B. below:

1. The registrant is organized under the laws of the United States or any State or Territory or the District of Columbia and has its principal business operations in the United States or its territories.

2. The registrant has a class of securities registered pursuant to Section 12(b) of the Securities Exchange Act of 1934 ("Exchange Act") or a class of equity securities registered pursuant to Section 12(g) of the Exchange Act or is required to file reports pursuant to Section 15(d) of the Exchange Act.

3. The registrant:

(a) has been subject to the requirements of Section 12 or 15(d) of the Exchange Act and has filed all the material required to be filed pursuant to Section 13, 14 or 15(d) for a period of at least twelve calendar months immediately preceding the filing of the registration statement on this Form; and

(b) has filed in a timely manner all reports required to be filed during the twelve calendar months and any portion of a month immediately preceding the filing of the registration statement, other than a report that is required solely pursuant to Item 1.01, 1.02, 2.03, 2.04, 2.05, 2.06 or 4.02(a) of Form 8-K (§ 249.308 of this chapter). If the registrant has used (during the twelve calendar months and any portion of a month immediately preceding the filing of the registration statement) Rule 12b-25(b) (§ 240.12b-25(b) of this chapter) under the Exchange Act with respect to a report or a portion of a report, that report or portion thereof has actually been filed within the time period prescribed by that rule.

4. The provisions of paragraphs A.2. and A.3.(a) above do not apply to any registered offerings of investment grade asset-backed securities as defined in I.B.5. below.

5. Neither the registrant nor any of its consolidated or unconsolidated subsidiaries have, since the end of the last fiscal year for which certified financial statements of the registrant and its consolidated subsidiaries were included in a report filed pursuant to Section 13(a) or 15(d) of the Exchange Act: (a) failed to pay any dividend or sinking fund installment on preferred stock; or (b) defaulted (i) on any installment or installments on indebtedness for borrowed money, or (ii) on any rental on one or more long term leases, which defaults in the aggregate are material to the financial position of the registrant and its consolidated and unconsolidated subsidiaries, taken as a whole.

6. A foreign issuer other than a foreign government, which satisfies all of the above provisions of these registrant eligibility requirements except the provisions in I.A. 1. relating to organization and principal business shall be deemed to have met these registrant eligibility requirements provided that such foreign issuer files the same reports with the Commission under Section 13(a) or 15(d) of the Exchange Act as a domestic registrant pursuant to I.A. 3. above.

7. If the registrant is a successor registrant, it shall be deemed to have met conditions 1., 2., 3., and 5, above if: (a) its predecessor and it, taken together, do so, provided that the succession was primarily for the purpose of changing the state of incorporation of the predecessor or forming a holding company and that the assets and liabilities of the successor at the time of succession were substantially the same as those of the predecessor, or (b) if all predecessors met the conditions at the time of succession and the registrant has continued to do so since the succession.

8. *Electronic filings:* In addition to satisfying the foregoing conditions, a registrant subject to the electronic filing requirements of Rule 101 of Regulation S-T (§ 232.101 of this chapter) shall have filed with the Commission all required electronic filings, including confirming electronic copies of documents submitted in paper pursuant to a hardship exemption as provided by Rule 201 or Rule 202(d) of Regulation S-T (§ § 232.201 or 232.202(d) of this chapter).

B. *Transaction Requirements.* Security offerings meeting any of the following conditions and made by a registrant meeting the Registrant Requirements specified in I.A. above may be registered on this Form:

1. *Primary Offerings by Certain Registrants.* Securities to be offered for cash by or on behalf of a registrant, or outstanding securities to be offered for cash for the account of any person other than the registrant, including securities acquired by standby underwriters in connection with the call or redemption by the registrant of warrants or a class of convertible securities; *provided* that the aggregate market value of the voting and non-voting common equity held by non-affiliates of the registrant is $75 million or more.

Instruction. For the purposes of this Form, "common equity" is as defined in Securities Act Rule 405 (§ 230.405 of this chapter). The aggregate market value of the registrant's outstanding voting and non-voting common equity shall be computed by use of the price at which the common equity was last sold, or the average of the bid and asked prices of such common equity, in the principal market for such common equity as of a date within 60 days prior to the date of filing. See the definition of "affiliate" in Securities Act Rule 405.

2. *Primary Offerings of Non-convertible Investment Grade Securities.* Non-convertible securities to be offered for cash by or on behalf of a registrant, provided such securities at the time of sale are "investment grade securities," as defined below. A non-convertible security is an "investment grade security" if, at the time of sale, at least one nationally recognized statistical rating organization (as that term is used in Rule 15c3-1(c)(2)(vi)(F) under the Securities Exchange Act of 1934 (§ 240.15c3-1(c)(2)(vi)(F) of this chapter)) has rated the security in one of its generic rating categories which signifies investment grade; typically, the four highest rating categories (within which there may be sub-categories or gradations indicating relative standing) signify investment grade.

3. *Transactions Involving Secondary Offerings.* Outstanding securities to be offered for the account of any person other than the issuer, including securities acquired by standby underwriters in connection with the call or redemption by the issuer of warrants or a class of convertible securities, if securities of the same class are listed and registered on a national securities exchange or are quoted on the automated quotation system of a national securities association. (In addition, attention is directed to General Instruction C to Form S-8 (§ 239.16b) for the registration of employee benefit plan securities for resale.)

4. *Rights Offerings, Dividend or Interest Reinvestment Plans, and Conversions, Warrants and Options.*

(a) Securities to be offered (1) upon the exercise of outstanding rights granted by the issuer of the securities to be offered, if such rights are granted on a pro rata basis to all existing security holders of the class of securities to which the rights attach, (2) under a dividend or interest reinvestment plan, or (3) upon the conversion of outstanding convertible securities or the exercise of outstanding warrants or options issued by the issuer of the securities to be offered, or an affiliate of that issuer.

(b) However, Form S-3 is available for registering these securities only if the issuer has sent, within the twelve calendar months immediately before the registration statement is filed, material containing the information required by Rule 14a-3(b) (§ 240.14a-3(b) of this chapter) under the Exchange Act to:

(1) all record holders of the rights,

(2) all participants in the plans, or

(3) all record holders of the convertible securities, warrants or options, respectively.

(c) The issuer also must have provided, within the twelve calendar months immediately before the Form S-3 registration statement is filed, the information required by Items 401, 402 and 403 of Regulation S-K (§ § 229.401-229.403 of this chapter) to:

(1) holders of rights exercisable for common stock,

(2) holders of securities convertible into common stock, and

(3) participants in plans that may invest in common stock, securities convertible into common stock, or warrants or options exercisable for common stock, respectively.

5. *Offerings of Investment Grade Asset-backed Securities.* Asset-backed securities to be offered for cash, provided the securities are "investment grade securities," as defined in I.B.2 above (Primary Offerings of Non-convertivle Investment Grade Securities). For purposes of this Form, the term "asset-backed security" means a security that is primarily serviced by the cashflows of a discrete pool of receivables or other financial assets, either fixed or revolving, that by their terms convert into cash within a finite time period plus any rights or other assets designed to assure the servicing or timely distribution of proceeds to the securityholders.

C. *Majority-owned Subsidiaries.* If a registrant is a majority-owned subsidiary, security offerings may be registered on this Form if:

1. the registrant-subsidiary itself meets the Registrant Requirements and the applicable Transaction Requirement;

2. the parent of the registrant-subsidiary meets the Registrant Requirements and the conditions of Transaction Requirement B. 2. (Primary Offerings of Non-convertible Investment Grade Securities) are met; or

3. the parent of the registrant-subsidiary meets the Registrant Requirements and the applicable Transaction Requirement, and fully and unconditionally guarantees the payment obligations on the securities being registered, and the securities being registered are non-convertible securities. Note: In such an instance, the parent-guarantor is the issuer of a separate security consisting if the guarantee which must be concurrently registered but may be registered on the same registration statement as are the guaranteed securities.

II. Application of General Rules and Regulations

A. Attention is directed to the General Rules and Regulations under the Securities Act, particularly Regulation C thereunder (17 CFR 230.400 to 230.494). That Regulation contains general requirements regarding the preparation and filing of registration statements

B. Attention is directed to Regulation S-K (17 CFR Part 229) for the requirements applicable to the content of the non-financial statement portions of registration statements under the Securities Act. Where this Form directs the registrant to furnish information required by Regulation S-K and the item of Regulation S-K so provides, information need only be furnished to the extent appropriate. Notwithstanding Item 501 and 502 of Regulation S-K, no table of contents is required to be included in the prospectus or registration statement prepared on this form. In addition to the information expressly required to be included in a registration statement on this Form S-3, registrants also may provide such other information as they deem appropriate.

C. A "small business issuer," defined in Rule 405 (17 CFR 230.405), that is eligible to use Form S-3 shall refer to the disclosure items in Regulation S-B (17 CFR 228.10 *et seq.*) and not Regulation S-K. For example, while Item 1 of Form S-3 requires the information required by Item 501 of Regulation S-K, small business issuers shall provide the information in Item 501 of Regulation S-B. Where Regulation S-B does not contain a comparable Item, for example there is no Item "301" in Regulation S-B, then small business issuers may omit the Item. Small business issuers shall provide the financial information called for by Item 310 of Regulation S-B in lieu of the financial information called for by Item 11.

D. Where two or more classes of securities being registered on this Form pursuant to General Instruction I.B.1. or I.B.2. are to be offered on a delayed or continuous basis pursuant to §230.415(a)(1)(x), §230.457(o) under the Securities Act permits the registration fee to be calculated on the basis of the maximum offering price of all the securities listed in the "Calculation of Registration Fee" Table ("Fee Table"). In this event, while the Fee Table would list each of the classes of securities being registered and the aggregate proceeds to be raised, the Fee Table need not specify by each class information as to the amount to be registered, proposed maximum offering price per unit, and proposed maximum aggregate offering price.

III. Dividend or Interest Reinvestment Plans: Filing and Effectiveness of Registration Statement; Requests for Confidential Treatment

A registration statement on this Form S-3 relating solely to securities offered pursuant to a dividend or interest reinvestment plan will become effective automatically (Rule 462, §230.462 of this chapter) upon filing (Rule 456, §230.456 of this chapter). Post-effective amendments to such a registration statement on this Form shall become effective upon filing (Rule 464, §230.464 of this chapter). All filings made on or in connection with this Form become public upon filing with the Commission. As a result, requests for confidential treatment made under Rule 406 (§230.406 of this chapter) must be processed with the Commission staff prior to the filing of such a registration statement. The number of copies of the registration statement and of each amendment required by rules 402 and 472 (§§230.402 and 230.472 of this chapter) shall be filed with the Commission: *provided, however,* That the number of additional copies referred to in Rule 402(b) may be reduced from ten to three and the number of additional copies referred to in Rule 472(a) may be reduced from eight to three, one of which shall be marked clearly and precisely to indicate changes.

IV. Registration of Additional Securities

With respect to the registration of additional securities for an offering pursuant to Rule 462(b) under the Securities Act, the registrant may file a registration statement consisting only of the following: the facing page; a statement that the contents of the earlier registration statement, identified by file number, are incorporated by reference; required opinions and consents; the signature page; and any price-related information omitted from the earlier registration statement in reliance on Rule 430A that the registrant chooses to include in the new registration statement. The information contained in such a Rule 462(b) registration statement shall be deemed to be a part of the earlier registration statement as of the date of effectiveness of the Rule 462(b) registration statement. Any opinion or consent required in the Rule 462(b) registration statement may be incorporated by reference from the earlier registration statement with respect to the offering, if: (i) such opinion or consent expressly provides for such incorporation; and (ii) such opinion relates to the securities registered pursuant to Rule 462(b). *See* Rule 411(c) and Rule 439(b) under the Securities Act.

PART I
INFORMATION REQUIRED IN PROSPECTUS

Item 1. Forepart of the Registration Statement and Outside Front Cover Page of Prospectus

Set forth in the forepart of the registration statement and on the outside from cover page of the prospectus the information required by Item 501 of Regulation S-K (§ 229.501 of this chapter).

Item 2. Inside Front and Outside Back Cover Pages of Prospectus

Set forth on the inside front cover page of the prospectus or, where permitted, on the outside back cover page, the information required by Item 502 of Regulation S-K (§ 229.502 of this chapter).

Item 3. Summary Information, Risk Factors and Ratio of Earnings to Fixed Charges

Furnish the information required by Item 503 of Regulation S-K (§ 229.503 of this chapter).

Item 4. Use of Proceeds

Furnish the information required by Item 504 of Regulation S-K (§ 229.504 of this chapter).

Item 5. Determination of Offering Price

Furnish the information required by Item 505 of Regulation S-K (§ 229.505 of this chapter).

Item 6. Dilution

Furnish the information required by Item 506 of Regulation S-K (§ 229.506 of this chapter).

Item 7. Selling Security Holders

Furnish the information required by Item 507 of Regulation S-K (§ 229.507 of this chapter).

Item 8. Plan of Distribution

Furnish the information required by Item 508 of Regulation S-K (§ 229.508 of this chapter).

Item 9. Description of Securities to be Registered

Furnish the information required by Item 202 of Regulation S-K (§ 229.202 of this chapter), unless capital stock is to be registered and securities of the same class are registered pursuant to Section 12 of the Exchange Act.

Item 10. Interests of Named Experts and Counsel

Furnish the information required by Item 509 of Regulation S-K (§ 229.509 of this chapter).

Item 11. Material Changes

(a) Describe any and all material changes in the registrant's affairs which have occurred since the end of the latest fiscal year for which certified financial statements were included in the latest annual report to security holders and which have not been described in a report on Form 10-Q (§ 249.308a of this chapter) and Form 10-QSB (§ 249.308b of this chapter) or Form 8-K (§ 249.308 of this chapter) filed under the Exchange Act.

(b) Include in the prospectus, if not incorporated by reference therein from the reports filed under the Exchange Act specified in Item 12(a), a proxy or information statement filed pursuant to Section 14 of the Exchange Act, a prospectus previously filed pursuant to Rule 424(b) or (c) under the Securities Act (§ 230.424(b) or (c) of this chapter) or, where no prospectus was required to be filed pursuant to Rule 424(b), the prospectus included in the registration statement at effectiveness, or a Form 8-K filed during either of the two preceeding years: (i) information required by Rule 3-05 and Article 11 of Regulation S-X (17 CFR Part 210); (ii) restated financial statements prepared in accordance with Regulation S-X if there has been a change in accounting principles or a correction in an error where such change or correction requires a material retroactive restatement of financial statements; (iii) restated financial statements prepared in accordance with

Regulation S-X where one or more business combinations accounted for by the pooling of interest method of accounting have been consummated subsequent to the most recent fiscal year and the acquired businesses, considered in the aggregate, are significant pursuant to Rule 11-01(b), or (iv) any financial information required because of a material disposition of assets outside the normal course of business.

Item 12. Incorporation of Certain Information by Reference

(a) the documents listed in (1) and (2) below shall be specifically incorporated by reference into the prospectus, by means of a statement to that effect in the prospectus listing all such documents.

(1) the registrant's latest annual report on Form 10-K (17 CFR 249.310) and Form 10-KSB (17 CFR 249.310b) filed pursuant to Section 13(a) or 215(d) of the Exchange Act which contains financial statements for the registrant's latest fiscal year for which a Form 10-K and Form 10-KSB was required to have been filed; and

(2) all other reports filed pursuant to Section 13(a) or 15(d) of the Exchange Act since the end of the fiscal year covered by the annual report referred to in (1) above; and

(3) if capital stock is to be registered and securities of the same class are registered under Section 12 of the Exchange Act, the description of such class of securities which is contained in a registration statement filed under the Exchange Act, including any amendment or reports filed for the purpose of updating such description.

(b) The prospectus shall also state that all documents subsequently filed by the registrant pursuant to Sections 13(a), 13(c), 14 or 15(d) of the Exchange Act, prior to the termination of the offering shall be deemed to be incorporated by reference into the prospectus.

(c) (1) You must state (i) that you will provide to each person, including any beneficial owner, to whom a prospectus is delivered, a copy of any or all of the information that has been incorporated by reference in the prospectus but not delivered with the prospectus;

(ii) that you will provide this information upon written or oral request;

(iii) that you will provide this information at no cost to the requester; and

(iv) the name, address, and telephone number to which the request for this information must be made.

Note to Item 12(c) (1)

If you send any of the information that is incorporated by reference in the prospectus to security holders, you also must send any exhibits that are specifically incorporated by reference in that information.

(2) You must (i) identify the reports and other information that you file with the SEC; and

(ii) state that the public may read and copy any materials you file with the SEC at the SEC's Public Reference Room at 450 Fifth Street, N.W., Washington, D.C. 20549. State that the public may obtain information on the operation of the Public Reference Room by calling the SEC at 1-800-SEC-0330. If you are an electronic filer, state that the SEC maintains an Internet site that contains reports, proxy and information statements, and other information regarding issuers that file electronically with the SEC and state the address of that site (www.sec.gov). You are encouraged to give your Internet address, if available.

Instruction—Attention is directed to Rule 439 (§ 230.439 of this chapter) regarding consent to use of material incorporated by reference.

Item 13. Disclosure of Commission Position on Indemnification for Securities Act Liabilities

Furnish the information required by Item 510 of Regulation S-K (§ 229.510 of this chapter).

PART II
INFORMATION NOT REQUIRED IN PROSPECTUS

Item 14. Other Expenses of Issuance and Distribution

Furnish the information required by Item 511 of Regulation S-K (§ 229.511 of this chapter).

Item 15. Indemnification of Directors and Officers

Furnish the information required by Item 702 of Regulation S-K (§ 229.702 of this chapter).

Item 16. Exhibits

Subject to the rules regarding incorporation by reference, furnish the exhibits required by Item 601 of Regulation S-K (§ 229.601 of this chapter).

Item 17. Undertakings

Furnish the undertakings required by Item 512 of Regulation S-K (§ 229.512 of this chapter).

SIGNATURES

Pursuant to the requirements of the Securities Act of 1933, the registrant certifies that it has reasonable grounds to believe that it meets all of the requirements for filing on Form S-3 and has duly caused this registration statement to be signed on its behalf by the undersigned, thereunto duly authorized in the City of . . . ., State of . . . . ,

on . . . ., 19. . . . . (Registrant) . . . .

By (Signature and Title) . . . .

Pursuant to the requirements of the Securities Act of 1933, this registration statement has been signed by the following persons in the capacities and on the dates indicated.

(Signature) . . . .

(Title) . . . .

(Date) . . . .

Instructions. 1. The registration statement shall be signed by the registrant, its principal executive officer or officers, its principal financial officer, its controller or principal accounting officer, and by at least a majority of the board of directors or persons performing similar functions. If the registrant is a foreign person, the registration statement shall also be signed by its authorized representative in the United States. Where the registrant is a limited partnership, the registration statement shall be signed by a majority of the board of directors of any corporate general partner signing the registration statement.

2. The name of each person who signs the registration statement shall be typed or printed beneath his signature. Any person who occupies more than one of the specified positions shall indicate each capacity in which he signs the registration statement. Attention is directed to Rule 402 concerning manual signatures and Item 601 of Regulation S-K concerning signatures pursuant to powers of attorney.

3. Where eligibility for use of the Form is based on the assignment of a security rating pursuant to Transaction Requirement B.2. or B.5., the registrant may sign the registration statement notwithstanding the fact that such security rating has not been assigned by the filing date, provided that the registrant reasonably believes, and so states, that the security rating requirement will be met by the time of sale.

FORM S-8

UNITED STATES SECURITIES AND EXCHANGE COMMISSION

Washington, D.C. 20549

FORM S-8

REGISTRATION STATEMENT UNDER THE SECURITIES ACT OF 1933

(Exact name of registrant as specified in its charter)

(State or other jurisdiction of incorporation or organization)

(I.R.S. Employer Identification No.)

(Address of Principal Executive Offices)   (Zip Code)

(Full title of the plan)

(Name and address of agent for service)

(Telephone number, including area code, of agent for service)

CALCULATION OF REGISTRATION FEE

Title of securities to be registered	Amount to be registered	Proposed maximum offering price per share	Proposed maximum aggregate offering price	Amount of registration fee

Notes:

1. If plan interests are being registered, include the following: In addition, pursuant to Rule 416(c) under the Securities Act of 1933, this registration statement also covers an indeterminate amount of interests to be offered or sold pursuant to the employee benefit plan(s) described herein.

2. Specific details relating to the fee calculation shall be furnished in notes to the table, including references to provisions of Rule 457 (§ 230,457 of this chapter) relied upon, if the basis of the calculation is not otherwise evident from the information presented in the table.

GENERAL INSTRUCTIONS

A. Rule as to Use of Form S-8

1. Any registrant that, immediately prior to the time of filing a registration statement on this Form, is subject to the requirement to file reports pursuant to Section 13 or 15(d) of the Securities Exchange Act of 1934 ("Exchange Act"), and has filed all reports and other materials required to be filed by such requirements during the preceding 12 months (or for such shorter period that the registrant was required to file such reports and materials), may use this Form for registration under the Securities Act of 1933 ("Act") of the following securities:

(a) Securities of the registrant to be offered under any employee benefit plan to its employees or employees of its subsidiaries or parents. For purposes of this form, the term "employee benefit plan" is defined in Rule 405 of Regulation C (230.405).

(1) For purposes of this form, the term "employee" is defined as any employee, director, general partner, trustee (where the registrant is a business trust), officer, or consultant or advisor. Form S-8 is available for the issuance of securities to consultants or advisors only if:

(i) they are natural persons;

(ii) They provide bona fide services to the registrant; and

(iii) the services are not in connection with the offer or sale of securities in a capital-raising transaction, and do not directly or indirectly promote or maintain a market for the registrant's securities.

(2) In addition, the term "employee" includes insurance agents who are exclusive agents of the registrant, its subsidiaries or parents, or derive more than 50% of their annual income from those entities.

(3) The term "employee" also includes former employees as well as executors, administrators or beneficiaries of the estates of deceased employees, guardians or members of a committee for incompetent former employees, or similar persons duly authorized by law to administer the estate or assets of former employees. The inclusion of all individuals described in the preceding sentence in the term "employee" is only to permit registration on Form S-8 of:

(i) the exercise of employee benefit plan stock options and the subsequent sale of the securities, if these exercises and sales are permitted under the terms of the plan; and

(ii) the acquisition of registrant securities pursuant to intra-plan transfers among plan funds, if these transfers are permitted under the terms of the plan.

(4) The term "registrant" as used in this Form means the company whose securities are to be offered pursuant to the plan, and also may mean the plan itself.

(5) The form also is available for the exercise of employee benefit plan options and the subsequent resale of the underlying securities by an employee's family member who has acquired the options from the employee through a gift or a domestic relations order. For purposes of this form, "family member" includes any child, stepchild, grandchild, parent, stepparent, grandparent, spouse, former spouse, sibling, niece, nephew, mother-in-law, father-in-law, son-in-law, daughter-in-law, brother-in-law, or sister-in-law, including adoptive relationships, any person sharing the employees household (other than a tenant or employee), a trust in which these persons have more than fifty percent of the beneficial interest, a foundation in which these persons (or the employee) control the management of assets, and any other entity in which these persons (or the employee) own more than fifty percent of the voting interests. Form S-8 is not available for the exercise of options transferred for value. The following transactions are not prohibited transfers for value:

(i) a transfer under a domestic relations order in settlement of marital property rights; and

(ii) a transfer to an entity in which more than fifty percent of the voting interests are owned by family members (or the employee) in exchange for an interest in that entity.

(b) Interests in the above plans, if such interests constitute securities and are required to be registered under the Act. (*See* Release No. 33-6188 (February 1, 1980) and Section 3(a)(2) of the Act.)

2. Where interests in a plan are being registered and the plan's latest annual report filed pursuant to Section 15(d) of the Exchange Act is to be incorporated by reference pursuant to the requirements of Form S-8, the plan shall either: (i) have been subject to the requirement to file reports pursuant to Section 15(d) and shall have filed all reports required to be filed by such requirements during the preceding 12 months (or for such shorter period that the plan was required to file such reports); or (ii) if the plan has not previously been subject to the reporting requirements of Section 15(d), concurrently with the filing of the registration statement on Form S-8, the plan shall file an annual report for its latest fiscal year (or if the plan has not yet completed its first fiscal year, then for a period ending not more than 90 days prior to the filing of this registration statement), *provided that* if the plan has not been in existence for at least 90 days prior to the filing date, the requirement to file an employee plan annual report concurrently with the Form S-8 registration statement shall not apply.

3. *Electronic filings.* In addition to satisfying the foregoing conditions, a registrant subject to the electronic filing requirements of Rule 101 of Regulation S-T (§ 232.101 of this chapter) shall have filed with the Commission all required electronic filings, including confirming electronic copies of documents submitted in paper pursuant to a hardship exemption as provided in Rule 201 or 202(d) of Regulation S-T (§ 232.201 or § 232.202(d) of this chapter).

B. Application of General Rules and Regulations

1. Attention is directed to the General Rules and Regulations under the Act, particularly those comprising Regulation C thereunder (17 CFR §§ 230.400 to 230.499). That Regulation contains general requirements regarding the preparation and filing of registration statements. However, any provision in this Form covering the same subject matter as any such requirement shall be controlling unless otherwise specifically provided in Regulation C (*see* § 230.400).

2. Attention is directed to Regulation S-K (17 CFR Part 229) for the requirements applicable to the content of the non-financial portions of registration statements under the Act. Where this Form directs the registrant to furnish information required by any item of Regulation S-K, information need only be furnished to the extent appropriate.

3. A "small business issuer," defined in § 230.405, shall refer to the disclosure items in Regulation S-B (17 CFR 228.10 *et seq.*) and not Regulation S-K (17 CFR 229.10 *et seq.*).

C. Reoffers and Resales

1. *Securities.* Reoffers and resales of the following securities may be made on a continuous or delayed basis in the future, as provided by Rule 415 (§ 230.415), pursuant to a registration statement on this Form by means of a separate prospectus ("reoffer prospectus"), which is prepared in accordance with the requirements of Part I of Form S-3 (or, if the registrant is a foreign private issuer, in accordance with Part I of Form F-3), and filed with the registration statement on Form S-8 or, in the case of control securities, a post-effective amendment thereto:

(a) *Control securities,* which are defined for purposes of this General Instruction C as securities acquired under a Securities Act registration statement held by affiliates of the registrant as defined in Rule 405 (§ 230.405). Control securities may be included in a reoffer prospectus only if they have been or will be acquired by the selling security holder pursuant to an employee benefit plan; or

(b) *Restricted securities,* which are defined for purposes of this General Instruction C as securities issued under any employee benefit plan of the registrant meeting the definition of, "restricted securities" in Rule 144(a)(3) (§ 230.144(a)(3)), whether or not held by affiliates of the registrant. Restricted securities may be included in a reoffer prospectus only if they have been acquired by the selling security holder prior to the filing of the registration statement.

2. *Limitations.* The reoffer prospectus may be used as follows:

(a) If the registrant, at the time of filing such prospectus, satisfies the registrant requirements for use of Form S-3 (or if the registrant is a foreign private issuer, the registrant requirements for use of Form F-3), then control and restricted securities may be registered for reoffer and resale without any limitations.

(b) If the registrant, at the time of filing such prospectus, does not satisfy the registrant requirements for use of Form S-3 or F-3, as appropriate, then the following limitation shall apply with respect to both control securities and restricted securities: the amount of securities to be offered or resold by means of the reoffer prospectus, by each person, and any other person with whom he or she is acting in concert for the purpose of selling securities of the registrant, may not exceed, during any three month period, the amount specified in Rule 144(e) (§ 230. 144(e)).

3. *Selling Security Holders.*

(a) *Control Securities.* If the names of the security holders who intend to resell are not known by the registrant at the time of filing the Form S-8 registration statement, the registrant may either: (1) refer to the selling security holders in a generic manner in the reoffer prospectus; later, as their names and the amounts of securities to be reoffered become known, the registrant must supplement the reoffer prospectus with that information; or (2) name in the reoffer prospectus all persons eligible to resell and the amounts of securities available to be resold, whether or not they have a present intent to do so; any additional persons must be added by prospectus supplement. Prospectus supplements must be filed with the Commission as required by Rule 424(b) (§ 230.424(b)). The registrant may file a reoffer prospectus covering control securities as part of the initial registration statement or by means of a post-effective amendment to the Form S-8 registration statement.

(b) *Restricted Securities.* All persons (including non-affiliates) holding restricted securities registered for reoffer or resale pursuant to a reoffer prospectus are to be named as selling shareholders in the reoffer prospectus; *provided, however,* that any non-affiliate who holds less than the lesser of 1000 shares or 1% of the shares issuable under the plan to which the Form S-8 registration statement relates need not be named if the reoffer prospectus indicates that certain unnamed non-affiliates, each of whom may sell up to that amount, may use the reoffer prospectus for reoffers and resales. The reoffer prospectus covering restricted securities must be filed with the initial registration statement, not a post-effective amendment thereto.

Notes to General Instruction C

1. The term "person" as used in this General Instruction C shall be the same as set forth in Rule 144(a)(2) (§ 230.144(a)(2)).

2. If the conditions of this General Instruction C are not satisfied, registration of reoffers or resales must be made by means of a separate registration statement using whichever form is applicable.

D. Filing and Effectiveness of Registration Statement; Requests for Confidential Treatment; Number of Copies

A registration statement on this Form S-8 will become effective automatically (Rule 462, § 230.462) upon filing (Rule 456. § 230.456). In addition, post-effective amendments on this Form shall become effective upon filing (Rules 464, § 230.464 and 456). Delaying amendments are not permitted in connection with any registration statement on this Form (Rule 473(d), § 230.473(d)), and any attempt to interpose a delaying amendment of any kind will be ineffective. All filings made on or in connection with this Form become public upon filing with the Commission. As a result, requests for confidential treatment made under either Rule 406 (§ 230.406), or Exchange Act Rule 24b-2 (§ 240.24b-2) in connection with documents incorporated by reference, must be acted upon, *i.e.*, granted or denied, by the Commission staff prior to the filing of the registration statement. The number of copies of the filing required by Rules 402(c) and 472(d) (§ 230.402(c), § 230.472(d)) shall be filed with the Commission.

E. Registration of Additional Securities

With respect to the registration of additional securities of the same class as other securities for which a registration statement filed on this Form relating to an employee benefit plan is effective, the registrant may file a registration statement consisting only of the following: the facing page; a statement that the contents of the earlier registration statement, identified by file number, are incorporated by reference, required opinions and consents; the signature page; and any information required in the new registration statement that is not in the earlier registration statement. If the new registration statement covers restricted securities being offered for resale, it shall include the required reoffer prospectus. If the earlier registration statement included a reoffer prospectus, the new registration statement shall be deemed to include that reoffer prospectus, *provided, however,* that a revised reoffer prospectus shall be filed. if the reoffer prospectus is substantively different from that filed in the earlier registration statement. The filing fee required by the Act and Rule 457 (§ 230.457) shall be paid with respect to the additional securities only.

F. Registration of Plan Interests

Where a registration statement on this Form relates to securities to be offered pursuant to an employee stock purchase, savings, or similar plan, the registration statement shall be deemed to register an indeterminate amount of interests in such plan that are separate securities and required to be registered under the Securities Act. *See* Rule 416(c) (§ 230.416(c)).

G. Updating

Updating of information constituting the Section 10(a) prospectus pursuant to Rule 428(a) (§ 230.428(a)) during the offering of the securities shall be accomplished as follows:

1. Plan information specified by Item 1 of Form S-8 required to be sent or given to employees shall be updated as specified in Rule 428(b)(1) (§ 230.428(b)(1)). Such information need not be filed with the Commission.

2. Registrant information shall be updated by the filing of Exchange Act reports, which are incorporated by reference in the registration statement and the Section 10(a) prospectus. Any material changes in the registrant's affairs required to be disclosed in the registration statement but not required to be included in a specific Exchange Act report shall be reported on Form 8-K (§ 249.308) pursuant to Item 5 thereof (or, if the registrant is a foreign private issuer, on Form 6-K (§ 249.306)).

3. An employee plan annual report incorporated by reference in the registration statement from Form 11-K (or Form 10-K, as permitted by Rule 15d-21 (§ 240.15d-21)) shall be updated by the filing of a subsequent plan annual report on Form 11-K or 10-K.

Part I
INFORMATION REQUIRED IN THE SECTION 10(a) PROSPECTUS

Note:

The document(s) containing the information specified in this Part I will be sent or given to employees as specified by Rule 428(b)(1) (§ 230.428(b)(1)). Such documents need not be filed with the Commission either as part of this registration statement or us prospectuses or prospectus supplements pursuant to Rule 424 (§ 230.424). These documents and the documents incorporated by reference in the registration statement pursuant to Item 3 of Part II of this Form, taken together, constitute a prospectus that meets the requirements of Section 10(a) of the Securities Act. See Rule 428 (§ 230.428(a)(1)).

Item 1. Plan Information

The registrant shall deliver or cause to be delivered to each participant material information regarding the plan and its operations that will enable participants to make an informed decision regarding investment in the plan. This information shall include, to the extent material to the particular plan being described, but not be limited to, the disclosure specified in (a) through (j) below. Any unusual risks associated with participation in the plan not described pursuant to a specified item shall be prominently disclosed, as, for example, when the plan imposes a substantial restriction on the ability of a participant to withdraw contributions, or when plan participation may obligate the participant's general credit in connection with purchases on a margin basis. The information may be in one or several documents, provided that it is presented in a clear, concise and understandable manner. *See* Rule 421 (§ 230.421).

(a) General Plan Information

(1) Give the title of the plan and the name of the registrant whose securities are to be offered pursuant to the plan.

(2) Briefly state the general nature and purpose of the plan, its duration, and any provisions for its modification, earlier termination or extension to the extent that they affect the participants.

(3) Indicate whether the plan is subject to any provisions of the Employee Retirement Income Security Act of 1974 ("ERISA"), and if so, the general nature of those provisions to which it is subject.

(4) Give an address and a telephone number, including area code, which participants may use to obtain additional information about the plan and its administrators. State the capacity in which the plan administrators act (*e.g.*, trustees or managers) and the functions that they perform. If any person other than a participating employee has discretion with respect to the investment of all or any part of the assets of the plan in one or more investment media, name such person and describe the policies followed and to be followed with respect to the type and proportion of securities or other property in which funds of the plan may be invested. If the plan is not subject to ERISA: (i) state the nature of any material relationship between the administrators and the employees, the registrant or its affiliates; and (ii) describe the manner in which the plan administrators are selected, their term of office, and the manner in which they may be removed from office.

(b) Securities to be Offered

(1) State the title and total amount of securities to be offered pursuant to the plan.

(2) Furnish the information required by Item 202 of Regulation S-K (§ 229.202), except that if common stock registered under Section 12 of the Exchange Act is offered, such information is unnecessary. If plan interests are being registered, they need not be described pursuant to this item.

(c) Employees Who May Participate In the Plan

Indicate each class or group of employees that may participate in the plan and the basis upon which the eligibility of employees to participate therein is to be determined.

(d) Purchase of Securities Pursuant to the Plan and Payment for Securities Offered

(1) State the period of time within which employees may elect to participate in the plan, the price at which the securities may be purchased or the basis upon which such price is to be determined, and any terms regarding the amount of securities that an eligible employee can purchase.

(2) State when and the manner in which employees are to pay for the securities purchased pursuant to the plan, if payment is to be made by payroll deductions or other installment payments, state the percentage of wages or salaries or other basis for computing such payments, and the time and manner in which an employee may alter the amount of such deduction or payment.

(3) State the amount each employee is required or permitted to contribute or, if not a fixed amount, the percentage of wages or salaries or other basis of computing contributions.

(4) If contributions are to be made under the plan by the registrant or any employer, state who is to make such contributions, when they are to be made and the nature and amount of each contribution: If such contributions are not a fixed amount, state the basis for computing contributions.

(5) State the nature and frequency of any reports to be made to participating employees as to the amount and status of their accounts.

(6) If the plan is not subject to ERISA, state whether securities are to be purchased in the open market or otherwise. If they are not to be purchased in the open market, then state from whom they are to be purchased and describe the fees, commissions or other charges paid. If the employer or any of its affiliates, or any person having a material relationship with the employer or any of its affiliates, directly or indirectly, receives any part of the aggregate purchase price (including fees, commissions or other charges), explain the basis for compensation.

Note:

If the plan is one under which credit is extended to finance the acquisition of securities, consideration should be given to the applicability of Regulation G (12 CFR Part 207) or T (12 CFR Part 220).

(e) Resale Restrictions

Describe briefly any restriction on resale of the securities purchased under the plan which may be imposed upon the employee purchaser.

(f) Tax Effects of Plan Participation

Describe briefly the tax effect that may accrue to employees as a result of plan participation as well as the tax effects, if any, upon the registrant and whether or not the plan is qualified under Section 401(a) of the Internal Revenue Code.

Note:

If the plan is not qualified under Section 401 of the Internal Revenue Code of 1986, as amended, consideration should be given to the applicability of the Investment Company Act of 1940. *See* Securities Act Release No. 4790 (July 13, 1965).

(g) Investment of Funds

If participating employees may direct all or any part of the assets under the plan to two or more investment media, furnish a brief description of the provisions of the plan with respect to the alternative investment media; and provide a tabular or other meaningful presentation of financial data for each of the past three fiscal years (or such lesser period for which the data with respect to each investment medium is available) that, in the opinion of the registrant, will apprise employees of material trends and significant changes in the performance of alternative investment media and enable them to make informed investment decisions. Financial data shall be presented for any additional fiscal years necessary to keep the information from being misleading or that the registrant deems appropriate, but the total period presented need not exceed five years.

(h) Withdrawal from the Plan; Assignment of Interest

(1) Describe the terms and conditions under which a participating employee may (i) withdraw from the plan and terminate his or her interest therein; or (ii) withdraw funds or investments held for the employee's account without terminating his or her interest in the plan.

(2) State whether, and the terms and conditions upon which, the plan permits an employee to assign or hypothecate his or her interest in the plan.

(3) No information need be provided as to the effect of a qualified domestic relations order as defined in ERISA Section 206(d) (29 U.S.C. 1056(d)).

(i) Forfeitures and Penalties

Describe briefly every event which could, under the plan, result in a forfeiture by, or a penalty to, a participant, and the consequences thereof.

(j) Charges and Deductions and Liens Therefor

(1) Describe all charges and deductions (other than deductions described in paragraph (d) and taxes) that may be made against employees participating in the plan or against funds. securities or other property held under the plan and indicate who will receive, directly or indirectly, any part thereof. Such description should include charges and deductions that may be made upon the termination of an employee's interest in the plan, or upon partial withdrawals from the employee's account thereunder.

(2) State whether or not under the plan, or pursuant to any contract in connection therewith, any person has or may create a lien on any funds, securities, or other property held under the plan. If so, describe fully the circumstances under which the lien was or may be created.

(3) No information need be provided as to the effect of a qualified domestic relations order as defined in ERISA Section 206(d) (29 U.S.C. 1056(d)).

Item 2. Registrant Information and Employee Plan Annual Information

The registrant shall provide a written statement to participants advising them of the availability without charge, upon written or oral request, of the documents incorporated by reference in Item 3 of Part II of the registration statement, and stating that these documents are incorporated by reference in the Section 10(a) prospectus. The statement also shall indicate the availability without charge, upon written or oral request, of other documents required to be delivered to employees pursuant to Rule 428(b) (§ 230.428(b)). The statement shall include the address (giving title or department) and telephone number to which the request is to be directed.

Part II
INFORMATION REQUIRED IN THE REGISTRATION STATEMENT

Item 3. Incorporation of Documents by Reference

The registrant, and where interests in the plan are being registered, the plan, shall state that the documents listed in (a) through (c) below are incorporated by reference in the registration statement; and shall state that all documents subsequently filed by it pursuant to Sections 13(a), 13(c), 14 and 15(d) of the Securities Exchange Act of 1934, prior to the filing of a post-effective amendment which indicates that all securities offered have been sold or which deregisters all securities then remaining unsold, shall be deemed to be incorporated by reference in the registration statement and to be part thereof from the date of filing of such documents. Copies of these documents are not required to be filed with the registration statement.

(a) The registrant's latest annual report. and where interests in the plan are being registered, the plan's latest annual report, filed pursuant to Section 13(a) or 15(d) of the Exchange Act, or in the case of the registrant either (1) the latest prospectus filed pursuant to Rule 424(b) under the Act that contains audited financial statements for the registrant's latest fiscal year for which such statements have been filed, or (2) the registrant's effective registration statement on Form 10, Form 20-F or, in the case of registrants described in General Instruction A.(2) of Form 40-F, on Form 40-F filed under the Exchange Act containing audited financial statements for the registrant's latest fiscal year.

(b) All other reports filed pursuant to Section 13(a) or 15(d) of the Exchange Act since the end of the fiscal year covered by the registrant document referred to in (a) above.

(c) If the class of securities to be offered is registered under Section 12 of the Exchange Act, the description of such class of securities contained in a registration statement filed under such Act, including any amendment or report filed for the purpose of updating such description.

Item 4. Description of Securities

If the class of securities to be offered is not registered under Section 12 of the Exchange Act, set forth the information required by Item 202 of Regulation S-K (§ 229.202 of this chapter). If plan interests are being registered, they need not be described pursuant to this item.

Item 5. Interests of Named Experts and Counsel

Furnish the information required by Item 509 of Regulation S-K (§ 229.509 of this chapter).

Item 6. Indemnification of Directors and Officers

Furnish the information required by Item 702 of Regulation S-K (§ 229.702 of this chapter).

Item 7. Exemption from Registration Claimed

With respect to restricted securities to be reoffered or resold pursuant to this registration statement, the registrant shall indicate the section of the Act or Rule of the Commission under which exemption from registration was claimed and set forth briefly the facts relied upon to make the exemption available.

Item 8. Exhibits

Furnish the exhibits required by Item 601 Regulation S-K (§ 229.601 of this chapter), except that with respect to Item 601(b)(5):

(a) An opinion of counsel as to the legality of the securities being registered is required only with respect to original issuance securities.

(b) Neither an opinion of counsel concerning compliance with the requirements of ERISA nor an Internal Revenue Service determination letter that the plan is qualified under Section 401 of the Internal Revenue Code shall be required if, in lieu thereof, the response to this Item 8 includes an undertaking that the registrant will submit or has submitted the plan and any amendment thereto to the Internal Revenue Service ("IRS") in a timely manner and has made or will make all changes required by the IRS in order to qualify the plan.

Item 9. Undertakings

Furnish the undertakings required by Item 512(a), (b) and (h) of Regulation S-K (§ 229.512(a), (b) and (h) of this chapter), as well as any other applicable undertakings in Item 512.

Notes to Item 9:

(1) The Regulation S-K Item 512(a) undertakings are usually required pursuant to this item since most registration statements on Form S-8 involve the continuous offering and sale of securities under Rule 415 (§ 230.415 of this chapter).

(2) With respect to registration statements filed on this Form, foreign private issuers are not required to furnish the Item 512(a)(4) undertaking.

SIGNATURES

The Registrant. Pursuant to the requirements of the Securities Act of 1933, the registrant certifies that it has reasonable grounds to believe that it meets all of the requirements for filing on Form S-8 and has duly caused this registration statement to be signed on its behalf by the undersigned, thereunto duly authorized, in the City of_____

State of _____,

on _____, 19 ___.

(Registrant)_____

By (Signature and Title)_____

Pursuant to the requirements of the Securities Act of 1933, this registration statement has been signed by the following persons in the capacities and on the date indicated.

(Signature)_____

(Title)_____

(Date)_____

The Plan. Pursuant to the requirements of the Securities Act of 1933, the trustees (or other persons who administer the employee benefit plan) have duly caused this registration statement to be signed on its behalf by the undersigned, thereunto duly authorized,

in the City of_____

State of _____

on_____ 19_____

(Plan)_____

By (Signature and Title)_____

Instructions.

1. The registration statement shall be signed by the registrant, its principal executive officer or officers, its principal financial officer, its controller or principal accounting officer, and at least a majority of the board of directors or persons performing similar functions. Where interests in the plan are being registered, the registration statement shall be signed by the plan. If the signing person is a foreign person, the registration statement shall also be signed by its authorized representative in the United States. Where the signing person is a limited partnership, the registration statement shall be signed by a majority of the board of directors of any corporate general partner signing the registration statement.

2. The name of each person who signs the registration statement shall be typed or printed beneath the signature. Any person who occupies more than one of the specified positions shall indicate each capacity in which he or she signs the registration statement. Attention is directed to Rule 402 (§ 230.402) concerning manual signatures and Item 601 (§ 229.601) of Regulation S-K concerning signatures pursuant to powers of attorney.

FORM SB-1

UNITED STATES SECURITIES AND EXCHANGE COMMISSION

Washington, D.C. 20549

FORM SB-1

REGISTRATION STATEMENT UNDER THE SECURITIES ACT OF 1933
(Amendment No. ——)

. . . .

(Name of small business issuer in its charter)

. . . .

(State or jurisdiction of incorporation or organization

. . . .

(Primary Standard Industrial Classification Code Number

. . . .

(I.R.S. Employer Identification No.)

. . . .

(Address and telephone number of principal executive offices)

. . . .

(Address of principal place of business or intended principal place of business)

. . . .

(Name, address, and telephone number of agent for service)

. . . .

Approximate date of proposed sale to the public

If this Form is filed to register additional securities for an offering pursuant to Rule 462(b) under the Securities Act, check the following box and list the Securities Act registration statement number of the earlier effective registration statement for the same offering. ☐

. . . .

If this Form is a post-effective amendment filed pursuant to Rule 462(c) under the Securities Act, check the following box and list the Securities Act registration statement number of the earlier effective registration statement for the same offering. ☐

. . . .

If this Form is a post-effective amendment filed pursuant to Rule 462(d) under the Securities Act, check the following box and list the Securities Act registration statement number of the earlier effective registration statement for the same offering. ☐

. . . .

If delivery of the prospectus is expected to be made pursuant to Rule 434, check the following box. ☐

Calculation of Registration Fee

Title of each class of securities to be registered	Dollar amount to be registered	Proposed maximum offering price per unit	Amount of registration fee

Note: If the filing fee is calculated pursuant to Rule 457(o) under the Securities Act, only the title of the class of securities to be registered, the proposed maximum aggregate offering price for that class of securities and the amount of registration fee need to appear in the Calculation of Registration Fee table. Any difference between the dollar amount of securities registered for such offerings and the dollar amount of securities sold may be carried forward on a future registration statement pursuant to Rule 429 under the Securities Act.

The following delaying amendment is optional, but see Rule 473 before omitting it: The registrant hereby amends this registration statement on such date or dates as may be necessary to delay its effective date until the registrant shall file a further amendment which specifically states that this registration statement shall thereafter become effective in accordance with Section 8(a) of the Securities Act of 1933 or until the registration statement shall become effective on such date as the Commission, acting pursuant to said Section 8(a), may determine.

Disclosure alternative used (check one): Alternative 1_; Alternative 2_

GENERAL INSTRUCTIONS

A. Use of Form and Place of Filing

1. (a) A "small business issuer," defined in *Rule 405* of the Securities Act of 1933 (the "Securities Act") may use this form to register up to $10,000,000 of securities to be sold for cash, if they have not registered more than $10,000,000 in securities offerings in any continuous 12-month period, including the transaction being registered. In calculating the $10,000,000 ceiling, issuers should include all offerings which were registered under the Securities Act, other than any amounts registered on Form S-8.

(b) A small business issuer may use this form until it (1) registers more than $10 million under the Securities Act in any continuous 12-month period (other than securities registered on Form S-8), (2) elects to file on a non-transitional disclosure document (other than the proxy statement disclosure in Schedule 14A), or (3) no longer meets the definition of small business issuer. Non-transitional disclosure documents include: (1) Securities Act registration statement forms other than Forms SB-1, S-3 (if the issuer incorporates by reference transitional Exchange Act reports), S-8 and S-4 (if the issuer relies upon the transitional disclosure format in that form); (2) Exchange Act periodic reporting Forms 10-K and 10-Q; (3) Exchange Act registration statement Form 10; and (4) reports or registration statements on Forms *10-KSB, 10-QSB* or *10-SB* which do not use the transitional disclosure document format. A reporting company may not return to the transitional disclosure forms.

2. The small business issuer shall file the registration statement in the Washington, D.C. office.

3. If the small business issuer is a reporting company or a holding company of a bank (see the definition of "bank" in section 12(i) of the Securities Exchange Act of 1934), it should file the registration statement in the Commission's Washington, D.C. headquarters.

B. General Requirements

1. In preparing a registration statement on this Form, reference should be made to the General Rules and Regulations under the Securities Act, particularly *Regulation C* which sets forth requirements for the preparation and filing of a registration statement such as paper type and size.

2. Issuers registering securities for the first time should be aware of Form SR and *Rule 463* under the Securities Act concerning sales of registered securities and the use of proceeds. First-time issuers also should be aware of Exchange Act Rule 15c2-8 (§ 240.15c2-8), which requires broker-dealers to deliver a prospectus 48 hours before a sale of securities can be confirmed.

3. Issuers engaged in real estate, banking, insurance, oil and gas or mining activities should consult the Industry Guides in *Item 801 of Regulation S-K* (17 CFR 229.801). Real estate companies also should refer to Item 13 [Investment Policies of Registrant], Item 14 [Description of Real Estate], and Item 15 [Operating Data] of Form S-11 (17 CFR 239.18).

C. Preparation and Filing of the Registration Statement

Part I of this form, which relates to the content of certain information about the issuer, provides alternative disclosure formats. The registrant may elect either of these alternative formats.

D. Financial Statement Requirements

Regardless of the disclosure model used, all registrants shall furnish the financial statements required by Part F/S of this Form SB-1.

E. Composition of Prospectus

The information required by Part I and Part F/S of this registration statement shall comprise the prospectus.

F. Cover Page of Registration Statement

Issuers electing Alternative 1 should furnish the information required by *Item 501 of Regulation S-B* in lieu of the information required by Alternative 1 with respect to the cover page of the registration statement. Issuers electing Alternative 2 should furnish the information required by Item 501 of Regulation S-B in lieu of the information required by Item 1 of Alternative 2.

G. Canadian Issuer—Consent of Service

Canadian issuers eligible to use this Form should file as an exhibit to this registration statement a written irrevocable consent and power of attorney on Form F-X (§ 239.42 of this title).

H. Registration of Additional Securities

With respect to the registration of additional securities for an offering pursuant to *Rule 462(b)* under the Securities Act, the registrant may file a registration statement consisting only of the following: the facing page; a statement that the contents of the earlier registration statement, identified by file number, are incorporated by reference; required opinions and consents; the signature page; and any price-related information omitted from the earlier registration statement in reliance on *Rule 430A* that the registrant chooses to include in the new registration statement. The information contained in such a *Rule 462(b)* registration statement shall be deemed to be a part of the earlier registration statement as of the date of effectiveness of the Rule 462(b) registration statement. Any opinion or consent required in the Rule 462(b) registration statement may be incorporated by reference from the earlier registration statement with respect to the offering, if: (i) such opinion or consent expressly provides for such incorporation; and (ii) such opinion relates to the securities registered pursuant to Rule 462(b). *See Rule 411(c)* and *Rule 439(b)* under the Securities Act.

PART I—Narrative Information Required in Prospectus

Alternative 1

Corporate issuers may elect to furnish the information required by Model A of Form 1-A, as well as the following information.

Item 1. Inside Front and Outside Back Cover Pages of Prospectus

Furnish the information required by *Item 502 of Regulation S-B*.

Item 2. Significant Parties

List the full names and business and residential addresses, as applicable, for the following persons:

(1) the issuer's directors;

(2) the issuer's officers;

(3) the issuer's general partners;

(4) record owners of 5 percent or more of any class of the issuer's equity securities;

(5) beneficial owners of 5 percent or more of any class of the issuer's equity securities;

(6) promoters of the issuer;

(7) affiliates of the issuer;

(8) counsel to the issuer with respect to the proposed offering;

(9) each underwriter with respect to the proposed offering;

(10) the underwriter's directors;

(11) the underwriter's officers;

(12) the underwriter's general partners; and

(13) counsel to the underwriter.

Item 3. Relationship with Issuer of Experts Named in Registration Statement

Furnish the information required by *Item 509 of Regulation S-B,* if applicable.

Item 4. Selling Security Holders

Furnish the information required by *Item 507 of Regulation S-B,* if applicable.

Item 5. Changes in and Disagreements with Accountants

Furnish the information required by *Item 304 of Regulation S-B,* if applicable.

Item 6. Disclosure of Commission position on Indemnification for Securities Act Liabilities

Furnish the information required by *Item 510 of Regulation S-B.*

Alternative 2

Any issuer may elect to furnish the information required by Model B of Part II of Form 1-A, as well as the following information.

Item 1. Inside Front and Outside Back Cover Pages of Prospectus

Furnish the information required by *Item 502 of Regulation S-B.*

Item 2. Significant Parties

List the full names and business and residential addresses, as applicable, for the following persons:

(1) the issuer's directors;

(2) the issuer's officers;

(3) the issuer's general partners;

(4) record owners of 5 percent or more of any class of the issuer's equity securities;

(5) beneficial owners of 5 percent or more of any class of the issuer's equity securities;

(6) promoters of the issuer;

(7) affiliates of the issuer;

(8) counsel to the issuer with respect to the proposed offering;

(9) each underwriter with respect to the proposed offering;

(10) the underwriter's directors;

(11) the underwriter's officers;

(12) the underwriter's general partners; and

(13) counsel to the underwriter.

Item 3. Relationship with Issuer of Experts Named in Registration Statement

Furnish the information required by *Item 509 of Regulation S-B,* if applicable.

Item 4. Legal Proceedings

Furnish the information required by *Item 103 of Regulation S-B.*

Item 5. Changes in and Disagreements with Accountants

Furnish the information required by *Item 304 of Regulation S-B,* if applicable.

Item 6. Disclosure of Commission position on Indemnification for Securities Act Liabilities

Furnish the information required by *Item 510 of Regulation S-B.*

Part F/S—Financial Information Required in Prospectus

Furnish the information required by *Item 310 of Regulation S-B.*

Part II—Information Not Required in Prospectus

Item 1. Indemnification of Directors and Officers

Furnish the information required by *Item 702 of Regulation S-B.*

Item 2. Other Expenses of Issuance and Distribution

Furnish the information required by *Item 511 of Regulation S-B.*

Item 3. Undertakings

Furnish the undertakings required by *Item 512 of Regulation S-B.*

Item 4. Unregistered Securities Issued or Sold Within One Year

(a) As to any unregistered securities issued by the issuer or any of its predecessors or affiliated issuers within one year prior to the filing of this Form SB-1, state:

(1) the name of such issuer;

(2) the title and amount of securities issued;

(3) the aggregate offering price or other consideration for which they were issued and the basis for computing the amount thereof;

(4) the names and identities of the persons to whom the securities were issued.

(b) As to any unregistered securities of the issuer or any of its predecessors or affiliated issuers which were sold within one year prior to the filing of this Form SB-1 by or for the account of any person who at the time was a director, officer, promoter or principal security holder of the issuer of such securities, or was an underwriter of any securities of such issuer, furnish the information specified in subsections (1) through (4) of paragraph (a).

(c) Indicate the section of the Securities Act or Commission rule or regulation relied upon for exemption from the registration requirements of such Act and state briefly the facts relied upon for such exemption.

Item 5. Index to Exhibits

(a) An index to the exhibits should be presented.

(b) Each exhibit should be listed in the exhibit index according to the number assigned to it in Part III of Form 1-A or Item 6, below.

(c) The index to exhibits should identify the location of the exhibit under the sequential page numbering system for this Form SB-1.

(d) Where exhibits are incorporated by reference, the reference shall be made in the index of exhibits.

Instructions:

1. Any document or part thereof filed with the Commission pursuant to any Act administered by the Commission may, subject to the limitations of Rule 24 of the Commission's Rules of Practice, be incorporated by reference as an exhibit to any registration statement.

2. If any modification has occurred in the text of any document incorporated by reference since the filing thereof, the issuer shall file with the reference a statement containing the text of such modification and the date thereof.

3. Procedurally, the techniques specified in *Rule 411(d) of Regulation C* shall be followed.

Item 6. Description of Exhibits

As appropriate, the issuer should file as exhibits those documents required to be filed under Part III of Form 1A. Part III of Form 1-A lists 10 exhibits. The registrant also shall file:

(11) *Opinion re legality*—An opinion of counsel as to the legality of the securities covered by the Registration Statement, indicating whether they will, when sold, be legally issued, fully paid and non-assessable, and if debt securities, whether they will be binding obligations of the issuer.

(12) *Additional exhibits*—Any additional exhibits which the issuer may wish to file, which shall be so marked as to indicate clearly the subject matters to which they refer.

(13) *Form F-X*—Canadian issuers shall file a written irrevocable consent and power of attorney on Form F-X.

SIGNATURES

In accordance with the requirements of the Securities Act of 1933, the registrant certifies that it has reasonable grounds to believe that it meets all of the requirements of filing on Form SB-1 and authorized this registration statement to be signed on its behalf by the undersigned, in the City of
_____ State   of   _____ on
_____, 19_____

(Registrant)_____

By (Signatures and Title)_____

In accordance with the requirements of the Securities Act of 1933, this registration statement was signed by the following persons in the capacities and on the dates stated:

(Signature)_____

(Title)_____

(Date)_____

Instructions for signatures.

(1) Who must sign: the small business issuer, its principal executive officer or officers, its principal financial officer, its controller or principal accounting officer and at least the majority of the board of directors or persons performing similar functions. If the issuer is a limited partnership then the general partner and a majority of its board of directors if a corporation.

(2) Beneath each signature, type or print the name of each signatory. Any person who occupies more than one of the specified positions shall indicate each capacity in which he or she signs the registration statement. *See Rule 402 of Regulation C* concerning manual signatures and *Item 601 of Regulation S-B* concerning signatures by powers of attorney.

FORM SB-2

UNITED STATES SECURITIES AND EXCHANGE COMMISSION
Washington, D.C. 20549
FORM SB-2

REGISTRATION STATEMENT UNDER THE SECURITIES ACT OF 1933
(Amendment No. ———)

. . . .

(Name of small business issuer in its charter)

. . . .

(State or jurisdiction of incorporation or organization)

. . . .

(Primary Standard Industrial Classification Code Number)

. . . .

(I.R.S. Employer Identification No.)

. . . .

(Address and telephone number of principal executive offices)

. . . .

(Address of principal place of business or intended principal place of business)

. . . .

(Name, address and telephone number of agent for service)

. . . .

Approximate date of proposed sale to the public

If this Form is filed to register additional securities for an offering pursuant to Rule 462(b) under the Securities Act, check the following box and list the Securities Act registration statement number of the earlier effective registration statement for the same offering. ☐

. . . .

If this Form is a post-effective amendment filed pursuant to Rule 462(c) under the Securities Act, check the following box and list the Securities Act registration statement number of the earlier effective registration statement for the same offering. ☐

. . . .

If this Form is a post-effective amendment filed pursuant to Rule 462(d) under the Securities Act, check the following box and list the Securities Act registration statement number of the earlier effective registration statement for the same offering. ☐

. . . .

If delivery of the prospectus is expected to be made pursuant to Rule 434, check the following box. ☐

Calculation of Registration Fee

Title of each class of securities to be registered	Amount to be registered	Proposed maximum offering price per unit	Proposed maximum aggregate offering price	Amount of registration fee

Note: Specific details relating to the fee calculation shall be furnished in notes to the table, including references to provisions of Rule 457 (§ 230.457 of this chapter) relied upon, if the basis of the calculation is not otherwise evident from the information presented in the table. If the filing fee is calculated pursuant to Rule 457(o) under the Securities Act, only the title of the class of securities to be registered, the proposed maximum aggregate offering price for that class of securities and the amount of registration fee need to appear in the Calculation of Registration Fee table. Any difference between the dollar amount of securities registered for such offerings and the dollar amount of securities sold may be carried forward on a future registration statement pursuant to Rule 429 under the Securities Act.

The registrant hereby amends this registration statement on such date or dates as may be necessary to delay its effective date until the registrant shall file a further amendment which specifically states that this registration statement shall thereafter become effective in accordance with Section 8(a) of the Securities Act of 1933 or until the registration statement shall become effective on such date as the Commission, acting pursuant to said Section 8(a), may determine.

GENERAL INSTRUCTIONS

A. Use of Form and Place of Filing

1. A "small business issuer," defined in *Rule 405* of the Securities Act of 1933 (the "Securities Act") may use this form to register securities to be sold for cash. See also *Item 10(a) of Regulation S-B* (17 CFR 228.10 et seq.)

2. Offerings on Form SB-2 shall be filed in the Washington, D.C. office.

3. If the small business issuer is a reporting company or a holding company of a bank (see the definition of "bank" in section 12(i) of the Exchange Act), it should file the registration statement in the Commission's Washington, D.C. headquarters.

B. General Requirements

1. Issuers registering securities for the first time should be aware of Form SR and *Rule 463* under the Securities Act concerning sales of registered securities and the use of proceeds. First time issuers also should be aware of Exchange Act Rule 15c2-8 (§ 240.15c2-8) which requires broker dealers to deliver a prospectus 48 hours before a sale of securities can be confirmed.

2. Issuers engaged in real estate, oil and gas or mining activities should consult the Industry Guides in *Item 801 of Regulation S-K* (17 CFR 229.801). Real estate companies also should refer to Item 13 [Investment Policies of Registrant], Item 14 [Description of Real Estate], and Item 15 [Operating Data] of Form S-11 (17 CFR 239.18).

3. If the issuer is not organized under the laws of any of the states of or the United States of America, it shall at the time of filing this registration statement, file with the Commission a written irrevocable consent and power of attorney on Form F-X [§ 239.42]. Any change to the name or address of the agent for service of the issuer shall be communicated promptly to the Commission through amendment of the requisite form and referencing the file number of the registration statement.

C. Registration of Additional Securities

With respect to the registration of additional securities for an offering pursuant to *Rule 462(b)* under the Securities Act, the registrant may file a registration statement consisting only of the following: the facing page; a statement that the contents of the earlier registration statement, identified by file number, are incorporated by reference; required opinions and consents; the signature page; and any price-related information omitted from the earlier registration statement in reliance on *Rule 430A* that the registrant chooses to include in the new registration statement. The information contained in such a *Rule 462(b)* registration statement shall be deemed to be a part of the earlier registration statement as of the date of effectiveness of the Rule 462(b) registration statement. Any opinion or consent required in the Rule 462(b) registration statement may be incorporated by reference from the earlier registration statement with respect to the offering, if: (i) such opinion or consent expressly provides for such incorporation; and (ii) such opinion relates to the securities registered pursuant to Rule 462(b). *See Rule 411(c)* and *Rule 439(b)* under the Securities Act.

PART I—INFORMATION REQUIRED IN PROSPECTUS

Item 1. Front of Registration Statement and Outside Front Cover of Prospectus

Furnish the information required by *Item 501 of Regulation S-B.*

Item 2. Inside Front and Outside Back Cover Pages of Prospectus

Furnish the information required by *Item 502 of Regulation S-B.*

Item 3. Summary Information and Risk Factors

Furnish the information required by *Item 503 of Regulation S-B.*

Item 4. Use of Proceeds

Furnish the information required by *Item 504 of Regulation S-B.*

Item 5. Determination of Offering Price

Furnish the information required by *Item 505 of Regulation S-B.*

Item 6. Dilution

Furnish the information required by *Item 506 of Regulation S-B.*

Item 7. Selling Security Holders

Furnish the information required by *Item 507 of Regulation S-B.*

Item 8. Plan of Distribution

Furnish the information required by *Item 508 of Regulation S-B.*

Item 9. Legal Proceedings

Furnish the information required by *Item 103 of Regulation S-B.*

Item 10. Directors, Executive Officers, Promoters and Control Persons

Furnish the information required by *Item 401 of Regulation S-B.*

Item 11. Security Ownership of Certain Beneficial Owners and Management

Furnish the information required by *Item 403 of Regulation S-B.*

Item 12. Description of Securities

Furnish the information required by *Item 202 of Regulation S-B.*

Item 13. Interest of Named Experts and Counsel

Furnish the information required by *Item 509 of Regulation S-B.*

Item 14. Disclosure of Commission Position of Indemnification for Securities Act Liabilities

Furnish the information required by *Item 510 of Regulation S-B.*

Item 15. Organization Within Last Five Years

Furnish the information required by *Item 404 of Regulation S-B.*

Item 16. Description of Business

Furnish the information required by *Item 101 of Regulation S-B.*

Item 17. Management's Discussion and Analysis or Plan of Operation

Furnish the information required by *Item 303 of Regulation S-B.*

Item 18. Description of Property

Furnish the information required by *Item 102 of Regulation S-B.*

Item 19. Certain Relationships and Related Transactions

Furnish the information required by *Item 404 of Regulation S-B.*

Item 20. Market for Common Equity and Related Stockholder Matters

Furnish the information required by *Item 201 of Regulation S-B.*

Item 21. Executive Compensation

Furnish the information required by *Item 402 of Regulation S-B.*

Item 22. Financial Statements

Furnish the information required by *Item 310 of Regulation S-B.*

Item 23. Changes In and Disagreements With Accountants on Accounting and Financial Disclosure

Furnish the information required by *Item 304 of Regulation S-B.*

PART II—INFORMATION NOT REQUIRED IN PROSPECTUS

Item 24. Indemnification of Directors and Officers

Furnish the information required by *Item 702 of Regulation S-B.*

Item 25. Other Expenses of Issuance and Distribution

Furnish the information required by *Item 511 of Regulation S-B.*

Item 26. Recent Sales of Unregistered Securities

Furnish the information required by *Item 701 of Regulation S-B.*

Item 27. Exhibits

Furnish the information required by *Item 601 of Regulation S-B.*

Item 28. Undertakings

Furnish the information required by *Item 512 of Regulation S-B.*

SIGNATURES

In accordance with the requirements of the Securities Act of 1933, the registrant certifies that it has reasonable grounds to believe that it meets all of the requirements of filing on Form SB-2 and authorized this registration statement to be signed on its behalf by the undersigned, in the City of _____ State   of   _____   on _____, 19_____

(Registrant)_____

By (Signatures and Title)_____

In accordance with the requirements of the Securities Act of 1933, this registration statement was signed by the following persons in the capacities and on the dates stated:

(Signature)_____

(Title)_____

(Date)_____

Instructions for signatures

1. Who must sign: the small business issuer, its principal executive officer or officers, its principal financial officer, its controller or principal accounting officer and at least the majority of

the board of directors or persons performing similar functions. If the issuer is a limited partnership then the general partner and a majority of its board of directors if a corporation.

2. Beneath each signature, type or print the name of each signatory. Any person who occupies more than one of the specified positions shall indicate each capacity in which he or she signs the registration statement. *See Rule 402 of Regulation C* concerning manual signatures and *Item 601 of Regulation S-B* concerning signatures by powers of attorney.

FORM 1-A

UNITED STATES SECURITIES AND EXCHANGE COMMISSION

Washington, D.C. 20549

FORM 1-A

REGULATION A OFFERING STATEMENT UNDER THE SECURITIES ACT OF 1933

. . . .

(Exact name of issuer as specified in its charter)

. . . .

(State or other jurisdiction of incorporation or organization)

. . . .

(Address, including zip code, and telephone number,
including area code of issuer's principal executive offices)

. . . .

(Name, address, including zip code, and telephone number,
including area code, of agent for service)

. . . .

| (Primary standard Industrial Classification Code Number) | (I.R.S. Employer Identification Number) |

The following delaying notation is optional, but see Rule 252(g) before omitting it:

This offering statement shall only be qualified upon order of the Commission, unless a subsequent amendment is filed indicating the intention to become qualified by operation of the terms of Regulation A.

GENERAL INSTRUCTIONS

I. Eligibility Requirements for Use of Form 1-A

This form is to be used for securities offerings made pursuant to Regulation A, 17 CFR 230.251 *et seq.* Careful attention should be directed to the terms, conditions and requirements of the regulation, especially Rule 251, inasmuch as the exemption is not available to all issuers or to every type of securities transaction. Further, the aggregate offering amount of securities which may be sold in any 12 month period is strictly limited to $5 million.

II. Preparation and Filing of the Offering Statement

An offering statement shall be prepared by all persons seeking exemption pursuant to the provisions of Regulation A. Parts I, II and III shall be addressed by all issuers. Part II of the form which relates to the content of the required offering circular provides several alternate formats depending upon the nature and/or business of the issuer; only one format needs to be followed and provided in the offering statement. General information regarding the preparation, format, content of, and where to file the offering statement is contained in Rule 252. Requirements relating to the offering circular are contained in Rules 253 and 255. The offering statement may be printed, mimeographed, lithographed, or typewritten or prepared by any similar process which will result in clearly legible copies.

III. Supplemental Information

The following information shall be furnished to the Commission as supplemental information:

(1) A statement as to whether or not the amount of compensation to be allowed or paid to the underwriter has been cleared with the NASD.

(2) Any engineering, management or similar report referenced in the offering circular.

(3) Such other information as requested by the staff in support of statements, representations and other assertions contained in the offering statement.

PART I—NOTIFICATION

The information requested shall be provided in the order which follows specifying each item number; the text of each item as presented in this form may be omitted. All items shall be addressed and negative responses should be included.

ITEM 1. Significant Parties

List the full names and business and residential addresses, as applicable, for the following persons:

(a) the issuer's directors;

(b) the issuer's officers;

(c) the issuer's general partners;

(d) record owners of 5 percent or more of any class of the issuer's equity securities;

(e) beneficial owners of 5 percent or more of any class of the issuer's equity securities;

(f) promoters of the issuer;

(g) affiliates of the issuer;

(h) counsel to the issuer with respect to the proposed offering;

(i) each underwriter with respect to the proposed offering;

(j) the underwriter's directors;

(k) the underwriter's officers;

(l) the underwriter's general partners; and

(m) counsel to the underwriter.

ITEM 2. Application of Rule 262

(a) State whether any of the persons identified in response to Item 1 are subject to any of the disqualification provisions set forth in Rule 262.

(b) If any such person is subject to these provisions, provide a full description including pertinent names, dates and other details, as well as whether or not an application has been made pursuant to Rule 262 for a waiver of such disqualification and whether or not such application has been granted or denied.

ITEM 3. Affiliate Sales

If any part of the proposed offering involves the resale of securities by affiliates of the issuer, confirm that the following description does not apply to the issuer.

The issuer has not had a net income from operations of the character in which the issuer intends to engage for at least one of its last two fiscal years.

ITEM 4. Jurisdictions in Which Securities Are to be Offered

(a) List the jurisdiction in which the securities are to be offered by underwriters, dealers or salespersons.

(b) List the jurisdictions in which the securities are to be offered other than by underwriters, dealers or salesmen and state the method by which such securities are to be offered.

ITEM 5. Unregistered Securities Issued or Sold Within One Year

(a) As to any unregistered securities issued by the issuer or any of its predecessors or affiliated issuers within one year prior to the filing of this Form 1-A, state:

(1) the name of such issuer;

(2) the title and amount of securities issued;

(3) the aggregate offering price or other consideration for which they were issued and the basis for computing the amount thereof;

(4) the names and identities of the persons to whom the securities were issued.

(b) As to any unregistered securities of the issuer or any of its predecessors or affiliated issuers which were sold within one year prior to the filing of this Form 1-A by or for the account of any person who at the time was a director, officer, promoter or principal security holder of the issuer of such securities, or was an underwriter of any securities of such issuer, furnish the information specified in subsections (1) through (4) of paragraph (a).

(c) Indicate the section of the Securities Act or Commission rule or regulation relied upon for exemption from the registration requirements of such Act and state briefly the facts relied upon for such exemption.

ITEM 6. Other Present or Proposed Offerings

State whether or not the issuer or any of its affiliates is currently offering or contemplating the offering of any securities in addition to those covered by this Form 1-A. If so, describe fully the present or proposed offering.

ITEM 7. Marketing Arrangements

(a) Briefly describe any arrangement known to the issuer or to any person named in response to Item 1 above or to any selling securityholder in the offering covered by this Form 1-A for any of the following purposes:

(1) To limit or restrict the sale of other securities of the same class as those to be offered for the period of distribution;

(2) To stabilize the market for any of the securities to be offered;

(3) For withholding commissions, or otherwise to hold each underwriter or dealer responsible for the distribution of its participation.

(b) Identify any underwriter that intends to confirm sales to any accounts over which it exercises discretionary authority and include an estimate of the amount of securities so intended to be confirmed.

ITEM 8. Relationship with Issuer of Experts Named in Offering Statement

If any expert named in the offering statement as having prepared or certified any part thereof was employed for such purpose on a contingent basis or, at the time of such preparation or certification or at any time thereafter, had a material interest in the issuer or any of its parents or subsidiaries or was connected with the issuer or any of its subsidiaries as a promoter, underwriter, voting trustee, director, officer or employee furnish a brief statement of the nature of such contingent basis, interest or connection.

ITEM 9. Use of a Solicitation of Interest Document

Indicate whether or not a written document or broadcast script authorized by Rule 254 was used prior to the filing of this notification. If so, indicate the date(s) of such use.

PART II—OFFERING CIRCULAR

Financial Statement requirements, regardless of the applicable disclosure model, are specified in Part F/S of this Form 1-A.

The Commission encourages the use of management's projections of future economic performance that have a reasonable basis and are presented in an appropriate format. See 17 CFR 228.10(e), 17 CFR 229.10. The Commission's safe harbor provision relative to projections is contained in Rule 175, 17 CFR 230.175.

The narrative disclosure contents of offering circulars are specified as follows:

A: For all corporate issuers—the information required by Model A of this Part II of Form 1-A.

B: For all other issuers and for any issuer that so chooses—the information required by either Part I of Form SB-2, 17 CFR 239.10, except for the financial statements called for there, or Model B of this Part II of Form 1-A. Offering circulars prepared pursuant to this instruction need not follow the order of the items or other requirements of the disclosure form. Such information shall not, however, be set forth in such a fashion as to obscure any of the required information or any information necessary to keep the required information from being incomplete or misleading. Information requested to be presented in a specified tabular format shall be given in substantially the tabular form specified in the item.

OFFERING CIRCULAR MODEL A

GENERAL INSTRUCTIONS:

Each question in each paragraph of this part shall be responded to; and each question and any notes, but not any instructions thereto, shall be restated in its entirety. If the question or series of questions is inapplicable, so state. If the space provided in the format is insufficient, additional space should be created by cutting and pasting the format to add more lines.

Be very careful and precise in answering all questions. Give full and complete answers so that they are not misleading under the circumstances involved. Do not discuss any future performance or other anticipated event unless you have a reasonable basis to believe that it will actually occur within the foreseeable future. If any answer requiring significant information is materially inaccurate, incomplete or misleading, the Company, its management and principal shareholders may have liability to investors. The selling agents should exercise appropriate diligence to determine that no such inaccuracy or incompleteness has occurred, or they may be liable.

COVER PAGE

. . . .

(Exact name of Company as set forth in Charter)

Type of securities offered: . . . .

Maximum number of securities offered:. . . . .

Minimum number of securities offered: . . . .

Price per security: $ . . . .

Total proceeds: If maximum sold: $ . . . . If minimum sold: $ . . . .

(See Questions 9 and 10)

Is a commissioned selling agent selling the securities in this offering?

    [ ] Yes [ ] No

If yes, what percent is commission of price to public? . . . .%.

Is there other compensation to selling agent(s)?

    [ ] Yes [ ] No

Is there a finder's fee or similar payment to any person?

    [ ] Yes [ ] No (See Question No. 22)

Is there an escrow of proceeds until minimum is obtained?

[ ] Yes [ ] No (See Question No. 26)

Is this offering limited to members of a special group, such as employees of the Company or individuals?

[ ] Yes [ ] No (See Question No. 25)

Is transfer of the securities restricted?

[ ] Yes [ ] No (See Question No. 25)

INVESTMENT IN SMALL BUSINESSES INVOLVES A HIGH DEGREE OF RISK, AND INVESTORS SHOULD NOT INVEST ANY FUNDS IN THIS OFFERING UNLESS THEY CAN AFFORD TO LOSE THEIR ENTIRE INVESTMENT. SEE QUESTION NO. 2 FOR THE RISK FACTORS THAT MANAGEMENT BELIEVES PRESENT THE MOST SUBSTANTIAL RISKS TO AN INVESTOR IN THIS OFFERING.

IN MAKING AN INVESTMENT DECISION INVESTORS MUST RELY ON THEIR OWN EXAMINATION OF THE ISSUER AND THE TERMS OF THE OFFERING, INCLUDING THE MERITS AND RISKS INVOLVED. THESE SECURITIES HAVE NOT BEEN RECOMMENDED OR APPROVED BY ANY FEDERAL OR STATE SECURITIES COMMISSION OR REGULATORY AUTHORITY. FURTHERMORE, THESE AUTHORITIES HAVE NOT PASSED UPON THE ACCURACY OR ADEQUACY OF THIS DOCUMENT. ANY REPRESENTATION TO THE CONTRARY IS A CRIMINAL OFFENSE.

THE U.S. SECURITIES AND EXCHANGE COMMISSION DOES NOT PASS UPON THE MERITS OF ANY SECURITIES OFFERED OR THE TERMS OF THE OFFERING, NOR DOES IT PASS UPON THE ACCURACY OR COMPLETENESS OF ANY OFFERING CIRCULAR OR SELLING LITERATURE. THESE SECURITIES ARE OFFERED UNDER AN EXEMPTION FROM REGISTRATION; HOWEVER, THE COMMISSION HAS NOT MADE AN INDEPENDENT DETERMINATION THAT THESE SECURITIES ARE EXEMPT FROM REGISTRATION.

This Company:

[ ] Has never conducted operations.

[ ] Is in the development stage.

[ ] Is currently conducting operations.

[ ] Has shown a profit in the last fiscal year.

[ ] Other (Specify): ....

(Check at least one, as appropriate)

This offering has been registered for offer and sale in the following states:

State	State File No.	Effective Date
....		
....		
....		

INSTRUCTION: The Cover Page of the Offering Circular is a summary of certain essential information and should be kept on one page if at all possible. For purposes of characterizing the Company on the cover page, the term "development stage" has the same meaning as that set forth in Statement of Financial Accounting Standards No. 7 (June 1, 1975).

TABLE OF CONTENTS

THIS OFFERING CIRCULAR CONTAINS ALL OF THE REPRESENTATIONS BY THE COMPANY CONCERNING THIS OFFERING, AND NO PERSON SHALL MAKE DIFFERENT OR BROADER STATEMENTS THAN THOSE CONTAINED HEREIN. INVESTORS ARE CAUTIONED NOT TO RELY UPON ANY INFORMATION NOT EXPRESSLY SET FORTH IN THIS OFFERING CIRCULAR.

This Offering Circular, together with Financial Statements and other Attachments, consists of a total of . . . . pages.

THE COMPANY

1. Exact corporate name: . . . .

State and date of incorporation: . . . .

Street address of principal office:

. . . .

Company Telephone Number: ( ) . . . .

Fiscal year: . . . .

(month)   (day)

Person(s) to contact at Company with respect to offering:

. . . .

Telephone Number (if different from above):

( ) . . . .

RISK FACTORS

2. List in the order of importance the factors which the Company considers to be the most substantial risks to an investor in this offering in view of all facts and circumstances or which otherwise make the offering one of high risk or speculative (i.e., those factors which constitute the greatest threat that the investment will be lost in whole or in part, or not provide an adequate return).

(1) . . . .

(2) . . . .

(3) . . . .

(4) . . . .

(5) . . . .

(6) . . . .

(7) . . . .

(8) . . . .

(9) . . . .

(10) . . . .

(11) . . . .

(12) . . . .

(13) . . . .

(14) . . . .

(15) . . . .

(16) . . . .

Note: In addition to the above risks, businesses are often subject to risks not foreseen or fully appreciated by management. In reviewing this Offering Circular potential investors should keep in mind other possible risks that could be important.

INSTRUCTION: The Company should avoid generalized statements and include only those factors which are unique to the Company. No specific number of risk factors is required to be identified. If more than 16 significant risk factors exist, add additional lines and number as appropriate. Risk factors may be due to such matters as cash flow and liquidity problems, inexperience of management in managing a business in the particular industry, dependence of the Company on an unproven product, absence of an existing market for the product (even though management may believe a need exists), absence of an operating history of the Company, absence of profitable operations in recent periods, an erratic financial history, the financial position of the Company, the nature of the business in which the Company is engaged or proposes to engage, conflicts of interest with management, arbitrary establishment of offering price, reliance on the efforts of a single individual, or absence of a trading market if a trading market is not expected to develop. Cross references should be made to the Questions where details of the risks are described.

BUSINESS AND PROPERTIES

3. With respect to the business of the Company and its properties:

(a) Describe in detail *what* business the Company does and proposes to do, including what products or goods are or will be produced or services that are or will be rendered.

(b) Describe *how* these products or services are to be produced or rendered and how and when the Company intends to carry out its activities. If the Company plans to offer a new product(s), state the present stage of development, including whether or not a working proto-type(s) is in existence. Indicate if completion of development of the product would require a material amount of the resources of the Company, and the estimated amount. If the Company is or is expected to be dependent upon one or a limited number of suppliers for essential raw materials, energy or other items, describe. Describe any major existing supply contracts.

(c) Describe the industry in which the Company is selling or expects to sell its products or services and, where applicable, any recognized trends within that industry. Describe that part of the industry and the geographic area in which the business competes or will compete.

Indicate whether competition is or is expected to be by price, service, or other basis. Indicate (by attached table if appropriate) the current or anticipated prices or price ranges for the Company's products or services, or the formula for determining prices, and how these prices compare with those of competitiors' products or services, including a description of any variations in product or service features. Name the principal competitors that the Company has or expects to have in its area of competition. Indicate the relative size and financial and market strengths of the Company's competitors in the area of competition in which the Company is or will be operating. State why the Company believes it can effectively compete with these and other companies in its area of competition.

Note: Because this Offering Circular focuses primarily on details concerning the Company rather than the industry in which the Company operates or will operate, potential investors may wish to conduct their own separate investigation of the Company's industry to obtain broader insight in assessing the Company's prospects.

(d) Describe specifically the marketing strategies the Company is employing or will employ in penetrating its market or in developing a new market. Set forth in response to Question 4 below the timing and size of the results of this effort which will be necessary in order for the Company to be profitable. Indicate how and by whom its products or services are or will be marketed (such as by advertising, personal contact by sales representatives, etc.), how its marketing structure operates or will operate and the basis of its marketing approach, including any market studies. Name any customers that account for, or based upon existing orders will account for a major portion (20% or more) of the Company's sales. Describe any major existing sales contracts.

(e) State the backlog of written firm orders for products and/or services as of a recent date (within the last 90 days) and compare it with the backlog of a year ago from that date.

As of:. . . . ./. . . . ./. . . . . $. . . . .
    (a recent date)
As of:. . . . ./. . . . ./. . . . . $. . . . .
    (one year earlier)

Explain the reason for significant variations between the two figures, if any. Indicate what types and amounts of orders are included in the backlog figures. State the size of typical orders. if the Company's sales are seasonal or cyclical, explain.

(f) State the number of the Company's present employees and the number of employees it anticipates it will have within the next 12 months. Also, indicate the number by type of employee (i.e., clerical, operations, administrative, etc.) the Company will use, whether or not any of them are subject to collective bargaining agreements, and the expiration date(s) of any collective bargaining agreement(s). If the Company's employees are on strike, or have been in the past three years, or are threatening to strike, describe the dispute. Indicate any supplemental benefits or incentive arrangements the Company has or will have with its employees.

(g) Describe generally the principal properties (such as real estate, plant and equipment, patents, etc.) that the Company owns, indicating also what properties it leases and a summary of the terms under those leases, including the amount of payments, expiration dates and the terms of any renewal options. Indicate what properties the Company intends to acquire in the immediate future, the cost of such acquisitions and the sources of financing it expects to use in obtaining these properties, whether by purchase, lease or otherwise.

(h) Indicate the extent to which the Company's operations depend or are expected to depend upon patents, copyrights, trade secrets, know-how or other proprietary information and the steps undertaken to secure and protect this intellectual property, including any use of confidentiality agreements, covenants-not-to-compete and the like. Summarize the principal terms and expiration dates of any significant license agreements. Indicate the amounts expended by the Company for research and development during the last fiscal year, the amount expected to be spent this year and what percentage of revenues research and development expenditures were for the last fiscal year.

(i) If the Company's business, products, or properties are subject to material regulation (including environmental regulation) by federal, state, or local governmental agencies, indicate the nature and extent of regulation and its effects or potential effects upon the Company.

(j) State the names of any subsidiaries of the Company, their business purposes and ownership, and indicate which are included in the Financial Statements attached hereto. If not included, or if included but not consolidated, please explain.

(k) Summarize the material events in the development of the Company (including any material mergers or acquisitions) during the past five years, or for whatever lesser period the Company has been in existence. Discuss any pending or anticipated mergers, acquisitions, spin-offs or recapitalizations. If the Company has recently undergone a stock split, stock dividend or recapitalization in anticipation of this offering, describe (and adjust historical per share figures elsewhere in this Offering Circular accordingly).

4.(a) If the Company was not profitable during its last fiscal year, list below in chronological order the events which in management's opinion must or should occur or the milestones which in management's opinion the Company must or should reach in order for the Company to become profitable, and indicate the expected manner of occurrence or the expected method by which the Company will achieve the milestones.

	Event or Milestone	Expected manner of occurrence or method of achievement	Date or number of months after receipt of proceeds when should be accomplished
(1)	_____	_____	_____
	_____	_____	
	_____	_____	
	_____	_____	
	_____	_____	
	_____	_____	
(2)	_____	_____	_____
	_____	_____	
	_____	_____	
	_____	_____	
	_____	_____	
	_____	_____	
(3)	_____	_____	_____
	_____	_____	
	_____	_____	
	_____	_____	
	_____	_____	
	_____	_____	
(4)	_____	_____	_____
	_____	_____	
	_____	_____	
	_____	_____	
	_____	_____	
(5)	_____	_____	_____
	_____	_____	
	_____	_____	
	_____	_____	

Event or Milestone	Expected manner of occurrence or method of achievement	Date or number of months after receipt of proceeds when should be accomplished
_____	_____	
_____	_____	

(b) State the probable consequences to the Company of delays in achieving each of the events or milestones within the above time schedule, and particularly the effect of any delays upon the Company's liquidity in view of the Company's then anticipated level of operating costs. (See Question Nos. 11 and 12)

Note: After reviewing the nature and timing of each event or milestone, potential investors should reflect upon whether achievement of each within the estimated time frame is realistic and should assess the consequences of delays or failure of achievement in making an investment decision.

INSTRUCTION: The inquiries under Business and Properties elicit information concerning the nature of the business of the Company and its properties. Make clear what aspects of the business are presently in operation and what aspects are planned to be in operation in the future. The description of principal properties should provide information which will reasonably inform investors as to the suitability, adequacy, productive capacity and extent of utilization of the facilities used in the enterprise. Detailed descriptions of the physical characteristics of the individual properties or legal descriptions by metes and bounds are not required and should not be given.

As to Question 4, if more than five events or milestones exist, add additional lines as necessary. A "milestone" is a significant point in the Company's development or an obstacle which the Company must overcome in order to become profitable.

OFFERING PRICE FACTORS

If the securities offered are common stock, or are exercisable for or convertible into common stock, the following factors may be relevant to the price at which the securities are being offered.

5. What were net, after-tax earnings for the last fiscal year?

Total $. . . . . ($. . . . . per share)

6. If the Company had profits, show offering price as a multiple of earnings. Adjust to reflect for any stock splits or recapitalizations, and use conversion or exercise price in lieu of offering price, if applicable.

$$\frac{\text{Offering Price Per Share}}{\text{Net After-Tax Earnings Last Year Per Share}} = \underline{\qquad\qquad} \text{(price/earnings multiple)}$$

7.(a) what is the net tangible book value of the Company? (If deficit, show in parenthesis.) For this purpose, net tangible book value means total assets (exclusive of copyrights, patents, goodwill, research and development costs and similar intangible items) minus total liabilities.

$. . . . . ($. . . . . per share)

If the net tangible book value per share is substantially less than this offering (or exercise or conversion) price per share, explain the reasons for the variation.

(b) State the dates on which the Company sold or otherwise issued securities during the last 12 months, the amount of such securities sold, the number of persons to whom they were sold, any relationship of such persons to the company at the time of sale, the price at which they were sold and, if not sold for cash, a concise description of the consideration. (Exclude bank debt.)

8.(a) What percentage of the outstanding shares of the Company will the investors in this offering have? Assume exercise of outstanding options, warrants or rights and conversion of convertible securities, if the respective exercise or conversion prices are at or less than the offering price. Also assume exercise of any options, warrants or rights and conversions of any convertible securities offered in this offering.)

If the maximum is sold: . . . .%

If the minimum is sold: . . . .%

(b) What post-offering value is management implicitly attributing to the entire Company by establishing the price per security set forth on the cover page (or exercise or conversion price if common stock is not offered)? (Total outstanding shares after offering times offering price, or exercise or conversion price if common stock is not offered.)

If maximum is sold: $ . . . .*

If minimum is sold: $ . . . .*

(For above purposes, assume outstanding options are exercised in determining "shares" if the exercise prices are at or less than the offering price. All convertible securities, including outstanding convertible securities, shall be assumed converted and any options, warrants or rights in this offering shall be assumed exercised.)

* These values assume that the Company's capital structure would be changed to reflect any conversions of outstanding convertible securities and any use of outstanding securities as payment in the exercise of outstanding options, warrants or rights included in the calculation. The type and amount of convertible or other securities thus eliminated would be: . . . . These values also assume an increase in cash in the Company by the amount of any cash payments that would be made upon cash exercise of options, warrants or rights included in the calculations. The amount of such cash would be: $ . . . .

Note: After reviewing the above, potential investors should consider whether or not the offering price (or exercise or conversion price, if applicable) for the securities is appropriate at the present stage of the Company's development.

INSTRUCTION: Financial information in response to Questions 5, 6 and 7 should be consistent with the Financial Statements. Earnings per share for purposes of Question 5 should be calculated by dividing earnings for the last fiscal year by the weighted average of outstanding shares during that year. No calculations should be shown for periods of less than one year or if earnings are negative or nominal. For purposes of Question 8, the "offering price" of any options, warrants or rights or convertible securities in the offering is the respective exercise or conversion price.

USE OF PROCEEDS

9. (a) The following table sets forth the use of the proceeds from this offering:

	If Minimum Sold		If Maximum Sold	
	Amount	**%**	**Amount**	**%**
Total Proceeds				
	$_____		$_____	
Less: Offering Expenses	100%		100%	
Commissions & Finders Fees				
Legal & Accounting	_____		_____	
Copying & Advertising	_____		_____	
Other (Specify):	_____		_____	
_____	_____		_____	
_____	_____		_____	
Net Proceeds from Offering	_____		_____	

	If Minimum Sold	If Maximum Sold
	Amount %	Amount %
Use of Net Proceeds	_____	_____
	_____	_____
_____	_____	_____
_____	$_____	$_____
_____	_____	_____
_____	_____	_____
_____	_____	_____
_____	$_____	_____
_____	_____	_____
_____	_____	_____
Total Use of Net Proceeds	_____	_____
	_____	_____
	_____	_____
	_____	_____
	_____	_____
	_____	_____
	_____	_____
	_____	_____
	$_____	$_____
	100%	100%

(b) If there is no minimum amount of proceeds that must be raised before the Company may use the proceeds of the offering, describe the order of priority in which the proceeds set forth above in the column "If Maximum Sold" will be used.

Note: After reviewing the portion of the offering allocated to the payment of offering expenses, and to the immediate payment to management and promoters of any fees, reimbursements, past salaries or similar payments, a potential investor should consider whether the remaining portion of his investment, which would be that part available for future development of the Company's business and operations, would be adequate.

10. (a) If material amounts of funds from sources other than this offering are to be used in conjunction with the proceeds from this offering, state the amounts and sources of such other funds, and whether funds are firm or contingent. If contingent, explain.

(b) If any material part of the proceeds is to be used to discharge indebtedness, describe the terms of such indebtedness, including interest rates. If the indebtedness to be discharged was incurred within the current or previous fiscal year, describe the use of proceeds of such indebtedness.

(c) If any material amount of proceeds is to be used to acquire assets, other than in the ordinary course of business, briefly describe and state the cost of the assets and other material terms of the acquisitions. If the assets are to be acquired from officers, directors, employees or principal stockholders of the Company or their associates, give the names of the persons from whom the assets are to be acquired and set forth the cost to the Company, the method followed in determining the cost, and any profit to such persons.

(d) If any amount of the proceeds is to be used to reimburse any officer, director, employee or stockholder for services already rendered, assets previously transferred, or monies loaned or advanced, or otherwise, explain:

11. Indicate whether the Company is having or anticipates having within the next 12 months any cash flow or liquidity problems and whether or not it is in default or in breach of any note, loan, lease or other indebtedness or financing arrangement requiring the Company to make payments. Indicate if a significant amount of the Company's tradepayables have not been paid within the stated trade term. State whether the Company is subject to any unsatisfied judgments, liens or settlement obligations and the amounts thereof. Indicate the Company's plans to resolve any such problems.

12. Indicate whether proceeds from this offering will satisfy the Company's cash requirements for the next 12 months, and whether it will be necessary to raise additional funds. State the source of additional funds, if known.

INSTRUCTION: Use of net proceeds should be stated with a high degree of specificity. Suggested (but not mandatory) categories are: leases, rent, utilities, payroll (by position or type), purchase or lease of specific items of equipment or inventory, payment of notes, accounts payable, etc., marketing or advertising costs, taxes, consulting fees, permits, professional fees, insurance and supplies. Categories will vary depending on the Company's plans. Use of footnotes or other explanation is recommended where appropriate. Footnotes should be used to indicate those items of offering expenses that are estimates. Set forth in separate categories all payments which will be made immediately to the Company's executive officers, directors and promoters, indicating by footnote that these payments will be so made to such persons. If a substantial amount is allocated to working capital, set forth separate sub-categories for use of the funds in the Company's business.

If any substantial portion of the proceeds has not been allocated for particular purposes, a statement to that effect as one of the Use of Net Proceeds categories should be included together with a statement of the amount of proceeds not so allocated and a footnote explaining how the Company expects to employ such funds not so allocated.

CAPITALIZATION

13. Indicate the capitalization of the Company as of the most recent balance sheet date (adjusted to reflect any subsequent stock splits, stock dividends, recapitalizations or refinancings) and as adjusted to reflect the sale of the minimum and maximum amount of securities in this offering and the use of the net proceeds therefrom:

	Amount Outstanding		
	As of:	As Adjusted	
	/ / (date)	Minimum	Maximum
Debt:			
Short-term debt (average interest rate ____%)	$_____	$_____	$_____
Long-term debt (average interest rate ____%)	$_____	$_____	$_____
Total debt	$_____	$_____	$_____
Stockholders equity (deficit):			
Preferred stock - par or stated value (by class of preferred in order of preferences)			
_____	$_____	$_____	$_____

Amount Outstanding

	As of: / / (date)	As Adjusted	
		Minimum	Maximum
_____	$_____	$_____	$_____
_____	$_____	$_____	$_____
Common stock - par or stated value	$_____	$_____	$_____
Additional paid in capital	$_____	$_____	$_____
Retained earnings (deficit)	$_____	$_____	$_____
Total stockholders equity (deficit)	$_____	$_____	$_____
Total Capitalization	$_____	$_____	$_____

Number of preferred shares
authorized to be outstanding:

Class of Preferred	Number of Shares Authorized	Par Value Per Share
_____	_____	$_____
_____	_____	$_____
_____	_____	$_____

Number of common shares authorized: . . . . shares. Par or stated value per share, if any: $ . . . .

Number of common shares reserved to meet conversion requirements or for the issuance upon exercise of options, warrants or rights: . . . . shares.

INSTRUCTION: Capitalization should be shown as of a date no earlier than that of the most recent Financial Statements provided pursuant to Question 46. If the Company has mandatory redeemable preferred stock, include the amount thereof in "long term debt" and so indicate by footnote to that category in the capitalization table.

DESCRIPTION OF SECURITIES

14. The securities being offered hereby are:

[ ] Common Stock

[ ] Preferred or Preference Stock

[ ] Notes or Debentures

[ ] Units of two or more types of securities composed of: . . . .

[ ] Other: . . . .

15. These securities have:

Yes	No	
[ ]	[ ]	Cumulative voting rights
[ ]	[ ]	Other special voting rights
[ ]	[ ]	Preemptive rights to purchase in new issues of shares
[ ]	[ ]	Preference as to dividends or interest
[ ]	[ ]	Preference upon liquidation
[ ]	[ ]	Other special rights or preferences (specify):

Explain:

16. Are the securities convertible? [ ] Yes [ ] No

If so, state conversion price or formula. . . . .

Date when conversion becomes effective: . . ./. . ./. . .

Date when conversion expires: . . ./. . .

17.(a) If securities are notes or other types of debt securities:

(1) What is the interest rate? . . . .%

If interest rate is variable or multiple rates, describe: . . . .

(2) What is the maturity date? . . ./. . ./. . .

If serial maturity dates, describe: . . . .

(3) Is there a mandatory sinking fund?

[ ] Yes [ ] No

Describe:. . . . .

(4) Is there a trust indenture? [ ] Yes [ ] No

Name, address and telephone number of Trustee

(5) Are the securities callable or subject to redemption? [ ] Yes [ ] No

Describe, including redemption prices:. . . . .

(6) Are the securities collateralized by real or personal property?

[ ] Yes [ ] No Describe: . . . .

(7) If these securities are subordinated in right of payment of interest or principal, explain the terms of such subordination.

How much currently outstanding indebtedness of the Company is senior to the securities in right of payment of interest or principal? $ . . . .

How much indebtedness shares in right of payment on an equivalent (pari passu) basis? $ . . . .

How much indebtedness is junior (subordinated) to the securities? $ . . . .

(b) If notes or other types of debt securities are being offered and the Company had earnings during its last fiscal year, show the ratio of earnings to fixed charges on an actual and pro forma basis for that fiscal year. "Earnings" means pretax income from continuing operations plus fixed charges and capitalized interest. "Fixed charges" means interest (including capitalized interest), amortization of debt discount, premium and expense, preferred stock dividend requirements of majority owned subsidiary, and such portion of rental expense as can be demonstrated to be representative of the interest factor in the particular case. The pro forma ratio of earnings to fixed charges should include incremental interest expense as a result of the offering of the notes or other debt securities.

		Last Fiscal Year		
		Actual	Pro Forma	
			Minimum	Maximum
"Earnings"	=	_____	_____	_____
"Fixed Charges"				
If no earnings show "Fixed Charges" only		_____	_____	_____

Note: Care should be exercised in interpreting the significance of the ratio of earnings to fixed charges as a measure of the "coverage" of debt service, as the existence of earnings does not necessarily mean that the Company's liquidity at any given time will permit payment of debt service requirements to be timely made. See Question Nos. 11 and 12. See also the Financial Statements and especially the Statement of Cash Flows.

18. If securities are Preference or Preferred stock:

Are unpaid dividends cumulative? [ ] Yes [ ] No

Are securities callable? [ ] Yes [ ] No

Explain:

Note: Attach to this Offering Circular copies or a summary of the charter, bylaw or contractual provision or document that gives rise to the rights of holders of Preferred or Preference Stock, notes or other securities being offered.

19. If securities are capital stock of any type, indicate restrictions on dividends under loan or other financing arrangements or otherwise:

20. Current amount of assets available for payment of dividends if deficit must be first made up, show deficit in parenthesis): $. . . . .

PLAN OF DISTRIBUTION

21. The selling agents (that is, the persons selling the securities as agent for the Company for a commission or other compensation) in this offering are:

Name:	. . . .	Name:	. . . .
Address:.		Address:	. . . .
Telephone No.( )		Telephone No. ( )	

22. Describe any compensation to selling agents or finders, including cash, securities, contracts or other consideration, in addition to the cash commission set forth as a percent of the offering price on the cover page of this Offering Circular. Also indicate whether the Company will indemnify the selling agents or finders against liabilities under the securities laws. ("Finders" are persons who for compensation act as intermediaries in obtaining selling agents or other-wise making introductions in furtherance of this offering.)

23. Describe any material relationships between any of the selling agents or finders and the Company or its management.

Note: After reviewing the amount of compensation to the selling agents or finders for selling the securities, and the nature of any relationship between the selling agents or finders and the Company, a potential investor should assess the extent to which it may be inappropriate to rely upon any recommendation by the selling agents or finders to buy the securities.

24. If this offering is not being made through selling agents, the names of persons at the Company through which this offering is being made:

Name:	. . . .	Name:	. . . .
Address:.		Address:	. . . .
Telephone No.( )		Telephone No. ( )	

25. If this offering is limited to a special group, such as employees of the Company, or is limited to a certain number of individuals (as required to qualify under Subchapter S of the Internal Revenue Code) or is subject to any other limitations, describe the limitations and any restrictions on resale that apply:

Will the certificates bear a legend notifying holders of such restrictions?

[ ] Yes [ ] No

26. (a) Name, address and telephone number of independent bank or savings and loan association or other similar depository institution acting as escrow agent if proceeds are escrowed until minimum proceeds are raised:

(b) Date at which funds will be returned by escrow agent if minimum proceeds are not raised:

Will interest on proceeds during escrow period be paid to investors? [ ] Yes [ ] No

27. Explain the nature of any resale restrictions on presently outstanding shares, and when those restrictions will terminate, if this can be determined:

Note: Equity investors should be aware that unless the Company is able to complete a further public offering or the Company is able to be sold for cash or merged with a public company that their investment in the Company may be illiquid indefinitely.

DIVIDENDS, DISTRIBUTIONS AND REDEMPTIONS

28. If the Company has within the last five years paid dividends, made distributions upon its stock or redeemed any securities, explain how much and when:

OFFICERS AND KEY PERSONNEL OF THE COMPANY

29. Chief Executive Officer: Title: . . . .

Name: . . . .   Age: . . . .

Office Street Address: Telephone No.:

. . . . ( )   -

Name of employers, titles and dates of positions held during past five years with an indication of job responsibilities.

Education (degrees, schools, and dates):

Also a Director of the Company [ ] Yes [ ] No

Indicate amount of time to be spent on Company matters if less than full time:

30. Chief Operating Officer: Title: . . . .

Name: . . . .   Age: . . . .

Office Street Address: Telephone No.:

. . . . ( )   -

Names of employers, titles and dates of positions held during past five years with an indication of job responsibilities.

Education (degrees, schools, and dates): . . . .

Also a Director of the Company? [ ] Yes [ ] No

Indicate amount of time to be spent on Company matters if less than full time:

31. Chief Financial Officer: Title: . . . .

Name: . . . .   Age: . . . .

Office Street Address: Telephone No.:

. . . . ( )   -

Names of employers, titles and dates of positions held during past five years with an indication of job responsibilities.

Education (degrees, schools, and dates): . . . .

Also a Director of the Company? [ ] Yes [ ] No

Indicate amount of time to be spent on Company matters if less than full time:

32. Other Key Personnel:

(A) Name: . . . .   Age: . . . .

Title: . . . .

Office Street Address: Telephone No.:
                                               ( )   -

Names of employers, titles and dates of positions held during past five years with an indication of job responsibilities.

Education (degrees, schools, and dates): . . . .

Also a Director of the Company? [ ] Yes [ ] No

Indicate amount of time to be spent on Company matters if less than full time:

(B) Name: ....   Age: ....
    Title: ....
    Office Street Address: Telephone No.:
    ....( )   -

Names of employers, titles and dates of positions held during past five years with an indication of job responsibilities.

Education (degrees, schools, and dates): ....

Also a Director of the Company? [ ] Yes [ ] No

Indicate amount of time to be spent on Company matters if less than full time:

INSTRUCTION: The term "Chief Executive Officer" means the officer of the Company who has been delegated final authority by the board of directors to direct all aspects of the Company's affairs. The term "Chief Operating Officer" means the officer in charge of the actual day-to-day operations of the Company's business. The term "Chief Financial Officer" means the officer having accounting skills who is primarily in charge of assuring that the Company's financial books and records are properly kept and maintained and financial statements prepared.

The term "key personnel" means persons such as vice presidents, production managers, sales managers, or research scientists and similar persons, who are not included above, but who make or are expected to make significant contributions to the business of the Company, whether as employees, independent contractors, consultants or otherwise.

DIRECTORS OF THE COMPANY

33. Number of Directors:........ If Directors are not elected annually, or are elected under a voting trust or other arrangement, explain:

34. Information concerning outside or other Directors (i.e. those not described above):

(A) Name: ....   Age: ....
    Office Street Address: Telephone No.:
    ....( )   -

Names of employers, titles and dates of positions held during past five years with an indication of job responsibilities.

Education (degrees, schools, and dates): ....

(B) Name: ....   Age: ....
    Office Street Address: Telephone No.:
    ....( )   -

Names of employers, titles and dates of positions held during past five years with an indication of job responsibilities.

Education (degrees, schools, and dates): ....

(C) Name: ....   Age: ....
    Office Street Address: Telephone No.:
    ....( )   -

Names of employers, titles and dates of positions held during past five years with an indication of job responsibilities.

Education (degrees, schools, and dates): ....

35. (a) Have any of the Officers or Directors ever worked for or managed a company (including a separate subsidiary or division of a larger enterprise) in the same business as the Company?

[ ] Yes [ ] No

Explain:

(b) If any of the Officers, Directors or other key personnel have ever worked for or managed a company in the same business or industry as the Company or in a related business or industry, describe what precautions, if any, (including the obtaining of releases or consents from prior employers) have been taken to preclude claims by prior employers for conversion or theft of trade secrets, know-how or other proprietary information.

(c) If the Company has never conducted operations or is otherwise in the development stage, indicate whether any of the Officers or Directors has ever managed any other company in the start-up or development stage and describe the circumstances, including relevant dates.

(d) If any of the Company's key personnel are not employees but are consultants or other independent contractors, state the details of their engagement by the Company.

(e) If the Company has key man life insurance policies on any of its Officers, Directors or key personnel, explain, including the names of the persons insured, the amount of insurance, whether the insurance proceeds are payable to the Company and whether there are arrangements that require the proceeds to be used to redeem securities or pay benefits to the estate of the insured person or a surviving spouse.

36. If a petition under the Bankruptcy Act or any State insolvency law was filed by or against the Company or its Officers, Directors or other key personnel, or a receiver, fiscal agent or similar officer was appointed by a court for the business or property of any such persons, or any partnership in which any of such persons was a general partner at or within the past five years, or any corporation or business association of which any such person was an executive officer at or within the past five years, set forth below the name of such persons, and the nature and date of such actions.

Note: After reviewing the information concerning the background of the Company's Officers, Directors and other key personnel, potential investors should consider whether or not these persons have adequate background and experience to develop and operate this Company and to make it successful. In this regard, the experience and ability of management are often considered the most significant factors in the success of a business.

PRINCIPAL STOCKHOLDERS

37. Principal owners of the Company (those who beneficially own directly or indirectly 10% or more of the common and preferred stock presently outstanding) starting with the largest common stockholder. Include separately all common stock issuable upon conversion of convertible securities (identifying them by asterisk) and show average price per share as if conversion has occurred. Indicate by footnote if the price paid was for a consideration other than cash and the nature of any such consideration.

Class of Shares	Average Price Per Share	No. of Shares Now Held	% of Total	No. of Shares Held After Offering if All Securities Sold	% of Total

Name:
_____   _____   _____   _____   _____   _____
_____   _____   _____   _____   _____   _____

Office Street Address:
_____
_____
_____

Telephone No.

(____) ____ - _____

220

Class of Shares	Average Price Per Share	No. of Shares Now Held	% of Total	No. of Shares Held After Offering if All Securities Sold	% of Total

Principal occupation: _____

38. Number of shares beneficially owned by Officers and Directors as a group:

Before offering: . . . . shares (. . . . .% of total outstanding)

After offering: a) Assuming minimum securities sold:

. . . . shares (. . . . .% of total outstanding)

b) Assuming maximum securities sold:

. . . . shares (. . . . .% of total outstanding)

(Assume all options exercised and all convertible securities converted.)

INSTRUCTION: If shares are held by family members, through corporations or partnerships, or otherwise in a manner that would allow a person to direct or control the voting of the shares (or share in such direction or control—as, for example, a co-trustee) they should be included as being "beneficially owned." An explanation of these circumstances should be set forth in a footnote to the "Number of Shares Now Held."

MANAGEMENT RELATIONSHIPS, TRANSACTIONS AND REMUNERATION

39.(a) If any of the Officers, key personnel or principal stockholders are related by blood or marriage, please describe.

(b) If the Company has made loans to or is doing business with any of its Officers, Directors, key personnel or 10% stockholders, or any of their relatives (or any entity controlled directly or indirectly by any such persons) within the last two years, or proposes to do so within the future, explain. (This includes sales or lease of goods, property or services to or from the Company, employment or stock purchase contracts, etc.) State the principal terms of any significant loans, agreements, leases, financing or other arrangements.

(c) If any of the Company's Officers, Directors, key personnel or 10% stockholders has guaranteed or co-signed any of the Company's bank debt or other obligations, including any indebtedness to be retired from the proceeds of this offering, explain and state the amounts involved.

40.(a) List all remuneration by the Company to Officers, Directors and key personnel for the last fiscal year:

	Cash	Other
Chief Executive Officer	$_____	$_____
Chief Operating Officer	_____	_____
Chief Accounting Officer	_____	_____
Key Personnel:		
_____	_____	_____
_____	_____	_____
_____	_____	_____
Others:		
_____	_____	_____
_____	_____	_____

	Cash	**Other**
Total:	$_____	$_____
Directors as a group (number of persons__)	$_____	$_____

(b) If remuneration is expected to change or has been unpaid in prior years, explain:

(c) If any employment agreements exist or are contemplated, describe:

41.(a) Number of shares subject to issuance under presently outstanding stock purchase agreements, stock options, warrants or rights: . . . . shares (% of total shares to be outstanding after the completion of the offering if all securities sold, assuming exercise of options and conversion of convertible securities). Indicate which have been approved by shareholders. State the expiration dates, exercise prices and other basic terms for these securities:

(b) Number of common shares subject to issuance existing stock purchase or option plans but not yet covered by outstanding purchase agreements, options or warrants: . . . . shares.

(c) Describe the extent to which future stock purchase agreements, stock options, warrants or rights must be approved by shareholders.

42. If the business is highly dependent on the services of certain key personnel, describe any arrangement to assure that these persons will remain with the Company and not compete upon any termination:

Note: After reviewing the above, potential investors should consider whether or not the compensation to management and other key personnel directly or indirectly, is reasonable in view of the present stage of the Company's development.

INSTRUCTION: For purposes of Question 39(b), a person directly or indirectly controls an entity if he is part of the group that directs or is able to direct the entity's activities or affairs. A person is typically a member of a control group if he is an officer, director, general partner, trustee or beneficial owner of a 10% or greater interest in the entity. In Question 40, the term "Cash" should indicate salary, bonus, consulting fees, non-accountable expense accounts and the like. The column captioned "Other" should include the value of any options or securities given, any annuity, pension or retirement benefits, bonus or profit-sharing plans, and personal benefits (club memberships, company cars, insurance benefits not generally available to employees, etc.). The nature of these benefits should be explained in a footnote to this column.

LITIGATION

43. Describe any past, pending or threatened litigation or administrative action which has held or may have a material effect upon the Company's business, financial condition, or operations, including any litigation or action involving the Company's Officers, Directors or other key personnel. State the names of the principal parties, the nature and current status of the matters, and amounts involved. Give an evaluation by managment or counsel, to the extent feasible, of the merits of the proceedings or litigation and the potential impact on the Company's business, financial condition, or operations.

FEDERAL TAX ASPECTS

44. If the Company is an S corporation under the Internal Revenue Code of 1986, and it is anticipated that any significant tax benefits will be available to investors in the offering, indicate the nature and amount of such anticipated tax benefits and the material risks of their disallowance. Also, state the name, address and telephone number of any tax advisor that has passed upon these tax benefits. Attach any opinion or description of the tax consequences of an investment in the securities by the tax advisor.

Name of Tax Advisor: . . . .

Address: ....

Telephone No. (   )   -

Note: Potential investors are encouraged to have their own personal tax consultant contact the tax advisor to review details of the tax benefits and the extent that the benefits would be available and advantageous to the particular investor.

MISCELLANEOUS FACTORS

45. Describe any other material factors, either adverse or favorable, that will or could affect the Company or its business (for example, discuss any defaults under major contracts, any breach of bylaw provisions, etc.) or which are necessary to make any other information in this Offering Circular not misleading or incomplete.

FINANCIAL STATEMENTS

46. Provide the financial statements required by Part F/S of this Offering Circular section of Form 1-A.

MANAGEMENT'S DISCUSSION AND ANALYSIS OF CERTAIN RELEVANT FACTORS

47. If the Company's financial statements show losses from operations, explain the causes underlying these losses and what steps the Company has taken or is taking to address these causes.

48. Describe any trends in the Company's historical operating results. Indicate any changes now occurring in the underlying economics of the industry or the Company's business which, in the opinion of Management, will have a significant impact (either favorable or adverse) upon the Company's results of operations within the next 12 months, and give a rough estimate of the probable extent of the impact, if possible.

49. If the Company sells a product or products and has had significant sales during its last fiscal year, state the existing gross margin (net sales less cost of such sales as presented in accordance with generally accepted accounting principles) as a percentage of sales for the last fiscal year: ... .%. What is the anticipated gross margin for next year of operations? Approximately ....%. If this is expected to change, explain. Also, if reasonably current gross margin figures are available for the industry, indicate these figures and the source or sources from which they are obtained.

50. Foreign sales as a percent of total sales for last fiscal year: ....%. Domestic government sales as a percent of total domestic sales for last fiscal year: ....%. Explain the nature of these sales, including any anticipated changes:

OFFERING CIRCULAR MODEL B.

Item 1. Cover Page

The cover page of the offering circular shall include the following information:

(a) Name of the issuer;

(b) The mailing address of the issuer's principal executive offices including the zip code and the issuer's telephone number;

(c) Date of the offering circular;

(d) Description and amount of securities offered (*Note:* this description should include, for example, appropriate disclosure of redemption and conversion features of debt securities);

(e) The statement required by Rule 253;

(f) The table(s) required by Item 2;

(g) The name of the underwriter or underwriters;

(h) Any materials required by the law of any state in which the securities are to be offered;

(i) If applicable, identify material risks in connection with the purchase of the securities; and

(j) Approximate date of commencement of proposed sale to the public.

Instruction: Where the name of the issuer is the same as the name of another well-known company or indicates a line of business in which the issuer is not engaged or is engaged to only a limited extent, a statement should be furnished to that effect. In some circumstances, however, disclosure may not be sufficient, and a change of name may be the only way to cure its misleading character.

Item 2. Distribution Spread

(a) The information called for by the following table shall be given, in substantially the tabular form indicated, on the outside front cover page of the offering circular as to all securities being offered (estimate, if necessary).

	Price to public	Underwriting discount and commissions	Proceeds to issuer or other persons
Per unit	_____	_____	_____
Total	_____	_____	_____

If the securities are to be offered on a best efforts basis, the cover page should set forth the termination date, if any, of the offering, any minimum required sale and any arrangements to place the funds received in an escrow, trust, or similar arrangement. The following tabular presentation of the total maximum and minimum securities to be offered should be combined with the table required above.

	Price to public	Underwriting discount and commissions	Proceeds to issuer or other persons
Total Minimum	_____	_____	_____
Total Maximum	_____	_____	_____

Instructions

1. The term "commissions" shall include all cash, securities, contracts, or anything else of value, paid, to be set aside, disposed of, or understandings with or for the benefit of any other persons in which any underwriter is interested, made in connection with the sale of such security.

2. Only commissions paid by the issuer in cash are to be indicated in the table. Commissions paid by other persons or any form of non-cash compensation shall be briefly identified in a note to the table with a cross-reference to a more complete description elsewhere in the offering circular.

3. Prior to the commencement of sales pursuant to Regulation A, the issuer shall inform the Commission whether or not the amount of compensation to be allowed or paid to the underwriters, as described in the offering statement, has been cleared with the National Association of Securities Dealers, Inc.

4. If the securities are not to be offered for cash, state the basis upon which the offering is to be made.

5. If it is impracticable to state the price to the public, the method by which it is to be determined shall be explained.

(b) Any finder's fees or similar payments shall be disclosed on the cover page with a reference to a more complete discussion in the offering circular. Such disclosure should identify the finder, the nature of the services rendered and the nature of any relationship between the finder and the issuer, its officers, directors, promoters, principal stockholders and underwriters (including any affiliates thereof.)

(c) The amount of the expenses of the offering borne by the issuer, including underwriting expenses to be borne by the issuer, should be disclosed in a footnote to the table.

Item 3. Summary Information, Risk Factors and Dilution

(a) Where appropriate to a clear understanding by investors, there should be set forth in the forepart of the offering circular, under an appropriate caption, a carefully organized series of short, concise paragraphs, summarizing the principal factors which make the offering one of high risk or speculative. *Note:* These factors may be due to such matters as an absence of an operating history of the issuer, an absence of profitable operations in recent periods, an erratic financial history, the financial position of the issuer, the nature of the business in which the issuer is engaged or proposed to engage, conflicts of interest with management, reliance on the efforts of a single individual, or the method of determining the market price where no market currently exists. Issuers should *avoid* generalized statements and include only those factors which are unique to the issuer.

(b) Where there is a material disparity between the public offering price and the effective cash cost to officers, directors, promoters and affiliated persons for shares acquired by them in a transaction during the past three years, or which they have a right to acquire, there should be included a comparison of the public contribution under the proposed public offering and the effective cash contribution of such persons. In such cases, and in other instances where the extent of the dilution makes is appropriate, the following shall be given: (1) the net tangible book value per share before and after the distribution; (2) the amount of the increase in such net tangible book value per share attributable to the cash payment made by purchasers of the shares being offered; and (3) the amount of the immediate dilution from the public offering price which will be absorbed by such purchasers.

Item 4. Plan of Distribution

(a) If the securities are to be offered through underwriters, give the names of the principal underwriters, and state the respective amounts underwritten. Identify each such underwriter having a material relationship to the issuer and state the nature of the relationship. State briefly the nature of the underwriters' obligation to take the securities.

(b) State briefly the discounts and commissions to be allowed or paid to dealers, including all cash, securities, contracts or other consideration to be received by any dealer in connection with the sale of the securities.

(c) Outline briefly the plan of distribution of any securities being issued which are to be offered through the selling efforts of brokers or dealers or otherwise than through underwriters.

(d) If any of the securities are to be offered for the account of security holders, indicate on the cover page the total amount to be offered for their account and include a cross-reference to a fuller discussion elsewhere in the offering circular. Such discussion should identify each selling security holder, state the amount owned by him, the amount offered for his account and the amount to be owned after the offering.

(e) (1) Describe any arrangements for the return of funds to subscribers if all of the securities to be offered are not sold; if there are no such arrangements, so state.

(2) If there will be a material delay in the payment of the proceeds of the offering by the underwriter to the issuer, the salient provisions in this regard and the effects on the issuer should be stated.

Instruction:

Attention is directed to the provisions of Rules 10b-9 [17 CFR § 240.10b-9] and 15c2-4 [17 CFR § 240.15c2-4] under the Securities Exchange Act of 1934. These rules outline, among other things, antifraud provisions concerning the return of funds to subscribers and the transmission of proceeds of an offering to a seller.

Item 5. Use of Proceeds to Issuer

State the principal purposes for which the net proceeds to the issuer from the securities to be offered are intended to be used, and the approximate amount intended to be used for each such purpose.

Instructions:

1. If any substantial portion of the proceeds has not been allocated for particular purposes, a statement to that effect shall be made together with a statement of the amount of proceeds not so allocated and how the registrant expects to employ such funds not so allocated.

2. Include a statement as to the use of the actual proceeds if they are not sufficient to accomplish the purpose set forth and the order of priority in which they will be applied. However, such statement need not be made if the underwriting arrangements are such that, if any securities are sold to the public, it can be reasonably expected that the actual proceeds of the issue will not be substantially less than the estimated aggregate proceeds to the issuer as shown under Item 2.

3. If any material amounts of other funds are to be used in conjunction with the proceeds, state the amounts and sources of such other funds.

4. If any material part of the proceeds is to be used to discharge indebtedness, describe the terms of such indebtedness. If the indebtedness to be discharged was incurred within one year, describe the use of the proceeds of such indebtedness.

5. If any material amount of the proceeds is to be used to acquire assets, otherwise than in the ordinary course of business, briefly describe and state the cost of the assets. If the assets are to be acquired from affiliates of the issuer or their associates, give the names of the persons from whom they are to be acquired and set forth the principle followed in determining the cost to the issuer.

6. The issuer may reserve the right to change the use of proceeds provided that such reservation is due to certain contingencies which are adequately disclosed.

Item 6. Description of Business

(a) Narrative description of business.

(1) Describe the business done and intended to be done by the issuer and its subsidiaries and the general development of the business during the past five years or such shorter period as the issuer may have been in business. Such description should include, but not be limited to, a discussion of the following factors if such factors are material to an understanding of the issuer's business:

(i) The principal products produced and services rendered and the principal markets for and method of distribution of such products and services.

(ii) The status of a product or service if the issuer has made public information about a new product or service which would require the investment of a material amount of the assets of the issuer or is otherwise material.

(iii) The estimated amount spent during each of the last two fiscal years on company-sponsored research and development activities determined in accordance with generally accepted accounting principles. In addition, state the estimated dollar amount spent during each of such years on material customer-sponsored research activities relating to the development of new products, services or techniques or the improvement of existing products, services or techniques.

(iv) The number of persons employed by the issuer, indicating the number employed full time.

(v) The material effects that compliance with Federal, State and Local provisions which have been enacted or adopted regulating the discharge of materials into the environment, may have upon the capital expenditures, earnings and competitive position of the issuer and its subsidiaries. The issuer shall disclose any material estimated capital expenditures for environmental control facilities for the remainder of its current fiscal year and for such further periods as the issuer may deem material.

(2) The issuer should also describe those distinctive or special characteristics of the issuer's operation or industry which may have a material impact upon the issuer's future financial performance. Examples of factors which might be discussed include dependence on one or a few major customers or suppliers (including suppliers of raw materials or financing), existing or probable governmental regulation, material terms of and/or expiration of material labor contracts or patents, trademarks, licenses, franchises, concessions or royalty agreements, unusual competitive conditions in the industry, cyclicality of the industry and anticipated raw material or energy shortages to the extent management may not be able to secure a continuing source of supply.

(3) The following requirement in subparagraph (i) applies only to issuers (including predecessors) which have not received revenue from operations during each of the three fiscal years immediately prior to the filing of the offering statement.

(i) Describe, if formulated, the issuer's plan of operation for the twelve months following the commencement of the proposed offering. If such information is not available, the reasons for its unavailability shall be stated. Disclosure relating to any plan should include, among other things, a statement indicating whether, in the issuer's opinion, the proceeds from the offering will satisfy its cash requirements and whether, in the next six months, it will be necessary to raise additional funds.

(ii) Any engineering, management or similar reports which have been prepared or provided for external use by the issuer or by a principal underwriter in connection with the proposed offering should be furnished to the Commission at the time of filing the offering statement or as soon as practicable thereafter. There should also be furnished at the same time a statement as to the actual or proposed use and distribution of such report or memorandum. Such statement should identify each class of persons who have received or will receive the report or memorandum, and state the number of copies distributed to each such class. If no such report or memorandum has been prepared, the Commission should be so informed in writing at the time the report or memorandum would otherwise have been submitted.

(b) Segment Data. If the issuer is required to include segment information in its financial statements, an appropriate cross-reference shall be included in the description of business.

Item 7. Description of Property

State briefly the location and general character of the principal plants, and other materially important physical properties of the issuer and its subsidiaries. If any such property is not held in fee or is held subject to any major encumbrance, so state and briefly describe how held.

Instruction:

What is required is information essential to an investor's appraisal of the securities being offered. Such information should be furnished as will reasonably inform investors as to the suitability, adequacy, productive capacity and extent of utilization of the facilities used in the enterprise. Detailed descriptions of the physical characteristics of individual properties or legal descriptions by metes and bounds are not required and should not be given.

Item 8. Directors, Executive Officers and Significant Employees

(a) List the names and ages of each of the following persons stating his term of office and any periods during which he has served as such and briefly describe any arrangement or understanding between him and any other person(s) (naming such person(s)) pursuant to which he was or is to be selected to his office or position:

(1) directors;

(2) persons nominated to become directors;

(3) executive officers;

(4) persons chosen to become executive officers;

(5) significant employees.

Instructions:

1. No nominee or person chosen to become a director or person chosen to be an executive officer who has not consented to act as such should be named in response to this item.

2. The term "executive officer" means the president, secretary, treasurer, any vice-president in charge of a principal business function (such as sales, administration, or finance) and any other person who performs similar policy making functions for the issuer.

3. The term "significant employee" means persons such as production managers, sales managers, or research scientists, who are not executive officers, but who make or are expected to make significant contributions to the business of the issuer.

(b) Family relationships. State the nature of any family relationship between any director, executive officer, person nominated or chosen by the issuer to become a director or executive officer or any significant employee.

Instruction:

The term "family relationship" means any relationship by blood, marriage, or adoption, not more remote than first cousin.

(c) Business experience. Give a brief account of the business experience during the past five years of each director, person nominated or chosen to become a director or executive officer, and each significant employee, including his principal occupations and employment during that period and the name and principal business of any corporation or other organization in which such occupations and employment were carried on. When an executive officer or significant employee has been employed by the issuer for less than five years, a brief explanation should be included as to the nature of the responsibilities undertaken by the individual in prior positions to provide adequate disclosure of this prior business experience. What is required is information relating to the level of his professional competence which may include, depending upon the circumstances, such specific information as the size of the operation supervised.

(d) Involvement in certain legal proceedings. Describe any of the following events which occurred during the past five years and which are material to an evaluation of the ability or integrity of any director, person nominated to become a director or executive officer of the issuer.

(1) A petition under the Bankruptcy Act or any State insolvency law was filed by or against, or a receiver, fiscal agent or similar officer was appointed by a court for the business or property of such person, or any partnership in which he was general partner at or within 2 years before the time of such filing, or any corporation or business association of which he was an executive officer at or within two years before the time of such filing;

(2) Such person was convicted in a criminal proceeding (excluding traffic violations and other minor offenses).

Item 9. Remuneration of Directors and Officers

(a) Furnish, in substantially the tabular form indicated, the aggregate annual remuneration of each of the three highest paid persons who are officers or directors as a group during the issuer's last fiscal year. State the number of persons in the group referred to above without naming them.

Name of individual or identity of group	Capacities in remuneration was received	Aggregate remuneration

Instructions:

1. In case of remuneration paid or to be paid otherwise than in cash, if it is impracticable to determine the cash value thereof, state in a note to the table the nature and amount thereof.

2. This item is to be answered on an accrual basis if practicable; if not so answered, state the basis used.

(b) Briefly describe all remuneration payments proposed to be made in the future pursuant to any ongoing plan or arrangement to the individuals and group specified in Item 9(a). The description should include a summary of how each plan operates, any performance formula or measure in effect (or the criteria used to determine payment amounts), the time periods over which the measurements of benefits will be determined, payment schedules, and any recent material amendments to the plan. Information need not be furnished with respect to any group life, health, hospitalization, or medical reimbursement plans which do not discriminate in scope, terms or operation in favor of officers or directors of the registrant and which are available generally to all salaried employees.

Item 10. Security Ownership of Management and Certain Securityholders

(a) Voting securities and principal holders thereof. Furnish the following information, in substantially the tabular form indicated, with respect to voting securities held of record by:

(1) each of the three highest paid persons who are officers and directors of the issuer; *Note—* In the event none of the issuer's officers or directors have received a salary in the past twelve months, this item should be responded to for every officer and director;

(2) all officers and directors as a group;

(3) each shareholder who owns more than 10% of any class of the issuer's securities, including those shares subject to outstanding options.

(1) Title of Class	(2) Name and address of owner	(3) Amount owned before the offering	(4) Amount owned after the offering	(5) Percent of Class

Instruction:

Column (4) need not be responded to if the information would be the same as that appearing under column (3).

(b) If, to the knowledge of the issuer, any other person holds or shares the power to vote or direct the voting of securities described pursuant to subsection (a) above, appropriate disclosure should be made. In addition, if any person other than those named pursuant to subsection (a) holds or shares the power to vote 10% or more of the issuer's voting securities, the information required by the table should be provided with respect to such person.

(c) Non-voting securities and principal holders thereof. Furnish the same information as required in subsection (a) above with respect to securities that are not entitled to vote.

(d) Options, warrants, and rights. Furnish the information required by the table as to options, warrants or rights to purchase securities from the issuer or any of its subsidiaries held by each of the individuals and referred to in subsection (a) above:

Name of holder	Title and amount securities called for by options, warrants or rights	Exercise price	Date of Exercise

Instruction:

Where the total market value of securities called for by all outstanding options, warrants or rights does not exceed $10,000 for any officer, director, or principal shareholder named in answer to this item, or $50,000 for all officers and directors as a group, this item need not be answered with respect to options, warrants or rights held by such person or group. If the issuer cannot ascertain the market value of its securities, the offering price may be used for purposes of this subsection. If, as is the case with offerings of debt securities, the offering price cannot be determined at the time of filing the offering statement, the issuer may utilize any reasonable method of valuation.

(e) List all parents of the issuer, showing the basis of control and as to each parent the percentage of voting securities owned or other basis of control by its immediate parent, if any.

Item 11. Interest of Management and Others in Certain Transactions

Describe briefly any transactions during the previous two years or any presently proposed transactions, to which the issuer or any of its subsidiaries was or is to be a party, in which any of the following persons had or is to have a direct or indirect material interest, naming such person and stating his relationship to the issuer, the nature of his interest in the transaction and, where practicable, the amount of such interest:

(1) Any director or officer of the issuer;

(2) Any nominee for election as a director;

(3) Any principal securityholder named in answer to Item 10(a);

(4) If the issuer was incorporated or organized within the past three years, any promoter of the issuer;

(5) Any relative or spouse of any of the foregoing persons, or any relative of such spouse, who has the same house as such person or who is a director or officer of any parent or subsidiary of the issuer.

Instructions:

1. No information need be given in answer to this item as to any transaction where:

(a) The rates of charges involved in the transaction are determined by competitive bids, or the transaction involves the rendering of services as a common or contract carrier fixed in conformity with law or governmental authority;

(b) The transaction involves services as a bank depositary of funds, transfer agent, registrar, trustee under a trust indenture, or similar services;

(c) The amount involved in the transaction or a series of similar transactions, including all periodic installments in the case of any lease or other agreement providing for periodic payments or installments does not exceed $50,000; or

(d) The interest of the specified person arises solely from the ownership of securities of the issuer and the specified person receives no extra or special benefit not shared on a pro-rata basis by all of the holders of securities of the class.

2. It should be noted that this Item calls for disclosure of indirect as well as direct material interests in transactions. A person who has a position or relationship with a firm, corporation, or other entity which engages in a transaction with the issuer or its subsidiaries may have an indirect interest in such transaction by reason of such position or relationship. However, a person shall be deemed not to have a material indirect interest in a transaction within the meaning of this Item where:

(a) the interest arises only (i) from such person's position as a director of another corporation or organization (other than a partnership) which is a party to the transaction, or (ii) from the direct or indirect ownership by such person and all other persons specified in subparagraphs (1) through (5) above, in the aggregate, of less than a 10 percent equity interest in another person (other than a partnership) which is a party to the transaction, or (iii) from both such position and ownership;

(b) the interest arises only from such person's position as a limited partner in a partnership in which he and all other persons specified in (1) through (5) above had an interest of less than 10 percent; or

(c) the interest of such person arises solely from the holding of an equity interest (including a limited partnership interest but excluding a general partnership interest) or a creditor interest in another person which is a party to the transaction with the issuer or any of its subsidiaries and the transaction is not material to such other person.

3. Include the name of each person whose interest in any transaction is described and the nature of the relationships by reason of which such interest is required to be described. The amount of the interest of any specified person shall be computed without regard to the amount of the profit or loss involved in the transaction. Where it is not practicable to state the approximate amount of the interest, the approximate amount involved in the transaction shall be disclosed.

4. Information should be included as to any material underwriting discounts and commissions upon the sale of securities by the issuer where any of the specified persons was or is to be a principal underwriter or is a controlling person, or member, of a firm which was or is to be a principal underwriter. Information need not be given concerning ordinary management fees paid by underwriters to a managing underwriter pursuant to an agreement among underwriters the parties to which do not include the issuer or its subsidiaries.

5. As to any transaction involving the purchase or sale of assets by or to any issuer or any subsidiary, otherwise than in the ordinary course of business, state the cost of the assets to the purchaser and, if acquired by the seller within two years prior to the transaction, the cost thereof to the seller.

6. Information shall be furnished in answer to this Item with respect to transactions not excluded above which involve remuneration from the issuer or its subsidiaries, directly or indirectly, to any of the specified persons for services in any capacity unless the interest of such persons arises solely from the ownership individually and in the aggregate of less than 10 percent of any class of equity securities of another corporation furnishing the services to the issuer or its subsidiaries.

Item 12. Securities Being Offered

(a) If capital stock is being offered, state the title of the class and furnish the following information:

(1) Outline briefly: (i) dividend rights; (ii) voting rights; (iii) liquidation rights; (iv) preemptive rights; (v) conversion rights; (vi) redemption provisions; (vii) sinking fund provisions; and (viii) liability to further calls or to assessment by the issuer.

(2) Briefly describe potential liabilities imposed on shareholders under state statutes or foreign law, e.g., to laborers, servants or employees of the registrant, unless such disclosure would be immaterial because the financial resources of the registrant are such as to make it unlikely that the liability will ever be imposed.

(b) If debt securities are being offered, outline briefly the following:

(1) Provisions with respect to interest, conversion, maturity, redemption, amortization, sinking fund or retirement.

(2) Provisions with respect to the kind and priority of any lien securing the issue, together with a brief identification of the principal properties subject to such lien.

(3) Provisions restricting the declaration of dividends or requiring the maintenance of any ratio of assets, the creation or maintenance of reserves or the maintenance of properties.

(4) Provisions permitting or restricting the issuance of additional securities, the withdrawal of cash deposited against such issuance, the incurring of additional debt, the release or substitution of assets securing the issue, the modification of the terms of the security, and similar provisions.

Instruction:

In the case of secured debt there should be stated (i) the approximate amount of unbonded property available for use against the issuance of bonds, as of the most recent practicable date, and (ii) whether the securities being issued are to be issued against such property, against the deposit of cash, or otherwise.

(c) If securities described are to be offered pursuant to warrants, rights, or convertible securities, state briefly:

(1) the amount of securities called for by such warrants, convertible securities or rights;

(2) the period during which and the price at which the warrants, convertible securities or rights are exercisable;

(3) the amounts of warrants, convertible securities or rights outstanding; and

(4) any other material terms of such securities.

(d) In the case of any other kind of securities, appropriate information of a comparable character.

PART F/S

The following financial statements of the issuer, or the issuer and its predecessors or any businesses to which the issuer is a successor shall be filed as part of the offering statement and included in the offering circular which is distributed to investors.

Such financial statements shall be prepared in accordance with generally accepted accounting principles (GAAP) in the United States. If the issuer is a Canadian company, a reconciliation to GAAP in the United States shall be filed as part of the financial statements.

Issuers which have audited financial statements because they prepare them for other purposes, shall provide them.

The Commission's Regulation S-X, 17 CFR 210.1 et seq. relating to the form, content of and requirements for financial statements shall not apply to the financial statements required by this part, except that if audited financial statements are filed, the qualifications and reports of an independent auditor shall comply with the requirements of Article 2 of Regulation S-X.

Issuers which are limited partners are required to also file the balance sheets of general partners: (1) if such general partner is a corporation, the balance sheet shall be as of the end of its most recently completed fiscal year; receivables from a parent or affiliate of such general partner (including notes receivable, but excluding trade receivables) should be deductions from shareholders equity of the general partner; where a parent or affiliate has committed to increase or maintain the general partner's capital, there shall also be filed the balance sheet of such parent or affiliate as of the end of its most recently completed fiscal year; (2) if such general partner is a partnership, its balance sheet as of the end of its most recently completed fiscal year; (3) if such general partner is a natural person, the net worth of such general partner(s) based on the estimated fair market value of their assets and liabilities, singly or in the aggregate shall be disclosed in the offering circular, and balance sheets of each of the individual general partners supporting such net worth shall be provided as supplemental information.

(1) **Balance Sheet**—as of a date within 90 days prior to filing the offering statement or such longer time, not exceeding 6 months, as the Commission may permit at the written request of the issuer upon a showing of good cause; for filings made after 90 days subsequent to the issuer's most recent fiscal year, the balance sheet shall be dated as of the end of the most recent fiscal year.

(2) **Statements of income, cash flows, and other stockholders equity**—for each of the 2 fiscal years preceding the date of the most recent balance sheet being filed, and for any interim period between the end of the most recent of such fiscal years and the date of the most recent balance sheet being filed, or for the period of the issuer's existence if less than the period above.

Income statements shall be accompanied by a statement that in the opinion of management all adjustments necessary for a fair statement of results for the interim period have been included. If all such adjustments are of a normal recurring nature, a statement to that effect shall be made. If otherwise, there shall be furnished as supplemental information and not as part of the offering statement, a letter describing in detail the nature and amount of any adjustments other than normal recurring adjustments entering into the determination of results shown.

(3) Financial Statements of Businesses Acquired or to be Acquired.

(a) Financial statements for the periods specified in (c) below should be furnished if any of the following conditions exist:

(i) Consummation of a significant business combination accounted for as a purchase has occurred or is probable (for purposes of this rule, the term "purchase" encompasses the purchase of an interst in a business accounted for by the equity method); or

(ii) Consummation of a significant business combination to be accounted for as a pooling is probable.

(b) A business combination shall be considered significant if a comparison of the most recent annual financial statements of the business acquired or to be acquired and the registrant's most recent annual consolidated financial statements filed at or prior to the date of acquisition indicates that the business would be a significant subsidiary pursuant to the conditions specified in Rule 405 of Regulation C, 17 CFR § 230.405.

(c) (i) The financial statements shall be furnished for the periods up to the date of acquisition, for those periods for which the registrant is required to furnish financial statements.

(ii) These financial statements need not be audited.

(iii) The separate balance sheet of the acquired business is not required when the registrant's most recent balance sheet filed is for a date after the acquisition was consummated.

(iv) If none of the conditions in the definitions of significant subsidiary in Rule 405 exceeds 40%, income statements of the acquired business for only the most recent fiscal year and interim period need be filed, unless such statements are readily available.

(d) If consummation of more than one transaction has occurred or is probable, the tests of significance shall be made using the aggregate impact of the businesses and the required financial statements may be presented on a combined basis, if appropriate.

(e) This paragraph (3) shall not apply to a business which is totally held by the registrant prior to consummation of the transaction.

(4) Pro Forma Financial Information.

(a) Pro forma information shall be furnished if any of the following conditions exist (for purposes of this rule, the term "purchase" encompasses the purchase of an interst in a business accounted for by the equity method);

(i) During the most recent fiscal year or subsequent interim period for which a balance sheet of the registrant is required, a singificant business combination accounted for as a purchase has occurred;

(ii) After the date of the registrant's most recent balance sheet, consummation of a significant business combination to be accounted for by either the purchase method or pooling of interests method of accounting has occurred or is probable.

(b) The provisions of paragraph (3)(b), (d) and (e) apply to this paragraph (4).

(c) Pro forma statements shall ordinarily be in columnar form showing condensed historical statements, pro forma adjustments, and the pro forma results and should include the following:

(i) If the transaction was consummated during the most recent fiscal year or in the subsequent interim period, pro forma statements of income reflecting the combined operations of the entities for the latest fiscal year and interim period, if any, or

(ii) If consummation of the transaction has occurred or is probable after the date of the most recent balance sheet, a pro forma balance sheet giving effect to the combination as of the date of the most recent balance sheet required by paragraph (b). For a purchase, pro forma statements of income reflecting the combined operations of the entities for the latest fiscal year and interim period, if any, and for a pooling of interests, pro forma statements of income for all periods for which income statements of the registrant are required.

PART III—EXHIBITS

Item 1. Index to Exhibits

(a) An index to the exhibits filed should be presented immediately following the cover page to Part III.

(b) Each exhibit should be listed in the exhibit index according to the number assigned to it under Item 2 below.

(c) The index to exhibits should identify the location of the exhibit under the sequential page numbering system for this Form 1-A.

(d) Where exhibits are incorporated by reference, the reference shall be made in the index of exhibits.

Instructions:

1. Any document or part thereof filed with the Commission pursuant to any Act administered by the Commission may, subject to the limitations of Rule 24 of the Commission's Rule of Practice, be incorporated by reference as an exhibit to any offering statement.

2. If any modification has occurred in the text of any document incorporated by reference since the filing thereof, the issuer shall file with the reference a statement containing the text of such modification and the date thereof.

3. Procedurally, the techniques specified in Rule 411(d) of Regulation C shall be followed.

Item 2. Description of Exhibits

As appropriate, the following documents should be filed as exhibits to the offering statement.

(1) *Underwriting Agreement*—Each underwriting contract or agreement with a principal underwriter or letter pursuant to which the securities are to be distributed; where the terms have yet to be finalized, proposed formats may be provided.

(2) *Charter and by-laws*—The charter and by-laws of the issuer or instruments corresponding thereto as presently in effect and any amendments thereto.

(3) *Instruments defining the rights of security holders*—(a) All instruments defining the rights of any holder of the issuer's securities, including but not limited to (i) holders of equity or debt securities being issued; (ii) holders of long-term debt of the issuer, and of all subsidiaries for which consolidated or unconsolidated financial statements are required to be filed.

(b) The following instruments need not be filed if the issuer agrees to provide them to the Commission upon request: (i) instruments defining the rights of holders of long-term debt of the issuer and all of its subsidiaries for which consolidated financial statements are required to be filed if such debt is not being issued pursuant to this Regulation A offering and the total amount of such authorized issuance does not exceed 5% of the total assets of the issuer and its subsidiaries on a consolidated basis; (ii) any instrument with respect to a class of securities which is to be retired or redeemed prior to the issuance or upon delivery of the securities being issued pursuant to this Regulation A offering and appropriate steps have been taken to assure such retirement or redemption; and (iii) copies of instruments evidencing scrip certificates or fractions of shares.

(4) *Subscription agreement*—The form of any subscription agreement to be used in connection with the purchase of securities in this offering.

(5) *Voting trust agreement*—Any voting trust agreements and amendments thereto.

(6) *Material contracts*—(a) Every contract not made in the ordinary course of business which is material to the issuer and is to be performed in whole or in part at or after the filing of the offering statement or was entered into not more than 2 years before such filing. Only contracts need be filed as to which the issuer or subsidiary of the issuer is a party or has succeeded to a party by assumption or assignment or in which the issuer or such subsidiary has a beneficial interest.

(b) If the contract is such as ordinarily accompanies the kind of business conducted by the issuer and its subsidiaries, it is made in the ordinary course of business and need not be filed unless it falls within one or more of the following categories, in which case it should be filed except where immaterial in amount or significance: (i) any contract to which directors, officers, promoters, voting trustees, security holders named in the offering statement, or underwriters are parties except where the contract merely involves the purchase or sale of current assets having a determinable market price, at such market price; (ii) any contract upon which the issuer's business is substantially dependent, as in the case of continuing contracts to sell the major part of the issuer's products or services or to purchase the major part of the issuer's requirements of goods, services or raw materials or any franchise or license or other agreement to use a patent, formula, trade secret, process or trade name upon which the issuer's business depends to a material extent; (iii) any contract calling for the acquisition or sale of any property, plant or equipment for a consideration exceeding 15% of such fixed assets of the issuer on a consolidated basis; or (iv) any material lease under which a part of the property described in the offering statement is held by the issuer.

(c) Any management contract or any compensatory plan, contract or arrangement including but not limited to plans relating to options, warrants or rights, pension, retirement or deferred compensation or bonus, incentive or profit sharing (or if not set forth in any formal document, a written description thereof) shall be deemed material and shall be filed except for the following: (i) ordinary purchase and sales agency agreements; (ii) agreements with managers of stores in a chain organization or similar organization; (iii) contracts providing for labor or salesmen's bonuses or payments to a class of security holders, as such; (iv) any compensatory plan, contract or arrangement which pursuant to its terms is available to employees generally and which in operation provides for the same method of allocation of benefits between management and non-management participants.

(7) *Material foreign patents*—Each material foreign patent for an invention not covered by a United States patent. If a substantial part of the securities to be offered or if the proceeds therefrom have been or are to be used for the particular purposes of acquiring, developing or exploiting one or more material foreign patents or patent rights, furnish a list showing the number and a brief identification of each such patent or patent right.

(8) *Plan of acquisition, reorganization, arrangement, liquidation, or succession*—Any material plan of acquisition, disposition, reorganization, readjustment, succession, liquidation or arrangement and any amendments thereto described in the offering statement. Schedules (or similar attachments) to these exhibits shall not be filed unless such schedules contain information which is material to an investment decision and which is not otherwise disclosed in the agreement or the offering statement. The plan filed shall contain a list briefly identifying the contents of all omitted schedules, together with an agreement to furnish supplementally a copy of any omitted schedule to the Commission upon request.

(9) *Escrow agreements*—Any escrow agreement or similar arrangement which has been executed in connection with the Regulation A offering.

(10) *Consents*—(a) Experts: The written consent of (i) any account, engineer, geologist, appraiser or any person whose profession gives authority to a statement made by them and who is

named in the offering statement as having prepared or certified any part of the document or is named as having prepared or certified a report or evaluation whether or not for use in connection with the offering statement; (ii) the expert that authored any portion of a report quoted or summarized as such in the offering statement, expressly stating their consent to the use of such quotation or summary; (iii) any persons who are referenced as having reviewed or passed upon any information in the offering statement, and that such information is being included on the basis of their authority or in reliance upon their status as experts.

(b) Underwriters: A written consent and certification in the form which follows signed by each underwriter of the securities proposed to be offered. All underwriters may, with appropriate modifications, sign the same consent and certification or separate consents and certifications may be signed by any underwriter or group of underwriters.

CONSENT AND CERTIFICATION BY UNDERWRITER

1. The undersigned hereby consents to being named as underwriter in an offering statement filed with the Securities and Exchange Commission by [insert name of issuer] pursuant to Regulation A in connection with a proposed offering of [insert title of securities] to the public.

2. The undersigned hereby certifies that it furnished the statements and information set forth in the offering statement with respect to the undersigned, its directors and officers or partners, that such statements and information are accurate, complete and fully responsive to the requirements of Parts I, II and III of the Offering Statement thereto, and do not omit any information required to be stated therein with respect of any such persons, or necessary to make the statements and information therein with respect to any of them not misleading.

3. If Preliminary Offering Circulars are distributed, the undersigned hereby undertakes to keep an accurate and complete record of the name and address of each person furnished a Preliminary Offering Circular and, if such Preliminary Offering Circular is inaccurate or inadequate in any material respect, to furnish a revised Preliminary Offering Circular or a Final Offering Circular to all persons to whom the securities are to be sold at least 48 hours prior to the mailing of any confirmation of sale to such persons, or to send such a circular to such persons under circumstances that it would normally be received by them 48 hours prior to their receipt of confirmation of the sale.

. . . .

(Underwriter)

By

. . . .

Date   /   /

(c) All written consents shall be dated and manually signed.

(11) *Opinion re legality*—An opinion of counsel as to the legality of the securities covered by the Offering Statement, indicating whether they will, when sold, be legally issued, fully paid and non-assessable, and if debt securities, whether they will be binding obligations of the issuer.

(12) *Sales Material*—Any material required to be filed by virtue of Rule 256.

(13) *"Test the Water" Material*—Any written document or broadcast script used under the authorization of Rule 254.

(14) *Appointment of Agent for Service of Process*—A Canadian issuer shall provide Form F-X.

(15) *Additional exhibits*—Any additional exhibits which the issuer may wish to file, which shall be so marked to indicate clearly the subject matters to which they refer.

SIGNATURES

The issuer has duly caused this offering statement to be signed on its behalf by the undersigned, thereunto duly authorized, in the City of ...., State of ...., on ...., 19....

(Issuer) ....

By (Signature and Title) ....

This offering statement has been signed by the following persons in the capacities and on the dates indicated.

(Signature)..

(Title) ....

(Selling security holder) ....

(Date)..

Instructions:

1. The offering statement shall be signed by the issuer, its Chief Executive Officer, Chief Financial Officer, a majority of the members of its board of directors or other governing instrumentality, and each person, other than the issuer, for whose account any of the securities are to be offered. If a signature is by a person on behalf of any other person, evidence of authority to sign shall be filed with the offering statement, except where an executive officer signs on behalf of the issuer. If the issuer is Canadian, its authorized representative in the United States also shall sign. Where the issuer is a limited partnership, the offering statement shall also be signed by a majority of the board of directors of any corporate general partner.

2. The name of each person signing the offering statement shall be typed or printed beneath the signature.

FORM 2-A

UNITED STATES SECURITIES AND EXCHANGE COMMISSION
Washington, D.C. 20549
FORM 2-A

REPORT OF SALES AND USES OF PROCEEDS PURSUANT TO RULE 257 OF REGULATION A

File No. 24-   -_

For period ending   /   /_

      Indicate whether the report is an   initial report [   ]

                     amendment [   ]

                     or final report [   ]

      If the report is an amendment, indicate the number of such amendment. ☐☐

         If the offering has terminated, indicate the date of termination   /   /

General Instructions:

The report shall be filed in accordance with the provisions of Rule 257 of Regulation A.

Answer each item in the box(es) or spaces provided. If additional space is required for any response, continue the response on an attached sheet.

If the issuer is required to file any report(s) on this form subsequent to its initial filing, each subsequent filing shall be deemed to be an amendment to the initial filing. Do not report in any amendment responses to Items 3-11 unless the information has changed.

No fee is required to accompany this filing.

Seven copies of the form shall be filed with the main office of the Commission in Washington, D.C. At least one copy of the form shall be manually signed; other copies may bear typed or printed signatures.

1. . . . .

      Exact name of issuer as specified in its charter.

2. Date of qualification of the offering statement:

      ☐☐☐☐☐

3. Has the offering commenced? [ ] Yes [ ] No.

    If yes, date of commencement: ☐☐☐☐☐

    If no, explain briefly:

. . . .

4. Did the offering terminate before any securities were sold? [ ] Yes [ ] No.

    If yes, explain briefly:

. . . .

    If "yes", do not answer Items 5-11.

5. Did the offering terminate prior to the sale of all the securities qualified under Regulation A? [ ] Yes [ ] No.

    If yes, explain briefly:

. . . .

6. Indicate the total number of shares or other units offered and sold to date:

      . . . . (issuer's account)   . . . . (selling securityholders)

    Indicate the number of shares or other units still being offered:

      . . . . (issuer's account)   . . . . (selling securityholders)

7. Total amount of dollars received from the public to date. $ . . . .

    Total amount allocable to selling securityholders: $ . . . .

          Underwriting discount or commission allowed $ . . . .

          Underwriting expenses paid $ . . . .

          Finders' Fees $ . . . .

          Other expenses paid to date by or for issuer:

              Legal (including organization) $ . . . .

              Accounting $ . . . .

              Engineering $ . . . .

              Printing and Advertising $ . . . .

Other (specify)_____ $........
     $........
     $........
     $........

Total costs and expenses $........
Total net proceeds remaining. $........

8. Uses of net proceeds to date.

Instructions:

1. Do not include any amount in "working capital" to which a more specific category is applicable.

2. Round all amounts to the nearest dollar.

3. Specify under "other purposes" any purpose for which at least 5% of the issuer's proceeds or $50,000, whichever is less, has been used.

Salaries and fees $........
Construction of plant, building and facilities $........
Purchases and installation of machinery and equipment $........
Purchase of real estate $........
Acquisition of other business(es) $........
Repayment of indebtedness $........
Working capital $........
Development expense (product development, research, patent costs, etc.) $........
Temporary investment (specify) .... $........
     $........
     $........
     $........

Other purposes (specify)
     $........
     $........
     $........
     $........
     $........
     $........
     $........
     $........

9. Do the use(s) of proceeds in Item 8 represent a material change in the use(s) of proceeds described in the offering circular? [ ] Yes [ ] No.

If yes, explain briefly:

....

10. State the number of shares held by each promoter, director, officer or controlling person of the issuer, if different from the amount stated in the offering circular.

....

11. List the names and addresses of all brokers and dealers who have, to the knowledge of the issuer or underwriters, participated in the distribution of the securities during the period covered by this report.

....

SIGNATURE

Pursuant to the requirements of Rule 257 and Regulation A, ...
.... has caused this report to be signed on its behalf by the undersigned thereunto duly authorized.

....
Issuer

.........................By ....
Date   Signature

Instruction:

The report shall be signed by an executive officer, general partner or counsel of the issuer or by any other duly authorized person. The name and any title of the person who signs the report shall be typed or printed beneath the signature.

FORM D

FORM D

UNITED STATES
SECURITIES AND EXCHANGE COMMISSION
Washington, D.C. 20549

FORM D

NOTICE OF SALE OF SECURITIES
PURSUANT TO REGULATION D,
SECTION 4(6), AND/OR
UNIFORM LIMITED OFFERING EXEMPTION

OMB APPROVAL	
OMB Number:	3235-0076
Expires:	May 31, 2002
Estimated average burden hours per response . . . 16.00	

SEC USE ONLY	
Prefix	Serial
DATE RECEIVED	

Name of Offering   (☐ check if this is an amendment and name has changed, and indicate change.)

Filing Under (Check box(es) that apply):   ☐ Rule 504   ☐ Rule 505   ☐ Rule 506   ☐ Section 4(6)   ☐ ULOE

Type of Filing: ☐ New Filing   ☐ Amendment

A. BASIC IDENTIFICATION DATA

1. Enter the information requested about the issuer

Name of Issuer   (☐ check if this is an amendment and name has changed, and indicate change.)

Address of Executive Offices (Number and Street, City, State, Zip Code)	Telephone Number (Including Area Code)
Address of Principal Business Operations (Number and Street, City, State, Zip Code) (if different from Executive Offices)	Telephone Number (Including Area Code)

Brief Description of Business

Type of Business Organization
   ☐ corporation   ☐ limited partnership, already formed   ☐ other (please specify):
   ☐ business trust   ☐ limited partnership, to be formed

Month   Year
Actual or Estimated Date of Incorporation or Organization: ☐☐ ☐☐   ☐ Actual   ☐ Estimated
Jurisdiction of Incorporation or Organization: (Enter two-letter U.S. Postal Service abbreviation for State:
               CN for Canada; FN for other foreign jurisdiction) ☐☐

GENERAL INSTRUCTIONS

Federal:

Who Must File: All issuers making an offering of securities in reliance on an exemption under Regulation D or Section 4(6), 17 CFR 230.501 et seq. or 15 U.S.C. 77d(6).

When To File: A notice must be filed no later than 15 days after the first sale of securities in the offering. A notice is deemed filed with the U.S. Securities and Exchange Commission (SEC) on the earlier of the date it is received by the SEC at the address given below or, if received at that address after the date on which it is due, on the date it was mailed by United States registered or certified mail to that address.

Where to File: U.S. Securities and Exchange Commission, 450 Fifth Street, N.W., Washington, D.C. 20549.

Copies Required: Five (5) copies of this notice must be filed with the SEC, one of which must be manually signed. Any copies not manually signed must be photocopies of the manually signed copy or bear typed or printed signatures.

Information Required: A new filing must contain all information requested. Amendments need only report the name of the issuer and offering, any changes thereto, the information requested in Part C, and any material changes from the information previously supplied in Parts A and B. Part E and the Appendix need not be filed with the SEC.

Filing Fee: There is no federal filing fee.

State:

This notice shall be used to indicate reliance on the Uniform Limited Offering Exemption (ULOE) for sales of securities in those states that have adopted ULOE and that have adopted this form. Issuers relying on ULOE must file a separate notice with the Securities Administrator in each state where sales are to be, or have been made. If a state requires the payment of a fee as a precondition to the claim for the exemption, a fee in the proper amount shall accompany this form. This notice shall be filed in the appropriate states in accordance with state law. The Appendix to the notice constitutes a part of this notice and must be completed.

——— **ATTENTION** ———
Failure to file notice in the appropriate states will not result in a loss of the federal exemption. Conversely, failure to file the appropriate federal notice will not result in a loss of an available state exemption unless such exemption is predicated on the filing of a federal notice.

Potential persons who are to respond to the collection of information contained in this form are not required to respond unless the form displays a currently valid OMB control number.   SEC 1972 (7-00) 1 of 8

CCH S10225 0331

A. BASIC IDENTIFICATION DATA

2. Enter the information requested for the following:

- Each promoter of the issuer, if the issuer has been organized within the past five years;
- Each beneficial owner having the power to vote or dispose, or direct the vote or disposition of, 10% or more of a class of equity securities of the issuer;
- Each executive officer and director of corporate issuers and of corporate general and managing partners of partnership issuers; and
- Each general and managing partner of partnership issuers.

Check Box(es) that Apply: ☐ Promoter   ☐ Beneficial Owner   ☐ Executive Officer   ☐ Director   ☐ General and/or Managing Partner

Full Name (Last name first, if individual)

Business or Residence Address   (Number and Street, City, State, Zip Code)

Check Box(es) that Apply: ☐ Promoter   ☐ Beneficial Owner   ☐ Executive Officer   ☐ Director   ☐ General and/or Managing Partner

Full Name (Last name first, if individual)

Business or Residence Address   (Number and Street, City, State, Zip Code)

Check Box(es) that Apply: ☐ Promoter   ☐ Beneficial Owner   ☐ Executive Officer   ☐ Director   ☐ General and/or Managing Partner

Full Name (Last name first, if individual)

Business or Residence Address   (Number and Street, City, State, Zip Code)

Check Box(es) that Apply: ☐ Promoter   ☐ Beneficial Owner   ☐ Executive Officer   ☐ Director   ☐ General and/or Managing Partner

Full Name (Last name first, if individual)

Business or Residence Address   (Number and Street, City, State, Zip Code)

Check Box(es) that Apply: ☐ Promoter   ☐ Beneficial Owner   ☐ Executive Officer   ☐ Director   ☐ General and/or Managing Partner

Full Name (Last name first, if individual)

Business or Residence Address   (Number and Street, City, State, Zip Code)

Check Box(es) that Apply: ☐ Promoter   ☐ Beneficial Owner   ☐ Executive Officer   ☐ Director   ☐ General and/or Managing Partner

Full Name (Last name first, if individual)

Business or Residence Address   (Number and Street, City, State, Zip Code)

Check Box(es) that Apply: ☐ Promoter   ☐ Beneficial Owner   ☐ Executive Officer   ☐ Director   ☐ General and/or Managing Partner

Full Name (Last name first, if individual)

Business or Residence Address   (Number and Street, City, State, Zip Code)

(Use blank sheet, or copy and use additional copies of this sheet, as necessary.)

CCH S10226 0331   2 of 8

242

B. INFORMATION ABOUT OFFERING

	Yes	No
1. Has the issuer sold, or does the issuer intend to sell, to non-accredited investors in this offering?	☐	☐

Answer also in Appendix, Column 2, if filing under ULOE.

2. What is the minimum investment that will be accepted from any individual? . . . . $ _____

	Yes	No
3. Does the offering permit joint ownership of a single unit?	☐	☐

4. Enter the information requested for each person who has been or will be paid or given, directly or indirectly, any commission or similar remuneration for solicitation of purchasers in connection with sales of securities in the offering. If a person to be listed is an associated person or agent of a broker or dealer registered with the SEC and/or with a state or states, list the name of the broker or dealer. If more than five (5) persons to be listed are associated persons of such a broker or dealer, you may set forth the information for that broker or dealer only..

Full Name (Last name first, if individual)

Business or Residence Address (Number and Street, City, State, Zip Code)

Name of Associated Broker or Dealer

States in Which Person Listed Has Solicited or Intends to Solicit Purchasers

(Check "All States" or check individual States) . . . . ☐ All States

[AL]	[AK]	[AZ]	[AR]	[CA]	[CO]	[CT]	[DE]	[DC]	[FL]	[GA]	[HI]	[ID]
[IL]	[IN]	[IA]	[KS]	[KY]	[LA]	[ME]	[MD]	[MA]	[MI]	[MN]	[MS]	[MO]
[MT]	[NE]	[NV]	[NH]	[NJ]	[NM]	[NY]	[NC]	[ND]	[OH]	[OK]	[OR]	[PA]
[RI]	[SC]	[SD]	[TN]	[TX]	[UT]	[VT]	[VA]	[WA]	[WV]	[WI]	[WY]	[PR]

Full Name (Last name first, if individual)

Business or Residence Address (Number and Street, City, State, Zip Code)

Name of Associated Broker or Dealer

States in Which Person Listed Has Solicited or Intends to Solicit Purchasers

(Check "All States" or check individual States) . . . . ☐ All States

[AL]	[AK]	[AZ]	[AR]	[CA]	[CO]	[CT]	[DE]	[DC]	[FL]	[GA]	[HI]	[ID]
[IL]	[IN]	[IA]	[KS]	[KY]	[LA]	[ME]	[MD]	[MA]	[MI]	[MN]	[MS]	[MO]
[MT]	[NE]	[NV]	[NH]	[NJ]	[NM]	[NY]	[NC]	[ND]	[OH]	[OK]	[OR]	[PA]
[RI]	[SC]	[SD]	[TN]	[TX]	[UT]	[VT]	[VA]	[WA]	[WV]	[WI]	[WY]	[PR]

Full Name (Last name first, if individual)

Business or Residence Address (Number and Street, City, State, Zip Code)

Name of Associated Broker or Dealer

States in Which Person Listed Has Solicited or Intends to Solicit Purchasers

(Check "All States" or check individual States) . . . . ☐ All States

[AL]	[AK]	[AZ]	[AR]	[CA]	[CO]	[CT]	[DE]	[DC]	[FL]	[GA]	[HI]	[ID]
[IL]	[IN]	[IA]	[KS]	[KY]	[LA]	[ME]	[MD]	[MA]	[MI]	[MN]	[MS]	[MO]
[MT]	[NE]	[NV]	[NH]	[NJ]	[NM]	[NY]	[NC]	[ND]	[OH]	[OK]	[OR]	[PA]
[RI]	[SC]	[SD]	[TN]	[TX]	[UT]	[VT]	[VA]	[WA]	[WV]	[WI]	[WY]	[PR]

(Use blank sheet, or copy and use additional copies of this sheet, as necessary.)

3 of 8

C. OFFERING PRICE, NUMBER OF INVESTORS, EXPENSES AND USE OF PROCEEDS

1. Enter the aggregate offering price of securities included in this offering and the total amount already sold. Enter "0" if answer is "none" or "zero." If the transaction is an exchange offering, check this box ☐ and indicate in the columns below the amounts of the securities offered for exchange and already exchanged.

Type of Security	Aggregate Offering Price	Amount Already Sold
Debt	$_____	$_____
Equity	$_____	$_____
☐ Common ☐ Preferred		
Convertible Securities (including warrants)	$_____	$_____
Partnership Interests	$_____	$_____
Other (Specify_____)	$_____	$_____
Total	$_____	$_____

Answer also in Appendix, Column 3, if filing under ULOE.

2. Enter the number of accredited and non-accredited investors who have purchased securities in this offering and the aggregate dollar amounts of their purchases. For offerings under Rule 504, indicate the number of persons who have purchased securities and the aggregate dollar amount of their purchases on the total lines. Enter "0" if answer is "none" or "zero."

	Number Investors	Aggregate Dollar Amount of Purchases
Accredited Investors.	_____	$_____
Non-accredited Investors	_____	$_____
Total (for filings under Rule 504 only)	_____	$_____

Answer also in Appendix, Column 4, if filing under ULOE.

3. If this filing is for an offering under Rule 504 or 505, enter the information requested for all securities sold by the issuer, to date, in offerings of the types indicated, in the twelve (12) months prior to the first sale of securities in this offering. Classify securities by type listed in Part C - Question 1.

Type of offering	Type of Security	Dollar Amount Sold
Rule 505	_____	$_____
Regulation A	_____	$_____
Rule 504	_____	$_____
Total	_____	$_____

4. a.   Furnish a statement of all expenses in connection with the issuance and distribution of the securities in this offering. Exclude amounts relating solely to organization expenses of the issuer. The information may be given as subject to future contingencies. If the amount of an expenditure is not known, furnish an estimate and check the box to the left of the estimate.

Transfer Agent's Fees	☐	$_____
Printing and Engraving Costs	☐	$_____
Legal Fees	☐	$_____
Accounting Fees	☐	$_____
Engineering Fees	☐	$_____
Sales Commissions (specify finders' fees separately)	☐	$_____
Other Expenses (identify) _____	☐	$_____
Total	☐	$_____

CCH S10228 0331

C. OFFERING PRICE, NUMBER OF INVESTORS, EXPENSES AND USE OF PROCEEDS

b.   Enter the difference between the aggregate offering price given in response to Part C - Question 1 and total expenses furnished in response to Part C - Question 4.a. This difference is the "adjusted gross proceeds to the issuer." .... $_____

5. Indicate below the amount of the adjusted gross proceeds to the issuer used or proposed to be used for each of the purposes shown. If the amount for any purpose is not known, furnish an estimate and check the box to the left of the estimate. The total of the payments listed must equal the adjusted gross proceeds to the issuer set forth in response to Part C - Question 4.b above.

	Payments to Officers, Directors, & Affiliates	Payments To Others
Salaries and fees	☐ $_____	☐ $_____
Purchase of real estate	☐ $_____	☐ $_____
Purchase, rental or leasing and installation of machinery and equipment	☐ $_____	☐ $_____
Construction or leasing of plant buildings and facilities	☐ $_____	☐ $_____
Acquisition of other businesses (including the value of securities involved in this offering that may be used in exchange for the assets or securities of another issuer pursuant to a merger)	☐ $_____	☐ $_____
Repayment of indebtedness	☐ $_____	☐ $_____
Working capital	☐ $_____	☐ $_____
Other (specify): _____	☐ $_____	☐ $_____
_____		
_____	☐ $_____	☐ $_____
Column Totals	☐ $_____	☐ $_____
Total Payments Listed (column totals added)...............................	☐ $_____	

D. FEDERAL SIGNATURE

The issuer has duly caused this notice to be signed by the undersigned duly authorized person. If this notice is filed under Rule 505, the following signature constitutes an undertaking by the issuer to furnish to the U.S. Securities and Exchange Commission, upon written request of its staff, the information furnished by the issuer to any non-accredited investor pursuant to paragraph (b)(2) of Rule 502.

Issuer (Print or Type)	Signature	Date
Name of Signer (Print or Type)	Title of Signer (Print or Type)	

─────── **ATTENTION** ───────
Intentional misstatements or omissions of fact constitute federal criminal violations. (See 18 U.S.C. 1001.)

CCH S10229 0331

E. STATE SIGNATURE

1. Is any party described in 17 CFR 230.262 presently subject to any of the disqualification provisions of such rule? . . . .

Yes   No
☐   ☐

See Appendix, Column 5, for state response.

2. The undersigned issuer hereby undertakes to furnish to any state administrator of any state in which this notice is filed, a notice on Form D (17 CFR 239.500) at such times as required by state law.

3. The undersigned issuer hereby undertakes to furnish to the state administrators, upon written request, information furnished by the issuer to offerees.

4. The undersigned issuer represents that the issuer is familiar with the conditions that must be satisfied to be entitled to the Uniform limited Offering Exemption (ULOE) of the state in which this notice is filed and understands that the issuer claiming the availability of this exemption has the burden of establishing that these conditions have been satisfied.

The issuer has read this notification and knows the contents to be true and has duly caused this notice to be signed on its behalf by the undersigned duly authorized person.

Issuer (Print or Type)	Signature	Date
Name (Print or Type)	Title (Print or Type)	

Instruction:
Print the name and title of the signing representative under his signature for the state portion of this form. One copy of every notice on Form D must be manually signed. Any copies not manually signed must be photocopies of the manually signed copy or bear typed or printed signatures.

6 of 8

CCH S10230 0331

246

APPENDIX									
1	2		3	4				5	
	Intend to sell to non-accredited investors in State (Part B-Item 1)		Type of security and aggregate offering price offered in state (Part C-Item 1)	Type of investor and amount purchased in State (Part C-Item 2)				Disqualification under State ULOE (if yes, attach explanation of waiver granted) (Part E-Item 1)	
State	Yes	No		Number of Accredited Investors	Amount	Number of Non-Accredited Investors	Amount	Yes	No
AL									
AK									
AZ									
AR									
CA									
CO									
CT									
DE									
DC									
FL									
GA									
HI									
ID									
IL									
IN									
IA									
KS									
KY									
LA									
ME									
MD									
MA									
MI									
MN									
MS									
MO									

CCH S10231 0331

APPENDIX									
1	2		3	4				5	
	Intend to sell to non-accredited investors in State (Part B-Item 1)		Type of security and aggregate offering price offered in state (Part C-Item l)	Type of investor and amount purchased in State (Part C-Item 2)				Disqualification under State ULOE (if yes, attach explanation of waiver granted) (Part E-Item l)	
State	Yes	No		Number of Accredited Investors	Amount	Number of Non-Accredited Investors	Amount	Yes	No
M T									
N E									
N V									
N H									
N J									
N M									
N Y									
N C									
N D									
O H									
O K									
O R									
P A									
R I									
S C									
S D									
T N									
T X									
U T									
V T									
V A									
W A									
W V									
W I									
W Y									
P R									

CCH B10232 0331

Form 144

UNITED STATES
SECURITIES AND EXCHANGE COMMISSION
Washington, D.C. 20549

FORM 144

NOTICE OF PROPOSED SALE OF SECURITIES
PURSUANT TO RULE 144 UNDER THE SECURITIES ACT OF 1933

ATTENTION: Transmit for filing 3 copies of this form concurrently with either placing an order with a broker to execute sale or executing a sale directly with a market maker.

SEC USE ONLY
DOCUMENT SEQUENCE NO.
CUSIP NUMBER

1 (a) NAME OF ISSUER (Please type or print)		(b) IRS IDENT. NO.	(c) S.E.C. FILE NO.

1 (d) ADDRESS OF ISSUER	STREET	CITY	STATE	ZIP CODE	WORK LOCATION

(e) TELEPHONE NO.
AREA CODE   NUMBER

2 (a) NAME OF PERSON FOR WHOSE ACCOUNT THE SECURITIES ARE TO BE SOLD	(b) IRS IDENT. NO.	(c) RELATIONSHIP TO ISSUER	(d) ADDRESS STREET	CITY	STATE	ZIP CODE

INSTRUCTION: The person filing this notice should contact the issuer to obtain the I.R.S. Identification Number and the S.E.C. File Number.

3 (a) Title of the Class of Securities To Be Sold	(b) Name and Address of Each Broker Through Whom the Securities are to be Offered or Each Market Maker who is Acquiring the Securities	(c) Broker-Dealer File Number [SEC USE ONLY]	(c) Number of Shares or Other Units To Be Sold (See instr. 3(c))	(d) Aggregate Market Value (See instr. 3(d))	(e) Number of Shares or Other Units Outstanding (See instr. 3(e))	(f) Approximate Date of Sale (See instr. 3(f)) (MO. DAY YR.)	(g) Name of Each Securities Exchange (See instr. 3(g))

INSTRUCTIONS:

1. (a) Name of issuer
   (b) Issuer's I.R.S. Identification Number
   (c) Issuer's S.E.C. file number, if any
   (d) Issuer's address, including zip code
   (e) Issuer's telephone number, including area code

2. (a) Name of person for whose account the securities are to be sold
   (b) Such person's I.R.S. identification number, if such person is an entity
   (c) Such person's relationship to the issuer (e.g., officer, director, 10% stockholder, or member of immediate family of any of the foregoing)
   (d) Such person's address, including zip code

3. (a) Title of the class of securities to be sold
   (b) Name and address of each broker through whom the securities are intended to be sold
   (c) Number of shares or other units to be sold (if debt securities, give the aggregate face amount)
   (d) Aggregate market value of the securities to be sold as of a specified date within 10 days prior to the filing of this notice
   (e) Number of shares or other units of the class outstanding, or if debt securities the face amount thereof outstanding, as shown by the most recent report or statement published by the issuer
   (f) Approximate date on which the securities are to be sold
   (g) Name of each securities exchange, if any, on which the securities are intended to be sold

TABLE I — SECURITIES TO BE SOLD

Furnish the following information with respect to the acquisition of the securities to be sold
and with respect to the payment of all or any part of the purchase price or other consideration therefor:

Title of the Class	Date you Acquired	Nature of Acquisition Transaction	Name of Person from Whom Acquired (If gift, also give date donor acquired)	Amount of Securities Acquired	Date of Payment	Nature of Payment

INSTRUCTIONS: If the securities were purchased and full payment therefor was not made in cash at the time of purchase, explain in the table or in a note thereto the nature of the consideration given. If the consideration consisted of any note or other obligation, or if payment was made in installments describe the arrangement and state when the note or other obligation was discharged in full or the last installment paid.

TABLE II — SECURITIES SOLD DURING THE PAST 3 MONTHS

Furnish the following information as to all securities of the issuer sold during the past 3 months by the person for whose account the securities are to be sold.

Name and Address of Seller	Title of Securities Sold	Date of Sale	Amount of Securities Sold	Gross Proceeds

REMARKS:

INSTRUCTIONS:
See the definition of "person" in paragraph (a) of Rule 144. Information is to be given not only as to the person for whose account the securities are to be sold but also as to all other persons included in that definition. In addition, information shall be given as to sales by all persons whose sales are required by paragraph (e) of Rule 144 to be aggregated with sales for the account of the person filing this notice.

ATTENTION:
The person for whose account the securities to which this notice relates are to be sold hereby represents by signing this notice that he does not know any material adverse information in regard to the current and prospective operations of the Issuer of the securities to be sold which has not been publicly disclosed.

_____
(SIGNATURE)

_____
DATE OF NOTICE

The notice shall be signed by the person for whose account the securities are to be sold. At least one copy of the notice shall be manually signed. Any copies not manually signed shall bear typed or printed signatures.

ATTENTION: Intentional misstatements or omission of facts constitute Federal Criminal Violations (See 18 U.S.C. 1001)

SECURITIES EXCHANGE ACT OF 1934
15 U.S.C. §§ 78a et seq.

Section	15 U.S.C. Section	Subject
1	78a	Short title
2	78b	Necessity for regulation as provided in this title
3(a)	78c	Definitions and application of title
(1)		Exchange
(2)		Facility
(3)		Member
(4)		Broker
(5)		Dealer
(6)		Bank
(7)		Director
(8)		Issuer
(9)		Person
(10)		Security
(11)		Equity security
(12)		Exempted security or exempted securities
(13)		Buy, purchase
(14)		Sale, sell
(15)		Commission
(16)		State
(17)		Interstate commerce
(18)		Person associated with a broker or dealer
(19)		Investment company
(20)		Investment adviser
(21)		Person associated with a member
(22)		Securities information processor
(23)		Clearing agency
(24)		Participant
(25)		Transfer agent
(26)		Self-regulatory organization
(27)		Rules of an exchange
(28)		Rules of a self-regulatory organization

Section	15 U.S.C. Section	Subject
(29)		Municipal securities
(30)		Municipal securities dealer
(31)		Municipal securities broker
(32)		Person associated with a municipal securities dealer
(33)		Municipal securities investment portfolio
(34)		Appropriate regulatory agency
(35)		Investment discretion
(36)		Equal regulation
(37)		Records
(38)		Market maker
(39)		Statutory disqualification
(40)		Financial responsibility rules
(41)		Mortgage related security
(42)		Government securities
(43)		Government securities broker
(44)		Government securities dealer
(45)		Person associated with a government securities broker or government securities dealer
(46)		Financial institution
(47)		Securities laws
(48)		Registered broker or dealer
(49)		Person associated with a transfer agent
(50)		Foreign securities authority
(51)		Penny stock
(52)		Foreign financial regulatory authority
(53)		Small business related security
(54)		Qualified investor
(55)		Security future; narrow-based security index
(56)		Security futures product
(57)		Margin; margin level; higher margin level
(58)		Audit committee
(59)		Registered public accounting firm
3(b)		Power to define terms
3(c)		Exemption of government departments and agencies
3(d)		Issuer of municipal securities
3(e)		Charitable organizations
3(f)		Consideration of promotion of efficency, competition, and capital formation
3(g)		Church plans
3A	78c-1	Swap Agreements
4	78d	Securities and Exchange Commission

Section	15 U.S.C. Section	Subject
4A	78d-1	Delegation of functions by Commission
4B	78d-2	Transfer of functions with respect to assignment of personnel to Chairman
4C	78d-3	Appearance and practice before the Commission
5	78e	Transactions on unregistered exchanges
6	78f	National securities exchanges
7	78g	Margin requirements
8	78h	Restrictions on borrowing by members, brokers, and dealers
9	78i	Prohibition against manipulation of security prices
10	78j	Regulation of the use of manipulative and deceptive devices
10A	78j-1	Audit requirements
11	78k	Trading by members of exchanges, brokers and dealers
11A	78k-1	National market system for securities; securities information processors
12	78l	Registration requirements for securities
13	78m	Periodical and other reports
14	78n	Proxies
15	78o	Registration and regulation of brokers and dealers
15A	78o-3	Registered securities associations
15B	78o-4	Municipal securities
15C	78o-5	Government securities brokers and dealers
15D	78o-6	Securities analysts and research reports
16	78p	Directors, officers, and principal stockholders
17	78q	Accounts and records, reports, examinations of exchanges, members, and others
17A	78q-1	National system for clearance and settlement of securities transactions
17B	78q-2	Automated quotation systems for penny stocks
18	78r	Liability for misleading statements
19	78s	Registration, responsibilities, and oversight of self-regulatory organizations
20	78t	Liability of controlling persons and persons who aid and abet violations
20A	78t-1	Liability to contemporaneous traders for insider trading
21	78u	Investigations; injunctions and prosecution of offenses
21A	78u-1	Civil penalties
21B	78u-2	Civil remedies in administrative proceedings
21C	78u-3	Cease-and-desist proceedings
21D	78u-4	Private securities Litigation
21E	78u-5	Application of safe harbor for forward-looking statements
22	78v	Hearings by Commission
23	78w	Rules, regulations and orders; annual reports

Section	15 U.S.C. Section	Subject
24	78x	Public availability of information
25	78y	Court review of orders and rules
26	78z	Unlawful representations
27	78aa	Jurisdiction of offenses and suits
27A	78aa-1	Special provision relating to statute of limitations on private causes of action
28	78bb	Effect on existing law
29	78cc	Validity of contracts
30	78dd	Foreign securities exchanges
30A	78dd-1	Prohibited foreign trade practices by issuers
31	78ee	Transaction fees
32	78ff	Penalties
33	78gg	Separability of provisions
34	78hh	Effective date
35	78kk	Authorization of appropriations
35A	78ll	Requirements for the EDGAR system
36	78mm	General exemptive authority
201-209		Amendments to Securities Act of 1933
210		Securities and Exchange Commission successor to Federal Trade Commission

TITLE I
Regulation of Securities Exchanges

Sec. 1. SHORT TITLE

This Act may be cited as the "Securities Exchange Act of 1934."

Sec. 2. NECESSITY FOR REGULATION AS PROVIDED IN THIS TITLE

For the reasons hereinafter enumerated, transactions in securities as commonly conducted upon securities exchanges and over-the-counter markets are affected with a national public interest which makes it necessary to provide for regulation and control of such transactions and of practices and matters related thereto, including transactions by officers, directors, and principal security holders, to require appropriate reports, to remove impediments to and perfect the mechanisms of a national market system for securities and a national system for the clearance and settlement of securities transactions and the safeguarding of securities and funds related thereto, and to impose requirements necessary to make such regulation and control reasonably complete and effective, in order to protect interstate commerce, the national credit, the Federal taxing power, to protect and make more effective the national banking system and Federal Reserve System, and to insure the maintenance of fair and honest markets in such transactions:

(1) Such transactions (a) are carried on in large volume by the public generally and in large part originate outside the States in which the exchanges and over-the-counter markets are located and/or are effected by means of the mails and instrumentalities of interstate commerce; (b) constitute an important part of the current of interstate commerce; (c) involve in large part the securities of issuers engaged in interstate commerce; (d) involve the use of credit, directly affect

the financing of trade, industry, and transportation in interstate commerce, and directly affect and influence the volume of interstate commerce; and affect the national credit.

(2) The prices established and offered in such transactions are generally disseminated and quoted throughout the United States and foreign countries and constitute a basis for determining and establishing the prices at which securities are bought and sold, the amount of certain taxes owing to the United States and to the several States by owners, buyers, and sellers of securities, and the value of collateral for bank loans.

(3) Frequently the prices of securities on such exchanges and markets are susceptible to manipulation and control, and the dissemination of such prices gives rise to excessive speculation, resulting in sudden and unreasonanble fluctuations in the prices of securities which (a) cause alternately unreasonable expansion and unreasonable contraction of the volume of credit available for trade, transportation, and industry in interstate commerce, (b) hinder the proper appraisal of the value of securities and thus prevent a fair calculation of taxes owing to the United States and to the several States by owners, buyers, and sellers of securities, and (c) prevent the fair valuation of collateral for bank loans and/or obstruct the effective operation of the national banking system and Federal Reserve System.

(4) National emergencies, which produce widespread unemployment and the dislocation of trade, transportation, and industry, and which burden interstate commerce and adversely affect the general welfare, are precipitated, intensified, and prolonged by manipulation and sudden and unreasonable fluctuations of security prices and by excessive speculation on such exchanges and markets, and to meet such emergencies the Federal Government is put to such great expense as to burden the national credit.

Sec. 3. DEFINITIONS AND APPLICATION OF TITLE

(a) When used in this title, unless the context otherwise requires—

(1) [Exchange]

The term "exchange" means any organization, association, or group of persons, whether incorporated or unincorporated, which constitutes, maintains, or provides a market place or facilities for bringing together purchasers and sellers of securities or for otherwise performing with respect to securities the functions commonly performed by a stock exchange as that term is generally understood, and includes the market place and the market facilities maintained by such exchange.

(2) [Facility]

The term "facility" when used with respect to an exchange includes its premises, tangible or intangible property whether on the premises or not, any right to the use of such premises or property or any service thereof for the purpose of effecting or reporting a transaction on an exchange (including, among other things, any system of communication to or from the exchange, by ticker or otherwise, maintained by or with the consent of the exchange), and any right of the exchange to the use of any property or service.

(3) [Member]

(A) The term "member" when used with respect to a national securities exchange means (i) any natural person permitted to effect transactions on the floor of the exchange without the services of another person acting as broker, (ii) any registered broker or dealer with which such a natural person is associated, (iii) any registered broker or dealer permitted to designate as a representative such a natural person, and (iv) any other registered broker or dealer which agrees to be regulated by such exchange and with respect to which the exchange undertakes to enforce compliance with the provisions of this title, the rules and regulations thereunder, and its own rules. For purposes of sections 6(b)(1), 6(b)(4), 6(b)(6), 6(b)(7), 6(d), 17(d), 19(d), 19(e), 19(g), 19(h), and 21 of this title, the term "member" when used with respect to a national securities exchange also means, to the extent of the rules of the exchange specified by the Commission, any person required by the Commission to comply with such rules pursuant to section 6(f) of this title.

(B) The term "member" when used with respect to a registered securities association means any broker or dealer who agrees to be regulated by such association and with respect to whom the association undertakes to enforce compliance with the provisions of this title, the rules and regulations thereunder, and its own rules.

(4) [Broker]

(A) IN GENERAL.—The term 'broker' means any person engaged in the business of effecting transactions in securities for the account of others.

(B) EXCEPTION FOR CERTAIN BANK ACTIVITIES.—A bank shall not be considered to be a broker because the bank engages in any one or more of the following activities under the conditions described:

(i) THIRD PARTY BROKERAGE ARRANGEMENTS.—The bank enters into a contractual or other written arrangement with a broker or dealer registered under this title under which the broker or dealer offers brokerage services on or off the premises of the bank if—

(I) such broker or dealer is clearly identified as the person performing the brokerage services;

(II) the broker or dealer performs brokerage services in an area that is clearly marked and, to the extent practicable, physically separate from the routine deposit-taking activities of the bank;

(III) any materials used by the bank to advertise or promote generally the availability of brokerage services under the arrangement clearly indicate that the brokerage services are being provided by the broker or dealer and not by the bank;

(IV) any materials used by the bank to advertise or promote generally the availability of brokerage services under the arrangement are in compliance with the Federal securities laws before distribution;

(V) bank employees (other than associated persons of a broker or dealer who are qualified pursuant to the rules of a self-regulatory organization) perform only clerical or ministerial functions in connection with brokerage transactions including scheduling appointments with the associated persons of a broker or dealer, except that bank employees may forward customer funds or securities and may describe in general terms the types of investment vehicles available from the bank and the broker or dealer under the arrangement;

(VI) bank employees do not receive incentive compensation for any brokerage transaction unless such employees are associated persons of a broker or dealer and are qualified pursuant to the rules of a self-regulatory organization, except that the bank employees may receive compensation for the referral of any customer if the compensation is a nominal one-time cash fee of a fixed dollar amount and the payment of the fee is not contingent on whether the referral results in a transaction;

(VII) such services are provided by the broker or dealer on a basis in which all customers that receive any services are fully disclosed to the broker or dealer;

(VIII) the bank does not carry a securities account of the customer except as permitted under clause (ii) or (viii) of this subparagraph; and

(IX) the bank, broker, or dealer informs each customer that the brokerage services are provided by the broker or dealer and not by the bank and that the securities are not deposits or other obligations of the bank, are not guaranteed by the bank, and are not insured by the Federal Deposit Insurance Corporation.

(ii) TRUST ACTIVITIES.—The bank effects transactions in a trustee capacity, or effects transactions in a fiduciary capacity in its trust department or other department that is regularly examined by bank examiners for compliance with fiduciary principles and standards, and—

(I) is chiefly compensated for such transactions, consistent with fiduciary principles and standards, on the basis of an administration or annual fee (payable on a monthly, quarterly, or other basis), a percentage of assets under management, or a flat or capped per order processing fee equal to not more than the cost incurred by the bank in connection with executing securities transactions for trustee and fiduciary customers, or any combination of such fees; and

(II) does not publicly solicit brokerage business, other than by advertising that it effects transactions in securities in conjunction with advertising its other trust activities.

(iii) PERMISSIBLE SECURITIES TRANSACTIONS.—The bank effects transactions in—

(I) commercial paper, bankers acceptances, or commercial bills;

(II) exempted securities;

(III) qualified Canadian government obligations as defined in section 5136 of the Revised Statutes, in conformity with section 15C of this title and the rules and regulations thereunder, or obligations of the North American Development Bank; or

(IV) any standardized, credit enhanced debt security issued by a foreign government pursuant to the March 1989 plan of then Secretary of the Treasury Brady, used by such foreign government to retire outstanding commercial bank loans.

(iv) CERTAIN STOCK PURCHASE PLANS.—

(I) EMPLOYEE BENEFIT PLANS.—The bank effects transactions, as part of its transfer agency activities, in the securities of an issuer as part of any pension, retirement, profit-sharing, bonus, thrift, savings, incentive, or other similar benefit plan for the employees of that issuer or its affiliates (as defined in section 2 of the Bank Holding Company Act of 1956), if the bank does not solicit transactions or provide investment advice with respect to the purchase or sale of securities in connection with the plan.

(II) DIVIDEND REINVESTMENT PLANS.—The bank effects transactions, as part of its transfer agency activities, in the securities of an issuer as part of that issuer's dividend reinvestment plan, if—

(aa) the bank does not solicit transactions or provide investment advice with respect to the purchase or sale of securities in connection with the plan; and

(bb) the bank does not net shareholders' buy and sell orders, other than for programs for odd-lot holders or plans registered with the Commission.

(III) ISSUER PLANS.—The bank effects transactions, as part of its transfer agency activities, in the securities of an issuer as part of a plan or program for the purchase or sale of that issuer's shares, if—

(aa) the bank does not solicit transactions or provide investment advice with respect to the purchase or sale of securities in connection with the plan or program; and

(bb) the bank does not net shareholders' buy and sell orders, other than for programs for odd-lot holders or plans registered with the Commission.

(IV) PERMISSIBLE DELIVERY OF MATERIALS.—The exception to being considered a broker for a bank engaged in activities described in subclauses (I), (II), and (III) will not be affected by delivery of written or electronic plan materials by a bank to employees of the issuer, shareholders of the issuer, or members of affinity groups of the issuer, so long as such materials are—

(aa) comparable in scope or nature to that permitted by the Commission as of the date of the enactment of the Gramm-Leach-Bliley Act; or

(bb) otherwise permitted by the Commission.

(v) SWEEP ACCOUNTS.—The bank effects transactions as part of a program for the investment or reinvestment of deposit funds into any no-load, open-end management investment company registered under the Investment Company Act of 1940 that holds itself out as a money market fund.

(vi) AFFILIATE TRANSACTIONS.—The bank effects transactions for the account of any affiliate of the bank (as defined in section 2 of the Bank Holding Company Act of 1956) other than—

(I) a registered broker or dealer; or

(II) an affiliate that is engaged in merchant banking, as described in section 4(k)(4)(H) of the Bank Holding Company Act of 1956.

(vii) PRIVATE SECURITIES OFFERINGS.—The bank—

(I) effects sales as part of a primary offering of securities not involving a public offering, pursuant to section 3(b), 4(2), or 4(6) of the Securities Act of 1933 or the rules and regulations issued thereunder;

(II) at any time after the date that is 1 year after the date of the enactment of the Gramm-Leach-Bliley Act, is not affiliated with a broker or dealer that has been registered for more than 1 year in accordance with this Act, and engages in dealing, market making, or underwriting activities, other than with respect to exempted securities; and

(III) if the bank is not affiliated with a broker or dealer, does not effect any primary offering described in subclause (I) the aggregate amount of which exceeds 25 percent of the capital of the bank, except that the limitation of this subclause shall not apply with respect to any sale of government securities or municipal securities.

(viii) SAFEKEEPING AND CUSTODY ACTIVITIES.—

(I) IN GENERAL.—The bank, as part of customary banking activities—

(aa) provides safekeeping or custody services with respect to securities, including the exercise of warrants and other rights on behalf of customers;

(bb) facilitates the transfer of funds or securities, as a custodian or a clearing agency, in connection with the clearance and settlement of its customers' transactions in securities;

(cc) effects securities lending or borrowing transactions with or on behalf of customers as part of services provided to customers pursuant to division (aa) or (bb) or invests cash collateral pledged in connection with such transactions;

(dd) holds securities pledged by a customer to another person or securities subject to purchase or resale agreements involving a customer, or facilitates the pledging or transfer of such securities by book entry or as otherwise provided under applicable law, if the bank maintains records separately identifying the securities and the customer; or

(ee) serves as a custodian or provider of other related administrative services to any individual retirement account, pension, retirement, profit sharing, bonus, thrift savings, incentive, or other similar benefit plan.

(II) EXCEPTION FOR CARRYING BROKER ACTIVITIES.—The exception to being considered a broker for a bank engaged in activities described in subclause (I) shall not apply if the bank, in connection with such activities, acts in the United States as a carrying broker (as such term, and different formulations thereof, are used in section 15(c)(3) of this title and the rules and regulations thereunder) for any broker or dealer, unless such carrying broker activities are engaged in with respect to government securities (as defined in paragraph (42) of this subsection).

(ix) IDENTIFIED BANKING PRODUCTS.—The bank effects transactions in identified banking products as defined in section 206 of the Gramm-Leach-Bliley Act.

(x) MUNICIPAL SECURITIES.—The bank effects transactions in municipal securities.

(xi) DE MINIMIS EXCEPTION.—The bank effects, other than in transactions referred to in clauses (i) through (x), not more than 500 transactions in securities in any calendar year, and such transactions are not effected by an employee of the bank who is also an employee of a broker or dealer.

(C) EXECUTION BY BROKER OR DEALER.—The exception to being considered a broker for a bank engaged in activities described in clauses (ii), (iv), and (viii) of subparagraph (B) shall not apply if the activities described in such provisions result in the trade in the United States of any security that is a publicly traded security in the United States, unless—

(i) the bank directs such trade to a registered broker or dealer for execution;

(ii) the trade is a cross trade or other substantially similar trade of a security that—

(I) is made by the bank or between the bank and an affiliated fiduciary; and

(II) is not in contravention of fiduciary principles established under applicable Federal or State law; or

(iii) the trade is conducted in some other manner permitted under rules, regulations, or orders as the Commission may prescribe or issue.

(D) FIDUCIARY CAPACITY.—For purposes of subparagraph (B)(ii), the term 'fiduciary capacity' means—

(i) in the capacity as trustee, executor, administrator, registrar of stocks and bonds, transfer agent, guardian, assignee, receiver, or custodian under a uniform gift to minor act, or as an investment adviser if the bank receives a fee for its investment advice;

(ii) in any capacity in which the bank possesses investment discretion on behalf of another; or

(iii) in any other similar capacity.

(E) EXCEPTION FOR ENTITIES SUBJECT TO SECTION 15(e).—The term 'broker' does not include a bank that—

(i) was, on the day before the date of enactment of the Gramm-Leach-Bliley Act, subject to section 15(e); and

(ii) is subject to such restrictions and requirements as the Commission considers appropriate.

(5) [Dealer]

(A) IN GENERAL.—The term 'dealer' means any person engaged in the business of buying and selling securities for such person's own account through a broker or otherwise.

(B) EXCEPTION FOR PERSON NOT ENGAGED IN THE BUSINESS OF DEALING.—The term 'dealer' does not include a person that buys or sells securities for such person's own account, either individually or in a fiduciary capacity, but not as a part of a regular business.

(C) EXCEPTION FOR CERTAIN BANK ACTIVITIES.—A bank shall not be considered to be a dealer because the bank engages in any of the following activities under the conditions described:

(i) PERMISSIBLE SECURITIES TRANSACTIONS.—The bank buys or sells—

(I) commercial paper, bankers acceptances, or commercial bills;

(II) exempted securities;

(III) qualified Canadian government obligations as defined in section 5136 of the Revised Statutes of the United States, in conformity with section 15C of this title and the rules and regulations thereunder, or obligations of the North American Development Bank; or

(IV) any standardized, credit enhanced debt security issued by a foreign government pursuant to the March 1989 plan of then Secretary of the Treasury Brady, used by such foreign government to retire outstanding commercial bank loans.

(ii) INVESTMENT, TRUSTEE, AND FIDUCIARY TRANSACTIONS.—The bank buys or sells securities for investment purposes—

(I) for the bank; or

(II) for accounts for which the bank acts as a trustee or fiduciary.

(iii) ASSET-BACKED TRANSACTIONS.—The bank engages in the issuance or sale to qualified investors, through a grantor trust or other separate entity, of securities backed by or representing an interest in notes, drafts, acceptances, loans, leases, receivables, other obligations (other than securities of which the bank is not the issuer), or pools of any such obligations predominantly originated by—

(I) the bank;

(II) an affiliate of any such bank other than a broker or dealer; or

(III) a syndicate of banks of which the bank is a member, if the obligations or pool of obligations consists of mortgage obligations or consumer-related receivables.

(iv) IDENTIFIED BANKING PRODUCTS.—The bank buys or sells identified banking products, as defined in section 206 of the Gramm-Leach-Bliley Act.

(6) [Bank]

The term "bank" means (A) a banking institution organized under the laws of the United States, (B) a member bank of the Federal Reserve System, (C) any other banking institution, whether incorporated or not, doing business under the laws of any State or of the United States, a substantial portion of the business of which consists of receiving deposits or exercising a fiduciary power similar to those permitted to national banks under the authority of the Comptroller of the Currency pursuant to the first section of Public Law 87-722 (12 U.S.C. 92a), and which is supervised and examined by State or Federal authority having supervision over banks, and which is not operated for the purpose of evading the provisions of this title, and (D) a receiver, conservator, or other liquidating agent of any institution or firm included in clauses (A), (B), or (C) of this paragraph.

(7) [Director]

The term "director" means any director of a corporation or any person performing similar functions with respect to any organization, whether incorporated or unincorporated.

(8) [Issuer]

The term "issuer" means any person who issues or proposes to issue any security; except that with respect to certificates of deposit for securities, voting-trust certificates, or collateral-trust certificates, or with respect to certificates of interest or shares in an unincorporated investment trust not having a board of directors or of the fixed, restricted management, or unit type, the term "issuer" means the person or persons performing the acts and assuming the duties of depositor or manager pursuant to the provisions of the trust or other agreement or instrument under which such securities are issued; and except that with respect to equipment-trust certificates or like securities, the term "issuer" means the person by whom the equipment or property is, or is to be, used.

(9) [Person]

The term "person" means a natural person, company, government, or political subdivision, agency, or instrumentality of a government.

(10) [Security]

The term "security" means any note, stock, treasury stock, security future, bond, debenture, certificate of interest or participation in any profit-sharing agreement or in any oil, gas, or other mineral royalty or lease, any collateral-trust certificate, preorganization certificate or subscription, transferable share, investment contract, voting-trust certificate, certificate of deposit for a security, any put, call, straddle, option, or privilege on any security, certificate of deposit, or group or index of securities (including any interest therein or based on the value thereof), or any put, call, straddle, option, or privilege entered into on a national securities exchange relating to foreign currency, or in general, any instrument commonly known as a "security"; or any certificate of interest or participation in, temporary or interim certificate for, receipt for, or warrant or right to subscribe to or purchase, any of the foregoing; but shall not include currency or any note, draft, bill of exchange, or banker's acceptance which has a maturity at the time of issuance of not exceeding nine months, exclusive of days of grace, or any renewal thereof the maturity of which is likewise limited.

[handwritten: short term note (but most read to be only commercial paper like 33 Act)]

(11) [Equity Security]

The term 'equity security' means any stock or similar security; or any security future on any such security; or any security convertible, with or without consideration, into such a security, or carrying any warrant or right to subscribe to or purchase such a security; or any such warrant or right; or any other security which the Commission shall deem to be of similar nature and consider necessary or appropriate, by such rules and regulations as it may prescribe in the public interest or for the protection of investors, to treat as an equity security.

(12) [Exempted Security or Exempted Securities]

(A) The term "exempted security" or "exempted securities" includes—

(i) government securities, as defined in paragraph (42) of this subsection;

(ii) municipal securities, as defined in paragraph (29) of this subsection;

(iii) any interest or participation in any common trust fund or similar fund that is excluded from the definition of the term 'investment company' under section 3(c)(3) of the Investment Company Act of 1940;

(iv) any interest or participation in a single trust fund, or a collective trust fund maintained by a bank, or any security arising out of a contract issued by an insurance company, which interest, participation, or security is issued in connection with a qualified plan as defined in subparagraph (C) of this paragraph;

(v) any security issued by or any interest or participation in any pooled income fund, collective trust fund, collective investment fund, or similar fund that is excluded from the definition of an investment company under section 3(c)(10)(B) of the Investment Company Act of 1940;

(vi) solely for purposes of sections 12, 13, 14, and 16 of this title, any security issued by or any interest or participation in any church plan, company, or account that is excluded from the definition of an investment company under section 3(c)(14) of the Investment Company Act of 1940; and

(vii) such other securities (which may include, among others, unregistered securities, the market in which is predominantly intrastate) as the Commission may, by such rules and regulations as it deems consistent with the public interest and the protection of investors, either unconditionally or upon specified terms and conditions or for stated periods, exempt from the operation of any one or more provisions of this title which by their terms do not apply to an "exempted security" or to "exempted securities."

(B)(i) Notwithstanding subparagraph (A)(i) of this paragraph, government securities shall not be deemed to be "exempted securities" for the purposes of section 17A of this title.

(ii) Notwithstanding subparagraph (A)(ii) of this paragraph, municipal securities shall not be deemed to be "exempted securities" for the purposes of sections 15 and 17A of this title.

(C) For purposes of subparagraph (A)(iv) of this paragraph, the term "qualified plan" means (i) a stock bonus, pension, or profit-sharing plan which meets the requirements for qualification under section 401 of the Internal Revenue Code of 1954, (ii) an annuity plan which meets the requirements for the deduction of the employer's contribution under section 404(a)(2) of such Code, or (iii) a governmental plan as defined in section 414(d) of such Code which has been established by an employer for the exclusive benefit of its employees or their beneficiaries for the purpose of distributing to such employees or their beneficiaries the corpus and income of the funds accumulated under such plan, if under such plan it is impossible, prior to the satisfaction of all liabilities with respect to such employees and their beneficiaries, for any part of the corpus or income to be used for, or diverted to, purposes other than the exclusive benefit of such employees or their beneficiaries, other than any plan described in clause (i), (ii), or (iii) of this subparagraph which (I) covers employees some or all of whom are employees within the meaning of section 401(c) of such Code, or (II) is a plan funded by an annuity contract described in section 403(b) of such Code.

(13) [Buy, Purchase]

The terms "buy" and "purchase" each include any contract to buy, purchase, or otherwise acquire. For security futures products, such term includes any contract, agreement, or transaction for future delivery.

(14) [Sale, Sell]

The terms "sale" and "sell" each include any contract to sell or otherwise dispose of. For security futures products, such term includes any contract, agreement, or transaction for future delivery.

(15) [Commission]

The term "Commission" means the Securities and Exchange Commission established by section 4 of this title.

(16) [State]

The term "State" means any State of the United States, the District of Columbia, Puerto Rico, the Virgin Islands, or any other possession of the United States.

(17) [Interstate Commerce]

The term "interstate commerce" means trade, commerce, transportation, or communication among the several States, or between any foreign country and any State, or between any State and any place or ship outside thereof. The term includes intrastate use of (A) any facility of a national securities exchange or of a telephone or other interstate means of communication, or (B) any other interstate instrumentality.

(18) [Person Associated with Broker]

The term "person associated with a broker or dealer" or "associated person of a broker or dealer" means any partner, officer, director, or branch manager of such broker or dealer (or any person occupying a similar status or performing similar functions), any person directly or indirectly controlling, controlled by, or under common control with such broker or dealer, or any employee of such broker or dealer, except that any person associated with a broker or dealer whose functions are solely clerical or ministerial shall not be inclued in the meaning of such term for purposes of section 15(b) of this title (other than paragraph (6) thereof).

(19) [Investment Company]

The terms "investment company", "affiliated person", "insurance company", "separate account", and "company" have the same meanings as in the Investment Company Act of 1940.

(20) [Investment Adviser]

The terms "investment adviser" and "underwriter" have the same meaning as in the Investment Advisers Act of 1940.

(21) [Person Associated with Member]

The term "person associated with a member" or "associated person of a member" when used with respect to a member of a national securities exchange or registered securities association means any partner, officer, director, or branch manager of such member (or any person occupying a similar status or performing similar functions), any person directly or indirectly controlling, controlled by, or under common control with such member, or any employee of such member.

(22) [Securities Information Processor]

(A) The term "securities information processor" means any person engaged in the business of (i) collecting, processing, or preparing for distribution or publication, or assisting, participating in, or coordinating the distribution or publication of, information with respect to transactions in or quotations for any security (other than an exempted security) or (ii) distributing or publishing (whether by means of a ticker tape, a communications network, a terminal display device, or otherwise) on a current and continuing basis, information with respect to such transactions or quotations. The term "securities information processor" does not include any bona fide newspaper, news magazine, or business or financial publication of general and regular circulation, any self-regulatory organization, any bank, broker, dealer, building and loan, savings and loan, or homestead association, or cooperative bank, if such bank, broker, dealer, association, or cooperative bank would be deemed to be a securities information processor solely by reason of functions performed by such institutions as part of customary banking, brokerage, dealing, association, or cooperative bank activities, or any common carrier, as defined in section 3 of the Communications Act of 1934, subject to the jurisdiction of the Federal Communications Commission or a State commission, as defined in section 3 of that Act, unless the Commission determines that such carrier is engaged in the business of collecting, processing, or preparing for distribution or publication, information with respect to transactions in or quotations for any security.

(B) The term "exclusive processor" means any securities information processor or self-regulatory organization which, directly or indirectly, engages on an exclusive basis on behalf of any national securities exchange or registered securities association or, any national securities exchange or registered securities association which engages on an exclusive basis on its own behalf, in collecting, processing, or preparing for distribution or publication any information with respect to (i) transactions or quotations on or effected or made by means of any facility of such exchange or (ii) quotations distributed or published by means of any electronic system operated or controlled by such association.

(23) [Clearing Agency]

(A) The term "clearing agency" means any person who acts as a intermediary in making payments or deliveries or both in connection with transactions in securities or who provides facilities for comparison of data respecting the terms of settlement of securities transactions, to reduce the number of settlements of securities transactions, or for the allocation of securities settlement responsibilities. Such term also means any person, such as a securities depository, who (i) acts as a custodian of securities in connection with a system for the central handling of securities whereby all securities of a particular class or series of any issuer deposited within the system are treated as fungible and may be transferred, loaned, or pledged by bookkeeping entry without physical delivery of securities certificates, or (ii) otherwise permits or facilitates the settlement of securities transactions or the hypothecation or lending of securities without physical delivery of securities certificates.

(B) The term "clearing agency" does not include (i) any Federal Reserve bank, Federal home loan bank, or Federal land bank; (ii) any national securities exchange or registered securities association solely by reason of its providing facilities for comparison of data respecting the terms of settlement of securities transactions effected on such exchange or by means of any electronic system operated or controlled by such association; (iii) any bank, broker, dealer, building and loan, savings and loan, or homestead association, or cooperative bank if such bank, broker, dealer, association, or cooperative bank would be deemed to be a clearing agency solely by reason of functions performed by such institution as part of customary banking, brokerage, dealing, association, or cooperative banking activities, or solely by reason of acting on behalf of a clearing agency or a participant therein in connection with the furnishing by the clearing agency of services to its participants or the use of services of the clearing agency by its participants, unless the Commission, by rule otherwise provides as necessary or appropriate to assure the prompt and accurate clearance and settlement of securities transactions or to prevent evasion of this title; (iv) any life insurance company, its registered separate accounts, or a subsidiary of such insurance company solely by reason of functions commonly performed by such entities in connection with variable annuity contracts or variable life policies issued by such insurance company or its separate accounts; (v) any registered open-end investment company or unit investment trust solely by reason of functions commonly performed by it in connection with shares in such registered open-end investment company or unit investment trust, or (vi) any person solely by reason of its performing functions described in paragraph 25(E) of this subsection.

(24) [Participant]

The term "participant" when used with respect to a clearing agency means any person who uses a clearing agency to clear or settle securities transactions or to transfer, pledge, lend, or hypothecate securities. Such term does not include a person whose only use of a clearing agency is (A) through another person who is a participant or (B) as a pledgee of securities.

(25) [Transfer Agent]

The term "transfer agent" means any person who engages on behalf of an issuer of securities or on behalf of itself as an issuer of securities in (A) countersigning such securities upon issuance; (B) monitoring the issuance of such securities with a view to preventing unauthorized issuance, a function commonly performed by a person called a registrar; (C) registering the transfer of such securities; (D) exchanging or converting such securities; or (E) transferring record ownership of securities by bookkeeping entry without physical issuance of securities certificates. The term "transfer agency" does not include any insurance company or separate account which performs such functions solely with respect to variable annuity contracts or variable life policies which it issues or any registered clearing agency which performs such functions solely with respect to options contracts which it issues.

(26) [Self-Regulatory Organization]

The term "self-regulatory organization" means any national securities exchange, registered securities association, or registered clearing agency, or (solely for purposes of sections 19(b), 19(c), and 23(b) of this title) the Municipal Securities Rulemaking Board established by section 15B of this title.

(27) [Rules of an Exchange]

The term "rules of an exchange", "rules of an association", or "rules of a clearing agency" means the constitution, articles of incorporation, bylaws, and rules, or instruments corresponding to the foregoing, of an exchange, association of brokers and dealers, or clearing agency, respectively, and such of the stated policies, practices, and interpretations of such exchange, association, or clearing agency as the Commission, by rule, may determine to be necessary or appropriate in the public interest or for the protection of investors to be deemed to be rules of such exchange, association or clearing agency.

(28) [Rules of a Self-Regulatory Organization]

The term "rules of a self-regulatory organization" means the rules of an exchange which is a national securities exchange, the rules of an association of brokers and dealers which is a registered securities association, the rules of a clearing agency which is a registered clearing agency, or the rules of the Municipal Securities Rulemaking Board.

(29) [Municipal Securities]

The term "municipal securities" means securities which are direct obligations of, or obligations guaranteed as to principal or interest by, a State or any political subdivision thereof, or any agency or instrumentality of a State or any political subdivision thereof, or any municipal corporate instrumentality of one or more States, or any security which is an industrial development bond (as defined in section 103(c)(2) of the Internal Revenue Code of 1954) the interest on which is excludable from gross income under section 103(a)(1) of such Code if, by reason of the application of paragraph (4) or (6) of section 103(c) of such Code (determined as if paragraphs 4(A), (5), and (7) were not included in such section 103(c)), paragraph (1) of such section 103(c) does not apply to such security.

(30) [Municipal Securities Dealer]

The term "municipal securities dealer" means any person (including a separately identifiable department or division of a bank) engaged in the business of buying and selling municipal securities for his own account, through a broker or otherwise, but does not include—

(A) any person insofar as he buys or sells such securities for his own account, either individually or in some fiduciary capacity, but not as a part of a regular business; or

(B) a bank, unless the bank is engaged in the business of buying and selling municipal securities for its own account other than in a fiduciary capacity, through a broker or otherwise: *Provided, however,* That if the bank is engaged in such business through a separately identifiable department or division (as defined by the Municipal Securities Rulemaking Board in accordance with Section 15B(b)(2)(H) of this title), the department or division and not the bank itself shall be deemed to be the municipal securities dealer.

(31) [Municipal Securities Broker]

The term "municipal securities broker" means a broker engaged in the business of effecting transactions in municipal securities for the account of others.

(32) [Person Associated with a Municipal Securities Dealer]

The term "person associated with a municipal securities dealer" when used with respect to a municipal securities dealer which is a bank or a division or department of a bank means any person directly engaged in the management, direction, supervision, or performance of any of the municipal securities dealer's activities with respect to municipal securities, and any person directly or indirectly controlling such activities or controlled by the municipal securities dealer in connection with such activities.

(33) [Municipal Securities Investment Portfolio]

The term "municipal securities investment portfolio" means all municipal securities held for investment and not for sale as part of a regular business by a municipal securities dealer or by a person, directly or indirectly, controlling, controlled by, or under common control with a municipal securities dealer.

(34) [Appropriate Regulatory Agency]

The term "appropriate regulatory agency" means—

(A) When used with respect to a municipal securities dealer:

(i) the Comptroller of the Currency, in the case of a national bank or a bank operating under the Code of Law for the District of Columbia, or a subsidiary or a department or division of any such bank;

(ii) the Board of Governors of the Federal Reserve System, in the case of a State member bank of the Federal Reserve System, a subsidiary or a department or division thereof, a bank holding company, a subsidiary of a bank holding company which is a bank other than a bank specified in clause (i) or (iii) of this subparagraph, or a subsidiary or a department or division of such subsidiary;

(iii) the Federal Deposit Insurance Corporation, in the case of a bank insured by the Federal Deposit Insurance Corporation (other than a member of the Federal Reserve System), or a subsidiary or department or division thereof; and

(iv) the Commission in the case of all other municipal securities dealers.

(B) When used with respect to a clearing agency or transfer agent:

(i) the Comptroller of the Currency, in the case of a national bank or a bank operating under the Code of Law for the District of Columbia, or a subsidiary of any such bank;

(ii) the Board of Governors of the Federal Reserve System, in the case of a State member bank of the Federal Reserve System, a subsidiary thereof, a bank holding company, or a subsidiary of a bank holding company which is a bank other than a bank specified in clause (i) or (iii) of this subparagraph;

(iii) the Federal Deposit Insurance Corporation, in the case of a bank insured by the Federal Deposit Insurance Corporation (other than a member of the Federal Reserve System), or a subsidiary thereof; and

(iv) the Commission in the case of all other clearing agencies and transfer agents.

(C) When used with respect to a participant or applicant to become a participant in a clearing agency or a person requesting or having access to services offered by a clearing agency:

(i) the Comptroller of the Currency, in the case of a national bank or a bank operating under the Code of Law for the District of Columbia when the appropriate regulatory agency for such clearing agency is not the Commission;

(ii) the Board of Governors of the Federal Reserve System in the case of a State member bank of the Federal Reserve System, a bank holding company, or a subsidiary of a bank holding company, or a subsidiary of a bank holding company which is a bank other than a bank specified in clause (i) or (iii) of this subparagraph when the appropriate regulatory agency for such clearing agency is not the Commission;

(iii) the Federal Deposit Insurance Corporation, in the case of a bank insured by the Federal Deposit Insurance Corporation (other than a member of the Federal Reserve System) when the appropriate regulatory agency for such clearing agency is not the Commission; and

(iv) the Commission in all other cases.

(D) When used with respect to an institutional investment manager which is a bank the deposits of which are insured in accordance with the Federal Deposit Insurance Act:

(i) the Comptroller of the Currency, in the case of a national bank or a bank operating under the Code of Law for the District of Columbia;

(ii) the Board of Governors of the Federal Reserve System, in the case of any other member bank of the Federal Reserve System; and

(iii) the Federal Deposit Insurance Corporation, in the case of any other insured bank.

(E) When used with respect to a national securities exchange or registered securities association, member thereof, person associated with a member thereof, applicant to become a member thereof or to become associated with a member thereof, or person requesting or having access to services offered by such exchange or association or member thereof, or the Municipal Securities Rulemaking Board, the Commission.

(F) When used with respect to a person exercising investment discretion with respect to an account:

(i) the Comptroller of the Currency, in the case of a national bank or a bank operating under the Code of Law for the District of Columbia;

(ii) the Board of Governors of the Federal Reserve System in the case of any other member bank of the Federal Reserve System;

(iii) the Federal Deposit Insurance Corporation, in the case of any other bank the deposits of which are insured in accordance with the Federal Deposit Insurance Act; and

(iv) the Commission in the case of all other such persons.

(G) When used with respect to a government securities broker or government securities dealer, or person associated with a government securities broker or government securities dealer:

(i) the Comptroller of the Currency, in the case of a national bank, a bank in the District of Columbia examined by the Comptroller of the Currency, or a Federal branch or Federal agency of a foreign bank (as such terms are used in the International Banking Act of 1978);

(ii) the Board of Governors of the Federal Reserve System, in the case of a State member bank of the Federal Reserve System, a foreign bank, an uninsured State branch or State agency of a foreign bank, a commercial lending company owned or controlled by a foreign bank (as such terms are used in the International Banking Act of 1978), or a corporation organized or having an agreement with the Board of Governors of the Federal Reserve System pursuant to section 25 or section 25A of the Federal Reserve Act;

(iii) the Federal Deposit Insurance Corporation, in the case of a bank insured by the Federal Deposit Insurance Corporation (other than a member of the Federal Reserve System or a Federal savings bank) or an insured State branch of a foreign bank (as such terms are used in the International Banking Act of 1978);

(iv) the Director of the Office of Thrift Supervision, in the case of a savings association (as defined in section 3(b) of the Federal Deposit Insurance Act) the deposits of which are insured by the Federal Deposit Insurance Corporation;

(v) the Commission, in the case of all other government securities brokers and government securities dealers."

As used in this paragraph, the terms "bank holding company" and "subsidiary of a bank holding company" have the meanings given them in section 2 of the Bank Holding Company Act of 1956, and the term "District of Columbia savings and loan association" means any association subject to examination and supervision by the Office of Thrift Supervision under section 8 of the Home Owners' Loan Act of 1933.

(H) When used with respect to an institution described in subparagraph (D), (F), or (G) of section 2(c)(2), or held under section 4(f), of the Bank Holding Company Act of 1956—

(i) the Comptroller of the Currency, in the case of a national bank or a bank in the District of Columbia examined by the Comptroller of the Currency;

(ii) the Board of Governors of the Federal Reserve System, in the case of a State member bank of the Federal Reserve System or any corporation chartered under section 25A of the Federal Reserve Act;

(iii) the Federal Deposit Insurance Corporation, in the case of any other bank the deposits of which are insured in accordance with the Federal Deposit Insurance Act; or

(iv) the Commission in the case of all other such institutions.

(35) [Investment Discretion]

A person exercises "investment discretion" with respect to an account if, directly or indirectly, such person (A) is authorized to determine what securities or other property shall be purchased or sold or for the account, (B) makes decisions as to what securities or other property shall be purchased or sold by or for the account even though some other person may have responsibility for such investment decisions, or (C) otherwise exercises such influence with respect to the purchase and sale of securities or other property by or for the account as the Commission, by rule, determines, in the public interest or for the protection of investors, should be subject to the operation of the provisions of this title and the rules and regulations thereunder.

(36) [Equal Regulation]

A class of persons or markets is subject to "equal regulation" if no member of the class has a competitive advantage over any other member thereof resulting from a disparity in their regulation under this title which the Commission determines is unfair and not necessary or appropriate in furtherance of the purposes of this title.

(37) [Records]

The term "records" means accounts, correspondence, memorandums, tapes, discs, papers, books, and other documents or transcribed information of any type, whether expressed in ordinary or machine language.

(38) [Market Maker]

The term "market maker" means any specialist permitted to act as a dealer, any dealer acting in the capacity of block positioner, and any dealer who, with respect to a security, holds himself out (by entering quotations in an inter-dealer communications system or otherwise) as being willing to buy and sell such security for his own account on a regular or continuous basis.

(39) [Statutory Disqualification]

A person is subject to a "statutory disqualification" with respect to membership or participation in, or association with a member of, a self-regulatory organization, if such person—

(A) has been and is expelled or suspended from membership or participation in, or barred or suspended from being associated with a member of, any self-regulatory organization, foreign equivalent of a self-regulatory organization, foreign or international securities exchange, contract market designated pursuant to section 5 of the Commodity Exchange Act (7 U.S.C. 7), or any substantially equivalent foreign statute or regulation or futures associates registered under section 17 of such Act (7 U.S.C. 21), or any substantially foreign statute or regulation or has been and is denied trading privileges on any such contract market or foreign equivalent;

(B) is subject to—

(i) an order of the Commission, other appropriate regulatory agency, or foreign financial regulatory authority—

(I) denying, suspending for a period not exceeding 12 months, or revoking his registration as a broker, dealer, municipal securities dealer, government securities broker, or government securities dealer or limiting his activities as a foreign person performing a function substantially equivalent to any of the above; or

(II) barring or suspending for a period not exceeding 12 months his being associated with a broker, dealer, municipal securities dealer, government securities broker, government securities dealer, or foreign person performing a function substantially equivalent to any of the above;

(ii) an order of the Commodity Futures Trading Commission denying, suspending, or revoking his registration under the Commodity Exchange Act (7 U.S.C. 1 et seq.); or

(iii) an order by a foreign financial regulatory authority denying, suspending, or revoking the person's authority to engage in transactions in contracts of sale of a commodity for future delivery or other instruments traded on or subject to the rules of a contract market, board of trade, or foreign equivalent thereof,

(C) by his conduct while associated with a broker, dealer, municipal securities dealer, government securities broker, or government securities dealer, or while associated with an entity or person required to be registered under the Commodity Exchange Act, has been found to be a cause of any effective suspension, expulsion, or order of the character described in subparagraph (A) or (B) of this paragraph, and in entering such a suspension, expulsion, or order, the Commission, an appropriate regulatory agency, or any such self-regulatory organization shall have jurisdiction to find whether or not any person was a cause thereof;

(D) by his conduct while associated with any broker, dealer, municipal securities dealer, government securities broker, government securities dealer, or any other entity engaged in transactions in securities, or while associated with an entity engaged in transactions in contracts of sale of a commodity for future delivery or other instruments traded on or subject to the rules of a contract market, board of trade, or foreign equivalent thereof, has been found to be a cause of any effective suspension, expulsion, or order by a foreign or international securities exchange or foreign financial regulatory authority empowered by a foreign government to administer or enforce its laws relating to financial transactions as described in subparagraphs (A) or (B) of this paragraph,

(E) has associated with him any person who is known, or in the exercise of reasonable care should be known, to him to be a person described by subparagraph (A), (B), (C), or (D) of this paragraph; or

(F) has committed or omitted any act enumerated in subparagraph (D), (E), or (G) of paragraph (4) of section 15(b) of this title, has been convicted of any offense specified in subparagraph (B) of such paragraph (4) or any other felony within ten years of the date of the filing of an application for membership or participation in, or to become associated with a member of, such self-regulatory organization, is enjoined from any action, conduct, or practice specified in subparagraph (C) of such paragraph (4), has willfully made or caused to be made in any application for membership or participation in, or to become associated with a member of, a self-regulatory organization, report required to be filed with a self-regulatory organization, or proceeding before a self-regulatory organization, any statement which was at the time, and in the light of the circumstances under which it was made, false or misleading with respect to any material fact, or has omitted to state in any such application, report, or proceeding any material fact which is required to be stated therein.

(40) [Financial Responsibility Rules]

The term "financial responsibility rules" means the rules and regulations of the Commission or the rules and regulations prescribed by any self-regulatory organization relating to financial responsibility and related practices which are designated by the Commission, by rule or regulation, to be financial responsiblity rules.

(41) [Mortgage Related Security]

The term "mortgage related security" means a security that is rated in one of the two highest rating categories by at least one nationally recognized statistical rating organization, and either:

(A) represents ownership of one or more promissory notes or certificates of interest or participation in such notes (including any rights designed to assure servicing of, or the receipt or timeliness of receipt by the holders of such notes, certificates, or participations of amounts payable under, such notes, certificates, or participations), which notes:

(i) are directly secured by a first lien on a single parcel of real estate, including stock allocated to a dwelling unit in a residential cooperative housing corporation, upon which is located a dwelling or mixed residential and commercial structure, on a residential manufactured home as defined in section 603(6) of the National Manufactured Housing Construction and Safety Standards Act of 1974, whether such manufactured home is considered real or personal property under the laws of the State in which it is to be located, or on one or more parcels of real estate upon which is located one or more commercial structures; and

(ii) were originated by a savings and loan association, savings bank, commercial bank, credit union, insurance company, or similar institution which is supervised and examined by a Federal or State authority, or by a mortgagee approved by the Secretary of Housing and Urban Development pursuant to sections 203 and 211 of the National Housing Act, or, where such notes involve a lien on the manufactured home, by any such institution or by any financial institution approved for insurance by the Secretary of Housing and Urban Development pursuant to section 2 of the National Housing Act; or

(B) is secured by one or more promissory notes or certificates of interest or participations in such notes (with or without recourse to the issuer thereof) and, by its terms, provides for payments of principal in relation to payments, or reasonable projections of payments, on notes meeting the requirements of subparagraphs (A)(i) and (ii) or certificates of interest or participations in promissory notes meeting such requirements.

For the purpose of this paragraph, the term "promissory note", when used in connection with a manufactured home, shall also include a loan, advance, or credit sale as evidence by a retail installment sales contract or other instrument.

(42) [Government Securities]

The term "government securities" means—

(A) securities which are direct obligations of, or obligations guaranteed as to principal or interest by, the United States;

(B) securities which are issued or guaranteed by corporations in which the United States has a direct or indirect interest and which are designated by the Secretary of the Treasury for exemption as necessary or appropriate in the public interest or for the protection of investors;

(C) securities issued or guaranteed as to principal or interest by any corporation the securities of which are designated, by statute specifically naming such corporation, to constitute exempt securities within the meaning of the laws administered by the Commission;

(D) for purposes of sections 15C and 17A, any put, call, straddle, option, or privilege on a security described in subparagraph (A), (B), or (C) other than a put, call, straddle, option, or privilege—

(i) that is traded on one or more national securities exchanges; or

(ii) for which quotations are disseminated through an automated quotation system operated by a registered securities association; or

(E) for purposes of sections 15, 15C, and 17A as applied to a bank, a qualified Canadian government obligation as defined in section 5136 of the Revised Statutes of the United States.

(43) [Government Securities Broker]

The term "government securities broker" means any person regularly engaged in the business of effecting transactions in government securities for the account of others, but does not include—

(A) any corporation the securities of which are government securities under subparagraph (B) or (C) of paragraph (42) of this subsection; or

(B) any person registered with the Commodity Futures Trading Commission, any contract market designated by the Commodity Futures Trading Commission, such contract market's affiliated clearing organization, or any floor trader on such contract market, solely because such person effects transactions in government securities that the Commission, after consultation with the Commodity Futures Trading Commission, has determined by rule or order to be incidental to such person's futures-related business.

(44) [Government Securities Dealer]

The term "government securities dealer" means any person engaged in the business of buying and selling government securities for his own account, through a broker or otherwise, but does not include—

(A) any person insofar as he buys or sells such securities for his own account, either individually or in some fiduciary capacity, but not as a part of a regular business;

(B) any corporation the securities of which are government securities under subparagraph (B) or (C) of paragraph (42) of this subsection;

(C) any bank, unless the bank is engaged in the business of buying and selling government securities for its own account other than in a fiduciary capacity, through a broker or otherwise; or

(D) any person registered with the Commodity Futures Trading Commission, any contract market designated by the Commodity Futures Trading Commission, such contract market's affiliated clearing organization, or any floor trader on such contract market, solely because such person effects transactions in government securities that the Commission, after consultation with the Commodity Futures Trading Commission, has determined by rule or order to be incidental to such person's futures-related business.

(45) [Person Associated with a Government Securities Broker or Government Securities Dealer]

The term "person associated with a government securities broker or government securities dealer" means any partner, officer, director, or branch manager of such government securities broker or government securities dealer (or any person occupying a similar status or performing similar functions), and any other employee of such government securities broker or government securities dealer who is engaged in the management, direction, supervision, or performance of any activities relating to government securities, and any person directly or indirectly controlling, controlled by, or under common control with such government securities broker or government securities dealer.

(46) [Financial Institution]

The term "financial institution" means—

(A) a bank (as defined in paragraph (6) of this subsection);

(B) a foreign bank (as such term is used in the International Banking Act of 1978); and

(C) a savings association (as defined in section 3(b) of the Federal Deposit Insurance Act) the deposits of which are insured by the Federal Deposit Insurance Corporation.

(47) [Securities Laws]

The term 'securities laws' means the Securities Act of 1933 (15 U.S.C. 77a et seq.), the Securites Exchange Act of 1934 (15 U.S.C. 78a et seq.), the Public Utility Holding Company Act of 1935 (15 U.S.C. 79a et seq.), the Trust Indenture Act of 1939 (15 U.S.C. 77aaa et seq.), the Investment Company Act of 1940 (15 U.S.C. 80a-1 et seq.), the Investment Advisers Act of 1940 (15 U.S.C. 80b et seq.), and the Securities Investor Protection Act of 1970 (15 U.S.C. 78aaa et seq.).

(48) [Registered Broker or Dealer]

The term "registered broker or dealer" means a broker or dealer registered or required to register pursuant to section 15 or 15B of this title, except that in paragraph (3) of this subsection and sections 6 and 15A the term means such a broker or dealer and a government securities broker or government securities dealer registered or required to register pursuant to section 15C(a)(1)(A) of this title.

(49) [Person Associated With a Transfer Agent]

The term "person associated with a transfer agent" and "associated person of a transfer agent" mean any person (except an employee whose functions are solely clerical or ministerial) directly engaged in the management, direction, supervision, or performance of any of the transfer agent's activities with respect to transfer agent functions, and any person directly or indirectly controlling such activities or controlled by the transfer agent in connection with such activities.

(50) [Foreign Securities Authority]

The term "foreign securities authority" means any foreign government, or any governmental body or regulatory organization empowered by a foreign government to administer or enforce its laws as they relate to securities matters.

(51) [Penny Stock]

(A) The term "penny stock" means any equity security other than a security that is—

(i) registered or approved for registration and traded on a national securities exchange that meets such criteria as the Commission shall prescribe by rule or regulation for purposes of this paragraph;

(ii) authorized for quotation on an automated quotation system sponsored by a registered securities association, if such system (I) was established and in operation before January 1, 1990, and (II) meets such criteria as the Commission shall prescribe by rule or regulation for purposes of this paragraph;

(iii) issued by an investment company registered under the Investment Company Act of 1940;

(iv) excluded, on the basis of exceeding a minimum price, net tangible assets of the issuer, or other relevant criteria, from the definition of such term by rule or regulation which the Commission shall prescribe for purposes of this paragraph; or

(v) exempted, in whole or in part, conditionally or unconditionally, from the definition of such term by rule, regulation, or order prescribed by the Commission.

(B) The Commission may, by rule, regulation, or order, designate any equity security or class of equity securities described in clause (i) or (ii) of subparagraph (A) as within the meaning of the term "penny stock" if such security or class of securities is traded other than on a national securities exchange or through an automated quotation system described in clause (ii) of subparagraph (A).

(C) In exercising its authority under this paragraph to prescribe rules, regulations, and orders, the Commission shall determine that such rule, regulation, or order is consistent with the public interest and the protection of investors.

(52) [Foreign Financial Regulatory Authority]

The term "foreign financial regulatory authority" means any (A) foreign securities authority, (B) other governmental body or foreign equivalent of a self-regulatory organization empowered by a foreign government to administer or enforce its laws relating to the regulation of fiduciaries, trusts, commercial lending, insurance, trading in contracts of sale of a commodity for future delivery, or other instruments traded on or subject to the rules of a contract market, board of trade, or foreign equivalent, or other financial activities, or (C) membership organization a function of which is to regulate participation of its members in activities listed above.

(53) [Small Business Related Security]

(A) The term "small business related security" means a security that is rated in 1 of the 4 highest rating categories by at least 1 nationally recognized statistical rating organization, and either—

(i) represents an interest in 1 or more promissory notes or leases of personal property evidencing the obligation of a small business concern and originated by an insured depository institution, insured credit union, insurance company, or similar institution which is supervised and examined by a Federal or State authority, or a finance company or leasing company; or

(ii) is secured by an interest in 1 or more promissory notes or leases of personal property (with or without recourse to the issuer or lessee) and provides for payments of principal in relation to payments, or reasonable projections of payments, on notes or leases described in clause (i).

(B) For purposes of this paragraph—

(i) an "interest in a promissory note or a lease of personal property" includes ownership rights, certificates of interest or participation in such notes or leases, and rights designed to assure servicing of such notes or leases, or the receipt or timely receipt of amounts payable under such notes or leases;

(ii) the term "small business concern" means a business that meets the criteria for a small business concern established by the Small Business Administration under section 3(a) of the Small Business Act;

(iii) the term "insured depository institution" has the same meaning as in section 3 of the Federal Deposit Insurance Act; and

(iv) the term "insured credit union" has the same meaning as in section 101 of the Federal Credit Union Act.

(54) [Qualified Investor]

QUALIFIED INVESTOR.—

(A) DEFINITION.—Except as provided in subparagraph (B), for purposes of this title, the term 'qualified investor' means—

(i) any investment company registered with the Commission under section 8 of the Investment Company Act of 1940;

(ii) any issuer eligible for an exclusion from the definition of investment company pursuant to section 3(c)(7) of the Investment Company Act of 1940;

(iii) any bank (as defined in paragraph (6) of this subsection), savings association (as defined in section 3(b) of the Federal Deposit Insurance Act), broker, dealer, insurance company (as defined in section 2(a)(13) of the Securities Act of 1933), or business development company (as defined in section 2(a)(48) of the Investment Company Act of 1940);

(iv) any small business investment company licensed by the United States Small Business Administration under section 301 (c) or (d) of the Small Business Investment Act of 1958;

(v) any State sponsored employee benefit plan, or any other employee benefit plan, within the meaning of the Employee Retirement Income Security Act of 1974, other than an individual retirement account, if the investment decisions are made by a plan fiduciary, as defined in section 3(21) of that Act, which is either a bank, savings and loan association, insurance company, or registered investment adviser;

(vi) any trust whose purchases of securities are directed by a person described in clauses (i) through (v) of this subparagraph;

(vii) any market intermediary exempt under section 3(c)(2) of the Investment Company Act of 1940;

(viii) any associated person of a broker or dealer other than a natural person;

(ix) any foreign bank (as defined in section 1(b)(7) of the International Banking Act of 1978);

(x) the government of any foreign country;

(xi) any corporation, company, or partnership that owns and invests on a discretionary basis, not less than $25,000,000 in investments;

(xii) any natural person who owns and invests on a discretionary basis, not less than $25,000,000 in investments;

(xiii) any government or political subdivision, agency, or instrumentality of a government who owns and invests on a discretionary basis not less than $50,000,000 in investments; or

(xiv) any multinational or supranational entity or any agency or instrumentality thereof.

(B) ALTERED THRESHOLDS FOR ASSET-BACKED SECURITIES AND LOAN PARTICIPATIONS.—For purposes of section 3(a)(5)(C)(iii) of this title and section 206(a)(5) of the Gramm-Leach-Bliley Act, the term 'qualified investor' has the meaning given such term by subparagraph (A) of this paragraph except that clauses (xi) and (xii) shall be applied by substituting '$10,000,000' for '$25,000,000'.

(C) ADDITIONAL AUTHORITY.—The Commission may, by rule or order, define a 'qualified investor' as any other person, taking into consideration such factors as the financial sophistication of the person, net worth, and knowledge and experience in financial matters.

(55) [Security Future; Narrow-based Security Index]

(A) The term 'security future' means a contract of sale for future delivery of a single security or of a narrow-based security index, including any interest therein or based on the value thereof, except an exempted security under section 3(a)(12) of the Securities Exchange Act of 1934 as in effect on the date of enactment of the Futures Trading Act of 1982 (other than any municipal security as defined in section 3(a)(29) as in effect on the date of enactment of the Futures Trading Act of 1982). The term 'security future' does not include any agreement, contract, or transaction excluded from the Commodity Exchange Act under section 2(c), 2(d), 2(f) or 2(g) of the Commodity Exchange Act (as in effect on the date of enactment of the Commodity Futures Modernization Act of 2000) or title IV of the Commodity Futures Modernization Act of 2000.

(B) The term 'narrow-based security index' means an index—

(i) that has 9 or fewer component securities;

(ii) in which a component security comprises more than 30 percent of the index's weighting;

(iii) in which the 5 highest weighted component securities in the aggregate comprise more than 60 percent of the index's weighting; or

(iv) in which the lowest weighted component securities comprising, in the aggregate, 25 percent of the index's weighting have an aggregate dollar value of average daily trading volume of less than $50,000,000 (or in the case of an index with 15 or more component securities, $30,000,000), except that if there are two or more securities with equal weighting that could be included in the calculation of the lowest weighted component securities comprising, in the aggregate, 25 percent of the index's weighting, such securities shall be ranked from lowest to highest dollar value of average daily trading volume and shall be included in the calculation based on their ranking starting with the lowest ranked security.

(C) Notwithstanding subparagraph (B), an index is not a narrow-based security index if—

(i)(I) it has at least 9 component securities;

(II) no component security comprises more than 30 percent of the index's weighting; and

(III) each component security is—

(aa) registered pursuant to section 12 of the Securities Exchange Act of 1934;

(bb) 1 of 750 securities with the largest market capitalization; and

(cc) 1 of 675 securities with the largest dollar value of average daily trading volume;

(ii) a board of trade was designated as a contract market by the Commodity Futures Trading Commission with respect to a contract of sale for future delivery on the index, before the date of enactment of the Commodity Futures Modernization Act of 2000;

(iii)(I) a contract of sale for future delivery on the index traded on a designated contract market or registered derivatives transaction execution facility for at least 30 days as a contract of sale for future delivery on an index that was not a narrow-based security index; and

(II) it has been a narrow-based security index for no more than 45 business days over 3 consecutive calendar months;

(iv) a contract of sale for future delivery on the index is traded on or subject to the rules of a foreign board of trade and meets such requirements as are jointly established by rule or regulation by the Commission and the Commodity Futures Trading Commission;

(v) no more than 18 months have passed since the date of enactment of the Commodity Futures Modernization Act of 2000 and—

(I) it is traded on or subject to the rules of a foreign board of trade;

(II) the offer and sale in the United States of a contract of sale for future delivery on the index was authorized before the date of the enactment of the Commodity Futures Modernization Act of 2000; and

(III) the conditions of such authorization continue to be met; or

(vi) a contract of sale for future delivery on the index is traded on or subject to the rules of a board of trade and meets such requirements as are jointly established by rule, regulation, or order by the Commission and the Commodity Futures Trading Commission.

(D) Within 1 year after the enactment of the Commodity Futures Modernization Act of 2000, the Commission and the Commodity Futures Trading Commission jointly shall adopt rules or regulations that set forth the requirements under clause (iv) of subparagraph (C).

(E) An index that is a narrow-based security index solely because it was a narrow-based security index for more than 45 business days over 3 consecutive calendar months pursuant to clause (iii) of subparagraph (C) shall not be a narrow-based security index for the 3 following calendar months.

(F) For purposes of subparagraphs (B) and (C) of this paragraph—

(i) the dollar value of average daily trading volume and the market capitalization shall be calculated as of the preceding 6 full calendar months; and

(ii) the Commission and the Commodity Futures Trading Commission shall, by rule or regulation, jointly specify the method to be used to determine market capitalization and dollar value of average daily trading volume.

(56) [Security Futures Product]

The term 'security futures product' means a security future or any put, call, straddle, option, or privilege on any security future.

(57) [Margin; Margin Level; Higher Margin Level]

(A) The term 'margin', when used with respect to a security futures product, means the amount, type, and form of collateral required to secure any extension or maintenance of credit, or the amount, type, and form of collateral required as a performance bond related to the purchase, sale, or carrying of a security futures product.

(B) The terms 'margin level' and 'level of margin', when used with respect to a security futures product, mean the amount of margin required to secure any extension or maintenance of credit, or the amount of margin required as a performance bond related to the purchase, sale, or carrying of a security futures product.

(C) The terms 'higher margin level' and 'higher level of margin', when used with respect to a security futures product, mean a margin level established by a national securities exchange registered pursuant to section 6(g) that is higher than the minimum amount established and in effect pursuant to section 7(c)(2)(B).

(58) [Audit Committee]

AUDIT COMMITTEE. The term 'audit committee' means—

(A) a committee (or equivalent body) established by and amongst the board of directors of an issuer for the purpose of overseeing the accounting and financial reporting processes of the issuer and audits of the financial statements of the issuer; and

(B) if no such committee exists with respect to an issuer, the entire board of directors of the issuer.

(59) [Registered Public Accounting Firm]

REGISTERED PUBLIC ACCOUNTING FIRM. The term 'registered public accounting firm' has the same meaning as in section 2 of the Sarbanes-Oxley Act of 2002.

(b) [Power to Define Terms]

The Commission and the Board of Governors of the Federal Reserve System, as to matters within their respective jurisdictions, shall have power by rules and regulations to define technical, trade, accounting, and other terms used in this title, consistently with the provisions and purposes of this title.

(c) [Exemption of Governmental Departments and Agencies from Act]

No provision of this title shall apply to, or be deemed to include, any executive department or independent establishment of the United States, or any lending agency which is wholly owned, directly or indirectly, by the United States, or any officer, agent, or employee of any such department, establishment, or agency, acting in the course of his official duty as such, unless such provision makes specific reference to such department, establishment, or agency.

(d) [Issuer of Municipal Securities]

No issuer of municipal securities or officer or employee thereof acting in the course of his official duties as such shall be deemed to be a "broker", "dealer", or "municipal securities dealer" solely by reason of buying, selling, or effecting transactions in the issuer's securities.

(e) [Charitable Organizations]

CHARITABLE ORGANIZATIONS.—

(1) EXEMPTION.—Notwithstanding any other provision of this title, but subject to paragraph (2) of this subsection, a charitable organization, as defined in section 3(c)(10)(D) of the Investment Company Act of 1940, or any trustee, director, officer, employee, or volunteer of such a charitable organization acting within the scope of such person's employment or duties with such organization, shall not be deemed to be a "broker", "dealer", "municipal securities broker", "municipal securities dealer", "government securities broker", or "government securities dealer" for purposes of this title solely because such organization or person buys, holds, sells, or trades in securities for its own account in its capacity as trustee or administrator of, or otherwise on behalf of or for the account of—

(A) such a charitable organization;

(B) a fund that is excluded from the definition of an investment company under section 3(c)(10)(B) of the Investment Company Act of 1940; or

(C) a trust or other donative instrument described in section 3(c)(10)(B) of the Investment Company Act of 1940, or the settlors (or potential settlors) or beneficiaries of any such trust or other instrument.

(2) LIMITATION ON COMPENSATION.—The exemption provided under paragraph (1) shall not be available to any charitable organization, or any trustee, director, officer, employee, or volunteer of such a charitable organization, unless each person who, on or after 90 days after the date of enactment of this subsection, solicits donations on behalf of such charitable organization from any donor to a fund that is excluded from the definition of an investment company under section 3(c)(10)(B) of the Investment Company Act of 1940, is either a volunteer or is engaged in the overall fund raising activities of a charitable organization and receives no commission or other special compensation based on the number or the value of donations collected for the fund.

(f) [Consideration of Promotion of Efficiency, Competition, and Capital Formation]

CONSIDERATION OF PROMOTION OF EFFICIENCY, COMPETITION, AND CAPITAL FORMATION. Whenever pursuant to this title the Commission is engaged in rulemaking, or in the review of a rule of a self-regulatory organization, and is required to consider or determine whether an action is necessary or appropriate in the public interest, the Commission shall also consider, in addition to the protection of investors, whether the action will promote efficiency, competition, and capital formation.

(g) [Church Plans]

CHURCH PLANS. No church plan described in section 414(e) of the Internal Revenue Code of 1986, no person or entity eligible to establish and maintain such a plan under the Internal Revenue Code of 1986, no company or account that is excluded from the definition of an investment company under section 3(c)(14) of the Investment Company Act of 1940, and no trustee, director, officer or employee of or volunteer for such plan, company, account person, or entity, acting within the scope of that person's employment or activities with respect to such plan, shall be deemed to be a "broker," "dealer," "municipal securities broker," "municipal securities dealer," "government securities broker," "government securities dealer," "clearing agency," or "transfer agent" for purposes of this title—

(1) solely because such plan, company, person, or entity buys, holds, sells, trades in, or transfers securities or acts as an intermediary in making payments in connection with transactions in securities for its own account in its capacity as trustee or administrator of, or otherwise on behalf of, or for the account of, any church plan, company, or account that is excluded from the definition of an investment company under section 3(c)(14) of the Investment Company Act of 1940; and

(2) if no such person or entity receives a commission or other transaction-related sales compensation in connection with any activities conducted in reliance on the exemption provided by this subsection.

Sec. 3A. SWAP AGREEMENTS

(a) NON-SECURITY-BASED SWAP AGREEMENTS.—The definition of 'security' in section 3(a)(10) of this title does not include any non-security-based swap agreement (as defined in section 206C of the Gramm-Leach-Bliley Act).

(b) SECURITY-BASED SWAP AGREEMENTS.—

(1) The definition of 'security' in section 3(a)(10) of this title does not include any security-based swap agreement (as defined in section 206B of the Gramm-Leach-Bliley Act).

(2) The Commission is prohibited from registering, or requiring, recommending, or suggesting, the registration under this title of any security-based swap agreement (as defined in section 206B of the Gramm-Leach-Bliley Act). If the Commission becomes aware that a registrant has filed a registration application with respect to such a swap agreement, the Commission shall promptly so notify the registrant. Any such registration with respect to such a swap agreement shall be void and of no force or effect.

(3) Except as provided in section 16(a) with respect to reporting requirements, the Commission is prohibited from—

(A) promulgating, interpreting, or enforcing rules; or

(B) issuing orders of general applicability; under this title in a manner that imposes or specifies reporting or recordkeeping requirements, procedures, or standards as prophylactic measures against fraud, manipulation, or insider trading with respect to any security-based swap agreement (as defined in section 206B of the Gramm-Leach-Bliley Act).

(4) References in this title to the 'purchase' or 'sale' of a security-based swap agreement (as defined in section 206B of the Gramm-Leach-Bliley Act) shall be deemed to mean the execution, termination (prior to its scheduled maturity date), assignment, exchange, or similar transfer or conveyance of, or extinguishing of rights or obligations under, a security-based swap agreement, as the context may require.

Sec. 4. SECURITIES AND EXCHANGE COMMISSION

(a) There is hereby established a Securities and Exchange Commission (hereinafter referred to as the "Commission") to be composed of five commissioners to be appointed by the President by and with the advice and consent of the Senate. Not more than three of such commissioners shall be members of the same political party, and in making appointments members of different political parties shall be appointed alternately as nearly as may be practicable. No commissioner shall engage in any other business, vocation, or employment than that of serving as commissioner, nor shall any commissioner participate, directly or indirectly, in any stock-market operations or transactions of a character subject to regulation by the Commission pursuant to this title. Each commissioner shall hold office for a term of five years and until his successor is appointed and has qualified, except that he shall not so continue to serve beyond the expiration of the next session of Congress subsequent to the expiration of said fixed term of office, and except (1) any Commissioner appointed to fill a vacancy occurring prior to the expiration of the term for which his predecessor was appointed shall be appointed for the remainder of such term, and (2) the terms of office of the Commissioners first taking office after the enactment of this title shall expire as designated by the President at the time of nomination, one at the end of one year, one at the end of two years, one at the end of three years, one at the end of four years, and one at the end of five years, after the date of the enactment of this title.

(b) APPOINTMENT AND COMPENSATION OF STAFF AND LEASING AUTHORITY.—

(1) APPOINTMENT AND COMPENSATION.—The Commission shall appoint and compensate officers, attorneys, economists, examiners, and other employees in accordance with section 4802 of title 5, United States Code.

(2) REPORTING OF INFORMATION.—In establishing and adjusting schedules of compensation and benefits for officers, attorneys, economists, examiners, and other employees of the Commission under applicable provisions of law, the Commission shall inform the heads of the agencies referred to under section 1206 of the Financial Institutions Reform, Recovery, and Enforcement Act of 1989 (12 U.S.C. 1833b) and Congress of such compensation and benefits and shall seek to maintain comparability with such agencies regarding compensation and benefits.

(3) LEASING AUTHORITY.—Notwithstanding any other provision of law, the Commission is authorized to enter directly into leases for real property for office, meeting, storage, and such other space as is necessary to carry out its functions, and shall be exempt from any General Services Administration space management regulations or directives.

(c) Notwithstanding any other provision of law, in accordance with regulations which the Commission shall prescribe to prevent conflicts of interest, the Commission may accept payment and reimbursement, in cash or in kind, from non-Federal agencies, organizations, and individuals for travel, subsistence, and other necessary expenses incurred by Commission members and employees in attending meetings and conferences concerning the functions or activities of the Commission. Any payment or reimbursement accepted shall be credited to the appropriated funds of the Commission. The amount of travel, subsistence, and other necessary expenses for members and employees paid or reimbursed under this subsection may exceed per diem amounts established in official travel regulations, but the Commission may include in its regulations under this subsection a limitation on such amounts.

(d) Notwithstanding any other provision of law, former employers of participants in the Commission's professional fellows programs may pay such participants their actual expenses for relocation to Washington, District of Columbia, to facilitate their participation in such programs, and program participants may accept such payments.

(e) Notwithstanding any other provision of law, whenever any fee is required to be paid to the Commission pursuant to any provision of the securities laws or any other law, the Commission may provide by rule that such fee shall be paid in a manner other than in cash and the Commission may also specify the time that such fee shall be determined and paid relative to the filing of any statement or document with the Commission.

(f) REIMBURSEMENT OF EXPENSES FOR ASSISTING FOREIGN SECURITIES AUTHORITIES.—Notwithstanding any other provision of law, the Commission may accept payment and reimbursement, in cash or in kind, from a foreign securities authority, or made on behalf of such authority, for necessary expenses incurred by the Commission, its members, and employees in carrying out any investigation pursuant to section 21(a)(2) of this title or in providing any other assistance to a foreign securities authority. Any payment or reimbursement accepted shall be considered a reimbursement to the appropriated funds of the Commission.

Sec. 4A. DELEGATION OF FUNCTIONS BY COMMISSION

(a) In addition to its existing authority, the Securities and Exchange Commission shall have the authority to delegate, by published order or rule, any of its functions to a division of the Commission, an individual Commissioner, an administrative law judge, or an employee or employee board, including functions with respect to hearing, determining, ordering, certifying, reporting, or otherwise acting as to any work, business, or matter. Nothing in this section shall be deemed to supersede the provisions of section 556(b) of title 5, or to authorize the delegation of the function of rule-making as defined in subchapter II of chapter 5 of title 5, United States Code, with reference to general rules as distinguished from rules of particular applicability, or of the making of any rule pursuant to section 19(c) of this title.

(b) With respect to the delegation of any of its functions, as provided in subsection (a) of this section, the Commission shall retain a discretionary right to review the action of any such division of the Commission, individual Commissioner, administrative law judge, employee, or employee board, upon its own initiative or upon petition of a party to or intervenor in such action, within such time and in such manner as the Commission by rule shall prescribe. The vote of one member of the Commission shall be sufficient to bring any such action before the Commission for review. A person or party shall be entitled to review by the Commission if he or it is adversely affected by action at a delegated level which (1) denies any request for action pursuant to section 8(a) or section 8(c) of the Securities Act of 1933 or the first sentence of section 12(d) of this title; (2) suspends trading in a security pursuant to section 12(k) of this title; or (3) is pursuant to any provision of this title in a case of adjudication, as defined in section 551 of title 5, United States Code, not required by this title to be determined on the record after notice and opportunity for hearing (except to the extent there is involved a matter described in section 554(a) (1) through (6) of such title 5).

(c) If the right to exercise such review is declined, or if no such review is sought within the time stated in the rules promulgated by the Commission, then the action of any such division of the Commission, individual Commissioner, administrative law judge, employee, or employee board, shall for all purposes, including appeal or review thereof, be deemed the action of the Commission.

Sec. 4B. TRANSFER OF FUNCTIONS WITH RESPECT TO ASSIGNMENT OF PERSONNEL TO CHAIRMAN

In addition to the functions transferred by the provisions of Reorganization Plan Numbered 10 of 1950 (64 Stat. 1265), there are hereby transferred from the Commission to the Chairman of the Commission the functions of the Commission with respect to the assignment of Commission personnel, including Commissioners, to perform such functions as may have been delegated by the Commission to the Commission personnel, including Commissioners, pursuant to section 4A of this title.

Sec. 4C. APPEARANCE AND PRACTICE BEFORE THE COMMISSION

(a) AUTHORITY TO CENSURE.—The Commission may censure any person, or deny, temporarily or permanently, to any person the privilege of appearing or practicing before the Commission in any way, if that person is found by the Commission, after notice and opportunity for hearing in the matter—

(1) not to possess the requisite qualifications to represent others;

(2) to be lacking in character or integrity, or to have engaged in unethical or improper professional conduct; or

(3) to have willfully violated, or willfully aided and abetted the violation of, any provision of the securities laws or the rules and regulations issued thereunder.

(b) DEFINITION.—With respect to any registered public accounting firm or associated person, for purposes of this section, the term "improper professional conduct" means—

(1) intentional or knowing conduct, including reckless conduct, that results in a violation of applicable professional standards; and

(2) negligent conduct in the form of—

(A) a single instance of highly unreasonable conduct that results in a violation of applicable professional standards in circumstances in which the registered public accounting firm or associated person knows, or should know, that heightened scrutiny is warranted; or

(B) repeated instances of unreasonable conduct, each resulting in a violation of applicable professional standards, that indicate a lack of competence to practice before the Commission.

Sec. 5. TRANSACTIONS ON UNREGISTERED EXCHANGES

It shall be unlawful for any broker, dealer, or exchange, directly or indirectly, to make use of the mails or any means or instrumentality of interstate commerce for the purpose of using any facility of an exchange within or subject to the jurisdiction of the United States to effect any transaction in a security or to report any such transaction, unless such exchange (1) is registered as a national securities exchange under section 6 of this title, or (2) is exempted from such registration upon application by the exchange because, in the opinion of the Commission, by reason of the limited volume of transactions effected on such exchange, it is not practicable and not necessary or appropriate in the public interest or for the protection of investors to require such registration.

Sec. 6. NATIONAL SECURITIES EXCHANGES

(a) An exchange may be registered as a national securities exchange under the terms and conditions hereinafter provided in this section and in accordance with the provisions of section 19(a) of this title, by filing with the Commission an application for registration in such form as the Commission, by rule, may prescribe containing the rules of the exchange and such other information and documents as the Commission, by rule, may prescribe as necessary or appropriate in the public interest or for the protection of investors.

(b) An exchange shall not be registered as a national securities exchange unless the Commission determines that—

(1) Such exchange is so organized and has the capacity to be able to carry out the purposes of this title and to comply, and (subject to any rule or order of the Commission pursuant to section 17(d) or 19(g)(2) of this title) to enforce compliance by its members and peron pursuant to section 17(d) or 19(g)(2) of this title) to enforce compliance by its members and persons associated with its members, with the provisions of this title, the rules and regulations thereunder, and the rules of the exchange.

(2) Subject to the provisions of subsection (c) of this section, the rules of the exchange provide that any registered broker or dealer or natural person associated with a registered broker or dealer may become a member of such exchange and any person may become associated with a member thereof.

(3) The rules of the exchange assure a fair representation of its members in the selection of its directors and administration of its affairs and provide that one or more directors shall be representative of issuers and investors and not be associated with a member of the exchange, broker, or dealer.

(4) The rules of the exchange provide for the equitable allocation of reasonable dues, fees, and other charges among its members and issuers and other persons using its facilities.

(5) The rules of the exchange are designed to prevent fraudulent and manipulative acts and practices, to promote just and equitable principles of trade, to foster cooperation and coordination with persons engaged in regulating, clearing, settling, processing information with respect to, and facilitating transactions in securities, to remove impediments to and perfect the mechanism of a free and open market and a national market system, and, in general, to protect investors and the public interest; and are not designed to permit unfair discrimination between customers, issuers,

brokers, or dealers, or to regulate by virtue of any authority conferred by this title matters not related to the purposes of this title or the administration of the exchange.

(6) The rules of the exchange provide that (subject to any rule or order to the Commission pursuant to section 17(d) or 19(g)(2) of this title) its members and persons associated with its members shall be appropriately disciplined for violation of the provisions of this title, the rules or regulations thereunder, or the rules of the exchange, by expulsion, suspension, limitation of activities, functions, and operations, fine, censure, being suspended or barred from being associated with a member, or any other fitting sanction.

(7) The rules of the exchange are in accordance with the provisions of subsection (d) of this section, and, in general, provide a fair procedure for the disciplining of members and persons associated with members, the denial of membership to any person seeking membership therein, the barring of any person from becoming associated with a member thereof, and the prohibition or limitation by the exchange of any person with respect to access to services offered by the exchange or a member thereof.

(8) The rules of the exchange do not impose any burden on competition not necessary or appropriate in furtherance of the purposes of this title.

(9) The rules of the exchange prohibit the listing of any security issued in a limited partnership rollup transaction (as such term is defined in paragraphs (4) and (5) of section 14(h)), unless such transaction was conducted in accordance with procedures designed to protect the rights of limited partners, including—

(A) the right of dissenting limited partners to one of the following:

(i) an appraisal and compensation:

(ii) retention of a security under substantially the same terms and conditions as the original issue;

(iii) approval of the limited partnership rollup transaction by not less than 75 percent of the outstanding securities of each of the participating limited partnerships;

(iv) the use of a committee of limited partners that is independent, as determined in accordance with rules prescribed by the exchange, of the general partner of sponsor, that has been approved by a majority of the outstanding units of each of the participating limited partnerships, and that has such authority as is necessary to protect, the interest of limited partners, including the authority to hire independent advisors, to negotiate with the general partner or sponsor on behalf of the limited partners, and to make a recommendation to the limited partners with respect to the proposed transaction; or

(v) other comparable rights that are prescribed by rule by the exchange and that are designed to protect dissenting limited partners;

(B) the right not to have their voting power unfairly reduced or abridged;

(C) the right not to bear an unfair protion of the costs of a proposed limited partnership rollup transaction that is rejected; and

(D) restrictions on the conversion of contingent interests of fees into non-contingent interests or fees and restrictions on the receipt of a non-contingent equity interest in exchange for fees for services which have not yet been provided.

As used in this paragraph, the term "dissenting limited partner" means a person who, on the date on which soliciting material is mailed to investors, is a holder of a beneficial interest in a limited partnership that is the subject of a limited partnership rollup transaction, and who casts a vote against the transaction and complies with procedures established by the exchange, except that for purposes of an exchange or tender offer, such person shall file an objection in writing under the rules of the exchange during the period during which the offer is outstanding.

(c)(1) A national securities exchange shall deny membership to (A) any person, other than a natural person, which is not a registered broker or dealer or (B) any natural person who is not, or is not associated with, a registered broker or dealer.

(2) A national securities exchange may, and in cases in which the Commission, by order, directs as necessary or appropriate in the public interest or for the protection of investors shall,

deny membership to any registered broker or dealer or natural person associated with a registered broker or dealer, and bar from becoming associated with a member any person, who is subject to a statutory disqualification. A national securities exchange shall file notice with the Commission not less than thirty days prior to admitting any person to membership or permitting any person to become associated with a member, if the exchange knew, or in the exercise of reasonable care should have known, that such person was subject to a statutory disqualification. The notice shall be in such form and contain such information as the Commission, by rule, may prescribe as necessary or appropriate in the public interest or for the protection of investors.

(3) (A) A national securities exchange may deny membership to, or condition the membership of, a registered broker or dealer if (i) such broker or dealer does not meet such standards of financial responsibility or operational capability or such broker or dealer or any natural persons associated with such broker or dealer does not meet such standards of training, experience, and competence as are prescribed by the rules of the exchange or (ii) such broker or dealer or person associated with such broker or dealer has engaged and there is a reasonable likelihood he will again engage in acts or practices inconsistent with just and equitable principles of trade. A national securities exchange may examine and verify the qualifications of an applicant to become a member and the natural persons associated with such an applicant in accordance with procedures established by the rules of the exchange.

(B) A national securities exchange may bar a natural person from becoming a member or associated with a member, or condition the membership of a natural person or association of a natural person with a member, if such natural person (i) does not meet such standards of training, experience, and competence as are prescribed by the rules of the exchange or (ii) has engaged and there is a reasonable likelihood he will again engage in acts or practices inconsistent with just and equitable principles of trade. A national securities exchange may examine and verify the qualifications of an applicant to become a person associated with a member in accordance with procedures established by the rules of the exchange and require any person associated with a member, or any class of such persons, to be registered with the exchange in accordance with procedures so established.

(C) A national securities exchange may bar any person from becoming associated with a member if such person does not agree (i) to supply the exchange with such information with respact to its relationship and dealings with the member as may be specified in the rules of the exchange and (ii) to permit the examination of its books and records to verify the accuracy of any information so supplied.

(4) A national securities exchange may limit (A) the number of members of the exchange and (B) the number of members and designated representatives of members permitted to effect transactions on the floor of the exchange without the services of another person acting as broker: Provided, however, That no national securities exchange shall have the authority to decrease the number of memberships in such exchange, or the number of members and designated representatives of members permitted to effect transactions on the floor of such exchange without the services of another person acting as broker, below such number in effect on May 1, 1975, or the date such exchange was registered with the Commission, whichever is later: And provided further, That the Commission, in accordance with the provisions of section 19(c) of this title, may amend the rules of any national securities exchange to increase (but not to decrease) or to remove any limitation on the number of memberships in such exchange or the number of members or designated representatives of members permitted to effect transactions on the floor of the exchange without the services of another person acting as broker, if the Commission finds that such limitation imposes a burden on competition not necessary or appropriate in furtherance of the purposes of this title.

(d) (1) In any proceeding by a national securities exchange to determine whether a member or person associated with a member should be disciplined (other than a summary proceeding pursuant to paragraph (3) of this subsection), the exchange shall bring specific charges, notify such member or person of, and give him an opportunity to defend against, such charges, and keep a record. A determination by the exchange to impose a disciplinary sanction shall be supported by a statement setting forth—

(A) any act or practice in which such member or person associated with a member has been found to have engaged, or which such member or person has been found to have omitted;

(B) the specific provision of this title, the rules or regulations thereunder, or the rules of the exchange which any such act or practice, or omission to act, is deemed to violate; and

(C) the sanction imposed and the reasons therefor.

(2) In any proceeding by a national securities exchange to determine whether a person shall be denied membership, barred from becoming associated with a member, or prohibited or limited with respect to access to services offered by the exchange or a member thereof (other than a summary proceeding pursuant to paragraph (3) of this subsection), the exchange shall notify such person of, and give him an opportunity to be heard upon, the specific grounds for denial, bar, or prohibition or limitation under consideration and keep a record. A determination by the exchange to deny membership, bar a person from becoming associated with a member, or prohibit or limit a person with respect to access to services offered by the exchange or a member thereof shall be supported by a statement setting forth the specific grounds on which the denial, bar, or prohibition or limitation is based.

(3) A national securities exchange may summarily (A) suspend a member or person associated with a member who has been and is expelled or suspended from any self-regulatory organization or barred or suspended from being associated with a member of any self-regulatory organization, (B) suspend a member who is in such financial or operating difficulty that the exchange determines and so notifies the Commission that the member cannot be permitted to continue to do business as a member with safety to investors, creditors, other members, or the exchange, or (C) limit or prohibit any person with respect to access to services offered by the exchange if subparagraaph (A) or (B) of this paragraph is applicable to such person or, in the case of a person who is not a member, if the exchange determines that such person does not meet the qualification reqirements or other prerequisites for such access and such person cannot be permitted to continue to have such access with safety to investors, creditors, members, or the exchange. Any person aggrieved by any such summary action shall be promptly afforded an opportunity for a hearing by the exchange in accordance with the provisions of paragraph (1) or (2) of this subsection. The Commission, by order, may stay any such summary action on its own motion or upon application by any person aggrieved thereby, if the Commission determines summarily or after notice and opportunity for hearing (which hearing may consist solely of the submission of affidavits or presentation of oral arguments) that such stay is consistent with the public interest and the protection of investors.

(e)(1) On and after the date of enactment of the Securities Acts Amendments of 1975, no national securities exchange may impose any schedule or fix rates of commissions, allowances, discounts, or other fees to be charged by its members: Provided, however, That until May 1, 1976, the preceding provisions of this paragraph shall not prohibit any such exchange from imposing or fixing any schedule of commissions, allowances, discounts, or other fees to be charged by its members for acting as broker on the floor of the exchange or as odd-lot dealer: And provided further, That the Commission, in accordance with the provisions of section 19(b) of this title as modified by the provisions of paragraph (3) of this subsection, may—

(A) permit a national securities exchange, by rule, to impose a reasonable schedule or fix reasonable rates of commissions, allowances, discounts, or other fees to be charged by its members for effecting transactions on such exchange prior to November 1, 1976, if the Commission finds that such schedule or fixed rates of commissions, allowances, discounts, or other fees are in the public interest; and

(B) permit a national securities exchange, by rule, to impose a schedule or fix rates of commissions, allowances, discounts, or other fees to be charged by its members for effecting transactions on such exchange after November 1, 1976, if the Commission finds that such schedule or fixed rates of commissions, allowances, discounts, or other fees (i) are reasonable in relation to the costs of providing the service for which such fees are charged (and the Commission publishes the standards employed in adjudging reasonableness) and (ii) do not impose any burden on competition not necessary or appropriate in furtherance of the purposes of this title, taking into consideration the competitive effects of permitting such schedule or fixed rates weighed against the competitive effects of other lawful actions which the Commission is authorized to take under this title.

(2) Notwithstanding the provisions of section 19(c) of this title, the Commission, by rule, may abrogate any exchange rule which imposes a schedule or fixes rates of commissions, allowances, discounts, or other fees, if the Commission determines that such schedule or fixed rates are no longer reasonable, in the public interest, or necessary to accomplish the purposes of this title.

(3)(A) Before approving or disapproving any proposed rule change submitted by a national securities exchange which would impose a schedule or fix rates of commissions, allowances, discounts, or other fees to be charged by its members for effecting transactions on such exchange, the Commission shall afford interested persons (i) an opportunity for oral presentation of data, views, and arguments and (ii) with respect to any such rule concerning transactions effected after November 1, 1976, if the Commission determines there are disputed issues of material fact, to present such rebuttal submissions and to conduct (or have conducted under subparagraph (B) of this paragraph) such cross-examination as the Commission determines to be appropriate and required for full disclosure and proper resolution of such disputed issues of material fact.

(B) The Commission shall prescribe rules and make rulings concerning any proceeding in accordance with subparagraph (A) of this paragraph designed to avoid unnecessary costs or delay. Such rules or rulings may (i) impose reasonable time limits on each interested person's oral presentations, and (ii) require any cross-examination to which a person may be entitled under subparagraph (A) of this paragraph to be conducted by the Commission on behalf of that person in such manner as the Commission determines to be appropriate and required for full disclosure and proper resolution of disputed issues of material fact.

(C)(i) If any class of persons, the members of which are entitled to conduct (or have conducted) cross-examination under subparagraphs (A) and (B) of this paragraph and which have, in the view of the Commission, the same or similar interests in the proceeding, cannot agree upon a single representative of such interests for purposes of cross-examination, the Commission may make rules and rulings specifying the manner in which such interests shall be represented and such cross-examination conducted.

(ii) No member of any class of persons with respect to which the Commission has specified the manner in which its interest shall be represented pursuant to clause (i) of this subparagraph shall be denied, pursuant to such clause (i), the opportunity to conduct (or have conducted) cross-examination as to issues affecting his particular interests if he satisfies the Commission that he has made a reasonable and good faith effort to reach agreement upon group representation and there are substantial and relevant issues which would not be presented adequately by group representation.

(D) A transcript shall be kept of any oral presentation and cross-examination.

(E) In addition to the bases specified in subsection 25(a), a reviewing Court may set aside an order of the Commission under section 19(b) approving an exchange rule imposing a schedule or fixing rates of commissions, allowances, discounts, or other fees, if the Court finds—

(1) a Commission determination under subparagraph (A) of this paragraph that an interested person is not entitled to conduct cross-examination or make rebuttal submissions, or

(2) a Commission rule or ruling under subparagraph (B) of this paragraph limiting the petitioner's cross-examination or rebuttal submissions,

has precluded full disclosure and proper resolution of disputed issues of material fact which were necessary for fair determination by the Commission.

(f) The Commission, by rule or order, as it deems necessary or appropriate in the public interest and for the protection of investors, to maintain fair and orderly markets, or to assure equal regulation, may require—

(1) any person not a member or a designated representative of a member of a national securities exchange effecting transactions on such exchange without the services of another person acting as a broker, or

(2) any broker or dealer not a member of a national securities exchange effecting transactions on such exchange on a regular basis,

to comply with such rules of such exchange as the Commission may specify.

(g) NOTICE REGISTRATION OF SECURITY FUTURES PRODUCT EXCHANGES.—

(1) REGISTRATION REQUIRED.—An exchange that lists or trades security futures products may register as a national securities exchange solely for the purposes of trading security futures products if—

(A) the exchange is a board of trade, as that term is defined by the Commodity Exchange Act (7 U.S.C. 1a(2)), that—

(i) has been designated a contract market by the Commodity Futures Trading Commission and such designation is not suspended by order of the Commodity Futures Trading Commission; or

(ii) is registered as a derivative transaction execution facility under section 5a of the Commodity Exchange Act and such registration is not suspended by the Commodity Futures Trading Commission; and

(B) such exchange does not serve as a market place for transactions in securities other than—

(i) security futures products; or

(ii) futures on exempted securities or groups or indexes of securities or options thereon that have been authorized under section 2(a)(1)(C) of the Commodity Exchange Act.

(2) REGISTRATION BY NOTICE FILING.—

(A) FORM AND CONTENT.—An exchange required to register only because such exchange lists or trades security futures products may register for purposes of this section by filing with the Commission a written notice in such form as the Commission, by rule, may prescribe containing the rules of the exchange and such other information and documents concerning such exchange, comparable to the information and documents required for national securities exchanges under section 6(a), as the Commission, by rule, may prescribe as necessary or appropriate in the public interest or for the protection of investors. If such exchange has filed documents with the Commodity Futures Trading Commission, to the extent that such documents contain information satisfying the Commission's informational requirements, copies of such documents may be filed with the Commission in lieu of the required written notice.

(B) IMMEDIATE EFFECTIVENESS.—Such registration shall be effective contemporaneously with the submission of notice, in written or electronic form, to the Commission, except that such registration shall not be effective if such registration would be subject to suspension or revocation.

(C) TERMINATION.—Such registration shall be terminated immediately if any of the conditions for registration set forth in this subsection are no longer satisfied.

(3) PUBLIC AVAILABILITY.—The Commission shall promptly publish in the Federal Register an acknowledgment of receipt of all notices the Commission receives under this subsection and shall make all such notices available to the public.

(4) EXEMPTION OF EXCHANGES FROM SPECIFIED PROVISIONS.—

(A) TRANSACTION EXEMPTIONS.—An exchange that is registered under paragraph (1) of this subsection shall be exempt from, and shall not be required to enforce compliance by its members with, and its members shall not, solely with respect to those transactions effected on such exchange in security futures products, be required to comply with, the following provisions of this title and the rules thereunder:

(i) Subsections (b)(2), (b)(3), (b)(4), (b)(7), (b)(9), (c), (d), and (e) of this section.

(ii) Section 8.

(iii) Section 11.

(iv) Subsections (d), (f), and (k) of section 17.

(v) Subsections (a), (f), and (h) of section 19.

(B) RULE CHANGE EXEMPTIONS.—An exchange that registered under paragraph (1) of this subsection shall also be exempt from submitting proposed rule changes pursuant to section 19(b) of this title, except that—

(i) such exchange shall file proposed rule changes related to higher margin levels, fraud or manipulation, recordkeeping, reporting, listing standards, or decimal pricing for security futures products, sales practices for security futures products for persons who effect transactions in security futures products, or rules effectuating such exchange's obligation to enforce the securities laws pursuant to section 19(b)(7);

(ii) such exchange shall file pursuant to sections 19(b)(1) and 19(b)(2) proposed rule changes related to margin, except for changes resulting in higher margin levels; and

(iii) such exchange shall file pursuant to section 19(b)(1) proposed rule changes that have been abrogated by the Commission pursuant to section 19(b)(7)(C).

(5) TRADING IN SECURITY FUTURES PRODUCTS.—

(A) IN GENERAL.—Subject to subparagraph (B), it shall be unlawful for any person to execute or trade a security futures product until the later of—

(i) 1 year after the date of enactment of the Commodity Futures Modernization Act of 2000; or

(ii) such date that a futures association registered under section 17 of the Commodity Exchange Act has met the requirements set forth in section 15A(k)(2) of this title.

(B) PRINCIPAL-TO-PRINCIPAL TRANSACTIONS.—Notwithstanding subparagraph (A), a person may execute or trade a security futures product transaction if—

(i) the transaction is entered into—

(I) on a principal-to-principal basis between parties trading for their own accounts or as described in section 1a(12)(B)(ii) of the Commodity Exchange Act; and

(II) only between eligible contract participants (as defined in subparagraphs (A), (B)(ii), and (C) of such section 1a(12)) at the time at which the persons enter into the agreement, contract, or transaction; and

(ii) the transaction is entered into on or after the later of—

(I) 8 months after the date of enactment of the Commodity Futures Modernization Act of 2000; or

(II) such date that a futures association registered under section 17 of the Commodity Exchange Act has met the requirements set forth in section 15A(k)(2) of this title.

(h) TRADING IN SECURITY FUTURES PRODUCTS.—

(1) TRADING ON EXCHANGE OR ASSOCIATION REQUIRED.—It shall be unlawful for any person to effect transactions in security futures products that are not listed on a national securities exchange or a national securities association registered pursuant to section 15A(a).

(2) LISTING STANDARDS REQUIRED.—Except as otherwise provided in paragraph (7), a national securities exchange or a national securities association registered pursuant to section 15A(a) may trade only security futures products that (A) conform with listing standards that such exchange or association files with the Commission under section 19(b) and (B) meet the criteria specified in section 2(a)(1)(D)(i) of the Commodity Exchange Act.

(3) REQUIREMENTS FOR LISTING STANDARDS AND CONDITIONS FOR TRADING.—Such listing standards shall—

(A) except as otherwise provided in a rule, regulation, or order issued pursuant to paragraph (4), require that any security underlying the security future, including each component security of a narrow-based security index, be registered pursuant to section 12 of this title;

(B) require that if the security futures product is not cash settled, the market on which the security futures product is traded have arrangements in place with a registered clearing agency for the payment and delivery of the securities underlying the security futures product;

(C) be no less restrictive than comparable listing standards for options traded on a national securities exchange or national securities association registered pursuant to section 15A(a) of this title;

(D) except as otherwise provided in a rule, regulation, or order issued pursuant to paragraph (4), require that the security future be based upon common stock and such other equity securities as the Commission and the Commodity Futures Trading Commission jointly determine appropriate;

(E) require that the security futures product is cleared by a clearing agency that has in place provisions for linked and coordinated clearing with other clearing agencies that clear security futures products, which permits the security futures product to be purchased on one market and offset on another market that trades such product;

(F) require that only a broker or dealer subject to suitability rules comparable to those of a national securities association registered pursuant to section 15A(a) effect transactions in the security futures product;

(G) require that the security futures product be subject to the prohibition against dual trading in section 4j of the Commodity Exchange Act (7 U.S.C. 6j) and the rules and regulations thereunder or the provisions of section 11(a) of this title and the rules and regulations thereunder, except to the extent otherwise permitted under this title and the rules and regulations thereunder;

(H) require that trading in the security futures product not be readily susceptible to manipulation of the price of such security futures product, nor to causing or being used in the manipulation of the price of any underlying security, option on such security, or option on a group or index including such securities;

(I) require that procedures be in place for coordinated surveillance among the market on which the security futures product is traded, any market on which any security underlying the security futures product is traded, and other markets on which any related security is traded to detect manipulation and insider trading;

(J) require that the market on which the security futures product is traded has in place audit trails necessary or appropriate to facilitate the coordinated surveillance required in subparagraph (I);

(K) require that the market on which the security futures product is traded has in place procedures to coordinate trading halts between such market and any market on which any security underlying the security futures product is traded and other markets on which any related security is traded; and

(L) require that the margin requirements for a security futures product comply with the regulations prescribed pursuant to section 7(c)(2)(B), except that nothing in this subparagraph shall be construed to prevent a national securities exchange or national securities association from requiring higher margin levels for a security futures product when it deems such action to be necessary or appropriate.

(4) AUTHORITY TO MODIFY CERTAIN LISTING STANDARD REQUIREMENTS.—

(A) AUTHORITY TO MODIFY.—The Commission and the Commodity Futures Trading Commission, by rule, regulation, or order, may jointly modify the listing standard requirements specified in subparagraph (A) or (D) of paragraph (3) to the extent such modification fosters the development of fair and orderly markets in security futures products, is necessary or appropriate in the public interest, and is consistent with the protection of investors.

(B) AUTHORITY TO GRANT EXEMPTIONS.—The Commission and the Commodity Futures Trading Commission, by order, may jointly exempt any person from compliance with the listing standard requirement specified in subparagraph (E) of paragraph (3) to the extent such exemption fosters the development of fair and orderly markets in security futures products, is necessary or appropriate in the public interest, and is consistent with the protection of investors.

(5) REQUIREMENTS FOR OTHER PERSONS TRADING SECURITY FUTURE PRODUCTS.—It shall be unlawful for any person (other than a national securities exchange or a national securities association registered pursuant to section 15A(a)) to constitute, maintain, or

provide a marketplace or facilities for bringing together purchasers and sellers of security future products or to otherwise perform with respect to security future products the functions commonly performed by a stock exchange as that term is generally understood, unless a national securities association registered pursuant to section 15A(a) or a national securities exchange of which such person is a member—

(A) has in place procedures for coordinated surveillance among such person, the market trading the securities underlying the security future products, and other markets trading related securities to detect manipulation and insider trading;

(B) has rules to require audit trails necessary or appropriate to facilitate the coordinated surveillance required in subparagraph (A); and

(C) has rules to require such person to coordinate trading halts with markets trading the securities underlying the security future products and other markets trading related securities.

(6) DEFERRAL OF OPTIONS ON SECURITY FUTURES TRADING.—No person shall offer to enter into, enter into, or confirm the execution of any put, call, straddle, option, or privilege on a security future, except that, after 3 years after the date of enactment of this subsection, the Commission and the Commodity Futures Trading Commission may by order jointly determine to permit trading of puts, calls, straddles, options, or privileges on any security future authorized to be traded under the provisions of this Act and the Commodity Exchange Act.

(7) DEFERRAL OF LINKED AND COORDINATED CLEARING.—

(A) Notwithstanding paragraph (2), until the compliance date, a national securities exchange or national securities association registered pursuant to section 15A(a) may trade a security futures product that does not—

(i) conform with any listing standard promulgated to meet the requirement specified in subparagraph (E) of paragraph (3); or

(ii) meet the criterion specified in section 2(a)(1)(D)(i)(IV) of the Commodity Exchange Act.

(B) The Commission and the Commodity Futures Trading Commission shall jointly publish in the Federal Register a notice of the compliance date no later than 165 days before the compliance date.

(C) For purposes of this paragraph, the term 'compliance date' means the later of—

(i) 180 days after the end of the first full calendar month period in which the average aggregate comparable share volume for all security futures products based on single equity securities traded on all national securities exchanges, any national securities associations registered pursuant to section 15A(a), and all other persons equals or exceeds 10 percent of the average aggregate comparable share volume of options on single equity securities traded on all national securities exchanges and any national securities associations registered pursuant to section 15A(a); or

(ii) 2 years after the date on which trading in any security futures product commences under this title.

(i) Consistent with this title, each national securities exchange registered pursuant to subsection (a) of this section shall issue such rules as are necessary to avoid duplicative or conflicting rules applicable to any broker or dealer registered with the Commission pursuant to section 15(b) (except paragraph (11) thereof), that is also registered with the Commodity Futures Trading Commission pursuant to section 4f(a) of the Commodity Exchange Act (except paragraph (2) thereof), with respect to the application of—

(1) rules of such national securities exchange of the type specified in section 15(c)(3)(B) involving security futures products; and

(2) similar rules of national securities exchanges registered pursuant to section 6(g) and national securities associations registered pursuant to section 15A(k) involving security futures products.

(j) PROCEDURES AND RULES FOR SECURITY FUTURE PRODUCTS.—A national securities exchange registered pursuant to subsection (a) shall implement the procedures specified in section 6(h)(5)(A) of this title and adopt the rules specified in subparagraphs (B) and (C) of section 6(h) (5) of this title not later than 8 months after the date of receipt of a request from an alternative trading system for such implementation and rules.

(k) (1) To the extent necessary or appropriate in the public interest, to promote fair competition, and consistent with the promotion of market efficiency, innovation, and expansion of investment opportunities, the protection of investors, and the maintenance of fair and orderly markets, the Commission and the Commodity Futures Trading Commission shall jointly issue such rules, regulations, or orders as are necessary and appropriate to permit the offer and sale of a security futures product traded on or subject to the rules of a foreign board of trade to United States persons.

(2) The rules, regulations, or orders adopted under paragraph (1) shall take into account, as appropriate, the nature and size of the markets that the securities underlying the security futures product reflect.

Sec. 7. MARGIN REQUIREMENTS

(a) For the purpose of preventing the excessive use of credit for the purchase or carrying of securities, the Board of Governors of the Federal Reserve System shall, prior to the effective date of this section and from time to time thereafter, prescribe rules and regulations with respect to the amount of credit that may be initially extended and subsequently maintained on any security (other than an exempted security or a security futures product). For the initial extension of credit, such rules and regulations shall be based upon the following standard: An amount not greater than whichever is the higher of—

(1) 55 per centum of the current market price of the security, or

(2) 100 per centum of the lowest market price of the security during the preceding thirty-six calendar months, but not more than 75 per centum of the current market price.

Such rules and regulations may make appropriate provision with respect to the carrying of undermargined accounts for limited periods and under specified conditions; the withdrawal of funds or securities; the substitution or additional purchases of securities; the transfer of accounts from one lender to another; special or different margin requirements for delayed deliveries, short sales, arbitrage transactions, and securities to which paragraph (2) of this subsection does not apply; the bases and the methods to be used in calculating loans, and margins and market prices; and similar administrative adjustments and details. For the purposes of paragraph (2) of this subsection, until July 1, 1936, the lowest price at which a security has sold on or after July 1, 1933, shall be considered as the lowest price at which such security has sold during the preceding thirty-six calendar months.

(b) Notwithstanding the provisions of subsection (a) of this section, the Board of Governors of the Federal Reserve System, may, from time to time, with respect to all or specified securities or transactions, or classes of securities, or classes of transactions, by such rules and regulations (1) prescribe such lower margin requirements for the initial extension or maintenance of credit as it deems necessary or appropriate for the accommodation of commerce and industry, having due regard to the general credit situation of the country, and (2) prescribe such higher margin requirements for the initial extension or maintenance of credit as it may deem necessary or appropriate to prevent the excessive use of credit to finance transactions in securities.

[Unlawful Credit Extension to Customers]

(c) Unlawful Credit Extension to Customers.—

(1) Prohibition.—It shall be unlawful for any member of a national securities exchange or any broker or dealer, directly or indirectly, to extend or maintain credit or arrange for the extension or maintenance of credit to or for any customer—

(A) on any security (other than an exempted security except as provided in paragraph (2)), in contravention of the rules and regulations which the Board of Governors of the Federal Reserve System (hereafter in this section referred to as the 'Board') shall prescribe under subsections (a) and (b); and

(B) without collateral or on any collateral other than securities, except in accordance with such rules and regulations as the Board may prescribe—

(i) to permit under specified conditions and for a limited period any such member, broker, or dealer to maintain a credit initially extended in conformity with the rules and regulations of the Board; and

(ii) to permit the extension or maintenance of credit in cases where the extension or maintenance of credit is not for the purpose of purchasing or carrying securities or of evading or circumventing the provisions of subparagraph (A).

(2) MARGIN REGULATIONS.—

(A) COMPLIANCE WITH MARGIN RULES REQUIRED.—It shall be unlawful for any broker, dealer, or member of a national securities exchange to, directly or indirectly, extend or maintain credit to or for, or collect margin from any customer on, any security futures product unless such activities comply with the regulations—

(i) which the Board shall prescribe pursuant to subparagraph (B); or

(ii) if the Board determines to delegate the authority to prescribe such regulations, which the Commission and the Commodity Futures Trading Commission shall jointly prescribe pursuant to subparagraph (B).

If the Board delegates the authority to prescribe such regulations under clause (ii) and the Commission and the Commodity Futures Trading Commission have not jointly prescribed such regulations within a reasonable period of time after the date of such delegation, the Board shall prescribe such regulations pursuant to subparagraph (B).

(B) CRITERIA FOR ISSUANCE OF RULES.—The Board shall prescribe, or, if the authority is delegated pursuant to subparagraph (A)(ii), the Commission and the Commodity Futures Trading Commission shall jointly prescribe, such regulations to establish margin requirements, including the establishment of levels of margin (initial and maintenance) for security futures products under such terms, and at such levels, as the Board deems appropriate, or as the Commission and the Commodity Futures Trading Commission jointly deem appropriate—

(i) to preserve the financial integrity of markets trading security futures products;

(ii) to prevent systemic risk;

(iii) to require that—

(I) the margin requirements for a security future product be consistent with the margin requirements for comparable option contracts traded on any exchange registered pursuant to section 6(a) of this title; and

(II) initial and maintenance margin levels for a security future product not be lower than the lowest level of margin, exclusive of premium, required for any comparable option contract traded on any exchange registered pursuant to section 6(a) of this title, other than an option on a security future;

except that nothing in this subparagraph shall be construed to prevent a national securities exchange or national securities association from requiring higher margin levels for a security future product when it deems such action to be necessary or appropriate; and

(iv) to ensure that the margin requirements (other than levels of margin), including the type, form, and use of collateral for security futures products, are and remain consistent with the requirements established by the Board, pursuant to subparagraphs (A) and (B) of paragraph (1).

(3) Exception.—This subsection and the rules and regulations issued under this subsection shall not apply to any credit extended, maintained, or arranged by a member of a national securities exchange or a broker or dealer to or for a member of a national securities exchange or a registered broker or dealer—

(A) a substantial portion of whose business consists of transactions with persons other than brokers or dealers; or

(B) to finance its activities as a market maker or an underwriter;

except that the Board may impose such rules and regulations, in whole or in part, on any credit otherwise exempted by this paragraph if the Board determines that such action is necessary or appropriate in the public interest or for the protection of investors.

[Extensions of Credit by Other Lenders]

(d) UNLAWFUL CREDIT EXTENSION IN VIOLATION OF RULES AND REGULATIONS; EXCEPTIONS TO APPLICATION OF RULES, ETC.—

(1) Prohibition.—It shall be unlawful for any person not subject to subsection (c) to extend or maintain credit or to arrange for the extension or maintenance of credit for the purpose of purchasing or carrying any security, in contravention of such rules and regulations as the Board shall prescribe to prevent the excessive use of credit for the purchasing or carrying of or trading in securities in circumvention of the other provisions of this section. Such rules and regulations may impose upon all loans made for the purpose of purchasing or carrying securities limitations similar to those imposed upon members, brokers, or dealers by subsection (c) and the rules and regulations thereunder.

(2) Exceptions.—This subsection and the rules and regulations issued under this subsection shall not apply to any credit extended, maintained, or arranged—

(A) by a person not in the ordinary course of business;

(B) on an exempted security;

(C) to or for a member of a national securities exchange or a registered broker or dealer—

(i) a substantial portion of whose business consists of transactions with persons other than brokers or dealers; or

(ii) to finance its activities as a market maker or an underwriter;

(D) by a bank on a security other than an equity security; or

(E) as the Board shall, by such rules, regulations, or orders as it may deem necessary or appropriate in the public interest or for the protection of investors, exempt, either unconditionally or upon specified terms and conditions or for stated periods, from the operation of this subsection and the rules and regulations thereunder.

(3) Board authority.—The Board may impose such rules and regulations, in whole or in part, on any credit otherwise exempted by subparagraph (C) if it determines that such action is necessary or appropriate in the public interest or for the protection of investors.

(e) The provisions of this section or the rules and regulations thereunder shall not apply on or before July 1, 1937, to any loan or extension of credit made prior to the enactment of this title or to the maintenance, renewal, or extension of any such loan or credit, except to the extent that the Board of Governors of the Federal Reserve System may by rules and regulations prescribe as necessary to prevent the circumvention of the provisions of this section or the rules and regulations thereunder by means of withdrawals of funds or securities, substitutions of securities, or additional purchases or by any other device.

(f) (1) It is unlawful for any United States person, or any foreign person controlled by a United States person or acting on behalf of or in conjunction with such person, to obtain, receive, or enjoy the beneficial use of a loan or other extension or credit from any lender (without regard to whether the lender's office or place of business is in a State or the transaction occurred in whole or in part within a State) for the purpose of (A) purchasing or carrying United States securities, or (B) purchasing or carrying within the United States of any other securities, if, under this section or rules and regulations prescribed thereunder, the loan or other credit transaction is prohibited or would be prohibited if it had been made or the transaction had otherwise occurred in a lender's office or other place of business in a State.

(2) For the purposes of this subsection—

(A) The term "United States person" includes a person which is organized or exists under the laws of any State or, in the case of a natural person, a citizen or resident of the United States; a domestic estate; or a trust in which one or more of the foregoing persons has a cumulative direct or indirect beneficial interest in excess of 50 per centum of the value of the trust.

(B) The term "United States security" means a security (other than an exempted security) issued by a person incorporated under the laws of any State, or whose principal place of business is within a State.

(C) The term "foreign person controlled by a United States person" includes any noncorporate entity in which United States persons directly or indirectly have more than a 50 per centum beneficial interest, and any corporation in which one or more United States persons, directly or indirectly, own stock possessing more than 50 per centum of the total combined voting power of all classes of stock entitled to vote, or more than 50 per centum of the total value of shares of all classes of stock.

(3) The Board of Governors of the Federal Reserve System may, in its discretion and with due regard for the purposes of this section, by rule or regulation exempt any class of United States persons or foreign persons controlled by a United States person from the application of this subsection.

(g) Subject to such rules and regulations as the Board of Governors of the Federal Reserve System may adopt in the public interest and for the protection of investors, no member of a national securities exchange or broker or dealer shall be deemed to have extended or maintained credit or arranged for the extension or maintenance of credit for the purpose of purchasing a security, within the meaning of this section, by reason of a bona fide agreement for delayed delivery of a mortgage related security or a small business related security against full payment of the purchase price thereof upon such delivery within one hundred and eighty days after the purchase, or within such shorter period as the Board of Governors of the Federal Reserve System may prescribe by rule or regulation.

Sec. 8. RESTRICTIONS ON BORROWING BY MEMBERS, BROKERS, AND DEALERS

It shall be unlawful for any registered broker or dealer, member of a national securities exchange, or broker or dealer who transacts a business in securities through the medium of any member of a national securities exchange, directly or indirectly—

[Hypothecation of Securities]

(a) In contravention of such rules and regulations as the Commission shall prescribe for the protection of investors to hypothecate or arrange for the hypothecation of any securities carried for the account of any customer under circumstances (1) that will permit the commingling of his securities without his written consent with the securities of any other customer, (2) that will permit such securities to be commingled with the securities of any person other than a bona fide customer, or (3) that will permit such securities to be hypothecated, or subjected to any lien or claim of the pledgee, for a sum in excess of the aggregate indebtedness of such customers in respect of such securities.

[Lending Securities Carried for Customers' Accounts]

(b) To lend or arrange for the lending of any securities carried for the account of any customer without the written consent of such customer or in contravention of such rules and regulations as the Commission shall prescribe for the protection of investors.

PROHIBITION AGAINST MANIPULATION OF SECURITY PRICES

Sec. 9. (a) It shall be unlawful for any person, directly or indirectly, by the use of the mails or any means or instrumentality of interstate commerce, or of any facility of any national securities exchange, or for any member of a national securities exchange—

(1) For the purpose of creating a false or misleading appearance of active trading in any security registered on a national securities exchange, or a false or misleading appearance with respect to the market for any such security, (A) to effect any transaction in such security which involves no change in the beneficial ownership thereof, or (B) to enter an order or orders for the purchase of such security with the knowledge that an order or orders of substantially the same size, at substantially the same time, and at substantially the same price, for the sale of any such security, has been or will be entered by or for the same or different parties, or (C) to enter any

order or orders for the sale of any such security with the knowledge that an order or orders of substantially the same size, at substantially the same time, and at substantially the same price, for the purchase of such security, has been or will be entered by or for the same or different parties.

(2) To effect, alone or with one or more other persons, a series of transactions in any security registered on a national securities exchange or in connection with any security-based swap agreement (as defined in section 206B of the Gramm-Leach-Bliley Act) with respect to such security creating actual or apparent active trading in such security, or raising or depressing the price of such security, for the purpose of inducing the purchase or sale of such security by others.

(3) If a dealer or broker, or other person selling or offering for sale or purchasing or offering to purchase the security or a security-based swap agreement (as defined in section 206B of the Gramm-Leach-Bliley Act) with respect to such security, to induce the purchase or sale of any security registered on a national securities exchange or any security-based swap agreement (as defined in section 206B of the Gramm-Leach-Bliley Act) with respect to such security by the circulation or dissemination in the ordinary course of business of information to the effect that the price of any such security will or is likely to rise or fall because of market operations of any one or more persons conducted for the purpose of raising or depressing the price of such security.

(4) If a dealer or broker, or the person selling or offering for sale or purchasing or offering to purchase the security or a security-based swap agreement (as defined in section 206B of the Gramm-Leach-Bliley Act) with respect to such security, to make, regarding any security registered on a national securities exchange or any security-based swap agreement (as defined in section 206B of the Gramm-Leach-Bliley Act) with respect to such security, for the purpose of inducing the purchase or sale of such security or such security-based swap agreement, any statement which was at the time and in the light of the circumstances under which it was made, false or misleading with respect to any material fact, and which he knew or had reasonable ground to believe was so false or misleading.

(5) For a consideration, received directly or indirectly from a dealer or broker, or other person selling or offering for sale or purchasing or offering to purchase the security or a security-based swap agreement (as defined in section 206B of the Gramm-Leach-Bliley Act) with respect to such security, to induce the purchase of any security registered on a national securities exchange or any security-based swap agreement (as defined in section 206B of the Gramm-Leach-Bliley Act) with respect to such security by the circulation or dissemination of information to the effect that the price of any such security will or is likely to rise or fall because of the market operations of any one or more persons conducted for the purpose of raising or depressing the price of such security.

(6) To effect either alone or with one or more other persons any series of transactions for the purchase and/or sale of any security registered on a national securities exchange for the purpose of pegging, fixing, or stabilizing the price of such security in contravention of such rules and regulations as the Commission may prescribe as necessary or appropriate in the public interest or for the protection of investors.

(b) It shall be unlawful for any person to effect, by use of any facility of a national securities exchange, in contravention of such rules and regulations as the Commission may prescribe as necessary or appropriate in the public interest or for the protection of investors—

(1) any transaction in connection with any security whereby any party to such transaction acquires (A) any put, call, straddle, or other option or privilege of buying the security from or selling the security to another without being bound to do so; or (B) any security futures product on the security; or

(2) any transaction in connection with any security with relation to which he has, directly or indirectly, any interest in any (A) such put, call, straddle, option, or privilege; or (B) such security futures product; or

(3) any transaction in any security for the account of any person who he has reason to believe has, and who actually has, directly or indirectly, any interest in any (A) such put, call, straddle, option, or privilege; or (B) such security futures product with relation to such security.

(c) It shall be unlawful for any member of a national securities exchange directly or indirectly to endorse or guarantee the performance of any put, call, straddle, option, or privilege in relation to any security registered on a national securities exchange, in contravention of such rules and regulations as the Commission may prescribe as necessary or appropriate in the public interest or for the protection of investors.

(d) The terms "put," "call," "straddle," "option," or "privilege" as used in this section shall not include any registered warrant, right, or convertible security.

(e) Any person who willfully participates in any act or transaction in violation of subsection (a), (b), or (c) of this section, shall be liable to any person who shall purchase or sell any security at a price which was affected by such act or transaction, and the person so injured may sue in law or in equity in any court of competent jurisdiction to recover the damages sustained as a result of any such act or transaction. In any such suit the court may, in its discretion, require an undertaking for the payment of the costs of such suit, and assess reasonable costs, including reasonable attorneys fees, against either party litigant. Every person who becomes liable to make any payment under this subsection may recover contribution as in cases of contract from any person who, if joined in the original suit, would have been liable to make the same payment. No action shall be maintained to enforce any liability created under this section, unless brought within one year after the discovery of the facts constituting the violation and within three years after such violation.

(f) The provisions of subsection (a) shall not apply to an exempted security.

(g) (1) Notwithstanding any other provision of law, the Commission shall have the authority to regulate the trading of any put, call, straddle, option, or privilege on any security, certificate of deposit, or group or index of securities (including any interest therein or based on the value thereof), or any put, call, straddle, option, or privilege entered into on a national securities exchange relating to foreign currency (but not, with respect to any of the foregoing, an option on a contract for future delivery other than a security futures product).

(2) Notwithstanding the Commodity Exchange Act, the Commission shall have the authority to regulate the trading of any security futures product to the extent provided in the securities laws.

(h) LIMITATIONS ON PRACTICES THAT AFFECT MARKET VOLATILITY.—It shall be unlawful for any person, by the use of the mails or any means or instrumentality of interstate commerce or of any facility of any national securities exchange, to use or employ any act or practice in connection with the purchase or sale of any equity security in contravention of such rules or regulations as the Commission may adopt, consistent with the public interest, the protection of investors, and the maintenance of fair and orderly markets—

(1) to prescribe means reasonably designed to prevent manipulation of price levels of the equity securities market or a substantial segment thereof; and

(2) to prohibit or constrain, during periods of extraordinary market volatility, any trading practice in connection with the purchase or sale of equity securities that the Commission determines (A) has previously contributed significantly to extraordinary levels of volatility that have threatened the maintenance of fair and orderly markets; and (B) is reasonably certain to engender such levels of volatility if not prohibited or constrained.

In adopting rules under paragraph (2), the Commission shall, consistent with the purposes of this subsection, minimize the impact on the normal operations of the market and a natural person's freedom to buy or sell any equity security.

(i) The authority of the Commission under this section with respect to security-based swap agreements shall be subject to the restrictions and limitations of section 3A(b) of this title.

REGULATION OF THE USE OF MANIPULATIVE AND DECEPTIVE DEVICES

Sec. 10. It shall be unlawful for any person, directly or indirectly, by the use of any means or instrumentality of interstate commerce or of the mails, or of any facility of any national securities exchange—

(a) (1) To effect a short sale, or to use or employ any stop-loss order in connection with the purchase or sale, of any security registered on a national securities exchange, in contravention of such rules and regulations as the Commission may prescribe as necessary or appropriate in the public interest or for the protection of investors.

(2) Paragraph (1) of this subsection shall not apply to security futures products.

(b) To use or employ, in connection with the purchase or sale of any security registered on a national securities exchange or any security not so registered, or any securities-based swap agreement (as defined in section 206B of the Gramm-Leach-Bliley Act), any manipulative or deceptive device or contrivance in contravention of such rules and regulations as the commission may prescribe as necessary or appropriate in the public interest or for the protection of investors.

Rules promulgated under subsection (b) that prohibit fraud, manipulation, or insider trading (but not rules imposing or specifying reporting or recordkeeping requirements, procedures, or standards as prophylactic measures against fraud, manipulation, or insider trading), and judicial precedents decided under subsection (b) and rules promulgated thereunder that prohibit fraud, manipulation, or insider trading, shall apply to security-based swap agreements (as defined in section 206B of the Gramm-Leach-Bliley Act) to the same extent as they apply to securities. Judicial precedents decided under section 17(a) of the Securities Act of 1933 and sections 9, 15, 16, 20, and 21A of this title, and judicial precedents decided under applicable rules promulgated under such sections, shall apply to security-based swap agreements (as defined in section 206B of the Gramm-Leach-Bliley Act) to the same extent as they apply to securities.

AUDIT REQUIREMENTS

Sec. 10A. (a) IN GENERAL.—Each audit required pursuant to this title of the financial statements of an issuer by a registered public accounting firm shall include, in accordance with generally accepted auditing standards, as may be modified or supplemented from time to time by the Commission—

(1) procedures designed to provide reasonable assurance of detecting illegal acts that would have a direct and material effect on the determination of financial statement amounts;

(2) procedures designed to identify related party transactions that are material to the financial statements or otherwise require disclosure therein; and

(3) an evaluation of whether there is substantial doubt about the ability of the issuer to continue as a going concern during the ensuing fiscal year.

(b) REQUIRED RESPONSE TO AUDIT DISCOVERIES.—

(1) INVESTIGATION AND REPORT TO MANAGEMENT.—If, in the course of conducting an audit pursuant to this title to which subsection (a) applies, the registered public accounting firm detects or otherwise becomes aware of information indicating that an illegal act (whether or not perceived to have a material effect on the financial statements of the issuer) has or may have occurred, the firm shall, in accordance with generally accepted auditing standards, as may be modified or supplemented from time to time by the Commission—

(A)(i) determine whether it is likely that an illegal act has occurred; and

(ii) if so, determine and consider the possible effect of the illegal act on the financial statements of the issuer, including any contingent monetary effects, such as fines, penalties, and damages; and

(B) as soon as practicable, inform the appropriate level of the management of the issuer and assure that the audit committee of the issuer, or the board of directors of the issuer in the absence of such a committee, is adequately informed with respect to illegal acts that have been detected or have otherwise come to the attention of such firm in the course of the audit, unless the illegal act is clearly inconsequential.

(2) Response to failure to take remedial action.—If, after determining that the audit committee of the board of directors of the issuer, or the board of directors of the issuer in the absence of an audit committee, is adequately informed with respect to illegal acts that have been detected or have otherwise come to the attention of the firm in the course of the audit of such firm, the registered public accounting firm concludes that—

(A) the illegal act has a material effect on the financial statements of the issuer;

(B) the senior management has not taken, and the board of directors has not caused senior management to take, timely and appropriate remedial actions with respect to the illegal act; and

(C) the failure to take remedial action is reasonably expected to warrant departure from a standard report of the auditor, when made, or warrant resignation from the audit engagement;

the registered public accounting firm shall, as soon as practicable, directly report its conclusions to the board of directors.

(3) Notice to commission; response to failure to notify.—An issuer whose board of directors receives a report under paragraph (2) shall inform the Commission by notice not later than 1 business day after the receipt of such report and shall furnish the registered public accounting firm making such report with a copy of the notice furnished to the Commission. If the registered public accounting firm fails to receive a copy of the notice before the expiration of the required 1-business-day period, the registered public accounting firm shall—

(A) resign from the engagement; or

(B) furnish to the Commission a copy of its report (or the documentation of any oral report given) not later than 1 business day following such failure to receive notice.

(4) Report after resignation.—If a registered public accounting firm resigns from an engagement under paragraph (3)(A), the firm shall, not later than 1 business day following the failure by the issuer to notify the Commission under paragraph (3), furnish to the Commission a copy of the report of the firm (or the documentation of any oral report given).

(c) AUDITOR LIABILITY LIMITATION.—No registered public accounting firm shall be liable in a private action for any finding, conclusion, or statement expressed in a report made pursuant to paragraph (3) or (4) of subsection (b), including any rule promulgated pursuant thereto.

(d) CIVIL PENALTIES IN CEASE-AND-DESIST PROCEEDINGS.—If the Commission finds, after notice and opportunity for hearing in a proceeding instituted pursuant to section 21C, that a registered public accounting firm has willfully violated paragraph (3) or (4) of subsection (b), the Commission may, in addition to entering an order under section 21C, impose a civil penalty against the registered public accounting firm and any other person that the Commission finds was a cause of such violation. The determination to impose a civil penalty and the amount of the penalty shall be governed by the standards set forth in section 21B.

(e) PRESERVATION OF EXISTING AUTHORITY.—Except as provided in subsection (d), nothing in this section shall be held to limit or otherwise affect the authority of the Commission under this title.

(f) DEFINITIONS.—As used in this section, the term "illegal act" means an act or omission that violates any law, or any rule or regulation having the force of law. As used in this section, the term "issuer" means an issuer (as defined in section 3), the securities of which are registered under section 12, or that is required to file reports pursuant to section 15(d), or that files or has filed a registration statement that has not yet become effective under the Securities Act of 1933 (15 U.S.C. 77a et seq.), and that it has not withdrawn.

(g) PROHIBITED ACTIVITIES.—Except as provided in subsection (h), it shall be unlawful for a registered public accounting firm (and any associated person of that firm, to the extent determined appropriate by the Commission) that performs for any issuer any audit required by this title or the rules of the Commission under this title or, beginning 180 days after the date of commencement of the operations of the Public Company Accounting Oversight Board established under section 101 of the Sarbanes-Oxley Act of 2002 (in this section referred to as the 'Board'), the rules of the Board, to provide to that issuer, contemporaneously with the audit, any non-audit service, including—

(1) bookkeeping or other services related to the accounting records or financial statements of the audit client;

(2) financial information systems design and implementation;

(3) appraisal or valuation services, fairness opinions, or contribution-in-kind reports;

(4) actuarial services;

(5) internal audit outsourcing services;

(6) management functions or human resources;

(7) broker or dealer, investment adviser, or investment banking services;

(8) legal services and expert services unrelated to the audit; and

(9) any other service that the Board determines, by regulation, is impermissible.

(h) PREAPPROVAL REQUIRED FOR NON-AUDIT SERVICES.—A registered public accounting firm may engage in any non-audit service, including tax services, that is not described in any of paragraphs (1) through (9) of subsection (g) for an audit client, only if the activity is approved in advance by the audit committee of the issuer, in accordance with subsection (i).

(i) PREAPPROVAL REQUIREMENTS.—

(1) IN GENERAL.—

(A) AUDIT COMMITTEE ACTION.—All auditing services (which may entail providing comfort letters in connection with securities underwritings or statutory audits required for insurance companies for purposes of State law) and non-audit services, other than as provided in subparagraph (B), provided to an issuer by the auditor of the issuer shall be preapproved by the audit committee of the issuer.

(B) DE MINIMUS EXCEPTION.—The preapproval requirement under subparagraph (A) is waived with respect to the provision of non-audit services for an issuer, if—

(i) the aggregate amount of all such non-audit services provided to the issuer constitutes not more than 5 percent of the total amount of revenues paid by the issuer to its auditor during the fiscal year in which the nonaudit services are provided;

(ii) such services were not recognized by the issuer at the time of the engagement to be non-audit services; and

(iii) such services are promptly brought to the attention of the audit committee of the issuer and approved prior to the completion of the audit by the audit committee or by 1 or more members of the audit committee who are members of the board of directors to whom authority to grant such approvals has been delegated by the audit committee.

(2) DISCLOSURE TO INVESTORS.—Approval by an audit committee of an issuer under this subsection of a non-audit service to be performed by the auditor of the issuer shall be disclosed to investors in periodic reports required by section 13(a).

(3) DELEGATION OF AUTHORITY.—The audit committee of an issuer may delegate to 1 or more designated members of the audit committee who are independent directors of the board of directors, the authority to grant preapprovals required by this subsection. The decisions of any member to whom authority is delegated under this paragraph to preapprove an activity under this subsection shall be presented to the full audit committee at each of its scheduled meetings.

(4) APPROVAL OF AUDIT SERVICES FOR OTHER PURPOSES.—In carrying out its duties under subsection (m)(2), if the audit committee of an issuer approves an audit service within the scope of the engagement of the auditor, such audit service shall be deemed to have been preapproved for purposes of this subsection.

(j) AUDIT PARTNER ROTATION.—It shall be unlawful for a registered public accounting firm to provide audit services to an issuer if the lead (or coordinating) audit partner (having primary responsibility for the audit), or the audit partner responsible for reviewing the audit, has performed audit services for that issuer in each of the 5 previous fiscal years of that issuer.

(k) REPORTS TO AUDIT COMMITTEES.—Each registered public accounting firm that performs for any issuer any audit required by this title shall timely report to the audit committee of the issuer—

(1) all critical accounting policies and practices to be used;

(2) all alternative treatments of financial information within generally accepted accounting principles that have been discussed with management officials of the issuer, ramifications of the use of such alternative disclosures and treatments, and the treatment preferred by the registered public accounting firm; and

(3) other material written communications between the registered public accounting firm and the management of the issuer, such as any management letter or schedule of unadjusted differences.

(l) CONFLICTS OF INTEREST.—It shall be unlawful for a registered public accounting firm to perform for an issuer any audit service required by this title, if a chief executive officer, controller, chief financial officer, chief accounting officer, or any person serving in an equivalent position for the issuer, was employed by that registered independent public accounting firm and participated in any capacity in the audit of that issuer during the 1-year period preceding the date of the initiation of the audit.

(m) STANDARDS RELATING TO AUDIT COMMITTEES.—

(1) COMMISSION RULES.—

(A) IN GENERAL.—Effective not later than 270 days after the date of enactment of this subsection, the Commission shall, by rule, direct the national securities exchanges and national securities associations to prohibit the listing of any security of an issuer that is not in compliance with the requirements of any portion of paragraphs (2) through (6).

(B) OPPORTUNITY TO CURE DEFECTS.—The rules of the Commission under subparagraph (A) shall provide for appropriate procedures for an issuer to have an opportunity to cure any defects that would be the basis for a prohibition under subparagraph (A), before the imposition of such prohibition.

(2) RESPONSIBILITIES RELATING TO REGISTERED PUBLIC ACCOUNTING FIRMS.—The audit committee of each issuer, in its capacity as a committee of the board of directors, shall be directly responsible for the appointment, compensation, and oversight of the work of any registered public accounting firm employed by that issuer (including resolution of disagreements between management and the auditor regarding financial reporting) for the purpose of preparing or issuing an audit report or related work, and each such registered public accounting firm shall report directly to the audit committee.

(3) INDEPENDENCE.—

(A) IN GENERAL.—Each member of the audit committee of the issuer shall be a member of the board of directors of the issuer, and shall otherwise be independent.

(B) CRITERIA.—In order to be considered to be independent for purposes of this paragraph, a member of an audit committee of an issuer may not, other than in his or her capacity as a member of the audit committee, the board of directors, or any other board committee—

(i) accept any consulting, advisory, or other compensatory fee from the issuer; or

(ii) be an affiliated person of the issuer or any subsidiary thereof.

(C) EXEMPTION AUTHORITY.—The Commission may exempt from the requirements of subparagraph (B) a particular relationship with respect to audit committee members, as the Commission determines appropriate in light of the circumstances.

(4) COMPLAINTS.—Each audit committee shall establish procedures for—

(A) the receipt, retention, and treatment of complaints received by the issuer regarding accounting, internal accounting controls, or auditing matters; and

(B) the confidential, anonymous submission by employees of the issuer of concerns regarding questionable accounting or auditing matters.

(5) AUTHORITY TO ENGAGE ADVISERS.—Each audit committee shall have the authority to engage independent counsel and other advisers, as it determines necessary to carry out its duties.

(6) FUNDING.—Each issuer shall provide for appropriate funding, as determined by the audit committee, in its capacity as a committee of the board of directors, for payment of compensation—

(A) to the registered public accounting firm employed by the issuer for the purpose of rendering or issuing an audit report; and

(B) to any advisers employed by the audit committee under paragraph (5).

TRADING BY MEMBERS OF EXCHANGES, BROKERS AND DEALERS

Sec. 11. (a)(1) It shall be unlawful for any member of a national securities exchange to effect any transaction on such exchange for its own account, the account of an associated person, or an account with respect to which it or an associated person thereof exercises investment discretion: Provided, however, That this paragraph shall not make unlawful—

(A) any transaction by a dealer acting in the capacity of market maker;

(B) any transaction for the account of an odd-lot dealer in a security in which he is so registered;

(C) any stabilizing transaction effected in compliance with rules under section 10(b) of this title to facilitate a distribution of a security in which the member effecting such transaction is participating;

(D) any bona fide arbitrage transaction, any bona fide hedge transaction involving a long or short position in an equity security and a long or short position in a security entitling the holder to acquire or sell such equity security, or any risk arbitrage transaction in connection with a merger, acquistion, tender offer, or similar transaction involving a recapitalization;

(E) any transaction for the account of a natural person, the estate of a natural person, or a trust created by a natural person for himself or another natural person:

(F) any transaction to offset a transaction made in error;

(G) any other transaction for a member's own account provided that (i) such member is primarily engaged in the business of underwriting and distributing securities issued by other persons, selling securities to customers, and acting as broker, or any one or more of such activities, and whose gross income normally is derived principally from such business and related activities and (ii) such transaction is effected in compliance with rules of the Commission which, as a minimum, assure that the transaction is not inconsistent with the maintenance of fair and orderly markets and yields priority, parity, and precedence in execution to order for the account of persons who are not members or associated with members of the exchange;

(H) any transaction for an account with respect to which such member or an associated person thereof exercises investment discretion if such member—

(i) has obtained, from the person or persons authorized to transact business for the account, express authorization for such member or associated person to effect such transactions prior to engaging in the practice of effecting such transactions;

(ii) furnishes the person or persons authorized to transact business for the account with a statement at least annually disclosing the aggregate compensation received by the exchange member in effecting such transactions; and

(iii) complies with any rules the Commission has prescribed with respect to the requirements of clauses (i) and (ii); and

(I) any other transaction of a kind which the Commission, by rule, determines is consistent with the purposes of this paragraph, the protection of investors, and the maintenance of fair and orderly markets.

(2) The Commission, by rule, as it deems necessary or appropriate in the public interest and for the protection of investors, to maintain fair and orderly markets, or to assure equal regulation of exchange markets and markets occurring otherwise than on an exchange, may regulate or prohibit:

(A) transactions on a national securities exchange not unlawful under paragraph (1) of this subsection effected by any member thereof for its own account (unless such member is acting in the capacity of market maker or odd-lot dealer), the account of an associated person, or an account with respect to which such member or an associated person thereof exercises investment discretion;

(B) transactions otherwise than on a national securities exchange effected by use of the mails or any means or instrumentality of interstate commerce by any member of a national securities exchange, broker, or dealer for the account of such member, broker, or dealer (unless such member, broker, or dealer is acting in the capacity of a market maker) the account of an associated person, or an account with respect to which such member, broker, or dealer or associated person thereof exercises investment discretion; and

(C) transactions on a national securities exchange effected by any broker or dealer not a member thereof for the account of such broker or dealer (unless such broker or dealer is acting in the capacity of market maker), the account of an associated person, or an account with respect to which such broker or dealer or associated person thereof exercises investment discretion.

(3) The provisions of paragraph (1) of this subsection insofar as they apply to transactions on a national securities exchange effected by a member thereof who was a member on Feburary 1, 1978 shall not become effective until February 1, 1979. Nothing in this paragraph shall be construed to impair or limit the authority of the Commission to regulate or prohibit such transactions prior to February 1, 1979, pursuant to paragraph (2) of this subsection.

(b) When not in contravention of such rules and regulations as the Commission may prescribe as necessary or appropriate in the public interest and for the protection of investors, to maintain fair and orderly markets, or to remove impediments to and perfect the mechanism of a national market system, the rules of a national securities exchange may permit (1) a member to be registered as an odd-lot dealer and as such to buy and sell for his own account so far as may be reasonably necessary to carry on such odd-lot transactions, and (2) a member to be registered as a specialist. Under the rules and regulations of the Commission a specialist may be permitted to act as a broker and dealer or limited to acting as a broker or dealer. It shall be unlawful for a specialist or an official of the exchange to disclose information in regard to orders placed with such specialist which is not available to all members of the exchange, to any person other than an official of the exchange, a representative of the Commission, or a specialist who may be acting for such specialist: Provided, however, That the Commission, by rule, may require disclosure to all members of the exchange of all orders placed with specialists, under such rules and regulations as the Commission may prescribe as necessary or appropriate in the public interest or for the protection of investors. It shall also be unlawful for a specialist permitted to act as a broker and dealer to effect on the exchange as broker any transaction except upon a market or limited price order.

(c) If because of the limited volume of transactions effected on an exchange, it is in the opinion of the Commission impracticable and not necessary or appropriate in the public interest or for the protection of investors to apply any of the foregoing provisions of this section or the rules and regulations thereunder, the Commission shall have power, upon application of the exchange and on a showing that the rules of such exchange are otherwise adequate for the protection of investors, to exempt such exchange and its members from any such provision or rules and regulations.

(d) It shall be unlawful for a member of a national securities exchange who is both a dealer and a broker, or for any person who both as a broker and a dealer transacts a business in securities through the medium of a member or otherwise, to effect through the use of any facility of a national securities exchange or of the mails or of any means or instrumentality of interstate commerce, or otherwise in the case of a member, (1) any transaction in connection with which, directly or indirectly, he extends or maintains or arranges for the extension or maintenance of credit to or for a customer on any security (other than an exempted security) which was a part of a new issue in the distribution of which he participated as a member of a selling syndicate or group within thirty days prior to such transaction: Provided, That credit shall not be deemed extended by reason of a bona fide delayed delivery of (i) any such security against full payment of the entire purchase price thereof upon such delivery within thirty-five days after such purchase or (ii) any mortgage related security or any small business related security against full payment of the entire purchase price thereof upon such delivery within one hundred and eighty days after such purchase, or within such shorter period as the Commission may prescribe by rule or regulation, or (2) any transaction with respect to any security (other than an exempted security) unless, if the transaction is with a customer, he discloses to such customer in writing at or before the completion of the transaction whether he is acting as a dealer for his own account, as a broker for such customer, or as a broker for some other person.

NATIONAL MARKET SYSTEM FOR SECURITIES; SECURITIES INFORMATION PROCESSORS

Sec. 11A. (a) (1) The Congress finds that—

(A) The securities markets are an important national asset which must be preserved and strengthened.

(B) New data processing and communications techniques create the opportunity for more efficient and effective market operations.

(C) It is in the public interest and appropriate for the protection of investors and the maintenance of fair and orderly markets to assure—

(i) economically efficient execution of securities transactions;

(ii) fair competition among brokers and dealers, among exchange markets, and between exchange markets and markets other than exchange markets;

(iii) the availability to brokers, dealers, and investors of information with respect to quotations for and transactions in securities;

(iv) the practicability of brokers executing investors' orders in the best market; and

(v) an opportunity, consistent with the provisions of clauses (i) and (iv) of this subparagraph, for investors' orders to be executed without the participation of a dealer.

(D) The linking of all markets for qualified securities through communication and data processing facilities will foster efficiency, enhance competition, increase the information available to brokers, dealers, and investors, facilitate the offsetting of investors' orders, and contribute to best execution of such orders.

(2) The Commission is directed, therefore, having due regard for the public interest, the protection of investors, and the maintenance of fair and orderly markets, to use its authority under this title to facilitate the establishment of a national market system for securities (which may include subsystems for particular types of securities with unique trading characteristics) in accordance with the findings and to carry out the objectives set forth in paragraph (1) of this subsection. The Commission, by rule, shall designate the securities or classes of securities qualified for trading in the national market system from among securities other than exempted securities. (Securities or classes of securities so designated hereinafter in this section referred to as "qualified securities".)

(3) The Commission is authorized in furtherance of the directive in paragraph (2) of this subsection—

(A) to create one or more advisory committees pursuant to the Federal Advisory Committee Act (which shall be in addition to the National Market Advisory Board established pursuant to subsection (d) of this section) and to employ one or more outside experts;

(B) by rule or order, to authorize or require self-regulatory organizations to act jointly with respect to matters as to which they share authority under this title in planning, developing, operating, or regulating a national market system (or a subsystem thereof) or one or more facilities thereof; and

(C) to conduct studies and make recommendations to the Congress from time to time as to the possible need for modifications of the scheme of self-regulation provided for in this title so as to adapt it to a national market system.

(b) (1) Except as otherwise provided in this section, it shall be unlawful for any securities information processor unless registered in accordance with this subsection, directly or indirectly, to make use of the mails or any means or instrumentality of interstate commerce to perform the functions of a securities information processor. The Commission, by rule or order, upon its own motion or upon application, may conditionally or unconditionally exempt any securities information processor or class of securities information processors or security or class of securities from any provision of this section or the rules or regulations thereunder, if the Commission finds that such exemption is consistent with the public interest, the protection of investors, and the purposes of this section, including the maintenance of fair and orderly markets in securities and the removal of impediments to and perfection of the mechanism of a national market system: Provided, however, That a securities information processor not acting as the exclusive processor of any information with respect to quotations for or transactions in securities is exempt from the requirement to register in accordance with this subsection unless the Commission, by rule, or order, finds that the registration of such securities information processor is necessary or appropriate in the public interest, for the protection of investors, or for the achievement of the purposes of this section.

(2) A securities information processor may be registered by filing with the Commission an application for registration in such form as the Commission, by rule, may prescribe containing the address of its principal office, or offices, the names of the securities and markets for which it is then acting and for which it proposes to act as a securities information processor, and such other information and documents as the Commission, by rule, may prescribe with regard to performance capability, standards and procedures for the collection, processing, distribution, and publication of information with respect to quotations for and transactions in securities, personnel qualifications, financial condition, and such other matters as the Commission determines to be germane to the provisions of this title and the rules and regulations thereunder, or necessary or appropriate in furtherance of the purposes of this section.

(3) The Commission shall, upon the filing of an application for registration pursuant to paragraph (2) of this subsection, publish notice of the filing and afford interested persons an opportunity to submit written data, views, and arguments concerning such application. Within ninety days of the date of the publication of such notice (or within such longer period as to which the applicant consents) the Commission shall—

(A) by order grant such registration, or

(B) institute proceedings to determine whether registration should be denied. Such proceedings shall include notice of the grounds for denial under consideration and opportunity for hearing and shall be concluded within one hundred eighty days of the date of publication of notice of the filing of the application for registration. At the conclusion of such proceedings the Commission, by order, shall grant or deny such registration. The Commission may extend the time for the conclusion of such proceedings for up to sixty days if it finds good cause for such extension and publishes its reasons for so finding or for such longer periods as to which the applicant consents.

The Commission shall grant the registration of a securities information processor if the Commission finds that such securities information processor is so organized, and has the capacity, to be able to assure the prompt, accurate, and reliable performance of its functions as a securities information processor, comply with the provisions of this title and the rules and regulations thereunder, carry out its functions in a manner consistent with the purposes of this section, and, insofar as it is acting as an exclusive processor, operate fairly and efficiently. The Commission shall deny the registration of a securities information processor if the Commission does not make any such finding.

(4) A registered securities information processor may, upon such terms and conditions as the Commission deems necessary or appropriate in the public interest or for the protection of investors, withdraw from registration by filing a written notice of withdrawal with the Commission. If the Commission finds that any registered securities information processor is no longer in existence or has ceased to do business in the capacity specified in its application for registration, the Commission, by order, shall cancel the registration.

(5) (A) If any registered securities information processor prohibits or limits any person in respect of access to services offered, directly or indirectly, by such securities information processor, the registered securities information processor shall promptly file notice thereof with the Commission. The notice shall be in such form and contain such information as the Commission, by rule, may prescribe as necessary or appropriate in the public interest or for the protection of investors. Any prohibition or limitation on access to services with respect to which a registered securities information processor is required by this paragraph to file notice shall be subject to review by the Commission on its own motion, or upon application by any person aggrieved thereby filed within thirty days after such notice has been filed with the Commission and received by such aggrieved person, or within such longer period as the Commission may determine. Application to the Commission for review, or the institution of review by the Commission on its

own motion, shall not operate as a stay of such prohibition or limitation, unless the Commission otherwise orders, summarily or after notice and opportunity for hearing on the question of a stay (which hearing may consist solely of the submission of affidavits or presentation of oral arguments). The Commission shall establish for appropriate cases an expedited procedure for consideration and determination of the question of a stay.

(B) In any proceeding to review the prohibition or limitation of any person in respect of access to services offered by a registered securities information processor, if the Commission finds after notice and opportunity for hearing, that such prohibition or limitation is consistent with the provisions of this title and the rules and regulations thereunder and that such person has not been discriminated against unfairly, the Commission, by order, shall dismiss the proceeding. If the Commission does not make any such finding or if it finds that such prohibition or limitation imposes any burden on competition not necessary or appropriate in furtherance of the purposes of this title, the Commission, by order, shall set aside the prohibition or limitation and require the registered securities information processor to permit such person access to services offered by the registered securities information processor.

(6) The Commission, by order, may censure or place limitations upon the activities, functions, or operations of any registered securities information processor or suspend for a period not exceeding twelve months or revoke the registration of any such processor, if the Commission finds, on the record after notice and opportunity for hearing, that such censure, placing of limitations, suspension, or revocation is in the public interest and necessary or appropriate for the protection of investors or to assure the prompt, accurate, or reliable performance of the functions of such securities information processor and that such securities information processor has violated or is unable to comply with any provision of this title or the rules or regulations thereunder.

(c)(1) No self-regulatory organization, member thereof, securities information processor, broker, or dealer shall make use of the mails or any means or instrumentality of interstate commerce to collect, process, distribute, publish, or prepare for distribution or publication any information with respect to quotations for or transactions in any security other than an exempted security, to assist, participate in, or coordinate the distribution or publication of such information, or to effect any transaction in, or to induce or attempt to induce the purchase or sale of, any such security in contravention of such rules and regulations as the Commission shall prescribe as necessary or appropriate in the public interest, for the protection of investors, or otherwise in furtherance of the purposes of this title to—

(A) prevent the use, distribution, or publication of fraudulent, deceptive, or manipulative information with respect to quotations for and transactions in such securities;

(B) assure the prompt, accurate, reliable, and fair collection, processing, distribution, and publication of information with respect to quotations for and transactions in such securities and the fairness and usefulness of the form and content of such information;

(C) assure that all securities information processors may, for purposes of distribution and publication, obtain on fair and reasonable terms such information with respect to quotations for and transactions in such securities as is collected, processed, or prepared for distribution or publication by any exclusive processor of such information acting in such capacity;

(D) assure that all exchange members, brokers, dealers, securities information processors, and, subject to such limitations as the Commission, by rule, may impose as necessary or appropriate for the protection of investors or maintenance of fair and orderly markets, all other persons may obtain on terms which are not unreasonably discriminatory such information with respect to quotations for and transactions in such securities as is published or distributed by any self-regulatory organization or securities information processor;

(E) assure that all exchange members, brokers, and dealers transmit and direct orders for the purchase or sale of qualified securities in a manner consistent with the establishment and operation of a national market system; and

(F) assure equal regulation of all markets for qualified securities and all exchange members, brokers, and dealers effecting transactions in such securities.

(2) The Commission, by rule, as it deems necessary or appropriate in the public interest or for the protection of investors, may require any person who has effected the purchase or sale of any qualified security by use of the mails or any means or instrumentality of interstate commerce to report such purchase or sale to a registered securities information processor, national securities exchange, or registered securities association and require such processor, exchange, or association to make appropriate distribution and publication of information with respect to such purchase or sale.

(3) (A) The Commission, by rule, is authorized to prohibit brokers and dealers from effecting transactions in securities registered pursuant to section 12(b) otherwise than on a national securities exchange, if the Commission finds, on the record after notice and opportunity for hearing, that—

(i) as a result of transactions in such securities effected otherwise than on a national securities exchange the fairness or orderliness of the markets for such securities has been affected in a manner contrary to the public interest or the protection of investors;

(ii) no rule of any national securities exchange unreasonably impairs the ability of any dealer to solicit or effect transactions in such securities for his own account or unreasonably restricts competition among dealers in such securities or betwwen dealers acting in the capacity of market makers who are specialists in such securities and such dealers who are not specialists in such securities, and

(iii) the maintenance or restoration of fair and orderly markets in such securities may not be assured through other lawful means under this title.

The Commission may conditionally or unconditionally exempt any security or transaction or any class of securities or transactions from any such prohibition if the Commission deems such exemption consistent with the public interest, the protection of investors, and the maintenance of fair and orderly markets.

(B) For the purposes of subparagraph (A) of this paragraph, the ability of a dealer to solicit or effect transactions in securities for his own account shall not be deemed to be unreasonably impaired by any rule of an exchange fairly and reasonably prescribing the sequence in which orders brought to the exchange must be executed or which has been adopted to effect compliance with a rule of the Commission promulgated under this title.

(4) The Commission is directed to review any and all rules of national securities exchanges which limit or condition the ability of members to effect transactions in securities otherwise than on such exchanges.

(5) No national securities exchange or registered securities association may limit or condition the participation of any member in any registered clearing agency.

(d) (1) Not later than one hundred eighty days after the date of enactment of the Securities Acts Amendments of 1975, the Commission shall establish a National Market Advisory Board (hereinafter in this section referred to as the "Advisory Board") to be composed of fifteen members, not all of whom shall be from the same geographical area of the United States, appointed by the Commission for a term specified by the Commission of not less than two years or more than five years. The Advisory Board shall consist of persons associated with brokers and dealers (who shall be a majority) and persons not so associated who are representative of the public and, to the extent feasible, have knowledge of the securities markets of the United States.

(2) It shall be the responsibility of the Advisory Board to formulate and furnish to the Commission its views on significant regulatory proposals made by the Commission or any self-regulatory organization concerning the establishment, operation, and regulation of the markets for securities in the United States.

(3) (A) The Advisory Board shall study and make recommendations to the Commission as to the steps it finds appropriate to facilitate the establishment of a national market system. In so doing, the Advisory Board shall assume the responsibilities of any advisory committee appointed to advise the Commission with respect to the national market system which is in existence at the time of the establishment of the Advisory Board.

(B) The Advisory Board shall study the possible need for modifications of the scheme of self-regulation provided for in this title so as to adapt it to a national market system, including the need for the establishment of a new self-regulatory organization (hereinafter in this section referred to as a "National Market Regulatory Board" or "Regulatory Board") to administer the national market system. In the event the Advisory Board determines a National Market Regulatory Board should be established, it shall make recommendations as to:

(i) the point in time at which a Regulatory Board should be established;

(ii) the composition of a Regulatory Board;

(iii) the scope of the authority of a Regulatory Board;

(iv) the relationship of a Regulatory Board to the Commission and to existing self-regulatory organizations; and

(v) the manner in which a Regulatory Board should be funded.

The Advisory Board shall report to the Congress, on or before December 31, 1976, the results of such study and its recommendations, including such recommendations for legislation as it deems appropriate.

(C) In carrying out its responsibilities under this paragraph, the Advisory Board shall consult with self-regulatory organizations, brokers, dealers, securities information processors, issuers, investors, representatives of Government agencies, and other persons interested or likely to participate in the establishment, operation, or regulation of the national market system.

(e) NATIONAL MARKETS SYSTEM FOR SECURITY FUTURES PRODUCTS.—

(1) CONSULTATION AND COOPERATION REQUIRED.—With respect to security futures products, the Commission and the Commodity Futures Trading Commission shall consult and cooperate so that, to the maximum extent practicable, their respective regulatory responsibilities may be fulfilled and the rules and regulations applicable to security futures products may foster a national market system for security futures products if the Commission and the Commodity Futures Trading Commission jointly determine that such a system would be consistent with the congressional findings in subsection (a)(1). In accordance with this objective, the Commission shall, at least 15 days prior to the issuance for public comment of any proposed rule or regulation under this section concerning security futures products, consult and request the views of the Commodity Futures Trading Commission.

(2) APPLICATION OF RULES BY ORDER OF CFTC.—No rule adopted pursuant to this section shall be applied to any person with respect to the trading of security futures products on an exchange that is registered under section 6(g) unless the Commodity Futures Trading Commission has issued an order directing that such rule is applicable to such persons.

REGISTRATION REQUIREMENTS FOR SECURITIES

Sec. 12. (a) It shall be unlawful for any member, broker, or dealer to effect any transaction in any security (other than an exempted security) on a national securities exchange unless a registration is effective as to such security for such exchange in accordance with the provisions of this title, and the rules and regulations thereunder. The provisions of this subsection shall not apply in respect of a security futures product traded on a national securities exchange.

(b) A security may be registered on a national securities exchange by the issuer filing an application with the exchange (and filing with the Commission such duplicate originals thereof as the Commission may require), which application shall contain—

(1) Such information, in such detail, as to the issuer and any person directly or indirectly controlling or controlled by, or under direct or indirect common control with, the issuer, and any guarantor of the security as to principal or interest or both, as the Commission may by rules and regulations require, as necessary or appropriate in the public interest or for the protection of investors, in respect of the following:

(A) the organization, financial structure and nature of the business;

(B) the terms, position, rights, and privileges of the different classes of securities outstanding;

(C) the terms on which their securities are to be, and during the preceding three years have been, offered to the public or otherwise;

(D) the directors, officers, and underwriters, and each security holder of record holding more than 10 per centum of any class of any equity security of the issuer (other than an exempted security), their remuneration and their interests in the securities of, and their material contracts with, the issuer and any person directly or indirectly controlling or controlled by, or under direct or indirect common control with, the issuer;

(E) remuneration to others than directors and officers exceeding $20,000 per annum;

(F) bonus and profit-sharing arrangements;

(G) management and service contracts;

(H) options existing or to be created in respect of their securities;

(I) material contracts, not made in the ordinary course of business, which are to be executed in whole or in part at or after the filing of the application or which were made not more than two years before such filing, and every material patent or contract for a material patent right shall be deemed a material contract;

(J) balance sheets for not more than the three preceding fiscal years, certified if required by the rules and regulations of the Commission by a registered public accounting firm;

(K) profit and loss statements for not more than the three preceding fiscal years, certified if required by the rules and regulations of the Commission by a registered public accounting firm; and

(L) any further financial statements which the Commission may deem necessary or appropriate for the protection of investors.

(2) Such copies of articles of incorporation, bylaws, trust indentures, or corresponding documents by whatever name known, underwriting arrangements, and other similar documents of, and voting trust agreements with respect to, the issuer and any person directly or indirectly controlling or controlled by, or under direct or indirect common control with, the issuer as the Commission may require as necessary or appropriate for the proper protection of investors and to insure fair dealing in the security.

(3) Such copies of material contracts, referred to in paragraph (1) (I) above, as the Commission may require as necessary or appropriate for the proper protection of investors and to insure fair dealing in the security.

(c) If in the judgment of the Commission any information required under subsection (b) is inapplicable to any specified class or classes of issuers, the Commission shall require in lieu thereof the submission of such other information of comparable character as it may deem applicable to such class of issuers.

(d) If the exchange authorities certify to the Commission that the security has been approved by the exchange for listing and registration, the registration shall become effective thirty days after the receipt of such certification by the Commission or within such shorter period of time as the Commission may determine. A security registered with a national securities exchange may be withdrawn or stricken from listing and registration in accordance with the rules of the exchange and, upon such terms as the Commission may deem necessary to impose for the protection of investors, upon application by the issuer or the exchange to the Commission; whereupon the issuer shall be relieved from further compliance with the provisions of this section and section 13 of this title and any rules or regulations under such sections as to the securities so withdrawn or stricken.

An unissued security may be registered only in accordance with such rules and regulations as the Commission may prescribe as necessary or appropriate in the public interest or for the protection of investors.

(e) Notwithstanding the foregoing provisions of this section, the Commission may by such rules and regulations as it deems necessary or appropriate in the public interest or for the protection of investors permit securities listed on any exchange at the time the registration of such exchange as a national securities exchange becomes effective, to be registered for a period ending not later than July 1, 1935, without complying with the provisions of this section.

(f)(1)(A) Notwithstanding the preceding subsections of this section, any national securities exchange, in accordance with the requirements of this subsection and the rules hereunder, may extend unlisted trading privileges to—

(i) any security that is listed and registered on a national securities exchange, subject to subparagraph (B); and

(ii) any security that is otherwise registered pursuant to this section, or that would be required to be so registered except for the exemption from registration provided in subparagraph (B) or (G) of subsection (g)(2), subject to subparagraph (E) of this paragraph.

(B) A national securities exchange may not extend unlisted trading privileges to a security described in subparagraph (A)(i) during such interval, if any, after the commencement of an initial public offering of such security, as is or may be required pursuant to subparagraph (C).

(C) Not later than 180 days after the date of enactment of the Unlisted Trading Privileges Act of 1994, the Commission shall prescribe, by rule or regulation, the duration of the interval referred to in subparagraph (B), if any, as the Commission determines to be necessary or appropriate for the maintenance of fair and orderly markets, the protection of investors and the public interest, or otherwise in furtherance of the purposes of this title. Until the earlier of the effective date of such rule or regulation or 240 days after such date of enactment, such interval shall begin at the opening of trading on the day on which such security commences trading on the national securities exchange with which such security is registered and end at the conclusion of the next day of trading.

(D) The Commission may prescribe, by rule or regulation such additional procedures or requirements for extending unlisted trading privileges to any security as the Commission deems necessary or appropriate for the maintenance of fair and orderly markets, the protection of investors and the public interest, or otherwise in furtherance of the purposes of this title.

(E) No extension of unlisted trading privileges to securities described in subparagraph (A)(ii) may occur except pursuant to a rule, regulation, or order of the Commission approving such extension or extensions. In promulgating such rule or regulation or in issuing such order, the Commission—

(i) shall find that such extension or extensions of unlisted trading privileges is consistent with the maintenance of fair and orderly markets, the protection of investors and the public interest, and otherwise in furtherance of the purposes of this title;

(ii) shall take account of the public trading activity in such securities, the character of such trading, the impact of such extension on the existing markets for such securities, and the desirability of removing impediments to and the progress that has been made toward the development of a national market system; and

(iii) shall not permit a national securities exchange to extend unlisted trading privileges to such securities if any rule of such national securities exchange would unreasonably impair the ability of a dealer to solicit or effect transactions in such securities for its own account, or would unreasonably restrict competition among dealers in such securities or between such dealers acting in the capacity of market makers who are specialists and such dealers who are not specialists.

(F) An exchange may continue to extend unlisted trading privileges in accordance with this paragraph only if the exchange and the subject security continue to satisfy the requirements for eligibility under this paragraph, including any rules and regulations issued by the Commission pursuant to this paragraph, except that unlisted trading privileges may continue with regard to securities which had been admitted on such exchange prior to July 1, 1964, notwithstanding the failure to satisfy such requirements. If unlisted trading privileges in a security are discontinued pursuant to this subparagraph, the exchange shall cease trading in that security, unless the exchange and the subject security thereafter satisfy the requirements of this paragraph and the rules issued hereunder.

(G) For purposes of this paragraph—

(i) a security is the subject of an initial public offering if—

(I) the offering of the subject security is registered under the Securities Act of 1933; and

(II) the issuer of the security, immediately prior to filing the registration statement with respect to the offering, was not subject to the reporting requirements of section 13 or 15(d) of this title; and

(ii) an initial public offering of such security commences at the opening of trading on the day on which such security commences trading on the national securities exchange with which such security is registered.

(2) (A) At any time within 60 days of commencement of trading on an exchange of a security pursuant to unlisted trading privileges, the Commission may summarily suspend such unlisted trading privileges on the exchange. Such suspension shall not be reviewable under section 25 of this title and shall not be deemed to be a final agency action for purposes of section 704 of title 5, United States Code. Upon such suspension—

(i) the exchange shall cease trading in the security by the close of business on the date of such suspension, or at such time as the Commission may prescribe by rule or order for the maintenance of fair and orderly markets, the protection of investors and the public interest, or otherwise in furtherance of the purposes of this title; and

(ii) if the exchange seeks to extend unlisted trading privileges to the security, the exchange shall file an application to reinstate its ability to do so with the Commission pursuant to such procedures as the Commission may prescribe by rule or order for the maintenance of fair and orderly markets, the protection of investors and the public interest, or otherwise in furtherance of the purposes of this title.

(B) A suspension under subparagraph (A) shall remain in effect until the Commission, by order, grants approval of an application to reinstate, as described in subparagraph (A) (ii).

(C) A suspension under subparagraph (A) shall not affect the validity or force of an extension of unlisted trading privileges in effect prior to such suspension.

(D) The Commission shall not approve an application by a national securities exchange to reinstate its ability to extend unlisted trading privileges to a security unless the Commission finds, after notice and opportunity for hearing, that the extension of unlisted trading privileges pursuant to such application is consistent with the maintenance of fair and orderly markets, the protection of investors and the public interest, and otherwise in furtherance of the purposes of this title. If the application is made to reinstate unlisted trading privileges to a security described in paragraph (1) (A) (ii), the Commission—

(i) shall take account of the public trading activity in such security, the character of such trading, the impact of such extension on the existing markets for such a security, and the desirability of removing impediments to and the progress that has been made toward the development of a national market system; and

(ii) shall not grant any such application if any rule of the national securities exchange making application under this subsection would unreasonably impair the ability of a dealer to solicit or effect transactions in such security for its own account, or would unreasonably restrict competition among dealers in such security or between such dealers acting in the capacity of marketmakers who are specialists and such dealers who are not specialists.

(3) Notwithstanding paragraph (2), the Commission shall by rules and regulations suspend unlisted trading privileges in whole or in part for any or all classes of securities for a period not exceeding twelve months, if it deems such suspension necessary or appropriate in the public interest or for the protection of investors or to prevent evasion of the purposes of this title.

(4) On the application of the issuer of any security for which unlisted trading privileges on any exchange have been continued or extended pursuant to this subsection, or of any broker or dealer who makes or creates a market for such security, or of any other person having a bona fide interest in the question of termination or suspension of such unlisted trading privileges, or on its own motion, the Commission shall by order terminate, or suspend for a period not exceeding

twelve months, such unlisted trading privileges for such security if the Commission finds, after appropriate notice and opportunity for hearing, that such termination or suspension is necessary or appropriate in the publc interest or for the protection of investors.

(5) In any proceeding under this subsection in which appropriate notice and opportunity for hearing are required, notice of not less than ten days to the applicant in such proceeding, to the issuer of the security involved, to the exchange which is seeking to continue or extend or has continued or extended unlisted trading privileges for such security, and to the exchange, if any, on which such security is listed and registered, shall be deemed adequate notice, and any broker or dealer who makes or creates a market for such security, and any other person having a bona fide interest in such proceeding, shall upon application be entitled to be heard.

(6) Any security for which unlisted trading privileges are continued or extended pursuant to this subsection shall be deemed to be registered on a national securities exchange within the meaning of this title. The powers and duties of the Commission under this title shall be applicable to the rules of an exchange in respect of any such security. The Commission may, by such rules and regulations as it deems necessary or appropriate in the public interest or for the protection of investors, either unconditionally or upon specified terms and conditions, or for stated periods, exempt such securities from the operation of any provision of section 13, 14, or 16 of this title.

(g)(1) Every issuer which is engaged in interstate commerce, or in a business affecting interstate commerce, or whose securities are traded by use of the mails or any means or instrumentality of interstate commerce shall—

(A) within one hundred and twenty days after the last day of its first fiscal year ended after the effective date of this subsection on which the issuer has total assets exceeding $1,000,000 and a class of equity security (other than an exempted security) held of record by seven hundred and fifty or more persons; and

(B) within one hundred and twenty days after the last day of its first fiscal year ended after two years from the effective date of this subsection on which the issuer has total assets exceeding $1,000,000 and a class of equity security (other than an exempted security) held of record by five hundred or more but less than seven hundred and fifty persons,

register such security by filing with the Commission a registration statement (and such copies thereof as the Commission may require) with respect to such security containing such information and documents as the Commission may specify comparable to that which is required in an application to register a security pursuant to subsection (b) of this section. Each such registration statement shall become effective sixty days after filing with the Commission or within such shorter period as the Commission may direct. Until such registration statement becomes effective it shall not be deemed filed for the purposes of section 18 of this title. Any issuer may register any class of equity security not required to be registered by filing a registration statement pursuant to the provisions of this paragraph. The Commission is authorized to extend the date upon which any issuer or class of issuers is required to register a security pursuant to the provisions of this paragraph.

(2) The provisions of this subsection shall not apply in respect of—

(A) any security listed and registered on a national securities exchange.

(B) any security issued by an investment company registered pursuant to section 8 of the Investment Company Act of 1940.

(C) any security, other than permanent stock, guaranty stock, permanent reserve stock, or any similar certificate evidencing nonwithdrawable capital, issued by a savings and loan association, building and loan association, cooperative bank, homestead association, or similar institution, which is supervised and examined by State or Federal authority having supervision over any such institution.

(D) any security of an issuer organized and operated exclusively for religious, educational, benevolent, fraternal, charitable, or reformatory purposes and not for pecuniary profit, and no part of the net earnings of which inures to the benefit of any private shareholder or individual; or any security of a fund that is excluded from the definition of an investment company under section 3(c)(10)(B) of the Investment Company Act of 1940.

(E) any security of an issuer which is a "cooperative association" as defined in the Agricultural Marketing Act, approved June 15, 1929, as amended, or a federation of such cooperative associations, if such federation possesses no greater powers or purposes than cooperative associations so defined.

(F) any security issued by a mutual or cooperative organization which supplies a commodity or service primarily for the benefit of its members and operates not for pecuniary profit, but only if the security is part of a class issuable only to persons who purchase commodities or services from the issuer, the security is transferable only to a successor in interest or occupancy of premises serviced or to be served by the issuer, and no dividends are payable to the holder of the security.

(G) any security issued by an insurance company if all of the following conditions are met:

(i) Such insurance company is required to and does file an annual statement with the Commissioner of Insurance (or other officer or agency performing a similar function) of its domiciliary State, and such annual statement conforms to that prescribed by the National Association of Insurance Commissioners or in the determination of such State commissioner, officer or agency substantially conforms to that so prescribed.

(ii) Such insurance company is subject to regulation by its domiciliary State of proxies, consents, or authorizations in respect of securities issued by such company and such regulation conforms to that prescribed by the National Association of Insurance Commissioners.

(iii) After July 1, 1966, the purchase and sales of securities issued by such insurance company by beneficial owners, directors, or officers of such company are subject to regulation (including reporting) by its domiciliary State substantially in the manner provided in section 16 of this title.

(H) any interest or participation in any collective trust funds maintained by a bank or in a separate account maintained by an insurance company which interest or participation is issued in connection with (i) a stock-bonus, pension, or profit-sharing plan which meets the requirements for qualification under section 401 of the Internal Revenue Code of 1954, or (ii) an annuity plan which meets the requirements for deduction of the employer's contribution under section 404(a)(2) of such Code.

(3) The Commission may by rules or regulations or, on its own motion, after notice and opportunity for hearing, by order, exempt from this subsection any security of a foreign issuer, including any certificate of deposit for such a security, if the Commission finds that such exemption is in the public interest and is consistent with the protection of investors.

(4) Registration of any class of security pursuant to this subsection shall be terminated ninety days, or such shorter period as the Commission may determine, after the issuer files a certification with the Commission that the number of holders of record of such class of security is reduced to less than three hundred persons. The Commission shall after notice and opportunity for hearing deny termination of registration if it finds that the certification is untrue. Termination of registration shall be deferred pending final determination on the question of denial.

(5) For the purposes of this subsection the term "class" shall include all securities of an issuer which are of substantially similar character and the holders of which enjoy substantially similar rights and privileges. The Commission may for the purpose of this subsection define by rules and regulations the terms "total assets" and "held of record" as it deems necessary or appropriate in the public interest or for the protection of investors in order to prevent circumvention of the provisions of this subsection. For purposes of this subsection, a security futures product shall not be considered a class of equity security of the issuer of the securities underlying the security futures product.

(h) The Commission may by rules and regulations, or upon application of an interested person, by order, after notice and opportunity for hearing, exempt in whole or in part any issuer or class of issuers from the provisions of subsection (g) of this section or from section 13, 14, or 15(d) or may exempt from section 16 any officer, director, or beneficial owner of securities of any issuer, any security of which is required to be registered pursuant to subsection (g) hereof, upon such terms and conditions and for such period as it deems necessary or appropriate, if the Commission finds, by reason of the number of public investors, amount of trading interest in the securities, the nature and extent of the activities of the issuer, income or assets of the issuer, or otherwise, that such action is not inconsistent with the public interest or the protection of investors. The Commission may, for the purposes of any of the above-mentioned sections or subsections of this title, classify issuers and prescribe requirements appropriate for each such class.

(i) In respect of any securities issued by banks and savings associations the deposits of which are insured in accordance with Federal Deposit Insurance Act, the powers, functions, and duties vested in the Commission to administer and enforce sections 10A(m), 12, 13, 14(a), 14(c), 14(d), 14(f), and 16 of this Act, and sections 302, 303, 304, 306, 401(b), 404, 406, and 407 of the Sarbanes-Oxley Act of 2002, (1) with respect to national banks and banks operating under the Code of Law for the District of Columbia are vested in the Comptroller of the Currency, (2) with respect to all other member banks of the Federal Reserve System are vested in the Board of Governors of the Federal Reserve System, (3) with respect to all other insured banks are vested in the Federal Deposit Insurance Corporation, and (4) with respect to savings associations the accounts of which are insured by the Federal Deposit Insurance Corporation are vested in the Office of Thrift Supervision. The Comptroller of the Currency, the Board of Governors of the Federal Reserve System, the Federal Deposit Insurance Corporation, and the Office of Thrift Supervision shall have the power to make such rules and regulations as may be necessary for the execution of the functions vested in them as provided in this subsection. In carrying out their responsibilities under this subsection, the agencies named in the first sentence of this subsection shall issue substantially similar regulations to regulations and rules issued by the Commission under sections 10A(m), 12, 13, 14(a), 14(c), 14(d), 14(f), and 16 of this Act, and sections 302, 303, 304, 306, 401(b), 404, 406, and 407 of the Sarbanes-Oxley Act of 2002, unless they find that implementation of substantially similar regulations with respect to insured banks and insured institutions are not necessary or appropriate in the public interest or for protection of investors, and publish such findings, and the detailed reasons therefor, in the Federal Register. Such regulations of the above-named agencies, or the reasons for failure to publish such substantially similar regulations to those of the Commission, shall be published in the Federal Register within 120 days of the date of enactment of this subsection, and, thereafter, within 60 days of any changes made by the Commission in its relevant regulations and rules.

(j) The Commission is authorized, by order, as it deems necessary or appropriate for the protection of investors to deny, to suspend the effective date of, to suspend for a period not exceeding twelve months, or to revoke the registration of a security, if the Commission finds, on the record after notice and opportunity for hearing, that the issuer of such security has failed to comply with any provision of this title or the rules and regulations thereunder. No member of a national securities exchange, broker, or dealer shall make use of the mails or any means or instrumentality of interstate commerce to effect any transaction in, or to induce the purchase or sale of, any security the registration of which has been and is suspended or revoked pursuant to the preceding sentence.

(k) TRADING SUSPENSIONS; EMERGENCY AUTHORITY.—

(1) TRADING SUSPENSIONS.—If in its opinion the public interest and the protection of investors so require, the Commission is authorized by order—

(A) summarily to suspend trading in any security (other than an exempted security) for a period not exceeding 10 business days, and

(B) summarily to suspend all trading on any national securities exchange or otherwise, in securities other than exempted securities, for a period not exceeding 90 calendar days.

The action described in subparagraph (B) shall not take effect unless the Commission notifies the President of its decision and the President notifies the Commission that the President does not disapprove of such decision.

If the actions described in subparagraph (A) or (B) involve a security futures product, the Commission shall consult with and consider the views of the Commodity Futures Trading Commission.

(2) EMERGENCY ORDERS.—(A) The Commission, in an emergency, may by order summarily take such action to alter, supplement, suspend, or impose requirements or restrictions with

respect to any matter or action subject to regulation by the Commission or a self-regulatory organization under this title, as the Commission determines is necessary in the public interest and for the protection of investors—

(i) to maintain or restore fair and orderly securities markets (other than markets in exempted securities); or

(ii) to ensure prompt, accurate, and safe clearance and settlement of transactions in securities (other than exempted securities).

(B) An order of the Commission under this paragraph (2) shall continue in effect for the period specified by the Commission, and may be extended, except that in no event shall the Commission's action continue in effect for more than 10 business days, including extensions. If the actions described in subparagraph (A) involve a security futures product, the Commission shall consult with and consider the views of the Commodity Futures Trading Commission. In exercising its authority under this paragraph, the Commission shall not be required to comply with the provisions of section 553 of title 5, United States Code, or with the provisions of section 19(c) of this title.

(3) TERMINATION OF EMERGENCY ACTIONS BY PRESIDENT.—The President may direct that action taken by the Commission under paragraph (1)(B) or paragraph (2) of this subsection shall not continue in effect.

(4) COMPLIANCE WITH ORDERS.—No member of a national securities exchange, broker, or dealer shall make use of the mails or any means or instrumentality of interstate commerce to effect any transaction in, or to induce the purchase or sale of, any security in contravention of an order of the Commission under this subsection unless such order has been stayed, modified, or set aside as provided in paragraph (5) of this subsection or has ceased to be effective upon direction of the President as provided in paragraph (3).

(5) LIMITATIONS ON REVIEW OF ORDERS.—An order of the Commission pursuant to this subsection shall be subject to review only as provided in section 25(a) of this title. Review shall be based on an examination of all the information before the Commission at the time such order was issued. The reviewing court shall not enter a stay, writ of mandamus, or similar relief unless the court finds, after notice and hearing before a panel of the court, that the Commission's action is arbitrary, capricious, an abuse of discretion, or otherwise not in accordance with law.

(6) DEFINITION OF EMERGENCY.—For purposes of this subsection, the term "emergency" means a major market disturbance characterized by or constituting—

(A) sudden and excessive fluctuations of securities prices generally, or a substantial threat thereof, that threaten fair and orderly markets, or

(B) a substantial disruption of the safe or efficient operation of the national system for clearance and settlement of securities, or a substantial threat thereof.

(l) It shall be unlawful for an issuer, any class of whose securities is registered pursuant to this section or would be required to be so registered except for the exemption from registration provided by subsection (g)(2)(B) or (g)(2)(G) of this section, by the use of any means or instrumentality of interstate commerce, or of the mails, to issue, either originally or upon transfer, any of such securities in a form or with a format which contravenes such rules and regulations as the Commission may prescribe as necessary or appropriate for the prompt and accurate clearance and settlement of transactions in securities. The provisions of this subsection shall not apply to variable annuity contracts or variable life policies issued by an insurance company or its separate accounts.

PERIODICAL AND OTHER REPORTS

Sec. 13. (a) Every issuer of a security registered pursuant to section 12 of this title shall file with the Commission, in accordance with such rules and regulations as the Commission may prescribe as necessary or appropriate for the proper protection of investors and to insure fair dealing in the security—

(1) such information and documents (and such copies thereof) as the Commission shall require to keep reasonably current the information and documents required to be included in or filed with an application or registration statement filed pursuant to section 12, except that the Commission may not require the filing of any material contract wholly executed before July 1, 1962.

(2) such annual reports (and such copies thereof), certified if required by the rules and regulations of the Commission by independent public accountants, and such quarterly reports (and such copies thereof), as the Commission may prescribe.

Every issuer of a security registered on a national securities exchange shall also file a duplicate original of such information, documents, and reports with the exchange.

(b) (1) The Commission may prescribe, in regard to reports made pursuant to this title, the form or forms in which the required information shall be set forth, the items or details to be shown in the balance sheet and the earnings statement, and the methods to be followed in the preparation of reports, in the appraisal or valuation of assets and liabilities, in the determination of depreciation and depletion, in the differentiation of recurring and nonrecurring income, in the differentiation of investment and operating income, and in the preparation, where the Commission deems it necessary or desirable, of separate and/or consolidated balance sheets or income accounts of any person directly or indirectly controlling or controlled by the issuer, or any person under direct or indirect common control with the issuer; but in the case of the reports of any person whose methods of accounting are prescribed under the provisions of any law of the United States, or any rule or regulation thereunder, the rules and regulations of the Commission with respect to reports shall not be inconsistent with the requirements imposed by such law or rule or regulation in respect of the same subject matter, (except that such rules and regulations of the Commission may be inconsistent with such requirements to the extent that the Commission determines that the public interest or the protection of investors so requires).

(2) Every issuer which has a class of securities registered pursuant to section 12 of this title and every issuer which is required to file reports pursuant to section 15(d) of this title shall—

(A) make and keep books, records, and accounts, which, in reasonable detail, accurately and fairly reflect the transactions and dispositions of the assets of the issuer;

(B) devise and maintain a system of internal accounting controls sufficient to provide reasonable assurances that—

(i) transactions are executed in accordance with management's general or specific authorization;

(ii) transactions are recorded as necessary (I) to permit preparation of financial statements in conformity with generally accepted accounting principles or any other criteria applicable to such statements, and (II) to maintain accountability for assets;

(iii) access to assets is permitted only in accordance with management's general or specific authorization; and

(iv) the recorded accountability for assets is compared with the existing assets at reasonable intervals and appropriate action is taken with respect to any differences; and

(C) notwithstanding any other provision of law, pay the allocable share of such issuer of a reasonable annual accounting support fee or fees, determined in accordance with section 109 of the Sarbanes-Oxley Act of 2002.

(3) (A) With respect to matters concerning the national security of the United States, no duty or liability under paragraph (2) of this subsection shall be imposed upon any person acting in cooperation with the head of any Federal department or agency responsible for such matters if such act in cooperation with such head of a department or agency was done upon the specific, written directive of the head of such department or agency pursuant to Presidential authority to issue such directives. Each directive issued under this paragraph shall set forth the specific facts and circumstances with respect to which the provisions of this paragraph are to be invoked. Each such directive shall, unless renewed in writing, expire one year after the date of issuance.

(B) Each head of a Federal department or agency of the United States who issues a directive pursuant to this paragraph shall maintain a complete file of all such directives and shall, on October 1 of each year, transmit a summary of matters covered by such directives in force at any time during the previous year to the Permanent Select Committee on Intelligence of the House of Representatives and the Select Committee on Intelligence of the Senate.

(4) No criminal liability shall be imposed for failing to comply with the requirements of paragraph (2) of this subsection except as provided in paragraph (5) of this subsection.

(5) No person shall knowingly circumvent or knowingly fail to implement a system of internal accounting controls or knowingly falsify any book, record, or account described in paragraph (2).

(6) Where an issuer which has a class of securities registered pursuant to section 12 of this title or an issuer which is required to file reports pursuant to section 15(d) of this title holds 50 per centum or less of the voting power with respect to a domestic or foreign firm, the provisions of paragraph (2) require only that the issuer proceed in good faith to use its influence, to the extent reasonable under the issuer's circumstances, to cause such domestic or foreign firm to devise and maintain a system of internal accounting controls consistent with paragraph (2). Such circumstances include the relative degree of the issuer's ownership of the domestic or foreign firm and the laws and practices governing the business operations of the country in which such firm is located. An issuer which demonstrates good faith efforts to use such influence shall be conclusively presumed to have complied with the requirements of paragraph (2).

(7) For the purpose of paragraph (2) of this subsection, the terms 'reasonable assurances' and 'reasonable detail' mean such level of detail and degree of assurance as would satisfy prudent officials in the conduct of their own affairs.

(c) If in the judgment of the Commission any report required under subsection (a) is inapplicable to any specified class or classes of issuers, the Commission shall require in lieu thereof the submission of such reports of comparable character as it may deem applicable to such class or classes of issuers.

(d)(1) Any person who, after acquiring directly or indirectly the beneficial ownership of any equity security of a class which is registered pursuant to section 12 of this title, or any equity security of an insurance company which would have been required to be so registered except for the exemption contained in section 12(g)(2)(G) of this title, or any equity security issued by a closed-end investment company registered under the Investment Company Act of 1940 or any equity security by a Native Corporation pursuant to section 37(d)(6) of the Alaska Native Claims Settlement Act, is directly or indirectly the beneficial owner of more than 5 per centum of such class shall, within ten days after such acquisition, send to the issuer of the security at its principal executive office, by registered or certified mail, send to each exchange where the security is traded, and file with the Commission, a statement containing such of the following information, and such additional information, as the Commission may by rules and regulations prescribe as necessary or appropriate in the public interest or for the protection of investors—

(A) The background, and identity, residence, and citizenship of, and the nature of such beneficial ownership by, such person and all other persons by whom or on whose behalf the purchases have been or are to be effected;

(B) the source and amount of the funds or other consideration used or to be used in making the purchases, and if any part of the purchase price or proposed purchase price is represented or is to be represented by funds or other consideration borrowed or otherwise obtained for the purpose of acquiring, holding, or trading such security, a description of the transaction and the names of the parties thereto, except that where a source of funds is a loan made in the ordinary course of business by a bank, as defined in section 3(a)(6) of this title, if the person filing such statement so requests, the name of the bank shall not be made available to the public;

(C) if the purpose of the purchases or prospective purchases is to acquire control of the business of the issuer of the securities, any plans or proposals which such persons may have to liquidate such issuer, to sell its assets to or merge it with any other persons, or to make any other major change in its business or corporate structure;

(D) the number of shares of such security which are beneficially owned, and the number of shares concerning which there is a right to acquire, directly or indirectly, by (i) such person, and (ii) by each associate of such person, giving the background, identity, residence and citizenship of each such associate; and

(E) information as to any contracts, arrangements, or understandings with any person with respect to any securities of the issuer, including but not limited to transfer of any of the securities, joint ventures, loan or option arrangements, puts or calls, guaranties of loans, guaranties against loss or guaranties of profits, division of losses or profits, or the giving or withholding of proxies, naming the persons with whom such contracts, arrangements, or understandings have been entered into, and giving the details thereof.

(2) If any material change occurs in the facts set forth in the statements to the issuer and the exchange, and in the statement filed with the Commission, an amendment shall be transmitted to the issuer and the exchange and shall be filed with the Commission, in accordance with such rules and regulations as the Commission may prescribe as necessary or appropriate in the public interest or for the protection of investors.

(3) When two or more persons act as a partnership, limited partnership, syndicate, or other group for the purpose of acquiring, holding, or disposing of securities of an issuer, such syndicate or group shall be deemed a "person" for the purposes of this subsection.

(4) In determining, for purposes of this subsection, any percentage of a class of any security, such class shall be deemed to consist of the amount of the outstanding securities of such class, exclusive of any securities of such class held by or for the account of the issuer or a subsidiary of the issuer.

(5) The Commission, by rule or regulation or by order, may permit any person to file in lieu of the statement required by paragraph (1) of this subsection or the rules and regulations thereunder, a notice stating the name of such person, the number of shares of any equity securities subject to paragraph (1) which are owned by him, the date of their acquisition and such other information as the Commission may specify, if it appears to the Commission that such securities were acquired by such person in the ordinary course of his business and were not acquired for the purpose of and do not have the effect of changing or influencing the control of the issuer nor in connection with or as a participant in any transaction having such purpose or effect.

(6) The provisions of this subsection shall not apply to—

(A) any acquisition or offer to acquire securities made or proposed to be made by means of a registration statement under the Securities Act of 1933;

(B) any acquisition of the beneficial ownership of a security which, together with all other acquisitions by the same person of securities of the same class during the preceding twelve months, does not exceed 2 per centum of that class;

(C) any acquisition of an equity security by the issuer of such security;

(D) any acquisition or proposed acquisition of a security which the Commission, by rules or regulations or by order, shall exempt from the provisions of this subsection as not entered into for the purpose of, and not having the effect of, changing or influencing the control of the issuer or otherwise as not comprehended within the purposes of this subsection.

(e) (1) It shall be unlawful for an issuer which has a class of equity securities registered pursuant to section 12 of this title, or which is a closed-end investment company registered under the Investment Company Act of 1940, to purchase any equity security issued by it if such purchase is in contravention of such rules and regulations as the Commission, in the public interest or for the protection of investors, may adopt (A) to define acts and practices which are fraudulent, deceptive, or manipulative, and (B) to prescribe means reasonably designed to prevent such acts and practices. Such rules and regulations may require such issuer to provide holders of equity securities of such class with such information relating to the reasons for such purchase, the source of funds, the number of shares to be purchased, the price to be paid for such securities, the method of purchase, and such additional information, as the Commission deems necessary or appropriate in the public interest or for the protection of investors, or which the Commission deems to be material to a determination whether such security should be sold.

(2) For the purpose of this subsection, a purchase by or for the issuer, or any person controlling, controlled by, or under the common control with the issuer, or a purchase subject to control of the issuer or any such person, shall be deemed to be a purchase by the issuer. The Commission shall have power to make rules and regulations implementing this paragraph in the public interest and for the protection of investors, including exemptive rules and regulations covering situations in which the Commission deems it unnecessary or inappropriate that a purchase of the type described in this paragraph shall be deemed to be a purchase by the issuer for purposes of some or all of the provisions of paragraph (1) of this subsection.

(3) At the time of filing such statement as the Commission may require by rule pursuant to paragraph (1) of this subsection, the person making the filing shall pay to the Commission a fee at a rate that, subject to paragraphs (5) and (6), is equal to $92 per $1,000,000 of the value of securities proposed to be purchased. The fee shall be reduced with respect to securities in an amount equal to any fee paid with respect to any securities issued in connection with the proposed transaction under section 6(b) of the Securities Act of 1933, or the fee paid under that section shall be reduced in an amount equal to the fee paid to the Commission in connection with such transaction under this paragraph.

(4) Offsetting Collections.—Fees collected pursuant to this subsection for any fiscal year shall be deposited and credited as offsetting collections to the account providing appropriations to the Commission, and, except as provided in paragraph (9), shall not be collected for any fiscal year except to the extent provided in advance in appropriation Acts. No fees collected pursuant to this subsection for fiscal year 2002 or any succeeding fiscal year shall be deposited and credited as general revenue of the Treasury.

(5) Annual Adjustment.—For each of the fiscal years 2003 through 2011, the Commission shall by order adjust the rate required by paragraph (3) for such fiscal year to a rate that is equal to the rate (expressed in dollars per million) that is applicable under section 6(b) of the Securities Act of 1933 for such fiscal year.

(6) Final Rate Adjustment.—For fiscal year 2012 and all of the succeeding fiscal years, the Commission shall by order adjust the rate required by paragraph (3) for all of such fiscal years to a rate that is equal to the rate (expressed in dollars per million) that is applicable under section 6(b) of the Securities Act of 1933 for all of such fiscal years.

(7) Pro Rata Application.—The rates per $1,000,000 required by this subsection shall be applied pro rata to amounts and balances of less than $1,000,000.

(8) Review And Effective Date.—In exercising its authority under this subsection, the Commission shall not be required to comply with the provisions of section 553 of title 5, United States Code. An adjusted rate prescribed under paragraph (5) or (6) and published under paragraph (10) shall not be subject to judicial review. Subject to paragraphs (4) and (9)—

(A) an adjusted rate prescribed under paragraph (5) shall take effect on the later of—

(i) the first day of the fiscal year to which such rate applies; or

(ii) five days after the date on which a regular appropriation to the Commission for such fiscal year is enacted; and

(B) an adjusted rate prescribed under paragraph (6) shall take effect on the later of—

(i) the first day of fiscal year 2012; or

(ii) five days after the date on which a regular appropriation to the Commission for fiscal year 2012 is enacted.

(9) Lapse of Appropriation.—If on the first day of a fiscal year a regular appropriation to the Commission has not been enacted, the Commission shall continue to collect fees (as offsetting collections) under this subsection at the rate in effect during the preceding fiscal year, until 5 days after the date such a regular appropriation is enacted.

(10) Publication.—The rate applicable under this subsection for each fiscal year is published pursuant to section 6(b)(10) of the Securities Act of 1933.

(f)(1) Every institutional investment manager which uses the mails, or any means or instrumentality of interstate commerce in the course of its business as an institutional investment manager and which exercises investment discretion with respect to accounts holding equity securities of a class described in section 13(d)(1) of this title having an aggregate fair market value on the last trading day in any of the preceding twelve months of at least $100,000,000 or such lesser amount (but in no case less than $10,000,000) as the Commission, by rule, may determine, shall file reports with the Commission in such form, for such periods, and at such times after the end of such periods as the Commission, by rule, may prescribe, but in no event shall such reports be filed for periods longer than one year or shorter than one quarter. Such reports shall include for each such equity security held on the last day of the reporting period by accounts (in aggregate or by type as the Commission, by rule, may prescribe) with respect to which the institutional investment manager exercises investment discretion (other than securities held in amounts which the Commission, by rule, determines to be insignificant for purposes of this subsection), the name of the issuer and the title, class, CUSIP number, number of shares or principal amount, and aggregate fair market value of each such security. Such reports may also include for accounts (in aggregate or by type) with respect to which the institutional investment manager exercises investment discretion such of the following information as the Commission, by rule, prescribes—

(A) the name of the issuer and the title, class, CUSIP number, number of shares or principal amount, and aggregate fair market value or cost or amortized cost of each other security (other than an exempted security) held on the last day of the reporting period by such accounts;

(B) the aggregate fair market value or cost or amortized cost of exempted securities (in aggregate or by class) held on the last day of the reporting period by such accounts;

(C) the number of shares of each equity security of a class described in section 13(d)(1) of this title held on the last day of the reporting period by such accounts with respect to which the institutional investment manager possesses sole or shared authority to exercise the voting rights evidenced by such securities;

(D) the aggregate purchases and aggregate sales during the reporting period of each security (other than an exempted security) effected by or for such accounts; and

(E) with respect to any transaction or series of transactions having a market value of at least $500,000 or such other amount as the Commission, by rule, may determine effected during the reporting period by or for such accounts in any equity security of a class described in section 13(d)(1) of this title—

(i) the name of the issuer and the title, class, and CUSIP number of the security;

(ii) the number of shares or principal amount of the security involved in the transaction;

(iii) whether the transaction was a purchase or sale;

(iv) the per share price or prices at which the transaction was effected;

(v) the date or dates of the transaction;

(vi) the date or dates of the settlement of the transaction;

(vii) the broker or dealer through whom the transaction was effected;

(viii) the market or markets in which the transaction was effected; and

(ix) such other related information as the Commission, by rule, may prescribe.

(2) The Commission, by rule or order, may exempt, conditionally or unconditionally, any institutional investment manager or security or any class of institutional investment managers or securities from any or all of the provisions of this subsection or the rules thereunder.

(3) The Commission shall make available to the public for a reasonable fee a list of all equity securities of a class described in section 13(d)(1) of this title, updated no less frequently than reports are required to be filed pursuant to paragraph (1) of this subsection. The Commission shall tabulate the information contained in any report filed pursuant to this subsection in a manner which will, in the view of the Commission, maximize the usefulness of the information to other Federal and State authorities and the public. Promptly after the filing of any such report, the Commission shall make the information contained therein conveniently available to the public for a reasonable fee in such form as the Commission, by rule, may prescribe, except that the Commission, as it determines to be necessary or appropriate in the public interest or for the

protection of investors, may delay or prevent public disclosure of any such information in accordance with section 552 of title 5, United States Code. Notwithstanding the preceding sentence, any such information identifying the securities held by the account of a natural person or an estate or trust (other than a business trust or investment company) shall not be disclosed to the public.

(4) In exercising its authority under this subsection, the Commission shall determine (and so state) that its action is necessary or appropriate in the public interest and for the protection of investors or to maintain fair and orderly markets or, in granting an exemption, that its action is consistent with the protection of investors and the purposes of this subsection. In exercising such authority the Commission shall take such steps as are within its power, including consulting with the Comptroller General of the United States, the Director of the Office of Management and Budget, the appropriate regulatory agencies, Federal and State authorities which, directly or indirectly, require reports from institutional investment managers of information substantially similar to that called for by this subsection, national securities exchanges, and registered securities associations, (A) to achieve uniform, centralized reporting of information concerning the securities holdings of and transactions by or for accounts with respect to which institutional investment managers exercise investment discretion, and (B) consistently with the objective set forth in the preceding subparagraph, to avoid unnecessarily duplicative reporting by, and minimize the compliance burden on, institutional investment managers. Federal authorities which, directly or indirectly, require reports from institutional investment managers of information substantially similar to that called for by this subsection shall cooperate with the Commission in the performance of its responsibilities under the preceding sentence. An institutional investment manager which is a bank, the deposits of which are insured in accordance with the Federal Deposit Insurance Act, shall file with the appropriate regulatory agency a copy of every report filed with the Commission pursuant to this subsection.

(5) (A) For purposes of this subsection the term "institutional investment manager" includes any person, other than a natural person, investing in or buying and selling securities for its own account, and any person exercising investment discretion with respect to the account of any other person.

(B) The Commission shall adopt such rules as it deems necessary or appropriate to prevent duplicative reporting pursuant to this subsection by two or more institutional investment managers exercising investment discretion with respect to the same amount.

(g) (1) Any person who is directly or indirectly the beneficial owner of more than 5 per centum of any security of a class described in subsection (d) (1) of this section shall send to the issuer of the security and shall file with the Commission a statement setting forth, in such form and at such time as the Commission may, by rule, prescribe—

(A) such person's identity, residence, and citizenship; and

(B) the number and description of the shares in which such person has an interest and the nature of such interest.

(2) If any material change occurs in the facts set forth in the statement sent to the issuer and filed with the Commission, an amendment shall be transmitted to the issuer and shall be filed with the Commission, in accordance with such rules and regulations as the Commission may prescribe as necessary or appropriate in the public interest or for the protection of investors.

(3) When two or more persons act as a partnership, limited partnership, syndicate, or other group for the purpose of acquiring, holding, or disposing of securities of an issuer, such syndicate or group shall be deemed a "person" for the purposes of this subsection.

(4) In determining, for purposes of this subsection, any percentage of a class of any security, such class shall be deemed to consist of the amount of the outstanding securities of such class, exclusive of any securities of such class held by or for the account of the issuer or a subsidiary of the issuer.

(5) In exercising its authority under this subsection, the Commission shall take such steps as it deems necessary or appropriate in the public interest or for the protection of investors (A) to achieve centralized reporting of information regarding ownership, (B) to avoid unnecessarily

duplicative reporting by and minimize the compliance burden on persons required to report, and (C) to tabulate and promptly make available the information contained in any report filed pursuant to this subsection in a manner which will, in the view of the Commission, maximize the usefulness of the information to other Federal and State agencies and the public.

(6) The Commission may, by rule or order, exempt, in whole or in part, any person or class of persons from any or all of the reporting requirements of this subsection as it deems necessary or appropriate in the public interest or for the protection of investors.

(h) LARGE TRADER REPORTING.—

(1) IDENTIFICATION REQUIREMENTS FOR LARGE TRADERS.—For the purpose of monitoring the impact on the securities markets of securities transactions involving a substantial volume or a large fair market value or exercise value and for the purpose of otherwise assisting the Commission in the enforcement of this title, each large trader shall—

(A) provide such information to the Commission as the Commission may by rule or regulation prescribe as necessary or appropriate, identifying such large trader and all accounts in or through which such large trader effects such transactions; and

(B) identify, in accordance with such rules or regulations as the Commission may prescribe as necessary or appropriate, to any registered broker or dealer by or through whom such large trader directly or indirectly effects securities transactions, such large trader and all accounts directly or indirectly maintained with such broker or dealer by such large trader in or through which such transactions are effected.

(2) RECORDKEEPING AND REPORTING REQUIREMENTS FOR BROKERS AND DEALERS.— Every registered broker or dealer shall make and keep for prescribed periods such records as the Commission by rule or regulation prescribes as necessary or appropriate in the public interest, for the protection of investors, or otherwise in furtherance of the purposes of this title, with respect to securities transactions that equal or exceed the reporting activity level effected directly or indirectly by or through such registered broker or dealer of or for any person that such broker or dealer knows is a large trader, or any person that such broker or dealer has reason to know is large trader on the basis of transactions in securities effected by or through such broker or dealer. Such records shall be available for reporting to the Commission, or any self-regulatory organization that the Commission shall designate to receive such reports, on the morning of the day following the day the transactions were effected, and shall be reported to the Commission or a self-regulatory organization designated by the Commission immediately upon request by the Commission or such a self-regulatory organization. Such records and reports shall be in a format and transmitted in a manner prescribed by the Commission (including, but not limited to, machine readable form).

(3) AGGREGATION RULES.—The Commission may prescribe rules or regulations governing the manner in which transactions and accounts shall be aggregated for the purpose of this subsection, including aggregation on the basis of common ownership or control.

(4) EXAMINATION OF BROKER AND DEALER RECORDS.—All records required to be made and kept by registered brokers and dealers pursuant to this subsection with respect to transactions effected by large traders are subject at any time, or from time to time, to such reasonable periodic, special, or other examinations by representatives of the Commission as the Commission deems necessary or appropriate in the public interest, for the protection of investors, or otherwise in furtherance of the purposes of this title.

(5) FACTORS TO BE CONSIDERED IN COMMISSION ACTIONS.—In exercising its authority under this subsection, the Commission shall take into account—

(A) existing reporting systems;

(B) the costs associated with maintaining information with respect to transactions effected by large traders and reporting such information to the Commission or self-regulatory organizations; and

(C) the relationship between the United States and international securities markets.

(6) EXEMPTIONS.—The Commission, by rule, regulation, or order, consistent with the purposes of this title, may exempt any person or class of persons or any transaction or class of

transactions, either conditionally or upon specified terms and conditions or for stated periods, from the operation of this subsection, and the rules and regulations thereunder.

(7) AUTHORITY OF COMMISSION TO LIMIT DISCLOSURE OF INFORMATION.—Notwithstanding any other provision of law, the Commission shall not be compelled to disclose any information required to be kept or reported under this subsection. Nothing in this subsection shall authorize the Commission to withhold information from Congress, or prevent the Commission from complying with a request for information from any other Federal department or agency requesting information for purposes within the scope of its jurisdiction, or complying with an order of a court of the United States in an action brought by the United States or the Commission. For purposes of section 552 of title 5, United States Code, this subsection shall be considered a statute described in subsection (b)(3)(B) of such section 552.

(8) DEFINITIONS.—For purposes of this subsection—

(A) the term "large trader" means every person who, for his own account or an account for which he exercises investment discretion, effects transactions for the purchase or sale of any publicly traded security or securities by use of any means or instrumentality of interstate commerce or of the mails, or of any facility of a national securities exchange, directly or indirectly by or through a registered broker or dealer in an aggregate amount equal to or in excess of the identifying activity level;

(B) the term "publicly traded security" means any equity security (including an option on individual equity securities, and an option on a group or index of such securities) listed, or admitted to unlisted trading privileges, on a national securities exchange, or quoted in an automated interdealer quotation system;

(C) the term "identifying activity level" means transactions in publicly traded securities at or above a level of volume, fair market value, or exercise value as shall be fixed from time to time by the Commission by rule or regulation, specifying the time interval during which such transactions shall be aggregated;

(D) the term "reporting activity level" means transactions in publicly traded securities at or above a level of volume, fair market value, or exercise value as shall be fixed from time to time by the Commission by rule, regulation, or order, specifying the time interval during which such transactions shall be aggregated; and

(E) the term 'person' has the meaning given in section 3(a)(9) of this title and also includes two or more persons acting as a partnership, limited partnership, syndicate, or other group, but does not include a foreign central bank.

(i) ACCURACY OF FINANCIAL REPORTS.—Each financial report that contains financial statements, and that is required to be prepared in accordance with (or reconciled to) generally accepted accounting principles under this title and filed with the Commission shall reflect all material correcting adjustments that have been identified by a registered public accounting firm in accordance with generally accepted accounting principles and the rules andregulations of the Commission.

(j) OFF-BALANCE SHEET TRANSACTIONS.—Not later than 180 days after the date of enactment of the Sarbanes-Oxley Act of 2002, the Commission shall issue final rules providing that each annual and quarterly financial report required to be filed with the Commission shall disclose all material off-balance sheet transactions, arrangements, obligations (including contingent obligations), and other relationships of the issuer with unconsolidated entities or other persons, that may have a material current or future effect on financial condition, changes in financial condition, results of operations, liquidity, capital expenditures, capital resources, or significant components of revenues or expenses.

(k) PROHIBITION ON PERSONAL LOANS TO EXECUTIVES.—

(1) IN GENERAL.—It shall be unlawful for any issuer (as defined in section 2 of the Sarbanes-Oxley Act of 2002), directly or indirectly, including through any subsidiary, to extend or maintain credit, to arrange for the extension of credit, or to renew an extension of credit, in the form of a personal loan to or for any director or executive officer (or equivalent thereof) of that issuer. An extension of credit maintained by the issuer on the date of enactment of this subsection shall not

be subject to the provisions of this subsection, provided that there is no material modification to any term of any such extension of credit or any renewal of any such extension of credit on or after that date of enactment.

(2) LIMITATION.—Paragraph (1) does not preclude any home improvement and manufactured home loans (as that term is defined in section 5 of the Home Owners' Loan Act (12 U.S.C. 1464)), consumer credit (as defined in section 103 of the Truth in Lending Act (15 U.S.C. 1602)), or any extension of credit under an open end credit plan (as defined in section 103 of the Truth in Lending Act (15 U.S.C. 1602)), or a charge card (as defined in section 127(c)(4)(e) of the Truth in Lending Act (15 U.S.C. 1637(c)(4)(e)), or any extension of credit by a broker or dealer registered under section 15 of this title to an employee of that broker or dealer to buy, trade, or carry securities, that is permitted under rules or regulations of the Board of Governors of the Federal Reserve System pursuant to section 7 of this title (other than an extension of credit that would be used to purchase the stock of that issuer), that is—

(A) made or provided in the ordinary course of the consumer credit business of such issuer;

(B) of a type that is generally made available by such issuer to the public; and

(C) made by such issuer on market terms, or terms that are no more favorable than those offered by the issuer to the general public for such extensions of credit.

(3) RULE OF CONSTRUCTION FOR CERTAIN LOANS.—Paragraph (1) does not apply to any loan made or maintained by an insured depository institution (as defined in section 3 of the Federal Deposit Insurance Act (12 U.S.C. 1813)), if the loan is subject to the insider lending restrictions of section 22(h) of the Federal Reserve Act (12 U.S.C. 375b).

(l) REAL TIME ISSUER DISCLOSURES.—Each issuer reporting under section 13(a) or 15(d) shall disclose to the public on a rapid and current basis such additional information concerning material changes in the financial condition or operations of the issuer, in plain English, which may include trend and qualitative information and graphic presentations, as the Commission determines, by rule, is necessary or useful for the protection of investors and in the public interest.

PROXIES

Sec. 14. (a) It shall be unlawful for any person, by the use of the mails or by any means or instrumentality of interstate commerce or of any facility of a national securities exchange or otherwise, in contravention of such rules and regulations as the Commission may prescribe as necessary or appropriate in the public interest or for the protection of investors, to solicit or to permit the use of his name to solicit any proxy or consent or authorization in respect of any security (other than an exempted security) registered pursuant to section 12 of this title.

(b)(1) It shall be unlawful for any member of a national securities exchange, or any broker or dealer registered under this title, or any bank, association, or other entity that exercises fiduciary powers, in contravention of such rules and regulations as the Commission may prescribe as necessary or appropriate in the public interest or for the protection of investors, to give, or to refrain from giving a proxy, consent, authorization, or information statement in respect of any security registered pursuant to section 12 of this title, or any security issued by an investment company registered under the Investment Company Act of 1940, and carried for the account of a customer.

(2) With respect to banks, the rules and regulations prescribed by the Commission under paragraph (1) shall not require the disclosure of the names of beneficial owners of securities in an account held by the bank on the date of enactment of this paragraph unless the beneficial owner consents to the disclosure. The provisions of this paragraph shall not apply in the case of a bank which the Commission finds has not made a good faith effort to obtain such consent from such beneficial owners.

(c) Unless proxies, consents, or authorizations in respect of a security registered pursuant to section 12 of this title, or a security issued by an investment company registered under the Investment Company Act of 1940, are solicited by or on behalf of the management of the issuer from the holders of record of such security in accordance with the rules and regulations prescribed under subsection (a) of this section, prior to any annual or other meeting of the holders of such security, such issuer shall, in accordance with rules and regulations prescribed by the Commission, file with the Commission and transmit to all holders of record of such security information substantially equivalent to the information which would be required to be transmitted if a solicitation were made, but no information shall be required to be filed or transmitted pursuant to this subsection before July 1, 1964.

(d) (1) It shall be unlawful for any person, directly or indirectly, by use of the mails or by any means or instrumentality of interstate commerce or of any facility of a national securities exchange or otherwise, to make a tender offer for, or a request or invitation for tenders of, any class of any equity security which is registered pursuant to section 12 of this title, or any equity of an insurance company which would have been required to be so registered except for the exemption contained in section 12(g)(2)(G) of this title, or any equity security issued by a closed-end investment company registered under the Investment Company Act of 1940, if, after consummation thereof, such person would, directly or indirectly, be the beneficial owner of more than 5 per centum of such class, unless at the time copies of the offer or request or invitation are first published or sent or given to security holders such person has filed with the Commission a statement containing such of the information specified in section 13(d) of this title, and such additional information as the Commission may by rules and regulations prescribe as necessary or appropriate in the public interest or for the protection of investors. All requests or invitations for tenders or advertisements making a tender offer or requesting or inviting tenders of such a security shall be filed as a part of such statement and shall contain such of the information contained in such statement as the Commission may by rules and regulations prescribe. Copies of any additional material soliciting or requesting such tender offers subsequent to the initial solicitation or request shall contain such information as the Commission may by rules and regulations prescribe as necessary or appropriate in the public interest or for the protection of investors, and shall be filed with the Commission not later than the time copies of such material are first published or sent or given to security holders. Copies of all statements, in the form in which such material is furnished to security holders and the Commission, shall be sent to the issuer not later than the date such material is first published or sent or given to any security holders.

(2) When two or more persons act as a partnership, limited partnership, syndicate, or other group for the purpose of acquiring, holding, or disposing of securities of an issuer, such syndicate or group shall be deemed a "person" for purposes of this subsection.

(3) In determining, for purposes of this subsection, any percentage of a class of any security, such class shall be deemed to consist of the amount of the outstanding securities of such class, exclusive of any securities of such class held by or for the account of the issuer or a subsidiary of the issuer.

(4) Any solicitation or recommendation to the holders of such a security to accept or reject a tender offer or request or invitation for tenders shall be made in accordance with such rules and regulations as the Commission may prescribe as necessary or appropriate in the public interest or for the protection of investors.

(5) Securities deposited pursuant to a tender offer or request or invitation for tenders may be withdrawn by or on behalf of the depositor at any time until the expiration of seven days after the time definitive copies of the offer or request or invitation are first published or sent or given to security holders, and at any time after sixty days from the date of the original tender offer or request or invitation, except as the Commission may otherwise prescribe by rules, regulations, or order as necessary or appropriate in the public interest or for the protection of investors.

(6) Where any person makes a tender offer, or request or invitation for tenders, for less than all the outstanding equity securities of a class, and where a greater number of securities is deposited pursuant thereto within ten days after copies of the offer or request or invitation are first published or sent or given to security holders than such person is bound or willing to take up and pay for, the securities taken up shall be taken up as nearly as may be pro rata, disregarding fractions, according to the number of securities deposited by each depositor. The provisions of this subsection shall also apply to securities deposited within ten days after notice of an increase in

the consideration offered to security holders, as described in paragraph (7), is first published or sent or given to security holders.

(7) Where any person varies the terms of a tender offer or request or invitation for tenders before the expiration thereof by increasing the consideration offered to holders of such securities, such person shall pay the increased consideration to each security holder whose securities are taken up and paid for pursuant to the tender offer or request or invitation for tenders whether or not such securities have been taken up by such person before the variation of the tender offer or request or invitation.

(8) The provisions of this subsection shall not apply to any offer for, or request or invitation for tenders of, any security—

(A) if the acquisition of such security, together with all other acquisitions by the same person of securities of the same class during the preceding twelve months, would not exceed 2 per centum of that class;

(B) by the issuer of such security; or

(C) which the Commission, by rules or regulations or by order, shall exempt from the provisions of this subsection as not entered into for the purpose of, and not having the effect of, changing or influencing the control of the issuer or otherwise as not comprehended within the purposes of this subsection.

(e) It shall be unlawful for any person to make any untrue statement of a material fact or omit to state any material fact necessary in order to make the statements made, in the light of the circumstances under which they are made, not misleading, or to engage in any fraudulent, deceptive, or manipulative acts or practices, in connection with any tender offer or request or invitation for tenders, or any solicitation of security holders in opposition to or in favor of any such offer, request, or invitation. The Commission shall, for the purposes of this subsection, by rules and regulations define, and prescribe means reasonably designed to prevent, such acts and practices as are fraudulent, deceptive, or manipulative.

(f) If, pursuant to any arrangement or understanding with the person or persons acquiring securities in a transaction subject to subsection (d) of this section or subsection (d) of section 13 of this title, any persons are to be elected or designated as directors of the issuer, otherwise than at a meeting of security holders, and the persons so elected or designated will constitute a majority of the directors of the issuer, then, prior to the time any such person takes office as a director, and in accordance with rules and regulations prescribed by the Commission, the issuer shall file with the Commission, and transmit to all holders of record of securities of the issuer who would be entitled to vote at a meeting for election of directors, information substantially equivalent to the information which would be required by subsection (a) or (c) of this section to be transmitted if such person or persons were nominees for election as directors at a meeting of such security holders.

(g) (1) (A) At the time of filing such preliminary proxy solicitation material as the Commission may require by rule pursuant to subsection (a) of this section that concerns an acquisition, merger, consolidation, or proposed sale or other disposition of substantially all the assets of a company, the person making such filing, other than a company registered under the Investment Company Act of 1940, shall pay to the Commission the following fees:

(i) for preliminary proxy solicitation material involving an acquisition, merger, or consolidation, if there is a proposed payment of cash or transfer of securities or property to shareholders, a fee at a rate that, subject to paragraphs (5) and (6), is equal to $92 per $1,000,000 of such proposed payment, or of the value of such securities or other property proposed to be transferred; and

(ii) for preliminary proxy solicitation material involving a proposed sale or other disposition of substantially all of the assets of a company, a fee at a rate that, subject to paragraphs (5) and (6), is equal to $92 per $1,000,000 of the cash or of the value of any securities or other property proposed to be received upon such sale or disposition.

(B) The fee imposed under subparagraph (A) shall be reduced with respect to securities in an amount equal to any fee paid to the Commission with respect to such securities in connection with the proposed transaction under section 6(b) of the Securities Act of 1933 (15 U.S.C. 77f(b)), or fee paid under that section shall be reduced in an amount equal to the fee paid to the Commission in connection with such transaction under this subsection. Where two or more companies involved in an acquisition, merger, consolidation, sale or other disposition of substantially all the assets of a company must file such proxy material with the Commission, each shall pay a proportionate share of such fee.

(2) At the time of filing such preliminary information statement as the Commission may require by rule pursuant to subsection (c) of this section, the issuer shall pay to the Commission the same fee as required for preliminary proxy solicitation material under paragraph (1) of this subsection.

(3) At the time of filing such statement as the Commission may require by rule pursuant to subsection (d)(1) of this section, the person making the filing shall pay to the Commission a fee at a rate that, subject to paragraphs (5) and (6), is equal to $92 per $1,000,000 of the aggregate amount of cash or of the value of securities or other property proposed to be offered. The fee shall be reduced with respect to securities in an amount equal to any fee paid with respect to such securities in connection with the proposed transaction under section 6(b) of the Securities Act of 1933 (15 U.S.C. 77f(b)), or the fee paid under that section shall be reduced in an amount equal to the fee paid to the Commission in connection with such transaction under this subsection.

(4) Offsetting Collections.—Fees collected pursuant to this subsection for any fiscal year shall be deposited and credited as offsetting collections to the account providing appropriations to the Commission, and, except as provided in paragraph (9), shall not be collected for any fiscal year except to the extent provided in advance in appropriation Acts. No fees collected pursuant to this subsection for fiscal year 2002 or any succeeding fiscal year shall be deposited and credited as general revenue of the Treasury.

(5) Annual Adjustment.—For each of the fiscal years 2003 through 2011, the Commission shall by order adjust each of the rates required by paragraphs (1) and (3) for such fiscal year to a rate that is equal to the rate (expressed in dollars per million) that is applicable under section 6(b) of the Securities Act of 1933 for such fiscal year.

(6) Final Rate Adjustment.—For fiscal year 2012 and all of the succeeding fiscal years, the Commission shall by order adjust each of the rates required by paragraphs (1) and (3) for all of such fiscal years to a rate that is equal to the rate (expressed in dollars per million) that is applicable under section 6(b) of the Securities Act of 1933 for all of such fiscal years.

(7) Pro Rata Application.—The rates per $1,000,000 required by this subsection shall be applied pro rata to amounts and balances of less than $1,000,000.

(8) Review And Effective Date.—In exercising its authority under this subsection, the Commission shall not be required to comply with the provisions of section 553 of title 5, United States Code. An adjusted rate prescribed under paragraph (5) or (6) and published under paragraph (10) shall not be subject to judicial review. Subject to paragraphs (4) and (9)—

(A) an adjusted rate prescribed under paragraph (5) shall take effect on the later of—

(i) the first day of the fiscal year to which such rate applies; or

(ii) five days after the date on which a regular appropriation to the Commission for such fiscal year is enacted; and

(B) an adjusted rate prescribed under paragraph (6) shall take effect on the later of—

(i) the first day of fiscal year 2012; or

(ii) five days after the date on which a regular appropriation to the Commission for fiscal year 2012 is enacted.

(9) Lapse of Appropriation.—If on the first day of a fiscal year a regular appropriation to the Commission has not been enacted, the Commission shall continue to collect fees (as offsetting collections) under this subsection at the rate in effect during the preceding fiscal year, until 5 days after the date such a regular appropriation is enacted.

(10) Publication.—The rate applicable under this subsection for each fiscal year is published pursuant to section 6(b)(10) of the Securities Act of 1933.

(11) Notwithstanding any other provision of law, the Commission may impose fees, charges, or prices for matters not involving any acquisition, merger, consolidation, sale, or other disposition of assets described in this subsection, as authorized by section 9701 of title 31, United States Code, or otherwise.

(h) PROXY SOLICITATIONS AND TENDER OFFERS IN CONNECTION WITH LIMITED PARTNERSHIP ROLLUP TRANSACTIONS.—

(1) PROXY RULES TO CONTAIN SPECIAL PROVISIONS.—It shall be unlawful for any person to solicit any proxy, consent, or authorization concerning a limited partnership rollup transaction, or to make any tender offer in furtherance of a limited partnership rollup transaction, unless such transaction is conducted in accordance with rules prescribed by the Commission under subsections (a) and (d) as required by this subsection. Such rules shall—

(A) permit any holder of a security that is the subject of the proposed limited partnership rollup transaction to engage in preliminary communications for the purpose of determining whether to solicit proxies, consents, or authorizations in opposition to the proposed limited partnership rollup transaction, without regard to whether any such communication would otherwise be considered a solicitation of proxies, and without being required to file soliciting material with the Commission prior to making that determination, except that—

(i) nothing in this subparagraph shall be construed to limit the application of any provision of this title prohibiting, or reasonably designed to prevent, fraudulent, deceptive, or manipulative acts or practices under this title; and

(ii) any holder of not less than 5 percent of the outstanding securities that are the subject of the proposed limited partnership rollup transaction who engages in the business of buying and selling limited partnership interests in the secondary market shall be required to disclose such ownership interests and any potential conflicts of interests in such preliminary communications;

(B) require the issuer to provide to holders of the securities that are the subject of the limited partnership rollup transaction such list of the holders of the issuer's securities as the Commission may determine in such form and subject to such terms and conditions as the Commission may specify;

(C) prohibit compensating any person soliciting proxies, consents, or authorizations directly from security holders concerning such a limited partnership rollup transaction—

(i) on the basis of whether the solicited proxy, consent, or authorization either approves or disapproves the proposed limited partnership rollup transaction; or

(ii) contingent on the approval, disapproval, or completion of the limited partnership rollup transaction;

(D) set forth disclosure requirements for soliciting material distributed in connection with a limited partnership rollup transaction, including requirements for clear, concise, and comprehensible disclosure with respect to—

(i) any changes in the business plan, voting rights, form of ownership interest, or the compensation of the general partner in the proposed limited partnership rollup transaction from each of the original limited partnerships;

(ii) the conflicts of interest, if any, of the general partner;

(iii) whether it is expected that there will be a significant difference between the exchange values of the limited partnerships and the trading price of the securities to be issued in the limited partnership rollup transaction;

(iv) the valuation of the limited partnerships and the method used to determine the value of the interests of the limited partners to be exchanged for the securities in the limited partnership rollup transaction;

(v) the differing risks and effects of the limited partnership rollup transaction for investors in different limited partnership proposed to be included, and the risks and effects of completing the limited partnership rollup transaction with less than all limited partnerships;

(vi) the statement by the general partner required under subparagraph (E);

(vii) such other matters deemed necessary or appropriate by the Commission;

(E) require a statement by the general partner as to whether the proposed limited partnership rollup transaction is fair or unfair to investors in each limited partnership, a discussion of the basis for that conclusion, and an evaluation and a description by the general partner of alternatives to the limited partnership rollup transaction, such as liquidation;

(F) provide that, if the general partner or sponsor has obtained any opinion (other than an opinion of counsel), appraisal, or report that is prepared by an outside party and that is materially related to the limited partnership rollup transaction, such soliciting materials shall contain or be accompanied by clear, concise, and comprehensible disclosure with respect to—

(i) the analysis of the transaction, scope of review, preparation of the opinion, and basis for and methods of arriving at conclusions, and any representations and undertakings with respect thereto;

(ii) the identity and qualifications of the person who prepared the opinion, the method of selection of such person, and any material past, existing, or contemplated relationships between the person or any of its affiliates and the general partner, sponsor, successor, or any other affiliate;

(iii) any compensation of the preparer of such opinion, appraisal, or report that is contingent on the transaction's approval or completion; and

(iv) any limitations imposed by the issuer on the access afforded to such preparer to the issuer's personnel, premises, and relevant books and records;

(G) provide that, if the general partner or sponsor has obtained any opinion, appraisal, or report as described in subparagraph (F) from any person whose compensation is contingent on the transaction's approval or completion or who has not been given access by the issuer to its personnel and premises and relevant books and records, the general partner or sponsor shall state the reasons therefor;

(H) provide that, if the general partner or sponsor has not obtained any opinion on the fairness of the proposed limited partnership rollup transaction to investors in each of the affected partnerships, such soliciting materials shall contain or be accompanied by a statement of such partner's or sponsor's reasons for concluding that such an opinion is not necessary in order to permit the limited partners to make an informed decision on the proposed transaction;

(I) require that the soliciting material include a clear, concise, and comprehensible summary of the limited partnership rollup transaction (including a summary of the matters referred to in clauses (i) through (vii) of subparagraph (D) and a summary of the matter referred to in subparagraphs (F), (G), and (H)), with the risks of the limited partnership rollup transaction set forth prominently in the fore part thereof;

(J) provide that any solicitation or offering period with respect to any proxy solicitation, tender offer, or information statement in a limited partnership rollup transaction shall be for not less than the lesser of 60 calendar days or the maximum number of days permitted under applicable State law; and

(K) contain such other provisions as the Commission determines to be necessary or appropriate for the protection of investors in limited partnership rollup transactions.

(2) EXEMPTIONS.—The Commission may, consistent with the public interest, the protection of investors, and the purposes of this title, exempt by rule or order any security or class of securities, any transaction or class of transactions, or any person or class of persons, in whole or in part, conditionally or unconditionally, from the requirements imposed pursuant to paragraph (1) or from the definition contained in paragraph (4).

(3) EFFECT ON COMMISSION AUTHORITY.—Nothing in this subsection limits the authority of the Commission under subsection (a) or (d) or any other provision of this title or precludes the Commission from imposing, under subsection (a) or (d) or any other provision of this title, a remedy or procedure required to be imposed under this subsection.

(4) DEFINITION OF LIMITED PARTNERSHIP ROLLUP TRANSACTION.—Except as provided in paragraph (5), as used in this subsection, the term "limited partnership rollup transaction" means a transaction involving the combination or reorganization of one or more limited partnerships, directly or indirectly, in which—

(A) some or all of the investors in any of such limited partnerships will receive new securities, or securities in another entity, that will be reported under a transaction reporting plan declared effective before the date of enactment of this subsection by the Commission under section 11A;

(B) any of the investors' limited partnership securities are not, as of the date of filing, reported under a transaction reporting plan declared effective before the date of enactment of this subsection by the Commission under section 11A;

(C) investors in any of the limited partnerships involved in the transaction are subject to a significant adverse change with respect to voting rights, the term of existence of the entity, management compensation, or investment objectives; and

(D) any of such investors are not provided an option to receive or retain a security under substantially the same terms and conditions as the original issue.

(5) EXCLUSIONS FROM DEFINITION.—Notwithstanding paragraph (4), the term "limited partnership rollup transaction" does not include—

(A) a transaction that involves only a limited partnership or partnerships having an operating policy or practice of retaining cash available for distribution and reinvesting proceeds from the sale, financing, or refinancing of assets in accordance with such criteria as the Commission determines appropriate;

(B) a transaction involving only limited partnerships wherein the interests of the limited partners are repurchased, recalled, or exchanged in accordance with the terms of the preexisting limited partnership agreements for securities in an operating company specifically identified at the time of the formation of the original limited partnership;

(C) a transaction in which the securities to be issued or exchanged are not required to be and are not registered under the Securities Act of 1933;

(D) a transaction that involves only issuers that are not required to register or report under section 12, both before and after the transaction;

(E) a transaction, except as the Commission may otherwise provide by rule for the protection of investors, involving the combination or reorganization of one or more limited partnerships in which a non-affiliated party succeeds to the interests of a general partner or sponsor, if—

(i) such action is approved by not less than 66 ⅔ percent of the outstanding units of each of the participating limited partnerships; and

(ii) as a result of the transaction, the existing general partners will receive only compensation to which they are entitled as expressly provided for in the preexisting limited partnership agreements; or

(F) a transaction, except as the Commission may otherwise provide by rule for the protection of investors, in which the securities offered to investors are securities of another entity that are reported under a transaction reporting plan declared effective before the date of enactment of this subsection by the Commission under section 11A, if—

(i) such other entity was formed, and such class of securities was reported and regularly traded, not less than 12 months before the date on which soliciting material is mailed to investors; and

(ii) the securities of that entity issued to investors in the transaction do not exceed 20 percent of the total outstanding securities of the entity, exclusive of any securities of such class held by or for the account of the entity or a subsidiary of the entity.

REGISTRATION AND REGULATION OF BROKERS AND DEALERS

Sec. 15. (a)(1) It shall be unlawful for any broker or dealer which is either a person other than a natural person or a natural person not associated with a broker or dealer which is a person other than a natural person (other than such a broker or dealer whose business is exclusively intrastate and who does not make use of any facility of a national securities exchange) to make use of the mails or any means or instrumentality of interstate commerce to effect any transactions in, or to induce or attempt to induce the purchase or sale of, any security (other than an exempted security or commercial paper, bankers' acceptances, or commercial bills) unless such broker or dealer is registered in accordance with subsection (b) of this section.

(2) The Commission, by rule or order, as it deems consistent with the public interest and the protection of investors, may conditionally or unconditionally exempt from paragraph (1) of this subsection any broker or dealer or class of broker[s] or dealer[s] specified in such rule or order.

(b)(1) A broker or dealer may be registered by filing with the Commission an application for registration in such form and containing such information and documents concerning such broker or dealer and any persons associated with such broker or dealer as the Commission, by rule, may prescribe as necessary or appropriate in the public interest or for the protection of investors. Within forty-five days of the date of the filing of such application (or within such longer period as to which the applicant consents), the Commission shall—

(A) by order grant registration, or

(B) institute proceedings to determine whether registration should be denied. Such proceedings shall include notice of the grounds for denial under consideration and opportunity for hearing and shall be concluded within one hundred twenty days of the date of the filing of the application for registration. At the conclusion of such proceedings, the Commission, by order, shall grant or deny such registration. The order granting registration shall not be effective until such broker or dealer has become a member of a registered securities association, or until such broker or dealer has become a member of a national securities exchange if such broker or dealer effects transactions solely on that exchange, unless the Commission has exempted such broker or dealer, by rule or order, from such membership. The Commission may extend the time for conclusion of such proceedings for up to ninety days if it finds good cause for such extension and publishes its reasons for so finding or for such longer period as to which the applicant consents.

The Commission shall grant such registration if the Commission finds that the requirements of this section are satisfied. The Commission shall deny such registration if it does not make such a finding or if it finds that if the applicant were so registered, its registration would be subject to suspension or revocation under paragraph (4) of this subsection.

(2)(A) An application for registration of a broker or dealer to be formed or organized may be made by a broker or dealer to which the broker or dealer to be formed or organized is to be the successor. Such application, in such form as the Commission, by rule, may prescribe, shall contain such information and documents concerning the applicant, the successor, and any persons associated with the applicant or the successor, as the Commission, by rule, may prescribe as necessary or appropriate in the public interest or for the protection of investors. The grant or denial of registration to such an applicant shall be in accordance with the procedures set forth in paragraph (1) of this subsection. If the Commission grants such registration, the registration shall terminate on the forty-fifth day after the effective date thereof, unless prior thereto the successor shall, in accordance with such rules and regulations as the Commission may prescribe, adopt the application for registration as its own.

(B) Any person who is a broker or dealer solely by reason of acting as a municipal securities dealer or municipal securities broker, who so acts through a separately identifiable department or division, and who so acted in such a manner on the date of enactment of the Securities Acts Amendments of 1975, may, in accordance with such terms and conditions as the Commission, by rule, prescribes as necessary and appropriate in the public interest and for the protection of investors, register such separately identifiable department or division in accordance with this subsection. If any such department or division is so registered, the department or division and not such person himself shall be the broker or dealer for purposes of this title.

(C) Within six months of the date of the granting of registration to a broker or dealer, the Commission, or upon the authorization and direction of the Commission, a registered securities association or national securities exchange of which such broker or dealer is a member, shall conduct an inspection of the broker or dealer to determine whether it is operating in conformity with the provisions of this title and the rules and regulations thereunder: Provided, however, That the Commission may delay such inspection of any class of brokers or dealers for a period not to exceed six months.

(3) Any provision of this title (other than section 5 and subsection (a) of this section) which prohibits any act, practice, or course of business if the mails or any means or instrumentality of interstate commerce is used in connection therewith shall also prohibit any such act, practice, or course of business by any registered broker or dealer or any person acting on behalf of such a broker or dealer, irrespective of any use of the mails or any means or instrumentality of interstate commerce in connection therewith.

(4) The Commission, by order, shall censure, place limitations on the activities, functions, or operations of, suspend for a period not exceeding twelve months, or revoke the registration of any broker or dealer if it finds, on the record after notice and opportunity for hearing, that such censure, placing of limitations, suspension, or revocation is in the public interest and that such broker or dealer, whether prior or subsequent to becoming such, or any person associated with such broker or dealer, whether prior or subsequent to becoming so associated—

(A) has willfully made or caused to be made in any application for registration or report required to be filed with the Commission or with any other appropriate regulatory agency under this title, or in any proceeding before the Commission with respect to registration, any statement which was at the time and in the light of the circumstances under which it was made false or misleading with respect to any material fact, or has omitted to state in any such application or report any material fact which is required to be stated therein.

(B) has been convicted within ten years preceding the filing of any application for registration or at any time thereafter of any felony or misdemeanor or of a substantially equivalent crime by a foreign court of competent jurisdiction which the Commission finds—

(i) involves the purchase or sale of any security, the taking of a false oath, the making of a false report, bribery, perjury, burglary, any substantially equivalent activity however denominated by the laws of the relevant foreign government or conspiracy to commit any such offense;

(ii) arises out of the conduct of the business of a broker, dealer, municipal securities dealer, government securities broker, government securities dealer, investment adviser, bank, insurance company, fiduciary, transfer agent, foreign person performing a function substantially equivalent to any of the above or entity or person required to be registered under the Commodity Exchange Act (7 U.S.C. 1 et seq.) or any substantially equivalent foreign statute or regulation;

(iii) involves the larceny, theft, robbery, extortion, forgery, counterfeiting, fraudulent conceal-ment, embezzlement, fraudulent conversion, or misappropriation of funds, or securities, or substantially equivalent activity however denominated by the laws of the relevant foreign govern-ment, or

(iv) involves the violation of section 152, 1341, 1342, or 1343 or chapter 25 or 47 of title 18, United States Code, or a violation of a substantially equivalent foreign statute.

(C) is permanently or temporarily enjoined by order, judgment, or decree of any court of competent jurisdiction from acting as an investment adviser, underwriter, broker, dealer, munici-pal securities dealer, government securities broker, government securities dealer, transfer agent, foreign person performing a function substantially equivalent to any of the above, or entity or person required to be registered with the Commodity Exchange Act or any substantially equivalent foreign statute or regulation, or as an affiliated person or employee of any investment company, bank, insurance company, foreign entity substantially equivalent to any of the above, or entity or person required to be registered under the Commodity Exchange Act or any substan-tially equivalent foreign statute or regulation, or from engaging in or continuing any conduct or practice in connection with any such activity, or in connection with the purchase or sale of any security.

(D) has willfully violated any provision of the Securities Act of 1933, the Investment Advisers Act of 1940, the Investment Company Act of 1940, the Commodity Exchange Act, this title, the rules or regulations under any of such statutes, or the rules of the Municipal Securities Rulemak-ing Board, or is unable to comply with any such provision.

(E) has willfully aided, abetted, counseled, commanded, induced, or procured the violation by any person of any provision of the Securities Act of 1933, the Investment Advisers Act of 1940, the Investment Company Act of 1940, the Commodity Exchange Act, this title, the rules or regulations under any of such statutes, or the rules of the Municipal Securities Rulemaking Board, or has failed reasonably to supervise, with a view to preventing violations of the provisions of such statutes, rules, and regulations, another person who commits such a violation, if such other person is subject to his supervision. For the purposes of this subparagraph (E) no person shall be deemed to have failed reasonably to supervise any other person, if—

(i) there have been established procedures, and a system for applying such procedures, which would reasonably be expected to prevent and detect, insofar as practicable, any such violation by such other person, and

(ii) such person has reasonably discharged the duties and obligations incumbent upon him by reason of such procedures and system without reasonable cause to believe that such procedures and system were not being complied with.

(F) is subject to any order of the Commission barring or suspending the right of the person to be associated with a broker or dealer;

(G) has been found a foreign financial regulatory authority to have—

(i) made or caused to made in any application for registration or report required to be filed with a foreign financial regulatory authority, or in any proceeding before a foreign financial regulatory authority with respect to registration, any statement that was at the time and in the light of the circumstances under which it was made false or misleading with respect to any material fact, or has omitted to state in any application or report to the foreign financial regulatory authority any material fact that is required to be stated therein;

(ii) violated any foreign statute or regulation regarding transactions in securities, or contracts of sale of a commodity for future delivery, traded on or subject to the rules of a contract market or any board of trade;

(iii) aided, abetted, counseled, commanded, induced, or procured the violation by any person of any provision of any statutory provisions enacted by a foreign government, or rules or regulations thereunder, empowering a foreign financial regulatory authority regarding transactions in securities, or contracts of sale of a commodity for future delivery, traded on or subject to the rules of a contract market or any board of trade, or has been found, by a foreign financial regulatory authority, to have failed reasonably to supervise, with a view to preventing violations of such statutory provisions, rules, and regulations, another person who commits such a violation, if such other person is subject to his supervision; or

(H) is subject to any final order of a State securities commission (or any agency or officer performing like functions), State authority that supervises or examines banks, savings associations, or credit unions, State insurance commission (or any agency or office performing like functions), an appropriate Federal banking agency (as defined in section 3 of the Federal Deposit Insurance Act (12 U.S.C. 1813(q))), or the National Credit Union Administration, that—

(i) bars such person from association with an entity regulated by such commission, authority, agency, or officer, or from engaging in the business of securities, insurance, banking, savings association activities, or credit union activities; or

(ii) constitutes a final order based on violations of any laws or regulations that prohibit fraudulent, manipulative, or deceptive conduct.

(5) Pending final determination whether any registration under this subsection shall be revoked, the Commission, by order, may suspend such registration, if such suspension appears to the Commission, after notice and opportunity for hearing, to be necessary or appropriate in the public interest or for the protection of investors. Any registered broker or dealer may, upon such terms and conditions as the Commission deems necessary or appropriate in the public interest or for the protection of investors, withdraw from registration by filing a written notice of withdrawal with the Commission. If the Commission finds that any registered broker or dealer is no longer in existence or has ceased to do business as a broker or dealer, the Commission, by order, shall cancel the registration of such broker or dealer.

(6) (A) With respect to any person who is associated, who is seeking to become associated, or, at the time of the alleged misconduct, who was associated or was seeking to become associated with a broker or dealer, or any person participating, or, at the time of the alleged

misconduct, who was participating, in an offering of any penny stock, the Commission, by order, shall censure, place limitations on the activities or functions of such person, or suspend for a period not exceeding 12 months, or bar such person from being associated with a broker or dealer, or from participating in an offering of penny stock, if the Commission finds, on the record after notice and opportunity for a hearing, that such censure, placing of limitations, suspension, or bar is in the public interest and that such person—

(i) has committed or omitted any act, or is subject to an order or finding, enumerated in subparagraph (A), (D), (E), (H), or (G) of paragraph (4) of this subsection;

(ii) has been convicted of any offense specified in subparagraph (B) of such paragraph (4) within 10 years of the commencement of the proceedings under this paragraph; or

(iii) is enjoined from any action, conduct, or practice specified in subparagraph (C) of such paragraph (4).

(B) It shall be unlawful—

(i) for any person as to whom an order under subparagraph (A) is in effect, without the consent of the Commission, willfully to become, or to be, associated with a broker or dealer in contravention of such order, or to participate in an offering of penny stock in contravention of such order;

(ii) for any broker or dealer to permit such a person, without the consent of the Commission, to become or remain, a person associated with the broker or dealer in contravention of such order, if such broker or dealer knew, or in the exercise of reasonable care should have known, of such order; or

(iii) for any broker or dealer to permit such a person, without the consent of the Commission, to participate in an offering of penny stock in contravention of such order, if such broker or dealer knew, or in the exercise of reasonable care should have known, of such order and of such participation.

(C) For purposes of this paragraph, the term "person participating in an offering of penny stock" includes any person acting as any promoter, finder, consultant, agent, or other person who engages in activities with a broker, dealer, or issuer for purposes of the issuance or trading in any penny stock, or inducing or attempting to induce the purchase or sale of any penny stock. The Commission may, by rule or regulation, define such term to include other activities, and may, by rule, regulation, or order, exempt any person or class of persons, in whole or in part, conditionally or unconditionally, from such term.

(7) No registered broker or dealer or government securities broker or government securities dealer registered (or required to register) under section 15C(a)(1)(A) shall effect any transaction in, or induce the purchase or sale of, any security unless such broker or dealer meets such standards of operational capability and such broker or dealer and all natural persons associated with such broker or dealer meet such standards of training, experience, competence, and such other qualifications as the Commission finds necessary or appropriate in the public interest or for the protection of investors. The Commission shall establish such standards by rules and regulations, which may—

(A) specify that all or any portion of such standards shall be applicable to any class of brokers and dealers and persons associated with brokers and dealers;

(B) require persons in any such class to pass tests prescribed in accordance with such rules and regulations, which tests shall, with respect to any class of partners, officers, or supervisory employees (which latter term may be defined by the Commission's rules and regulations and as so defined shall include branch managers of brokers or dealers) engaged in the management of the broker or dealer, include questions relating to bookkeeping, accounting, internal control over cash and securities, supervision of employees, maintenance of records, and other appropriate matters; and

(C) provide that persons in any such class other than brokers and dealers and partners, officers, and supervisory employees of brokers or dealers, may be qualified solely on the basis of compliance with such standards of training and such other qualifications as the Commission finds appropriate.

The Commission, by rule, may prescribe reasonable fees and charges to defray its costs in carrying out this paragraph, including, but not limited to, fees for any test administered by it or under its direction. The Commission may cooperate with registered securities associations and national securities exchanges in devising and administering tests and may require registered brokers and dealers and persons associated with such brokers and dealers to pass tests administered by or on behalf of any such association or exchange and to pay such association or exchange reasonable fees or charges to defray the costs incurred by such association or exchange in administering such tests.

(8) It shall be unlawful for any registered broker or dealer to effect any transaction in, or induce or attempt to induce the purchase or sale of, any security (other than commercial paper, bankers' acceptances, or commercial bills), unless such broker or dealer is a member of a securities association registered pursuant to section 15A of this title or effects transactions in securities solely on a national securities exchange of which it is a member.

(9) The Commission by rule or order, as it deems consistent with the public interest and the protection of investors, may conditionally or unconditionally exempt from paragraph (8) of this subsection any broker or dealer or class of brokers or dealers specified in such rule or order.

(10) For purposes of determining whether a person is subject to a statutory disqualification under section 6(c)(2), 15A(g)(2), or 17A(b)(4)(A) of this title, the term "Commission" in paragraph (4)(B) of this subsection shall mean "exchange", "association", or "clearing agency", respectively.

(11) BROKER/DEALER REGISTRATION WITH RESPECT TO TRANSACTIONS IN SECURITY FUTURES PRODUCTS.—

(A) NOTICE REGISTRATION.—

(i) CONTENTS OF NOTICE.—Notwithstanding paragraphs (1) and (2), a broker or dealer required to register only because it effects transactions in security futures products on an exchange registered pursuant to section 6(g) may register for purposes of this section by filing with the Commission a written notice in such form and containing such information concerning such broker or dealer and any persons associated with such broker or dealer as the Commission, by rule, may prescribe as necessary or appropriate in the public interest or for the protection of investors. A broker or dealer may not register under this paragraph unless that broker or dealer is a member of a national securities association registered under section 15A(k).

(ii) IMMEDIATE EFFECTIVENESS.—Such registration shall be effective contemporaneously with the submission of notice, in written or electronic form, to the Commission, except that such registration shall not be effective if the registration would be subject to suspension or revocation under paragraph (4).

(iii) SUSPENSION.—Such registration shall be suspended immediately if a national securities association registered pursuant to section 15A(k) of this title suspends the membership of that broker or dealer.

(iv) TERMINATION.—Such registration shall be terminated immediately if any of the above stated conditions for registration set forth in this paragraph are no longer satisfied.

(B) EXEMPTIONS FOR REGISTERED BROKERS AND DEALERS.—A broker or dealer registered pursuant to the requirements of subparagraph (A) shall be exempt from the following provisions of this title and the rules thereunder with respect to transactions in security futures products:

(i) Section 8.

(ii) Section 11.

(iii) Subsections (c)(3) and (c)(5) of this section.

(iv) Section 15B.

(v) Section 15C.

(vi) Subsections (d), (e), (f), (g), (h), and (i) of section 17.

(12) EXEMPTION FOR SECURITY FUTURES PRODUCT EXCHANGE MEMBERS.—

(A) REGISTRATION EXEMPTION.—A natural person shall be exempt from the registration requirements of this section if such person—

(i) is a member of a designated contract market registered with the Commission as an exchange pursuant to section 6(g);

(ii) effects transactions only in securities on the exchange of which such person is a member; and

(iii) does not directly accept or solicit orders from public customers or provide advice to public customers in connection with the trading of security futures products.

(B) OTHER EXEMPTIONS.—A natural person exempt from registration pursuant to subparagraph (A) shall also be exempt from the following provisions of this title and the rules thereunder:

(i) Section 8.

(ii) Section 11.

(iii) Subsections (c)(3), (c)(5), and (e) of this section.

(iv) Section 15B.

(v) Section 15C.

(vi) Subsections (d), (e), (f), (g), (h), and (i) of section 17.

(c)(1)(A) No broker or dealer shall make use of the mails or any means or instrumentality of interstate commerce to effect any transaction in, or to induce or attempt to induce the purchase or sale of, any security (other than commercial paper, bankers' acceptances, or commercial bills) otherwise than on a national securities exchange of which it is a member, or any security-based swap agreement (as defined in section 206B of the Gramm-Leach-Bliley Act), by means of any manipulative, deceptive, or other fraudulent device or contrivance.

(B) No municipal securities dealer shall make use of the mails or any means or instrumentality of interstate commerce to effect any transaction in, or to induce or attempt to induce the purchase or sale of, any municipal security or any security-based swap agreement (as defined in section 206B of the Gramm-Leach-Bliley Act) involving a municipal security by means of any manipulative, deceptive, or other fraudulent device or contrivance.

(C) No government securities broker or government securities dealer shall make use of the mails or any means or instrumentality of interstate commerce to effect any transaction in, or to induce or to attempt to induce the purchase or sale of, any government security or any security-based swap agreement (as defined in section 206B of the Gramm-Leach-Bliley Act) involving a government security by means of any manipulative, deceptive, or other fraudulent device or contrivance.

(2)(A) No broker or dealer shall make use of the mails or any means or instrumentality of interstate commerce to effect any transaction in, or to induce or attempt to induce the purchase or sale of, any security (other than an exempted security or commercial paper, bankers' acceptances, or commercial bills) otherwise than on a national securities exchange of which it is a member, in connection with which such broker or dealer engages in any fraudulent, deceptive, or manipulative act or practice, or makes any fictitious quotation.

(B) No municipal securities dealer shall make use of the mails or any means or instrumentality of interstate commerce to effect any transaction in, or to induce or attempt to induce the purchase or sale of, any municipal security in connection with which such municipal securities dealer engages in any fraudulent, deceptive, or manipulative act or practice, or makes any fictitious quotation.

(C) No government securities broker or government securities dealer shall make use of the mails or any means or instrumentality of interstate commerce to effect any transaction in, or induce or attempt to induce the purchase or sale of, any government security in connection with which such government securities broker or government securities dealer engages in any fraudulent, deceptive, or manipulative act or practice, or makes any fictitious quotation.

(D) The Commission shall, for the purposes of this paragraph, by rules and regulations define, and prescribe means reasonably designed to prevent, such acts and practices as are fraudulent, deceptive, or manipulative and such quotations as are fictitious.

(E) The Commission shall, prior to adopting any rule or regulation under subparagraph (C), consult with and consider the views of the Secretary of the Treasury and each appropriate regulatory agency. If the Secretary of the Treasury or any appropriate regulatory agency comments in writing on a proposed rule or regulation of the Commission under such subparagraph (C) that has been published for comment, the Commission shall respond in writing to such written comment before adopting the proposed rule. If the Secretary of the Treasury determines, and notifies the Commission, that such rule or regulation, if implemented, would, or as applied does (i) adversely affect the liquidity or efficiency of the market for government securities; or (ii) impose any burden on competition not necessary or appropriate in furtherance of the purposes of this section, the Commission shall, prior to adopting the proposed rule or regulation, find that such rule or regulation is necessary and appropriate in furtherance of the purposes of this section notwithstanding the Secretary's determination.

(3)(A) No broker or dealer (other than a government securities broker or government securities dealer, except a registered broker or dealer) shall make use of the mails or any means or instrumentality of interstate commerce to effect any transaction in, or to induce or attempt to induce the purchase or sale of, any security (other than an exempted security (except a government security) or commercial paper, bankers' acceptances, or commercial bills) in contravention of such rules and regulations as the Commission shall prescribe as necessary or appropriate in the public interest or for the protection of investors to provide safeguards with respect to the financial responsibility and related practices of brokers and dealers including, but not limited to, the acceptance of custody and use of customers' securities and the carrying and use of customers' deposits or credit balances. Such rules and regulations shall (A) require the maintenance of reserves with respect to customers' deposits or credit balances, and (B) no later than September 1, 1975, establish minimum financial responsibility requirements for all brokers and dealers.

(B) Consistent with this title, the Commission, in consultation with the Commodity Futures Trading Commission, shall issue such rules, regulations, or orders as are necessary to avoid duplicative or conflicting regulations applicable to any broker or dealer registered with the Commission pursuant to section 15(b) (except paragraph (11) thereof), that is also registered with the Commodity Futures Trading Commission pursuant to section 4f(a) of the Commodity Exchange Act (except paragraph (2) thereof), with respect to the application of (i) the provisions of section 8, section 15(c)(3), and section 17 of this title and the rules and regulations thereunder related to the treatment of customer funds, securities, or property, maintenance of books and records, financial reporting, or other financial responsibility rules, involving security futures products and (ii) similar provisions of the Commodity Exchange Act and rules and regulations thereunder involving security futures products.

(4) If the Commission finds, after notice and opportunity for a hearing, that any person subject to the provisions of sections 12, 13, 14, or subsection (d) of section 15 of this title or any rule or regulation thereunder has failed to comply with any such provision, rule, or regulation in any material respect, the Commission may publish its findings and issue an order requiring such person, and any person who was a cause of the failure to comply due to an act or omission the person knew or should have known would contribute to the failure to comply, to comply, or to take steps to effect compliance, with such provision or such rule or regulation thereunder upon such terms and conditions and within such time as the Commission may specify in such order.

(5) No dealer (other than a specialist registered on a national securities exchange) acting in the capacity of market maker or otherwise shall make use of the mails or any means or instrumentality of interstate commerce to effect any transaction in, or to induce or attempt to induce the purchase or sale of, any security (other than an exempted security or a municipal security) in contravention of such specified and appropriate standards with respect to dealing as the Commission, by rule, shall prescribe as necessary or appropriate in the public interest and for the protection of investors, to maintain fair and orderly markets, or to remove impediments to and

perfect the mechanism of a national market system. Under the rules of the Commission a dealer in a security may be prohibited from acting as a broker in that security.

(6) No broker or dealer shall make use of the mails or any means or instrumentality of interstate commerce to effect any transaction in, or to induce or attempt to induce the purchase or sale of, any security (other than an exempted security, municipal security, commercial paper, bankers' acceptances, or commercial bills) in contravention of such rules and regulations as the Commission shall prescribe as necessary or appropriate in the public interest and for the protection of investors or to perfect or remove impediments to a national system for the prompt and accurate clearance and settlement of securities transactions, with respect to the time and method of, and the form and format of documents used in connection with, making settlements of and payments for transactions in securities, making transfers and deliveries of securities, and closing accounts. Nothing in this paragraph shall be construed (A) to affect the authority of the Board of Governors of the Federal Reserve System, pursuant to section 7 of this title, to prescribe rules and regulations for the purpose of preventing the excessive use of credit for the purchase or carrying of securities, or (B) to authorize the Commission to prescribe rules or regulations for such purpose.

(7) In connection with any bid for or purchase of a government security related to an offering of government securities by or on behalf of an issuer, no government securities broker, government securities dealer, or bidder for or purchaser of securities in such offering shall knowingly or willfully make any false or misleading written statement or omit any fact necessary to make any written statement made not misleading.

(8) PROHIBITION OF REFERRAL FEES.—No broker or dealer, or person associated with a broker or dealer, may solicit or accept, directly or indirectly, remuneration for assisting an attorney in obtaining the representation of any person in any private action arising under this title or under the Securities Act of 1933.

(d) Each issuer which has filed a registration statement containing an undertaking which is or becomes operative under this subsection as in effect prior to the date of enactment of the Securities Acts Amendments of 1964, and each issuer which shall after such date file a registration statement which has become effective pursuant to the Securities Act of 1933, as amended, shall file with the Commission, in accordance with such rules and regulations as the Commission may prescribe as necessary or appropriate in the public interest or for the protection of investors, such supplementary and periodic information, documents, and reports as may be required pursuant to section 13 of this title in respect of a security registered pursuant to section 12 of this title. The duty to file under this subsection shall be automatically suspended if and so long as any issue of securities of such issuer is registered pursuant to section 12 of this title. The duty to file under this subsection shall also be automatically suspended as to any fiscal year, other than the fiscal year within which such registration statement became effective, if, at the beginning of such fiscal year, the securities of each class to which the registration statement relates are held of record by less than three hundred persons. For the purposes of this subsection, the term "class" shall be construed to include all securities of an issuer which are of substantially similar character and the holders of which enjoy substantially similar rights and privileges. The Commission may, for the purpose of this subsection, define by rules and regulations the term "held of record" as it deems necessary or appropriate in the public interest or for the protection of investors in order to prevent circumvention of the provisions of this subsection. Nothing in this subsection shall apply to securities issued by a foreign government or political subdivision thereof.

(e) The Commission, by rule, as it deems necessary or appropriate in the public interest and for the protection of investors or to assure equal regulation, may require any member of a national securities exchange not required to register under section 15 of this title and any person associated with any such member to comply with any provision of this title (other than section 15(a)) or the rules or regulations thereunder which by its terms regulates or prohibits any act, practice, or course of business by a "broker or dealer" or "registered broker or dealer" or a "person associated with a broker or dealer," respectively.

(f) Every registered broker or dealer shall establish, maintain, and enforce written policies and procedures reasonably designed, taking into consideration the nature of such broker's or dealer's business, to prevent the misuse in violation of this title, or the rule or regulations thereunder, of material, nonpublic information by such broker or dealer or any person associated with such broker or dealer. The Commission, as it deems necessary or appropriate in the public interest or for the protection of investors, shall adopt rules or regulations to require specific policies or procedures reasonably designed to prevent misuse in violation of this title (or the rules or regulations thereunder) of material, nonpublic information.

(g) REQUIREMENTS FOR TRANSACTIONS IN PENNY STOCKS.—

(1) IN GENERAL.—No broker or dealer shall make use of the mails or any means or instrumentality of interstate commerce to effect any transaction in, or to induce or attempt to induce the purchase or sale of, any penny stock by any customer except in accordance with the requirements of this subsection and the rules and regulations prescribed under this subsection.

(2) RISK DISCLOSURE WITH RESPECT TO PENNY STOCKS.—Prior to effecting any transaction in any penny stock, a broker or dealer shall give the customer a risk disclosure document that—

(A) contains a description of the nature and level of risk in the market for penny stocks in both public offerings and secondary trading;

(B) contains a description of the broker's or dealer's duties to the customer and of the rights and remedies available to the customer with respect to violations of such duties or other requirements of Federal securities laws;

(C) contains a brief, clear, narrative description of a dealer market, including 'bid' and 'ask' prices for penny stocks and the significance of the spread between the bid and ask prices;

(D) contains the toll free telephone number for inquiries on disciplinary actions established pursuant to section 15A(i) of this title;

(E) defines significant terms used in the disclosure document or in the conduct of trading in penny stocks; and

(F) contains such other information, and is in such form (including language, type size, and format), as the Commission shall require by rule or regulation.

(3) COMMISSION RULES RELATING TO DISCLOSURE.—The Commission shall adopt rules setting forth additional standards for the disclosure by brokers and dealers to customers of information concerning transactions in penny stocks. Such rules—

(A) shall require brokers and dealers to disclose to each customer, prior to effecting any transaction in, and at the time of confirming any transaction with respect to any penny stock, in accordance with such procedures and methods as the Commission may require consistent with the public interest and the protection of investors—

(i) the bid and ask prices for penny stock, or such other information as the Commission may, by rule, require to provide customers with more useful and reliable information relating to the price of such stock;

(ii) the number of shares to which such bid and ask prices apply, or other comparable information relating to the depth and liquidity of the market for such stock; and

(iii) the amount and a description of any compensation that the broker or dealer and the associated person thereof will receive or has received in connection with such transaction;

(B) shall require brokers and dealers to provide, to each customer whose account with the broker or dealer contains penny stocks, a monthly statement indicating the market value of the penny stocks in that account or indicating that the market value of such stock cannot be determined because of the unavailability of firm quotes; and

(C) may, as the Commission finds necessary or appropriate in the public interest or for the protection of investors, require brokers and dealers to disclose to customers additional information concerning transactions in penny stocks.

(4) EXEMPTIONS.—The Commission, as it determines consistent with the public interest and the protection of investors, may by rule, regulation, or order exempt in whole or in part, conditionally or unconditionally, any person or class of persons, or any transaction or class of transactions, from the requirements of this subsection. Such exemptions shall include an exemp-

tion for brokers and dealers based on the minimal percentage of the broker's or dealer's commissions, commission-equivalents, and markups received from transactions in penny stocks.

(5) REGULATIONS.—It shall be unlawful for any person to violate such rules and regulations as the Commission shall prescribe in the public interest or for the protection of investors or to maintain fair and orderly markets—

(A) as necessary or appropriate to carry out this subsection; or

(B) as reasonably designed to prevent fraudulent, deceptive, or manipulative acts and practices with respect to penny stocks.

(h) LIMITATIONS ON STATE LAW.—

(1) Capital, margin, books and records, bonding, and reports.—No law, rule, regulation, or order, or other administrative action of any State or political subdivision thereof shall establish capital, custody, margin, financial responsibility, making and keeping records, bonding, or financial or operational reporting requirements for brokers, dealers, municipal securities dealers, government securities brokers, or government securities dealers that differ from, or are in addition to, the requirements in those areas established under this title. The Commission shall consult periodically the securities commissions (or any agency or office performing like functions) of the States concerning the adequacy of such requirements as established under this title.

(2) De minimis transactions by associated persons.—No law, rule, regulation, or order, or other administrative action of any State or political subdivision thereof may prohibit an associated person of a broker or dealer from effecting a transaction described in paragraph (3) for a customer in such State if—

(A) such associated person is not ineligible to register with such State for any reason other than such a transaction;

(B) such associated person is registered with a registered securities association and at least one State; and

(C) the broker or dealer with which such person is associated is registered with such State.

(3) Described transactions.—

(A) In general.—A transaction is described in this paragraph if—

(i) such transaction is effected—

(I) on behalf of a customer that, for 30 days prior to the day of the transaction, maintained an account with the broker or dealer; and

(II) by an associated person of the broker or dealer—

(aa) to which the customer was assigned for 14 days prior to the day of the transaction; and

(bb) who is registered with a State in which the customer was a resident or was present for at least 30 consecutive days during the 1-year period prior to the day of the transaction; or

(ii) the transaction is effected—

(I) on behalf of a customer that, for 30 days prior to the day of the transaction, maintained an account with the broker or dealer; and

(II) during the period beginning on the date on which such associated person files an application for registration with the State in which the transaction is effected and ending on the earlier of—

(aa) 60 days after the date on which the application is filed; or

(bb) the date on which such State notifies the associated person that it has denied the application for registration or has stayed the pendency of the application for cause.

(B) Rules of construction.—For purposes of subparagraph (A)(i)(II)—

(i) each of up to 3 associated persons of a broker or dealer who are designated to effect transactions during the absence or unavailability of the principal associated person for a customer may be treated as an associated person to which such customer is assigned; and

(ii) if the customer is present in another State for 30 or more consecutive days or has permanently changed his or her residence to another State, a transaction is not described in this paragraph, unless the associated person of the broker or dealer files an application for registration with such State not later than 10 business days after the later of the date of the transaction, or the date of the discovery of the presence of the customer in the other State for 30 or more consecutive days or the change in the customer's residence.

(i) RULEMAKING TO EXTEND REQUIREMENTS TO NEW HYBRID PRODUCTS.—

(1) CONSULTATION.—Prior to commencing a rulemaking under this subsection, the Commission shall consult with and seek the concurrence of the Board concerning the imposition of broker or dealer registration requirements with respect to any new hybrid product. In developing and promulgating rules under this subsection, the Commission shall consider the views of the Board, including views with respect to the nature of the new hybrid product; the history, purpose, extent, and appropriateness of the regulation of the new product under the Federal banking laws; and the impact of the proposed rule on the banking industry.

(2) LIMITATION.—The Commission shall not—

(A) require a bank to register as a broker or dealer under this section because the bank engages in any transaction in, or buys or sells, a new hybrid product; or

(B) bring an action against a bank for a failure to comply with a requirement described in subparagraph (A), unless the Commission has imposed such requirement by rule or regulation issued in accordance with this section.

(3) CRITERIA FOR RULEMAKING.—The Commission shall not impose a requirement under paragraph (2) of this subsection with respect to any new hybrid product unless the Commission determines that—

(A) the new hybrid product is a security; and

(B) imposing such requirement is necessary and appropriate in the public interest and for the protection of investors.

(4) CONSIDERATIONS.—In making a determination under paragraph (3), the Commission shall consider—

(A) the nature of the new hybrid product; and

(B) the history, purpose, extent, and appropriateness of the regulation of the new hybrid product under the Federal securities laws and under the Federal banking laws.

(5) OBJECTION TO COMMISSION REGULATION.—

(A) FILING OF PETITION FOR REVIEW.—The Board may obtain review of any final regulation described in paragraph (2) in the United States Court of Appeals for the District of Columbia Circuit by filing in such court, not later than 60 days after the date of publication of the final regulation, a written petition requesting that the regulation be set aside. Any proceeding to challenge any such rule shall be expedited by the Court of Appeals.

(B) TRANSMITTAL OF PETITION AND RECORD.—A copy of a petition described in subparagraph (A) shall be transmitted as soon as possible by the Clerk of the Court to an officer or employee of the Commission designated for that purpose. Upon receipt of the petition, the Commission shall file with the court the regulation under review and any documents referred to therein, and any other relevant materials prescribed by the court.

(C) EXCLUSIVE JURISDICTION.—On the date of the filing of the petition under subparagraph (A), the court has jurisdiction, which becomes exclusive on the filing of the materials set forth in subparagraph (B), to affirm and enforce or to set aside the regulation at issue.

(D) STANDARD OF REVIEW.—The court shall determine to affirm and enforce or set aside a regulation of the Commission under this subsection, based on the determination of the court as to whether—

(i) the subject product is a new hybrid product, as defined in this subsection;

(ii) the subject product is a security; and

(iii) imposing a requirement to register as a broker or dealer for banks engaging in transactions in such product is appropriate in light of the history, purpose, and extent of regulation under the Federal securities laws and under the Federal banking laws, giving deference neither to the views of the Commission nor the Board.

(E) JUDICIAL STAY.—The filing of a petition by the Board pursuant to subparagraph (A) shall operate as a judicial stay, until the date on which the determination of the court is final (including any appeal of such determination).

(F) OTHER AUTHORITY TO CHALLENGE.—Any aggrieved party may seek judicial review of the Commission's rulemaking under this subsection pursuant to section 25 of this title.

(6) DEFINITIONS.—For purposes of this subsection:

(A) NEW HYBRID PRODUCT.—The term 'new hybrid product' means a product that—

(i) was not subjected to regulation by the Commission as a security prior to the date of the enactment of the Gramm-Leach-Bliley Act;

(ii) is not an identified banking product as such term is defined in section 206 of such Act; and

(iii) is not an equity swap within the meaning of section 206(a)(6) of such Act.

(B) BOARD.—The term 'Board' means the Board of Governors of the Federal Reserve System.

(i) The authority of the Commission under this section with respect to security-based swap agreements (as defined in section 206B of the Gramm-Leach-Bliley Act) shall be subject to the restrictions and limitations of section 3A(b) of this title.

REGISTERED SECURITIES ASSOCIATIONS

Sec. 15A. (a) An association of brokers and dealers may be registered as a national securities association pursuant to subsection (b), or as an affiliated securities association pursuant to subsection (d), under the terms and conditions hereinafter provided in this section and in accordance with the provisions of section 19(a) of this title, by filing with the Commission an application for registration in such form as the Commission, by rule, may prescribe containing the rules of the association and such other information and documents as the Commission, by rule, may prescribe as necessary or appropriate in the public interest or for the protection of investors.

(b) An association of brokers and dealers shall not be registered as a national securities association unless the Commission determines that—

(1) By reason of the number and geographical distribution of its members and the scope of their transactions, such association will be able to carry out the purposes of this section.

(2) Such association is so organized and has the capacity to be able to carry out the purposes of this title and to comply, and (subject to any rule or order of the Commission pursuant to section 17(d) or 19(g)(2) of this title) to enforce compliance by its members and persons associated with its members, with the provisions of this title, the rules and regulations thereunder, the rules of the Municipal Securities Rulemaking Board, and the rules of the association.

(3) Subject to the provisions of subsection (g) of this section, the rules of the association provide that any registered broker or dealer may become a member of such association and any person may become associated with a member thereof.

(4) The rules of the association assure a fair representation of its members in the selection of its directors and administration of its affairs and provide that one or more directors shall be representative of issuers and investors and not be associated with a member of the association, broker, or dealer.

(5) The rules of the association provide for the equitable allocation of reasonable dues, fees, and other charges among members and issuers and other persons using any facility or system which the association operates or controls.

(6) The rules of the association are designed to prevent fraudulent and manipulative acts and practices, to promote just and equitable principles of trade, to foster cooperation and coordination with persons engaged in regulating, clearing, settling, processing information with respect to, and facilitating transactions in securities, to remove impediments to and perfect the mechanism of a

free and open market and a national market system, and, in general, to protect investors and the public interest; and are not designed to permit unfair discrimination between customers, issuers, brokers, or dealers, to fix minimum profits, to impose any schedule or fix rates of commissions, allowances, discounts, or other fees to be charged by its members, or to regulate by virtue of any authority conferred by this title matters not related to the purposes of this title or the administration of the association.

(7) The rules of the association provide that (subject to any rule or order of the Commission pursuant to section 17(d) or 19(g)(2) of this title) its members and persons associated with its members shall be appropriately disciplined for violation of any provision of this title, the rules or regulations thereunder, the rules of the Municipal Securities Rulemaking Board, or the rules of the association, by expulsion, suspension, limitation of activities, functions, and operations, fine, censure, being suspended or barred from being associated with a member, or any other fitting sanction.

(8) The rules of the association are in accordance with the provisions of subsection (h) of this section, and, in general, provide a fair procedure for the disciplining of members and persons associated with members, the denial of membership to any person seeking membership therein, the barring of any person from becoming associated with a member thereof, and the prohibition or limitation by the association of any person with respect to access to services offered by the association or a member thereof.

(9) The rules of the association do not impose any burden on competition not necessary or appropriate in furtherance of the purposes of this title.

(10) The requirements of subsection (c), insofar as these may be applicable, are satisfied.

(11) The rules of the association include provisions governing the form and content of quotations relating to securities sold otherwise than on a national securities exchange which may be distributed or published by any member or person associated with a member, and the persons to whom such quotations may be supplied. Such rules relating to quotations shall be designed to produce fair and informative quotations, to prevent fictitious or misleading quotations, and to promote orderly procedures for collecting, distributing, and publishing quotations.

(12) The rules of the association to promote just and equitable principles of trade, as required by paragraph (6), include rules to prevent members of the association from participating in any limited partnership rollup transaction (as such term is defined in paragraphs (4) and (5) of section 14(h)) unless such transaction was conducted in accordance with procedures designed to protect the rights of limited partners, including—

(A) the right of dissenting limited partners to one of the following:

(i) an appraisal and compensation;

(ii) retention of a security under substantially the same terms and conditions as the original issue;

(iii) approval of the limited partnership rollup transaction by not less than 75 percent of the outstanding securities of each of the participating limited partnerships;

(iv) the use of a committee that is independent, as determined in accordance with rules prescribed by the association, of the general partner or sponsor, that has been approved by a majority of the outstanding securities of each of the participating partnerships, and that has such authority as is necessary to protect the interest of limited partners, including the authority to hire independent advisors, to negotiate with the general partner or sponsor on behalf of the limited partners, and to make a recommendation to the limited partners with respect to the proposed transaction; or

(v) other comparable rights that are prescribed by rule by the association and that are designed to protect dissenting limited partners;

(B) the right not to have their voting power unfairly reduced or abridged;

(C) the right not to bear an unfair portion of the costs of a proposed limited partnership rollup transaction that is rejected; and

(D) restrictions on the conversion of contingent interests or fees into non-contingent interests or fees and restrictions on the receipt of a non-contingent equity interest in exchange for fees for services which have not yet been provided.

As used in this paragraph, the term "dissenting limited partner" means a person who, on the date on which soliciting material is mailed to investors, is a holder of a beneficial interest in a limited partnership that is the subject of a limited partnership rollup transaction, and who casts a vote against the transaction and complies with procedures established by the association, except that for purposes of an exchange or tender offer, such person shall file an objection in writing under the rules of the association during the period in which the offer is outstanding.

(13) The rules of the association prohibit the authorization for quotation on an automated interdealer quotation system sponsored by the association of any security designated by the Commission as a national market system security resulting from a limited partnership rollup transaction (as such term is defined in paragraphs (4) and (5) of section 14(h)), unless such transaction was conducted in accordance with procedures designed to protect the rights of limited partners including—

(A) the right of dissenting limited partners to one of the following:

(i) an appraisal and compensation;

(ii) retention of a security under substantially the same terms and conditions as the original issue;

(iii) approval of the limited partnership rollup transaction by not less than 75 percent of the outstanding securities of each of the participating limited partnerships;

(iv) the use of a committee that is independent, as determined in accordance with rules prescribed by the association, of the general partner or sponsor, that has been approved by a majority of the outstanding securities of each of the participating partnerships, and that has such authority as is necessary to protect the interest of limited partners, including the authority to hire independent advisors, to negotiate with the general partner or sponsor on behalf of the limited partners, and to make a recommendation to the limited partners with respect to the proposed transaction; or

(v) other comparable rights that are prescribed by rule by the association and that are designed to protect dissenting limited partners;

(B) the right not to have their voting power unfairly reduced or abridged;

(C) the right not to bear an unfair portion of the costs of a proposed limited partnership rollup transaction that is rejected; and

(D) restrictions on the conversion of contingent interests or fees into non-contingent interests or fees and restrictions on the receipt of a non-contingent equity interest in exchange for fees for services which have not yet been provided.

As used in this paragraph, the term "dissenting limited partner" means a person who, on the date on which soliciting material is mailed to investors, is a holder of a beneficial interest in a limited partnership that is the subject of a limited partnership rollup transaction, and who casts a vote against the transaction and complies with procedures established by the association, except that for purposes of an exchange or tender offer, such person shall file an objection in writing under the rules of the association during the period during which the offer is outstanding.

(c) The Commission may permit or require the rules of an association applying for registration pursuant to subsection (b), to provide for the admission of an association registered as an affiliated securities association pursuant to subsection (d), to participation in said applicant association as an affiliate thereof, under terms permitting such powers and responsibilities to such affiliate, and under such other appropriate terms and conditions, as may be provided by the rules of said applicant association, if such rules appear to the Commission to be necessary or appropriate in the public interest or for the protection of investors and to carry out the purposes of this section. The duties and powers of the Commission with respect to any national securities association or any affiliated association shall in no way be limited by reason of any such affiliation.

(d) An applicant association shall not be registered as an affiliated securities association unless it appears to the Commission that—

(1) such association, notwithstanding that it does not satisfy the requirements set forth in paragraph (1) of subsection (b), will, forthwith upon the registration thereof, be admitted to affiliation with an association registered as a national securities association pursuant to said subsection (b), in the manner and under the terms and conditions provided by the rules of said national securities association in accordance with subsection (c); and

(2) such association and its rules satisfy the requirements set forth in paragraphs (2) to (10) inclusive and paragraph (12), of subsection (b); except that in the case of any such association any restrictions upon membership therein of the type authorized by paragraph (3) of subsection (b) shall not be less stringent than in the case of the national securities association with which such association is to be affiliated.

(e)(1) The rules of a registered securities association may provide that no member thereof shall deal with any nonmember professional (as defined in paragraph (2) of this subsection) except at the same prices, for the same commissions or fees, and on the same terms and conditions as are by such member accorded to the general public.

(2) For the purposes of this subsection, the term "nonmember professional" shall include (A) with respect to transactions in securities other than municipal securities, any registered broker or dealer who is not a member of any registered securities association, except such a broker or dealer who deals exclusively in commercial paper, bankers' acceptances, and commercial bills, and (B) with respect to transactions in municipal securities, any municipal securities dealer (other than a bank or division or department of a bank) who is not a member of any registered securities association and any municipal securities broker who is not a member of any such association.

(3) Nothing in this subsection shall be so construed or applied as to prevent (A) any member of a registered securities association from granting to any other member of any registered securities association any dealer's discount, allowance, commission, or special terms, in connection with the purchase or sale of securities, or (B) any member of a registered securities association or any municipal securities dealer which is a bank or a division or department of a bank from granting to any member of any registered securities association or any such municipal securities dealer any dealer's discount, allowance, commission, or special terms in connection with the purchase or sale of municipal securities: Provided, however, That the granting of any such discount, allowance, commission, or special terms in connection with the purchase or sale of municipal securities shall be subject to rules of the Municipal Securities Rulemaking Board adopted pursuant to section 15B(b)(2)(K) of this title.

(f) Nothing in subsection (b)(6) or (b)(11) of this section shall be construed to permit a registered securities association to make rules concerning any transaction by a registered broker or dealer in a municipal security.

(g)(1) A registered securities association shall deny membership to any person who is not a registered broker or dealer.

(2) A registered securities association may, and in cases in which the Commission, by order, directs as necessary or appropriate in the public interest or for the protection of investors shall, deny membership to any registered broker or dealer, and bar from becoming associated with a member any person, who is subject to a statutory disqualification. A registered securities association shall file notice with the Commission not less than thirty days prior to admitting any registered broker or dealer to membership or permitting any person to become associated with a member, if the association knew, or in the exercise of reasonable care should have known, that such broker or dealer or person was subject to a statutory disqualification. The notice shall be in such form and contain such information as the Commission, by rule, may prescribe as necessary or appropriate in the public interest or for the protection of investors.

(3)(A) A registered securities association may deny membership to, or condition the membership of, a registered broker or dealer if (i) such broker or dealer does not meet such standards of financial responsibility or operational capability or such broker or dealer or any natural person associated with such broker or dealer does not meet such standards of training, experience, and competence as are prescribed by the rules of the association or (ii) such broker or dealer or person associated with such broker or dealer has engaged and there is a reasonable likelihood he will again engage in acts or practices inconsistent with just and equitable principles of trade. A registered securities association may examine and verify the qualifications of an applicant to become a member and the natural persons associated with such an applicant in accordance with procedures established by the rules of the association.

(B) A registered securities association may bar a natural person from becoming associated with a member or condition the association of a natural person with a member if such natural person (i) does not meet such standards of training, experience, and competence as are prescribed by the rules of the association or (ii) has engaged and there is a reasonable likelihood he will again engage in acts or practices inconsistent with just and equitable principles of trade. A registered securities association may examine and verify the qualifications of an applicant to become a person associated with a member in accordance with procedures established by the rules of the association and require a natural person associated with a member, or any class of such natural persons, to be registered with the association in accordance with procedures so established.

(C) A registered securities association may bar any person from becoming associated with a member if such person does not agree (i) to supply the association with such information with respect to its relationship and dealings with the member as may be specified in the rules of the association and (ii) to permit examination of its books and records to verify the accuracy of any information so supplied.

(D) Nothing in subparagraph (A), (B), or (C) of this paragraph shall be construed to permit a registered securities association to deny membership to or condition the membership of, or bar any person from becoming associated with or condition the association of any person with, a broker or dealer that engages exclusively in transactions in municipal securities.

(4) A registered securities association may deny membership to a registered broker or dealer not engaged in a type of business in which the rules of the association require members to be engaged: Provided, however, That no registered securities association may deny membership to a registered broker or dealer by reason of the amount of such type of business done by such broker or dealer or the other types of business in which he is engaged.

(h)(1) In any proceeding by a registered securities association to determine whether a member or person associated with a member should be disciplined (other than a summary proceeding pursuant to paragraph (3) of this subsection) the association shall bring specific charges, notify such member or person of, and give him an opportunity to defend against, such charges, and keep a record. A determination by the association to impose a disciplinary sanction shall be supported by a statement setting forth—

(A) any act or practice in which such member or person associated with a member has been found to have engaged, or which such member or person has been found to have omitted;

(B) the specific provision of this title, the rules or regulations thereunder, the rules of the Municipal Securities Rulemaking Board, or the rules of the association which any such act or practice, or omission to act, is deemed to violate; and

(C) the sanction imposed and the reason therefor.

(2) In any proceeding by a registered securities association to determine whether a person shall be denied membership, barred from becoming associated with a member, or prohibited or limited with respect to access to services offered by the association or a member thereof (other than a summary proceeding pursuant to paragraph (3) of this subsection), the association shall notify such person of and give him an opportunity to be heard upon, the specific grounds for denial, bar, or prohibition or limitation under consideration and keep a record. A determination by the association to deny membership, bar a person from becoming associated with a member, or prohibit or limit a person with respect to access to services offered by the association or a member thereof shall be supported by a statement setting forth the specific grounds on which the denial, bar, or prohibition or limitation is based.

(3) A registered securities association may summarily (A) suspend a member or person associated with a member who has been and is expelled or suspended from any self-regulatory organization or barred or suspended from being associated with a member of any self-regulatory organization, (B) suspend a member who is in such financial or operating difficulty that the association determines and so notifies the Commission that the member cannot be permitted to continue to do business as a member with safety to investors, creditors, other members, or the association, or (C) limit or prohibit any person with respect to access to services offered by the association if subparagraph (A) or (B) of this paragraph is applicable to such person or, in the case of a person who is not a member, if the association determines that such person does not meet the qualification requirements or other prerequisites for such access and such person cannot be permitted to continue to have such access with safety to investors, creditors, members, or the association. Any person aggrieved by any such summary action shall be promptly afforded an opportunity for a hearing by the association in accordance with the provisions of paragraph (1) or (2) of this subsection. The Commission, by order, may stay any such summary action on its own motion or upon application by any person aggrieved thereby, if the Commission determines summarily or after notice and opportunity for hearing (which hearing may consist solely of the submission of affidavits or presentation of oral arguments) that such stay is consistent with the public interest and the protection of investors.

(i) A registered securities association shall, within one year from the date of enactment of this section, (1) establish and maintain a toll-free telephone listing to receive inquiries regarding disciplinary actions involving its members and their associated persons, and (2) promptly respond to such inquiries in writing. Such association may charge persons, other than individual investors, reasonable fees for written responses to such inquiries. Such an association shall not have any liability to any person for any actions taken or omitted in good faith under this paragraph.

(j) REGISTRATION FOR SALES OF PRIVATE SECURITIES OFFERINGS.—A registered securities association shall create a limited qualification category for any associated person of a member who effects sales as part of a primary offering of securities not involving a public offering, pursuant to section 3(b), 4(2), or 4(6) of the Securities Act of 1933 and the rules and regulations thereunder, and shall deem qualified in such limited qualification category, without testing, any bank employee who, in the six month period preceding the date of the enactment of the Gramm-Leach-Bliley Act, engaged in effecting such sales.

(k) LIMITED PURPOSE NATIONAL SECURITIES ASSOCIATION.—

(1) REGULATION OF MEMBERS WITH RESPECT TO SECURITY FUTURES PRODUCTS.—A futures association registered under section 17 of the Commodity Exchange Act shall be a registered national securities association for the limited purpose of regulating the activities of members who are registered as brokers or dealers in security futures products pursuant to section 15(b)(11).

(2) REQUIREMENTS FOR REGISTRATION.—Such a securities association shall—

(A) be so organized and have the capacity to carry out the purposes of the securities laws applicable to security futures products and to comply, and (subject to any rule or order of the Commission pursuant to section 19(g)(2)) to enforce compliance by its members and persons associated with its members, with the provisions of the securities laws applicable to security futures products, the rules and regulations thereunder, and its rules;

(B) have rules that—

(i) are designed to prevent fraudulent and manipulative acts and practices, to promote just and equitable principles of trade, and, in general, to protect investors and the public interest, including rules governing sales practices and the advertising of security futures products reasonably comparable to those of other national securities associations registered pursuant to subsection (a) that are applicable to security futures products; and

(ii) are not designed to regulate by virtue of any authority conferred by this title matters not related to the purposes of this title or the administration of the association;

(C) have rules that provide that (subject to any rule or order of the Commission pursuant to section 19(g)(2)) its members and persons associated with its members shall be appropriately disciplined for violation of any provision of the securities laws applicable to security futures products, the rules or regulations thereunder, or the rules of the association, by expulsion, suspension, limitation of activities, functions, and operations, fine, censure, being suspended or barred from being associated with a member, or any other fitting sanction; and

(D) have rules that ensure that members and natural persons associated with members meet such standards of training, experience, and competence necessary to effect transactions in security futures products and are tested for their knowledge of securities and security futures products.

(3) EXEMPTION FROM RULE CHANGE SUBMISSION.—Such a securities association shall be exempt from submitting proposed rule changes pursuant to section 19(b) of this title, except that—

(A) the association shall file proposed rule changes related to higher margin levels, fraud or manipulation, recordkeeping, reporting, listing standards, or decimal pricing for security futures products, sales practices for, advertising of, or standards of training, experience, competence, or other qualifications for security futures products for persons who effect transactions in security futures products, or rules effectuating the association's obligation to enforce the securities laws pursuant to section 19(b)(7);

(B) the association shall file pursuant to sections 19(b)(1) and 19(b)(2) proposed rule changes related to margin, except for changes resulting in higher margin levels; and

(C) the association shall file pursuant to section 19(b)(1) proposed rule changes that have been abrogated by the Commission pursuant to section 19(b)(7)(C).

(4) OTHER EXEMPTIONS.—Such a securities association shall be exempt from and shall not be required to enforce compliance by its members, and its members shall not, solely with respect to their transactions effected in security futures products, be required to comply, with the following provisions of this title and the rules thereunder:

(A) Section 8.

(B) Subsections (b)(1), (b)(3), (b)(4), (b)(5), (b)(8), (b)(10), (b)(11), (b)(12), (b)(13), (c), (d), (e), (f), (g), (h), and (i) of this section.

(C) Subsections (d), (f), and (k) of section 17.

(D) Subsections (a), (f), and (h) of section 19.

(l) Consistent with this title, each national securities association registered pursuant to subsection (a) of this section shall issue such rules as are necessary to avoid duplicative or conflicting rules applicable to any broker or dealer registered with the Commission pursuant to section 15(b) (except paragraph (11) thereof), that is also registered with the Commodity Futures Trading Commission pursuant to section 4f(a) of the Commodity Exchange Act (except paragraph (2) thereof), with respect to the application of—

(1) rules of such national securities association of the type specified in section 15(c)(3)(B) involving security futures products; and

(2) similar rules of national securities associations registered pursuant to subsection (k) of this section and national securities exchanges registered pursuant to section 6(g) involving security futures products.

(m) PROCEDURES AND RULES FOR SECURITY FUTURE PRODUCTS.—A national securities association registered pursuant to subsection (a) shall, not later than 8 months after the date of enactment of the Commodity Futures Modernization Act of 2000, implement the procedures specified in section 6(h)(5)(A) of this title and adopt the rules specified in subparagraphs (B) and (C) of section 6(h)(5) of this title.

MUNICIPAL SECURITIES

Sec. 15B. (a)(1) it shall be unlawful for any municipal securities dealer (other than one registered as a broker or dealer under section 15 of this title) to make use of the mails or any means or instrumentality of interstate commerce to effect any transaction in, or to induce or attempt to induce the purchase or sale of, any municipal security unless such municipal securities dealer is registered in accordance with this subsection.

(2) A municipal securities dealer may be registered by filing with the Commission an application for registration in such form and containing such information and documents concerning such municipal securities dealer and any persons associated with such municipal securities dealer as the Commission, by rule, may prescribe as necessary or appropriate in the public interest or for the protection of investors. Within forty-five days of the date of the filing of such application (or within such longer period as to which the applicant consents), the Commission shall—

(A) by order grant registration, or

(B) institute proceedings to determine whether registration should be denied. Such proceedings shall include notice of the grounds for denial under consideration and opportunity for hearing and shall be concluded within one hundred twenty days of the date of the filing of the application for registration. At the conclusion of such proceedings the Commission, by order, shall grant or deny such registration. The Commission may extend the time for the conclusion of such proceedings for up to ninety days if it finds good cause for such extension and publishes its reasons for so finding or for such longer period as to which the applicant consents.

The Commission shall grant the registration of a municipal securities dealer if the Commission finds that the requirements of this section are satisfied. The Commission shall deny such registration if it does not make such a finding or if it finds that if the applicant were so registered, its registration would be subject to suspension or revocation under subsection (c) of this section.

(3) Any provision of this title (other than section 5 or paragraph (1) of this subsection) which prohibits any act, practice, or course of business if the mails or any means or instrumentality of interstate commerce is used in connection therewith shall also prohibit any such act, practice, or course of business by any registered municipal securities dealer or any person acting on behalf of such municipal securities dealer, irrespective of any use of the mails or any means or instrumentality of interstate commerce in connection therewith.

(4) The Commission, by rule or order, upon its own motion or upon application, may conditionally or unconditionally exempt any broker, dealer, or municipal securities dealer or class of brokers, dealers, or municipal securities dealers from any provision of this section or the rules or regulations thereunder, if the Commission finds that such exemption is consistent with the public interest, the protection of investors, and the purposes of this section.

(b)(1) Not later than one hundred twenty days after the date of enactment of the Securities Acts Amendments of 1975, the Commission shall establish a Municipal Securities Rulemaking Board (hereinafter in this section referred to as the "Board") to be composed initially of fifteen members appointed by the Commission, which shall perform the duties set forth in this section. The initial members of the Board shall serve as members for a term of two years, and shall consist of (A) five individuals who are not associated with any broker, dealer, or municipal securities dealer (other than by reason of being under common control with, or indirectly controlling, any broker or dealer which is not a municipal securities broker or municipal securities dealer), at least one of whom shall be representative of investors in municipal securities, and at least one of whom shall be representative of issuers of municipal securities (which members are hereinafter referred to as "public representatives"); (B) five individuals who are associated with and representative of municipal securities brokers and municipal securities dealers which are not banks or subsidiaries or departments or divisions of banks (which members are hereinafter referred to as "broker-dealer representatives"); and (C) five individuals who are associated with and representative of municipal securities dealers which are banks or subsidiaries or departments or divisions of banks (which members are hereinafter referred to as "bank representatives"). Prior to the expiration of the terms of office of the initial members of the Board, and election shall be held under rules adopted by the Board (pursuant to subsection (b)(2)(B) of this section) of the members to succeed such initial members.

(2) The Board shall propose and adopt rules to effect the purposes of this title with respect to transactions in municipal securities effected by brokers, dealers, and municipal securities dealers.

(Such rules are hereinafter collectively referred to in this title as "rules of the Board".) The rules of the Board, as a minimum, shall:

(A) provide that no municipal securities broker or municipal securities dealer shall effect any transaction in, or induce or attempt to induce the purchase or sale of, any municipal security unless such municipal securities broker or municipal securities dealer meets such standards of operational capability and such municipal securities broker or municipal securities dealer and every natural person associated with such municipal securities broker or municipal securities dealer meets such standards of training, experience, competence, and such other qualifications as the Board finds necessary or appropriate in the public interest or for the protection of investors. In connection with the definition and application of such standards the Board may—

(i) appropriately classify municipal securities brokers and municipal securities dealers (taking into account relevant matters, including types of business done, nature of securities other than municipal securities sold, and character of business organization), and persons associated with municipal securities brokers and municipal securities dealers;

(ii) specify that all or any portion of such standards shall be applicable to any such class;

(iii) require persons in any such class to pass tests administered in accordance with subsection (c) (7) of this section; and

(iv) provide that persons in any such class other than municipal securities brokers and municipal securities dealers and partners, officers, and supervisory employees of municipal securities brokers or municipal securities dealers, may be qualified solely on the basis of compliance with such standards of training and such other qualifications as the Board finds appropriate.

(B) establish fair procedures for the nomination and election of members of the Board and assure fair representation in such nominations and elections of municipal securities brokers and municipal securities dealers. Such rules shall provide that the membership of the Board shall at all times be equally divided among public representatives, broker-dealer representatives, and bank representatives, and that the public representatives shall be subject to approval by the Commission to assure that no one of them is associated with any broker, dealer, or municipal securities dealer (other than by reason of being under common control with, or indirectly controlling, any broker or dealer which is not a municipal securities broker or municipal securities dealer) and that at least one is representative of investors in municipal securities and at least one is representative of issuers of municipal securities. Such rules shall also specify the term members shall serve and may increase the number of members which shall constitute the whole Board provided that such number is an odd number.

(C) be designed to prevent fraudulent and manipulative acts and practices, to promote just and equitable principles of trade, to foster cooperation and coordination with persons engaged in regulating, clearing, settling, processing information with respect to, and facilitating transactions in municipal securities, to remove impediments to and perfect the mechanism of a free and open market in municipal securities, and, in general, to protect investors and the public interest; and not be designed to permit unfair discrimination between customers, issuers, municipal securities brokers, or municipal securities dealers, to fix minimum profits, to impose any schedule or fix rates of commissions, allowances, discounts, or other fees to be charged by municipal securities brokers or municipal securities dealers, to regulate by virtue of any authority conferred by this title matters not related to the purposes of this title or the administration of the Board, or to impose any burden on competition not necessary or appropriate in furtherance of the purpose of this title.

(D) if the Board deems appropriate, provide for the arbitration of claims, disputes, and controversies relating to transactions in municipal securities: Provided, however, That no person other than a municipal securities broker, municipal securities dealer, or person associated with such a municipal securities broker or municipal securities dealer may be compelled to submit to such arbitration except at his instance and in accordance with section 29 of this title.

(E) provide for the periodic examination in accordance with subsection (c) (7) of this section of municipal securities brokers and municipal securities dealers to determine compliance with applicable provisions of this title, the rules and regulations thereunder, and the rules of the Board. Such rules shall specify the minimum scope and frequency of such examinations and shall be designed to avoid unnecessary regulatory duplication or undue regulatory burdens for any such municipal securities broker or municipal securities dealer.

(F) include provisions governing the form and content of quotations relating to municipal securities which may be distributed or published by any municipal securities broker, municipal securities dealer, or person associated with such a municipal securities broker or municipal securities dealer, and the persons to whom such quotations may be supplied. Such rules relating to quotations shall be designed to produce fair and informative quotations, to prevent fictitious or misleading quotations, and to promote orderly procedures for collecting, distributing, and publishing quotations.

(G) prescribe records to be made and kept by municipal securities brokers and municipal securities dealers and the periods for which such records shall be preserved.

(H) define the term "separately identifiable department or division", as that term is used in section 3(a)(30) of this title, in accordance with specified and appropriate standards to assure that a bank is not deemed to be engaged in the business of buying and selling municipal securities through a separately identifiable department or division unless such department or division is organized and administered so as to permit independent examination and enforcement of applicable provisions of this title, the rules and regulations thereunder and the rules of the Board. A separately identifiable department or division of a bank may be engaged in activities other than those relating to municipal securities.

(I) provide for the operation and administration of the Board, including the selection of a Chairman from among the members of the Board, the compensation of the members of the Board, and the appointment and compensation of such employees, attorneys, and consultants as may be necessary or appropriate to carry out the Board's functions under this section.

(J) provide that each municipal securities broker and each municipal securities dealer shall pay to the Board such reasonable fees and charges as may be necessary or appropriate to defray the costs and expenses of operating and administering the Board. Such rules shall specify the amount of such fees and charges.

(K) establish the terms and conditions under which any municipal securities dealer may sell, or prohibit any municipal securities dealer from selling, any part of a new issue of municipal securities to a municipal securities investment portfolio during the underwriting period.

(3) Nothing in this section shall be construed to impair or limit the power of the Commission under this title.

(c)(1) No broker, dealer, or municipal securities dealer shall make use of the mails or any means or instrumentality of interstate commerce to effect any transaction in, or to induce or attempt to induce the purchase or sale of, any municipal security in contravention of any rule of the Board.

(2) The Commission, by order, shall censure, place limitations on the activities, functions, or operations, suspend for a period not exceeding twelve months, or revoke the registration of any municipal securities dealer, if it finds, on the record after notice and opportunity for hearing, that such censure, placing of limitations, denial, suspension, or revocation, is in the public interest and that such municipal securities dealer has committed or omitted any act, or is subject to an order or finding, enumerated in subparagraph (A), (D), (E), or (H), (G) of paragraph (4) of section 15(b) of this title, has been convicted of any offense specified in subparagraph (B) of such paragraph (4) within ten years of the commencement of the proceedings under this paragraph, or is enjoined from any action, conduct, or practice specified in subparagraph (C) of such paragraph (4).

(3) Pending final determination whether any registration under this section shall be revoked, the Commission, by order, may suspend such registration, if such suspension appears to the Commission, after notice and opportunity for hearing, to be necessary or appropriate in the public interest or for the protection of investors. Any registered municipal securities dealer may, upon such terms and conditions as the Commission may deem necessary in the public interest or for the protection of investors, withdraw from registration by filing a written notice of withdrawal with

the Commission. If the Commission finds that any registered municipal securities dealer is no longer in existence or has ceased to do business as a municipal securities dealer, the Commission, by order, shall cancel the registration of such municipal securities dealer.

(4) The Commission, by order, shall censure or place limitations on the activities or functions of any person associated, seeking to become associated, or, at the time of the alleged misconduct, associated or seeking to become associated with a municipal securities dealer, or suspend for a period not exceeding twelve months or bar any such person from being associated with a municipal securities dealer, if the Commission finds, on the record after notice and opportunity for hearing, that such censure, placing of limitations, suspension, or bar is in the public interest and that such person has committed any act, or is subject to an order or finding, enumerated in subparagraph (A), (D), (E), (H), or (G) of paragraph (4) of section 15(b) of this title, has been convicted of any offense specified in subparagraph (B) of such paragraph (4) within ten years of the commencement of the proceedings under this paragraph, or is enjoined from any action, conduct, or practice specified in subparagraph (C) of such paragraph (4). It shall be unlawful for any person as to whom an order entered pursuant to this paragraph or paragraph (5) of this subsection suspending or barring him from being associated with a municipal securities dealer is in effect willfully to become, or to be, associated with a municipal securities dealer without the consent of the Commission, and it shall be unlawful for any municipal securities dealer to permit such a person to become, or remain, a person associated with him without the consent of the Commission, if such municipal securities dealer knew, or, in the exercise of reasonable care should have known, of such order.

(5) With respect to any municipal securities dealer for which the Commission is not the appropriate regulatory agency, the appropriate regulatory agency for such municipal securities dealer may sanction any such municipal securities dealer in the manner and for the reasons specified in paragraph (2) of this subsection and any person associated with such municipal securities dealer in the manner and for the reasons specified in paragraph (4) of this subsection. In addition, such appropriate regulatory agency may, in accordance with section 8 of the Federal Deposit Insurance Act (12 U.S.C. 1818), enforce compliance by such municipal securities dealer or any person associated with such municipal securities dealer with the provisions of this section, section 17 of this title, the rules of the Board, and the rules of the Commission pertaining to municipal securities dealers, persons associated with municipal securities dealers, and transactions in municipal securities. For purposes of the preceding sentence, any violation of any such provision shall constitute adequate basis for the issuance of any order under section 8(b) or 8(c) of the Federal Deposit Insurance Act, and the customers of any such municipal securities dealer shall be deemed to be "depositors" as that term is used in section 8(c) of that Act. Nothing in this paragraph shall be construed to affect in any way the powers of such appropriate regulatory agency to proceed against such municipal securities dealer under any other provision of law.

(6) (A) The Commission, prior to the entry of an order of investigation, or commencement of any proceedings, against any municipal securities dealer, or person associated with any municipal securities dealer, for which the Commission is not the appropriate regulatory agency, for violation of any provision of this section, section 15(c)(1) or 15(c)(2) of this title, any rule or regulation under any such section, or any rule of the Board, shall (i) give notice to the appropriate regulatory agency for such municipal securities dealer of the identity of such municipal securities dealer or person associated with such municipal securities dealer, the nature of and basis for such proposed action, and whether the Commission is seeking a monetary penalty against such municipal securities dealer or such associated person pursuant to section 21B of this title; and (ii) consult with such appropriate regulatory agency concerning the effect of such proposed action on sound banking practices and the feasibility and desirability of coordinating such action with any proceeding or proposed proceeding by such appropriate regulatory agency against such municipal securities dealer or associated person.

(B) The appropriate regulatory agency for a municipal securities dealer (if other than the Commission), prior to the entry of an order of investigation, or commencement of any proceedings, against such municipal securities dealer or person associated with such municipal securities dealer, for violation of any provision of this section, the rules of the Board, or the rules or regulations of the Commission pertaining to municipal securities dealers, persons associated with municipal securities dealers, or transactions in municipal securities shall (i) give notice to the Commission of the identity of such municipal securities dealer or person associated with such municipal securities dealer and the nature of and basis for such proposed action and (ii) consult with the Commission concerning the effect of such proposed action on the protection of investors and the feasibility and desirability of coordinating such action with any proceeding or proposed proceeding by the Commission against such municipal securities dealer or associated person.

(C) Nothing in this paragraph shall be construed to impair or limit (other than by the requirement of prior consultation) the power of the Commission or the appropriate regulatory agency for a municipal securities dealer to initiate any action of a class described in this paragraph or to affect in any way the power of the Commission or such appropriate regulatory agency to initiate any other action pursuant to this title or any other provision of law.

(7) (A) Tests required pursuant to subsection (b) (2) (A) (iii) of this section shall be administered by or on behalf of and periodic examinations pursuant to subsection (b) (2) (E) of this section shall be conducted by—

(i) a registered securities association, in the case of municipal securities brokers and municipal securities dealers who are members of such association; and

(ii) the appropriate regulatory agency for any municipal securities broker or municipal securities dealer, in the case of all other municipal securities brokers and municipal securities dealers.

(B) A registered securities association shall make a report of any examination conducted pursuant to subsection (b) (2) (E) of this section and promptly furnish the Commission a copy thereof and any data supplied to it in connection with such examination. Subject to such limitations as the Commission, by rule, determines to be necessary or appropriate in the public interest or for the protection of investors, the Commission shall, on request, make available to the Board a copy of any report of an examination of a municipal securities broker or municipal securities dealer made by or furnished to the Commission pursuant to this paragraph or section 17 (c) (3) of this title.

(8) The Commission is authorized, by order, if in its opinion such action is necessary or appropriate in the public interest, for the protection of investors, or otherwise, in furtherance of the purposes of this title, to remove from office or censure any member or employee of the Board, who, the Commission finds, on the record after notice and opportunity for hearing, has willfully (A) violated any provision of this title, the rules and regulations thereunder, or the rules of the Board or (B) abused his authority.

(d) (1) Neither the Commission nor the Board is authorized under this title, by rule or regulation, to require any issuer of municipal securities, directly or indirectly through a purchaser or prospective purchaser of securities from the issuer, to file with the Commission or the Board prior to the sale of such securities by the issuer any application, report, or document in connection with the issuance, sale, or distribution of such securities.

(2) The Board is not authorized under this title to require any issuer of municipal securities, directly or indirectly through a municipal securities broker or municipal securities dealer or otherwise, to furnish to the Board or to a purchaser or prospective purchaser of such securities any application, report, document, or information with respect to such issuer: *Provided, however,* That the Board may require municipal securities brokers and municipal securities dealers to furnish to the Board or purchaser or prospective purchasers of municipal securities applications, reports, documents, and information with respect to the issuer thereof which [are] generally available from a source other than such issuer. Nothing in this paragraph shall be construed to impair or limit the power of the Commission under any provision of this title.

GOVERNMENT SECURITIES BROKERS AND DEALERS

Sec. 15C. (a) (1) (A) It shall be unlawful for any government securities broker or government securities dealer (other than a registered broker or dealer or a financial institution) to make use of the mails or any means or instrumentality of interstate commerce to effect any transaction in, or to induce or attempt to induce the purchase or sale of, any government security unless such government securities broker or government securities dealer is registered in accordance with paragraph (2) of this subsection.

(B) (i) It shall be unlawful for any government securities broker or government securities dealer that is a registered broker or dealer or a financial institution to make use of the mails or any means or instrumentality of interstate commerce to effect any transaction in, or to induce or attempt to induce the purchase or sale of, any government security unless such government securities broker or government securities dealer has filed with the appropriate regulatory agency written notice that it is a government securities broker or government securities dealer. When such a government securities broker or government securities dealer ceases to act as such it shall file with the appropriate regulatory agency a written notice that it is no longer acting as a government securities broker or government securities dealer.

(ii) Such notices shall be in such form and contain such information concerning a government securities broker or government securities dealer that is a financial institution and any persons associated with such government securities broker or government securities dealer as the Board of Governors of the Federal Reserve System shall, by rule, after consultation with each appropriate regulatory agency (including the Commission), prescribe as necessary or appropriate in the public interest or for the protection of investors. Such notices shall be in such form and contain such information concerning a government securities broker or government securities dealer that is a registered broker or dealer and any persons associated with such government securities broker or government securities dealer as the Commission shall, by rule, prescribe as necessary or appropriate in the public interest or for the protection of investors.

(iii) Each appropriate regulatory agency (other than the Commission) shall make available to the Commission the notices which have been filed with it under this subparagraph, and the Commission shall maintain and make available to the public such notices and the notices it receives under this subparagraph.

(2) A government securities broker or a government securities dealer subject to the registration requirement of paragraph (1) (A) of this subsection may be registered by filing with the Commission an application for registration in such form and containing such information and documents concerning such government securities broker or government securities dealer and any persons associated with such government securities broker or government securities dealer as the Commission, by rule, may prescribe as necessary or appropriate in the public interest or for the protection of investors. Within 45 days of the date of filing of such application (or within such longer period as to which the applicant consents), the Commission shall—

(i) by order grant registration, or

(ii) institute proceedings to determine whether registration should be denied. Such proceedings shall include notice of the grounds for denial under consideration and opportunity for hearing and shall be concluded within 120 days of the date of the filing of the application for registration. At the conclusion of such proceedings, the Commission, by order, shall grant or deny such registration. The order granting registration shall not be effective until such government securities broker or government securities dealer has become a member of a national securities exchange registered under section 6 of this title, or a securities association registered under section 15A of this title, unless the Commission has exempted such government securities broker or government securities dealer, by rule or order, from such membership. The Commission may extend the time for the conclusion of such proceedings for up to 90 days if it finds good cause for such extension and publishes its reasons for so finding or for such longer period as to which the applicant consents.

The Commission shall grant the registration of a government securities broker or a government securities dealer if the Commission finds that the requirements of this section are satisfied. The Commission shall deny such registration if it does not make such a finding or if it finds that if the applicant were so registered, its registration would be subject to suspension or revocation under subsection (c) of this section.

(3) Any provision of this title (other than section 5 or paragraph (1) of this subsection) which prohibits any act, practice, or course of business if the mails or any means or instrumentality of interstate commerce is used in connection therewith shall also prohibit any such act, practice, or course of business by any government securities broker or government securities dealer registered or having filed notice under paragraph (1) of this subsection or any person acting on behalf of such government securities broker or government securities dealer, irrespective of any use of the mails or any means or instrumentality of interstate commerce in connection therewith.

(4) No government securities broker or government securities dealer that is required to register under paragraph (1)(A) and that is not a member of the Securities Investor Protection Corporation shall effect any transaction in any security in contravention of such rules as the Commission shall prescribe pursuant to this subsection to assure that its customers receive complete, accurate, and timely disclosure of the inapplicability of Securities Investor Protection Corporation coverage to their accounts.

(5) The Secretary of the Treasury (hereinafter in this section referred to as the "Secretary"), by rule or order, upon the Secretary's own motion or upon application, may conditionally or unconditionally exempt any government securities broker or government securities dealer, or class of government securities brokers or government securities dealers, from any provision of subsection (a), (b), or (d) of this section, other than subsection (d)(3), or the rules thereunder, if the Secretary finds that such exemption is consistent with the public interest, the protection of investors, and the purposes of this title.

(b)(1) The Secretary shall propose and adopt rules to effect the purposes of this title with respect to transactions in government securities effected by government securities brokers and government securities dealers as follows:

(A) Such rules shall provide safeguards with respect to the financial responsibility and related practices of government securities brokers and government securities dealers including, but not limited to, capital adequacy standards, the acceptance of custody and use of customers' securities, the carrying and use of customers' deposits or credit balances, and the transfer and control of government securities subject to repurchase agreements and in similar transactions.

(B) Such rules shall require every government securities broker and government securities dealer to make reports to and furnish copies of records to the appropriate regulatory agency, and to file with the appropriate regulatory agency, annually or more frequently, a balance sheet and income statement certified by an independent public accountant, prepared on a calendar or fiscal year basis, and such other financial statements (which shall, as the Secretary specifies, be certified) and information concerning its financial condition as required by such rules.

(C) Such rules shall require records to be made and kept by government securities brokers and government securities dealers and shall specify the periods for which such records shall be preserved.

(2) RISK ASSESSMENT FOR HOLDING COMPANY SYSTEMS.—

(A) OBLIGATIONS TO OBTAIN, MAINTAIN, AND REPORT INFORMATION.—Every person who is registered as a government securities broker or government securities dealer under this section shall obtain such information and make and keep such records as the Secretary by rule prescribes concerning the registered person's policies, procedures, or systems for monitoring and controlling financial and operational risks to it resulting from the activities of any of its associated persons, other than a natural person. Such records shall describe, in the aggregate, each of the financial and securities activities conducted by, and customary sources of capital and funding of, those of its associated persons whose business activities are reasonably likely to have a material impact on the financial or operational condition of such registered person, including its capital, its liquidity, or its ability to conduct or finance its operations. The Secretary, by rule, may require summary reports of such information to be filed with the registered person's appropriate regulatory agency no more frequently than quarterly.

(B) AUTHORITY TO REQUIRE ADDITIONAL INFORMATION.—If, as a result of adverse market conditions or based on reports provided pursuant to subparagraph (A) of this paragraph or other available information, the appropriate regulatory agency reasonably concludes that it has concerns regarding the financial or operational condition of any government securities broker or government securities dealer registered under this section, such agency may require the registered person to make reports concerning the financial and securities activities of any of such person's associated persons, other than a natural person, whose business activities are reasonably likely to have a material impact on the financial or operational condition of such registered person. The appropriate regulatory agency, in requiring reports pursuant to this subparagraph, shall specify the information required, the period for which it is required, the time and date on which the information must be furnished, and whether the information is to be furnished directly to the appropriate regulatory agency or to a self-regulatory organization with primary responsibility for examining the registered person's financial and operational condition.

(C) SPECIAL PROVISIONS WITH RESPECT TO ASSOCIATED PERSONS SUBJECT TO FEDERAL BANKING AGENCY REGULATION.—

(i) COOPERATION IN IMPLEMENTATION.—In developing and implementing reporting requirements pursuant to subparagraph (A) of this paragraph with respect to associated persons subject to examination by or reporting requirements of a Federal banking agency, the Secretary shall consult with and consider the views of each such Federal banking agency. If a Federal banking agency comments in writing on a proposed rule of the Secretary under this paragraph that has been published for comment, the Secretary shall respond in writing to such written comment before adopting the proposed rule. The Secretary shall, at the request of a Federal banking agency, publish such comment and response in the Federal Register at the time of publishing the adopted rule.

(ii) USE OF BANKING AGENCY REPORTS.—A registered government securities broker or government securities dealer shall be in compliance with any recordkeeping or reporting requirement adopted pursuant to subparagraph (A) of this paragraph concerning an associated person that is subject to examination by or reporting requirements of a Federal banking agency if such government securities broker or government securities dealer utilizes for such recordkeeping or reporting requirement copies of reports filed by the associated person with the Federal banking agency pursuant to section 5211 of the Revised Statutes, section 9 of the Federal Reserve Act, section 7(a) of the Federal Deposit Insurance Act, section 10(b) of the Home Owners' Loan Act, or section 8 of the Bank Holding Company Act of 1956. The Secretary may, however, by rule adopted pursuant to subparagraph (A), require any registered government securities broker or government securities dealer filing such reports with the appropriate regulatory agency to obtain, maintain, or report supplemental information if the Secretary makes an explicit finding, based on information provided by the appropriate regulatory agency, that such supplemental information is necessary to inform the appropriate regulatory agency regarding potential risks to such government securities broker or government securities dealer. Prior to requiring any such supplemental information, the Secretary shall first request the Federal banking agency to expand its reporting requirements to include such information.

(iii) PROCEDURE FOR REQUIRING ADDITIONAL INFORMATION.—Prior to making a request pursuant to subparagraph (B) of this paragraph for information with respect to an associated person that is subject to examination by or reporting requirements of a Federal banking agency, the appropriate regulatory agency shall—

(I) notify such banking agency of the information required with respect to such associated person; and

(II) consult with such agency to determine whether the information required is available from such agency and for other purposes, unless the appropriate regulatory agency determines that any delay resulting from such consultation would be inconsistent with ensuring the financial and operational condition of the government securities broker or government securities dealer or the stability or integrity of the securities markets.

(iv) EXCLUSION FOR EXAMINATION REPORTS.—Nothing in this subparagraph shall be construed to permit the Secretary or an appropriate regulatory agency to require any registered government securities broker or government securities dealer to obtain, maintain, or furnish any examination report of any Federal banking agency or any supervisory recommendations or analysis contained therein.

(v) CONFIDENTIALITY OF INFORMATION PROVIDED.—No information provided to or obtained by an appropriate regulatory agency from any Federal banking agency pursuant to a request under clause (iii) of this subparagraph regarding any associated person which is subject to examination by or reporting requirements of a Federal banking agency may be disclosed to any other person (other than a self-regulatory organization), without the prior written approval of the Federal banking agency. Nothing in this clause shall authorize the Secretary or any appropriate regulatory agency to withhold information from Congress, or prevent the Secretary or any appropriate regulatory agency from complying with a request for information from any other Federal department or agency requesting the information for purposes within the scope of its jurisdiction, or complying with an order of a court of the United States in an action brought by the United States or the Commission.

(vi) NOTICE TO BANKING AGENCIES CONCERNING FINANCIAL AND OPERATIONAL CONDITION CONCERNS.—The Secretary or appropriate regulatory agency shall notify the Federal banking agency of any concerns of the Secretary or the appropriate regulatory agency regarding significant financial or operational risks resulting from the activities of any government securities broker or government securities dealer to any associated person thereof which is subject to examination by or reporting requirements of the Federal banking agency.

(vii) DEFINITION.—For purposes of this subparagraph, the term 'Federal banking agency' shall have the same meaning as the term 'appropriate Federal banking agency' in section 3(q) of the Federal Deposit Insurance Act (12 U.S.C. 1813(q)).

(D) EXEMPTIONS.—The Secretary by rule or order may exempt any person or class of persons, under such terms and conditions and for such periods as the Secretary shall provide in such rule or order, from the provisions of this paragraph, and the rules thereunder. In granting such exemptions, the Secretary shall consider, among other factors—

(i) whether information of the type required under this paragraph is available from a supervisory agency (as defined in section 1101(6) of the Right to Financial Privacy Act of 1978 (12 U.S.C. 3401(6))), a State insurance commission or similar State agency, the Commodity Futures Trading Commission, or a similar foreign regulator;

(ii) the primary business of any associated person;

(iii) the nature and extent of domestic or foreign regulation of the associated person's activities;

(iv) the nature and extent of the registered person's securities transactions; and

(v) with respect to the registered person and its associated persons, on a consolidated basis, the amount and proportion of assets devoted to, and revenues derived from, activities in the United States securities markets.

(E) CONFORMITY WITH REQUIREMENTS UNDER SECTION 17(h).—In exercising authority pursuant to subparagraph (A) of this paragraph concerning information with respect to associated persons of government securities brokers and government securities dealers who are also associated persons of registered brokers or dealers reporting to the Commission pursuant to section 17(h) of this title, the requirements relating to such associated persons shall conform, to the greatest extent practicable, to the requirements under section 17(h).

(F) AUTHORITY TO LIMIT DISCLOSURE OF INFORMATION.—Notwithstanding any other provision of law, the Secretary and any appropriate regulatory agency shall not be compelled to disclose any information required to be reported under this paragraph, or any information supplied to the Secretary or any appropriate regulatory agency by any domestic or foreign regulatory agency that relates to the financial or operational condition of any associated person of a registered government securities broker or a government securities dealer. Nothing in this paragraph shall authorize the Secretary or any appropriate regulatory agency to withhold information from Congress, or prevent the Secretary or any appropriate regulatory agency from complying with a request for information from any other Federal department or agency requesting the information for purposes within the scope of its jurisdiction, or complying with an order of a court of the United States in an action brought by the United States or the Commission. For purposes of section 552 of title 5, United States Code, this paragraph shall be considered a statute described in subsection (b)(3)(B) of such section 552.

(3)(A) With respect to any financial institution that has filed notice as a government securities broker or government securities dealer or that is required to file notice under subsection (a)(1)(B), the appropriate regulatory agency for such government securities broker or government securities dealer may issue such rules and regulations with respect to transactions in government securities as may be necessary to prevent fraudulent and manipulative acts and practices and to promote just and equitable principles of trade. If the Secretary of the Treasury determines, and notifies the appropriate regulatory agency, that such rule or regulation, if implemented, would, or as applied does (i) adversely affect the liquidity or efficiency of the market for government securities; or (ii) impose any burden on competition not necessary or appropriate in furtherance of the purposes of this section, the appropriate regulatory agency shall, prior to adopting the proposed rule or regulation, find that such rule or regulation is necessary and appropriate in furtherance of the purposes of this section notwithstanding the Secretary's determination.

(B) The appropriate regulatory agency shall consult with and consider the views of the Secretary prior to approving or amending a rule or regulation under this paragraph, except where the appropriate regulatory agency determines that an emergency exists requiring expeditious and summary action and publishes its reasons therefor. If the Secretary comments in writing to the appropriate regulatory agency on a proposed rule or regulation that has been published for comment, the appropriate regulatory agency shall respond in writing to such written comment before approving the proposed rule or regulation.

(C) In promulgating rules under this section, the appropriate regulatory agency shall consider the sufficiency and appropriateness of then existing laws and rules applicable to government securities brokers, government securities dealers, and persons associated with government securities brokers and government securities dealers.

(4) Rules promulgated and orders issued under this section shall—

(A) be designed to prevent fraudulent and manipulative acts and practices and to protect the integrity, liquidity, and efficiency of the market for government securities, investors, and the public interest; and

(B) not be designed to permit unfair discrimination between customers, issuers, government securities brokers, or government securities dealers, or to impose any burden on competition not necessary or appropriate in furtherance of the purposes of this title.

(5) In promulgating rules and issuing orders under this section, the Secretary—

(A) may appropriately classify government securities brokers and government securities dealers (taking into account relevant matters, including types of business done, nature of securities other than government securities purchased or sold, and character of business organization) and persons associated with government securities brokers and government securities dealers;

(B) may determine, to the extent consistent with paragraph (2) of this subsection and with the public interest, the protection of investors, and the purposes of this title, not to apply, in whole or in part, certain rules under this section, or to apply greater, lesser, or different standards, to certain classes of government securities brokers, government securities dealers, or persons associated with government securities brokers or government securities dealers;

(C) shall consider the sufficiency and appropriateness of then existing laws and rules applicable to government securities brokers, government securities dealers, and persons associated with government securities brokers and government securities dealers; and

(D) shall consult with and consider the views of the Commission and the Board of Governors of the Federal Reserve System, except where the Secretary determines that an emergency exists requiring expeditious or summary action and publishes its reasons for such determination.

(6) If the Commission or the Board of Governors of the Federal Reserve System comments in writing on a proposed rule of the Secretary that has been published for comment, the Secretary shall respond in writing to such written comment before approving the proposed rule.

(7) No goverment securities broker or government securities dealer shall make use of the mails or any means or instrumentality of interstate commerce to effect any transaction in, or to induce or attempt to induce the purchase or sale of, any government security in contravention of any rule under this section.

(c)(1) With respect to any government securities broker or government securities dealer registered or required to register under subsection (a)(1)(A) of this section—

(A) The Commission, by order, shall censure, place limitations on the activities, functions, or operations of, suspend for a period not exceeding 12 months, or revoke the registration of such government securities broker or government securities dealer, if it finds, on the record after notice and opportunity for hearing, that such censure, placing of limitations, suspension, or revocation is in the public interest and that such government securities broker or government securities dealer, or any person associated with such government securities broker or government securities dealer (whether prior or subsequent to becoming so associated), has committed or omitted any act, or is subject to an order or finding, enumerated in subparagraph (A), (D), (E), (H), or (G) of paragraph (4) of section 15(b) of this title, has been convicted of any offense specified in subparagraph (B) of such paragraph (4) within 10 years of the commencement of the proceedings under this paragraph, or is enjoined from any action, conduct, or practice specified in subparagraph (C) of such paragraph (4).

(B) Pending final determination whether registration of any government securities broker or government securities dealer shall be revoked, the Commission, by order, may suspend such registration, if such suspension appears to the Commission, after notice and opportunity for hearing, to be necessary or appropriate in the public interest or for the protection of investors. Any registered government securities broker or registered government securities dealer may, upon such terms and conditions as the Commission may deem necessary in the public interest or for the protection of investors, withdraw from registration by filing a written notice of withdrawal with the Commission. If the Commission finds that any registered government securities broker or registered government securities dealer is no longer in existence or has ceased to do business as a government securities broker or government securities dealer, the Commission, by order, shall cancel the registration of such government securities broker or government securities dealer.

(C) The Commission, by order, shall censure or place limitations on the activities or functions of any person associated, or seeking to become associated, with a government securities broker or government securities dealer registered or required to register under subsection (a)(1)(A) of this section or suspend for a period not exceeding 12 months or bar any such person from being associated with such a government securities broker or government securities dealer, if the Commission finds, on the record after notice and opportunity for hearing, that such censure, placing of limitations, suspension, or bar is in the public interest and that such person has committed or omitted any act, or is subject to an order or finding, enumerated in subparagraph (A), (D), (E), (H), or (G) of paragraph (4) of section 15(b) of this title, has been convicted of any offense specified in subparagraph (B) of such paragraph (4) within 10 years of the commencement of the proceedings under this paragraph, or is enjoined from any action, conduct, or practice specified in subparagraph (C) of such paragraph (4).

(2)(A) With respect to any government securities broker or government securities dealer which is not registered or required to register under subsection (a)(1)(A) of this section, the appropriate regulatory agency for such government securities broker or government securities dealer may, in the manner and for the reasons specified in paragraph (1)(A) of this subsection, censure, place limitations on the activities, functions, or operations of, suspend for a period not exceeding 12 months, or bar from acting as a government securities broker or government securities dealer any such government securities broker or government securities dealer, and may sanction any person associated with such government securities broker or government securities dealer in the manner and for the reasons specified in paragraph (1)(C) of this subsection.

(B) In addition, where applicable, such appropriate regulatory agency may, in accordance with section 8 of the Federal Deposit Insurance Act (12 U.S.C. 1818), section 5 of the Home Owners' Loan Act of 1933 (12 U.S.C. 1464), or section 407 of the National Housing Act (12 U.S.C.

1730), enforce compliance by such government securities broker or government securities dealer or any person associated with such government securities broker or government securities dealer with the provisions of this section and the rules thereunder.

(C) For purposes of subparagraph (B) of this paragraph, any violation of any such provision shall constitute adequate basis for the issuance of any order under section 8(b) or 8(c) of the Federal Deposit Insurance Act, section 5(d)(2) or 5(d)(3) of the Home Owners' Loan Act of 1933, or section 407(e) or 407(f) of the National Housing Act, and the customers of any such government securities broker or government securities dealer shall be deemed, respectively, 'depositors' as that term is used in section 8(c) of the Federal Deposit Insurance Act, 'savings account holders' as that term is used in section 5(d)(3) of the Home Owners' Loan Act of 1933, or 'insured members' as that term is used in section 407(f) of the National Housing Act.

(D) Nothing in this paragraph shall be construed to affect in any way the powers of such appropriate regulatory agency to proceed against such government securities broker or government securities dealer under any other provision of law.

(E) Each appropriate regulatory agency (other than the Commission) shall promptly notify the Commission after it has imposed any sanction under this paragraph on a government securities broker or government securities dealer, or a person associated with a government securities broker or government securities dealer, and the Commission shall maintain, and make available to the public, a record of such sanctions and any sanctions imposed by it under this subsection.

(3) It shall be unlawful for any person as to whom an order entered pursuant to paragraph (1) or (2) of this subsection suspending or barring him from being associated with a government securities broker or government securities dealer is in effect willfully to become, or to be, associated with a government securities broker or government securities dealer without the consent of the appropriate regulatory agency, and it shall be unlawful for any government securities broker or government securities dealer to permit such a person to become, or remain, a person associated with it without the consent of the appropriate regulatory agency, if such government securities broker or government securities dealer knew, or, in the exercise of reasonable care should have known, of such order.

(d)(1) All records of a government securities broker or government securities dealer are subject at any time, or from time to time, to such reasonable periodic, special, or other examinations by representatives of the appropriate regulatory agency for such government securities broker or government securities dealer as such appropriate regulatory agency deems necessary or appropriate in the public interest, for the protection of investors, or otherwise in furtherance of the purposes of this title.

(2) Information received by an appropriate regulatory agency, the Secretary, or the Commission from or with respect to any government securities broker, government securities dealer, any person associated with a government securities broker or government securities dealer, or any other person subject to this section or rules promulgated thereunder, may be made available by the Secretary or the recipient agency to the Commission, the Secretary, the Department of Justice, the Commodity Futures Trading Commission, any appropriate regulatory agency, any self-regulatory organization, or any Federal Reserve Bank.

(3) GOVERNMENT SECURITIES TRADE RECONSTRUCTION.—

(A) FURNISHING RECORDS.—Every government securities broker and government securities dealer shall furnish to the Commission on request such records of government securities transactions, including records of the date and time of execution of trades, as the Commission may require to reconstruct trading in the course of a particular inquiry or investigation being conducted by the Commission for enforcement or surveillance purposes. In requiring information pursuant to this paragraph, the Commission shall specify the information required, the period for which it is required, the time and date on which the information must be furnished, and whether the information is to be furnished directly to the Commission, to the Federal Reserve Bank of New York, or to an appropriate regulatory agency or self-regulatory organization with responsibility for examining the government securities broker or government securities dealer. The Commission may require that such information be furnished in machine readable form notwithstanding any limitation in subparagraph (B). In utilizing its authority to require information in machine readable form, the Commission shall minimize the burden such requirement may place on small government securities brokers and dealers.

(B) LIMITATION; CONSTRUCTION.—The Commission shall not utilize its authority under this paragraph to develop regular reporting requirements, except that the Commission may require information to be furnished under this paragraph as frequently as necessary for particular inquiries or investigations for enforcement or surveillance purposes. This paragraph shall not be construed as requiring, or as authorizing the Commission to require, any government securities broker or government securities dealer to obtain or maintain any information for purposes of this paragraph which is not otherwise maintained by such broker or dealer in accordance with any other provision of law or usual and customary business practice. The Commission shall, where feasible, avoid requiring any information to be furnished under this paragraph that the Commission may obtain from the Federal Reserve Bank of New York.

(C) PROCEDURES FOR REQUIRING INFORMATION.—At the time the Commission requests any information pursuant to subparagraph (A) with respect to any government securities broker or government securities dealer for which the Commission is not the appropriate regulatory agency, the Commission shall notify the appropriate regulatory agency for such government securities broker or government securities dealer and, upon request, furnish to the appropriate regulatory agency any information supplied to the Commission.

(D) CONSULTATION.—Within 90 days after the date of enactment of this paragraph, and annually thereafter, or upon the request of any other appropriate regulatory agency, the Commission shall consult with the other appropriate regulatory agencies to determine the availability of records that may be required to be furnished under this paragraph and, for those records available directly from the other appropriate regulatory agencies, to develop a procedure for furnishing such records expeditiously upon the Commission's request.

(E) EXCLUSION FOR EXAMINATION REPORTS.—Nothing in this paragraph shall be construed so as to permit the Commission to require any government securities broker or government securities dealer to obtain, maintain, or furnish any examination report of any appropriate regulatory agency other than the Commission or any supervisory recommendations or analysis contained in any such examination report.

(F) AUTHORITY TO LIMIT DISCLOSURE OF INFORMATION.—Notwithstanding any other provision of law, the Commission and the appropriate regulatory agencies shall not be compelled to disclose any information required or obtained under this paragraph. Nothing in this paragraph shall authorize the Commission or any appropriate regulatory agency to withhold information from Congress, or prevent the Commission or any appropriate regulatory agency from complying with a request for information from any other Federal department or agency requesting information for purposes within the scope of its jurisdiction, or from complying with an order of a court of the United States in an action brought by the United States, the Commission, or the appropriate regulatory agency. For purposes of section 552 of title 5, United States Code, this subparagraph shall be considered a statute described in subsection (b)(3)(B) of such section 552.

(e)(1) It shall be unlawful for any government securities broker or government securities dealer registered or required to register with the Commission under subsection (a)(1)(A) to effect any transaction in, or induce or attempt to induce the purchase or sale of, any government security, unless such government securities broker or government securities dealer is a member of a national securities exchange registered under section 6 of this title or a securities association registered under section 15A of this title.

(2) The Commission, after consultation with the Secretary, by rule or order, as it deems consistent with the public interest and the protection of investors, may conditionally or unconditionally exempt from paragraph (1) of this subsection any government securities broker or government securities dealer or class of government securities brokers or government securities dealers specified in such rule or order.

(f) LARGE POSITION REPORTING.—

(1) REPORTING REQUIREMENTS.—The Secretary may adopt rules to require specified persons holding, maintaining, or controlling large positions in to-be-issued or recently issued Treasury securities to file such reports regarding such positions as the Secretary determines to be necessary and appropriate for the purpose of monitoring the impact in the Treasury securities market of concentrations of positions in Treasury securities and for the purpose of otherwise assisting the Commission in the enforcement of this title, taking into account any impact of such rules on the efficiency and liquidity of the Treasury securities market and the cost to taxpayers of funding the Federal debt. Unless otherwise specified by the Secretary, reports required under this subsection shall be filed with the Federal Reserve Bank of New York, acting as agent for the Secretary. Such reports shall, on a timely basis, be provided directly to the Commission by the person with whom they are filed.

(2) RECORDKEEPING REQUIREMENTS.—Rules under this subsection may require persons holding, maintaining, or controlling large positions in Treasury securities to make and keep for prescribed periods such records as the Secretary determines are necessary or appropriate to ensure that such persons can comply with reporting requirements under this subsection.

(3) AGGREGATION RULES.—Rules under this subsection—

(A) may prescribe the manner in which positions and accounts shall be aggregated for the purpose of this subsection, including aggregation on the basis of common ownership or control; and

(B) may define which persons (individually or as a group) hold, maintain, or control large positions.

(4) DEFINITIONAL AUTHORITY; DETERMINATION OF REPORTING THRESHOLD.—

(A) In prescribing rules under this subsection, the Secretary may, consistent with the purpose of this subsection, define terms used in this subsection that are not otherwise defined in section 3 of this title.

(B) Rules under this subsection shall specify—

(i) the minimum size of positions subject to reporting under this subsection, which shall be no less than the size that provides the potential for manipulation or control of the supply or price, or the cost of financing arrangements, of an issue or the portion thereof that is available for trading;

(ii) the types of positions (which may include financing arrangements) to be reported;

(iii) the securities to be covered; and

(iv) the form and manner in which reports shall be transmitted, which may include transmission in machine readable form.

(5) EXEMPTIONS.—Consistent with the public interest and the protection of investors, the Secretary by rule or order may exempt in whole or in part, conditionally or unconditionally, any person or class of persons, or any transaction or class of transactions, from the requirements of this subsection.

(6) LIMITATION ON DISCLOSURE OF INFORMATION.—Notwithstanding any other provision of law, the Secretary and the Commission shall not be compelled to disclose any information required to be kept or reported under this subsection. Nothing in this subsection shall authorize the Secretary or the Commission to withhold information from Congress, or prevent the Secretary or the Commission from complying with a request for information from any other Federal department or agency requesting information for purposes within the scope of its jurisdiction, or from complying with an order of a court of the United States in an action brought by the United States, the Secretary, or the Commission. For purposes of section 552 of title 5, United States Code, this paragraph shall be considered a statute described in subsection (b)(3)(B) of such section 552.

(g)(1) Nothing in this section except paragraph (2) of this subsection shall be construed to impair or limit the authority under any other provision of law of the Commission, the Secretary of the Treasury, the Board of Governors of the Federal Reserve System, the Comptroller of the Currency, the Federal Deposit Insurance Corporation, the Director of the Office of Thrift

Supervision, the Federal Savings and Loan Insurance Corporation, the Secretary of Housing and Urban Development, and the Government National Mortgage Association.

(2) Notwithstanding any other provision of this title, the Commission shall not have any authority to make investigations of, require the filing of a statement by, or take any other action under this title against a government securities broker or government securities dealer, or any person associated with a government securities broker or government securities dealer, for any violation or threatened violation of the provisions of this section, other than subsection (d)(3) or the rules or regulations thereunder, unless the Commission is the appropriate regulatory agency for such government securities broker or government securities dealer. Nothing in the preceding sentence shall be construed to limit the authority of the Commission with respect to violations or threatened violations of any provision of this title other than this section (except subsection (d)(3)), the rules or regulations under any such other provision, or investigations pursuant to section 21(a)(2) of this title to assist a foreign securities authority.

SECURITIES ANALYSTS AND RESEARCH REPORTS

Sec. 15D. (a) ANALYST PROTECTIONS.—The Commission, or upon the authorization and direction of the Commission, a registered securities association or national securities exchange, shall have adopted, not later than 1 year after the date of enactment of this section, rules reasonably designed to address conflicts of interest that can arise when securities analysts recommend equity securities in research reports and public appearances, in order to improve the objectivity of research and provide investors with more useful and reliable information, including rules designed—

(1) to foster greater public confidence in securities research, and to protect the objectivity and independence of securities analysts, by—

(A) restricting the prepublication clearance or approval of research reports by persons employed by the broker or dealer who are engaged in investment banking activities, or persons not directly responsible for investment research, other than legal or compliance staff;

(B) limiting the supervision and compensatory evaluation of securities analysts to officials employed by the broker or dealer who are not engaged in investment banking activities; and

(C) requiring that a broker or dealer and persons employed by a broker or dealer who are involved with investment banking activities may not, directly or indirectly, retaliate against or threaten to retaliate against any securities analyst employed by that broker or dealer or its affiliates as a result of an adverse, negative, or otherwise unfavorable research report that may adversely affect the present or prospective investment banking relationship of the broker or dealer with the issuer that is the subject of the research report, except that such rules may not limit the authority of a broker or dealer to discipline a securities analyst for causes other than such research report in accordance with the policies and procedures of the firm;

(2) to define periods during which brokers or dealers who have participated, or are to participate, in a public offering of securities as underwriters or dealers should not publish or otherwise distribute research reports relating to such securities or to the issuer of such securities;

(3) to establish structural and institutional safeguards within registered brokers or dealers to assure that securities analysts are separated by appropriate informational partitions within the firm from the review, pressure, or oversight of those whose involvement in investment banking activities might potentially bias their judgment or supervision; and

(4) to address such other issues as the Commission, or such association or exchange, determines appropriate.

(b) DISCLOSURE.—The Commission, or upon the authorization and direction of the Commission, a registered securities association or national securities exchange, shall have adopted, not later than 1 year after the date of enactment of this section, rules reasonably designed to require each securities analyst to disclose in public appearances, and each registered broker or dealer to disclose in each research report, as applicable, conflicts of interest that are known or should have been known by the securities analyst or the broker or dealer, to exist at the time of the appearance or the date of distribution of the report, including—

(1) the extent to which the securities analyst has debt or equity investments in the issuer that is the subject of the appearance or research report;

(2) whether any compensation has been received by the registered broker or dealer, or any affiliate thereof, including the securities analyst, from the issuer that is the subject of the appearance or research report, subject to such exemptions as the Commission may determine appropriate and necessary to prevent disclosure by virtue of this paragraph of material non-public information regarding specific potential future investment banking transactions of such issuer, as is appropriate in the public interest and consistent with the protection of investors;

(3) whether an issuer, the securities of which are recommended in the appearance or research report, currently is, or during the 1-year period preceding the date of the appearance or date of distribution of the report has been, a client of the registered broker or dealer, and if so, stating the types of services provided to the issuer;

(4) whether the securities analyst received compensation with respect to a research report, based upon (among any other factors) the investment banking revenues (either generally or specifically earned from the issuer being analyzed) of the registered broker or dealer; and

(5) such other disclosures of conflicts of interest that are material to investors, research analysts, or the broker or dealer as the Commission, or such association or exchange, determines appropriate.

(c) DEFINITIONS.—In this section—

(1) the term "securities analyst" means any associated person of a registered broker or dealer that is principally responsible for, and any associated person who reports directly or indirectly to a securities analyst in connection with, the preparation of the substance of a research report, whether or not any such person has the job title of "securities analyst"; and

(2) the term "research report" means a written or electronic communication that includes an analysis of equity securities of individual companies or industries, and that provides information reasonably sufficient upon which to base an investment decision.

[DIRECTORS, OFFICERS, AND PRINCIPAL STOCKHOLDERS]

Sec. 16. (a) DISCLOSURES REQUIRED.—

(1) DIRECTORS, OFFICERS, AND PRINCIPAL STOCKHOLDERS REQUIRED TO FILE.—Every person who is directly or indirectly the beneficial owner of more than 10 percent of any class of any equity security (other than an exempted security) which is registered pursuant to section 12, or who is a director or an officer of the issuer of such security, shall file the statements required by this subsection with the Commission (and, if such security is registered on a national securities exchange, also with the exchange).

(2) TIME OF FILING.—The statements required by this subsection shall be filed—

(A) at the time of the registration of such security on a national securities exchange or by the effective date of a registration statement filed pursuant to section 12(g);

(B) within 10 days after he or she becomes such beneficial owner, director, or officer;

(C) if there has been a change in such ownership, or if such person shall have purchased or sold a securitybased swap agreement (as defined in section 206(b) of the Gramm-Leach-Bliley Act (15 U.S.C. 78c note)) involving such equity security, before the end of the second business day following the day on which the subject transaction has been executed, or at such other time as the Commission shall establish, by rule, in any case in which the Commission determines that such 2-day period is not feasible.

(3) CONTENTS OF STATEMENTS.—A statement filed—

(A) under subparagraph (A) or (B) of paragraph (2) shall contain a statement of the amount of all equity securities of such issuer of which the filing person is the beneficial owner; and

(B) under subparagraph (C) of such paragraph shall indicate ownership by the filing person at the date of filing, any such changes in such ownership, and such purchases and sales of the security-based swap agreements as have occurred since the most recent such filing under such subparagraph.

(4) ELECTRONIC FILING AND AVAILABILITY.—Beginning not later than 1 year after the date of enactment of the Sarbanes-Oxley Act of 2002—

(A) a statement filed under subparagraph (C) of paragraph (2) shall be filed electronically;

(B) the Commission shall provide each such statement on a publicly accessible Internet site not later than the end of the business day following that filing; and

(C) the issuer (if the issuer maintains a corporate website) shall provide that statement on that corporate website, not later than the end of the business day following that filing.

(b) For the purpose of preventing the unfair use of information which may have been obtained by such beneficial owner, director, or officer by reason of his relationship to the issuer, any profit realized by him from any purchase and sale, or any sale and purchase, of any equity security of such issuer (other than an exempted security) or a security-based swap agreement (as defined in section 206B of the Gramm-Leach-Bliley Act) involving any such equity security within any period of less than six months, unless such security or security-based swap agreement was acquired in good faith in connection with a debt previously contracted, shall inure to and be recoverable by the issuer, irrespective of any intention on the part of such beneficial owner, director, or officer in entering into such transaction of holding the security or security-based swap agreement purchased or of not repurchasing the security or security-based swap agreement sold for a period exceeding six months. Suit to recover such profit may be instituted at law or in equity in any court of competent jurisdiction by the issuer, or by the owner of any security of the issuer in the name and in behalf of the issuer if the issuer shall fail or refuse to bring such suit within sixty days after request or shall fail diligently to prosecute the same thereafter; but no such suit shall be brought more than two years after the date such profit was realized. This subsection shall not be construed to cover any transaction where such beneficial owner was not such both at the time of the purchase and sale, or the sale and purchase, of the security or security-based swap agreement (as defined in section 206B of the Gramm-Leach-Bliley Act) involved, or any transaction or transactions which the Commission by rules and regulations may exempt as not comprehended within the purpose of this subsection.

(c) It shall be unlawful for any such beneficial owner, director, or officer, directly or indirectly, to sell any equity security of such issuer (other than an exempted security), if the person selling the security or his principal (1) does not own the security sold, or (2) if owning the security, does not deliver it against such sale within twenty days thereafter, or does not within five days after such sale deposit it in the mails or other usual channels of transportation; but no person shall be deemed to have violated this subsection if he proves that notwithstanding the exercise of good faith he was unable to make such delivery or deposit within such time, or that to do so would cause undue inconvenience or expense.

(d) The provisions of subsection (b) of this section shall not apply to any purchase and sale, or sale and purchase, and the provisions of subsection (c) of this section shall not apply to any sale, of an equity security not then or theretofore held by him in an investment account, by a dealer in the ordinary course of his business and incident to the establishment or maintenance by him of a primary or secondary market (otherwise than on a national securities exchange or an exchange exempted from registration under section 5 of this title) for such security. The Commission may, by such rules and regulations as it deems necessary or appropriate in the public interest, define and prescribe terms and conditions with respect to securities held in an investment account and transactions made in the ordinary course of business and incident to the establishment or maintenance of a primary or secondary market.

(e) The provisions of this section shall not apply to foreign or domestic arbitrage transactions unless made in contravention of such rules and regulations as the Commission may adopt in order to carry out the purposes of this section.

(f) TREATMENT OF TRANSACTIONS IN SECURITY FUTURES PRODUCTS.—The provisions of this section shall apply to ownership of and transactions in security futures products.

(g) The authority of the Commission under this section with respect to security-based swap agreements (as defined in section 206B of the Gramm-Leach-Bliley Act) shall be subject to the restrictions and limitations of section 3A(b) of this title.

ACCOUNTS AND RECORDS, REPORTS, EXAMINATIONS OF EXCHANGES, MEMBERS, AND OTHERS

Sec. 17. (a)(1) Every national securities exchange, member thereof, broker or dealer who transacts a business in securities through the medium of any such member, registered securities association, registered broker or dealer, registered municipal securities dealer, registered securities information processor, registered transfer agent, and registered clearing agency and the Municipal Securities Rulemaking Board shall make and keep for prescribed periods such records, furnish such copies thereof, and make and disseminate such reports as the Commission, by rule, prescribes as necessary or appropriate in the public interest, for the protection of investors, or otherwise in furtherance of the purposes of this title.

(2) Every registered clearing agency shall also make and keep for prescribed period such records, furnish such copies thereof, and make and disseminate such reports, as the appropriate regulatory agency for such clearing agency, by rule, prescribes as necessary or appropriate for the safeguarding of securities and funds in the custody or control of such clearing agency or for which it is responsible.

(3) Every registered transfer agent shall also make and keep for prescribed periods such records, furnish such copies thereof, and make such reports as the appropriate regulatory agency for such transfer agent, by rule, prescribes as necessary or appropriate in furtherance of the purposes of section 17A of this title.

(b) RECORDS SUBJECT TO EXAMINATION.—

(1) PROCEDURES FOR COOPERATION WITH OTHER AGENCIES.—All records of persons described in subsection (a) of this section are subject at any time, or from time to time, to such reasonable periodic, special, or other examinations by representatives of the Commission and the appropriate regulatory agency for such persons as the Commission or the appropriate regulatory agency for such persons deems necessary or appropriate in the public interest, for the protection of investors, or otherwise in furtherance of the purposes of this title: Provided, however, That the Commission shall, prior to conducting any such examination of a—

(A) registered clearing agency, registered transfer agent, or registered municipal securities dealer for which it is not the appropriate regulatory agency, give notice to the appropriate regulatory agency for such clearing agency, transfer agent, or municipal securities dealer of such proposed examination and consult with such appropriate regulatory agency concerning the feasibility and desirability of coordinating such examination with examinations conducted by such appropriate regulatory agency with a view to avoiding unnecessary regulatory duplication or undue regulatory burdens for such clearing agency, transfer agent, or municipal securities dealer; or

(B) broker or dealer registered pursuant to section 15(b)(11), exchange registered pursuant to section 6(g), or national securities association registered pursuant to section 15A(k) gives notice to the Commodity Futures Trading Commission of such proposed examination and consults with the Commodity Futures Trading Commission concerning the feasibility and desirability of coordinating such examination with examinations conducted by the Commodity Futures Trading Commission in order to avoid unnecessary regulatory duplication or undue regulatory burdens for such broker or dealer or exchange.

(2) FURNISHING DATA AND REPORTS TO CFTC.—The Commission shall notify the Commodity Futures Trading Commission of any examination conducted of any broker or dealer registered pursuant to section 15(b)(11), exchange registered pursuant to section 6(g), or national securities association registered pursuant to section 15A(k) and, upon request, furnish to the

Commodity Futures Trading Commission any examination report and data supplied to, or prepared by, the Commission in connection with such examination.

(3) USE OF CFTC REPORTS.—Prior to conducting an examination under paragraph (1), the Commission shall use the reports of examinations, if the information available therein is sufficient for the purposes of the examination, of—

(A) any broker or dealer registered pursuant to section 15(b)(11);

(B) exchange registered pursuant to section 6(g); or

(C) national securities association registered pursuant to section 15A(k);

that is made by the Commodity Futures Trading Commission, a national securities association registered pursuant to section 15A(k), or an exchange registered pursuant to section 6(g).

(4) RULES OF CONSTRUCTION.—

(A) Notwithstanding any other provision of this subsection, the records of a broker or dealer registered pursuant to section 15(b)(11), an exchange registered pursuant to section 6(g), or a national securities association registered pursuant to section 15A(k) described in this subparagraph shall not be subject to routine periodic examinations by the Commission.

(B) Any recordkeeping rules adopted under this subsection for a broker or dealer registered pursuant to section 15(b)(11), an exchange registered pursuant to section 6(g), or a national securities association registered pursuant to section 15A(k) shall be limited to records with respect to persons, accounts, agreements, contracts, and transactions involving security futures products.

(C) Nothing in the proviso in paragraph (1) shall be construed to impair or limit (other than by the requirement of prior consultation) the power of the Commission under this subsection to examine any clearing agency, transfer agent, or municipal securities dealer or to affect in any way the power of the Commission under any other provision of this title or otherwise to inspect, examine, or investigate any such clearing agency, transfer agent, or municipal securities dealer.

(c)(1) Every clearing agency, transfer agent, and municipal securities dealer for which the Commission is not the appropriate regulatory agency shall (A) file with the appropriate regulatory agency for such clearing agency, transfer agent, or municipal securities dealer a copy of any application, notice, proposal, report, or document filed with the Commission by reason of its being a clearing agency, transfer agent, or municipal securities dealer and (B) file with the Commission a copy of any application, notice, proposal, report, or document filed with such appropriate regulatory agency by reason of its being a clearing agency, transfer agent, or municipal securities dealer. The Municipal Securities Rulemaking Board shall file with each agency enumerated in section 3(a)(34)(A) of this title copies of every proposed rule change filed with the Commission pursuant to section 19(b) of this title.

(2) The appropriate regulatory agency for a clearing agency, transfer agent, or municipal securities dealer for which the Commission is not the appropriate regulatory agency shall file with the Commission notice of the commencement of any proceeding and a copy of any order entered by such appropriate regulatory agency against any clearing agency, transfer agent, municipal securities dealer, or person associated with a transfer agent or municipal securities dealer, and the Commission shall file with such appropriate regulatory agency, if any, notice of the commencement of any proceeding and a copy of any order entered by the Commission against the clearing agency, transfer agent, or municipal securities dealer, or against any person associated with a transfer agent or municipal securities dealer for which the agency is the appropriate regulatory agency.

(3) The Commission and the appropriate regulatory agency for a clearing agency, transfer agent, or municipal securities dealer for which the Commission is not the appropriate regulatory agency shall each notify the other and make a report of any examination conducted by it of such clearing agency, transfer agent, or municipal securities dealer, and, upon request, furnish to the other a copy of such report and any data supplied to it in connection with such examination.

(4) The Commission or the appropriate regulatory agency may specify that documents required to be filed pursuant to this subsection with the Commission or such agency, respectively,

may be retained by the originating clearing agency, transfer agent, or municipal securities dealer, or filed with another appropriate regulatory agency. The Commission or the appropriate regulatory agency (as the case may be) making such a specification shall continue to have access to the document on request.

(d) (1) The Commission, by rule or order, as it deems necessary or appropriate in the public interest and for the protection of investors, to foster cooperation and coordination among self-regulatory organizations, or to remove impediments to and foster the development of a national market system and national system for the clearance and settlement of securities transactions, may—

(A) with respect to any person who is a member of or participant in more than one self-regulatory organization, relieve any such self-regulatory organization of any responsibility under this title (i) to receive regulatory reports from such person, (ii) to examine such person for compliance, or to enforce compliance by such person, with specified provisions of this title, the rules and regulations thereunder, and its own rules, or (iii) to carry out other specified regulatory functions with respect to such person, and

(B) allocate among self-regulatory organizations the authority to adopt rules with respect to matters as to which, in the absence of such allocation, such self-regulatory organizations share authority under this title.

In making any such rule or entering any such order, the Commission shall take into consideration the regulatory capabilities and procedures of the self-regulatory organizations, availability of staff, convenience of location, unnecessary regulatory duplication, and such other factors as the Commission may consider germane to the protection of investors, cooperation and coordination among self-regulatory organizations, and the development of a national market system and a national system for the clearance and settlement of securities transactions. The Commission, by rule or order, as it deems necessary or appropriate in the public interest and for the protection of investors, may require any self-regulatory organization relieved of any responsibility pursuant to this paragraph, and any person with respect to whom such responsibility relates, to take such steps as are specified in any such rule or order to notify customers of, and persons doing business with, such person of the limited nature of such self-regulatory organization's responsibility for such person's acts, practices, and course of business.

(2) A self-regulatory organization shall furnish copies of any report of examination of any person who is a member of or a participant in such self-regulatory organization to any other self-regulatory organization of which such person is a member or in which such person is a participant upon the request of such person, such other self-regulatory organization, or the Commission.

(e) (1) (A) Every registered broker or dealer shall annually file with the Commission a balance sheet and income statement certified by a registered public accounting firm, prepared on a calendar or fiscal year basis, and such other financial statements (which shall, as the Commission specifies, be certified) and information concerning its financial condition as the Commission, by rule may prescribe as necessary or appropriate in the public interest or for the protection of investors.

(B) Every registered broker and dealer shall annually send to its customers its certified balance sheet and such other financial statements and information concerning its financial condition as the Commission, by rule, may prescribe pursuant to subsection (a) of this section.

(C) The Commission, by rule or order, may conditionally or unconditionally exempt any registered broker or dealer, or class of such brokers or dealers, from any provision of this paragraph if the Commission determines that such exemption is consistent with the public interest and the protection of investors.

(2) The Commission, by rule, as it deems necessary or appropriate in the public interest or for the protection of investors, may prescribe the form and content of financial statements filed pursuant to this title and the accounting principles and accounting standards used in their preparation.

(f) (1) Every national securities exchange, member thereof, registered securities association, broker, dealer, municipal securities dealer, government securities broker, government securities dealer, registered transfer agent, registered clearing agency, participant therein, member of the Federal Reserve System, and bank whose deposits are insured by the Federal Deposit Insurance Corporation shall—

(A) report to the Commission or other person designated by the Commission and, in the case of government securities, to the Secretary of the Treasury such information about missing, lost, counterfeit, or stolen securities, in such form and within such time as the Commission, by rule, determines is necessary or appropriate in the public interest or for the protection of investors; such information shall be available on request for a reasonable fee, to any such exchange, member, association, broker, dealer, municipal securities dealer, transfer agent, clearing agency, participant, member of the Federal Reserve System, or insured bank, and such other persons as the Commission, by rule, designates; and

(B) make such inquiry with respect to information reported pursuant to this subsection as the Commission, by rule, prescribes as necessary or appropriate in the public interest or for the protection of investors, to determine whether securities in their custody or control, for which they are responsible, or in which they are effecting, clearing, or settling a transaction have been reported as missing, lost, counterfeit, or stolen.

(2) Every member of a national securities exchange, broker, dealer, registered transfer agent, and registered clearing agency, shall require that each of its partners, directors, officers, and employees be fingerprinted and shall submit such fingerprints, or cause the same to be submitted, to the Attorney General of the United States for identification and appropriate processing. The Commission, by rule, may exempt from the provisions of this paragraph upon specified terms, conditions, and periods, any class of partners, directors, officers, or employees of any such member, broker, dealer, transfer agent, or clearing agency, if the Commission finds that such action is not inconsistent with the public interest or the protection of investors.

Notwithstanding any other provision of law, in providing identification and processing functions, the Attorney General shall provide the Commission and self-regulatory organizations designated by the Commission with access to all criminal history record information.

(3) (A) In order to carry out the authority under paragraph (1) above, the Commission or its designee may enter into agreement with the Attorney General to use the facilities of the National Crime Information Center ("NCIC") to receive, store, and disseminate information in regard to missing, lost, counterfeit, or stolen securities and to permit direct inquiry access to NCIC's file on such securities for the financial community.

(B) In order to carry out the authority under paragraph (1) of this subsection, the Commission or its designee and the Secretary of the Treasury shall enter into an agreement whereby the Commission or its designee will receive, store, and disseminate information in the possession, and which comes into the possession, of the Department of the Treasury in regard to missing, lost, counterfeit, or stolen securities.

(4) In regard to paragraphs (1), (2), and (3), above insofar as such paragraphs apply to any bank or member of the Federal Reserve System, the Commission may delegate its authority to:

(A) the Comptroller of the Currency as to national banks and banks operating under the Code of Law for the District of Columbia;

(B) the Federal Reserve Board in regard to any member of the Federal Reserve System which is not a national bank or a bank operating under the Code of Law for the District of Columbia; and

(C) the Federal Deposit Insurance Corporation for any State bank which is insured by the Federal Deposit Insurance Corporation but which is not a member of the Federal Reserve System.

(5) The Commission shall encourage the insurance industry to require their insured to report expeditiously instances of missing, lost, counterfeit, or stolen securities to the Commission or to such other person as the Commission may, by rule, designate to receive such information.

(g) Any broker, dealer, or other person extending credit who is subject to the rules and regulations prescribed by the Board of Governors of the Federal Reserve System pursuant to this title shall make such reports to the Board as it may require as necessary or appropriate to enable it to perform the functions conferred upon it by this title. If any such broker, dealer, or other person shall fail to make any such report or fail to furnish full information therein, or, if in the judgment of the Board it is otherwise necessary, such broker, dealer, or other person shall permit such inspections to be made by the Board with respect to the business operations of such broker, dealer, or other person as the Board may deem necessary to enable it to obtain the required information.

(h) RISK ASSESSMENT FOR HOLDING COMPANY SYSTEMS.—

(1) OBLIGATIONS TO OBTAIN, MAINTAIN, AND REPORT INFORMATION.—Every person who is (A) a registered broker or dealer, or (B) a registered municipal securities dealer for which the Commission is the appropriate regulatory agency, shall obtain such information and make and keep such records as the Commission by rule prescribes concerning the registered person's policies, procedures, or systems for monitoring and controlling financial and operational risks to it resulting from the activities of any of its associated persons, other than a natural person. Such records shall describe, in the aggregate, each of the financial and securities activities conducted by, and the customary sources of capital and funding of, those of its associated persons whose business activities are reasonably likely to have a material impact on the financial or operational condition of such registered person, including its net capital, its liquidity, or its ability to conduct or finance its operations. The Commission, by rule, may require summary reports of such information to be filed with the Commission no more frequently than quarterly.

(2) AUTHORITY TO REQUIRE ADDITIONAL INFORMATION.—If, as a result of adverse market conditions or based on reports provided to the Commission pursuant to paragraph (1) of this subsection or other available information, the Commission reasonably concludes that it has concerns regarding the financial or operational condition of (A) any registered broker or dealer, or (B) any registered municipal securities dealer, government securities broker, or government securities dealer for which the Commission is the appropriate regulatory agency, the Commission may require the registered person to make reports concerning the financial and securities activities of any of such person's associated persons, other than a natural person, whose business activities are reasonably likely to have a material impact on the financial or operational condition of such registered person. The Commission, in requiring reports pursuant to this paragraph, shall specify the information required, the period for which it is required, the time and date on which the information must be furnished, and whether the information is to be furnished directly to the Commission or to a self-regulatory organization with primary responsibility for examining the registered person's financial and operational condition.

(3) SPECIAL PROVISIONS WITH RESPECT TO ASSOCIATED PERSONS SUBJECT TO FEDERAL BANKING AGENCY REGULATION.—

(A) COOPERATION IN IMPLEMENTATION.—In developing and implementing reporting requirements pursuant to paragraph (1) of this subsection with respect to associated persons subject to examination by or reporting requirements of a Federal banking agency, the Commission shall consult with and consider the views of each such Federal banking agency. If a Federal banking agency comments in writing on a proposed rule of the Commission under this subsection that has been published for comment, the Commission shall respond in writing to such written comment before adopting the proposed rule. The Commission shall, at the request of the Federal banking agency, publish such comment and response in the Federal Register at the time of publishing the adopted rule.

(B) USE OF BANKING AGENCY REPORTS.—A registered broker, dealer, or municipal securities dealer shall be in compliance with any recordkeeping or reporting requirement adopted pursuant to paragraph (1) of this subsection concerning an associated person that is subject to examination by or reporting requirements of a Federal banking agency if such broker, dealer, or municipal securities dealer utilizes for such recordkeeping or reporting requirement copies of reports filed by the associated person with the Federal banking agency pursuant to section 5211 of the Revised Statutes, section 9 of the Federal Reserve Act, section 7(a) of the Federal Deposit Insurance Act, section 10(b) of the Home Owners' Loan Act, or section 8 of the Bank Holding Company Act of 1956. The Commission may, however, by rule adopted pursuant to paragraph (1), require any broker, dealer, or municipal securities dealer filing such reports with the Commission to obtain, maintain, or report supplemental information if the Commission makes an explicit finding that such supplemental information is necessary to inform the Commission regarding potential risks to such broker, dealer, or municipal securities dealer. Prior to requiring any such supplemental information, the Commission shall first request the Federal banking agency to expand its reporting requirements to include such information.

(C) PROCEDURE FOR REQUIRING ADDITIONAL INFORMATION.—Prior to making a request pursuant to paragraph (2) of this subsection for information with respect to an associated person that is subject to examination by or reporting requirements of a Federal banking agency, the Commission shall—

(i) notify such agency of the information required with respect to such associated person; and

(ii) consult with such agency to determine whether the information required is available from such agency and for other purposes, unless the Commission determines that any delay resulting from such consultation would be inconsistent with ensuring the financial and operational condition of the broker, dealer, municipal securities dealer, government securities broker, or government securities dealer or the stability or integrity of the securities markets.

(D) EXCLUSION FOR EXAMINATION REPORTS.—Nothing in this subsection shall be construed to permit the Commission to require any registered broker or dealer, or any registered municipal securities dealer, government securities broker, or government securities dealer for which the Commission is the appropriate regulatory agency, to obtain, maintain, or furnish any examination report of any Federal banking agency or any supervisory recommendations or analysis contained therein.

(E) CONFIDENTIALITY OF INFORMATION PROVIDED.—No information provided to or obtained by the Commission from any Federal banking agency pursuant to a request by the Commission under subparagraph (C) of this paragraph regarding any associated person which is subject to examination by or reporting requirements of a Federal banking agency may be disclosed to any other person (other than a self-regulatory organization), without the prior written approval of the Federal banking agency. Nothing in this subsection shall authorize the Commission to withhold information from Congress, or prevent the Commission from complying with a request for information from any other Federal department or agency requesting the information for purposes within the scope of its jurisdiction, or complying with an order of a court of the United States in an action brought by the United States or the Commission.

(F) NOTICE TO BANKING AGENCIES CONCERNING FINANCIAL AND OPERATIONAL CONDITION CONCERNS.— The Commission shall notify the Federal banking agency of any concerns of the Commission regarding significant financial or operational risks resulting from the activities of any registered broker or dealer, or any registered municipal securities dealer, government securities broker, or government securities dealer for which the Commission is the appropriate regulatory agency, to any associated person thereof which is subject to examination by or reporting requirements of the Federal banking agency.

(G) DEFINITION.—For purposes of this paragraph, the term "Federal banking agency" shall have the same meaning as the term "appropriate Federal bank agency" in section 3(q) of the Federal Deposit Insurance Act (12 U.S.C. 1813(q)).

(4) EXEMPTIONS.—The Commission by rule or order may exempt any person or class of persons, under such terms and conditions and for such periods as the Commission shall provide in such rule or order, from the provisions of this subsection, and the rules thereunder. In granting such exemptions, the Commission shall consider, among other factors—

(A) whether information of the type required under this subsection is available from a supervisory agency (as defined in section 1101(6) of the Right to Financial Privacy Act of 1978 (12 U.S.C. 3401(6))), a State insurance commission or similar State agency, the Commodity Futures Trading Commission, or a similar foreign regulator;

(B) the primary business of any associated person;

(C) the nature and extent of domestic or foreign regulation of the associated person's activities;

(D) the nature and extent of the registered person's securities activities; and

(E) with respect to the registered person and its associated persons, on a consolidated basis, the amount and proportion of assets devoted to, and revenues derived from, activities in the United States securities markets.

(5) AUTHORITY TO LIMIT DISCLOSURE OF INFORMATION.—Not withstanding any other provision of law, the Commission shall not be compelled to disclose any information required to be reported under this subsection, or any information supplied to the Commission by any domestic or foreign regulatory agency that relates to the financial or operational condition of any associated person of a registered broker, dealer, government securities broker, government securities dealer, or municipal securities dealer. Nothing in this subsection shall authorize the Commission to withhold information from Congress, or prevent the Commission from complying with a request for information from any other Federal department or agency requesting the information for purposes withn the scope of its jurisdiction, or complying with an order of a court of the United States in an action brought by the United States or the Commission. For purposes of section 552 of title 5, United States Code, this subsection shall be considered a statute described in subsection (b)(3)(B) of such section 552. In prescribing regulatiions to carry out the requirements of this subsection, the Commission shall designate information described in or obtained pursuant to subparagraph (B) or (C) of paragraph (3) of this subsection as confidential information for purposes of section 24(b)(2) of this title.

(i) INVESTMENT BANK HOLDING COMPANIES.—

(1) ELECTIVE SUPERVISION OF AN INVESTMENT BANK HOLDING COMPANY NOT HAVING A BANK OR SAVINGS ASSOCIATION AFFILIATE.—

(A) IN GENERAL.—An investment bank holding company that is not—

(i) an affiliate of an insured bank (other than an institution described in subparagraph (D), (F), or (G) of section 2(c)(2), or held under section 4(f), of the Bank Holding Company Act of 1956), or a savings association;

(ii) a foreign bank, foreign company, or company that is described in section 8(a) of the International Banking Act of 1978; or

(iii) a foreign bank that controls, directly or indirectly, a corporation chartered under section 25A of the Federal Reserve Act,

may elect to become supervised by filing with the Commission a notice of intention to become supervised, pursuant to subparagraph (B) of this paragraph. Any investment bank holding company filing such a notice shall be supervised in accordance with this section and comply with the rules promulgated by the Commission applicable to supervised investment bank holding companies.

(B) NOTIFICATION OF STATUS AS A SUPERVISED INVESTMENT BANK HOLDING COMPANY.—An investment bank holding company that elects under subparagraph (A) to become supervised by the Commission shall file with the Commission a written notice of intention to become supervised by the Commission in such form and containing such information and documents concerning such investment bank holding company as the Commission, by rule, may prescribe as necessary or appropriate in furtherance of the purposes of this section. Unless the Commission finds that such supervision is not necessary or appropriate in furtherance of the purposes of this section, such supervision shall become effective 45 days after the date of receipt of such written notice by the Commission or within such shorter time period as the Commission, by rule or order, may determine.

(2) ELECTION NOT TO BE SUPERVISED BY THE COMMISSION AS AN INVESTMENT BANK HOLDING COMPANY.—

(A) VOLUNTARY WITHDRAWAL.—A supervised investment bank holding company that is supervised pursuant to paragraph (1) may, upon such terms and conditions as the Commission deems necessary or appropriate, elect not to be supervised by the Commission by filing a written notice of withdrawal from Commission supervision. Such notice shall not become effective until 1 year after receipt by the Commission, or such shorter or longer period as the Commission deems necessary or appropriate to ensure effective supervision of the material risks to the supervised investment bank holding company and to the affiliated broker or dealer, or to prevent evasion of the purposes of this section.

(B) DISCONTINUATION OF COMMISSION SUPERVISION.—If the Commission finds that any supervised investment bank holding company that is supervised pursuant to paragraph (1) is no longer in existence or has ceased to be an investment bank holding company, or if the Commission finds that continued supervision of such a supervised investment bank holding company is not consistent with the purposes of this section, the Commission may discontinue the supervision pursuant to a rule or order, if any, promulgated by the Commission under this section.

(3) SUPERVISION OF INVESTMENT BANK HOLDING COMPANIES.—

(A) RECORDKEEPING AND REPORTING.—

(i) IN GENERAL.—Every supervised investment bank holding company and each affiliate thereof shall make and keep for prescribed periods such records, furnish copies thereof, and make such reports, as the Commission may require by rule, in order to keep the Commission informed as to—

(I) the company's or affiliate's activities, financial condition, policies, systems for monitoring and controlling financial and operational risks, and transactions and relationships between any broker or dealer affiliate of the supervised investment bank holding company; and

(II) the extent to which the company or affiliate has complied with the provisions of this Act and regulations prescribed and orders issued under this Act.

(ii) FORM AND CONTENTS.—Such records and reports shall be prepared in such form and according to such specifications (including certification by a registered public accounting firm), as the Commission may require and shall be provided promptly at any time upon request by the Commission. Such records and reports may include—

(I) a balance sheet and income statement;

(II) an assessment of the consolidated capital of the supervised investment bank holding company;

(III) an independent auditor's report attesting to the supervised investment bank holding company's compliance with its internal risk management and internal control objectives; and

(IV) reports concerning the extent to which the company or affiliate has complied with the provisions of this title and any regulations prescribed and orders issued under this title.

(B) USE OF EXISTING REPORTS.—

(i) IN GENERAL.—The Commission shall, to the fullest extent possible, accept reports in fulfillment of the requirements under this paragraph that the supervised investment bank holding company or its affiliates have been required to provide to another appropriate regulatory agency or self-regulatory organization.

(ii) AVAILABILITY.—A supervised investment bank holding company or an affiliate of such company shall provide to the Commission, at the request of the Commission, any report referred to in clause (i).

(C) EXAMINATION AUTHORITY.—

(i) FOCUS OF EXAMINATION AUTHORITY.—The Commission may make examinations of any supervised investment bank holding company and any affiliate of such company in order to—

(I) inform the Commission regarding—

(aa) the nature of the operations and financial condition of the supervised investment bank holding company and its affiliates;

(bb) the financial and operational risks within the supervised investment bank holding company that may affect any broker or dealer controlled by such supervised investment bank holding company; and

(cc) the systems of the supervised investment bank holding company and its affiliates for monitoring and controlling those risks; and

(II) monitor compliance with the provisions of this subsection, provisions governing transactions and relationships between any broker or dealer affiliated with the supervised investment bank holding company and any of the company's other affiliates, and applicable provisions of subchapter II of chapter 53, title 31, United States Code (commonly referred to as the 'Bank Secrecy Act') and regulations thereunder.

(ii) RESTRICTED FOCUS OF EXAMINATIONS.—The Commission shall limit the focus and scope of any examination of a supervised investment bank holding company to—

(I) the company; and

(II) any affiliate of the company that, because of its size, condition, or activities, the nature or size of the transactions between such affiliate and any affiliated broker or dealer, or the centralization of functions within the holding company system, could, in the discretion of the Commission, have a materially adverse effect on the operational or financial condition of the broker or dealer.

(iii) DEFERENCE TO OTHER EXAMINATIONS.—For purposes of this subparagraph, the Commission shall, to the fullest extent possible, use the reports of examination of an institution described in subparagraph (D), (F), or (G) of section 2(c)(2), or held under section 4(f), of the Bank Holding Company Act of 1956 made by the appropriate regulatory agency, or of a licensed insurance company made by the appropriate State insurance regulator.

(4) FUNCTIONAL REGULATION OF BANKING AND INSURANCE ACTIVITIES OF SUPERVISED INVESTMENT BANK HOLDING COMPANIES.—The Commission shall defer to—

(A) the appropriate regulatory agency with regard to all interpretations of, and the enforcement of, applicable banking laws relating to the activities, conduct, ownership, and operations of banks, and institutions described in subparagraph (D), (F), and (G) of section 2(c)(2), or held under section 4(f), of the Bank Holding Company Act of 1956; and

(B) the appropriate State insurance regulators with regard to all interpretations of, and the enforcement of, applicable State insurance laws relating to the activities, conduct, and operations of insurance companies and insurance agents.

(5) DEFINITIONS.—For purposes of this subsection:

(A) The term 'investment bank holding company' means—

(i) any person other than a natural person that owns or controls one or more brokers or dealers; and

(ii) the associated persons of the investment bank holding company.

(B) The term 'supervised investment bank holding company' means any investment bank holding company that is supervised by the Commission pursuant to this subsection.

(C) The terms 'affiliate', 'bank', 'bank holding company', 'company', 'control', and 'savings association' have the same meanings as given in section 2 of the Bank Holding Company Act of 1956 (12 U.S.C. 1841).

(D) The term 'insured bank' has the same meaning as given in section 3 of the Federal Deposit Insurance Act.

(E) The term 'foreign bank' has the same meaning as given in section 1(b)(7) of the International Banking Act of 1978.

(F) The terms 'person associated with an investment bank holding company' and 'associated person of an investment bank holding company' mean any person directly or indirectly controlling, controlled by, or under common control with, an investment bank holding company.

(j) AUTHORITY TO LIMIT DISCLOSURE OF INFORMATION.—Notwithstanding any other provision of law, the Commission shall not be compelled to disclose any information required to be reported under subsection (h) or (i) or any information supplied to the Commission by any domestic or foreign regulatory agency that relates to the financial or operational condition of any associated person of a broker or dealer, investment bank holding company, or any affiliate of an investment bank holding company. Nothing in this subsection shall authorize the Commission to withhold information from Congress, or prevent the Commission from complying with a request for information from any other Federal department or agency or any self-regulatory organization requesting the information for purposes within the scope of its jurisdiction, or complying with an order of a court of the United States in an action brought by the United States or the Commission. For purposes of section 552 of title 5, United States Code, this subsection shall be considered a statute described in subsection (b)(3)(B) of such section 552. In prescribing regulations to carry out the requirements of this subsection, the Commission shall designate information described in or obtained pursuant to subparagraphs (A), (B), and (C) of subsection (i)(5) as confidential information for purposes of section 24(b)(2) of this title.".

(k) COORDINATION OF EXAMINING AUTHORITIES.—

(1) Elimination of duplication.—The Commission and the examining authorities, through cooperation and coordination of examination and oversight activities, shall eliminate any unnecessary and burdensome duplication in the examination process.

(2) Coordination of examinations.—The Commission and the examining authorities shall share such information, including reports of examinations, customer complaint information, and other nonpublic regulatory information, as appropriate to foster a coordinated approach to regulatory oversight of brokers and dealers that are subject to examination by more than one examining authority.

(3) Examinations for cause.—At any time, any examining authority may conduct an examination for cause of any broker or dealer subject to its jurisdiction.

(4) Confidentiality.—

(A) In general.—Section 24 shall apply to the sharing of information in accordance with this subsection. The Commission shall take appropriate action under section 24(c) to ensure that such information is not inappropriately disclosed.

(B) Appropriate disclosure not prohibited.—Nothing in this paragraph authorizes the Commission or any examining authority to withhold information from the Congress, or prevent the Commission or any examining authority from complying with a request for information from any other Federal department or agency requesting the information for purposes within the scope of its jurisdiction, or complying with an order of a court of the United States in an action brought by the United States or the Commission.

(5) Definition.—For purposes of this subsection, the term 'examining authority' means a self-regulatory organization registered with the Commission under this title (other than a registered clearing agency) with the authority to examine, inspect, and otherwise oversee the activities of a registered broker or dealer.

NATIONAL SYSTEM FOR CLEARANCE AND SETTLEMENT OF SECURITIES TRANSACTIONS

Sec. 17A. (a)(1) The Congress finds that—

(A) The prompt and accurate clearance and settlement of securities transactions, including the transfer of record ownership and the safeguarding of securities and funds related thereto, are necessary for the protection of investors and persons facilitating transactions by and acting on behalf of investors.

(B) Inefficient procedures for clearance and settlement impose unnecessary costs on investors and persons facilitating transactions by and acting on behalf of investors.

(C) New data processing and communications techniques create the opportunity for more efficient, effective, and safe procedures for clearance and settlement.

(D) The linking of all clearance and settlement facilities and the development of uniform standards and procedures for clearance and settlement will reduce unnecessary costs and increase the protection of investors and persons facilitating transactions by and acting on behalf of investors.

(2)(A) The Commission is directed, therefore, having due regard for the public interest, the protection of investors, the safeguarding of securities and funds, and maintenance of fair competition among brokers and dealers, clearing agencies, and transfer agents, to use its authority under this title—

(i) to facilitate the establishment of a national system for the prompt and accurate clearance and settlement of transactions in securities (other than exempt securities); and

(ii) to facilitate the establishment of linked or coordinated facilities for clearance and settlement of transactions in securities, securities options, contracts of sale for future delivery and options thereon, and commodity options;

in accordance with the findings and to carry out the objectives set forth in paragraph (1) of this subsection.

(B) The Commission shall use its authority under this title to assure equal regulation under this title of registered clearing agencies and registered transfer agents. In carrying out its responsibilities set forth in subparagraph (A)(ii) of this paragraph, the Commission shall coordinate with the Commodity Futures Trading Commission and consult with the Board of Governors of the Federal Reserve System.

(b)(1) Except as otherwise provided in this section, it shall be unlawful for any clearing agency, unless registered in accordance with this subsection, directly or indirectly, to make use of the mails or any means or instrumentality of interstate commerce to perform the functions of a clearing agency with respect to any security (other than an exempted security). The Commission, by rule or order, upon its own motion or upon application, may conditionally or unconditionally exempt any clearing agency or security or any class of clearing agencies or securities from any provisions of this section or the rules or regulations thereunder, if the Commission finds that such exemption is consistent with the public interest, the protection of investors, and the purposes of this section, including the prompt and accurate clearance and settlement of securities transactions and the safeguarding of securities and funds. A clearing agency or transfer agent shall not perform the functions of both a clearing agency and a transfer agent unless such clearing agency or transfer agent is registered in accordance with this subsection and subsection (c) of this section.

(2) A clearing agency may be registered under the terms and conditions hereinafter provided in this subsection and in accordance with the provisions of section 19(a) of this title, by filing with the Commission an application for registration in such form as the Commission, by rule, may prescribe containing the rules of the clearing agency and such other information and documents as the Commission, by rule, may prescribe as necessary or appropriate in the public interest or for the prompt and accurate clearance and settlement of securities transactions.

(3) A clearing agency shall not be registered unless the Commission determines that—

(A) Such clearing agency is so organized and has the capacity to be able to facilitate the prompt and accurate clearance and settlement of securities transactions and derivative agreements, contracts, and transactions for which it is responsible, to safeguard securities and funds in its custody or control or for which it is responsible, to comply with the provisions of this title and the rules and regulations thereunder, to enforce (subject to any rule or order of the Commission pursuant to section 17(d) or 19(g)(2) of this title) compliance by its participants with the rules of the clearing agency, and to carry out the purposes of this section.

(B) Subject to the provisions of paragraph (4) of this subsection, the rules of the clearing agency provide that any (i) registered broker or dealer, (ii) other registered clearing agency, (iii) registered investment company, (iv) bank, (v) insurance company, or (vi) other person or class of persons as the Commission, by rule, may from time to time designate as appropriate to the development of a national system for the prompt and accurate clearance and settlement of securities transactions may become a participant in such clearing agency.

(C) The rules of the clearing agency assure a fair representation of its shareholders (or members) and participants in the selection of its directors and administration of its affairs. (The Commission may determine that the representation of participants is fair if they are afforded a reasonable opportunity to acquire voting stock of the clearing agency, directly or indirectly, in reasonable proportion to their use of such clearing agency.)

(D) The rules of the clearing agency provide for the equitable allocation of reasonable dues, fees and other charges among its participants.

(E) The rules of the clearing agency do not impose any schedule of prices, or fix rates or other fees, for services rendered by its participants.

(F) The rules of the clearing agency are designed to promote the prompt and accurate clearance and settlement of securities transactions and, to the extent applicable, derivative agreements, contracts, and transactions, to assure the safeguarding of securities and funds which are in the custody or control of the clearing agency or for which it is responsible, to foster cooperation and coordination with persons engaged in the clearance and settlement of securities transactions, to remove impediments to and perfect the mechanism of a national system for the prompt and accurate clearance and settlement of securities transactions, and, in general, to protect investors and the public interest; and are not designed to permit unfair discrimination in the admission of participants or among participants in the use of the clearing agency, or to regulate by virtue of any authority conferred by this title matters not related to the purposes of this section or the administration of the clearing agency.

(G) The rules of the clearing agency provide that (subject to any rule or order of the Commission pursuant to section 17(d) or 19(g)(2) of this title) its participants shall be appropriately disciplined for violation of any provision of the rules of the clearing agency by expulsion, suspension, limitation of activities, functions, and operations, fine, censure, or any other fitting sanction.

(H) The rules of the clearing agency are in accordance with the provisions of paragraph (5) of this subsection, and, in general, provide a fair procedure with respect to the disciplining of participants, the denial of participation to any person seeking participation therein, and the prohibition or limitation by the clearing agency of any person with respect to access to services offered by the clearing agency.

(I) The rules of the clearing agency do not impose any burden on competition not necessary or appropriate in furtherance of the purpose of this title.

(4)(A) A registered clearing agency may, and in cases in which the Commission, by order, directs as appropriate in the public interest shall, deny participation to any person subject to a statutory disqualification. A registered clearing agency shall file notice with the Commission not less than thirty days prior to admitting any person to participation, if the clearing agency knew, or in the exercise of reasonable care should have known, that such person was subject to a statutory disqualification. The notice shall be in such form and contain such information as the Commission, by rule, may prescribe as necessary or appropriate in the public interest or for the protection of investors.

(B) A registered clearing agency may deny participation to, or condition the participation of, any person if such person does not meet such standards of financial responsibility, operational capability, experience, and competence as are prescribed by the rules of the clearing agency. A registered clearing agency may examine and verify the qualifications of an applicant to be a participant in accordance with procedures established by the rules of the clearing agency.

(5)(A) In any proceeding by a registered clearing agency to determine whether a participant should be disciplined (other than a summary proceeding pursuant to subparagraph (C) of this paragraph), the clearing agency shall bring specific charges, notify such participant of, and give him an opportunity to defend against such charges, and keep a record. A determination by the clearing agency to impose a disciplinary sanction shall be supported by a statement setting forth—

(i) any act or practice in which such participant has been found to have engaged, or which such participant has been found to have omitted;

(ii) the specific provisions of the rules of the clearing agency which any such act or practice, or omission to act, is deemed to violate; and

(iii) the sanction imposed and the reasons therefor.

(B) In any proceeding by a registered clearing agency to determine whether a person shall be denied participation or prohibited or limited with respect to access to services offered by the clearing agency, the clearing agency shall notify such person of, and give him an opportunity to be heard upon the specific grounds for denial or prohibition or limitation under consideration and keep a record. A determination by the clearing agency to deny participation or prohibit or limit a person with respect to access to services offered by the clearing agency shall be supported by a statement setting forth the specific grounds on which the denial or prohibition or limitation is based.

(C) A registered clearing agency may summarily suspend and close the accounts of a participant who (i) has been and is expelled or suspended from any self-regulatory organization, (ii) is in default of any delivery of funds or securities to the clearing agency, or (iii) is in such financial or operating difficulty that the clearing agency determines and so notifies the appropriate regulatory agency for such participant that such suspension and closing of accounts are necessary for the protection of the clearing agency, its participants, creditors, or investors. A participant so summarily suspended shall be promptly afforded an opportunity for a hearing by the clearing agency in accordance with the provisions of subparagraph (A) of this paragraph. The appropriate regulatory agency for such participant, by order, may stay any such summary suspension on its own motion or upon application by any person aggrieved thereby, if such appropriate regulatory agency determines summarily or after notice and opportunity for hearing (which hearing may consist solely of the submission of affidavits or presentation of oral arguments) that such stay is consistent with the public interest and the protection of investors.

(6) No registered clearing agency shall prohibit or limit access by any person to services offered by any participant therein.

(7) (A) A clearing agency that is regulated directly or indirectly by the Commodity Futures Trading Commission through its association with a designated contract market for security futures products that is a national securities exchange registered pursuant to section 6(g), and that would be required to register pursuant to paragraph (1) of this subsection only because it performs the functions of a clearing agency with respect to security futures products effected pursuant to the rules of the designated contract market with which such agency is associated, is exempted from the provisions of this section and the rules and regulations thereunder, except that if such a clearing agency performs the functions of a clearing agency with respect to a security futures product that is not cash settled, it must have arrangements in place with a registered clearing agency to effect the payment and delivery of the securities underlying the security futures product.

(B) Any clearing agency that performs the functions of a clearing agency with respect to security futures products must coordinate with and develop fair and reasonable links with any and all other clearing agencies that perform the functions of a clearing agency with respect to security futures products, in order to permit, as of the compliance date (as defined in section 6(h)(6)(C)), security futures products to be purchased on one market and offset on another market that trades such products.

(8) A registered clearing agency shall be permitted to provide facilities for the clearance and settlement of any derivative agreements, contracts, or transactions that are excluded from the Commodity Exchange Act, subject to the requirements of this section and to such rules and regulations as the Commission may prescribe as necessary or appropriate in the public interest, for the protection of investors, or otherwise in furtherance of the purposes of this title.

(c) (1) Except as otherwise provided in this section, it shall be unlawful for any transfer agent, unless registered in accordance with this section, directly or indirectly, to make use of the mails or any means or instrumentality of interstate commerce to perform the function of a transfer agent with respect to any security registered under section 12 of this title or which would be required to be registered except for the exemption from registration provided by subsection (g)(2)(B) or (g)(2)(G) of that section. The appropriate regulatory agency, by rule or order, upon its own motion or upon application, may conditionally or unconditionally exempt any person or security or class of persons or securities from any provision of this section or any rule or regulation prescribed under this section, if the appropriate regulatory agency finds (A) that such exemption is in the public interest and consistent with the protection of investors and the purposes of this section, including the prompt and accurate clearance and settlement of securities transactions and the safeguarding of securities and funds, and (B) the Commission does not object to such exemption.

(2) A transfer agent may be registered by filing with the appropriate regulatory agency for such transfer agent an application for registration in such form and containing such information and documents concerning such transfer agent and any persons associated with the transfer agent as such appropriate regulatory agency may prescribe as necessary or appropriate in furtherance of

the purposes of this section. Except as hereinafter provided, such registration shall become effective 45 days after receipt of such application by such appropriate regulatory agency or within such shorter period of time as such appropriate regulatory agency may determine.

(3) The appropriate regulatory agency for a transfer agent, by order, shall deny registration to, censure, place limitations on the activities, functions, or operations of, suspend for a period not exceeding 12 months, or revoke the registration of such transfer agent, if such appropriate regulatory agency finds, on the record after notice and opportunity for hearing, that such denial, censure, placing of limitations, suspension, or revocation is in the public interest and that such transfer agent, whether prior or subsequent to becoming such, or any person associated with such transfer agent, whether prior or subsequent to becoming so associated—

(A) has committed or omitted any act, or is subject to an order or finding, enumerated in subparagraph (A), (D), (E), (H), or (G) of paragraph (4) of section 15(b) of this title, has been convicted of any offense specified in subparagraph (B) of such paragraph (4) within ten years of the commencement of the proceedings under this paragraph, or is enjoined from any action, conduct, or practice specified in subparagraph (C) of such paragraph (4); or

(B) is subject to an order entered pursuant to subparagraph (C) of paragraph (4) of this subsection barring or suspending the right of such person to be associated with a transfer agent.

(4)(A) Pending final determination whether any registration by a transfer agent under this subsection shall be denied, the appropriate regulatory agency for such transfer agent, by order, may postpone the effective date of such registration for a period not to exceed fifteen days, but if, after notice and opportunity for hearing (which may consist solely of affidavits and oral arguments), it shall appear to such appropriate regulatory agency to be necessary or appropriate in the public interest or for the protection of investors to postpone the effective date of such registration until final determination, such appropriate regulatory agency shall so order. Pending final determination whether any registration under this subsection shall be revoked, such appropriate regulatory agency, by order, may suspend such registration, if such suspension appears to such appropriate regulatory agency, after notice and opportunity for hearing, to be necessary or appropriate in the public interest or for the protection of investors.

(B) A registered transfer agent may, upon such terms and conditions as the appropriate regulatory agency for such transfer agent deems necessary or appropriate in the public interest, for the protection of investors, or in furtherance of the purposes of this section, withdraw from registration by filing a written notice of withdrawal with such appropriate regulatory agency. If such appropriate regulatory agency finds that any transfer agent for which it is the appropriate regulatory agency, is no longer in existence or has ceased to do business as a transfer agent, such appropriate regulatory agency, by order, shall cancel or deny the registration.

(C) The appropriate regulatory agency for a transfer agent, by order, shall censure or place limitations on the activities or functions of any person associated, seeking to become associated, or, at the time of the alleged misconduct, associated or seeking to become associated with the transfer agent, or suspend for a period not exceeding twelve months or bar any such person from being associated with the transfer agent, if the appropriate regulatory agency finds, on the record after notice and opportunity for hearing, that such censure, placing of limitations, suspension, or bar is in the public interest and that such person has committed or omitted any act, or is subject to an order or finding, enumerated in subparagraph (A), (D), (E), (H), or (G) of paragraph (4) of section 15(b) of this title, has been convicted of any offense specified in subparagraph (B) of such paragraph (4) within ten years of the commencement of the proceedings under this paragraph, or is enjoined from any action, conduct, or practice specified in subparagraph (C) of such paragraph (4). It shall be unlawful for any person as to whom such an order suspending or barring him from being associated with a transfer agent is in effect willfully to become, or to be, associated with a transfer agent without the consent of the appropriate regulatory agency that entered the order and the appropriate regulatory agency for that transfer agent. It shall be unlawful for any transfer agent to permit such a person to become, or remain, a person associated with it without the consent of such appropriate regulatory agencies, if the transfer agent knew, or in the exercise of reasonable care should have known, of such order. The Commission may establish, by rule, procedures by which a transfer agent reasonably can determine whether a person associated or seeking to become associated with it is subject to any such order, and may require, by rule, that any transfer agent comply with such procedures.

(d) (1) No registered clearing agency or registered transfer agent shall, directly or indirectly, engage in any activity as clearing agency or transfer agent in contravention of such rules and regulations (A) as the Commission may prescribe as necessary or appropriate in the public interest, for the protection of investors, or otherwise in furtherance of the purposes of this title, or (B) as the appropriate regulatory agency for such clearing agency or transfer agent may prescribe as necessary or appropriate for the safeguarding of securities and funds.

(2) With respect to any clearing agency or transfer agent for which the Commission is not the appropriate regulatory agency, the appropriate regulatory agency for such clearing agency or transfer agent may, in accordance with section 8 of the Federal Deposit Insurance Act (12 U.S.C. 1818), enforce compliance by such clearing agency or transfer agent with the provisions of this section, sections 17 and 19 of this title, and the rules and regulations thereunder. For purposes of the preceding sentence, any violation of any such provision shall constitute adequate basis for the issuance of an order under section 8(b) or 8(c) of the Federal Deposit Insurance Act, and the participants in any such clearing agency and the persons doing business with any such transfer agent shall be deemed to be "depositors" as that term is used in section 8(c) of that Act.

(3) (A) With respect to any clearing agency or transfer agent for which the Commission is not the appropriate regulatory agency, the Commission and the appropriate regulatory agency for such clearing agency or transfer agent shall consult and cooperate with each other, and, as may be appropriate, with State banking authorities having supervision over such clearing agency or transfer agent toward the end that, to the maximum extent practicable, their respective regulatory responsibilities may be fulfilled and the rules and regulations applicable to such clearing agency or transfer agent may be in accord with both sound banking practices and a national system for the prompt and accurate clearance and settlement of securities transactions. In accordance with this objective—

(i) the Commission and such appropriate regulatory agency shall, at least fifteen days prior to the issuance for public comment of any proposed rule or regulation or adoption of any rule or regulation concerning such clearing agency or transfer agent, consult and request the views of the other; and

(ii) such appropriate regulatory agency shall assume primary responsibility to examine and enforce compliance by such clearing agency or transfer agent with the provisions of this section and sections 17 and 19 of this title.

(B) Nothing in the preceding subparagraph or elsewhere in this title shall be construed to impair or limit (other than by the requirement of notification) the Commission's authority to make rules under any provision of this title or to enforce compliance pursuant to any provision of this title by any clearing agency, transfer agent, or person associated with a transfer agent with the provisions of this title and the rules and regulations thereunder.

(4) Nothing in this section shall be construed to impair the authority of any State banking authority or other State or Federal regulatory authority having jurisdiction over a person registered as a clearing agency, transfer agent, or person associated with a transfer agent, to make and enforce rules governing such person which are not inconsistent with this title and the rules and regulations thereunder.

(5) A registered transfer agent may not, directly or indirectly, engage in any activity in connection with the guarantee of a signature of an endorser of a security, including the acceptance or rejection of such guarantee, in contravention of such rules and regulations as the Commission may prescribe as necessary or appropriate in the public interest, for the protection of investors, to facilitate the equitable treatment of financial institutions which issue such guarantees, or otherwise in furtherance of the purposes of this title.

(e) The Commission shall use its authority under this title to end the physical movement of securities certificates in connection with the settlement among brokers and dealers of transactions in securities consummated by means of the mails or any means or instrumentalities of interstate commerce.

(f) (1) Notwithstanding any provision of State law, except as provided in paragraph (3), if the Commission makes each of the findings described in paragraph (2) (A), the Commission may adopt rules concerning—

(A) the transfer of certificated or uncertificated securities (other than government securities issued pursuant to chapter 31 of title 31, United States Code, or securities otherwise processed within a book-entry system operated by the Federal Reserve banks pursuant to a Federal book-entry regulation) or limited interests (including security interests) therein; and

(B) rights and obligations of purchasers, sellers, owners, lenders, borrowers, and financial intermediaries (including brokers, dealers, banks, and clearing agencies) involved in or affected by such transfers, and the rights of third parties whose interests in such securities devolve from such transfers.

(2) (A) The findings described in this paragraph are findings by the Commission that—

(i) such rule is necessary or appropriate for the protection of investors or in the public interest and is reasonably designed to promote the prompt, accurate, and safe clearance and settlement of securities transactions;

(ii) in the absence of a uniform rule, the safe and efficient operation of the national system for clearance and settlement of securities transactions will be, or is, substantially impeded; and

(iii) to the extent such rule will impair or diminish, directly or indirectly, rights of persons specified in paragraph (1) (B) under State law concerning transfers of securities (or limited interests therein), the benefits of such rule outweigh such impairment or diminution of rights.

(B) In making the findings described in subparagraph (A), the Commission shall give consideration to the recommendations of the Advisory Committee established under paragraph (4), and it shall consult with and consider the views of the Secretary of the Treasury and the Board of Governors of the Federal Reserve System. If the Secretary of the Treasury objects, in writing, to any proposed rule of the Commission on the basis of the Secretary's view on the issues described in clauses (i), (ii), and (iii) of subparagraph (A), the Commission shall consider all feasible alternatives to the proposed rule, and it shall not adopt any such rule unless the Commission makes an explicit finding that the rule is the most practicable method for achieving safe and efficient operation of the national clearance and settlement system.

(3) Any State may, prior to the expiration of 2 years after the Commission adopts a rule under this subsection, enact a statute that specifically refers to this subsection and the specific rule thereunder and establishes, prospectively from the date of enactment of the State statute, a provision that differs from that applicable under the Commission's rule.

(4) (A) Within 90 days after the date of enactment of this subsection, the Commission shall (and at such times thereafter as the Commission may determine, the Commission may), after consultation with the Secretary of the Treasury and the Board of Governors of the Federal Reserve System, establish an advisory committee under the Federal Advisory Committee Act (5 U.S.C. App.). The Advisory Committee shall be directed to consider and report to the Commission on such matters as the Commission, after consultation with the Secretary of the Treasury and the Board of Governors of the Federal Reserve System, determines, including the areas, if any, in which State commercial laws and related Federal laws concerning the transfer of certificated or uncertificated securities, limited interests (including security interests) in such securities, or the creation or perfection of security interests in such securities do not provide the necessary certainty, uniformity, and clarity for purchasers, sellers, owners, lenders, borrowers, and financial intermediaries concerning their respective rights and obligations.

(B) The Advisory Committee shall consist of 15 members, of which—

(i) 11 shall be designated by the Commission in accordance with the Federal Advisory Committee Act; and

(ii) 2 each shall be designated by the Board of Governors of the Federal Reserve System and the Secretary of the Treasury.

(C) The Advisory Committee shall conduct its activities in accordance with the Federal Advisory Committee Act. Within 6 months of its designation, or such longer time as the

Commission may designate, the Advisory Committee shall issue a report to the Commission, and shall cause copies of that report to be delivered to the Secretary of the Treasury and the Chairman of the Board of Governors of the Federal Reserve System.

AUTOMATED QUOTATION SYSTEMS FOR PENNY STOCKS

Sec. 17B. (a) FINDINGS.—The Congress finds that—

(1) the market for penny stocks suffers from a lack of reliable and accurate quotation and last sale information available to investors and regulators;

(2) it is in the public interest and appropriate for the protection of investors and the maintenance of fair and orderly markets to improve significantly the information available to brokers, dealers, investors, and regulators with respect to quotations for and transactions in penny stocks; and

(3) a fully implemented automated quotation system for penny stocks would meet the information needs of investors and market participants and would add visibility and regulatory and surveillance data to that market.

(b) MANDATE TO FACILITATE THE ESTABLISHMENT OF AUTOMATED QUOTATION SYSTEMS.—

(1) IN GENERAL.—The Commission shall facilitate the wide-spread dissemination of reliable and accurate last sale and quotation information with respect to penny stocks in accordance with the findings set forth in subsection (a), with a view toward establishing, at the earliest feasible time, one or more automated quotation systems that will collect and disseminate information regarding all penny stocks.

(2) CHARACTERISTICS OF SYSTEMS.—Each such automated quotation system shall—

(A) be operated by a registered securities association or a national securities exchange in accordance with such rules as the Commission and these entities shall prescribe;

(B) collect and disseminate quotation and transaction information;

(C) except as provided in subsection (c), provide bid and ask quotations of participating brokers or dealers, or comparably accurate and reliable pricing information, which shall constitute firm bids or offers for at least such minimum numbers of shares or minimum dollar amounts as the Commission and the registered securities association or national securities exchange shall require; and

(D) provide for the reporting of the volume of penny stock transactions, including last sale reporting, when the volume reaches appropriate levels that the Commission shall specify by rule or order.

(c) EXEMPTIVE AUTHORITY.—The Commission may, by rule or order, grant such exemptions, in whole or in part, conditionally or unconditionally, to any penny stock or class of penny stocks from the requirements of subsection (b) as the Commission determines to be consistent with the public interest, the protection of investors, and the maintenance of fair and orderly markets.

(d) COMMISSION REPORTING REQUIREMENTS.—The Commission shall, in each of the first 5 annual reports (under section 23(b)(1) of this title) submitted more than 12 months after the date of enactment of this section, include a description of the status of the penny stock automated quotation system or systems required by subsection (b). Such description shall include—

(1) a review of the development, implementation, and progress of the project, including achievement of significant milestones and current project schedule; and

(2) a review of the activities of registered securities associations and national securities exchanges in the development of the system.

LIABILITY FOR MISLEADING STATEMENTS

Sec. 18. (a) Any person who shall make or cause to be made any statement in any application, report, or document filed pursuant to this title or any rule or regulation thereunder or any undertaking contained in a registration statement as provided in subsection (d) of section 15 of this title, which statement was at the time and in the light of the circumstances under which it was made false or misleading with respect to any material fact, shall be liable to any person (not knowing that such statement was false or misleading) who, in reliance upon such statement, shall have purchased or sold a security at a price which was affected by such statement, for damages caused by such reliance, unless the person sued shall prove that he acted in good faith and had no knowledge that such statement was false or misleading. A person seeking to enforce such liability may sue at law or in equity in any court of competent jurisdiction. In any such suit the court may, in its discretion, require an undertaking for the payment of the costs of such suit, and assess reasonable costs, including reasonable attorneys' fees, against either party litigant.

(b) Every person who becomes liable to make payment under this section may recover contribution as in cases of contract from any person who, if joined in the original suit, would have been liable to make the same payment.

(c) No action shall be maintained to enforce any liability created under this section unless brought within one year after the discovery of the facts constituting the cause of action and within three years after such cause of action accrued.

REGISTRATION, RESPONSIBILITIES, AND OVERSIGHT OF SELF-REGULATORY ORGANIZATIONS

Sec. 19. (a)(1) The Commission shall, upon the filing of an application for registration as a national securities exchange, registered securities association, or registered clearing agency, pursuant to section 6, 15A or 17A of this title, respectively, publish notice of the filing and afford interested persons an opportunity to submit written data, views, and arguments concerning such application. Within ninety days of the date of publication of such notice (or within such longer period as to which the applicant consents), the Commission shall—

(A) by order grant such registration, or

(B) institute proceedings to determine whether registration should be denied. Such proceedings shall include notice of the grounds for denial under consideration and opportunity for hearing and shall be concluded within one hundred eighty days of the date of publication of notice of the filing of the application for registration. At the conclusion of such proceedings the Commission, by order, shall grant or deny such registration. The Commission may extend the time for conclusion of such proceedings for up to ninety days if it finds good cause for such extension and publishes its reasons for so finding or for such longer period as to which the applicant consents.

The Commission shall grant such registration if it finds that the requirements of this title and the rules and regulations thereunder with respect to the applicant are satisfied. The Commission shall deny such registration if it does not make such finding.

(2) With respect to an application for registration filed by a clearing agency for which the Commission is not the appropriate regulatory agency—

(A) The Commission shall not grant registration prior to the sixtieth day after the date of publication of notice of the filing of such application unless the appropriate regulatory agency for such clearing agency has notified the Commission of such appropriate regulatory agency's determination that such clearing agency is so organized and has the capacity to be able to safeguard securities and funds in its custody or control or for which it is responsible and that the rules of such clearing agency are designed to assure the safeguarding of such securities and funds.

(B) The Commission shall institute proceedings in accordance with paragraph (1)(B) of this subsection to determine whether registration should be denied if the appropriate regulatory agency for such clearing agency notifies the Commission within sixty days of the date of publication of notice of the filing of such application of such appropriate regulatory agency's (i) determination that such clearing agency may not be so organized or have the capacity to be able to safeguard securities or funds in its custody or control or for which it is responsible or that the rules of such clearing agency may not be designed to assure the safeguarding of such securities and funds and (ii) reasons for such determination.

(C) The Commission shall deny registration if the appropriate regulatory agency for such clearing agency notifies the Commission prior to the conclusion of proceedings instituted in accordance with paragraph (1)(B) of this subsection of such appropriate regulatory agency's (i) determination that such clearing agency is not so organized or does not have the capacity to be able to safeguard securities or funds in its custody or control or for which it is responsible or that the rules of such clearing agency are not designed to assure the safeguarding of such securities or funds and (ii) reasons for such determination.

(3) A self-regulatory organization may, upon such terms and conditions as the Commission, by rule, deems necessary or appropriate in the public interest or for the protection of investors, withdraw from registration by filing a written notice of withdrawal with the Commission. If the Commission finds that any self-regulatory organization is no longer in existence or has ceased to do business in the capacity specified in its application for registration, the Commission, by order, shall cancel its registration. Upon the withdrawal of a national securities association from registration or the cancellation, suspension, or revocation of the registration of a national securities association, the registration of any association affiliated therewith shall automatically terminate.

(b)(1) Each self-regulatory organization shall file with the Commission, in accordance with such rules as the Commission may prescribe, copies of any proposed rule or any proposed change in, addition to, or deletion from the rules of such self-regulatory organization (hereinafter in this subsection collectively referred to as a "proposed rule change") accompanied by a concise general statement of the basis and purpose of such proposed rule change. The Commission shall, upon the filing of any proposed rule change, publish notice thereof together with the terms of substance of the proposed rule change or a description of the subjects and issues involved. The Commission shall give interested persons an opportunity to submit written data, views, and arguments concerning such proposed rule change. No proposed rule change shall take effect unless approved by the Commission or otherwise permitted in accordance with the provisions of this subsection.

(2) Within thirty-five days of the date of publication of notice of the filing of a proposed rule change in accordance with paragraph (1) of this subsection, or within such longer period as the Commission may designate up to ninety days of such date if it finds such longer period to be appropriate and publishes its reasons for so finding or as to which the self-regulatory organization consents, the Commission shall—

(A) by order approve such proposed rule change, or

(B) institute proceedings to determine whether the proposed rule change should be disapproved. Such proceedings shall include notice of the grounds for disapproval under consideration and opportunity for hearing and be concluded within one hundred eighty days of the date of publication of notice of the filing of the proposed rule change. At the conclusion of such proceedings the Commission, by order, shall approve or disapprove such proposed rule change. The Commission may extend the time for conclusion of such proceedings for up to sixty days if it finds good cause for such extension and publishes its reasons for so finding or for such longer period as to which the self-regulatory organization consents.

The Commission shall approve a proposed rule change of a self-regulatory organization if it finds that such proposed rule change is consistent with the requirements of this title and the rules and regulations thereunder applicable to such organization. The Commission shall disapprove a proposed rule change of a self-regulatory organization if it does not make such finding. The Commission shall not approve any proposed rule change prior to the thirtieth day after the date of publication of notice of the filing thereof, unless the Commission finds good cause for so doing and publishes its reasons for so finding.

(3)(A) Notwithstanding the provisions of paragraph (2) of this subsection, a proposed rule change may take effect upon filing with the Commission if designated by the self-regulatory organization as (i) constituting a stated policy, practice, or interpretation with respect to the meaning, administration, or enforcement of an existing rule of the self-regulatory organization, (ii) establishing or changing a due, fee, or other charge imposed by the self-regulatory organization, or (iii) concerned solely with the administration of the self-regulatory organization or other matters which the Commission, by rule, consistent with the public interest and the purposes of this subsection, may specify as without the provisions of such paragraph (2).

(B) Notwithstanding any other provision of this subsection, a proposed rule change may be put into effect summarily if it appears to the Commission that such action is necessary for the protection of investors, the maintenance of fair and orderly markets, or the safeguarding of securities or funds. Any proposed rule change so put into effect shall be filed promptly thereafter in accordance with the provisions of paragraph (1) of this subsection.

(C) Any proposed rule change of a self-regulatory organization which has taken effect pursuant to subparagraph (A) or (B) of this paragraph may be enforced by such organization to the extent it is not inconsistent with the provisions of this title, the rules and regulations thereunder, and applicable Federal and State law. At any time within sixty days of the date of filing of such a proposed rule change in accordance with the provisions of paragraph (1) of this subsection, the Commission summarily may abrogate the change in the rules of the self-regulatory organization made thereby and require that the proposed rule change be refiled in accordance with the provisions of paragraph (1) of this subsection and reviewed in accordance with the provisions of paragraph (2) of this subsection, if it appears to the Commission that such action is necessary or appropriate in the public interest, for the protection of investors, or otherwise in furtherance of the purposes of this title. Commission action pursuant to the preceding sentence shall not affect the validity or force of the rule change during the period it was in effect and shall not be reviewable under section 25 of this title nor deemed to be "final agency action" for purposes of section 704 of title 5, United States Code.

(4) With respect to a proposed rule change filed by a registered clearing agency for which the Commission is not the appropriate regulatory agency—

(A) The Commission shall not approve any such proposed rule change prior to the thirtieth day after the date of publication of notice of the filing thereof unless the appropriate regulatory agency for such clearing agency has notified the Commission of such appropriate regulatory agency's determination that the proposed rule change is consistent with the safeguarding of securities and funds in the custody or control of such clearing agency or for which it is responsible.

(B) The Commission shall institute proceedings in accordance with paragraph (2)(B) of this subsection to determine whether any such proposed rule change should be disapproved, if the appropriate regulatory agency for such clearing agency notifies the Commission within thirty days of the date of publication of notice of the filing of the proposed rule change of such appropriate regulatory agency's (i) determination that the proposed rule change may be inconsistent with the safeguarding of securities or funds in the custody or control of such clearing agency or for which it is responsible and (ii) reasons for such determination.

(C) The Commission shall disapprove any such proposed rule change if the appropriate regulatory agency for such clearing agency notifies the Commission prior to the conclusion of proceedings instituted in accordance with paragraph (2)(B) of this subsection of such appropriate regulatory agency's (i) determination that the proposed rule change is inconsistent with the safeguarding of securities or funds in the custody or control of such clearing agency or for which it is responsible and (ii) reasons for such determination.

(D) The Commission shall abrogate any change in the rules of such a clearing agency made by a proposed rule change which has taken effect pursuant to paragraph (3) of this subsection, require that the proposed rule change be refiled in accordance with the provisions of paragraph (1) of this subsection, and reviewed in accordance with the provisions of paragraph (2) of this subsection, if the appropriate regulatory agency for such clearing agency notifies the Commission within thirty days of the date of filing of such proposed rule change of such appropriate regulatory agency's (i) determination that the rules of such clearing agency as so changed may be inconsistent with the safeguarding of securities or funds in the custody or control of such clearing agency or for which it is responsible and (ii) reasons for such determination.

(5) The Commission shall consult with and consider the views of the Secretary of the Treasury prior to approving a proposed rule filed by a registered securities association that

primarily concerns conduct related to transactions in government securities, except where the Commission determines that an emergency exists requiring expeditious or summary action and publishes its reasons therefor. If the Secretary of the Treasury comments in writing to the Commission on a proposed rule that has been published for comment, the Commission shall respond in writing to such written comment before approving the proposed rule. If the Secretary of the Treasury determines, and notifies the Commission, that such rule, if implemented, would, or as applied does (i) adversely affect the liquidity or efficiency of the market for government securities; or (ii) impose any burden on competition not necessary or appropriate in furtherance of the purposes of this section, the Commission shall, prior to adopting the proposed rule, find that such rule is necessary and appropriate in furtherance of the purposes of this section notwithstanding the Secretary's determination.

(6) In approving rules described in paragraph (5), the Commission shall consider the sufficiency and appropriateness of then existing laws and rules applicable to government securities brokers, government securities dealers, and persons associated with government securities brokers and government securities dealers.

(7) SECURITY FUTURES PRODUCT RULE CHANGES.—

(A) FILING REQUIRED.—A self-regulatory organization that is an exchange registered with the Commission pursuant to section 6(g) of this title or that is a national securities association registered pursuant to section 15A(k) of this title shall file with the Commission, in accordance with such rules as the Commission may prescribe, copies of any proposed rule change or any proposed change in, addition to, or deletion from the rules of such self-regulatory organization (hereinafter in this paragraph collectively referred to as a 'proposed rule change') that relates to higher margin levels, fraud or manipulation, recordkeeping, reporting, listing standards, or decimal pricing for security futures products, sales practices for security futures products for persons who effect transactions in security futures products, or rules effectuating such self-regulatory organization's obligation to enforce the securities laws. Such proposed rule change shall be accompanied by a concise general statement of the basis and purpose of such proposed rule change. The Commission shall, upon the filing of any proposed rule change, promptly publish notice thereof together with the terms of substance of the proposed rule change or a description of the subjects and issues involved. The Commission shall give interested persons an opportunity to submit data, views, and arguments concerning such proposed rule change.

(B) FILING WITH CFTC.—A proposed rule change filed with the Commission pursuant to subparagraph (A) shall be filed concurrently with the Commodity Futures Trading Commission. Such proposed rule change may take effect upon filing of a written certification with the Commodity Futures Trading Commission under section 5c(c) of the Commodity Exchange Act, upon a determination by the Commodity Futures Trading Commission that review of the proposed rule change is not necessary, or upon approval of the proposed rule change by the Commodity Futures Trading Commission.

(C) ABROGATION OF RULE CHANGES.—Any proposed rule change of a self-regulatory organization that has taken effect pursuant to subparagraph (B) may be enforced by such self-regulatory organization to the extent such rule is not inconsistent with the provisions of this title, the rules and regulations thereunder, and applicable Federal law. At any time within 60 days of the date of the filing of a written certification with the Commodity Futures Trading Commission under section 5c(c) of the Commodity Exchange Act, the date the Commodity Futures Trading Commission determines that review of such proposed rule change is not necessary, or the date the Commodity Futures Trading Commission approves such proposed rule change, the Commission, after consultation with the Commodity Futures Trading Commission, may summarily abrogate the proposed rule change and require that the proposed rule change be refiled in accordance with the provisions of paragraph (1), if it appears to the Commission that such proposed rule change unduly burdens competition or efficiency, conflicts with the securities laws, or is inconsistent with the public interest and the protection of investors. Commission action pursuant to the preceding sentence shall not affect the validity or force of the rule change during the period it was in effect and shall not be reviewable under section 25 of this title nor deemed to be a final agency action for purposes of section 704 of title 5, United States Code.

(D) REVIEW OF RESUBMITTED ABROGATED RULES.—

(i) PROCEEDINGS.—Within 35 days of the date of publication of notice of the filing of a proposed rule change that is abrogated in accordance with subparagraph (C) and refiled in accordance with paragraph (1), or within such longer period as the Commission may designate up to 90 days after such date if the Commission finds such longer period to be appropriate and publishes its reasons for so finding or as to which the self-regulatory organization consents, the Commission shall—

(I) by order approve such proposed rule change; or

(II) after consultation with the Commodity Futures Trading Commission, institute proceedings to determine whether the proposed rule change should be disapproved. Proceedings under subclause (II) shall include notice of the grounds for disapproval under consideration and opportunity for hearing and be concluded within 180 days after the date of publication of notice of the filing of the proposed rule change. At the conclusion of such proceedings, the Commission, by order, shall approve or disapprove such proposed rule change. The Commission may extend the time for conclusion of such proceedings for up to 60 days if the Commission finds good cause for such extension and publishes its reasons for so finding or for such longer period as to which the self-regulatory organization consents.

(ii) GROUNDS FOR APPROVAL.—The Commission shall approve a proposed rule change of a self-regulatory organization under this subparagraph if the Commission finds that such proposed rule change does not unduly burden competition or efficiency, does not conflict with the securities laws, and is not inconsistent with the public interest or the protection of investors. The Commission shall disapprove such a proposed rule change of a self-regulatory organization if it does not make such finding. The Commission shall not approve any proposed rule change prior to the 30th day after the date of publication of notice of the filing thereof, unless the Commission finds good cause for so doing and publishes its reasons for so finding.

(8) DECIMAL PRICING.—Not later than 9 months after the date on which trading in any security futures product commences under this title, all self-regulatory organizations listing or trading security futures products shall file proposed rule changes necessary to implement decimal pricing of security futures products. The Commission may not require such rules to contain equal minimum increments in such decimal pricing.

(9) CONSULTATION WITH CFTC.—

(A) CONSULTATION REQUIRED.—The Commission shall consult with and consider the views of the Commodity Futures Trading Commission prior to approving or disapproving a proposed rule change filed by a national securities association registered pursuant to section 15A(a) or a national securities exchange subject to the provisions of subsection (a) that primarily concerns conduct related to transactions in security futures products, except where the Commission determines that an emergency exists requiring expeditious or summary action and publishes its reasons therefor.

(B) RESPONSES TO CFTC COMMENTS AND FINDINGS.—If the Commodity Futures Trading Commission comments in writing to the Commission on a proposed rule that has been published for comment, the Commission shall respond in writing to such written comment before approving or disapproving the proposed rule. If the Commodity Futures Trading Commission determines, and notifies the Commission, that such rule, if implemented or as applied, would—

(i) adversely affect the liquidity or efficiency of the market for security futures products; or

(ii) impose any burden on competition not necessary or appropriate in furtherance of the purposes of this section,

the Commission shall, prior to approving or disapproving the proposed rule, find that such rule is necessary and appropriate in furtherance of the purposes of this section notwithstanding the Commodity Futures Trading Commission's determination.

(c) The Commission, by rule, may abrogate, add to, and delete from (hereinafter in this subsection collectively referred to as "amend") the rules of a self-regulatory organization (other than a registered clearing agency) as the Commission deems necessary or appropriate to insure the fair administration of the self-regulatory organization, to conform its rules to requirements of this title and the rules and regulations thereunder applicable to such organization, or otherwise in furtherance of the purposes of this title, in the following manner:

(1) The Commission shall notify the self-regulatory organization and publish notice of the proposed rulemaking in the Federal Register. The notice shall include the text of the proposed amendment to the rules of the self-regulatory organization and a statement of the Commission's reasons, including any pertinent facts, for commencing such proposed rulemaking.

(2) The Commission shall give interested persons an opportunity for the oral presentation of data, views, and arguments, in addition to an opportunity to make written submissions. A transcript shall be kept of any oral presentation.

(3) A rule adopted pursuant to this subsection shall incorporate the text of the amendment to the rules of the self-regulatory organization and a statement of the Commission's basis for and purpose in so amending such rules. This statement shall include an identification of any facts on which the Commission considers its determination so to amend the rules of the self-regulatory agency to be based, including the reasons for the Commission's conclusions as to any of such facts which were disputed in the rulemaking.

(4) (A) Except as provided in paragraphs (1) through (3) of this subsection, rulemaking under this subsection shall be in accordance with the procedures specified in section 553 of title 5, United States Code, for rulemaking not on the record.

(B) Nothing in this subsection shall be construed to impair or limit the Commission's power to make, or to modify or alter the procedures the Commission may follow in making rules and regulations pursuant to any other authority under this title.

(C) Any amendment to the rules of a self-regulatory organization made by the Commission pursuant to this subsection shall be considered for all purposes of this title to be part of the rules of such self-regulatory organization and shall not be considered to be a rule of the Commission.

(5) With respect to rules described in subsection (b) (5), the Commission shall consult with and consider the views of the Secretary of the Treasury before abrogating, adding to, and deleting from such rules, except where the Commission determines that an emergency exists requiring expeditious or summary action and publishes its reasons therefor.

(d) (1) If any self-regulatory organization imposes any final disciplinary sanction on any member thereof or participant therein, denies membership or participation to any applicant, or prohibits or limits any person in respect to access to services offered by such organization or member thereof or if any self-regulatory organization (other than a registered clearing agency) imposes any final disciplinary sanction on any person associated with a member, or bars any person from becoming associated with a member, the self-regulatory organization shall promptly file notice thereof with the appropriate regulatory agency for the self-regulatory organization and (if other than the appropriate regulatory agency for the self-regulatory organization) the appropriate regulatory agency for such member, participant, applicant, or other person. The notice shall be in such form and contain such information as the appropriate regulatory agency for the self-regulatory organization, by rule, may prescribe as necessary or appropriate in furtherance of the purposes of this title.

(2) Any action with respect to which a self-regulatory organization is required by paragraph (1) of this subsection to file notice shall be subject to review by the appropriate regulatory agency for such member, participant, applicant, or other person, on its own motion, or upon application by any person aggrieved thereby filed within thirty days after the date such notice was filed with such appropriate regulatory agency and received by such aggrieved person, or within such longer period as such appropriate regulatory agency may determine. Application to such appropriate regulatory agency for review, or the institution of review by such appropriate regulatory agency on its own motion, shall not operate as a stay of such action unless such appropriate regulatory agency otherwise orders, summarily or after notice and opportunity for hearing on the question of a stay (which hearing may consist solely of the submission of affidavits or presentation of oral arguments). Each appropriate regulatory agency shall establish for appropriate cases an expedited procedure for consideration and determination of the question of a stay.

(3) The provisions of this subsection shall apply to an exchange registered pursuant to section 6(g) of this title or a national securities association registered pursuant to section 15A(k) of this title only to the extent that such exchange or association imposes any final disciplinary sanction for—

(A) a violation of the Federal securities laws or the rules and regulations thereunder; or

(B) a violation of a rule of such exchange or association, as to which a proposed change would be required to be filed under section 19 of this title, except that, to the extent that the exchange or association rule violation relates to any account, agreement, contract, or transaction, this subsection shall apply only to the extent such violation involves a security futures product.

(e)(1) In any proceeding to review a final disciplinary sanction imposed by a self-regulatory organization on a member thereof or participant therein or a person associated with such a member, after notice and opportunity for hearing (which hearing may consist solely of consideration of the record before the self-regulatory organization and opportunity for the presentation of supporting reasons to affirm, modify, or set aside the sanction)—

(A) if the appropriate regulatory agency for such member, participant, or person associated with a member finds that such member, participant, or person associated with a member has engaged in such acts or practices, or has omitted such acts, as the self-regulatory organization has found him to have engaged in or omitted, that such acts or practices, or omissions to act, are in violation of such provisions of this title, the rules or regulations thereunder, the rules of the self-regulatory organization, or, in the case of a registered securities association, the rules of the Municipal Securities Rulemaking Board as have been specified in the determination of the self-regulatory organization, and that such provisions are, and were applied in a manner, consistent with the purposes of this title, such appropriate regulatory agency, by order, shall so declare and, as appropriate, affirm the sanction imposed by the self-regulatory organization, modify the sanction in accordance with paragraph (2) of this subsection, or remand to the self-regulatory organization for further proceedings; or

(B) if such appropriate regulatory agency does not make any such finding it shall, by order, set aside the sanction imposed by the self-regulatory organization and, if appropriate, remand to the self-regulatory organization for further proceedings.

(2) If the appropriate regulatory agency for a member, participant, or person associated with a member, having due regard for the public interest and the protection of investors, finds after a proceeding in accordance with paragraph (1) of this subsection that a sanction imposed by a self-regulatory organization upon such member, participant, or person associated with a member imposes any burden on competition not necessary or appropriate in furtherance of the purposes of this title or is excessive or oppressive, the appropriate regulatory agency may cancel, reduce, or require the remission of such sanction.

(f) In any proceeding to review the denial of membership or participation in a self-regulatory organization to any applicant, the barring of any person from becoming associated with a member of a self-regulatory organization, or the prohibition or limitation by a self-regulatory organization of any person with respect to access to services offered by the self-regulatory organization or any member thereof if the appropriate regulatory agency for such applicant or person, after notice and opportunity for hearing (which hearing may consist solely of consideration of the record before the self-regulatory organization and opportunity for the presentation of supporting reasons to dismiss the proceeding or set aside the action of the self-regulatory organization) finds that the specific grounds on which such denial, bar, or prohibition or limitation is based exist in fact, that such denial, bar, or prohibition or limitation is in accordance with the rules of the self-regulatory organization, and that such rules are, and were applied in a manner consistent with the purposes of this title, such appropriate regulatory agency, by order, shall dismiss the proceeding. If such appropriate regulatory agency does not make any such finding or if it finds that such denial, bar, or prohibition or limitation imposes any burden on competition not necessary or appropriate in furtherance of the purposes of this title, such appropriate regulatory agency, by order, shall set aside the action of the self-regulatory organization and require it to admit such applicant to membership or participation, permit such person to become associated with a member, or grant such person access to services offered by the self-regulatory organization or member thereof.

(g)(1) Every self-regulatory organization shall comply with the provisions of this title, the rules and regulations thereunder, and its own rules, and (subject to the provisions of section 17(d) of this title, paragraph (2) of this subsection, and the rules thereunder) absent reasonable justification or excuse enforce compliance—

(A) in the case of a national securities exchange, with such provisions by its members and persons associated with its members;

(B) in the case of a registered securities association, with such provisions and the provisions of the rules of the Municipal Securities Rulemaking Board by its members and persons associated with its members; and

(C) in the case of a registered clearing agency, with its own rules by its participants.

(2) The Commission, by rule, consistent with the public interest, the protection of investors, and the other purposes of this title, may relieve any self-regulatory organization of any responsibility under this title to enforce compliance with any specified provision of this title or the rules or regulations thereunder by any member of such organization or person associated with such a member, or any class of such members or persons associated with a member.

(h)(1) The appropriate regulatory agency for a self-regulatory organization is authorized, by order, if in its opinion such action is necessary or appropriate in the public interest, for the protection of investors, or otherwise in furtherance of the purposes of this title, to suspend for a period not exceeding twelve months or revoke the registration of such self-regulatory organization, or to censure or impose limitations upon the activities, functions, and operations of such self-regulatory organization, if such appropriate regulatory agency finds, on the record after notice and opportunity for hearing, that such self-regulatory organization has violated or is unable to comply with any provisions of this title, the rules or regulations thereunder, or its own rules or without reasonable justification or excuse has failed to enforce compliance—

(A) in the case of a national securities exchange, with any such provision by a member thereof or a person associated with a member thereof;

(B) in the case of a registered securities association, with any such provision or any provision of the rules of the Municipal Securities Rulemaking Board by a member thereof or a person associated with a member thereof; or

(C) in the case of a registered clearing agency, with any provision of its own rules by a participant therein.

(2) The appropriate regulatory agency for a self-regulatory organization is authorized, by order, if in its opinion such action is necessary or appropriate in the public interest, for the protection of investors, or otherwise in furtherance of the purposes of this title, to suspend for a period not exceeding twelve months or expel from such self-regulatory organization any member thereof or participant therein, if such member or participant is subject to an order of the Commission pursuant to section 15(b)(4) of this title or if such appropriate regulatory agency finds, on the record after notice and opportunity for hearing, that such member or participant has willfully violated or has effected any transaction for any other person who, such member or participant had reason to believe, was violating with respect to such transaction—

(A) in the case of a national securities exchange, any provision of the Securities Act of 1933, the Investment Advisers Act of 1940, the Investment Company Act of 1940, this title, or the rules or regulations under any of such statutes;

(B) in the case of a registered securities association, any provision of the Securities Act of 1933, the Investment Advisers Act of 1940, the Investment Company Act of 1940, this title, or the rules or regulations under any of such statutes, or the rules of the Municipal Securities Rulemaking Board; or

(C) in the case of a registered clearing agency, any provision of the rules of the clearing agency.

(3) The appropriate regulatory agency for a national securities exchange or registered securities association is authorized, by order, if in its opinion such action is necessary or appropriate in the public interest, for the protection of investors, or otherwise in furtherance of the

purposes of this title, to suspend for a period not exceeding twelve months or to bar any person from being associated with a member of such national securities exchange or registered securities association, if such person is subject to an order of the Commission pursuant to section 15(b)(6) or if such appropriate regulatory agency finds, on the record after notice and opportunity for hearing, that such person has willfully violated or has effected any transaction for any other person who, such person associated with a member had reason to believe, was violating with respect to such transaction—

(A) in the case of a national securities exchange, any provision of the Securities Act of 1933, the Investment Advisers Act of 1940, the Investment Company Act of 1940, this title, or the rules or regulations under any of such statutes; or

(B) in the case of a registered securities association, any provision of the Securities Act of 1933, the Investment Advisers Act of 1940, the Investment Company Act of 1940, this title, the rules or regulations under any of the statutes, or the rules of the Municipal Securities Rulemaking Board.

(4) The appropriate regulatory agency for a self-regulatory organization is authorized by order, if in its opinion such action is necessary or appropriate in the public interest, for the protection of investors, or otherwise in furtherance of the purposes of this title, to remove from office or censure any officer or director of such self-regulatory organization, if such appropriate regulatory agency finds, on the record after notice and opportunity for hearing, that such officer or director has willfully violated any provision of this title, the rules or regulations thereunder, or the rules of such self-regulatory organization, willfully abused his authority, or without reasonable justification or excuse has failed to enforce compliance—

(A) in the case of a national securities exchange, with any such provision by any member or person associated with a member;

(B) in the case of a registered securities association, with any such provision or any provision of the rules of the Municipal Securities Rulemaking Board by any member or person associated with a member; or

(C) in the case of a registered clearing agency, with any provision of the rules of the clearing agency by any participant.

(i) If a proceeding under subsection (h)(1) of this section results in the suspension or revocation of the registration of a clearing agency, the appropriate regulatory agency for such clearing agency may, upon notice to such clearing agency, apply to any court of competent jurisdiction specified in section 21(d) or 27 of this title for the appointment of a trustee. In the event of such an application, the court may, to the extent it deems necessary or appropriate, take exclusive jurisdiction of such clearing agency and the records and assets thereof, wherever located; and the court shall appoint the appropriate regulatory agency for such clearing agency or a person designated by such appropriate regulatory agency as trustee with power to take possession and continue to operate or terminate the operations of such clearing agency in an orderly manner for the protection of participants and investors, subject to such terms and conditions as the court may prescribe.

LIABILITY OF CONTROLLING PERSONS AND PERSONS WHO AID AND ABET VIOLATIONS

Sec. 20. (a) Every person who, directly or indirectly, controls any person liable under any provision of this title or of any rule or regulation thereunder shall also be liable jointly and severally with and to the same extent as such controlled person to any person to whom such controlled person is liable, unless the controlling person acted in good faith and did not directly or indirectly induce the act or acts constituting the violation or cause of action.

(b) It shall be unlawful for any person, directly or indirectly, to do any act or thing which it would be unlawful for such person to do under the provisions of this title or any rule or regulation thereunder through or by means of any other person.

(c) It shall be unlawful for any director or officer of, or any owner of any securities issued by, any issuer required to file any document, report, or information under this title or any rule or regulation thereunder without just cause to hinder, delay, or obstruct the making or filing of any such document, report, or information.

(d) Wherever communicating, or purchasing or selling a security while in possession of, material nonpublic information would violate, or result in liability to any purchaser or seller of the security under any provisions of this title, or any rule or regulation thereunder, such conduct in connection with a purchase or sale of a put, call, straddle, option, privilege or security-based swap agreement (as defined in section 206B of the Gramm-Leach-Bliley Act) with respect to such security or with respect to a group or index of securities including such security, shall also violate and result in comparable liability to any purchaser or seller of that security under such provision, rule, or regulation.

(e) PROSECUTION OF PERSONS WHO AID AND ABET VIOLATIONS.—For purposes of any action brought by the Commission under paragraph (1) or (3) of section 21(d), any person that knowingly provides substantial assistance to another person in violation of a provision of this title, or of any rule or regulation issued under this title, shall be deemed to be in violation of such provision to the same extent as the person to whom such assistance is provided.

(f) The authority of the Commission under this section with respect to security-based swap agreements (as defined in section 206B of the Gramm-Leach-Bliley Act) shall be subject to the restrictions and limitations of section 3A(b) of this title.

LIABILITY TO CONTEMPORANEOUS TRADERS FOR INSIDER TRADING

Sec. 20A. (a) PRIVATE RIGHTS OF ACTION BASED ON CONTEMPORANEOUS TRADING.— Any person who violates any provision of this title or the rules or regulations thereunder by purchasing or selling a security while in possession of material, nonpublic information shall be liable in an action in any court of competent jurisdiction to any person who, contemporaneously with the purchase or sale of securities that is the subject of such violation, has purchased (where such violation is based on a sale of securities) or sold (where such violation is abased on a purchase of securities) securities of the same class.

(b) LIMITATIONS ON LIABILITY.—

(1) CONTEMPORANEOUS TRADING ACTIONS LIMITED TO PROFIT GAINED OR LOSS AVOIDED.—The total amount of damages imposed under subsection (a) shall not exceed the profit gained or loss avoided in the transaction or transactions that are the subject of the violation.

(2) OFFSETTING DISGORGEMENTS AGAINST LIABILITY.—The total amount of damages imposed against any person under subsection (a) shall be diminished by the amounts, if any, that such person may be required to disgorge, pursuant to a court order obtained at the instance of the Commission, in a proceeding brought under section 21(d) of this title relating to the same transaction or transactions.

(3) CONTROLLING PERSON LIABILITY.—No person shall be liable under this section solely by reason of employing another person who is liable under this section, but the liability of a controlling person under this section shall be subject to section 20(a) of this title.

(4) STATUTE OF LIMITATIONS.—No action may be brought under this section more than 5 years after the date of the last transaction that is the subject of the violation.

(c) JOINT AND SEVERAL LIABILITY FOR COMMUNICATING.—Any person who violates any provision of this title or the rules or regulations thereunder by communicating material, nonpublic information shall be jointly and severally liable under subsection (a) with, and to the same extent as, any person or persons liable under subsection (a) to whom the communication was directed.

(d) AUTHORITY NOT TO RESTRICT OTHER EXPRESS OR IMPLIED RIGHTS OF ACTION.— Nothing in this section shall be construed to limit or condition the right of any person to bring an action to enforce a requirement of this title or the availability of any cause of action implied from a provision of this title.

(e) PROVISIONS NOT TO AFFECT PUBLIC PROSECUTIONS.—This section shall not be construed to bar or limit in any manner any action by the Commission or the Attorney General under any other provision of this title, nor shall it bar or limit in any manner any action to recover penalties, or to seek any other order regarding penalties.

INVESTIGATIONS; INJUNCTIONS AND PROSECUTION OF OFFENSES

Sec. 21. (a) (1) The Commission may, in its discretion, make such investigations as it deems necessary to determine whether any person has violated, is violating, or is about to violate any provision of this title, the rules or regulations thereunder, the rules of a national securities exchange or registered securities association of which such person is a member or a person associated with a member, the rules of a registered clearing agency in which such person is a participant, the rules of the Public Company Accounting Oversight Board, of which such person is a registered public accounting firm or a person associated with such a firm, or the rules of the Municipal Securities Rulemaking Board, and may require or permit any person to file with it a statement in writing, under oath or otherwise as the Commission shall determine, as to all the facts and circumstances concerning the matter to be investigated. The Commission is authorized, in its discretion, to publish information concerning any such violations, and to investigate any facts, conditions, practices, or matters which it may deem necessary or proper to aid in the enforcement of such provisions, in the prescribing of rules and regulations under this title, or in securing information to serve as a basis for recommending further legislation concerning the matters to which this title relates.

(2) On request from a foreign securities authority, the Commission may provide assistance in accordance with this paragraph if the requesting authority states that the requesting authority is conducting an investigation which it deems necessary to determine whether any person has violated, is violating, or is about to violate any laws or rules relating to securities matters that the requesting authority administers or enforces. The Commission may, in its discretion, conduct such investigation as the Commission deems necessary to collect information and evidence pertinent to the request for assistance. Such assistance may be provided wihtout regard to whether the facts stated in the request would also constitute a violation of the laws of the United States. In deciding whether to provide such assistance, the Commission shall consider whether (A) the requesting authority has agreed to provide reciprocal assistance in securities matters to the Commission; and (B) compliance with the request would prejudice the public interest of the United States.

(b) For the purpose of any such investigation, or any other proceeding under this title, any member of the Commission or any officer designated by it is empowered to administer oaths and affirmations, subpena witnesses, compel their attendance, take evidence, and require the production of any books, papers, correspondence, memoranda, or other records which the Commission deems relevant or material to the inquiry. Such attendance of witnesses and the production of any such records may be required from any place in the United States or any State at any designated place of hearing.

(c) In case of contumacy by, or refusal to obey a subpena issued to, any person, the Commission may invoke the aid of any court of the United States within the jurisdiction of which such investigation or proceeding is carried on, or where such person resides or carries on business, in requiring the attendance and testimony of witnesses and the production of books, papers, correspondence, memoranda, and other records. And such court may issue an order requiring such person to appear before the Commission or member or officer designated by the Commission, there to produce records, if so ordered, or to give testimony touching the matter under investigation or in question; and any failure to obey such order of the court may be punished by such court as a contempt thereof. All process in any such case may be served in the judicial district whereof such person is an inhabitant or wherever he may be found. Any person who shall, without just cause, fail or refuse to attend and testify or to answer any lawful inquiry or to produce books, papers, correspondence, memoranda, and other records, if in his power so to do, in obedience to the subpena of the Commission, shall be guilty of a misdemeanor and, upon conviction, shall be subject to a fine of not more than $1,000 or to imprisonment for a term of not more than one year, or both.

(d) (1) Whenever it shall appear to the Commission that any person is engaged or is about to engage in any acts or practices constituting a violation of any provision of this title, the rules or regulations thereunder, the rules of a national securities exchange or registered securities association of which such person is a member or a person associated with a member, the rules of a registered clearing agency in which such person is a participant, the rules of the Public Company Accounting Oversight Board, of which such person is a registered public accounting firm or a person associated with such a firm, or the rules of the Municipal Securities Rulemaking Board, it may in its discretion bring an action in the proper district court of the United States, the United States District Court for the District of Columbia, or the United States courts of any territory or other place subject to the jurisdiction of the United States, to enjoin such acts or practices, and upon a proper showing a permanent or temporary injunction or restraining order shall be granted without bond. The Commission may transmit such evidence as may be available concerning such acts or practices as may constitute a violation of any provision of this title or the rules or regulations thereunder to the Attorney General, who may, in his discretion, institute the necessary criminal proceedings under this title.

(2) AUTHORITY OF A COURT TO PROHIBIT PERSONS FROM SERVING AS OFFICERS AND DIRECTORS.—In any proceeding under paragraph (1) of this subsection, the court may prohibit, conditionally or unconditionally, and permanently or for such period of time as it shall determine, any person who violated section 10(b) of this title or the rules or regulations thereunder from acting as an officer or director of any issuer that has a class of securities registered pursuant to section 12 of this title or that is required to file reports pursuant to section 15(d) of this title if the person's conduct demonstrates unfitness to serve as an officer or director of any such issuer.

(3) MONEY PENALTIES IN CIVIL ACTIONS.—

(A) AUTHORITY OF COMMISSION.—Whenever it shall appear to the Commission that any person has violated any provision of this title, the rules or regulations thereunder, or a cease-and-desist order entered by the Commission pursuant to section 21C of this title, other than by committing a violation subject to a penalty pursuant to section 21A, the Commission may bring an action in a United States district court to seek, and the court shall have jurisdiction to impose, upon a proper showing, a civil penalty to be paid by the person who committed such violation.

(B) AMOUNT OF PENALTY.—

(i) FIRST TIER.—The amount of the penalty shall be determined by the court in light of the facts and circumstances. For each violation, the amount of the penalty shall not exceed the greater of (I) $5,000 for a natural person or $50,000 for any other person, or (II) the gross amount of pecuniary gain to such defendant as a result of the violation.

(ii) SECOND TIER.—Notwithstanding clause (i), the amount of penalty for each such violation shall not exceed the greater of (I) $50,000 for a natural person or $250,000 for any other person, or (II) the gross amount of pecuniary gain to such defendant as a result of the violation, if the violation described in subparagraph (A) involved fraud, deceit, manipulation, or deliberate or reckless disregard of a regulatory requirement.

(iii) THIRD TIER.—Notwithstanding clauses (i) and (ii), the amount of penalty for each such violation shall not exceed the greater of (I) $100,000 for a natural person or $500,000 for any other person, or (II) the gross amount of pecuniary gain to such defendant as a result of the violation, if—

(aa) the violation described in subparagraph (A) involved fraud, deceit, manipulation, or deliberate or reckless disregard of a regulatory requirement; and

(bb) such violation directly or indirectly resulted in substantial losses or created a significant risk of substantial losses to other persons.

(C) PROCEDURES FOR COLLECTION.—

(i) PAYMENT OF PENALTY TO TREASURY.—A penalty imposed under this section shall be payable into the Treasury of the United States, except as otherwise provided in section 308 of the Sarbanes-Oxley Act of 2002.

(ii) COLLECTION OF PENALTIES.—If a person upon whom such a penalty is imposed shall fail to pay such penalty within the time prescribed in the court's order, the Commission may refer the matter to the Attorney General who shall recover such penalty by action in the appropriate United States district court.

(iii) REMEDY NOT EXCLUSIVE.—The actions authorized by this paragraph may be brought in addition to any other action that the Commission or the Attorney General is entitled to bring.

(iv) JURISDICTION AND VENUE.—For purposes of section 27 of this title, action under this paragraph shall be actions to enforce a liability or a duty created by this title.

(D) SPECIAL PROVISIONS RELATING TO A VIOLATION OF A CEASE-AND-DESIST ORDER.— In an action to enforce a cease-and-desist order entered by the Commission pursuant to section 21C, each separate violation of such order shall be a separate offense, except that in the case of a violation through a continuing failure to comply with the order, each day of the failure to comply shall be deemed a separate offense.

(4) PROHIBITION OF ATTORNEYS' FEES PAID FROM COMMISSION DISGORGEMENT FUNDS.—Except as otherwise ordered by the court upon motion by the Commission, or, in the case of an administrative action, as otherwise ordered by the Commission, funds disgorged as the result of an action brought by the Commission in Federal court, or as a result of any Commission administrative action, shall not be distributed as payment for attorneys' fees or expenses incurred by private parties seeking distribution of the disgorged funds.

(5) EQUITABLE RELIEF.—In any action or proceeding brought or instituted by the Commission under any provision of the securities laws, the Commission may seek, and any Federal court may grant, any equitable relief that may be appropriate or necessary for the benefit of investors.

(6) AUTHORITY OF A COURT TO PROHIBIT PERSONS FROM PARTICIPATING IN AN OFFERING OF PENNY STOCK.—

(A) IN GENERAL.—In any proceeding under paragraph (1) against any person participating in, or, at the time of the alleged misconduct who was participating in, an offering of penny stock, the court may prohibit that person from participating in an offering of penny stock, conditionally or unconditionally, and permanently or for such period of time as the court shall determine.

(B) DEFINITION.—For purposes of this paragraph, the term "person participating in an offering of penny stock" includes any person engaging in activities with a broker, dealer, or issuer for purposes of issuing, trading, or inducing or attempting to induce the purchase or sale of, any penny stock. The Commission may, by rule or regulation, define such term to include other activities, and may, by rule, regulation, or order, exempt any person or class of persons, in whole or in part, conditionally or unconditionally, from inclusion in such term.

(e) Upon application of the Commission the district courts of the United States and the United States courts of any territory or other place subject to the jurisdiction of the United States shall also have jurisdiction to issue writs of mandamus, injunctions, and orders commanding (1) any person to comply with the provisions of this title, the rules, regulations, and orders thereunder, the rules of a national securities exchange or registered securities association of which such person is a member or person associated with a member, the rules of a registered clearing agency in which such person is a participant, the rules of the Public Company Accounting Oversight Board, of which such person is a registered public accounting firm or a person associated with such a firm, and the rules of the Municipal Securities Rulemaking Board, or any undertaking contained in a registration statement as provided in subsection (d) of section 15 of this title, (2) any national securities exchange or registered securities association to enforce compliance by its members and persons associated with its members with the provisions of this title, the rules, regulations, and orders thereunder, and the rules of such exchange or association, or (3) any registered clearing agency to enforce compliance by its participants with the provisions of the rules of such clearing agency.

(f) Notwithstanding any other provision of this title, the Commission shall not bring any action pursuant to subsection (d) or (e) of this section against any person for violation of, or to command compliance with, the rules of a self-regulatory organization or the Public Company Accounting Oversight Board unless it appears to the Commission that (1) such self-regulatory organization or the Public Company Accounting Oversight Board is unable or unwilling to take appropriate action against such person in the public interest and for the protection of investors, or (2) such action is otherwise necessary or appropriate in the public interest or for the protection of investors.

(g) Notwithstanding the provisions of section 1407(a) of title 28, United States Code, or any other provision of law, no action for equitable relief instituted by the Commission pursuant to the securities laws shall be consolidated or coordinated with other actions not brought by the Commission, even though such other actions may involve common questions of fact, unless such consolidation is consented to by the Commission.

(h) (1) The Right to Financial Privacy Act of 1978 shall apply with respect to the Commission, except as otherwise provided in this subsection.

(2) Nothwithstanding section 1105 or 1107 of the Right to Financial Privacy Act of 1978, the Commission may have access to and obtain copies of, or the information contained in financial records of a customer from a financial institution without prior notice to the customer upon an ex parte showing to an approprite United States district court that the Commission seeks such financial records pursuant to a subpoena issued in conformity with the requirements of section 19(b) of the Securities Act of 1933, section 21(b) of the Securities Exchange Act of 1934, section 18(c) of the Public Utility Holding Company Act of 1935, section 42(b) of the Investment Company Act of 1940, or section 209(b) of the Investment Advisers Act of 1940, and that the Commission has reason to believe that—

(A) delay in obtaining access to such financial records, or the required notice, will result in—

(i) flight from prosecution;

(ii) destruction of or tampering with evidence;

(iii) transfer of assets or records outside the territorial limits of the United States;

(iv) improper conversion of investor assets; or

(v) impeding the ability of the Commission to identify or trace the source or disposition of funds involved in any securities transaction;

(B) such financial records are necessary to identify or trace the record or beneficial ownership interest in any security;

(C) the acts, practices or course of conduct under investigation involve—

(i) the dissemination of materially false or misleading informatioin concerning any security, issuer, or market, or the failure to make disclosures required under the securities law, which remain uncorrected; or

(ii) a financial loss to investors or other persons protected under the securities laws which remains substantially uncompensated; or

(D) the acts, practices or course of conduct under investigation—

(i) involve significant financial speculation in securities; or

(ii) endanger the stability of any financial or investment intermediary.

(3) Any application under paragraph (2) for a delay in notice shall be made with reasonable specificity.

(4)(A) Upon a showing described in paragraph (2), the presiding judge or magistrate shall enter an ex parte order granting the requested delay for a period not to exceed ninety days and an order prohibiting the financial institution involved from disclosing that records have been obtained or that a request for records has been made.

(B) Extensions of the period of delay of notice provided in subparagraph (A) of up to ninety days each may be granted by the court upon application, but only in accordance with this subsection or section 1109(a), (b)(1), or (b)(2) of the Right to Financial Privacy Act of 1978.

(C) Upon expiration of the period of delay of notification ordered under subparagraph (A) or (B), the customer shall be served with or mailed a copy of the subpoena insofar as it applies to the customer together with the following notice which shall describe with reasonable specificity the nature of the investigation for which the Commission sought the financial records:

"Records or information concerning your transactions which are held by the financial institutions named in the attached subpoena were supplied to the Securities and Exchange Commission on (date), Notification was, withheld pursuant to a determination by the (title of court so ordering) under section 21(h) of the Securities Exchange Act of 1934 that (state reason). The purpose of the investigation or official proceeding was (state purpose)".

(5) Upon application by the Commission, all proceedings pursuant to paragraphs (2) and (4) shall be held in camera and the records thereof sealed until expiration of the period of delay or such other date as the presiding judge or magistrate may permit.

(6) The Commission shall compile an annual tabulation of the occasions on which the Commission used each separate subparagraph or clause of paragraph (2) of this subsection or the provisions of the Right to Financial Privacy Act of 1978 to obtain access to financial records of a customer and include it in its annual report to the Congress. Section 1121(b) of the Right to Financial Privacy Act of 1978 shall not apply with respect to the Commission.

(7)(A) Following the expiration of the period of delay of notification ordered by the court pursuant to paragraph (4) of this subsection, the customer may, upon motion, reopen the proceeding in the district court which issued the order. If the presiding judge or magistrate finds that the movant is the customer to whom the records obtained by the Commission pertain, and that the Commission has obtained financial records or information contained therein in violation of this subsection, other than paragraph (1), it may order that the customer be granted civil penalties against the Commission in an amount equal to the sum of—

(i) $100 without regard to the volume of records involved;

(ii) any out-of-pocket damages sustained by the customer as a direct result of the disclosure; and

(iii) if the violation is found to have been willful, intentional, and without good faith, such punitive damages as the court may allow, together with the costs of the action and reasonable attorneys' fees as determined by the court.

(B) Upon a finding that the Commission has obtained financial records or information contained therein in violaton of this subsection, other than paragraph (1), the court, in its discretion, may also or in the alternative issue injunctive relief to require the Commission to comply with this subsection with respect to any subpoena which the Commission issues in the future for financial records of such customer for purposes of the same investigation.

(C) Whenever the court determines that the Commission has failed to comply with this subsection, other than paragraph (1), and the court finds that the circumstances raise questions of whether an officer or employee of the Commission acted in a willful and intentional manner and without good faith with respect to the violation, the Office of Personnel Management shall promptly initiate a proceeding to determine whether disciplinary action is warranted against the agent or employee who was primarily responsible for the violation. After investigating and considering the evidence submitted, the Office of Personnel Management shall submit its findings and recommendations to the Commission and shall send copies of the findings and recommendations to the officer or employee or his representative. The Commission shall take the corrective action that the Office of Personnel Management recommends.

(8) The relief described in paragraphs (7) and (10) shall be the only remedies or sanctions available to a customer for a violation of this subsection, other than paragraph (1), and nothing herein or in the Right to Financial Privacy Act of 1978 shall be deemed to prohibit the use of any investigation or proceeding of financial records, or the information contained therein obtained by a subpoena issued by the Commission. In the case of an unsuccessful action under paragraph (7), the court shall award the costs of the action and attorneys' fees to the Commission if the presiding judge or magistrate finds that the customer's claims were made in bad faith.

(9)(A) The Commission may transfer financial records or the information contained therein to any government authority if the Commission proceeds as a transferring agency in accordance with section 1112 of the Right to Financial Privacy Act of 1978, except that the customer notice required under section 1112(b) or (c) of such Act may be delayed upon a showing by the

Commission, in accordance with the procedure set forth in paragraphs (4) and (5), that one or more of subparagraphs (A) through (B) of paragraph (2) apply.

(B) The Commission may, without notice to the customer pursuant to section 1112 of the Right to Financial Privacy Act of 1978, transfer financial records or the information contained therein to a State securities agency or to the Department of Justice. Financial records or information transferred by the Commission to the Department of Justice or to a State securities agency pursuant to the provisions of this subparagraph may be disclosed or used only in an admininstrative, civil, or criminal action or investigation by the Department of Justice or the State securities agency which arises out of or relates to the acts, practices, or courses of conduct investigated by the Commission, except that if the Department of Justice or the State securities agency determines that the information should be disclosed or used for any other purpose, it may do so if it notifies the customer, except as otherwise provided in the Right to Financial Privacy Act of 1978, within 30 days of its determination, or complies with the requirements of section 1109 of such Act regarding delay of notice.

(10) Any government authority violating paragraph (9) shall be subject to the procedures and penalties applicable to the Commission under paragraph (7)(A) with respect to a violation by the Commission in obtaining financial records.

(11) Notwithstanding the provisions of this subsection, the Commission may obtain financial records from a financial institution or transfer such records in accordance with provisions of the Right to Financial Privacy Act of 1978.

(12) Nothing in this subsection shall enlarge or restrict any rights of a financial institution to challenge requests for records made by the Commission under existing law. Nothing in this subsection shall entitle a customer to assert any rights of a financial institution.

(13) Unless the context otherwise requires, all terms defined in the Right to Financial Privacy Act of 1978 which are common to this subsection shall have the same meaning as in such Act.

(i) INFORMATION TO CFTC.—The Commission shall provide the Commodity Futures Trading Commission with notice of the commencement of any proceeding and a copy of any order entered by the Commission against any broker or dealer registered pursuant to section 15(b)(11), any exchange registered pursuant to section 6(g), or any national securities association registered pursuant to section 15A(k).

CIVIL PENALTIES FOR INSIDER TRADING

Sec. 21A. (a) AUTHORITY TO IMPOSE CIVIL PENALTIES.—

(1) JUDICIAL ACTIONS BY COMMISSION AUTHORIZED.—Whenever it shall appear to the Commission that any person has violated any provision of this title or the rules or regulations thereunder by purchasing or selling a security or security-based swap agreement (as defined in section 206B of the Gramm-Leach-Bliley Act) while in possession of material, nonpublic information in, or has violated any such provision by communicating such information in connection with, a transaction on or through the facilities of a national securities exchange or from or through a broker or dealer, and which is not part of a public offering by an issuer of securities other than standardized options or security futures products, the Commission—

(A) may bring an action in a United States district court to seek, and the court shall have jurisdiction to impose, a civil penalty to be paid by the person who committed such violation; and

(B) may, subject to subsection (b)(1), bring an action in a United States district court to seek, and the court shall have jurisdiction to impose, a civil penalty to be paid by a person who, at the time of the violation, directly or indirectly controlled the person who committed such violation.

(2) AMOUNT OF PENALTY FOR PERSON WHO COMMITTED VIOLATION.—The amount of the penalty which may be imposed on the person who committed such violation shall be determined by the court in light of the facts and circumstances, but shall not exceed three times the profit gained or loss avoided as a result of such unlawful purchase, sale, or communication.

(3) AMOUNT OF PENALTY FOR CONTROLLING PERSON.—The amount of the penalty which may be imposed on any person who, at the time of the violation, directly or indirectly controlled the

person who committed such violation, shall be determined by the court in light of the facts and circumstances, but shall not exceed the greater of $1,000,000, or three times the amount of the profit gained or loss avoided as a result of such controlled person's violation. If such controlled person's violation was a violation by communication, the profit gained or loss avoided as a result of the violation shall, for purposes of this paragraph only, be deemed to be limited to the profit gained or loss avoided by the person or persons to whom the controlled person directed such communication.

(b) LIMITATIONS ON LIABILITY.—

(1) LIABILITY OF CONTROLLING PERSONS.—No controlling person shall be subject to a penalty under subsection (a)(1)(B) unless the Commission establishes that—

(A) such controlling person knew or recklessly disregarded the fact that such controlled person was likely to engage in the act or acts constituting the violation and failed to take appropriate steps to prevent such act or acts before they occurred; or

(B) such controlling person knowingly or recklessly failed to establish, maintain, or enforce any policy or procedure required under section 15(f) of this title or section 204A of the Investment Advisers Act of 1940 and such failure substantially contributed to or permitted the occurrence of the act or acts constituting the violation.

(2) ADDITIONAL RESTRICTIONS ON LIABILITY.—No person shall be subject to a penalty under subsection (a) solely by reason of employing another person who is subject to a penalty under such subsection, unless such employing person is liable as a controlling person under paragraph (1) of this subsection. Section 20(a) of this title shall not apply to actions under subsection (a) of this section.

(c) AUTHORITY OF COMMISSION.—The Commissioner, by such rules, regulations, and orders as it considers necessary or appropriate in the public interest or for the protection of investors, may exempt, in whole or in part, either unconditionally or upon specific terms and conditions, any person or transaction or class of persons or transactions from this section.

(d) PROCEDURES FOR COLLECTION.—

(1) PAYMENT OF PENALTY TO TREASURY.—A penalty imposed under this section shall (subject to subsection (e)) be payable into the Treasury of the United States, except as otherwise provided in section 308 of the Sarbanes-Oxley Act of 2002.

(2) COLLECTION OF PENALTIES.—If a person upon whom such a penalty is imposed shall fail to pay such penalty within the time prescribed in the court's order, the Commission may refer the matter to the Attorney General who shall recover such penalty by action in the appropriate United States district court.

(3) REMEDY NOT EXCLUSIVE.—The actions authorized by this section may be brought in addition to any other actions that the Commission or the Attorney General are entitled to bring.

(4) JURISDICTION AND VENUE.—For purposes of section 27 of this title, actions under this section shall be actions to enforce a liability or a duty created by this title.

(5) STATUTE OF LIMITATIONS.—No action may be brought under this section more than 5 years after the date of the purchase or sale. This section shall not be construed to bar or limit in any manner any action by the Commission or the Attorney General under any other provision of this title, nor shall it bar or limit in any manner any action to recover penalties, or to seek any other order regarding penalties, imposed in an action commenced within 5 years of such transaction.

(e) AUTHORITY TO AWARD BOUNTIES TO INFORMANTS.—Notwithstanding the provisions of subsection (d)(1), there shall be paid from amounts imposed as a penalty under this section and recovered by the Commission or the Attorney General, such sums, not to exceed 10 percent of such amounts, as the Commission deems appropriate, to the person or persons who provide information leading to the imposition of such penalty. Any determinations under this subsection, including whether, to whom, or in what amount to make payments, shall be in the sole discretion of the Commission, except that no such payment shall be made to any member, officer, or employee of any appropriate regulatory agency, the Department of Justice, or a self-regulatory organization. Any such determination shall be final and not subject to judicial review.

(f) DEFINITION.—For purposes of this section, 'profit gained' or 'loss avoided' is the difference between the purchase or sale price of the security and the value of that security as measured by the trading price of the security a reasonable period after public dissemination of the nonpublic information.

(g) The authority of the Commission under this section with respect to security-based swap agreements (as defined in section 206B of the Gramm-Leach-Bliley Act) shall be subject to the restrictions and limitations of section 3A(b) of this title.

CIVIL REMEDIES IN ADMINISTRATIVE PROCEEDINGS

Sec. 21B. (a) COMMISSION AUTHORITY TO ASSESS MONEY PENALTIES.—In any proceeding instituted pursuant to sections 15(b)(4), 15(b)(6), 15D, 15B, 15C, or 17A of this title against any person, the Commission or the appropriate regulatory agency may impose a civil penalty if it finds, on the record after notice and opportunity for hearing, that such person—

(1) has willfully violated any provision of the Securities Act of 1933, the Investment Company Act of 1940, the Investment Advisers Act of 1940, or this title, or the rules or regulations thereunder, or the rules of the Municipal Securities Rulemaking Board;

(2) has willfully aided, abetted, counseled, commanded, induced, or procured such a violation by any other person;

(3) has willfully made or caused to be made in any application for registration or report required to be filed with the Commission or with any other appropriate regulatory agency under this title, or in any proceeding before the Commission with respect to registration, any statement which was, at the time and in the light of the circumstances under which it was made, false or misleading with respect to any material fact, or has omitted to state in any such application or report any material fact which is required to be stated therein; or

(4) has failed reasonably to supervise, within the meaning of section 15(b)(4)(E) of this title, with a view to preventing violations of the provisions of such statutes, rules and regulations, another person who commits such a violation, if such other person is subject to his supervision;

and that such penalty is in the public interest.

(b) MAXIMUM AMOUNT OF PENALTY.—

(1) FIRST TIER.—The maximum amount of penalty for each act or omission described in subsection (a) shall be $5,000 for a natural person or $50,000 for any other person.

(2) SECOND TIER.—Notwithstanding paragraph (1), the maximum amount of penalty for each such act or omission shall be $50,000 for a natural person or $250,000 for any other person if the act or omission described in subsection (a) involved fraud, deceit, manipulation, or deliberate or reckless disregard of a regulatory requirement.

(3) THIRD TIER.—Notwithstanding paragraphs (1) and (2), the maximum amount of penalty for each such act or omission shall be $100,000 for a natural person or $500,000 for any other person if—

(A) The act or omission described in subsection (a) involved fraud, deceit, manipulation, or deliberate or reckless disregard of a regulatory requirement; and

(B) such act or omission directly or indirectly resulted in substantial losses or created a significant risk of substantial losses to other persons or resulted in substantial pecuniary gain to the person who committed the act or omission.

(c) DETERMINATION OF PUBLIC INTEREST.—In considering under this section whether a penalty is in the public interest, the Commission or the appropriate regulatory agency may consider—

(1) whether the act or omission for which such penalty is assessed involved fraud, deceit, manipulation, or deliberate or reckless disregard of a regulatory requirement;

(2) the harm to other persons resulting either directly or indirectly from such act or omission;

(3) the extent to which any person was unjustly enriched, taking into account any restitution made to persons injured by such behavior;

(4) whether such person previously has been found by the Commission, another appropriate regulatory agency, or a self-regulatory organization to have violated the Federal securities laws, State securities laws, or the rules of a self-regulatory organization, has been enjoined by a court of competent jurisdiction from violations of such laws or rules, or has been convicted by a court of competent jurisdiction of violations of such laws or of any felony or misdemeanor described in section 15(b)(4)(B) of this title;

(5) the need to deter such person and other persons from committing such acts or omissions; and

(6) such other matters as justice may require.

(d) EVIDENCE CONCERNING ABILITY TO PAY.—In any proceeding in which the Commission or the appropriate regulatory agency may impose a penalty under this section, a respondent may present evidence of the respondent's ability to pay such penalty. The Commission or the appropriate regulatory agency may, in its discretion, consider such evidence in determining whether such penalty is in the public interest. Such evidence may relate to the extent of such person's ability to continue in business and the collectability of a penalty, taking into account any other claims of the United States or third parties upon such person's assets and the amount of such person's assets.

(e) AUTHORITY TO ENTER AN ORDER REQUIRING AN ACCOUNTING AND DISGORGEMENT.—In any proceeding in which the Commission or the appropriate regulatory agency may impose a penalty under this section, the Commission or the appropriate regulatory agency may enter an order requiring accounting and disgorgement, including reasonable interest. The Commission is authorized to adopt rules, regulations, and orders concerning payments to investors, rates of interest, periods of accrual, and such other matters as it deems appropriate to implement this subsection.

CEASE-AND-DESIST PROCEEDINGS

Sec. 21C. (a) AUTHORITY OF THE COMMISSION.—If the Commission finds, after notice and opportunity for hearing, that any person is violating, has violated, or is about to violate any provision of this title, or any rule or regulation thereunder, the Commission may publish its findings and enter an order requiring such person, and any other person that is, was, or would be a cause of the violation, due to an act or omission the person knew or should have known would contribute to such violation, to cease and desist from committing or causing such violation and any future violation of the same provision, rule, or regulation. Such order may, in addition to requiring a person to cease and desist from committing or causing a violation, require such person to comply, or to take steps to effect compliance, with such provision, rule, or regulation, upon such terms and conditions and within such time as the Commission may specify in such order. Any such order may, as the Commission deems appropriate, require future compliance or steps to effect future compliance, either permanently or for such period of time as the Commission may specify, with such provision, rule, or regulation with respect to any security, any issuer, or any other person.

(b) HEARING.—The notice instituting proceedings pursuant to subsection (a) shall fix a hearing date not earlier than 30 days nor later than 60 days after service of the notice unless an earlier or a later date is set by the Commission with the consent of any respondent so served.

(c) TEMPORARY ORDER.—

(1) IN GENERAL.—Whenever the Commission determines that the alleged violation or threatened violation specified in the notice instituting proceedings pursuant to subsection (a), or the continuation thereof, is likely to result in significant dissipation or conversion of assets, significant harm to investors, or substantial harm to the public interest, including, but not limited to, losses to the Securities Investor Protection Corporation, prior to the completion of the proceedings, the Commission may enter a temporary order requiring the respondent to cease and desist from the violation or threatened violation and to take such action to prevent the violation or threatened violation and to prevent dissipation or conversion of assets, significant harm to investors, or substantial harm to the public interest as the Commission deems appropriate pending completion of such proceedings. Such an order shall be entered only after notice and

opportunity for a hearing, unless the Commission determines that notice and hearing prior to entry would be impracticable or contrary to the public interest. A temporary order shall become effective upon service upon the respondent and, unless set aside, limited, or suspended by the Commission or a court of competent jurisdiction, shall remain effective and enforceable pending the completion of the proceedings.

(2) APPLICABILITY.—[Paragraph (1)] shall apply only to a respondent that acts, or, at the time of the alleged misconduct acted, as a broker, dealer, investment adviser, investment company, municipal securities dealer, government securities broker, government securities dealer, registered public accounting firm (as defined in section 2 of the Sarbanes-Oxley Act of 2002), or transfer agent, or is, or was at the time of the alleged misconduct, an associated person of, or a person seeking to become associated with, any of the foregoing.

(3) TEMPORARY FREEZE.—

(A) IN GENERAL.—

(i) ISSUANCE OF TEMPORARY ORDER.—Whenever, during the course of a lawful investigation involving possible violations of the Federal securities laws by an issuer of publicly traded securities or any of its directors, officers, partners, controlling persons, agents, or employees, it shall appear to the Commission that it is likely that the issuer will make extraordinary payments (whether compensation or otherwise) to any of the foregoing persons, the Commission may petition a Federal district court for a temporary order requiring the issuer to escrow, subject to court supervision, those payments in an interest-bearing account for 45 days.

(ii) STANDARD.—A temporary order shall be entered under clause (i), only after notice and opportunity for a hearing, unless the court determines that notice and hearing prior to entry of the order would be impracticable or contrary to the public interest.

(iii) EFFECTIVE PERIOD.—A temporary order issued under clause (i) shall—

(I) become effective immediately;

(II) be served upon the parties subject to it; and

(III) unless set aside, limited or suspended by a court of competent jurisdiction, shall remain effective and enforceable for 45 days.

(iv) EXTENSIONS AUTHORIZED.—The effective period of an order under this subparagraph may be extended by the court upon good cause shown for not longer than 45 additional days, provided that the combined period of the order shall not exceed 90 days.

(B) PROCESS ON DETERMINATION OF VIOLATIONS.—

(i) VIOLATIONS CHARGED.—If the issuer or other person described in subparagraph (A) is charged with any violation of the Federal securities laws before the expiration of the effective period of a temporary order under subparagraph (A) (including any applicable extension period), the order shall remain in effect, subject to court approval, until the conclusion of any legal proceedings related thereto, and the affected issuer or other person, shall have the right to petition the court for review of the order.

(ii) VIOLATIONS NOT CHARGED.—If the issuer or other person described in subparagraph (A) is not charged with any violation of the Federal securities laws before the expiration of the effective period of a temporary order under subparagraph (A) (including any applicable extension period), the escrow shall terminate at the expiration of the 45-day effective period (or the expiration of any extension period, as applicable), and the disputed payments (with accrued interest) shall be returned to the issuer or other affected person.

(d) REVIEW OF TEMPORARY ORDERS.—

(1) COMMISSION REVIEW.—At any time after the respondent has been served with a temporary cease-and-desist order pursuant to subsection (c), the respondent may apply to the Commission to have the order set aside, limited, or suspended. If the respondent has been served with a temporary cease-and-desist order entered without a prior Commission hearing, the respondent may, within 10 days after the date on which the order was served, request a hearing on such application and the Commission shall hold a hearing and render a decision on such application at the earliest possible time.

(2) JUDICIAL REVIEW.—Within—

(A) 10 days ater the date the respondent was served with a temporary cease-and-desist order entered with a prior Commission hearing, or

(B) 10 days after the Commission renders a decision on an application and hearing under paragraph (1), with respect to any temporary cease-and-desist order entered without a prior Commission hearing,

the respondent may apply to the United States district court for the district in which the respondent resides or has its principal place of business, or for the District of Columbia, for an order setting aside, limiting, or suspending the effectiveness or enforcement of the order, and the court shall have jurisdiction to enter such an order. A respondent served with a temporary cease-and-desist order entered without a prior Commission hearing may not apply to the court except after hearing and decision by the Commission on the respondent's application under paragraph (1) of this subsection.

(3) No AUTOMATIC STAY OF TEMPORARY ORDER.—The commencement of proceedings under paragraph (2) of this subsection shall not, unless specifically ordered by the court, operate as a stay of the Commission's order.

(4) EXCLUSIVE REVIEW.—Section 25 of this title shall not apply to a temporary order entered pursuant to this section.

(e) AUTHORITY TO ENTER AN ORDER REQUIRING AN ACCOUNTING AND DISGORGEMENT.—In any cease-and-desist proceeding under subsection (a), the Commission may enter an order requiring accounting and disgorgement, including reasonable interest. The Commission is authorized to adopt rules, regulations, and orders concerning payments to investors, rates of interest, periods of accrual, and such other matters as it deems appropriate to implement this subsection.

(f) AUTHORITY OF THE COMMISSION TO PROHIBIT PERSONS FROM SERVING AS OFFICERS OR DIREC- TORS.—In any cease-and-desist proceeding under subsection (a), the Commission may issue an order to prohibit, conditionally or unconditionally, and permanently or for such period of time as it shall determine, any person who has violated section 10(b) or the rules or regulations thereunder, from acting as an officer or director of any issuer that has a class of securities registered pursuant to section 12, or that is required to file reports pursuant to section 15(d), if the conduct of that person demonstrates unfitness to serve as an officer or director of any such issuer.

PRIVATE SECURITIES LITIGATION

Sec. 21D. (a) PRIVATE CLASS ACTIONS.—

(1) IN GENERAL.—The provisions of this subsection shall apply in each private action arising under this title that is brought as a plaintiff class action pursuant to the Federal Rules of Civil Procedure.

(2) CERTIFICATION FILED WITH COMPLAINT.—

(A) IN GENERAL.—Each plaintiff seeking to serve as a representative party on behalf of a class shall provide a sworn certification, which shall be personally signed by such plaintiff and filed with the complaint, that—

(i) states that the plaintiff has reviewed the complaint and authorized its filing;

(ii) states that the plaintiff did not purchase the security that is the subject of the complaint at the direction of plaintiff's counsel or in order to participate in any private action arising under this title;

(iii) states that the plaintiff is willing to serve as a representative party on behalf of a class, including providing testimony at deposition and trial, if necessary;

(iv) sets forth all of the transactions of the plaintiff in the security that is the subject of the complaint during the class period specified in the complaint;

(v) identifies any other action under this title, filed during the 3-year period preceding the date on which the certification is signed by the plaintiff, in which the plaintiff has sought to serve as a representative party on behalf of a class; and

(vi) states that the plaintiff will not accept any payment for serving as a representative party on behalf of a class beyond the plaintiff's pro rata share of any recovery, except as ordered or approved by the court in accordance with paragraph (4).

(B) NONWAIVER OF ATTORNEY-CLIENT PRIVILEGE.—The certification filed pursuant to subparagraph (A) shall not be construed to be a waiver of the attorney-client privilege.

(3) APPOINTMENT OF LEAD PLAINTIFF.—

(A) EARLY NOTICE TO CLASS MEMBERS.—

(i) IN GENERAL.—Not later than 20 days after the date on which the complaint is filed, the plaintiff or plaintiffs shall cause to be published, in a widely circulated national business-oriented publication or wire service, a notice advising members of the purported plaintiff class—

(I) of the pendency of the action, the claims asserted therein, and the purported class period; and

(II) that, not later than 60 days after the date on which the notice is published, any member of the purported class may move the court to serve as lead plaintiff of the purported class.

(ii) MULTIPLE ACTIONS.—If more than one action on behalf of a class asserting substantially the same claim or claims arising under this title is filed, only the plaintiff or plaintiffs in the first filed action shall be required to cause notice to be published in accordance with clause (i).

(iii) ADDITIONAL NOTICES MAY BE REQUIRED UNDER FEDERAL RULES.—Notice required under clause (i) shall be in addition to any notice required pursuant to the Federal Rules of Civil Procedure.

(B) APPOINTMENT OF LEAD PLAINTIFF.—

(i) IN GENERAL.—Not later than 90 days after the date on which a notice is published under subparagraph (A)(i), the court shall consider any motion made by a purported class member in response to the notice, including any motion by a class member who is not individually named as a plaintiff in the complaint or complaints, and shall appoint as lead plaintiff the member or members of the purported plaintiff class that the court determines to be most capable of adequately representing the interests of class members (hereafter in this paragraph referred to as the "most adequate plaintiff") in accordance with this subparagraph.

(ii) CONSOLIDATED ACTIONS.—If more than one action on behalf of a class asserting substantially the same claim or claims arising under this title has been filed, and any party has sought to consolidate those actions for pretrial purposes or for trial, the court shall not make the determination required by clause (i) until after the decision on the motion to consolidate is rendered. As soon as practicable after such decision is rendered, the court shall appoint the most adequate plaintiff as lead plaintiff for the consolidated actions in accordance with this paragraph.

(iii) REBUTTABLE PRESUMPTION.—

(I) IN GENERAL.—Subject to subclause (II), for purposes of clause (i), the court shall adopt a presumption that the most adequate plaintiff in any private action arising under this title is the person or group of persons that—

(aa) has either filed the complaint or made a motion in response to a notice under subparagraph (A)(i);

(bb) in the determination of the court, has the largest financial interest in the relief sought by the class; and

(cc) otherwise satisfies the requirements of Rule 23 of the Federal Rules of Civil Procedure.

(II) REBUTTAL EVIDENCE.—The presumption described in subclause (I) may be rebutted only upon proof by a member of the purported plaintiff class that the presumptively most adequate plaintiff—

(aa) will not fairly and adequately protect the interests of the class; or

(bb) is subject to unique defenses that render such plaintiff incapable of adequately representing the class.

(iv) DISCOVERY.—For purposes of this subparagraph, discovery relating to whether a member or members of the purported plaintiff class is the most adequate plaintiff may be conducted by a plaintiff only if the plaintiff first demonstrates a reasonable basis for a finding that the presumptively most adequate plaintiff is incapable of adequately representing the class.

(v) SELECTION OF LEAD COUNSEL.—The most adequate plaintiff shall, subject to the approval of the court, select and retain counsel to represent the class.

(vi) RESTRICTIONS ON PROFESSIONAL PLAINTIFFS.—Except as the court may otherwise permit, consistent with the purposes of this section, a person may be a lead plaintiff, or an officer, director, or fiduciary of a lead plaintiff, in no more than 5 securities class actions brought as plaintiff class actions pursuant to the Federal Rules of Civil Procedure during any 3-year period.

(4) RECOVERY BY PLAINTIFFS.—The share of any final judgment or of any settlement that is awarded to a representative party serving on behalf of a class shall be equal, on a per share basis, to the portion of the final judgment or settlement awarded to all other members of the class. Nothing in this paragraph shall be construed to limit the award of reasonable costs and expenses (including lost wages) directly relating to the representation of the class to any representative party serving on behalf of a class.

(5) RESTRICTIONS ON SETTLEMENTS UNDER SEAL.—The terms and provisions of any settlement agreement of a class action shall not be filed under seal, except that on motion of any party to the settlement, the court may order filing under seal for those portions of a settlement agreement as to which good cause is shown for such filing under seal. For purposes of this paragraph, good cause shall exist only if publication of a term or provision of a settlement agreement would cause direct and substantial harm to any party.

(6) RESTRICTIONS ON PAYMENT OF ATTORNEYS' FEES AND EXPENSES.—Total attorneys' fees and expenses awarded by the court to counsel for the plaintiff class shall not exceed a reasonable percentage of the amount of any damages and prejudgment interest actually paid to the class.

(7) DISCLOSURE OF SETTLEMENT TERMS TO CLASS MEMBERS.—Any proposed or final settlement agreement that is published or otherwise disseminated to the class shall include each of the following statements, along with a cover page summarizing the information contained in such statements:

(A) STATEMENT OF PLAINTIFF RECOVERY.—The amount of the settlement proposed to be distributed to the parties to the action, determined in the aggregate and on an average per share basis.

(B) STATEMENT OF POTENTIAL OUTCOME OF CASE.—

(i) AGREEMENT ON AMOUNT OF DAMAGES.—If the settling parties agree on the average amount of damages per share that would be recoverable if the plaintiff prevailed on each claim alleged under this title, a statement concerning the average amount of such potential damages per share.

(ii) DISAGREEMENT ON AMOUNT OF DAMAGES.—If the parties do not agree on the average amount of damages per share that would be recoverable if the plaintiff prevailed on each claim alleged under this title, a statement from each settling party concerning the issue or issues on which the parties disagree.

(iii) INADMISSIBILITY FOR CERTAIN PURPOSES.—A statement made in accordance with clause (i) or (ii) concerning the amount of damages shall not be admissible in any Federal or State judicial action or administrative proceeding, other than an action or proceeding arising out of such statement.

(C) STATEMENT OF ATTORNEYS' FEES OR COSTS SOUGHT.—If any of the settling parties or their counsel intend to apply to the court for an award of attorneys' fees or costs from any fund established as part of the settlement, a statement indicating which parties or counsel intend to make such an application, the amount of fees and costs that will be sought (including the amount of such fees and costs determined on an average per share basis), and a brief explanation supporting the fees and costs sought. Such information shall be clearly summarized on the cover page of any notice to a party of any proposed or final settlement agreement.

(D) IDENTIFICATION OF LAWYERS' REPRESENTATIVES.—The name, telephone number, and address of one or more representatives of counsel for the plaintiff class who will be reasonably available to answer questions from class members concerning any matter contained in any notice of settlement published or otherwise disseminated to the class.

(E) REASONS FOR SETTLEMENT.—A brief statement explaining the reasons why the parties are proposing the settlement.

(F) OTHER INFORMATION.—Such other information as may be required by the court.

(8) SECURITY FOR PAYMENT OF COSTS IN CLASS ACTIONS.—In any private action arising under this title that is certified as a class action pursuant to the Federal Rules of Civil Procedure, the court may require an undertaking from the attorneys for the plaintiff class, the plaintiff class, or both, or from the attorneys for the defendant, the defendant, or both, in such proportions and at such times as the court determines are just and equitable, for the payment of fees and expenses that may be awarded under this subsection.

(9) ATTORNEY CONFLICT OF INTEREST.—If a plaintiff class is represented by an attorney who directly owns or otherwise has a beneficial interest in the securities that are the subject of the litigation, the court shall make a determination of whether such ownership or other interest constitutes a conflict of interest sufficient to disqualify the attorney from representing the plaintiff class.

(b) REQUIREMENTS FOR SECURITIES FRAUD ACTIONS.—

(1) MISLEADING STATEMENTS AND OMISSIONS.—In any private action arising under this title in which the plaintiff alleges that the defendant—

(A) made an untrue statement of a material fact; or

(B) omitted to state a material fact necessary in order to make the statements made, in the light of the circumstances in which they were made, not misleading;

the complaint shall specify each statement alleged to have been misleading, the reason or reasons why the statement is misleading, and, if an allegation regarding the statement or omission is made on information and belief, the complaint shall state with particularity all facts on which that belief is formed.

(2) REQUIRED STATE OF MIND.—In any private action arising under this title in which the plaintiff may recover money damages only on proof that the defendant acted with a particular state of mind, the complaint shall, with respect to each act or omission alleged to violate this title, state with particularity facts giving rise to a strong inference that the defendant acted with the required state of mind.

(3) MOTION TO DISMISS; STAY OF DISCOVERY.—

(A) DISMISSAL FOR FAILURE TO MEET PLEADING REQUIREMENTS.—In any private action arising under this title, the court shall, on the motion of any defendant, dismiss the complaint if the requirements of paragraphs (1) and (2) are not met.

(B) STAY OF DISCOVERY.—In any private action arising under this title, all discovery and other proceedings shall be stayed during the pendency of any motion to dismiss, unless the court finds upon the motion of any party that particularized discovery is necessary to preserve evidence or to prevent undue prejudice to that party.

(C) PRESERVATION OF EVIDENCE.—

(i) IN GENERAL.—During the pendency of any stay of discovery pursuant to this paragraph, unless otherwise ordered by the court, any party to the action with actual notice of the allegations contained in the complaint shall treat all documents, data compilations (including electronically recorded or stored data), and tangible objects that are in the custody or control of such person and that are relevant to the allegations, as if they were the subject of a continuing request for production of documents from an opposing party under the Federal Rules of Civil Procedure.

(ii) SANCTION FOR WILLFUL VIOLATION.—A party aggrieved by the willful failure of an opposing party to comply with clause (i) may apply to the court for an order awarding appropriate sanctions.

(D) CIRCUMVENTION OF STAY OF DISCOVERY.—Upon a proper showing, a court may stay discovery proceedings in any private action in a State court, as necessary in aid of its jurisdiction, or to protect or effectuate its judgments, in an action subject to a stay of discovery pursuant to this paragraph.

(4) LOSS CAUSATION.—In any private action arising under this title, the plaintiff shall have the burden of proving that the act or omission of the defendant alleged to violate this title caused the loss for which the plaintiff seeks to recover damages.

(c) SANCTIONS FOR ABUSIVE LITIGATION.—

(1) MANDATORY REVIEW BY COURT.—In any private action arising under this title, upon final adjudication of the action, the court shall include in the record specific findings regarding compliance by each party and each attorney representing any party with each requirement of Rule 11(b) of the Federal Rules of Civil Procedure as to any complaint, responsive pleading, or dispositive motion.

(2) MANDATORY SANCTIONS.—If the court makes a finding under paragraph (1) that a party or attorney violated any requirement of Rule 11(b) of the Federal Rules of Civil Procedure as to any complaint, responsive pleading, or dispositive motion, the court shall impose sanctions on such party or attorney in accordance with Rule 11 of the Federal Rules of Civil Procedure. Prior to making a finding that any party or attorney has violated Rule 11 of the Federal Rules of Civil Procedure, the court shall give such party or attorney notice and an opportunity to respond.

(3) PRESUMPTION IN FAVOR OF ATTORNEYS' FEES AND COSTS.—

(A) IN GENERAL.—Subject to subparagraphs (B) and (C), for purposes of paragraph (2), the court shall adopt a presumption that the appropriate sanction—

(i) for failure of any responsive pleading or dispositive motion to comply with any requirement of Rule 11(b) of the Federal Rules of Civil Procedure is an award to the opposing party of the reasonable attorneys' fees and other expenses incurred as a direct result of the violation; and

(ii) for substantial failure of any complaint to comply with any requirement of Rule 11(b) of the Federal Rules of Civil Procedure is an award to the opposing party of the reasonable attorneys' fees and other expenses incurred in the action.

(B) REBUTTAL EVIDENCE.—The presumption described in subparagraph (A) may be rebutted only upon proof by the party or attorney against whom sanctions are to be imposed that—

(i) the award of attorneys' fees and other expenses will impose an unreasonable burden on that party or attorney and would be unjust, and the failure to make such an award would not impose a greater burden on the party in whose favor sanctions are to be imposed; or

(ii) the violation of Rule 11(b) of the Federal Rules of Civil Procedure was de minimis.

(C) SANCTIONS.—If the party or attorney against whom sanctions are to be imposed meets its burden under subparagraph (B), the court shall award the sanctions that the court deems appropriate pursuant to Rule 11 of the Federal Rules of Civil Procedure.

(d) DEFENDANT'S RIGHT TO WRITTEN INTERROGATORIES.—In any private action arising under this title in which the plaintiff may recover money damages, the court shall, when requested by a defendant, submit to the jury a written interrogatory on the issue of each such defendant's state of mind at the time the alleged violation occurred.

(e) LIMITATION ON DAMAGES.—

(1) IN GENERAL.—Except as provided in paragraph (2), in any private action arising under this title in which the plaintiff seeks to establish damages by reference to the market price of a security, the award of damages to the plaintiff shall not exceed the difference between the purchase or sale price paid or received, as appropriate, by the plaintiff for the subject security and the mean trading price of that security during the 90-day period beginning on the date on which the information correcting the misstatement or omission that is the basis for the action is disseminated to the market.

(2) EXCEPTION.—In any private action arising under this title in which the plaintiff seeks to establish damages by reference to the market price of a security, if the plaintiff sells or repurchases the subject security prior to the expiration of the 90-day period described in paragraph (1), the plaintiff's damages shall not exceed the difference between the purchase or sale price paid or received, as appropriate, by the plaintiff for the security and the mean trading price of the security during the period beginning immediately after dissemination of information correcting the mis-

statement or omission and ending on the date on which the plaintiff sells or repurchases the security.

(3) DEFINITION.—For purposes of this subsection, the "mean trading price" of a security shall be an average of the daily trading price of that security, determined as of the close of the market each day during the 90-day period referred to in paragraph (1).

(f) PROPORTIONATE LIABILITY.—

(1) APPLICABILITY.—Nothing in this subsection shall be construed to create, affect, or in any manner modify, the standard for liability associated with any action arising under the securities laws.

(2) LIABILITY FOR DAMAGES.—

(A) JOINT AND SEVERAL LIABILITY.—Any covered person against whom a final judgment is entered in a private action shall be liable for damages jointly and severally only if the trier of fact specifically determines that such covered person knowingly committed a violation of the securities laws.

(B) PROPORTIONATE LIABILITY.—

(i) IN GENERAL.—Except as provided in subparagraph (A), a covered person against whom a final judgment is entered in a private action shall be liable solely for the portion of the judgment that corresponds to the percentage of responsibility of that covered person, as determined under paragraph (3).

(ii) RECOVERY BY AND COSTS OF COVERED PERSON.—In any case in which a contractual relationship permits, a covered person that prevails in any private action may recover the attorney's fees and costs of that covered person in connection with the action.

(3) DETERMINATION OF RESPONSIBILITY.—

(A) IN GENERAL.—In any private action, the court shall instruct the jury to answer special interrogatories, or if there is no jury, shall make findings, with respect to each covered person and each of the other persons claimed by any of the parties to have caused or contributed to the loss incurred by the plaintiff, including persons who have entered into settlements with the plaintiff or plaintiffs, concerning—

(i) whether such person violated the securities laws;

(ii) the percentage of responsibility of such person, measured as a percentage of the total fault of all persons who caused or contributed to the loss incurred by the plaintiff; and

(iii) whether such person knowingly committed a violation of the securities laws.

(B) CONTENTS OF SPECIAL INTERROGATORIES OR FINDINGS.—The responses to interrogatories, or findings, as appropriate, under subparagraph (A) shall specify the total amount of damages that the plaintiff is entitled to recover and the percentage of responsibility of each covered person found to have caused or contributed to the loss incurred by the plaintiff or plaintiffs.

(C) FACTORS FOR CONSIDERATION.—In determining the percentage of responsibility under this paragraph, the trier of fact shall consider—

(i) the nature of the conduct of each covered person found to have caused or contributed to the loss incurred by the plaintiff or plaintiffs; and

(ii) the nature and extent of the causal relationship between the conduct of each such person and the damages incurred by the plaintiff or plaintiffs.

(4) UNCOLLECTIBLE SHARE.—

(A) IN GENERAL.—Notwithstanding paragraph (2)(B), upon motion made not later than 6 months after a final judgment is entered in any private action, the court determines that all or part of the share of the judgment of the covered person is not collectible against that covered person, and is also not collectible against a covered person described in paragraph (2)(A), each covered person described in paragraph (2)(B) shall be liable for the uncollectible share as follows:

(i) PERCENTAGE OF NET WORTH.—Each covered person shall be jointly and severally liable for the uncollectible share if the plaintiff establishes that—

(I) the plaintiff is an individual whose recoverable damages under the final judgment are equal to more than 10 percent of the net worth of the plaintiff; and

(II) the net worth of the plaintiff is equal to less than $200,000.

(ii) OTHER PLAINTIFFS.—With respect to any plaintiff not described in subclauses (I) and (II) of clause (i), each covered person shall be liable for the uncollectible share in proportion to the percentage of responsibility of that covered person, except that the total liability of a covered person under this clause may not exceed 50 percent of the proportionate share of that covered person, as determined under paragraph (3)(B).

(iii) NET WORTH.—For purposes of this subparagraph, net worth shall be determined as of the date immediately preceding the date of the purchase or sale (as applicable) by the plaintiff of the security that is the subject of the action, and shall be equal to the fair market value of assets, minus liabilities, including the net value of the investments of the plaintiff in real and personal property (including personal residences).

(B) OVERALL LIMIT.—In no case shall the total payments required pursuant to subparagraph (A) exceed the amount of the uncollectible share.

(C) COVERED PERSONS SUBJECT TO CONTRIBUTION.—A covered person against whom judgment is not collectible shall be subject to contribution and to any continuing liability to the plaintiff on the judgment.

(5) RIGHT OF CONTRIBUTION.—To the extent that a covered person is required to make an additional payment pursuant to paragraph (4), that covered person may recover contribution—

(A) from the covered person originally liable to make the payment;

(B) from any covered person liable jointly and severally pursuant to paragraph (2)(A);

(C) from any covered person held proportionately liable pursuant to this paragraph who is liable to make the same payment and has paid less than his or her proportionate share of that payment; or

(D) from any other person responsible for the conduct giving rise to the payment that would have been liable to make the same payment.

(6) NONDISCLOSURE TO JURY.—The standard for allocation of damages under paragraphs (2) and (3) and the procedure for reallocation of uncollectible shares under paragraph (4) shall not be disclosed to members of the jury.

(7) SETTLEMENT DISCHARGE.—

(A) IN GENERAL.—A covered person who settles any private action at any time before final verdict or judgment shall be discharged from all claims for contribution brought by other persons. Upon entry of the settlement by the court, the court shall enter a bar order constituting the final discharge of all obligations to the plaintiff of the settling covered person arising out of the action. The order shall bar all future claims for contribution arising out of the action—

(i) by any person against the settling covered person; and

(ii) by the settling covered person against any person, other than a person whose liability has been extinguished by the settlement of the settling covered person.

(B) REDUCTION.—If a covered person enters into a settlement with the plaintiff prior to final verdict or judgment, the verdict or judgment shall be reduced by the greater of—

(i) an amount that corresponds to the percentage of responsibility of that covered person; or

(ii) the amount paid to the plaintiff by that covered person.

(8) CONTRIBUTION.—A covered person who becomes jointly and severally liable for damages in any private action may recover contribution from any other person who, if joined in the original action, would have been liable for the same damages. A claim for contribution shall be determined based on the percentage of responsibility of the claimant and of each person against whom a claim for contribution is made.

(9) STATUTE OF LIMITATIONS FOR CONTRIBUTION.—In any private action determining liability, an action for contribution shall be brought not later than 6 months after the entry of a final, nonappealable judgment in the action, except that an action for contribution brought by a covered

person who was required to make an additional payment pursuant to paragraph (4) may be brought not later than 6 months after the date on which such payment was made.

(10) DEFINITIONS.—For purposes of this subsection—

(A) a covered person "knowingly commits a violation of the securities laws"—

(i) with respect to an action that is based on an untrue statement of material fact or omission of a material fact necessary to make the statement not misleading, if—

(I) that covered person makes an untrue statement of a material fact, with actual knowledge that the representation is false, or omits to state a fact necessary in order to make the statement made not misleading, with actual knowledge that, as a result of the omission, one of the material representations of the covered person is false; and

(II) persons are likely to reasonably rely on that misrepresentation or omission; and

(ii) with respect to an action that is based on any conduct that is not described in clause (i), if that covered person engages in that conduct with actual knowledge of the facts and circumstances that make the conduct of that covered person a violation of the securities laws;

(B) reckless conduct by a covered person shall not be construed to constitute a knowing commission of a violation of the securities laws by that covered person;

(C) the term "covered person" means—

(i) a defendant in any private action arising under this title; or

(ii) a defendant in any private action arising under section 11 of the Securities Act of 1933, who is an outside director of the issuer of the securities that are the subject of the action; and

(D) the term "outside director" shall have the meaning given such term by rule or regulation of the Commission.

APPLICATION OF SAFE HARBOR FOR FORWARD-LOOKING STATEMENTS

Sec. 21E. (a) APPLICABILITY.—This section shall apply only to a forward-looking statement made by—

(1) an issuer that, at the time that the statement is made, is subject to the reporting requirements of section 13(a) or section 15(d);

(2) a person acting on behalf of such issuer;

(3) an outside reviewer retained by such issuer making a statement on behalf of such issuer; or

(4) an underwriter, with respect to information provided by such issuer or information derived from information provided by such issuer.

(b) EXCLUSIONS.—Except to the extent otherwise specifically provided by rule, regulation, or order of the Commission, this section shall not apply to a forward-looking statement—

(1) that is made with respect to the business or operations of the issuer, if the issuer—

(A) during the 3-year period preceding the date on which the statement was first made—

(i) was convicted of any felony or misdemeanor described in clauses (i) through (iv) of section 15(b)(4)(B); or

(ii) has been made the subject of a judicial or administrative decree or order arising out of a governmental action that—

(I) prohibits future violations of the antifraud provisions of the securities laws;

(II) requires that the issuer cease and desist from violating the antifraud provisions of the securities laws; or

(III) determines that the issuer violated the antifraud provisions of the securities laws;

(B) makes the forward-looking statement in connection with an offering of securities by a blank check company;

(C) issues penny stock;

(D) makes the forward-looking statement in connection with a rollup transaction; or

(E) makes the forward-looking statement in connection with a going private transaction; or

(2) that is—

(A) included in a financial statement prepared in accordance with generally accepted accounting principles;

(B) contained in a registration statement of, or otherwise issued by, an investment company;

(C) made in connection with a tender offer;

(D) made in connection with an initial public offering;

(E) made in connection with an offering by, or relating to the operations of, a partnership, limited liability company, or a direct participation investment program; or

(F) made in a disclosure of beneficial ownership in a report required to be filed with the Commission pursuant to section 13(d).

(c) SAFE HARBOR.—

(1) IN GENERAL.—Except as provided in subsection (b), in any private action arising under this title that is based on an untrue statement of a material fact or omission of a material fact necessary to make the statement not misleading, a person referred to in subsection (a) shall not be liable with respect to any forward-looking statement, whether written or oral, if and to the extent that—

(A) the forward-looking statement is—

(i) identified as a forward-looking statement, and is accompanied by meaningful cautionary statements identifying important factors that could cause actual results to differ materially from those in the forward-looking statement; or

(ii) immaterial; or

(B) the plaintiff fails to prove that the forward-looking statement—

(i) if made by a natural person, was made with actual knowledge by that person that the statement was false or misleading; or

(ii) if made by a business entity; was—

(I) made by or with the approval of an executive officer of that entity; and

(II) made or approved by such officer with actual knowledge by that officer that the statement was false or misleading.

(2) ORAL FORWARD-LOOKING STATEMENTS.—In the case of an oral forward-looking statement made by an issuer that is subject to the reporting requirements of section 13(a) or section 15(d), or by a person acting on behalf of such issuer, the requirement set forth in paragraph (1)(A) shall be deemed to be satisfied—

(A) if the oral forward-looking statement is accompanied by a cautionary statement—

(i) that the particular oral statement is a forward-looking statement; and

(ii) that the actual results might differ materially from those projected in the forward-looking statement; and

(B) if—

(i) the oral forward-looking statement is accompanied by an oral statement that additional information concerning factors that could cause actual results to materially differ from those in the forward-looking statement is contained in a readily available written document, or portion thereof;

(ii) the accompanying oral statement referred to in clause (i) identifies the document, or portion thereof, that contains the additional information about those factors relating to the forward-looking statement; and

(iii) the information contained in that written document is a cautionary statement that satisfies the standard established in paragraph (1)(A).

(3) AVAILABILITY.—Any document filed with the Commission or generally disseminated shall be deemed to be readily available for purposes of paragraph (2).

(4) EFFECT ON OTHER SAFE HARBORS.—The exemption provided for in paragraph (1) shall be in addition to any exemption that the Commission may establish by rule or regulation under subsection (g).

(d) DUTY TO UPDATE.—Nothing in this section shall impose upon any person a duty to update a forward-looking statement.

(e) DISPOSITIVE MOTION.—On any motion to dismiss based upon subsection (c)(1), the court shall consider any statement cited in the complaint and any cautionary statement accompanying the forward-looking statement, which are not subject to material dispute, cited by the defendant.

(f) STAY PENDING DECISION ON MOTION.—In any private action arising under this title, the court shall stay discovery (other than discovery that is specifically directed to the applicability of the exemption provided for in this section) during the pendency of any motion by a defendant for summary judgment that is based on the grounds that—

(1) the statement or omission upon which the complaint is based is a forward-looking statement within the meaning of this section; and

(2) the exemption provided for in this section precludes a claim for relief.

(g) EXEMPTION AUTHORITY.—In addition to the exemptions provided for in this section, the Commission may, by rule or regulation, provide exemptions from or under any provision of this title, including with respect to liability that is based on a statement or that is based on projections or other forward-looking information, if and to the extent that any such exemption is consistent with the public interest and the protection of investors, as determined by the Commission.

(h) EFFECT ON OTHER AUTHORITY OF COMMISSION.—Nothing in this section limits, either expressly or by implication, the authority of the Commission to exercise similar authority or to adopt similar rules and regulations with respect to forward-looking statements under any other statute under which the Commission exercises rulemaking authority.

(i) DEFINITIONS.—For purposes of this section, the following definitions shall apply:

(1) FORWARD-LOOKING STATEMENT.—The term "forward-looking statement" means—

(A) a statement containing a projection of revenues, income (including income loss), earnings (including earnings loss) per share, capital expenditures, dividends, capital structure, or other financial items;

(B) a statement of the plans and objectives of management for future operations, including plans or objectives relating to the products or services of the issuer;

(C) a statement of future economic performance, including any such statement contained in a discussion and analysis of financial condition by the management or in the results of operations included pursuant to the rules and regulations of the Commission;

(D) any statement of the assumptions underlying or relating to any statement described in subparagraph (A), (B), or (C);

(E) any report issued by an outside reviewer retained by an issuer, to the extent that the report assesses a forward-looking statement made by the issuer; or

(F) a statement containing a projection or estimate of such other items as may be specified by rule or regulation of the Commission.

(2) INVESTMENT COMPANY.—The term "investment company" has the same meaning as in section 3(a) of the Investment Company Act of 1940.

(3) GOING PRIVATE TRANSACTION.—The term "going private transaction" has the meaning given that term under the rules or regulations of the Commission issued pursuant to section 13(e).

(4) PERSON ACTING ON BEHALF OF AN ISSUER.—The term "person acting on behalf of an issuer" means any officer, director, or employee of such issuer.

(5) OTHER TERMS.—The terms "blank check company", "rollup transaction", "partnership", "limited liability company", "executive officer of an entity" and "direct participation investment program", have the meanings given those terms by rule or regulation of the Commission.

HEARINGS BY COMMISSION

Sec. 22. Hearings may be public and may be held before the Commission, any member or members thereof, or any officer or officers of the Commission designated by it, and appropriate records thereof shall be kept.

RULES, REGULATIONS, AND ORDERS; ANNUAL REPORTS

Sec. 23. (a)(1) The Commission, the Board of Governors of the Federal Reserve System, and the other agencies enumerated in section 3(a)(34) of this title shall each have power to make such rules and regulations as may be necessary or appropriate to implement the provisions of this title for which they are responsible or for the execution of the functions vested in them by this title, and may for such purposes classify persons, securities, transactions, statements, applications, reports, and other matters within their respective jurisdictions, and prescribe greater, lesser, or different requirements for different classes thereof. No provision of this title imposing any liability shall apply to any act done or omitted in good faith in conformity with a rule, regulation, or order of the Commission, the Board of Governors of the Federal Reserve System, other agency enumerated in section 3(a)(34) of this title, or any self-regulatory organization, notwithstanding that such rule, regulation, or order may thereafter be amended or rescinded or determined by judicial or other authority to be invalid for any reason.

(2) The Commission and the Secretary of the Treasury, in making rules and regulations pursuant to any provisions of this title, shall consider among other matters the impact any such rule or regulation would have on competition. The Commission and the Secretary of the Treasury shall not adopt any such rule or regulation which would impose a burden on competition not necessary or appropriate in furtherance of the purposes of this title. The Commission and the Secretary of the Treasury shall include in the statement of basis and purpose incorporated in any rule or regulation adopted under this title, the reasons for the Commission's or the Secretary's determination that any burden on competition imposed by such rule or regulation is necessary or appropriate in furtherance of the purposes of this title.

(3) The Commission and the Secretary, in making rules and regulations pursuant to any provision of this title, considering any application for registration in accordance with section 19(a) of this title, or reviewing any proposed rule change of a self-regulatory organization in accordance with section 19(b) of this title, shall keep in a public file and make available for copying all written statements filed with the Commission and the Secretary and all written communications between the Commission or the Secretary and any person relating to the proposed rule, regulation, application, or proposed rule change; Provided, however, That the Commission and the Secretary shall not be required to keep in a public file or make available for copying any such statement or communication which it may withhold from the public in accordance with the provisions of section 552 of title 5, United States Code.

(c) The Commission, by rule, shall prescribe the procedure applicable to every case pursuant to this title of adjudication (as defined in section 551 of title 5, United States Code) not required to be determined on the record after notice and opportunity for hearing. Such rules shall, as a minimum, provide that prompt notice shall be given of any adverse action or final disposition and that such notice and the entry of any order shall be accompanied by a statement of written reasons.

(d) CEASE-AND-DESIST PROCEDURES.—Within 1 year after the date of enactment of this subsection, the Commission shall establish regulations providing for the expeditious conduct of hearings and rendering of decisions under section 21C of this title, section 8A of the Securities Act of 1933, section 9(f) of the Investment Company Act of 1940, and section 203(k) of the Investment Advisers Act of 1940.

PUBLIC AVAILABILITY OF INFORMATION

Sec. 24. (a) For purposes of section 552 of title 5, United States Code, the term "records" includes all applications, statements, reports, contracts, correspondence, notices, and other documents filed with or otherwise obtained by the Commission pursuant to this title or otherwise.

(b) It shall be unlawful for any member, officer, or employee of the Commission to disclose to any person other than a member, officer, or employee of the Commission, or to use for personal benefit, any information contained in any application, statement, report, contract, correspondence, notice, or other document filed with or otherwise obtained by the Commission (1) in contravention of the rules and regulations of the Commission under section 552 of title 5, United States

Code, or (2) in circumstances where the Commission has determined pursuant to such rules to accord confidential treatment to such information.

(c) CONFIDENTIAL DISCLOSURES.—The Commission may, in its discretion and a showing that such information is needed, provide all 'records' (as defined in subsection (a)) and other information in its possession to such persons, both domestic and foreign, as the Commission by rule deems appropriate if the person receiving such records or information provides such assurances of confidentiality as the Commission deems appropriate.

(d) RECORDS OBTAINED FROM FOREIGN SECURITIES AUTHORITIES.—Except as provided in subsection (e), the Commission shall not be compelled to disclose records obtained from a foreign securities authority if (1) the foreign securities authority has in good faith determined and represented to the Commission that public disclosure of such records would violate the laws applicable to that foreign securities authority, and (2) the Commission obtains such records pursuant to (A) such procedure as the Commission may authorize for use in connection with the administration or enforcement of the securities laws, or (B) a memorandum of understanding. For purposes of section 552 of title 5, United States Code, this subsection shall be considered a statute described in subsection (b)(3)(B) of such section 552.

(e) SAVINGS PROVISIONS.—Nothing in this section shall—

(1) alter the Commission's responsibilities under the Right to Financial Privacy Act (12 U.S.C. 3401 et seq.), as limited by section 21(h) of this Act, with respect to transfers of records covered by such statutes, or

(2) authorize the Commission to withhold information from the Congress or prevent the Commission from complying with an order of a court of the United States in an action commenced by the United States or the Commission.

COURT REVIEW OF ORDERS AND RULES

Sec. 25. (a)(1) A person aggrieved by a final order of the Commission entered pursuant to this title may obtain review of the order in the United States Court of Appeals for the circuit in which he resides or has his principal place of business, or for the District of Columbia Circuit, by filing in such court, within sixty days after the entry of the order, a written petition requesting that the order be modified or set aside in whole or in part.

(2) A copy of the petition shall be transmitted forthwith by the clerk of the court to a member of the Commission or an officer designated by the Commission for that purpose. Thereupon the Commission shall file in the court the record on which the order complained of is entered, as provided in section 2112 of title 28, United States Code, and the Federal Rules of Appellate Procedure.

(3) On the filing of the petition, the court has jurisdiction, which becomes exclusive on the filing of the record, to affirm or modify and enforce or to set aside the order in whole or in part.

(4) The findings of the Commission as to the facts, if supported by substantial evidence, are conclusive.

(5) If either party applies to the court for leave to adduce additional evidence and shows to the satisfaction of the court that the additional evidence is material and that there was reasonable ground for failure to adduce it before the Commission, the court may remand the case to the Commission for further proceedings, in whatever manner and on whatever conditions the court considers appropriate. If the case is remanded to the Commission, it shall file in the court a supplemental record containing any new evidence, any further or modified findings, and any new order.

(b)(1) A person adversely affected by a rule of the Commission promulgated pursuant to section 6, 9(h)(2), 11, 11A, 15(c)(5) or (6), 15A, 17, 17A, or 19 of this title may obtain review of this rule in the United States Court of Appeals for the circuit in which he resides or has his principal place of business or for the District of Columbia Circuit, by filing in such court, within sixty days after the promulgation of the rule, a written petition requesting that the rule be set aside.

(2) A copy of the petition shall be transmitted forthwith by the clerk of the court to a member of the Commission or an officer designated for that purpose. Thereupon, the Commission shall file in the court the rule under review and any documents referred to therein, the Commission's notice of proposed rulemaking and any documents referred to therein, all written submissions and the transcript of any oral presentations in the rulemaking, factual information not included in the foregoing that was considered by the Commission in the promulgation of the rule or proffered by the Commission as pertinent to the rule, the report of any advisory committee received or considered by the Commission in the rulemaking, and any other materials prescribed by the court.

(3) On the filing of the petition, the court has jurisdiction, which becomes exclusive on the filing of the materials set forth in paragraph (2) of this subsection, to affirm and enforce or to set aside the rule.

(4) The findings of the Commission as to the facts identified by the Commission as the basis, in whole or in part, of the rule, if supported by substantial evidence, are conclusive. The court shall affirm and enforce the rule unless the Commission's action in promulgating the rule is found to be arbitrary, capricious, an abuse of discretion, or otherwise not in accordance with law; contrary to constitutional right, power, privilege or immunity; in excess of statutory jurisdiction, authority, or limitations, or short of statutory right; or without observance of procedure required by law.

(5) If proceedings have been instituted under this subsection in two or more courts of appeals with respect to the same rule, the Commission shall file the materials set forth in paragraph (2) of this subsection in that court in which a proceeding was first instituted. The other courts shall thereupon transfer all such proceedings to the court in which the materials have been filed. For the convenience of the parties in the interest of justice that court may thereafter transfer all the proceedings to any other court of appeals.

(c) (1) No objection to an order or rule of the Commission, for which review is sought under this section, may be considered by the court unless it was urged before the Commission or there was reasonable ground for failure to do so.

(2) The filing of a petition under this section does not operate as a stay of the Commission's order or rule. Until the court's jurisdiction becomes exclusive, the Commission may stay its order or rule pending judicial review if it finds that justice so requires. After the filing of a petition under this section, the court, on whatever conditions may be required and to the extent necessary to prevent irreparable injury, may issue all necessary and appropriate process to stay the order or rule or to preserve status or rights pending its review; but (notwithstanding section 705 of title 5, United States Code) no such process may be issued by the court before the filing of the record or the materials set forth in subsection (b)(2) of this section unless: (A) the Commission has denied a stay or failed to grant requested relief, (B) a reasonable period has expired since the filing of an application for a stay without a decision by the Commission, or (C) there was reasonable ground for failure to apply to the Commission.

(3) When the same order or rule is the subject of one or more petitions for review filed under this section and an action for enforcement filed in a district court of the United States under section 21 (d) or (e) of this title, that court in which the petition or the action is first filed has jurisdiction with respect to the order or rule to the exclusion of any other court, and thereupon all such proceedings shall be transferred to that court; but, for the convenience of the parties in the interest of justice, that court may thereafter transfer all the proceedings to any other court of appeals or district court of the United States, whether or not a petition for review or an action for enforcement was originally filed in the transferee court. The scope of review by a district court under section 21 (d) or (e) of this title is in all cases the same as by a court of appeals under this section.

(d) (1) For purposes of the preceding subsections of this section, the term "Commission" includes the agencies enumerated in section 3(a)(34) of this title insofar as such agencies are acting pursuant to this title and the Secretary of the Treasury insofar as he is acting pursuant to section 15C of this title.

(2) For purposes of subsection (a)(4) of this section and section 706 of title 5, United States Code, an order of the Commission pursuant to section 19(a) of this title denying registration to a clearing agency for which the Commission is not the appropriate regulatory agency or pursuant to section 19(b) of this title disapproving a proposed rule change by such a clearing agency shall be deemed to be an order of the appropriate regulatory agency for such clearing agency insofar as such order was entered by reason of a determination by such appropriate regulatory agency pursuant to section 19(a)(2)(C) or 19(b)(4)(C) of this title that such registration or proposed rule change would be inconsistent with the safeguarding of securities or funds.

UNLAWFUL REPRESENTATIONS

Sec. 26. No action or failure to act by the Commission or the Board of Governors of the Federal Reserve System, in the administration of this title shall be construed to mean that the particular authority has in any way passed upon the merits of, or given approval to, any security or any transaction or transactions therein, nor shall such action or failure to act with regard to any statement or report filed with or examined by such authority pursuant to this title or rules and regulations thereunder, be deemed a finding by such authority that such statement or report is true and accurate on its face or that it is not false or misleading. It shall be unlawful to make, or cause to be made, to any prospective purchaser or seller of a security any representation that any such action or failure to act by any such authority is to be so construed or has such effect.

JURISDICTION OF OFFENSES AND SUITS

Sec. 27. The district courts of the United States and the United States courts of any Territory or other place subject to the jurisdiction of the United States shall have exclusive jurisdiction of violations of this title or the rules and regulations thereunder, and of all suits in equity and actions at law brought to enforce any liability or duty created by this title or the rules and regulations thereunder. Any criminal proceeding may be brought in the district wherein any act or transaction constituting the violation occurred. Any suit or action to enforce any liability or duty created by this title or rules and regulations thereunder, or to enjoin any violation of such title or rules and regulations, may be brought in any such district or in the district wherein the defendant is found or is an inhabitant or transacts business, and process in such cases may be served in any other district of which the defendant is an inhabitant or wherever the defendant may be found. Judgments and decrees so rendered shall be subject to review as provided in sections 1254, 1291, 1292, and 1294 of title 28, United States Code. No costs shall be assessed for or against the Commission in any proceeding under this title brought by or against it in the Supreme Court or such other courts.

SPECIAL PROVISION RELATING TO STATUTE OF LIMITATIONS ON PRIVATE CAUSES OF ACTION

Sec. 27A. (a) Effect on Pending Causes of Action.—The limitation period for any private civil action implied under section 10(b) of this Act that was commenced on or before June 19, 1991, shall be the limitation period provided by the laws applicable in the jurisdiction, including principles of retroactivity, as such laws existed on June 19, 1991.

(b) Effect on Dismissed Causes of Action.—Any private civil action implied under section 10(b) of this Act that was commenced on or before June 19, 1991—

(1) which was dismissed as time barred subsequent to June 19, 1991, and

(2) which would have been timely filed under the limitation period provided by the laws applicable in the jurisdiction, including principles of retroactivity, as such laws existed on June 19, 1991,

shall be reinstated on motion by the plaintiff not later than 60 days after the date of enactment of this section.

EFFECT ON EXISTING LAW

Sec. 28. (a) Except as provided in subsection (f), the rights and remedies provided by this title shall be in addition to any and all other rights and remedies that may exist at law or in equity; but no person permitted to maintain a suit for damages under the provisions of this title shall recover, through satisfaction of judgment in one or more actions, a total amount in excess of his actual damages on account of the act complained of. Except as otherwise specifically provided in this title, nothing in this title shall affect the jurisdiction of the securities commission (or any agency or officer performing like functions) of any State over any security or any person insofar as it does not conflict with the provisions of this title or the rules and regulations thereunder. No State law which prohibits or regulates the making or promoting of wagering or gaming contracts, or the operation of "bucket shops" or other similar or related activities, shall invalidate any put, call, straddle, option, privilege, or other security subject to this title, or apply to any activity which is incidental or related to the offer, purchase, sale, exercise, settlement, or closeout of any such security. No provision of State law regarding the offer, sale, or distribution of securities shall apply to any transaction in a security futures product, except that this sentence shall not be construed as limiting any State antifraud law of general applicability.

(b) Nothing in this title shall be construed to modify existing law with regard to the binding effect (1) on any member of or participant in any self-regulatory organization of any action taken by the authorities of such organization to settle disputes between its members or participants, (2) on any municipal securities dealer or municipal securities broker of any action taken pursuant to a procedure established by the Municipal Securities Rulemaking Board to settle disputes between municipal securities dealers and municipal securities brokers, or (3) of any action described in paragraph (1) or (2) on any person who has agreed to be bound thereby.

(c) The stay, setting aside, or modification pursuant to section 19(e) of this title of any disciplinary sanction imposed by a self-regulatory organization on a member thereof, person associated with a member, or participant therein, shall not affect the validity or force of any action taken as a result of such sanction by the self-regulatory organization prior to such stay, setting aside, or modification: Provided, That such action is not inconsistent with the provisions of this title or the rules or regulations thereunder. The rights of any person acting in good faith which arise out of any such action shall not be affected in any way by such stay, setting aside, or modification.

(d) No State or political subdivision thereof shall impose any tax on any change in beneficial or record ownership of securities effected through the facilities of a registered clearing agency or registered transfer agent or any nominee thereof or custodian therefor or upon the delivery or transfer of securities to or through or receipt from such agency or agent or any nominee thereof or custodian therefor, unless such change in beneficial or record ownership or such transfer or delivery or receipt would otherwise be taxable by such State or political subdivision if the facilities of such registered clearing agency, registered transfer agent, or any nominee thereof or custodian therefor were not physically located in the taxing State or political subdivision. No State or political subdivision thereof shall impose any tax on securities which are deposited in or retained by a registered clearing agency, registered transfer agent, or any nominee thereof or custodian therefor, unless such securities would otherwise be taxable by such State or political subdivision if the facilities of such registered clearing agency, registered transfer agent, or any nominee thereof or custodian therefor were not physically located in the taxing State or political subdivision.

(e)(1) No person using the mails, or any means or instrumentality of interstate commerce, in the exercise of investment discretion with respect to an account shall be deemed to have acted unlawfully or to have breached a fiduciary duty under State or Federal law unless expressly provided to the contrary by a law enacted by the Congress or any State subsequent to the date of enactment of the Securities Acts Amendments of 1975 solely by reason of his having caused the account to pay a member of an exchange, broker, or dealer an amount of commission for effecting a securities transaction in excess of the amount of commission another member of an exchange, broker, or dealer would have charged for effecting that transaction, if such person determined in good faith that such amount of commission was reasonable in relation to the value of the brokerage and research services provided by such member, broker, or dealer, viewed in terms of either that particular transaction or his overall responsibilities with respect to the accounts as to which he exercises investment discretion. This subsection is exclusive and plenary insofar as conduct is covered by the foregoing, unless otherwise expressly provided by contract: Provided, however, That nothing in this subsection shall be construed to impair or limit the power of the Commission under any other provision of this title or otherwise.

(2) A person exercising investment discretion with respect to an account shall make such disclosure of his policies and practices with respect to commissions that will be paid for effecting securities transactions, at such times and in such manner, as the appropriate regulatory agency, by rule, may prescribe as necessary or appropriate in the public interest or for the protection of investors.

(3) For purposes of this subsection a person provides brokerage and research services insofar as he—

(A) furnishes advice, either directly or through publications or writings, as to the value of securities, the advisability of investing in, purchasing, or selling securities, and the availability of securities or purchasers or sellers of securities;

(B) furnishes analyses and reports concerning issuers, industries, securities, economic factors and trends, portfolio strategy, and the performance of accounts; or

(C) effects securities transactions and performs functions incidental thereto (such as clearance, settlement, and custody) or required in connection therewith by rules of the Commission or a self-regulatory organization of which such person is a member or person associated with a member or in which such person is a participant.

(4) The provisions of this subsection shall not apply with regard to securities that are security futures products.

(f) LIMITATIONS ON REMEDIES.—

(1) CLASS ACTION LIMITATIONS.—No covered class action based upon the statutory or common law of any State or subdivision thereof may be maintained in any State or Federal court by any private party alleging—

(A) a misrepresentation or omission of a material fact in connection with the purchase or sale of a covered security; or

(B) that the defendant used or employed any manipulative or deceptive device or contrivance in connection with the purchase or sale of a covered security.

(2) REMOVAL OF COVERED CLASS ACTIONS.—Any covered class action brought in any State court involving a covered security, as set forth in paragraph (1), shall be removable to the Federal district court for the district in which the action is pending, and shall be subject to paragraph (1).

(3) PRESERVATION OF CERTAIN ACTIONS.—

(A) Actions under state law of state of incorporation.—

(i) Actions preserved.—Notwithstanding paragraph (1) or (2), a covered class action described in clause (ii) of this subparagraph that is based upon the statutory or common law of the State in which the issuer is incorporated (in the case of a corporation) or organized (in the case of any other entity) may be maintained in a State or Federal court by a private party.

(ii) Permissible actions.—A covered class action is described in this clause if it involves—

(I) the purchase or sale of securities by the issuer or an affiliate of the issuer exclusively from or to holders of equity securities of the issuer; or

(II) any recommendation, position, or other communication with respect to the sale of securities of an issuer that—

(aa) is made by or on behalf of the issuer or an affiliate of the issuer to holders of equity securities of the issuer; and

(bb) concerns decisions of such equity holders with respect to voting their securities, acting in response to a tender or exchange offer, or exercising dissenters' or appraisal rights.

(B) State actions.—

(i) In general.—Notwithstanding any other provision of this subsection, nothing in this subsection may be construed to preclude a State or political subdivision thereof or a State pension plan from bringing an action involving a covered security on its own behalf, or as a member of a class comprised solely of other States, political subdivisions, or State pension plans that are named plaintiffs, and that have authorized participation, in such action.

(ii) State pension plan defined.—For purposes of this subparagraph, the term 'State pension plan' means a pension plan established and maintained for its employees by the government of a State or political subdivision thereof, or by any agency or instrumentality thereof.

(C) Actions under contractual agreements between issuers and indenture trustees.—Notwithstanding paragraph (1) or (2), a covered class action that seeks to enforce a contractual agreement between an issuer and an indenture trustee may be maintained in a State or Federal court by a party to the agreement or a successor to such party.

(D) Remand of removed actions.—In an action that has been removed from a State court pursuant to paragraph (2), if the Federal court determines that the action may be maintained in State court pursuant to this subsection, the Federal court shall remand such action to such State court.

(4) PRESERVATION OF STATE JURISDICTION.—The securities commission (or any agency or office performing like functions) of any State shall retain jurisdiction under the laws of such State to investigate and bring enforcement actions.

(5) DEFINITIONS.—For purposes of this subsection, the following definitions shall apply:

(A) Affiliate of the issuer.—The term 'affiliate of the issuer' means a person that directly or indirectly, through one or more intermediaries, controls or is controlled by or is under common control with, the issuer.

(B) Covered class action.—The term 'covered class action' means—

(i) any single lawsuit in which—

(I) damages are sought on behalf of more than 50 persons or prospective class members, and questions of law or fact common to those persons or members of the prospective class, without reference to issues of individualized reliance on an alleged misstatement or omission, predominate over any questions affecting only individual persons or members; or

(II) one or more named parties seek to recover damages on a representative basis on behalf of themselves and other unnamed parties similarly situated, and questions of law or fact common to those persons or members of the prospective class predominate over any questions affecting only individual persons or members; or

(ii) any group of lawsuits filed in or pending in the same court and involving common questions of law or fact, in which—

(I) damages are sought on behalf of more than 50 persons; and

(II) the lawsuits are joined, consolidated, or otherwise proceed as a single action for any purpose.

(C) Exception for derivative actions.—Notwithstanding subparagraph (B), the term 'covered class action' does not include an exclusively derivative action brought by one or more shareholders on behalf of a corporation.

(D) Counting of certain class members.—For purposes of this paragraph, a corporation, investment company, pension plan, partnership, or other entity, shall be treated as one person or prospective class member, but only if the entity is not established for the purpose of participating in the action.

(E) Covered security.—The term 'covered security' means a security that satisfies the standards for a covered security specified in paragraph (1) or (2) of section 18(b) of the Securities Act of 1933, at the time during which it is alleged that the misrepresentation, omission, or manipulative or deceptive conduct occurred, except that such term shall not include any debt security that is exempt from registration under the Securities Act of 1933 pursuant to rules issued by the Commission under section 4(2) of that Act.

(F) Rule of construction.—Nothing in this paragraph shall be construed to affect the discretion of a State court in determining whether actions filed in such court should be joined, consolidated, or otherwise allowed to proceed as a single action.

VALIDITY OF CONTRACTS

Sec. 29. (a) Any condition, stipulation, or provision binding any person to waive compliance with any provision of this title or of any rule or regulation thereunder, or of any rule of an exchange required thereby shall be void.

(b) Every contract made in violation of any provision of this title or of any rule or regulation thereunder, and every contract (including any contract for listing a security on an exchange) heretofore or hereafter made the performance of which involves the violation of, or the continuance of any relationship or practice in violation of, any provision of this title or any rule or regulation thereunder, shall be void (1) as regards the rights of any person who, in violation of any such provision, rule, or regulation, shall have made or engaged in the performance of any such contract, and (2) as regards the rights of any person who, not being a party to such contract, shall have acquired any right thereunder with actual knowledge of the facts by reason of which the making or performance of such contract was in violation of any such provision, rule, or regulation: *Provided,* (A) That no contract shall be void by reason of this subsection because of any violation of any rule or regulation prescribed pursuant to paragraph (3) of subsection (c) of section 15 of this title, and (B) that no contract shall be deemed to be void by reason of this subsection in any action maintained in reliance upon this subsection, by any person to or for whom any broker or dealer sells, or from or for whom any broker or dealer purchases, a security in violation of any rule or regulation prescribed pursuant to paragraph (1) or (2) of subsection (c) of section 15 of this title, unless such action is brought within one year after the discovery that such sale or purchase involves such violation and within 3 years after such violation. The Commission may, in a rule or regulation prescribed pursuant to such paragraph (2), of such section 15(c), designate such rule or regulation, or portion thereof, as a rule or regulation, or portion thereof, a contract in violation of which shall not be void by reason of this subsection.

(c) Nothing in this title shall be construed (1) to affect the validity of any loan or extension of credit (or any extension or renewal thereof) made or of any lien created prior or subsequent to the enactment of this title, unless at the time of the making of such loan or extension of credit (or extension or renewal thereof) or the creating of such lien, the person making such loan or extension of credit (or extension or renewal thereof) or acquiring such lien shall have actual knowledge of facts by reason of which the making of such loan or extension of credit (or extension or renewal thereof) or the acquisition of such lien is a violation of the provisions of this title or any rule or regulation thereunder, or (2) to afford a defense to the collection of any debt or obligation or the enforcement of any lien by any person who shall have acquired such debt, obligation, or lien in good faith for value and without actual knowledge of the violation of any provision of this title or any rule or regulation thereunder affecting the legality of such debt, obligation, or lien.

FOREIGN SECURITIES EXCHANGES

Sec. 30. (a) It shall be unlawful for any broker or dealer, directly or indirectly, to make use of the mails or of any means or instrumentality of interstate commerce for the purpose of effecting on an exchange not within or subject to the jurisdiction of the United States, any transaction in any security the issuer of which is a resident of, or is organized under the laws of, or has its principal place of business in, a place within or subject to the jurisdiction of the United States, in contravention of such rules and regulations as the Commission may prescribe as necessary or appropriate in the public interest or for the protection of investors or to prevent the evasion of this chapter.

(b) The provisions of this chapter or of any rule or regulation thereunder shall not apply to any person insofar as he transacts a business in securities without the jurisdiction of the United

States, unless he transacts such business in contravention of such rules and regulations as the Commission may prescribe as necessary or appropriate to prevent the evasion of this chapter.

PROHIBITED FOREIGN TRADE PRACTICES BY ISSUERS

Sec. 30A. (a) PROHIBITION.—It shall be unlawful for any issuer which has a class of securities registered pursuant to section 12 of this title or which is required to file reports under section 15(d) of this title, or for any officer, director, employee, or agent of such issuer or any stockholder thereof acting on behalf of such issuer, to make use of the mails or any means of instrumentality of interstate commerce corruptly in furtherance of an offer, payment, promise to pay, or authorization of the payment of any money, or offer, gift, promise to give, or authorization of the giving of anything of value to—

(1) any foreign official for purposes of—

(A)(i) influencing any act or decision of such foreign official in his official capacity, (ii) inducing such foreign official to do or omit to do any act in violation of the lawful duty of such official, or (iii) securing any improper advantage; or

(B) inducing such foreign official to use his influence with a foreign government or instrumentality thereof to affect or influence any act or decision of such government or instrumentality,

in order to assist such issuer in obtaining or retaining business for or with, or directing business to, any person;

(2) any foreign political party or official thereof or any candidate for foreign political office for purposes of—

(A)(i) influencing any act or decision of such party, official, or candidate in its or his official capacity, (ii) inducing such party, official, or candidate to do or omit to do an act in violation of the lawful duty of such party, official, or candidate, or (iii) securing any improper advantage; or

(B) inducing such party, official, or candidate to use its or his influence with a foreign government or instrumentality thereof to affect or influence any act or decision of such government or instrumentality,

in order to assist such issuer in obtaining or retaining business for or with, or directing business to, any person; or

(3) any person, while knowing that all or a portion of such money or thing of value will be offered, given, or promised, directly or indirectly, to any foreign official, to any foreign political party or official thereof, or to any candidate for foreign political office, for purposes of—

(A)(i) influencing any act or decision of such foreign official, political party, party official, or candidate in his or its official capacity, (ii) inducing such foreign official, political party, party official, or candidate to do or omit to do any act in violation of the lawful duty of such foreign official, political party, party official, or candidate, or (iii) securing any improper advantage;

(B) inducing such foreign official, political party, party official, or candidate to use his or its influence with a foreign government or instrumentality thereof to affect or influence any act or decision of such government or instrumentality,

in order to assist such issuer in obtaining or retaining business for or with, or directing business to, any person.

(b) EXCEPTION FOR ROUTINE GOVERNMENTAL ACTION.—Subsections (a) and (g) shall not apply to any facilitating or expediting payment to a foreign official, political party, or party official the purpose of which is to expedite or to secure the performance of a routine governmental action by a foreign official, political party, or party official.

(c) AFFIRMATIVE DEFENSES.—It shall be an affirmative defense to actions under subsection (a) or (g) that—

(1) the payment, gift, offer, or promise of anything of value that was made, was lawful under the written laws and regulations of the foreign official's, political party's, party official's, or candidate's country; or

(2) the payment, gift, offer, or promise of anything of value that was made, was a reasonable and bona fide expenditure, such as travel and lodging expenses, incurred by or on behalf of a foreign official, party, party official, or candidate and was directly related to—

(A) the promotion, demonstration, or explanation of products or services; or

(B) the execution or performance of a contract with a foreign government or agency thereof.

(d) GUIDELINES BY THE ATTORNEY GENERAL.—Not later than one year after the date of the enactment of the Foreign Corrupt Practices Act Amendments of 1988, the Attorney General, after consultation with the Commission, the Secretary of Commerce, the United States Trade Representative, the Secretary of State, and the Secretary of the Treasury, and after obtaining the views of all interested persons through public notice and comment procedures, shall determine to what extent compliance with this section would be enhanced and the business community would be assisted by further clarification of the preceding provisions of this section and may, based on such determination and to the extent necessary and appropriate, issue—

(1) guidelines describing specific types of conduct, associated with common types of export sales arrangments and business contracts, which for purposes of the Department of Justice's present enforcement policy, the Attorney General determines would be in conformance with the preceding providisions of this section; and

(2) general precautionary procedures which issuers may use on a voluntary basis to conform their conduct to the Department of Justice's present enforcement policy regarding the preceding provisions of this section.

The Attorney General shall issue the guidelines and procedures referred to in the preceding sentence in accordance with the provisions of subchapter II of chapter 5 of title 5, United States Code, and those guidelines and procedures shall be subject to the provisions of chapter 7 of that title.

(e) OPINIONS OF THE ATTORNEY GENERAL.—(1) The Attorney General, after consultation with appropriate departments and agencies of the United States and after obtaining the views of all interested persons through public notice and comment procedures, shall establish a procedure to provide responses to specific inquiries by issuers concerning conformance of their conduct with the Department of Justice's present enforcement policy regarding the preceding provisions of this section. The Attorney General shall, within 30 days after receiving such a request, issue an opinion in response to that request. The opinion shall state whether or not certain specified prospective conduct would, for purposes of the Department of Justice's present enforcement policy, violate the preceding provisions of this section. Additional requests for opinions may be filed with the Attorney General regarding other specified prospective conduct that is beyond the scope of conduct specified in previous requests. In any action brought under the applicable provisions of this section, there shall be a rebuttable presumption that conduct, which is specified in a request by an issuer and for which the Attorney General has issued an opinion that such conduct is in conformity with the Department of Justice's present enforcement policy, is in compliance with the preceding provisions of this section. Such a presumption may be rebutted by a preponderance of the evidence. In considering the presumption for purposes of this paragraph, a court shall weigh all relevant factors, including but not limited to whether the information submitted to the Attorney General was accurate and complete and whether it was within the scope of the conduct specified in any request received by the Attorney General. The Attorney General shall establish the procedure required by this paragraph in accordance with the provisions of subchapter II of chapter 5 of title 5, United States Code, and that procedure shall be subject to the provisions of chapter 7 of that title.

(2) Any document or other material which is provided to, received by, or prepared in the Department of Justice or any other department or agency of the United States in connection with a request by an issuer under the procedure established under paragraph (1), shall be exempt from disclosure under section 552 of title 5, United States Code, and shall not, except with the consent of the issuer, be made publicly available, regardless of whether the Attorney General responds to such a request or the issuer withdraws such request before receiving a response.

(3) Any issuer who has made a request to the Attorney General under paragraph (1) may withdraw such request prior to the time the Attorney General issues an opinion in response to such request. Any request so withdrawn shall have no force or effect.

(4) The Attorney General shall, to the maximum extent practicable, provide timely guidance concerning the Department of Justice's present enforcement policy with respect to the preceding provisions of this section to potential exporters and small businesses that are unable to obtain specialized counsel on issues pertaining to such provisions. Such guidance shall be limited to responses to requests under paragraph (1) concerning conformity of specified prospective conduct with the Department of Justice's present enforcement policy regarding the preceding provisions of this section and general explanations of compliance responsibilities and of potential liabilities under the preceding provisions of this section.

(f) DEFINITIONS.—For purposes of this section:

(1) The term 'foreign official' means any officer or employee of a foreign government or any department, agency, or instrumentality thereof, or of a public international organization, or any person acting in an official capacity for or on behalf of any such government or department, agency, or instrumentality, or for or on behalf of any such public international organization.

(B) For purposes of subparagraph (A), the term 'public international organization' means—

(i) an organization that is designated by Executive order pursuant to section 1 of the International Organizations Immunities Act (22 U.S.C. 288); or

(ii) any other international organization that is designated by the President by Executive order for the purposes of this section, effective as of the date of publication of such order in the Federal Register.

(2) (A) A person's state of mind is 'knowing' with respect to conduct, a circumstance, or a result if—

(i) such person is aware that such person is engaging in such conduct, that such circumstance exists, or that such result is substantially certain to occur; or

(ii) such person has a firm belief that such circumstance exists or that such result is substantially certain to occur.

(B) When knowledge of the existence of a particular circumstance is required for an offense, such knowledge is established if a person is aware of a high probability of the existence of such circumstance, unless the person actually believes that such circumstance does not exist.

(3) (A) The term 'routine governmental action' means only an action which is ordinarily and commonly performed by a foreign official in—

(i) obtaining permits, licenses, or other official documents to qualify a person to do business in a foreign country;

(ii) processing governmental papers, such as visas and work orders;

(iii) providing police protection, mail pick-up and delivery, or scheduling inspections associated with contract performance or inspections related to transit of goods across country;

(iv) providing phone service, power and water supply, loading and unloading cargo, or protecting perishable products or commodities from deterioration; or

(v) actions of a similar nature.

(B) The term "routine governmental action" does not include any decision by a foreign official whether, or on what terms, to award new business to or to continue business with a particular party, or any action taken by a foreign official involved in the decisionmaking process to encourage a decision to award new business to or continue business with a particular party.

(g) ALTERNATIVE JURISDICTION.—

(1) It shall also be unlawful for any issuer organized under the laws of the United States, or a State, territory, possession, or commonwealth of the United States or a political subdivision thereof and which has a class of securities registered pursuant to section 12 of this title or which is required to file reports under section 15(d) of this title, or for any United States person that is an officer, director, employee, or agent of such issuer or a stockholder thereof acting on behalf of

such issuer, to corruptly do any act outside the United States in furtherance of an offer, payment, promise to pay, or authorization of the payment of any money, or offer, gift, promise to give, or authorization of the giving of anything of value to any of the persons or entities set forth in paragraphs (1), (2), and (3) of subsection (a) of this section for the purposes set forth therein, irrespective of whether such issuer or such officer, director, employee, agent, or stockholder makes use of the mails or any means or instrumentality of interstate commerce in furtherance of such offer, gift, payment, promise, or authorization.

(2) As used in this subsection, the term 'United States person' means a national of the United States (as defined in section 101 of the Immigration and Nationality Act (8 U.S.C. 1101)) or any corporation, partnership, association, joint-stock company, business trust, unincorporated organization, or sole proprietorship organized under the laws of the United States or any State, territory, possession, or commonwealth of the United States, or any political subdivision thereof.

TRANSACTION FEES

Sec. 31. (a) Recovery of Cost of Services.—The Commission shall, in accordance with this section, collect transaction fees and assessments that are designed to recover the costs to the Government of the supervision and regulation of securities markets and securities professionals, and costs related to such supervision and regulation, including enforcement activities, policy and rulemaking activities, administration, legal services, and international regulatory activities.

(b) Exchange-Traded Securities.—Subject to sub-section (j), each national securities exchange shall pay to the Commission a fee at a rate equal to $15 per $1,000,000 of the aggregate dollar amount of sales of securities (other than bonds, debentures, other evidences of indebtedness, security futures products, and options on securities indexes (excluding a narrow-based security index)) transacted on such national securities exchange.

(c) Off-Exchange Trades of Exchange Registered and Last-Sale-Reported Securities.—Subject to subsection (j), each national securities association shall pay to the Commission a fee at a rate equal to $15 per $1,000,000 of the aggregate dollar amount of sales transacted by or through any member of such association otherwise than on a national securities exchange of securities (other than bonds, debentures, other evidences of indebtedness, security futures products, and options on securities indexes (excluding a narrow-based security index)) registered on a national securities exchange or subject to prompt last sale reporting pursuant to the rules of the Commission or a registered national securities association.

(d) Assessments on Security Futures Transactions.—Each national securities exchange and national securities association shall pay to the Commission an assessment equal to $0.009 for each round turn transaction (treated as including one purchase and one sale of a contract of sale for future delivery) on a security future traded on such national securities exchange or by or through any member of such association otherwise than on a national securities exchange, except that for fiscal year 2007 and each succeeding fiscal year such assessment shall be equal to $0.0042 for each such transaction.

(e) Dates for Payments.—The fees and assessments required by subsections (b), (c), and (d) of this section shall be paid—

(1) on or before March 15, with respect to transactions and sales occurring during the period beginning on the preceding September 1 and ending at the close of the preceding December 31; and

(2) on or before September 30, with respect to transactions and sales occurring during the period beginning on the preceding January 1 and ending at the close of the preceding August 31.

(f) Exemptions.—The Commission, by rule, may exempt any sale of securities or any class of sales of securities from any fee or assessment imposed by this section, if the Commission finds that such exemption is consistent with the public interest, the equal regulation of markets and brokers and dealers, and the development of a national market system.

(g) Publication.—The Commission shall publish in the Federal Register notices of the fee and assessment rates applicable under this section for each fiscal year not later than April 30 of the fiscal year preceding the fiscal year to which such rate applies, together with any estimates or projections on which such fees are based.

(h) Pro Rata Application.—The rates per $1,000,000 required by this section shall be applied pro rata to amounts and balances of less than $1,000,000.

(i) Deposit of Fees.—

(1) Offsetting Collections.—Fees collected pursuant to subsections (b), (c), and (d) for any fiscal year—

(A) shall be deposited and credited as offsetting collections to the account providing appropriations to the Commission; and

(B) except as provided in subsection (k), shall not be collected for any fiscal year except to the extent provided in advance in appropriation Acts.

(2) General Revenues Prohibited.—No fees collected pursuant to subsections (b), (c), and (d) for fiscal year 2002 or any succeeding fiscal year shall be deposited and credited as general revenue of the Treasury.

(j) Recapture of Projection Windfalls for Further Rate Reductions.—

(1) Annual Adjustment.—For each of the fiscal years 2003 through 2011, the Commission shall by order adjust each of the rates applicable under subsections (b) and (c) for such fiscal year to a uniform adjusted rate that, when applied to the baseline estimate of the aggregate dollar amount of sales for such fiscal year, is reasonably likely to produce aggregate fee collections under this section (including assessments collected under subsection (d)) that are equal to the target offsetting collection amount for such fiscal year.

(2) Mid-Year Adjustment.—For each of the fiscal years 2002 through 2011, the Commission shall determine, by March 1 of such fiscal year, whether, based on the actual aggregate dollar volume of sales during the first 5 months of such fiscal year, the baseline estimate of the aggregate dollar volume of sales used under paragraph (1) for such fiscal year (or $48,800,000,000,000 in the case of fiscal year 2002) is reasonably likely to be 10 percent (or more) greater or less than the actual aggregate dollar volume of sales for such fiscal year. If the Commission so determines, the Commission shall by order, no later than such March 1, adjust each of the rates applicable under subsections (b) and (c) for such fiscal year to a uniform adjusted rate that, when applied to the revised estimate of the aggregate dollar amount of sales for the remainder of such fiscal year, is reasonably likely to produce aggregate fee collections under this section (including fees collected during such 5-month period and assessments collected under subsection (d)) that are equal to the target offsetting collection amount for such fiscal year. In making such revised estimate, the Commission shall, after consultation with the Congressional Budget Office and the Office of Management and Budget, use the same methodology required by subsection (l)(2).

(3) Final Rate Adjustment.—For fiscal year 2012 and all of the succeeding fiscal years, the Commission shall by order adjust each of the rates applicable under subsections (b) and (c) for all of such fiscal years to a uniform adjusted rate that, when applied to the baseline estimate of the aggregate dollar amount of sales for fiscal year 2012, is reasonably likely to produce aggregate fee collections under this section in fiscal year 2012 (including assessments collected under subsection (d)) equal to the target offsetting collection amount for fiscal year 2011.

(4) Review and Effective Date.—In exercising its authority under this subsection, the Commission shall not be required to comply with the provisions of section 553 of title 5, United States Code. An adjusted rate prescribed under paragraph (1), (2), or (3) and published under subsection (g) shall not be subject to judicial review. Subject to subsections (i)(1)(B) and (k)—

(A) an adjusted rate prescribed under paragraph (1) shall take effect on the later of—

(i) the first day of the fiscal year to which such rate applies; or

(ii) thirty days after the date on which a regular appropriation to the Commission for such fiscal year is enacted;

(B) an adjusted rate prescribed under paragraph (2) shall take effect on April 1 of the fiscal year to which such rate applies; and

(C) an adjusted rate prescribed under paragraph (3) shall take effect on the later of—

(i) the first day of fiscal year 2012; or

(ii) thirty days after the date on which a regular appropriation to the Commission for fiscal year 2012 is enacted.

(k) Lapse of Appropriation.—If on the first day of a fiscal year a regular appropriation to the Commission has not been enacted, the Commission shall continue to collect (as offsetting collections) the fees and assessments under subsections (b), (c), and (d) at the rate in effect during the preceding fiscal year, until 30 days after the date such a regular appropriation is enacted.

(l) Definitions.—For purposes of this section:

(1) Target Offsetting Collection Amount.—The target offsetting collection amount for each of the fiscal years 2002 through 2011 is determined according to the following table:

"Fiscal year:	Target offsetting collection amount
2002	$732,000,000
2003	$849,000,000
2004	$1,028,000,000
2005	$1,220,000,000
2006	$1,435,000,000
2007	$881,000,000
2008	$892,000,000
2009	$1,023,000,000
2010	$1,161,000,000
2011	$1,321,000,000

(2) Baseline Estimate of the Aggregate Dollar Amount of Sales.—The baseline estimate of the aggregate dollar amount of sales for any fiscal year is the baseline estimate of the aggregate dollar amount of sales of securities (other than bonds, debentures, other evidences of indebtedness, security futures products, and options on securities indexes (excluding a narrow-based security index)) to be transacted on each national securities exchange and by or through any member of each national securities association (otherwise than on a national securities exchange) during such fiscal year as determined by the Commission, after consultation with the Congressional Budget Office and the Office of Management and Budget, using the methodology required for making projections pursuant to section 257 of the Balanced Budget and Emergency Deficit Control Act of 1985.

PENALTIES

Sec. 32. (a) Any person who willfully violates any provision of this title (other than section 30A), or any rule or regulation thereunder the violation of which is made unlawful or the observance of which is required under the terms of this title, or any person who willfully and knowingly makes, or causes to be made, any statement in any application, report, or document required to be filed under this title or any rule or regulation thereunder or any undertaking contained in a registration statement as provided in subsection (d) of section 15 of this title or by any self-regulatory organization in connection with an application for membership or participation therein or to become associated with a member thereof, which statement was false or misleading with respect to any material fact, shall upon conviction be fined not more than $5,000,000, or imprisoned not more than 20 years, or both, except that when such person is a person other than a natural person, a fine not exceeding $25,000,000 may be imposed; but no person shall be subject to imprisonment under this section for the violation of any rule or regulation if he proves that he had no knowledge of such rule or regulation.

(b) Any issuer which fails to file information, documents, or reports required to be filed under subsection (d) of section 15 of this title or any rule or regulation thereunder shall forfeit to the United States the sum of $100 for each and every day such failure to file shall continue. Such forfeiture, which shall be in lieu of any criminal penalty for such failure to file which might be deemed to arise under subsection (a) of this section, shall be payable into the Treasury of the United States and shall be recoverable in a civil suit in the name of the United States.

(c)(1)(A) Any issuer that violates subsection (a) or (g) of section 30A shall be fined not more than $2,000,000.

(B) Any issuer that violates subsection (a) or (g) of section 30A(a) shall be subject to a civil penalty of not more than $10,000 imposed in an action brought by the Commission.

(2)(A) Any officer, director, employee, or agent of an issuer, or stockholder acting on behalf of such issuer, who willfully violates subsection (a) or (g) of section 30A of this title shall be fined not more than $100,000, or imprisoned not more than 5 years, or both.

(B) Any officer, director, employee, or agent of an issuer, or stockholder acting on behalf of such issuer, who violates subsection (a) or (g) of section 30A of this title shall be subject to a civil penalty of not more than $10,000 imposed in an action brought by the Commission.

(3) Whenever a fine is imposed under paragraph (2) upon any officer, director, employee, agent, or stockholder of an issuer, such fine may not be paid, directly or indirectly, by such issuer.

SEPARABILITY OF PROVISIONS

Sec. 33. If any provision of this Act, or the application of such provision to any person or circumstances, shall be held invalid, the remainder of the Act, and the application of such provision to persons or circumstances other than those as to which it is held invalid, shall not be affected thereby.

EFFECTIVE DATE

Sec. 34. This Act shall become effective on July 1, 1934, except that sections 6 and 12(b), (c), (d), and (e) shall become effective on September 1, 1934; and sections 5, 7, 8, 9(a)(6), 10, 11, 12(a), 13, 14, 15, 16, 17, 18, 19, and 30 shall become effective on October 1, 1934.

AUTHORIZATION OF APPROPRIATIONS

Sec. 35. In addition to any other funds authorized to be appropriated to the Commission, there are authorized to be appropriated to carry out the functions, powers, and duties of the Commission, $776,000,000 for fiscal year 2003, of which—

(1) $102,700,000 shall be available to fund additional compensation, including salaries and benefits, as authorized in the Investor and Capital Markets Fee Relief Act (Public Law 107-123; 115 Stat. 2390 et seq.);

(2) $108,400,000 shall be available for information technology, security enhancements, and recovery and mitigation activities in light of the terrorist attacks of September 11, 2001; and

(3) $98,000,000 shall be available to add not fewer than an additional 200 qualified professionals to provide enhanced oversight of auditors and audit services required by the Federal securities laws, and to improve Commission investigative and disciplinary efforts with respect to such auditors and services, as well as for additional professional support staff necessary to strengthen the programs of the Commission involving Full Disclosure and Prevention and Suppression of Fraud, risk management, industry technology review, compliance, inspections, examinations, market regulation, and investment management.

REQUIREMENTS FOR THE EDGAR SYSTEM

Sec. 35A. The Commission, by rule or regulation—

(1) shall provide that any information in the EDGAR system that is required to be disseminated by the contractor—

(A) may be sold or disseminated by the contractor only pursuant to a uniform schedule of fees prescribed by the Commission;

(B) may be obtained by a purchaser by direct interconnection with the EDGAR system;

(C) shall be equally available on equal terms to all persons; and

(D) may be used, resold, or redisseminated by any person who has lawfully obtained such information without restriction and without payment of additional fees or royalties; and

(2) shall require that persons, or classes of persons, required to make filings with the Commission submit such filings in a form and manner suitable for entry into the EDGAR system and shall specify the date that such requirement is effective with respect to that person or class; except that the Commission may exempt persons or classes of persons, or filings or classes of filings, from such rules or regulations in order to prevent hardships or to avoid imposing unreasonable burdens or as otherwise may be necessary or appropriate.

GENERAL EXEMPTIVE AUTHORITY

Sec. 36. General Exemptive Authority.

(a) AUTHORITY.—

(1) In general.—Except as provided in subsection (b), but notwithstanding any other provision of this title, the Commission, by rule, regulation, or order, may conditionally or unconditionally exempt any person, security, or transaction, or any class or classes of persons, securities, or transactions, from any provision or provisions of this title or of any rule or regulation thereunder, to the extent that such exemption is necessary or appropriate in the public interest, and is consistent with the protection of investors.

(2) Procedures.—The Commission shall, by rule or regulation, determine the procedures under which an exemptive order under this section shall be granted and may, in its sole discretion, decline to entertain any application for an order of exemption under this section.

(b) LIMITATION.—The Commission may not, under this section, exempt any person, security, or transaction, or any class or classes of persons, securities, or transactions from section 15C or the rules or regulations issued thereunder or (for purposes of section 15C and the rules and regulations issued thereunder) from any definition in paragraph (42), (43), (44), or (45) of section 3(a).

TITLE II

AMENDMENTS TO SECURITIES ACT OF 1933

Sec. 201. [Sec. 201 amends Sec. 2(1), (4), 10 of the Securities Act of 1933.]

Sec. 202. [Sec. 202 amends Sec. 3a(2), (4) of the Securities Act of 1933 and adds Sec. 3a(9), (10), (11).]

Sec. 203. [Sec. 203 amends Sec. 4(1) and repeals Sec. 4(3) of the Securities Act of 1933.]

Sec. 204. [Sec. 204 repeals Sec. 5c of the Securities Act of 1933.]

Sec. 205. [Sec. 205 amends Sec. 10b(1) of the Securities Act of 1933.]

Sec. 206. [Sec. 206 amends Sec. 11a, b, c, e of the Securities Act of 1933.]

Sec. 207. [Sec. 207 amends Sec. 13 of the Securities Act of 1933.]

Sec. 208. [Sec. 208 amends Sec. 15 of the Securities Act of 1933.]

Sec. 209. [Sec. 209 amends Sec. 19a of the Securities Act of 1933.]

SECURITIES AND EXCHANGE COMMISSION SUCCESSOR TO FEDERAL TRADE COMMISSION

Sec. 210. Upon the expiration of sixty days after the date upon which a majority of the members of the Securities and Exchange Commission appointed under section 4 of title I of this Act have qualified and taken office, all powers, duties, and functions of the Federal Trade Commission under the Securities Act of 1933 shall be transferred to such Commission, together with all property, books, records, and unexpended balances of appropriations used by or available to the Federal Trade Commission for carrying out its functions under the Securities Act of 1933. All proceedings, hearings, or investigations commenced or pending before the Federal Trade Commission arising under the Securities Act of 1933 shall be continued by the Securities and Exchange Commission. All orders, rules, and regulations which have been issued by the Federal

Trade Commission under the Securities Act of 1933 and which are in effect shall continue in effect until modified, superseded, revoked, or repealed. All rights and interests accruing or to accrue under the Securities Act of 1933, or any provision of any regulation relating to or out of action taken by, the Federal Trade Commission under such Act, shall be followed in all respects and may be exercised and enforced.

EXCHANGE ACT RULES—SELECTED PROVISIONS

17 C.F.R. §§ 240.0-4 to 240.19b-4

Rule	Subject
12g-2	Securities deemed to be registered pursuant to Section 12(g)(1) upon termination of exemption pursuant to Section 12(g)(2) (A) or (B)
12g-3	Registration of securities of successor issuers under Section 12(b) or 12(g)
12g3-2	Exemptions for American depositary receipts and certain foreign securities
12g-4	Certification of termination of registration under Section 12(g)
12g5-1	Definition of securities "held of record"
12g5-2	Definition of "total assets"
12h-1	Exemptions from registration under Section 12(g) of the Act
12h-3	Suspension of duty to file reports under Section 15(d)

Regulation 13A—Reports of Issues of Securities Registered Pursuant to Section 12

Rule	Subject
13a-1	Requirement of annual reports
13a-11	Current reports on Form 8-K
13a-13	Quarterly reports on Form 10-Q and Form 10-QSB (§ 249.308a and § 249.308b of this chapter)
13a-14	Certification of disclosure in annual and quarterly reports
13a-15	Controls and Procedures

Regulation 13B-2: Maintenance of Records and Preparation of Required Reports

Rule	Subject
13b2-1	Falsification of accounting records
13b2-2	Representations and conduct in connection with the preparation of required reports and documents

Regulation 13D-G

Rule	Subject
13d-1	Filing of Schedules 13D and 13G
13d-2	Filing of amendments to Schedules 13D or 13G
13d-3	Determination of beneficial ownership
13d-4	Disclaimer of beneficial ownership
13d-5	Acquisition of securities
13d-6	Exemption of certain acquisitions
13d-7	Dissemination
13e-1	Purchase of securities by the issuer during a third-party tender offer
13e-3	Going private transactions by certain issuers or their affiliates

Regulation 14A—Solicitation of Proxies

Rule	Subject
14a-1	Definitions
14a-2	Solicitations to which § 240.14a-3 to § 240.14a-15 apply
14a-3	Information to be furnished security holders
14a-4	Requirements as to proxy
14a-5	Presentation of information in proxy statement
14a-6	Filing requirements
14a-7	Obligations of registrants to provide a list of, or mail soliciting material to, security holders
14a-8	Shareholder proposals
14a-9	False or misleading statements

Rule	Subject
15g-8	Sales of escrowed securities of blank check companies
15g-9	Sales practice requirements for certain low-priced securities

Reports of Directors, Officers, and Principal Stockholders

Rule	Subject
16a-1	Definition of terms
16a-2	Persons and transactions subject to Section 16
16a-3	Reporting transactions and holdings
16a-4	Derivative securities
16a-6	Small acquisitions
16a-8	Trusts
16a-10	Exemptions under Section 16(a)

Exemption of Certain Transactions From Section 16(b)

Rule	Subject
16b-3	Transactions between an issuer and its officers or directors
16b-5	Bona fide gifts and inheritance
16b-6	Derivative securities
16b-7	Mergers, reclassifications, and consolidations

Membership on National Securities Exchanges

Rule	Subject
19b-4	Filings with respect to proposed rule changes by self-regulatory organizations

RULES OF GENERAL APPLICATION

Rule 0-4. Non-disclosure of Information Obtained in the Course of Examinations and Investigations

Information or documents obtained by officers or employees of the Commission in the course of any examination or investigation pursuant to Section 17(a) or 21(a) shall, unless made a matter of public record, be deemed confidential. Except as provided by 17 CFR 203.2, officers and employees are hereby prohibited from making such confidential information or documents or any other non-public records of the Commission available to anyone other than a member, officer or employee of the Commission, unless the Commission or the General Counsel, pursuant to delegated authority, authorizes the disclosure of such information or the production of such documents as not being contrary to the public interest. Any officer or employee who is served with a subpoena requiring the disclosure of such information or the production of such documents shall appear in court and, unless the authorization described in the preceding sentence shall have been given, shall respectfully decline to disclose the information or produce the documents called for, basing his refusal upon this rule. Any officer or employee who is served with such a subpoena shall promptly advise the General Counsel of the service of such subpoena, the nature of the information or documents sought, and any circumstances which may bear upon the desirability of making available such information or documents.

Rule 3a1-1. Exemption from the Definition of the "Exchange" under Section 3(a)(1) of the Act

(a) An organization, association, or group of persons shall be exempt from the definition of the term "exchange" under Section 3(a)(1) of the Act, (15 U.S.C. 78c(a)(1)), if such organization, association, or group of persons:

(1) Is operated by a national securities association;

(2) Is in compliance with Regulation ATS, 17 CFR 242.300 through 242.303; or

(3) Pursuant to paragraph (a) of §242.301 of Regulation ATS, 17 CFR 242.301(a), is not required to comply with Regulation ATS, 17 CFR 242.300 through 242.303.

(b) Notwithstanding paragraph (a) of this section, an organization, association, or group of persons shall not be exempt under this section from the definition of "exchange," if:

(1) During three of the preceding four calendar quarters such organization, association, or group of persons had:

(i) Fifty percent or more of the average daily dollar trading volume in any security and five percent or more of the average daily dollar trading volume in any class of securities; or

(ii) Forty percent or more of the average daily dollar trading volume in any class of securities; and

(2) The Commission determines, after notice to the organization, association, or group of persons, and an opportunity for such organization, association, or group of persons to respond, that such an exemption would not be necessary or appropriate in the public interest or consistent with the protection of investors taking into account the requirements for exchange registration under Section 6 of the Act, (15 U.S.C. 78f), and the objectives of the national market system under Section 11A of the Act, (15 U.S.C 78k-1).

(3) For purposes of paragraph (b) of this section, each of the following shall be considered a "class of securities" :

(i) Equity securities, which shall have the same meaning as in §240.3a11-1;

(ii) Listed options, which shall mean any options traded on a national securities exchange or automated facility of a national securities exchange;

(iii) Unlisted options, which shall mean any options other than those traded on a national securities exchange or automated facility of a national securities association;

(iv) Municipal securities, which shall have the same meaning as in Section 3(a)(29) of the Act, (15 U.S.C. 78c(a)(29));

(v) Investment grade corporate debt securities, which shall mean any security that:

(A) Evidences a liability of the issuer of such security;

(B) Has a fixed maturity date that is at least one year following the date of issuance;

(C) Is rated in one of the four highest ratings categories by at least one Nationally Recognized Statistical Ratings Organization; and

(D) Is not an exempted security, as defined in Section 3(a)(12) of the Act, (15 U.S.C. 78c(a)(12));

(vi) Non-investment grade corporate debt securities, which shall mean any security that:

(A) Evidences a liability of the issuer of such security;

(B) Has a fixed maturity date that is at least one year following the date of issuance;

(C) Is not rated in one of the four highest ratings categories by at least one Nationally Recognized Statistical Ratings Organization; and

(D) Is not an exempted security, as defined in Section 3(a)(12) of the Act, (15 U.S.C. 78o);

(vii) Foreign corporate debt securities, which shall mean any security that:

(A) Evidences a liability of the issuer of such debt security;

(B) Is issued by a corporation or other organization incorporated or organized under the laws of any foreign country; and

(C) Has a fixed maturity date that is at least one year following the date of issuance; and

(viii) Foreign sovereign debt securities, which shall mean any security that:

(A) Evidences a liability of the issuer of such debt security;

(B) Is issued or guaranteed by the government of a foreign country, any political subdivision of a foreign country, or any supranational entity; and

(C) Does not have a maturity date of a year or less following the date of issuance.

DEFINITION OF "EQUITY SECURITY" AS USED IN
SECTIONS 12(g) AND 16

Rule 3a11-1. Definition of the Term "Equity Security"

The term *equity security* is hereby defined to include any stock or similar security, certificate of interest or participation in any profit sharing agreement, preorganization certificate or subscription, transferable share, voting trust certificate or certificate of deposit for an equity security, limited partnership interest, interest in a joint venture, or certificate of interest in a business trust; any security future on any such security; or any security convertible, with or without consideration into such a security, or carrying any warrant or right to subscribe to or purchase such a security; or any such warrant or right; or any put, call, straddle, or other option or privilege of buying such a security from or selling such a security to another without being bound to do so.

MISCELLANEOUS EXEMPTIONS

Rule 3a12-3. Exemption from Sections 14(a), 14(b), 14(c), 14(f) and 16 for Securities of Certain Foreign Issuers

(a) Securities for which the filing of securities on Form 18 [17 CFR 249.218] are authorized shall be exempt from the operation of sections 14 and 16 of the Act.

(b) Securities registered by a foreign private issuer, as defined in Rule 3b-4 (§ 240.3b-4 of this chapter), shall be exempt from sections 14(a), 14(b), 14(c), 14(f) and 16 of the Act.

DEFINITIONS

Rule 3a51-1. Definition of "Penny Stock"

For purposes of Section 3(a)(51) of the Act, the term "penny stock" shall mean any equity security other than a security:

(a) that is a reported security, as defined in 17 CFR 240.11Aa3-1(a) of this chapter;

except that a security that is registered on the American Stock Exchange, Inc. pursuant to the listing criteria of the Emerging Company Marketplace, but that does not otherwise satisfy the requirements of paragraphs (b), (c), or (d) of this section, shall be a penny stock for purposes of Section 15(b)(6) of the Act;

(b) that is issued by an investment company registered under the Investment Company Act of 1940;

(c) that is a put or call option issued by the Options Clearing Corporation;

(d) except for purposes of Section 7(b) of the Securities Act and Rule 419 (17 CFR 230.419), that has a price of five dollars or more;

(1) For purposes of paragraph (d) of this section:

(i) a security has a price of five dollars or more for a particular transaction if the security is purchased or sold in that transaction at a price of five dollars or more, excluding any broker or dealer commission, commission equivalent, mark-up, or mark-down; and

(ii) other than in connection with a particular transaction, a security has a price of five dollars or more at a given time if the inside bid quotation is five dollars or more; *provided, however,* that if there is no such inside bid quotation, a security has a price of five dollars or more at a given time if the average of three or more interdealer bid quotations at specified prices displayed at that time in an interdealer quotation system, as defined in 17 CFR 240.15c2-7(c)(1), by three or more market makers in the security, is five dollars or more.

(iii) The term "inside bid quotation" shall mean the highest bid quotation for the security displayed by a market maker in the security on an automated interdealer quotation system that has the characteristics set forth in Section 17B(b)(2) of the Act, or such other automated interdealer quotation system designated by the Commission for purposes of this section, at any time in which at least two market makers are contemporaneously displaying on such system bid and offer quotations for the security at specified prices.

(2) If a security is a unit composed of one or more securities, the unit price divided by the number of shares of the unit that are not warrants, options, rights, or similar securities must be five dollars or more, as determined in accordance with paragraph (d)(1) of this section, and any share of the unit that is a warrant, option, right, or similar security, or a convertible security, must have an exercise price or conversion price of five dollars or more;

(e) that is registered, or approved for registration upon notice of issuance, on a national securities exchange that makes transaction reports available pursuant to 17 CFR 240.11Aa3-1 of this chapter, provided that:

(1) price and volume information with respect to transactions in that security is required to be reported on a current and continuing basis and is made available to vendors of market information pursuant to the rules of the national securities exchange; and

(2) the security is purchased or sold in a transaction that is effected on or through the facilities of the national securities exchange, or that is part of a distribution of the security;

except that a security that satisfies the requirements of this paragraph, but that does not otherwise satisfy the requirements of paragraphs (a), (b), (c), or (d) of this section, shall be a penny stock for purposes of Section 15(b)(6) of the Act;

(f) that is authorized, or approved for authorization upon notice of issuance, for quotation in the National Association of Securities Dealers' Automated Quotation system (NASDAQ), provided that price and volume information with respect to transactions in that security is required to be reported on a current and continuing basis and is made available to vendors of market information pursuant to the rules of the National Association of Securities Dealers, Inc.;

except that a security that satisfies the requirements of this paragraph, but that does not otherwise satisfy the requirements of paragraphs (a), (b), (c), or (d) of this section, shall be a penny stock for purposes of Section 15(b)(6) of the Act; or

(g) whose issuer has:

(1) net tangible assets (*i.e.*, total assets less intangible assets and liabilities) in excess of $2,000,000, if the issuer has been in continuous operation for at least three years, or $5,000,000, if the issuer has been in continuous operation for less than three years; or

(2) average revenue of at least $6,000,000 for the last three years.

(3) For purposes of paragraph (g) of this section, net tangible assets or average revenues must be demonstrated by financial statements dated less than fifteen months prior to the date of the transaction that the broker or dealer has reviewed and has a reasonable basis for believing are accurate in relation to the date of the transaction, and:

(i) if the issuer is other than a foreign private issuer, are the most recent financial statements for the issuer that have been audited and reported on by an independent public accountant in accordance with the provisions of 17 CFR 210.2-02; or

(ii) if the issuer is a foreign private issuer, are the most recent financial statements for the issuer that have been filed with the Commission or furnished to the Commission pursuant to 17 CFR 240.12g3-2(b) of this chapter; *provided, however,* that if financial statements for the issuer dated less than fifteen months prior to the date of the transaction have not been filed with or furnished to the Commission, financial statements dated within fifteen months prior to the transaction shall be prepared in accordance with generally accepted accounting principles in the country of incorporation, audited in compliance with the requirements of that jurisdiction, and reported on by an accountant duly registered and in good standing in accordance with the regulations of that jurisdiction;

(4) The broker or dealer shall preserve, as part of its records, copies of the financial statements required by paragraph (g)(3) of this section for the period specified in 17 CFR 240.17a-4(b) of this chapter.

Rule 3b-2. Definition of "Officer"

The term "officer" means a president, vice president, secretary, treasurer or principal financial officer, comptroller or principal accounting officer, and any person routinely performing corresponding functions with respect to any organization whether incorporated or unincorporated.

Rule 3b-3. Definition of "Short Sale"

The term "short sale" means any sale of a security which the seller does not own or any sale which is consummated by the delivery of a security borrowed by, or for the account of, the seller. A person shall be deemed to own a security if (1) he or his agent has title to it; or (2) he has purchased, or has entered into an unconditional contract, binding on both parties thereto, to purchase it but has not yet received it; or (3) he owns a security convertible into or exchangeable for it and has tendered such security for conversion or exchange; or (4) he has an option to purchase or acquire it and has exercised such option; or (5) he has rights or warrants to subscribe to it and has exercised such rights or warrants: *Provided however,* That a person shall be deemed to own securities only to the extent that he has a net long position in such securities.

Rule 3b-4. Definition of "foreign government", "foreign issuer" and "foreign private issuer"

(a) The term "foreign government" means the government of any foreign country or of any political subdivision of a foreign country.

(b) The term "foreign issuer" means any issuer which is a foreign government, a national of any foreign country or a corporation or other organization incorporated or organized under the laws of any foreign country.

(c) The term *foreign private issuer* means any foreign issuer other than a foreign government except an issuer meeting the following conditions:

(1) More than 50 percent of the issuer's outstanding voting securities are directly or indirectly held of record by residents of the United States; and

(2) Any of the following:

(i) The majority of the executive officers or directors are United States citizens or residents;

(ii) More than 50 percent of the assets of the issuer are located in the United States; or

(iii) The business of the issuer is administered principally in the United States.

Instruction to paragraph (c) (1): To determine the percentage of outstanding voting securities held by U.S. residents:

A. Use the method of calculating record ownership in Rule 12g3-2(a) under the Act (§ 240.12g3-2(a)), except that your inquiry as to the amount of shares represented by accounts of customers resident in the United States may be limited to brokers, dealers, banks and other nominees located in (1) the United States, (2) your jurisdiction of incorporation, and (3) the jurisdiction that is the primary trading market for your voting securities, if different than your jurisdiction of incorporation.

B. If, after reasonable inquiry, you are unable to obtain information about the amount of shares represented by accounts of customers resident in the United States, you may assume, for purposes of this definition, that the customers are residents of the jurisdiction in which the nominee has its principal place of business.

C. Count shares of voting securities beneficially owned by residents of the United States as reported on reports of beneficial ownership provided to you or filed publicly and based on information otherwise provided to you.

Rule 3b-6. Liability for Certain Statements by Issuers

(a) A statement within the coverage of paragraph (b) of this section which is made by or on behalf of an issuer or by an outside reviewer retained by the issuer shall be deemed not to be a fraudulent statement (as defined in paragraph (d) of this section), unless it is shown that such statement was made or reaffirmed without a reasonable basis or was disclosed other than in good faith.

(b) This rule applies to the following statements:

(1) A forward-looking statement (as defined in paragraph (c) of this section) made in a document filed with the Commission, in Part I of a quarterly report on Form 10–Q and Form 10–QSB, § 249.308a of this chapter, or in an annual report to share–holders meeting the requirements of Rules 14a–3(b) and (c) or 14c–3(a) and (b) under the Securities Exchange Act of 1934, a statement reaffirming such forward-looking statement subsequent to the date the document was filed or the annual report was made publicly available, or a forward-looking statement made prior to the date the document was filed or the date the annual report was made publicly available if such statement is reaffirmed in a filed document, in Part I of a quarterly report on Form 10–Q and Form 10–QSB, or in an annual report made publicly available within a reasonable time after the making of such forward-looking statement; *Provided,* That:

(i) At the time such statements are made or reaffirmed, either the issuer is subject to the reporting requirements of section 13(a) or 15(d) of the Securities Exchange Act of 1934 and has complied with the requirements of Rule 13a–1 or 15d–1 thereunder, if applicable, to file its most recent annual report on Form 10–K and Form 10–KSB or Form 20–F or Form 40–F; or if the issuer is not subject to the reporting requirements of section 13(a) or 15(d) of the Securities Exchange Act of 1934, the statements are made in a registration statement filed under the Securities Act of 1933 offering statement or solicitation of interest written document or broadcast script under Regulation A or pursuant to section 12(b) or (g) of the Securities Exchange Act of 1934, and

(ii) The statements are not made by or on behalf of an issuer that is an investment company registered under the Investment Company Act of 1940; and

(2) Information which is disclosed in a document filed with the Commission in Part I of a quarterly report on Form 10–Q and Form 10–QSB (§ 249.308a of this chapter) or in an annual report to shareholders meeting the requirements of Rules 14a–3 (b) and (c) or 14c–3 (a) and (b) under the Securities Exchange Act of 1934 (§§ 240.14a–3 (b) and (c) or 240.14c–3 (a) and (b) of this chapter) and which relates to (i) the effects of changing prices on the business enterprise, presented voluntarily or pursuant to Item 303 of Regulation S–K (§ 229.303 of this chapter) or Regulation S–B (§ 228.303 of this chapter), "Management's Discussion and Analysis of Financial Condition and Results of Operations," or Item 5 of Form 20-F, Operating and Financial Review and Prospects," or Item 302 of Regulation S–K (§ 229.302 of this chapter), "Supplementary financial information," or Rule 3–20(c) of Regulation S–X (§ 210.3–20(c)) of this chapter) or (ii) the value of proved oil and gas reserves (such as a standardized measure of discounted future net cash flows relating to proved oil and gas reserves as set forth in paragraphs 30–34 of Statement of Financial Accounting Standards No. 69) presented voluntarily or pursuant to Item 302 of Regulation S–K (§ 229.302 of this chapter).

(c) For the purpose of this rule, the term *forward-looking statement* shall mean and shall be limited to:

(1) A statement containing a projection of revenues, income (loss), earnings (loss) per share, capital expenditures, dividends, capital structure or other financial items;

(2) A statement of management's plans and objectives for future operations;

(3) A statement of future economic performance contained in management's discussion and analysis of financial condition and results of operations included pursuant to Item 303 of Regulation S–K (§ 229.303 of this chapter) or Item 5 of Form 20–F or

(4) Disclosed statements of the assumptions underlying or relating to any of the statements described in paragraphs (c) (1), (2), or (3) of this section.

(d) For the purpose of this rule the term *fraudulent statement* shall mean a statement which is an untrue statement of a material fact, a statement false or misleading with respect to any material fact, an omission to state a material fact necessary to make a statement not misleading, or which constitutes the employment of a manipulative, deceptive, or fraudulent device, contrivance, scheme, transaction, act, practice, course of business, or an artifice to defraud, as those terms are used in the Securities Exchange Act of 1934 or the rules or regulations promulgated thereunder.

Rule 3b-7. Definition of "Executive Officer"

The term "executive officer," when used with reference to a registrant, means its president, any vice president of the registrant in charge of a principal business unit, division or function (such as sales, administration, or finance), any other officer who performs a policy making function or any other person who performs similar policy making functions for the registrant. Executive officers of subsidiaries may be deemed executive officers of the registrant if they perform such policy making functions for the registrant.

MANIPULATIVE AND DECEPTIVE DEVICES AND CONTRIVANCES

Rule 10b-5. Employment of Manipulative and Deceptive Devices

It shall be unlawful for any person, directly or indirectly, by the use of any means or instrumentality of interstate commerce, or of the mails, or of any facility of any national securities exchange,

(a) to employ any device, scheme, or artifice to defraud,

(b) to make any untrue statement of a material fact or to omit to state a material fact necessary in order to make the statements made, in the light of the circumstances under which they were made, not misleading, or

(c) to engage in any act, practice, or course of business which operates or would operate as a fraud or deceit upon any person, in connection with the purchase or sale of any security.

Rule 10b5-1. Trading "on the basis of" Material Nonpublic Information in Insider Trading Cases

Preliminary Note to § 240.10b5-1: This provision defines when a purchase or sale constitutes trading "on the basis of" material nonpublic information in insider trading cases brought under Section 10(b) of the Act and Rule 10b-5 thereunder. The law of insider trading is otherwise defined by judicial opinions construing Rule 10b-5, and Rule 10b5-1 does not modify the scope of insider trading law in any other respect.

(a) General. The "manipulative and deceptive devices" prohibited by Section 10(b) of the Act (15 U.S.C. 78j) and § 240.10b-5 thereunder include, among other things, the purchase or sale of a security of any issuer, on the basis of material nonpublic information about that security or issuer, in breach of a duty of trust or confidence that is owed directly, indirectly, or derivatively, to the issuer of that security or the shareholders of that issuer, or to any other person who is the source of the material nonpublic information.

(b) Definition of "on the basis of." Subject to the affirmative defenses in paragraph (c) of this section, a purchase or sale of a security of an issuer is "on the basis of" material nonpublic information about that security or issuer if the person making the purchase or sale was aware of the material nonpublic information when the person made the purchase or sale.

(c) Affirmative defenses. (1)(i) Subject to paragraph (c)(1)(ii) of this section, a person's purchase or sale is not "on the basis of" material nonpublic information if the person making the purchase or sale demonstrates that:

(A) Before becoming aware of the information, the person had:

(1) Entered into a binding contract to purchase or sell the security,

(2) Instructed another person to purchase or sell the security for the instructing person's account, or

(3) Adopted a written plan for trading securities;

(B) The contract, instruction, or plan described in paragraph (c)(1)(i)(A) of this Section:

(1) Specified the amount of securities to be purchased or sold and the price at which and the date on which the securities were to be purchased or sold;

(2) Included a written formula or algorithm, or computer program, for determining the amount of securities to be purchased or sold and the price at which and the date on which the securities were to be purchased or sold; or

(3) Did not permit the person to exercise any subsequent influence over how, when, or whether to effect purchases or sales; provided, in addition, that any other person who, pursuant to the contract, instruction, or plan, did exercise such influence must not have been aware of the material nonpublic information when doing so; and

(C) The purchase or sale that occurred was pursuant to the contract, instruction, or plan. A purchase or sale is not "pursuant to a contract, instruction, or plan" if, among other things, the person who entered into the contract, instruction, or plan altered or deviated from the contract, instruction, or plan to purchase or sell securities (whether by changing the amount, price, or timing of the purchase or sale), or entered into or altered a corresponding or hedging transaction or position with respect to those securities.

(ii) Paragraph (c)(1)(i) of this section is applicable only when the contract, instruction, or plan to purchase or sell securities was given or entered into in good faith and not as part of a plan or scheme to evade the prohibitions of this section.

(iii) This paragraph (c)(1)(iii) defines certain terms as used in paragraph (c) of this Section.

(A) Amount. "Amount" means either a specified number of shares or other securities or a specified dollar value of securities.

(B) Price. "Price" means the market price on a particular date or a limit price, or a particular dollar price.

(C) Date. "Date" means, in the case of a market order, the specific day of the year on which the order is to be executed (or as soon thereafter as is practicable under ordinary principles of best execution). "Date" means, in the case of a limit order, a day of the year on which the limit order is in force.

(2) A person other than a natural person also may demonstrate that a purchase or sale of securities is not "on the basis of" material nonpublic information if the person demonstrates that:

(i) The individual making the investment decision on behalf of the person to purchase or sell the securities was not aware of the information; and

(ii) The person had implemented reasonable policies and procedures, taking into consideration the nature of the person's business, to ensure that individuals making investment decisions would not violate the laws prohibiting trading on the basis of material nonpublic information. These policies and procedures may include those that restrict any purchase, sale, and causing any purchase or sale of any security as to which the person has material nonpublic information, or those that prevent such individuals from becoming aware of such information.

Rule 10b5-2. Duties of Trust or Confidence in Misappropriation Insider Trading Cases

Preliminary Note to § 240.10b5-2: This section provides a non-exclusive definition of circumstances in which a person has a duty of trust or confidence for purposes of the "misappropriation" theory of insider trading under Section 10(b) of the Act and Rule 10b-5. The law of insider trading is otherwise defined by judicial opinions construing Rule 10b-5, and Rule 10b5-2 does not modify the scope of insider trading law in any other respect.

(a) Scope of Rule. This section shall apply to any violation of Section 10(b) of the Act (15 U.S.C. 78j(b)) and § 240.10b-5 thereunder that is based on the purchase or sale of securities on the basis of, or the communication of, material nonpublic information misappropriated in breach of a duty of trust or confidence.

(b) Enumerated "duties of trust or confidence." For purposes of this section, a "duty of trust or confidence" exists in the following circumstances, among others:

(1) Whenever a person agrees to maintain information in confidence;

(2) Whenever the person communicating the material nonpublic information and the person to whom it is communicated have a history, pattern, or practice of sharing confidences, such that the recipient of the information knows or reasonably should know that the person communicating the material nonpublic information expects that the recipient will maintain its confidentiality; or

(3) Whenever a person receives or obtains material nonpublic information from his or her spouse, parent, child, or sibling; provided, however, that the person receiving or obtaining the information may demonstrate that no duty of trust or confidence existed with respect to the

information, by establishing that he or she neither knew nor reasonably should have known that the person who was the source of the information expected that the person would keep the information confidential, because of the parties' history, pattern, or practice of sharing and maintaining confidences, and because there was no agreement or understanding to maintain the confidentiality of the information.

Rule 10b-10. Confirmation of Transactions

Preliminary Note. This section requires broker-dealers to disclose specified information in writing to customers at or before completion of a transaction. The requirements under this section that particular information be disclosed is not determinative of a broker-dealer's obligation under the general antifraud provisions of the federal securities laws to disclose additional information to a customer at the time of the customer's investment decision.

(a) *Disclosure Requirement.* It shall he unlawful for any broker or dealer to effect for or with an account of a customer any transaction in, or to induce the purchase or sale by such customer of, any security (other than U.S. Savings Bonds or municipal securities) unless such broker or dealer, at or before completion of such transaction, gives or sends to such customer written notification disclosing:

(1) The date and time of the transaction (or the fact that the time of the transaction will be furnished upon written request to such customer) and the identity, price, and number of shares or units (or principal amount) of such security purchased or sold by such customer; and

(2) Whether the broker or dealer is acting as agent for such customer, as agent for some other person, as agent for both such customer and some other person, or as principal for its own account; and if the broker or dealer is acting as principal, whether it is a market maker in the security (other than by reason of acting as a block positioner); and

(i) If the broker or dealer is acting as agent for such customer, for some other person, or for both such customer and some other person:

(A) The name of the person from whom the security was purchased, or to whom it was sold, for such customer or the fact that the information will be furnished upon written request of such customer; and

(B) The amount of any remuneration received or to be received by the broker from such customer in connection with the transaction unless remuneration paid by such customer is determined pursuant to written agreement with such customer, otherwise than on a transaction basis; and

(C) For a transaction in any subject security as defined in § 240.11Ac1-2 or a security authorized for quotation on an automated interdealer quotation system that has the characteristics set forth in Section 17B of this Act (15 U.S.C. § 78q-2), a statement whether payment for order flow is received by the broker or dealer for transactions in such securities and the fact that the source and nature of the compensation received in connection with the particular transaction will be furnished upon written request of the customer; provided, however, that brokers or dealers that do not receive payment for order flow in connection with any transaction have no disclosure obligation under this paragraph; and

(D) The source and amount of any other remuneration received or to be received by the broker in connection with the transaction: *Provided, however,* that if, in the case of a purchase, the broker was not participating in a distribution, or in the case of a sale, was not participating in a tender offer, the written notification may state whether any other remuneration has been or will be received and the fact that the source and amount of such other remuneration will be furnished upon written request of such customer; or

(ii) If the broker or dealer is acting as principal for its own account:

(A) In the case where such broker or dealer is not a market maker in an equity security and, if, after having received an order to buy from a customer, the broker or dealer purchased the equity security from another person to offset a contemporaneous sale to such customer or, after having received an order to sell from a customer, the broker or dealer sold the security to another person to offset a contemporaneous purchase from such customer, the difference between the price to the customer and the dealer's contemporaneous purchase (for customer purchases) or sale price (for customer sales); or

(B) In the case of any other transaction in a reported security, or an equity security that is quoted on NASDAQ or traded on a national securities exchange and that is subject to last sale reporting, the reported trade price, the price to the customer in the transaction, and the difference, if any, between the reported trade price and the price to the customer.

(3) Whether any odd-lot differential or equivalent fee has been paid by such customer in connection with the execution of an order for an odd-lot number of shares or units (or principal amount) of a security and the fact that the amount of any such differential or fee will be furnished upon oral or written request: *Provided, however*, that such disclosure need not be made if the differential or fee is included in the remuneration disclosure, or exempted from disclosure, pursuant to paragraph (a)(2)(i)(B) of this section; and

(4) In the case of any transaction in a debt security subject to redemption before maturity, a statement to the effect that such debt security may be redeemed in whole or in part before maturity, that such a redemption could affect the yield represented and the fact that additional information is available upon request; and

(5) In the case of a transaction in a debt security effected exclusively on the basis of a dollar price:

(i) The dollar price at which the transaction was effected, and

(ii) The yield to maturity calculated from the dollar price: *Provided, however*, that this paragraph (a)(5)(ii) shall not apply to a transaction in a debt security that either:

(A) Has a maturity date that may be extended by the issuer thereof, with a variable interest payable thereon; or

(B) Is an asset-backed security, that represents an interest in or is secured by a pool of receivables or other financial assets that are subject continuously to prepayment; and

(6) In the case of a transaction in a debt security effected on the basis of yield:

(i) The yield at which the transaction was effected, including the percentage amount and its characterization (*e.g.*, current yield, yield to maturity, or yield to call) and if effected at yield to call, the type of call, the call date and call price; and

(ii) The dollar price calculated from the yield at which the transaction was effected; and

(iii) If effected on a basis other than yield to maturity and the yield to maturity is lower than the represented yield, the yield to maturity as well as the represented yield; *Provided, however*, that this paragraph (a)(6)(iii) shall not apply to a transaction in a debt security that either:

(A) Has a maturity date that may be extended by the issuer thereof, with a variable interest rate payable thereon; or

(B) Is an asset-backed security, that represents an interest in or is secured by a pool of receivables or other financial assets that are subject continuously to prepayment; and

(7) In the case of a transaction in a debt security that is an asset-backed security, which represents an interest in or is secured by a pool of receivables or other financial assets that are subject continuously to prepayment, a statement indicating that the actual yield of such asset-backed security may vary according to the rate at which the underlying receivables or other financial assets are prepaid and a statement of the fact that information concerning the factors that affect yield (including at a minimum estimated yield, weighted average life, and the prepayment assumptions underlying yield) will be furnished upon written request of such customer; and

(8) In the case of a transaction in a debt security, other than a government security, that the security is unrated by a nationally recognized statistical rating organization, if such is the case; and

(9) That the broker or dealer is not a member of the Securities Investor Protection Corporation (SIPC), or that the broker or dealer clearing or carrying the customer account is not a member of SIPC, if such is the case: *Provided, however*, that this paragraph (a)(9) shall not apply in the case of a transaction in shares of a registered open-end investment company or unit investment trust if:

(i) The customer sends funds or securities directly to, or received funds or securities directly from, the registered open-end investment company or unit investment trust, its transfer agent, its custodian, or other designated agent, and such person is not an associated person of the broker or dealer required by paragraph (a) of this section to send written notification to the customer; and

(ii) The written notification required by paragraph (a) of this section is sent on behalf of the broker or dealer to the customer by a person described in paragraph (a)(9)(i) of this section.

(b) *Alternative Periodic Reporting.* A broker or dealer may effect transactions for or with the account of a customer without giving or sending to such customer the written notification described in paragraph (a) of this section if:

(1) Such transactions are effected pursuant to a periodic plan or an investment company plan, or effected in shares of any open-end management investment company registered under the Investment Company Act of 1940 that holds itself out as a money market fund and attempts to maintain a stable net asset value per share: *Provided, however*, that no sales load is deducted upon the purchase or redemption of shares in the money market fund; and

(2) Such broker or dealer gives or sends to such customer within five business days after the end of each *quarterly* period, for transactions involving investment company and periodic plans, and after the end of each *monthly* period, for other transactions described in paragraph (b)(1) of this section, a written statement disclosing each purchase or redemption, effected for or with, and each dividend or distribution credited to or reinvested for, the account of such customer during the month; the date of such transaction; the identity, number, and price of any securities purchased or redeemed by such customer in each such transaction; the total number of shares of such securities in such customer's account; any remuneration received or to be received by the broker or dealer in connection therewith; and that any other information required by paragraph (a) of this section will be furnished upon written request: *Provided, however*, that the written statement may be delivered to some other person designated by the customer for distribution to the customer; and

(3) Such customer is provided with prior notification in writing disclosing the intention to send the written information referred to in paragraph (b)(1) of this section in lieu of an immediate confirmation.

(c) A broker or dealer shall give or send to a customer information requested pursuant to this rule within 5 business days of receipt of the request; *Provided, however,* That in the case of information pertaining to a transaction effected more than 30 days prior to receipt of the request, the information shall be given or sent to the customer within 15 business days.

(d) *Definitions.* For the purposes of this section:

(1) *Customer* shall not include a broker or dealer;

(2) *Completion of the transaction* shall have the meaning provided in Rule 15c1-1 under the Act;

(3) *Time of the transaction* means the time of execution, to the extent feasible, of the customer's order;

(4) *Debt security* as used in paragraphs (a)(3), (4), and (5) only, means any security, such as a bond, debenture, note, or any other similar instrument which evidences a liability of the issuer (including any such security that is convertible into stock or a similar security) and fractional or participation interests in one or more of any of the foregoing; *Provided, however,* that securities issued by an investment company registered under the Investment Company Act of 1940 shall not be included in this definition;

(5) *Periodic plan* means any written authorization for a broker acting as agent to purchase or sell for a customer a specific security or securities (other than securities issued by an open end investment company or unit investment trust registered under the Investment Company Act of 1940), in specific amounts (calculated in security units or dollars), at specific time intervals and setting forth the commissions or charges to be paid by the customer in connection therewith (or the manner of calculating them); and

(6) *Investment company plan* means any plan under which securities issued by an open-end investment company or unit investment trust registered under the Investment Company Act of

1940 are purchased by a customer (the payments being made directly to, or made payable to, the registered investment company, or the principal underwriter, custodian, trustee, or other designated agent of the registered investment company), or sold by a customer pursuant to:

(i) An individual retirement or individual pension plan qualified under the Internal Revenue Code;

(ii) A contractual or systematic agreement under which the customer purchases at the applicable public offering price, or redeems at the applicable redemption price, such securities in specified amounts (calculated in security units or dollars) at specified time intervals and setting forth the commissions or charges to be paid by such customer in connection therewith (or the manner of calculating them); or

(iii) Any other arrangement involving a group of two or more customers and contemplating periodic purchases of such securities by each customer through a person designated by the group; *Provided,* That such arrangement requires the registered investment company or its agent—

(A) To give or send to the designated person, at or before the completion of the transaction for the purchase of such securities, a written notification of the receipt of the total amount paid by the group;

(B) To send to anyone in the group who was a customer in the prior quarter and on whose behalf payment has not been received in the current quarter a quarterly written statement reflecting that a payment was not received on his behalf; and

(C) To advise each customer in the group if a payment is not received from the designated person on behalf of the group within 10 days of a date certain specified in the arrangement for delivery of that payment by the designated person and thereafter to send to each such customer the written notification described in paragraph (a) of this section for the next three succeeding payments.

(7) *Reported security* shall have the meaning provided in Rule 11Aa3-1 under the Act.

(8) *Effective transaction reporting plan* shall have the meaning provided in Rule 11Aa3-1 under the Act.

(9) *Payment for order flow* shall mean any monetary payment, service, property, or other benefit that results in remuneration, compensation, or consideration to a broker or dealer from any broker or dealer, national securities exchange, registered securities association, or exchange member in return for the routing of customer orders by such broker or dealer to any broker or dealer, national securities exchange, registered securities association, or exchange member for execution, including but not limited to: research, clearance, custody, products or services; reciprocal agreements for the provision of order flow; adjustment of a broker or dealer's unfavorable trading errors; offers to participate as underwriter in public offerings; stock loans or shared interest accrued thereon; discounts, rebates, or any other reductions of or credits against any fee to, or expense or other financial obligation of, the broker or dealer routing a customer order that exceeds that fee, expense or financial obligation.

(10) *Asset-backed security* means a security that is primarily serviced by the cashflows of a discrete pool of receivables or other financial assets, either fixed or revolving, that by their terms convert into cash within a finite time period plus any rights or other assets designed to assure the servicing or timely distribution of proceeds to the security holders.

(e) *Security futures products.* The provisions of paragraphs (a) and (b) of this section shall not apply to a broker or dealer registered pursuant to section 15(b)(11)(A) of the Act (15 U.S.C. 78*o* (b)(11)(A)) to the extent that it effects transactions for customers in security futures products in a futures account (as that term is defined in § 240.15c3-3(a)(15)) and a broker or dealer registered pursuant to section 15(b)(1) of the Act (15 U.S.C. 78*o* (b)(1)) that is also a futures commission merchant registered pursuant to section 4f(a)(1) of the Commodity Exchange Act (7 U.S.C. 6f(a)(1)), to the extent that it effects transactions for customers in security futures products in a futures account (as that term is defined in § 240.15c3-3(a)(15)), *Provided* that:

(1) The broker or dealer that effects any transaction for a customer in security futures products in a futures account gives or sends to the customer no later than the next business day after execution of any futures securities product transaction, written notification disclosing:

(i) The date the transaction was executed, the identity of the single security or narrow-based security index underlying the contract for the security futures product, the number of contracts of such security futures product purchased or sold, the price, and the delivery month;

(ii) The source and amount of any remuneration received or to be received by the broker or dealer in connection with the transaction, including, but not limited to, markups, commissions, costs, fees, and other charges incurred in connection with the transaction, provided, however, that if no remuneration is to be paid for an initiating transaction until the occurrence of the corresponding liquidating transaction, that the broker or dealer may disclose the amount of remuneration only on the confirmation for the liquidating transaction;

(iii) The fact that information about the time of the execution of the transaction, the identity of the other party to the contract, and whether the broker or dealer is acting as agent for such customer, as agent for some other person, as agent for both such customer and some other person, or as principal for its own account, and if the broker or dealer is acting as principal, whether it is engaging in a block transaction or an exchange of security futures products for physical securities, will be available upon written request of the customer; and

(iv) Whether payment for order flow is received by the broker or dealer for such transactions, the amount of this payment and the fact that the source and nature of the compensation received in connection with the particular transaction will be furnished upon written request of the customer; provided, however, that brokers or dealers that do not receive payment for order flow have no disclosure obligation under this paragraph.

(2) *Transitional provision.*

(i) Broker-dealers are not required to comply with paragraph (e)(1)(iii) of this section until June 1, 2003, *Provided* that, if, not withstanding the absence of the disclosure required in that paragraph, the broker-dealer receives a written request from a customer for the information described in paragraph (e)(1)(iii) of this section, the broker-dealer must make the information available to the customer; and

(ii) Broker-dealers are not required to comply with paragraph (e)(1)(iv) of this section until June 1, 2003.

(f) The Commission may exempt any broker or dealer from the requirements of paragraphs (a) and (b) of this section with regard to specific transactions or specific classes of transactions for which the broker or dealer will provide alternative procedures to effect the purposes of this section; any such exemption may be granted subject to compliance with such alternative procedures and upon such other stated terms and conditions as the Commission may impose.

Rule 10b-16. Disclosure of Credit Terms in Margin Transactions

(a) It shall be unlawful for any broker or dealer to extend credit, directly or indirectly, to any customer in connection with any securities transaction unless such broker or dealer has established procedures to assure that each customer

(1) is given or sent at the time of opening the account, a written statement or statements disclosing (i) the conditions under which an interest charge will be imposed; (ii) the annual rate or rates of interest that can be imposed; (iii) the method of computing interest; (iv) if rates of interest are subject to change without prior notice, the specific conditions under which they can be changed; (v) the method of determining the debit balance or balances on which interest is to be charged and whether credit is to be given for credit balances in cash accounts; (vi) what other charges resulting from the extension of credit, if any, will be made and under what conditions; and (vii) the nature of any interest or lien retained by the broker or dealer in the security or other property held as collateral and the conditions under which additional collateral can be required; *provided, however,* that the requirements of this Paragraph (a)(1) will be met in any case where the account is opened by telephone if the information required to be disclosed is orally communicated to the customer at that time and the required written statement or statements are sent to the

customer immediately thereafter; and *provided, further,* that in the case of customers to whom credit is already being extended on the effective date of this Rule, the written statement or statements required hereunder must be given or sent to said customers within 90 days after the effective date of this Rule; and

(2) is given or sent a written statement or statements, at least quarterly, for each account in which credit was extended, disclosing (i) the balance at the beginning of the period; the date, amount and a brief description of each debit and credit entered during such period; the closing balance; and, if interest is charged for a period different from the period covered by the statement, the balance as of the last day of the interest period; (ii) the total interest charge for the period during which interest is charged (or, if interest is charged separately for separate accounts, the total interest charge for each such account), itemized to show the dates on which the interest period began and ended; the annual rate or rates of interest charged and the interest charge for each such different annual rate of interest; and either each different debit balance on which an interest calculation was based or the average debit balance for the interest period, except that if an average debit balance is used, a separate average debit balance must be disclosed for each interest rate applied; and (iii) all other charges resulting from the extension of credit in that account; *provided, however,* that if the interest charge disclosed on a statement is for a period different from the period covered by the statement, there must be printed on the statement appropriate language to the effect that it should be retained for use in conjunction with the next statement containing the remainder of the required information; and *provided further,* that in the case of "equity funding programs" registered under the Securities Act of 1933, the requirements of this Paragraph (a)(2) will be met if the broker or dealer furnishes to the customer, within one month after each extension of credit, a written statement or statements containing the information required to be disclosed under this Paragraph (a)(2).

(b) It shall be unlawful for any broker or dealer to make any changes in the terms and conditions under which credit charges will be made (as described in the initial statement made under Paragraph (a) of this Rule), unless the customer shall have been given not less than thirty (30) days written notice of such changes, except that no such prior notice shall be necessary where such changes are required by law; *provided, however,* that if any change for which prior notice would otherwise be required under this paragraph results in a lower interest charge to the customer than would have been imposed before the change, notice of such change may be given within a reasonable time after the effective date of the change.

Rule 10b-18. Purchases of Certain Equity Securities by the Issuer and Others
Preliminary Notes

1. Section 240.10b-18 provides an issuer (and its affiliated purchasers) with a "safe harbor" from liability for manipulation under sections 9(a)(2) of the Act and §240.10b-5 under the Act *solely* by reason of the manner, timing, price, and volume of their repurchases when they repurchase the issuer's common stock in the market in accordance with the section's manner, timing, price, and volume conditions. As a safe harbor, compliance with §240.10b-18 is voluntary. To come within the safe harbor, however, an issuer's repurchases must satisfy (on a daily basis) each of the section's four conditions. Failure to meet any one of the four conditions will remove all of the issuer's repurchases from the safe harbor for that day. The safe harbor, moreover, is not available for repurchases that, although made in technical compliance with the section, are part of a plan or scheme to evade the federal securities laws.

2. Regardless of whether the repurchases are effected in accordance with §240.10b-18, reporting issuers must report their repurchasing activity as required by Item 703 of Regulations S-K and S-B (17 CFR 229.703 and 228.703) and Item 15(e) of Form 20-F (17 CFR 249.220f) (regarding foreign private issuers), and closed-end management investment companies that are registered under the Investment Company Act of 1940 must report their repurchasing activity as required by Item 8 of Form N-CSR (17 CFR 249.331; 17 CFR 274.128).

(a) *Definitions.* Unless otherwise provided, all terms used in this section shall have the same meaning as in the Act. In addition, the following definitions shall apply:

443

(1) *ADTV* means the average daily trading volume reported for the security during the four calendar weeks preceding the week in which the Rule 10b-18 purchase is to be effected.

(2) *Affiliate* means any person that directly or indirectly controls, is controlled by, or is under common control with, the issuer.

(3) *Affiliated purchaser* means:

(i) A person acting, directly or indirectly, in concert with the issuer for the purpose of acquiring the issuer's securities; or

(ii) An affiliate who, directly or indirectly, controls the issuer's purchases of such securities, whose purchases are controlled by the issuer, or whose purchases are under common control with those of the issuer; *Provided, however,* that "affiliated purchaser" shall not include a broker, dealer, or other person solely by reason of such broker, dealer, or other person effecting Rule 10b-18 purchases on behalf of the issuer or for its account, and shall not include an officer or director of the issuer solely by reason of that officer or director's participation in the decision to authorize Rule 10b-18 purchases by or on behalf of the issuer.

(4) *Agent independent of the issuer* has the meaning contained in § 242.100 of this chapter.

(5) *Block* means a quantity of stock that either:

(i) Has a purchase price of $200,000 or more; or

(ii) Is at least 5,000 shares and has a purchase price of at least $50,000; or

(iii) Is at least 20 round lots of the security and totals 150 percent or more of the trading volume for that security or, in the event that trading volume data are unavailable, is at least 20 round lots of the security and totals at least one-tenth of one percent (.001) of the outstanding shares of the security, exclusive of any shares owned by any affiliate;

Provided, however, That a block under paragraph (a)(5)(i), (ii), and (iii) shall not include any amount a broker or dealer, acting as principal, has accumulated for the purpose of sale or resale to the issuer or to any affiliated purchaser of the issuer if the issuer or such affiliated purchaser knows or has reason to know that such amount was accumulated for such purpose, nor shall it include any amount that a broker or dealer has sold short to the issuer or to any affiliated purchaser of the issuer if the issuer or such affiliated purchaser knows or has reason to know that the sale was a short sale.

(6) *Consolidated system* means a consolidated transaction or quotation reporting system that collects and publicly disseminates on a current and continuous basis transaction or quotation information in common equity securities pursuant to an effective transaction reporting plan (as defined in § 240.11Aa3-1) or a national market system plan (as defined in § 240.11Aa3-2).

(7) *Market-wide trading suspension* means a market-wide trading halt of 30 minutes or more that is:

(i) Imposed pursuant to the rules of a national securities exchange or a national securities association in response to a market-wide decline during a single trading session; or

(ii) Declared by the Commission pursuant to its authority under section 12(k) of the Act (15 U.S.C. 78*l* (k)).

(8) *Plan* has the meaning contained in § 242.100 of this chapter.

(9) *Principal market* for a security means the single securities market with the largest reported trading volume for the security during the six full calendar months preceding the week in which the Rule 10b-18 purchase is to be effected.

(10) *Public float value* has the meaning contained in § 242.100 of this chapter.

(11) *Purchase price* means the price paid per share as reported, exclusive of any commission paid to a broker acting as agent, or commission equivalent, mark-up, or differential paid to a dealer.

(12) *Riskless principal transaction* means a transaction in which a broker or dealer after having received an order from an issuer to buy its security, buys the security as principal in the market at the same price to satisfy the issuer's buy order. The issuer's buy order must be effected at the same price per-share at which the broker or dealer bought the shares to satisfy the issuer's buy order, exclusive of any explicitly disclosed markup or markdown, commission equivalent, or other fee. In addition, only the first leg of the transaction, when the broker or dealer buys the

security in the market as principal, is reported under the rules of a self-regulatory organization or under the Act. For purposes of this section, the broker or dealer must have written policies and procedures in place to assure that, at a minimum, the issuer's buy order was received prior to the offsetting transaction; the offsetting transaction is allocated to a riskless principal account or the issuer's account within 60 seconds of the execution; and the broker or dealer has supervisory systems in place to produce records that enable the broker or dealer to accurately and readily reconstruct, in a time-sequenced manner, all orders effected on a riskless principal basis.

(13) *Rule 10b-18 purchase* means a purchase (or any bid or limit order that would effect such purchase) of an issuer's common stock (or an equivalent interest, including a unit of beneficial interest in a trust or limited partnership or a depository share) by or for the issuer or any affiliated purchaser (including riskless principal transactions). However, it does *not* include any purchase of such security:

(i) Effected during the applicable restricted period of a distribution that is subject to § 242.102 of this chapter;

(ii) Effected by or for an issuer plan by an agent independent of the issuer;

(iii) Effected as a fractional share purchase (a fractional interest in a security) evidenced by a script certificate, order form, or similar document;

(iv) Effected during the period from the time of public announcement (as defined in § 230.165(f)) of a merger, acquisition, or similar transaction involving a recapitalization, until the earlier of the completion of such transaction or the completion of the vote by target shareholders.This exclusion does *not* apply to Rule 10b-18 purchases:

(A) Effected during such transaction in which the consideration is solely cash and there is no valuation period; or

(B) Where:

(*1*) The total volume of Rule 10b-18 purchases effected on any single day does not exceed the lesser of 25% of the security's four-week ADTV or the issuer's average daily Rule 10b-18 purchases during the three full calendar months preceding the date of the announcement of such transaction;

(*2*) The issuer's block purchases effected pursuant to paragraph (b)(4) of this section do not exceed the average size and frequency of the issuer's block purchases effected pursuant to paragraph (b)(4) of this section during the three full calendar months preceding the date of the announcement of such transaction; and

(*3*) Such purchases are not otherwise restricted or prohibited;

(v) Effected pursuant to § 240.13e-1;

(vi) Effected pursuant to a tender offer that is subject to § 240.13e-4 or specifically excepted from § 240.13e-4; or

(vii) Effected pursuant to a tender offer that is subject to section 14(d) of the Act (15 U.S.C. 78n(d)) and the rules and regulations thereunder.

(b) *Conditions to be met.* Rule 10b-18 purchases shall not be deemed to have violated the anti-manipulation provisions of sections 9(a)(2) or 10(b) of the Act (15 U.S.C. 78i(a)(2) or 78j(b)), or § 240.10b-5 under the Act, solely by reason of the time, price, or amount of the Rule 10b-18 purchases, or the number of brokers or dealers used in connection with such purchases, if the issuer or affiliated purchaser of the issuer effects the Rule 10b-18 purchases according to each of the following conditions:

(1) *One broker or dealer.* Rule 10b-18 purchases must be effected from or through only one broker or dealer on any single day; *Provided, however,* that:

(i) The "one broker or dealer" condition shall not apply to Rule 10b-18 purchases that are not solicited by or on behalf of the issuer or its affiliated purchaser(s);

(ii) Where Rule 10b-18 purchases are effected by or on behalf of more than one affiliated purchaser of the issuer (or the issuer and one or more of its affiliated purchasers) on a single day, the issuer and all affiliated purchasers must use the same broker or dealer; and

(iii) Where Rule 10b-18 purchases are effected on behalf of the issuer by a broker-dealer that is not an electronic communication network (ECN) or other alternative trading system (ATS), that broker-dealer can access ECN or other ATS liquidity in order to execute repurchases on behalf of the issuer (or any affiliated purchaser of the issuer) on that day.

(2) *Time of purchases.* Rule 10b-18 purchases must not be:

(i) The opening (regular way) purchase reported in the consolidated system;

(ii) Effected during the 10 minutes before the scheduled close of the primary trading session in the principal market for the security, and the 10 minutes before the scheduled close of the primary trading session in the market where the purchase is effected, for a security that has an ADTV value of $1 million or more and a public float value of $150 million or more; and

(iii) Effected during the 30 minutes before the scheduled close of the primary trading session in the principal market for the security, and the 30 minutes before the scheduled close of the primary trading session in the market where the purchase is effected, for all other securities;

(iv) However, for purposes of this section, Rule 10b-18 purchases may be effected following the close of the primary trading session until the termination of the period in which last sale prices are reported in the consolidated system so long as such purchases are effected at prices that do not exceed the lower of the closing price of the primary trading session in the principal market for the security and any lower bids or sale prices subsequently reported in the consolidated system, and all of this section's conditions are met. However, for purposes of this section, the issuer may use one broker or dealer to effect Rule 10b-18 purchases during this period that may be different from the broker or dealer that it used during the primary trading session. However, the issuer's Rule 10b-18 purchase may not be the opening transaction of the session following the close of the primary trading session.

(3) *Price of purchases.* Rule 10b-18 purchases must be effected at a purchase price that:

(i) Does not exceed the highest independent bid or the last independent transaction price, whichever is higher, quoted or reported in the consolidated system at the time the Rule 10b-18 purchase is effected;

(ii) For securities for which bids and transaction prices are not quoted or reported in the consolidated system, Rule 10b-18 purchases must be effected at a purchase price that does not exceed the highest independent bid or the last independent transaction price, whichever is higher, displayed and disseminated on any national securities exchange or on any inter-dealer quotation system (as defined in § 240.15c2-11) that displays at least two priced quotations for the security, at the time the Rule 10b-18 purchase is effected; and

(iii) For all other securities, Rule 10b-18 purchases must be effected at a price no higher than the highest independent bid obtained from three independent dealers.

(4) *Volume of purchases.* The total volume of Rule 10b-18 purchases effected by or for the issuer and any affiliated purchasers effected on any single day must not exceed 25 percent of the ADTV for that security; *However*, once each week, in lieu of purchasing under the 25 percent of ADTV limit for that day, the issuer or an affiliated purchaser of the issuer may effect one block purchase if:

(i) No other Rule 10b-18 purchases are effected that day, and

(ii) The block purchase is *not* included when calculating a security's four week ADTV under this section.

(c) *Alternative conditions.* The conditions of paragraph (b) of this section shall apply in connection with Rule 10b-18 purchases effected during a trading session following the imposition of a market-wide trading suspension, except:

(1) That the time of purchases condition in paragraph (b)(2) of this section shall not apply, either:

(i) From the reopening of trading until the scheduled close of trading on the day that the market-wide trading suspension is imposed; or

(ii) At the opening of trading on the next trading day until the scheduled close of trading that day, if a market-wide trading suspension was in effect at the close of trading on the preceding day; and

(2) The volume of purchases condition in paragraph (b)(4) of this section is modified so that the amount of Rule 10b-18 purchases must not exceed 100 percent of the ADTV for that security.

(d) *Other purchases.* No presumption shall arise that an issuer or an affiliated purchaser has violated the anti-manipulation provisions of sections 9(a)(2) or 10(b) of the Act (15 U.S.C. 78i(a)(2) or 78j(b)), or §240.10b-5 under the Act, if the Rule 10b-18 purchases of such issuer or affiliated purchaser do not meet the conditions specified in paragraph (b) or (c) of this section.

NOTICE PURSUANT TO SECTION 10A OF THE ACT

Rule 10A-1. Notice to the Commission Pursuant to Section 10A of the Act

(a)(1) If any issuer with a reporting obligation under the Act receives a report requiring a notice to the Commission in accordance with section 10A(b)(3) of the Act, 15 U.S.C. 78j-1(b)(3), the issuer shall submit such notice to the Commission's Office of the Chief Accountant within the time period prescribed in that section. The notice may be provided by facsimile, telegraph, personal delivery, or any other means, provided it is received by the Office of the Chief Accountant within the required time period.

(2) The notice specified in paragraph (a)(1) of this section shall be in writing and:

(i) Shall identify the issuer (including the issuer's name, address, phone number, and file number assigned to the issuer's filings by the Commission) and the independent accountant (including the independent accountant's name and phone number, and the address of the independent accountant's principal office);

(ii) Shall state the date that the issuer received from the independent accountant the report specified in section 10A(b)(2) of the Act, 15 U.S.C. 78j-1(b)(2);

(iii) Shall provide, at the election of the issuer, either:

(A) A summary of the independent accountant's report, including a description of the act that the independent accountant has identified as a likely illegal act and the possible effect of that act on all affected financial statements of the issuer or those related to the most current three-year period, whichever is shorter; or

(B) A copy of the independent accountant's report; and

(iv) May provide additional information regarding the issuer's views of and response to the independent accountant's report.

(3) Reports of the independent accountant submitted by the issuer to the Commission's Office of the Chief Accountant in accordance with paragraph (a)(2)(iii)(B) of this section shall be deemed to have been made pursuant to section 10A(b)(3) or section 10A(b)(4) of the Act, 15 U.S.C. 78j-1(b)(3) or 78j-1(b)(4), for purposes of the safe harbor provided by section 10A(c) of the Act, 15 U.S.C. 78j-1(c).

(4) Submission of the notice in paragraphs (a)(1) and (a)(2) of this section shall not relieve the issuer from its obligations to comply fully with all other reporting requirements, including, without limitation:

(i) The filing requirements of Form 8-K, §249.308 of this chapter, and Form N-SAR, §274.101 of this chapter, regarding a change in the issuer's certifying accountant and

(ii) The disclosure requirements of item 304 of Regulation S-B or item 304 of Regulation S-K, §§228.304 or 229.304 of this chapter.

(b)(1) Any independent accountant furnishing to the Commission a copy of a report (or the documentation of any oral report) in accordance with section 10A(b)(3) or section 10A(b)(4) of the Act, 15 U.S.C. 78j-1(b)(3) or 78j-1(b)(4), shall submit that report (or documentation) to the Commission's Office of the Chief Accountant within the time period prescribed by the appropriate section of the Act. The report (or documentation) may be submitted to the Commission's Office of the Chief Accountant by facsimile, telegraph, personal delivery, or any other means, provided it is received by the Office of the Chief Accountant within the time period set forth in section 10A(b)(3) or 10A(b)(4) of the Act, 15 U.S.C. 78j-1(b)(3) or 78j-1(b)(4), whichever is applicable in the circumstances.

(2) If the report (or documentation) submitted to the Office of the Chief Accountant in accordance with paragraph (b)(1) of this section does not clearly identify both the issuer (including the issuer's name, address, phone number, and file number assigned to the issuer's

filings with the Commission) and the independent accountant (including the independent accountant's name and phone number, and the address of the independent accountant's principal office), then the independent accountant shall place that information in a prominent attachment to the report (or documentation) and shall submit that attachment to the Office of the Chief Accountant at the same time and in the same manner as the report (or documentation) is submitted to that Office.

(3) Submission of the report (or documentation) by the independent accountant as described in paragraphs (b)(1) and (b)(2) of this section shall not replace, or otherwise satisfy the need for, the newly engaged and former accountants' letters under items 304(a)(2)(D) and 304(a)(3) of Regulation S-K, §§ 229.304(a)(2)(D) and 229.304(a)(3) of this chapter, respectively, and under items 304(a)(2)(D) and 304(a)(3) of Regulation S-B, §§ 228.304(a)(2)(D) and 228.304(a)(3) of this chapter, respectively, and shall not limit, reduce, or affect in any way the independent accountant's obligations to comply fully with all other legal and professional responsibilities, including, without limitation, those under generally accepted auditing standards and the rules or interpretations of the Commission that modify or supplement those auditing standards.

(c) A notice or report submitted to the Office of the Chief Accountant in accordance with paragraphs (a) and (b) of this section shall be deemed to be an investigative record and shall be non-public and exempt from disclosure pursuant to the Freedom of Information Act to the same extent and for the same periods of time that the Commission's investigative records are non-public and exempt from disclosure under, among other applicable provisions, 5 U.S.C. 552(b)(7) and § 200.80(b)(7) of this chapter. Nothing in this paragraph, however, shall relieve, limit, delay, or affect in any way, the obligation of any issuer or any independent accountant to make all public disclosures required by law, by any Commission disclosure item, rule, report, or form, or by any applicable accounting, auditing, or professional standard.

Instruction to paragraph (c).

Issuers and independent accountants may apply for additional bases for confidential treatment for a notice, report, or part thereof, in accordance with § 200.83 of this chapter. That section indicates, in part, that any person who, pursuant to any requirement of law, submits any information or causes or permits any information to be submitted to the Commission, may request that the Commission afford it confidential treatment by reason of personal privacy or business confidentiality, or for any other reason permitted by Federal law.

Rule 10A-2. Auditor Independence

It shall be unlawful for an auditor not to be independent under § 210.2-01(c)(2)(iii)(B), (c)(4), (c)(6), (c)(7), and § 210.2-07.

Rule 10A-3. Listing Standards Relating to Audit Committees

(a) Pursuant to section 10A(m) of the Act (15 U.S.C. 78j-1(m)) and section 3 of the Sarbanes-Oxley Act of 2002 (15 U.S.C. 7202):

(1) *National securities exchanges.* The rules of each national securities exchange registered pursuant to section 6 of the Act (15 U.S.C. 78f) must, in accordance with the provisions of this section, prohibit the initial or continued listing of any security of an issuer that is not in compliance with the requirements of any portion of paragraph (b) or (c) of this section.

(2) *National securities associations.* The rules of each national securities association registered pursuant to section 15A of the Act (15 U.S.C. 78o-3) must, in accordance with the provisions of this section, prohibit the initial or continued listing in an automated inter-dealer quotation system of any security of an issuer that is not in compliance with the requirements of any portion of paragraph (b) or (c) of this section.

(3) *Opportunity to cure defects.* The rules required by paragraphs (a)(1) and (a)(2) of this section must provide for appropriate procedures for a listed issuer to have an opportunity to cure any defects that would be the basis for a prohibition under paragraph (a) of this section, before the imposition of such prohibition. Such rules also may provide that if a member of an audit committee ceases to be independent in accordance with the requirements of this section for

reasons outside the member's reasonable control, that person, with notice by the issuer to the applicable national securities exchange or national securities association, may remain an audit committee member of the listed issuer until the earlier of the next annual shareholders meeting of the listed issuer or one year from the occurrence of the event that caused the member to be no longer independent.

(4) *Notification of noncompliance.* The rules required by paragraphs (a)(1) and (a)(2) of this section must include a requirement that a listed issuer must notify the applicable national securities exchange or national securities association promptly after an executive officer of the listed issuer becomes aware of any material noncompliance by the listed issuer with the requirements of this section.

(5) *Implementation.*

(i) The rules of each national securities exchange or national securities association meeting the requirements of this section must be operative, and listed issuers must be in compliance with those rules, by the following dates:

(A) July 31, 2005 for foreign private issuers and small business issuers (as defined in § 240.12b-2); and

(B) For all other listed issuers, the earlier of the listed issuer's first annual shareholders meeting after January 15, 2004, or October 31, 2004.

(ii) Each national securities exchange and national securities association must provide to the Commission, no later than July 15, 2003, proposed rules or rule amendments that comply with this section.

(iii) Each national securities exchange and national securities association must have final rules or rule amendments that comply with this section approved by the Commission no later than December 1, 2003.

(b) *Required standards.*

(1) *Independence.*

(i) Each member of the audit committee must be a member of the board of directors of the listed issuer, and must otherwise be independent; provided that, where a listed issuer is one of two dual holding companies, those companies may designate one audit committee for both companies so long as each member of the audit committee is a member of the board of directors of at least one of such dual holding companies.

(ii) *Independence requirements for non-investment company issuers.* In order to be considered to be independent for purposes of this paragraph (b)(1), a member of an audit committee of a listed issuer that is not an investment company may not, other than in his or her capacity as a member of the audit committee, the board of directors, or any other board committee:

(A) Accept directly or indirectly any consulting, advisory, or other compensatory fee from the issuer or any subsidiary thereof, provided that, unless the rules of the national securities exchange or national securities association provide otherwise, compensatory fees do not include the receipt of fixed amounts of compensation under a retirement plan (including deferred compensation) for prior service with the listed issuer (provided that such compensation is not contingent in any way on continued service); or

(B) Be an affiliated person of the issuer or any subsidiary thereof.

(iii) *Independence requirements for investment company issuers.* In order to be considered to be independent for purposes of this paragraph (b)(1), a member of an audit committee of a listed issuer that is an investment company may not, other than in his or her capacity as a member of the audit committee, the board of directors, or any other board committee:

(A) Accept directly or indirectly any consulting, advisory, or other compensatory fee from the issuer or any subsidiary thereof, provided that, unless the rules of the national securities exchange or national securities association provide otherwise, compensatory fees do not include the receipt of fixed amounts of compensation under a retirement plan (including deferred compensation) for prior service with the listed issuer (provided that such compensation is not contingent in any way on continued service); or

(B) Be an "interested person" of the issuer as defined in section 2(a)(19) of the Investment Company Act of 1940 (15 U.S.C. 80a-2(a)(19)).

(iv) *Exemptions from the independence requirements.*

(A) For an issuer listing securities pursuant to a registration statement under section 12 of the Act (15 U.S.C. 78*l*), or for an issuer that has a registration statement under the Securities Act of 1933 (15 U.S.C. 77a *et seq.*) covering an initial public offering of securities to be listed by the issuer, where in each case the listed issuer was not, immediately prior to the effective date of such registration statement, required to file reports with the Commission pursuant to section 13(a) or 15(d) of the Act (15 U.S.C. 78m(a) or 78o(d)):

(*1*) All but one of the members of the listed issuer's audit committee may be exempt from the independence requirements of paragraph (b)(1)(ii) of this section for 90 days from the date of effectiveness of such registration statement; and

(*2*) A minority of the members of the listed issuer's audit committee may be exempt from the independence requirements of paragraph (b)(1)(ii) of this section for one year from the date of effectiveness of such registration statement.

(B) An audit committee member that sits on the board of directors of a listed issuer and an affiliate of the listed issuer is exempt from the requirements of paragraph (b)(1)(ii)(B) of this section if the member, except for being a director on each such board of directors, otherwise meets the independence requirements of paragraph (b)(1)(ii) of this section for each such entity, including the receipt of only ordinary-course compensation for serving as a member of the board of directors, audit committee or any other board committee of each such entity.

(C) An employee of a foreign private issuer who is not an executive officer of the foreign private issuer is exempt from the requirements of paragraph (b)(1)(ii) of this section if the employee is elected or named to the board of directors or audit committee of the foreign private issuer pursuant to the issuer's governing law or documents, an employee collective bargaining or similar agreement or other home country legal or listing requirements.

(D) An audit committee member of a foreign private issuer may be exempt from the requirements of paragraph (b)(1)(ii)(B) of this section if that member meets the following requirements:

(*1*) The member is an affiliate of the foreign private issuer or a representative of such an affiliate;

(*2*) The member has only observer status on, and is not a voting member or the chair of, the audit committee; and

(*3*) Neither the member nor the affiliate is an executive officer of the foreign private issuer.

(E) An audit committee member of a foreign private issuer may be exempt from the requirements of paragraph (b)(1)(ii)(B) of this section if that member meets the following requirements:

(*1*) The member is a representative or designee of a foreign government or foreign governmental entity that is an affiliate of the foreign private issuer; and

(*2*) The member is not an executive officer of the foreign private issuer.

(F) In addition to paragraphs (b)(1)(iv)(A) through (E) of this section, the Commission may exempt from the requirements of paragraphs (b)(1)(ii) or (b)(1)(iii) of this section a particular relationship with respect to audit committee members, as the Commission determines appropriate in light of the circumstances.

(2) *Responsibilities relating to registered public accounting firms.* The audit committee of each listed issuer, in its capacity as a committee of the board of directors, must be directly responsible for the appointment, compensation, retention and oversight of the work of any registered public accounting firm engaged (including resolution of disagreements between management and the auditor regarding financial reporting) for the purpose of preparing or issuing an audit report or performing other audit, review or attest services for the listed issuer, and each such registered public accounting firm must report directly to the audit committee.

(3) *Complaints.* Each audit committee must establish procedures for:

(i) The receipt, retention, and treatment of complaints received by the listed issuer regarding accounting, internal accounting controls, or auditing matters; and

(ii) The confidential, anonymous submission by employees of the listed issuer of concerns regarding questionable accounting or auditing matters.

(4) *Authority to engage advisers.* Each audit committee must have the authority to engage independent counsel and other advisers, as it determines necessary to carry out its duties.

(5) *Funding.* Each listed issuer must provide for appropriate funding, as determined by the audit committee, in its capacity as a committee of the board of directors, for payment of:

(i) Compensation to any registered public accounting firm engaged for the purpose of preparing or issuing an audit report or performing other audit, review or attest services for the listed issuer;

(ii) Compensation to any advisers employed by the audit committee under paragraph (b)(4) of this section; and

(iii) Ordinary administrative expenses of the audit committee that are necessary or appropriate in carrying out its duties.

(c) *General exemptions.*

(1) At any time when an issuer has a class of securities that is listed on a national securities exchange or national securities association subject to the requirements of this section, the listing of other classes of securities of the listed issuer on a national securities exchange or national securities association is not subject to the requirements of this section.

(2) At any time when an issuer has a class of common equity securities (or similar securities) that is listed on a national securities exchange or national securities association subject to the requirements of this section, the listing of classes of securities of a direct or indirect consolidated subsidiary or an at least 50% beneficially owned subsidiary of the issuer (except classes of equity securities, other than non-convertible, non-participating preferred securities, of such subsidiary) is not subject to the requirements of this section.

(3) The listing of securities of a foreign private issuer is not subject to the requirements of paragraphs (b)(1) through (b)(5) of this section if the foreign private issuer meets the following requirements:

(i) The foreign private issuer has a board of auditors (or similar body), or has statutory auditors, established and selected pursuant to home country legal or listing provisions expressly requiring or permitting such a board or similar body;

(ii) The board or body, or statutory auditors is required under home country legal or listing requirements to be either:

(A) Separate from the board of directors; or

(B) Composed of one or more members of the board of directors and one or more members that are not also members of the board of directors;

(iii) The board or body, or statutory auditors, are not elected by management of such issuer and no executive officer of the foreign private issuer is a member of such board or body, or statutory auditors;

(iv) Home country legal or listing provisions set forth or provide for standards for the independence of such board or body, or statutory auditors, from the foreign private issuer or the management of such issuer;

(v) Such board or body, or statutory auditors, in accordance with any applicable home country legal or listing requirements or the issuer's governing documents, are responsible, to the extent permitted by law, for the appointment, retention and oversight of the work of any registered public accounting firm engaged (including, to the extent permitted by law, the resolution of disagreements between management and the auditor regarding financial reporting) for the purpose of preparing or issuing an audit report or performing other audit, review or attest services for the issuer; and

(vi) The audit committee requirements of paragraphs (b)(3), (b)(4) and (b)(5) of this section apply to such board or body, or statutory auditors, to the extent permitted by law.

(4) The listing of a security futures product cleared by a clearing agency that is registered pursuant to section 17A of the Act (15 U.S.C. 78q-1) or that is exempt from the registration requirements of section 17A pursuant to paragraph (b)(7)(A) of such section is not subject to the requirements of this section.

(5) The listing of a standardized option, as defined in § 240.9b-1(a)(4), issued by a clearing agency that is registered pursuant to section 17A of the Act (15 U.S.C. 78q-1) is not subject to the requirements of this section.

(6) The listing of securities of the following listed issuers are not subject to the requirements of this section:

(i) Asset-Backed Issuers (as defined in § 240.13a-14(g) and § 240.15d-14(g));

(ii) Unit investment trusts (as defined in 15 U.S.C. 80a-4(2)); and

(iii) Foreign governments (as defined in § 240.3b-4(a)).

(7) The listing of securities of a listed issuer is not subject to the requirements of this section if:

(i) The listed issuer, as reflected in the applicable listing application, is organized as a trust or other unincorporated association that does not have a board of directors or persons acting in a similar capacity; and

(ii) The activities of the listed issuer that is described in paragraph (c)(7)(i) of this section are limited to passively owning or holding (as well as administering and distributing amounts in respect of) securities, rights, collateral or other assets on behalf of or for the benefit of the holders of the listed securities.

(d) *Disclosure.* Any listed issuer availing itself of an exemption from the independence standards contained in paragraph (b)(1)(iv) of this section (except paragraph (b)(1)(iv)(B) of this section), the general exemption contained in paragraph (c)(3) of this section or the last sentence of paragraph (a)(3) of this section, must:

(1) Disclose its reliance on the exemption and its assessment of whether, and if so, how, such reliance would materially adversely affect the ability of the audit committee to act independently and to satisfy the other requirements of this section in any proxy or information statement for a meeting of shareholders at which directors are elected that is filed with the Commission pursuant to the requirements of section 14 of the Act (15 U.S.C. 78n); and

(2) Disclose the information specified in paragraph (d)(1) of this section in, or incorporate such information by reference from such proxy or information statement filed with the Commission into, its annual report filed with the Commission pursuant to the requirements of section 13(a) or 15(d) of the Act (15 U.S.C. 78m(a) or 78o(d)).

(e) *Definitions.* Unless the context otherwise requires, all terms used in this section have the same meaning as in the Act. In addition, unless the context otherwise requires, the following definitions apply for purposes of this section:

(1)(i) The term *affiliate* of, or a person *affiliated* with, a specified person, means a person that directly, or indirectly through one or more intermediaries, controls, or is controlled by, or is under common control with, the person specified.

(ii)(A) A person will be deemed not to be in control of a specified person for purposes of this section if the person:

(*1*) Is not the beneficial owner, directly or indirectly, of more than 10% of any class of voting equity securities of the specified person; and

(*2*) Is not an executive officer of the specified person.

(B) Paragraph (e)(1)(ii)(A) of this section only creates a safe harbor position that a person does not control a specified person. The existence of the safe harbor does not create a presumption in any way that a person exceeding the ownership requirement in paragraph (e)(1)(ii)(A)(*1*) of this section controls or is otherwise an affiliate of a specified person.

(iii) The following will be deemed to be affiliates:

(A) An executive officer of an affiliate;

(B) A director who also is an employee of an affiliate;

(C) A general partner of an affiliate; and

(D) A managing member of an affiliate.

(iv) For purposes of paragraph (e)(1)(i) of this section, dual holding companies will not be deemed to be affiliates of or persons affiliated with each other by virtue of their dual holding company arrangements with each other, including where directors of one dual holding company are also directors of the other dual holding company, or where directors of one or both dual holding companies are also directors of the businesses jointly controlled, directly or indirectly, by the dual holding companies (and, in each case, receive only ordinary-course compensation for serving as a member of the board of directors, audit committee or any other board committee of the dual holding companies or any entity that is jointly controlled, directly or indirectly, by the dual holding companies).

(2) In the case of foreign private issuers with a two-tier board system, the term *board of directors* means the supervisory or non-management board.

(3) In the case of a listed issuer that is a limited partnership or limited liability company where such entity does not have a board of directors or equivalent body, the term board of directors means the board of directors of the managing general partner, managing member or equivalent body.

(4) The term *control* (including the terms *controlling, controlled by* and under *common control with*) means the possession, direct or indirect, of the power to direct or cause the direction of the management and policies of a person, whether through the ownership of voting securities, by contract, or otherwise.

(5) The term *dual holding companies* means two foreign private issuers that:

(i) Are organized in different national jurisdictions;

(ii) Collectively own and supervise the management of one or more businesses which are conducted as a single economic enterprise; and

(iii) Do not conduct any business other than collectively owning and supervising such businesses and activities reasonably incidental thereto.

(6) The term *executive officer* has the meaning set forth in § 240.3b-7.

(7) The term *foreign private issuer* has the meaning set forth in § 240.3b-4(c).

(8) The term *indirect* acceptance by a member of an audit committee of any consulting, advisory or other compensatory fee includes acceptance of such a fee by a spouse, a minor child or stepchild or a child or stepchild sharing a home with the member or by an entity in which such member is a partner, member, an officer such as a managing director occupying a comparable position or executive officer, or occupies a similar position (except limited partners, non-managing members and those occupying similar positions who, in each case, have no active role in providing services to the entity) and which provides accounting, consulting, legal, investment banking or financial advisory services to the issuer or any subsidiary of the issuer.

(9) The terms *listed* and *listing* refer to securities listed on a national securities exchange or listed in an automated inter-dealer quotation system of a national securities association or to issuers of such securities.

Instructions to § 240.10A-3.

1. The requirements in paragraphs (b)(2) through (b)(5), (c)(3)(v) and (c)(3)(vi) of this section do not conflict with, and do not affect the application of, any requirement or ability under a listed issuer's governing law or documents or other home country legal or listing provisions that requires or permits shareholders to ultimately vote on, approve or ratify such requirements. The requirements instead relate to the assignment of responsibility as between the audit committee and management. In such an instance, however, if the listed issuer provides a recommendation or nomination regarding such responsibilities to shareholders, the audit committee of the listed issuer, or body performing similar functions, must be responsible for making the recommendation or nomination.

2. The requirements in paragraphs (b)(2) through (b)(5), (c)(3)(v), (c)(3)(vi) and Instruction 1 of this section do not conflict with any legal or listing requirement in a listed issuer's home jurisdiction that prohibits the full board of directors from delegating such responsibilities to the

listed issuer's audit committee or limits the degree of such delegation. In that case, the audit committee, or body performing similar functions, must be granted such responsibilities, which can include advisory powers, with respect to such matters to the extent permitted by law, including submitting nominations or recommendations to the full board.

3. The requirements in paragraphs (b)(2) through (b)(5), (c)(3)(v) and (c)(3)(vi) of this section do not conflict with any legal or listing requirement in a listed issuer's home jurisdiction that vests such responsibilities with a government entity or tribunal. In that case, the audit committee, or body performing similar functions, must be granted such responsibilities, which can include advisory powers, with respect to such matters to the extent permitted by law.

4. For purposes of this section, the determination of a person's beneficial ownership must be made in accordance with § 240.13d-3.

CONDUCT OF SPECIALISTS

Rule 11b-1. Regulation of Specialists

(a)(1) The rules of a national securities exchange may permit a member of such exchange to register as a specialist and to act as a dealer.

(2) The rules of a national securities exchange permitting a member of such exchange to register as a specialist and to act as a dealer shall include:

(i) Adequate minimum capital requirements in view of the markets for securities on such exchange;

(ii) Requirements, as a condition of a specialist's registration, that a specialist engage in a course of dealings for his own account to assist in the maintenance, so far as practicable, of a fair and orderly market, and that a finding by the exchange of any substantial or continued failure by a specialist to engage in such a course of dealings will result in the suspension or cancellation of such specialist's registration in one or more of the securities in which such specialist is registered;

(iii) Provisions restricting his dealings so far as practicable to those reasonably necessary to permit him to maintain a fair and orderly market or necessary to permit him to act as an odd-lot dealer;

(iv) Provisions stating the responsibilities of a specialist acting as a broker in securities in which he is registered; and

(v) Procedures to provide for the effective and systematic surveillance of the activities of specialists.

(b) If after appropriate notice and opportunity for hearing the Commission finds that a member of a national securities exchange registered with such exchange as a specialist in specified securities has, for any account in which he, his member organization, or any participant therein has any beneficial interest, direct or indirect, effected transactions in such securities which were not part of a course of dealings reasonably necessary to permit such specialist to maintain a fair and orderly market, or to act as an odd-lot dealer, in the securities in which he is registered and were not effected in a manner consistent with the rules adopted by such exchange pursuant to paragraph (a)(2)(iii) of this section, the Commission may by order direct such exchange to cancel, or to suspend for such period as the Commission may determine, such specialist's registration in one or more of the securities in which such specialist is registered: *Provided, however,* If such exchange has itself suspended or cancelled such specialist's registration is one or more of the securities in which such specialist is registered, no further sanction shall be imposed pursuant to this paragraph (b) except in a case where the Commission finds substantial or continued misconduct by a specialist; *And provided, further,* That the provisions of this paragraph (b) shall not apply to a member of a national securities exchange exempted pursuant to the provisions of paragraph (d) of this section.

(c) For the purposes of this rule, the term "rules" of an exchange shall mean its constitution, articles of incorporation, by-laws, or rules or instruments corresponding thereto, whatever the name, and its stated policies.

(d) Any national securities exchange may apply for an exemption from the provisions of this rule in compliance with the provisions of Section 11(c) of the Act.

REGULATION 12B—REGISTRATION AND REPORTING

General Requirements as to Contents

Rule 12b-20. Additional Information

In addition to the information expressly required to be included in a statement or report, there shall be added such further material information, if any, as may be necessary to make the required statements, in the light of the circumstances under which they are made not misleading.

Rule 12b-21. Information Unknown or Not Available

Information required need be given only insofar as it is known or reasonably available to the registrant. If any required information is unknown and not reasonably available to the registrant, either because the obtaining thereof would involve unreasonable effort or expense, or because it rests peculiarly within the knowledge of another person not affiliated with the registrant, the information may be omitted, subject to the following conditions:

(a) The registrant shall give such information on the subject as it possesses or can acquire without unreasonable effort or expense, together with the sources thereof.

(b) The registrant shall include a statement either showing that unreasonable effort or expense would be involved or indicating the absence of any affiliation with the person within whose knowledge the information rests and stating the result of a request made to such person for the information.

Rule 12b-22. Disclaimer of Control

If the existence of control is open to reasonable doubt in any instance, the registrant may disclaim the existence of control and any admission thereof; in such case, however, the registrant shall state the material facts pertinent to the possible existence of control.

Rule 12b-25. Notification of Inability to Timely File All or Any Required Portion of a Form 10-K, 10-KSB, 20-F, 11-K, N-SAR, N-CSR, 10-Q or 10-QSB

(a) If all or any required portion of an annual or transition report on Form 10-K, 10-KSB, 20-F or 11-K (17 CFR 249.310, 249.310b, 249.220f or 249.311), or a quarterly or transition report on Form 10-Q or 10-QSB (17 CFR 249.308a or 249.308b) required to be filed pursuant to sections 13 or 15(d) of the Act (15 U.S.C. 78m or 78o(d)) and rules thereunder, or if all or any required portion of a semi-annual, annual or transition report on Form N-CSR (17 CFR 249.331; 17 CFR 274.128) or Form N-SAR (17 CFR 249.330; 17 CFR 274.101) required to be filed pursuant to sections 13 or 15(d) of the Act or section 30 of the Investment Company Act of 1940 (15 U.S.C. 80a-29) and the rules thereunder, is not filed within the time period prescribed for such report, the registrant, no later than one business day after the due date for such report, shall file a Form 12b-25 (17 CFR 249.322) with the Commission which shall contain disclosure of its inability to file the report timely and the reasons therefor in reasonable detail.

(b) With respect to any report or portion of any report described in paragraph (a) of this section which is not timely filed because the registrant is unable to do so without unresaonable effort or expense, such report shall be deemed to be filed on the prescribed due date for such report if:

(1) The registrant files the Form 12b-25 in compliance with paragraph (a) of this section and, when applicable, furnishes the exhibit required by paragraph (c) of this section;

(2) The registrant represents in the Form 12b-25 that:

(i) The reason(s) causing the inability to file timely could not be eliminated by the registrant without unreasonable effort or expense; and

(ii) The subject annual report, semi-annual report or transition report on Form 10-K, 10-KSB, 20-F, 11-K, N-SAR, or N-CSR, or portion thereof, will be filed no later than the fifteenth calendar day following the prescribed due date; or the subject quarterly report or transition report on Form 10-Q or 10-QSB, or portion thereof, will be filed no later than the fifth calendar day following the prescribed due date; and

(3) The report/portion thereof is actually filed within the period specified by paragraph (b)(2)(ii) of this section.

(c) If paragraph (b) of this section is applicable and the reason the subject report/portion thereof cannot be filed timely without unreasonable effort or expense relates to the inability of any person, other than the registrant, to furnish any required opinion, report or certification, the Form 12b-25 shall have attached as an exhibit a statement signed by such person stating the specific reasons why such person is unable to furnish the required opinion, report or certification on or before the date such report must be filed.

(d) Notwithstanding paragraph (b) of this section, a registrant will not be eligible to use any registration statement form under the Securities Act of 1933 the use of which is predicated on timely filed reports until the subject report is actually filed pursuant to paragraph (b)(3) of this section.

(e) If a Form 12b-25 filed pursuant to paragraph (a) of this section relates only to a portion of a subject report, the registrant shall:

(1) File the balance of such report and indicate on the cover page thereof which disclosure items are omitted; and

(2) Include, on the upper right corner of the amendment to the report which includes the previously omitted information, the following statement:

The following items were the subject of a Form 12b-25 and are included herein: (*List Item Numbers*)

(f) The provisions of this section shall not apply to financial statements to be filed by amendment to a form 10-K and Form 10-KSB as provided for by paragraph (a) of § 210.3-09 or schedules to be filed by amendment in accordance with General Instruction A to form 10-K and Form 10-KSB.

(g) *Electronic filings.* The provisions of this section shall not apply to reports required to be filed in electronic format if the sole reason the report is not filed within the time period prescribed is that the filer is unable to file the report in electronic format. Filers unable to submit a report in electronic format within the time period prescribed solely due to difficulties with electronic filing should comply with either Rule 201 or 202 of Regulation S-T (§ 232.201 and § 232.202 of this chapter), or apply for an adjustment of filing date pursuant to Rule 13(b) of Regulation S-T (232.13(b) of this chapter).

EXTENSIONS AND TEMPORARY EXEMPTIONS—DEFINITIONS

Rule 12g-1. Exemptions from Section 12(g)

An issuer shall be exempt from the requirement to register any class of equity securities pursuant to section 12(g)(1) if on the last day of its most recent fiscal year the issuer had total assets not exceeding $10,000,000 and, with respect to a foreign private issuer, such securities were not quoted in an automated inter-dealer quotation system.

Rule 12g-2. Securities Deemed to Be Registered Pursuant to Section 12(g)(1) upon Termination of Exemption Pursuant to Section 12(g)(2)(A) or (B)

Any class of securities which would have been required to be registered pursuant to section 12(g)(1) of the Act except for the fact that it was exempt from such registration by section 12(g)(2)(A) because it was listed and registered on a national securities exchange, or by section 12(g)(2)(B) because it was issued by an investment company registered pursuant to section 8 of the Investment Company Act of 1940, shall upon the termination of the listing and registration of such class or the termination of the registration of such company and without the filing of an additional registration statement be deemed to be registered pursuant to said section 12(g)(1) if at the time of such termination (i) the issuer of such class of securities has elected to be regulated as a business development company pursuant to section 55 through 65 of the Investment Company Act of 1940 and such election has not been withdrawn, or (ii) securities of the class are not exempt from such registration pursuant to section 12 or rules thereunder and all securities of such class are held of record by 300 or more persons.

Rule 12g-3. Registration of Securities of Successor Issuers Under Section 12(b) or 12(g)

(a) Where in connection with a succession by merger, consolidation, exchange of securities, acquisition of assets or otherwise, securities of an issuer that are not already registered pursuant to section 12 of the Act (15 U.S.C. 78l) are issued to the holders of any class of securities of another issuer that is registered pursuant to either section 12(b) or (g) of the Act (15 U.S.C. 78l(b) or (g)), the class of securities so issued shall be deemed to be registered under the same paragraph of section 12 of the Act unless upon consummation of the succession:

(1) Such class is exempt from such registration other than by § 240.12g3-2;

(2) All securities of such class are held of record by less than 300 persons; or

(3) The securities issued in connection with the succession were registered on Form F-8 or Form F-80 (§ 239.38 or § 239.41 of this chapter) and following succession the successor would not be required to register such class of securities under section 12 of the Act (15 U.S.C. 78l) but for this section.

(b) Where in connection with a succession by merger, consolidation, exchange of securities, acquisition of assets or otherwise, securities of an issuer that are not already registered pursuant to section 12 of the Act (15 U.S.C. 78l) are issued to the holders of any class of securities of another issuer that is required to file a registration statement pursuant to either section 12(b) or (g) of the Act (15 U.S.C. 78l(b) or (g)) but has not yet done so, the duty to file such statement shall be deemed to have been assumed by the issuer of the class of securities so issued. The successor issuer shall file a registration statement pursuant to the same paragraph of section 12 of the Act with respect to such class within the period of time the predecessor issuer would have been required to file such a statement unless upon consummation of the succession:

(1) Such class is exempt from such registration other than by § 240.12g3-2;

(2) All securities of such class are held of record by less than 300 persons; or

(3) The securities issued in connection with the succession were registered on Form F-8 or Form F-80 (§ 239.38 or § 239.41 of this chapter) and following the succession the successor would not be required to register such class of securities under section 12 of the Act (15 U.S.C. 78l) but for this section.

(c) Where in connection with a succession by merger, consolidation, exchange of securities, acquisition of assets or otherwise, securities of an issuer that are not already registered pursuant to section 12 of the Act (15 U.S.C. 78l) are issued to the holders of classes of securities of two or more other issuers that are each registered pursuant to section 12 of the Act, the class of securities so issued shall be deemed to be registered under section 12 of the Act unless upon consummation of the succession:

(1) Such class is exempt from such registration other than by § 240.12g3-2;

(2) All securities of such class are held of record by less than 300 persons; or

(3) The securities issued in connection with the succession were registered on Form F-8 or Form F-80 (§ 239.38 or § 239.41 of this chapter) and following succession the successor would not be required to register such class of securities under section 12 of the Act (15 U.S.C. 78l) but for this section.

(d) If the classes of securities issued by two or more predecessor issuers (as described in paragraph (c) of this section) are registered under the same paragraph of section 12 of the Act (15 U.S.C. 78l), the class of securities issued by the successor issuer shall be deemed registered under the same paragraph of section 12 of the Act. If the classes of securities issued by the predecessor issuers are not registered under the same paragraph of section 12 of the Act, the class of securities issued by the successor issuer shall be deemed registered under section 12(g) of the Act (15 U.S.C. 78l(g)).

(e) An issuer that is deemed to have a class of securities registered pursuant to section 12 of the Act (15 U.S.C. 78l) according to paragraph (a), (b), (c) or (d) of this section shall file reports on the same forms and such class of securities shall be subject to the provisions of sections 14 and 16 of the Act (15 U.S.C. 78n and 78p) to the same extent as the predecessor issuers, except as follows:

(1) An issuer that is not a foreign issuer shall not be eligible to file on Form 20-F (§ 249.220f of this chapter) or to use the exemption in § 240.3a12-3.

(2) A foreign private issuer shall be eligible to file on Form 20-F (§ 249.220f of this chapter) and to use the exemption in § 240.3a12-3.

(f) An issuer that is deemed to have a class of securities registered pursuant to section 12 of the Act (15 U.S.C. 78l) according to paragraphs (a), (b), (c) or (d) of this section shall indicate in the Form 8-K (§ 249.308 of this chapter) report filed with the Commission in connection with the succession, pursuant to the requirements of Form 8-K, the paragraph of section 12 of the Act under which the class of securities issued by the successor issuer is deemed registered by operation of paragraphs (a), (b), (c) or (d) of this section. If a successor issuer that is deemed registered under section 12(g) of the Act (15 U.S.C. 78l(g)) by paragraph (d) of this section intends to list a class of securities on a national securities exchange, it must file a registration statement pursuant to section 12(b) of the Act (15 U.S.C. 78l(b)) with respect to that class of securities.

(g) An issuer that is deemed to have a class of securities registered pursuant to section 12 of the Act (15 U.S.C. 78l) according to paragraph (a), (b), (c) or (d) of this section shall file an annual report for each fiscal year beginning on or after the date as of which the succession occurred. Annual reports shall be filed within the period specified in the appropriate form. Each such issuer shall file an annual report for each of its predecessors that had securities registered pursuant to section 12 of the Act (15 U.S.C. 78l) covering the last full fiscal year of the predecessor before the registrant's succession, unless such report has been filed by the predecessor. Such annual report shall contain information that would be required if filed by the predecessor.

Rule 12g3-2. Exemptions for American Depositary Receipts and Certain Foreign Securities

(a) Securities of any class issued by any foreign private issuer shall be exempt from section 12(g) (15 U.S.C. 78l (g)) of the Act if the class has fewer than 300 holders resident in the United States. This exemption shall continue until the next fiscal year end at which the issuer has a class of equity securities held by 300 or more persons resident in the United States. For the purpose of determining whether a security is exempt pursuant to this paragraph:

(1) Securities held of record by persons resident in the United States shall be determined as provided in § 240.12g5-1 except that securities held of record by a broker, dealer, bank or nominee for any of them for the accounts of customers resident in the United States shall be counted as held in the United States by the number of separate accounts for which the securities are held. The issuer may rely in good faith on information as to the number of such separate accounts supplied by all owners of the class of its securities which are brokers, dealers, or banks or a nominee for any of them.

(2) Persons in the United States who hold the security only through a Canadian Retirement Account (as that term is defined in rule 237(a)(2) under the Securities Act of 1933 (§ 230.237(a)(2) of this chapter)), shall not be counted as holders resident in the United States.

(b)(1) Securities of any foreign private issuer shall be exempt from section 12(g) of the Act if the issuer, or a government official or agency of the country of the issuer's domicile or in which it is incorporated or organized:

(i) Shall furnish to the Commission whatever information in each of the following categories the issuer since the beginning of its last fiscal year (A) has made or is required to make public pursuant to the law of the country of its domicile or in which it is incorporated or organized, (B) has filed or is required to file with a stock exchange on which its securities are traded and which was made public by such exchange, or (C) has distributed or is required to distribute to its security holders;

(ii) Shall furnish to the Commission a list identifying the information referred to in paragraph (b)(1)(i) of this section and stating when and by whom it is required to be made public, filed with any such exchange, or distributed to security holders;

(iii) Shall furnish to the Commission, during each subsequent fiscal year, whatever information is made public as described in (A), (B) or (C) of paragraph (b)(1)(i) of this section promptly after such information is made or required to be made public as described therein;

(iv) Shall, promptly after the end of any fiscal year in which any changes occur in the kind of information required to be published as referred to in the list furnished under paragraph (b)(1)(ii) of this section or any subsequent list, furnish to the Commission a revised list reflecting such changes; and

(v) Shall furnish to the Commission in connection with the initial submission the following information to the extent known or which can be obtained without unreasonable effort or expense: the number of holders of each class of equity securities resident in the United States, the amount and percentage of each class of outstanding equity securities held by residents in the United States, the circumstances in which such securities were acquired, and the date and circumstances of the most recent public distribution of securities by the issuer or an affiliate thereof.

(2) The information required to be furnished under paragraphs (b)(1)(i) and (b)(1)(ii) of this section shall be furnished on or before the date on which a registration statement under section 12(g) of the Act would otherwise be required to be filed. Any issuer furnishing information under paragraph (b)(1)(i) of this section shall notify the Commission that it is furnished under that paragraph.

(3) The information required to be furnished under this paragraph (b) is information material to an investment decision such as: the financial condition or results of operations; changes in business; acquisitions or dispositions of assets; issuance, redemption or acquisitions of their securities; changes in management or control; the granting of options or the payment of other compensation to directors or officers; and transactions with directors, officers or principal security holders.

(4) Only one complete copy of any information or document need be furnished under paragraph (b)(1) of this section. Such information and documents need not be under cover of any prescribed form and shall not be deemed to be "filed" with the Commission or otherwise subject to the liabilities of section 18 of the Act. Press releases and all other communications or materials distributed directly to securityholders of each class of securities to which the exemption relates shall be in English. English versions or adequate summaries in English may be furnished in lieu of original English translations. No other documents need be furnished unless the issuer has prepared or caused to be prepared, English translations, versions, or summaries of them. If no English translations, versions, or summaries have been prepared, a brief description in English of any such documents shall be furnished. Information or documents in a language other than English are not required to be furnished. If practicable, the Commission file number shall appear on the information furnished or in an accompanying letter. Any information or document previously sent to the Commission under cover of Form 40-F or Form 6-K need not be furnished under paragraph b(1) of this section.

(5) The furnishing of any information or document under paragraph (b) of this rule shall not constitute an admission for any purpose that the issuer is subject to the Act.

(c) Depositary Shares registered on Form F-6 (§ 239.36 of this chapter), but not the underlying deposited securities, are exempt from section 12(g) of the Act under this paragraph (c).

(d) The exemption provided by paragraph (b) of this rule shall not be available for the following securities:

(1) Securities of a foreign private issuer that has or has had during the prior eighteen months any securities registered under section 12 of the Act or a reporting obligation (suspended or

active) under section 15(d) of the Act (other than arising solely by virtue of the use of Form F-7, F-8, F-9, F-10 or F-80);

(2) Securities of a foreign private issuer issued in a transaction (other than a transaction registered on Form F-8, F-9, F-10 or F-80) to acquire by merger, consolidation, exchange of securities, or acquisition of assets, another issuer that had securities registered under section 12 of the Act or a reporting obligation (suspended or active) under section 15(d) of the Act; and

(3) Securities quoted in an "automated inter-dealer quotation system" or securities represented by American Depositary Receipts so quoted unless all the following conditions are met:

(i) Such securities were so quoted on October 5, 1983 and have been continuously traded since;

(ii) The issuer is in compliance with the exemption in paragraph (b) on October 5, 1983 and has continuously maintained the exemption since; and

(iii) After January 2, 1986, the issuer is organized under the laws of any country except Canada or a political subdivision thereof.

Rule 12g-4. Certifications of Termination of Registration under Section 12(g)

(a) Termination of registration of a class of securities shall take effect in 90 days, or such shorter period as the Commission may determine, after the issuer certifies to the Commission on Form 15 that:

(1) Such class of securities is held of record by: (i) less than 300 persons; or (ii) by less than 500 persons, where the total assets of the issuer have not exceeded $10,000,000 on the last day of each of the issuer's three most recent fiscal years; or

(2) Such class of securities of a foreign private issuer, as defined in Rule 3b-4 [§ 240.3b-4], is held of record by: (i) less than 300 persons resident in the United States or (ii) less than 500 persons resident in the United States where the total assets of the issuer have not exceeded $10,000,000 on the last day of each of the issuer's most recent three fiscal years. For purposes of this paragraph, the number of persons resident in the United States shall be determined in accordance with the provisions of rule 12g3-2(a) [§ 240.12g3-2(a)].

(b) The issuer's duty to file any reports required under section 13(a) shall be suspended immediately upon filing a certification on Form 15. *Provided, however,* That if the certification on Form 15 is subsequently withdrawn or denied, the issuer shall, within 60 days after the date of such withdrawal or denial, file with the Commission all reports which would have been required had the certification on Form 15 not been filed. If the suspension resulted from the issuer's merger into, or consolidation with, another issuer or issuers, the certification shall be filed by the successor issuer.

Rule 12g5-1. Definition of Securities "Held of Record"

(a) For the purpose of determining whether an issuer is subject to the provisions of Sections 12(g) and 15(d) of the Act, securities shall be deemed to be "held of record" by each person who is identified as the owner of such securities on records of security holders maintained by or on behalf of the issue, subject to the following:

(1) In any case where the records of security holders have not been maintained in accordance with accepted practice, any additional person who would be identified as such an owner on such records if they had been maintained in accordance with accepted practice shall be included as a holder of record.

(2) Securities identified as held of record by a corporation, a partnership, a trust whether or not the trustees are named, or other organization shall be included as so held by one person.

(3) Securities identified as held of record by one or more persons as trustees, executors, guardians, custodians or in other fiduciary capacities with respect to a single trust, estate or account shall be included as held of record by one person.

(4) Securities held by two or more persons as co-owners shall be included as held by one person.

(5) Each outstanding unregistered or bearer certificate shall be included as held of record by a separate person, except to the extent that the issuer can establish that, if such securities were registered, they would be held of record, under the provisions of this rule, by a lesser number of persons.

(6) Securities registered in substantially similar names where the issuer has reason to believe because of the address or other indications that such names represent the same person, may be included as held of record by one person.

(b) Notwithstanding paragraph (a) of this section:

(1) Securities held, to the knowledge of the issuer, subject to a voting trust, deposit agreement or similar arrangement shall be included as held of record by the record holders of the voting trust certificates, certificates of deposit, receipts or similar evidences of interest in such securities; *Provided however,* That the issuer may rely in good faith on such information as is received in response to its request from a non-affiliated issuer of the certificates or evidences of interest.

(2) Whole or fractional securities issued by a savings and loan association, building and loan association, cooperative bank, homestead association, or similar institution for the sole purpose of qualifying a borrower for membership in the issuer, and which are to be redeemed or repurchased by the issuer when the borrower's loan is terminated, shall not be included as held of record by any person.

(3) If the issuer knows or has reason to know that the form of holding securities of record is used primarily to circumvent the provisions of Section 12(g) or 15(d) of the Act, the beneficial owners of such securities shall be deemed to be the record owners thereof.

Rule 12g5-2. Definition of "Total Assets"

For the purpose of Section 12(g)(1) of the Act, the term "total assets" shall mean the total assets as shown on the issuer's balance sheet or the balance sheet of the issuer and its subsidiaries consolidated, whichever is larger, as required to be filed on the form prescribed for registration under this section and prepared in accordance with the pertinent provisions of Regulation S-X. Where the security is a certificate of deposit, voting trust certificate, or certificate or other evidence of interest in a similar trust or agreement, the "total assets" of the issuer of the security held under the trust or agreement shall be deemed to be the "total assets" of the issuer of such certificate or evidence of interest.

Rule 12h-1. Exemptions from Registration under Section 12(g) of the Act

Issuers shall be exempt from the provisions of Section 12(g) of the Act with respect to the following securities:

(a) Any interest or participation in an employee stock bonus, stock purchase, profit sharing, pension, retirement, incentive, thrift, savings or similar plan which is not transferable by the holder except in the event of death or mental incompetency, or any security issued solely to fund such plans;

(b) Any interest or participation in any common trust fund or similar fund maintained by a bank exclusively for the collective investment and reinvestment of monies contributed thereto by the bank in its capacity as a trustee, executor, administrator, or guardian. For purposes of this paragraph (b), the term "common trust fund" shall include a common trust fund which is maintained by a bank which is a member of an affiliated group, as defined in section 1504(a) of the Internal Revenue Code of 1954 [26 U.S.C. 1504(a)], and which is maintained exclusively for the investment and reinvestment of monies contributed thereto by one or more bank members of such affiliated group in the capacity of trustee, executor, administrator, or guardian, provided that:

(1) the common trust fund is operated in compliance with the same state and federal regulatory requirements as would apply if the bank maintaining such fund and any other contributing banks were the same entity; and

(2) the rights of persons for whose benefit a contributing bank acts as trustee, executor, administrator or guardian would not be diminished by reason of the maintenance of such common trust fund by another bank member of the affiliated group

(c) Any class of equity security which would not be outstanding 60 days after a registration statement would be required to be filed with respect thereto;

(d) Any standardized option, as that term is defined in section 240.9b-1(a)(4), that is issued by a clearing agency registered under section 17A of the Act (15 U.S.C. 78q-1) and traded on a national securities exchange registered pursuant to section 6(a) of the Act (15 U.S.C. 78f(a)) or on a national securities association registered pursuant to section 15A(a) of the Act (15 U.S.C. 78o-3(a)); and

(e) Any security futures product that is traded on a national securities exchange registered pursuant to section 6 of the Act (15 U.S.C. 78f) or on a national securities association registered pursuant to section 15A(a) of the Act (15 U.S.C. 78o-3(a)) and cleared by a clearing agency that is registered pursuant to section 17A of the Act (15 U.S.C. 78q-1) or is exempt from registration under section 17A(b)(7) of the Act (15 U.S.C. 78q-1(b)(7)).

Rule 12h-3. Suspension of Duty to File Reports under Section 15(d)

(a) Subject to paragraphs (c) and (d) of this section, the duty under section 15(d) to file reports required by section 13(a) of the Act with respect to a class of securities specified in paragraph (b) of this section shall be suspended for such class of securities immediately upon filing with the Commission a certification on Form 15 [17 CFR 249.323] if the issuer of such class has filed all reports required by Section 13(a), without regard to Rule 12b-25 [17 CFR 249.322], for the shorter of its most recent three fiscal years and the portion of the current year preceding the date of filing Form 15, or the period since the issuer became subject to such reporting obligation. If the certification on Form 15 is subsequently withdrawn or denied, the issuer shall, within 60 days, file with the Commission all reports which would have been required if such certification had not been filed.

(b) The classes of securities eligible for the suspension provided in paragraph (a) of this section are:

(1) Any class of securities held of record by: (i) less than 300 persons; or (ii) by less than 500 persons, where the total assets of the issuer have not exceeded $10,000,000 on the last day of each of the issuer's three most recent fiscal years;

(2) Any class of securities of a foreign private issuer, as defined in Rule 3b-4 [§ 240.3b-4], held of record by: (i) less than 300 persons resident in the United States or (ii) less than 500 persons resident in the United States where the total assets of the issuer have not exceeded $10,000,000 on the last day of each of the issuer's three most recent fiscal years. For purposes of this paragraph, the number of persons resident in the United States shall be determined in accordance with the provisions of Rule 12g3-2(a) [§ 240.12g3-2(a)]; and

(3) Any class of securities deregistered pursuant to section 12(d) of the Act if such class would not thereupon be deemed registered under section 12(g) of the Act or the rules thereunder.

(c) This section shall not be available for any class of securities for a fiscal year in which a registration statement relating to that class becomes effective under the Securities Act of 1933, or is required to be updated pursuant to section 10(a)(3) of the Act, and, in the case of paragraphs (b)(1)(ii) and (b)(2)(ii), the two succeeding fiscal years. *Provided, however,* That this paragraph shall not apply to the duty to file reports which arises solely from a registration statement filed by an issuer with no significant assets, for the reorganization of a non-reporting issuer into a one subsidiary holding company in which equity security holders receive the same proportional interest in the holding company as they held in the non-reporting issuer, except for changes resulting from the exercise of dissenting shareholder rights under state law.

(d) The suspension provided by this rule relates only to the reporting obligation under section 15(d) with respect to a class of securities, does not affect any other duties imposed on that class of securities, and shall continue as long as criteria (i) or (ii) in either paragraph (b)(1) or (b)(2) is met on the first day of any subsequent fiscal year. *Provided, however,* That such criteria need not be met if the duty to file reports arises solely from a registration statement filed by an issuer with no significant assets in a reorganization of a non-reporting company into a one subsidiary holding company in which equity security holders receive the same proportional interest in the holding company as they held in the non-reporting issuer except for changes resulting from the exercise of dissenting shareholder rights under state law.

(e) If the suspension provided by this rule is discontinued because a class of securities does not meet the eligibility criteria of paragraph (b) on the first day of an issuer's fiscal year, then the issuer shall resume periodic reporting pursuant to section 15(d) by filing an annual report on Form 10-K and Form 10-KSB for its preceding fiscal year, not later than 120 days after the end of such fiscal year.

REGULATION 13A—REPORTS OF ISSUERS OF SECURITIES REGISTERED PURSUANT TO SECTION 12

Annual Reports

Rule 13a-1. Requirements of Annual Reports

Every issuer having securities registered pursuant to section 12 of the Act (15 U.S.C. 78l) shall file an annual report on the appropriate form authorized or prescribed therefor for each fiscal year after the last full fiscal year for which financial statements were filed in its registration statement. Annual reports shall be filed within the period specified in the appropriate form.

Other Reports

Rule 13a-11. Current Reports on Form 8-K

(a) Except as provided in paragraph (b) of this section, every registrant subject to §240.13a-1 shall file a current report on Form 8-K within the period specified in that form, unless substantially the same information as that required by Form 8-K has been previously reported by the registrant.

(b) This section shall not apply to foreign governments, foreign private issuers required to make reports on Form 6-K (17 CFR 249.306) pursuant to §240.13a-16, issuers of American Depositary Receipts for securities of any foreign issuer, or investment companies required to file reports pursuant to §270.30b1-1 of this chapter under the Investment Company Act of 1940, except where such investment companies are required to file notice of a blackout period pursuant to §245.104 of this chapter.

(c) No failure to file a report on Form 8-K that is required solely pursuant to Item 1.01, 1.02, 2.03, 2.04, 2.05, 2.06 or 4.02(a) of Form 8-K shall be deemed to be a violation of 15 U.S.C. 78j(b) and §240.10b-5.

Rule 13a-13. Quarterly Reports on Form 10-Q and Form 10-QSB (§249.308a and §249.308b of This Chapter)

(a) Except as provided in paragraphs (b) and (c) of this section, every issuer that has securities registered pursuant to Section 12 of the Act and is required to file annual reports pursuant to Section 13 of the Act, and has filed or intends to file such reports on Form 10-K and Form 10-KSB (§249.310 and §249.310b of this chapter) or U5S (§259.5s of this chapter), shall file a quarterly report on Form 10-Q Form 10-QSB (§249.308a and §249.308b of this chapter) within the period specified in General Instruction A.1. to that form, for each of the first three quarters of each fiscal year of the issuer, commencing with the first fiscal quarter following the most recent fiscal year for which full financial statements were included in the registration statement, or, if the registration statement included financial statements for an interim period subsequent to the most recent fiscal year end meeting the requirements of Article 10 of Regulation S-X, for the first fiscal quarter subsequent to the quarter reported upon in the registration statement. The first quarterly report of the issuer shall be filed either within 45 days after the effective date of the registration statement or on or before the date on which such report would have been required to be filed if the issuer had been required to file reports on Form 10-Q and Form 10-QSB as of its last fiscal quarter, whichever is later.

(b) The provisions of this rule shall not apply to the following issuers:

(1) Investment companies required to file reports pursuant to § 270.30b1-1;

(2) Foreign private issuers required to file reports pursuant to § 240.13a-16.

(c) Part I of the quarterly reports on Form 10-Q or Form 10-QSB need not be filed by:

(1) Mutual life insurance companies; or

(2) Mining companies not in the production stage but engaged primarily in the exploration for the development of mineral deposits other than oil, gas or coal, if all the following conditions are met:

(i) The registrant has not been in production during the current fiscal year or the two years immediately prior thereto; except that being in production for an aggregate period of not more than eight months over the three-year period shall not be a violation of this condition.

(ii) Receipts from the sale of mineral products or from the operations of mineral producing properties by the registrant and its subsidiaries combined have not exceeded $500,000 in any of the most recent six years and have not aggregated more than $1,500,000 in the most recent six fiscal years.

(d) Notwithstanding the foregoing provisions of this section, the financial information required by Part I of Form 10-Q and Form 10-QSB shall not be deemed to be "filed" for the purpose of section 18 of the Act or otherwise subject to the liabilities of that section of the Act but shall be subject to all other provisions of the Act.

Rule 13a-14. Certification of Disclosure in Annual and Quarterly Reports

(a) Each report, including transition reports, filed on Form 10-Q, Form 10-QSB, Form 10-K, Form 10-KSB, Form 20-F or Form 40-F (§§ 249.308a, 249.308b, 249.310, 249.310b, 249.220f or 249.240f of this chapter) under section 13(a) of the Act (15 U.S.C. 78m(a)), other than a report filed by an Asset-Backed Issuer (as defined in paragraph (g) of this section), must include certifications in the form specified in the applicable exhibit filing requirements of such report and such certifications must be filed as an exhibit to such report. Each principal executive and principal financial officer of the issuer, or persons performing similar functions, at the time of filing of the report must sign a certification.

(b) Each periodic report containing financial statements filed by an issuer pursuant to section 13(a) of the Act (15 U.S.C. 78m(a)) must be accompanied by the certifications required by Section 1350 of Chapter 63 of Title 18 of the United States Code (18 U.S.C. 1350) and such certifications must be furnished as an exhibit to such report as specified in the applicable exhibit requirements for such report. Each principal executive and principal financial officer of the issuer (or equivalent thereof) must sign a certification. This requirement may be satisfied by a single certification signed by an issuer's principal executive and principal financial officers.

(c) A person required to provide a certification specified in paragraph (a) or (b) of this section may not have the certification signed on his or her behalf pursuant to a power of attorney or other form of confirming authority.

(d) Each annual report filed by an Asset-Backed Issuer (as defined in paragraph (g) of this section) under section 13(a) of the Act (15 U.S.C. 78m(a)) must include a certification addressing the following items:

(1) Review by the certifying officer of the annual report and other reports containing distribution information for the period covered by the annual report;

(2) The absence in these reports, to the best of the certifying officer's knowledge, of any untrue statement of material fact or omission of a material fact necessary to make the statements made, in light of the circumstances under which such statements were made, not misleading;

(3) The inclusion in these reports, to the best of the certifying officer's knowledge, of the financial information required to be provided to the trustee under the governing documents of the issuer; and

(4) Compliance by the servicer with its servicing obligations and minimum servicing standards.

(e) With respect to Asset-Backed Issuers, the certification required by paragraph (d) of this section must be signed by the trustee of the trust (if the trustee signs the annual report) or the senior officer in charge of securitization of the depositor (if the depositor signs the annual report). Alternatively, the senior officer in charge of the servicing function of the master servicer (or entity performing the equivalent functions) may sign the certification.

(f) [Reserved]

(g) For purposes of this section, the term Asset-Backed Issuer means any issuer whose reporting obligation results from the registration of securities it issued that are primarily serviced by the cash flows of a discrete pool of receivables or other financial assets, either fixed or revolving, that by their terms convert into cash within a finite time period plus any rights or other assets designed to assure the servicing or timely distribution of proceeds to security holders.

Rule 13a-15. Controls and Procedure

(a) Every issuer that has a class of securities registered pursuant to section 12 of the Act (15 U.S.C. 78*l*), other than an Asset-Backed Issuer (as defined in § 240.13a-14(g)), a small business investment company registered on Form N-5 (§ § 239.24 and 274.5 of this chapter), or a unit investment trust as defined by section 4(2) of the Investment Company Act of 1940 (15 U.S.C. 80a-4(2)), must maintain disclosure controls and procedures (as defined in paragraph (e) of this section) and internal control over financial reporting (as defined in paragraph (f) of this section).

(b) Each such issuer's management must evaluate, with the participation of the issuer's principal executive and principal financial officers, or persons performing similar functions, the effectiveness of the issuer's disclosure controls and procedures, as of the end of each fiscal quarter, except that management must perform this evaluation:

(1) In the case of a foreign private issuer (as defined in § 240.3b-4) as of the end of each fiscal year; and

(2) In the case of an investment company registered under section 8 of the Investment Company Act of 1940 (15 U.S.C. 80a-8), within the 90-day period prior to the filing date of each report requiring certification under § 270.30a-2 of this chapter.

(c) The management of each such issuer, other than an investment company registered under section 8 of the Investment Company Act of 1940, must evaluate, with the participation of the issuer's principal executive and principal financial officers, or persons performing similar functions, the effectiveness, as of the end of each fiscal year, of the issuer's internal control over financial reporting. The framework on which management's evaluation of the issuer's internal control over financial reporting is based must be a suitable, recognized control framework that is established by a body or group that has followed due-process procedures, including the broad distribution of the framework for public comment.

(d) The management of each such issuer, other than an investment company registered under section 8 of the Investment Company Act of 1940, must evaluate, with the participation of the issuer's principal executive and principal financial officers, or persons performing similar functions, any change in the issuer's internal control over financial reporting, that occurred during each of the issuer's fiscal quarters, or fiscal year in the case of a foreign private issuer, that has materially affected, or is reasonably likely to materially affect, the issuer's internal control over financial reporting.

(e) For purposes of this section, the term *disclosure controls and procedures* means controls and other procedures of an issuer that are designed to ensure that information required to be disclosed by the issuer in the reports that it files or submits under the Act (15 U.S.C. 78a *et seq*.) is recorded, processed, summarized and reported, within the time periods specified in the Commission's rules and forms. Disclosure controls and procedures include, without limitation, controls and procedures designed to ensure that information required to be disclosed by an issuer in the reports that it files or submits under the Act is accumulated and communicated to the issuer's management, including its principal executive and principal financial officers, or persons performing similar functions, as appropriate to allow timely decisions regarding required disclosure.

(f) The term *internal control over financial reporting* is defined as a process designed by, or under the supervision of, the issuer's principal executive and principal financial officers, or persons performing similar functions, and effected by the issuer's board of directors, management and other personnel, to provide reasonable assurance regarding the reliability of financial reporting and the preparation of financial statements for external purposes in accordance with generally accepted accounting principles and includes those policies and procedures that:

(1) Pertain to the maintenance of records that in reasonable detail accurately and fairly reflect the transactions and dispositions of the assets of the issuer;

(2) Provide reasonable assurance that transactions are recorded as necessary to permit preparation of financial statements in accordance with generally accepted accounting principles, and that receipts and expenditures of the issuer are being made only in accordance with authorizations of management and directors of the issuer; and

(3) Provide reasonable assurance regarding prevention or timely detection of unauthorized acquisition, use or disposition of the issuer's assets that could have a material effect on the financial statements.

REGULATION 13B-2: MAINTENANCE OF RECORDS AND PREPARATION OF REQUIRED REPORTS

Rule 13b2-1. Falsification of Accounting Records

No person shall, directly or indirectly, falsify or cause to be falsified, any book, record or account subject to Section 13(b)(2)(A) of the Securities Exchange Act

Rule 13b2-2. Representations and conduct in connection with the preparation of required reports and documents

(a) No director or officer of an issuer shall, directly or indirectly:

(1) Make or cause to be made a materially false or misleading statement to an accountant in connection with; or

(2) Omit to state, or cause another person to omit to state, any material fact necessary in order to make statements made, in light of the circumstances under which such statements were made, not misleading, to an accountant in connection with:

(i) Any audit, review or examination of the financial statements of the issuer required to be made pursuant to this subpart; or

(ii) The preparation or filing of any document or report required to be filed with the Commission pursuant to this subpart or otherwise.

(b)(1) No officer or director of an issuer, or any other person acting under the direction thereof, shall directly or indirectly take any action to coerce, manipulate, mislead, or fraudulently influence any independent public or certified public accountant engaged in the performance of an audit or review of the financial statements of that issuer that are required to be filed with the Commission pursuant to this subpart or otherwise if that person knew or should have known that such action, if successful, could result in rendering the issuer's financial statements materially misleading.

(2) For purposes of paragraphs (b)(1) and (c)(2) of this section, actions that,"if successful, could result in rendering the issuer's financial statements materially misleading" include, but are not limited to, actions taken at any time with respect to the professional engagement period to coerce, manipulate, mislead, or fraudulently influence an auditor:

(i) To issue or reissue a report on an issuer's financial statements that is not warranted in the circumstances (due to material violations of generally accepted accounting principles, generally accepted auditing standards, or other professional or regulatory standards);

(ii) Not to perform audit, review or other procedures required by generally accepted auditing standards or other professional standards;

(iii) Not to withdraw an issued report; or

(iv) Not to communicate matters to an issuer's audit committee.

(c) In addition, in the case of an investment company registered under section 8 of the Investment Company Act of 1940 (15 U.S.C. 80a-8), or a business development company as defined in section 2(a)(48) of the Investment Company Act of 1940 (15 U.S.C. 80a-2(a)(48)), no officer or director of the company's investment adviser, sponsor, depositor, trustee, or administrator (or, in the case of paragraph (c)(2) of this section, any other person acting under the direction thereof) shall, directly or indirectly:

(1)(i) Make or cause to be made a materially false or misleading statement to an accountant in connection with; or

(ii) Omit to state, or cause another person to omit to state, any material fact necessary in order to make statements made, in light of the circumstances under which such statements were made, not misleading to an accountant in connection with:

(A) Any audit, review, or examination of the financial statements of the investment company required to be made pursuant to this subpart; or

(B) The preparation or filing of any document or report required to be filed with the Commission pursuant to this subpart or otherwise; or

(2) Take any action to coerce, manipulate, mislead, or fraudulently influence any independent public or certified public accountant engaged in the performance of an audit or review of the financial statements of that investment company that are required to be filed with the Commission pursuant to this subpart or otherwise if that person knew or should have known that such action, if successful, could result in rendering the investment company's financial statements materially misleading.

REGULATION 13D-G

Rule 13d-1. Filing of Schedules 13D and 13G

(a) Any person who, after acquiring directly or indirectly the beneficial ownership of any equity security of a class which is specified in paragraph (i) of this section, is directly or indirectly the beneficial owner of more than five percent of the class shall, within 10 days after the acquisition, file with the Commission, a statement containing the information required by Schedule 13D (§ 240.13d-101).

(b)(1) A person who would otherwise be obligated under paragraph (a) of this section to file a statement on Schedule 13D (§ 240.13d-101) may, in lieu thereof, file with the Commission, a short-form statement on Schedule 13G (§ 240.13d-102), *Provided*, That:

(i) Such person has acquired such securities in the ordinary course of his business and not with the purpose nor with the effect of changing or influencing the control of the issuer, nor in connection with or as a participant in any transaction having such purpose or effect, including any transaction subject to Rule 13d-3(b) (§ 240.13d-3(b)); and

(ii) Such person is:

(A) A broker or dealer registered under section 15 of the Act (15 U.S.C. 78o);

(B) A bank as defined in section 3(a)(6) of the Act (15 U.S.C. 78c);

(C) An insurance company as defined in section 3(a)(19) of the Act (15 U.S.C. 78c);

(D) An investment company registered under section 8 of the Investment Company Act of 1940 (15 U.S.C. 80a-8);

(E) Any person registered as an investment adviser under Section 203 of the Investment Advisers Act of 1940 (15 U.S.C. 80b-3) or under the laws of any state;

(F) An employee benefit plan as defined in Section 3(3) of the Employee Retirement Income Security Act of 1974, as amended, 29 U.S.C. 1001 et seq. ("ERISA") that is subject to the provisions of ERISA, or any such plan that is not subject to ERISA that is maintained primarily for the benefit of the employees of a state or local government or instrumentality, or an endowment fund;

(G) A parent holding company or control person, provided the aggregate amount held directly by the parent or control person, and directly and indirectly by their subsidiaries or affiliates that are not persons specified in § 240.13d-1 (b) (1) (ii) (A) through (I), does not exceed one percent of the securities of the subject class;

(H) A savings association as defined in Section 3 (b) of the Federal Deposit Insurance Act (12 U.S.C. 1813);

(I) A church plan that is excluded from the definition of an investment company under section 3 (c) (14) of the Investment Company Act of 1940 (15 U.S.C. 80a-3); and

(J) A group, provided that all the members are persons specified in § 240.13d-1 (b) (1) (ii) (A) through (I); and

(iii) Such person has promptly notified any other person (or group within the meaning of Section 13 (d) (3) of the Act) on whose behalf it holds, on a discretionary basis, securities exceeding five percent of the class, of any acquisition or transaction on behalf of such other person which might be reportable by that person under Section 13 (d) of the Act. This paragraph only requires notice to the account owner of information which the filing person reasonably should be expected to know and which would advise the account owner of an obligation he may have to file a statement pursuant to Section 13 (d) of the Act or an amendment thereto.

(2) The Schedule 13G filed pursuant to paragraph (b) (1) of this section shall be filed within 45 days after the end of the calendar year in which the person became obligated under paragraph (b) (1) of this section to report the person's beneficial ownership as of the last day of the calendar year, *Provided, That* it shall not be necessary to file a Schedule 13G unless the percentage of the class of equity security specified in paragraph (i) of this section beneficially owned as of the end of the calendar year is more than five percent; However, if the person's direct or indirect beneficial ownership exceeds 10 percent of the class of equity securities prior to the end of the calendar year, the initial Schedule 13G shall be filed within 10 days after the end of the first month in which the person's direct or indirect beneficial ownership exceeds 10 percent of the class of equity securities, computed as of the last day of the month.

(c) A person who would otherwise be obligated under paragraph (a) of this section to file a statement on Schedule 13D (§ 240.13d-101) may, in lieu thereof, file with the Commission, within 10 days after an acquisition described in paragraph (a) of this section, a short-form statement on Schedule 13G (§ 240.13d-102). *Provided,* That the person:

(1) Has not acquired the securities with any purpose, or with the effect of, changing or influencing the control of the issuer, or in connection with or as a participant in any transaction having that purpose or effect, including any transaction subject to § 240.13d-3 (b);

(2) Is not a person reporting pursuant to paragraph (b) (1) of this section; and

(3) Is not directly or indirectly the beneficial owner of 20 percent or more of the class.

(d) Any person who, as of the end of any calendar year, is or becomes directly or indirectly the beneficial owner of more than five percent of any equity security of a class specified in paragraph (i) of this section and who is not required to file a statement under paragraph (a) of this section by virtue of the exemption provided by Section 13 (d) (6) (A) or (B) of the Act (15 U.S.C. 78m (d) (6) (A) or 78m (d) (6) (B)), or because the beneficial ownership was acquired prior to December 22, 1970, or because the person otherwise (except for the exemption provided by Section 13 (d) (6) (C) of the Act (15 U.S.C. 78m (d) (6) (C))) is not required to file a statement, shall file with the Commission, within 45 days after the end of the calendar year in which the person became obligated to report under this paragraph (d), a statement containing the information required by Schedule 13G (§ 240.13d-102).

(e) (1) Notwithstanding paragraphs (b) and (c) of this section and § 240.13d-2 (b), a person that has reported that it is the beneficial owner of more than five percent of a class of equity securities in a statement on Schedule 13G (§ 240.13d-102) pursuant to paragraph (b) or (c) of this section, or is required to report the acquisition but has not yet filed the schedule, shall immediately become subject to §§ 240.13d-1 (a) and 240.13d-2 (a) and shall file a statement on Schedule 13D (§ 240.13d-101) within 10 days if, and shall remain subject to those requirements for so long as, the person:

(i) Has acquired or holds the securities with a purpose or effect of changing or influencing control of the issuer, or in connection with or as a participant in any transaction having that purpose or effect, including any transaction subject to § 240.13d-3(b); and

(ii) Is at that time the beneficial owner of more than five percent of a class of equity securities described in § 240.13d-1(i).

(2) From the time the person has acquired or holds the securities with a purpose or effect of changing or influencing control of the issuer, or in connection with or as a participant in any transaction having that purpose or effect until the expiration of the tenth day from the date of the filing of the Schedule 13D (§ 240.13d-101) pursuant to this section, that person shall not:

(i) Vote or direct the voting of the securities described therein; or

(ii) Acquire an additional beneficial ownership interest in any equity securities of the issuer of the securities, nor of any person controlling the issuer.

(f) (1) Notwithstanding paragraph (c) of this section and § 240.13d-2(b), persons reporting on Schedule 13G (§ 240.13d-102) pursuant to paragraph (c) of this section shall immediately become subject to §§ 240.13d-1(a) and 240.13d-2(a) and shall remain subject to those requirements for so long as, and shall file a statement on Schedule 13D (§ 240.13d-101) within 10 days of the date on which, the person's beneficial ownership equals or exceeds 20 percent of the class of equity securities.

(2) From the time of the acquisition of 20 percent or more of the class of equity securities until the expiration of the tenth day from the date of the filing of the Schedule 13D (§ 240.13d-101) pursuant to this section, the person shall not:

(i) Vote or direct the voting of the securities described therein, or

(ii) Acquire an additional beneficial ownership interest in any equity securities of the issuer of the securities, nor of any person controlling the issuer.

(g) Any person who has reported an acquisition of securities in a statement on Schedule 13G (§ 240.13d-102) pursuant to paragraph (b) of this section, or has become obligated to report on the Schedule 13G (§ 240.13d-102) but has not yet filed the Schedule, and thereafter ceases to be a person specified in paragraph (b)(1)(ii) of this section or determines that it no longer has acquired or holds the securities in the ordinary course of business shall immediately become subject to § 240.13d-1(a) or § 240.13d-1(c) (if the person satisfies the requirements specified in § 240.13d-1(c)), and §§ 240.13d-2(a), (b) or (d), and shall file, within 10 days thereafter, a statement on Schedule 13D (§ 240.13d-101) or amendment to Schedule 13G, as applicable, if the person is a beneficial owner at that time of more than five percent of the class of equity securities.

(h) Any person who has filed a Schedule 13D (§ 240.13d-101) pursuant to paragraph (e), (f) or (g) of this section may again report its beneficial ownership on Schedule 13G (§ 240.13d-102) pursuant to paragraphs (b) or (c) of this section provided the person qualifies thereunder, as applicable, by filing a Schedule 13G (§ 240.13d-102) once the person determines that the provisions of paragraph (e), (f) or (g) of this section no longer apply.

(i) For the purpose of this regulation, the term "equity security" means any equity security of a class which is registered pursuant to Section 12 of that Act, or any equity security of any insurance company which would have been required to be so registered except for the exemption contained in Section 12(g)(2)(G) of the Act, or any equity security issued by a closed-end investment company registered under the Investment Company Act of 1940: provided, such term shall not include securities of a class of non-voting securities.

(j) For the purposes of Sections 13(d) and 13(g), any person, in determining the amount of outstanding securities of a class of equity securities, may rely upon information set forth in the issuer's most recent quarterly or annual report, and any current report subsequent thereto, filed with the Commission pursuant to this Act, unless he knows or has reason to believe that the information contained therein is inaccurate.

(k) (1) Whenever two or more persons are required to file a statement containing the information required by Schedule 13D or Schedule 13G with respect to the same securities, only one statement need be filed, provided that:

(i) Each person on whose behalf the statement is filed is individually eligible to use the Schedule on which the information is filed;

(ii) Each person on whose behalf the statement is filed is responsible for the timely filing of such statement and any amendments thereto, and for the completeness and accuracy of the information concerning such person contained therein; such person is not responsible for the completeness or accuracy of the information concerning the other persons making the filing, unless such person knows or has reason to believe that such information is inaccurate; and

(iii) Such statement identifies all such persons, contains the required information with regard to each such person, indicates that such statement is filed on behalf of all such persons, and includes, as an exhibit, their agreement in writing that such a statement is filed on behalf of each of them.

(2) A group's filing obligation may be satisfied either by a single joint filing or by each of the group's members making an individual filing. If the group's members elect to make their own filings, each such filing should identify all members of the group but the information provided concerning the other persons making the filing need only reflect information which the filing person knows or has reason to know.

Rule 13d-2. Filing of Amendments to Schedules 13D or 13G

(a) If any material change occurs in the facts set forth in the Schedule 13D (§ 240.13d-101) required by § 240.13d-1(a), including, but not limited to, any material increase or decrease in the percentage of the class beneficially owned, the person or persons who were required to file the statement shall promptly file or cause to be filed with the Commission an amendment disclosing that change. An acquisition or disposition of beneficial ownership of securities in an amount equal to one percent or more of the class of securities shall be deemed "material" for purposes of this section; acquisitions or dispositions of less than those amounts may be material, depending upon the facts and circumstances.

(b) Notwithstanding paragraph (a) of this section, and provided that the person filing a Schedule 13G (§ 240.13d-102) pursuant to § 240.13d-1(b) or § 240.13d-1(c) continues to meet the requirements set forth therein, any person who has filed a Schedule 13G (§ 240.13d-102) pursuant to § 240.13d-1(b), § 240.13d-1(c) or § 240.13d-1(d) shall amend the statement within forty-five days after the end of each calendar year if, as of the end of the calendar year, there are any changes in the information reported in the previous filing on that Schedule; *Provided, however,* That an amendment need not be filed with respect to a change in the percent of class outstanding previously reported if the change results solely from a change in the aggregate number of securities outstanding. Once an amendment has been filed reflecting beneficial ownership of five percent or less of the class of securities, no additional filings are required unless the person thereafter becomes the beneficial owner of more than five percent of the class and is required to file pursuant to § 240.13d-1.

(c) Any person relying on § 240.13d-1(b) that has filed its initial Schedule 13G (§ 240.13d-102) pursuant to that paragraph shall, in addition to filing any amendments pursuant to § 240.13d-2(b), file an amendment on Schedule 13G (§ 240.13d-102) within 10 days after the end of the first month in which the person's direct or indirect beneficial ownership, computed as of the last day of the month, exceeds 10 percent of the class of equity securities. Thereafter, that person shall, in addition to filing any amendments pursuant to § 240.13d-2(b), file an amendment on Schedule 13G (§ 240.13d-102) within 10 days after the end of the first month in which the person's direct or indirect beneficial ownership, computed as of the last day of the month, increases or decreases by more than five percent of the class of equity securities. Once an amendment has been filed reflecting beneficial ownership of five percent or less of the class of securities, no additional filings are required by this paragraph (c).

(d) Any person relying on § 240.13d-1(c) and has filed its initial Schedule 13G (§ 240.13d-102) pursuant to that paragraph shall, in addition to filing any amendments pursuant to § 240.13d-2(b), file an amendment on Schedule 13G (§ 240.13d-102) promptly upon acquiring, directly or indirectly, greater than 10 percent of a class of equity securities specified in § 240.13d-1(d), and thereafter promptly upon increasing or decreasing its beneficial ownership by more than five percent of the class of equity securities. Once an amendment has been filed reflecting beneficial ownership of five percent or less of the class of securities, no additional filings are required by this paragraph (d).

(e) The first electronic amendment to a paper format Schedule 13D (§ 240.13d-101 of this chapter) or Schedule 13G (§ 240.13d-102 of this chapter) shall restate the entire text of the Schedule 13D or 13G, but previously filed paper exhibits to such Schedules are not required to be restated electronically. See Rule 102 of Regulation S-T (§ 232.102 of this chapter) regarding amendments to exhibits previously filed in paper format. Notwithstanding the foregoing, if the sole purpose of filing the first electronic Schedule 13D or 13G amendment is to report a change in beneficial ownership that would terminate the filer's obligation to report, the amendment need not include a restatement of the entire text of the Schedule being amended.

Note to § 240.13d-2: For persons filing a short-form statement pursuant to Rule 13d-1(b) or (c), see also Rules 13d-1(e), (f), and (g).

Rule 13d-3. Determination of Beneficial Ownership

(a) For the purposes of Sections 13(d) and 13(g) of the Act a beneficial owner of a security includes any person who, directly or indirectly, through any contract, arrangement, understanding, relationship, or otherwise has or shares:

(1) Voting power which includes the power to vote, or to direct the voting of, such security; and/or

(2) Investment power which includes the power to dispose, or to direct the disposition of, such security.

(b) Any person who, directly or indirectly, creates or uses a trust, proxy, power of attorney, pooling arrangement or any other contract, arrangement, or device with the purpose or effect of divesting such person of beneficial ownership of a security or preventing the vesting of such beneficial ownership as part of a plan or scheme to evade the reporting requirements of Section 13(d) or 13(g) of the Act shall be deemed for purposes of such sections to be the beneficial owner of such security.

(c) All securities of the same class beneficially owned by a person, regardless of the form which such beneficial ownership takes, shall be aggregated in calculating the number of shares beneficially owned by such person.

(d) Notwithstanding the provisions of paragraphs (a) and (c) of this rule:

(1)(i) A person shall be deemed to be the beneficial owner of a security, subject to the provisions of paragraph (b) of this rule, if that person has the right to acquire beneficial ownership of such security, as defined in Rule 13d-3(a) (§ 240.13d-3(a)) within sixty days, including but not limited to any right to acquired: (A) through the exercise of any option, warrant or right; (B) through the conversion of a security; (C) pursuant to the power to revoke a trust, discretionary account, or similar arrangement; or (D) pursuant to the automatic termination of a trust, discretionary account or similar arrangement; provided, however, any person who acquires a security or power specified in paragraphs (A), (B) or (C), above, with the purpose or effect of changing or influencing the control of the issuer, or in connection with or as a participant in any transaction having such purpose or effect, immediately upon such acquisition shall be deemed to be the beneficial owner of the securities which may be acquired through the exercise or conversion of such security or power. Any securities not outstanding which are subject to such options, warrants, rights or conversion privileges shall be deemed to be outstanding for the purpose of computing the percentage of outstanding securities of the class owned by such person but shall not be deemed to be outstanding for the purpose of computing the percentage of the class by any other person.

(ii) Paragraph (d)(1)(i) of this section remains applicable for the purpose of determining the obligation to file with respect to the underlying security even though the option, warrant, right or convertible security is of a class of equity security, as defined in § 240.13d-1(i), and may therefore give rise to a separate obligation to file.

(2) A member of a national securities exchange shall not be deemed to be a beneficial owner of securities held directly or indirectly by it on behalf of another person solely because such member is the record holder of such securities and, pursuant to the rules of such exchange, may direct the vote of such securities, without instruction, on other than contested matters or matters that may affect substantially the rights or privileges of the holders of the securities to be voted, but is otherwise precluded by the rules of such exchange from voting without instruction.

(3) A person who in the ordinary course of business is a pledgee of securities under a written pledge agreement shall not be deemed to be the beneficial owner of such pledged securities until the pledgee has taken all formal steps necessary which are required to declare a default and determines that the power to vote or to direct to vote or to dispose or to direct the disposition of such pledged securities will be exercised, provided that:

(i) The pledgee agreement is bona fide and was not entered into with the purpose nor with the effect of changing or influencing the control of the issuer, nor in connection with any transaction having such purpose or effect, including any transaction subject to Rule 13d-3(b);

(ii) The pledgee is a person specified in Rule 13d-1(b)(ii), including persons meeting the conditions set forth in paragraph (G) thereof; and

(iii) The pledgee agreement, prior to default, does not grant to the pledgee:

(A) The power to vote or to direct the vote of the pledged securities; or

(B) The power to dispose or direct the disposition of the pledged securities, other than the grant of such power(s) pursuant to a pledge agreement under which credit is extended subject to Regulation T (12 CFR 220.1 to 220.8) and in which the pledgee is a broker or dealer registered under section 15 of the Act.

(4) A person engaged in business as an underwriter of securities who acquires securities through his participation in good faith in a firm commitment underwriting registered under the Securities Act of 1933 shall not be deemed to be the beneficial owner of such securities until the expiration of forty days after the date of such acquisition.

Rule 13d-4. Disclaimer of Beneficial Ownership

Any person may expressly declare in any statement filed that the filing of such statement shall not be construed as an admission that such person is, for the purposes of section 13(d), or 13(g) of the Act, the beneficial owner of any securities covered by the statement.

Rule 13d-5. Acquisition of Securities

(a) A person who becomes a beneficial owner of securities shall be deemed to have acquired such securities for purposes of Section 13(d)(1) of the Act, whether such acquisition was through purchase or otherwise. However, executors or administrators of a decedent's estate generally will be presumed not to have acquired beneficial ownership of the securities in the decedent's estate until such time as such executors or administrators are qualified under local law to perform their duties.

(b)(1) When two or more persons agree to act together for the purpose of acquiring, holding, voting or disposing of equity securities of an issuer, the group formed thereby shall be deemed to have acquired beneficial ownership, for purposes of Sections 13(d) and 13(g) of the Act, as of the date of such agreement, of all equity securities of that issuer beneficially owned by any such persons.

(2) Notwithstanding the previous paragraph, a group shall be deemed not to have acquired any equity securities beneficially owned by the other members of the group solely by virtue of their concerted actions relating to the purchase of equity securities directly from an issuer in a transaction not involving a public offering, provided that:

(i) All the members of the group are persons specified in Rule 13d-1(b)(1)(ii);

(ii) The purchase is in the ordinary course of each member's business and not with the purpose nor with the effect of changing or influencing control of the issuer, nor in connection with or as a participant in any transaction having such purpose or effect, including any transaction subject to Rule 13d-3(b);

(iii) There is no agreement among, or between any members of the group to act together with respect to the issuer or its securities except for the purpose of facilitating the specific purchase involved; and

(iv) The only actions among or between any members of the group with respect to the issuer or its securities subsequent to the closing date of the non-public offering are those which are necessary to conclude ministerial matters directly related to the completion of the offer or sale of the securities.

Rule 13d-6. Exemption of Certain Acquisitions

The acquisition of securities of an issuer by a person who, prior to such acquisition, was a beneficial owner of more than five percent of the outstanding securities of the same class as those acquired shall be exempt from section 13(d) of the Act, provided that:

(a) The acquisition is made pursuant to preemptive subscription rights in an offering made to all holders of securities of the class to which the preemptive subscription rights pertain;

(b) Such person does not acquire additional securities except through the exercise of his pro rata share of the preemptive subscription rights; and

(c) The acquisition is duly reported, if required, pursuant to section 16(a) of the Act and the rules and regulations thereunder.

Rule 13d-7. Dissemination

One copy of the Schedule filed pursuant to §§ 240.13d-1 and 240.13d-2 shall be sent to the issuer of the security at its principal executive office, by registered or certified mail. A copy of Schedules filed pursuant to §§ 240.13d-1(a) and 240.13d-2(a) shall also be sent to each national securities exchange where the security is traded.

Rule 13e-1. Purchase of Securities by the Issuer During a Third-Party Tender Offer

An issuer that has received notice that it is the subject of a tender offer made under Section 14(d) (1) of the Act (15 U.S.C. 78n), that has commenced under § 240.14d-2 must not purchase any of its equity securities during the tender offer unless the issuer first:

(a) Files a statement with the Commission containing the following information:

(1) The title and number of securities to be purchased;

(2) The names of the persons or classes of persons from whom the issuer will purchase the securities;

(3) The name of any exchange, inter-dealer quotation system or any other market on or through which the securities will be purchased;

(4) The purpose of the purchase;

(5) Whether the issuer will retire the securities, hold the securities in its treasury, or dispose of the securities. If the issuer intends to dispose of the securities, describe how it intends to do so; and

(6) The source and amount of funds or other consideration to be used to make the purchase. If the issuer borrows any funds or other consideration to make the purchase or enters any agreement for the purpose of acquiring, holding, or trading the securities, describe the transaction and agreement and identify the parties; and

(b) Pays the fee required by § 240.0-11 when it files the initial statement.

(c) This section does not apply to periodic repurchases in connection with an employee benefit plan or other similar plan of the issuer so long as the purchases are made in the ordinary course and not in response to the tender offer.

Instruction to § 240.13e-1:

File eight copies if paper filing is permitted.

Rule 13e-3. Going Private Transactions by Certain Issuers or Their Affiliates

(a) *Definitions.* Unless indicated otherwise or the context requires, all terms used in this section and in Schedule 13E-3 [§ 240.13e-100] shall have the same meaning as in the Act or elsewhere in the General Rules and Regulations thereunder. In addition, the following definitions apply:

(1) An "affiliate" of an issuer is a person that directly or indirectly through one or more intermediaries controls, is controlled by, or is under common control with such issuer. For the purposes of this section only, a person who is not an affiliate of an issuer at the commencement of such person's tender offer for a class of equity securities of such issuer will not be deemed an affiliate of such issuer prior to the stated termination of such tender offer and any extensions thereof;

(2) The term "purchase" means any acquisition for value including, but not limited to, (i) any acquisition pursuant to the dissolution of an issuer subsequent to the sale or other disposition of substantially all the assets of such issuer to its affiliate, (ii) any acquisition pursuant to a merger, (iii) any acquisition of fractional interests in connection with a reverse stock split, and (iv) any acquisition subject to the control of an issuer or an affiliate of such issuer;

(3) A "Rule 13e-3 transaction" is any transaction or series of transactions involving one or more of the transactions described in paragraph (a)(3)(i) of this section which has either a reasonable likelihood or a purpose of producing, either directly or indirectly, any of the effects described in paragraph (a)(3)(ii) of this section;

(i) The transactions referred to in paragraph (a)(3) of this section are:

(A) A purchase of any equity security by the issuer of such security or by an affiliate of such issuer;

(B) A tender offer for or request or invitation for tenders of any equity security made by the issuer of such class of securities or by an affiliate of such issuer; or

(C) A solicitation subject to Regulation 14A [§§ 240.14a-1 to 240.14b-1] of any proxy, consent or authorization of, or a distribution subject to Regulation 14C [§§ 240.14c-1 to 240.14c-101] of information statements to, any equity security holder by the issuer of the class of securities or by an affiliate of such issuer, in connection with: a merger, consolidation, reclassification, recapitalization, reorganization or similar corporate transaction of an issuer or between an issuer (or its subsidiaries) and its affiliate; a sale of substantially all the assets of an issuer to its affiliate or group of affiliates; or a reverse stock split of any class of equity securities of the issuer involving the purchase of fractional interests.

(ii) The effects referred to in paragraph (a)(3) of this section are:

(A) Causing any class of equity securities of the issuer which is subject to section 12(g) or section 15(d) of the Act to be held of record by less than 300 persons; or

(B) Causing any class of equity securities of the issuer which is either listed on a national securities exchange or authorized to be quoted in an inter-dealer quotation system of a registered national securities association to be neither listed on any national securities exchange nor authorized to be quoted on an inter-dealer quotation system of any registered national securities association.

(4) An "unaffiliated security holder" is any security holder of an equity security subject to a Rule 13e-3 transaction who is not an affiliate of the issuer of such security.

(b) *Application of section to an issuer (or an affiliate of such issuer) subject to section 12 of the Act.*

(1) It shall be a fraudulent, deceptive or manipulative act or practice, in connection with a Rule 13e-3 transaction, for an issuer which has a class of equity securities registered pursuant to Section 12 of the Act or which is a closed-end investment company registered under the Investment Company Act of 1940, or an affiliate of such issuer, directly or indirectly.

(i) To employ any device, scheme or artifice to defraud any person;

(ii) To make any untrue statement of a material fact or to omit to state a material fact necessary in order to make the statements made, in light of the circumstances under which they were made, not misleading; or

(iii) To engage in any act, practice or course of business which operates or would operate as a fraud or deceit upon any person.

(2) As a means reasonably designed to prevent fraudulent, deceptive or manipulative acts or practices in connection with any Rule 13e-3 transaction, it shall be unlawful for an issuer which has a class of equity securities registered pursuant to Section 12 of the Act, or an affiliate of such issuer, to engage, directly or indirectly, in a Rule 13e-3 transaction unless:

(i) Such issuer or affiliate complies with the requirements of paragraphs (d), (e) and (f) of this Section; and

(ii) The Rule 13e-3 transaction is not in violation of paragraph (b)(1) of this section.

(c) *Application of section to an issuer (or an affiliate of such issuer) subject to Section 15(d) of the Act.*

(1) It shall be unlawful as a fraudulent, deceptive or manipulative act or practice for an issuer which is required to file periodic reports pursuant to Section 15(d) of the Act, or an affiliate of such issuer, to engage, directly or indirectly, in a Rule 13e-3 transaction unless such issuer or affiliate complies with the requirements of paragraphs (d), (e) and (f) of this section.

(2) An issuer or affiliate which is subject to paragraph (c)(1) of this section and which is soliciting proxies or distributing information statements in connection with a transaction described in paragraph (a)(3)(i)(A) of this section may elect to use the timing procedures for conducting a solicitation subject to Regulation 14A (§§ 240.14a-1 to 240.14b-1) or a distribution subject to Regulation 14C (§§ 240.14c-1 to 240.14c-101) in complying with paragraphs (d), (e) and (f) of this section, provided that if an election is made, such solicitation or distribution is conducted in accordance with the requirements of the respective regulations, including the filing of preliminary copies of soliciting materials or an information statement at the time specified in Regulation 14A or 14C, respectively.

(d) *Material required to be filed.* The issuer or affiliate engaging in a Rule 13e-3 transaction must file with the Commission:

(1) A Schedule 13E-3 (§ 240.13e-100), including all exhibits;

(2) An amendment to Schedule 13E-3 reporting promptly any material changes in the information set forth in the schedule previously filed; and

(3) A final amendment to Schedule 13E-3 reporting promptly the results of the Rule 13e-3 transaction.

(e) *Disclosure of information to security holders.*

(1) In addition to disclosing the information required by any other applicable rule or regulation under the federal securities laws, the issuer or affiliate engaging in a § 240.13e-3 transaction must disclose to security holders of the class that is the subject of the transaction, as specified in paragraph (f) of this section, the following:

(i) The information required by Item 1 of Schedule 13E-3 (§ 240.13e-100) (Summary Term Sheet);

(ii) The information required by Items 7, 8 and 9 of Schedule 13E-3, which must be prominently disclosed in a "Special Factors" section in the front of the disclosure document;

(iii) A prominent legend on the outside front cover page that indicates that neither the Securities and Exchange Commission nor any state securities commission has: approved or disapproved of the transaction; passed upon the merits or fairness of the transaction; or passed upon the adequacy or accuracy of the disclosure in the document. The legend also must make it clear that any representation to the contrary is a criminal offense;

(iv) The information concerning appraisal rights required by § 229.1016(f) of this chapter; and

(v) The information required by the remaining items of Schedule 13E-3, except for § 229.1016 of this chapter (exhibits), or a fair and adequate summary of the information.

Instructions to paragraph (e)(1):

1. If the Rule 13e-3 transaction also is subject to Regulation 14A (§§ 240.14a-1 through 240.14b-2) or 14C (§§ 240.14c-1 through 240.14c-101), the registration provisions and rules of the Securities Act of 1933, Regulation 14D or § 240.13e-4, the information required by paragraph (e)

(1) of this section must be combined with the proxy statement, information statement, prospectus or tender offer material sent or given to security holders.

2. If the Rule 13e-3 transaction involves a registered securities offering, the legend required by § 229.501(b)(7) of this chapter must be combined with the legend required by paragraph (e)(1)(iii) of this section.

3. The required legend must be written in clear, plain language.

(2) If there is any material change in the information previously disclosed to security holders, the issuer or affiliate must disclose the change promptly to security holders as specified in paragraph (f)(1)(iii) of this section.

(f) *Dissemination of information to security holders.* (1) If the Rule 13e-3 transaction involves a purchase as described in paragraph (a)(3)(i)(A) of this section or a vote, consent, authorization, or distribution of information statements as described in paragraph (a)(3)(i)(C) of this section, the issuer or affiliate engaging in the Rule 13e-3 transaction shall:

(i) Provide the information required by paragraph (e) of this section: (A) in accordance with the provisions of any applicable federal or state law, but in no event later than 20 days prior to; any such purchase; any such vote, consent or authorization; or with respect to the distribution of information statements, the meeting date, or if corporate action is to be taken by means of the written authorization or consent of security holders, the earliest date on which corporate action may be taken: *Provided, however,* That if the purchase subject to this section is pursuant to a tender offer excepted from Rule 13e-4 by paragraph (g)(5) of Rule 13e-4, the information required by paragraph (e) of this section shall be disseminated in accordance with paragraph (e) of Rule 13e-4 no later than 10 business days prior to any purchase pursuant to such tender offer, (B) to each person who is a record holder of a class of equity security subject to the Rule 13e-3 transaction as of a date not more than 20 days prior to the date of dissemination of such information.

(ii) If the issuer or affiliate knows that securities of the class of securities subject to the Rule 13e-3 transaction are held of record by a broker, dealer, bank or voting trustee or their nominees, such issuer or affiliate shall (unless Rule 14a-13(a) [§ 240.14a-13(a)] or 14c-7 [§ 240.14c-7] is applicable) furnish the number of copies of the information required by paragraph (e) of this section that are requested by such persons (pursuant to inquiries by or on behalf of the issuer or affiliate), instruct such persons to forward such information to the beneficial owners of such securities in a timely manner and undertake to pay the reasonable expenses incurred by such persons in forwarding such information; and

(iii) Promptly disseminate disclosure of material changes to the information required by paragraph (d) of this section in a manner reasonably calculated to inform security holders.

(2) If the Rule 13e-3 transaction is a tender offer or a request or invitation for tenders of equity securities which is subject to Regulation 14D [§§ 240.14d-1 to 240.14d-101] or Rule 13e-4 [§ 240.13e-4], the tender offer containing the information required by paragraph (e) of this section, and any material change with respect thereto, shall be published, sent or given in accordance with Regulation 14D or Rule 13e-4, respectively, to security holders of the class of securities being sought by the issuer or affiliate.

(g) *Exceptions.* This section shall not apply to:

(1) Any Rule 13e-3 transaction by or on behalf of a person which occurs within one year of the date of termination of a tender offer in which such person was the bidder and became an affiliate of the issuer as a result of such tender offer *provided* that the consideration offered to unaffiliated security holders in such Rule 13e-3 transaction is at least equal to the highest consideration offered during such tender offer and *provided further* that:

(i) If such tender offer was made for any or all securities of a class of the issuer:

(A) Such tender offer fully disclosed such person's intention to engage in a Rule 13e-3 transaction, the form and effect of such transaction and, to the extent known, the proposed terms thereof; and

(B) Such Rule 13e-3 transaction is substantially similar to that described in such tender offer; or

(ii) If such tender offer was made for less than all the securities of a class of the issuer:

(A) Such tender offer fully disclosed a plan of merger, a plan of liquidation or a similar binding agreement between such person and the issuer with respect to a Rule 13e-3 transaction; and

(B) Such Rule 13e-3 transaction occurs pursuant to the plan of merger, plan of liquidation or similar binding agreement disclosed in the bidder's tender offer.

(2) Any Rule 13e-3 transaction in which the security holders are offered or receive only an equity security *provided* That:

(i) such equity security has substantially the same rights as the equity security which is the subject of the Rule 13e-3 transaction including, but not limited to, voting, dividends, redemption and liquidation rights except that this requirement shall be deemed to be satisfied if unaffiliated security holders are offered common stock;

(ii) such equity security is registered pursuant to section 12 of the Act or reports are required to be filed by the issuer thereof pursuant to section 15(d) of the Act; and

(iii) if the security which is the subject of the Rule 13e-3 transaction was either listed on a national securities exchange or authorized to be quoted in an inter-dealer quotation system of a registered national securities association, such equity security is either listed on a national securities exchange or authorized to be quoted in an inter-dealer quotation system of a registered national securities association.

(3) Transactions by a holding company registered under the Public Utility Holding Company Act of 1935 in compliance with the provisions of that Act;

(4) Redemptions, calls or similar purchases of an equity security by an issuer pursuant to specific provisions set forth in the instrument(s) creating or governing that class of equity securities; or

(5) Any solicitation by an issuer with respect to a plan of reorganization under Chapter XI of the Bankruptcy Act, as amended, if made after the entry of an order approving such plan pursuant to section 1125(b) of that Act and after, or concurrently with, the transmittal of information concerning such plan as required by section 1125(b) of that Act.

(6) Any tender offer or business combination made in compliance with § 230.802 of this chapter, § 240.13e-4(h)(8) or § 240.14d-1(c).

PROXY RULES

REGULATION 14A—SOLICITATION OF PROXIES

Rule 14a-1. Definitions

Unless the context otherwise requires, all terms used in this regulation have the same meanings as in the Act or elsewhere in the general rules and regulations thereunder. In addition, the following definitions apply unless the context otherwise requires:

(a) *Associate.* The term "associate," used to indicate a relationship with any person, means (1) any corporation or organization (other than the registrant or a majority owned subsidiary of the registrant) of which such person is an officer or partner or is, directly or indirectly, the beneficial owner of 10 percent or more of any class of equity securities; (2) any trust or other estate in which such person has a substantial beneficial interest or as to which such person serves as trustee or in a similar fiduciary capacity; and (3) any relative or spouse of such person, or any relative of such spouse, who has the same home as such person or who is a director or officer of the registrant or any of its parents or subsidiaries.

(b) *Employee benefit plan.* For purposes of §§ 240.14a-13, 240.14b-1 and 240.14b-2, the term "employee benefit plan" means any purchase, savings, option, bonus, appreciation, profit sharing, thrift, incentive, pension or similar plan primarily for employees, directors, trustees or officers.

(c) *Entity that exercises fiduciary powers.* The term "entity that exercises fiduciary powers" means any entity that holds securities in nominee name or otherwise on behalf of a beneficial owner but does not include a clearing agency registered pursuant to section 17A of the Act or a broker or a dealer.

(d) *Exempt employee benefit plan securities.* For purposes of §§ 240.14a-13, 240.14b-1 and 240.14b-2, the term "exempt employee benefit plan securities" means: (1) securities of the registrant held by an employee benefit plan, as defined in paragraph (b) of this section, where such plan is established by the registrant; or (2) if notice regarding the current solicitation has been given pursuant to § 240.14a-13(a)(1)(ii)(C) or if notice regarding the current request for a list of names, addresses and securities positions of beneficial owners has been given pursuant to § 240.14a-13(b)(3), securities of the registrant held by an employee benefit plan, as defined in paragraph (b) of this section, where such plan is established by an affiliate of the registrant.

(e) *Last fiscal year.* The term "last fiscal year" of the registrant means the last fiscal year of the registrant ending prior to the date of the meeting for which proxies are to be solicited or if the solicitation involves written authorizations or consents in lieu of a meeting, the earliest date they may be used to effect corporate action.

(f) *Proxy.* The term "proxy" includes every proxy, consent or authorization within the meaning of section 14(a) of the Act. The consent or authorization may take the form of failure to object or to dissent.

(g) *Proxy statement.* The term "proxy statement" means the statement required by § 240.14a-3(a) whether or not contained in a single document.

(h) *Record date.* The term "record date" means the date as of which the record holders of securities entitled to vote at a meeting or by written consent or authorization shall be determined.

(i) *Record holder.* For purposes of §§ 240.14a-13, 240.14b-1 and 240.14b-2, the term "record holder" means any broker, dealer, voting trustee, bank, association or other entity that exercises fiduciary powers which holds securities of record in nominee name or otherwise or as a participant in a clearing agency registered pursuant to section 17A of the Act.

(j) *Registrant.* The term "registrant" means the issuer of the securities in respect of which proxies are to be solicited.

(k) *Respondent bank.* For purposes of §§ 240.14a-13, 240.14b-1 and 240.14b-2, the term "respondent bank" means any bank, association or other entity that exercises fiduciary powers which holds securities on behalf of beneficial owners and deposits such securities for safekeeping with another bank, association or other entity that exercises fiduciary powers.

(l) *Solicitation.* (1) The terms "solicit" and "solicitation" include:

(i) Any request for a proxy whether or not accompanied by or included in a form of proxy;

(ii) Any request to execute or not to execute, or to revoke, a proxy; or

(iii) The furnishing of a form of proxy or other communication to security holders under circumstances reasonably calculated to result in the procurement, withholding or revocation of a proxy.

(2) The terms do not apply, however, to:

(i) The furnishing of a form of proxy to a security holder upon the unsolicited request of such security holder;

(ii) The performance by the registrant of acts required by § 240.14a-7;

(iii) The performance by any person of ministerial acts on behalf of a person soliciting a proxy; or

(iv) A communication by a security holder who does not otherwise engage in a proxy solicitation (other than a solicitation exempt under § 240.14a-2) starting how the security holder intends to vote and the reasons therefor, provided that the communication:

(A) is made by means of speeches in public forums, press releases, published or broadcast opinions, statements, or advertisements appearing in a broadcast media, or newspaper, magazine or other bona fide publication disseminated on a regular basis,

(B) is directed to persons to whom the security holder owes a fiduciary duty in connection with the voting of securities of a registrant held by the security holder, or

(C) is made in response to unsolicited requests for additional information with respect to a prior communication by the security holder made pursuant to this paragraph (*l*)(2)(iv).

Rule 14a-2. Solicitations to Which §240.14a-3 to §240.14a-15 Apply

Sections 240.14a-3 to 240.14a-15, except as specified below, apply to every solicitation of a proxy with respect to securities registered pursuant to Section 12 of the Act (15 U.S.C. 78*l*), whether or not trading in such securities has been suspended. To the extent specified below, certain of these sections also apply to roll-up transactions that do not involve an entity with securities registered pursuant to Section 12 of the Act.

(a) Sections 240.14a-3 to 240.14a-15 do not apply to the following:

(1) Any solicitation by a person in respect to securities carried in his name or in the name of his nominee (otherwise than as voting trustee) or held in his custody, if such person—

(i) Receives no commission or remuneration for such solicitation, directly or indirectly, other than reimbursement of reasonable expenses,

(ii) Furnishes promptly to the person solicited (or such person's household in accordance with §240.14a-3(e)(1)) a copy of all soliciting material with respect to the same subject matter or meeting received from all persons who shall furnish copies thereof for such purpose and who shall, if requested, defray the reasonable expenses to be incurred in forwarding such material, and

(iii) In addition, does no more than impartially instruct the person solicited to forward a proxy to the person, if any, to whom the person solicited desires to give a proxy, or impartially request from the person solicited instructions as to the authority to be conferred by the proxy and state that a proxy will be given if no instructions are received by a certain date.

(2) Any solicitation by a person in respect of securities of which he is the beneficial owner;

(3) Any solicitation involved in the offer and sale of securities registered under the Securities Act of 1933: *Provided,* That this paragraph shall not apply to securities to be issued in any transaction of the character specified in paragraph (a) of Rule 145 under that Act;

(4) Any solicitation with respect to a plan of reorganization under Chapter 11 of the Bankruptcy Reform Act of 1978, as amended, if made after the entry of an order approving the written disclosure statement concerning a plan of reorganization pursuant to section 1125 of said Act and after, or concurrently with, the transmittal of such disclosure statement as required by section 1125 of said Act;

(5) Any solicitation which is subject to Rule 62 under the Public Utility Holding Company Act of 1935; and

(6) Any solicitation through the medium of a newspaper advertisement which informs security holders of a source from which they may obtain copies of a proxy statement, form of proxy and any other soliciting material and does no more than (i) name the registrant, (ii) state the reason for the advertisement, and (iii) identify the proposal or proposals to be acted upon by security holders.

(b) Sections 240.14a-3 to 240.14a-6 (other than 14a-6(g)), 240.14a-8, and 240.14a-10 to 14a-15 do not apply to the following:

(1) Any solicitation by or on behalf of any person who does not, at any time during such solicitation, seek directly or indirectly, either on its own or another's behalf, the power to act as proxy for a security holder and does not furnish or otherwise request, or act on behalf of a person who furnishes or requests, a form of revocation, abstention, consent or authorization. *Provided, however,* that the exemption set forth in this paragraph shall not apply to:

(i) the registrant or an affiliate or associate of the registrant (other than an officer or director or any person serving in a similar capacity);

(ii) an officer or director of the registrant or any person serving in a similar capacity engaging in a solicitation financed directly or indirectly by the registrant;

(iii) an officer, director, affiliate or associate of a person that is ineligible to rely on the exemption set forth in this paragraph (other than persons specified in paragraph (b)(1)(i) of this section), or any person serving in a similar capacity;

(iv) any nominee for whose election as a director proxies are solicited;

(v) any person soliciting in opposition to a merger, recapitalization, reorganization, sale of assets or other extraordinary transaction recommended or approved by the board of directors of the registrant who is proposing or intends to propose an alternative transaction to which such person or one of its affiliates is a party;

(vi) any person who is required to report beneficial ownership of the registrant's equity securities on a Schedule 13D [§ 240.13d-101], unless such person has filed a Schedule 13D and has not disclosed pursuant to Item 4 thereto an intent, or reserved the right, to engage in a control transaction, or any contested solicitation for the election of directors;

(vii) any person who receives compensation from an ineligible person directly related to the solicitation of proxies, other than pursuant to § 240.14a-13;

(viii) where the registrant is an investment company registered under the Investment Company Act of 1940 [15 U.S.C. 80a-1 et seq.], an "interested person" of that investment company, as that term is defined in Section 2(a)(19) of the investment Company Act [15 U.S.C. 80a-2];

(ix) any person who, because of a substantial interest in the subject matter of the solicitation, is likely to receive a benefit from a successful solicitation that would not be shared pro rata by all other holders of the same class of securities, other than a benefit arising from the person's employment with the registrant; and

(x) any person acting on behalf of any of the foregoing.

(2) Any solicitation made otherwise than on behalf of the registrant where the total number of persons solicited is not more than ten; and

(3) The furnishing of proxy voting advice by any person (the "advisor") to any other person with whom the advisor has a business relationship, if:

(i) The advisor renders financial advice in the ordinary course of his business;

(ii) The advisor discloses to the recipient of the advice any significant relationship with the registrant or any of its affiliates, or a security holder proponent of the matter on which advice is given, as well as any material interest of the advisor in such matter.

(iii) The advisor receives no special commission or remuneration for furnishing the proxy voting advice from any person other than a recipient of the advice and other persons who receive similar advice under this subsection; and

(iv) The proxy voting advice is not furnished on behalf of any person soliciting proxies or on behalf of a participant in an election subject to the provisions of Rule 14a-11.

(4) Any solicitation in connection with a roll-up transaction as defined in Item 901(c) of Regulation S-K (§ 229.901 of this chapter) in which the holder of a security that is the subject of a proposed roll-up transaction engages in preliminary communications with other holders of securities that are the subject of the same limited partnership roll-up transaction for the purpose of determining whether to solicit proxies, consents, or authorizations in opposition to the proposed limited partnership roll-up transaction; *provided, however*, that:

(i) This exemption shall not apply to a security holder who is an affiliate of the registrant or general partner or sponsor; and

(ii) This exemption shall not apply to a holder of five percent (5%) or more of the outstanding securities of a class that is the subject of the proposed roll-up transaction who engages in the business of buying and selling limited partnership interests in the secondary market unless that holder discloses to the persons to whom the communications are made such ownership interest and any relations of the holder to the parties of the transaction or to the transaction itself, as required by § 240.14a-6(n)(1) and specified in the Notice of Exempt Preliminary Roll-up Communication (§ 240.14a-104). If the communication is oral, this disclosure may be provided to the security holder orally. Whether the communication is written or oral, the notice required by § 240.14a-6(n) and § 240.14a-104 shall be furnished to the Commission.

Rule 14a-3. Information to Be Furnished Security Holders

(a) No solicitation subject to this regulation shall be made unless each person solicited is concurrently furnished or has previously been furnished with a publicly-filed preliminary or definitive written proxy statement containing the information specified in Schedule 14A (§ 240.14a-101) or with a preliminary or definitive written proxy statement included in a registration statement filed under the Securities Act of 1933 on Form S-4 or F-4 (§ 239.25 or § 239.34 of this chapter) or Form N-14 (§ 239.23) and containing the information specified in such Form.

(b) If the solicitation is made on behalf of the registrant, other than an investment company registered under the Investment Company Act of 1940, and relates to an annual (or special meeting in lieu of the annual) meeting of security holders, or written consent in lieu of such meeting, at which directors are to be elected, each proxy statement furnished pursuant to paragraph (a) of this section shall be accompanied or preceded by an annual report to security holders as follows:

Note to Small Business Issuers. A "small business issuer," defined under Rule 12b-2 of the Exchange Act (§ 240.12b-2), shall refer to the disclosure items in Regulation S-B (§ 228.10–702 of this chapter) rather than Regulation S-K (§ 229.10–702 of this chapter). If there is no comparable disclosure item in Regulation S-B, a small business issuer need not provide the information requested. A small business issuers shall provide the information in Item 310(a) of Regulation S-B in lieu of the financial information required by Rule 14a-3(b)(1) (§ 240.14a-3(b)(1)). Small business issuers using the transitional small business issuers disclosure format in the filing of their most recent annual report on Form 10-KSB (§ 249.310b of this chapter) need not provide the information specified below. Rather, those small business issuers shall provide only the financial statements required to be filed in their most recent Form 10-KSB. The inclusion of additional information, including information required of non-transitional small business issuers, in the annual report to security holders will not cause the issuer to be ineligible for the transitional disclosure forms.

(1) The report shall include, for the registrant and its subsidiaries consolidated, audited balance sheets as of the end of each of the two most recent fiscal years and audited statements of income and cash flows for each of the three most recent fiscal years prepared in accordance with Regulation S-X (Part 210 of this chapter), except that the provisions of Article 3 (other than § 210.3-03(e), 210.3-04 and 210.3-20) and Article 11 shall not apply. Any financial statement schedules or exhibits or separate financial statements which may otherwise be required in filings with the Commission may be omitted. If the financial statements of the registrant and its subsidiaries consolidated in the annual report filed or to be filed with the Commission are not required to be audited, the financial statements required by this paragraph may be unaudited.

Note 1: If the financial statements for a period prior to the most recently completed fiscal year have been examined by a predecessor accountant, the separate report of the predecessor accountant may be omitted in the report to security holders provided the registrant has obtained from the predecessor accountant a reissued report covering the prior period presented and the successor accountant clearly indicates in the scope paragraph of his report (a) that the financial statements of the prior period were examined by other accountants, (b) the date of their report, (c) the type of opinion expressed by the predecessor accountant, and (d) the substantive reasons therefor, if it was other than unqualified. It should be noted, however, that the separate report of any predecessor accountant is required in filings with the Commission. If, for instance, the financial statements in the annual report to security holders are incorporated by reference in a Form 10-K and Form 10-KSB, the separate report of a predecessor accountant shall be filed in Part II or in Part IV as a financial statement schedule.

Note 2: For purposes of complying with § 240.14a-3, if the registrant has changed its fiscal closing date, financial statements covering two years and one period of nine to 12 months shall be deemed to satisfy the requirements for statements of income and cash flows for the three most recent fiscal years.

(2)(i) Financial statements and notes thereto shall be presented in roman type at least as large and as legible as 10-point modern type. If necessary for convenient presentation, the financial statements may be in roman type as large and as legible as 8-point modern type. All type shall be leaded at least 2-point.

(ii) Where the annual report to security holders is delivered through an electronic medium, issuers may satisfy legibility requirements applicable to printed documents, such as type size and font, by presenting all required information in a format readily communicated to investors.

(3) The report shall contain the supplementary financial information required by Item 302 of Regulation S-K (§ 229.302 of this chapter).

(4) The report shall contain information concerning changes in and disagreements with accountants on accounting and financial disclosure required by Item 304 of Regulation S-K (§ 229.304 of this chapter).

(5) (i) The report shall contain the selected financial data required by Item 301 of Regulation S-K (§ 229.301 of this chapter).

(ii) The report shall contain management's discussion and analysis of financial condition and results of operations required by Item 303 of Regulation S-K (§ 229.303 of this chapter) or, if applicable, a plan of operation required by Item 303(a) of Regulation S-B (§ 228.303(a) of this chapter).

(iii) The report shall contain the quantitative and qualitative disclosures about market risk required by Item 305 of Regulation S-K (§ 229.305 of this chapter).

(6) The report shall contain a brief description of the business done by the registrant and its subsidiaries during the most recent fiscal year which will, in the opinion of management, indicate the general nature and scope of the business of the registrant and its subsidiaries.

(7) The report shall contain information relating to the registrant's industry segments, classes of similar products or services, foreign and domestic operations and exports sales required by paragraphs (b), (c)(1)(i) and (d) of Item 101 of Regulation S-K (§ 229.101 of this chapter).

(8) The report shall identify each of the registrant's directors and executive officers, and shall indicate the principal occupation or employment of each such person and the name and principal business of any organization by which such person is employed.

(9) The report shall contain the market price of and dividends on the registrant's common equity and related security holder matters required by Item 201(a), (b) and (c) of Regulation S-K (§ 229.201(a), (b) and (c) of this chapter).

(10) The registrant's proxy statement, or the report, shall contain an undertaking in bold face or otherwise reasonably prominent type to provide without charge to each person solicited upon the written request of any such person, a copy of the registrant's annual report on Form 10-K and Form 10-KSB, including the financial statements and the financial statement schedules, required to be filed with the Commission pursuant to Rule 13a-1 under the Act for the registrant's most recent fiscal year, and shall indicate the name and address (including title or department) of the person to whom such a written request is to be directed. In the discretion of management, a registrant need not undertake to furnish without charge copies of all exhibits to its Form 10-K and Form 10-KSB provided that the copy of the annual report on Form 10-K and Form 10-KSB furnished without charge to requesting security holders is accompanied by a list briefly describing all the exhibits not contained therein and indicating that the registrant will furnish any exhibit upon the payment of a specified reasonable fee which fee shall be limited to the registrant's reasonable expenses in furnishing such exhibit. If the registrant's annual report to security holders complies with all of the disclosure requirements of Form 10-K and Form 10-KSB and is filed with the Commission in satisfaction of its Form 10-K and Form 10-KSB filing requirements, such registrant need not furnish a separate Form 10-K and Form 10-KSB to security holders who receive a copy of such annual report.

Note: Pursuant to the undertaking required by paragraph (b)(10) of this section, a registrant shall furnish a copy of its annual report on Form 10-K (§ 249.310 of this chapter) and Form 10-KSB (§ 249.310b of this chapter) to a beneficial owner of its securities upon receipt of a written request from such person. Each request must set forth a good faith representation that, as of the record date for the solicitation requiring the furnishing of the annual report to security holders pursuant to paragraph (b) of this section, the person making the request was a beneficial owner of securities entitled to vote.

(11) Subject to the foregoing requirements, the report may be in any form deemed suitable by management and the information required by paragraphs (b)(5) to (b)(10) of this section may

be presented in an appendix or other separate section of the report, provided that the attention of security holders is called to such presentation.

Note: Registrants are encouraged to utilize tables, schedules, charts and graphic illustrations of present financial information in an understandable manner. Any presentation of financial information must be consistent with the data in the financial statements contained in the report and, if appropriate, should refer to relevant portions of the financial statements and notes thereto.

(12) [Removed and reserved in Release No. 34-34832, effective November 23, 1994, 59 F.R. 52689.]

(13) Paragraph (b) of this section shall not apply, however, to solicitations made on behalf of the registrant before the financial statements are available if a solicitation is being made at the same time in opposition to the registrant and if the registrant's proxy statement includes an undertaking in bold face type to furnish such annual report to all persons being solicited at least 20 calendar days before the date of the meeting or, if the solicitation refers to a written consent or authorization in lieu of a meeting, at least 20 calendar days prior to the earliest date on which it may be used to effect corporate action.

(c) Seven copies of the report sent to security holders pursuant to this rule shall be mailed to the Commission, solely for its information, not later than the date on which such report is first sent or given to security holders or the date on which preliminary copies, or definitive copies, if preliminary filing was not required, of solicitation material are filed with the Commission pursuant to Rule 14a-6, whichever date is later. The report is not deemed to be "soliciting material" or to be "filed" with the Commission or subject to this regulation otherwise than as provided in this Rule, or to the liabilities of section 18 of the Act, except to the extent that the registrant specifically requests that it be treated as a part of the proxy soliciting material or incorporates it in the proxy statement or other filed report by reference.

(d) An annual report to security holders prepared on an integrated basis pursuant to General Instruction H to Form 10-K (§ 249.310) and Form 10-KSB (§ 249-310a) may also be submitted in satisfaction of this rule. When filed as the annual report on Form 10-K and Form 10-KSB, responses to the Items of that form are subject to section 18 of the Act notwithstanding paragraph (c).

(e) Notwithstanding paragraphs (a) and (b) of this section:

(e)(1)(i) A registrant will be considered to have delivered an annual report or proxy statement to all security holders of record who share an address if:

(A) The registrant delivers one annual report or proxy statement, as applicable, to the shared address;

(B) The registrant addresses the annual report or proxy statement, as applicable, to the security holders as a group (for example, "ABC Fund [or Corporation] Security Holders," "Jane Doe and Household," "The Smith Family"), to each of the security holders individually (for example, "John Doe and Richard Jones") or to the security holders in a form to which each of the security holders has consented in writing;

Note to paragraph (e)(1)(i)(B):

Unless the company addresses the annual report or proxy statement to the security holders as a group or to each of the security holders individually, it must obtain, from each security holder to be included in the householded group, a separate affirmative written consent to the specific form of address the company will use.

(C) The security holders consent, in accordance with paragraph (e)(1)(ii) of this section, to delivery of one annual report or proxy statement, as applicable;

(D) With respect to delivery of the proxy statement, the registrant delivers, together with or subsequent to delivery of the proxy statement, a separate proxy card for each security holder at the shared address; and

(E) The registrant includes an undertaking in the proxy statement to deliver promptly upon written or oral request a separate copy of the annual report or proxy statement, as applicable, to a security holder at a shared address to which a single copy of the document was delivered.

(ii) *Consent.*

(A) *Affirmative written consent.* Each security holder must affirmatively consent, in writing, to delivery of one annual report or proxy statement, as applicable. A security holder's affirmative written consent will only be considered valid if the security holder has been informed of:

(*1*) The duration of the consent;

(*2*) The specific types of documents to which the consent will apply;

(*3*) The procedures the security holder must follow to revoke consent; and

(*4*) The registrant's obligation to begin sending individual copies to a security holder within thirty days after the security holder revokes consent.

(B) *Implied consent.* The registrant need not obtain affirmative written consent from a security holder for purposes of paragraph (e)(1)(ii)(A) of this section if all of the following conditions are met:

(*1*) The security holder has the same last name as the other security holders at the shared address or the registrant reasonably believes that the security holders are members of the same family;

(*2*) The registrant has sent the security holder a notice at least 60 days before the registrant begins to rely on this section concerning delivery of annual reports and proxy statements to that security holder. The notice must:

(*i*) Be a separate written document;

(*ii*) State that only one annual report or proxy statement, as applicable, will be delivered to the shared address unless the registrant receives contrary instructions;

(*iii*) Include a toll-free telephone number, or be accompanied by a reply form that is pre-addressed with postage provided, that the security holder can use to notify the registrant that the security holder wishes to receive a separate annual report or proxy statement;

(*iv*) State the duration of the consent;

(*v*) Explain how a security holder can revoke consent;

(*vi*) State that the registrant will begin sending individual copies to a security holder within thirty days after the security holder revokes consent; and

(*vii*) Contain the following prominent statement, or similar clear and understandable statement, in bold-face type: "Important Notice Regarding Delivery of Security Holder Documents." This statement also must appear on the envelope in which the notice is delivered. Alternatively, if the notice is delivered separately from other communications to security holders, this statement may appear either on the notice or on the envelope in which the notice is delivered.

Note to paragraph (e)(1)(ii)(B)(2):

The notice should be written in plain English. See § 230.421(d)(2) of this chapter for a discussion of plain English principles.

(*3*) The registrant has not received the reply form or other notification indicating that the security holder wishes to continue to receive an individual copy of the annual report or proxy statement, as applicable, within 60 days after the registrant sent the notice; and

(*4*) The registrant delivers the document to a post office box or residential street address.

Note to paragraph (e)(1)(ii)(B)(4):

The registrant can assume that a street address is residential unless the registrant has information that indicates the street address is a business.

(iii) *Revocation of consent.* If a security holder, orally or in writing, revokes consent to delivery of one annual report or proxy statement to a shared address, the registrant must begin sending individual copies to that security holder within 30 days after the registrant receives revocation of the security holder's consent.

(iv) *Definition of address.* Unless otherwise indicated, for purposes of this section, *address* means a street address, a post office box number, an electronic mail address, a facsimile telephone number or other similar destination to which paper or electronic documents are delivered, unless otherwise provided in this section. If the registrant has reason to believe that the address is a street address of a multi-unit building, the address must include the unit number.

Note to paragraph (e) (1).

A person other than the registrant making a proxy solicitation may deliver a single proxy statement to security holders of record or beneficial owners who have separate accounts and share an address if: (a) the registrant or intermediary has followed the procedures in this section; and (b) the registrant or intermediary makes available the shared address information to the person in accordance with § 240.14a-7(a) (2) (i) and (ii).

(2) Notwithstanding paragraphs (a) and (b) of this section, unless state law requires otherwise, a registrant is not required to send an annual report or proxy statement to a security holder if:

(i) An annual report and a proxy statement for two consecutive annual meetings; or

(ii) All, and at least two, payments (if sent by first class mail) of dividends or interest on securities, or dividend reinvestment confirmations, during a twelve month period, have been mailed to such security holder's address and have been returned as undeliverable. If any such security holder delivers or causes to be delivered to the registrant written notice setting forth his then current address for security holder communications purposes, the registrant's obligation to deliver an annual report or a proxy statement under this section is reinstated.

(f) The provisions of paragraph (a) of this section shall not apply to a communication made by means of speeches in public forums, press releases, published or broadcast opinions, statements, or advertisements appearing in a broadcast media, newspaper, magazine or other bona fide publication disseminated on a regular basis, provided that:

(1) No form of proxy, consent or authorization or means to execute the same is provided to a security holder in connection with the communication; and

(2) At the time the communication is made, a definitive proxy statement is on file with the Commission pursuant to § 240.14a-6(b).

Rule 14a-4. Requirements as to Proxy

(a) The form of proxy (1) shall indicate in bold-face type whether or not the proxy is solicited on behalf of the registrant's board of directors or, if provided other than by a majority of the board of directors, shall indicate in bold-face type on whose behalf the solicitation is made; (2) shall provide a specifically designated blank space for dating the proxy card; and (3) shall identify clearly and impartially each separate matter intended to be acted upon, whether or not related to or conditioned on the approval of other matters, and whether proposed by the registrant or by security holders. No reference need be made, however, to proposals as to which discretionary authority is conferred pursuant to paragraph (c) of this section.

Note to paragraph (a) (3) (electronic filers): Electronic filers shall satisfy the filing requirements of Rule 14a-6(a) or (b) (§ 240.14a-6(a) or (b)) with respect to the form of proxy by filing the form of proxy as an appendix at the end of the proxy statement. Forms of proxy shall not be filed as exhibits or separate documents within an electronic submission.

(b) (1) Means shall be provided in the form of proxy whereby the person solicited is afforded an opportunity to specify by boxes a choice between approval or disapproval of, or abstention with respect to each separate matter referred to therein as intended to be acted upon, other than elections to office. A proxy may confer discretionary authority with respect to matters as to which a choice is not specified by the security holder provided that the form of proxy states in bold-face type how it is intended to vote the shares represented by the proxy in each such case.

(2) A form of proxy which provides for the election of directors shall set forth the names of persons nominated for election as directors. Such form of proxy shall clearly provide any of the following means for security holders to withhold authority to vote for each nominee:

(i) a box opposite the name of each nominee which may be marked to indicate that authority to vote for such nominee is withheld; or

(ii) an instruction in bold-face type which indicates that the security holder may withhold authority to vote for any nominee by lining through or otherwise striking out the name of any nominee; or

(iii) designated blank spaces in which the security holder may enter the names of nominees with respect to whom the shareholder chooses to withhold authority to vote; or

(iv) any other similar means, provided that clear instructions are furnished indicating how the security holder may withhold authority to vote for any nominee.

Such form of proxy also may provide a means for the security holder to grant authority to vote for the nominees set forth, as a group, provided that there is a similar means for the security holder to withhold authority to vote for such group of nominees. Any such form of proxy which is executed by the security holder in such manner as not to withhold authority to vote for the election of any nominee shall be deemed to grant such authority, provided that the form of proxy so states in bold-face type.

Instructions. 1. Paragraph (2) does not apply in the case of a merger, consolidation or other plan if the election of directors is an integral part of the plan.

2. If applicable state law gives legal effect to votes cast against a nominee, then in lieu of, or in addition to, providing a means for security holders to withhold authority to vote, the issuer should provide a similar means for security holders to vote against each nominee.

(c) A proxy may confer discretionary authority to vote on any of the following matters:

(1) For an annual meeting of shareholders, if the registrant did not have notice of the matter at least 45 days before the date on which the registrant first mailed its proxy materials for the prior year's annual meeting of shareholders (or date specified by an advance notice provision), and a specific statement to that effect is made in the proxy statement or form of proxy. If during the prior year the registrant did not hold an annual meeting, or if the date of the meeting has changed more than 30 days from the prior year, then notice must not have been received a reasonable time before the registrant mails its proxy materials for the current year.

(2) In the case in which the registrant has received timely notice in connection with an annual meeting of shareholders (as determined under paragraph (c)(1) of this section), if the registrant includes, in the proxy statement, advice on the nature of the matter and how the registrant intends to exercise its discretion to vote on each matter. However, even if the registrant includes this information in its proxy statement, it may not exercise discretionary voting authority on a particular proposal if the proponent:

(i) Provides the registrant with a written statement, within the time-frame determined under paragraph (c)(1) of this section, that the proponent intends to deliver a proxy statement and form of proxy to holders of at least the percentage of the company's voting shares required under applicable law to carry the proposal;

(ii) Includes the same statement in its proxy materials filed under § 240.14a-6; and

(iii) Immediately after soliciting the percentage of shareholders required to carry the proposal, provides the registrant with a statement from any solicitor or other person with knowledge that the necessary steps have been taken to deliver a proxy statement and form of proxy to holders of at least the percentage of the company's voting shares required under applicable law to carry the proposal.

(3) For solicitations other than for annual meetings or for solicitations by persons other than the registrant, matters which the persons making the solicitation do not know, a reasonable time before the solicitation, are to be presented at the meeting, if a specific statement to that effect is made in the proxy statement or form of proxy.

(4) Approval of the minutes of the prior meeting if such approval does not amount to ratification of the action taken at that meeting;

(5) The election of any person to any office for which a bona fide nominee is named in the proxy statement and such nominee is unable to serve or for good cause will not serve.

(6) Any proposal omitted from the proxy statement and form of proxy pursuant to § 240.14a-8 or § 240.14a-9 of this chapter.

(7) Matters incident to the conduct of the meeting.

(d) No proxy shall confer authority (1) to vote for the election of any person to any office for which a bona fide nominee is not named in the proxy statement, (2) to vote at any annual meeting other than the next annual meeting (or any adjournment thereof) to be held after the date on which the proxy statement and form of proxy are first sent or given to security holders, (3) to vote with respect to more than one meeting (and any adjournment thereof) or more than one consent solicitation or (4) to consent to or authorize any action other than the action proposed to be taken in the proxy statement, or matters referred to in paragraph (c) of this rule. A person shall not be deemed to be a bona fide nominee and he shall not be named as such unless he has consented to being named in the proxy statement and to serve if elected. *Provided, however*, that nothing in this section 240.14a-4 shall prevent any person soliciting in support of nominees who, if elected, would constitute a minority of the board of directors, from seeking authority to vote for nominees named in the registrant's proxy statement, so long as the soliciting party:

(i) seeks authority to vote in the aggregate for the number of director positions then subject to election;

(ii) represents that it will vote for all the registrant nominees, other than those registrant nominees specified by the soliciting party;

(iii) provides the security holder an opportunity to withhold authority with respect to any other registrant nominee by writing the name of that nominee on the form of proxy; and

(iv) states on the form of proxy and in the proxy statement that there is no assurance that the registrant's nominees will serve if elected with any of the soliciting party's nominees.

(e) The proxy statement or form of proxy shall provide, subject to reasonable specified conditions, that the shares represented by the proxy will be voted and that where the person solicited specifies by means of a ballot provided pursuant to paragraph (b) a choice with respect to any matter to be acted upon, the shares will be voted in accordance with the specifications so made.

(f) No person conducting a solicitation subject to this regulation shall deliver a form of proxy, consent or authorization to any security holder unless the security holder concurrently receives, or has previously received, a definitive proxy statement that has been filed with the Commission pursuant to § 240.14a-6(b).

Rule 14a-5. Presentation of Information in Proxy Statement

(a) The information included in the proxy statement shall be clearly presented and the statements made shall be divided into groups according to subject matter and the various groups of statements shall be preceded by appropriate headings. The order of items and sub-items in the schedule need not be followed. Where practicable and appropriate, the information shall be presented in tabular form. All amounts shall be stated in figures. Information required by more than one applicable item need not be repeated. No statement need be made in response to any item or sub-item which is inapplicable.

(b) Any information required to be included in the proxy statement as to terms of securities or other subject matter which from a standpoint of practical necessity must be determined in the future may be stated in terms of present knowledge and intention. To the extent practicable, the authority to be conferred concerning each such matter shall be confined within limits reasonably related to the need for discretionary authority. Subject to the foregoing, information which is not known to the persons on whose behalf the solicitation is to be made and which it is not reasonably within the power of such persons to ascertain or procure may be omitted, if a brief statement of the circumstances rendering such information unavailable is made.

(c) Any information contained in any other proxy soliciting material which has been furnished to each person solicited in connection with the same meeting or subject matter may be omitted from the proxy statement, if a clear reference is made to the particular document containing such information.

(d)(1) All printed proxy statements shall be in roman type at least as large and as legible as 10-point modern type, except that to the extent necessary for convenient presentation financial statements and other tabular data, but not the notes thereto, may be in roman type at least as large and as legible as 8-point modern type. All such type shall be leaded at least 2 points.

(2) Where a proxy statement is delivered through an electronic medium, issuers may satisfy legibility requirements applicable to printed documents, such as type size and font, by presenting all required information in a format readily communicated to investors.

(e) All proxy statements shall disclose, under an appropriate caption, the following dates:

(1) The deadline for submitting shareholder proposals for inclusion in the registrant's proxy statement and form of proxy for the registrant's next annual meeting, calculated in the manner provided in § 240.14a-8(e) (Question 5); and

(2) The date after which notice of a shareholder proposal submitted outside the processes of § 240.14a-8 is considered untimely, either calculated in the manner provided by § 240.14a-4(c) (1) or as established by the registrant's advance notice provision, if any, authorized by applicable state law.

(f) If the date of the next annual meeting is subsequently advanced or delayed by more than 30 calendar days from the date of the annual meeting to which the proxy statement relates, the registrant shall, in a timely manner, inform shareholders of such change, and the new dates referred to in paragraphs (e)(1) and (e)(2) of this section, by including a notice, under Item 5, in its earliest possible quarterly report on Form 10-Q (§ 249.308a of this chapter) or Form 10-QSB (§ 249.308b of this chapter), or, in the case of investment companies, in a shareholder report under § 270.30d-1 of this chapter under the Investment Company Act of 1940, or, if impracticable, any means reasonably calculated to inform shareholders.

Rule 14a-6. Filing Requirements

(a) *Preliminary proxy statement.* Five preliminary copies of the proxy statement and form of proxy shall be filed with the Commission at least 10 calendar days prior to the date definitive copies of such material are first sent or given to security holders, or such shorter period prior to that date as the Commission may authorize upon a showing of good cause thereunder. A registrant, however, shall not file with the Commission a preliminary proxy statement, form of proxy or other soliciting material to be furnished to security holders concurrently therewith if the solicitation relates to an annual (or special meeting in lieu of the annual) meeting, or for an investment company registered under the Investment Company Act of 1940 (15 U.S.C. 80a-1 *et seq.*) or a business development company, if the solicitation relates to any meeting of security holders at which the only matters to be acted upon are:

(1) the election of directors;

(2) the election, approval or ratification of accountant(s);

(3) a security holder proposal included pursuant to Rule 14a-8 (§ 240.14a-8 of this chapter);

(4) the approval or ratification of a plan as defined in paragraph (a)(7)(ii) of Item 402 of Regulation S-K (§ 229.402(a)(7)(ii) of this chapter) or amendments to such a plan;

(5) with respect to an investment company registered under the Investment Company Act of 1940 or a business development company, a proposal to continue, without change, any advisory or other contract or agreement that previously has been the subject of a proxy solicitation for which proxy material was filed with the Commission pursuant to this section; and/or

(6) with respect to an open-end investment company registered under the Investment Company Act of 1940, a proposal to increase the number of shares authorized to be issued.

This exclusion from filing preliminary proxy material does not apply if the registrant comments upon or refers to a solicitation in opposition in connection with the meeting in its proxy material.

Note 1: The filing of revised material does not recommence the ten day time period unless the revised material contains material revisions or material new proposal(s) that constitute a fundamental change in the proxy material.

Note 2: The official responsible for the preparation of the proxy material should make every effort to verify the accuracy and completeness of the information required by the applicable rules. The preliminary material should be filed with the Commission at the earliest practicable date.

Note 3. Solicitation in Opposition. For purposes of the exclusion from filing preliminary proxy material, a "solicitation in opposition" includes: (a) any solicitation opposing a proposal supported by the registrant; and (b) any solicitation supporting a proposal that the registrant does not expressly support, other than a security holder proposal included in the registrant's proxy material pursuant to Rule 14a-8 [§ 240.14a-8 of this chapter]. The inclusion of a security holder proposal in the registrant's proxy material pursuant to Rule 14a-8 does not constitute a "solicitation in opposition," even if the registrant opposes the proposal and/or includes a statement in opposition to the proposal.

Note 4: A registrant that is filing proxy material in preliminary form only because the registrant has commented on or referred to a solicitation in opposition should indicate that fact in a transmittal letter when filing the preliminary material with the Commission.

(b) *Definitive proxy statement and other soliciting material.* Eight definitive copies of the proxy statement, form of proxy and all other soliciting materials, in the same form as the materials sent to security holders, must be filed with the Commission no later than the date they are first sent or given to security holders. Three copies of these materials also must be filed with, or mailed for filing to, each national securities exchange on which the registrant has a class of securities listed and registered.

(c) *Personal solicitation materials.* If part or all of the solicitation involves personal solicitation, then eight copies of all written instructions or other materials that discuss, review or comment on the merits of any matter to be acted on, that are furnished to persons making the actual solicitation for their use directly or indirectly in connection with the solicitation, must be filed with the Commission no later than the date the materials are first sent or given to these persons.

(d) *Release dates.* All preliminary proxy statements and forms of proxy filed pursuant to paragraph (a) of this section shall be accompanied by a statement of the date on which definitive copies thereof filed pursuant to paragraph (b) of this section are intended to be released to security holders. All definitive material filed pursuant to paragraph (b) of this section shall be accompanied by a statement of the date on which copies of such material were released to security holders, or, if not released, the date on which copies thereof are intended to be released. All material filed pursuant to paragraph (c) of this section shall be accompanied by a statement of the date on which copies thereof are released to the individual who will make the actual solicitation or if not released, the date on which copies thereof are intended to be released.

(e)(1) *Public availability of information.* All copies of preliminary proxy statements and forms of proxy filed pursuant to paragraph (a) of this section shall be clearly marked "Preliminary Copies," and shall be deemed available for public inspection unless confidential treatment is obtained pursuant to paragraph (e)(2) of this section.

(2) *Confidential treatment.* If action will be taken on any matter specified in Item 14 of Schedule 14A (§ 240.14a-101), all copies of the preliminary proxy statement and form of proxy filed under paragraph (a) of this section will be for the information of the Commission only and will not be deemed available for public inspection until filed with the Commission in definitive form so long as:

(i) The proxy statement does not relate to a matter or proposal subject to § 240.13e-3 or a roll-up transaction as defined in Item 901(c) of Regulation S-K (§ 229.901(c) of this chapter);

(ii) Neither the parties to the transaction nor any persons authorized to act on their behalf have made any public communications relating to the transaction except for statements where the content is limited to the information specified in § 230.135 of this chapter; and

(iii) The materials are filed in paper and marked "Confidential, For Use of the Commission Only." In all cases, the materials may be disclosed to any department or agency of the United States Government and to the Congress, and the Commission may make any inquiries or investigation into the materials as may be necessary to conduct an adequate review by the Commission.

Instruction to paragraph (e)(2): If communications are made publicly that go beyond the information specified in § 230.135 of this chapter, the preliminary proxy materials must be re-filed promptly with the Commission as public materials.

(f) *Communications not required to be filed.* Copies of replies to inquiries from security holders requesting further information and copies of communications which do no more than request that forms of proxy theretofore solicited be signed and returned need not be filed pursuant to this rule.

(g) *Solicitations subject to § 240.14a-2(b)(1).*

(1) Any person who:

(i) engages in a solicitation pursuant to § 240.14a-2(b)(1), and

(ii) at the commencement of that solicitation owns beneficially securities of the class which is the subject of the solicitation with a market value of over $5 million, shall furnish or mail to the Commission, not later than three days after the date the written solicitation is first sent or given to any security holder, five copies of a statement containing the information specified in the Notice of Exempt Solicitation [§ 240.14a-103] which statement shall attach as an exhibit all written soliciting materials. Five copies of an amendment to such statement shall be furnished or mailed to the Commission, in connection with dissemination of any additional communications, not later than three days after the date the additional material is first sent or given to any security holder. Three copies of the Notice of Exempt Solicitation and amendments thereto shall, at the same time the materials are furnished or mailed to the Commission, be furnished or mailed to each national securities exchange upon which any class of securities of the registrant is listed and registered.

(2) Notwithstanding paragraph (g)(1) of this section, no such submission need be made with respect to oral solicitations (other than with respect to scripts used in connection with such oral solicitations), speeches delivered in a public forum, press releases, published or broadcast opinions, statements, and advertisements appearing in a broadcast media, or a newspaper, magazine or other bona fide publication disseminated on a regular basis.

(h) *Revised material.* Where any proxy statement, form of proxy or other material filed pursuant to this rule is amended or revised, two of the copies of such amended or revised material filed pursuant to this rule (or in the case of investment companies registered under the Investment Company Act of 1940, three of such copies) shall be marked to indicate clearly and precisely the changes effected therein. If the amendment or revision alters the text of the material the change in such text shall be indicated by means of underscoring or in some other appropriate manner.

(i) *Fees.* At the time of filing the proxy solicitation material, the persons upon whose behalf the solicitation is made, other than investment companies registered under the Investment Company Act of 1940, shall pay to the Commission the following applicable fee:

(1) For preliminary proxy material involving acquisitions, mergers, spinoffs, consolidations or proposed sales or other dispositions of substantially all the assets of the company, a fee established in accordance with Rule 0-11 (§ 240.0-11 of this chapter) shall be paid. No refund shall be given.

(2) For all other proxy submissions and submissions made pursuant to § 240.14a-6(g), no fee shall be required.

(j) *Merger proxy materials.* Any proxy statement, form of proxy or other soliciting material required to be filed by this section that also is either: (i) included in a registration statement filed under the Securities Act of 1933 on Forms S-4 (§ 239.25 of this chapter), F-4 (§ 239.34 of this chapter) or N-14 (§ 239.23 of this chapter); or (ii) filed under § 230.424, § 230.425 or § 230.497 of this chapter is required to be filed only under the Securities Act, and is deemed filed under this section. In that case, the fee required under paragraph (i) of this section need not be paid.

(k) *Computing time periods.* In computing time periods beginning with the filing date specified in Regulation 14A (§ § 240.14a-1 to 240.14b-1 of this chapter), the filing date shall be counted as the first day of the time period and midnight of the last day shall constitute the end of the specified time period.

(*l*) *Roll-up transactions.* If a transaction is a roll-up transaction as defined in Item 901(c) of Regulation S-K (17 CFR 229.901(c)) and is registered (or authorized to be registered) on Form S-4 (17 CFR 229.25) or Form F-4 (17 CFR 229.34), the proxy statement of the sponsor or the general partner as defined in Item 901(d) and Item 901(a), respectively, of Regulation S-K (17 CFR 229.901) must be distributed to security holders no later than the lesser of 60 calendar days prior to the date on which the meeting of security holders no later than the lesser of 60 calendar days prior to the date on which the meeting of security holders is held or action is taken, or the maximum number of days permitted for giving notice under applicable state law.

(m) *Cover Page.* Proxy materials filed with the Commission shall include a cover page in the form set in Schedule 14A (§ 240.14a-101 of this chapter). The cover page required by this paragraph need not be distributed to security holders.

(n) *Solicitations subject to § 240.14a-2(b)(4).* Any person who:

(1) Engages in a solicitation pursuant to § 240.14a-2(b)(4), and

(2) At the commencement of that solicitation both owns five percent (5%) or more of the outstanding securities of a class that is the subject of the proposed roll-up transaction, and engages in the business of buying and selling limited partnership interests in the secondary market, shall furnish or mail to the Commission, not later than three days after the date an oral or written solicitation by that person is first made, sent or provided to any security holder, five copies of a statement containing the information specified in the Notice of Exempt Preliminary Roll-up Communication (§ 240.14a-104). Five copies of any amendment to such statement shall be furnished or mailed to the Commission not later than three days after a communication containing revised material is first made, sent or provided to any security holder.

(o) *Solicitations before furnishing a definitive proxy statement.* Solicitations that are published, sent or given to security holders before they have been furnished a definitive proxy statement must be made in accordance with § 240.14a-12 unless there is an exemption available under § 240.14a-2.

Rule 14a-7. Obligations of Registrants to Provide a List of, or Mail Soliciting Material to, Security Holders

(a) If the registrant has made or intends to make a proxy solicitation in connection with a security holder meeting or action by consent or authorization, upon the written request by any record or beneficial holder of securities of the class entitled to vote at the meeting or to execute a consent or authorization to provide a list of security holders or to mail the requesting security holder's materials, regardless of whether the request references this section, the registrant shall:

(1) deliver to the requesting security holder within five business days after receipt of the request:

(i) notification as to whether the registrant has elected to mail the security holder's soliciting materials or provide a security holder list if the election under paragraph (b) is to be made by the registrant;

(ii) a statement of the approximate number of record holders and beneficial holders, separated by type of holder and class, owning securities in the same class or classes as holders which have been or are to be solicited on management's behalf, or any more limited group of such holders designated by the security holder if available or retrievable under the registrant's or its transfer agent's security holder data systems; and

(iii) the estimated cost of mailing a proxy statement, form of proxy or other communication to such holders, including to the extent known or reasonably available, the estimated costs of any bank, broker, and similar person through whom the registrant has solicited or intends to solicit beneficial owners in connection with the security holder meeting or action.

(2) perform the acts set forth in either paragraphs (a)(2)(i) or (a)(2)(ii) of this section, at the registrant's or requesting security holder's option, as specified in paragraph (b) of this section:

(i) Mail copies of any proxy statement, form of proxy or other soliciting material furnished by the security holder to the record holders, including banks, brokers, and similar entities, designated by the security holder. A sufficient number of copies must be mailed to the banks, brokers, and similar entities for distribution to all beneficial owners designated by the security holder. If the registrant has received affirmative written or implied consent to deliver a single proxy statement to security holders at a shared address in accordance with the procedures in § 240.14a-3(e)(1), a single copy of the proxy statement furnished by the security holder shall be mailed to that address. The registrant shall mail the security holder material with reasonable promptness after tender of the material to be mailed, envelopes or other containers therefor, postage or payment for postage and other reasonable expenses of effecting such mailing. The registrant shall not be responsible for the content of the material; or

(ii) Deliver the following information to the requesting security holder within five business days of receipt of the request: a reasonably current list of the names, addresses and security positions of the record holders, including banks, brokers and similar entities holding securities in the same class or classes as holders which have been or are to be solicited on management's behalf, or any more limited group of such holders designated by the security holder if available or retrievable under the registrant's or its transfer agent's security holder data systems; the most recent list of names, addresses and security positions of beneficial owners as specified in §240.14a-13(b), in the possession, or which subsequently comes into the possession, of the registrant; and the names of security holders at a shared address that have consented to delivery of a single copy of proxy materials to a shared address, if the registrant has received written or implied consent in accordance with §240.14a-3(e)(1). All security holder list information shall be in the form requested by the security holder to the extent that such form is available to the registrant without undue burden or expense. The registrant shall furnish the security holder with updated record holder information on a daily basis or, if not available on a daily basis, at the shortest reasonable intervals, provided, however, the registrant need not provide beneficial or record holder information more current than the record date for the meeting or action.

(b)(1) The requesting security holder shall have the options set forth in paragraph (a)(2) of this section, and the registrant shall have corresponding obligations, if the registrant or general partner or sponsor is soliciting or intends to solicit with respect to:

(i) A proposal that is subject to §240.13e-3;

(ii) A roll-up transaction as defined in Item 901(c) of Regulation S-K (§229.901(c) of this chapter) that involves an entity with securities registered pursuant to Section 12 of the Act (15 U.S.C. 78*l*); or

(iii) A roll-up transaction as defined in Item 901(c) of Regulation S-K (§229.901(c) of this chapter) that involves a limited partnership, unless the transaction involves only:

(A) Partnership whose investors will receive new securities or securities in another entity that are not reported under a transaction reporting plan declared effective before December 17, 1993 by the Commission under Section 11A of the Act (15 U.S.C. 78k-1); or

(B) Partnerships whose investors' securities are reported under a transaction reporting plan declared effective before December 17, 1993 by the Commission under Section 11A of the Act (15 U.S.C. 78k-1).

(2) With respect to all other requests pursuant to this section, the registrant shall have the option to either mail the security holder's material or furnish the security holder list as set forth in this section.

(c) At the time of a list request, the security holder making the request shall:

(1) if holding the registrant's securities through a nominee, provide the registrant with a statement by the nominee or other independent third party, or a copy of a current filing made with the Commission and furnished to the registrant, confirming such holder's beneficial ownership; and

(2) provide the registrant with an affidavit, declaration, affirmation or other similar document provided for under applicable state law identifying the proposal or other corporate action that will be the subject of the security holder's solicitation or communication and attesting that:

(i) the security holder will not use the list information for any purpose other than to solicit security holders with respect to the same meeting or action by consent or authorization for which the registrant is soliciting or intends to solicit or to communicate with security holders with respect to a solicitation commenced by the registrant; and

(ii) the security holder will not disclose such information to any person other than a beneficial owner for whom the request was made and an employee or agent to the extent necessary to effectuate the communication or solicitation.

(d) The security holder shall not use the information furnished by the registrant pursuant to paragraph (a)(2)(ii) of this section for any purpose other than to solicit security holders with respect to the same meeting or action by consent or authorization for which the registrant is soliciting or intends to solicit or to communicate with security holders with respect to a solicitation commenced by the registrant; or disclose such information to any person other than an employee, agent, or beneficial owner for whom a request was made to the extent necessary to effectuate the communication or solicitation. The security holder shall return the information provided pursuant to paragraph (a)(2)(ii) of this section and shall not retain any copies thereof or of any information derived from such information after the termination of the solicitation.

(e) The security holder shall reimburse the reasonable expenses incurred by the registrant in performing the acts requested pursuant to paragraph (a) of this section.

Notes to § 240.14a-7.

1. Reasonably prompt methods of distribution to security holders may be used instead of mailing. If an alternative distribution method is chosen, the costs of that method should be considered where necessary rather than the costs of mailing.

2. When providing the information required by § 240.14a-7(a)(1)(ii), if the registrant has received affirmative written or implied consent to delivery of a single copy of proxy materials to a shared address in accordance with § 240.14a-3(e)(1), it shall exclude from the number of record holders those to whom it does not have to deliver a separate proxy statement.

Rule 14a-8. Shareholder Proposals

This section addresses when a company must include a shareholder's proposal in its proxy statement and identify the proposal in its form of proxy when the company holds an annual or special meeting of shareholders. In summary, in order to have your shareholder proposal included on a company's proxy card, and included along with any supporting statement in its proxy statement, you must be eligible and follow certain procedures. Under a few specific circumstances, the company is permitted to exclude your proposal, but only after submitting its reasons to the Commission. We structured this section in a question-and-answer format so that it is easier to understand. The references to "you" are to a shareholder seeking to submit the proposal.

(a) **Question 1: What is a proposal?**

A shareholder proposal is your recommendation or requirement that the company and/or its board of directors take action, which you intend to present at a meeting of the company's shareholders. Your proposal should state as clearly as possible the course of action that you believe the company should follow. If your proposal is placed on the company's proxy card, the company must also provide in the form of proxy means for shareholders to specify by boxes a choice between approval or disapproval, or abstention. Unless otherwise indicated, the word "proposal" as used in this section refers both to your proposal, and to your corresponding statement in support of your proposal (if any).

(b) **Question 2: Who is eligible to submit a proposal, and how do I demonstrate to the company that I am eligible?**

(1) In order to be eligible to submit a proposal, you must have continuously held at least $2,000 in market value, or 1%, of the company's securities entitled to be voted on the proposal at the meeting for at least one year by the date you submit the proposal. You must continue to hold those securities through the date of the meeting.

(2) If you are the registered holder of your securities, which means that your name appears in the company's records as a shareholder, the company can verify your eligibility on its own, although you will still have to provide the company with a written statement that you intend to continue to hold the securities through the date of the meeting of shareholders. However, if like many shareholders you are not a registered holder, the company likely does not know that you are a shareholder, or how many shares you own. In this case, at the time you submit your proposal, you must prove your eligibility to the company in one of two ways:

(i) The first way is to submit to the company a written statement from the "record" holder of your securities (usually a broker or bank) verifying that, at the time you submitted your proposal, you continuously held the securities for at least one year. You must also include your own written statement that you intend to continue to hold the securities through the date of the meeting of shareholders; or

(ii) The second way to prove ownership applies only if you have filed a Schedule 13D (§ 240.13d-101), Schedule 13G (§ 240.13d-102), Form 3 (§ 249.103 of this chapter), Form 4 (§ 249.104 of this chapter) and/or Form 5 (§ 249.105 of this chapter), or amendments to those documents or updated forms, reflecting your ownership of the shares as of or before the date on which the one-year eligibility period begins. If you have filed one of these documents with the SEC, you may demonstrate your eligibility by submitting to the company:

(A) A copy of the schedule and/or form, and any subsequent amendments reporting a change in your ownership level;

(B) Your written statement that you continuously held the required number of shares for the one-year period as of the date of the statement; and

(C) Your written statement that you intend to continue ownership of the shares through the date of the company's annual or special meeting.

(c) **Question 3: How many proposals may I submit?**

Each shareholder may submit no more than one proposal to a company for a particular shareholders' meeting.

(d) **Question 4: How long can my proposal be?**

The proposal, including any accompanying supporting statement, may not exceed 500 words.

(e) **Question 5: What is the deadline for submitting a proposal?** (1) If you are submitting your proposal for the company's annual meeting, you can in most cases find the deadline in last year's proxy statement. However, if the company did not hold an annual meeting last year, or has changed the date of its meeting for this year more than 30 days from last year's meeting, you can usually find the deadline in one of the company's quarterly reports on Form 10-Q (§ 249.308a of this chapter) or 10-QSB (§ 249.308b of this chapter), or in shareholder reports of investment companies under § 270.30d-1 of this chapter of the Investment Company Act of 1940. In order to avoid controversy, shareholders should submit their proposals by means, including electronic means, that permit them to prove the date of delivery.

(2) The deadline is calculated in the following manner if the proposal is submitted for a regularly scheduled annual meeting. The proposal must be received at the company's principal executive offices not less than 120 calendar days before the date of the company's proxy statement released to shareholders in connection with the previous year's annual meeting. However, if the company did not hold an annual meeting the previous year, or if the date of this year's annual meeting has been changed by more than 30 days from the date of the previous year's meeting, then the deadline is a reasonable time before the company begins to print and mail its proxy materials.

(3) If you are submitting your proposal for a meeting of shareholders other than a regularly scheduled annual meeting, the deadline is a reasonable time before the company begins to print and mail its proxy materials.

(f) **Question 6: What if I fail to follow one of the eligibility or procedural requirements explained in answers to Questions 1 through 4 of this section?**

(1) The company may exclude your proposal, but only after it has notified you of the problem, and you have failed adequately to correct it. Within 14 calendar days of receiving your proposal, the company must notify you in writing of any procedural or eligibility deficiencies, as well as of the time frame for your response. Your response must be postmarked , or transmitted electronically, no later than 14 days from the date you received the company's notification. A company need not provide you such notice of a deficiency if the deficiency cannot be remedied, such as if you fail to submit a proposal by the company's properly determined deadline. If the company intends to exclude the proposal, it will later have to make a submission under § 240.14a-8 and provide you with a copy under Question 10 below, § 240.14a-8(j).

(2) If you fail in your promise to hold the required number of securities through the date of the meeting of shareholders, then the company will be permitted to exclude all of your proposals from its proxy materials for any meeting held in the following two calendar years.

(g) **Question 7: Who has the burden of persuading the Commission or its staff that my proposal can be excluded?**

Except as otherwise noted, the burden is on the company to demonstrate that it is entitled to exclude a proposal.

(h) **Question 8: Must I appear personally at the shareholders' meeting to present the proposal?**

(1) Either you, or your representative who is qualified under state law to present the proposal on your behalf, must attend the meeting to present the proposal. Whether you attend the meeting yourself or send a qualified representative to the meeting in your place, you should make sure that you, or your representative, follow the proper state law procedures for attending the meeting and/ or presenting your proposal.

(2) If the company holds its shareholder meeting in whole or in part via electronic media, and the company permits you or your representative to present your proposal via such media, then you may appear through electronic media rather than traveling to the meeting to appear in person.

(3) If you or your qualified representative fail to appear and present the proposal, without good cause, the company will be permitted to exclude all of your proposals from its proxy materials for any meetings held in the following two calendar years.

(i) **Question 9: If I have complied with the procedural requirements, on what other bases may a company rely to exclude my proposal?**

(1) *Improper under state law:* If the proposal is not a proper subject for action by shareholders under the laws of the jurisdiction of the company's organization;

Note to paragraph (i) (1): Depending on the subject matter, some proposals are not considered proper under state law if they would be binding on the company if approved by shareholders. In our experience, most proposals that are cast as recommendations or requests that the board of directors take specified action are proper under state law. Accordingly, we will assume that a proposal drafted as a recommendation or suggestion is proper unless the company demonstrates otherwise.

(2) *Violation of law:* If the proposal would, if implemented, cause the company to violate any state, federal, or foreign law to which it is subject;

Note to paragraph (i) (2): We will not apply this basis for exclusion to permit exclusion of a proposal on grounds that it would violate foreign law if compliance with the foreign law would result in a violation of any state or federal law.

(3) *Violation of proxy rules:* If the proposal or supporting statement is contrary to any of the Commission's proxy rules, including § 240.14a-9, which prohibits materially false or misleading statements in proxy soliciting materials;

(4) *Personal grievance; special interest:* If the proposal relates to the redress of a personal claim or grievance against the company or any other person, or if it is designed to result in a benefit to you, or to further a personal interest, which is not shared by the other shareholders at large;

(5) *Relevance:* If the proposal relates to operations which account for less than 5 percent of the company's total assets at the end of its most recent fiscal year, and for less than 5 percent of its net earnings and gross sales for its most recent fiscal year, and is not otherwise significantly related to the company's business;

(6) *Absence of power/authority:* If the company would lack the power or authority to implement the proposal;

(7) *Management functions:* If the proposal deals with a matter relating to the company's ordinary business operations;

(8) *Relates to election:* If the proposal relates to an election for membership on the company's board of directors or analogous governing body;

(9) *Conflicts with company's proposal:* If the proposal directly conflicts with one of the company's own proposals to be submitted to shareholders at the same meeting;

Note to paragraph (i) (9): A company's submission to the Commission under this section should specify the points of conflict with the company's proposal.

(10) *Substantially implemented:* If the company has already substantially implemented the proposal;

(11) *Duplication:* If the proposal substantially duplicates another proposal previously submitted to the company by another proponent that will be included in the company's proxy materials for the same meeting;

(12) *Resubmissions:* If the proposal deals with substantially the same subject matter as another proposal or proposals that has or have been previously included in the company's proxy materials within the preceding 5 calendar years, a company may exclude it from its proxy materials for any meeting held within 3 calendar years of the last time it was included if the proposal received:

(i) Less than 3% of the vote if proposed once within the preceding 5 calendar years;

(ii) Less than 6% of the vote on its last submission to shareholders if proposed twice previously within the preceding 5 calendar years; or

(iii) Less than 10% of the vote on its last submission to shareholders if proposed three times or more previously within the preceding 5 calendar years; and

(13) *Specific amount of dividends:* If the proposal relates to specific amounts of cash or stock dividends.

(j) **Question 10: What procedures must the company follow if it intends to exclude my proposal?**

(1) If the company intends to exclude a proposal from its proxy materials, it must file its reasons with the Commission no later than 80 calendar days before it files its definitive proxy statement and form of proxy with the Commission. The company must simultaneously provide you with a copy of its submission. The Commission staff may permit the company to make its submission later than 80 days before the company files its definitive proxy statement and form of proxy, if the company demonstrates good cause for missing the deadline.

(2) The company must file six paper copies of the following:

(i) The proposal;

(ii) An explanation of why the company believes that it may exclude the proposal, which should, if possible, refer to the most recent applicable authority, such as prior Division letters issued under the rule; and

(iii) A supporting opinion of counsel when such reasons are based on matters of state or foreign law.

(k) **Question 11: May I submit my own statement to the Commission responding to the company's arguments?**

Yes, you may submit a response, but it is not required. You should try to submit any response to us, with a copy to the company, as soon as possible after the company makes its submission. This way, the Commission staff will have time to consider fully your submission before it issues its response. You should submit six paper copies of your response.

(l) **Question 12: If the company includes my shareholder proposal in its proxy materials, what information about me must it include along with the proposal itself?**

(1) The company's proxy statement must include your name and address, as well as the number of the company's voting securities that you hold. However, instead of providing that information, the company may instead include a statement that it will provide the information to shareholders promptly upon receiving an oral or written request.

(2) The company is not responsible for the contents of your proposal or supporting statement.

(m) **Question 13: What can I do if the company includes in its proxy statement reasons why it believes shareholders should not vote in favor of my proposal, and I disagree with some of its statements?**

(1) The company may elect to include in its proxy statement reasons why it believes shareholders should vote against your proposal. The company is allowed to make arguments reflecting its own point of view, just as you may express your own point of view in your proposal's supporting statement.

(2) However, if you believe that the company's opposition to your proposal contains materially false or misleading statements that may violate our anti-fraud rule, §240.14a-9, you should promptly send to the Commission staff and the company a letter explaining the reasons for your view, along with a copy of the company's statements opposing your proposal. To the extent possible, your letter should include specific factual information demonstrating the inaccuracy of the company's claims. Time permitting, you may wish to try to work out your differences with the company by yourself before contacting the Commission staff.

(3) We require the company to send you a copy of its statements opposing your proposal before it mails its proxy materials, so that you may bring to our attention any materially false or misleading statements, under the following timeframes:

(i) If our no-action response requires that you make revisions to your proposal or supporting statement as a condition to requiring the company to include it in its proxy materials, then the company must provide you with a copy of its opposition statements no later than 5 calendar days after the company receives a copy of your revised proposal; or

(ii) In all other cases, the company must provide you with a copy of its opposition statements no later than 30 calendar days before its files definitive copies of its proxy statement and form of proxy under §240.14a-6.

Rule 14a-9. False or Misleading Statements

(a) No solicitation subject to this regulation shall be made by means of any proxy statement, form of proxy, notice of meeting or other communication, written or oral, containing any statement which, at the time and in the light of the circumstances under which it is made, is false or misleading with respect to any material fact, or which omits to state any material fact necessary in order to make the statements therein not false or misleading or necessary to correct any statement in any earlier communication with respect to the solicitation of a proxy for the same meeting or subject matter which has become false or misleading.

(b) The fact that a proxy statement, form of proxy or other soliciting material has been filed with or examined by the Commission shall not be deemed a finding by the Commission that such material is accurate or complete or not false or misleading, or that the Commission has passed upon the merits of or approved any statement contained therein or any matter to be acted upon by security holders. No representation contrary to the foregoing shall be made.

Note: The following are some examples of what, depending upon particular facts and circumstances, may be misleading within the meaning of this section.

(a) Predictions as to specific future market values.

(b) Material which directly or indirectly impugns character, integrity or personal reputation, or directly or indirectly makes charges concerning improper, illegal or immoral conduct or associations, without factual foundation.

(c) Failure to so identify a proxy statement, form of proxy and other soliciting material as to clearly distinguish it from the soliciting material of any other person or persons soliciting for the same meeting or subject matter.

(d) Claims made prior to a meeting regarding the results of a solicitation.

Rule 14a-10. Prohibition of Certain Solicitations

No person making a solicitation which is subject to §§240.14a-1 to 240.14a-10 shall solicit:

(a) any undated or post-dated proxy, or

(b) any proxy which provides that it shall be deemed to be dated as of any date subsequent to the date on which it is signed by the security holder.

Rule 14a-11. Special Provisions Applicable to Election Contests

[Removed and Reserved in Release No. 33-7760, effective January 24, 2000, 64 F.R. 61408.]

Rule 14a-12. Solicitation Before Furnishing a Proxy Statement

(a) Notwithstanding the provisions of § 240.14a-3(a), a solicitation may be made before furnishing security holders with a proxy statement meeting the requirements of Reg. 240.14a-3(a) if:

(1) Each written communication includes:

(i) The identity of the participants in the solicitation (as defined in Instruction 3 to Item 4 of Schedule 14A (§ 240.14a-101)) and a description of their direct or indirect interests, by security holdings or otherwise, or a prominent legend in clear, plain language advising security holders where they can obtain that information; and

(ii) A prominent legend in clear, plain language advising security holders to read the proxy statement when it is available because it contains important information. The legend also must explain to investors that they can get the proxy statement, and any other relevant documents, for free at the Commission's web site and describe which documents are available free from the participants; and

(2) A definitive proxy statement meeting the requirements of § 240.14a-3(a) is sent or given to security holders solicited in reliance on this section before or at the same time as the forms of proxy, consent or authorization are furnished to or requested from security holders.

(b) Any soliciting material published, sent or given to security holders in accordance with paragraph (a) of this section must be filed with the Commission no later than the date the material is first published, sent or given to security holders. Three copies of the material must at the same time be filed with, or mailed for filing to, each national securities exchange upon which any class of securities of the registrant is listed and registered. The soliciting material must include a cover page in the form set forth in Schedule 14A (§ 240.14a-101) and the appropriate box on the cover page must be marked. Soliciting material in connection with a registered offering is required to be filed only under § 230.424 or § 230.425 of this chapter, and will be deemed filed under this section.

(c) Solicitations by any person or group of persons for the purpose of opposing a solicitation subject to this regulation by any other person or group of persons with respect to the election or removal of directors at any annual or special meeting of security holders also are subject to the following provisions:

(1) *Application of this rule to annual report.* Notwithstanding the provisions of § 240.14a-3(b) and (c), any portion of the annual report referred to in § 240.14a-3(b) that comments upon or refers to any solicitation subject to this rule, or to any participant in the solicitation, other than the solicitation by the management, must be filed with the Commission as proxy material subject to this regulation. This must be filed in electronic format unless an exemption is available under Rules 201 or 202 of Regulation S-T (§ 232.201 or § 232.202 of this chapter).

(2) *Use of reprints or reproductions.* In any solicitation subject to this § 240.14a-12(c), soliciting material that includes, in whole or part, any reprints or reproductions of any previously published material must:

(i) State the name of the author and publication, the date of prior publication, and identify any person who is quoted without being named in the previously published material.

(ii) Except in the case of a public or official document or statement, state whether or not the consent of the author and publication has been obtained to the use of the previously published material as proxy soliciting material.

(iii) If any participant using the previously published material, or anyone on his or her behalf, paid, directly or indirectly, for the preparation or prior publication of the previously published material, or has made or proposes to make any payments or give any other consideration in connection with the publication or republication of the material, state the circumstances.

Instructions to § 240.14a-12:

1. If paper filing is permitted, file eight copies of the soliciting material with the Commission, except that only three copies of the material specified by § 240.14a-12(c)(1) need be filed.

2. Any communications made under this section after the definitive proxy statement is on file but before it is disseminated also must specify that the proxy statement is publicly available and the anticipated date of dissemination.

Rule 14a-13. Obligation of Registrants in Communicating with Beneficial Owners

(a) If the registrant knows that securities of any class entitled to vote at a meeting (or by written consents or authorizations if no meeting is held) with respect to which the registrant intends to solicit proxies, consents or authorizations are held of record by a broker, dealer, voting trustee, bank, association, or other entity that exercises fiduciary powers in nominee name or otherwise, the registrant shall:

(1) By first class mail or other equally prompt means: (i) inquire of each such record holder: (A) whether other persons are the beneficial owners of such securities and if so, the number of copies of the proxy and other soliciting material necessary to supply such material to such beneficial owners; (B) in the case of an annual (or special meeting in lieu of the annual) meeting, or written consents in lieu of such meeting, at which directors are to be elected, the number of copies of the annual report to security holders necessary to supply such report to beneficial owners to whom such reports are to be distributed by such record holder or its nominee and not by the registrant; and (C) if the record holder has an obligation under § 240.14b-1(b)(3) or § 240.14b-2(b)(4)(ii) and (iii), whether an agent has been designated to act on its behalf in fulfilling such obligation and, if so, the name and address of such agent; and (D) whether it holds the registrant's securities on behalf of any respondent bank and, if so, the name and address of each such respondent bank; and (ii) indicate to each such record holder: (A) whether the registrant, pursuant to paragraph (c) of this section, intends to distribute the annual report to security holders to beneficial owners of its securities whose names, addresses and securities positions are disclosed pursuant to § 240.14b-1(c) and § 240.14b-2(e)(2) and (3); (B) the record date; and (C) at the option of the registrant, any employee benefit plan established by an affiliate of the registrant that holds securities of the registrant that the registrant elects to treat as exempt employee benefit plan securities;

(2) Upon receipt of a record holder's or respondent bank's response indicating, pursuant to § 240.14b-2(b)(1)(i), the names and addresses of its respondent banks, within one business day after the date such response is received, make an inquiry of and give notification to each such respondent bank in the same manner required by paragraph (a)(1) of this section; *Provided, however,* the inquiry required by paragraphs (a)(1) and (a)(2) of this section shall not cover beneficial owners of exempt employee benefit plan securities;

(3) Make the inquiry required by paragraph (a)(1) of this section at least 20 business days prior to the record date of the meeting of security holders, or (i) if such inquiry is impracticable 20 business days prior to the record date of a special meeting, as many days before the record date of such meeting as is practicable or, (ii) if consents or authorizations are solicited, and such inquiry is impracticable 20 business days before the earliest date on which they may be used to effect corporate action, as many days before that date as is practicable, or (iii) at such later time as the rules of a national securities exchange on which the class of securities in question is listed may permit for good cause shown; *Provided, however,* that if a record holder or respondent bank has informed the registrant that a designated office(s) or department(s) is to receive such inquiries, the inquiry shall be made to such designated office(s) or department(s); and

(4) Supply, in a timely manner, each record holder and respondent bank of whom the inquiries required by paragraphs (a)(1) and (a)(2) of this section are made with copies of the proxy, other proxy soliciting material, and/or the annual report to security holders, in such quantities, assembled in such form and at such place(s), as the record holder or respondent bank may reasonably request in order to send such material to each beneficial owner of securities who is to be furnished with such material by the record holder or respondent bank; and

(5) Upon the request of any record holder or respondent bank that is supplied with proxy soliciting material and/or annual reports to security holders pursuant to paragraph (a)(4) of this section, pay its reasonable expenses for completing the mailing of such material to beneficial owners.

Note 1.—If the registrant's list of security holders indicates that some of its securities are registered in the name of a clearing agency registered pursuant to section 17A of the Act (*e.g.,* "Cede & Co.," nominee for the Depository Trust Company), the registrant shall make appropriate inquiry of the clearing agency and thereafter of the participants in such clearing agency who may hold on behalf of a beneficial owner or respondent bank, and shall comply with the above paragraph with respect to any such participant (see § 240.14a-1(i)).

Note 2.—The attention of registrants is called to the fact that each broker, dealer, bank, association, and other entity that exercises fiduciary powers has an obligation pursuant to § 240.14b-1 and § 240.14b-2 (except as provided therein with respect to exempt employee benefit plan securities held in nominee name) and, with respect to brokers and dealers, applicable self-regulatory organization requirements to obtain and forward, within the time periods prescribed therein, (a) proxies (or in lieu thereof requests for voting instructions) and proxy soliciting materials to beneficial owners on whose behalf it holds securities, and (b) annual reports to security holders to beneficial owners on whose behalf it holds securities, unless the registrant has notified the record holder or respondent bank that it has assumed responsibility to mail such material to beneficial owners whose names, addresses, and securities positions are disclosed pursuant to § 240.14b-1(b)(3) and § 240.14b-2(b)(4)(ii) and (iii).

Note 3.—The attention of registrants is called to the fact that registrants have an obligation, pursuant to paragraph (d) of this section, to cause proxies (or in lieu thereof requests for voting instructions), proxy soliciting material and annual reports to security holders to be furnished, in a timely manner, to beneficial owners of exempt employee benefit plan securities.

(b) Any registrant requesting pursuant to § 240.14b-1(c) and § 240.14b-2(e)(2) and (3) a list of names, addresses and securities positions of beneficial owners of its securities who either have consented or have not objected to disclosure of such information shall:

(1) By first class mail or other equally prompt means, inquire of each record holder and each respondent bank identified to the registrant pursuant to § 240.14b-2(b)(4)(i) whether such record holder or respondent bank holds the registrant's securities on behalf of any respondent banks and, if so, the name and address of each such respondent bank.

(2) Request such list to be compiled as of a date no earlier than five business days after the date the registrant's request is received by the record holder or respondent bank; *Provided, however,* that if the record holder or respondent bank has informed the registrant that a designated office(s) or department(s) is to receive such requests, the request shall be made to such designated office(s) or department(s);

(3) Make such request to the following persons that hold the registrant's securities on behalf of beneficial owners: all brokers, dealers, banks, associations and other entities that exercise fiduciary powers; *Provided, however,* such request shall not cover beneficial owners of exempt employee benefit plan securities as defined in § 240.14a-1(d)(1); and, at the option of the registrant, such request may give notice of any employee benefit plan established by an affiliate of the registrant that holds securities of the registrant that the registrant elects to treat as exempt employee benefit plan securities;

(4) Use the information furnished in response to such request exclusively for purposes of corporate communications; and

(5) Upon the request of any record holder or respondent bank to whom such request is made, pay the reasonable expenses, both direct and indirect, of providing beneficial owner information.

Note.—A registrant will be deemed to have satisfied its obligations under paragraph (b) of this section by requesting consenting and non-objecting beneficial owner lists from a designated agent acting on behalf of the record holder or respondent bank and paying to that designated agent the reasonable expenses of providing the beneficial owner information.

(c) A registrant, at its option, may mail its annual report to security holders to the beneficial owners whose identifying information is provided by record holders and respondent banks, pursuant to § 240.14b-1(c) and § 240.14b-2(e)(2) and (3), provided that such registrant notifies the record holders and respondent banks, at the time it makes the inquiry required by paragraph (a) of this section, that the registrant will mail the annual report to security holders to the beneficial owners so identified.

(d) If a registrant solicits proxies, consents or authorizations from record holders and respondent banks who hold securities on behalf of beneficial owners, the registrant shall cause proxies (or in lieu thereof requests for voting instructions), proxy soliciting material and annual reports to security holders to be furnished, in a timely manner, to beneficial owners of exempt employee benefit plan securities.

REGULATION 14D

Disclosure Requirements and Minimum Time for Tender Offers

Rule 14d-1. Scope of and Definitions Applicable to Regulations 14D and 14E

(a) *Scope.* Regulation 14D (§§ 240.14d-1 through 240.14d-101) shall apply to any tender offer which is subject to section 14(d)(1) of the Act, including, but not limited to, any tender offer for securities of a class described in that section which is made by an affiliate of the issuer of such class. Regulation 14E (§§ 240.14e-1 and 240.14e-2) shall apply to any tender offer for securities (other than exempted securities) unless otherwise noted therein.

(b) The requirements imposed by sections 14(d)(1) through 14(d)(7) of the Act, Regulation 14D and Schedules TO and 14D-9 thereunder, and Rule 14e-1 of Regulation 14E under the Act, shall be deemed satisfied with respect to any tender offer, including any exchange offer, for the securities of an issuer incorporated or organized under the laws of Canada or any Canadian province or territory, if such issuer is a foreign private issuer and is not an investment company registered or required to be registered under the Investment Company Act of 1940, if less than 40 percent of the class of securities outstanding that is the subject of the tender offer is held by U.S. holders, and the tender offer is subject to, and the bidder complies with, the laws, regulations and policies of Canada and/or any of its provinces or territories governing the conduct of the offer (unless the bidder has received an exemption(s) from, and the tender offer does not comply with, requirements that otherwise would be prescribed by Regulation 14D or 14E), *provided that:*

(1) In the case of tender offers subject to section 14(d)(1) of the Act, where the consideration for a tender offer subject to this section consists solely of cash, the entire disclosure document or documents required to be furnished to holders of the class of securities to be acquired shall be filed with the Commission on Schedule 14D-1F (§ 240.14d-102) and disseminated to shareholders of the subject company residing in the United States in accordance with such Canadian laws, regulations and policies; or

(2) Where the consideration for a tender offer subject to this section includes securities of the bidder to be issued pursuant to the offer, any registration statement and/or prospectus relating thereto shall be filed with the Commission along with the Schedule 14D-1F referred to in paragraph (b)(1) of this section, and shall be disseminated, together with the home jurisdiction document(s) accompanying such Schedule, to shareholders of the subject company residing in the United States in accordance with such Canadian laws, regulations and policies.

NOTES: 1. For purposes of any tender offer, including any exchange offer, otherwise eligible to proceed in accordance with Rule 14d-1(b) under the Act, the issuer of the subject securities will be presumed to be a foreign private issuer and U.S. holders will be presumed to hold less than 40 percent of such outstanding securities, *unless* (a) the aggregate trading volume of that class on national securities exchanges in the United States and on NASDAQ exceeded its aggregate trading volume on securities exchanges in Canada and on the Canadian Dealing Network, Inc. ("CDN") over the 12 calendar month period prior to commencement of this offer, or if commenced in response to a prior offer, over the 12 calendar month period prior to the commencement of the initial offer (based on volume figures published by such exchanges and NASDAQ and CDN); (b) the most recent annual report or annual information form filed or submitted by the issuer with securities regulators of Ontario, Quebec, British Columbia or Alberta (or, if the issuer of the subject securities is not a reporting issuer in any of such provinces, with any other Canadian securities regulator) or with the Commission indicates that U.S. holders hold 40 percent or more of the outstanding subject class of securities; or (c) the offeror has actual knowledge that the level of U.S. ownership equals or exceeds 40 percent of such securities.

2. Notwithstanding the grant of an exemption from one or more of the applicable Canadian regulatory provisions imposing requirements that otherwise would be prescribed by Regulation 14D or 14E, the tender offer will be eligible to proceed in accordance with the requirements of this section if the Commission by order determines that the applicable Canadian regulatory provisions are adequate to protect the interest of investors.

(c) *Tier I.* Any tender offer for the securities of a foreign private issuer as defined in § 240.3b-4 is exempt from the requirements of Sections 14(d)(1) through 14(d)(7) of the Act (15 U.S.C. 78n(d)(1) through 78n(d)(7)), Regulation 14D (§ 240.14d-1 through § 240.14d-10) and Schedules TO (§ 240.14d-100) and 14D-9 (§ 240.14d-101) thereunder, and § 240.14e-1 and § 240.14e-2 of Regulation 14E under the Act if the following conditions are satisfied:

(1) *U.S. ownership limitation.* Except in the case of a tender offer which is commenced during the pendency of a tender offer made by a prior bidder in reliance on this paragraph or § 240.13e-4(h)(8), U.S. holders do not hold more than 10 percent of the class of securities sought in the offer (as determined under Instruction 2 to paragraphs (c) and (d) of this section).

(2) *Equal treatment.* The bidder must permit U.S. holders to participate in the offer on terms at least as favorable as those offered any other holder of the same class of securities that is the subject of the tender offer; however:

(i) *Registered exchange offers.* If the bidder offers securities registered under the Securities Act of 1933 (15 U.S.C. 77a *et seq.*), the bidder need not extend the offer to security holders in those states or jurisdictions that prohibit the offer or sale of the securities after the bidder has made a good faith effort to register or qualify the offer and sale of securities in that state or jurisdiction, except that the bidder must offer the same cash alternative to security holders in any such state or jurisdiction that it has offered to security holders in any other state or jurisdiction.

(ii) *Exempt exchange offers.* If the bidder offers securities exempt from registration under § 230.802 of this chapter, the bidder need not extend the offer to security holders in those states or jurisdictions that require registration or qualification, except that the bidder must offer the same cash alternative to security holders in any such state or jurisdiction that it has offered to security holders in any other state or jurisdiction.

(iii) *Cash only consideration.* The bidder may offer U.S. holders only a cash consideration for the tender of the subject securities, notwithstanding the fact that the bidder is offering security holders outside the United States a consideration that consists in whole or in part of securities of the bidder, so long as the bidder has a reasonable basis for believing that the amount of cash is substantially equivalent to the value of the consideration offered to non-U.S. holders, and either of the following conditions are satisfied:

(A) The offered security is a "margin security" within the meaning of Regulation T (12 CFR 220.2) and the issuer undertakes to provide, upon the request of any U.S. holder or the Commission staff, the closing price and daily trading volume of the security on the principal trading market for the security as of the last trading day of each of the six months preceding the announcement of the offer and each of the trading days thereafter; or

(B) If the offered security is not a "margin security" within the meaning of Regulation T (12 CFR 220.2) the issuer undertakes to provide, upon the request of any U.S. holder or the Commission staff, an opinion of an independent expert stating that the cash consideration offered to U.S. holders is substantially equivalent to the value of the consideration offered security holders outside the United States.

(iv) *Disparate tax treatment.* If the bidder offers loan notes solely to offer sellers tax advantages not available in the United States and these notes are neither listed on any organized securities market nor registered under the Securities Act of 1933 (15 U.S.C. 77a *et seq.*), the loan notes need not be offered to U.S. holders.

(3) *Informational documents.* (i) The bidder must disseminate any informational document to U.S. holders, including any amendments thereto, in English, on a comparable basis to that provided to security holders in the home jurisdiction.

(ii) If the bidder disseminates by publication in its home jurisdiction, the bidder must publish the information in the United States in a manner reasonably calculated to inform U.S. holders of the offer.

(iii) In the case of tender offers for securities described in Section 14(d)(1) of the Act (15 U.S.C. 78n(d)(1)), if the bidder publishes or otherwise disseminates an informational document to the holders of the securities in connection with the tender offer, the bidder must furnish that informational document, including any amendments thereto, in English, to the Commission on Form CB (§ 249.480 of this chapter) by the first business day after publication or dissemination. If the bidder is a foreign company, it must also file a Form F-X (§ 239.42 of this chapter) with the Commission at the same time as the submission of Form CB to appoint an agent for service in the United States.

(4) *Investment companies.* The issuer of the securities that are the subject of the tender offer is not an investment company registered or required to be registered under the Investment Company Act of 1940 (15 U.S.C. 80a-1 *et seq.*), other than a registered closed-end investment company.

(d) *Tier II.* A person conducting a tender offer (including any exchange offer) that meets the conditions in paragraph (d)(1) of this section shall be entitled to the exemptive relief specified in paragraph (d)(2) of this section provided that such tender offer complies with all the requirements of this section other than those for which an exemption has been specifically provided in paragraph (d)(2) of this section:

(1) *Conditions.* (i) The subject company is a foreign private issuer as defined in § 240.3b-4 and is not an investment company registered or required to be registered under the Investment Company Act of 1940 (15 U.S.C. 80a-1 *et seq.*), other than a registered closed-end investment company;

(ii) Except in the case of a tender offer which is commenced during the pendency of a tender offer made by a prior bidder in reliance on this paragraph or § 240.13e-4(i), U.S. holders do not hold more than 40 percent of the class of securities sought in the offer (as determined under Instruction 2 to paragraphs (c) and (d) of this section); and

(iii) The bidder complies with all applicable U.S. tender offer laws and regulations, other than those for which an exemption has been provided for in paragraph (d)(2) of this section.

(2) *Exemptions.* (i) *Equal treatment - loan notes.* If the bidder offers loan notes solely to offer sellers tax advantages not available in the United States and these notes are neither listed on any organized securities market nor registered under the Securities Act of 1933 (15 U.S.C. 77a *et seq.*), the loan notes need not be offered to U.S. holders, notwithstanding § 240.14d-10.

(ii) *Equal treatment - separate U.S. and foreign offers.* Notwithstanding the provisions of § 240.14d-10, a bidder conducting a tender offer meeting the conditions of paragraph (d)(1) of this section may separate the offer into two offers: one offer made only to U.S. holders and another offer made only to non-U.S. holders. The offer to U.S. holders must be made on terms at least as favorable as those offered any other holder of the same class of securities that is the subject of the tender offers.

(iii) *Notice of extensions.* Notice of extensions made in accordance with the requirements of the home jurisdiction law or practice will satisfy the requirements of § 240.14e-1(d).

(iv) *Prompt payment.* Payment made in accordance with the requirements of the home jurisdiction law or practice will satisfy the requirements of § 240.14e-1(c).

(v) *Subsequent offering period/Withdrawal rights.* A bidder will satisfy the announcement and prompt payment requirements of § 240.14d-11(d), if the bidder announces the results of the tender offer, including the approximate number of securities deposited to date, and pays for tendered securities in accordance with the requirements of the home jurisdiction law or practice and the subsequent offering period commences immediately following such announcement. Notwithstanding Section 14(d)(5) of the Act (15 U.S.C. 78n(d)(5)), the bidder need not extend withdrawal rights following the close of the offer and prior to the commencement of the subsequent offering period.

Instructions to paragraphs (c) and (d):

1. Home jurisdiction means both the jurisdiction of the subject company's incorporation, organization or chartering and the principal foreign market where the subject company's securities are listed or quoted.

2. *U.S. holder* means any security holder resident in the United States. Except as otherwise provided in Instruction 3 below, to determine the percentage of outstanding securities held by U.S. holders:

i. Calculate the U.S. ownership as of 30 days before the commencement of the tender offer;

ii. Include securities underlying American Depositary Shares convertible or exchangeable into the securities that are the subject of the tender offer when calculating the number of subject securities outstanding, as well as the number held by U.S. holders. Exclude from the calculations other types of securities that are convertible or exchangeable into the securities that are the subject of the tender offer, such as warrants, options and convertible securities. Exclude from those calculations securities held by persons who hold more than 10 percent of the subject securities, or that are held by the bidder;

iii. Use the method of calculating record ownership in Rule 12g3-2(a) under the Act (§ 240.12g3-2(a) of this chapter), except that your inquiry as to the amount of securities represented by accounts of customers resident in the United States may be limited to brokers, dealers, banks and other nominees located in the United States, the subject company's jurisdiction of incorporation or that of each participant in a business combination, and the jurisdiction that is the primary trading market for the subject securities, if different than the subject company's jurisdiction of incorporation;

iv. If, after reasonable inquiry, you are unable to obtain information about the amount of securities represented by accounts of customers resident in the United States, you may assume, for purposes of this definition, that the customers are residents of the jurisdiction in which the nominee has its principal place of business; and

v. Count securities as beneficially owned by residents of the United States as reported on reports of beneficial ownership that are provided to you or publicly filed and based on information otherwise provided to you.

3. In a tender offer by a bidder other than an affiliate of the issuer of the subject securities, the issuer of the subject securities will be presumed to be a foreign private issuer and U.S. holders will be presumed to hold 10 percent or less (40 percent or less in the case of 14d-1(d)) of such outstanding securities, unless:

i. The tender offer is made pursuant to an agreement with the issuer of the subject securities;

ii. The aggregate trading volume of the subject class of securities on all national securities exchanges in the United States, on the Nasdaq market, or on the OTC market, as reported to the NASD, over the 12-calendar-month period ending 30 days before commencement of the offer, exceeds 10 percent (40 percent in the case of 14d-1(d)) of the worldwide aggregate trading volume of that class of securities over the same period;

iii. The most recent annual report or annual information filed or submitted by the issuer with securities regulators of the home jurisdiction or with the Commission indicates that U.S. holders hold more than 10 percent (40 percent in the case of 14d-1(d)) of the outstanding subject class of securities; or

iv. The bidder knows or has reason to know that the level of U.S. ownership exceeds 10 percent (40 percent in the case of 14d-1(d)) of such securities.

4. *United States. United States* means the United States of America, its territories and possessions, any State of the United States, and the District of Columbia.

5. The exemptions provided by paragraphs (c) and (d) of this section are not available for any securities transaction or series of transactions that technically complies with paragraph (c) or (d) of this section but are part of a plan or scheme to evade the provisions of Regulations 14D or 14E.

(e) Notwithstanding paragraph (a) of this section, the requirements imposed by sections 14(d)(1) through 14(d)(7) of the Act [15 U.S.C. 78n(d)(1) through 78n(d)(7)], Regulation 14D promulgated thereunder (§§ 240.14d-1 through 240.14d-10), and §§ 240.14e-1 and 240.14e-2 shall not apply by virtue of the fact that a bidder for the securities of a foreign private issuer, as defined in § 240.3b-4, the subject company of such a tender offer, their representatives, or any other person specified in § 240.14d-9(d), provides any journalist with access to its press conferences held outside of the United States, to meetings with its representatives conducted outside of the United States, or to written press-related materials released outside the United States, at or in which a present or proposed tender offer is discussed, if:

(1) Access is provided to both U.S. and foreign journalists; and

(2) With respect to any written press-related materials released by the bidder or its representatives that discuss a present or proposed tender offer for equity securities registered under Section 12 of the Act [15 U.S.C. 78l], the written press-related materials must state that these written press-related materials are not an extension of a tender offer in the United States for a class of equity securities of the subject company. If the bidder intends to extend the tender offer in the United States at some future time, a statement regarding this intention, and that the procedural and filing requirements of the Williams Act will be satisfied at that time, also must be included in these written press-related materials. No means to tender securities, or coupons that could be returned to indicate interest in the tender offer, may be provided as part of, or attached to, these written press-related materials.

(f) For the purpose of § 240.14d-1(e), a bidder may presume that a target company qualifies as a foreign private issuer if the target company is a foreign issuer and files registration statements or reports on the disclosure forms specifically designated for foreign private issuers, claims the exemption from registration under the Act pursuant to § 240.12g3-2(b), or is not reporting in the United States.

(g) *Definitions.* Unless the context otherwise requires, all terms used in Regulation 14D and Regulation 14E have the same meaning as in the Act and in Rule 12b-2 (§ 240.12b-2) promulgated thereunder. In addition, for purposes of section 14(d) and 14(e) of the Act and Regulations 14D and 14E, the following definitions apply:

(1) The term "beneficial owner" shall have the same meaning as that set forth in Rule 13d-3: *Provided, however,* That, except with respect to Rule 14d-3 and Rule 14d-9(d), the term shall not include a person who does not have or share investment power or who is deemed to be a beneficial owner by virtue of Rule 13d-3(d)(1) (§ 240.13d-3(d)(1));

(2) The term "bidder" means any person who makes a tender offer or on whose behalf a tender offer is made: *Provided, however,* That the term does not include an issuer which makes a tender offer for securities of any class of which it is the issuer;

(3) The term "business day" means any day, other than Saturday, Sunday or a federal holiday, and shall consist of the time period from 12:01 a.m. through 12:00 midnight Eastern time. In computing any time period under section 14(d)(5) or section 14(d)(6) of the Act or under Regulation 14D or Regulation 14E, the date of the event which begins the running of such time period shall be included *except that* if such event occurs on other than a business day such period shall begin to run on and shall include the first business day thereafter; and

(4) The term *initial offering period* means the period from the time the offer commences until all minimum time periods, including extensions, required by Regulations 14D (§§ 240.14d-1 through 240.14d-103) and 14E (§§ 240.14e-1 through 240.14e-8) have been satisfied and all conditions to the offer have been satisfied or waived within these time periods.

(5) The term "security holders" means holders of record and beneficial owners of securities which are the subject of a tender offer;

(6) The term "security position listing" means, with respect to securities of any issuer held by a registered clearing agency in the name of the clearing agency or its nominee, a list of those participants in the clearing agency on whose behalf the clearing agency holds the issuer's securities and of the participants' respective positions in such securities as of a specified date.

(7) The term "subject company" means any issuer of securities which are sought by a bidder pursuant to a tender offer;

(8) The term *subsequent offering period* means the period immediately following the initial offering period meeting the conditions specified in § 240.14d-11.

(9) The term "tender offer material" means:

(i) The bidder's formal offer, including all the material terms and conditions of the tender offer and all amendments thereto;

(ii) The related transmittal letter (whereby securities of the subject company which are sought in the tender offer may be transmitted to the bidder or its depositary) and all amendments thereto; and

(iii) Press releases, advertisements, letters and other documents published by the bidder or sent or given by the bidder to security holders which, directly or indirectly, solicit, invite or request tenders of the securities being sought in the tender offer;

(h) *Signatures.* Where the Act or the rules, forms, reports or schedules thereunder require a document filed with or furnished to the Commission to be signed, such document shall be manually signed, or signed using either typed signatures or duplicated or facsimile versions of manual signatures. Where typed, duplicated or facsimile signatures are used, each signatory to the filing shall manually sign a signature page or other document authenticating, acknowledging or otherwise adopting his or her signature that appears in the filing. Such document shall be executed before or at the time the filing is made and shall be retained by the filer for a period of five years. Upon request, the filer shall furnish to the Commission or its staff a copy of any or all documents retained pursuant to this section.

Rule 14d-2. Commencement of a Tender Offer

(a) *Date of commencement.* A bidder will have commenced its tender offer for purposes of section 14(d) of the Act (15 U.S.C. 78n) and the rules under that section at 12:01 a.m. on the date when the bidder has first published, sent or given the means to tender to security holders. For purposes of this section, the means to tender includes the transmittal form or a statement regarding how the transmittal form may be obtained.

(b) *Pre-commencement communications.* A communication by the bidder will not be deemed to constitute commencement of a tender offer if:

(1) It does not include the means for security holders to tender their shares into the offer; and

(2) All written communications relating to the tender offer, from and including the first public announcement, are filed under cover of Schedule TO (§ 240.14d-100) with the Commission no later than the date of the communication. The bidder also must deliver to the subject company and any other bidder for the same class of securities the first communication relating to the transaction that is filed, or required to be filed, with the Commission.

Instructions to paragraph (b)(2): 1. The box on the front of Schedule TO indicating that the filing contains pre-commencement communications must be checked.

2. Any communications made in connection with an exchange offer registered under the Securities Act of 1933 need only be filed under § 230.425 of this chapter and will be deemed filed under this section.

3. Each pre-commencement written communication must include a prominent legend in clear, plain language advising security holders to read the tender offer statement when it is available because it contains important information. The legend also must advise investors that they can get the tender offer statement and other filed documents for free at the Commission's web site and explain which documents are free from the offeror.

4. See Regs. 230.135, 230.165 and 230.166 of this chapter for pre-commencement communications made in connection with registered exchange offers.

5. "Public announcement" is any oral or written communication by the bidder, or any person authorized to act on the bidder's behalf, that is reasonably designed to, or has the effect of, informing the public or security holders in general about the tender offer.

(c) *Filing and other obligations triggered by commencement.* As soon as practicable on the date of commencement, a bidder must comply with the filing requirements of § 240.14d-3(a), the dissemination requirements of § 240.14d-4(a) or (b), and the disclosure requirements of § 240.14d-6(a).

Rule 14d-3. Filing and Transmission of Tender Offer Statement

(a) *Filing and transmittal.* No bidder shall make a tender offer if, after consummation thereof, such bidder would be the beneficial owner of more than 5 percent of the class of the subject company's securities for which the tender offer is made, unless as soon as practicable on the date of the commencement of the tender offer such bidder:

(1) Files with the Commission a Tender Offer Statement on Schedule TO (§ 240.14d-100), including all exhibits thereto;

(2) Delivers a copy of such Schedule TO, including all exhibits thereto:

(i) To the subject company at its principal executive office; and

(ii) To any other bidder, which has filed a Schedule TO with the Commission relating to a tender offer which has not yet terminated for the same class of securities of the subject company, at such bidder's principal executive office or at the address of the person authorized to receive notices and communications (which is disclosed on the cover sheet of such other bidder's Schedule TO);

(3) Gives telephonic notice of the information required by Rule 14d-6(e)(2)(i) and (ii) (§ 240.14d-6(e)(2)(i) and (ii)) and mails by means of first class mail a copy of such Schedule TO, including all exhibits thereto:

(i) To each national securities exchange where such class of the subject company's securities is registered and listed for trading (which may be based upon information contained in the subject company's most recent Annual Report on Form 10-K and Form 10-KSB (§ 249.310 and § 249.310b) filed with the Commission unless the bidder has reason to believe that such information is not current) which telephonic notice shall be made when practicable prior to the opening of each such exchange; and

(ii) To the National Association of Securities Dealers, Inc. ("NASD") if such class of the subject company's securities is authorized for quotation in the NASDAQ interdealer quotation system.

(b) *Post-commencement amendments and additional materials.* The bidder making the tender offer must file with the Commission:

(1) An amendment to Schedule TO (§ 240.14d-100) reporting promptly any material changes in the information set forth in the schedule previously filed and including copies of any additional tender offer materials as exhibits; and

(2) A final amendment to Schedule TO (§ 240.14d-100) reporting promptly the results of the tender offer.

Instruction to paragraph (b):

A copy of any additional tender offer materials or amendment filed under this section must be sent promptly to the subject company and to any exchange and/or NASD, as required by paragraph (a) of this section, but in no event later than the date the materials are first published, sent or given to security holders.

(c) *Certain announcements.* Notwithstanding the provisions of paragraph (b) of this section, if the additional tender offer material or an amendment to Schedule TO discloses only the number of shares deposited to date, and/or announces an extension of the time during which shares may be tendered, then the bidder may file such tender offer material or amendment and send a copy of such tender offer material or amendment to the subject company, any exchange and/or the NASD, as required by paragraph (a) of this section, promptly after the date such tender offer material is first published or sent or given to security holders.

Rule 14d-4. Dissemination of Tender Offers to Security Holders

As soon as practicable on the date of commencement of a tender offer, the bidder must publish, send or give the disclosure required by § 240.14d-6 to security holders of the class of securities that is the subject of the offer, by complying with all of the requirements of any of the following:

(a) *Cash tender offers and exempt securities offers.* For tender offers in which the consideration consists solely of cash and/or securities exempt from registration under section 3 of the Securities Act of 1933 (15 U.S.C. 77c):

(1) *Long-form publication.* The bidder makes adequate publication in a newspaper or newspapers of long-form publication of the tender offer.

(2) *Summary publication.*

(i) If the tender offer is not subject to Rule 13e-3 (§ 240.13e-3), the bidder makes adequate publication in a newspaper or newspaper of a summary advertisement of the tender offer; and

(ii) Mails by first class mail or otherwise furnishes with reasonable promptness the bidder's tender offer materials to any security holder who requests such tender offer materials pursuant to the summary advertisement or otherwise.

(3) *Use of stockholder lists and security position listings.* Any bidder using stockholder lists and security position listings under § 240.14d-5 must comply with paragraph (a)(1) or (2) of this section on or before the date of the bidder's request under § 240.14d-5(a).

Instruction to paragraph (a): Tender offers may be published or sent or given to security holders by other methods, but with respect to summary publication and the use of stockholder lists and security position listings under § 240.14d-5, paragraphs (a)(2) and (a)(3) of this section are exclusive.

(b) *Registered securities offers.* For tender offers in which the consideration consists solely or partially of securities registered under the Securities Act of 1933, a registration statement containing all of the required information, including pricing information, has been filed and a preliminary prospectus or a prospectus that meets the requirements of Section 10(a) of the Securities Act (15 U.S.C. 77j(a)), including a letter of transmittal, is delivered to security holders. However, for going-private transactions (as defined by § 240.13e-3) and roll-up transactions (as described by Item 901 of Regulation S-K (§ 229.901 of this chapter)), a registration statement registering the securities to be offered must have become effective and only a prospectus that meets the requirements of Section 10(a) of the Securities Act may be delivered to security holders on the date of commencement.

Instructions to paragraph (b): 1. If the prospectus is being delivered by mail, mailing on the date of commencement is sufficient.

2. A preliminary prospectus used under this section may not omit information under § 230.430 or § 230.430A of this chapter.

3. If a preliminary prospectus is used under this section and the bidder must disseminate material changes, the tender offer must remain open for the period specified in paragraph (d)(2) of this section.

4. If a preliminary prospectus is used under this section, tenders may be requested in accordance with § 230.162(a) of this chapter.

(c) *Adequate publication.* Depending on the facts and circumstances involved, adequate publication of a tender offer pursuant to this section may require publication in a newspaper with a national circulation or may only require publication in a newspaper with metropolitan or regional circulation or may require publication in a combination thereof: *Provided, however,* That publication in all editions of a daily newspaper with a national circulation shall be deemed to constitute adequate publication.

(d)(1) *Publication of changes and extension of the offer.* If a tender offer has been published or sent or given to security holders by one or more of the methods enumerated in this section, a material change in the information published, sent or given to security holders shall be promptly disseminated to security holders in a manner reasonably designed to inform security holders of such change; *Provided, however,* That if the bidder has elected pursuant to Rule 14d-5(f)(1) of this section to require the subject company to disseminate amendments disclosing material changes to the tender offer materials pursuant to Rule 14d-5, the bidder shall disseminate material changes in the information published or sent or given to security holders at least pursuant to Rule 14d-5.

(2) In a registered securities offer where the bidder disseminates the preliminary prospectus as permitted by paragraph (b) of this section, the offer must remain open from the date that material changes to the tender offer materials are disseminated to security holders, as follows:

(i) Five business days for a prospectus supplement containing a material change other than price or share levels;

(ii) Ten business days for a prospectus supplement containing a change in price, the amount of securities sought, the dealer's soliciting fee, or other similarly significant change;

(iii) Ten business days for a prospectus supplement included as part of a post-effective amendment; and

(iv) Twenty business days for a revised prospectus when the initial prospectus was materially deficient.

Rule 14d-5. Dissemination of Certain Tender Offers by the Use of Stockholder Lists and Security Position Listings

(a) *Obligations of the subject company.* Upon receipt by a subject company at its principal executive offices of a bidder's written request, meeting the requirements of paragraph (e) of this section, the subject company shall comply with the following sub-paragraphs.

(1) The subject company shall notify promptly transfer agents and any other person who will assist the subject company in complying with the requirements of this section of the receipt by the subject company of a request by a bidder pursuant to this section.

(2) The subject company shall promptly ascertain whether the most recently prepared stockholder list, written or otherwise, within the access of the subject company was prepared as of a date earlier than ten business days before the date of the bidder's request and, if so, the subject company shall promptly prepare or cause to be prepared a stockholder list as of the most recent practicable date which shall not be more than ten business days before the date of the bidder's request.

(3) The subject company shall make an election to comply and shall comply with all of the provisions of either paragraph (b) or paragraph (c) of this section. The subject company's election once made shall not be modified or revoked during the bidder's tender offer and extensions thereof.

(4) No later than the second business day after the date of the bidder's request, the subject company shall orally notify the bidder, which notification shall be confirmed in writing, of the subject company's election made pursuant to paragraph (a)(3) of this section. Such notification shall indicate (i) the approximate number of security holders of the class of securities being sought by the bidder and, (ii) if the subject company elects to comply with paragraph (b) of this section, appropriate information concerning the location for delivery of the bidder's tender offer materials and the approximate direct costs incidental to the mailing to security holders of the bidder's tender offer materials computed in accordance with paragraph (g)(2) of this section.

(b) *Mailing of tender offer materials by the subject company.* A subject company which elects pursuant to paragraph (a)(3) of this section to comply with the provisions of this paragraph shall perform the acts prescribed by the following subparagraphs.

(1) The subject company shall promptly contact each participant named on the most recent security position listing of any clearing agency within the access of the subject company and make inquiry of each such participant as to the approximate number of beneficial owners of the subject company securities being sought in the tender offer held by each such participant.

(2) No later than the third business day after delivery of the bidder's tender offer materials pursuant to paragraph (g)(1) of this section, the subject company shall begin to mail or cause to be mailed by means of first class mail a copy of the bidder's tender offer materials to each person whose name appears as a record holder of the class of securities for which the offer is made on the most recent stockholder list referred to in paragraph (a)(2) of this section. The subject company shall use its best efforts to complete the mailing in a timely manner but in no event shall such mailing be completed in a substantially greater period of time than the subject company would complete a mailing to security holders of its own materials relating to the tender offer.

(3) No later than the third business day after the delivery of the bidder's tender offer materials pursuant to paragraph (g)(1) of this section, the subject company shall begin to transmit or cause to be transmitted a sufficient number of sets of the bidder's tender offer materials to the participants named on the security position listings described in paragraph (b)(1) of this section. The subject company shall use its best efforts to complete the transmittal in a timely manner but in no event shall such transmittal be completed in a substantially greater period of time than the subject company would complete a transmittal to such participants pursuant to security position listings of clearing agencies of its own material relating to the tender offer.

(4) The subject company shall promptly give oral notification to the bidder, which notification shall be confirmed in writing, of the commencement of the mailing pursuant to paragraph (b)(2) of this section and of the transmittal pursuant to paragraph (b)(3) of this section.

(5) During the tender offer and any extension thereof the subject company shall use reasonable efforts to update the stockholder list and shall mail or cause to be mailed promptly following each update a copy of the bidder's tender offer materials (to the extent sufficient sets of such materials have been furnished by the bidder) to each person who has become a record holder since the later of (i) the date of preparation of the most recent stockholder list referred to in paragraph (a)(2) of this section or (ii) the last preceding update.

(6) If the bidder has elected pursuant to paragraph (f)(1) of this section to require the subject company to disseminate amendments disclosing material changes to the tender offer materials pursuant to this section, the subject company, promptly following delivery of each such amendment, shall mail or cause to be mailed a copy of each such amendment to each record holder whose name appears on the shareholder list described in paragraphs (a)(2) and (b)(5) of this section and shall transmit or cause to be transmitted sufficient copies of such amendment to each participant named on security position listings who received sets of the bidder's tender offer materials pursuant to paragraph (b)(3) of this section.

(7) The subject company shall not include any communication other than the bidder's tender offer materials or amendments thereto in the envelopes or other containers furnished by the bidder.

(8) Promptly following the termination of the tender offer, the subject company shall reimburse the bidder the excess, if any, of the amounts advanced pursuant to paragraph (f)(3)(iii) over the direct costs incidental to compliance by the subject company and its agents in performing the acts required by this section computed in accordance with paragraph (g)(2) of this section.

(c) *Delivery of stockholder lists and security position listings.* A subject company which elects pursuant to paragraph (a)(3) of this section to comply with the provisions of this paragraph shall perform the acts prescribed by the following subparagraphs.

(1) No later than the third business day after the date of the bidder's request, the subject company must furnish to the bidder at the subject company's principal executive office a copy of the names and addresses of the record holders on the most recent stockholder list referred to in paragraph (a) (2) of this section; the names and addresses of participants identified on the most recent security position listing of any clearing agency that is within the access of the subject company; and the most recent list of names, addresses and security positions of beneficial owners as specified in § 240.14a-13(b), in the possession of the subject company, or that subsequently comes into its possession. All security holder list information must be in the format requested by the bidder to the extent the format is available to the subject company without undue burden or expense.

(2) If the bidder has elected pursuant to paragraph (f)(1) of this section to require the subject company to disseminate amendments disclosing material changes to the tender offer materials, the subject company shall update the stockholder list by furnishing the bidder with the name and address of each record holder named on the stockholder list, and not previously furnished to the bidder, promptly after such information becomes available to the subject company during the tender offer and any extensions thereof.

(d) *Liability of subject company and others.* Neither the subject company nor any affiliate or agent of the subject company nor any clearing agency shall be:

(1) Deemed to have made a solicitation or recommendation respecting the tender offer within the meaning of section 14(d)(4) based solely upon the compliance or noncompliance by the subject company or any affiliate or agent of the subject company with one or more requirements of this section;

(2) Liable under any provision of the Federal securities laws to the bidder or to any security holder based solely upon the inaccuracy of the current names or addresses on the stockholder list or security position listing, unless such inaccuracy results from a lack of reasonable care on the part of the subject company or any affiliate or agent of the subject company;

(3) Deemed to be an "underwriter" within the meaning of section (2)(11) of the Securities Act of 1933 for any purpose of that Act or any rule or regulation promulgated thereunder based solely upon the compliance or noncompliance by the subject company or any affiliate or agent of the subject company with one or more of the requirements of this section;

(4) Liable under any provision of the Federal securities laws for the disclosure in the bidder's tender offer materials, including any amendment thereto, based solely upon the compliance or noncompliance by the subject company or any affiliate or agent of the subject company with one or more of the requirements of this section.

(e) *Content of the bidder's request.* The bidder's written request referred to in paragraph (a) of this section shall include the following:

(1) The identity of the bidder;

(2) The title of the class of securities which is the subject of the bidder's tender offer;

(3) A statement that the bidder is making a request to the subject company pursuant to paragraph (a) of this section for the use of the stockholder list and security position listings for the purpose of disseminating a tender offer to security holders;

(4) A statement that the bidder is aware of and will comply with the provisions of paragraph (f) of this section;

(5) A statement as to whether or not it has elected pursuant to paragraph (f)(1) of this section to disseminate amendments disclosing material changes to the tender offer materials pursuant to this section; and

(6) The name, address and telephone number of the person whom the subject company shall contact pursuant to paragraph (a)(4) of this section.

(f) *Obligations of the bidder.* Any bidder who requests that a subject company comply with the provisions of paragraph (a) of this section shall comply with the following subparagraphs.

(1) The bidder shall make an election whether or not to require the subject company to disseminate amendments disclosing material changes to the tender offer materials pursuant to this section, which election shall be included in the request referred to in paragraph (a) of this section and shall not be revocable by the bidder during the tender offer and extensions thereof.

(2) With respect to a tender offer subject to section 14(d)(1) of the Act in which the consideration consists solely of cash and/or securities exempt from registration under section 3 of the Securities Act of 1933, the bidder shall comply with the requirements of Rule 14d-4(a)(3).

(3) If the subject company elects to comply with paragraph (b) of this section,

(i) The bidder shall promptly deliver the tender offer materials after receipt of the notification from the subject company as provided in paragraph (a)(4) of this section;

(ii) The bidder shall promptly notify the subject company of any amendment to the bidder's tender offer materials requiring compliance by the subject company with paragraph (b)(6) of this section and shall promptly deliver such amendment to the subject company pursuant to paragraph (g)(1) of this section;

(iii) The bidder shall advance to the subject company an amount equal to the approximate cost of conducting mailings to security holders computed in accordance with paragraph (g)(2) of this section;

(iv) The bidder shall promptly reimburse the subject company for the direct costs incidental to compliance by the subject company and its agents in performing the acts required by this section computed in accordance with paragraph (g)(2) of this section which are in excess of the amount advanced pursuant to paragraph (f)(2)(iii) of this section; and

(v) The bidder shall mail by means of first class mail or otherwise furnish with reasonable promptness the tender offer materials to any security holder who requests such materials.

(4) If the subject company elects to comply with paragraph (c) of this section,

(i) The subject company shall use the stockholder list and security position listings furnished to the bidder pursuant to paragraph (c) of this section exclusively in the dissemination of tender offer materials to security holders in connection with the bidder's tender offer and extensions thereof;

(ii) The bidder shall return the stockholder lists and security position listings furnished to the bidder pursuant to paragraph (c) of this section promptly after the termination of the bidder's tender offer;

(iii) The bidder shall accept, handle and return the stockholder lists and security position listings furnished to the bidder pursuant to paragraph (c) of this section to the subject company on a confidential basis;

(iv) The bidder shall not retain any stockholder list or security position listing furnished by the subject company pursuant to paragraph (c) of this section, or any copy thereof, nor retain any information derived from any such list or listing or copy thereof after the termination of the bidder's tender offer;

(v) The bidder shall mail by means of first class mail, at its own expense, a copy of its tender offer materials to each person whose identity appears on the stockholder list as furnished and updated by the subject company pursuant to paragraphs (c)(1) and (c)(2) of this section;

(vi) The bidder shall contact the participants named on the security position listing of any clearing agency, make inquiry of each participant as to the approximate number of sets of tender offer materials required by each such participant, and furnish, at its own expense, sufficient sets of tender offer materials and any amendment thereto to each such participant for subsequent transmission to the beneficial owners of the securities being sought by the bidder;

(vii) The bidder shall mail by means of first class mail or otherwise furnish with reasonable promptness the tender offer materials to any security holder who requests such materials; and

(viii) The bidder shall promptly reimburse the subject company for direct costs incidental to compliance by the subject company and its agents in performing the acts required by this section computed in accordance with paragraph (g)(2) of this section.

(g) *Delivery of materials, computation of direct costs.*

(1) Whenever the bidder is required to deliver tender offer materials or amendments to tender offer materials, the bidder shall deliver to the subject company at the location specified by the subject company in its notice given pursuant to paragraph (a)(4) of this section a number of sets of the materials or of the amendment, as the case may be, at least equal to the approximate number of security holders specified by the subject company in such notice, together with appropriate envelopes or other containers therefor: *Provided, however,* That such delivery shall be deemed not to have been made unless the bidder has complied with paragraph (f)(3)(iii) of this section at the time the materials or amendments, as the case may be, are delivered.

(2) The approximate direct cost of mailing the bidder's tender offer materials shall be computed by adding (i) the direct cost incidental to the mailing of the subject company's last annual report to shareholders (excluding employee time), less the cost of preparation and printing of the report, and postage, plus (ii) the amount of first class postage required to mail the bidder's tender offer materials. The approximate direct costs incidental to the mailing of the amendments to the bidder's tender offer materials shall be computed by adding (iii) the estimated direct costs of preparing mailing labels, of updating shareholder lists and of third party handling charges plus (iv) the amount of first class postage required to mail the bidder's amendment. Direct costs incidental to the mailing of the bidder's tender offer materials and amendments thereto when finally computed may include all reasonable charges paid by the subject company to third parties for supplies or services, including costs attendant to preparing shareholder lists, mailing labels, handling the bidder's materials, contacting participants named on security position listings and for postage, but shall exclude indirect costs, such as employee time which is devoted to either

contesting or supporting the tender offer on behalf of the subject company. The final billing for direct costs shall be accompanied by an appropriate accounting in reasonable detail.

Note to § 240.14d-5. Reasonably prompt methods of distribution to security holders may be used instead of mailing. If alternative methods are chosen, the approximate direct costs of distribution shall be computed by adding the estimated direct costs of preparing the document for distribution through the chosen medium (including updating of shareholder lists) plus the estimated reasonable cost of distribution through that medium. Direct costs incidental to the distribution of tender offer materials and amendments thereto may include all reasonable charges paid by the subject company to third parties for supplies or services, including costs attendant to preparing shareholder lists, handling the bidder's materials, and contacting participants named on security position listings, but shall not include indirect costs, such as employee time which is devoted to either contesting or supporting the tender offer on behalf of the subject company.

Rule 14d-6. Disclosure of Tender Offer Information to Security Holders

(a) *Information required on date of commencement.*

(1) *Long-form publication.* If a tender offer is published, sent or given to security holders on the date of commencement by means of long-form publication under § 240.14d-4(a)(1), the long-form publication must include the information required by paragraph (d)(1) of this section.

(2) *Summary publication.* If a tender offer is published, sent or given to security holders on the date of commencement by means of summary publication under § 240.14d-4(a)(2):

(i) The summary advertisement must contain at least the information required by paragraph (d)(2) of this section; and

(ii) The tender offer materials furnished by the bidder upon request of any security holder must include the information required by paragraph (d)(1) of this section.

(3) *Use of stockholder lists and security position listings.* If a tender offer is published, sent or given to security holders on the date of commencement by the use of stockholder lists and security position listings under § 240.14d-4(a)(3):

(i) The summary advertisement must contain at least the information required by paragraph (d)(2) of this section; and

(ii) The tender offer materials transmitted to security holders pursuant to such lists and security position listings and furnished by the bidder upon the request of any security holder must include the information required by paragraph (d)(1) of this section.

(4) *Other tender offers.* If a tender offer is published or sent or given to security holders other than pursuant to § 240.14d-4(a), the tender offer materials that are published or sent or given to security holders on the date of commencement of such offer must include the information required by paragraph (d)(1) of this section.

(b) *Information required in other tender offer materials published after commencement.* Except for tender offer materials described in paragraphs (a)(2)(ii) and (a)(3)(ii) of this section, additional tender offer materials published, sent or given to security holders after commencement must include:

(1) The identities of the bidder and subject company;

(2) The amount and class of securities being sought;

(3) The type and amount of consideration being offered; and

(4) The scheduled expiration date of the tender offer, whether the tender offer may be extended and, if so, the procedures for extension of the tender offer.

Instruction to paragraph (b): If the additional tender offer materials are summary advertisements, they also must include the information required by paragraphs (d)(2)(v) of this section.

(c) *Material changes.* A material change in the information published or sent or given to security holders must be promptly disclosed to security holders in additional tender offer materials.

(d) *Information to be included.*

(1) *Tender offer materials other than summary publication.* The following information is required by paragraphs (a)(1), (a)(2)(ii), (a)(3)(ii) and (a)(4) of this section:

(i) The information required by Item 1 of Schedule TO (§ 240.14d-100) (Summary Term Sheet); and

(ii) The information required by the remaining items of Schedule TO (§ 240.14d-100) for third-party tender offers, except for Item 12 (exhibits) of Schedule TO (§ 240.14d-100), or a fair and adequate summary of the information.

(2) *Summary Publication.* The following information is required in a summary advertisement under paragraphs (a)(2)(i) and (a)(3)(i) of this section:

(i) The identity of the bidder and the subject company;

(ii) The information required by Item 1004(a)(1) of Regulation M-A (§ 229.1004(a)(1) of this chapter);

(iii) If the tender offer is for less than all of the outstanding securities of a class of equity securities, a statement as to whether the purpose or one of the purposes of the tender offer is to acquire or influence control of the business of the subject company;

(iv) A statement that the information required by paragraph (d)(1) of this section is incorporated by reference into the summary advertisement;

(v) Appropriate instructions as to how security holders may obtain promptly, at the bidder's expense, the bidder's tender offer materials; and

(vi) In a tender offer published or sent or given to security holders by use of stockholder lists and security position listings under § 240.14d-4(a)(3), a statement that a request is being made for such lists and listings. The summary publication also must state that tender offer materials will be mailed to record holders and will be furnished to brokers, banks and similar persons whose name appears or whose nominee appears on the list of security holders or, if applicable, who are listed as participants in a clearing agency's security position listing for subsequent transmittal to beneficial owners of such securities. If the list furnished to the bidder also included beneficial owners pursuant to § 240.14d-5(c)(1) and tender offer materials will be mailed directly to beneficial holders, include a statement to that effect.

(3) *No transmittal letter.* Neither the initial summary advertisement nor any subsequent summary advertisement may include a transmittal letter (the letter furnished to security holders for transmission of securities sought in the tender offer) or any amendment to the transmittal letter.

Rule 14d-7. Additional Withdrawal Rights

(a)(1) *Rights.* In addition to the provisions of section 14(d)(5) of the Act, any person who has deposited securities pursuant to a tender offer has the right to withdraw any such securities during the period such offer request or invitation remains open.

(a)(2) *Exemption during subsequent offering period.* Notwithstanding the provisions of Section 14 (d)(5) of the Act (15 U.S.C. 78n(d)(5)) and paragraph (a) of this section, the bidder need not offer withdrawal rights during a subsequent offering period.

(b) *Notice of withdrawal.* Notice of withdrawal pursuant to this section shall be deemed to be timely upon the receipt by the bidder's depositary of a written notice of withdrawal specifying the name(s) of the tendering stockholder(s), the number or amount of the securities to be withdrawn and the name(s) in which the certificate(s) is (are) registered, if different from that of the tendering security holder(s). A bidder may impose other reasonable requirements, including certificate numbers and a signed request for withdrawal accompanied by a signature guarantee, as conditions precedent to the physical release of withdrawn securities.

Rule 14d-8. Exemption from Statutory Pro Rata Requirement

Notwithstanding the pro rata provisions of Section 14(d)(6) of the Act, if any person makes a tender offer or request or invitation for tenders, for less than all of the outstanding equity securities of a class, and if a greater number of securities are deposited pursuant thereto than such person is bound or willing to take up and pay for, the securities taken up and paid for shall be taken up and paid for as nearly as may be pro rata, disregarding fractions, according to the number of securities deposited by each depositor during the period such offer, request or invitation remains open.

Rule 14d-9. Recommendation or Solicitation by the Subject Company and Others

(a) *Pre-commencement communications.*

A communication by a person described in paragraph (e) of this section with respect to a tender offer will not be deemed to constitute a recommendation or solicitation under this section if:

(1) The tender offer has not commenced under § 240.14d-2; and

(2) The communication is filed under cover of Schedule 14D-9 (§ 240.14d-101) with the Commission no later than the date of the communication.

Instructions to paragraph (a)(2):

1. The box on the front of Schedule 14D-9 (§ 240.14d-101) indicating that the filing contains pre-commencement communications must be checked.

2. Any communications made in connection with an exchange offer registered under the Securities Act of 1933 need only be filed under § 230.425 of this chapter and will be deemed filed under this section.

3. Each pre-commencement written communication must include a prominent legend in clear, plain language advising security holders to read the company's solicitation/ recommendation statement when it is available because it contains important information. The legend also must advise investors that they can get the recommendation and other filed documents for free at the Commission's web site and explain which documents are free from the filer.

4. See Sections 230.135, 230.165 and 230.166 of this chapter for pre-commencement communications made in connection with registered exchange offers.

(b) *Post-commencement communications.*

After commencement by a bidder under § 240.14d-2, no solicitation or recommendation to security holders may be made by any person described in paragraph (e) of this section with respect to a tender offer for such securities unless as soon as practicable on the date such solicitation or recommendation is first published or sent or given to security holders such person complies with the following:

(1) Such person shall file with the Commission a Tender Offer Solicitation/ Recommendation Statement on Schedule 14D-9 (240.14d-101), including all exhibits thereto; and

(2) If such person is either the subject company or an affiliate of the subject company,

(i) Such person shall hand deliver a copy of the Schedule 14D-9 to the bidder at its principal office or at the address of the person authorized to receive notices and communications (which is set forth on the cover sheet of the bidder's Schedule TO (§ 240.14d-100) filed with the Commission; and

(ii) Such person shall give telephonic notice (which notice to the extent possible shall be given prior to the opening of the market) of the information required by Items 1003(d) and 1012(a) of Regulation M-A (§ 229.1005(d) and § 229.1012(a)) and shall mail a copy of the Schedule to each national securities exchange where the class of securities is registered and listed for trading and, if the class is authorized for quotation in the NASDAQ interdealer quotation system, to the National Association of Securities Dealers, Inc. ("NASD").

(3) If such person is neither the subject company nor an affiliate of the subject company,

(i) Such person shall mail a copy of the schedule to the bidder at its principal office or at the address of the person authorized to receive notices and communications (which is set forth on the cover sheet of the bidder's Schedule TO (§ 240.14d-100) filed with the Commission); and

(ii) Such person shall mail a copy of the Schedule to the subject company at its principal office.

(c) *Amendments.* If any material change occurs in the information set forth in the Schedule 14D-9 (§ 240.14d-101) required by this section, the person who filed such Schedule 14D-9 shall:

(1) File with the Commission eight copies of an amendment on Schedule 14D-9 (§ 240.14d-101) disclosing such change promptly, but not later than the date such material is first published, sent or given to security holders; and

(2) Promptly deliver copies and give notice of the amendment in the same manner as that specified in paragraph (b) (2) or (3) of this section, whichever is applicable; and

(3) Promptly disclose and disseminate such change in a manner reasonably designed to inform security holders of such change.

(d) *Information required in solicitation or recommendation.*

Any solicitation or recommendation to holders of a class of securities referred to in section 14 (d) (1) of the Act with respect to a tender offer for such securities shall include the name of the person making such solicitation or recommendation and the information required by Items 1 through 8 of Schedule 14D-9 (§ 240.14d-101) or a fair and adequate summary thereof: *Provided, however,* That such solicitation or recommendation may omit any of such information previously furnished to security holders of such class of securities by such person with respect to such tender offer.

(e) *Applicability.*

(1) Except as is provided in paragraphs (e) (2) and (f) of this section, this section shall only apply to the following persons:

(i) The subject company, any director, officer, employee, affiliate or subsidiary of the subject company;

(ii) Any record holder or beneficial owner of any security issued by the subject company, by the bidder, or by any affiliate of either the subject company or the bidder; and

(iii) Any person who makes a solicitation or recommendation to security holders on behalf of any of the foregoing or on behalf of the bidder other than by means of a solicitation or recommendation to security holders which has been filed with the Commission pursuant to this section or Rule 14d-3 (§ 240.14d-3).

(2) Notwithstanding paragraph (e) (1) of this section, this section shall not apply to the following persons:

(i) A bidder who has filed a Schedule TO (§ 240.14d-100) pursuant to Rule 14d-3 (§ 240.14d-3);

(ii) Attorneys, banks, brokers, fiduciaries or investment advisers who are not participating in a tender offer in more than a ministerial capacity and who furnish information and/or advice regarding such tender offer to their customers or clients on the unsolicited request of such customers or clients or solely pursuant to a contract or a relationship providing for advice to the customer or client to whom the information and/or advice is given.

(iii) Any person specified in paragraph (e) (1) of this section if:

(A) The subject company is the subject of a tender offer conducted under § 240.14d-1 (c);

(B) Any person specified in paragraph (e) (1) of this section furnishes to the Commission on Form CB (§ 249.480 of this chapter) the entire informational document it publishes or otherwise disseminates to holders of the class of securities in connection with the tender offer no later than the next business day after publication or dissemination;

(C) Any person specified in paragraph (e) (1) of this section disseminates any informational document to U.S. holders, including any amendments thereto, in English, on a comparable basis to that provided to security holders in the issuer's home jurisdiction; and

(D) Any person specified in paragraph (e) (1) of this section disseminates by publication in its home jurisdiction, such person must publish the information in the United States in a manner reasonably calculated to inform U.S. security holders of the offer.

(f) *Stop-look-and-listen communication.* This section shall not apply to the subject company with respect to a communication by the subject company to its security holders which only:

(1) Identifies the tender offer by the bidder;

(2) States that such tender offer is under consideration by the subject company's board of directors and/or management;

(3) States that on or before a specified date (which shall be no later than 10 business days from the date of commencement of such tender offer) the subject company will advise such security holders of (i) whether the subject company recommends acceptance or rejection of such tender offer; expresses no opinion and remains neutral toward such tender offer; or is unable to take a position with respect to such tender offer and (ii) the reason(s) for the position taken by the subject company with respect to the tender offer (including the inability to take a position); and

(4) Requests such security holders to defer making a determination whether to accept or reject such tender offer until they have been advised of the subject company's position with respect thereto pursuant to paragraph (f)(3) of this section.

(g) *Statement of management's position.* A statement by the subject company of its position with respect to a tender offer which is required to be published or sent or given to security holders pursuant to Rule 14e-2 shall be deemed to constitute a solicitation or recommendation within the meaning of this section and section 14(d)(4) of the Act.

Rule 14d-10. Equal Treatment of Security Holders

(a) No bidder shall make a tender offer unless:

(1) The tender offer is open to all security holders of the class of securities subject to the tender offer; and

(2) The consideration paid to any security holder pursuant to the tender offer is the highest consideration paid to any other security holder during such tender offer.

(b) Paragraph (a)(1) of this section shall not:

(1) Affect dissemination under Rule 14d-4 (§ 240.14d-4); or

(2) Prohibit a bidder from making a tender offer excluding all security holders in a state where the bidder is prohibited from making the tender offer by administrative or judicial action pursuant to a state statute after a good faith effort by the bidder to comply with such statute.

(c) Paragraph (a)(2) of this section shall not prohibit the offer of more than one type of consideration in a tender offer, provided that:

(1) Security holders are afforded equal right to elect among each of the types of consideration offered; and

(2) The highest consideration of each type paid to any security holder is paid to any other security holder receiving that type of consideration.

(d) If the offer and sale of securities constituting consideration offered in a tender offer is prohibited by the appropriate authority of a state after a good faith effort by the bidder to register or qualify the offer and sale of such securities in such state:

(1) The bidder may offer security holders in such state an alternative form of consideration; and

(2) Paragraph (c) of this section shall not operate to require the bidder to offer or pay the alternative form of consideration to security holders in any other state.

(e) This section shall not apply to any tender offer with respect to which the Commission, upon written request or upon its own motion, either unconditionally or on specified terms and conditions, determines that compliance with this section is not necessary or appropriate in the public interest or for the protection of investors.

Rule 14d-11. Subsequent Offering Period

A bidder may elect to provide a subsequent offering period of three business days to 20 business days during which tenders will be accepted if:

(a) The initial offering period of at least 20 business days has expired;

(b) The offer is for all outstanding securities of the class that is the subject of the tender offer, and if the bidder is offering security holders a choice of different forms of consideration, there is no ceiling on any form of consideration offered;

(c) The bidder immediately accepts and promptly pays for all securities tendered during the initial offering period;

(d) The bidder announces the results of the tender offer, including the approximate number and percentage of securities deposited to date, no later than 9:00 a.m. Eastern time on the next business day after the expiration date of the initial offering period and immediately begins the subsequent offering period;

(e) The bidder immediately accepts and promptly pays for all securities as they are tendered during the subsequent offering period; and

(f) The bidder offers the same form and amount of consideration to security holders in both the initial and the subsequent offering period.

Note § 240.14d-11: No withdrawal rights apply during the subsequent offering period in accordance with § 240.14d-7(a)(2).

REGULATION 14E

Note: For the scope of and definitions applicable to Regulation 14E refer to § 240.14d-1.

Rule 14e-1. Unlawful Tender Offer Practices

As a means reasonably designed to prevent fraudulent, deceptive or manipulative acts or practices within the meaning of section 14(e) of the Act, no person who makes a tender offer shall:

(a) Hold such tender offer open for less than twenty business days from the date such tender offer is first published or sent to security holders; provided, however, that if the tender offer involves a roll-up transaction as defined in Item 901(c) of Regulation S-K (17 CFR 229.901(c)) and the securities being offered are registered (or authorized to be registered) on Form S-4 (17 CFR 229.25) or Form F-4 (17 CFR 229.34), the offer shall not be open for less than sixty calendar days from the date the tender offer is first published or sent to security holders;

(b) Increase or decrease the percentage of the class of securities being sought or the consideration offered or the dealer's soliciting fee to be given in a tender offer unless such tender offer remains open for at least ten business days from the date that notice of such increase or decrease is first published or sent or given to security holders;

Provided, however, That, for purposes of this paragraph, the acceptance for payment of an additional amount of securities not to exceed two percent of the class of securities that is the subject of the tender offer shall not be deemed to be an increase. For purposes of this paragraph, the percentage of a class of securities shall be calculated in accordance with section 14(d)(3) of the Act.

(c) Fail to pay the consideration offered or return the securities deposited by or on behalf of security holders promptly after the termination or withdrawal of a tender offer. This paragraph does not prohibit a bidder electing to offer a subsequent offering period under § 240.14d-11 from paying for securities during the subsequent offering period in accordance with that section.

(d) Extend the length of a tender offer without issuing a notice of such extension by press release or other public announcement, which notice shall include disclosure of the approximate number of securities deposited to date and shall be issued no later than the earlier of (i) 9:00 a.m. Eastern time, on the next business day after the scheduled expiration date of the offer or (ii), if the class of securities which is the subject of the tender offer is registered on one or more national securities exchanges, the first opening of any one of such exchanges on the next business day after the scheduled expiration date of the offer.

(e) The periods of time required by paragraphs (a) and (b) of this section shall be tolled for any period during which the bidder has failed to file in electronic format, absent a hardship exemption (§§ 232.201 and 232.202 of this chapter), the Schedule 14D-1 Tender Offer Statement (§ 240.14d-100 of this chapter), any tender offer material specified in paragraph (a) of Item 11 of that Schedule, and any amendments thereto. If such documents were filed in paper pursuant to a hardship exemption (see § 232.201 and § 232.202(d) of this chapter), the minimum offering periods shall be tolled for any period during which a required confirming electronic copy of such Schedule and tender offer material is delinquent.

Rule 14e-2. Position of a Subject Company with Respect to a Tender Offer

(a) *Position of subject company.* As a means reasonably designed to prevent fraudulent, deceptive or manipulative acts or practices within the meaning of section 14(e) of the Act, the subject company, no later than 10 business days from the date the tender offer is first published or sent or given, shall publish, send or give to security holders a statement disclosing that the subject company:

(1) Recommends acceptance or rejection of the bidder's tender offer;

(2) Expresses no opinion and is remaining neutral toward the bidder's tender offer; or

(3) Is unable to take a position with respect to the bidder's tender offer.

Such statement shall also include the reason(s) for the position (including the inability to take a position) disclosed therein.

(b) *Material change.* If any material change occurs in the disclosure required by paragraph (a) of this section, the subject company shall promptly publish, send or give a statement disclosing such material change to security holders.

(c) Any issuer, a class of the securities of which is the subject of a tender offer filed with the Commission on Schedule 14D-1F and conducted in reliance upon and in conformity with Rule 14d-1(b) under the Act, and any director or officer of such issuer where so required by the laws, regulations and policies of Canada and/or any of its provinces or territories, in lieu of the statements called for by paragraph (a) of this section and Rule 14d-9 under the Act, shall file with the Commission on Schedule 14D-9F the entire disclosure document(s) required to be furnished to holders of securities of the subject issuer by the laws, regulations and policies of Canada and/or any of its provinces or territories governing the conduct of the tender offer, and shall disseminate such document(s) in the United States in accordance with such laws, regulations and policies.

(d) *Exemption for cross-border tender offers.* The subject company shall be exempt from this section with respect to a tender offer conducted under § 240.14d-1(c).

Rule 14e-3. Transactions in Securities on the Basis of Material, Nonpublic Information in the Context of Tender Offers

(a) If any person has taken a substantial step or steps to commence, or has commenced, a tender offer (the "offering person"), it shall constitute a fraudulent, deceptive or manipulative act or practice within the meaning of section 14(e) of the Act for any other person who is in possession of material information relating to such tender offer which information he knows or has reason to know is nonpublic and which he knows or has reason to know has been acquired directly or indirectly from (1) the offering person, (2) the issuer of the securities sought or to be sought by such tender offer, or (3) any officer, director, partner or employee or any other person acting on behalf of the offering person or such issuer, to purchase or sell or cause to be purchased or sold any of such securities or any securities convertible into or exchangeable for any such securities or any option or right to obtain or to dispose of any of the foregoing securities, unless within a reasonable time prior to any purchase or sale such information and its source are publicly disclosed by press release or otherwise.

(b) A person other than a natural person shall not violate paragraph (a) of this section if such persons shows that:

(1) The individual(s) making the investment decision on behalf of such person to purchase or sell any security described in paragraph (a) or to cause any such security to be purchased or sold by or on behalf of others did not know the material, nonpublic information; and

(2) Such person had implemented one or a combination of policies and procedures, reasonable under the circumstances, taking into consideration the nature of the person's business, to ensure that individual(s) making investment decision(s) would not violate paragraph (a), which policies and procedures may include, but are not limited to, (i) those which restrict any purchase, sale and causing any purchase and sale of any such security or (ii) those which prevent such individual(s) from knowing such information.

(c) Notwithstanding anything in paragraph (a) to the contrary, the following transactions shall not be violations of paragraph (a) of this section:

(1) Purchase(s) of any security described in paragraph (a) by a broker or by another agent on behalf of an offering person; or

(2) Sale(s) by any person of any security described in paragraph (a) to the offering person.

(d) (1) As a means reasonably designed to prevent fraudulent, deceptive or manipulative acts or practices within the meaning of section 14(e) of the Act, it shall be unlawful for any person described in paragraph (d)(2) of this section to communicate material, nonpublic information relating to a tender offer to any other person under circumstances in which it is reasonably foreseeable that such communication is likely to result in a violation of this section *except* that this paragraph shall not apply to a communication made in good faith,

(i) To the officers, directors, partners or employees of the offering person, to its advisors or to other persons, involved in the planning, financing, preparation or execution of such tender offer;

(ii) To the issuer whose securities are sought or to be sought by such tender offer, to its officers, directors, partners, employees or advisors or to other persons, involved in the planning, financing, preparation or execution of the activities of the issuer with respect to such tender offer; or

(iii) To any person pursuant to a requirement of any statute or rule or regulation promulgated thereunder.

(2) The persons referred to in paragraph (d)(1) of this section are:

(i) The offering person or its officers, directors, partners, employees or advisers;

(ii) The issuer of the securities sought or to be sought by such tender offer or its officers, directors, partners, employees or advisors;

(iii) Anyone acting on behalf of the persons in paragraph (d)(2)(i) or the issuer or persons in paragraph (d)(2)(ii); and

(iv) Any person in possession of material information relating to a tender offer which information he knows or has reason to know is nonpublic and which he knows or has reason to know has been acquired directly or indirectly from any of the above.

Rule 14e-4. Prohibited Transactions In Connection With Partial Tender Offers

(a) Definitions. For purposes of this section:

(1) The amount of a person's "net long position" in a subject security shall equal the excess, if any, of such person's "long position" over such person's "short position." For the purposes of determining the net long position as of the end of the proration period and for tendering concurrently to two or more partial tender offers, securities that have been tendered in accordance with the Rule and not withdrawn are deemed to be part of the person's long position.

(i) Such person's "long position," is the amount of subject securities that such person:

(A) or his agent has title to or would have title to but for having lent such securities; or

(B) has purchased, or has entered into an unconditional contract, binding on both parties thereto, to purchase but has not yet received; or

(C) has exercised a standardized call option for; or

(D) has converted, exchanged, or exercised an equivalent security for; or

(E) is entitled to receive upon conversion, exchange, or exercise of an equivalent security.

(ii) Such person's "short position," is the amount of subject securities or subject securities underlying equivalent securities that such person:

(A) has sold, or has entered into an unconditional contract, binding on both parties thereto, to sell; or

(B) has borrowed; or

(C) has written a non-standardized call option, or granted any other right pursuant to which his shares may be tendered by another person; or

(D) is obligated to deliver upon exercise of a standardized call option sold on or after the date that a tender offer is first publicly announced or otherwise made known by the bidder to holders of the security to be acquired, if the exercise price of such option is lower than the highest tender offer price or stated amount of the consideration offered for the subject security. For the purpose of this paragraph, if one or more tender offers for the same security are ongoing on such date, the announcement date shall be that of the first announced offer.

(2) The term "equivalent security" means (i) any security (including any option, warrant, or other right to purchase the subject security), issued by the person whose securities are the subject of the offer, that is immediately convertible into, or exchangeable or exercisable for, a subject security, or (ii) any other right or option (other than a standardized call option) that entitles the holder thereof to acquire a subject security, but only if the holder thereof reasonably believes that the maker or writer of the right or option has title to and possession of the subject security and upon exercise will promptly deliver the subject security.

(3) The term "subject security" means a security that is the subject of any tender offer or request or invitation for tenders.

(4) For purposes of this rule, a person shall be deemed to "tender" a security if he (i) delivers a subject security pursuant to an offer, (ii) causes such delivery to be made, (iii) guarantees delivery of a subject security pursuant to a tender offer, (iv) causes a guarantee of such delivery to be given by another person, or (v) uses any other method by which acceptance of a tender offer may be made.

(5) The term "partial tender offer" means a tender offer or request or invitation for tenders for less than all of the outstanding securities subject to the offer in which tenders are accepted either by lot or on a *pro rata* basis for a specified period, or a tender offer for all of the outstanding shares that offers a choice of consideration in which tenders for different forms of consideration may be accepted either by lot or on a *pro rata* basis for a specified period.

(6) The term "standardized call option" means any call option that is traded on an exchange, or for which quotation information is disseminated in an electronic interdealer quotation system of a registered national securities association.

(b) It shall be unlawful for any person acting alone or in concert with others, directly or indirectly, to tender any subject security in a partial tender offer:

(1) For his own account unless at the time of tender, and at the end of the proration period or period during which securities are accepted by lot (including any extensions thereof), he has a net long position equal to or greater than the amount tendered in:

(i) the subject security and will deliver or cause to be delivered such security for the purpose of tender to the person making the offer within the period specified in the offer; or

(ii) an equivalent security and, upon the acceptance of his tender will acquire the subject security by conversion, exchange, or exercise of such equivalent security to the extent required by the terms of the offer, and will deliver or cause to be delivered the subject security so acquired for the purpose of tender to the person making the offer within the period specified in the offer; or

(2) For the account of another person unless the person making the tender (i) possesses the subject security or an equivalent security, or (ii) has a reasonable belief that, upon information furnished by the person on whose behalf the tender is made, such person owns the subject security or an equivalent security and will promptly deliver the subject security or such equivalent security for the purpose of tender to the person making the tender.

(c) This rule shall not prohibit any transaction or transactions which the Commission, upon written request or upon its own motion, exempts, either unconditionally or on specified terms and conditions.

Rule 14e-5. Prohibiting Purchases Outside of a Tender Offer

(a) *Unlawful activity.* As a means reasonably designed to prevent fraudulent, deceptive or manipulative acts or practices in connection with a tender offer for equity securities, no covered person may directly or indirectly purchase or arrange to purchase any subject securities or any related securities except as part of the tender offer. This prohibition applies from the time of public announcement of the tender offer until the tender offer expires. This prohibition does not apply to any purchases or arrangements to purchase made during the time of any subsequent offering period as provided for in § 240.14d-11 if the consideration paid or to be paid for the purchases or arrangements to purchase is the same in form and amount as the consideration offered in the tender offer.

(b) *Excepted activity.* The following transactions in subject securities or related securities are not prohibited by paragraph (a) of this section:

(1) *Exercises of securities.* Transactions by covered persons to convert, exchange, or exercise related securities into subject securities, if the covered person owned the related securities before public announcement;

(2) *Purchases for plans.* Purchases or arrangements to purchase by or for a plan that are made by an agent independent of the issuer;

(3) *Purchases during odd-lot offers.* Purchases or arrangements to purchase if the tender offer is excepted under § 240.13e-4(h)(5);

(4) *Purchases as intermediary.* Purchases by or through a dealer-manager or its affiliates that are made in the ordinary course of business and made either:

(i) On an agency basis not for a covered person; or

(ii) As principal for its own account if the dealer-manager or its affiliate is not a market maker, and the purchase is made to offset a contemporaneous sale after having received an unsolicited order to buy from a customer who is not a covered person;

(5) *Basket transactions.* Purchases or arrangements to purchase a basket of securities containing a subject security or a related security if the following conditions are satisfied:

(i) The purchase or arrangement to purchase is made in the ordinary course of business and not to facilitate the tender offer;

(ii) The basket contains 20 or more securities; and

(iii) Covered securities and related securities do not comprise more than 5% of the value of the basket;

(6) *Covering transactions.* Purchases or arrangements to purchase that are made to satisfy an obligation to deliver a subject security or a related security arising from a short sale or from the exercise of an option by a non-covered person if:

(i) The short sale or option transaction was made in the ordinary course of business and not to facilitate the offer;

(ii) In the case of a short sale, the short sale was entered into before public announcement of the tender offer; and

(iii) In the case of an exercise of an option, the covered person wrote the option before public announcement of the tender offer;

(7) *Purchases pursuant to contractual obligations.* Purchases or arrangements to purchase pursuant to a contract if the following conditions are satisfied:

(i) The contract was entered into before public announcement of the tender offer;

(ii) The contract is unconditional and binding on both parties; and

(iii) The existence of the contract and all material terms including quantity, price and parties are disclosed in the offering materials;

(8) *Purchases or arrangements to purchase by an affiliate of the dealer-manager.* Purchases or arrangements to purchase by an affiliate of a dealer-manager if the following conditions are satisfied:

(i) The dealer-manager maintains and enforces written policies and procedures reasonably designed to prevent the flow of information to or from the affiliate that might result in a violation of the federal securities laws and regulations;

(ii) The dealer-manager is registered as a broker or dealer under Section 15(a) of the Act;

(iii) The affiliate has no officers (or persons performing similar functions) or employees (other than clerical, ministerial, or support personnel) in common with the dealer-manager that direct, effect, or recommend transactions in securities; and

(iv) The purchases or arrangements to purchase are not made to facilitate the tender offer;

(9) *Purchases by connected exempt market makers or connected exempt principal traders.* Purchases or arrangements to purchase if the following conditions are satisfied:

(i) The issuer of the subject security is a foreign private issuer, as defined in § 240.3b-4(c);

(ii) The tender offer is subject to the United Kingdom's City Code on Takeovers and Mergers;

(iii) The purchase or arrangement to purchase is effected by a connected exempt market maker or a connected exempt principal trader, as those terms are used in the United Kingdom's City Code on Takeovers and Mergers;

(iv) The connected exempt market maker or the connected exempt principal trader complies with the applicable provisions of the United Kingdom's City Code on Takeovers and Mergers; and

(v) The tender offer documents disclose the identity of the connected exempt market maker or the connected exempt principal trader and disclose, or describe how U.S. security holders can obtain, information regarding market making or principal purchases by such market maker or principal trader to the extent that this information is required to be made public in the United Kingdom; and

(10) *Purchases during cross-border tender offers.* Purchases or arrangements to purchase if the following conditions are satisfied:

(i) The tender offer is excepted under § 240.13e-4(h)(8) or § 240.14d-1(c);

(ii) The offering documents furnished to U.S. holders prominently disclose the possibility of any purchases, or arrangements to purchase, or the intent to make such purchases;

(iii) The offering documents disclose the manner in which any information about any such purchases or arrangements to purchase will be disclosed;

(iv) The offeror discloses information in the United States about any such purchases or arrangements to purchase in a manner comparable to the disclosure made in the home jurisdiction, as defined in § 240.13e-4(i)(3); and

(v) The purchases comply with the applicable tender offer laws and regulations of the home jurisdiction.

(c) *Definitions.* For purposes of this section, the term:

(1) *Affiliate* has the same meaning as in § 240.12b-2;

(2) *Agent independent of the issuer* has the same meaning as in § 242.100(b) of this chapter;

(3) *Covered person* means:

(i) The offeror and its affiliates;

(ii) The offeror's dealer-manager and its affiliates;

(iii) Any advisor to any of the persons specified in paragraph (c)(3)(i) and (ii) of this section, whose compensation is dependent on the completion of the offer; and

(iv) Any person acting, directly or indirectly, in concert with any of the persons specified in this paragraph (c)(3) in connection with any purchase or arrangement to purchase any subject securities or any related securities;

(4) *Plan* has the same meaning as in § 242.100(b) of this chapter;

(5) *Public announcement* is any oral or written communication by the offeror or any person authorized to act on the offeror's behalf that is reasonably designed to, or has the effect of, informing the public or security holders in general about the tender offer;

(6) *Related securities* means securities that are immediately convertible into, exchangeable for, or exercisable for subject securities; and

(7) *Subject securities* has the same meaning as in § 229.1000 of this chapter.

(d) *Exemptive authority.* Upon written application or upon its own motion, the Commission may grant an exemption from the provisions of this section, either unconditionally or on specified terms or conditions, to any transaction or class of transactions or any security or class of security, or any person or class of persons.

RULES RELATING TO OVER-THE-COUNTER MARKETS

Rule 15c1-1. Definitions

As used in any rule adopted pursuant to Section 15(c)(1) of the Act:

(a) The term "customer" shall not include a broker or dealer or a municipal securities dealer; provided, however, that the term "customer" shall include a municipal securities dealer (other than a broker or dealer) with respect to transactions in securities other than municipal securities.

(b) The term "the completion of the transaction" means:

(1) In the case of a customer who purchases a security through or from a broker, dealer or municipal securities dealer, except as provided in subparagraph (2) of this paragraph, the time when such customer pays the broker, dealer or municipal securities dealer any part of the purchase price, or, if payment is effected by a bookkeeping entry, the time when such bookkeeping entry is made by the broker, dealer or municipal securities dealer for any part of the purchase price;

(2) In the case of a customer who purchases a security through or from a broker, dealer or municipal securities dealer and who makes payment therefor prior to the time when paymet is requested or notification is given that payment is due, the time when such broker, dealer or municipal securities dealer delivers the security to or into the account of such customer;

(3) In the case of a customer who sells a security through or to a broker, dealer or municipal securities dealer except as provided in subparagraph (4) of this paragraph, if the security is not in the custody of the broker, dealer or municipal securities dealer at the time of sale, the time when the security is delivered to the broker, dealer or municipal securities dealer, and if the security is in the custody of the broker, dealer or municipal securities dealer at the time of sale, the time when the broker, dealer or municipal securities dealer transfers the security from the account of such customer;

(4) In the case of a customer who sells a security through or to a broker, dealer or municipal securities dealer and who delivers such security to such broker, dealer or municipal securities dealer prior to the time when delivery is requested or notification is given that delivery is due, the time when such broker, dealer or municipal securities dealer makes payment to or into the account of such customer.

Rule 15c1-2. Fraud and Misrepresentation

(a) The term "manipulative, deceptive, or other fraudulent device or contrivance," as used in Section 15(c)(1) of the Act, is hereby defined to include any act, practice, or course of business which operates or would operate as a fraud or deceit upon any person.

(b) The term "manipulative, deceptive, or other fraudulent device or contrivance," as used in Section 15(c)(1) of the Act, is hereby defined to include any untrue statement of a material fact and any omission to state a material fact necessary in order to make the statements made, in the light of the circumstances under which they are made, not misleading, which statement or omission is made with knowledge or reasonable grounds to believe that it is untrue or misleading.

(c) The scope of this rule shall not be limited by any specific definitions of the term "manipulative, deceptive, or other fraudulent device or contrivance" contained in other rules adopted pursuant to Section 15(c)(1) of the Act.

Rule 15c1-6. Disclosure of Interest in Distribution

The term "manipulative, deceptive, or other fraudulent device or contrivance," as used in Section 15(c)(1) of the Act, is hereby defined to include any act of any broker who is acting for a customer or for both such customer and some other person, or of any dealer or municipal securities dealer who receives or has promise of receiving a fee from a customer for advising such customer with respect to securities, designed to effect with or for the account of such customer any transaction in, or to induce the purchase or sale by such customer of, any security in the primary or secondary distribution of which such broker, dealer or municipal securities dealer is participating or is otherwise financially interested unless such broker, dealer or municipal securities dealer, at or before the completion of each such transaction gives or sends to such customer written notification of the existence of such participation or interest.

524

Rule 15c2-1. Hypothecation of Customers' Securities

(a) *General Provisions.* The term "fraudulent, deceptive, or manipulative act or practice," as used in section 15(c)(2) of the Act, is hereby defined to include the direct or indirect hypothecation by a broker or dealer, or his arranging for or permitting, directly, or indirectly, the continued hypothecation of any securities carried for the account of any customer under circumstances—

(1) that will permit the commingling of securities carried for the account of any such customer with securities carried for the account of any other customer, without first obtaining the written consent of each such customer to such hypothecation;

(2) that will permit such securities to be commingled with securities carried for the account of any person other than a bona fide customer of such broker or dealer under a lien for a loan made to such broker or dealer; or

(3) that will permit securities carried for the account of customers to be hypothecated, or subjected to any lien or liens or claim or claims of the pledgee or pledgees, for a sum which exceeds the aggregate indebtedness of all customers in respect of securities carried for their accounts; except that this clause shall not be deemed to be violated by reason of an excess arising on any day through the reduction of the aggregate indebtedness of customers on such day, provided that funds or securities in an amount sufficient to eliminate such excess are paid or placed in transfer to pledgees for the purpose of reducing the sum of the liens or claims to which securities carried for the account of customers are subjected as promptly as practicable after such reduction occurs, but before the lapse of one-half hour after the commencement of banking hours on the next banking day at the place where the largest principal amount of loans of such broker or dealer are payable and, in any event, before such broker or dealer on such day has obtained or increased any bank loan collateralized by securities carried for the account of customers.

(b) *Definitions.* For the purposes of this rule—

(1) The term *customer* shall not include any general or special partner or any director or officer of such broker or dealer, or any participant, as such, in any joint, group or syndicate account with such broker or dealer or with any partner, officer or director thereof. The term also shall not include a counterparty who has delivered collateral to an OTC derivatives dealer pursuant to a transaction in an eligible OTC derivative instrument, or pursuant to the OTC derivatives dealer's cash management securities activities or ancillary portfolio management securities activities, and who has received a prominent written notice from the OTC derivatives dealer that:

(i) Except as otherwise agreed in writing by the OTC derivatives dealer and the counterparty, the dealer may repledge or otherwise use the collateral in its business;

(ii) In the event of the OTC derivatives dealer's failure, the counterparty will likely be considered an unsecured creditor of the dealer as to that collateral;

(iii) The Securities Investor Protection Act of 1970 (15 U.S.C 78aaa through 78lll) does not protect the counterparty; and

(iv) The collateral will not be subject to the requirements of §240.8c-1, §240.15c2-1, §240.15c3-2, or §240.15c3-3;

(2) the term "securities carried for the account of any customer" shall be deemed to mean:

(i) securities received by or on behalf of such broker or dealer for the account of any customer;

(ii) securities sold and appropriated by such broker or dealer to a customer, except that if such securities were subject to a lien when appropriated to a customer they shall not be deemed to be "securities carried for the account of any customer" pending their release from such lien as promptly as practicable;

(iii) securities sold, but not appropriated, by such broker or dealer to a customer who has made any payment therefor, to the extent that such broker or dealer owns and has received delivery of securities of like kind, except that if such securities were subject to a lien when such payment was made they shall not be deemed to be "securities carried for the account of any customer" pending their release from such lien as promptly as practicable;

(3) "aggregate indebtedness" shall not be deemed to be reduced by reason of uncollected items. In computing aggregate indebtedness, related guaranteed and guarantor accounts shall be treated as a single account and considered on a consolidated basis, and balances in accounts carrying both long and short positions shall be adjusted by treating the market value of the securities required to cover such short positions as though such market value were a debit; and

(4) in computing the sum of the liens or claims to which securities carried for the account of customers of a broker or dealer are subject, any rehypothecation of such securities by another broker or dealer who is subject to this section or to § 240.8c-1 shall be disregarded.

(c) *Exemption for Cash Accounts.* The provisions of paragraph (a) (1) hereof shall not apply to any hypothecation of securities carried for the account of a customer in a special cash account within the meaning of Section 4(c) of Regulation T of the Board of Governors of the Federal Reserve System, provided that at or before the completion of the transaction of purchase of such securities for, or of sale of such securities to, such customer, written notice is given or sent to such customer disclosing that such securities are or may be hypothecated under circumstances which will permit the commingling thereof with securities carried for the account of other customers. The term "the completion of the transaction" shall have the meaning given to such term by § 240.15c1-1(b).

(d) *Exemption for Clearing House Liens.* The provisions of paragraphs (a) (2), (a) (3), and (f) hereof shall not apply to any lien or claim of the clearing corporation, or similar department or association, of a national securities exchange or a registered national securities association, for a loan made and to be repaid on the same calendar day, which is incidental to the clearing of transactions in securities or loans through such corporation, department or association: Provided, however, that for the purpose of paragraph (a) (3) hereof, "aggregate indebtedness of all customers in respect of securities carried for their accounts" shall not include indebtedness in respect of any securities subject to any lien or claim exempted by this paragraph.

(e) *Exemption for Certain Liens on Securities of Noncustomers.* The provisions of paragraph (a) (2) hereof shall not be deemed to prevent such broker or dealer from permitting securities not carried for the account of a customer to be subjected (i) to a lien for a loan made against securities carried for the account of customers, or (ii) to a lien for a loan made and to be repaid on the same calendar day. For the purpose of this exemption, a loan shall be deemed to be "made against securities carried for the account of customers" if only securities carried for the account of customers are used to obtain or to increase such loan or as substitute for other securities carried for the account of customers.

(f) *Notice and Certification Requirements.* No person subject to this rule shall hypothecate any security carried for the account of a customer unless, at or prior to the time of each such hypothecation, he gives written notice to the pledgee that the security pledged is carried for the account of a customer and that such hypothecation does not contravene any provision of this rule, except that in the case of an omnibus account the broker or dealer for whom such account is carried may furnish a signed statement to the person carrying such account that all securities carried therein by such broker or dealer will be securities carried for the account of his customers and that the hypothecation thereof by such broker or dealer will not contravene any provision of this rule. The provisions of this clause shall not apply to any hypothecation of securities under any lien or claim of a pledgee securing a loan made and to be repaid on the same calendar day.

(g) The fact that securities carried for the accounts of customers and securities carried for the accounts of others are represented by one or more certificates in the custody of a clearing corporation or other subsidiary organization of either a national securities exchange or of a registered national securities association, or of a custodian bank, in accordance with a system for the central handling of securities established by a national securities exchange or a registered national securities association, pursuant to which system the hypothecation of such securities is effected by bookkeeping entries without physical delivery of such securities, shall not, in and of itself, result in a commingling of securities prohibited by paragraph (a) (1) or (a) (2) hereof, whenever a participating member, broker or dealer hypothecates securities in accordance with such system, *provided, however,* that (i) any such custodian of any securities held by or for such system shall agree that it will not for any reason, including the assertion of any claim, right or lien of any kind, refuse or refrain from promptly delivering any such securities (other than securities then hypothecated in accordance with such system) to such clearing corporation or other subsidiary organization or as directed by it, except that nothing in such agreement shall be deemed to require the custodian to deliver any securities in contravention of any notice of levy, seizure or similar notice, or order, or judgment, issued or directed by a governmental agency or court, or officer thereof, having jurisdiction over such custodian, which on its face affects such securities; (ii) such system shall have safeguards in the handling, transfer and delivery of securities and provisions for fidelity bond coverage of the employees and agents of the clearing corporation or other subsidiary organization and for periodic examinations by independent public accountants; and (iii) the pro visi ons of this subparagraph (g) shall not be effective with respect to any particular system unless the agreement required by (i) and the safeguards and provisions required by (ii) shall have been deemed adequate by the Commission for the protection of investors, and unless any subsequent amendments to such agreement, safeguards or provisions shall have been deemed adequate by the Commission for the protection of investors.

Rule 15c2-8. Delivery of Prospectus

(a) It shall constitute a deceptive act or practice, as those terms are used in Section 15(c)(2) of the Act, for a broker or dealer to participate in a distribution of securities with respect to which a registration statement has been filed under the Securities Act of 1933 unless he complies with the requirements set forth in paragraphs (b) through (g) below. For the purposes of this rule a broker or dealer participating in the distribution shall mean any underwriter and any member or proposed member of the selling group.

(b) In connection with an issue of securities, the issuer of which has not previously been required to file reports pursuant to sections 13(a) or 15(d) of the Securities Exchange Act of 1934, unless such issuer has been exempted from the requirement to file reports thereunder pursuant to section 12(h) of the Act, such broker or dealer shall deliver a copy of the preliminary prospectus to any person who is expected to receive a confirmation of sale at least 48 hours prior to the sending of such confirmation.

(c) Such broker or dealer shall take reasonable steps to furnish to any person who makes written request for a preliminary prospectus between the filing date and a reasonable time prior to the effective date of the registration statement to which such prospectus relates, a copy of the latest preliminary prospectus on file with the Commission. Reasonable steps shall include receiving an undertaking by the managing underwriter or underwriters to send such copy to the address given in the requests.

(d) Such broker or dealer shall take reasonable steps to comply promptly with the written request of any person for a copy of the final prospectus relating to such securities during the period between the effective date of the registration statement and the later of either the termination of such distribution, or the expiration of the applicable 40 or 90 day period under Section 4(3) of the Securities Act of 1933. Reasonable steps shall include receiving an undertaking by the managing underwriter or underwriters to send such copy to the address given in the requests. (The 40-day and 90-day periods referred to above shall be deemed to apply for purposes of this rule irrespective of the provisions of paragraphs (b) and (d) of Rule 174 under the Securities Act of 1933).

(e) Such broker or dealer shall take reasonable steps (i) to make available a copy of the preliminary prospectus relating to such securities to each of his associated persons who is expected, prior to the effective date, to solicit customers' orders for such securities before the making of any such solicitation by such associated persons and (ii) to make available to each such associated person a copy of any amended preliminary prospectus promptly after the filing thereof.

(f) Such broker or dealer shall take reasonable steps to make available a copy of the final prospectus relating to such securities to each of his associated persons who is expected, after the effective date, to solicit customers orders for such securities prior to the making of any such solicitation by such associated persons, unless a preliminary prospectus which is substantially the same as the final prospectus except for matters relating to the price of the stock has been so made available.

(g) If the broker or dealer is a managing underwriter of such distribution, he shall take reasonable steps to see to it that all other brokers or dealers participating in such distribution are promptly furnished with sufficient copies, as requested by them, of each preliminary prospectus, each amended preliminary prospectus and the final prospectus to enable them to comply with paragraphs (b), (c), (d) and (e) above.

(h) If the broker or dealer is a managing underwriter of such distribution, he shall take reasonable steps to see that any broker or dealer participating in the distribution or trading in the registered security is furnished reasonable quantities of the final prospectus relating to such securities, as requested by him, in order to enable him to comply with the prospectus delivery requirements of Section 5(b)(1) and (2) of the Securities Act of 1933.

(i) This rule shall not require the furnishing of prospectuses in any state where such furnishing would be unlawful under the laws of such state; provided, however, that this provisions is not to be construed to relieve a broker-dealer from complying with the requirements of Section 5(b)(1) and (2) of the Securities Act of 1933. Prospectuses shall not be furnished pursuant to this rule while the registration statement is subject to an examination, proceeding, or stop order pursuant to Section 8 of the Securities Act of 1933.

(j) For purposes of this section, the term *preliminary prospectus* shall include the term *prospectus subject to completion* as used in 17 CFR 230.434(a), and the term *final prospectus* shall include the term *Section 10(a) prospectus* as used in 17 CFR 230.434(a).

Rule 15c2-11. Initiation or Resumption of Quotations without Specified Information

Preliminary Note: Brokers and dealers may wish to refer to Securities Exchange Act Release No. 29094 (April 17, 1991), for a discussion of procedures for gathering and reviewing the information required by this rule and the requirement that a broker or dealer have a reasonable basis for believing that the information is accurate and obtained from reliable sources.

(a) As a means reasonably designed to prevent fraudulent, deceptive, or manipulative acts or practices, it shall be unlawful for a broker or dealer to publish any quotation for a security or, directly or indirectly, to submit any such quotation for publication, in any quotation medium (as defined in this section) unless such broker or dealer has in its records the documents and information required by this paragraph (for purposes of this section, "paragraph (a) information"), and, based upon a review of the paragraph (a) information together with any other documents and information required by paragraph (b) of this section, has a reasonable basis under the circumstances for believing that the paragraph (a) information is accurate in all material respects, and that the sources of the paragraph (a) information are reliable. The information required pursuant to this paragraph is:

(1) A copy of the prospectus specified by section 10(a) of the Securities Act of 1933 for an issuer that has filed a registration statement under the Securities Act of 1933, other than a registration statement on Form F-6, which became effective less than 90 calendar days prior to the day on which such broker or dealer publishes or submits the quotation to the quotation medium, *Provided* That such registration statement has not thereafter been the subject of a stop order which is still in effect when the quotation is published or submitted; or

(2) A copy of the offering circular provided for under Regulation A under the Securities Act of 1933 for an issuer that has filed a notification under Regulation A which became effective less than 40 calendar days prior to the day on which such broker or dealer publishes or submits the quotation to the quotation medium, *Provided* That the offering circular provided for under Regulation A has not thereafter become the subject of a suspension order which is still in effect when the quotation is published or submitted; or

(3) A copy of the issuer's most recent annual report filed pursuant to Section 13 or 15(d) of the Act or a copy of the annual statement referred to in Section 12(g)(2)(G)(i) of the Act, in the case of an issuer required to file reports pursuant to Section 13 or 15(d) of the Act or an issuer of a security covered by section 12(g)(2)(B) or (G) of the Act, together with any quarterly and current reports that have been filed under the provisions of the Act by the issuer after such annual report or annual statement; *Provided, however,* That until such issuer has filed its first annual report pursuant to Section 13 or 15(d) of the Act or annual statement referred to in Section

12(g)(2)(G)(i) of the Act, the broker or dealer has in its records a copy of the prospectus specified by Section 10(a) of the Securities Act of 1933 included in a registration statement filed by the issuer under the Securities Act of 1933, other than a registration statement on Form F-6, that became effective within the prior 16 months or a copy of any registration statement filed by the issuer under Section 12 of the Act that became effective within the prior 16 months, together with any quarterly and current reports filed thereafter under section 13 or 15(d) of the Act; and *Provided Further* That the broker or dealer has a reasonable basis under the circumstances for believing that the issuer is current in filing annual, quarterly, and current reports filed pursuant to section 13 or 15(d) of the Act, or, in the case of an insurance company exempted from section 12(g) of the Act by reason of section 12(g)(2)(G) thereof, the annual statement referred in section 12(g)(2)(G)(i) of the Act; or

(4) The information furnished to the Commission pursuant to § 240.12g3-2(b) since the beginning of the issuer's last fiscal year, in the case of an issuer exempt from Section 12(g) of the Act by reason of compliance with the provisions of § 240.12g3-2(b), which information the broker or dealer shall make reasonably available upon request to any person expressing an interest in a proposed transaction in the security with such broker or dealer; or

(5) The following information, which shall be reasonably current in relation to the day the quotation is submitted and which the broker or dealer shall make reasonably available upon request to any person expressing an interest in a proposed transaction in the security with such broker or dealer:

(i) the exact name of the issuer and its predecessor (if any);

(ii) the address of its principal executive offices;

(iii) the state of incorporation, if it is a corporation;

(iv) the exact title and class of the security;

(v) the par or stated value of the security;

(vi) the number of shares or total amount of the securities outstanding as of the end of the issuer's most recent fiscal year;

(vii) the name and address of the transfer agent;

(viii) the nature of the issuer's business;

(ix) the nature of products or services offered;

(x) the nature and extent of the issuer's facilities;

(xi) the name of the chief executive officer and members of the board of directors;

(xii) the issuer's most recent balance sheet and profit and loss and retained earnings statements;

(xiii) similar financial information for such part of the two preceding fiscal years as the issuer or its predecessor has been in existence;

(xiv) whether the broker or dealer or any associated person is affiliated, directly or indirectly with the issuer;

(xv) whether the quotation is being published or submitted on behalf of any other broker or dealer, and, if so, the name of such broker or dealer; and,

(xvi) whether the quotation is being submitted or published directly or indirectly on behalf of the issuer, or any director, officer or any person, directly or indirectly the beneficial owner of more than 10 per cent of the outstanding units or shares of any equity security of the issuer, and, if so, the name of such person, and the basis for any exemption under the federal securities laws for any sales of such securities on behalf of such person.

If such information is made available to others upon request pursuant to this paragraph, such delivery, unless otherwise represented, shall not constitute a representation by such broker or dealer that such information is accurate, but shall constitute a representation by such broker or dealer that the information is reasonably current in relation to the day the quotation is submitted, that the broker or dealer has a reasonable basis under the circumstances for believing the information is accurate in all material respects, and that the information was obtained from sources which the broker or dealer has a reasonable basis for believing are reliable. This paragraph (a)(5) shall not apply to any security of an issuer included in paragraph (a)(3) of this section unless a report or statement of such issuer described in paragraph (a) (3) of this section is not reasonably available to the broker or dealer. A report or statement of an issuer described in paragraph (a) (3) of this section shall be "reasonably available" when such report or statement is filed with the Commission.

(b) With respect to any security the quotation of which is within the provisions of this section, the broker or dealer submitting or publishing such quotation shall have in its records the following documents and information:

(1) A record of the circumstances involved in the submission of publication of such quotation, including the identity of the person or persons for whom the quotation is being submitted or published and any information regarding the transactions provided to the broker or dealer by such person or persons;

(2) A copy of any trading suspension order issued by the Commission pursuant to Section 12(k) of the Act respecting any securities of the issuer or its predecessor (if any) during the 12 months preceding the date of the publication or submission of the quotation, or a copy of the public release issued by the Commission announcing such trading suspension order; and

(3) A copy or a written record of any other material information (including adverse information) regarding the issuer which comes to the broker's or dealer's knowledge or possession before the publication or submission of the quotation.

(c) The broker or dealer shall preserve the documents and information required under paragraphs (a) and (b) of this section for a period of not less than three years, the first two years in an easily accessible place.

(d) (1) For any security of an issuer included in paragraph (a) (5) of this section, the broker or dealer submitting the quotation shall furnish to the interdealer quotation system (as defined in paragraph (e) (2) of this section), in such form as such system shall prescribe, at least 3 business days before the quotation is published or submitted, the information regarding the security and the issuer which such broker or dealer is required to maintain pursuant to said paragraph (a) (5) of this section.

(2) For any security of an issuer included in paragraph (a) (3) of this section, (i) a broker-dealer shall be in compliance with the requirement to obtain current reports filed by the issuer if the broker-dealer obtains all current reports filed with the Commission by the issuer as of a date up to five business days in advance of the earlier of the date of submission of the quotation to the quotation medium and the date of submission of paragraph (a) information pursuant to Schedule H of the By-Laws of the National Association of Securities Dealers, Inc.; and (ii) a broker-dealer shall be in compliance with the requirements to obtain the annual, quarterly, and current reports filed by the issuer, if the broker-dealer has made arrangements to receive all such reports when filed by the issuer and it has regularly received reports from the issuer on a timely basis, unless the broker-dealer has a reasonable basis under the circumstances for believing that the issuer has failed to file a required report or has filed a report but has not sent it to the broker-dealer.

(e) For purposes of this rule:

(1) "Quotation medium" shall mean any "inter-dealer quotation system" or any publication or electronic communications network or other device which is used by brokers or dealers to make known to others their interest in transactions in any security, including offers to buy or sell at a stated price or otherwise, or invitations of offers to buy or sell.

(2) "inter-dealer quotation system" shall mean any system of general circulation to brokers or dealers which regularly disseminates quotations of identified brokers or dealers.

(3) Except as otherwise specified in this rule, "quotation" shall mean any bid or offer at a specified price with respect to a security, or any indication of interest by a broker or dealer in receiving bids or offers from others for a security, or any indication by a broker or dealer that he wishes to advertise his general interest in buying or selling a particular security.

(4) "Issuer," in the case of quotations represented by American Depositary Receipts, shall mean the issuer of the deposited shares represented by such American Depositary Receipts.

(f) The provisions of this rule shall not apply to:

(1) The publication or submission of a quotation respecting a security admitted to trading on a national securities exchange and which is traded on such an exchange on the same day as, or on the business day next preceding, the day the quotation is published or submitted.

(2) The publication or submission by a broker or dealer, solely on behalf of a customer (other than a person acting as or for a dealer), of a quotation that represents the customer's indication of interest and does not involve the solicitation of the customer's interest; *Provided, however,* That this paragraph (f)(2) shall not apply to a quotation consisting of both a bid and an offer, each of which is at a specified price, unless the quotation medium specifically identifies the quotation as representing such an unsolicited customer interest.

(3)(i) The publication or submission, in an interdealer quotation system that specifically identifies as such unsolicited customer indications of interest of the kind described in paragraph (f)(2) of this section, of a quotation respecting a security which has been the subject of quotations (exclusive of any identified customer interests) in such a system on each of at least 12 days within the previous 30 calendar days, with no more than 4 business days in succession without a quotation; or

(ii) The publication or submission, in an interdealer quotation system that does not so identify any such unsolicited customer indications of interest, of a quotation respecting a security which has been the subject of both bid and ask quotations in an interdealer quotation system at specified prices on each of at least 12 days within the previous 30 calendar days, with no more than 4 business days in succession without such a two-way quotation;

(iii) A dealer acting in the capacity of market maker, as defined in section 3(a)(38) of the Act, that has published or submitted a quotation respecting a security in an interdealer quotation system and such quotation has qualified for an exception provided in this paragraph (f)(3), may continue to publish or submit quotations for such security in the interdealer quotation system without compliance with this section unless and until such dealer ceases to submit or publish a quotation or ceases to act in the capacity of market maker respecting such security.

(4) The publication or submission of a quotation respecting a municipal security.

(5) The publication or submission of a quotation respecting a security that is authorized for quotation in the NASDAQ system (as defined in § 240.11Ac1-2(a)(3) of this chapter), and such authorization is not suspended, terminated or prohibited.

(g) The requirement in subparagraph (a)(5) that the information with respect to the issuer be "reasonably current" will be presumed to be satisfied, unless the broker or dealer has information to the contrary, if:

(1) the balance sheet is as of a date less than 16 months before the publication or submission of the quotation, the statements of profit and loss and retained earnings are for the 12 months preceding the date of such balance sheet, and if such balance sheet is not as of a date less than 6 months before the publication or submission of the quotation, it shall be accompanied by additional statements of profit and loss and retained earnings for the period from the date of such balance sheet to a date less than 6 months before the publication or submission of the quotation.

(2) other information regarding the issuer specified in subparagraph (a)(5) is as of a date within 12 months prior to the publication or submission of the quotation.

(h) This rule shall not prohibit any publication or submission of any quotation if the Commission, upon written request or upon its own motion, exempts such quotation either unconditionally or on specific terms and conditions, as not constituting a fraudulent, manipulative or deceptive practice comprehended within the purpose of this rule.

Rule 15c2-12. Municipal Securities Disclosure

Preliminary Note: For a discussion of disclosure obligations relating to municipal securities, issuers, brokers, dealers, and municipal securities dealers should refer to Securities Act Release No. 7049, Securities Exchange Act Release No. 33741, FR-42 (March 9, 1994). For a discussion of the obligations of underwriters to have a reasonable basis for recommending municipal securities, brokers, dealers, and municipal securities dealers should refer to Securities Exchange Act Release No. 26100 (Sept. 22, 1988) and Securities Exchange Act Release No. 26985 (June 28, 1989).

(a) *General.* As a means reasonably designed to prevent fraudulent, deceptive, or manipulative acts or practices, it shall be unlawful for any broker, dealer, or municipal securities dealer (a "Participating Underwriter" when used in connection with an Offering) to act as an underwriter in a primary offering of municipal securities with an aggregate principal amount of $1,000,000 or more (an "Offering") unless the Participating Underwriter complies with the requirements of this section or is exempted from the provisions of this section.

(b) *Requirements.*

(1) Prior to the time the Participating Underwriter bids for, purchases, offers, or sells municipal securities in an Offering, the Participating Underwriter shall obtain and review an official statement that an issuer of such securities deems final as of its date, except for the omission of no more than the following information: the offering price(s), interest rate(s), selling compensation, aggregate principal amount, principal amount per maturity, delivery dates, any other terms or provisions required by an issuer of such securities to be specified in a competitive bid, ratings, other terms of the securities depending on such matters, and the identity of the underwriter(s).

(2) Except in competitively bid offerings, from the time the Participating Underwriter has reached an understanding with an issuer of municipal securities that it will become a Participating Underwriter in an Offering until a final official statement is available, the Participating Underwriter shall send no later than the next business day, by first class mail or other equally prompt means, to any potential customer, on request, a single copy of the most recent preliminary official statement, if any.

(3) The Participating Underwriter shall contract with an issuer of municipal securities or its designated agent to receive, within seven business days after any final agreement to purchase, offer, or sell the municipal securities in an Offering and in sufficient time to accompany any confirmation that requests payment from any customer, copies of a final official statement in sufficient quantity to comply with paragraph (b)(4) of this rule and the rules of the Municipal Securities Rulemaking Board.

(4) From the time the final official statement becomes available until the earlier of (i) ninety days from the end of the underwriting period or (ii) the time when the official statement is available to any person from a nationally recognized municipal securities information repository, but in no case less than twenty five days following the end of the underwriting period, the Participating Underwriter in an Offering shall send no later than the next business day, by first class mail or other equally prompt means, to any potential customer, on request, a single copy of the final official statement.

(5)(i) A Participating Underwriter shall not purchase or sell municipal securities in connection with an Offering unless the Participating Underwriter has reasonably determined that an issuer of municipal securities, or an obligated person for whom financial or operating data is presented in the final official statement has undertaken, either individually or in combination with other issuers of such municipal securities or obligated persons, in a written agreement or contract for the benefit of holders of such securities, to provide, either directly or indirectly through an indenture trustee or a designated agent:

(A) To each nationally recognized municipal securities information repository and to the appropriate state information depository, if any, annual financial information for each obligated person for whom financial information or operating data is presented in the final official statement, or, for each obligated person meeting the objective criteria specified in the undertaking and used to select the obligated persons for whom financial information or operating data is presented in the final official statement, except that, in the case of pooled obligations, the undertaking shall specify such objective criteria;

(B) If not submitted as part of the annual financial information, then when and if available, to each nationally recognized municipal securities information repository and to the appropriate state information depository, audited financial statements for each obligated person covered by paragraph (b)(5)(i)(A) of this section;

(C) In a timely manner, to each nationally recognized municipal securities information repository or to the Municipal Securities Rulemaking Board, and to the appropriate state information depository, if any, notice of any of the following events with respect to the securities being offered in the Offering, if material:

(*1*) Principal and interest payment delinquencies;

(*2*) Non-payment related defaults;

(*3*) Unscheduled draws on debt service reserves reflecting financial difficulties;

(*4*) Unscheduled draws on credit enhancements reflecting financial difficulties;

(*5*) Substitution of credit or liquidity providers, or their failure to perform;

(*6*) Adverse tax opinions or events affecting the tax-exempt status of the security;

(*7*) Modifications to rights of security holders;

(*8*) Bond calls;

(*9*) Defeasances;

(*10*) Release, substitution, or sale of property securing repayment of the securities;

(*11*) Rating changes; and

(D) In a timely manner, to each nationally recognized municipal securities information repository or to the Municipal Securities Rulemaking Board, and to the appropriate state information depository, if any, notice of a failure of any person specified in paragraph (b)(5)(i)(A) of this section to provide required annual financial information, on or before the date specified in the written agreement or contract.

(ii) The written agreement or contract for the benefit of holders of such securities also shall identify each person for whom annual financial information and notices of material events will be provided, either by name or by the objective criteria used to select such persons, and, for each such person shall:

(A) Specify, in reasonable detail, the type of financial information and operating data to be provided as part of annual financial information;

(B) Specify, in reasonable detail, the accounting principles pursuant to which financial statements will be prepared, and whether the financial statements will be audited; and

(C) Specify the date on which the annual financial information for the preceding fiscal year will be provided, and to whom it will be provided.

(iii) Such written agreement or contract for the benefit of holders of such securities also may provide that the continuing obligation to provide annual financial information and notices of events may be terminated with respect to any obligated person, if and when such obligated person no longer remains an obligated person with respect to such municipal securities.

(c) *Recommendations.* As a means reasonably designed to prevent fraudulent, deceptive, or manipulative acts or practices, it shall be unlawful for any broker, dealer, or municipal securities dealer to recommend the purchase or sale of a municipal security unless such broker, dealer, or municipal securities dealer has procedures in place that provide reasonable assurance that it will receive prompt notice of any event disclosed pursuant to paragraph (b)(5)(i)(C), paragraph (b)(5)(i)(D), and paragraph (d)(2)(ii)(B) of this section with respect to that security.

(d) *Exemptions.* (1) This section shall not apply to a primary offering of municipal securities in authorized denominations of $100,000 or more, if such securities:

(i) Are sold to no more than thirty-five persons each of whom the Participating Underwriter reasonably believes:

(A) Has such knowledge and experience in financial and business matters that it is capable of evaluating the merits and risks of the prospective investment; and

(B) Is not purchasing for more than one account or with a view to distributing the securities; or

(ii) Have a maturity of nine months or less; or

(iii) At the option of the holder thereof may be tendered to an issuer of such securities or its designated agent for redemption or purchase at par value or more at least as frequently as every nine months until maturity, earlier redemption, or purchase by an issuer or its designated agent.

(2) Paragraph (b)(5) of this section shall not apply to an Offering of municipal securities if, at such time as an issuer of such municipal securities delivers the securities to the Participating Underwriters:

(i) No obligated person will be an obligated person with respect to more than $10,000,000 in aggregate amount of outstanding municipal securities, including the offered securities and excluding municipal securities that were offered in a transaction exempt from this section pursuant to paragraph (d)(1) of this section;

(ii) An issuer of municipal securities or obligated person has undertaken, either individually or in combination with other issuers of municipal securities or obligated persons, in a written agreement or contract for the benefit of holders of such municipal securities, to provide:

(A) Upon request to any person or at least annually to the appropriate state information depository, if any, financial information or operating data regarding each obligated person for which financial information or operating data is presented in the final official statement, as specified in the undertaking, which financial information and operating data shall include, at a minimum, that financial information and operating data which is customarily prepared by such obligated person and is publicly available; and

(B) In a timely manner, to each nationally recognized municipal securities information repository or to the Municipal Securities Rulemaking Board, and to the appropriate state information depository, if any, notice of events specified in paragraph (b)(5)(i)(C) of this section with respect to the securities that are the subject of the Offering, if material; and

(iii) the final official statement identifies by name, address, and telephone number the persons from which the foregoing information, data, and notices can be obtained.

(3) The provisions of paragraph (b)(5) of this section, other than paragraph (b)(5)(i)(C) of this section, shall not apply to an Offering of municipal securities, if such municipal securities have a stated maturity of 18 months or less.

(4) The provisions of paragraph (c) of this section shall not apply to municipal securities:

(i) Sold in an Offering to which paragraph (b)(5) of this section did not apply, other than Offerings exempt under paragraph (d)(2)(ii) of this section; or

(ii) Sold in an Offering exempt from this section under paragraph (d)(1) of this section.

(e) *Exemptive Authority.* The Commission, upon written request, or upon its own motion, may exempt any broker, dealer, or municipal securities dealer, whether acting in the capacity of a Participating Underwriter or otherwise, that is a participant in a transaction or class of transactions from any requirement of this section, either unconditionally or on specified terms and conditions, if the Commission determines that such an exemption is consistent with the public interest and the protection of investors.

(f) *Definitions.* For the purposes of this rule—

(1) The term "authorized denominations of $100,000 or more" means municipal securities with a principal amount of $100,000 or more and with restrictions that prevent the sale or transfer of such securities in principal amounts of less than $100,000 other than through a primary offering; except that, for municipal securities with an original issue discount of 10 percent or more, the term means municipal securities with a minimum purchase price of $100,000 or more and with restrictions that prevent the sale or transfer of such securities, in principal amounts that are less than the original principal amount at the time of the primary offering, other than through a primary offering.

(2) The term "end of the underwriting period" means the later of such time as (i) the issuer of municipal securities delivers the securities to the Participating Underwriters or (ii) the Participating Underwriter does not retain, directly or as a member or an underwriting syndicate, an unsold balance of the securities for sale to the public.

(3) The term *final official statement* means a document or set of documents prepared by an issuer of municipal securities or its representatives that is complete as of the date delivered to the Participating Underwriter(s) and that sets forth information concerning the terms of the proposed issue of securities; information, including financial information or operating data, concerning such issuers of municipal securities and those other entities, enterprises, funds, accounts, and other

persons material to an evaluation of the Offering; and a description of the undertakings to be provided pursuant to paragraph (b)(5)(i), paragraph (d)(2)(ii), and paragraph (d)(2)(iii) of this section, if applicable, and of any instances in the previous five years in which each person specified pursuant to paragraph (b)(5)(ii) of this section failed to comply, in all material respects, with any previous undertakings in a written contract or agreement specified in paragraph (b)(5)(i) of this section. Financial information or operating data may be set forth in the document or set of documents, or may be included by specific reference to documents previously provided to each nationally recognized municipal securities information repository, and to a state information depository, if any, or filed with the Commission. If the document is a final official statement, it must be available from the Municipal Securities Rulemaking Board.

(4) The term "issuer of municipal securities" means the governmental issuer specified in section 3(a)(29) of the Act and the issuer of any separate security, including a separate security as defined in rule 3b-5(a) under the Act.

(5) The term "potential customer" means (i) any person contacted by the Participating Underwriter concerning the purchase of municipal securities that are intended to be offered or have been sold in an Offering, (ii) any person who has expressed an interest to the Participating Underwriter in possibly purchasing such municipal securities, and (iii) any person who has a customer account with the Participating Underwriter.

(6) The term "preliminary official statement" means an official statement prepared by or for an issuer of municipal securities for dissemination to potential customers prior to the availability of the final official statement.

(7) The term "primary offering" means an offering of municipal securities directly or indirectly by or on behalf of an issuer of such securities, including any remarketing of municipal securities (i) that is accompanied by a change in the authorized denomination of such securities from $100,000 or more to less than $100,000, or (ii) that is accompanied by a change in the period during which such securities may be tendered to an issuer of such securities or its designated agent for redemption or purchase from a period of nine months or less to a period of more than nine months.

(8) The term "underwriter" means any person who has purchased from an issuer of municipal securities with a view to, or offers or sells for an issuer of municipal securities in connection with, the offering of any municipal security, or participates or has a direct or indirect participating in any such undertaking, or participates or has a participation in the direct or indirect underwriting of any such undertaking; except, that such term shall not include a person whose interest is limited to a commission, concession, or allowance from an underwriter, broker, dealer, or municipal securities dealer not in excess of the usual and customary distributors' or sellers' commission, concession, or allowance.

(9) The term *annual financial information* means financial information or operating data, provided at least annually, of the type included in the final official statement with respect to an obligated person, or in the case where no financial information or operating data was provided in the final official statement with respect to such obligated person, of the type included in the final official statement with respect to those obligated persons that meet the objective criteria applied to select the persons for which financial information or operating data will be provided on an annual basis. Financial information or operating data may be set forth in the document or set of documents, or may be included by specific reference to documents previously provided to each nationally recognized municipal securities information repository, and to a state information depository, if any, or filed with the Commission. If the document is a final official statement, it must be available from the Municipal Securities Rulemaking Board.

(10) The term *obligated person* means any person, including an issuer of municipal securities, who is either generally or through an enterprise, fund, or account of such person committed by contract or other arrangement to support payment of all, or part of the obligations on the municipal securities to be sold in the Offering (other than providers of municipal bond insurance, letters of credit, or other liquidity facilities).

(g) *Transitional Provision.* If on July 28, 1989 a Participating Underwriter was contractually committed to act as underwriter in an Offering of municipal securities originally issued before July

29, 1989, and requirements of paragraphs (b)(3) and (b)(4) shall not apply to the Participating Underwriter in connection with such an Offering. Paragraph (b)(5) of this section shall not apply to a Participating Underwriter that has contractually committed to act as an underwriter in an Offering of municipal securities before July 3, 1995; *except that* paragraph (b)(5)(i)(A) and paragraph (b)(5)(i)(B) shall not apply with respect to fiscal years ending prior to January 1, 1996. Paragraph (c) shall become effective on January 1, 1996. Paragraph (d)(2)(ii) and paragraph (d)(2)(iii) of this section shall not apply to an Offering of municipal securities commencing prior to January 1, 1996.

PENNY STOCK DISCLOSURES

Rule 15g-1. Exemptions for Certain Transactions

The following transactions shall be exempt from 17 CFR 240.15g-2, 17 CFR 240.15g-3, 17 CFR 240.15g-4, 17 CFR 240.15g-5, and 17 CFR 240.15g-6:

(a) Transactions by a broker or dealer:

(1) whose commissions, commission equivalents, mark-ups, and mark-downs from transactions in penny stocks during each of the immediately preceding three months and during eleven or more of the preceding twelve months, or during the immediately preceding six months, did not exceed five percent of its total commissions, commission equivalents, mark-ups, and mark-downs from transactions in securities during those months; and

(2) who has not been a market maker in the penny stock that is the subject of the transaction in the immediately preceding twelve months.

Note: Prior to April 28, 1993, commissions, commission equivalents, mark-ups, and mark-downs from transactions in designated securities, as defined in 17 CFR 240.15c2-6(d)(2) as of April 15, 1992, may be considered to be commissions, commission equivalents, mark-ups, mark-downs from transactions in penny stocks for purposes of paragraph (a)(1) of this section.

(b) Transactions in which the customer is an institutional accredited investor, as defined in 17 CFR 230.501(a)(1), (2), (3), (7) or (8) of this chapter.

(c) Transactions that meet the requirements of Regulation D (17 CFR 230.501—230.508 of this chapter), or transactions with an issuer not involving any public offering pursuant to Section 4(2) of the Securities Act of 1933.

(d) Transactions in which the customer is the issuer, or a director, officer, general partner, or direct or indirect beneficial owner of more than five percent of any class of equity security of the issuer, of the penny stock that is the subject of the transaction.

(e) Transactions that are not recommended by the broker or dealer.

(f) Any other transaction or class of transactions or persons or class of persons that, upon prior written request or upon its own motion, the Commission conditionally or unconditionally exempts by order as consistent with the public interest and the protection of investors.

Rule 15g-2. Risk Disclosure Document Relating to the Penny Stock Market

(a) It shall be unlawful for a broker or dealer to effect a transaction in any penny stock for or with the account of a customer unless, prior to effecting such transaction, the broker or dealer has furnished to the customer a document containing the information set forth in Schedule 15G, 17 CFR 240.15g-100, and has obtained from the customer a manually signed and dated written acknowledgement of receipt of the document.

(b) The broker or dealer shall preserve, as part of its records, a copy of the written acknowledgment required by paragraph (a) of this section for the period specified in 17 CFR 240.17a-4(b) of this chapter.

Rule 15g-3. Broker or Dealer Disclosure of Quotations and Other Information Relating to the Penny Stock Market

(a) *Requirement.* It shall be unlawful for a broker or dealer to effect a transaction in any penny stock with or for the account of a customer unless such broker or dealer discloses to such customer, within the time periods and in the manner required by paragraph (b) of this section, the following information:

(1) The inside bid quotation and the inside offer quotation for the penny stock.

(2) If paragraph (a)(1) of this section does not apply because of the absence of an inside bid quotation and an inside offer quotation:

(i) With respect to a transaction effected with or for a customer on a principal basis (other than as provided in paragraph (a)(2)(ii) of this section):

(A) The dealer shall disclose its offer price for the security:

(1) if during the previous five days the dealer has effected no fewer than three *bona fide* sales to other dealers consistently at its offer price for the security current at the time of those sales, and

(2) if the dealer reasonably believes in good faith at the time of the transaction with the customer that its offer price accurately reflects the price at which it is willing to sell one or more round lots to another dealer.

For purposes of this paragraph (a)(2)(i)(A), "consistently" shall constitute, at a minimum, seventy-five percent of the dealer's *bona fide* interdealer sales during the previous five-day period, and, if the dealer has effected only three *bona fide* inter-dealer sales during such period, all three of such sales.

(B) The dealer shall disclose its bid price for the security:

(1) if during the previous five days the dealer has effected no fewer than three *bona fide* purchases from other dealers consistently at its bid price for the security current at the time of those purchases, and

(2) if the dealer reasonably believes in good faith at the time of the transaction with the customer that its bid price accurately reflects the price at which it is willing to buy one or more round lots from another dealer.

For purposes of this paragraph (a)(2)(i)(B), "consistently" shall constitute, at a minimum, seventy-five percent of the dealer's *bona fide* interdealer purchases during the previous five-day period, and, if the dealer has effected only three *bona fide* inter-dealer purchases during such period, all three of such purchases.

(C) If the dealer's bid or offer prices to the customer do not satisfy the criteria of paragraphs (a)(2)(i)(A) or (a)(2)(i)(B) of this section, the dealer shall disclose to the customer:

(1) that it has not effected inter-dealer purchases or sales of the penny stock consistently at its bid or offer price, and

(2) the price at which it last purchased the penny stock from, or sold the penny stock to, respectively, another dealer in a *bona fide* transaction.

(ii) With respect to transactions effected by a broker or dealer with or for the account of the customer:

(A) on an agency basis or

(B) on a basis other than as a market maker in the security, where, after having received an order from the customer to purchase a penny stock, the dealer effects the purchase from another person to offset a contemporaneous sale of the penny stock to such customer, or, after having received an order from the customer to sell the penny stock, the dealer effects the sale to another person to offset a contemporaneous purchase from such customer, the broker or dealer shall disclose the best independent interdealer bid and offer prices for the penny stock that the broker or dealer obtains through reasonable diligence. A broker-dealer shall be deemed to have exercised reasonable diligence if it obtains quotations from three market makers in the security (or all known market makers if there are fewer than three).

(3) With respect to bid or offer prices and transaction prices disclosed pursuant to paragraph (a) of this section, the broker or dealer shall disclose the number of shares to which the bid and offer prices apply.

(b) *Timing.* (1) The information described in paragraph (a) of this section:

(i) shall be provided to the customer orally or in writing prior to effecting any transaction with or for the customer for the purchase or sale of such penny stock; and

(ii) shall be given or sent to the customer in writing, at or prior to the time that any written confirmation of the transaction is given or sent to the customer pursuant to 17 CFR 240.10b-10 of this chapter.

(2) A broker or dealer, at the time of making the disclosure pursuant to paragraph (b)(1)(i) of this section, shall make and preserve as part of its records, a record of such disclosure for the period specified in 17 CFR 240.17a-4(b) of this chapter.

(c) *Definitions*. For purposes of this section:

(1) The term "bid price" shall mean the price most recently communicated by the dealer to another broker or dealer at which the dealer is willing to purchase one or more round lots of the penny stock, and shall not include indications of interest.

(2) The term "offer price" shall mean the price most recently communicated by the dealer to another broker or dealer at which the dealer is willing to sell one or more round lots of the penny stock, and shall not include indications of interest.

(3) The term "inside bid quotation" for a security shall mean the highest bid quotation for the security displayed by a market maker in the security on a Qualifying Electronic Quotation System, at any time in which at least two market makers are contemporaneously displaying on such system bid and offer quotations for the security at specified prices.

(4) The term "inside offer quotation" for a security shall mean the lowest offer quotation for the security displayed by a market maker in the security on a Qualifying Electronic Quotation System, at any time in which at least two market makers are contemporaneously displaying on such system bid and offer quotations for the security at specified prices.

(5) The term "Qualifying Electronic Quotation System" shall mean an automated interdealer quotation system that has the characteristics set forth in Section 17B(b)(2) of the Act, or such other automated interdealer quotation system designated by the Commission for purposes of this section.

Rule 15g-4. Disclosure of Compensation to Brokers or Dealers

Preliminary Note: Brokers and dealers may wish to refer to Securities Exchange Act Release No. 30608 (April 20, 1992) for a discussion of the procedures for computing compensation in active and competitive markets, inactive and competitive markets, and dominated and controlled markets.

(a) *Disclosure Requirement*. It shall be unlawful for any broker or dealer to effect a transaction in any penny stock for or with the account of a customer unless such broker or dealer discloses to such customer, within the time periods and in the manner required by paragraph (b) of this section, the aggregate amount of any compensation received by such broker or dealer in connection with such transaction.

(b) *Timing*. (1) The information described in paragraph (a) of this section:

(i) shall be provided to the customer orally or in writing prior to effecting any transaction with or for the customer for the purchase or sale of such penny stock; and

(ii) shall be given or sent to the customer in writing, at or prior to the time that any written confirmation of the transaction is given or sent to the customer pursuant to 17 CFR 240.10b-10 of this chapter.

(2) A broker or dealer, at the time of making the disclosure pursuant to paragraph (b)(1)(i) of this section, shall make and preserve as part of its records, a record of such disclosure for the period specified in 17 CFR 240.17a-4(b) of this chapter.

(c) *Definition of Compensation*. For purposes of this section, "compensation" means, with respect to a transaction in a penny stock:

(1) if a broker is acting as agent for a customer, the amount of any remuneration received or to be received by it from such customer in connection with such transaction;

(2) if, after having received a buy order from a customer, a dealer other than a market maker purchased the penny stock as principal from another person to offset a contemporaneous sale to such customer or, after having received a sell order from a customer, sold the penny stock as principal to another person to offset a contemporaneous purchase from such customer, the

difference between the price to the customer and such contemporaneous purchase or sale price; or

(3) if the dealer otherwise is acting as principal for its own account, the difference between the price to the customer and the prevailing market price.

(d) *"Active and competitive" market.* For purposes of this section only, a market may be deemed to be "active and competitive" in determining the prevailing market price with respect to a transaction by a market maker in a penny stock if the aggregate number of transactions effected by such market maker in the penny stock in the five business days preceding such transaction is less than twenty percent of the aggregate number of all transactions in the penny stock reported on a Qualifying Electronic Quotation System (as defined in 17 CFR 240.15g-3(c)(5)) during such five-day period. No presumption shall arise that a market is not "active and competitive" solely by reason of a market maker not meeting the conditions specified in this paragraph.

Rule 15g-5. Disclosure of Compensation of Associated Persons in Connection with Penny Stock Transactions

(a) *General.* (1) It shall be unlawful for a broker or dealer to effect a transaction in any penny stock for or with the account of a customer unless the broker or dealer discloses to such customer, within the time periods and in the manner required by paragraph (b) of this section, the aggregate amount of cash compensation that any associated person of the broker or dealer who is a natural person and has communicated with the customer concerning the transaction at or prior to receipt of the customer's transaction order, other than any person whose function is solely clerical or ministerial, has received or will receive from any source in connection with the transaction and that is determined at or prior to the time of the transaction, including separate disclosure, if applicable, of the source and amount of such compensation that is not paid by the broker or dealer.

(b) *Timing.* (1) The information described in paragraph (a) of this section:

(i) shall be provided to the customer orally or in writing prior to effecting any transaction with or for the customer for the purchase or sale of such penny stock; and

(ii) shall be given or sent to the customer in writing, at or prior to the time that any written confirmation of the transaction is given or sent to the customer pursuant to 17 CFR 240.10b-10 of this chapter.

(2) A broker or dealer, at the time of making the disclosure pursuant to paragraph (b)(1)(i) of this section, shall make and preserve as part of its records, a record of such disclosure for the period specified in 17 CFR 240.17a-4(b) of this chapter.

(c) *Contingent Compensation Arrangements.* Where a portion or all of the cash or other compensation that the associated person may receive in connection with the transaction may be determined and paid following the transaction based on aggregate sales volume levels or other contingencies, the written disclosure required by paragraph (b)(1)(ii) of this section shall state that fact and describe the basis upon which such compensation is determined.

Rule 15g-6. Account Statements for Penny Stock Customers

(a) *Requirement.* It shall be unlawful for any broker or dealer that has effected the sale to any customer, other than in a transaction that is exempt pursuant to 17 CFR 240.15g-1 of this chapter, of any security that is a penny stock on the last trading day of any calendar month, or any successor of such broker or dealer, to fail to give or send to such customer a written statement containing the information described in paragraphs (c) and (d) of this section with respect to each such month in which such security is held for the customer's account with the broker or dealer, within ten days following the end of such month.

(b) *Exemptions.* A broker or dealer shall be exempted from the requirement of paragraph (a) of this section under either of the following circumstances:

(1) If the broker or dealer does not effect any transactions in penny stocks for or with the account of the customer during a period of six consecutive calendar months, then the broker or dealer shall not be required to provide monthly statements for each quarterly period that is

immediately subsequent to such six-month period and in which the broker or dealer does not effect any transaction in penny stocks for or with the account of the customer, *provided* that the broker or dealer gives or sends to the customer written statements containing the information described in paragraphs (d) and (e) of this section on a quarterly basis, within ten days following the end of each such quarterly period.

(2) If, on all but five or fewer trading days of any quarterly period, a security has a price of five dollars or more, the broker or dealer shall not be required to provide a monthly statement covering the security for subsequent quarterly periods, until the end of any such subsequent quarterly period on the last trading day of which the price of the security is less than five dollars.

(c) *Price Determinations.* For purposes of paragraphs (a) and (b) of this section, the price of a security on any trading day shall be determined at the close of business in accordance with the provisions of 17 CFR 240.3a51-1(d)(1) of this chapter.

(d) *Market and Price Information.* The statement required by paragraph (a) of this section shall contain at least the following information with respect to each penny stock covered by paragraph (a) of this section, as of the last trading day of the period to which the statement relates:

(1) The identity and number of shares or units of each such security held for the customer's account; and

(2) The estimated market value of the security, to the extent that such estimated market value can be determined in accordance with the following provisions:

(i) The highest inside bid quotation for the security on the last trading day of the period to which the statement relates, multiplied by the number of shares or units of the security held for the customer's account; or

(ii) If paragraph (d)(2)(i) of this section is not applicable because of the absence of an inside bid quotation, and if the broker or dealer furnishing the statement has effected at least ten separate Qualifying Purchases in the security during the last five trading days of the period to which the statement relates, the weighted average price per share paid by the broker or dealer in all Qualifying Purchases effected during such five-day period, multiplied by the number of shares or units of the security held for the customer's account; or

(iii) If neither of paragraphs (d)(2)(i) nor (d)(2)(ii) of this section is applicable, a statement that there is "no estimated market value" with respect to the security.

(e) *Legend.* In addition to the information required by paragraph (d) of this section, the written statement required by paragraph (a) of this section shall include a conspicuous legend that is identified with the penny stocks described in the statement and that contains the following language:

IF THIS STATEMENT CONTAINS AN ESTIMATED VALUE, YOU SHOULD BE AWARE THAT THIS VALUE MAY BE BASED ON A LIMITED NUMBER OF TRADES OR QUOTES. THEREFORE, YOU MAY NOT BE ABLE TO SELL THESE SECURITIES AT A PRICE EQUAL OR NEAR TO THE VALUE SHOWN. HOWEVER, THE BROKER-DEALER FURNISHING THIS STATEMENT MAY NOT REFUSE TO ACCEPT YOUR ORDER TO SELL THESE SECURITIES. ALSO, THE AMOUNT YOU RECEIVE FROM A SALE GENERALLY WILL BE REDUCED BY THE AMOUNT OF ANY COMMISSIONS OR SIMILAR CHARGES. IF AN ESTIMATED VALUE IS NOT SHOWN FOR A SECURITY, A VALUE COULD NOT BE DETERMINED BECAUSE OF A LACK OF INFORMATION.

(f) *Preservation of Records.* Any broker or dealer subject to this section shall preserve, as part of its records, copies of the written statements required by paragraph (a) of this section and keep such records for the periods specified in 17 CFR 240.17a-4(b) of this chapter.

(g) *Definitions.* For purposes of this section:

(1) The term "Quarterly period" shall mean any period of three consecutive full calendar months.

(2) The "inside bid quotation" for a security shall mean the highest bid quotation for the security displayed by a market maker in the security on a Qualifying Electronic Quotation System,

at any time in which at least two market makers are contemporaneously displaying on such system bid and offer quotations for the security at specified prices.

(3) The term "Qualifying Electronic Quotation System" shall mean an automated interdealer quotation system that has the characteristics set forth in Section 17B(b)(2) of the Act, or such other automated interdealer quotation system designated by the Commission for purposes of this section.

(4) The term "Qualifying Purchases" shall mean *bona fide* purchases by a broker or dealer of a penny stock for its own account, each of which involves at least 100 shares, but excluding any block purchase involving more than one percent of the outstanding shares or units of the security.

Rule 15g-8. Sales of Escrowed Securities of Blank Check Companies

As a means reasonably designed to prevent fraudulent, deceptive, or manipulative acts or practices, it shall be unlawful for any person to sell or offer to sell any security that is deposited and held in an escrow or trust account pursuant to Rule 419 under the Securities Act of 1933 [17 CFR 230.419], or any interest in or related to such security, other than pursuant to a qualified domestic relations order as defined by the Internal Revenue Code of 1986, as amended [26 U.S.C. 1 *et seq.*], or Title I of the Employee Retirement Income Security Act [29 U.S.C. 1001 *et seq.*], or the rules thereunder.

Rule 15g-9. Sales Practice Requirements for Certain Low-Priced Securities

(a) As a means reasonably designed to prevent fraudulent, deceptive, or manipulative acts or practices, it shall be unlawful for a broker or dealer to sell a penny stock to, or to effect the purchase of a penny stock by, any person unless:

(1) the transaction is exempt under paragraph (c) of this section; or

(2) prior to the transaction:

(i) the broker or dealer has approved the person's account for transactions in penny stocks in accordance with the procedures set forth in paragraph (b) of this section; and

(ii) the broker or dealer has received from the person a written agreement to the transaction setting forth the identity and quantity of the penny stock to be purchased.

(b) In order to approve a person's account for transactions in penny stocks, the broker or dealer must:

(1) obtain from the person information concerning the person's financial situation, investment experience, and investment objectives;

(2) reasonably determine, based on the information required by paragraph (b)(1) of this section and any other information known by the broker-dealer, that transactions in penny stocks are suitable for the person, and that the person (or the person's independent adviser in these transactions) has sufficient knowledge and experience in financial matters that the person (or the person's independent adviser in these transactions) reasonably may be expected to be capable of evaluating the risks of transactions in penny stocks;

(3) deliver to the person a written statement:

(i) setting forth the basis on which the broker or dealer made the determination required by paragraph (b)(2) of this section;

(ii) stating in a highlighted format that it is unlawful for the broker or dealer to effect a transaction in a penny stock subect to the provisions of paragraph (a)(2) of this section unless the broker or dealer has received, prior to the transaction, a written agreement to the transaction from the person; and

(iii) stating in a highlighted format immediately preceding the customer signature line that:

(A) the broker or dealer is required by this section to provide the person with the written statement; and

(B) the person should not sign and return the written statement to the broker or dealer if it does not accurately reflect the person's financial situation, investment experience, and investment objectives; and

(4) obtain from the person a manually signed and dated copy of the written statement required by paragraph (b)(3) of this section.

(c) For purposes of this section, the following transactions shall be exempt:

(1) Transactions that are exempt under 17 CFR 240.15g-1(a), (b), (d), (e), and (f).

(2) Transactions that meet the requirements of 17 CFR 230.505 or 230.506 (including, where applicable, the requirements of 17 CFR 230.501 through 230.503, and 230.507 through 230.508), or transactions with an issuer not involving any public offering pursuant to Section 4(2) of the Securities Act of 1933.

(3) Transactions in which the purchaser is an established customer of the broker or dealer.

(d) For purposes of this section:

(1) The term "penny stock" shall have the same meaning as in 17 CFR 240.3a51-1.

(2) The term "established customer" shall mean any person for whom the broker or dealer, or a clearing broker on behalf of such broker or dealer, carries an account, and who in such account:

(i) has effected a securities transaction, or made a deposit of funds or securities, more than one year previously; or

(ii) has made three purchases of penny stocks that occurred on separate days and involved different issuers.

REPORTS OF DIRECTORS, OFFICERS, AND PRINCIPAL STOCKHOLDERS

Rule 16a-1. Definition of Terms

Terms defined in this Rule shall apply solely to Section 16 of the Act and the rules thereunder. These terms shall not be limited to Section 16(a) of the Act but also shall apply to all other subsections under Section 16 of the Act.

(a) The term "beneficial owner" shall have the following applications:

(1) Solely for purposes of determining whether a person is a beneficial owner of more than ten percent of any class of equity securities registered pursuant to Section 12 of the Act, the term "beneficial owner" shall mean any person who is deemed a beneficial owner pursuant to Section 13(d) of the Act and the rules thereunder; *provided, however,* that the following institutions or persons shall not be deemed the beneficial owner of securities of such class held for the benefit of third parties or in customer or fiduciary accounts in the ordinary course of business (or in the case of an employee benefit plan specified in subparagraph (vi) below, of securities of such class allocated to plan participants where participants have voting power) as long as such shares are acquired by such institutions or persons without the purpose or effect of changing or influencing control of the issuer or engaging in any arrangement subject to Rule 13d-3(b) (§ 240.13d-3(b)):

(i) A broker or dealer registered under section 15 of the Act (15 U.S.C. 78o);

(ii) A bank as defined in section 3(a)(6) of the Act (15 U.S.C. 78c);

(iii) An insurance company as defined in section 3(a)(19) of the Act (15 U.S.C. 78c);

(iv) An investment company registered under section 8 of the Investment Company Act of 1940 (15 U.S.C. 80a-8);

(v) Any person registered as an investment adviser under Section 203 of the Investment Advisers Act of 1940 (15 U.S.C. 80b-3) or under the laws of any state;

(vi) An employee benefit plan as defined in Section 3(3) of the Employee Retirement Income Security Act of 1974, as amended, 29 U.S.C. 1001 et seq. ("ERISA") that is subject to the provisions of ERISA, or any such plan that is not subject to ERISA that is maintained primarily for the benefit of the employees of a state or local government or instrumentality, or an endowment fund;

(vii) A parent holding company or control person, provided the aggregate amount held directly by the parent or control person, and directly and indirectly by their subsidiaries or affiliates that are not persons specified in paragraphs (a)(1)(i) through (ix), does not exceed one percent of the securities of the subject class;

(viii) A savings association as defined in Section 3(b) of the Federal Deposit Insurance Act (12 U.S.C. 1813);

(ix) A church plan that is excluded from the definition of an investment company under section 3(c)(14) of the Investment Company Act of 1940 (15 U.S.C. 80a-3); and

(x) A group, provided that all the members are persons specified in §240.16a-1(a)(1)(i) through (ix).

(xi) A group, provided that all the members are persons specified in §240.16a-1(a)(1)(i) through (vii).

Note to paragraph (a). Pursuant to this section, a person deemed a beneficial owner of more than ten percent of any class of equity securities registered under Section 12 of the Act would file a Form 3 (§249.103), but the securities holdings disclosed on Form 3, and changes in beneficial ownership reported on subsequent Forms 4 (§249.104) or 5 (§249.105), would be determined by the definition of "beneficial owner" in paragraph (a)(2) of this section.

(2) Other than for purposes of determining whether a person is a beneficial owner of more than ten percent of any class of equity securities registered under Section 12 of the Act, the term "beneficial owner" shall mean any person who, directly or indirectly, through any contract, arrangement, understanding, relationship or otherwise, has or shares a direct or indirect pecuniary interest in the equity securities, subject to the following:

(i) The term "pecuniary interest" in any class of equity securities shall mean the opportunity, directly or indirectly, to profit or share in any profit derived from a transaction in the subject securities.

(ii) The term "indirect pecuniary interest" in any class of equity securities shall include, but not be limited to:

(A) securities held by members of a person's immediate family sharing the same household *provided, however,* that the presumption of such beneficial ownership may be rebutted; *see* also §240.16a-1(a)(4);

(B) a general partner's proportionate interest in the portfolio securities held by a general or limited partnership. The general partner's proportionate interest, as evidenced by the partnership agreement in effect at the time of the transaction and the partnership's most recent financial statements, shall be the greater of:

(*1*) the general partner's share of the partnership's profits, including profits attributed to any limited partnership interests held by the general partner and any other interests in profits that arise from the purchase and sale of the partnership's portfolio securities; or

(*2*) the general partner's share of the partnership capital account, including the share attributable to any limited partnership interest held by the general partner.

(C) a performance-related fee, other than an asset-based fee, received by any broker, dealer, bank, insurance company, investment company, investment adviser, investment manager, trustee or person or entity performing a similar function; *provided, however,* that no pecuniary interest shall be present where:

(*1*) the performance-related fee, regardless of when payable, is calculated based upon net capital gains and/or net capital appreciation generated from the portfolio or from the fiduciary's overall performance over a period of one year or more; and

(*2*) equity securities of the issuer do not account for more than ten percent of the market value of the portfolio. A right to a nonperformance-related fee alone shall not represent a pecuniary interest in the securities;

(D) A person's right to dividends that is separated or separable from the underlying securities. Otherwise, a right to dividends alone shall not represent a pecuniary interest in the securities;

(E) A person's interest in securities held by a trust, as specified in §240.16a-8(b); and

(F) A person's right to acquire equity securities through the exercise or conversion of any derivative security, whether or not presently exercisable.

(iii) A shareholder shall not be deemed to have a pecuniary interest in the portfolio securities held by a corporation or similar entity in which the person owns securities if the shareholder is not a controlling shareholder of the entity and does not have or share investment control over the entity's portfolio.

(3) Where more than one person subject to section 16 of the Act is deemed to be a beneficial owner of the same equity securities, all such persons must report as beneficial owners of the securities, either separately or jointly, as provided in § 240.16a-3(j). In such cases, the amount of short-swing profit recoverable shall not be increased above the amount recoverable if there were only one beneficial owner.

(4) Any person filing a statement pursuant to Section 16(a) of the Act may state that the filing shall not be deemed an admission that such person is, for purposes of Section 16 of the Act or otherwise, the beneficial owner of any equity securities covered by the statement.

(5) The following interests are deemed not to confer beneficial ownership for purposes of Section 16 of the Act:

(i) Interests in portfolio securities held by any holding company registered under the Public Utility Holding Company Act of 1935 (15 U.S.C. § 79a *et seq.*);

(ii) Interests in portfolio securities held by any investment company registered under the Investment Company Act of 1940 (15 U.S.C. § 80a-1 *et seq.*); and

(iii) Interests in securities comprising part of a broad-based, publicly traded market basket or index of stocks, approved for trading by the appropriate federal governmental authority.

(b) The term "call equivalent position" shall mean a derivative security position that increases in value as the value of the underlying equity increases, including, but not limited to, a long convertible security, a long call option, and a short put option position.

(c) The term "derivative securities" shall mean any option, warrant, convertible security, stock appreciation right, or similar right with an exercise or conversion privilege at a price related to an equity security, or similar securities with a value derived from the value of an equity security, but shall not include:

(1) rights of a pledgee of securities to sell the pledged securities;

(2) rights of all holders of a class of securities of an issuer to receive securities pro rata, or obligations to dispose of securities, as a result of a merger, exchange offer, or consolidation involving the issuer of the securities;

(3) Rights or obligations to surrender a security, or have a security withheld, upon the receipt or exercise of a derivative security or the receipt or vesting of equity securities, in order to satisfy the exercise price or the tax withholding consequences of receipt, exercise or vesting;

(4) interests in broad-based index options, broad-based index futures, and broad-based publicly traded market baskets of stocks approved for trading by the appropriate federal governmental authority;

(5) interests or rights to participate in employee benefit plans of the issuer; or

(6) rights with an exercise or conversion privilege at a price that is not fixed; or

(7) Options granted to an underwriter in a registered public offering for the purpose of satisfying over-allotments in such offering.

(d) The term "equity security of such issuer" shall mean any equity security or derivative security relating to an issuer, whether or not issued by that issuer.

(e) The term "immediate family" shall mean any child, stepchild, grandchild, parent, steppar-ent, grandparent, spouse, sibling, mother-in-law, father-in-law, son-in-law, daughter-in-law, brother-in-law, or sister-in-law, and shall include adoptive relationships.

(f) The term "officer" shall mean an issuer's president, principal financial officer, principal accounting officer (or, if there is no such accounting officer, the controller), any vice-president of the issuer in charge of a principal business unit, division or function (such as sales, administration or finance), any other officer who performs a policy-making function, or any other person who performs similar policy-making functions for the issuer. Officers of the issuer's parent(s) or subsidiaries shall be deemed officers of the issuer if they perform such policy-making functions for the issuer. In addition, when the issuer is a limited partnership, officers or employees of the general partner(s) who perform policy-making functions for the limited partnership are deemed officers of the limited partnership. When the issuer is a trust, officers or employees of the trustee(s) who perform policy-making functions for the trust are deemed officers of the trust.

Note: "Policy-making function" is not intended to include policy-making functions that are not significant. If pursuant to Item 401(b) of Regulation S-K (§ 229.401(b)) the issuer identifies a person as an "executive officer," it is presumed that the Board of Directors has made that judgment and that the persons so identified are the officers for purposes of Section 16 of the Act, as are such other persons enumerated in this paragraph (f) but not in Item 401(b).

(g) The term "portfolio securities" shall mean all securities owned by an entity, other than securities issued by the entity.

(h) The term "put equivalent position" shall mean a derivative security position that increases in value as the value of the underlying equity decreases, including, but not limited to, a long put option and a short call option position.

Rule 16a-2. Persons and Transactions Subject to Section 16

Any person who is the beneficial owner, directly or indirectly, of more than ten percent of any class of equity securities ("ten percent beneficial owner") registered pursuant to section 12 of the Act (15 U.S.C. 78*l*), any director or officer of the issuer of such securities, and any person specified in section 17(a) of the Public Utility Holding Company Act of 1935 (15 U.S.C. 79q(a)) or section 30(h) of the Investment Company Act of 1940 (15 U.S.C. 80a-29(h)), including any person specified in § 240.16a-8, shall be subject to the provisions of section 16 of the Act (15 U.S.C. 78p). The rules under Section 16 of the Act apply to any class of equity securities of an issuer whether or not registered under Section 12 of the Act. The rules under Section 16 of the Act also apply to non-equity securities as provided by the Public Utility Holding Company Act of 1935 and the Investment Company Act of 1940. With respect to transactions by persons subject to Section 16 of the Act:

(a) A transaction(s) carried out by a director or officer in the six months prior to the director or officer becoming subject to Section 16 of the Act shall be subject to Section 16 of the Act and reported on the first required Form 4 only if the transaction(s) occurred within six months of the transaction giving rise to the Form 4 filing obligation and the director or officer became subject to Section 16 of the Act solely as a result of the issuer registering a class of equity securities pursuant to Section 12 of the Act.

(b) A transaction(s) following the cessation of director or officer status shall be subject to section 16 of the Act only if:

(1) Executed within a period of less than six months of an opposite transaction subject to section 16(b) of the Act that occurred while that person was a director or officer; and

(2) Not otherwise exempted from section 16(b) of the Act pursuant to the provisions of this chapter.

Note to paragraph (b): For purposes of this paragraph, an acquisition and a disposition each shall be an opposite transaction with respect to the other.

(c) The transaction that results in a person becoming a ten percent beneficial owner is not subject to Section 16 of the Act unless the person otherwise is subject to Section 16 of the Act. A ten percent beneficial owner not otherwise subject to Section 16 of the Act must report only those transactions conducted while the beneficial owner of more than ten percent of a class of equity securities of the issuer registered pursuant to Section 12 of the Act.

(d)(1) Transactions by a person or entity shall be exempt from the provisions of Section 16 of the Act for the 12 months following appointment and qualification, to the extent such person or entity is acting as:

(i) Executor or administrator of the estate of a decedent;

(ii) Guardian or member of a committee for an incompetent;

(iii) Receiver, trustee in bankruptcy, assignee for the benefit of creditors, conservator, liquidating agent, or other similar person duly authorized by law to administer the estate or assets of another person; or

(iv) Fiduciary in a similar capacity.

(2) Transactions by such person or entity acting in a capacity specified in paragraph (d)(1) of this section after the period specified in that paragraph shall be subject to section 16 of the Act only where the estate, trust or other entity is a beneficial owner of more than ten percent of any class of equity security registered pursuant to section 12 of the Act.

Rule 16a-3. Reporting Transactions and Holdings

(a) Initial statements of beneficial ownership of equity securities required by Section 16(a) of the Act shall be filed on Form 3. Statements of changes in beneficial ownership required by that Section shall be filed on Form 4. Annual statements shall be filed on Form 5. At the election of the reporting person, any transaction required to be reported on Form 5 may be reported on an earlier filed Form 4. All such statements shall be prepared and filed in accordance with the requirements of the applicable form.

(b) A person filing statements pursuant to Section 16(a) of the Act with respect to any class of equity securities registered pursuant to Section 12 of the Act need not file an additional statement on Form 3:

(1) When an additional class of equity securities of the same issuer becomes registered pursuant to Section 12 of the Act; or

(2) When such person assumes a different or an additional relationship to the same issuer (for example, when an officer becomes a director).

(c) Any issuer that has equity securities listed on more than one national securities exchange may designate one exchange as the only exchange with which reports pursuant to Section 16(a) of the Act need be filed. Such designation shall be made in writing and shall be filed with the Commission and with each national securities exchange on which any equity security of the issuer is listed at the time of such election. The reporting person's obligation to file reports with each national securities exchange on which any equity security of the issuer is listed shall be satisfied by filing with the exchange so designated.

(d) Any person required to file a statement with respect to securities of a single issuer under both section 16(a) of the Act (15 U.S.C. 78p(a)) and either section 17(a) of the Public Utility Holding Company Act of 1935 (15 U.S.C. 79q(a)) or section 30(h) of the Investment Company Act of 1940 (15 U.S.C. 80a-29(h)) may file a single statement containing the required information, which will be deemed to be filed under both Acts.

(e) Any person required to file a statement under Section 16(a) of the Act shall, not later than the time the statement is transmitted for filing with the Commission, send or deliver a duplicate to the person designated by the issuer to receive such statements, or, in the absence of such a designation, to the issuer's corporate secretary or person performing equivalent functions.

(f)(1) A Form 5 shall be filed by every person who at any time during the issuer's fiscal year was subject to Section 16 of the Act with respect to such issuer, except as provided in paragraph (2) below. The Form shall be filed within 45 days after the issuer's fiscal year end, and shall disclose the following holdings and transactions not reported previously on Forms 3, 4 or 5:

(i) All transactions during the most recent fiscal year that were exempt from section 16(b) of the Act, except:

(A) Exercises and conversions of derivative securities exempt under either § 240.16b-3 or § 240.16b-6(b), and any transaction exempt under § 240.16b-3(d), § 240.16b-3(e), or § 240.16b-3(f) (these are required to be reported on Form 4);

(B) Transactions exempt from section 16(b) of the Act pursuant to § 240.16b-3(c), which shall be exempt from section 16(a) of the Act; and

(C) Transactions exempt from section 16(a) of the Act pursuant to another rule;

(ii) Transactions that constituted small acquisitions pursuant to § 240.16a-6(a);

(iii) all holdings and transactions that should have been reported during the most recent fiscal year, but were not; and

(iv) with respect to the first Form 5 requirement for a reporting person, all holdings and transactions that should have been reported in each of the issuer's last two fiscal years but were not, based on the reporting person's reasonable belief in good faith in the completeness and accuracy of the information.

(2) Notwithstanding the above, no Form 5 shall be required where all transactions otherwise required to be reported on the Form 5 have been reported before the due date of the Form 5.

Note: Persons no longer subject to Section 16 of the Act, but who were subject to the Section at any time during the issuer's fiscal year, must file a Form 5 unless paragraph (f)(2) is satisfied. *See also* § 240.16a-2(b) regarding the reporting obligations of persons ceasing to be officers or directors.

(g)(1) A Form 4 must be filed to report: all transactions not exempt from section 16(b) of the Act; all transactions exempt from section 16(b) of the Act pursuant to § 240.16b-3(d), § 240.16b-3(e), or § 240.16b-3(f); and all exercises and conversions of derivative securities, regardless of whether exempt from section 16(b) of the Act. Form 4 must be filed before the end of the second business day following the day on which the subject transaction has been executed.

(2) Solely for purposes of section 16(a)(2)(C) of the Act and paragraph (g)(1) of this section, the date on which the executing broker, dealer or plan administrator notifies the reporting person of the execution of the transaction is deemed the date of execution for a transaction where the following conditions are satisfied:

(i) the transaction is pursuant to a contract, instruction or written plan for the purchase or sale of equity securities of the issuer (as defined in § 16a-1(d)) that satisfies the affirmative defense conditions of § 240.10b5-1(c) of this chapter; and

(ii) the reporting person does not select the date of execution.

(3) Solely for purposes of section 16(a)(2)(C) of the Act and paragraph (g)(1) of this section, the date on which the plan administrator notifies the reporting person that the transaction has been executed is deemed the date of execution for a discretionary transaction (as defined in § 16b-3(b)(1)) for which the reporting person does not select the date of execution.

(4) In the case of the transactions described in paragraphs (g)(2) and (g)(3) of this section, if the notification date is later than the third business day following the trade date of the transaction, the date of execution is deemed to be the third business day following the trade date of the transaction.

(5) At the option of the reporting person, transactions that are reportable on Form 5 may be reported on Form 4, so long as the Form 4 is filed no later than the due date of the Form 5 on which the transaction is otherwise required to be reported.

(h) The date of filing with the Commission shall be the date of receipt by the Commission.

(i) *Signatures.* Where Section 16 of the Act, or the rules or forms thereunder, require a document filed with or furnished to the Commission to be signed, such document shall be manually signed, or signed using either typed signatures or duplicated or facsimile versions of manual signatures. Where typed, duplicated or facsimile signatures are used, each signatory to the filing shall manually sign a signature page or other document authenticating, acknowledging or otherwise adopting his or her signature that appears in the filing. Such document shall be executed before or at the time the filing is made and shall be retained by the filer for a period of five years. Upon request, the filer shall furnish to the Commission or its staff a copy of any or all documents retained pursuant to this section.

(j) Where more than one person subject to section 16 of the Act is deemed to be a beneficial owner of the same equity securities, all such persons must report as beneficial owners of the securities, either separately or jointly. Where persons in a group are deemed to be beneficial owners of equity securities pursuant to § 240.16a-1(a)(1) due to the aggregation of holdings, a single Form 3, 4 or 5 may be filed on behalf of all persons in the group. Joint and group filings must include all required information for each beneficial owner, and such filings must be signed by each beneficial owner, or on behalf of such owner by an authorized person.

(k) Any issuer that maintains a corporate website shall post on that website by the end of the business day after filing any Form 3, 4 or 5 filed under section 16(a) of the Act as to the equity securities of that issuer. Each such form shall remain accessible on such issuer's website for at least a 12-month period. In the case of an issuer that is an investment company and that does not maintain its own website, if any of the issuer's investment adviser, sponsor, depositor, trustee, administrator, principal underwriter, or any affiliated person of the investment company maintains a website that includes the name of the issuer, the issuer shall comply with the posting requirements by posting the forms on one such website.

Rule 16a-4. Derivative Securities

(a) For purposes of Section 16 of the Act, both derivative securities and the underlying securities to which they relate shall be deemed to be the same class of equity securities, *except that* the acquisition or disposition of any derivative security shall be separately reported.

(b) The exercise or conversion of a call equivalent position shall be reported on Form 4 and treated for reporting purposes as:

(1) A purchase of the underlying security; and

(2) A closing of the derivative security position.

(c) The exercise or conversion of a put equivalent position shall be reported on Form 4 and treated for reporting purposes as:

(1) A sale of the underlying security; and

(2) A closing of the derivative security position.

(d) The disposition or closing of a long derivative security position, as a result of cancellation or expiration, shall be exempt from section 16(a) of the Act if exempt from section 16(b) of the Act pursuant to § 240.16b-6(d).

Note to § 240.16a-4: A purchase or sale resulting from an exercise or conversion of a derivative security may be exempt from section 16(b) of the Act pursuant to § 240.16b-3 or § 240.16b6(b).

Rule 16a-6. Small Acquisitions

(a) Any acquisition of an equity security or the right to acquire such securities, other than an acquisition from the issuer (including an employee benefit plan sponsored by the issuer), not exceeding $10,000 in market value shall be reported on Form 5, subject to the following conditions:

(1) Such acquisition, when aggregated with other acquisitions of securities of the same class (including securities underlying derivative securities, but excluding acquisitions exempted by rule from section 16(b) or previously reported on Form 4 or Form 5) within the prior six months, does not exceed a total of $10,000 in market value; and

(2) The person making the acquisition does not within six months thereafter make any disposition, other than by a transaction exempt from section 16(b) of the Act.

(b) If an acquisition no longer qualifies for the reporting deferral in paragraph (a) of this section, all such acquisitions that have not yet been reported must be reported on Form 4 before the end of the second business day following the day on which the conditions of paragraph (a) of this section are no longer met.

Rule 16a-8. Trusts

(a) *Persons Subject to Section 16.*

(1) *Trusts.* A trust shall be subject to section 16 of the Act with respect to securities of the issuer if the trust is a beneficial owner, pursuant to § 240.16a-1(a)(1), of more than ten percent of any class of equity securities of the issuer registered pursuant to section 12 of the Act ("ten percent beneficial owner").

(2) *Trustees, Beneficiaries, and Settlors.* In determining whether a trustee, beneficiary, or settlor is a ten percent beneficial owner with respect to the issuer:

(i) such persons shall be deemed the beneficial owner of the issuer's securities held by the trust, to the extent specified by § 240.16a-1(a)(1); and

(ii) settlors shall be deemed the beneficial owner of the issuer's securities held by the trust where they have the power to revoke the trust without the consent of another person.

(b) *Trust Holdings and Transactions*. Holdings and transactions in the issuer's securities held by a trust shall be reported by the trustee on behalf of the trust, if the trust is subject to Section 16 of the Act, except as provided below. Holdings and transactions in the issuer's securities held by a trust (whether or not subject to Section 16 of the Act) may be reportable by other parties as follows:

(1) *Trusts*. The trust need not report holdings and transactions in the issuer's securities held by the trust in an employee benefit plan subject to the Employee Retirement Income Security Act over which no trustee exercises investment control.

(2) *Trustees*. If, as provided by § 240.16a-1(a)(2), a trustee subject to Section 16 of the Act has a pecuniary interest in any holding or transaction in the issuer's securities held by the trust, such holding or transaction shall be attributed to the trustee and shall be reported by the trustee in the trustee's individual capacity, as well as on behalf of the trust. With respect to performance fees and holdings of the trustee's immediate family, trustees shall be deemed to have a pecuniary interest in the trust holdings and transactions in the following circumstances:

(i) a performance fee is received that does not meet the proviso of § 240.16a-1(a)(2)(ii)(C); or

(ii) at least one beneficiary of the trust is a member of the trustee's immediate family. The pecuniary interest of the immediate family member(s) shall be attributed to and reported by the trustee.

(3) *Beneficiaries*. A beneficiary subject to Section 16 of the Act shall have or share reporting obligations with respect to transactions in the issuer's securities held by the trust, if the beneficiary is a beneficial owner of the securities pursuant to § 240.16a-1(a)(2), as follows:

(i) If a beneficiary shares investment control with the trustee with respect to a trust transaction, the transaction shall be attributed to and reported by both the beneficiary and the trust;

(ii) If a beneficiary has investment control with respect to a trust transaction without consultation with the trustee, the transaction shall be attributed to and reported by the beneficiary only; and

(iii) In making a determination as to whether a beneficiary is the beneficial owner of the securities pursuant to § 240.16a-1(a)(2), beneficiaries shall be deemed to have a pecuniary interest in the issuer's securities held by the trust to the extent of their pro rata interest in the trust where the trustee does not exercise exclusive investment control.

Note to paragraph (b)(3): Transactions and holdings attributed to a trust beneficiary may be reported by the trustee on behalf of the beneficiary, provided that the report is signed by the beneficiary or other authorized person. Where the transactions and holdings are attributed both to the trustee and trust beneficiary, a joint report may be filed in accordance with § 240.16a-3(j).

(4) *Settlors*. If a settlor subject to Section 16 of the Act reserves the right to revoke the trust without the consent of another person, the trust holdings and transactions shall be attributed to and reported by the settlor instead of the trust; *provided, however*, that if the settlor does not exercise or share investment control over the issuer's securities held by the trust, the trust holdings and transactions shall be attributed to and reported by the trust instead of the settlor.

(c) *Remainder interests*. Remainder interests in a trust are deemed not to confer beneficial ownership for purposes of Section 16 of the Act, provided that the persons with the remainder interests have no power, directly or indirectly, to exercise or share investment control over the trust.

(d) A trust, trustee, beneficiary or settlor becoming subject to Section 16(a) of the Act pursuant to this Rule also shall be subject to Sections 16(b) and 16(c) of the Act.

Rule 16a-10. Exemptions Under Section 16(a)

Except as provided in § 240.16a-6, any transaction exempted from the requirements of Section 16(a) of the Act, insofar as it is otherwise subject to the provisions of Section 16(b), shall be likewise exempt from Section 16(b) of the Act.

EXEMPTION OF CERTAIN TRANSACTIONS FROM SECTION 16(b)

Rule 16b-3. Transactions between an issuer and its officers or directors

(a) *General.* A transaction between the issuer (including an employee benefit plan sponsored by the issuer) and an officer or director of the issuer that involves issuer equity securities shall be exempt from section 16(b) of the Act if the transaction satisfies the applicable conditions set forth in this section.

(b) *Definitions.* (1) A Discretionary Transaction shall mean a transaction pursuant to an employee benefit plan that:

(i) Is at the volition of a plan participant;

(ii) Is not made in connection with the participant's death, disability, retirement or termination of employment;

(iii) Is not required to be made available to a plan participant pursuant to a provision of the Internal Revenue Code; and

(iv) Results in either an intra-plan transfer involving an issuer equity securities fund, or a cash distribution funded by a volitional disposition of an issuer equity security.

(2) An Excess Benefit Plan shall mean an employee benefit plan that is operated in conjunction with a Qualified Plan, and provides only the benefits or contributions that would be provided under a Qualified Plan but for any benefit or contribution limitations set forth in the Internal Revenue Code of 1986, or any successor provisions thereof.

(3) (i) A Non-Employee Director shall mean a director who:

(A) Is not currently an officer (as defined in § 240.16a-1(f)) of the issuer or a parent or subsidiary of the issuer, or otherwise currently employed by the issuer or a parent or subsidiary of the issuer;

(B) Does not receive compensation, either directly or indirectly, from the issuer or a parent or subsidiary of the issuer, for services rendered as a consultant or in any capacity other than as a director, except for an amount that does not exceed the dollar amount for which disclosure would be required pursuant to § 229.404(a) of this chapter;

(C) Does not possess an interest in any other transaction for which disclosure would be required pursuant to § 229.404(a) of this chapter; and

(D) Is not engaged in a business relationship for which disclosure would be required pursuant to § 229.404(b) of this chapter.

(ii) Notwithstanding paragraph (b)(3)(i) of this section, a Non-Employee Director of a closedend investment company shall mean a director who is not an "interested person" of the issuer, as that term is defined in Section 2(a)(19) of the Investment Company Act of 1940.

(4) A Qualified Plan shall mean an employee benefit plan that satisfies the coverage and participation requirements of sections 410 and 401(a)(26) of the Internal Revenue Code of 1986, or any successor provisions thereof.

(5) A Stock Purchase Plan shall mean an employee benefit plan that satisfies the coverage and participation requirements of sections 423(b)(3) and 423(b)(5), or section 410, of the Internal Revenue Code of 1986, or any successor provisions thereof.

(c) *Tax-conditioned plans.* Any transaction (other than a Discretionary Transaction) pursuant to a Qualified Plan, an Excess Benefit Plan, or a Stock Purchase Plan shall be exempt without condition.

(d) *Grants, awards and other acquisitions from the issuer.* Any transaction involving a grant, award or other acquisition from the issuer (other than a Discretionary Transaction) shall be exempt if:

(1) The transaction is approved by the board of directors of the issuer, or a committee of the board of directors that is composed solely of two or more Non-Employee Directors;

(2) The transaction is approved or ratified, in compliance with section 14 of the Act, by either: the affirmative votes of the holders of a majority of the securities of the issuer present, or represented, and entitled to vote at a meeting duly held in accordance with the applicable laws of

the state or other jurisdiction in which the issuer is incorporated; or the written consent of the holders of a majority of the securities of the issuer entitled to vote; provided that such ratification occurs no later than the date of the next annual meeting of shareholders; or

(3) The issuer equity securities so acquired are held by the officer or director for a period of six months following the date of such acquisition, provided that this condition shall be satisfied with respect to a derivative security if at least six months elapse from the date of acquisition of the derivative security to the date of disposition of the derivative security (other than upon exercise or conversion) or its underlying equity security.

(e) *Dispositions to the issuer.* Any transaction involving the disposition to the issuer of issuer equity securities (other than a Discretionary Transaction) shall be exempt, provided that the terms of such disposition are approved in advance in the manner prescribed by either paragraph (d)(1) or paragraph (d)(2) of this section.

(f) *Discretionary Transactions.* A Discretionary Transaction shall be exempt only if effected pursuant to an election made at least six months following the date of the most recent election, with respect to any plan of the issuer, that effected a Discretionary Transaction that was:

(i) An acquisition, if the transaction to be exempted would be a disposition; or

(ii) A disposition, if the transaction to be exempted would be an acquisition.

Notes to § 240.16b-3:

Note (1): The exercise or conversion of a derivative security that does not satisfy the conditions of this section is eligible for exemption from section 16(b) of the Act to the extent that the conditions of § 240.16b-6(b) are satisfied.

Note (2): Section 16(a) reporting requirements applicable to transactions exempt pursuant to this section are set forth in § 240.16a-3(f) and (g) and § 240.16a-4.

Note (3): The approval conditions of paragraphs (d)(1), (d)(2) and (e) of this section require the approval of each specific transaction, and are not satisfied by approval of a plan in its entirety except for the approval of a plan pursuant to which the terms and conditions of each transaction are fixed in advance, such as a formula plan. Where the terms of a subsequent transaction (such as the exercise price of an option, or the provision of an exercise or tax with-holding right) are provided for in a transaction as initially approved pursuant to paragraphs (d)(1), (d)(2) or (e), such subsequent transaction shall not require further specific approval.

Rule 16b-5. Bona Fide Gifts and Inheritance

Both the acquisition and the disposition of equity securities shall be exempt from the operation of Section 16(b) of the Act if they are: (a) bona fide gifts; or (b) transfers of securities by will or the laws of descent and distribution.

Rule 16b-6. Derivative Securities

(a) The establishment of or increase in a call equivalent position or liquidation of or decrease in a put equivalent position shall be deemed a purchase of the underlying security for purposes of Section 16(b) of the Act, and the establishment of or increase in a put equivalent position or liquidation of or decrease in a call equivalent position shall be deemed a sale of the underlying securities for purposes of Section 16(b) of the Act; *provided, however,*that if the increase or decrease occurs as a result of the fixing of the exercise price of a right initially issued without a fixed price, where the date the price is fixed is not known in advance and is outside the control of the recipient, the increase or decrease shall be exempt from Section 16(b) of the Act with respect to any offsetting transaction within the six months prior to the date the price is fixed.

(b) The closing of a derivative security position as a result of its exercise or conversion shall be exempt from the operation of Section 16(b) of the Act, and the acquisition of underlying securities at a fixed exercise price due to the exercise or conversion of a call equivalent position or the disposition of underlying securities at a fixed exercise price due to the exercise of a put equivalent position shall be exempt from the operation of Section 16(b) of the Act; *provided, however,* that the acquisition of underlying securities from the exercise of an out-of-the-money option, warrant, or right shall not be exempt unless the exercise is necessary to comport with the sequential exercise provisions of the Internal Revenue Code (26 U.S.C. § 422A).

Note to Paragraph (b): The exercise or conversion of a derivative security that does not satisfy the conditions of this section is eligible for exemption from section 16(b) of the Act to the extent that the conditions of § 240.16b-3 are satisfied.

(c) In determining the short-swing profit recoverable pursuant to Section 16(b) of the Act from transactions involving the purchase and sale or sale and purchase of derivative and other securities, the following rules apply:

(1) Short-swing profits in transactions involving the purchase and sale or sale and purchase of derivative securities that have identical characteristics (*e.g.*, purchases and sales of call options of the same strike price and expiration date, or purchases and sales of the same series of convertible debentures) shall be measured by the actual prices paid or received in the short-swing transactions.

(2) Short-swing profits in transactions involving the purchase and sale or sale and purchase of derivative securities having different characteristics but related to the same underlying security (*e.g.*, the purchase of a call option and the sale of a convertible debenture) or derivative securities and underlying securities shall not exceed the difference in price of the underlying security on the date of purchase or sale and the date of sale or purchase. Such profits may be measured by calculating the short-swing profits that would have been realized had the subject transactions involved purchases and sales solely of the derivative security that was purchased or solely of the derivative security that was sold, valued as of the time of the matching purchase or sale, and calculated for the lesser of the number of underlying securities actually purchased or sold.

(d) Upon cancellation or expiration of an option within six months of the writing of the option, any profit derived from writing the option shall be recoverable under Section 16(b) of the Act. The profit shall not exceed the premium received for writing the option. The disposition or closing of a long derivative security position, as a result of cancellation or expiration, shall be exempt from Section 16(b) of the Act where no value is received from the cancellation or expiration.

Rule 16b-7. Mergers, Reclassifications, and Consolidations

(a) The following transactions shall be exempt from the provisions of Section 16(b) of the Act:

(1) The acquisition of a security of a company, pursuant to a merger or consolidation, in exchange for a security of a company which, prior to the merger or consolidation, owned 85 percent or more of either

(i) the equity securities of all other companies involved in the merger or consolidation, or; in the case of a consolidation, the resulting company; or

(ii) the combined assets of all the companies involved in the merger or consolidation, computed according to their book values prior to the merger or consolidation as determined by reference to their most recent available financial statements for a 12 month period prior to the merger or consolidation, or such shorter time as the company has been in existence.

(2) The disposition of a security, pursuant to a merger or consolidation, of a company which, prior to the merger or consolidation, owned 85 percent or more of either

(i) the equity securities of all other companies involved in the merger or consolidation or; in the case of a consolidation, the resulting company; or

(ii) the combined assets of all the companies undergoing merger or consolidation, computed according to their book values prior to the merger or consolidation as determined by reference to their most recent available financial statements for a 12 month period prior to the merger or consolidation.

(b) A merger within the meaning of this section shall include the sale or purchase of substantially all the assets of one company by another in exchange for equity securities which are then distributed to the security holders of the company that sold its assets.

(c) Notwithstanding the foregoing, if a person subject to Section 16 of the Act makes any non-exempt purchase of a security in any company involved in the merger or consolidation and any non-exempt sale of a security in any company involved in the merger or consolidation within any period of less than six months during which the merger or consolidation took place, the exemption provided by this Rule shall be unavailable to the extent of such purchase and sale.

MEMBERSHIP ON NATIONAL SECURITIES EXCHANGES

Rule 19b-4. Filings with Respect to Proposed Rule Changes by Self-Regulatory Organizations

(a) Filings with respect to proposed rule changes by a self-regulatory organization, except filings with respect to proposed rule changes by self-regulatory organizations submitted pursuant to Section 19(b)(7) of the Act (15 U.S.C. 78s(b)(7)), shall be made on Form 19b-4 (§ 249.819 of this chapter).

(b) The term "stated policy, practice, or interpretation" means (1) any material aspect of the operation of the facilities of the self-regulatory organization or (2) any statement made generally available to the membership of, to all participants in, or to persons having or seeking access (including, in the case of national securities exchanges or registered securities associations, through a member) to facilities of, the self-regulatory organization ("specified persons"), or to a group or category of specified persons, that establishes or changes any standard, limit, or guideline with respect to (i) the rights, obligations, or privileges of specified persons or, in the case of national securities exchanges or registered securities associations, persons associated with specified persons, or (ii) the meaning, administration, or enforcement of an existing rule.

(c) A stated policy, practice, or interpretation of the self-regulatory organization shall be deemed to be a proposed rule change unless (1) it is reasonably and fairly implied by an existing rule of the self-regulatory organization or (2) it is concerned solely with the administration of the self-regulatory organization and is not a stated policy, practice, or interpretation with respect to the meaning, administration, or enforcement of an existing rule of the self-regulatory organization.

(d) Regardless of whether it is made generally available, an interpretation of an existing rule of the self-regulatory organization shall be deemed to be a proposed rule change if

(1) it is approved or ratified by the governing body of the self-regulatory organization and

(2) it is not reasonably and fairly implied by that rule.

(e) For the purposes of this paragraph, *new derivative securities product* means any type of option, warrant, hybrid securities product or any other security whose value is based, in whole or in part, upon the performance of, or interest in, an underlying instrument.

(1) The listing and trading of a new derivative securities product by a self-regulatory organization shall not be deemed a proposed rule change, pursuant to paragraph (c)(1) of this section, if the Commission has approved, pursuant to Section 19(b) of the Act (15 U.S.C. 78s(b)), the self-regulatory organization's trading rules, procedures and listing standards for the product class that would include the new derivative securities product and the self-regulatory organization has a surveillance program for the product class.

(2) *Recordkeeping and Reporting.*

(i) Self-regulatory organizations shall retain at their principal place of business a file, available to Commission staff for inspection, of all relevant records and information pertaining to each new derivative securities product traded pursuant to this paragraph (e) for a period of not less than five years, the first two years in an easily accessible place, as prescribed in § 240.17a-1.

(ii) When relying on this paragraph (e), a self-regulatory organization shall submit Form 19b-4(e) (17 CFR 249.820) to the Commission within five business days after commencement of trading a new derivative securities product.

(f) A proposed rule change may take effect upon filing with the Commission pursuant to Section 19(b)(3)(A) of the Act, 15 U.S.C. 78s(b)(3)(A), if properly designated by the self-regulatory organization as:

(1) Constituting a stated policy, practice, or interpretation with respect to the meaning, administration, or enforcement of an existing rule;

(2) Establishing or changing a due, fee, or other charge;

(3) Concerned solely with the administration of the self-regulatory organization;

(4) Effecting a change in an existing service of a registered clearing agency that:

(i) Does not adversely affect the safeguarding of securities or funds in the custody or control of the clearing agency or for which it is responsible; and

(ii) Does not significantly affect the respective rights or obligations of the clearing agency or persons using the service;

(5) Effecting a change in an existing order-entry or trading system of a self-regulatory organization that:

(i) Does not significantly affect the protection of investors or the public interest;

(ii) Does not impose any significant burden on competition; and

(iii) Does not have the effect of limiting the access to or availability of the system; or

(6) Effecting a change that:

(i) Does not significantly affect the protection of investors or the public interest;

(ii) Does not impose any significant burden on competition; and

(iii) By its terms, does not become operative for 30 days after the date of the filing, or such shorter time as the Commission may designate if consistent with the protection of investors and the public interest; provided that the self-regulatory organization has given the Commission written notice of its intent to file the proposed rule change, along with a brief description and text of the proposed rule change, at least five business days prior to the date of filing of the proposed rule change, or such shorter time as designated by the Commission.

(g) After instituting a proceeding to determine whether a proposed rule change should be disapproved, the Commission will afford the self-regulatory organization and interested persons an opportunity to submit additional written data, views, and arguments and may afford, in the discretion of the Commission, an opportunity to make oral presentations.

(h) Notice of orders issued pursuant to Section 19(b) of the Act will be given by prompt publication thereof, together with a statement of written reasons therefor.

(i) Self-regulatory organizations shall retain at their principal place of business a file, available to interested persons for public inspection and copying, of all filings made pursuant to this section and all correspondence and other communications reduced to writing (including comment letters) to and from such self-regulatory organization concerning any such filing, whether such correspondence and communications are received or prepared before or after the filing of the proposed rule change.

SECURITIES EXCHANGE ACT OF 1934—SELECTED FORMS

Selected Forms and Schedules

Form	Subject
10-Q	Quarterly reports pursuant to Section 13 or 15(d) of the Securities and Exchange Act of 1934
8-K	Current report pursuant to Section 13 or 15(d) of the Securities and Exchange Act of 1934
10-K	Annual report pursuant to Section 13 or 15(d) of the Securities and Exchange Act of 1934
Schedule 13D	Information required in beneficial ownership report filed pursuant to Rule 13d-1
Schedule 13E-3	Transaction statement under Section 13(e) of the Securities and Exchange Act of 1934 and Rule 13E-3
Schedule 14A	Information required in proxy statement
Schedule TO	Tender offer statement pursuant to section 14(d)(1) of the Securities Exchange Act of 1934
Schedule 14D-9	Solicitation/recommendation statement under Section 14(d)(4) of the Securities and Exchange Act of 1934
Schedule 15G	Information to be included in the document distributed pursuant to 17 CFR 240.15g-2
Form 4	Statement of changes of beneficial ownership of securities

FORM 10-Q
UNITED STATES
SECURITIES AND EXCHANGE COMMISSION
Washington, D.C. 20549
FORM 10-Q
GENERAL INSTRUCTIONS

A. Rule as to Use of Form 10-Q.

1. Form 10-Q shall be used for quarterly reports under Section 13 or 15(d) of the Securities Exchange Act of 1934 (15 U.S.C. 78m or 78o(d)), filed pursuant to Rule 13a-13 (17 CFR 240.13a-13) or Rule 15d-13 (17 CFR 240.15d-13). A quarterly report on this form pursuant to Rule 13a-13 or Rule 15d-13 shall be filed within the following period after the end of each of the first three fiscal quarters of each fiscal year, but no report need be filed for the fourth quarter of any fiscal year:

a. For accelerated filers (as defined in 17 CFR 240.12b-2):

(i) 45 days after the end of the fiscal quarter for fiscal years ending on or after December 15, 2002 and before December 15, 2004;

(ii) 40 days after the end of the fiscal quarter for fiscal years ending on or after December 15, 2004 and before December 15, 2005; and

(iii) 35 days after the end of the fiscal quarter for fiscal years ending on or after December 15, 2005; and

b. 45 days after the end of the fiscal quarter for all other issuers.

2. Form 10-Q also shall be used for transition and quarterly reports under Section 13 or 15(d) of the Securities Exchange Act of 1934, filed pursuant to Rule 13a-10 (17 CFR 240.13a-10) or Rule 15d-10 (17 CFR 240.15d-10). Such transition or quarterly reports shall be filed in accordance with the requirements set forth in Rule 13a-10 or Rule 15d-10 applicable when the registrant changes its fiscal year end.

B. Application of General Rules and Regulations.

1. The General Rules and Regulations under the Act contain certain general requirements which are applicable to reports on any form. These general requirements should be carefully read and observed in the preparation and filing of reports on this form.

2. Particular attention is directed to Regulation 12B which contains general requirements regarding matters such as the kind and size of paper to be used, the legibility of the report, the information to be given whenever the title of securities is required to be stated, and the filing of the report. The definitions contained in Rule 12b-2 (17 CFR 240.12b-2) should be especially noted. See also Regulations 13A and 15D.

C. Preparation of Report.

1. This is not a blank form to be filled in. It is a guide copy to be used in preparing the report in accordance with Rules 12b-11 (17 CFR 240.12b-11) and 12b-12 (17 CFR 240.12b-12). The Commission does not furnish blank copies of this form to be filled in for filing.

2. These general instructions are not to be filed with the report. The instructions to the various captions of the form are also to be omitted from the report as filed.

D. Incorporation by Reference.

1. If the registrant makes available to its stockholders or otherwise publishes, within the period prescribed for filing the report, a document or statement containing information meeting some or all of the requirements of Part I of this form, the information called for may be incorporated by reference from such published document or statement, in answer or partial

answer to any item or items of Part I of this form, provided copies thereof are filed as an exhibit to Part I of the report on this form.

2. Other information may be incorporated by reference in answer or partial answer to any item or items of Part II of this form in accordance with the provisions of Rule 12b-23 (17 CFR 240.12b-23).

3. If any information required by Part I or Part II is incorporated by reference into an electronic format document from the quarterly report to security holders as provided in General Instruction D, any portion of the quarterly report to security holders incorporated by reference shall be filed as an exhibit in electronic format, as required by Item 601(b)(13) of Regulation S-K.

E. Integrated Reports to Security Holders.

Quarterly reports to security holders may be combined with the required information of Form 10-Q and will be suitable for filing with the Commission if the following conditions are satisfied:

1. The combined report contains full and complete answers to all items required by Part I of this form. When responses to a certain item of required disclosure are separated within the combined report, an appropriate cross-reference should be made.

2. If not included in the combined report, the cover page, appropriate responses to Part II, and the required signatures shall be included in the Form 10-Q. Additionally, as appropriate, a cross-reference sheet should be filed indicating the location of information required by the items of the form.

3. If an electronic filer files any portion of a quarterly report to security holders in combination with the required information of Form 10-Q, as provided in this instruction, only such portions filed in satisfaction of the Form 10-Q requirements shall be filed in electronic format.

F. Filed Status of Information Presented.

1. Pursuant to Rule 13a-13(d) and Rule 15d-13(d), the information presented in satisfaction of the requirements of Items 1, 2, and 3 of Part I of this form, whether included directly in a report on this form, incorporated therein by reference from a report, document or statement filed as an exhibit to Part I of this form pursuant to Instruction D(1) above, included in an integrated report pursuant to Instruction E above, or contained in a statement regarding computation of per share earnings or a letter regarding a change in accounting principles filed as an exhibit to Part I pursuant to Item 601 of Regulation S-K (§ 229.601 of this chapter), except as provided by Instruction F(2) below, shall not be deemed filed for the purpose of Section 18 of the Act or otherwise subject to the liabilities of that section of the Act but shall be subject to the other provisions of the Act.

2. Information presented in satisfaction of the requirements of this form other than those of Items 1, 2, and 3 of Part I shall be deemed filed for the purpose of Section 18 of the Act; except that, where information presented in response to Item 1 or 2 of Part I (or as an exhibit thereto) is also used to satisfy Part II requirements through incorporation by reference, only that portion of Part I (or exhibit thereto) consisting of the information required by Part II shall be deemed so filed.

G. Signature and Filing of Report.

If the report is filed in paper pursuant to a hardship exemption from electronic filing (see Item 201 et seq. of Regulation S-T (17 CFR 232.201 et seq.), three complete copies of the report, including any financial statements, exhibits or other papers or documents filed as a part thereof, and five additional copies which need not include exhibits must be filed with the Commission. At least one complete copy of the report, including any financial statements, exhibits or other papers or documents filed as a part thereof, must be filed with each exchange on which any class of securities of the registrant is registered. At least one complete copy of the report filed with the Commission and one such copy filed with each exchange must be manually signed on the registrant's behalf by a duly authorized officer of the registrant and by the principal financial or chief accounting officer of the registrant. (See Rule 12b-11(d) (17 CFR 240.12b-11(d).) Copies not manually signed must bear typed or printed signatures. In the case where the principal executive officer, principal financial officer or chief accounting officer is also duly authorized to sign on behalf of the registrant, one signature is acceptable provided that the registrant clearly indicates the dual responsibilities of the signatory.

H. Omission of Information by Certain Wholly-Owned Subsidiaries.

If on the date of the filing of its report on Form 10-Q, the registrant meets the conditions specified in paragraph (1) below, then such registrant may omit the information called for in the items specified in paragraph (2) below.

1. Conditions for availability of the relief specified in paragraph (2) below:

a. All of the registrant's equity securities are owned, either directly or indirectly, by a single person which is a reporting company under the Act and which has filed all the material required to be filed pursuant to section 13, 14 or 15(d) thereof, as applicable;

b. During the preceding thirty-six calendar months and any subsequent period of days, there has not been any material default in the payment of principal, interest, a sinking or purchase fund installment, or any other material default not cured within thirty days, with respect to any indebtedness of the registrant or its subsidiaries, and there has not been any material default in the payment of rentals under material long-term leases; and

c. There is prominently set forth, on the cover page of the Form 10-Q, a statement that the registrant meets the conditions set forth in General Instruction H(1)(a) and (b) of Form 10-Q and is therefore filing this form with the reduced disclosure format.

2. Registrants meeting the conditions specified in paragraph (1) above are entitled to the following relief:

a. Such registrants may omit the information called for by Item 2 of Part I, Management's Discussion and Analysis of Financial Condition and Results of Operations, provided that the registrant includes in the Form 10-Q a management's narrative analysis of the results of operations explaining the reasons for material changes in the amount of revenue and expense items between the most recent fiscal year-to-date period presented and the corresponding year-to-date period in the preceding fiscal year. Explanations of material changes should include, but not be limited to, changes in the various elements which determine revenue and expense levels such as unit sales volume, prices charged and paid, production levels, production cost variances, labor costs and discretionary spending programs. In addition, the analysis should include an explanation of the effect of any changes in accounting principles and practices or method of application that have a material effect on net income as reported.

b. Such registrants may omit the information called for in the following Part II Items: Item 2, Changes in Securities; Item 3, Defaults Upon Senior Securities; and Item 4, Submission of Matters to a Vote of Security Holders.

c. Such registrants may omit the information called for by Item 3 of Part I, Quantitative and Qualitative Disclosures About Market Risk.

UNITED STATES
SECURITIES AND EXCHANGE COMMISSION
Washington, D.C. 20549

FORM 10-Q

(Mark One)

[ ]   QUARTERLY REPORT PURSUANT TO SECTION 13 OR 15(d) OF THE SECURITIES EXCHANGE ACT OF 1934

For the quarterly period ended . . . .

OR

[ ]   TRANSITION REPORT PURSUANT TO SECTION 13 OR 15(d) OF THE SECURITIES EXCHANGE ACT OF 1934

For the transition period from . . . . to . . . .
. . . .

Commission file number . . . .

. . . .
(Exact name of registrant as specified in its charter)

. . . .
(State or other jurisdiction of incorporation or
organization)   (I.R.S. Employer Identification No.)

. . . .
(Address of principal executive offices)
(Zip Code)

. . . .
(Registrant's telephone number, including area code)

. . . .
(Former name, former address and former fiscal year, if changesd since last report)

Indicate by check mark whether the registrant (1) has filed all reports required to be filed by Section 13 or 15(d) of the Securities Exchange Act of 1934 during the preceding 12 months (or for such shorter period that the registrant was required to file such reports), and (2) has been subject to such filing requirements for the past 90 days.

Yes. . . . . No. . . . .

Indicate by check mark whether the registrant is an accelerated filer (as defined in Rule 12b-2 of the Exchange Act.).

Yes. . . . . No. . . . .

APPLICABLE ONLY TO ISSUERS INVOLVED IN BANKRUPTCY

PROCEEDINGS DURING THE PRECEDING FIVE YEARS:

Indicate by check mark whether the registrant has filed all documents and reports required to be filed by Sections 12, 13 or 15(d) of the Securities Exchange Act of 1934 subsequent to the distribution of securities under a plan confirmed by a court.

Yes. . . . . No. . . . .

APPLICABLE ONLY TO CORPORATE ISSUERS:

Indicate the number of shares outstanding of each of the issuer's classes of common stock, as of the latest practicable date.

PART I—FINANCIAL INFORMATION

Item 1. Financial Statements.

Provide the information required by Rule 10-01 of Regulation S-X (17 CFR Part 210).

Item 2. Management's Discussion and Analysis of Financial Condition and Results of Operations.

Furnish the information required by Item 303 of Regulation S-K (§ 229.303 of this chapter).

Item 3. Quantitative and Qualitative Disclosures About Market Risk.

Furnish the information required by Item 305 of Regulation S-K (§ 229.305 of this chapter).

Item 4. Controls and Procedures.

Furnish the information required by Items 307 of Regulation S-K (17 CFR 229.307) and 308(c) of Regulation S-K (17 CFR 229.308(c)).

PART II—OTHER INFORMATION

Instruction. The report shall contain the item numbers and captions of all applicable items of Part II, but the text of such items may be omitted provided the responses clearly indicate the coverage of the item. Any item which is inapplicable or to which the answer is negative may be omitted and no reference thereto need be made in the report. If substantially the same information has been previously reported by the registrant, an additional report of the information on this form need not be made. The term "previously reported" is defined in Rule 12b-2 (17 CFR 240.12b-2). A separate response need not be presented in Part II where information called for is already disclosed in the financial information provided in Part I and is incorporated by reference into Part II of the report by means of a statement to that effect in Part II which specifically identifies the incorporated information.

Item 1. Legal Proceedings.

Furnish the information required by Item 103 of Regulation S-K (§ 229.103 of this chapter). As to such proceedings which have been terminated during the period covered by the report, provide similar information, including the date of termination and a description of the disposition thereof with respect to the registrant and its subsidiaries.

Instruction. A legal proceeding need only be reported in the 10-Q filed for the quarter in which it first became a reportable event and in subsequent quarters in which there have been material developments. Subsequent Form 10-Q filings in the same fiscal year in which a legal proceeding or a material development is reported should reference any previous reports in that year.

Item 2. Unregistered Sales of Equity Securities and Use of Proceeds.

(a) Furnish the information required by Item 701 of Regulation S-K (17 CFR 229.701) as to all equity securities of the registrant sold by the registrant during the period covered by the report that were not registered under the Securities Act. If the Item 701 information previously has been included in a Current Report on Form 8-K (17 CFR 249.308), however, it need not be furnished.

(b) If required pursuant to Rule 463 (17 CFR 230.463) of the Securities Act of 1933, furnish the information required by Item 701(f) of Regulation S-K (229.701(f) of this chapter).

(c) Furnish the information required by Item 703 of Regulation S-K (§ 229.703 of this chapter) for any repurchase made in the quarter covered by the report. Provide disclosures covering repurchases made on a monthly basis. For example, if the quarter began on January 16 and ended on April 15, the chart would show repurchases for the months from January 16 through February 15, February 16 through March 15, and March 16 through April 15.

Instruction. Working capital restrictions and other limitations upon the payment of dividends are to be reported hereunder.

Item 3. Defaults Upon Senior Securities.

(a) If there has been any material default in the payment of principal, interest, a sinking or purchase fund installment, or any other material default not cured within 30 days, with respect to any indebtedness of the registrant or any of its significant subsidiaries exceeding 5 percent of the total assets of the registrant and its consolidated subsidiaries, identify the indebtedness and state the nature of the default. In the case of such a default in the payment of principal, interest, or a sinking or purchase fund installment, state the amount of the default and the total arrearage on the date of filing this report.

Instruction. This paragraph refers only to events which have become defaults under the governing instruments, i.e., after the expiration of any period of grace and compliance with any notice requirements.

(b) If any material arrearage in the payment of dividends has occurred or if there has been any other material delinquency not cured within 30 days, with respect to any class of preferred stock of the registrant which is registered or which ranks prior to any class of registered securities, or with respect to any class of preferred stock of any significant subsidiary of the registrant, give the title of the class and state the nature of the arrearage or delinquency. In the case of an arrearage in the payment of dividends, state the amount and the total arrearage on the date of filing this report.

Instructions to Item 3

1. Item 3 need not be answered as to any default or arrearage with respect to any class of securities all of which is held by or for the account of the registrant or its totally held subsidiaries.

2. The information required by Item 3 need not be made if previously disclosed on a report on Form 8-K (17 CFR 249.308).

Item 4. Submission of Matters to a Vote of Security Holders.

If any matter has been submitted to a vote of security holders during the period covered by this report, through the solicitation of proxies or otherwise, furnish the following information:

(a) The date of the meeting and whether it was an annual or special meeting.

(b) If the meeting involved the election of directors, the name of each director elected at the meeting and the name of each other director whose term of office as a director continued after the meeting.

(c) A brief description of each matter voted upon at the meeting and state the number of votes cast for, against or withheld, as well as the number of abstentions and broker non-votes, as to each such matter, including a separate tabulation with respect to each nominee for office.

(d) A description of the terms of any settlement between the registrant and any other participant (as defined in Rule 14a-11 (17 CFR 240.14a-11) of Regulation 14A under the Act) terminating any solicitation subject to Rule 14a-11, including the cost or anticipated cost to the registrant.

Instructions:

1. If any matter has been submitted to a vote of security holders otherwise than at a meeting of such security holders, corresponding information with respect to such submission shall be furnished. The solicitation of any authorization or consent (other than a proxy to vote at a stockholders' meeting) with respect to any matter shall be deemed a submission of such matter to a vote of security holders within the meaning of this item.

2. Paragraph (a) need be answered only if paragraph (b) or (c) is required to be answered.

3. Paragraph (b) need not be answered if (i) proxies for the meeting were solicited pursuant to Regulation 14 under the Act, (ii) there was no solicitation in opposition to the management's nominees as listed in the proxy statement, and (iii) all of such nominees were elected. If the registrant did not solicit proxies and the board of directors as previously reported to the

Commission was re-elected in its entirety, a statement to that effect in answer to paragraph (b) will suffice as an answer thereto.

4. Paragraph (c) must be answered for all matters voted upon at the meeting, including both contested and uncontested elections of directors.

5. If the registrant has furnished to its security holders proxy soliciting material containing the information called for by paragraph (d), the paragraph may be answered by reference to the information contained in such material.

6. If the registrant has published a report containing all of the information called for by this item, the item may be answered by a reference to the information contained in such report.

Item 5. Other Information.

(a) The registrant must disclose under this item any information required to be disclosed in a report on Form 8-K during the period covered by this Form 10-Q, but not reported, whether or not otherwise required by this Form 10-Q. If disclosure of such information is made under this item, it need not be repeated in a report on Form 8-K which would otherwise be required to be filed with respect to such information or in a subsequent report on Form 10-Q.

(b) Furnish the information required by Item 401 (j) of Regulation S-K (§ 229.401).

Item 6. Exhibits.

Furnish the exhibits required by Item 601 of Regulation S-K (§ 229.601 of this chapter).

SIGNATURES*

Pursuant to the requirements of the Securities Exchange Act of 1934, the registrant has duly caused this report to be signed on its behalf by the undersigned thereunto duly authorized.

. . . .

(Registrant) . . . .

Date . . . .

(Signature)**

Date . . . .

(Signature) ** . . . .

** Print name and title of the signing officer under his signature.

FORM 8-K

UNITED STATES

SECURITIES AND EXCHANGE COMMISSION

Washington, D.C. 20549

FORM 8-K
CURRENT REPORT

Pursuant to Section 13 or 15(d) of the Securities Exchange Act of 1934

Date of Report (Date of earliest event reported) . . . .

. . . .

(Exact name of registrant as specified in its charter)

. . . .

		(IRS Employer File
(State or other jurisdiction of		Number) 70,Identification
incorporation)	(Commission	No.)

. . . .

(Address of principal executive
offices)   (Zip Code)

Registrant's telephone number, including area code . . . .

. . . .

(Former name or former address, if changed since last report.)

Check the appropriate box below if the Form 8-K filing is intended to simultaneously satisfy the filing obligation of the registrant under any of the following provisions (see General Instruction A.2. below):

[ ] Written communications pursuant to Rule 425 under the Securities Act (17 CFR 230.425)

[ ] Soliciting material pursuant to Rule 14a-12 under the Exchange Act (17 CFR 240.14a-12)

[ ] Pre-commencement communications pursuant to Rule 14d-2(b) under the Exchange Act (17 CFR 240.14d-2(b))

[ ] Pre-commencement communications pursuant to Rule 13e-4(c) under the Exchange Act (17 CFR 240.13e-4(c))

GENERAL INSTRUCTIONS

A. Rule as to Use of Form 8-K

1. Form 8-K shall be used for current reports under Section 13 or 15(d) of the Securities Exchange Act of 1934, filed pursuant to Rule 13a-11 or Rule 15d-11, and for reports of nonpublic information required to be disclosed by Regulation FD (17 CFR 243.100 and 243.101).

2. Form 8-K may be used by a registrant to satisfy its filing obligations pursuant to Rule 425 under the Securities Act, regarding written communications related to business combination transactions, or Rules 14a-12(b) or Rule 14d-2(b) under the Exchange Act, relating to soliciting materials and pre-commencement communications pursuant to tender offers, respectively, provided that the Form 8-K filing satisfies all the substantive requirements of those rules (other than the Rule 425(c) requirement to include certain specified information in any prospectus filed pursuant to such rule). Such filing is also deemed to be filed pursuant to any rule for which the box is checked. A registrant is not required to check the box in connection with Rule 14a-12(b) or Rule 14d-2(b) if the communication is filed pursuant to Rule 425. Communications filed pursuant to Rule 425 are deemed filed under the other applicable sections. See Note 2 to Rule 425, Rule 14a-12(b) and Instruction 2 to Rule 14d-2(b)(2).

B. Events to be Reported and Time for Filing of Reports

1. A report on this form is required to be filed or furnished, as applicable, upon the occurrence of any one or more of the events specified in the items in Sections 1 - 6 and 9 of this form. Unless otherwise specified, a report is to be filed or furnished within four business days after occurrence of the event. If the event occurs on a Saturday, Sunday or holiday on which the Commission is not open for business, then the four business day period shall begin to run on, and include, the first business day thereafter. A registrant either furnishing a report on this form under Item 7.01 (Regulation FD Disclosure) or electing to file a report on this form under Item 8.01 (Other Events) solely to satisfy its obligations under Regulation FD (17 CFR 243.100 and 243.101) must furnish such report or make such filing, as applicable, in accordance with the requirements of Rule 100(a) of Regulation FD (17 CFR 243.100(a)), including the deadline for furnishing or filing such report.

2. The information in a report furnished pursuant to Item 2.02 (Results of Operations and Financial Condition) or Item 7.01 (Regulation FD Disclosure) shall not be deemed to be "filed" for purposes of Section 18 of the Exchange Act or otherwise subject to the liabilities of that section, unless the registrant specifically states that the information is to be considered " filed" under the Exchange Act or incorporates it by reference into a filing under the Securities Act or the Exchange Act. If a report on Form 8-K contains disclosures under Item 2.02 or Item 7.01, whether or not the report contains disclosures regarding other items, all exhibits to such report relating to Item 2.02 or Item 7.01 will be deemed furnished, and not filed, unless the registrant specifies, under Item 9.01 (Financial Statements and Exhibits), which exhibits, or portions of exhibits, are intended to be deemed filed rather than furnished pursuant to this instruction.

3. If the registrant previously has reported substantially the same information as required by this form, the registrant need not make an additional report of the information on this form. To the extent that an item calls for disclosure of developments concerning a previously reported event or transaction, any information required in the new report or amendment about the previously reported event or transaction may be provided by incorporation by reference to the previously filed report. The term *previously reported* is defined in Rule 12b-2 (17 CFR 240.12b-2).

4. Copies of agreements, amendments or other documents or instruments required to be filed pursuant to Form 8-K are not required to be filed or furnished as exhibits to the Form 8-K unless specifically required to be filed or furnished by the applicable Item. This instruction does not affect the requirement to otherwise file such agreements, amendments or other documents or instruments, including as exhibits to registration statements and periodic reports pursuant to the requirements of Item 601 of Regulation S-K or Item 601 of Regulation S-B, as applicable.

5. When considering current reporting on this form, particularly of other events of material importance pursuant to Item 7.01 (Regulation FD Disclosure) and Item 8.01(Other Events), registrants should have due regard for the accuracy, completeness and currency of the information in registration statements filed under the Securities Act which incorporate by reference information in reports filed pursuant to the Exchange Act, including reports on this form.

6. A registrant's report under Item 7.01 (Regulation FD Disclosure) or Item 8.01 (Other Events) will not be deemed an admission as to the materiality of any information in the report that is required to be disclosed solely by Regulation FD.

C. Application of General Rules and Regulations

1. The General Rules and Regulations under the Act (17 CFR Part 240) contain certain general requirements which are applicable to reports on any form. These general requirements should be carefully read and observed in the preparation and filing of reports on this form.

2. Particular attention is directed to Regulation 12B (17 CFR 240.12b-1 *et seq.*) which contains general requirements regarding matters such as the kind and size of paper to be used, the legibility of the report, the information to be given whenever the title of securities is required to be stated, and the filing of the report. The definitions contained in Rule 12b-2 should be especially noted. See also Regulations 13A (17 CFR 240.13a-1 *et seq.*) and 15D (17 CFR 240.15d-1 *et seq.*).

3. A "small business issuer," defined under Rule 12b-2 of the Exchange Act (§ 240.12b-2 of this chapter), shall refer to the disclosure items in Regulation S-B (17 CFR 228.10 *et seq.*) and not Regulation S-K. If there is no comparable disclosure item in Regulation S-B, a small business issuer need not provide the information requested. A small business issuer shall provide the information required by Item 310 (c) and (d) of Regulation S-B in lieu of the financial information required by Item 7 of this Form.

D. Preparation of Report

This form is not to be used as a blank form to be filled in, but only as a guide in the preparation of the report on paper meeting the requirements of Rule 12b-12 (17 CFR 240.12b-12). The report shall contain the numbers and captions of all applicable items, but the text of such items may be omitted, provided the answers thereto are prepared in the manner specified in Rule 12b-13 (17 CFR 240.12b-13). All items that are not required to be answered in a particular report may be omitted and no reference thereto need be made in the report. All instructions should also be omitted.

E. Signature and Filing of Report

Three complete copies of the report, including any financial statements, exhibits or other papers or documents filed as a part thereof, and five additional copies which need not include exhibits, shall be filed with the Commission. At least one complete copy of the report, including any financial statements, exhibits or other papers or documents filed as a part thereof, shall be filed, with each exchange on which any class of securities of the registrant is registered. At least one complete copy of the report filed with the Commission and one such copy filed with each exchange shall be manually signed. Copies not manually signed shall bear typed or printed signatures.

F. Incorporation by Reference

If the registrant makes available to its stockholders or otherwise publishes, within the period prescribed for filing the report, a press release or other document or statement containing information meeting some or all of the requirements of this form, the information called for may be incorporated by reference to such published document or statement, in answer or partial answer to any item or items of this form, provided copies thereof are filed as an exhibit to the report on this form.

INFORMATION TO BE INCLUDED IN THE REPORT

Section 1 - Registrant's Business and Operations
Item 1.01 Entry into a Material Definitive Agreement.

(a) If the registrant has entered into a material definitive agreement not made in the ordinary course of business of the registrant, or into any amendment of such agreement that is material to the registrant, disclose the following information:

(1) the date on which the agreement was entered into or amended, the identity of the parties to the agreement or amendment and a brief description of any material relationship between the registrant or its affiliates and any of the parties, other than in respect of the material definitive agreement or amendment; and

(2) a brief description of the terms and conditions of the agreement or amendment that are material to the registrant.

(b) For purposes of this Item 1.01, a *material definitive agreement* means an agreement that provides for obligations that are material to and enforceable against the registrant, or rights that are material to the registrant and enforceable by the registrant against one or more other parties to the agreement, in each case whether or not subject to conditions.

Instructions.

1. Any material definitive agreement of the registrant not made in the ordinary course of the registrant's business must be disclosed under this Item 1.01. An agreement is deemed to be not made in the ordinary course of a registrant's business even if the agreement is such as ordinarily

accompanies the kind of business conducted by the registrant if it involves the subject matter identified in Item 601(b)(10)(ii)(A) - (D) of Regulation S-K (17 CFR 229.601(b)(10)(ii)(A) - (D)). An agreement involving the subject matter identified in Item 601(b)(10)(iii)(A) or (B) also must be disclosed unless Item 601(b)(10)(iii)(C) would not require the registrant to file a material agreement involving the same subject matter as an exhibit.

2. A registrant must provide disclosure under this Item 1.01 if the registrant succeeds as a party to the agreement or amendment to the agreement by assumption or assignment (other than in connection with a merger or acquisition or similar transaction).

Item 1.02 Termination of a Material Definitive Agreement.

(a) If a material definitive agreement which was not made in the ordinary course of business of the registrant and to which the registrant is a party is terminated otherwise than by expiration of the agreement on its stated termination date, or as a result of all parties completing their obligations under such agreement, and such termination of the agreement is material to the registrant, disclose the following information:

(1) the date of the termination of the material definitive agreement, the identity of the parties to the agreement and a brief description of any material relationship between the registrant or its affiliates and any of the parties other than in respect of the material definitive agreement;

(2) a brief description of the terms and conditions of the agreement that are material to the registrant;

(3) a brief description of the material circumstances surrounding the termination; and

(4) any material early termination penalties incurred by the registrant.

(b) For purposes of this Item 1.02, the term *material definitive agreement* shall have the same meaning as set forth in Item 1.01(b).

Instructions.

1. No disclosure is required solely by reason of this Item 1.02 during negotiations or discussions regarding termination of a material definitive agreement unless and until the agreement has been terminated.

2. No disclosure is required solely by reason of this Item 1.02 if the registrant believes in good faith that the material definitive agreement has not been terminated, unless the registrant has received a notice of termination pursuant to the terms of agreement.

Item 1.03 Bankruptcy or Receivership.

(a) If a receiver, fiscal agent or similar officer has been appointed for a registrant or its parent, in a proceeding under the U.S. Bankruptcy Code or in any other proceeding under state or federal law in which a court or governmental authority has assumed jurisdiction over substantially all of the assets or business of the registrant or its parent, or if such jurisdiction has been assumed by leaving the existing directors and officers in possession but subject to the supervision and orders of a court or governmental authority, disclose the following information:

(1) the name or other identification of the proceeding;

(2) the identity of the court or governmental authority;

(3) the date that jurisdiction was assumed; and

(4) the identity of the receiver, fiscal agent or similar officer and the date of his or her appointment.

(b) If an order confirming a plan of reorganization, arrangement or liquidation has been entered by a court or governmental authority having supervision or jurisdiction over substantially all of the assets or business of the registrant or its parent, disclose the following;

(1) the identity of the court or governmental authority;

(2) the date that the order confirming the plan was entered by the court or governmental authority;

(3) a summary of the material features of the plan and, pursuant to Item 9.01 (Financial Statements and Exhibits), a copy of the plan as confirmed;

(4) the number of shares or other units of the registrant or its parent issued and outstanding, the number reserved for future issuance in respect of claims and interests filed and allowed under the plan, and the aggregate total of such numbers; and

(5) information as to the assets and liabilities of the registrant or its parent as of the date that the order confirming the plan was entered, or a date as close thereto as practicable.

Instruction.

The information called for in paragraph (b)(5) of this Item 1.03 may be presented in the form in which it was furnished to the court or governmental authority.

Section 2 - Financial Information

Item 2.01 Completion of Acquisition or Disposition of Assets.

If the registrant or any of its majority-owned subsidiaries has completed the acquisition or disposition of a significant amount of assets, otherwise than in the ordinary course of business, disclose the following information:

(a) the date of completion of the transaction;

(b) a brief description of the assets involved;

(c) the identity of the person(s) from whom the assets were acquired or to whom they were sold and the nature of any material relationship, other than in respect of the transaction, between such person(s) and the registrant or any of its affiliates, or any director or officer of the registrant, or any associate of any such director or officer;

(d) the nature and amount of consideration given or received for the assets and, if any material relationship is disclosed pursuant to paragraph (c) of this Item 2.01, the formula or principle followed in determining the amount of such consideration; and

(e) if the transaction being reported is an acquisition and if a material relationship exists between the registrant or any of its affiliates and the source(s) of the funds used in the acquisition, the identity of the source(s) of the funds unless all or any part of the consideration used is a loan made in the ordinary course of business by a bank as defined by Section 3(a)(6) of the Act, in which case the identity of such bank may be omitted provided the registrant:

(1) has made a request for confidentiality pursuant to Section 13(d)(1)(B) of the Act; and

(2) states in the report that the identity of the bank has been so omitted and filed separately with the Commission.

Instructions.

1. No information need be given as to:

(i) any transaction between any person and any wholly-owned subsidiary of such person;

(ii) any transaction between two or more wholly-owned subsidiaries of any person; or

(iii) the redemption or other acquisition of securities from the public, or the sale or other disposition of securities to the public, by the issuer of such securities or by a wholly-owned subsidiary of that issuer.

2. The term *acquisition* includes every purchase, acquisition by lease, exchange, merger, consolidation, succession or other acquisition, except that the term does not include the construction or development of property by or for the registrant or its subsidiaries or the acquisition of materials for such purpose. The term *disposition* includes every sale, disposition by lease, exchange, merger, consolidation, mortgage, assignment or hypothecation of assets, whether for the benefit of creditors or otherwise, abandonment, destruction, or other disposition.

3. The information called for by this Item 2.01 is to be given as to each transaction or series of related transactions of the size indicated. The acquisition or disposition of securities is deemed the

indirect acquisition or disposition of the assets represented by such securities if it results in the acquisition or disposition of control of such assets.

4. An acquisition or disposition shall be deemed to involve a significant amount of assets:

(i) if the registrant's and its other subsidiaries' equity in the net book value of such assets or the amount paid or received for the assets upon such acquisition or disposition exceeded 10% of the total assets of the registrant and its consolidated subsidiaries; or

(ii) if it involved a business (see 17 CFR 210.11-01(d)) that is significant (see 17 CFR 210.11-01(b)).

Acquisitions of individually insignificant businesses are not required to be reported pursuant to this Item 2.01 unless they are related businesses (see 17 CFR 210.3-05(a)(3)) and are significant in the aggregate.

5. Attention is directed to the requirements in Item 9.01 (Financial Statements and Exhibits) with respect to the filing of:

(i) financial statements of businesses acquired;

(ii) *pro forma* financial information; and

(iii) copies of the plans of acquisition or disposition as exhibits to the report.

Item 2.02 Results of Operations and Financial Condition.

(a) If a registrant, or any person acting on its behalf, makes any public announcement or release (including any update of an earlier announcement or release) disclosing material non-public information regarding the registrant's results of operations or financial condition for a completed quarterly or annual fiscal period, the registrant shall disclose the date of the announcement or release, briefly identify the announcement or release and include the text of that announcement or release as an exhibit.

(b) A Form 8-K is not required to be furnished to the Commission under this Item 2.02 in the case of disclosure of material non-public information that is disclosed orally, telephonically, by webcast, by broadcast, or by similar means if:

(1) the information is provided as part of a presentation that is complementary to, and initially occurs within 48 hours after, a related, written announcement or release that has been furnished on Form 8-K pursuant to this Item 2.02 prior to the presentation;

(2) the presentation is broadly accessible to the public by dial-in conference call, by webcast, by broadcast or by similar means;

(3) the financial and other statistical information contained in the presentation is provided on the registrant's website, together with any information that would be required under 17 CFR 244.100; and

(4) the presentation was announced by a widely disseminated press release, that included instructions as to when and how to access the presentation and the location on the registrant's website where the information would be available.

Instructions.

1. The requirements of this Item 2.02 are triggered by the disclosure of material non-public information regarding a completed fiscal year or quarter. Release of additional or updated material non-public information regarding a completed fiscal year or quarter would trigger an additional Item 2.02 requirement.

2. The requirements of paragraph (e)(1)(i) of Item 10 of Regulation S-K (17 CFR 229.10(e)(1)(i)) (or paragraph (h)(1)(i) of Item 10 of Regulation S-B (17 CFR 228.10(h)(1)(i)) in the case of a small business issuer) shall apply to disclosures under this Item 2.02.

3. Issuers that make earnings announcements or other disclosures of material non-public information regarding a completed fiscal year or quarter in an interim or annual report to shareholders are permitted to specify which portion of the report contains the information required to be furnished under this Item 2.02.

4. This Item 2.02 does not apply in the case of a disclosure that is made in a quarterly report filed with the Commission on Form 10-Q (17 CFR 249.308a) (or Form 10-QSB (17 CFR 249.308b)) or an annual report filed with the Commission on Form 10-K (17 CFR 249.310) (or Form 10-KSB (17 CFR 249.310b)).

Item 2.03 Creation of a Direct Financial Obligation or an Obligation under an Off-Balance Sheet Arrangement of a Registrant.

(a) If the registrant becomes obligated on a direct financial obligation that is material to the registrant, disclose the following information:

(1) the date on which the registrant becomes obligated on the direct financial obligation and a brief description of the transaction or agreement creating the obligation;

(2) the amount of the obligation, including the terms of its payment and, if applicable, a brief description of the material terms under which it may be accelerated or increased and the nature of any recourse provisions that would enable the registrant to recover from third parties; and

(3) a brief description of the other terms and conditions of the transaction or agreement that are material to the registrant.

(b) If the registrant becomes directly or contingently liable for an obligation that is material to the registrant arising out of an off-balance sheet arrangement, disclose the following information:

(1) the date on which the registrant becomes directly or contingently liable on the obligation and a brief description of the transaction or agreement creating the arrangement and obligation;

(2) a brief description of the nature and amount of the obligation of the registrant under the arrangement, including the material terms whereby it may become a direct obligation, if applicable, or may be accelerated or increased and the nature of any recourse provisions that would enable the registrant to recover from third parties;

(3) the maximum potential amount of future payments (undiscounted) that the registrant may be required to make, if different; and

(4) a brief description of the other terms and conditions of the obligation or arrangement that are material to the registrant.

(c) For purposes of this Item 2.03, *direct financial obligation* means any of the following:

(1) a long-term debt obligation, as defined in Item 303(a)(5)(ii)(A) of Regulation S-K (17 CFR 229.303(a)(5)(ii)(A));

(2) a capital lease obligation, as defined in Item 303(a)(5)(ii)(B) of Regulation S-K (17 CFR 229.303(a)(5)(ii)(B));

(3) an operating lease obligation, as defined in Item 303(a)(5)(ii)(C) of Regulation S-K (17 CFR 229.303(a)(5)(ii)(C)); or

(4) a short-term debt obligation that arises other than in the ordinary course of business.

(d) For purposes of this Item 2.03, *off-balance sheet arrangement* has the meaning set forth in Item 303(a)(4)(ii) of Regulation S-K (17 CFR 229.303(a)(4)(ii)) or Item 303(c)(2) of Regulation S-B (17 CFR 228.303(c)(2)), as applicable.

(e) For purposes of this Item 2.03, *short-term debt obligation* means a payment obligation under a borrowing arrangement that is scheduled to mature within one year, or, for those registrants that use the operating cycle concept of working capital, within a registrant's operating cycle that is longer than one year, as discussed in Accounting Research Bulletin No. 43, Chapter 3A, *Working Capital*.

Instructions.

1. A registrant has no obligation to disclose information under this Item 2.03 until the registrant enters into an agreement enforceable against the registrant, whether or not subject to conditions, under which the direct financial obligation will arise or be created or issued. If there is no such agreement, the registrant must provide the disclosure within four business days after the occurrence of the closing or settlement of the transaction or arrangement under which the direct financial obligation arises or is created.

2. A registrant must provide the disclosure required by paragraph (b) of this Item 2.03 whether or not the registrant is also a party to the transaction or agreement creating the contingent obligation arising under the off-balance sheet arrangement. In the event that neither the registrant nor any affiliate of the registrant is also a party to the transaction or agreement creating the contingent obligation arising under the off-balance sheet arrangement in question, the four business day period for reporting the event under this Item 2.03 shall begin on the earlier of (i) the fourth business day after the contingent obligation is created or arises, and (ii) the day on which an executive officer, as defined in 17 CFR 240.3b-7, of the registrant becomes aware of the contingent obligation.

3. In the event that an agreement, transaction or arrangement requiring disclosure under this Item 2.03 comprises a facility, program or similar arrangement that creates or may give rise to direct financial obligations of the registrant in connection with multiple transactions, the registrant shall:

(i) disclose the entering into of the facility, program or similar arrangement if the entering into of the facility is material to the registrant; and

(ii) as direct financial obligations arise or are created under the facility or program, disclose the required information under this Item 2.03 to the extent that the obligations are material to the registrant (including when a series of previously undisclosed individually immaterial obligations become material in the aggregate).

4. For purposes of Item 2.03(b)(3), the maximum amount of future payments shall not be reduced by the effect of any amounts that may possibly be recovered by the registrant under recourse or collateralization provisions in any guarantee agreement, transaction or arrangement.

5. If the obligation required to be disclosed under this Item 2.03 is a security, or a term of a security, that has been or will be sold pursuant to an effective registration statement of the registrant, the registrant is not required to file a Form 8-K pursuant to this Item 2.03, *provided* that the prospectus relating to that sale contains the information required by this Item 2.03 and is filed within the required time period under Securities Act Rule 424 (§ 230.424 of this chapter).

Item 2.04 Triggering Events That Accelerate or Increase a Direct Financial Obligation or an Obligation under an Off-Balance Sheet Arrangement.

(a) If a triggering event causing the increase or acceleration of a direct financial obligation of the registrant occurs and the consequences of the event, taking into account those described in paragraph (a)(4) of this Item 2.04, are material to the registrant, disclose the following information:

(1) the date of the triggering event and a brief description of the agreement or transaction under which the direct financial obligation was created and is increased or accelerated;

(2) a brief description of the triggering event;

(3) the amount of the direct financial obligation, as increased if applicable, and the terms of payment or acceleration that apply; and

(4) any other material obligations of the registrant that may arise, increase, be accelerated or become direct financial obligations as a result of the triggering event or the increase or acceleration of the direct financial obligation.

(b) If a triggering event occurs causing an obligation of the registrant under an off-balance sheet arrangement to increase or be accelerated, or causing a contingent obligation of the registrant under an off-balance sheet arrangement to become a direct financial obligation of the registrant, and the consequences of the event, taking into account those described in paragraph (b)(4) of this Item 2.04, are material to the registrant, disclose the following information:

(1) the date of the triggering event and a brief description of the off-balance sheet arrangement;

(2) a brief description of the triggering event;

(3) the nature and amount of the obligation, as increased if applicable, and the terms of payment or acceleration that apply; and

(4) any other material obligations of the registrant that may arise, increase, be accelerated or become direct financial obligations as a result of the triggering event or the increase or acceleration of the obligation under the off-balance sheet arrangement or its becoming a direct financial obligation of the registrant.

(c) For purposes of this Item 2.04, the term *direct financial obligation* has the meaning provided in Item 2.03 of this form, but shall also include an obligation arising out of an off-balance sheet arrangement that is accrued under FASB Statement of Financial Accounting Standards No. 5 *Accounting for Contingencies* (SFAS No. 5) as a probable loss contingency.

(d) For purposes of this Item 2.04, the term *off-balance sheet arrangement* has the meaning provided in Item 2.03 of this form.

(e) For purposes of this Item 2.04, a *triggering event* is an event, including an event of default, event of acceleration or similar event, as a result of which a direct financial obligation of the registrant or an obligation of the registrant arising under an off-balance sheet arrangement is increased or becomes accelerated or as a result of which a contingent obligation of the registrant arising out of an off-balance sheet arrangement becomes a direct financial obligation of the registrant.

Instructions.

1. Disclosure is required if a triggering event occurs in respect of an obligation of the registrant under an off-balance sheet arrangement and the consequences are material to the registrant, whether or not the registrant is also a party to the transaction or agreement under which the triggering event occurs.

2. No disclosure is required under this Item 2.04 unless and until a triggering event has occurred in accordance with the terms of the relevant agreement, transaction or arrangement, including, if required, the sending to the registrant of notice of the occurrence of a triggering event pursuant to the terms of the agreement, transaction or arrangement and the satisfaction of all conditions to such occurrence, except the passage of time.

3. No disclosure is required solely by reason of this Item 2.04 if the registrant believes in good faith that no triggering event has occurred, unless the registrant has received a notice described in Instruction 2 to this Item 2.04.

4. Where a registrant is subject to an obligation arising out of an off-balance sheet arrangement, whether or not disclosed pursuant to Item 2.03 of this form, if a triggering event occurs as a result of which under that obligation an accrual for a probable loss is required under SFAS No. 5, the obligation arising out of the off-balance sheet arrangement becomes a direct financial obligation as defined in this Item 2.04. In that situation, if the consequences as determined under Item 2.04(b) are material to the registrant, disclosure is required under this Item 2.04.

Item 2.05 Costs Associated with Exit or Disposal Activities.

If the registrant's board of directors, a committee of the board of directors or the officer or officers of the registrant authorized to take such action if board action is not required, commits the registrant to an exit or disposal plan, or otherwise disposes of a long-lived asset or terminates employees under a plan of termination described in paragraph 8 of FASB Statement of Financial Accounting Standards No. 146 *Accounting for Costs Associated with Exit or Disposal Activities*

(SFAS No. 146), under which material charges will be incurred under generally accepted accounting principles applicable to the registrant, disclose the following information:

(a) the date of the commitment to the course of action and a description of the course of action, including the facts and circumstances leading to the expected action and the expected completion date;

(b) for each major type of cost associated with the course of action (for example, one-time termination benefits, contract termination costs and other associated costs), an estimate of the total amount or range of amounts expected to be incurred in connection with the action;

(c) an estimate of the total amount or range of amounts expected to be incurred in connection with the action; and

(d) the registrant's estimate of the amount or range of amounts of the charge that will result in future cash expenditures, *provided, however*, that if the registrant determines that at the time of filing it is unable in good faith to make a determination of an estimate required by paragraphs (b), (c) or (d) of this Item 2.05, no disclosure of such estimate shall be required; *provided further, however*, that in any such event, the registrant shall file an amended report on Form 8-K under this Item 2.05 within four business days after it makes a determination of such an estimate or range of estimates.

Item 2.06 Material Impairments.

If the registrant's board of directors, a committee of the board of directors or the officer or officers of the registrant authorized to take such action if board action is not required, concludes that a material charge for impairment to one or more of its assets, including, without limitation, impairments of securities or goodwill, is required under generally accepted accounting principles applicable to the registrant, disclose the following information:

(a) the date of the conclusion that a material charge is required and a description of the impaired asset or assets and the facts and circumstances leading to the conclusion that the charge for impairment is required;

(b) the registrant's estimate of the amount or range of amounts of the impairment charge; and

(c) the registrant's estimate of the amount or range of amounts of the impairment charge that will result in future cash expenditures, *provided, however*, that if the registrant determines that at the time of filing it is unable in good faith to make a determination of an estimate required by paragraphs (b) or (c) of this Item 2.06, no disclosure of such estimate shall be required; *provided further, however*, that in any such event, the registrant shall file an amended report on Form 8-K under this Item 2.06 within four business days after it makes a determination of such an estimate or range of estimates.

Instruction.

No filing is required under this Item 2.06 if the conclusion is made in connection with the preparation, review or audit of financial statements required to be included in the next periodic report due to be filed under the Exchange Act, the periodic report is filed on a timely basis and such conclusion is disclosed in the report.

Section 3 - Securities and Trading Markets

Item 3.01 Notice of Delisting or Failure to Satisfy a Continued Listing Rule or Standard; Transfer of Listing.

(a) If the registrant has received notice from the national securities exchange or national securities association (or a facility thereof) that maintains the principal listing for any class of the registrant's common equity (as defined in Exchange Act Rule 12b-2 (17 CFR 240.12b-2)) that:

- the registrant or such class of the registrant's securities does not satisfy a rule or standard for continued listing on the exchange or association;

- the exchange has submitted an application under Exchange Act Rule 12d2-2 (17 CFR 240.12d2-2) to the Commission to delist such class of the registrant's securities; or

- the association has taken all necessary steps under its rules to delist the security from its automated inter-dealer quotation system,

the registrant must disclose:

(i) the date that the registrant received the notice;

(ii) the a rule or standard for continued listing on the national securities exchange or national securities association that the registrant fails, or has failed to, satisfy; and

(iii) any action or response that, at the time of filing, the registrant has determined to take in response to the notice.

(b) If the registrant has notified the national securities exchange or national securities association (or a facility thereof) that maintains the principal listing for any class of the registrant's common equity (as defined in Exchange Act Rule 12b-2 (17 CFR 240.12b-2) that the registrant is aware of any material noncompliance with a rule or standard for continued listing on the exchange or association, the registrant must disclose:

(i) the date that the registrant provided such notice to the exchange or association;

(ii) the rule or standard for continued listing on the exchange or association that the registrant fails, or has failed, to satisfy; and

(iii) any action or response that, at the time of filing, the registrant has determined to take regarding its noncompliance.

(c) If the national securities exchange or national securities association (or a facility thereof) that maintains the principal listing for any class of the registrant's common equity (as defined in Exchange Act Rule 12b-2 (17 CFR 240.12b-2)), in lieu of suspending trading in or delisting such class of the registrant's securities, issues a public reprimand letter or similar communication indicating that the registrant has violated a rule or standard for continued listing on the exchange or association, the registrant must state the date, and summarize the contents of the letter or communication.

(d) If the registrant's board of directors, a committee of the board of directors or the officer or officers of the registrant authorized to take such action if board action is not required, has taken definitive action to cause the listing of a class of its common equity to be withdrawn from the national securities exchange, or terminated from the automated inter-dealer quotation system of a registered national securities association, where such exchange or association maintains the principal listing for such class of securities, including by reason of a transfer of the listing or quotation to another securities exchange or quotation system, describe the action taken and state the date of the action.

Instructions.

1. The registrant is not required to disclose any information required by paragraph (a) of this Item 3.01 where the delisting is a result of one of the following:

- the entire class of the security has been called for redemption, maturity or retirement; appropriate notice thereof has been given; if required by the terms of the securities, funds sufficient for the payment of all such securities have been deposited with an agency authorized to make such payments; and such funds have been made available to security holders;

- the entire class of the security has been redeemed or paid at maturity or retirement;

- the instruments representing the entire class of securities have come to evidence, by operation of law or otherwise, other securities in substitution therefor and represent no other right, except, if true, the right to receive an immediate cash payment (the right of dissenters to receive the appraised or fair value of their holdings shall not prevent the application of this provision); or

- all rights pertaining to the entire class of the security have been extinguished; *provided, however*, that where such an event occurs as the result of an order of a court or other governmental authority, the order shall be final, all applicable appeal periods shall have expired and no appeals shall be pending.

2. A registrant must provide the disclosure required by paragraph (a) or (b) of this Item 3.01, as applicable, regarding any failure to satisfy a rule or standard for continued listing on the national securities exchange or national securities association (or a facility thereof) that maintains the principal listing for any class of the registrant's common equity (as defined in Exchange Act Rule 12b-2 (17 CFR 240.12b-2)) even if the registrant has the benefit of a grace period or similar extension period during which it may cure the deficiency that triggers the disclosure requirement.

3. Notices or other communications subsequent to an initial notice sent to, or by, a registrant under Item 3.01(a), (b) or (c) that continue to indicate that the registrant does not comply with the same rule or standard for continued listing that was the subject of the initial notice are not required to be filed, but may be filed voluntarily.

4. Registrants whose securities are quoted exclusively (i.e., the securities are not otherwise listed on an exchange or association) on automated inter-dealer quotation systems are not subject to this Item 3.01 and such registrants are thus not required to file a Form 8-K pursuant to this Item 3.01 if the securities are no longer quoted on such quotation system. If a security is listed on an exchange or association and is also quoted on an automated inter-dealer quotation system, the registrant is subject to the disclosure obligations of Item 3.01 if any of the events specified in Item 3.01 occur.

Item 3.02 Unregistered Sales of Equity Securities.

(a) If the registrant sells equity securities in a transaction that is not registered under the Securities Act, furnish the information set forth in paragraphs (a) and (c) through (e) of Item 701 of Regulation S-K or Regulation S-B, as applicable (17 CFR 229.701(a) and (c) through (e) and 228.701(a) and (c) through (e), respectively). For purposes of determining the required filing date for the Form 8-K under this Item 3.02(a), the registrant has no obligation to disclose information under this Item 3.02 until the registrant enters into an agreement enforceable against the registrant, whether or not subject to conditions, under which the equity securities are to be sold. If there is no such agreement, the registrant must provide the disclosure within four business days after the occurrence of the closing or settlement of the transaction or arrangement under which the equity securities are to be sold.

(b) No report need be filed under this Item 3.02 if the equity securities sold, in the aggregate since its last report filed under this Item 3.02 or its last periodic report, whichever is more recent, constitute less than 1% of the number of shares outstanding of the class of equity securities sold. In the case of a small business issuer, no report need be filed if the equity securities sold, in the aggregate since its last report filed under this Item 3.02 or its last periodic report, whichever is more recent, constitute less than 5% of the number of shares outstanding of the class of equity securities sold.

Instructions.

1. For purposes of this Item 3.02, "the number of shares outstanding" refers to the actual number of shares of equity securities of the class outstanding and does not include outstanding securities convertible into or exchangeable for such equity securities.

2. Small business issuer is defined under Item 10(a)(1) of Regulation S-B (17 CFR 228.10(a)(1)).

Item 3.03 Material Modification to Rights of Security Holders.

(a) If the constituent instruments defining the rights of the holders of any class of registered securities of the registrant have been materially modified, disclose the date of the modification, the title of the class of securities involved and briefly describe the general effect of such modification upon the rights of holders of such securities.

(b) If the rights evidenced by any class of registered securities have been materially limited or qualified by the issuance or modification of any other class of securities by the registrant, briefly disclose the date of the issuance or modification, the general effect of the issuance or modification of such other class of securities upon the rights of the holders of the registered securities.

Instruction.

Working capital restrictions and other limitations upon the payment of dividends must be reported pursuant to this Item 3.03.

Section 4 - Matters Related to Accountants and Financial Statements

Item 4.01 Changes in Registrant's Certifying Accountant.

(a) If an independent accountant who was previously engaged as the principal accountant to audit the registrant's financial statements, or an independent accountant upon whom the principal accountant expressed reliance in its report regarding a significant subsidiary, resigns (or indicates that it declines to stand for re-appointment after completion of the current audit) or is dismissed, disclose the information required by Item 304(a)(1) of Regulation S-K or Item 304(a)(1) of Regulation S-B, as applicable, including compliance with Item 304(a)(3) of Regulation S-K or Item 304(a)(3) of Regulation S-B (17 CFR 229.304(a)(1) and (a)(3) or 228.304(a)(1) and (a)(3), respectively).

(b) If a new independent accountant has been engaged as either the principal accountant to audit the registrant's financial statements or as an independent accountant on whom the principal accountant is expected to express reliance in its report regarding a significant subsidiary, the registrant must disclose the information required by Item 304(a)(2) of Regulation S-K or Item 304(a)(2) of Regulation S-B, as applicable (17 CFR 229.304(a)(2) or 228.304(a)(2), respectively).

Instruction.

The resignation or dismissal of an independent accountant, or its refusal to stand for re-appointment, is a reportable event separate from the engagement of a new independent accountant. On some occasions, two reports on Form 8-K are required for a single change in accountants, the first on the resignation (or refusal to stand for re-appointment) or dismissal of the former accountant and the second when the new accountant is engaged. Information required in the second Form 8-K in such situations need not be provided to the extent that it has been reported previously in the first Form 8-K.

Item 4.02 Non-Reliance on Previously Issued Financial Statements or a Related Audit Report or Completed Interim Review.

(a) If the registrant's board of directors, a committee of the board of directors or the officer or officers of the registrant authorized to take such action if board action is not required, concludes that any previously issued financial statements, covering one or more years or interim periods for which the registrant is required to provide financial statements under Regulation S-X (17 CFR 210) or Regulation S-B (17 CFR 228), should no longer be relied upon because of an error in such financial statements as addressed in Accounting Principles Board Opinion No. 20, as may be modified, supplemented or succeeded, disclose the following information:

(1) the date of the conclusion regarding the non-reliance and an identification of the financial statements and years or periods covered that should no longer be relied upon;

(2) a brief description of the facts underlying the conclusion to the extent known to the registrant at the time of filing; and

(3) a statement of whether the audit committee, or the board of directors in the absence of an audit committee, or authorized officer or officers, discussed with the registrant's independent accountant the matters disclosed in the filing pursuant to this Item 4.02(a).

(b) If the registrant is advised by, or receives notice from, its independent accountant that disclosure should be made or action should be taken to prevent future reliance on a previously issued audit report or completed interim review related to previously issued financial statements, disclose the following information:

(1) the date on which the registrant was so advised or notified;

(2) identification of the financial statements that should no longer be relied upon;

(3) a brief description of the information provided by the accountant; and

(4) a statement of whether the audit committee, or the board of directors in the absence of an audit committee, or authorized officer or officers, discussed with the independent accountant the matters disclosed in the filing pursuant to this Item 4.02(b).

(c) If the registrant receives advisement or notice from its independent accountant requiring disclosure under paragraph (b) of this Item 4.02, the registrant must:

(1) provide the independent accountant with a copy of the disclosures it is making in response to this Item 4.02 that the independent accountant shall receive no later than the day that the disclosures are filed with the Commission;

(2) request the independent accountant to furnish to the registrant as promptly as possible a letter addressed to the Commission stating whether the independent accountant agrees with the statements made by the registrant in response to this Item 4.02 and, if not, stating the respects in which it does not agree; and

(3) amend the registrant's previously filed Form 8-K by filing the independent accountant's letter as an exhibit to the filed Form 8-K no later than two business days after the registrant's receipt of the letter.

Section 5 - Corporate Governance and Management

Item 5.01 Changes in Control of Registrant.

(a) If, to the knowledge of the registrant's board of directors, a committee of the board of directors or authorized officer or officers of the registrant, a change in control of the registrant has occurred, furnish the following information:

(1) the identity of the person(s) who acquired such control;

(2) the date and a description of the transaction(s) which resulted in the change in control;

(3) the basis of the control, including the percentage of voting securities of the registrant now beneficially owned directly or indirectly by the person(s) who acquired control;

(4) the amount of the consideration used by such person(s);

(5) the source(s) of funds used by the person(s), *unless* all or any part of the consideration used is a loan made in the ordinary course of business by a bank as defined by Section 3(a)(6) of the Act, in which case the identity of such bank may be omitted provided the person who acquired control:

(i) has made a request for confidentiality pursuant to Section 13(d)(1)(B) of the Act; and

(ii) states in the report that the identity of the bank has been so omitted and filed separately with the Commission.

(6) the identity of the person(s) from whom control was assumed; and

(7) any arrangements or understandings among members of both the former and new control groups and their associates with respect to election of directors or other matters.

(b) Furnish the information required by Item 403(c) of Regulation S-K (17 CFR 229.403(c)) or Item 403(c) of Regulation S-B (17 CFR 228.403(c)), as applicable.

Item 5.02 Departure of Directors or Principal Officers; Election of Directors; Appointment of Principal Officers.

(a)(1) If a director has resigned or refuses to stand for re-election to the board of directors since the date of the last annual meeting of shareholders because of a disagreement with the registrant, known to an executive officer of the registrant, as defined in 17 CFR 240.3b-7, on any matter relating to the registrant's operations, policies or practices, or if a director has been removed for cause from the board of directors, disclose the following information:

(i) the date of such resignation, refusal to stand for re-election or removal;

(ii) any positions held by the director on any committee of the board of directors at the time of the director's resignation, refusal to stand for re-election or removal; and

(iii) a brief description of the circumstances representing the disagreement that the registrant believes caused, in whole or in part, the director's resignation, refusal to stand for re-election or removal.

(2) If the director has furnished the registrant with any written correspondence concerning the circumstances surrounding his or her resignation, refusal or removal, the registrant shall file a copy of the document as an exhibit to the report on Form 8-K.

(3) The registrant also must:

(i) provide the director with a copy of the disclosures it is making in response to this Item 5.02 no later than the day the registrant file the disclosures with the Commission;

(ii) provide the director with the opportunity to furnish the registrant as promptly as possible with a letter addressed to the registrant stating whether he or she agrees with the statements made by the registrant in response to this Item 5.02 and, if not, stating the respects in which he or she does not agree; and

(iii) file any letter received by the registrant from the director with the Commission as an exhibit by an amendment to the previously filed Form 8-K within two business days after receipt by the registrant.

(b) If the registrant's principal executive officer, president, principal financial officer, principal accounting officer, principal operating officer or any person performing similar functions retires, resigns or is terminated from that position, or if a director retires, resigns, is removed, or refuses to stand for re-election (except in circumstances described in paragraph (a) of this Item 5.02), disclose the fact that the event has occurred and the date of the event.

(c) If the registrant appoints a new principal executive officer, president, principal financial officer, principal accounting officer, principal operating officer or person performing similar functions, disclose the following information with respect to the newly appointed officer:

(1) the name and position of the newly appointed officer and the date of the appointment;

(2) the information required by Items 401(b), (d), (e) and Item 404(a) of Regulation S-K (17 CFR 229.401(b), (d), (e) and 229.404(a)), or, in the case of a small business issuer, Items 401(a)(4), (a)(5), (c), and Items 404(a) and (b) of Regulation S-B (17 CFR 228.401(a)(4), (a)(5), (c), and 228.404(a) and (b), respectively); and

(3) a brief description of the material terms of any employment agreement between the registrant and that officer.

Instruction to paragraph (c).

If the registrant intends to make a public announcement of the appointment other than by means of a report on Form 8-K, the registrant may delay filing the Form 8-K containing the disclosures required by this Item 5.02(c) until the day on which the registrant otherwise makes public announcement of the appointment of such officer.

(d) If the registrant elects a new director, except by a vote of security holders at an annual meeting or special meeting convened for such purpose, disclose the following information:

(1) the name of the newly elected director and the date of election;

(2) a brief description of any arrangement or understanding between the new director and any other persons, naming such persons, pursuant to which such director was selected as a director;

(3) the committees of the board of directors to which the new director has been, or at the time of this disclosure is expected to be, named; and

(4) the information required by Item 404(a) of Regulation S-K or Item 404(a) of Regulation S-B, as applicable (17 CFR 229.404(a) or 228.404(a), respectively).

Instructions to Item 5.02.

1. The disclosure requirements of this Item 5.02 do not apply to a registrant that is a wholly-owned subsidiary of an issuer with a class of securities registered under Section 12 of the Exchange Act (15 U.S.C. 78l), or that is required to file reports under Section 15(d) of the Exchange Act (15 U.S.C. 78o(d)).

2. To the extent that any information called for in Item 5.02(c)(3) or Item 5.02(d)(3) or Item 5.02(d)(4) is not determined or is unavailable at the time of the required filing, the registrant shall include a statement this effect in the filing and then must file an amendment to its Form 8-K filing under this Item 5.02 containing such information within four business days after the information is determined or becomes available.

Item 5.03 Amendments to Articles of Incorporation or Bylaws; Change in Fiscal Year.

(a) If a registrant with a class of equity securities registered under Section 12 of the Exchange Act (15 U.S.C. 78l) amends its articles of incorporation or bylaws and a proposal for the amendment was not disclosed in a proxy statement or information statement filed by the registrant, disclose the following information:

(1) the effective date of the amendment; and

(2) a description of the provision adopted or changed by amendment and, if applicable, the previous provision.

(b) If the registrant determines to change the fiscal year from that used in its most recent filing with the Commission other than by means of:

(1) a submission to a vote of security holders through the solicitation of proxies or otherwise; or

(2) an amendment to its articles of incorporation or bylaws,

disclose the date of such determination, the date of the new fiscal year end and the form (for example, Form 10-K, Form 10-KSB, Form 10-Q or Form 10-QSB) on which the report covering the transition period will be filed.

Instruction to Item 5.03.

Refer to Item 601(b)(3) of Regulation S-K or Regulation S-B (17 CFR 229.601(b)(3) and 228.601(b)(3)), as applicable, regarding the filing of exhibits to this Item 5.03.

Item 5.04 Temporary Suspension of Trading Under Registrant's Employee Benefit Plans.

(a) No later than the fourth business day after which the registrant receives the notice required by section 101(i)(2)(E) of the Employment Retirement Income Security Act of 1974 (29 U.S.C. 1021(i)(2)(E)), or, if such notice is not received by the registrant, on the same date by which the registrant transmits a timely notice to an affected officer or director within the time period prescribed by Rule 104(b)(2)(i)(B) or 104(b)(2)(ii) of Regulation BTR (17 CFR 245.104(b)(2)(i)(B) or 17 CFR 245.104(b)(2)(ii)), provide the information specified in Rule 104(b) (17 CFR 245.104(b)) and the date the registrant received the notice required by section 101(i)(2)(E) of the Employment Retirement Income Security Act of 1974 (29 U.S.C. 1021(i)(2)(E)), if applicable.

(b) On the same date by which the registrant transmits a timely updated notice to an affected officer or director, as required by the time period under Rule 104(b)(2)(iii) of Regulation BTR (17 CFR 245.104(b)(2)(iii)), provide the information specified in Rule 104(b)(3)(iii) (17 CFR 245.104(b)(2)(iii)).

Item 5.05 Amendments to the Registrant's Code of Ethics, or Waiver of a Provision of the Code of Ethics.

(a) Briefly describe the date and nature of any amendment to a provision of the registrant's code of ethics that applies to the registrant's principal executive officer, principal financial officer, principal accounting officer or controller or persons performing similar functions and that relates to any element of the code of ethics definition enumerated in Item 406(b) of Regulations S-K and S-B (17 CFR 229.406(b) and 228.406(b), respectively).

(b) If the registrant has granted a waiver, including an implicit waiver, from a provision of the code of ethics to an officer or person described in paragraph (a) of this Item 5.05, and the waiver relates to one or more of the elements of the code of ethics definition referred to in paragraph (a) of this Item 5.05, briefly describe the nature of the waiver, the name of the person to whom the waiver was granted, and the date of the waiver.

(c) The registrant does not need to provide any information pursuant to this Item 5.05 if it discloses the required information on its Internet website within four business days following the date of the amendment or waiver and the registrant has disclosed in its most recently filed annual report its Internet address and intention to provide disclosure in this manner. If the registrant elects to disclose the information required by this Item 5.05 through its website, such information must remain available on the website for at least a 12-month period. Following the 12-month period, the registrant must retain the information for a period of not less than five years. Upon request, the registrant must furnish to the Commission or its staff a copy of any or all information retained pursuant to this requirement.

Instructions.

1. The registrant does not need to disclose technical, administrative or other non-substantive amendments to its code of ethics.

2. For purposes of this Item 5.05:

(i) The term *waiver* means the approval by the registrant of a material departure from a provision of the code of ethics; and

(ii) The term *implicit waiver* means the registrant's failure to take action within a reasonable period of time regarding a material departure from a provision of the code of ethics that has been made known to an executive officer, as defined in Rule 3b-7 (17 CFR 240.3b-7) of the registrant.

Section 6 -[Reserved]

Section 7 - Regulation FD

Item 7.01 Regulation FD Disclosure.

Unless filed under Item 8.01, disclose under this item only information that the registrant elects to disclose through Form 8-K pursuant to Regulation FD (17 CFR 243.100 through 243.103).

Section 8 -Other Events

Item 8.01 Other Events.

The registrant may, at its option, disclose under this Item 8.01 any events, with respect to which information is not otherwise called for by this form, that the registrant deems of importance to security holders. The registrant may, at its option, file a report under this Item 8.01 disclosing the nonpublic information required to be disclosed by Regulation FD (17 CFR 243.100 through 243.103).

Section 9 - Financial Statements and Exhibits

Item 9.01 Financial Statements and Exhibits.

List below the financial statements, pro forma financial information and exhibits, if any, filed as a part of this report.

(a) *Financial statements of businesses acquired.*

(1) For any business acquisition required to be described in answer to Item 2.01 of this form, financial statements of the business acquired shall be filed for the periods specified in Rule 3-05(b) of Regulation S-X (17 CFR 210.3-05(b)).

(2) The financial statements shall be prepared pursuant to Regulation S-X except that supporting schedules need not be filed. A manually signed accountant's report should be provided pursuant to Rule 2-02 of Regulation S-X (17 CFR 210.2-02).

(3) With regard to the acquisition of one or more real estate properties, the financial statements and any additional information specified by Rule 3-14 of Regulation S-X (17 CFR 210.3-14) shall be filed.

(4) Financial statements required by this item may be filed with the initial report, or by amendment not later than 71 calendar days after the date that the initial report on Form 8-K must be filed. If the financial statements are not included in the initial report, the registrant should so indicate in the Form 8-K report and state when the required financial statements will be filed. The registrant may, at its option, include unaudited financial statements in the initial report on Form 8-K.

(b) *Pro forma financial information.*

(1) For any transaction required to be described in answer to Item 2.01 of this form, furnish any pro forma financial information that would be required pursuant to Article 11 of Regulation S-X (17 CFR 210).

(2) The provisions of paragraph (a)(4) of this Item 9.01 shall also apply to pro forma financial information relative to the acquired business.

(c) *Exhibits.* The exhibits shall be deemed to be filed or furnished, depending on the relevant item requiring such exhibit, in accordance with the provisions of Item 601 of Regulation S-K (17 CFR 229.601), or Item 601 of Regulation S-B (17 CFR 228.601) and Instruction B.2 to this form.

Instruction.

During the period after a registrant has reported a business combination pursuant to Item 2.01 of this form, until the date on which the financial statements specified by this Item 9.01 must be filed, the registrant will be deemed current for purposes of its reporting obligations under Section 13(a) or 15(d) of the Exchange Act (15 U.S.C. 78m or 78o(d)). With respect to filings under the Securities Act, however, registration statements will not be declared effective and post-effective amendments to registrations statements will not be declared effective unless financial statements meeting the requirements of Rule 3-05 of Regulation S-X (17 CFR 210.3-05) are provided. In addition, offerings should not be made pursuant to effective registration statements, or pursuant to Rules 505 and 506 of Regulation D (17 CFR 230.505 and 230.506) where any purchasers are not accredited investors under Rule 501(a) of that Regulation, until the audited financial statements required by Rule 3-05 of Regulation S-X (17 CFR 210.3-05) are filed; *provided, however,* that the following offerings or sales of securities may proceed notwithstanding that financial statements of the acquired business have not been filed:

(a) offerings or sales of securities upon the conversion of outstanding convertible securities or upon the exercise of outstanding warrants or rights;

(b) dividend or interest reinvestment plans;

(c) employee benefit plans;

(d) transactions involving secondary offerings; or

(e) sales of securities pursuant to Rule 144 (17 CFR 230.144).

SIGNATURES

Pursuant to the requirements of the Securities Exchange Act of 1934, the registrant has duly caused this report to be signed on its behalf by the undersigned hereunto duly authorized.

. . . .

(Registrant)

Date . . . .

(Signature)*

_____

* Print name and title of the signing officer under his signature.

FORM 10-K

SECURITIES AND EXCHANGE COMMISSION

Washington, D.C. 20549

FORM 10-K

Annual Report Pursuant to Section 13 or 15(d) of the Securities Exchange Act of 1934

GENERAL INSTRUCTIONS

A. Rule as to Use of Form 10-K.

(1) This Form shall be used for annual reports pursuant to Section 13 or 15(d) of the Securities Exchange Act of 1934 (15 U.S.C. 78m or 78o(d)) (the "Act") for which no other form is prescribed. This Form also shall be used for transition reports filed pursuant to Section 13 or 15(d) of the Act.

(2) Annual reports on this Form shall be filed within the following period:

(a) For accelerated filers (as defined in 17 CFR 240.12b-2):

(i) 90 days after the end of the fiscal year covered by the report for fiscal years ending on or after December 15, 2002 and before December 15, 2003;

(ii) 75 days after the end of the fiscal year covered by the report for fiscal years ending on or after December 15, 2003 and before December 15, 2004; and

(iii) 60 days after the end of the fiscal year covered by the report for fiscal years ending on or after December 15, 2004; and

(b) 90 days after the end of the fiscal year covered by the report for all other registrants.

(3) Transition reports on this Form shall be filed in accordance with the requirements set forth in Rule 13a-10 (17 CFR 240.13a-10) or Rule 15d-10 (17 CFR 240.15d-10) applicable when the registrant changes its fiscal year end.

(4) Notwithstanding paragraphs (2) and (3) of this General Instruction A., all schedules required by Article 12 of Regulation S-X (17 CFR 210.12-01 - 210.12-29) may, at the option of the registrant, be filed as an amendment to the report not later than 30 days after the applicable due date of the report.

B. Application of General Rules and Regulations.

(1) The General Rules and Regulations under the Act (17 CFR 240) contain certain general requirements which are applicable to reports on any form. These general requirements should be carefully read and observed in the preparation and filing of reports on this Form.

(2) Particular attention is directed to Regulation 12B which contains general requirements regarding matters such as the kind and size of paper to be used, the legibility of the report, the information to be given whenever the title of securities is required to be stated, and the filing of the report. The definitions contained in Rule 12b-2 should be especially noted. *See also* Regulations 13A and 15D.

C. Preparation of Report.

(1) This Form is not to be used as a blank form to be filled in, but only as a guide in the preparation of the report on paper meeting the requirements of Rule 12b-12. Except as provided in General Instruction G, the answers to the items shall be prepared in the manner specified in Rule 12b-13.

(2) Except where information is required to be given for the fiscal year or as of a specified date, it shall be given as of the latest practicable date.

(3) Attention is directed to Rule 12b-20, which states: "In addition to the information expressly required to be included in a statement or report, there shall be added such further

material information, if any, as may be necessary to make the required statements, in the light of the circumstances under which they are made, not misleading."

D. Signature and Filing of Report.

(1) Three complete copies of the report, including financial statements, financial statement schedules, exhibits, and all other papers and documents filed as a part thereof, and five additional copies which need not include exhibits, shall be filed with the Commission. At least one complete copy of the report, including financial statements, financial statement schedules, exhibits, and all other papers and documents filed as a part thereof, shall be filed with each exchange on which any class of securities of the registrant is registered. At least one complete copy of the report filed with the Commission and one such copy filed with each exchange shall be manually signed. Copies not manually signed shall bear typed or printed signatures.

(2) (a) The report must be signed by the registrant, and on behalf of the registrant by its principal executive officer or officers, its principal financial officer or officers, its controller or principal accounting officer, and by at least the majority of the board of directors or persons performing similar functions. Where the registrant is a limited partnership, the report must be signed by the majority of the board of directors of any corporate general partner who signs the report.

(b) The name of each person who signs the report shall be typed or printed beneath his signature. Any person who occupies more than one of the specified positions shall indicate each capacity in which he signs the report. Attention is directed to Rule 12b-11 (17 CFR 240.12b-11) concerning manual signatures and signatures pursuant to powers of attorney.

(3) Registrants are requested to indicate in a transmittal letter with the Form 10-K whether the financial statements in the report reflect a change from the preceding year in any accounting principles or practices, or in the method of applying any such principles or practices.

E. Disclosure With Respect to Foreign Subsidiaries.

Information required by any item or other requirement of this form with respect to any foreign subsidiary may be omitted to the extent that the required disclosure would be detrimental to the registrant. However, financial statements and financial statement schedules, otherwise required, shall not be omitted pursuant to this Instruction. Where information is omitted pursuant to this Instruction, a statement shall be made that such information has been omitted and the names of the subsidiaries involved shall be separately furnished to the Commission. The Commission may, in its discretion, call for justification that the required disclosure would be detrimental.

F. Information as to Employee Stock Purchase, Savings and Similar Plans.

Attention is directed to Rule 15d-21 which provides that separate annual and other reports need not be filed pursuant to Section 15(d) of the Act with respect to any employee stock purchase, savings or similar plan if the issuer of the stock or other securities offered to employees pursuant to the plan furnishes to the Commission the information and documents specified in the Rule.

G. Information to be Incorporated by Reference.

(1) Attention is directed to Rule 12b-23 which provides for the incorporation by reference of information contained in certain documents in answer or partial answer to any item of a report.

(2) The information called for by Parts I and II of this Form (Items 1 through 9A or any portion thereof) may, at the registrant's option, be incorporated by reference from the registrant's annual report to security holders furnished to the Commission pursuant to Rule 14a-3(b) or Rule 14c-3(a) or from the registrant's annual report to security holders, even if not furnished to the Commission pursuant to Rule 14a-3(b) or Rule 14c-3(a), provided such annual report contains the information required by Rule 14a-3.

Note 1.—In order to fulfill the requirements of Part 1 of Form 10-K, the incorporated portion of the annual report to security holders must contain the information required by Items 1-3 of Form 10-K, to the extent applicable.

Note 2.—If any information required by Part I or Part II is incorporated by reference into an electronic format document from the annual report to security holders as provided in General Instruction G, any portion of the annual report to security holders incorporated by reference shall be filed as en exhibit in electronic format, as required by Item 601(b)(13) of Regulation S-K.

(3) The information required by Part III (Items 10, 11, 12, 13 and 14) may be incorporated by reference from the registrant's definitive proxy statement (filed or to be filed pursuant to Regulation 14A) or definitive information statement (filed or to be filed pursuant to Regulation 14C) which involves the election of directors, if such definitive proxy statement or information statement is filed with the Commission not later than 120 days after the end of the fiscal year covered by the Form 10-K. However, if such definitive proxy statement or information statement is not filed with the Commission in the 120-day period or is not required to be filed with the Commission by virtue of Rule 3a12-3(b) under the Exchange Act, the Items comprising the Part III information must be filed as part of the Form 10-K, or as an amendment to the Form 10-K, not later than the end of the 120-day period. It should be noted that the information regarding executive officers required by Item 401 of Regulation S-K (§ 229.401 of this chapter) may be included in Part I of Form 10-K under an appropriate caption. See Instruction 3 to Item 401(b) of Regulation S-K (§-229.401(b) of this chapter).

(4) No item numbers of captions of items need be contained in the material incorporated by reference into the report. However, the registrant's attention is directed to Rule 12b-23(e) (17 CFR 240.12b(e)) regarding the specific disclosure required in the report concerning information incorporated by reference. When the registrant combines all of the information in Parts I and II of this Form (Items 1 through 9A) by incorporation by reference from the registrant's annual report to security holders and all of the information in Part III of this Form (Items 10 through 14) by incorporating by reference from a definitive proxy statement or information statement involving the election of directors, then, notwithstanding General Instruction C(1), this Form shall consist of the facing or cover page, those sections incorporated from the annual report to security holders, the proxy or information statement, and the information, if any, required by Part IV of this Form, signatures, and a cross-reference sheet setting forth the item numbers and captions in Parts I, II and III of this Form and the page and/or pages in the referenced materials where the corresponding information appears.

H. Integrated Reports to Security Holders.

Annual reports to security holders may be combined with the required information of Form 10-K and will be suitable for filing with the Commission if the following conditions are satisfied:

(1) The combined report contains full and complete answers to all items required by Form 10-K. When responses to a certain item of required disclosure are separated within the combined report, an appropriate cross-reference should be made. If the information required by Part III of Form 10-K is omitted by virtue of General Instruction G, a definitive proxy or information statement shall be filed.

(2) The cover page and the required signatures are included. As appropriate, a cross-reference sheet should be filed indicating the location of information required by the items of the Form.

(3) If an electronic filer files any portion of an annual report to security holders in combination with the required information of Form 10-K, as provided in this instruction, only such portions filed in satisfaction of the Form 10-K requirements shall be filed in electronic format.

I. Omission of Information by Certain Wholly-Owned Subsidiaries.

If, on the date of the filing of its report on Form 10-K, the registrant meets the conditions specified in paragraph (1) below, then such registrant may furnish the abbreviated narrative disclosure specified in paragraph (2) below.

(1) Conditions for availability of the relief specified in paragraph (2) below.

(a) All of the registrant's equity securities are owned, either directly or indirectly, by a single person which is a reporting company under the Act and which has filed all the material required to be filed pursuant to section 13, 14, or 15(d) thereof, as applicable, and which is named in conjunction with the registrant's description of its business;

(b) During the preceding thirty-six calendar months and any subsequent period of days, there has not been any material default in the payment of principal, interest, a sinking or purchase fund installment, or any other material default not cured within thirty days, with respect to any indebtedness of the registrant or its subsidiaries, and there has not been any material default in the payment of rentals under material long-term leases; and

(c) There is prominently set forth, on the cover page of the Form 10-K, a statement that the registrant meets the conditions set forth in General Instruction (I)(1)(a) and (b) of Form 10-K and is therefore filing this Form with the reduced disclosure format.

(2) Registrants meeting the conditions specified in paragraph (1) above are entitled to the following relief:

(a) Such registrants may omit the information called for by Item 6, Selected Financial Data, and Item 7, Management's Discussion and Analysis of Financial Condition and Results of Operations provided that the registrant includes in the Form 10-K a management's narrative analysis of the results of operations explaining the reasons for material changes in the amount of revenue and expense items between the most recent fiscal year presented and the fiscal year immediately preceding it. Explanations of material changes should include, but not be limited to, changes in the various elements which determine revenue and expense levels such as unit sales volume, prices charged and paid, production levels, production cost variances, labor costs and discretionary spending programs. In addition, the analysis should include an explanation of the effect of any changes in accounting principles and practices or method of application that have a material effect on net income as reported.

(b) Such registrants may omit the list of subsidiaries exhibit required by Item 601 of Regulation S-K (§ 229.601 of this chapter).

(c) Such registrants may omit the information called for by the following otherwise required Items: Item 4, Submission of Matters to a Vote of Security Holders; Item 10, Directors and Executive Officers of the Registrant; Item 11, Executive Compensation; Item 12, Security Ownership of Certain Beneficial Owners and Management; and Item 13, Certain Relationships and Related Transactions.

(d) In response to Item 1, Business, such registrant only need furnish a brief description of the business done by the registrant and its subsidiaries during the most recent fiscal year which will, in the opinion of management, indicate the general nature and scope of the business of the registrant and its subsidiaries, and in response to Item 2, Properties, such registrant only need furnish a brief description of the material properties of the registrant and its subsidiaries to the extent, in the opinion of the management, necessary to an understanding of the business done by the registrant and its subsidiaries.

UNITED STATES
SECURITIES AND EXCHANGE COMMISSION
Washington, D.C. 20549

FORM 10-K

(Mark One)

[ ]   ANNUAL REPORT PURSUANT TO SECTION 13 OR 15(d) OF THE SECURITIES EXCHANGE ACT
OF 1934

For the fiscal year ended . . . .

OR

[ ]   TRANSITION REPORT PURSUANT TO SECTION 13 OR 15(d) OF THE SECURITIES EXCHANGE
ACT OF 1934

For the transition period from . . . . to . . . .

Commission file number . . . .

. . . .

(Exact name of registrant as specified in its charter)

. . . . State or other jurisdiction of   (I.R.S. Employer . . . .
. . . . incorporation or organization   Identification No.) . . . .
. . . .
(Address of principal executive offices) . . . .   (Zip Code) . . . . . .

Registrant's telephone number, including area code . . . .

Securities registered pursuant to Section 12(b) of the Act:

Title of each class   Name of each exchange on which registered

. . . .
. . . .

Securities registered pursuant to section 12(g) of the Act:

. . . .
(Title of class)

. . . .
(Title of class)

. . . .

Indicate by check mark whether the registrant (1) has filed all reports required to be filed by Section 13 or 15(d) of the Securities Exchange Act of 1934 during the preceding 12 months (or for such shorter period that the registrant was required to file such reports), and (2) has been subject to such filing requirements for the past 90 days. Yes . . . . No . . . .

Indicate by check mark if disclosure of delinquent filers pursuant to Item 405 of Regulation S-K (§ 229.405 of this chapter) is not contained herein, and will not be contained, to the best of registrant's knowledge, in definitive proxy or information statements incorporated by reference in Part III of this Form 10-K or any amendment to this Form 10-K. [   ]

Indicate by check mark whether the registrant is an accelerated filer (as defined in Rule 12b-2 of the Act).

Yes ___. No ___.

State the aggregate market value of the voting and non-voting common equity held by non-affiliates computed by reference to the price at which the common equity was last sold, or the average bid and asked price of such common equity, as of the last business day of the registrant's most recently completed second fiscal quarter.

Note.—If a determination as to whether a particular person or entity is an affiliate cannot be made without involving unreasonable effort and expense, the aggregate market value of the common stock held by non-affiliates may be calculated on the basis of assumptions reasonable under the circumstances, provided that the assumptions are set forth in this Form.

APPLICABLE ONLY TO REGISTRANTS INVOLVED IN BANKRUPTCY

PROCEEDINGS DURING THE PRECEDING FIVE YEARS:

Indicate by check mark whether the registrant has filed all documents and reports required to be filed by Section 12, 13 or 15(d) of the Securities Exchange Act of 1934 subsequent to the distribution of securities under a plan confirmed by a court.

YES . . . . NO . . . .

(APPLICABLE ONLY TO CORPORATE REGISTRANTS)

Indicate the number of shares outstanding of each of the registrant's classes of common stock, as of the latest practicable date.

DOCUMENTS INCORPORATED BY REFERENCE

List hereunder the following documents if incorporated by reference and the Part of the Form 10-K (e.g., Part I, Part II, etc.) into which the document is incorporated: (1) Any annual report to security holders; (2) Any proxy or information statement; and (3) Any prospectus filed pursuant to Rule 424(b) or (c) under the Securities Act of 1933. The listed documents should be clearly described for identification purposes (e.g., annual report to security holders for fiscal year ended December 24, 1980).

PART I

[See General Instruction G(2)]

Item 1. Business.

Furnish the information required by Item 101 of Regulation S-K (§ 229.101 of this chapter) except that the discussion of the development of the registrant's business need only include developments since the beginning of the fiscal year for which this report is filed.

Item 2. Properties.

Furnish the information required by Item 102 of Regulation S-K (§ 229.102 of this chapter).

Item 3. Legal Proceedings.

(a) Furnish the information required by Item 103 of Regulation S-K (§ 229.103 of this chapter).

(b) As to any proceeding that was terminated during the fourth quarter of the fiscal year covered by this report, furnish information similar to that required by Item 103 of Regulation S-K (§ 229.103 of this chapter), including the date of termination and a description of the disposition thereof with respect to the registrant and its subsidiaries.

Item 4. Submission of Matters to a Vote of Security Holders.

If any matter was submitted during the fourth quarter of the fiscal year covered by this report to a vote of security holders, through the solicitation of proxies or otherwise, furnish the following information:

(a) The date of the meeting and whether it was an annual or special meeting.

(b) If the meeting involved the election of directors, the name of each director elected at the meeting and the name of each other director whose term of office as a director continued after the meeting.

(c) A brief description of each matter voted upon at the meeting and state the number of votes cast for, against or withheld, as well as the number of abstentions and broker non-votes as to each such matter, including a separate tabulation with respect to each nominee for office.

(d) A description of the terms of any settlement between the registrant and any other participant (as defined in Rule 14a-11 (17 CFR 240.14a-11) of Regulation 14A under the Act) terminating any solicitation subject to Rule 14a-11, including the cost or anticipated cost to the registrant.

Instructions:

1. If any matter has been submitted to a vote of security holders otherwise than at a meeting of such security holders, corresponding information with respect to such submission shall be furnished. The solicitation of any authorization or consent (other than a proxy to vote at a stockholders' meeting) with respect to any matter shall be deemed a submission of such matter to a vote of security holders within the meaning of this item.

2. Paragraph (a) need be answered only if paragraph (b) or (c) is required to be answered.

3. Paragraph (b) need not be answered if (i) proxies for the meeting were solicited pursuant to Regulation 14A under the Act, (ii) there was no solicitation in opposition to the management's nominees as listed in the proxy statement, and (iii) all of such nominees were elected. If the registrant did not solicit proxies and the board of directors as previously reported to the Commission was re-elected in its entirety, a statement to that effect in answer to paragraph (b) will suffice as an answer thereto.

4. Paragraph (c) must be answered for all matters voted upon at the meeting, including both contested and uncontested elections of directors.

5. If the registrant has furnished to its security holders proxy soliciting material containing the information called for by paragraph (d), the paragraph may be answered by reference to the information contained in such material.

6. If the registrant has published a report containing all of the information called for by this item, the item may be answered by a reference to the information contained in such report.

PART II

[See General Instruction G(2)]

Item 5. Market for Registrant's Common Equity, Related Stockholder Matters and Issuer Purchases of Equity Securities.

(a) Furnish the information required by Item 201 of Regulation S-K (17 CFR 229.201) and Item 701 of Regulation S-K (17 CFR 229.701) as to all equity securities of the registrant sold by the registrant during the period covered by the report that were not registered under the Securities Act. If the Item 701 information previously has been included in a Quarterly Report on Form 10-Q or 10-QSB (17 CFR 249.308a or 249.308b), or in a Current Report on Form 8-K (17 CFR 249.308), it need not be furnished.

(b) If required pursuant to Rule 463 (17 CFR 230.463) of the Securities Act of 1933, furnish the information required by Item 701(f) of Regulation S-K (229.701(f) of this chapter).

(c) Furnish the information required by Item 703 of Regulation S-K (§ 229.703 of this chapter) for any repurchase made in a month within the fourth quarter of the fiscal year covered by the report. Provide disclosures covering repurchases made on a monthly basis. For example, if the fourth quarter began on January 16 and ended on April 15, the chart would show repurchases for the months from January 16 through February 15, February 16 through March 15, and March 16 through April 15.

Item 6. Selected Financial Data.

Furnish the information required by Item 301 of Regulation S-K (§ 229.301 of this chapter).

Item 7. Management's Discussion and Analysis of Financial Condition and Results of Operation.

Furnish the information required by Item 303 of Regulation S-K (§ 229.303 of this chapter).

Item 7A. Quantitative and Qualitative Disclosures About Market Risk.

Furnish the information required by Item 305 of Regulation S-K (§ 229.305 of this chapter).

Item 8. Financial Statements and Supplementary Data.

Furnish financial statements meeting the requirements of Regulation S-X (§ 210 of this chapter), except § 210.3-05 and Article 11 thereof, and the supplementary financial information required by Item 302 of Regulation S-K (§ 229.302 of this chapter). Financial statements of the registrant and its subsidiaries consolidated (as required by Rule 14a-3(b)) shall be filed under this item. Other financial statements and schedules required under Regulation S-X may be filed as "Financial Statement Schedules" pursuant to Item 13, Exhibits, Financial Statement Schedules, and Reports on Form 8-K, of this Form.

Notwithstanding the above, if the issuer is subject to the reporting provisions of Section 15(d) and such obligation results solely from the issuer having filed a registration statement on Form S-18 which became effective under the Securities Act of 1933 during the last fiscal year, or such obligation applies as to the first or second fiscal year after the registration statement on Form S-18 became effective solely because the issuer had on the first day of the pertinent fiscal year 300 or more record holders of any of its securities to which the Form S-18 related, audited financial statements for the issuer, or for the issuer and its predecessors, may be presented as provided below. The report of the independent accountant shall in all events comply with the requirements of Article 2 of Regulation S-X.

(a) A Form 10-K filed for the fiscal year during which the registrant had a registration statement on Form S-18 become effective may include the following financial statements prepared in accordance with generally accepted accounting principles:

(1) A balance sheet as of the end of each of the two most recent fiscal years; and

(2) Consolidated statements of income, statements of cash flows, and statements of other stockholders' equity for each of the two fiscal years preceding the date of the most recent audited balance sheet being filed.

(b) A Form 10-K filed for the first fiscal year after the registrant had a registration statement on Form S-18 become effective may include financial statements prepared as follows:

(1) Financial statements for the most recent fiscal year prepared in accordance with Regulation S-X, Form and Content of and Requirements for Financial Statements; and

(2) Financial statements previously disclosed in accordance with paragraph (a) for the prior year. These statements do not need to include the compliance items and schedules of Regulation S-X, but should be recast to show the same line items as are set forth for the most recent fiscal year.

(c) A Form 10-K filed for the second fiscal year after the registrant had a registration statement on Form S-18 become effective may include financial statements for the two most recent fiscal years prepared in accordance with Regulation S-X (17 CFR 210).

Item 9. Changes in and Disagreements With Accountants on Accounting and Financial Disclosure.

Furnish the information required by Item 304(b) of Regulation S-K (§ 229.304(b) of this chapter).

Item 9A. Controls and Procedures.

Furnish the information required by Items 307 and 308 of Regulation S-K (17 CFR 229.307 and 229.308).

Item 9B. Other Information.

The registrant must disclose under this item any information required to be disclosed in a report on Form 8-K during the fourth quarter of the year covered by this Form 10-K, but not reported, whether or not otherwise required by this Form 10-K. If disclosure of such information is made under this item, it need not be repeated in a report on Form 8-K which would otherwise be required to be filed with respect to such information or in a subsequent report on Form 10-K.

PART III

[See General Instruction G(3)]

Item 10. Directors and Executive Officers of the Registrant.

Furnish the information required by Items 401, 405 and 406 of Regulation S-K (§§ 229.401, 229.405 and 229.406 of this chapter).

Instruction

Checking the box provided on the cover page of this Form to indicate that Item 405 disclosure of delinquent Form 3, 4, or 5 filers is not contained herein is intended to facilitate Form processing and review. Failure to provide such indication will not create liability for violation of the federal securities laws. The space should be checked only if there is no disclosure in this Form of reporting person delinquencies in response to Item 405 and the registrant, at the time of filing the Form 10-K, has reviewed the information necessary to ascertain, and has determined that, Item 405 disclosure is not expected to be contained in Part III of the Form 10-K or incorporated by reference.

Item 11. Executive Compensation.

Furnish the information required by Item 402 of Regulations S-K (§ 229.402) of this chapter.

Item 12. Security Ownership of Certain Beneficial Owners and Management and Related Stockholder Matters.

Furnish the information required by Item 201(d) of Regulation S-K (§ 229.201(d) of this chapter) and by Item 403 of Regulation S-K (§ 229.403 of this chapter).

Item 13. Certain Relationships and Related Transactions.

Furnish the information required by Item 404 of Regulation S-K (§ 229.404 of this chapter).

Item 14. Principal Accountant Fees and Services.

Furnish the information required by Item 9(e) of Schedule 14A (-240.14a-101 of this chapter).

(1) Disclose, under the caption *Audit Fees*, the aggregate fees billed for each of the last two fiscal years for professional services rendered by the principal accountant for the audit of the registrant's annual financial statements and review of financial statements included in the registrant's Form 10-Q (17 CFR 249.308a) or 10-QSB (17 CFR 249.308b) or services that are normally provided by the accountant in connection with statutory and regulatory filings or engagements for those fiscal years.

(2) Disclose, under the caption *Audit-Related Fees*, the aggregate fees billed in each of the last two fiscal years for assurance and related services by the principal accountant that are reasonably related to the performance of the audit or review of the registrant's financial statements and are not reported under Item 9(e)(1) of Schedule 14A. Registrants shall describe the nature of the services comprising the fees disclosed under this category.

(3) Disclose, under the caption *Tax Fees*, the aggregate fees billed in each of the last two fiscal years for professional services rendered by the principal accountant for tax compliance, tax advice, and tax planning. Registrants shall describe the nature of the services comprising the fees disclosed under this category.

(4) Disclose, under the caption *All Other Fees*, the aggregate fees billed in each of the last two fiscal years for products and services provided by the principal accountant, other than the services reported in Items 9(e)(1) through 9(e)(3) of Schedule 14A. Registrants shall describe the nature of the services comprising the fees disclosed under this category.

(5)(i) Disclose the audit committee's pre-approval policies and procedures described in paragraph (c)(7)(i) of Rule 2-01 of Regulation S-X.

(ii) Disclose the percentage of services described in each of Items 9(e)(2) through 9(e)(4) of Schedule 14A that were approved by the audit committee pursuant to paragraph (c)(7)(i)(C) of Rule 2-01 of Regulation S-X.

(6) If greater than 50 percent, disclose the percentage of hours expended on the principal accountant's engagement to audit the registrant's financial statements for the most recent fiscal year that were attributed to work performed by persons other than the principal accountant's full-time, permanent employees.

Instruction to Item 14.

A registrant that is an Asset-Backed Issuer (as defined in § 240.13a-14(g) and § 240.15d-14(g) of this chapter) is not required to disclose the information required by this Item.

PART IV

Item 15. Exhibits and Financial Statement Schedules.

(a) List the following documents filed as a part of the report:

1. All financial statements;

2. Those financial statement schedules required to be filed by Item 8 of this form, and by paragraph (d) below.

(3) Those exhibits required by Item 601 of Regulation S-K (17 CFR 229.601 of this chapter) and by paragraph (c) below. Identify in the list each management contract or compensatory plan or arrangement required to be filed as an exhibit to this form pursuant to Item 14(c) of this report.

(b) Registrants shall file, as exhibits to this Form, the exhibits required by Item 601 of Regulation S-K (§ 229.601 of this chapter).

(c) Registrants shall file, as financial statement schedules to this Form, the financial statements required by Regulation S-X (17 CFR 210) which are excluded from the annual report to shareholders by Rule 14a-3(b) including (1) separate financial statements of subsidiaries not consolidated and fifty percent or less owned persons; (2) separate financial statements of affiliates whose securities are pledged as collateral; and (3) schedules.

SIGNATURES

[See General Instruction D]

Pursuant to the requirements of Section 13 or 15(d) of the Securities Exchange Act of 1934, the registrant has duly caused this report to be signed on its behalf by the undersigned, thereunto duly authorized.

(Registrant) . . . .

By (Signature and Title)* . . . .

Date . . . .

Pursuant to the requirements of the Securities Exchange Act of 1934, this report has been signed below by the following persons on behalf of the registrant and in the capacities and on the dates indicated.

By (Signature and Title)* . . . .

Date . . . .

By (Signature and Title)* . . . .

Date . . . .

Supplemental Information to be Furnished With Reports Filed Pursuant to Section 15(d) of the Act by Registrants Which Have Not Registered Securities Pursuant to Section 12 of the Act

(a) Except to the extent that the materials enumerated in (1) and/or (2) below are specifically incorporated into this Form by reference (in which case *see* Rule 12b-23(d)), every registrant

---

* Print the name and title of each signing officer under his signature.

which files an annual report on this Form pursuant to Section 15(d) of the Act shall furnish to the Commission for its information, at the time of filing its report on this Form, four copies of the following:

(1) Any annual report to security holders covering the registrant's last fiscal year; and

(2) Every proxy statement, form of proxy or other proxy soliciting material sent to more than ten of the registrant's security holders with respect to any annual or other meeting of security holders.

(b) The foregoing material shall not be deemed to be "filed" with the Commission or otherwise subject to the liabilities of Section 18 of the Act, except to the extent that the registrant specifically incorporates it in its annual report on this Form by reference.

(c) If no such annual report or proxy material has been sent to security holders, a statement to that effect shall be included under this caption. If such report or proxy material is to be furnished to security holders subsequent to the filing of the annual report of this Form, the registrant shall so state under this caption and shall furnish copies of such material to the Commission when it is sent to security holders.

SCHEDULE 13D

Schedule 13D Information to be Included in Statements Filed Pursuant to §240.13d-1(a) and Amendments Thereto Filed Pursuant to §240.13d-2(a).

SECURITIES AND EXCHANGE COMMISSION
Washington, D.C. 20549
SCHEDULE 13D

Under the Securities Exchange Act of 1934 (Amendment No.)*

. . . .

(Name of Issuer)

. . . .

(Title of Class of Securities)

. . . .

(CUSIP Number)

. . . .

(Name, Address and Telephone Number of Person Authorized to Receive Notices and Communications)

. . . .

(Date of Event which Requires Filing of this Statement)

If the filing person has previously filed a statement on Schedule 13G to report the acquisition that is the subject of this Schedule 13D, and is filing this schedule because of §§240.13d-1(e), 240.13d-1(f) or 240.13d-1(g), check the following box. [ ]

NOTE: Schedules filed in paper format shall include a signed original and five copies of the schedule, including all exhibits. See Rule 13d-7 for other parties to whom copies are to be sent.

*The remainder of this cover page shall be filled out for a reporting person's initial filing on this form with respect to the subject class of securities, and for any subsequent amendment containing information which would alter disclosures provided in a prior cover page.

The information required on the remainder of this cover page shall not be deemed to be "filed" for the purpose of Section 18 of the Securities Exchange Act of 1934 ("Act") or otherwise subject to the liabilities of that section of the Act but shall be subject to all other provisions of the Act (however, see the Notes).

CUSIP No. . . . .

	1)	Names of Reporting Persons. . . . . I.R.S. Identification Nos. of Above Persons (entities only) . . . .
	2)	Check the Appropriate Box if a Member of a Group (See Instructions) . . . . . . (a) . . . . (b) . . . .
	3)	SEC Use Only . . . .
	4)	Source of Funds (See Instructions) . . . .
	5)	Check if Disclosure of Legal Proceedings is Required Pursuant to Items 2(d) or 2(e) . . . .
	6)	Citizenship or Place of Organization . . . .
Number of		(7) Sole Voting Power . . . .

Shares Bene-		
ficially	(8) Shared Voting Power	
Owned by		
Each Report-	(9) Sole Dispositive Power	
ing Person		
With	(10) Shared Dispositive Power	

11)	Aggregate Amount Beneficially Owned by Each Reporting Person ....
12)	Check if the Aggregate Amount in Row (11) Excludes Certain Shares (See Instructions) ....
13)	Percent of Class Represented by Amount in Row (11) ....
14)	Type of Reporting Person (See Instructions) ....

Instructions for Cover Page

(1) Names and I.R.S. Identification Numbers of Reporting Persons. Furnish the full legal name of each person for whom the report is filed—i.e., each person required to sign the schedule itself—including each member of a group. Do not include the name of a person required to be identified in the report but who is not a reporting person. Reporting persons that are entities are also requested to furnish their I.R.S. identification numbers, although disclosure of such numbers is voluntary, not mandatory (see "SPECIAL INSTRUCTIONS FOR COMPLYING WITH SCHEDULE 13-D" below).

(2) If any of the shares beneficially owned by a reporting person are held as a member of a group and the membership is expressly affirmed, please check row 2(a). If the reporting person disclaims membership in a group or describes a relationship with other person but does not affirm the existence of a group, please check row 2(b) [unless it is a joint filing pursuant to Rule 13d-1(k)(1) in which case it may not be necessary to check row 2 (b)].

(3) The 3rd row is for SEC internal use; please leave blank.

(4) Classify the source of funds or other consideration used or to be used in making the purchases as required to be disclosed pursuant to Item 3 of Schedule 13D and insert the appropriate symbol (or symbols if more than one is necessary in row (4):

Category of Source	Symbol
Subject Company (Company whose securities are being acquired)	SC
Bank	BK
Affiliate (of reporting person)	AF
Working Capital (of reporting person)	WC

Category of Source	Symbol
Personal Funds (of reporting person)	PF
Other	OO

(5) If disclosure of legal proceedings or actions is required pursuant to either Items 2(d) or 2(e) of Schedule 13D, row 5 should be checked.

(6) *Citizenship or Place of Organization*—Furnish citizenship if the named reporting person is a natural person. Otherwise, furnish place of organization. (See Item 2 of Schedule 13D).

(7)-(11), (13) *Aggregate Amount Beneficially Owned by Each Reporting Person, etc.*—Rows (7) through (11), inclusive, and (13) are to be completed in accordance with the provisions of Item 5 of Schedule 13D. All percentages are to be rounded off to nearest tenth (one place after decimal point).

(12) Check if the aggregate amount reported as beneficially owned in row (11) does not include shares which the reporting person discloses in the report but as to which beneficial ownership is disclaimed pursuant to Rule 13d-4 [17 CFR 240.13d-4] under the Securities Exchange Act of 1934.

(14) *Type of Reporting Person*—Please classify each "reporting person" according to the following breakdown and place the appropriate symbol (or symbols, i.e., if more than one is applicable, insert all applicable symbols) on the form:

Category	Symbol
Broker Dealer	BD
Bank	BK
Insurance Company	IC
Investment Company	IV
Investment Adviser	IA
Employee Benefit Plan or Endowment Fund	EP
Parent Holding Company/Control Person	HC
Savings Association	SA
Church Plan	CP
Corporation	CO
Partnership	PN
Individual	IN
Other	OO

Note: Attach additional pages if needed.

Notes:

Attach as many copies of the second part of the cover page as are needed, one reporting person per page.

Filing persons may, in order to avoid unnecessary duplication, answer items on the schedules (Schedule 13D, 13G or 14D-1) by appropriate cross references to an item or items on the cover page(s). This approach may only be used where the cover page item or items provide all the disclosure required by the schedule item. Moreover, such a use of a cover page item will result in the item becoming a part of the schedule and accordingly being considered as "filed" for purposes of Section 18 of the Securities Exchange Act or otherwise subject to the liabilities of that section of the Act.

Reporting persons may comply with their cover page filing requirements by filing either completed copies of the blank forms available from the Commission, printed or typed facsimiles, or computer printed facsimiles, provided the documents filed have identical formats to the forms prescribed in the Commission's regulations and meet existing Securities Exchange Act rules as to such matters as clarity and size (Securities Exchange Act Rule 12b-12).

SPECIAL INSTRUCTIONS FOR COMPLYING WITH SCHEDULE 13D

Under Sections 13(d) and 23 of the Securities Exchange Act of 1934 and the rules and regulations thereunder, the Commission is authorized to solicit the information required to be supplied by this schedule by certain security holders of certain issuers.

Disclosure of the information specified in this schedule is mandatory, except for I.R.S. identification numbers, disclosure of which is voluntary. The information will be used for the primary purpose of determining and disclosing the holdings of certain beneficial owners of certain equity securities. This statement will be made a matter of public record. Therefore, any information given will be available for inspection by any member of the public.

Because of the public nature of the information, the Commission can utilize it for a variety of purposes, including referral to other governmental authorities or securities self-regulatory organizations for investigatory purposes or in connection with litigation involving the Federal securities laws or other civil, criminal or regulatory statutes or provisions. I.R.S. identification numbers, if furnished, will assist the Commission in identifying security holders and, therefore, in promptly processing statements of beneficial ownership of securities.

Failure to disclose the information requested by this schedule, except for I.R.S. identification numbers, may result in civil or criminal action against the persons involved for violation of the Federal securities laws and rules promulgated thereunder.

General Instructions

A. The item numbers and captions of the items shall be included but the text of the items is to be omitted. The answers to the items shall be so prepared as to indicate clearly the coverage of the items without referring to the text of the items. Answer every item. If an item is inapplicable or the answer is in the negative, so state.

B. Information contained in exhibits to the statement may be incorporated by reference in answer or partial answer to any item or sub-item of the statement unless it would render such answer misleading, incomplete, unclear or confusing. Matter incorporated by reference shall be clearly identified in the reference by page, paragraph, caption or otherwise. An express statement that the specified matter is incorporated by reference shall be made at the particular place in the statement where the information is required. A copy of any information or a copy of the pertinent pages of a document containing such information which is incorporated by reference shall be submitted with this statement as an exhibit and shall be deemed to be filed with the Commission for all purposes of the Act.

C. If the statement is filed by a general or limited partnership, syndicate, or other group, the information called for by Items 2-6, inclusive, shall be given with respect to (i) each partner of such general partnership; (ii) each partner who is denominated as a general partner or who functions as a general partner of such limited partnership; (ii) each member of such syndicate or group; and (iv) each person controlling such partner or member. If the statement is filed by a corporation or if a person referred to in (i), (ii), (iii) or (iv) of this Instruction is a corporation, the information called for by the above mentioned items shall be given with respect to (a) each executive officer and director of such corporation; (b) each person controlling such corporation; and (c) each executive officer and director of any corporation or other person ultimately in control of such corporation.

Item 1. Security and Issuer

State the title of the class of equity securities to which this statement relates and the name and address of the principal executive offices of the issuer of such securities.

Item 2. Identity and Background

If the person filing this statement or any person enumerated in Instruction C of this statement is a corporation, general partnership, limited partnership, syndicate or other group of persons, state its name, the state or other place of its organization, its principal business, the address of its principal business, the address of its principal office and the information required by (d) and (e) of this Item. If the person filing this statement or any person enumerated in Instruction C is a natural person, provide the information specified in (a) through (f) of this Item with respect to such person(s).

(a) Name;

(b) Residence or business address;

(c) Present principal occupation or employment and the name, principal business and address of any corporation or other organization in which such employment is conducted;

(d) Whether or not, during the last five years, such person has been convicted in a criminal proceeding (excluding traffic violations or similar misdemeanors) and, if so, give the dates, nature of conviction, name and location of court, any penalty imposed, or other disposition of the case;

(e) Whether or not, during the last five years, such person was a party to a civil proceeding of a judicial or administrative body of competent jurisdiction and as a result of such proceeding was or is subject to a judgment, decree or final order enjoining future violations of, or prohibiting or mandating activities subject to, federal or state securities laws or finding any violation with respect to such laws; and, if so, identify and describe such proceedings and summarize the terms of such judgment, decree or final order; and

(f) Citizenship.

Item 3. Source and Amount of Funds or Other Consideration

State the source and the amount of funds or other consideration used or to be used in making the purchases, and if any part of the purchase price is or will be represented by funds or other consideration borrowed or otherwise obtained for the purpose of acquiring, holding, trading or voting the securities, a description of the transaction and the names of the parties thereto. Where material, such information should also be provided with respect to prior acquisitions not previously reported pursuant to this regulation. If the source of all or any part of the funds is a loan made in the ordinary course of business by a bank, as defined in Section 3(a)(6) of the Act, the name of the bank shall not be made available to the public if the person at the time of filing the statement so requests in writing and files such request, naming such bank, with the Secretary of the Commission. If the securities were acquired other than by purchase, describe the method of acquisition.

Item 4. Purpose of Transaction

State the purpose or purposes of the acquisition of securities of the issuer. Describe any plans or proposals which the reporting persons may have which relate to or would result in:

(a) The acquisition by any person of additional securities of the issuer, or the disposition of securities of the issuer;

(b) An extraordinary corporate transaction, such as a merger, reorganization or liquidation, involving the issuer or any of its subsidiaries;

(c) A sale or transfer of a material amount of assets of the issuer or any of its subsidiaries;

(d) Any change in the present board of directors or management of the issuer, including any plans or proposals to change the number of term of directors or to fill any existing vacancies on the board;

(e) Any material change in the present capitalization or dividend policy of the issuer;

(f) Any other material change in the issuer's business or corporate structure including but not limited to, if the issuer is a registered closed-end investment company, any plans or proposals to make any changes in its investment policy for which a vote is required by section 13 of the Investment Company Act of 1940;

(g) Changes in the issuer's charter, bylaws or instruments corresponding thereto or other actions which may impede the acquisition of control of the issuer by any person;

(h) Causing a class of securities of the issuer to be delisted from a national securities exchange or to cease to be authorized to be quoted in an inter-dealer quotation system of a registered national securities association;

(i) A class of equity securities of the issuer becoming eligible for termination of registration pursuant to Section 12(g)(4) of the Act; or

(j) Any action similar to any of those enumerated above.

Item 5. Interest in Securities of the Issuer

(a) State the aggregate number and percentage of the class of securities identified pursuant to Item 1 (which may be based on the number of securities outstanding as contained in the most recently available filing with the Commission by the issuer unless the filing person has reason to believe such information is not current) beneficially owned (identifying those shares which there is a right to acquire) by each person named in Item 2. The above mentioned information should also be furnished with respect to persons who, together with any of the persons named in Item 2, comprise a group within the meaning of Section 13(d)(3) of the Act;

(b) For each person named in response to paragraph (a), indicate the number of shares as to which there is sole power to vote or to direct the vote, shared power to vote or to direct the vote, sole power to dispose or to direct the disposition, or shared power to dispose or to direct the disposition. Provide the applicable information required by Item 2 with respect to each person with whom the power to vote or to direct the vote or to dispose or direct the disposition is shared;

(c) Describe any transactions in the class of securities reported on that were effected during the past sixty days or since the most recent filing on Schedule 13D (§ 240.13d-191), whichever is less, by the persons named in response to paragraph (a).

Instruction. The description of a transaction required by Item 5(c) shall include, but not necessarily be limited to: (1) the identity of the person covered by Item 5(c) who effected the transaction; (2) the date of the transaction; (3) the amount of securities involved; (4) the price per share or unit; and (5) where and how the transaction was effected.

(d) If any other person is known to have the right to receive or the power to direct the receipt of dividends from, or the proceeds from the sale of, such securities, a statement to that effect should be included in response to this item and, if such interest relates to more than five percent of the class, such person should be identified. A listing of the shareholders of an investment company registered under the Investment Company Act of 1940 or the beneficiaries of an employee benefit plan, pension fund or endowment fund is not required.

(e) If applicable, state the date on which the reporting person ceased to be the beneficial owner of more than five percent of the class of securities.

Instruction. For computations regarding securities which represent a right to acquire an underlying security, see Rule 13d-3(d)(1) and the note thereto.

Item 6. Contracts, Arrangements, Understandings or Relationships with Respect to Securities of the Issuer

Describe any contracts, arrangements, understandings or relationships (legal or otherwise) among the persons named in Item 2 and between such persons and any person with respect to any securities of the issuer, including but not limited to transfer or voting of any of the securities, finder's fees, joint ventures, loan or option arrangements, put or calls, guarantees of profits, division of profits or loss, or the giving or withholding of proxies, naming the persons with whom such contracts, arrangements, understandings or relationships have been entered into. Include such information for any of the securities that are pledged or otherwise subject to a contingency the occurrence of which would give another person voting power or investment power over such securities except that disclosure of standard default and similar provisions contained in loan agreements need not be included.

Item 7. Material to Be Filed as Exhibits

The following shall be filed as exhibits: copies of written agreements relating to the filing of joint acquisition statements as required by Rule 13d-1(k) and copies of all written agreements, contracts, arrangements, understandings, plans or proposals relating to (1) the borrowing of funds to finance the acquisition as disclosed in Item 3; (2) the acquisition of issuer control, liquidation, sale of assets, merger, or change in business or corporate structure or any other matter as disclosed in Item 4; and (3) the transfer or voting of the securities, finder's fees, joint ventures, options, puts, calls, guarantees of loans, guarantees against loss or of profit, or the giving or withholding of any proxy as disclosed in Item 6.

Signature.

After reasonable inquiry and to the best of my knowledge and belief, I certify that the information set forth in this statement is true, complete and correct.

. . . .

Date

. . . .

Signature

. . . .

Name/Title

The original statement shall be signed by each person on whose behalf the statement is filed or his authorized representative. If the statement is signed on behalf of a person by his authorized representative (other than an executive officer or general partner of this filing person), evidence of the representative's authority to sign on behalf of such person shall be filed with the statement, provided, however, that a power of attorney for this purpose which is already on file with the Commission may be incorporated by reference. The name and any title of each person who signs the statement shall be typed or printed beneath his signature.

Attention: Intentional misstatements or omissions of fact constitute Federal criminal violations (See 18 U. S. C. 1001).

SCHEDULE 13E-3
Schedule 13E-3 Transaction Statement under Section 13(e) of the Securities Exchange Act of 1934 and Rule 13e-3 (§ 240.13e-3) thereunder.

SECURITIES AND EXCHANGE COMMISSION

Washington, D.C. 20549

Rule 13e-3 Transaction Statement under Section 13(e) of the Securities Exchange Act of 1934

[Amendment No........................]

. . . .

(Name of the Issuer)

. . . .

(Name of Person(s) Filing Statement)

. . . .

(Title of Class of Securities)

. . . .

(CUSIP Number of Class of Securities)

. . . .

(Name, Address and Telephone Numbers of Person Authorized to Receive Notices and Communications on Behalf of Persons Filing Statement)

This statement is filed in connection with (check the appropriate box):

a. [ ] The filing of solicitation materials or an information statement subject to Regulation 14A (§§ 240.14a-1 through 240.14b-2), Regulation 14C (§§ 240.14c-1 through 240.14c-101) or Rule 13e-3(c) (§ 240.13e-3(c)) under the Securities Exchange Act of 1934 ("the Act").

b. [ ] The filing of a registration statement under the Securities Act of 1933.

c. [ ] A tender offer.

d. [ ] None of the above.

Check the following box if the soliciting materials or information statement referred to in checking box (a) are preliminary copies: []

Check the following box if the filing is a final amendment reporting the results of the transaction: [ ]

Calculation of Filing Fee

Transaction valuation*	Amount of filing fee

*Set forth the amount on which the filing fee is calculated and state how it was determined.

[ ] Check the box if any part of the fee is offset as provided by § 240.0-11(a)(2) and identify the filing with which the offsetting fee was previously paid. Identify the previous filing by registration statement number, or the Form or Schedule and the date of its filing.

Amount Previously Paid:_____

Form or Registration No.:————————

Filing Party:————————

Date Filed:————————

General Instructions:

A. File eight copies of the statement, including all exhibits, with the Commission if paper filing is permitted.

B. This filing must be accompanied by a fee payable to the Commission as required by § 240.0-11(b)

C. If the statement is filed by a general or limited partnership, syndicate or other group, the information called for by Items 3, 5, 6, 10 and 11 must be given with respect to: (i) each partner of the general partnership; (ii) each partner who is, or functions as, a general partner of the limited partnership; (iii) each member of the syndicate or group; and (iv) each person controlling the partner or member. If the statement is filed by a corporation or if a person referred to in (i), (ii), (iii) or (iv) of this Instruction is a corporation, the information called for by the items specified above must be given with respect to: (a) each executive officer and director of the corporation; (b) each person controlling the corporation; and (c) each executive officer and director of any corporation or other person ultimately in control of the corporation.

D. Depending on the type of Rule 13e-3 transaction (§ 240.13e-3(a)(3)), this statement must be filed with the Commission:

1. At the same time as filing preliminary or definitive soliciting materials or an information statement under Regulations 14A or 14C of the Act;

2. At the same time as filing a registration statement under the Securities Act of 1933;

3. As soon as practicable on the date a tender offer is first published, sent or given to security holders; or

4. At least 30 days before any purchase of securities of the class of securities subject to the Rule 13e-3 transaction, if the transaction does not involve a solicitation, an information statement, the registration of securities or a tender offer, as described in paragraphs 1, 2 or 3 of this Instruction; and

5. If the Rule 13e-3 transaction involves a series of transactions, the issuer or affiliate must file this statement at the time indicated in paragraphs 1 through 4 of this Instruction for the first transaction and must amend the schedule promptly with respect to each subsequent transaction.

E. If an item is inapplicable or the answer is in the negative, so state. The statement published, sent or given to security holders may omit negative and not applicable responses, except that responses to Items 7, 8 and 9 of this schedule must be provided in full. If the schedule includes any information that is not published, sent or given to security holders, provide that information or specifically incorporate it by reference under the appropriate item number and heading in the schedule. Do not recite the text of disclosure requirements in the schedule or any document published, sent or given to security holders. Indicate clearly the coverage of the requirements without referring to the text of the items.

F. Information contained in exhibits to the statement may be incorporated by reference in answer or partial answer to any item unless it would render the answer misleading, incomplete, unclear or confusing. A copy of any information that is incorporated by reference or a copy of the pertinent pages of a document containing the information must be submitted with this statement as an exhibit, unless it was previously filed with the Commission electronically on EDGAR. If an exhibit contains information responding to more than one item in the schedule, all information in that exhibit may be incorporated by reference once in response to the several items in the schedule for which it provides an answer. Information incorporated by reference is deemed filed with the Commission for all purposes of the Act.

G. If the Rule 13e-3 transaction also involves a transaction subject to Regulation 14A (§§ 240.14a-1 through 240.14b-2) or 14C (§§ 240.14c-1 through 240.14c-101) of the Act, the registration of securities under the Securities Act of 1933 and the General Rules and Regulations of that Act, or a tender offer subject to Regulation 14D (§§ 240.14d-1 through 240.14d-101) or § 240.13e-4, this statement must incorporate by reference the information contained in the proxy, information, registration or tender offer statement in answer to the items of this statement.

H. The information required by the items of this statement is intended to be in addition to any disclosure requirements of any other form or schedule that may be filed with the Commission in connection with the Rule 13e-3 transaction. If those forms or schedules require less information on any topic than this statement, the requirements of this statement control.

I. If the Rule 13e-3 transaction involves a tender offer, then a combined statement on Schedules 13E-3 and TO may be filed with the Commission under cover of Schedule TO (§ 240.14d-100). See Instruction J of Schedule TO (§ 240.14d-100).

J. Amendments disclosing a material change in the information set forth in this statement may omit any information previously disclosed in this statement.

Item 1. *Summary Term Sheet*

Furnish the information required by Item 1001 of Regulation M-A (§ 229.1001 of this chapter) unless information is disclosed to security holders in a prospectus that meets the requirements of § 230.421(d) of this chapter.

Item 2. *Subject Company Information*

Furnish the information required by Item 1002 of Regulation M-A (§ 229.1002 of this chapter).

Item 3. *Identity and Background of Filing Person*

Furnish the information required by Item 1003(a) through (c) of Regulation M-A (§ 229.1003 of this chapter).

Item 4. *Terms of the Transaction*

Furnish the information required by Item 1004(a) and (c) through (f) of Regulation M-A (§ 229.1004 of this chapter).

Item 5. *Past Contacts, Transactions, Negotiations and Agreements*

Furnish the information required by Item 1005(a) through (c) and (e) of Regulation M-A (§ 229.1005 of this chapter).

Item 6. *Purposes of the Transaction and Plans or Proposals*

Furnish the information required by Item 1006(b) and (c)(1) through (8) of Regulation M-A (§ 229.1006 of this chapter).

Instruction to Item 6:

In providing the information specified in Item 1006(c) for this item, discuss any activities or transactions that would occur after the Rule 13e-3 transaction.

Item 7. *Purposes, Alternatives, Reasons and Effects*

Furnish the information required by Item 1013 of Regulation M-A (§ 229.1013 of this chapter).

Item 8. *Fairness of the Transaction*

Furnish the information required by Item 1014 of Regulation M-A (§ 229.1014 of this chapter).

Item 9. *Reports, Opinions, Appraisals and Negotiations*

Furnish the information required by Item 1015 of Regulation M-A (§ 229.1015 of this chapter).

Item 10. *Source and Amounts of Funds or Other Consideration*

Furnish the information required by Item 1007 of Regulation M-A (§ 229.1007 of this chapter).

Item 11. *Interest in Securities of the Subject Company*

Furnish the information required by Item 1008 of Regulation M-A (§ 229.1008 of this chapter).

Item 12. *The Solicitation or Recommendation*

Furnish the information required by Item 1012(d) and (e) of Regulation M-A (§ 229.1012 of this chapter).

Item 13. *Financial Statements*

Furnish the information required by Item 1010(a) through (b) of Regulation M-A (§ 229.1010 of this chapter) for the issuer of the subject class of securities.

Instructions to Item 13:

1. The disclosure materials disseminated to security holders may contain the summarized financial information required by Item 1010(c) of Regulation M-A (§ 229.1010 of this chapter) instead of the financial information required by Item 1010(a) and (b). In that case, the financial information required by Item 1010(a) and (b) of Regulation M-A must be disclosed directly or incorporated by reference in the statement. If summarized financial information is disseminated to security holders, include appropriate instructions on how more complete financial information can be obtained. If the summarized financial information is prepared on the basis of a comprehensive body of accounting principles other than U.S. GAAP, the summarized financial information must be accompanied by a reconciliation as described in Instruction 2.

2. If the financial statements required by this Item are prepared on the basis of a comprehensive body of accounting principles other than U.S. GAAP, provide a reconciliation to U.S. GAAP in accordance with Item 17 of Form 20-F (§ 249.220f of this chapter).

3. The filing person may incorporate by reference financial statements contained in any document filed with the Commission, solely for the purposes of this schedule, if: (a) the financial statements substantially meet the requirements of this Item; (b) an express statement is made that the financial statements are incorporated by reference; (c) the matter incorporated by reference is clearly identified by page, paragraph, caption or otherwise; and (d) if the matter incorporated by reference is not filed with this Schedule, an indication is made where the information may be inspected and copies obtained. Financial statements that are required to be presented in comparative form for two or more fiscal years or periods may not be incorporated by reference unless the material incorporated by reference includes the entire period for which the comparative data is required to be given. *See* General Instruction F to this Schedule.

Item 14. *Persons/Assets, Retained, Employed, Compensated or Used*

Furnish the information required by Item 1009 of Regulation M-A (§ 229.1009 of this chapter).

Item 15. *Additional Information*

Furnish the information required by Item 1011(b) of Regulation M-A (§ 229.1011 of this chapter).

Item 16. *Exhibits*

File as an exhibit to the Schedule all documents specified in Item 1016(a) through (d), (f) and (g) of Regulation M-A (§ 229.1016 of this chapter).

Signature. After due inquiry and to the best of my knowledge and belief, I certify that the information set forth in this statement is true, complete and correct.

_____

(Signature)

_____

(Name and title)

_____

(Date)

Instruction to Signature:

The statement must be signed by the filing person or that person's authorized representative. If the statement is signed on behalf of a person by an authorized representative (other than an executive officer of a corporation or general partner of a partnership), evidence of the representative's authority to sign on behalf of the person must be filed with the statement. The name and any title of each person who signs the statement must be typed or printed beneath the signature. See § 240.12b-11 with respect to signature requirements.

Schedule 14A
Information Required in Proxy Statement
SCHEDULE 14A INFORMATION

Proxy Statement Pursuant to Section 14(a) of the Securities Exchange Act of 1934 (Amendment No.)

Filed by the Registrant [ ]

Filed by a Party other than the Registrant [ ]

Check the appropriate box:

[ ] Preliminary Proxy Statement

[ ] Confidential, for Use of the Commission Only (as permitted by Rule 14a-6(e)(2))

[ ] Definitive Proxy Statement

[ ] Definitive Additional Materials

[ ] Soliciting Material Pursuant to § 240.14a-12

. . . .

(Name of Registrant as Specified In Its Charter)

. . . .

(Name of Person(s) Filing Proxy Statement, if other than the Registrant)

Payment of Filing Fee (Check the appropriate box):

[ ] No fee required.

[ ] Fee computed on table below per Exchange Act Rules 14a-6(i)(1) and 0-11.

    1) Title of each class of securities to which transaction applies:

. . . .

    2) Aggregate number of securities to which transaction applies:

. . . .

    3) Per unit price or other underlying value of transaction computed pursuant to Exchange Act Rule 0-11 (set forth the amount on which the filing fee is calculated and state how it was determined):

. . . .

    4) Proposed maximum aggregate value of transaction:

. . . .

    5) Total fee paid:

. . . .

[ ] Fee paid previously with preliminary materials.

[ ] Check box if any part of the fee is offset as provided by Exchange Act Rule 0-11(a)(2) and identify the filing for which the offsetting fee was paid previously. Identify the previous filing by registration statement number, or the Form or Schedule and the date of its filing.

    1) Amount Previously Paid:

. . . .

    2) Form, Schedule or Registration Statement No.:

. . . .

    3) Filing Party:

. . . .

    4) Date Filed:

. . . .

Notes.—A. Where any item calls for information with respect to any matter to be acted upon and such matter involves other matters with respect to which information is called for by other items of this schedule, the information called for by such other items also shall be given. For example, where a solicitation of security holders is for the purpose of approving the authorization of additional securities which are to be used to acquire another specified company, and the registrants' security holders will not have a separate opportunity to vote upon the transaction, the solicitation to authorize the securities is also a solicitation with respect to the acquisition. Under those facts, information required by Items 11, 13 and 14 shall be furnished.

B. Where any item calls for information with respect to any matter to be acted upon at the meeting, such item need be answered in the registrant's soliciting material only with respect to proposals to be made by or on behalf of the registrant.

C. Except as otherwise specifically provided, where any item calls for information for a specified period with regard to directors, executive officers, officers or other persons holding specified positions or relationships, the information shall be given with regard to any person who held any of the specified positions or relationships at any time during the period. Information need not be included for any portion of the period during which such person did not hold any such position or relationship, provided a statement to that effect is made.

D. Information may be incorporated by reference only in the manner and to the extent specifically permitted in the items of this schedule. Where incorporation by reference is used, the following shall apply:

1. Any incorporation by reference of information pursuant to the provisions of this schedule shall be subject to the provisions of § 228.10(f) and § 229.10(d) restricting incorporation by reference of documents which incorporate by reference other information. A registrant incorporating any documents, or portions of documents, shall include a statement on the last page(s) of the proxy statement as to which documents, or portions of documents, are incorporated by reference. Information shall not be incorporated by reference in any case where such incorporation would render the statement incomplete, unclear or confusing.

2. If a document is incorporated by reference but not delivered to security holders, include an undertaking to provide, without charge, to each person to whom a proxy statement is delivered, upon written or oral request of such person and by first class mail or other equally prompt means within one business day of receipt of such request, a copy of any and all of the information that has been incorporated by reference in the proxy statement (not including exhibits to the information that is incorporated by reference unless such exhibits are specifically incorporated by reference into the information that the proxy statement incorporates), and the address (including title or department) and telephone numbers to which such a request is to be directed. This includes information contained in documents filed subsequent to the date on which definitive copies of the proxy statement are sent or given to security holders, up to the date of responding to the request.

3. If a document or portion of a document other than an annual report sent to security holders pursuant to the requirements of Rule 14a-3 (§ 240.14a-3 of this chapter) with respect to the same meeting or solicitation of consents or authorizations as that to which the proxy statement relates is incorporated by reference in the manner permitted by Item 13(b) or 14(e)(1) of this schedule, the proxy statement must be sent to security holders no later than 20 business days prior to the date on which the meeting of such security holders is held or, if no meeting is held, at least 20 business days prior to the date the votes, consents or authorizations may be used to effect the corporate action.

4. *Electronic filings.* If any of the information required by Items 13 or 14 of this Schedule is incorporated by reference from an annual or quarterly report to security holders, such report, or any portion thereof incorporated by reference, shall be filed in electronic format with the proxy statement. This provision shall not apply to registered investment companies.

E. In Items 13 of this Schedule, the reference to "meets the requirements of Form S-2" shall refer to a registrant which meets the requirements for use of Form S-2 (§ 239.12 of this chapter) and the reference to "meets the requirement of Form S-3" shall refer to a registrant which meets the following requirements:

(1) the registrant meets the requirements of General Instruction I.A. of Form S-3 (§ 239.13 of this chapter); and

(2) one of the following is met:

(i) the registrant meets the aggregate market value requirement of General Instruction I.B.1 of Form S-3; or

(ii) action is to be taken as described in Items 11, 12 and 14 of this schedule which concerns non-convertible debt or preferred securities which are "investment grade securities" as defined in General Instruction I.B.2 of Form S-3, except that the time by which the rating must be assigned shall be the date on which definitive copies of the proxy statement are first sent or given to security holders; or

(iii) the registrant is a majority-owned subsidiary and one of the conditions of General Instruction I.C. of Form S-3 is met.

F. *Note to Small Business Issuers*—Registrants and acquirees that meet the definition of "small business issuer" under Rule 12b-2 of the Exchange Act (§ 240.12b-2) shall refer to the disclosure items in Regulation S-B (§ 228.10 *et seq.* of this chapter) and not Regulation S-K (§ 229.10 *et seq.* of this chapter). If there is no comparable disclosure item in Regulation S-B, small business issuers need not provide the information requested. Small business issuers shall provide the financial information in Item 310 of Regulation S-B in lieu of the financial statements required in Schedule 14A.

G. *Special Note for Small Business Issuers.*

(1) Registrants and acquirees which meet the definition of "small business issuer" in Rule 12b-2 of the Exchange Act and filed their latest annual report in accordance with "Information Required in Annual Report of Transitional Small Business Issuers" in Form 10-KSB shall refer to this "Special Note for Small Business Issuers" with respect to the specified items in this Schedule. If paragraph G(2) or G(3), below, does not contain an alternative disclosure instruction, small business issuers should comply with the disclosure item in this schedule, as modified by Instruction F.

(2) Registrants and acquirees that relied upon Alternative 1 in their most recent Form 10-KSB may provide the following information (Question numbers are in reference to Model A of Form 1-A): (a) Questions 37 and 38 instead of Item 6(d); (b) Question 43 instead of Item 7(a); (c) Questions 29-36 and 39 instead of Item 7(b); (d) Questions 40-42 instead of Item 8; (e) Questions 40-42 instead of Item 10; (f) the information required in Part F/S of Form 10-SB instead of the financial statement requirements of Items 13 or 14; (g) Questions 4, 11, and 47-50 instead of Item 13(a)(1)(3); (h) Question 3 instead of the information specified in Items 101 and 102 of Regulation S-B (§ 228.101 and § 228.102 of this chapter); and (i) Questions 4, 11, and 47-50 instead of the information specified in Item 303 of Regulation S-B (§ 228.303 of this chapter).

(3) Registrants and acquirees that relied upon Alternative 2 in their most recent Form 10-KSB may provide the following information ("Model B" refers to Model B of Form 1-A): (a) Item 10 of Model B instead of Item 6(d) of Schedule 14A; (b) Item 8(d) of Model B instead of Item 7(a) of Schedule 14A; (c) Items 8(a)-8(c) and Item 11 of Model B instead of Item 7(b) of Schedule 14A; (d) Item 9 of Model B instead of Item 8 of Schedule 14A; (e) Item 9 of Model B instead of Item 10 of Schedule 14A; (f) the information required in Part F/S of Form 10-SB instead of the financial statements requirements of Items 13 or 14 of Schedule 14A; (g) Item 6(a)(3)(i) of Model B instead of Item 13(a)(1)(3) of Schedule 14A; (h) Items 6 and 7 of Model B instead of the information specified in Items 101 and 102 of Regulation S-B (§ 228.101 and § 228.102 of this chapter); and (i) Item 6(a)(3)(i) of Model B instead of the information specified in Item 303 of Regulation S-B (§ 228.303 of this chapter).

Item 1. Date, time and place information

(a) State the date, time and place of the meeting of security holders, and the complete mailing address, including ZIP Code, of the principal executive offices of the registrant, unless such information is otherwise disclosed in material furnished to security holders with or preceding the proxy statement. If action is to be taken by written consent, state the date by which consents are to be submitted if state law requires that such a date be specified or if the person soliciting intends to set a date.

(b) On the first page of the proxy statement, as delivered to security holders, state the approximate date on which the proxy statement and form of proxy are first sent or given to security holders.

(c) Furnish the information required to be in the proxy statement by Rule 14a-5(e) (§ 240.14a-5(e) of this chapter).

Item 2. Revocability of Proxy

State whether or not the person giving the proxy has the power to revoke it. If the right of revocation before the proxy is exercised is limited or is subject to compliance with any formal procedure, briefly describe such limitation or procedure.

Item 3. Dissenters' Right of Appraisal

Outline briefly the rights of appraisal or similar rights of dissenters with respect to any matter to be acted upon and indicate any statutory procedure required to be followed by dissenting security holders in order to perfect such rights. Where such rights may be exercised only within a limited time after the date of adoption of a proposal, the filing of a charter amendment or other similar act, state whether the persons solicited will be notifed of such date.

Instructions. 1. Indicate whether a security holder's failure to vote against a proposal will constitute a waiver of his appraisal or similar rights and whether a vote against a proposal will be deemed to satisfy any notice requirements under State law with respect to appraisal rights. If the State law is unclear, state what position will be taken in regard to these matters.

2. Open-end investment companies registered under the Investment Company Act of 1940 are not required to respond to this item.

Item 4. Persons Making the Solicitation

(a) *Solicitations not subject to Rule 14a-12(c) (§ 240.14a-12(c) of this chapter.)* (1) If the solicitation is made by the registrant, so state. Give the name of any director of the registrant who has informed the registrant in writing that he intends to oppose any action intended to be taken by the registrant and indicate the action which he intends to oppose.

(2) If the solicitation is made otherwise than by the registrant, so state and give the names of the participants in the solicitation, as defined in paragraphs (a)(iii), (iv), (v) and (vi) of Instruction 3 to this Item.

(3) If the solicitation is to be made otherwise than by the use of the mails, describe the methods to be employed. If the solicitation is to be made by specially engaged employees or paid solicitors, state (i) the material features of any contract or arrangement for such solicitation and identify the parties, and (ii) the cost or anticipated cost thereof.

(4) State the names of the persons by whom the cost of solicitation has been or will be borne, directly or indirectly.

(b) *Solicitations subject to Rule 14a-12(c) (§ 240.14a-12(c)).* (1) State by whom the solicitation is made and describe the methods employed and to be employed to solicit security holders.

(2) If regular employees of the registrant or any other participant in a solicitation have been or are to be employed to solicit security holders, describe the class or classes of employees to be so employed, and the manner and nature of their employment for such purpose.

(3) If specially engaged employees, representatives or other persons have been or are to be employed to solicit security holders, state (i) the material features of any contract or arrangement for such solicitation and the identity of the parties, (ii) the cost or anticipated cost thereof, and (iii) the approximate number of such employees or employees of any other person (naming such other person) who will solicit security holders).

(4) State the total amount estimated to be spent and the total expenditures to date for, in furtherance of, or in connection with the solicitation of security holders.

(5) State by whom the cost of the solicitation will be borne. If such cost is to be borne initially by any person other than the registrant, state whether reimbursement will be sought from the

registrant, and, if so, whether the question of such reimbursement will be submitted to a vote of security holders.

(6) If any such solicitation is terminated pursuant to a settlement between the registrant and any other participant in such solicitation, describe the terms of such settlement, including the cost or anticipated cost thereof to the registrant.

Instructions. 1. With respect to solicitations subject to Rule 14a-12(c) (§ 240.14a-12(c)), costs and expenditures within the meaning of this Item 4 shall include fees for attorneys, accountants, public relations or financial advisers, solicitors, advertising, printing, transportation, litigation and other costs incidental to the solicitation, except that the registrant may exclude the amount of such costs represented by the amount normally expended for a solicitation for an election of directors in the absence of a contest, and costs represented by salaries and wages of regular employees and officers, provided a statement to that effect is included in the proxy statement.

2. The information required pursuant to paragraph (b)(6) of this Item should be included in any amended or revised proxy statement or other soliciting materials relating to the same meeting or subject matter furnished to security holders by the registrant subsequent to the date of settlement.

3. For purposes of this Item 4 and Item 5 of this Schedule 14A: (a) The terms "participant" and "participant in a solicitation" include the following:

(i) the registrant;

(ii) any director of the registrant, and any nominee for whose election as a director proxies are solicited;

(iii) any committee or group which solicits proxies, any member of such committee or group, and any person whether or not named as a member who, acting alone or with one or more other persons, directly or indirectly takes the initiative, or engages, in organizing, directing, or arranging for the financing of any such committee or group;

(iv) any person who finances or joins with another to finance the solicitation of proxies, except persons who contribute not more than $500 and who are not otherwise participants;

(v) any person who lends money or furnishes credit or enters into any other arrangements, pursuant to any contract or understanding with a participant, for the purpose of financing or otherwise inducing the purchase, sale, holding or voting of securities of the registrant by any participant or other persons, in support of or in opposition to a participant; except that such terms do not include a bank, broker or dealer who, in the ordinary course of business, lends money or executes orders for the purchase or sale of securities and who is not otherwise a participant; and

(vi) any person who solicits proxies.

(b) The terms "participant" and "participant in a solicitation" do not include:

(i) any person or organization retained or employed by a participant to solicit security holders and whose activities are limited to the duties required to be performed in the course of such employment;

(ii) any person who merely transmits proxy soliciting material or performs other ministerial or clerical duties;

(iii) any person employed by a participant in the capacity of attorney, accountant, or advertising, public relations or financial adviser, and whose activities are limited to the duties required to be performed in the course of such employment;

(iv) any person regularly employed as an officer or employee of the registrant or any of its subsidiaries who is not otherwise a participant; or

(v) any officer or director of, or any person regularly employed by, any other participant, if such officer, director or employee is not otherwise a participant.

Item 5. Interest of Certain Persons in Matters to Be Acted Upon

(a) *Solicitations not subject to Rule 14a-12(c) (§ 240.14a-12(c) of this chapter)*. Describe briefly any substantial interest, direct or indirect, by security holdings or otherwise, of each of the following persons in any matter to be acted upon, other than elections to office:

(1) If the solicitation is made on behalf of the registrant, each person who has been a director or executive officer of the registrant at any time since the beginning of the last fiscal year.

(2) If the solicitation is made otherwise than on behalf of the registrant, each participation in the solicitation, as defined in paragraphs in the solicitation, as defined in paragraphs (a) (iii), (iv), (v), and (vi) of Instruction 3 to Item 4 of This Schedule 14A.

(3) Each nominee for election as a director of the registrant.

(4) Each associate of any of the foregoing persons.

Instruction. Except in the case of a solicitation subject to this regulation made in opposition to another solicitation subject to this regulation, the sub-item (a) shall not apply to any interest arising from the ownership of securities of the registrant where the security holder receives no extra or special benefit not shared on a pro rata basis by all other holders of the same class.

(b) *Solicitation subject to Rule 14a-12(c) (§ 240.14a-12(c) of this chapter)*. With respect to any solicitation subject to Rule 14a-12(c) (§ 240.14a-12(c)):

(1) Describe briefly any substantial interest, direct or indirect, by security holdings or otherwise, of each participant as defined in paragraphs (a) (ii), (iii), (iv), (v) and (vi) of Instruction 3 to Item 4 of this Schedule 14A, in any matter to be acted upon at the meeting, and include with respect to each participant the following information, or a fair and accurate summary thereof:

(i) Name and business address of the participant.

(ii) The participant's present principal occupation or employment and the name, principal business and address of any corporation or other organization in which such employment is carried on.

(iii) State whether or not, during the past ten years, the participant has been convicted in a criminal proceeding (excluding traffic violations or similar misdemeanors) and, if so, give dates, nature of conviction, name and location of court, and penalty imposed or other disposition of the case. A negative answer need not be included in the proxy statement or other soliciting material.

(iv) State the amount of each class of securities of the registrant which the participant owns beneficially, directly or indirectly.

(v) State the amount of each class of securities of the registrant which the participant owns of record but not beneficially.

(vi) State with respect to all securities of the registrant purchased or sold within the past two years, the dates on which they were purchased or sold and the amount purchased or sold on each such date.

(vii) If any part of the purchase price or market value of any of the shares specified in paragraph (b) (1) (vi) of this Item is represented by funds borrowed or otherwise obtained for the purpose of acquiring or holding such securities, so state and indicate the amount of the indebtedness as of the latest practicable date. If such funds were borrowed or obtained otherwise than pursuant to a margin account or bank loan in the regular course of business of a bank, broker or dealer, briefly describe the transaction, and state the names of the parties.

(viii) State whether or not the participant is, or was within the past year, a party to any contract, arrangements or understandings with any person with respect to any securities of the registrant, including, but not limited to joint ventures, loan or option arrangements, puts or calls, guarantees against loss or guarantees of profit, division of losses or profits, or the giving or withholding of proxies. If so, name the parties to such contracts, arrangements or understandings and give the details thereof.

(ix) State the amount of securities of the registrant owned beneficially, directly or indirectly, by each of the participant's associates and the name and address of each such associate.

(x) State the amount of each class of securities of any parent or subsidiary of the registrant which the participant owns beneficially, directly or indirectly.

(xi) Furnish for the participant and associates of the participant the information required by Item 404(a) of Regulation S-K (§ 229.404(a) of this chapter).

(xii) State whether or not the participant or any associates of the participant have any arrangement or understanding with any person—

(A) with respect to any future employment by the registrant or its affiliates; or

(B) with respect to any future transactions to which the registrant or any of its affiliates will or may be a party.

If so, describe such arrangement or understanding and state the names of the parties thereto.

(2) With respect to any person, other than a director or executive officer of the registrant acting solely in that capacity, who is a party to an arrangement or understanding pursuant to which a nominee for election as director is proposed to be elected, describe any substantial interest, direct or indirect, by security holdings or otherwise, that such person has in any matter to be acted upon at the meeting, and furnish the information called for by paragraphs (b)(1)(xi) and (xii) of this Item.

Instruction: For purposes of this Item 5, beneficial ownership shall be determined in accordance with Rule 13d-3 under the Act (Section 240.13d-3 of this chapter).

Item 6. Voting Securities and Principal Holders Thereof

(a) As to each class of voting securities of the registrant entitled to be voted at the meeting (or by written consents or authorizations if no meeting is held), state the number of shares outstanding and the number of votes to which each class is entitled.

(b) State the record date, if any, with respect to this solicitation. If the right to vote or give consent is not to be determined, in whole or in part, by reference to a record date, indicate the criteria for the determination of security holders entitled to vote or give consent.

(c) If action is to be taken with respect to the election of directors and if the persons solicited have cumulative voting rights: (1) Make a statement that they have such rights, (2) briefly describe such rights, (3) state briefly the conditions precedent to the exercise thereof, and (4) if discretionary authority to cumulate votes is solicited, so indicate.

(d) Furnish the information required by Item 403 of Regulation S-K (§ 229.403 of this chapter) to the extent known by the persons on whose behalf the solicitation if made.

(e) If, to the knowledge of the persons on whose behalf the solicitation is made, a change in control of the registrant has occurred since the beginning of its last fiscal year, state the name of the person(s) who acquired such control, the amount and the source of the consideration used by such person or persons; the basis of the control, the date and a description of the transaction(s) which resulted in the change of control and the percentage of voting securities of the registrant now beneficially owned directly or indirectly by the person(s) who acquired control; and the identity of the person(s) from whom control was assumed. If the source of all or any part of the consideration used is a loan made in the ordinary course of business by a bank as defined by section 3(a)(6) of the Act, the identity of such bank shall be omitted provided a request for confidentiality has been made pursuant to section 13(d)(1)(B) of the Act by the person(s) who acquired control. In lieu thereof, the material shall indicate that the identity of the bank has been so omitted and filed separately with the Commission.

Instruction. 1. State the terms of any loans or pledges obtained by the new control group for the purposes of acquiring control, and the names of the lenders or pledgees.

2. Any arrangements or understandings among members of both the former and new control groups and their associates with respect to election of directors or other matters should be described.

Item 7. Directors and Executive Officers

If action is to be taken with respect to the election of directors, furnish the following information in tabular form to the extent practicable. If, however, the solicitation is made on behalf of persons other than the registrant, the information required need be furnished only as to nominees of the persons making the solicitation.

(a) The information required by instruction 4 to Item 103 of Regulation S-K (§ 229.103 of this chapter) with respect to directors and executive officers.

(b) The information required by Items 401, 404(a) and (c), and 405 of Regulation S-K (§ 229.401, § 229.404 and § 229.405 of this chapter).

(c) The information required by Item 404(b) of Regulation S-K (§ 229.404 of this chapter).

(d) (1) State whether or not the registrant has standing audit, nominating and compensation committees of the Board of Directors, or committees performing similar functions. If the registrant has such committees, however designated, identify each committee member, state the number of committee meetings held by each such committee during the last fiscal year and describe briefly the functions performed by such committees. Such disclosure need not be provided to the extent it is duplicative of disclosure provided in accordance with Item 401(i) of Regulation S-K (-229.401(i) of this chapter).

(2)(i) If the registrant does not have a standing nominating committee or committee performing similar functions, state the basis for the view of the board of directors that it is appropriate for the registrant not to have such a committee and identify each director who participates in the consideration of director nominees;

(ii) Provide the following information regarding the registrant's director nomination process:

(A) If the nominating committee has a charter, disclose whether a current copy of the charter is available to security holders on the registrant's website. If the nominating committee has a charter and a current copy of the charter is available to security holders on the registrant's website, provide the registrant's website address. If the nominating committee has a charter and a current copy of the charter is not available to security holders on the registrant's website, include a copy of the charter as an appendix to the registrant's proxy statement at least once every three fiscal years. If a current copy of the charter is not available to security holders on the registrant's website, and is not included as an appendix to the registrant's proxy statement, identify in which of the prior fiscal years the charter was so included in satisfaction of this requirement;

(B) If the nominating committee does not have a charter, state that fact;

(C) If the registrant is a listed issuer (as defined in § 240.10A-3) whose securities are listed on a national securities exchange registered pursuant to section 6(a) of the Act (15 U.S.C. 78f(a)) or in an automated inter-dealer quotation system of a national securities association registered pursuant to section 15A(a) of the Act (15 U.S.C. 78o-3(a)) that has independence requirements for nominating committee members, disclose whether the members of the nominating committee are independent, as independence for nominating committee members is defined in the listing standards applicable to the listed issuer;

(D) If the registrant is not a listed issuer (as defined in § 240.10A-3), disclose whether each of the members of the nominating committee is independent. In determining whether a member is independent, the registrant must use a definition of independence of a national securities exchange registered pursuant to section 6(a) of the Act (15 U.S.C. 78f(a)) or a national securities association registered pursuant to section 15A(a) of the Act (15 U.S.C. 78o-3(a)) that has been approved by the Commission (as that definition may be modified or supplemented), and state which definition it used. Whatever definition the registrant chooses, it must apply that definition consistently to all members of the nominating committee and use the independence standards of the same national securities exchange or national securities association for purposes of nominating committee disclosure under this requirement and audit committee disclosure required under paragraph (d)(3)(iv) of Item 7 of Schedule 14A (§ 240.14a-101);

(E) If the nominating committee has a policy with regard to the consideration of any director candidates recommended by security holders, provide a description of the material elements of that policy, which shall include, but need not be limited to, a statement as to whether the committee will consider director candidates recommended by security holders;

(F) If the nominating committee does not have a policy with regard to the consideration of any director candidates recommended by security holders, state that fact and state the basis for the view of the board of directors that it is appropriate for the registrant not to have such a policy;

(G) If the nominating committee will consider candidates recommended by security holders, describe the procedures to be followed by security holders in submitting such recommendations;

(H) Describe any specific, minimum qualifications that the nominating committee believes must be met by a nominating committee-recommended nominee for a position on the registrant's board of directors, and describe any specific qualities or skills that the nominating committee believes are necessary for one or more of the registrant's directors to possess;

(I) Describe the nominating committee's process for identifying and evaluating nominees for director, including nominees recommended by security holders, and any differences in the manner in which the nominating committee evaluates nominees for director based on whether the nominee is recommended by a security holder;

(J) With regard to each nominee approved by the nominating committee for inclusion on the registrant's proxy card (other than nominees who are executive officers or who are directors standing for re-election), state which one or more of the following categories of persons or entities recommended that nominee: security holder, non-management director, chief executive officer, other executive officer, third-party search firm, or other, specified source. With regard to each such nominee approved by a nominating committee of an investment company, state which one or more of the following additional categories of persons or entities recommended that nominee: security holder, director, chief executive officer, other executive officer, or employee of the investment company's investment adviser, principal underwriter, or any affiliated person of the investment adviser or principal underwriter;

(K) If the registrant pays a fee to any third party or parties to identify or evaluate or assist in identifying or evaluating potential nominees, disclose the function performed by each such third party; and

(L) If the registrant's nominating committee received, by a date not later than the 120th calendar day before the date of the registrant's proxy statement released to security holders in connection with the previous year's annual meeting, a recommended nominee from a security holder that beneficially owned more than 5% of the registrant's voting common stock for at least one year as of the date the recommendation was made, or from a group of security holders that beneficially owned, in the aggregate, more than 5% of the registrant's voting common stock, with each of the securities used to calculate that ownership held for at least one year as of the date the recommendation was made, identify the candidate and the security holder or security holder group that recommended the candidate and disclose whether the nominating committee chose to nominate the candidate, provided, however, that no such identification or disclosure is required without the written consent of both the security holder or security holder group and the candidate to be so identified.

Instructions to paragraph (d) (2) (ii) (L):

1. For purposes of Item 7(d)(2)(ii)(L), the percentage of securities held by a nominating security holder may be determined using information set forth in the registrant's most recent quarterly or annual report, and any current report subsequent thereto, filed with the Commission pursuant to this Act (or, in the case of a registrant that is an investment company registered under the Investment Company Act of 1940, the registrant's most recent report on Form N-CSR (§ § 249.331 and 274.128)), unless the party relying on such report knows or has reason to believe that the information contained therein is inaccurate.

2. For purposes of the registrant's obligation to provide the disclosure specified in Item 7(d)(2)(ii)(L), where the date of the annual meeting has been changed by more than 30 days from the date of the previous year's meeting, the obligation under that Item will arise where the

registrant receives the security holder recommendation a reasonable time before the registrant begins to print and mail its proxy materials.

3. For purposes of Item 7(d)(2)(ii)(L), the percentage of securities held by a recommending security holder, as well as the holding period of those securities, may be determined by the registrant if the security holder is the registered holder of the securities. If the security holder is not the registered owner of the securities, he or she can submit one of the following to the registrant to evidence the required ownership percentage and holding period:

A. A written statement from the "record" holder of the securities (usually a broker or bank) verifying that, at the time the security holder made the recommendation, he or she had held the required securities for at least one year; or

B. If the security holder has filed a Schedule 13D (§ 240.13d-101), Schedule 13G (§ 240.13d-102), Form 3 (§ 249.103), Form 4 (§ 249.104), and/or Form 5 (§ 249.105), or amendments to those documents or updated forms, reflecting ownership of the securities as of or before the date of the recommendation, a copy of the schedule and/or form, and any subsequent amendments reporting a change in ownership level, as well as a written statement that the security holder continuously held the securities for the one-year period as of the date of the recommendation.

4. For purposes of the registrant's obligation to provide the disclosure specified in Item 7(d)(2)(ii)(L), the security holder or group must have provided to the registrant, at the time of the recommendation, the written consent of all parties to be identified and, where the security holder or group members are not registered holders, proof that the security holder or group satisfied the required ownership percentage and holding period as of the date of the recommendation.

Instruction to paragraph (d)(2)(ii): For purposes of Item 7(d)(2)(ii), the term "nominating committee" refers not only to nominating committees and committees performing similar functions, but also to groups of directors fulfilling the role of a nominating committee, including the entire board of directors.

(3) If the registrant has an audit committee:

(i) Provide the information required by Item 306 of Regulation S-K (17 CFR 229.306).

(ii) State whether the registrant's Board of Directors has adopted a written charter for the audit committee.

(iii) Include a copy of the written charter, if any, as an appendix to the registrant's proxy statement, unless a copy has been included as an appendix to the registrant's proxy statement within the registrant's past three fiscal years.

(iv) (A) If the registrant is a listed issuer, as defined in § 240.10A-3:

(*1*) Disclose whether the members of the audit committee are independent, as independence for audit committee members is defined in the listing standards applicable to the listed issuer. If the registrant does not have a separately designated audit committee, or committee performing similar functions, the registrant must provide the disclosure with respect to all members of its board of directors.

(*2*)) If the listed issuer's board of directors determines, in accordance with the listing standards applicable to the listed issuer, to appoint a director to the audit committee who is not independent (apart from the requirements in § 240.10A-3) because of exceptional or limited or similar circumstances, disclose the nature of the relationship that makes that individual not independent and the reasons for the board of directors' determination.

(B) If the registrant, including a small business issuer, is not a listed issuer, disclose whether the registrant has an audit committee established in accordance with section 3(a)(58)(A) of the Act (15 U.S.C. 78c(a)(58)(A)) and, if so, whether the members of the committee are independent. In determining whether a member is independent, the registrant must use a definition for audit committee member independence of a national securities exchange registered pursuant to section 6(a) of the Act (15 U.S.C. 78f(a)) or a national securities association registered pursuant to section 15A(a) of the Act (15 U.S.C. 78o-3(a)) that has been approved by the Commission (as such definition may be modified or supplemented), and state which definition was used. Whichever definition is chosen must be applied consistently to all members of the audit committee.

(v) The information required by paragraph (d)(3) of this Item shall not be deemed to be "soliciting material," or to be "filed" with the Commission or subject to Regulation 14A or 14C (17 CFR 240.14a-1 *et seq.* or 240.14c-1 *et seq.*), other than as provided in this Item, or to the liabilities of section 18 of the Exchange Act (15 U.S.C. §78r), except to the extent that the registrant specifically requests that the information be treated as soliciting material or specifically incorporates it by reference into a document filed under the Securities Act or the Exchange Act. Such information will not be deemed to be incorporated by reference into any filing under the Securities Act or the Exchange Act, except to the extent that the registrant specifically incorporates it by reference.

(vi) The disclosure required by this paragraph (d)(3) need only be provided one time during any fiscal year.

(vii) Investment companies registered under the Investment Company Act of 1940 (15 U.S.C. §80a-1 *et seq.*), other than closed-end investment companies, need not provide the information required by this paragraph (d)(3).

(e) In lieu of paragraphs (a) through (d)(1) and (d)(2)(ii)(D) of this Item, investment companies registered under the Investment Company Act of 1940 (15 U.S.C. 80a) must furnish the information required by Item 22(b) of this Schedule 14A.

(f) State the total number of meetings of the board of directors (including regularly scheduled and special meetings) which were held during the last full fiscal year. Name each incumbent director who during the last full fiscal year attended fewer than 75 percent of the aggregate of (1) the total number of meetings of the board of directors (held during the period for which he has been a director) and (2) the total number of meetings held by all committees of the board on which he served (during the periods that he served).

(g) If a director has resigned or declined to stand for re-election to the board of directors since the date of the last annual meeting of security holders because of a disagreement with the registrant on any matter relating to the registrant's operations, policies or practices, and if the director has furnished the registrant with a letter describing such disagreement and requesting that the matter be disclosed, the registrant shall state the date of resignation or declination to stand for re-election and summarize the director's description of the disagreement.

If the registrant believes that the description provided by the director is incorrect or incomplete, it may include a brief statement presenting its views of the disagreement.

(h)(1) State whether or not the registrant's board of directors provides a process for security holders to send communications to the board of directors and, if the registrant does not have such a process for security holders to send communications to the board of directors, state the basis for the view of the board of directors that it is appropriate for the registrant not to have such a process;

(2) If the registrant has a process for security holders to send communications to the board of directors:

(i) Describe the manner in which security holders can send communications to the board and, if applicable, to specified individual directors; and

(ii) If all security holder communications are not sent directly to board members, describe the registrant's process for determining which communications will be relayed to board members; and

Instruction to paragraph (h)(2)(ii): For purposes of the disclosure required by this paragraph, a registrant's process for collecting and organizing security holder communications, as well as similar or related activities, need not be disclosed provided that the registrant's process is approved by a majority of the independent directors or, in the case of a registrant that is an investment company, a majority of the directors who are not "interested persons" of the investment company as defined in section 2(a)(19) of the Investment Company Act of 1940 (15 U.S.C. 80a-2(a)(19)).

(3) Describe the registrant's policy, if any, with regard to board members' attendance at annual meetings and state the number of board members who attended the prior year's annual meeting.

Instruction to paragraphs (h)(2) and (h)(3): In lieu of providing the information required by paragraphs (h)(2) and (h)(3) in the proxy statement, the registrant may instead provide the registrant's website address where such information appears.

Instructions to paragraph (h):

1. For purposes of this paragraph, communications from an officer or director of the registrant will not be viewed as "security holder communications." Communications from an employee or agent of the registrant will be viewed as "security holder communications" for purposes of this paragraph only if those communications are made solely in such employee's or agent's capacity as a security holder.

2. For purposes of this paragraph, security holder proposals submitted pursuant to § 240.14a-8, and communications made in connection with such proposals, will not be viewed as "security holder communications."

Item 8. Compensation of Directors and Executive Officers

Furnish the information required by Item 402 (§ 229.402 of this chapter) of Regulation S-K if action is to be taken with regard to:

(a) the election of directors;

(b) any bonus, profit sharing or other compensation plan, contract or arrangement in which any director, nominee for election as a director, or executive officer of the registrant will participate;

(c) any pension or retirement plan in which any such person will participate; or

(d) the granting or extension to any such person of any options, warrants or rights to purchase any securities, other than warrants or rights issued to security holders as such, on a pro rata basis.

However, if the solicitation is made on behalf of persons other than the registrant, the information required need be furnished only as to nominees of the persons making the solicitation and associates of such nominees. In the case of investment companies registered under the Investment Company Act of 1940 and registrants that have elected to be regulated as business development companies, furnish the information required by Item 22(b)(13) of this Schedule.

Instruction. If an otherwise reportable compensation plan became subject to such requirements because of an acquisition or merger and, within one year of the acquisition or merger, such plan was terminated for purposes of prospective eligibility, the registrant may furnish a description of its obligation to the designated individuals pursuant to the compenation plan. Such description may be furnished in lieu of a description of the compensation plan in the proxy statement.

Item 9. Independent Public Accountants

If the solicitation is made on behalf of the registrant and relates to (1) the annual (or special meeting in lieu of annual) meeting of security holders at which directors are to be elected, or a solicitation of consents or authorizations in lieu of such meeting or (2) the election, approval or ratification of the registrant's accountant, furnish the following information describing the registrant's relationship with its independent public accountant:

(a) The name of the principal accountant selected or being recommended to security holders for election, approval or ratification for the current year. If no accountant has been selected or recommended, so state and briefly describe the reasons therefor.

(b) The name of the principal accountant for the fiscal year most recently completed if different from the accountant selected or recommended for the current year of if no accountant has yet been selected or recommended for the current year.

(c) The proxy statement shall indicate (1) whether or not representatives of the principal accountant for the current year and for the most recently completed fiscal year are expected to be present at the security holders' meeting, (2) whether or not they will have the opportunity to make a statement if they desire to do so and (3) whether or not such representatives are expected to be available to respond to appropriate questions.

(d) If during the registrant's two most recent fiscal years or any subsequent interim period, (1) an independent accountant who was previously engaged as the principal accountant to audit the registrant's financial statements, or an independent accountant on whom the principal accountant expressed reliance in its report regarding a significant subsidiary, has resigned (or indicated it has declined to stand for re-election after the completion of the current audit) or was dismissed, or (2) a new independent accountant has been engaged as either the principal accountant to audit the registrant's financial statements or as an independent accountant on whom the principal accountant has expressed or is expected to express reliance in its report regarding a significant subsidiary, then, notwithstanding any previous disclosure, provide the information required by Item 304(a) of Regulation S-K (§ 229.304 of this chapter).

(e)(1) Disclose, under the caption *Audit Fees*, the aggregate fees billed for each of the last two fiscal years for professional services rendered by the principal accountant for the audit of the registrant's annual financial statements and review of financial statements included in the registrant's Form 10-Q (17 CFR 249.308a) or 10-QSB (17 CFR 249.308b) or services that are normally provided by the accountant in connection with statutory and regulatory filings or engagements for those fiscal years.

(2) Disclose, under the caption *Audit-Related Fees*, the aggregate fees billed in each of the last two fiscal years for assurance and related services by the principal accountant that are reasonably related to the performance of the audit or review of the registrant's financial statements and are not reported under paragraph (e)(1) of this section. Registrants shall describe the nature of the services comprising the fees disclosed under this category.

(3) Disclose, under the caption *Tax Fees*, the aggregate fees billed in each of the last two fiscal years for professional services rendered by the principal accountant for tax compliance, tax advice, and tax planning. Registrants shall describe the nature of the services comprising the fees disclosed under this category.

(4) Disclose, under the caption *All Other Fees*, the aggregate fees billed in each of the last two fiscal years for products and services provided by the principal accountant, other than the services reported in paragraphs (e)(1) through (e)(3) of this section. Registrants shall describe the nature of the services comprising the fees disclosed under this category.

(5)(i) Disclose the audit committee's pre-approval policies and procedures described in 17 CFR 210.2-01(c)(7)(i).

(ii) Disclose the percentage of services described in each of paragraphs (e)(2) through (e)(4) of this section that were approved by the audit committee pursuant to 17 CFR 210.2-01(c)(7)(i)(C).

(6) If greater than 50 percent, disclose the percentage of hours expended on the principal accountant's engagement to audit the registrant's financial statements for the most recent fiscal year that were attributed to work performed by persons other than the principal accountant's full-time, permanent employees.

(7) If the registrant is an investment company, disclose the aggregate non-audit fees billed by the registrant's accountant for services rendered to the registrant, and to the registrant's investment adviser (not including any subadviser whose role is primarily portfolio management and is subcontracted with or overseen by another investment adviser), and any entity controlling, controlled by, or under common control with the adviser that provides ongoing services to the registrant for each of the last two fiscal years of the registrant.

(8) If the registrant is an investment company, disclose whether the audit committee of the board of directors has considered whether the provision of non-audit services that were rendered to the registrant's investment adviser (not including any subadviser whose role is primarily portfolio management and is subcontracted with or overseen by another investment adviser), and any entity controlling, controlled by, or under common control with the investment adviser that provides ongoing services to the registrant that were not pre-approved pursuant to 17 CFR 210.2-01(c)(7)(ii) is compatible with maintaining the principal accountant's independence.

Instruction to Item 9(e).

For purposes of Item 9(e)(2), (3), and (4), registrants that are investment companies must disclose fees billed for services rendered to the registrant and separately, disclose fees required to be approved by the investment company registrant's audit committee pursuant to 17 CFR 210.2-01(c)(7)(ii). Registered investment companies must also disclose the fee percentages as required by item 9(e)(5)(ii) for the registrant and separately, disclose the fee percentages as required by item 9(e)(5)(ii) for the fees required to be approved by the investment company registrant's audit committee pursuant to 17 CFR 210.2-01(c)(7)(ii).

Item 10. Compensation Plans

If action is to be taken with respect to any plan pursuant to which cash or noncash compensation may be paid or distributed, furnish the following information:

(a) *Plans Subject to Securityholder Action.*

(1) Describe briefly the material features of the plan being acted upon, identify each class of persons who will be eligible to participate therein, indicate the approximate number of persons in each such class and state the basis of such participation.

(2)(i) In the tabular format specified below, disclose the benefits or amounts that will be received by or allocated to each of the following under the plan being acted upon, if such benefits or amounts are determinable:

NEW PLAN BENEFITS
Plan Name

Name and Position	Dollar Value ($)	Number of Units
CEO		
A		
B		
C		
D		
Executive Group		
Non-Executive Director Group		
Non-Executive Officer Employee Group		

(ii) The table required by paragraph (a)(2)(i) of this Item shall provide information as to the following persons:

(A) Each person (stating name and position) specified in paragraph (a) (3) of Item 402 of Regulation S-K (§ 229.402 (a) (3) of this chapter);

Instruction: In the case of investment companies registered under the Investment Company Act of 1940, furnish the information for Compensated Persons as defined in Item 22 (b) (13) of this Schedule in lieu of the persons specified in paragraph (a) (3) of Item 402 of Regulation S-K (§ 229.402 (a) (3) of this chapter).

(B) All current executive officers as a group;

(C) All current directors who are not executive officers as a group; and

(D) All employees, including all current officers who are not executive officers, as a group.

Instruction to New Plan Benefits Table.

Additional columns should be added for each plan with respect to which securityholder action is to be taken.

(iii) If the benefits or amounts specified in paragraph (a) (2) (i) of this Item are not determinable, state the benefits or amounts which would have been received by or allocated to each of the following for the last completed fiscal year if the plan had been in effect, if such benefits or amounts may be determined in the table specified in paragraph (a) (2) (i) of this Item:

(A) Each person (stating name and position) specified in paragraph (a) (3) of Item 402 of Regulation S-K (§ 229.402 (a) (3) of this chapter);

(B) All current executive officers as a group;

(C) All current directors who are not executive officers as a group; and

(D) All employees, including all current officers who are not executive officers, as a group.

(3) If the plan to be acted upon can be amended, otherwise than by a vote of securityholders, to increase the cost thereof to the registrant or to alter the allocation of the benefits as between the persons and groups specified in paragraph (2) (a) of this item, state the nature of the amendments which can be so made.

(b) *Additional Information Regarding Specific Plans Subject to Securityholder Action.*

(1) With respect to any pension or retirement plan submitted for securityholder action, state:

(i) The approximate total amount necessary to fund the plan with respect to past services, the period over which such amount is to be paid and the estimated annual payments necessary to pay the total amount over such period; and

(ii) The estimated annual payment to be made with respect to current services. In the case of a pension or retirement plan, information called for by paragraph (a) (2) of this Item may be furnished in the format specified by paragraph (f) (1) of Item 402 of Regulation S-K (§ 229.402 (f) (1) of this chapter).

Instruction. In the case of investment companies registered under the Investment Company Act of 1940, refer to instruction 4 in Item 22 (b) (13) (i) of this Schedule in lieu of paragraph (f) (1) of Item 402 of Regulation S-K (§ 229.402 (f) (1) of this chapter).

(2) (i) With respect to any specific grant of or any plan containing options, warrants or rights submitted for security holder action, state:

(A) The title and amount of securities underlying such options, warrants or rights;

(B) The prices, expiration dates and other material conditions upon which the options, warrants or rights may be exercised;

(C) The consideration received or to be received by the registrant or subsidiary for the granting or extension of the options, warrants or rights;

(D) The market value of the securities underlying the options, warrants or rights as of the latest practicable date; and

618

(E) In the case of options, the federal income tax consequences of the issuance and exercise of such options to the recipient and the registrant; and

(ii) State separately the amount of such options received or to be received by the following persons if such benefits or amounts are determinable:

(A) Each person (stating name and position) specified in paragraph (a) (3) of Item 402 of Regulation S-K (§ 229.402 (a) (3) of this chapter);

(B) All current executive officers as a group;

(C) All current directors who are not executive officers as a group;

(D) Each nominee for election as a director;

(E) Each associate of any of such directors, executive officer or nominees;

(F) Each other person who received or is to receive 5 percent of such options, warrants or rights; and

(G) All employees, including all current officers who are not executive officers, as a group.

(c) *Information regarding plans and other arrangements not subject to security holder action.* Furnish the information required by Item 201 (d) of Regulation S-K (§ 229.201 (d) of this chapter).

Instructions to paragraph (c).

1. If action is to be taken as described in paragraph (a) of this Item with respect to the approval of a new compensation plan under which equity securities of the registrant are authorized for issuance, information about the plan shall be disclosed as required under paragraphs (a) and (b) of this Item and shall not be included in the disclosure required by Item 201 (d) of Regulation S-K (§ 229.201 (d) of this chapter). If action is to be taken as described in paragraph (a) of this Item with respect to the amendment or modification of an existing plan under which equity securities of the registrant are authorized for issuance, the registrant shall include information about securities previously authorized for issuance under the plan (including any outstanding options, warrants and rights previously granted pursuant to the plan and any securities remaining available for future issuance under the plan) in the disclosure required by Item 201 (d) of Regulation S-K (§ 229.201 (d) of this chapter). Any additional securities that are the subject of the amendments or modification of the existing plan shall be disclosed as required under paragraphs (a) and (b) of this Item and shall not be included in the Item 201 (d) disclosure.

Instructions

1. The term "plan" as used in this Item means any plan as defined in paragraph (a) (7) (ii) of Item 402 of Regulation S-K (§ 229.402 (a) (7) (ii) of this chapter).

2. If action is to be taken with respect to a material amendment or modification of an existing plan, the item shall be answered with respect to the plan as proposed to be amended or modified and shall indicate any material differences from the existing plan.

3. If the plan to be acted upon is set forth in a written document, three copies thereof shall be filed with the Commission at the time copies of the proxy statement and form of proxy are first filed pursuant to paragraph (a) or (b) of § 240.14a-6. Electronic filers shall file with the Commission a copy of such written plan document in electronic format as an appendix to the proxy statement. It need not be provided to security holders unless it is a part of the proxy statement.

4. Paragraphs (b) (2) (ii) does not apply to warrants or rights to be issued to security holders as such on a pro rata basis.

5. The Commission should be informed, as supplemental information, when the proxy statement is first filed, as to when the options, warrants, or rights and the shares called for thereby will be registered under the Securities Act or, if such registration is not contemplated, the section of the Securities Act or rule of the Commission under which exemption from such registration is claimed and the facts relied upon to make the exemption available.

Item 11. Authorization or Issuance of Securities Otherwise than for Exchange

If action is to be taken with respect to the authorization or issuance of any securities otherwise than for exchange for outstanding securities of the registrant, furnish the following information:

(a) State the title and amount of securities to be authorized or issued.

(b) Furnish the information required by Item 202 of Regulation S-K (§ 229.202 of this chapter). If the terms of the securities cannot be stated or estimated with respect to any or all of the securities to be authorized, because no offering thereof is contemplated in the proximate future, and if no further authorization by security holders for the issuance thereof is to be obtained, it should be stated that the terms of the securities to be authorized, including dividend or interest rates, conversion prices, voting rights, redemption prices, maturity dates, and similar matters will be determined by the board of directors. If the securities are additional shares of common stock of a class outstanding, the description may be omitted except for a statement of the preemptive rights, if any. Where the statutory provisions with respect to preemptive rights are so indefinite or complex that they cannot be stated in summarized form, it will suffice to make a statement in the form of an opinion of counsel as to the existence and extent of such rights.

(c) Describe briefly the transaction in which the securities are to be issued including a statement as to (1) the nature and approximate amount of consideration received or to be received by the registrant and (2) the approximate amount devoted to each purpose so far as determinable for which the net proceeds have been or are to be used. If it is impracticable to describe the transaction in which the securities are to be issued, state the reason, indicate the purpose of the authorization of the securities, and state whether further authorization for the issuance of the securities by a vote of security holders will be solicited prior to such issuance.

(d) If the securities are to be issued otherwise than in a public offering for cash, state the reasons for the proposed authorization or issuance and the general effect thereof upon the rights of existing security holders.

(e) Furnish the information required by Item 13(a) of this schedule.

Item 12. Modification or Exchange of Securities

If action is to be taken with respect to the modification of any class of securities of the registrant, or the issuance or authorization for issuance of securities of the registrant in exchange for outstanding securities of the registrant furnish the following information:

(a) If outstanding securities are to be modified, state the title and amount thereof. If securities are to be issued in exchange for outstanding securities, state the title and amount of securities to be so issued, the title and amount of outstanding securities to be exchanged therefor and the basis of the exchange.

(b) Describe any material differences between the outstanding securities and the modified or new securities in respect of any of the matters concerning which information would be required in the description of the securities in Item 202 of Regulation S- K (§ 229.202 of this chapter).

(c) State the reasons for the proposed modification or exchange and the general effect thereof upon the rights of existing security holders.

(d) Furnish a brief statement as to arrears in dividends or as to defaults in principal or interest in respect to the outstanding securities which are to be modified or exchanged and such other information as may be appropriate in the particular case to disclose adequately the nature and effect of the proposed action.

(e) Outline briefly any other material features of the proposed modification or exchange. If the plan of proposed action is set forth in a written document, file copies thereof with the Commission in accordance with § 240.14a-8.

(f) Furnish the information required by Item 13(a) of this Schedule.

Instruction. If the existing security is presently listed and registered on a national securities exchange, state whether the registrant intends to apply for listing and registration of the new or reclassified security on such exchange or any other exchange. If the registrant does not intend to make such application, state the effect of the termination of such listing and registration.

Item 13. Financial and Other Information

(*See* Notes D and E at the beginning of this Schedule.)

(a) *Information required.* If action is to be taken with respect to any matter specified in Item 11 or 12, furnish the following information:

(1) Financial statements meeting the requirements of Regulation S-X, including financial information required by Rule 3-05 and Article 11 of Regulation S-X with respect to transactions other than that pursuant to which action is to be taken as described in this proxy statement;

(2) Item 302 of Regulation S-K, supplementary financial information;

(3) Item 303 of Regulation S-K, management's discussion and analysis of financial condition and results of operations;

(4) Item 304 of Regulation S-K, changes in and disagreements with accountants on accounting and financial disclosure;

(5) Item 305 of Regulation S-K, quantitative and qualitative disclosures about market risk; and

(6) A statement as to whether or not representatives of the principal accountants for the current year and for the most recently completed fiscal year:

(i) are expected to be present at the security holders' meeting;

(ii) will have the opportunity to make a statement if they desire to do so; and

(iii) are expected to be available to respond to appropriate questions.

(b) *Incorporation by reference.* The information required pursuant to paragraph (a) of this Item may be incorporated by reference into the proxy statement as follows:

(1) *S-3 registrants.* If the registrant meets the requirements of Form S-3 (*see* Note E to this Schedule), it may incorporate by reference to previously-filed documents any of the information required by paragraph (a) of this Item, provided that the requirements of paragraph (c) are met. Where the registrant meets the requirements of Form S-3 and has elected to furnish the required information by incorporation by reference, the registrant may elect to update the information so incorporated by reference to information in subsequently-filed documents.

(2) *All registrants.* The registrant may incorporate by reference any of the information required by paragraph (a) of this Item, provided that the information is contained in an annual report to security holders or a previously-filed statement or report, such report or statement is delivered to security holders with the proxy statement and the requirements of paragraph (c) are met.

(c) *Certain conditions applicable to incorporation by reference.* Registrants eligible to incorporate by reference into the proxy statement the information required by paragraph (a) of this Item in the manner specified by paragraphs (b)(1) and (b)(2) may do so only if:

(1) the information is not required to be included in the proxy statement pursuant to the requirement of another Item;

(2) the proxy statement identifies on the last page(s) the information incorporated by reference; and

(3) the material incorporated by reference substantially meets the requirements of this Item or the appropriate portions of this Item.

Instructions to Item 13. 1. Notwithstanding the provisions of this Item, any or all of the information required by paragraph (a) of this Item, not material for the exercise of prudent judgment in regard to the matter to be acted upon may be omitted. In the usual case the information is deemed material to the exercise of prudent judgment where the matter to be acted upon is the authorization or issuance of a material amount of senior securities, but the information is not deemed material where the matter to be acted upon is the authorization or issuance of common stock, otherwise than in an exchange, merger, consolidation, acquisition or similar transaction, the authorization of preferred stock without present intent to issue or the authorization of preferred stock for issuance for cash in an amount constituting fair value.

2. In order to facilitate compliance with Rule 2-02(a) of Regulation S-X, one copy of the definitive proxy statement filed with the Commission shall include a manually signed copy of the accountant's report. If the financial statements are incorporated by reference, a manually signed copy of the accountant's report shall be filed with the definitive proxy statement.

3. Notwithstanding the provisions of Regulation S-X, no schedules other than those prepared in accordance with Rules 12-15, 12-28 and 12-29 (or, for management investment companies, Rules 12-12 through 12-14) of that regulation need be furnished in the proxy statement.

4. Unless registered on a national securities exchange or otherwise required to furnish such information, registered investment companies need not furnish the information required by paragraphs (a)(2) or (3) of this Item.

5. If the registrant submits preliminary proxy material incorporating by reference financial statements required by this Item, the registrant should furnish a draft of the financial statements if the document from which they are incorporated has not been filed with or furnished to the Commission.

6. A registered investment company need not comply with items (a)(2), (a)(3), and (a)(5) of this Item 13.

Item 14. Mergers, Consolidations, Acquisitions and Similar Matters

(Notes A, and D at the beginning of this Schedule.)

Instructions to Item 14.

1. In transactions in which the consideration offered to security holders consists wholly or in part of securities registered under the Securities Act of 1933, furnish the information required by Form S-4 (§ 239.25 of this chapter), Form F-4 (§ 239.34 of this chapter), or Form N-14 (§ 239.23 of this chapter), as applicable, instead of this Item. Only a Form S-4, Form F-4, or Form N-14 must be filed in accordance with § 240.14a-6(j).

2. (a) In transactions in which the consideration offered to security holders consists wholly of cash, the information required by paragraph (c)(1) of this Item for the acquiring company need not be provided unless the information is material to an informed voting decision (*e.g.*, the security holders of the target company are voting and financing is not assured).

(b) Additionally, if only the security holders of the target company are voting:

i. The financial information in paragraphs (b)(8) -(11) of this Item for the acquiring company and the target need not be provided; and

ii. The information in paragraph (c)(2) of this Item for the target company need not be provided.

If, however, the transaction is a going-private transaction (as defined by § 240.13e-3), then the information required by paragraph (c)(2) of this Item must be provided and to the extent that the going-private rules require the information specified in paragraph (b)(8) - (b)(11) of this Item, that information must be provided as well.

3. In transactions in which the consideration offered to security holders consists wholly of securities exempt from registration under the Securities Act of 1933 or a combination of exempt securities and cash, information about the acquiring company required by paragraph (c)(1) of this Item need not be provided if only the security holders of the acquiring company are voting, unless the information is material to an informed voting decision. If only the security holders of the target company are voting, information about the target company in paragraph (c)(2) of this Item need not be provided. However, the information required by paragraph (c)(2) of this Item must be provided if the transaction is a going-private (as defined by § 240.13e-3) or roll-up (as described by Item 901 of Regulation S-K (§ 229.901 of this chapter)) transaction.

4. The information required by paragraphs (b)(8)-(11) and (c) need not be provided if the plan being voted on involves only the acquiring company and one or more of its totally held subsidiaries and does not involve a liquidation or a spin-off.

5. To facilitate compliance with Rule 2-02(a) of Regulation S-X (§ 210.2-02(a) of this chapter) (technical requirements relating to accountants' reports), one copy of the definitive proxy statement filed with the Commission must include a signed copy of the accountant's report. If the financial statements are incorporated by reference, a signed copy of the accountant's report must be filed with the definitive proxy statement. Signatures may be typed if the document is filed electronically on EDGAR. *See* Rule 302 of Regulation S-T (§ 232.302 of this chapter).

6. Notwithstanding the provisions of Regulation S-X, no schedules other than those prepared in accordance with § 210.12-15, § 210.12-28 and § 210.12-29 of this chapter (or, for management investment companies, § § 210.12-12 through 210.12-14 of this chapter) of that regulation need be furnished in the proxy statement.

7. If the preliminary proxy material incorporates by reference financial statements required by this Item, a draft of the financial statements must be furnished to the Commission staff upon request if the document from which they are incorporated has not been filed with or furnished to the Commission.

(a) *Applicability.* If action is to be taken with respect to any of the following transactions, provide the information required by this Item:

(1) A merger or consolidation;

(2) An acquisition of securities of another person;

(3) An acquisition of any other going business or the assets of a going business;

(4) A sale or other transfer of all or any substantial part of assets; or

(5) A liquidation or dissolution.

(b) *Transaction information.* Provide the following information for each of the parties to the transaction unless otherwise specified:

(1) *Summary term sheet.* The information required by Item 1001 of Regulation M-A (§ 229.1001 of this chapter).

(2) *Contact information.* The name, complete mailing address and telephone number of the principal executive offices.

(3) *Business conducted.* A brief description of the general nature of the business conducted.

(4) *Terms of the transaction.* The information required by Item 1004(a)(2) of Regulation M-A (§ 229.1004 of this chapter).

(5) *Regulatory approvals.* A statement as to whether any federal or state regulatory requirements must be complied with or approval must be obtained in connection with the transaction and, if so, the status of the compliance or approval.

(6) *Reports, opinions, appraisals.* If a report, opinion or appraisal materially relating to the transaction has been received from an outside party, and is referred to in the proxy statement, furnish the information required by Item 1015(b) of Regulation M-A (§ 229.1015 of this chapter).

(7) *Past contacts, transactions or negotiations.* The information required by Items 1005(b) and 1011(a)(1) of Regulation M-A (§ 229.1005 of this chapter and § 229.1011 of this chapter), for the parties to the transaction and their affiliates during the periods for which financial statements are presented or incorporated by reference under this Item.

(8) *Selected financial data.* The selected financial data required by Item 301 of Regulation S-K (§ 229.301 of this chapter).

(9) *Pro forma selected financial data.* If material, the information required by Item 301 of Regulation S-K (§ 229.301 of this chapter) for the acquiring company, showing the pro forma effect of the transaction.

(10) *Pro forma information.* In a table designed to facilitate comparison, historical and pro forma per share data of the acquiring company and historical and equivalent pro forma per share data of the target company for the following Items:

(i) Book value per share as of the date financial data is presented pursuant to Item 301 of Regulation S-K (§ 229.301 of this chapter);

(ii) Cash dividends declared per share for the periods for which financial data is presented pursuant to Item 301 of Regulation S-K (§ 229.301 of this chapter); and

(iii) Income (loss) per share from continuing operations for the periods for which financial data is presented pursuant to Item 301 of Regulation S-K (§ 229.301 of this chapter).

Instructions to paragraphs (b)(8), (b)(9) and (b)(10):

1. For a business combination accounted for as a purchase, present the financial information required by paragraphs (b)(9) and (b)(10) only for the most recent fiscal year and interim period. For a business combination accounted for as a pooling, present the financial information required by paragraphs (b)(9) and (b)(10) (except for information with regard to book value) for the most recent three fiscal years and interim period. For purposes of these paragraphs, book value information need only be provided for the most recent balance sheet date.

2. Calculate the equivalent pro forma per share amounts for one share of the company being acquired by multiplying the exchange ratio times each of:

(i) The pro forma income (loss) per share before non-recurring charges or credits directly attributable to the transaction;

(ii) The pro forma book value per share; and

(iii) The pro forma dividends per share of the acquiring company.

3. Unless registered on a national securities exchange or otherwise required to furnish such information, registered investment companies need not furnish the information required by paragraphs (b)(8) and (b)(9) of this Item.

(11) *Financial information.* If material, financial information required by Article 11 of Regulation S-X (§§ 210.10-01 through 229.11-03 of this chapter) with respect to this transaction.

Instructions to paragraph (b)(11):

1. Present any Article 11 information required with respect to transactions other than those being voted upon (where not incorporated by reference) together with the pro forma information relating to the transaction being voted upon. In presenting this information, you must clearly distinguish between the transaction being voted upon and any other transaction.

2. If current pro forma financial information with respect to all other transactions is incorporated by reference, you need only present the pro forma effect of this transaction.

(c) *Information about the parties to the transaction.*

(1) *Acquiring company.* Furnish the information required by Part B (Registrant Information) of Form S-4 (§ 239.25 of this chapter) or Form F-4 (§ 239.34 of this chapter), as applicable, for the acquiring company. However, financial statements need only be presented for the latest two fiscal years and interim periods.

(2) *Acquired company.* Furnish the information required by Part C (Information with Respect to the Company Being Acquired) of Form S-4 (§ 239.25 of this chapter) or Form F-4 (§ 239.34 of this chapter), as applicable.

(d) *Information about parties to the transaction: registered investment companies and business development companies.*

If the acquiring company or the acquired company is an investment company registered under the Investment Company Act of 1940 or a business development company as defined by Section 2(a)(48) of the Investment Company Act of 1940, provide the following information for that company instead of the information specified by paragraph (c) of this Item:

624

(1) Information required by Item 101 of Regulation S-K (§ 229.101 of this chapter), description of business;

(2) Information required by Item 102 of Regulation S-K (§ 229.102 of this chapter), description of property;

(3) Information required by Item 103 of Regulation S-K (§ 229.103 of this chapter), legal proceedings;

(4) Information required by Item 201(a), (b) and (c) of Regulation S-K (§ 229.201(a), (b) and (c) of this chapter), market price of and dividends on the registrant's common equity and related stockholder matters;

(5) Financial statements meeting the requirements of Regulation S-X, including financial information required by Rule 3-05 and Article 11 of Regulation S-X (§ 210.3-05 and § 210.11-01 through § 210.11-03 of this chapter) with respect to transactions other than that as to which action is to be taken as described in this proxy statement;

(6) Information required by Item 301 of Regulation S-K (§ 229.301 of this chapter), selected financial data;

(7) Information required by Item 302 of Regulation S-K (§ 229.302 of this chapter), supplementary financial information;

(8) Information required by Item 303 of Regulation S-K (§ 229.303 of this chapter), management's discussion and analysis of financial condition and results of operations; and

(9) Information required by Item 304 of Regulation S-K (§ 229.304 of this chapter), changes in and disagreements with accountants on accounting and financial disclosure.

Instruction to paragraph (d) of Item 14:

Unless registered on a national securities exchange or otherwise required to furnish such information, registered investment companies need not furnish the information required by paragraphs (d)(6), (d)(7) and (d)(8) of this Item.

(e) *Incorporation by reference.*

(1) The information required by paragraph (c) of this section may be incorporated by reference into the proxy statement to the same extent as would be permitted by Form S-4 (§ 239.25 of this chapter) or Form F-4 (§ 239.34 of this chapter), as applicable.

(2) Alternatively, the registrant may incorporate by reference into the proxy statement the information required by paragraph (c) of this Item if it is contained in an annual report sent to security holders in accordance with § 240.14a-3 of this chapter with respect to the same meeting or solicitation of consents or authorizations that the proxy statement relates to and the information substantially meets the disclosure requirements of Item 14 or Item 17 of Form S-4 (§ 239.25 of this chapter) or Form F-4 (§ 239.34 of this chapter), as applicable.

Item 15. Acquisition or Disposition of Property

If action is to be taken with respect to the acquisition or disposition of any property, furnish the following information:

(a) Describe briefly the general character and location of the property.

(b) State the nature and amount of consideration to be paid or received by the registrant or any subsidiary. To the extent practicable, outline briefly the facts bearing upon the question of the fairness of the consideration.

(c) State the name and address of the transferer or transferee, as the case may be and the nature of any material relationship of such person to the registrant or any affiliate of the registrant.

(d) Outline briefly any other material features of the contract or transaction.

Item 16. Restatement of Accounts

If action is to be taken with respect to the restatement of any asset, capital, or surplus account of the registrant, furnish the following information:

(a) State the nature of the restatement and the date as of which it is to be effective.

(b) Outline briefly the reasons for the restatement and for the selection of the particular effective date.

(c) State the name and amount of each account (including any reserve accounts) affected by the restatement and the effect of the restatement thereon. Tabular presentation of the amounts shall be made when appropriate, particularly in the case of recapitalizations.

(d) To the extent practicable, state whether and the extent, if any, to which the restatement will, as of the date thereof, alter the amount available for distribution to the holders of equity securities.

Item 17. Action with Respect to Reports

If action is to be taken with respect to any report of the registrant or of its directors, officers or committees or any minutes of a meeting of its security holders furnish the following information:

(a) State whether or not such action is to constitute approval or disapproval of any of the matters referred to in such reports or minutes.

(b) Identify each of such matters which it is intended will be approved or disapproved, and furnish the information required by the appropriate item or items of this schedule with respect to each such matter.

Item 18. Matters Not Required to Be Submitted

If action is to be taken with respect to any matter which is not required to be submitted to a vote of security holders, state the nature of such matter, the reasons for submitting it to a vote of security holders and what action is intended to be taken by the registrant in the event of a negative vote on the matter by the security holders.

Item 19. Amendment of Charter, bylaws or Other Documents

If action is to be taken with respect to any amendment of the registrant's charter, bylaws or other documents as to which information is not required above, state briefly the reasons for and the general effect of such amendment.

Instructions. 1. Where the matter to be acted upon is the classification of directors, state whether vacancies which occur during the year may be filled by the board of directors to serve only until the next annual meeting or may be so filled for the remainder of the full term.

2. Attention is directed to the discussion of disclosure regarding anti-takeover and similar proposals in Release No. 34-15230 (October 13, 1978).

Item 20. Other Proposed Action

If action is to be taken on any matter not specifically referred to in this Schedule 14A, describe briefly the substance of each such matter in substantially the same degree of detail as is required by Items 5 to 19, inclusive, of this Schedule, and, with respect to investment companies registered under the Investment Company Act of 1940, Item 22 of this Schedule.

Item 21. Voting procedures

As to each matter which is to be submitted to a vote of security holders, furnish the following information:

(a) State the vote required for approval or election, other than for the approval of auditors.

(b) Disclose the method by which votes will be counted, including the treatment and effect of abstentions and broker non-votes under applicable state law as well as registrant charter and by-law provisions.

Item 22. Information Required in Investment Company Proxy Statement

(a) *General*.

(1) *Definitions*. Unless the context otherwise requires, terms used in this Item that are defined in § 240.14a-1 (with respect to proxy soliciting material), in § 240.14c-1 (with respect to information statements), and in the Investment Company Act of 1940 shall have the same meanings provided therein and the following terms shall also apply:

(i) *Administrator*. The term "Administrator" shall mean any person who provides significant administrative or business affairs management services to a Fund.

(ii) *Affiliated Broker*. The term "Affiliated Broker" shall mean any broker:

(A) That is an affiliated person of the Fund;

(B) That is an affiliated person of such person; or

(C) An affiliated person of which is an affiliated person of the Fund, its investment adviser, principal underwriter, or Administrator.

(iii) *Distribution Plan*. The term "Distribution Plan" shall mean a plan adopted pursuant to Rule 12b-1 under the Investment Company Act of 1940 (§ 270.12b-1 of this chapter).

(iv) *Family of Investment Companies*. The term "Family of Investment Companies" shall mean any two or more registered investment companies that:

(A) Share the same investment adviser or principal underwriter; and

(B) Hold themselves out to investors as related companies for purposes of investment and investor services.

(v) *Fund*. The term "Fund" shall mean a Registrant or, where the Registrant is a series company, a separate portfolio of the Registrant.

(vi) *Fund Complex*. The term "Fund Complex" shall mean two or more Funds that:

(A) Hold themselves out to investors as related companies for purposes of investment and investor services; or

(B) Have a common investment adviser or have an investment adviser that is an affiliated person of the investment adviser of any of the other Funds.

(vii) *Immediate Family Member*. The term "Immediate Family Member" shall mean a person's spouse; child residing in the person's household (including step and adoptive children); and any dependent of the person, as defined in section 152 of the Internal Revenue Code (26 U.S.C. 152).

(viii) *Officer*. The term "Officer" shall mean the president, vice-president, secretary, treasurer, controller, or any other officer who performs policy-making functions.

(ix) *Parent*. The term "Parent" shall mean the affiliated person of a specified person who controls the specified person directly or indirectly through one or more intermediaries.

(x) *Registrant*. The term "Registrant" shall mean an investment company registered under the Investment Company Act of 1940 (15 U.S.C. 80a) or a business development company as defined by section 2(a)(48) of the Investment Company Act of 1940 (15 U.S.C. 80a-2(a)(48)).

(xi) *Sponsoring Insurance Company*. The term "Sponsoring Insurance Company" of a Fund that is a separate account shall mean the insurance company that establishes and maintains the separate account and that owns the assets of the separate account.

(xii) *Subsidiary*. The term "Subsidiary" shall mean an affiliated person of a specified person who is controlled by the specified person directly, or indirectly through one or more intermediaries.

(2) [Removed and reserved in Release No. 34-37692, effective October 7, 1996, 61 F.R. 49957.]

(3) *General Disclosure*. Furnish the following information in the proxy statement of a Fund or Funds:

(i) State the name and address of the Fund's investment adviser, principal underwriter, and Administrator.

(ii) When a Fund proxy statement solicits a vote on proposals affecting more than one Fund or class of securities of a Fund (unless the proposal or proposals are the same and affect all Fund or class shareholders), present a summary of all of the proposals in tabular form on one of the first three pages of the proxy statement and indicate which Fund or class shareholders are solicited with respect to each proposal.

(iii) Unless the proxy statement is accompanied by a copy of the Fund's most recent annual report, state prominently in the proxy statement that the Fund will furnish, without charge, a copy of the annual report and the most recent semi-annual report succeeding the annual report, if any, to a shareholder upon request providing the name, address, and toll-free telephone number of the person to whom such request shall be directed (or, if no toll-free telephone number is provided, a self-addressed postage paid card for requesting the annual report). The Fund should provide a copy of the annual report and the most recent semi-annual report succeeding the annual report, if any, to the requesting shareholder by first class mail, or other means designed to assure prompt delivery, within three business days of the request.

(iv) If the action to be taken would, directly or indirectly, establish a new fee or expense or increase any existing fee or expense to be paid by the Fund or its shareholders, provide a table showing the current and pro forma fees (with the required examples) using the format prescribed in the appropriate registration statement form under the Investment Company Act of 1940 (for open-end management investment companies, Item 2 of Form N-1A (§ 239.15A); for closed-end management investment companies, Item 3 of Form N-2 (§ 239.14); and for separate accounts that offer variable annuity contracts, Item 3 of Form N-3 (§ 239.17a)).

Instructions. 1. Where approval is sought only for a change in asset breakpoints for a pre-existing fee that would not have increased the fee for the previous year (or have the effect of increasing fees or expenses, but for any other reason would not be reflected in a pro forma fee table), describe the likely effect of the change in lieu of providing pro forma fee information.

2. An action would indirectly establish or increase a fee or expense where, for example, the approval of a new investment advisory contract would result in higher custodial or transfer agency fees.

3. The tables should be prepared in a manner designed to facilitate understanding of the impact of any change in fees or expenses.

4. A Fund that offers its shares exclusively to one or more separate accounts and thus is not required to include a fee table in its prospectus (*see* Item 2(a)(ii) of Form N-1A (§ 239.15A)) should nonetheless prepare a table showing current and pro forma expenses and disclose that the table does not reflect separate account expenses, including sales load.

(v) If action is to be taken with respect to the election of directors or the approval of an advisory contract, describe any purchases or sales of securities of the investment adviser or its Parents, or Subsidiaries of either, since the beginning of the most recently completed fiscal year by any director or any nominee for election as a director of the Fund.

Instructions. 1. Identify the parties, state the consideration, the terms of payment and describe any arrangement or understanding with respect to the composition of the board of directors of the Fund or of the investment adviser, or with respect to the selection of appointment of any person to any office with either such company.

2. Transactions involving securities in an amount not exceeding one percent of the outstanding securities of any class of the investment adviser or any of its Parents or Subsidiaries may be omitted.

(b) *Election of Directors.* If action is to be taken with respect to the election of directors of a Fund, furnish the following information in the proxy statement in addition to the information (and in the format) required by paragraphs (d)(2) (other than (d).(2)(ii)(D)), (d)(3), (f), (g), and (h) of Item 7 of Schedule 14A.

Instructions to introductory text of paragraph (b). 1. Furnish information with respect to a prospective investment adviser to the extent applicable.

2. If the solicitation is made by or on behalf of a person other than the Fund or an investment adviser of the Fund, provide information only as to nominees of the person making the solicitation.

3. When providing information about directors and nominees for election as directors in response to this Item 22(b), furnish information for directors or nominees who are or would be "interested persons" of the Fund within the meaning of section 2(a)(19) of the Investment Company Act of 1940 (15 U.S.C. 80a-2(a)(19)) separately from the information for directors or nominees who are not or would not be interested persons of the Fund. For example, when furnishing information in a table, you should provide separate tables (or separate sections of a single table) for directors and nominees who are or would be interested persons and for directors or nominees who are not or would not be interested persons. When furnishing information in narrative form, indicate by heading or otherwise the directors or nominees who are or would be interested persons and the directors or nominees who are not or would not be interested persons.

4. No information need be given about any director whose term of office as a director will not continue after the meeting to which the proxy statement relates.

(1) Provide the information required by the following table for each director, nominee for election as director, Officer of the Fund, person chosen to become an Officer of the Fund, and, if the Fund has an advisory board, member of the board.

Explain in a footnote to the table any family relationship between the persons listed.

(1)	(2)	(3)	(4)	(5)	(6)
Name, Address, Position(s) Held and Age	Position(s) Held with Fund	Term of Office and Length of Time Served	Principal Occupation(s) During Past 5 Years	Number of Portfolios in Fund Complex Overseen by Director or Nominee for Director	Other Directorships Held by Director or Nominee for Director

Instructions to paragraph (b)(1). 1. For purposes of this paragraph, the term "family relationship" means any relationship by blood, marriage, or adoption, not more remote than first cousin.

2. No nominee or person chosen to become a director or Officer who has not consented to act as such may be named in response to this Item. In this regard, see Rule 14a-4(d) under the Exchange Act (§ 240.14a-4(d)).

3. If fewer nominees are named than the number fixed by or pursuant to the governing instruments, state the reasons for this procedure and that the proxies cannot be voted for a greater number of persons than the number of nominees named.

4. For each director or nominee for election as director who is or would be an "interested person" of the Fund within the meaning of section 2(a)(19) of the Investment Company Act of 1940 (15 U.S.C. 80a-2(a)(19)), describe, in a footnote or otherwise, the relationship, events, or transactions by reason of which the director or nominee is or would be an interested person.

5. State the principal business of any company listed under column (4) unless the principal business is implicit in its name.

6. Include in column (5) the total number of separate portfolios that a nominee for election as director would oversee if he were elected.

7. Indicate in column (6) directorships not included in column (5) that are held by a director or nominee for election as director in any company with a class of securities registered pursuant to section 12 of the Exchange Act (15 U.S.C. 78*l*), or subject to the requirements of section 15(d) of the Exchange Act (15 U.S.C. 78o(d)), or any company registered as an investment company

under the Investment Company Act of 1940 (15 U.S.C. 80a), as amended, and name the companies in which the directorships are held.

Where the other directorships include directorships overseeing two or more portfolios in the same Fund Complex, identify the Fund Complex and provide the number of portfolios overseen as a director in the Fund Complex rather than listing each portfolio separately.

(2) For each individual listed in column (1) of the table required by paragraph (b) (1) of this Item, except for any director or nominee for election as director who is not or would not be an "interested person" of the Fund within the meaning of section 2(a) (19) of the Investment Company Act of 1940 (15 U.S.C. 80a-2(a) (19)), describe any positions, including as an officer, employee, director, or general partner, held with affiliated persons or principal underwriters of the Fund.

Instruction to paragraph (b) (2). When an individual holds the same position(s) with two or more registered investment companies that are part of the same Fund Complex, identify the Fund Complex and provide the number of registered investment companies for which the position(s) are held rather than listing each registered investment company separately.

(3) Describe briefly any arrangement or understanding between any director, nominee for election as director, Officer, or person chosen to become an Officer, and any other person(s) (naming the person(s)) pursuant to which he was or is to be selected as a director, nominee, or Officer.

Instruction to paragraph (b) (3). Do not include arrangements or understandings with directors or Officers acting solely in their capacities as such.

(4) Unless disclosed in the table required by paragraph (b) (1) of this Item, describe any positions, including as an officer, employee, director, or general partner, held by any director or nominee for election as director, who is not or would not be an "interested person" of the Fund within the meaning of section 2(a) (19) of the Investment Company Act of 1940 (15 U.S.C. 80a-2(a) (19)), or Immediate Family Member of the director or nominee, during the past five years, with:

(i) The Fund;

(ii) An investment company, or a person that would be an investment company but for the exclusions provided by sections 3(c) (1) and 3(c) (7) of the Investment Company Act of 1940 (15 U.S.C. 80a-3(c) (1) and (c) (7)), having the same investment adviser, principal underwriter, or Sponsoring Insurance Company as the Fund or having an investment adviser, principal underwriter, or Sponsoring Insurance Company that directly or indirectly controls, is controlled by, or is under common control with an investment adviser, principal underwriter, or Sponsoring Insurance Company of the Fund;

(iii) An investment adviser, principal underwriter, Sponsoring Insurance Company, or affiliated person of the Fund; or

(iv) Any person directly or indirectly controlling, controlled by, or under common control with an investment adviser, principal underwriter, or Sponsoring Insurance Company of the Fund.

Instruction to paragraph (b) (4). When an individual holds the same position(s) with two or more portfolios that are part of the same Fund Complex, identify the Fund Complex and provide the number of portfolios for which the position(s) are held rather than listing each portfolio separately.

(5) For each director or nominee for election as director, state the dollar range of equity securities beneficially owned by the director or nominee as required by the following table:

(i) In the Fund; and

(ii) On an aggregate basis, in any registered investment companies overseen or to be overseen by the director or nominee within the same Family of Investment Companies as the Fund.

(1)	(2)	(3)
Name of Director or Nominee	Dollar Range of Equity Securities in the Fund	Aggregate Dollar Range of Equity Securities in All Funds Overseen *or* to be Overseen by Director or Nominee in Family of Investment Companies

Instructions to paragraph (b)(5). 1. Information should be provided as of the most recent practicable date. Specify the valuation date by footnote or otherwise.

2. Determine "beneficial ownership" in accordance with rule 16a-1(a)(2) under the Exchange Act (§ 240.16a-1(a)(2)).

3. If action is to be taken with respect to more than one Fund, disclose in column (2) the dollar range of equity securities beneficially owned by a director or nominee in each such Fund overseen or to be overseen by the director or nominee.

4. In disclosing the dollar range of equity securities beneficially owned by a director or nominee in columns (2) and (3), use the following ranges: none, $1-$10,000, $10,001-$50,000, $50,001-$100,000, or over $100,000.

(6) For each director or nominee for election as director who is not or would not be an "interested person" of the Fund within the meaning of section 2(a)(19) of the Investment Company Act of 1940 (15 U.S.C. 80a-2(a)(19), and his Immediate Family Members, furnish the information required by the following table as to each class of securities owned beneficially or of record in:

(i) An investment adviser, principal underwriter, or Sponsoring Insurance Company of the Fund; or

(ii) A person (other than a registered investment company) directly or indirectly controlling, controlled by, or under common control with an investment adviser, principal underwriter, or Sponsoring Insurance Company of the Fund:

(1)	(2)	(3)	(4)	(5)	(6)
Name of Director or Nominee	Name of Owners and Relationships to Director or Nominee	Company	Title of Class	Value of Securities	Percent of Class

Instructions to paragraph (b)(6). 1. Information should be provided as of the most recent practicable date. Specify the valuation date by footnote or otherwise.

2. An individual is a "beneficial owner" of a security if he is a "beneficial owner" under either rule 13d-3 or rule 16a-1(a)(2) under the Exchange Act (§§ 240.13d-3 or 240.16a-1(a)(2)).

3. Identify the company in which the director, nominee, or Immediate Family Member of the director or nominee owns securities in column (3). When the company is a person directly or indirectly controlling, controlled by, or under common control with an investment adviser, principal underwriter, or Sponsoring Insurance Company, describe the company's relationship with the investment adviser, principal underwriter, or Sponsoring Insurance Company.

4. Provide the information required by columns (5) and (6) on an aggregate basis for each director (or nominee) and his Immediate Family Members.

(7) Unless disclosed in response to paragraph (b)(6) of this Item, describe any direct or indirect interest, the value of which exceeds $60,000, of each director or nominee for election as

director who is not or would not be an "interested person" of the Fund within the meaning of section 2(a)(19) of the Investment Company Act of 1940 (15 U.S.C. 80a-2(a)(19)), or Immediate Family Member of the director or nominee, during the past five years, in:

(i) An investment adviser, principal underwriter, or Sponsoring Insurance Company of the Fund; or

(ii) A person (other than a registered investment company) directly or indirectly controlling, controlled by, or under common control with an investment adviser, principal underwriter, or Sponsoring Insurance Company of the Fund.

Instructions to paragraph (b)(7). 1. A director, nominee, or Immediate Family Member has an interest in a company if he is a party to a contract, arrangement, or understanding with respect to any securities of, or interest in, the company.

2. The interest of the director (or nominee) and the interests of his Immediate Family Members should be aggregated in determining whether the value exceeds $60,000.

(8) Describe briefly any material interest, direct or indirect, of any director or nominee for election as director who is not or would not be an "interested person" of the Fund within the meaning of section 2(a)(19) of the Investment Company Act of 1940 (15 U.S.C. 80a-2(a)(19)), or Immediate Family Member of the director or nominee, in any transaction, or series of similar transactions, since the beginning of the last two completed fiscal years of the Fund, or in any currently proposed transaction, or series of similar transactions, in which the amount involved exceeds $60,000 and to which any of the following persons was or is to be a party:

(i) The Fund;

(ii) An Officer of the Fund;

(iii) An investment company, or a person that would be an investment company but for the exclusions provided by sections 3(c)(1) and 3(c)(7) of the Investment Company Act of 1940 (15 U.S.C. 80a-3(c)(1) and (c)(7)), having the same investment adviser, principal underwriter, or Sponsoring Insurance Company as the Fund or having an investment adviser, principal underwriter, or Sponsoring Insurance Company that directly or indirectly controls, is controlled by, or is under common control with an investment adviser, principal underwriter, or Sponsoring Insurance Company of the Fund;

(iv) An Officer of an investment company, or a person that would be an investment company but for the exclusions provided by sections 3(c)(1) and 3(c)(7) of the Investment Company Act of 1940 (15 U.S.C. 80a-3(c)(1) and (c)(7)), having the same investment adviser, principal underwriter, or Sponsoring Insurance Company as the Fund or having an investment adviser, principal underwriter, or Sponsoring Insurance Company that directly or indirectly controls, is controlled by, or is under common control with an investment adviser, principal underwriter, or Sponsoring Insurance Company of the Fund;

(v) An investment adviser, principal underwriter, or Sponsoring Insurance Company of the Fund;

(vi) An Officer of an investment adviser, principal underwriter, or Sponsoring Insurance Company of the Fund;

(vii) A person directly or indirectly controlling, controlled by, or under common control with an investment adviser, principal underwriter, or Sponsoring Insurance Company of the Fund; or

(viii) An Officer of a person directly or indirectly controlling, controlled by, or under common control with an investment adviser, principal underwriter, or Sponsoring Insurance Company of the Fund.

Instructions to paragraph (b)(8). 1. Include the name of each director, nominee, or Immediate Family Member whose interest in any transaction or series of similar transactions is described and the nature of the circumstances by reason of which the interest is required to be described.

2. State the nature of the interest, the approximate dollar amount involved in the transaction, and, where practicable, the approximate dollar amount of the interest.

3. In computing the amount involved in the transaction or series of similar transactions, include all periodic payments in the case of any lease or other agreement providing for periodic payments.

4. Compute the amount of the interest of any director, nominee, or Immediate Family Member of the director or nominee without regard to the amount of profit or loss involved in the transaction(s).

5. As to any transaction involving the purchase or sale of assets, state the cost of the assets to the purchaser and, if acquired by the seller within two years prior to the transaction, the cost to the seller. Describe the method used in determining the purchase or sale price and the name of the person making the determination.

6. If the proxy statement relates to multiple portfolios of a series Fund with different fiscal years, then, in determining the date that is the beginning of the last two completed fiscal years of the Fund, use the earliest date of any series covered by the proxy statement.

7. Disclose indirect, as well as direct, material interests in transactions. A person who has a position or relationship with, or interest in, a company that engages in a transaction with one of the persons listed in paragraphs (b)(8)(i) through (b)(8)(viii) of this Item may have an indirect interest in the transaction by reason of the position, relationship, or interest. The interest in the transaction, however, will not be deemed "material" within the meaning of paragraph (b)(8) of this Item where the interest of the director, nominee, or Immediate Family Member arises solely from the holding of an equity interest (including a limited partnership interest, but excluding a general partnership interest) or a creditor interest in a company that is a party to the transaction with one of the persons specified in paragraphs (b)(8)(i) through (b)(8)(viii) of this Item, and the transaction is not material to the company.

8. The materiality of any interest is to be determined on the basis of the significance of the information to investors in light of all the circumstances of the particular case. The importance of the interest to the person having the interest, the relationship of the parties to the transaction with each other, and the amount involved in the transaction are among the factors to be considered in determining the significance of the information to investors.

9. No information need be given as to any transaction where the interest of the director, nominee, or Immediate Family Member arises solely from the ownership of securities of a person specified in paragraphs (b)(8)(i) through (b)(8)(viii) of this Item and the director, nominee, or Immediate Family Member receives no extra or special benefit not shared on a pro rata basis by all holders of the class of securities.

10. Transactions include loans, lines of credit, and other indebtedness. For indebtedness, indicate the largest aggregate amount of indebtedness outstanding at any time during the period, the nature of the indebtedness and the transaction in which it was incurred, the amount outstanding as of the latest practicable date, and the rate of interest paid or charged.

11. No information need be given as to any routine, retail transaction. For example, the Fund need not disclose that a director has a credit card, bank or brokerage account, residential mortgage, or insurance policy with a person specified in paragraphs (b)(8)(i) through (b)(8)(viii) of this Item unless the director is accorded special treatment.

(9) Describe briefly any direct or indirect relationship, in which the amount involved exceeds $60,000, of any director or nominee for election as director who is not or would not be an "interested person" of the Fund within the meaning of section 2(a)(19) of the Investment Company Act of 1940 (15 U.S.C. 80a-2(a)(19)), or Immediate Family Member of the director or nominee, that exists, or has existed at any time since the beginning of the last two completed fiscal years of the Fund, or is currently proposed, with any of the persons specified in paragraphs (b)(8)(i) through (b)(8)(viii) of this Item. Relationships include:

(i) Payments for property or services to or from any person specified in paragraphs (b)(8)(i) through (b)(8)(viii) of this Item;

(ii) Provision of legal services to any person specified in paragraphs (b)(8)(i) through (b)(8)(viii) of this Item;

(iii) Provision of investment banking services to any person specified in paragraphs (b)(8)(i) through (b)(8)(viii) of this Item, other than as a participating underwriter in a syndicate; and

(iv) Any consulting or other relationship that is substantially similar in nature and scope to the relationships listed in paragraphs (b)(9)(i) through (b)(9)(iii) of this Item.

Instructions to paragraph (b)(9). 1. Include the name of each director, nominee, or Immediate Family Member whose relationship is described and the nature of the circumstances by reason of which the relationship is required to be described.

2. State the nature of the relationship and the amount of business conducted between the director, nominee, or Immediate Family Member and the person specified in paragraphs (b)(8)(i) through (b)(8)(viii) of this Item as a result of the relationship since the beginning of the last two completed fiscal years of the Fund or proposed to be done during the Fund's current fiscal year.

3. In computing the amount involved in a relationship, include all periodic payments in the case of any agreement providing for periodic payments.

4. If the proxy statement relates to multiple portfolios of a series Fund with different fiscal years, then, in determining the date that is the beginning of the last two completed fiscal years of the Fund, use the earliest date of any series covered by the proxy statement.

5. Disclose indirect, as well as direct, relationships. A person who has a position or relationship with, or interest in, a company that has a relationship with one of the persons listed in paragraphs (b)(8)(i) through (b)(8)(viii) of this Item may have an indirect relationship by reason of the position, relationship, or interest.

6. In determining whether the amount involved in a relationship exceeds $60,000, amounts involved in a relationship of the director (or nominee) should be aggregated with those of his Immediate Family Members.

7. In the case of an indirect interest, identify the company with which a person specified in paragraphs (b)(8)(i) through (b)(8)(viii) of this Item has a relationship; the name of the director, nominee, or Immediate Family Member affiliated with the company and the nature of the affiliation; and the amount of business conducted between the company and the person specified in paragraphs (b)(8)(i) through (b)(8)(viii) of this Item since the beginning of the last two completed fiscal years of the Fund or proposed to be done during the Fund's current fiscal year.

8. In calculating payments for property and services for purposes of paragraph (b)(9)(i) of this Item, the following may be excluded:

A. Payments where the transaction involves the rendering of services as a common contract carrier, or public utility, at rates or charges fixed in conformity with law or governmental authority; or

B. Payments that arise solely from the ownership of securities of a person specified in paragraphs (b)(8)(i) through (b)(8)(viii) of this Item and no extra or special benefit not shared on a pro rata basis by all holders of the class of securities is received.

9. No information need be given as to any routine, retail relationship. For example, the Fund need not disclose that a director has a credit card, bank or brokerage account, residential mortgage, or insurance policy with a person specified in paragraphs (b)(8)(i) through (b)(8)(viii) of this Item unless the director is accorded special treatment.

(10) If an Officer of an investment adviser, principal underwriter, or Sponsoring Insurance Company of the Fund, or an Officer of a person directly or indirectly controlling, controlled by, or under common control with an investment adviser, principal underwriter, or Sponsoring Insurance Company of the Fund, serves, or has served since the beginning of the last two completed fiscal years of the Fund, on the board of directors of a company where a director of the Fund or nominee for election as director who is not or would not be an "interested person" of the Fund within the meaning of section 2(a)(19) of the Investment Company Act of 1940 (15 U.S.C.

80a-2(a)(19)), or Immediate Family Member of the director or nominee, is, or was since the beginning of the last two completed fiscal years of the Fund, an Officer, identify:

(i) The company;

(ii) The individual who serves or has served as a director of the company and the period of service as director;

(iii) The investment adviser, principal underwriter, or Sponsoring Insurance Company or person controlling, controlled by, or under common control with the investment adviser, principal underwriter, or Sponsoring Insurance Company where the individual named in paragraph (b)(10)(ii) of this Item holds or held office and the office held; and

(iv) The director of the Fund, nominee for election as director, or Immediate Family Member who is or was an Officer of the company; the office held; and the period of holding the office.

Instruction to paragraph (b)(10). If the proxy statement relates to multiple portfolios of a series Fund with different fiscal years, then, in determining the date that is the beginning of the last two completed fiscal years of the Fund, use the earliest date of any series covered by the proxy statement.

(11) Provide in tabular form, to the extent practicable, the information required by Items 401(f) and (g), 404(a) and (c), and 405 of Regulation S-K (§§ 229.401(f) and (g), 229.404(a) and (c), and 229.405 of this chapter).

Instruction to paragraph (b)(11). Information provided under paragraph (b)(8) of this Item 22 is deemed to satisfy the requirements of Items 404(a) and (c) of Regulation S-K for information about directors, nominees for election as directors, and Immediate Family Members of directors and nominees, and need not be provided under this paragraph (b)(11).

(12) Describe briefly any material pending legal proceedings, other than ordinary routine litigation incidental to the Fund's business, to which any director or nominee for director or affiliated person of such director or nominee is a party adverse to the Fund or any of its affiliated persons or has a material interest adverse to the Fund or any of its affiliated persons. Include the name of the court where the case is pending, the date instituted, the principal parties, a description of the factual basis alleged to underlie the proceeding, and the relief sought.

(13) For all directors, and for each of the three highest-paid Officers that have aggregate compensation from the Fund for the most recently completed fiscal year in excess of $60,000 ("Compensated Persons"):

(i) Furnish the information required by the following table for the last fiscal year:

Compensation Table

(1)	(2)	(3)	(4)	(5)
Name of Person, Position	Aggregate Compensation From Fund	Pension or Retirement Benefits Accrued as Part of Fund Expenses	Estimated Annual Benefits Upon Retirement	Total Compensation From Fund and Fund Complex Paid to Directors

Instructions to paragraph (b)(13)(i). 1. For column (1), indicate, if necessary, the capacity in which the remuneration is received. For Compensated Persons that are directors of the Fund, compensation is amounts received for service as a director.

2. If the Fund has not completed its first full year since its organization, furnish the information for the current fiscal year, estimating future payments that would be made pursuant to an existing agreement or understanding. Disclose in a footnote to the Compensation Table the period for which the information is furnished.

3. Include in column (2) amounts deferred at the election of the Compensated Person, whether pursuant to a plan established under Section 401(k) of the Internal Revenue Code (26 U.S.C. 401(k)) or otherwise, for the fiscal year in which earned. Disclose in a footnote to the Compensation Table the total amount of deferred compensation (including interest) payable to or accrued for any Compensated Person.

4. Include in columns (3) and (4) all pension or retirement benefits proposed to be paid under any existing plan in the event of retirement at normal retirement date, directly or indirectly, by the Fund or any of its Subsidiaries, or by other companies in the Fund Complex. Omit column (4) where retirement benefits are not determinable.

5. For any defined benefit or actuarial plan under which benefits are determined primarily by final compensation (or average final compensation) and years of service, provide the information required in column (4) in a separate table showing estimated annual benefits payable upon retirement (including amounts attributable to any defined benefit supplementary or excess pension award plans) in specified compensation and years of service classifications. Also provide the estimated credited years of service for each Compensated Person.

6. Include in column (5) only aggregate compensation paid to a director for service on the board and other boards of investment companies in a Fund Complex specifying the number of such other investment companies.

(ii) Describe briefly the material provisions of any pension, retirement, or other plan or any arrangement other than fee arrangements disclosed in paragraph (b)(13)(i) of this Item pursuant to which Compensated Persons are or may be compensated for any services provided, including amounts paid, if any, to the Compensated Person under any such arrangements during the most recently completed fiscal year.

Specifically include the criteria used to determine amounts payable under any plan, the length of service or vesting period required by the plan, the retirement age or other event that gives rise to payments under the plan, and whether the payment of benefits is secured or funded by the Fund.

(iii) With respect to each Compensated Person, business development companies must include the information required by Items 402(b)(2)(iv) and 402(c) of Regulation S-K (§§ 229.402(b)(2)(iv) and 229.402(c) of this chapter).

(14) State whether or not the Fund has a separately designated audit committee established in accordance with section 3(a)(58)(A) of the Act (15 U.S.C. 78c(a)(58)(A)). If the entire board of directors is acting as the Fund's audit committee as specified in section 3(a)(58)(B) of the Act (15 U.S.C. 78c(a)(58)(B)), so state. If applicable, provide the disclosure required by § 240.10A-3(d) regarding an exemption from the listing standards for audit committees. Identify the other standing committees of the Fund's board of directors, and provide the following information about each committee, including any separately designated audit committee:

(i) A concise statement of the functions of the committee;

(ii) The members of the committee and, in the case of a nominating committee, whether or not the members of the committee are "interested persons" of the Fund as defined in section 2(a)(19) of the Investment Company Act of 1940 (15 U.S.C. 80a-2(a)(19)); and

(iii) The number of committee meetings held during the last fiscal year.

Instruction to paragraph (b)(14): For purposes of Item 22(b)(14), the term "nominating committee" refers not only to nominating committees and committees performing similar functions, but also to groups of directors fulfilling the role of a nominating committee, including the entire board of directors.

(c) *Approval of Investment Advisory Contract.* If action is to be taken with respect to an investment advisory contract, include the following information in the proxy statement.

Instruction. Furnish information with respect to a prospective investment adviser to the extent applicable (including the name and address of the prospective adviser).

(1) With respect to the existing investment advisory contract:

(i) State the date of the contract and the date on which it was last submitted to a vote of security holders of the Fund, including the purpose of such submission;

(ii) Briefly describe the terms of the contract, including the rate of compensation of the investment adviser;

(iii) State the aggregate amount of the investment adviser's fee and the amount and purpose of any other material payments by the Fund to the investment adviser, or any affiliated person of the investment adviser, during the last fiscal year of the Fund;

(iv) If any person is acting as an investment adviser of the Fund other than pursuant to a written contract that has been approved by the security holders of the company, identify the person and describe the nature of the services and arrangements;

(v) Describe any action taken with respect to the investment advisory contract since the beginning of the Fund's last fiscal year by the board of directors of the Fund (unless described in response to paragraph (c)(1)(vi)) of this Item 22); and

(vi) If an investment advisory contract was terminated or not renewed for any reason, state the date of such termination or non-renewal, identify the parties involved, and describe the circumstances of such termination or non-renewal.

(2) State the name, address and principal occupation of the principal executive officer and each director or general partner of the investment adviser.

Instruction. If the investment adviser is a partnership with more than ten general partners, name:

(i) the general partners with the five largest economic interests in the partnership, and, if different, those general partners comprising the management or executive committee of the partnership or exercising similar authority;

(ii) the general partners with significant management responsibilities relating to the fund.

(3) State the names and addresses of all Parents of the investment adviser and show the basis of control of the investment adviser and each Parent by its immediate Parent.

Instructions. 1. If any person named is a corporation, include the percentage of its voting securities owned by its immediate Parent.

2. If any person named is a partnership, name the general partners having the three largest partnership interests (computed by whatever method is appropriate in the particular case).

(4) If the investment adviser is a corporation and if, to the knowledge of the persons mailing the solicitation or the persons on whose behalf the solicitation is made, any person not named in answer to paragraph (c)(3) of this Item 22 owns, of record or beneficially, ten percent or more of the outstanding voting securities of the investment adviser, indicate that fact and state the name and address of each such person.

(5) Name each officer or director of the Fund who is an officer, employee, director, general partner or shareholder of the investment adviser. As to any officer or director who is not a director or general partner of the investment adviser and who owns securities or has any other material direct or indirect interest in the investment adviser or any other person controlling, controlled by or under common control with the investment adviser, describe the nature of such interest.

(6) Describe briefly and state the approximate amount of, where practicable, any material interest, direct or indirect, of any director of the Fund in any material transactions since the beginning of the most recently completed fiscal year, or in any material proposed transactions, to which the investment adviser of the Fund, any Parent or Subsidiary of the investment adviser (other than another Fund), or any Subsidiary of the Parent of such entities was or is to be a party.

Instructions. 1. Include the name of each person whose interest in any transaction is described and the nature of the relationship by reason of which such interest is required to be described. Where it is not practicable to state the approximate amount of the interest, indicate the appropriate amount involved in the transaction.

2. As to any transaction involving the purchase or sale of assets by or to the investment adviser, state the cost of the assets to the purchaser and the cost thereof to the seller if acquired by the seller within two years prior to the transaction.

3. If the interest of any person arises from the position of the person as a partner in a partnership, the proportionate interest of such person in transactions to which the partnership is a party need not be set forth, but state the amount involved in the transaction with the partnership.

4. No information need be given in response to this paragraph (c)(6) of Item 22 with respect to any transaction that is not related to the business or operations of the Fund and to which neither the Fund nor any of its Parents or Subsidiaries is a party.

(7) Disclose any financial condition of the investment adviser that is reasonably likely to impair the financial ability of the adviser to fulfil its commitment to the fund under the proposed investment advisory contract.

(8) Describe the nature of the action to be taken on the investment advisory contract and the reasons therefor, the terms of the contract to be acted upon, and, if the action is an amendment to, or a replacement of, an investment advisory contract, the material differences between the current and proposed contract.

(9) If a change in the investment advisory fee is sought, state:

(i) The aggregate amount of the investment adviser's fee during the last year;

(ii) The amount that the adviser would have received had the proposed fee been in effect; and

(iii) The difference between the aggregate amounts stated in response to paragraphs (i) and (ii) this item (c)(9) as a percentage of the amount stated in response to paragraph (i) of this item (c)(9).

(10) If the investment adviser acts as such with respect to any other Fund having a similar investment objective, identify and state the size of such other Fund and the rate of the investment adviser's compensation. Also indicate for any Fund identified whether the investment adviser has waived, reduced, or otherwise agreed to reduce its compensation under any applicable contract.

Instruction. Furnish the information in response to this paragraph (c)(10) of Item 22 in tabular form.

(11) Discuss in reasonable detail the material factors and the conclusions with respect thereto that form the basis for the recommendation of the board of directors that the shareholders approve an investment advisory contract. Include the following in the discussion:

(i) Factors relating to both the board's selection of the investment adviser and approval of the advisory fee and any other amounts to be paid by the Fund under the contract. This would include, but not be limited to, a discussion of the nature, extent, and quality of the services to be provided by the investment adviser; the investment performance of the Fund and the investment adviser; the costs of the services to be provided and profits to be realized by the investment adviser and its affiliates from the relationship with the Fund; the extent to which economies of scale would be realized as the Fund grows; and whether fee levels reflect these economies of scale for the benefit of Fund investors. Also indicate in the discussion whether the board relied upon comparisons of the services to be rendered and the amounts to be paid under the contract with those under other investment advisory contracts, such as contracts of the same and other investment advisers with other registered investment companies or other types of clients (*e.g.*, pension funds and other institutional investors). If the board relied upon such comparisons, describe the comparisons that were relied on and how they assisted the board in determining to recommend that the shareholders approve the advisory contract; and

(ii) If applicable, any benefits derived or to be derived by the investment adviser from the relationship with the Fund such as soft dollar arrangements by which brokers provide research to the Fund or its investment adviser in return for allocating Fund brokerage.

Instructions. 1. Conclusory statements or a list of factors will not be considered sufficient disclosure. Relate the factors to the specific circumstances of the Fund and the investment advisory contract for which approval is sought and state how the board evaluated each factor. For example, it is not sufficient to state that the board considered the amount of the investment advisory fee without stating what the board concluded about the amount of the fee and how that affected its determination to recommend approval of the contract.

2. If any factor enumerated in paragraph (c)(11)(i) of this Item 22 is not relevant to the board's evaluation of the investment advisory contract for which approval is sought, note this and explain the reasons why that factor is not relevant.

(12) Describe any arrangement or understanding made in connection with the proposed investment advisory contract with respect to the composition of the board of directors of the Fund or the investment adviser or with respect to the selection or appointment of any person to any office with either such company.

(13) For the most recently completed fiscal year, state:

(i) The aggregate amount of commissions paid to any Affiliated Broker; and

(ii) The percentage of the Fund's aggregate brokerage commissions paid to any such Affiliated Broker.

Instruction. Identify each Affiliated Broker and the relationships that cause the broker to be an Affiliated Broker.

(14) Disclose the amount of any fees paid by the Fund to the investment adviser, its affiliated persons or any affiliated person of such person during the most recent fiscal year for services provided to the Fund (other than under the investment advisory contract or for brokerage commissions). State whether these services will continue to be provided after the investment advisory contract is approved.

(d) *Approval of Distribution Plan.* If action is to be taken with respect to a Distribution Plan, include the following information in the proxy statement.

Instruction. Furnish information on a prospective basis to the extent applicable.

(1) Describe the nature of the action to be taken on the Distribution Plan and the reason therefor, the terms of the Distribution Plan to be acted upon, and, if the action is an amendment to, or a replacement of, a Distribution Plan, the material differences between the current and proposed Distribution Plan.

(2) If the Fund has a Distribution Plan in effect:

(i) Provide the date that the Distribution Plan was adopted and the date of the last amendment, if any;

(ii) Disclose the persons to whom payments may be made under the Distribution Plan, the rate of the distribution fee and the purposes for which such fee may be used;

(iii) Disclose the amount of distribution fees paid by the Fund pursuant to the plan during its most recent fiscal year, both in the aggregate and as a percentage of the Fund's average net assets during the period;

(iv) Disclose the name of, and the amount of any payments made under the Distribution Plan by the Fund during its most recent fiscal year to, any person who is an affiliated person of the Fund, its investment adviser, principal underwriter, or Administrator, an affiliated person of such person, or a person that during the most recent fiscal year received 10% or more of the aggregate amount paid under the Distribution Plan by the Fund;

(v) Describe any action taken with respect to the Distribution Plan since the beginning of the Fund's most recent fiscal year by the board of directors of the Fund; and

(vi) If a Distribution Plan was or is to be terminated or not renewed for any reason, state the date or prospective date of such termination or non-renewal, identify the parties involved, and describe the circumstances of such termination or non-renewal.

(3) Describe briefly and state the approximate amount of, where practicable, any material interest, direct or indirect, of any director or nominee for election as a director of the Fund in any material transactions since the beginning of the most recently completed fiscal year, or in any material proposed transactions, to which any person identified in response to Item 22(d)(2)(iv) was or is to be a party.

Instructions. 1. Include the name of each person whose interest in any transaction is described and the nature of the relationship by reason of which such interest is required to be described. Where it is not practicable to state the approximate amount of the interest, indicate the approximate amount involved in the transaction.

2. As to any transaction involving the purchase or sale of assets, state the cost of the assets to the purchaser and the cost thereof to the seller if acquired by the seller within two years prior to the transaction.

3. If the interest of any person arises from the position of the person as a partner in a partnership, the proportionate interest of such person in transactions to which the partnership is a party need not be set forth but state the amount involved in the transaction with the partnership.

4. No information need be given in response to this paragraph (d)(3) of Item 22 with respect to any transaction that is not related to the business or operations of the Fund and to which neither the Fund nor any of its Parents or Subsidiaries is a party.

(4) Discuss in reasonable detail the material factors and the conclusions with respect thereto which form the basis for the conclusion of the board of directors that there is a reasonable likelihood that the proposed Distribution Plan (or amendment thereto) will benefit the Fund and its shareholders.

Instruction. Conclusory statements or a list of factors will not be considered sufficient disclosure.

Item 23. Delivery of Documents to Security Holders Sharing an Address

If one annual report or proxy statement is being delivered to two or more security holders who share an address in accordance with § 240.14a-3(e)(1), furnish the following information:

(a) State that only one annual report or proxy statement, as applicable, is being delivered to multiple security holders sharing an address unless the registrant has received contrary instructions from one or more of the security holders;

(b) Undertake to deliver promptly upon written or oral request a separate copy of the annual report or proxy statement, as applicable, to a security holder at a shared address to which a single copy of the documents was delivered and provide instructions as to how a security holder can notify the registrant that the security holder wishes to receive a separate copy of an annual report or proxy statement, as applicable;

(c) Provide the phone number and mailing address to which a security holder can direct a notification to the registrant that the security holder wishes to receive a separate annual report or proxy statement, as applicable, in the future; and

(d) Provide instructions how security holders sharing an address can request delivery of a single copy of annual reports or proxy statements if they are receiving multiple copies of annual reports or proxy statements.

Schedule TO
Tender offer statement pursuant to section 14(d)(1) of the Securities Exchange Act of 1934.

SECURITIES AND EXCHANGE COMMISSION
Washington, D.C. 20549
SCHEDULE TO

Tender Offer Statement under Section 14(d)(1) or 13(e)(1) of the Securities Exchange Act of 1934

(Amendment No. ___)*

_____

(Name of Subject Company (issuer))

_____

(Names of Filing Persons (identifying status as offeror, issuer or other person))

_____

(Title of Class of Securities)

_____

(CUSIP Number of Class of Securities)

(Name, address, and telephone numbers of person authorized to receive notices and communications on behalf of filing persons)

Calculation of Filing Fee

Transaction valuation*	Amount of filing fee

_____

* Set forth the amount on which the filing fee is calculated and state how it was determined.

[ ] Check the box if any part of the fee is offset as provided by Rule 0-11(a)(2) and identify the filing with which the offsetting fee was previously paid. Identify the previous filing by registration statement number, or the Form or Schedule and the date of its filing.

Amount Previously Paid:_____

Form or Registration No.:_____

Filing Party:_____

Date Filed:_____

[ ] Check the box if the filing relates solely to preliminary communications made before the commencement of a tender offer.

Check the appropriate boxes below to designate any transactions to which the statement relates:

[ ] third-party tender offer subject to Rule 14d-1.

[ ] issuer tender offer subject to Rule 13e-4.

[ ] going-private transaction subject to Rule 13e-3.

[ ] amendment to Schedule 13D under Rule 13d-2.

Check the following box if the filing is a final amendment reporting the results of the tender offer:[ ]

General Instructions:

A. File eight copies of the statement, including all exhibits, with the Commission if paper filing is permitted.

B. This filing must be accompanied by a fee payable to the Commission as required by § 240.0-11.

C. If the statement is filed by a general or limited partnership, syndicate or other group, the information called for by Items 3 and 5—8 for a third-party tender offer and Items 5—8 for an issuer tender offer must be given with respect to: (i) each partner of the general partnership; (ii) each partner who is, or functions as, a general partner of the limited partnership; (iii) each member of the syndicate or group; and (iv) each person controlling the partner or member. If the statement is filed by a corporation or if a person referred to in (i), (ii), (iii) or (iv) of this Instruction is a corporation, the information called for by the items specified above must be given with respect to: (a) each executive officer and director of the corporation; (b) each person controlling the corporation; and (c) each executive officer and director of any corporation or other person ultimately in control of the corporation.

D. If the filing contains only preliminary communications made before the commencement of a tender offer, no signature or filing fee is required. The filer need not respond to the items in the schedule. Any pre-commencement communications that are filed under cover of this schedule need not be incorporated by reference into the schedule.

E. If an item is inapplicable or the answer is in the negative, so state. The statement published, sent or given to security holders may omit negative and not applicable responses. If the schedule includes any information that is not published, sent or given to security holders, provide that information or specifically incorporate it by reference under the appropriate item number and heading in the schedule. Do not recite the text of disclosure requirements in the schedule or any document published, sent or given to security holders. Indicate clearly the coverage of the requirements without referring to the text of the items.

F. Information contained in exhibits to the statement may be incorporated by reference in answer or partial answer to any item unless it would render the answer misleading, incomplete, unclear or confusing. A copy of any information that is incorporated by reference or a copy of the pertinent pages of a document containing the information must be submitted with this statement as an exhibit, unless it was previously filed with the Commission electronically on EDGAR. If an exhibit contains information responding to more than one item in the schedule, all information in that exhibit may be incorporated by reference once in response to the several items in the schedule for which it provides an answer. Information incorporated by reference is deemed filed with the Commission for all purposes of the Act.

G. A filing person may amend its previously filed Schedule 13D (§ 240.13d-101) on Schedule TO (§ 240.14d-100) if the appropriate box on the cover page is checked to indicate a combined filing and the information called for by the fourteen disclosure items on the cover page of Schedule 13D (§ 240.13d-101) is provided on the cover page of the combined filing with respect to each filing person.

H. The final amendment required by § 240.14d-3(b)(2) and § 240.13e-4(c)(4) will satisfy the reporting requirements of section 13(d) of the Act with respect to all securities acquired by the offeror in the tender offer.

I. Amendments disclosing a material change in the information set forth in this statement may omit any information previously disclosed in this statement.

J. If the tender offer disclosed on this statement involves a going-private transaction, a combined Schedule TO (§ 240.14d-100) and Schedule 13E-3 (§ 240.13e-100) may be filed with the Commission under cover of Schedule TO. The Rule 13e-3 box on the cover page of the Schedule TO must be checked to indicate a combined filing. All information called for by both schedules must be provided except that Items 1†3, 5, 8 and 9 of Schedule TO may be omitted to the extent those items call for information that duplicates the item requirements in Schedule 13E-3.

K. For purposes of this statement, the following definitions apply:

(1) The term *offeror* means any person who makes a tender offer or on whose behalf a tender offer is made;

(2) The term *issuer tender offer* has the same meaning as in Rule 13e-4(a)(2); and

(3) The term *third-party tender offer* means a tender offer that is not an issuer tender offer.

SPECIAL INSTRUCTIONS FOR COMPLYING WITH SCHEDULE TO:

Under Sections 13(e), 14(d) and 23 of the Act and the rules and regulations of the Act, the Commission is authorized to solicit the information required to be supplied by this schedule.

Disclosure of the information specified in this schedule is mandatory, except for I.R.S. identification numbers, disclosure of which is voluntary. The information will be used for the primary purpose of disclosing tender offer and going-private transactions. This statement will be made a matter of public record. Therefore, any information given will be available for inspection by any member of the public.

Because of the public nature of the information, the Commission can use it for a variety of purposes, including referral to other governmental authorities or securities self-regulatory organizations for investigatory purposes or in connection with litigation involving the Federal securities laws or other civil, criminal or regulatory statutes or provisions. I.R.S. identification numbers, if furnished, will assist the Commission in identifying security holders and, therefore, in promptly processing tender offer and going-private statements.

Failure to disclose the information required by this schedule, except for I.R.S. identification numbers, may result in civil or criminal action against the persons involved for violation of the Federal securities laws and rules.

Item 1. *Summary Term Sheet.*

Furnish the information required by Item 1001 of Regulation M-A (§ 229.1001 of this chapter) unless information is disclosed to security holders in a prospectus that meets the requirements of § 230.421(d) of this chapter.

Item 2. *Subject Company Information.*

Furnish the information required by Item 1002(a) through (c) of Regulation M-A (§ 229.1002 of this chapter).

Item 3. *Identity and Background of Filing Person.*

Furnish the information required by Item 1003(a) through (c) of Regulation M-A (§ 229.1003 of this chapter) for a third-party tender offer and the information required by Item 1003(a) of Regulation M-A (§ 229.1003 of this chapter) for an issuer tender offer.

Item 4. *Terms of the Transaction.*

Furnish the information required by Item 1004(a) of Regulation M-A (§ 229.1004 of this chapter) for a third-party tender offer and the information required by Item 1004(a) through (b) of Regulation M-A (§ 229.1004 of this chapter) for an issuer tender offer.

Item 5. *Past Contacts, Transactions, Negotiations and Agreements.*

Furnish the information required by Item 1005(a) and (b) of Regulation M-A (§ 229.1005 of this chapter) for a third-party tender offer and the information required by Item 1005(e) of Regulation M-A (§ 229.1005) for an issuer tender offer.

Item 6. *Purposes of the Transaction and Plans or Proposals.*

Furnish the information required by Item 1006(a) and (c)(1) through (7) of Regulation M-A (§ 229.1006 of this chapter) for a third-party tender offer and the information required by Item 1006(a) through (c) of Regulation M-A (§ 229.1006 of this chapter) for an issuer tender offer.

Item 7. *Source and Amount of Funds or Other Consideration.*

Furnish the information required by Item 1007(a), (b) and (d) of Regulation M-A (§ 229.1007 of this chapter).

Item 8. *Interest in Securities of the Subject Company.*

Furnish the information required by Item 1008 of Regulation M-A (§ 229.1008 of this chapter).

Item 9. *Persons/Assets, Retained, Employed, Compensated or Used.*

Furnish the information required by Item 1009(a) of Regulation M-A (§ 229.1009 of this chapter).

Item 10. *Financial Statements.*

If material, furnish the information required by Item 1010(a) and (b) of Regulation M-A (§ 229.1010 of this chapter) for the issuer in an issuer tender offer and for the offeror in a third-party tender offer.

Instructions to Item 10:

1. Financial statements must be provided when the offeror's financial condition is material to security holder's decision whether to sell, tender or hold the securities sought. The facts and circumstances of a tender offer, particularly the terms of the tender offer, may influence a determination as to whether financial statements are material, and thus required to be disclosed.

2. Financial statements are *not* considered material when: (a) the consideration offered consists solely of cash; (b) the offer is not subject to any financing condition; *and* either: (c) the offeror is a public reporting company under Section 13(a) or 15(d) of the Act that files reports electronically on EDGAR, or (d) the offer is for all outstanding securities of the subject class. Financial information may be required, however, in a two-tier transaction. *See* Instruction 5 below.

3. The filing person may incorporate by reference financial statements contained in any document filed with the Commission, solely for the purposes of this schedule, if: (a) the financial statements substantially meet the requirements of this item; (b) an express statement is made that the financial statements are incorporated by reference; (c) the information incorporated by reference is clearly identified by page, paragraph, caption or otherwise; and (d) if the information incorporated by reference is not filed with this schedule, an indication is made where the information may be inspected and copies obtained. Financial statements that are required to be presented in comparative form for two or more fiscal years or periods may not be incorporated by reference unless the material incorporated by reference includes the entire period for which the comparative data is required to be given. *See* General Instruction F to this schedule.

4. If the offeror in a third-party tender offer is a natural person, and such person's financial information is material, disclose the net worth of the offeror. If the offeror's net worth is derived from material amounts of assets that are not readily marketable or there are material guarantees and contingencies, disclose the nature and approximate amount of the individual's net worth that consists of illiquid assets and the magnitude of any guarantees or contingencies that may negatively affect the natural person's net worth.

5. Pro forma financial information is required in a negotiated third-party cash tender offer when securities are intended to be offered in a subsequent merger or other transaction in which remaining target securities are acquired and the acquisition of the subject company is significant to the offeror under § 210.11-01(b)(1) of this chapter. The offeror must disclose the financial information specified in Item 3(f) and Item 5 of Form S-4 (§ 239.25 of this chapter) in the schedule filed with the Commission, but may furnish only the summary financial information specified in Item 3(d), (e) and (f) of Form S-4 in the disclosure document sent to security holders. If pro forma financial information is required by this instruction, the historical financial statements specified in Item 1010 of Regulation M-A (§ 229.1010 of this chapter) are required for the bidder.

6. The disclosure materials disseminated to security holders may contain the summarized financial information specified by Item 1010(c) of Regulation M-A (§ 229.1010 of this chapter) instead of the financial information required by Item 1010(a) and (b). In that case, the financial

information required by Item 1010(a) and (b) of Regulation M-A must be disclosed in the statement. If summarized financial information is disseminated to security holders, include appropriate instructions on how more complete financial information can be obtained. If the summarized financial information is prepared on the basis of a comprehensive body of accounting principles other than U.S. GAAP, the summarized financial information must be accompanied by a reconciliation as described in Instruction 8 of this Item.

7. If the offeror is not subject to the periodic reporting requirements of the Act, the financial statements required by this Item need not be audited if audited financial statements are not available or obtainable without unreasonable cost or expense. Make a statement to that effect and the reasons for their unavailability.

8. If the financial statements required by this Item are prepared on the basis of a comprehensive body of accounting principles other than U.S. GAAP, provide a reconciliation to U.S. GAAP in accordance with Item 17 of Form 20-F (§ 249.220f of this chapter), unless a reconciliation is unavailable or not obtainable without unreasonable cost or expense. At a minimum, however, when financial statements are prepared on a basis other than U.S. GAAP, a narrative description of all material variations in accounting principles, practices and methods used in preparing the non-U.S. GAAP financial statements from those accepted in the U.S. must be presented.

Item 11. *Additional Information.*

Furnish the information required by Item 1011 of Regulation M-A (§ 229.1011 of this chapter).

Item 12. *Exhibits.*

File as an exhibit to the Schedule all documents specified by Item 1016(a), (b), (d), (g) and (h) of Regulation M-A (§ 229.1016 of this chapter).

Item 13. *Information Required by Schedule 13E-3.*

If the Schedule TO is combined with Schedule 13E-3 (§ 240.13e-100), set forth the information required by Schedule 13E-3 that is not included or covered by the items in Schedule TO.

Signature. After due inquiry and to the best of my knowledge and belief, I certify that the information set forth in this statement is true, complete and correct.

_____

(Signature)

_____

(Name and title)

_____

(Date)

Instruction to Signature:

The statement must be signed by the filing person or that person's authorized representative. If the statement is signed on behalf of a person by an authorized representative (other than an executive officer of a corporation or general partner of a partnership), evidence of the representative's authority to sign on behalf of the person must be filed with the statement. The name and any title of each person who signs the statement must be typed or printed beneath the signature. See §§ 240.12b-11 and 240.14d-1(f) with respect to signature requirements.

The original statement shall be signed by each person on whose behalf the statement is filed or his authorized representative. If the statement is signed on behalf of a person by his authorized representative (other than an executive officer or general partner of the bidder), evidence of the representative's authority to sign on behalf of such person shall be filed with the statement. The name and any title of each person who signs the statement shall be typed or printed beneath his signature.

Schedule 14D-9
Solicitation/Recommendation Statement under Section 14(d)(4) of the Securities Exchange Act of 1934

SECURITIES AND EXCHANGE COMMISSION
Washington, D.C. 20549
SCHEDULE 14D-9

Solicitation/Recommendation Statement under Section 14(d)(4) of the Securities Exchange Act of 1934

(Amendment No.___)

_____

(Name of Subject Company)

_____

(Names of Persons Filing Statement)

_____

(Title of Class of Securities)

_____

(CUSIP Number of Class of Securities)

_____

(Name, address, and telephone numbers of person authorized to receive notices and communications on behalf of the persons filing statement)

[ ] Check the box if the filing relates solely to preliminary communications made before the commencement of a tender offer.

General Instructions:

A. File eight copies of the statement, including all exhibits, with the Commission if paper filing is permitted.

B. If the filing contains only preliminary communications made before the commencement of a tender offer, no signature is required. The filer need not respond to the items in the schedule. Any pre-commencement communications that are filed under cover of this schedule need not be incorporated by reference into the schedule.

C. If an item is inapplicable or the answer is in the negative, so state. The statement published, sent or given to security holders may omit negative and not applicable responses. If the schedule includes any information that is not published, sent or given to security holders, provide that information or specifically incorporate it by reference under the appropriate item number and heading in the schedule. Do not recite the text of disclosure requirements in the schedule or any document published, sent or given to security holders. Indicate clearly the coverage of the requirements without referring to the text of the items.

D. Information contained in exhibits to the statement may be incorporated by reference in answer or partial answer to any item unless it would render the answer misleading, incomplete, unclear or confusing. A copy of any information that is incorporated by reference or a copy of the pertinent pages of a document containing the information must be submitted with this statement as an exhibit, unless it was previously filed with the Commission electronically on EDGAR. If an exhibit contains information responding to more than one item in the schedule, all information in that exhibit may be incorporated by reference once in response to the several items in the schedule for which it provides an answer. Information incorporated by reference is deemed filed with the Commission for all purposes of the Act.

E. Amendments disclosing a material change in the information set forth in this statement may omit any information previously disclosed in this statement.

Item 1. *Subject Company Information.*

Furnish the information required by Item 1002(a) and (b) of Regulation M-A (§ 229.1002 of this chapter).

Item 2. *Identity and Background of Filing Person.*

Furnish the information required by Item 1003(a) and (d) of Regulation M-A (§ 229.1003 of this chapter).

Item 3. *Past Contacts, Transactions, Negotiations and Agreements.*

Furnish the information required by Item 1005(d) of Regulation M-A (§ 229.1005 of this chapter).

Item 4. *The Solicitation or Recommendation.*

Furnish the information required by Item 1012(a) through (c) of Regulation M-A (§ 229.1012 of this chapter).

Item 5. *Person/Assets, Retained, Employed, Compensated or Used.*

Furnish the information required by Item 1009(a) of Regulation M-A (§ 229.1009 of this chapter).

Item 6. *Interest in Securities of the Subject Company.*

Furnish the information required by Item 1008(b) of Regulation M-A (§ 229.1008 of this chapter).

Item 7. *Purposes of the Transaction and Plans or Proposals.*

Furnish the information required by Item 1006(d) of Regulation M-A (§ 229.1006 of this chapter).

Item 8. *Additional Information.*

Furnish the information required by Item 1011(b) of Regulation M-A (§ 229.1011 of this chapter).

Item 9. *Exhibits.*

File as an exhibit to the Schedule all documents specified by Item 1016(a), (e) and (g) of Regulation M-A (§ 229.1016 of this chapter).

Signature. After due inquiry and to the best of my knowledge and belief, I certify that the information set forth in this statement is true, complete and correct.

_____

(Signature)

_____

(Name and title)

_____

(Date)

Instruction to Signature:

The statement must be signed by the filing person or that person's authorized representative. If the statement is signed on behalf of a person by an authorized representative (other than an executive officer of a corporation or general partner of a partnership), evidence of the representative's authority to sign on behalf of the person must be filed with the statement. The name and any title of each person who signs the statement must be typed or printed beneath the signature. See § 240.14d-1(f) with respect to signature requirements.

Schedule 15G
Information to be included in the document distributed pursuant to 17 CFR 240.15g-2

SECURITIES AND EXCHANGE COMMISSION
Washington, D.C. 20549
SCHEDULE 15G
Under the Securities Exchange Act of 1934

Instructions to Schedule 15G

A. The information contained in Schedule 15G ("Schedule") must be reproduced in its entirety. No language of the document may be omitted, added to, or altered in any way. No material may be given to a customer that is intended in any way to detract from, rebut, or contradict the Schedule.

B. The document entitled "Important Information on Penny Stocks" must be distributed as the first page of Schedule 15G, and on one page only. The remainder of Schedule 15G, entitled "Further Information," explains the items discussed in the first page in greater detail.

C. The disclosures made through the Schedule are in addition to any other disclosure(s) that are required to be made under the federal securities laws, including without limitation the disclosures required pursuant to the rules adopted under Sections 15(c)(1), 15(c)(2), and 15(g) of the Securities Exchange Act of 1934, 15 U.S.C. 78o(c)(1) and (2), and 15 U.S.C. 78o(g), respectively.

D. The format and typeface of the document must be reproduced as presented in the Schedule. The document may be reproduced from the Schedule by photographic copying that is clear, complete, and at least satisfies the type-size requirements set forth below for printing. In the alternative, the document may be printed and must meet the following criteria regarding typeface:

1. Words appearing in capital letters in the Schedule must be reproduced in capital letters and printed in bold-face roman type at least as large as ten-point modern type and at least two points leaded.

2. Words appearing in lower-case letters must be reproduced in lower-case roman type at least as large as ten point modern type and at least two points leaded.

3. Words that are underlined in the document must be underlined in reproduction and appear in bold-faced roman type at least as large as ten point modern type and at least two points leaded, and meet the criteria for lower-case or capital letters in paragraphs (1) and (2) above, whichever is applicable.

E. Recipients of the document must not be charged any fee for the document.

F. The content of the Schedule is as follows:

IMPORTANT INFORMATION ON PENNY STOCKS

This statement is required by the U.S. Securities and Exchange Commission (SEC) and contains important information on penny stocks. You are urged to read it before making a purchase or sale.

This statement is required by the U.S. Securities and Exchange Commission (SEC) and contains important information on penny stocks. Your broker-dealer is required to obtain your signature to show that you have received this statement before your first trade in a penny stock. You are urged to read this statement before signing and before making a purchase or sale of a penny stock.

Penny stocks can be very risky.

- Penny stocks are low-priced shares of small companies not traded on an exchange or quoted on NASDAQ. Prices often are not available. Investors in penny stocks often are unable to sell stock back to the dealer that sold them the stock. Thus, you may lose your investment. Be cautious of newly issued penny stock.

• Your salesperson is not an impartial advisor but is paid to sell you the stock. Do not rely only on the salesperson, but seek outside advice before you buy any stock. If you have problems with a salesperson, contact the firm's compliance officer or the regulators listed below.

Information you should get.

• *Before you buy penny stock*, federal law requires your salesperson to tell you the *offer* and the "*bid*" on the stock, and the "*compensation*" the salesperson and the firm receive for the trade. The firm also must mail a confirmation of these prices to you after the trade.

• You will need this price information to determine what profit, if any, you will have when you sell your stock. The offer price is the wholesale price at which the dealer is willing to sell stock to other dealers. The bid price is the wholesale price at which the dealer is willing to buy the stock from other dealers. In its trade with you, the dealer may add a retail charge to these wholesale prices as compensation (called a "markup" or "markdown").

• The difference between the bid and the offer price is the dealer's "*spread.*" A spread that is large compared with the purchase price can make a resale of a stock very costly. To be profitable when you sell, the bid price of your stock must rise above the amount of this spread *and* the compensation charged by both your selling and purchasing dealers. If the dealer has no bid price, you may not be able to sell the stock after you buy it, and may lose your whole investment.

Brokers' duties and customer's rights and remedies.

• If you are a victim of fraud, you may have rights and remedies under state and federal law. You can get the disciplinary history of a salesperson or firm from the NASD at 1-800-289-9999, and additional information from your state securities official, at the North American Securities Administrators Association's central number: (202) 737-0900. You also may contact the SEC with complaints at (202) 272-7440.

FURTHER INFORMATION

THE SECURITIES BEING SOLD TO YOU HAVE NOT BEEN APPROVED OR DISAPPROVED BY THE SECURITIES AND EXCHANGE COMMISSION. MOREOVER, THE SECURITIES AND EXCHANGE COMMISSION HAS NOT PASSED UPON THE FAIRNESS OR THE MERITS OF THIS TRANSACTION NOR UPON THE ACCURACY OR ADEQUACY OF THE INFORMATION CONTAINED IN ANY PROSPECTUS OR ANY OTHER INFORMATION PROVIDED BY AN ISSUER OR A BROKER OR DEALER.

Generally, penny stock is a security that:

• is priced under five dollars;

• is *not* traded on a national stock exchange or on NASDAQ (the NASD's automated quotation system for actively traded stocks);

• may be listed in the "pink sheets" or the NASD OTC Bulletin Board;

• is issued by a company that has less than $5 million in net tangible assets and has been in business less than three years, by a company that has under $2 million in net tangible assets and has been in business for at least three years, or by a company that has revenues of $6 million for three years.

Use caution when investing in penny stocks:

1. *Do not make a hurried investment decision.* High-pressure sales techniques can be a warning sign of fraud. The salesperson is not an impartial advisor, but is paid for selling stock to you. The salesperson also does not have to watch your investment for you. Thus, you should think over the offer and seek outside advice. Check to see if the information given by the salesperson differs from other information you may have. Also, it is illegal for salespersons to promise that a stock will increase in value or is risk-free, or to guarantee against loss. If you think there is a problem, ask to speak with a compliance official at the firm, and, if necessary, any of the regulators referred to in this statement.

2. *Study the company issuing the stock.* Be wary of companies that have no operating history, few assets, or no defined business purpose. These may be sham or "shell" corporations. Read the prospectus for the company carefully before you invest. Some dealers fraudulently solicit investors' money to buy stock in sham companies, artificially inflate the stock prices, then cash in their profits before public investors can sell their stock.

3. *Understand the risky nature of these stocks.* You should be aware that you may lose part or all of your investment. Because of large dealer spreads, you will not be able to sell the stock immediately back to the dealer at the same price it sold the stock to you. In some cases, the stock may fall quickly in value. New companies, whose stock is sold in an "initial public offering," often are riskier investments. Try to find out if the shares the salesperson wants to sell you are part of such an offering. Your salesperson must give you a "prospectus" in an initial public offering, but the financial condition shown in the prospectus of new companies can change very quickly.

4. *Know the brokerage firm and the salespeople with whom you are dealing.* Because of the nature of the market for penny stock, you may have to rely solely on the original brokerage firm that sold you the stock for prices and to buy the stock back from you. Ask the National Association of Securities Dealers, Inc. (NASD) or your state securities regulator, which is a member of the North American Securities Administrators Association, Inc. (NASAA), about the licensing and disciplinary record of the brokerage firm and the salesperson contacting you. The telephone numbers of the NASD and NASAA are listed on the first page of this document.

5. *Be cautious if your salesperson leaves the firm.* If the salesperson who sold you the stock leaves his or her firm, the firm may reassign your account to a new salesperson. If you have problems, ask to speak to the firm's branch office manager or a compliance officer. Although the departing salesperson may ask you to transfer your stock to his or her new firm, you do not have to do so. Get information on the new firm. Be wary of requests to sell your securities when the salesperson transfers to a new firm. Also, you have the right to get your stock certificate from your selling firm. You do not have to leave the certificate with that firm or any other firm.

YOUR RIGHTS

Disclosures to you. Under penalty of federal law, your brokerage firm must tell you the following information at two different times—*before* you agree to buy or sell a penny stock, and after the trade, by *written confirmation:*

- *The bid and offer price quotes for penny stock, and the number of shares to which the quoted prices apply.* The *bid* and *offer* quotes are the wholesale prices at which dealers trade among themselves. These prices give you an idea of the market value of the stock. The dealer must tell you these price quotes if they appear on an automated quotation system approved by the SEC. If not, the dealer must use its own quotes or trade prices. You should calculate the *spread*, the difference between the bid and offer quotes, to help decide if buying the stock is a good investment.

A lack of quotes may mean that the market among dealers is not active. It thus may be difficult to resell the stock. You also should be aware that the actual price charged to you for the stock may differ from the price quoted to you for 100 shares. You should therefore determine, before you agree to a purchase, what the actual sales price (before the *markup*) will be for the exact number of shares you want to buy.

- *The brokerage firm's compensation for the trade.* A *markup* is the amount a dealer adds to the wholesale offer price of the stock and a *markdown* is the amount it subtracts from the wholesale bid price of the stock as *compensation*. A markup/markdown usually serves the same role as a broker's commission on a trade. Most of the firms in the penny stock market will be dealers, not brokers.

- *The compensation received by the brokerage firm's salesperson for the trade.* The brokerage firm must disclose to you, as a total sum, the cash compensation of your salesperson for the trade that is known at the time of the trade. The firm must describe in the written confirmation the nature of any other compensation of your salesperson that is unknown at the time of the trade.

In addition to the items listed above, your brokerage firm must send to you:

• *Monthly account statements.* In general, *your brokerage firm must send you a monthly statement* that gives an estimate of the value of each penny stock in your account, if there is enough information to make an estimate. If the firm has not bought or sold any penny stocks for your account for six months, it can provide these statements every three months.

• *A Written Statement of Your Financial Situation and Investment Goals.* In general, unless you have had an account with your brokerage firm for more than one year, or you have previously bought three different penny stocks from that firm, your brokerage firm must send you a written statement for you to sign that accurately describes your financial situation, your investment experience, and your investment goals, and that contains a statement of why your firm decided that penny stocks are a suitable investment for you. The firm also must get your written consent to buy the penny stock.

Legal remedies. If penny stocks are sold to you in violation of your rights listed above, or other federal or state securities laws, you may be able to cancel your purchase and get your money back. If the stocks are sold in a fraudulent manner, you may be able to sue the persons and firms that caused the fraud for damages. If you have signed an arbitration agreement, however, you may have to pursue your claim through arbitration. You may wish to contact an attorney. The SEC is not authorized to represent individuals in private litigation.

However, to protect yourself and other investors, you should report any violations of your brokerage firm's duties listed above and other securities laws to the SEC, the NASD, or your state securities administrator at the telephone numbers on the first page of this document. These bodies have the power to stop fraudulent and abusive activity of salespersons and firms engaged in the securities business. Or you can write to the SEC at 450 Fifth St., N.W., Washington, D.C. 20549; the NASD at 1735 K Street, N.W., Washington, D.C. 20006; or NASAA at 555 New Jersey Avenue, N.W., Suite 750, Washington, D.C. 20001. NASAA will give you the telephone number of your state's securities agency. If there is any disciplinary record of a person or a firm, the NASD, NASAA, or your state securities regulator will send you this information if you ask for it.

MARKET INFORMATION

The market for penny stocks. Penny stocks usually are not listed on an exchange or quoted on the NASDAQ system. Instead, they are traded between dealers on the telephone in the "over-the-counter" market. The NASD's OTC Bulletin Board also will contain information on some penny stocks. At times, however, price information for these stocks is not publicly available.

Market domination. In some cases, only one or two dealers, acting as "market makers," may be buying and selling a given stock. You should first ask if a firm is acting as a *broker* (your agent) or as a dealer. A *dealer* buys stock itself to fill your order or already owns the stock. A *market maker* is a dealer who holds itself out as ready to buy and sell stock on a regular basis. If the firm is a market maker, ask how many other market makers are dealing in the stock to see if the firm (or group of firms) dominates the market. When there are only one or two market makers, there is a risk that the dealer or group of dealers may control the market in that stock and set prices that are not based on competitive forces. In recent years, some market makers have created fraudulent markets in certain penny stocks, so that stock prices rose suddenly, but collapsed just as quickly, at a loss to investors.

Mark-ups and mark-downs. The actual price that the customer pays usually includes the mark-up or markdown. Markups and markdowns are direct profits for the firm and its salespeople, so you should be aware of such amounts to assess the overall value of the trade.

The "spread." The difference between the bid and offer price is the spread. Like a mark-up or mark-down, the spread is another source of profit for the brokerage firm and compensates the firm for the risk of owning the stock. A large spread can make a trade very expensive to an investor. For some penny stocks, the spread between the bid and offer may be a large part of the purchase price of the stock. Where the bid price is much lower than the offer price, the market value of the stock must rise substantially before the stock can be sold at a profit. Moreover, an investor may experience substantial losses if the stock must be sold immediately.

Example: If the bid is $0.04 per share and the offer is $0.10 per share, the spread (difference) is $0.06, which appears to be a small amount. But you would lose $0.06 on every share that you bought for $0.10 if you had to sell that stock immediately to the same firm. If you had invested $5,000 at the $0.10 offer price, the market maker's repurchase price, at $0.04 bid, would be only $2,000; thus you would lose $3,000, or more than half of your investment, if you decided to sell the stock. In addition, you would have to pay compensation (a "mark-up," "mark-down," or commission) to buy and sell the stock.

In addition to the amount of the spread, the price of your stock must rise enough to make up for the compensation that the dealer charged you when it first sold you the stock. Then, when you want to resell the stock, a dealer again will charge compensation, in the form of a markdown. The dealer subtracts the markdown from the price of the stock when it buys the stock from you. Thus, to make a profit, the bid price of your stock must rise above the amount of the original spread, the markup, and the markdown.

Primary offerings. Most penny stocks are sold to the public on an ongoing basis. However, dealers sometimes sell these stocks in initial public offerings. You should pay special attention to stocks of companies that have never been offered to the public before, because the market for these stocks is untested. Because the offering is on a first-time basis, there is generally no market information about the stock to help determine its value. The federal securities laws generally require broker-dealers to give investors a "prospectus," which contains information about the objectives, management, and financial condition of the issuer. In the absence of market information, investors should read the company's prospectus with special care to find out if the stocks are a good investment. However, the prospectus is only a description of the current condition of the company. The outlook of the start-up companies described in a prospectus often is very uncertain.

For more information about penny stocks, contact the Office of Filings, Information, and Consumer Services of the U.S. Securities and Exchange Commission, 450 Fifth Street, N.W., Washington, D.C. 20549, (202) 272-7440.

FORM 4

U.S. SECURITIES AND EXCHANGE COMMISSION
Washington, D.C. 20549

FORM 4

STATEMENT OF CHANGES IN BENEFICIAL OWNERSHIP OF SECURITIES

The Commission is authorized to solicit the information required by this form pursuant to Sections 16(a) and 23(a) of the Securities Exchange Act of 1934, Sections 17(a) and 20(a) of the Public Utility Holding Company Act of 1935, and Sections 30(h) and 38 of the Investment Company Act of 1940, and the rules and regulations thereunder.

Disclosure of information specified on this form is mandatory, except for disclosure of the IRS identification number of the reporting person if such person is an entity, which is voluntary. If such numbers are furnished, they will assist the Commission in distinguishing reporting persons with similar names and will facilitate the prompt processing of the form. The information will be used for the primary purpose of disclosing the transactions and holdings of directors, officers, and beneficial owners of registered companies. Information disclosed will be a matter of public record and available for inspection by members of the public. The Commission can use it in investigations or litigation involving the federal securities laws or other civil, criminal, or regulatory statutes or provisions, as well as for referral to other governmental authorities and self-regulatory organizations. Failure to disclose required information may result in civil or criminal action against persons involved for violations of the federal securities laws and rules.

GENERAL INSTRUCTIONS

1. When Form Must be Filed

(a) This Form must be filed before the end of the second business day following the day on which a transaction resulting in a change in beneficial ownership has been executed (see Rule 16a-1(a)(2) and Instruction 4 regarding the meaning of "beneficial owner," and Rule 16a-3(g) regarding determination of the date of execution for specified transactions). This Form and any amendment is deemed filed with the Commission or the Exchange on the date it is received by the Commission or the Exchange, respectively. See, however, Rule 16a-3(h) regarding delivery to a third party business that guarantees delivery of the filing no later than the specified due date.

(b) A reporting person no longer subject to section 16 of the Securities Exchange Act of 1934 ("Exchange Act") must check the exit box appearing on this Form. However, Form 4 and Form 5 obligations may continue to be applicable. *See* Rules 16a-3(f) and 16a-2(b). Form 5 transactions to date may be included on this Form and subsequent Form 5 transactions may be reported on a later Form 4 or Form 5, provided all transactions are reported by the required date.

(c) A separate Form shall be filed to reflect beneficial ownership of securities of each issuer, except that a single statement shall be filed with respect to the securities of a registered public utility holding company and all of its subsidiary companies.

(d) If a reporting person is not an officer, director, or 10% holder, the person should check "other" in Item 6 (Relationship of Reporting Person to Issuer) and describe the reason for reporting status in the space provided.

2. Where Form Must be Filed

(a) A reporting person must file this Form in electronic format via the Commission's Electronic Data Gathering Analysis and Retrieval System (EDGAR) in accordance with EDGAR rules set forth in Regulation S-T (17 CFR Part 232), except that a filing person that has obtained a hardship exception under Regulation S-T Rule 202 (17 CFR 232.202) may file the Form in paper. For assistance with technical questions about EDGAR or to request an access code, call the

EDGAR Filer Support Office at (202) 942-8900. For assistance with questions about the EDGAR rules, call the Office of EDGAR and Information Analysis at (202) 942-2940.

(b) At the time this Form or any amendment is filed with the Commission, file one copy with each Exchange on which any class of securities of the issuer is registered. If the issuer has designated a single Exchange to receive Section 16 filings, the copy shall be filed with that Exchange only.

(c) Any person required to file this Form or amendment shall, not later than the time the Form or amendment is transmitted for filing with the Commission, send or deliver a copy to the person designated by the issuer to receive the copy or, if no person is so designated, the issuer's corporate secretary (or person performing similar functions) in accordance with Rule 16a-3(e).

NOTE: If filing pursuant to a hardship exception under Regulation S-T Rule 202 (17 CFR 232.202), file three copies of this Form or any amendment, at least one of which is signed, with the Securities and Exchange Commission, 450 5th Street, NW, Washington, DC 20549. (Acknowledgement of receipt by the Commission may be obtained by enclosing a self-addressed stamped postcard identifying the Form or amendment filed.)

3. Class of Securities Reported

(a) (i) Persons reporting pursuant to Section 16(a) of the Exchange Act must report each transaction resulting in a change in beneficial ownership of any class of equity securities of the issuer and the beneficial ownership of that class of securities following the reported transaction(s), even though one or more of such classes may not be registered pursuant to Section 12 of the Exchange Act.

(ii) Persons reporting pursuant to Section 17(a) of the Public Utility Holding Company Act of 1935 must report each transaction resulting in a change in beneficial ownership of any class of securities (equity or debt) of the registered holding company and all of its subsidiary companies and the beneficial ownership of that class of securities following the reported transaction(s). Specify the name of the parent or subsidiary issuing the securities.

(iii) Persons reporting pursuant to Section 30(h) of the Investment Company Act of 1940 must report each transaction resulting in a change in beneficial ownership of any class of securities (equity or debt) of the registered closed-end investment company (other than "short-term paper" as defined in Section 2(a)(38) of the Investment Company Act) and the beneficial ownership of that class of securities following the reported transaction(s).

(b) The title of the security should clearly identify the class, even if the issuer has only one class of securities outstanding; for example, "Common Stock," "Class A Common Stock," "Class B Convertible Preferred Stock," etc.

(c) The amount of securities beneficially owned should state the face amount of debt securities (U.S. Dollars) or the number of equity securities, whichever is appropriate.

4. Transactions and Holdings Required to be Reported

(a) *General Requirements*

(i) Report, in accordance with Rule 16a-3(g): (1) all transactions not exempt from Section 16(b); (2) all transactions exempt from Section 16(b) pursuant to § 240.16b-3(d), § 240.16b-3(e), or § 240.16b-3(f); and (3) all exercises and conversions of derivative securities, regardless of whether exempt from Section 16(b) of the Act. Every transaction must be reported even though acquisitions and dispositions are equal. Report total beneficial ownership following the reported transaction(s) for each class of securities in which a transaction was reported.

Note: The amount of securities beneficially owned following the reported transaction(s) specified in Column 5 of Table I and Column 9 of Table II should reflect holdings reported or required to be reported by the date of the Form. Transactions and holdings eligible for deferred reporting on Form 5 need not be reflected in the month end total unless the transactions were reported earlier or are included on this Form.

(ii) Each transaction should be reported on a separate line. Transaction codes specified in Instruction 8 should be used to identify the nature of the transaction resulting in an acquisition or disposition of a security. A deemed execution date must be reported in Column 2A of Table I or Column 3A of Table II only if the execution date for the transaction is calculated pursuant to § 240.16a-3(g)(2) or § 240.16a-3(g)(3).

Note: Transactions reportable on Form 5 may, at the option of the reporting person, be reported on a Form 4 filed before the due date of the Form 5. (*See* Instruction 8 for the code for voluntarily reported transactions.)

(b) *Beneficial Ownership Reported (Pecuniary Interest)*

(i) Although for purposes of determining status as a ten percent holder, a person is deemed to beneficially own securities over which that person has voting or investment control (*see* Rule 16a-1(a)(1)), for reporting transactions and holdings, a person is deemed to be the beneficial owner of securities if that person has or shares the opportunity, directly or indirectly, to profit or share in any profit derived from a transaction in the securities ("pecuniary interest"). *See* Rule 16a-1(a)(2). *See also* Rule 16a-8 for the application of the beneficial ownership definition to trust holdings and transactions.

(ii) Both direct and indirect beneficial ownership of securities shall be reported. Securities beneficially owned directly are those held in the reporting person's name or in the name of a bank, broker or nominee for the account of the reporting person. In addition, securities held as joint tenants, tenants in common, tenants by the entirety, or as community property are to be reported as held directly. If a person has a pecuniary interest, by reason of any contract, understanding, or relationship (including a family relationship or arrangement), in securities held in the name of another person, that person is an indirect beneficial owner of the securities. *See* Rule 16a-1(a)(2)(ii) for certain indirect beneficial ownerships.

(iii) Report transactions in securities beneficially owned directly on separate lines from those beneficially owned indirectly. Report different forms of indirect ownership on separate lines. The nature of indirect ownership shall be stated as specifically as possible; for example, "By Self as Trustee for X," "By Spouse," "By X Trust," "By Y Corporation," etc.

(iv) In stating the amount of securities acquired, disposed of, or beneficially owned indirectly through a partnership, corporation, trust, or other entity, report the number of securities representing the reporting person's proportionate interest in transactions conducted by that entity or holdings of that entity. Alternatively, at the option of the reporting person, the entire amount of the entity's interest may be reported. *See* Rule 16a-1(a)(2)(ii) (B) and Rule 16a-1(a)(2)(iii).

(v) Where more than one beneficial owner of the same equity securities must report the same transaction on Form 4, such owners may file Form 4 individually or jointly. Joint and group filings may be made by any designated beneficial owner. Transactions with respect to securities owned separately by any joint or group filer are permitted to be included in the joint filing. Indicate only the name and address of the designated filer in Item 1 of Form 4 and attach a list of the names and addresses of each other reporting person. Joint and group filings must include all required information for each beneficial owner, and such filings must be signed by each beneficial owner, or on behalf of such owner by an authorized person.

If this Form is being filed in paper pursuant to a hardship exemption and the space provided for signatures is insufficient, attach a signature page. If this Form is being filed in paper, submit any attached listing of names or signatures on another Form 4, copy of Form 4 or separate page of 8 1/2 by 11 inch white paper, indicate the number of pages comprising the report (Form plus attachments) at the bottom of each report page (*e.g.*, 1 of 3, 2 of 3, 3 of 3), and include the name of the designated filer and information required by Items 2 and 3 of the Form on the attachment.

See Rule 16a-3(i) regarding signatures.

(c) *Non-Derivative and Derivative Securities*

(i) Report acquisitions or dispositions and holdings of non-derivative securities in Table I. Report acquisitions or dispositions and holdings of derivative securities (*e.g.*, puts, calls, options, warrants, convertible securities, or other rights or obligations to buy or sell securities) in Table II. Report the exercise or conversion of a derivative security in Table II (as a disposition of the derivative security) and report in Table I the holdings of the underlying security. Report acquisitions or dispositions and holdings of derivative securities that are both equity securities and convertible or exchangeable for other equity securities (*e.g.*, convertible preferred securities) only on Table II.

(ii) The title of a derivative security and the title of the equity security underlying the derivative security should be shown separately in the appropriate columns in Table II. The "puts" and "calls" reported in Table II include, in addition to separate puts and calls, any combination of the two, such as spreads and straddles. In reporting an option in Table II, state whether it represents a right to buy, a right to sell, an obligation to buy, or an obligation to sell the equity securities subject to the option.

(iii) Describe in the appropriate columns in Table II characteristics of derivative securities, including title, exercise or conversion price, date exercisable, expiration date, and the title and amount of securities underlying the derivative security. If the transaction reported is a purchase or sale of a derivative security, the purchase or sale price of that derivative security shall be reported in column 8. If the transaction is the exercise or conversion of a derivative security, leave column 8 blank and report the exercise or conversion price of the derivative security in column 2.

(iv) Securities constituting components of a unit shall be reported separately on the applicable table (*e.g.*, if a unit has a non-derivative security component and a derivative security component, the non-derivative security component shall be reported in Table I and the derivative security component shall be reported in Table II). The relationship between individual securities comprising the unit shall be indicated in the space provided for explanation of responses. When securities are purchased or sold as a unit, state the purchase or sale price per unit and other required information regarding the unit securities.

5. Price of Securities

(a) Prices of securities shall be reported in U.S. dollars on a per share basis, not an aggregate basis, except that the aggregate price of debt shall be stated. Amounts reported shall exclude brokerage commissions and other costs of execution.

(b) If consideration other than cash was paid for the security, describe the consideration, including the value of the consideration, in the space provided for explanation of responses.

6. Additional Information

(a) If the space provided in the line items on the electronic Form is insufficient, use the space provided for footnotes. If the space provided for footnotes is insufficient, create a footnote that refers to an exhibit to the form that contains the additional information

(b) If the space provided in the line items on the paper Form or space provided for additional comments is insufficient, attach another Form 4, copy of Form 4 or separate 8 1/2 by 11 inch white paper to Form 4, completed as appropriate to include the additional comments. Each attached page must include information required in Items 1, 2 and 3 of the Form. The number of pages comprising the report (Form plus attachments) shall be indicated at the bottom of each report page (*e.g.* 1 of 3, 2 of 3, 3 of 3).

(c) If one or more exhibits are included, whether due to a lack of space or because the exhibit is, by nature, a separate document (*e.g.*, a power of attorney), provide a sequentially numbered list of the exhibits in the Form. Use the number "24" for any power of attorney and the number "99" for any other exhibit. If there is more than one of either such exhibit, then use numerical subparts. If the exhibit is being filed as a confirming electronic copy under Regulation S-T Rule 202(d) (17 CFR 232.202(d)), then place the designation "CE" (confirming exhibit) next to the name of the exhibit in the exhibit list. If the exhibit is being filed in paper pursuant to a hardship exception under Regulation S-T Rule 202 (17 CFR 232.202), then place the designation "P" (paper) next to the name of the exhibit in the exhibit list.

(d) If additional information is not reported as provided in paragraph (a), (b) or (c) of this instruction, whichever apply, it will be assumed that no additional information was provided.

7. Signature

(a) If the Form is filed for an individual, it shall be signed by that person or specifically on behalf of the individual by a person authorized to sign for the individual. If signed on behalf of the individual by another person, the authority of such person to sign the Form shall be confirmed to the Commission in writing in an attachment to the Form or as soon as practicable in an amendment by the individual for whom the Form is filed, unless such a confirmation still in effect is on file with the Commission. The confirming statement need only indicate that the reporting person authorizes and designates the named person or persons to file the Form on the reporting person's behalf, and state the duration of the authorization.

(b) If the Form is filed for a corporation, partnership, trust, or other entity, the capacity in which the individual signed shall be set forth (*e.g.*, John Smith, Secretary, on behalf of X Corporation).

8. Transaction Codes

Use the codes listed below to indicate in Table I, Column 3 and Table II, Column 4 the character of the transaction reported. Use the code that most appropriately describes the transaction. If the transaction is not specifically listed, use transaction Code "J" and describe the nature of the transaction in the space for explanation of responses. If a transaction is voluntarily reported earlier than required, place "V" in the appropriate column to so indicate; otherwise, the column should be left blank. If a transaction involves an equity swap or instrument with similar characteristics, use transaction Code "K" in addition to the code(s) that most appropriately describes the transaction, *e.g.*, "S/K" or "P/K."

General Transaction Codes

P - Open market or private purchase of non-derivative or derivative security

S - Open market or private sale of non-derivative or derivative security

V - Transaction voluntarily reported earlier than required

Rule 16b-3 Transaction Codes

A - Grant, award or other acquisition pursuant to Rule 16b3(d)

D - Disposition to the issuer of issuer equity securities pursuant to Rule 16b-3(e)

F - Payment of exercise price or tax liability by delivering or withholding securities incident to the receipt, exercise, or vesting of a security issued in accordance with Rule 16b-3

I - Discretionary transaction in accordance with Rule 16b3(f) resulting in acquisition or disposition of issuer securities

M - Exercise or conversion of derivative security exempted pursuant to Rule 16b-3

Derivative Securities Codes (Except for transactions exempted pursuant to Rule 16b-3)

C - Conversion of derivative security

E - Expiration of short derivative position

H - Expiration (or cancellation) of long derivative position with value received

O - Exercise of out-of-the-money derivative security

X - Exercise of in-the-money or at-the-money derivative security

Other Section 16(b) Exempt Transactions and Small Acquisition Codes (except for Rule 16b-3 codes above)

G - Bona fide gift

L - Small acquisition under Rule 16a-6

W - Acquisition or disposition by will or laws of descent and distribution

Z - Deposit into or withdrawal from voting trust

Other Transaction Codes

J - Other acquisition or disposition (describe transaction)

K - Transaction in equity swap or instrument with similar characteristics

U - Disposition pursuant to a tender of shares in a change of control transaction

9. Amendments

(a) If this Form is filed as an amendment in order to add one or more lines of transaction information to Table I or Table II of the Form being amended, provide each line being added, together with one or more footnotes, as necessary, to explain the addition of the line or lines. Do not repeat lines of transaction information that were disclosed in the original Form and are not being amended.

(b) If this Form is filed as an amendment in order to amend one or more lines of transaction information that already were disclosed in Table I or Table II of the Form being amended, provide the complete line or lines being amended, as amended, together with one or more footnotes, as necessary, to explain the amendment of the line or lines. Do not repeat lines of transaction information that were disclosed in the original Form and are not being amended.

(c) If this Form is filed as an amendment for any purpose other than or in addition to the purposes described in paragraphs (a) and (b) of this General Instruction 9, provide one or more footnotes, as necessary, to explain the amendment.

Form 4

FORM 4

☐ Check this box if no longer
subject to Section 16. Form 4 or
Form 5 obligations may continue.
See Instruction 1(b).
(Print or Type Responses)

UNITED STATES SECURITIES AND EXCHANGE COMMISSION
Washington, D.C. 20549

STATEMENT OF CHANGES IN BENEFICIAL OWNERSHIP OF SECURITIES

Filed pursuant to Section 16(a) of the Securities Exchange Act of 1934, Section 17(a) of the Public Utility
Holding Company Act of 1935 or Section 30(h) of the Investment Company Act of 1940

1. Name and Address of Reporting Person*	2. Issuer Name and Ticker or Trading Symbol	5. Relationship of Reporting Person(s) to Issuer (Check all applicable)
(Last) (First) (Middle)	3. Date of Earliest Transaction Required to be Reported (Month/Day/Year)	_____ Director _____ 10% Owner _____ Officer (give _____ Other (specify title below) below)
(Street)	4. If Amendment, Date Original Filed (Month/Day/Year)	6. Individual or Joint/Group Filing (Check Applicable Line) _____ Form filed by One Reporting Person _____ Form filed by More than One Reporting Person
(City) (State) (Zip)		

Table I — Non-Derivative Securities Acquired, Disposed of, or Beneficially Owned

1. Title of Security (Instr. 3)	2. Transaction Date (Month/Day/Year)	2A. Deemed Execution Date, if any (Month/Day/Year)	3. Transaction Code (Instr. 8)		4. Securities Acquired (A) or Disposed of (D) (Instr. 3, 4 and 5)			5. Amount of Securities Beneficially Owned Following Reported Transaction(s) (Instr. 3 and 4)	6. Ownership Form: Direct (D) or Indirect (I) (Instr. 4)	7. Nature of Indirect Beneficial Ownership (Instr. 4)
			Code	V	Amount	(A) or (D)	Price			

Reminder: Report on a separate line for each class of securities beneficially owned directly or indirectly.

* If the form is filed by more than one reporting person, *see* Instruction 4(b)(v).

(Over)

FORM 4 (continued)

Table II — Derivative Securities Acquired, Disposed of, or Beneficially Owned
(*e.g.*, puts, calls, warrants, options, convertible securities)

1. Title of Derivative Security (Instr. 3)	2. Conversion or Exercise Price of Derivative Security	3. Transaction Date (Month/Day/Year)	3A. Deemed Execution Date, if any (Month/Day/Year)	4. Transaction Code (Instr. 8)		5. Number of Derivative Securities Acquired (A) or Disposed of (D) (Instr. 3, 4, and 5)		6. Date Exercisable and Expiration Date (Month/Day/Year)		7. Title and Amount of Underlying Securities (Instr. 3 and 4)		8. Price of Derivative Security (Instr. 5)	9. Number of derivative Securities Beneficially Owned Following Reported Transaction(s) (Instr. 4)	10. Ownership Form of Derivative Security: Direct (D) or Indirect (I) (Instr. 4)	11. Nature of Indirect Beneficial Ownership (Instr. 4)
				Code	V	(A)	(D)	Date Exercisable	Expiration Date	Title	Amount or Number of Shares				

Explanation of Responses:

_____   _____
**Signature of Reporting Person   Date

** Intentional misstatements or omissions of facts constitute Federal Criminal Violations. *See* 18 U.S.C. 1001 and 15 U.S.C. 78ff(a).

Note: File three copies of this Form, one of which must be manually signed. If space is insufficient, *see* Instruction 6 for procedure.

Potential persons who are to respond to the collection of information contained in this form are not required to respond unless the form displays a currently valid OMB Number.

REGULATION S-K—SELECTED PROVISIONS

17 C.F.R. §§ 229.10-229.802

Item	Subject

PART 229—STANDARD INSTRUCTIONS FOR FILING FORMS UNDER SECURITIES ACT OF 1933, SECURITIES EXCHANGE ACT OF 1934 AND ENERGY POLICY AND CONSERVATION ACT OF 1975— REGULATION S-K

Subpart 1—General

Item 10. General

(a) *Application of Regulation S-K.* This part (together with the General Rules and Regulations under the Securities Act of 1933, 15 U.S.C. 77a et seq., as amended ("Securities Act"), and the Securities Exchange Act of 1934, 15 U.S.C. 78a et seq., as amended ("Exchange Act") (Parts 230 and 240 of this chapter), the Interpretative Releases under these Acts (Parts 231 and 241 of this chapter) and the forms under these Acts (Parts 239 and 249 of this chapter)) states the requirements applicable to the content of the non-financial statement portions of:

(1) Registration statements under the Securities Act (Part 239 of this chapter) to the extent provided in the forms to be used for registration under such Act; and

(2) Registration statements under section 12 (subpart C of part 249 of this chapter), annual or other reports under sections 13 and 15(d) (subparts D and E of part 249 of this chapter), going-private transaction statements under section 13 (part 240 of this chapter), tender offer statements under sections 13 and 14 (part 240 of this chapter), annual reports to security holders and proxy and information statements under section 14 (part 240 of this chapter), and any other documents required to be filed under the Exchange Act, to the extent provided in the forms and rules under that Act.

(b) *Commission policy on projections.* The Commission encourages the use in documents specified in Rule 175 under the Securities Act (§ 230.175 of this chapter) and Rule 3b-6 under the Exchange Act (§ 240.3b-6 of this chapter) of management's projections of future economic performance that have a reasonable basis and are presented in an appropriate format. The guidelines set forth herein represent the Commission's views on important factors to be considered in formulating and disclosing such projections.

(1) *Basis for projections.* The Commission believes that management must have the option to present in Commission filings its good faith assessment of a registrant's future performance. Management, however, must have a reasonable basis for such an assessment. Although a history

664

of operations or experience in projecting may be among the factors providing a basis for management's assessment, the Commission does not believe that a registrant always must have had such a history or experience in order to formulate projections with a reasonable basis. An outside review of management's projections may furnish additional support for having a reasonable basis for a projection. If management decides to include a report of such a review in a Commission filing, there also should be disclosure of the qualifications of the reviewer, the extent of the review, the relationship between the reviewer and the registrant, and other material factors concerning the process by which any outside review was sought or obtained. Moreover, in the case of a registration statement under the Securities Act, the reviewer would be deemed an expert and an appropriate consent must be filed with the registration statement.

(2) *Format for projections.* In determining the appropriate format for projections included in Commission filings, consideration must be given to, among other things, the financial items to be projected, the period to be covered, and the manner of presentation to be used. Although traditionally projections have been given for three financial items generally considered to be of primary importance to investors (revenues, net income (loss) and earnings (loss) per share), projection information need not necessarily be limited to these three items. However, management should take care to assure that the choice of items projected is not susceptible of misleading inferences through selective projection of only favorable items. Revenues, net income (loss) and earnings (loss) per share usually are presented together in order to avoid any misleading inferences that may arise when the individual items reflect contradictory trends. There may be instances, however, when it is appropriate to present earnings (loss) from continuing operations, or income (loss) before extraordinary items in addition to or in lieu of net income (loss). It generally would be misleading to present sales or revenue projections without one of the foregoing measures of income. The period that appropriately may be covered by a projection depends to a large extent on the particular circumstances of the company involved. For certain companies in certain industries, a projection covering a two or three year period may be entirely reasonable. Other companies may not have a reasonable basis for projections beyond the current year. Accordingly, management should select the period most appropriate in the circumstances. In addition, management, in making a projection, should disclose what, in its opinion, is the most probable specific amount or the most reasonable range for each financial item projected based on the selected assumptions. Ranges, however, should not be so wide as to make the disclosures meaningless. Moreover, several pr ojections based on varying assumptions may be judged by management to be more meaningful than a single number or range and would be permitted.

(3) *Investor understanding.* (i) When management chooses to include its projections in a Commission filing, the disclosures accompanying the projections should facilitate investor understanding of the basis for and limitations of projections. In this regard investors should be cautioned against attributing undue certainty to management's assessment, and the Commission believes that investors would be aided by a statement indicating management's intention regarding the furnishing of updated projections. The Commission also believes that investor understanding would be enhanced by disclosure of the assumptions which in management's opinion are most significant to the projections or are the key factors upon which the financial results of the enterprise depend and encourages disclosure of assumptions in a manner that will provide a framework for analysis of the projection.

(ii) Management also should consider whether disclosure of the accuracy or inaccuracy of previous projections would provide investors with important insights into the limitations of projections. In this regard, consideration should be given to presenting the projections in a format that will facilitate subsequent analysis of the reasons for differences between actual and forecast results. An important benefit may arise from the systematic analysis of variances between projected and actual results on a continuing basis, since such disclosure may highlight for investors the most significant risk and profit-sensitive areas in a business operation.

(iii) With respect to previously issued projections, registrants are reminded of their responsibility to make full and prompt disclosure of material facts, both favorable and unfavorable, regarding their financial condition. This responsibility may extend to situations where management knows or has reason to know that its previously disclosed projections no longer have a reasonable basis.

(iv) Since a registrant's ability to make projections with relative confidence may vary with all the facts and circumstances, the responsibility for determining whether to discontinue or to resume making projections is best left to management. However, the Commission encourages registrants not to discontinue or to resume projections in Commission filings without a reasonable basis.

(c) *Commission policy on security ratings.* In view of the importance of security ratings ("ratings") to investors and the marketplace, the Commission permits registrants to disclose, on a voluntary basis, ratings assigned by rating organizations to classes of debt securities, convertible debt securities and preferred stock in registration statements and periodic reports. In addition, the Commission permits, pursuant to Rule 134(a)(14) under the Securities Act (§230.134(a)(14) of this chapter), voluntary disclosure of ratings assigned by any nationally recognized statistical rating organizations ("NRSROs") in certain communications deemed not to be a prospectus ("tombstone advertisements").

Set forth herein are the Commission's views on important matters to be considered in disclosing security ratings.

(1) *Securities Act filings.* (i) If a registrant includes in a registration statement filed under the Securities Act any rating(s) assigned to a class of securities, it should consider including: (A) any other rating intended for public dissemination assigned to such class by a NRSRO ("additional NRSRO rating") that is available on the date of the initial filing of the document and that is materially different from any rating disclosed; and (B) the name of each rating organization whose rating is disclosed; each such rating organization's definition or description of the category in which it rated the class of securities; the relative rank of each rating within the assigning rating organization's overall classification system; and a statement informing investors that a security rating is not a recommendation to buy, sell or hold securities, that it may be subject to revision or withdrawal at any time by the assigning rating organization, and that each rating should be evaluated independently of any other rating. The registrant also should include the written consent of any rating organization that is not a NRSRO whose rating is included. With respect to the written consent of any NRSRO whose rating is included, see Rule 436(g) under the Securities Act (§230.436(g) of this chapter). When the registrant has filed a registration statement on Form F-9 (§239.39 of this chapter), see Rule 436(g) (§230.436(g) of this chapter) under the Securities Act with respect to the written consent of any rating organization specified in the Instruction to paragraph (a)(2) of General Instruction I of Form F-9.

(ii) If a change in a rating already included is available subsequent to the filing of the registration statement, but prior to its effectiveness, the registrant should consider including such rating change in the final prospectus. If the rating change is material or if a materially different rating from any disclosed becomes available during this period, the registrant should consider amending the registration statement to include the rating change or additional rating and recirculating the preliminary prospectus.

(iii) If a materially different additional NRSRO rating or a material change in a rating already included becomes available during any period in which offers or sales are being made, the registrant should consider disclosing such additional rating or rating change by means of a post-effective amendment or sticker to the prospectus pursuant to Rule 424(b) under the Securities Act (§230.424(b) of this chapter), unless, in the case of a registration statement on Form S-3 (§239.13 of this chapter), it has been disclosed in a document incorporated by reference into the registration statement subsequent to its effectiveness and prior to the termination of the offering.

(2) *Exchange Act filings.* (i) If a registrant includes in a registration statement or periodic report filed under the Exchange Act any rating(s) assigned to a class of securities, it should consider including the information specified in paragraphs (c)(1)(i)(A) and (B) of this section.

(ii) If there is a material change in the rating(s) assigned by any NRSRO(s) to any outstanding class(es) of securities of a registrant subject to the reporting requirements of section 13(a) or 15(d) of the Exchange Act, the registrant should consider filing a report on Form 8-K (§249.308 of this chapter) or other appropriate report under the Exchange Act disclosing such rating change.

(d) *Incorporation by Reference.* Where rules, regulations, or instructions to forms of the Commission permit incorporation by reference, a document may be so incorporated by reference to the specific document and to the prior filing or submission in which such document was physically filed or submitted. Except where a registrant or issuer is expressly required to incorporate a document or documents by reference, reference may not be made to any document which incorporates another document by reference if the pertinent portion of the document containing the information or financial statements to be incorporated by reference includes an incorporation by reference to another document. No document on file with the Commission for more than five years may be incorporated by reference except:

(1) Documents contained in registration statements, which may be incorporated by reference as long as the registrant has a reporting requirement with the Commission; or

(2) Documents that the registrant specifically identifies by physical location by SEC file number reference, provided such materials have not been disposed of by the Commission pursuant to its Records Control Schedule (17 CFR 200.80f).

(e) *Use of non-GAAP financial measures in Commission filings.* (1) Whenever one or more non-GAAP financial measures are included in a filing with the Commission:

(i) The registrant must include the following in the filing:

(A) A presentation, with equal or greater prominence, of the most directly comparable financial measure or measures calculated and presented in accordance with Generally Accepted Accounting Principles (GAAP);

(B) A reconciliation (by schedule or other clearly understandable method), which shall be quantitative for historical non-GAAP measures presented, and quantitative, to the extent available without unreasonable efforts, for forward-looking information, of the differences between the non-GAAP financial measure disclosed or released with the most directly comparable financial measure or measures calculated and presented in accordance with GAAP identified in paragraph (e)(1)(i)(A) of this section;

(C) A statement disclosing the reasons why the registrant's management believes that presentation of the non-GAAP financial measure provides useful information to investors regarding the registrant's financial condition and results of operations; and

(D) To the extent material, a statement disclosing the additional purposes, if any, for which the registrant's management uses the non-GAAP financial measure that are not disclosed pursuant to paragraph (e)(1)(i)(C) of this section; and

(ii) A registrant must not:

(A) Exclude charges or liabilities that required, or will require, cash settlement, or would have required cash settlement absent an ability to settle in another manner, from non-GAAP liquidity measures, other than the measures earnings before interest and taxes (EBIT) and earnings before interest, taxes, depreciation, and amortization (EBITDA);

(B) Adjust a non-GAAP performance measure to eliminate or smooth items identified as non-recurring, infrequent or unusual, when the nature of the charge or gain is such that it is reasonably likely to recur within two years or there was a similar charge or gain within the prior two years;

(C) Present non-GAAP financial measures on the face of the registrant's financial statements prepared in accordance with GAAP or in the accompanying notes;

(D) Present non-GAAP financial measures on the face of any pro forma financial information required to be disclosed by Article 11 of Regulation S-X (17 CFR 210.11-01 through 210.11-03); or

(E) Use titles or descriptions of non-GAAP financial measures that are the same as, or confusingly similar to, titles or descriptions used for GAAP financial measures; and

(iii) If the filing is not an annual report on Form 10-K or Form 20-F (17 CFR 249.220f), a registrant need not include the information required by paragraphs (e)(1)(i)(C) and (e)(1)(i)(D) of this section if that information was included in its most recent annual report on Form 10-K or Form 20-F or a more recent filing, provided that the required information is updated to the extent necessary to meet the requirements of paragraphs (e)(1)(i)(C) and (e)(1)(i)(D) of this section at the time of the registrant's current filing.

(2) For purposes of this paragraph (e), a non-GAAP financial measure is a numerical measure of a registrant's historical or future financial performance, financial position or cash flows that:

(i) Excludes amounts, or is subject to adjustments that have the effect of excluding amounts, that are included in the most directly comparable measure calculated and presented in accordance with GAAP in the statement of income, balance sheet or statement of cash flows (or equivalent statements) of the issuer; or

(ii) Includes amounts, or is subject to adjustments that have the effect of including amounts, that are excluded from the most directly comparable measure so calculated and presented.

(3) For purposes of this paragraph (e), GAAP refers to generally accepted accounting principles in the United States, except that (i) in the case of foreign private issuers whose primary financial statements are prepared in accordance with non-U.S. generally accepted accounting principles, GAAP refers to the principles under which those primary financial statements are prepared; and (ii) in the case of foreign private issuers that include a non-GAAP financial measure derived from or based on a measure calculated in accordance with U.S. generally accepted accounting principles, GAAP refers to U.S. generally accepted accounting principles for purposes of the application of the requirements of this paragraph (e) to the disclosure of that measure.

(4) For purposes of this paragraph (e), non-GAAP financial measures exclude:

(i) operating and other statistical measures; and

(ii) ratios or statistical measures calculated using exclusively one or both of:

(A) Financial measures calculated in accordance with GAAP; and

(B) Operating measures or other measures that are not non-GAAP financial measures.

(5) For purposes of this paragraph (e), non-GAAP financial measures exclude financial measures required to be disclosed by GAAP, Commission rules, or a system of regulation of a government or governmental authority or self-regulatory organization that is applicable to the registrant. However, the financial measure should be presented outside of the financial statements unless the financial measure is required or expressly permitted by the standard-setter that is responsible for establishing the GAAP used in such financial statements.

(6) The requirements of paragraph (e) of this section shall not apply to a non-GAAP financial measure included in disclosure relating to a proposed business combination, the entity resulting therefrom or an entity that is a party thereto, if the disclosure is contained in a communication that is subject to § 230.425 of this chapter, § 240.14a-12 or § 240.14d-2(b)(2) of this chapter or § 229.1015 of this chapter.

(7) The requirements of paragraph (e) of this section shall not apply to investment companies registered under Section 8 of the Investment Company Act of 1940 (15 U.S.C. 80a-8).

Note to paragraph (e).

A non-GAAP financial measure that would otherwise be prohibited by paragraph (e)(1)(ii) of this section is permitted in a filing of a foreign private issuer if:

1. The non-GAAP financial measure relates to the GAAP used in the registrant's primary financial statements included in its filing with the Commission;

2. The non-GAAP financial measure is required or expressly permitted by the standard-setter that is responsible for establishing the GAAP used in such financial statements; and

3. The non-GAAP financial measure is included in the annual report prepared by the registrant for use in the jurisdiction in which it is domiciled, incorporated or organized or for distribution to its security holders.

Subpart 100—Business

Item 101. Description of Business

(a) *General development of business.* Describe the general development of the business of the registrant, its subsidiaries and any predecessor(s) during the past five years, or such shorter period as the registrant may have been engaged in business. Information shall be disclosed for earlier periods if material to an understanding of the general development of the business.

(1) In describing developments, information shall be given as to matters such as the following: the year in which the registrant was organized and its form of organization; the nature and results of any bankruptcy, receivership or similar proceedings with respect to the registrant or any of its significant subsidiaries; the nature and results of any other material reclassification, merger or consolidation of the registrant or any of its significant subsidiaries; the acquisition or disposition of any material amount of assets otherwise than in the ordinary course of business; and any material changes in the mode of conducting the business.

(2) Registrants, (i) filing a registration statement on Form S-1 (§ 239.11 of this chapter) under the Securities Act or on Form 10 and Form 10-SB (§ 249.210 and § 249.210b of this chapter) under the Exchange Act, (ii) not subject to the reporting requirements of section 13(a) or 15(d) of the Exchange Act immediately prior to the filing of such registration statement, and (iii) that (including predecessors) have not received revenue from operations during each of the three fiscal years immediately prior to the filing of registration statement, shall provide the following information: (A) if the registration statement is filed prior to the end of the registrant's second fiscal quarter, a description of the registrant's plan of operation for the remainder of the fiscal year; or (B) if the registration statement is filed subsequent to the end of the registrant's second fiscal quarter, a description of the registrant's plan of operation for the remainder of the fiscal year and for the first six months of the next fiscal year. If such information is not available, the reasons for its not being available shall be stated. Disclosure relating to any plan shall include such matters as:

(1) In the case of a registration statement on Form S-1, a statement in narrative form indicating the registrant's opinion as to the period of time that the proceeds from the offering will satisfy cash requirements and whether in the next six months it will be necessary to raise additional funds to meet the expenditures required for operating the business of the registrant; the specific reasons for such opinion shall be set forth and categories of expenditures and sources of cash resources shall be identified; however, amounts of expenditures and cash resources need not be provided; in addition, if the narrative statement is based on a cash budget, such budget shall be furnished to the Commission as supplemental information, but not as part of the registration statement;

(2) An explanation of material product research and development to be performed during the period covered in the plan;

(3) Any anticipated material acquisition of plant and equipment and the capacity thereof;

(4) Any anticipated material changes in number of employees in the various departments such as research and development, production, sales or administration; and

(5) Other material areas which may be peculiar to the registrant's business.

(b) *Financial information about segments.* Report for each segment, as defined by generally accepted accounting principles, revenues from external customers, a measure of profit or loss and total assets. A registrant must report this information for each of the last three fiscal years or for as long as it has been in business, whichever period is shorter. If the information provided in response to this paragraph (b) conforms with generally accepted accounting principles, a registrant may include in its financial statements a cross reference to this data in lieu of presenting duplicative information in the financial statements; conversely, a registrant may cross reference to the financial statements.

(1) If a registrant changes the structure of its internal organization in a manner that causes the composition of its reportable segments to change, the registrant must restate the corresponding information for earlier periods, including interim periods, unless it is impracticable to do so. Following a change in the composition of its reportable segments, a registrant shall disclose whether it has restated the corresponding items of segment information for earlier periods. If it has not restated the items from earlier periods, the registrant shall disclose in the year in which the change occurs segment information for the current period under both the old basis and the new basis of segmentation, unless it is impracticable to do so.

(2) If the registrant includes, or is required by Article 3 of Regulation S-X (17 CFR 210) to include, interim financial statements, discuss any facts relating to the performance of any of the segments during the period which, in the opinion of management, indicate that the three year

segment financial data may not be indicative of current or future operations of the segment. Comparative financial information shall be included to the extent necessary to the discussion.

(c) *Narrative description of business.* (1) Describe the business done and intended to be done by the registrant and its subsidiaries, focusing upon the registrant's dominant segment or each reportable segment about which financial information is presented in the financial statements. To the extent material to an understanding of the registrant's business taken as a whole, the description of each such segment shall include the information specified in paragraphs (c)(1)(i) through (x) of this Item. The matters specified in paragraphs (c)(1)(xi) through (xiii) of this Item shall be discussed with respect to the registrant's business in general; where material, the segments to which these matters are significant shall be identified.

(i) The principal products produced and services rendered by the registrant in the segment and the principal markets for, and methods of distribution of, the segment's principal products and services. In addition, state for each of the last three fiscal years the amount or percentage of total revenue contributed by any class of similar products or services which accounted for 10 percent or more of consolidated revenue in any of the last three fiscal years or 15 percent or more of consolidated revenue, if total revenue did not exceed $50,000,000 during any of such fiscal years.

(ii) A description of the status of a product or segment (*e.g.* whether in the planning stage, whether prototypes exist, the degree to which product design has progressed or whether further engineering is necessary), if there has been a public announcement of, or if the registrant otherwise has made public information about, a new product or segment that would require the investment of a material amount of the assets of the registrant or that otherwise is material. This paragraph is not intended to require disclosure of otherwise nonpublic corporate information the disclosure of which would affect adversely the registrant's competitive position.

(iii) The sources and availability of raw materials.

(iv) The importance to the segment and the duration and effect of all patents, trademarks, licenses, franchises and concessions held.

(v) The extent to which the business of the segment is or may be seasonal.

(vi) The practices of the registrant and the industry (respective industries) relating to working capital items (*e.g.,* where the registrant is required to carry significant amounts of inventory to meet rapid delivery requirements of customers or to assure itself of a continuous allotment of goods from suppliers; where the registrant provides rights to return merchandise; or where the registrant has provided extended payment terms to customers).

(vii) The dependence of the segment upon a single customer, or a few customers, the loss of any one or more of which would have a material adverse effect on the segment. The name of any customer and its relationship, if any, with the registrant or its subsidiaries shall be disclosed if sales to the customer by one or more segments are made in an aggregate amount equal to 10 percent or more of the registrant's consolidated revenues and the loss of such customer would have a material adverse effect on the registrant and its subsidiaries taken as a whole. The names of other customers may be included, unless in the particular case the effect of including the names would be misleading. For purposes of this paragraph, a group of customers under common control or customers that are affiliates of each other shall be regarded as a single customer.

(viii) The dollar amount of backlog orders believed to be firm, as of a recent date and as of a comparable date in the preceding fiscal year, together with an indication of the portion thereof not reasonably expected to be filled within the current fiscal year, and seasonal or other material aspects of the backlog. (There may be included as firm orders government orders that are firm but not yet funded and contracts awarded but not yet signed, provided an appropriate statement is added to explain the nature of such orders and the amount thereof. The portion of orders already included in sales or operating revenues on the basis of percentage of completion or program accounting shall be excluded.)

(ix) A description of any material portion of the business that may be subject to renegotiation of profits or termination of contracts or subcontracts at the election of the Government.

(x) Competitive conditions in the business involved including, where material, the identity of the particular markets in which the registrant competes, an estimate of the number of competitors and the registrant's competitive position, if known or reasonably available to the registrant.

Separate consideration shall be given to the principal products or services or classes of products or services of the segment, if any. Generally, the names of competitors need not be disclosed. The registrant may include such names, unless in the particular case the effect of including the names would be misleading. Where, however, the registrant knows or has reason to know that one or a small number of competitors is dominant in the industry it shall be identified. The principal methods of competition (*e.g.*, price, service, warranty or product performance) shall be identified, and positive and negative factors pertaining to the competitive position of the registrant, to the extent that they exist, shall be explained if known or reasonably available to the registrant.

(xi) If material, the estimated amount spent during each of the last three fiscal years on company-sponsored research and development activities determined in accordance with generally accepted accounting principles. In addition, state, if material, the estimated dollar amount spent during each of such years on customer-sponsored research activities relating to the development of new products, services or techniques or the improvement of existing products, services or techniques.

(xii) Appropriate disclosure also shall be made as to the material effects that compliance with Federal, State and local provisions which have been enacted or adopted regulating the discharge of materials into the environment, or otherwise relating to the protection of the environment, may have upon the capital expenditures, earnings and competitive position of the registrant and its subsidiaries. The registrant shall disclose any material estimated capital expenditures for environmental control facilities for the remainder of its current fiscal year and its succeeding fiscal year and for such further periods as the registrant may deem material.

(xiii) The number of persons employed by the registrant.

(d) *Financial information about geographic areas.* (1) State for each of the registrant's last three fiscal years, or for each fiscal year the registrant has been engaged in business, whichever period is shorter:

(i) Revenues from external customers attributed to:

(A) The registrant's country of domicile;

(B) All foreign countries, in total, from which the registrant derives revenues; and

(C) Any individual foreign country, if material. Disclose the basis for attributing revenues from external customers to individual countries.

(ii) Long-lived assets, other than financial instruments, long-term customer relationships of a financial institution, mortgage and other servicing rights, deferred policy acquisition costs, and deferred tax assets, located in:

(A) The registrant's country of domicile;

(B) All foreign countries, in total, in which the registrant holds assets; and

(C) Any individual foreign country, if material.

(2) A registrant shall report the amounts based on the financial information that it uses to produce the general-purpose financial statements. If providing the geographic information is impracticable, the registrant shall disclose that fact. A registrant may wish to provide, in addition to the information required by paragraph (d)(1) of this section, subtotals of geographic information about groups of countries. To the extent that the disclosed information conforms with generally accepted accounting principles, the registrant may include in its financial statements a cross reference to this data in lieu of presenting duplicative data in its financial statements; conversely, a registrant may cross-reference to the financial statements.

(3) A registrant shall describe any risks attendant to the foreign operations and any dependence on one or more of the registrant's segments upon such foreign operations, unless it would be more appropriate to discuss this information in connection with the description of one or more of the registrant's segments under paragraph (c) of this item.

(4) If the registrant includes, or is required by Article 3 of Regulation S-X (17 CFR 210), to include, interim financial statements, discuss any facts relating to the information furnished under this paragraph (d) that, in the opinion of management, indicate that the three year financial data for geographic areas may not be indicative of current or future operations. To the extent necessary to the discussion, include comparative information.

(e) *Available information.* Disclose the information in paragraphs (e)(1), (e)(2) and (e)(3) of this section in any registration statement you file under the Securities Act (15 U.S.C. 77a *et seq.*), and disclose the information in paragraphs (e)(3) and (e)(4) of this section if you are an accelerated filer (as defined in §240.12b-2 of this chapter) filing an annual report on Form 10-K (§249.310 of this chapter):

(1) Whether you file reports with the Securities and Exchange Commission. If you are a reporting company, identify the reports and other information you file with the SEC.

(2) That the public may read and copy any materials you file with the SEC at the SEC's Public Reference Room at 450 Fifth Street, NW, Washington, DC 20549. State that the public may obtain information on the operation of the Public Reference Room by calling the SEC at 1-800-SEC-0330. If you are an electronic filer, state that the SEC maintains an Internet site that contains reports, proxy and information statements, and other information regarding issuers that file electronically with the SEC and state the address of that site (http://www.sec.gov).

(3) You are encouraged to give your Internet address, if available, except that if you are an accelerated filer filing your annual report on Form 10-K, you must disclose your Internet address, if you have one.

(4)(i) Whether you make available free of charge on or through your Internet website, if you have one, your annual report on Form 10-K, quarterly reports on Form 10-Q (§249.308a of this chapter), current reports on Form 8-K (§249.308 of this chapter), and amendments to those reports filed or furnished pursuant to Section 13(a) or 15(d) of the Exchange Act (15 U.S.C. 78m(a) or 78o(d)) as soon as reasonably practicable after you electronically file such material with, or furnish it to, the SEC;

(ii) If you do not make your filings available in this manner, the reasons you do not do so (including, where applicable, that you do not have an Internet website); and

(iii) If you do not make your filings available in this manner, whether you voluntarily will provide electronic or paper copies of your filings free of charge upon request.

(f) *Reports to Security Holders.* Disclose the following information in any registration statement you file under the Securities Act:

(1) If the SEC's proxy rules or regulations, or stock exchange requirements, do not require you to send an annual report to security holders or to holders of American depository receipts, describe briefly the nature and frequency of reports that you will give to security holders. Specify whether the reports that you give will contain financial information that has been examined and reported on, with an opinion expressed "by" an independent public or certified public accountant.

(2) For a foreign private issuer, if the report will not contain financial information prepared in accordance with U.S. generally accepted accounting principles, you must state whether the report will include a reconciliation of this information with U.S. generally accepted accounting principles.

(g) *Enforceability of Civil Liabilities Against Foreign Persons.* Disclose the following if you are a foreign private issuer filing a registration statement under the Securities Act:

(1) Whether or not investors may bring actions under the civil liability provisions of the U.S. federal securities laws against the foreign private issuer, any of its officers and directors who are residents of a foreign country, any underwriters or experts named in the registration statement that are residents of a foreign country, and whether investors may enforce these civil liability provisions when the assets of the issuer or these other persons are located outside of the United States. The disclosure must address the following matters:

(i) The investor's ability to effect service of process within the United States on the foreign private issuer or any person;

(ii) The investor's ability to enforce judgments obtained in U.S. courts against foreign persons based upon the civil liability provisions of the U.S. federal securities laws;

(iii) The investor's ability to enforce, in an appropriate foreign court, judgments of U.S. courts based upon the civil liability provisions of the U.S. federal securities laws; and

(iv) The investor's ability to bring an original action in an appropriate foreign court to enforce liabilities against the foreign private issuer or any person based upon the U.S. federal securities laws.

(2) If you provide this disclosure based on an opinion of counsel, name counsel in the prospectus and file as an exhibit to the registration statement a signed consent of counsel to the use of its name and opinion.

Instructions to Item 101. 1. In determining what information about the segments is material to an understanding of the registrant's business taken as a whole and therefore required to be disclosed pursuant to paragraph (c) of this Item, the registrant should take into account both quantitative and qualitative factors such as the significance of the matter to the registrant (*e.g.,* whether a matter with a relatively minor impact on the registrant's business is represented by management to be important to its future profitability), the pervasiveness of the matter (*e.g.,* whether it affects or may affect numerous items in the segment information), and the impact of the matter (*e.g.,* whether it distorts the trends reflected in the segment information). Situations may arise when information should be disclosed about a segment, although the information in quantitative terms may not appear significant to the registrant's business taken as a whole.

2. Base the determination of whether information about segments is required for a particular year upon an evaluation of interperiod comparability. For instance, interperiod comparability would require a registrant to report segment information in the current period even if not material under the criteria for reportability of SFAS No. 131 if a segment has been significant in the immediately preceding period and the registrant expects it to be significant in the future.

(3) The Commission, upon written request of the registrant and where consistent with the protection of investors, may permit the omission of any of the information required by this Item or the furnishing in substitution thereof of appropriate information of comparable character.

Item 102. Description of Property

State briefly the location and general character of the principal plants, mines and other materially important physical properties of the registrant and its subsidiaries. In addition, identify the segment(s), as reported in the financial statements, that use the properties described. If any such property is not held in fee or is held subject to any major encumbrance, so state and describe briefly how held.

Instructions to Item 102. 1. What is required is such information as reasonably will inform investors as to the suitability, adequacy, productive capacity and extent of utilization of the facilities by the registrant. Detailed descriptions of the physical characteristics of individual properties or legal descriptions by metes and bounds are not required and shall not be given.

2. In determining whether properties should be described, the registrant should take into account both quantitative and qualitative factors. See Instruction 1 to Item 101 of Regulation S-K (§ 229.101).

3. In the case of an extractive enterprise, material information shall be given as to production, reserves, locations, development and the nature of the registrant's interest. If individual properties are of major significance to an industry segment:

A. More detailed information concerning these matters shall be furnished; and

B. Appropriate maps shall be used to disclose location data of significant properties except in cases for which numerous maps would be required.

4. A. If reserve estimates are referred to in the document, the staff of the Office of Engineering, Division of Corporation Finance of the Commission, shall be consulted. That Office may request that a copy of the full report of the engineer or other expert who estimated the reserves be furnished as supplemental information and not as part of the filing. See Rule 418 of Regulation C (§ 230.418 of this chapter) and Rule 12b-4 of Regulation 12B (§ 240.12b-4 of this chapter) with respect to the submission to, and return by, the Commission of supplemental information.

B. If the estimates of reserves, or any estimated valuation thereof, are represented as being based on estimates prepared or reviewed by independent consultants, those independent consultants shall be named in the document.

5. Estimates of oil or gas reserves other than proved or, in the case of other extractive reserves, estimates other than proved or probable reserves, and any estimated values of such reserves shall not be disclosed in any document publicly filed with the Commission, unless such information is required to be disclosed in the document by foreign or state law; provided, however, that where such estimates previously have been provided to a person (or any of its affiliates) that is offering to acquire, merge or consolidate with the registrant or otherwise to acquire the registrant's securities, such estimates may be included in documents relating to such acquisition.

6. The definitions in § 210.4-10(a) of Regulation S-X [17 CFR 210] shall apply to this Item with respect to oil and gas operations.

Item 103. Legal Proceedings

Describe briefly any material pending legal proceedings, other than ordinary routine litigation incidental to the business, to which the registrant or any of its subsidiaries is a party or of which any of their property is the subject. Include the name of the court or agency in which the proceedings are pending, the date instituted, the principal parties thereto, a description of the factual basis alleged to underlie the proceeding and the relief sought. Include similar information as to any such proceedings known to be contemplated by governmental authorities.

Instructions to Item 103. 1. If the business ordinarily results in actions for negligence or other claims, no such action or claim need be described unless it departs from the normal kind of such actions.

2. No information need be given with respect to any proceeding that involves primarily a claim for damages if the amount involved, exclusive of interest and costs, does not exceed 10 percent of the current assets of the registrant and its subsidiaries on a consolidated basis. However, if any proceeding presents in large degree the same legal and factual issues as other proceedings pending or known to be contemplated, the amount involved in such other proceedings shall be included in computing such percentage.

3. Notwithstanding Instructions 1 and 2, any material bankruptcy, receivership, or similar proceeding with respect to the registrant or any of its significant subsidiaries shall be described.

4. Any material proceedings to which any director, officer or affiliate of the registrant, any owner of record or beneficially of more than five percent of any class of voting securities of the registrant, or any associate of any such director, officer, affiliate of the registrant, or security holder is a party adverse to the registrant or any of its subsidiaries or has a material interest adverse to the registrant or any of its subsidiaries also shall be described.

5. Notwithstanding the foregoing, an administrative or judicial proceeding (including, for purposes of A and B of this Instruction, proceedings which present in large degree the same issues) arising under any Federal, State or local provisions that have been enacted or adopted regulating the discharge of materials into the environment or primary [primarily] for the purpose of protecting the environment shall not be deemed "ordinary routine litigation incidental to the business" and shall be described if:

A. Such proceeding is material to the business or financial condition of the registrant;

B. Such proceeding involves primarily a claim for damages, or involves potential monetary sanctions, capital expenditures, deferred charges or charges to income and the amount involved, exclusive of interest and costs, exceeds 10 percent of the current assets of the registrant and its subsidiaries on a consolidated basis; or

C. A governmental authority is a party to such proceeding and such proceeding involves potential monetary sanctions, unless the registrant reasonably believes that such proceeding will result in no monetary sanctions, or in monetary sanctions, exclusive of interest and costs, of less than $100,000; provided, however, that such proceedings which are similar in nature may be grouped and described generically.

Subpart 200—Securities of the Registrant

Item 201. Market Price of and Dividends on the Registrant's Common Equity and Related Stockholder Matters

(a) *Market information.* (1) (i) Identify the principal United States market or markets in which each class of the registrant's common equity is being traded. Where there is no established public trading market for a class of common equity, furnish a statement to that effect. For purposes of this Item the existence of limited or sporadic quotations should not of itself be deemed to constitute an "established public trading market." In the case of foreign registrants, also identify the principal established foreign public trading market, if any, for each class of the registrant's common equity.

(ii) If the principal United States market for such common equity is an exchange, state the high and low sales prices for the equity for each full quarterly period within the two most recent fiscal years and any subsequent interim period for which financial statements are included, or are required to be included by Article 3 of Regulation S-X [17 CFR 210], as reported in the consolidated transaction reporting system or, if not so reported, as reported on the principal exchange market for such equity.

(iii) If the principal United States market for such common equity is not an exchange, state the range of high and low bid information for the equity for each full quarterly period within the two most recent fiscal years and any subsequent interim period for which financial statements are included, or are required to be included by Article 3 of Regulation S-X, as regularly quoted in the automated quotation system of a registered securities association, or where the equity is not quoted in such a system, the range of reported high and low bid quotations, indicating the source of such quotations. Indicate, as applicable, that such over-the-counter market quotations reflect inter-dealer prices, without retail mark-up, mark-down or commission and may not necessarily represent actual transactions. Where there is an absence of an established public trading market, reference to quotations shall be qualified by appropriate explanation.

(iv) Where a foreign registrant has identified a principal established foreign trading market for its common equity pursuant to paragraph (a) (1) of this Item, also provide market price information comparable, to the extent practicable, to that required for the principal United States market, including the source of such information. Such prices shall be stated in the currency in which they are quoted. The registrant may translate such prices into United States currency at the currency exchange rate in effect on the date the price disclosed was reported on the foreign exchange. If the primary United States market for the registrant's common equity trades using American Depositary Receipts, the United States prices disclosed shall be on that basis.

(v) If the information called for by this Item is being presented in a registration statement filed pursuant to the Securities Act or a proxy or information statement filed pursuant to the Exchange Act, the document also shall include price information as of the latest practicable date, and, in the case of securities to be issued in connection with an acquisition, business combination or other reorganization, as of the date immediately prior to the public announcement of such transaction.

(2) If the information called for by this paragraph (a) is being presented in a registration statement on Form S-1 [§ 239.11 of this chapter] or Form SB-2 [§ 239.10 of this chapter] under the Securities Act or on Form 10 and Form 10-SB [§ 249.210 and § 249.210b of this chapter] under the Exchange Act relating to a class of common equity for which at the time of filing there is no established United States public trading market, indicate the amount(s) of common equity (i) that is subject to outstanding options or warrants to purchase, or securities convertible into, common equity of the registrant; (ii) that could be sold pursuant to Rule 144 under the Securities Act [§ 230.144 of this chapter] or that the registrant has agreed to register under the Securities Act for sale by security holders; or (iii) that is being, or has been publicly proposed to be, publicly offered by the registrant (unless such common equity is being offered pursuant to an employee benefit plan or dividend reinvestment plan), the offering of which could have a material effect on the market price of the registrant's common equity.

(b) *Holders.* (1) Set forth the approximate number of holders of each class of common equity of the registrant as of the latest practicable date.

(2) If the information called for by this paragraph (b) is being presented in a registration statement filed pursuant to the Securities Act or a proxy statement or information statement filed pursuant to the Exchange Act that relates to an acquisition, business combination or other reorganization, indicate the effect of such transaction on the amount and percentage of present holdings of the registrant's common equity owned beneficially by (i) any person (including any group as that term is used in section 13(d)(3) of the Exchange Act) who is known to the registrant to be the beneficial owner of more than five percent of any class of the registrant's common equity and (ii) each director and nominee and (iii) all directors and officers as a group, and the registrant's present commitments to such persons with respect to the issuance of shares of any class of its common equity.

(c) *Dividends.* (1) State the frequency and amount of any cash dividends declared on each class of its common equity by the registrant for the two most recent fiscal years and any subsequent interim period for which financial statements are required to be presented by § 210.3 of Regulation S-X. Where there are restrictions (including, where appropriate, restrictions on the ability of registrant's subsidiaries to transfer funds to the registrant in the form of cash dividends, loans or advances) that currently materially limit the registrant's ability to pay such dividends or that the registrant reasonably believes are likely to limit materially the future payment of dividends on the common equity so state and either (i) describe briefly (where appropriate quantify) such restrictions, or (ii) cross reference to the specific discussion of such restrictions in the Management's Discussion and Analysis of financial condition and operating results prescribed by Item 303 of Regulation S-K (§ 229.303) and the description of such restrictions required by Regulation S-X in the registrant's financial statements.

(2) Where registrants have a record of paying no cash dividends although earnings indicate an ability to do so, they are encouraged to consider the question of their intention to pay cash dividends in the foreseeable future and, if no such intention exists, to make a statement of that fact in the filing. Registrants which have a history of paying cash dividends also are encouraged to indicate whether they currently expect that comparable cash dividends will continue to be paid in the future and, if not, the nature of the change in the amount or rate of cash dividend payments.

(d) *Securities authorized for issuance under equity compensation plans.* (1) In the following tabular format, provide the information specified in paragraph (d)(2) of this Item as of the end of the most recently completed fiscal year with respect to compensation plans (including individual compensation arrangements) under which equity securities of the registrant are authorized for issuance, aggregated as follows:

(i) All compensation plans previously approved by security holders; and

(ii) All compensation plans not previously approved by security holders.

Equity Compensation Plan Information

Plan category	Number of securities to be issued upon exercise of outstanding options, warrants and rights	Weighted-average exercise price of outstanding options, warrants and rights	Number of securities remaining available for future issuance under equity compensation plans (excluding securities reflected in column (a))
	(a)	*(b)*	*(c)*
Equity compensation plans approved by security holders			
Equity compensation plans not approved by security holders			

Equity Compensation Plan Information

Plan category	Number of securities to be issued upon exercise of outstanding options, warrants and rights	Weighted-average exercise price of outstanding options, warrants and rights	Number of securities remaining available for future issuance under equity compensation plans (excluding securities reflected in column (a))
	(a)	*(b)*	*(c)*
Total			

(2) The table shall include the following information as of the end of the most recently completed fiscal year for each category of equity compensation plan described in paragraph (d)(1) of this Item:

(i) The number of securities to be issued upon the exercise of outstanding options, warrants and rights (column (a));

(ii) The weighted-average exercise price of the outstanding options, warrants and rights disclosed pursuant to paragraph (d)(2)(i) of this Item (column (b)); and

(iii) Other than securities to be issued upon the exercise of the outstanding options, warrants and rights disclosed in paragraph (d)(2)(i) of this Item, the number of securities remaining available for future issuance under the plan (column (c)).

(3) For each compensation plan under which equity securities of the registrant are authorized for issuance that was adopted without the approval of security holders, describe briefly, in narrative form, the material features of the plan.

Instructions to Paragraph (d).

1. Disclosure shall be provided with respect to any compensation plan and individual compensation arrangement of the registrant (or parent, subsidiary or affiliate of the registrant) under which equity securities of the registrant are authorized for issuance to employees or non-employees (such as directors, consultants, advisors, vendors, customers, suppliers or lenders) in exchange for consideration in the form of goods or services as described in Statement of Financial Accounting Standards No. 123, *Accounting for Stock-Based Compensation*, or any successor standard. No disclosure is required with respect to

(i) any plan, contract or arrangement for the issuance of warrants or rights to all security holders of the registrant as such on a pro rata basis (such as a stock rights offering) or

(ii) any employee benefit plan that is intended to meet the qualification requirements of Section 401(a) of the Internal Revenue Code (26 U.S.C. § 401(a)).

2. For purposes of this paragraph, an "individual compensation arrangement" includes, but is not limited to, the following: a written compensation contract within the meaning of "employee benefit plan" under § 230.405 of this chapter and a plan (whether or not set forth in any formal document) applicable to one person as provided under Item 402(a)(7)(ii) of Regulation S-K (§ 229.402(a)(7)(ii)).

3. If more than one class of equity security is issued under its equity compensation plans, a registrant should aggregate plan information for each class of security.

4. A registrant may aggregate information regarding individual compensation arrangements with the plan information required under paragraph (d)(1)(i) and (ii) of this item, as applicable.

5. A registrant may aggregate information regarding a compensation plan assumed in connection with a merger, consolidation or other acquisition transaction pursuant to which the registrant may make subsequent grants or awards of its equity securities with the plan information required under paragraph (d)(1)(i) and (ii) of this item, as applicable. A registrant shall disclose on an aggregated basis in a footnote to the table the information required under paragraph (d)(2)(i) and (ii) of this item with respect to any individual options, warrants or rights assumed in connection with a merger, consolidation or other acquisition transaction.

6. To the extent that the number of securities remaining available for future issuance disclosed in column (c) includes securities available for future issuance under any compensation

plan or individual compensation arrangement other than upon the exercise of an option, warrant or right, disclose the number of securities and type of plan separately for each such plan in a footnote to the table.

7. If the description of an equity compensation plan set forth in a registrant's financial statements contains the disclosure required by paragraph (d) (3) of this item, a cross-reference to such description will satisfy the requirements of paragraph (d) (3) of this item.

8. If an equity compensation plan contains a formula for calculating the number of securities available for issuance under the plan, including, without limitation, a formula that automatically increases the number of securities available for issuance by a percentage of the number of outstanding securities of the registrant, a description of this formula shall be disclosed in a footnote to the table.

9. Except where it is part of a document that is incorporated by reference into a prospectus, the information required by this paragraph need not be provided in any registration statement filed under the Securities Act.

Instructions to Item 201. 1. Registrants, the common equity of which is listed for trading on more than one securities exchange registered under the Exchange Act, are required to indicate each such exchange pursuant to paragraph (a) (1) (i) of this Item; such registrants, however, need only report one set of price quotations pursuant to paragraph (a) (1) (ii) of this Item; where available, these shall be the prices as reported in the consolidated transaction reporting system and, where the prices are not so reported, the prices on the most significant (in terms of volume) securities exchange for such shares.

2. Market prices and dividends reported pursuant to this Item shall be adjusted to give retroactive effect to material changes resulting from stock dividends, stock splits and reverse stock splits.

3. The computation of the approximate number of holders of registrant's common equity may be based upon the number of record holders or also may include individual participants in security position listings. See Rule 17Ad-8 under the Exchange Act. The method of computation that is chosen shall be indicated.

4. If the registrant is a foreign issuer, describe briefly:

A. Any governmental laws, decrees or regulations in the country in which the registrant is organized that restrict the export or import of capital, including, but not limited to, foreign exchange controls, or that affect the remittance of dividends or other payments to nonresident holders of the registrant's common equity; and

B. All taxes, including withholding provisions, to which United States common equity holders are subject under existing laws and regulations of the foreign country in which the registrant is organized. Include a brief description of pertinent provisions of any reciprocal tax treaty between such foreign country and the United States regarding withholding. If there is no such treaty, so state.

5. If the registrant is a foreign private issuer whose common equity of the class being registered is wholly or partially in bearer form, the response to this Item shall so indicate together with as much information as the registrant is able to provide with respect to security holdings in the United States. If the securities being registered trade in the United States in the form of American Depositary Receipts or similar certificates, the response to this Item shall so indicate together with the name of the depositary issuing such receipts and the number of shares or other units of the underlying security representing the trading units in such receipts.

Item 202. Description of Registrant's Securities

Note.—If the securities being described have been accepted for listing on an exchange, the exchange may be identified. The document should not however, convey the impression that the registrant may apply successfully for listing of the securities on an exchange or that, in the case of an underwritten offering, the underwriters may request the registrant to apply for such listing, unless there is reasonable assurance that the securities to be offered will be acceptable to a securities exchange for listing.

(a) *Capital stock.* If capital stock is to be registered, state the title of the class and describe such of the matters listed in paragraphs (a)(1) through (5) as are relevant. A complete legal description of the securities need not be given.

(1) Outline briefly: (i) dividend rights; (ii) terms of conversion; (iii) sinking fund provisions; (iv) redemption provisions; (v) voting rights, including any provisions specifying the vote required by security holders to take action; (vi) any classification of the Board of Directors, and the impact of such classification where cumulative voting is permitted or required; (vii) liquidation rights; (viii) preemption rights; and (ix) liability to further calls or to assessment by the registrant and for liabilities of the registrant imposed on its stockholders under state statutes (*e.g.,* to laborers, servants or employees of the registrant), unless such disclosure would be immaterial because the financial resources of the registrant or other factors make it improbable that liability under such state statutes would be imposed; (x) any restriction on alienability of the securities to be registered; and (xi) any provision discriminating against any existing or prospective holder of such securities as a result of such security holder owning a substantial amount of securities.

(2) If the rights of holders of such stock may be modified otherwise than by a vote of a majority or more of the shares outstanding, voting as a class, so state and explain briefly.

(3) If preferred stock is to be registered, describe briefly any restriction on the repurchase or redemption of shares by the registrant while there is any arrearage in the payment of dividends or sinking fund installments. If there is no such restriction, so state.

(4) If the rights evidenced by, or amounts payable with respect to, the shares to be registered are, or may be, materially limited or qualified by the rights of any other authorized class of securities, include the information regarding such other securities as will enable investors to understand such limitations or qualifications. No information need be given, however, as to any class of securities all of which will be retired, provided appropriate steps to ensure such retirement will be completed prior to or upon delivery by the registrant of the shares.

(5) Describe briefly or cross-reference to a description in another part of the document, any provision of the registrant's charter or by-laws that would have an effect of delaying, deferring or preventing a change in control of the registrant and that would operate only with respect to an extraordinary corporate transaction involving the registrant [or any of its subsidiaries], such as a merger, reorganization, tender offer, sale or transfer of substantially all of its assets, or liquidation. Provisions and arrangements required by law or imposed by governmental or judicial authority need not be described or discussed pursuant to this paragraph (a)(5). Provisions or arrangements adopted by the registrant to effect, or further, compliance with laws or governmental or judicial mandate are not subject to the immediately preceding sentence where such compliance did not require the specific provisions or arrangements adopted.

(b) *Debt securities.* If debt securities are to be registered, state the title of such securities, the principal amount being offered, and, if a series, the total amount authorized and the total amount outstanding as of the most recent practicable date; and describe such of the matter listed in paragraphs (b)(1) through (10) as are relevant. A complete legal description of the securities need not be given. For purposes solely of this Item, debt securities that differ from one another only as to the interest rate or maturity shall be regarded as securities of the same class. Outline briefly:

(1) Provisions with respect to maturity, interest, conversion, redemption, amortization, sinking fund, or retirement;

(2) Provisions with respect to the kind and priority of any lien securing the securities, together with a brief identification of the principal properties subject to such lien;

(3) Provisions with respect to the subordination of the rights of holders of the securities to other security holders or creditors of the registrant; where debt securities are designated as subordinated in accordance with Instruction 1 to this Item, set forth the aggregate amount of outstanding indebtedness as of the most recent practicable date that by the terms of such debt securities would be senior to such subordinated debt and describe briefly any limitation on the issuance of such additional senior indebtedness or state that there is no such limitation;

(4) Provisions restricting the declaration of dividends or requiring the maintenance of any asset ratio or the creation or maintenance of reserves;

(5) Provisions restricting the incurrence of additional debt or the issuance of additional securities; in the case of secured debt, whether the securities being registered are to be issued on the basis of unbonded bondable property, the deposit of cash or otherwise; as of the most recent practicable date, the approximate amount of unbonded bondable property available as a basis for the issuance of bonds; provisions permitting the withdrawal of cash deposited as a basis for the issuance of bonds; and provisions permitting the release or substitution of assets securing the issue; *Provided, however,* That provisions permitting the release of assets upon the deposit of equivalent funds or the pledge of equivalent property, the release of property no longer required in the business, obsolete property, or property taken by eminent domain or the application of insurance moneys, and other similar provisions need not be described;

(6) The general type of event that constitutes a default and whether or not any periodic evidence is required to be furnished as to the absence of default or as to compliance with the terms of the indenture;

(7) Provisions relating to modification of the terms of the security or the rights of security holders;

(8) If the rights evidenced by the securities to be registered are, or may be, materially limited or qualified by the rights of any other authorized class of securities, the information regarding such other securities as will enable investors to understand the rights evidenced by the securities[;] to the extent not otherwise disclosed pursuant to this Item; no information need be given, however, as to any class of securities all of which will be retired, provided appropriate steps to ensure such retirement will be completed prior to or upon delivery by the registrant of the securities;

(9) If debt securities are to be offered at a price such that they will be deemed to be offered at an "original issue discount" as defined in paragraph (a) of Section 1273 of the Internal Revenue Code (26 U.S.C. 1273), or if a debt security is sold in a package with another security and the allocation of the offering price between the two securities may have the effect of offering the debt security at such an original issue discount, the tax effects thereof pursuant to sections 1271—1278; and

(10) The name of the trustee(s) and the nature of any material relationship with the registrant or with any of its affiliates; the percentage of securities of the class necessary to require the trustee to take action; and what indemnification the trustee may require before proceeding to enforce the lien.

(c) *Warrants and rights.* If the securities described are to be offered pursuant to warrants or rights state:

(1) The amount of securities called for by such warrants or rights;

(2) The period during which and the price at which the warrants or rights are exercisable;

(3) The amount of warrants or rights outstanding;

(4) Provisions for changes to or adjustments in the exercise price; and

(5) Any other material terms of such rights on [or] warrants.

(d) *Other securities.* If securities other than capital stock, debt, warrants or rights are to be registered, include a brief description (comparable to that required in paragraphs (a), (b) and (c) of Item 202) of the rights evidenced thereby.

(e) *Market information for securities other than common equity.* If securities other than common equity are to be registered and there is an established public trading market for such securities (as that term is used in Item 201 of Regulation S-K (§ 229.201 of this chapter)) provide market information with respect to such securities comparable to that required by paragraph (a) of Item 201 of Regulation S-K (§ 229.201).

(f) *American Depositary Receipts.* If Depositary Shares represented by American Depositary Receipts are being registered, furnish the following information:

(1) The name of the depositary and the address of its principal executive office.

(2) State the title of the American Depositary Receipts and identify the deposited security. Describe briefly the terms of deposit, including the provisions, if any, with respect to: (i) the amount of deposited securities represented by one unit of American Depositary Receipts; (ii) the procedure for voting, if any, the deposited securities; (iii) the collection and distribution of

dividends; (iv) the transmission of notices, reports and proxy soliciting material; (v) the sale or exercise of rights; (vi) the deposit or sale of securities resulting from dividends, splits or plans of reorganization; (vii) amendment, extension or termination of the deposit; (viii) rights of holders of receipts to inspect the transfer books of the depositary and the list of holders of receipts; (ix) restrictions upon the right to deposit or withdraw the underlying securities; (x) limitation upon the liability of the depositary.

(3) Describe all fees and charges which may be imposed directly or indirectly against the holder of the American Depositary Receipts, indicating the type of service, the amount of fee or charges and to whom paid.

Instructions to Item 202. 1. Wherever the title of securities is required to be stated, there shall be given such information as will indicate the type and general character of the securities, including the following:

A. In the case of shares, the par or stated value, if any; the rate of dividends, if fixed, and whether cumulative or non-cumulative; a brief indication of the preference, if any; and if convertible or redeemable, a statement to that effect;

B. In the case of debt, the rate of interest; the date of maturity or, if the issue matures serially, a brief indication of the serial maturities, such as "maturing serially from 1955 to 1960"; if the payment of principal or interest is contingent, an appropriate indication of such contingency; a brief indication of the priority of the issue; and, if convertible or callable, a statement to that effect; or

C. In the case of any other kind of security, appropriate information of comparable character.

2. If the registrant is a foreign registrant, include (to the extent not disclosed in the document pursuant to Item 201 of Regulation S-K (§ 229.201) or otherwise) in the description of the securities:

A. A brief description of any limitations on the right of nonresident or foreign owners to hold or vote such securities imposed by foreign law or by the charter or other constituent document of the registrant, or if no such limitations are applicable, so state;

B. A brief description of any governmental laws, decrees or regulations in the country in which the registrant is organized affecting the remittance of dividends, interest and other payments to nonresident holders of the securities being registered;

C. A brief outline of all taxes, including withholding provisions, to which United States security holders are subject under existing laws and regulations of the foreign country in which the registrant is organized; and

D. A brief description of pertinent provisions of any reciprocal tax treaty between such foreign country and the United States regarding withholding or, if there is no such treaty, so state.

3. Section 305(a)(2) of the Trust Indenture Act of 1939, 15 U.S.C. 77aaa et seq., as amended ("Trust Indenture Act"), shall not be deemed to require the inclusion in a registration statement or in a prospectus of any information not required by this Item.

4. Where convertible securities or stock purchase warrants are being registered that are subject to redemption or call, the description of the conversion terms of the securities or material terms of the warrants shall disclose:

A. Whether the right to convert or purchase the securities will be forfeited unless it is exercised before the date specified in a notice of the redemption or call;

B. The expiration or termination date of the warrants;

C. The kinds, frequency and timing of notice of the redemption or call, including the cities or newspapers in which notice will be published (where the securities provide for a class of newspapers or group of cities in which the publication may be made at the discretion of the registrant, the registrant should describe such provision); and

D. In the case of bearer securities, that investors are responsible for making arrangements to prevent loss of the right to convert or purchase in the event of redemption of call, for example, by reading the newspapers in which the notice of redemption or call may be published.

5. The response to paragraph (f) shall include information with respect to fees and charges in connection with (A) the deposit or substitution of the underlying securities; (B) receipt and distribution of dividends; (C) the sale or exercise of rights; (D) the withdrawal of the underlying security; and (E) the transferring, splitting or grouping of receipts. Information with respect to the right to collect the fees and charges against dividends received and deposited securities shall be included in response to this item.

Subpart 300—Financial Information

Item 301. Selected Financial Data

Furnish in comparative columnar form the selected financial data for the registrant referred to below, for

(a) Each of the last five fiscal years of the registrant (or for the life of the registrant and its predecessors, if less), and

(b) Any additional fiscal years necessary to keep the information from being misleading.

Instructions to Item 301. 1. The purpose of the selected financial data shall be to supply in a convenient and readable format selected financial data which highlight certain significant trends in the registrant's financial condition and results of operations.

2. Subject to appropriate variation to conform to the nature of the registrant's business, the following items shall be included in the table of financial data: net sales or operating revenues; income (loss) from continuing operations; income (loss) from continuing operations per common share; total assets; long-term obligations and redeemable preferred stock (including long-term debt, capital leases, and redeemable preferred stock as defined in § 210.5-02.28(a) of Regulation S-X [17 CFR 210]; and cash dividends declared per common share. Registrants may include additional items which they believe would enhance an understanding of and would highlight other trends in their financial condition and results of operations.

Briefly describe, or cross-reference to a discussion thereof, factors such as accounting changes, business combinations or dispositions of business operations, that materially affect the comparability of the information reflected in selected financial data. Discussion of, or reference to, any material uncertainties should also be included where such matters might cause the data reflected herein not to be indicative of the registrant's future financial condition or results of operations.

3. All references to the registrant in the table of selected financial data and in this Item shall mean the registrant and its subsidiaries consolidated.

4. If interim period financial statements are included, or are required to be included by Article 3 of Regulation S-X, registrants should consider whether any or all of the selected financial data need to be updated for such interim periods to reflect a material change in the trends indicated; where such updating information is necessary, registrants shall provide the information on a comparative basis unless not necessary to an understanding of such updating information.

5. A foreign private issuer shall disclose also the following information in all filings containing financial statements:

A. In the forepart of the document and as of the latest practicable date, the exchange rate into U.S. currency of the foreign currency in which the financial statements are denominated;

B. A history of exchange rates for the five most recent years and any subsequent interim period for which financial statements are presented setting forth the rates for period end, the average rates, and the range of high and low rates for each year, and

C. If equity securities are being registered, a five year summary of dividends per share stated in both the currency in which the financial statements are denominated and United States currency based on the exchange rates at each respective payment date.

6. A foreign private issuer shall present the selected financial data in the same currency as its financial statements. The issuer may present the selected financial data on the basis of the accounting principles used in its primary financial statements but in such case shall present this data also on the basis of any reconciliations of such data to United States generally accepted accounting principles and Regulation S-X made pursuant to Rule 4-01 of Regulation S-X (§ 210.4-01 of this chapter).

7. For purposes of this rule, the rate of exchange means the noon buying rate in New York City for cable transfers in foreign currencies as certified for customs purposes by the Federal Reserve Bank of New York. The average rate means the average of the exchange rates on the last day of each month during a year.

Item 302. Supplementary Financial Information

(a) *Selected quarterly financial data.* Registrants specified in paragraph (a)(5) of this Item shall provide the information specified below.

(1) Disclosure shall be made of net sales, gross profit (net sales less costs and expenses associated directly with or allocated to products sold or services rendered), income (loss) before extraordinary items and cumulative effect of a change in accounting, per share data based upon such income (loss), and net income (loss), for each full quarter within the two most recent fiscal years and any subsequent interim period for which financial statements are included or are required to be included by Article 3 of Regulation S-X [17 CFR 210].

(2) When the data supplied pursuant to this paragraph (a) vary from the amounts previously reported on the Form 10-Q and Form 10-QSB (§ 249.308a and § 249.308b of this chapter) filed for any quarter, such as would be the case when a pooling of interests occurs or where an error is corrected, reconcile the amounts given with those previously reported and describe the reason for the difference.

(3) Describe the effect of any disposals of segments of a business, and extraordinary, unusual or infrequently occurring items recognized in each full quarter within the two most recent fiscal years and any subsequent interim period for which financial statements are included or are required to be included by Article 3 of Regulation S-X, as well as the aggregate effect and the nature of year-end or other adjustments which are material to the results of that quarter.

(4) If the financial statements to which this information relates have been reported on by an accountant, appropriate professional standards and procedures, as enumerated in the Statements of Auditing Standards issued by the Auditing Standards Board of the American Institute of Certified Public Accountants, shall be followed by the reporting accountant with regard to the data required by this paragraph (a).

(5) This paragraph (a) applies to any registrant, except a foreign private issuer, that has securities registered pursuant to sections 12(b) (15 U.S.C. § 78*l* (b)) (other than mutual life insurance companies) or 12(g) of the Exchange Act (15 U.S.C. § 78*l* (g)).

(b) *Information about oil and gas producing activities.* Registrants engaged in oil and gas producing activities shall present the information about oil and gas producing activities (as those activities are defined in Regulation S-X, § 210.4-10(a)) specified in paragraphs 9-34 of Statement of Financial Accounting Standards ("SFAS") No. 69, "Disclosures about Oil and Gas Producing Activities," if such oil and gas producing activities are regarded as significant under one or more of the tests set forth in paragraph 8 of SFAS No. 69.

Instructions to Paragraph (b). 1. (a) SFAS No. 69 disclosures that relate to annual periods shall be presented for each annual period for which an income statement is required, (b) SFAS No. 69 disclosures required as of the end of an annual period shall be presented as of the date of each audited balance sheet required, and (c) SFAS No. 69 disclosures required as of the beginning of an annual period shall be presented as of the beginning of each annual period for which an income statement is required.

2. This paragraph, together with § 210.4-10 of Regulation S-X, prescribes financial reporting standards for the preparation of accounts by persons engaged, in whole or in part, in the production of crude oil or natural gas in the United States, pursuant to Section 503 of the Energy Policy and Conservation Act of 1975 [42 U.S.C. 6383] ("EPCA") and Section 11(c) of the Energy

Supply and Environmental Coordination Act of 1974 [15 U.S.C. 796] ("ESECA") as amended by Section 506 of EPCA. The application of this paragraph to those oil and gas producing operations of companies regulated for ratemaking purposes on an individual-company-cost-of-service basis may, however, give appropriate recognition to differences arising because of the effect of the ratemaking process.

3. Any person exempted by the Department of Energy from any recordkeeping or reporting requirements pursuant to Section 11(c) of ESECA, as amended, is similarly exempted from the related provisions of this paragraph in the preparation of accounts pursuant to EPCA. This exemption does not affect the applicability of this paragraph to filings pursuant to the federal securities laws.

Item 303. Management's Discussion and Analysis of Financial Condition and Results of Operations

(a) *Full fiscal years.* Discuss registrant's financial condition, changes in financial condition and results of operations. The discussion shall provide information as specified in paragraphs (a)(1) through (5) of this item and also shall provide such other information that the registrant believes to be necessary to an understanding of its financial condition, changes in financial condition and results of operations. Discussions of liquidity and capital resources may be combined whenever the two topics are interrelated. Where in the registrant's judgment a discussion of segment information or of other subdivisions of the registrant's business would be appropriate to an understanding of such business, the discussion shall focus on each relevant, reportable segment or other subdivision of the business and on the registrant as a whole.

(1) *Liquidity.* Identify any known trends or any known demands, commitments, events or uncertainties that will result in or that are reasonably likely to result in the registrant's liquidity increasing or decreasing in any material way. If a material deficiency is identified, indicate the course of action that the registrant has taken or proposes to take to remedy the deficiency. Also identify and separately describe internal and external sources of liquidity, and briefly discuss any material unused sources of liquid assets.

(2) *Capital resources.* (i) Describe the registrant's material commitments for capital expenditures as of the end of the latest fiscal period, and indicate the general purpose of such commitments and the anticipated source of funds needed to fulfill such commitments.

(ii) Describe any known material trends, favorable or unfavorable, in the registrant's capital resources. Indicate any expected material changes in the mix and relative cost of such resources. The discussion shall consider changes between equity, debt and any off-balance sheet financing arrangements.

(3) *Results of operations.* (i) Describe any unusual or infrequent events or transactions or any significant economic changes that materially affected the amount of reported income from continuing operations and, in each case, indicate the extent to which income was so affected. In addition, describe any other significant components of revenues or expenses that, in the registrant's judgment, should be described in order to understand the registrant's results of operations.

(ii) Describe any known trends or uncertainties that have had or that the registrant reasonably expects will have a material favorable or unfavorable impact on net sales or revenues or income from continuing operations. If the registrant knows of events that will cause a material change in the relationship between costs and revenues (such as known future increases in costs of labor or materials or price increases or inventory adjustments), the change in the relationship shall be disclosed.

(iii) To the extent that the financial statements disclose material increases in net sales or revenues, provide a narrative discussion of the extent to which such increases are attributable to increases in prices or to increases in the volume or amount of goods or services being sold or to the introduction of new products or services.

(iv) For the three most recent fiscal years of the registrant, or for those fiscal years in which the registrant has been engaged in business, whichever period is shortest, discuss the impact of inflation and changing prices on the registrant's net sales and revenues and on income from continuing operations.

684

(4) *Off-balance sheet arrangements.* (i) In a separately-captioned section, discuss the registrant's off-balance sheet arrangements that have or are reasonably likely to have a current or future effect on the registrant's financial condition, changes in financial condition, revenues or expenses, results of operations, liquidity, capital expenditures or capital resources that is material to investors. The disclosure shall include the items specified in paragraphs (a)(4)(i)(A), (B), (C) and (D) of this Item to the extent necessary to an understanding of such arrangements and effect and shall also include such other information that the registrant believes is necessary for such an understanding.

(A) The nature and business purpose to the registrant of such off-balance sheet arrangements;

(B) The importance to the registrant of such off-balance sheet arrangements in respect of its liquidity, capital resources, market risk support, credit risk support or other benefits;

(C) The amounts of revenues, expenses and cash flows of the registrant arising from such arrangements; the nature and amounts of any interests retained, securities issued and other indebtedness incurred by the registrant in connection with such arrangements; and the nature and amounts of any other obligations or liabilities (including contingent obligations or liabilities) of the registrant arising from such arrangements that are or are reasonably likely to become material and the triggering events or circumstances that could cause them to arise; and

(D) Any known event, demand, commitment, trend or uncertainty that will result in or is reasonably likely to result in the termination, or material reduction in availability to the registrant, of its off-balance sheet arrangements that provide material benefits to it, and the course of action that the registrant has taken or proposes to take in response to any such circumstances.

(ii) As used in this paragraph (a)(4), the term *off-balance sheet arrangement* means any transaction, agreement or other contractual arrangement to which an entity unconsolidated with the registrant is a party, under which the registrant has:

(A) Any obligation under a guarantee contract that has any of the characteristics identified in paragraph 3 of FASB Interpretation No. 45, *Guarantor's Accounting and Disclosure Requirements for Guarantees, Including Indirect Guarantees of Indebtedness of Others* (November 2002) ("FIN 45"), as may be modified or supplemented, and that is not excluded from the initial recognition and measurement provisions of FIN 45 pursuant to paragraphs 6 or 7 of that Interpretation;

(B) A retained or contingent interest in assets transferred to an unconsolidated entity or similar arrangement that serves as credit, liquidity or market risk support to such entity for such assets;

(C) Any obligation, including a contingent obligation, under a contract that would be accounted for as a derivative instrument, except that it is both indexed to the registrant's own stock and classified in stockholders' equity in the registrant's statement of financial position, and therefore excluded from the scope of FASB Statement of Financial Accounting Standards No. 133, *Accounting for Derivative Instruments and Hedging Activities* (June 1998), pursuant to paragraph 11(a) of that Statement, as may be modified or supplemented; or

(D) Any obligation, including a contingent obligation, arising out of a variable interest (as referenced in FASB Interpretation No. 46, *Consolidation of Variable Interest Entities* (January 2003), as may be modified or supplemented) in an unconsolidated entity that is held by, and material to, the registrant, where such entity provides financing, liquidity, market risk or credit risk support to, or engages in leasing, hedging or research and development services with, the registrant.

(5) *Tabular disclosure of contractual obligations.* (i) In a tabular format, provide the information specified in this paragraph (a)(5) as of the latest fiscal year end balance sheet date with respect to the registrant's known contractual obligations specified in the table that follows this paragraph (a)(5)(i). The registrant shall provide amounts, aggregated by type of contractual obligation. The registrant may disaggregate the specified categories of contractual obligations using other categories suitable to its business, but the presentation must include all of the obligations of the registrant that fall within the specified categories. A presentation covering at least the periods specified shall be included. The tabular presentation may be accompanied by footnotes to describe provisions that create, increase or accelerate obligations, or other pertinent

data to the extent necessary for an understanding of the timing and amount of the registrant's specified contractual obligations.

		Payments due by period			
Contractual Obligations	*Total*	*Less than 1 year*	*1–3 years*	*3–5 years*	*More than 5 years*
[Long–Term Debt Obligations]					
[Capital (Finance) Lease Obligations]					
[Operating Lease Obligations]					
[Purchase Obligations]					
[Other Long–Term Liabilities Reflected on the Registrant's Balance Sheet under GAAP]					
Total					

(ii) *Definitions* : The following definitions apply to this paragraph (a) (5):

(A) *Long-Term Debt Obligation* means a payment obligation under long-term borrowings referenced in FASB Statement of Financial Accounting Standards No. 47 *Disclosure of Long-Term Obligations* (March 1981), as may be modified or supplemented.

(B) *Capital Lease Obligation* means a payment obligation under a lease classified as a capital lease pursuant to FASB Statement of Financial Accounting Standards No. 13 *Accounting for Leases* (November 1976), as may be modified or supplemented.

(C) *Operating Lease Obligation* means a payment obligation under a lease classified as an operating lease and disclosed pursuant to FASB Statement of Financial Accounting Standards No. 13 *Accounting for Leases* (November 1976), as may be modified or supplemented.

(D) *Purchase Obligation* means an agreement to purchase goods or services that is enforceable and legally binding on the registrant that specifies all significant terms, including: fixed or minimum quantities to be purchased; fixed, minimum or variable price provisions; and the approximate timing of the transaction.

Instructions to Paragraph 303(a). 1. The registrant's discussion and analysis shall be of the financial statements and of other statistical data that the registrant believes will enhance a reader's understanding of its financial condition, changes in financial condition and results of operations. Generally, the discussion shall cover the three year period covered by the financial statements and shall use year-to-year comparisons or any other formats that in the registrant's judgment enhance a reader's understanding. However, where trend information is relevant, reference to the five year selected financial data appearing pursuant to Item 301 of Regulation S-K (§ 229.301) may be necessary.

2. The purpose of the discussion and analysis shall be to provide to investors and other users information relevant to an assessment of the financial condition and results of operations of the registrant as determined by evaluating the amounts and certainty of cash flows from operations and from outside sources.

3. The discussion and analysis shall focus specifically on material events and uncertainties known to management that would cause reported financial information not to be necessarily indicative of future operating results or of future financial condition. This would include descriptions and amounts of (A) matters that would have an impact on future operations and have not had an impact in the past, and (B) matters that have had an impact on reported operations and are not expected to have an impact upon future operations.

4. Where the consolidated financial statements reveal material changes from year to year in one or more line items, the causes for the changes shall be described to the extent necessary to an understanding of the registrant's businesses as a whole; *Provided, however,* That if the causes for a change in one line item also relate to other line items, no repetition is required and a line-by-line analysis of the financial statements as a whole is not required or generally appropriate. Registrants need not recite the amounts of

changes from year to year which are readily computable from the financial statements. The discussion shall not merely repeat numerical data contained in the consolidated financial statements.

5. The term "liquidity" as used in this Item refers to the ability of an enterprise to generate adequate amounts of cash to meet the enterprise's needs for cash. Except where it is otherwise clear from the discussion, the registrant shall indicate those balance sheet conditions or income or cash flow items which the registrant believes may be indicators of its liquidity condition. Liquidity generally shall be discussed on both a long-term and short-term basis. The issue of liquidity shall be discussed in the context of the registrant's own business or businesses. For example a discussion of working capital may be appropriate for certain manufacturing, industrial or related operations but might be inappropriate for a bank or public utility.

6. Where financial statements presented or incorporated by reference in the registration statement are required by § 210.4-08(e)(3) of Regulation S-X [17 CFR Part 210] to include disclosure of restrictions on the ability of both consolidated and unconsolidated subsidiaries to transfer funds to the registrant in the form of cash dividends, loans or advances, the discussion of liquidity shall include a discussion of the nature and extent of such restrictions and the impact such restrictions have had and are expected to have on the ability of the parent company to meet its cash obligations.

7. Any forward-looking information supplied is expressly covered by the safe harbor rule for projections. See Rule 175 under the Securities Act [17 CFR 230.175], Rule 3b-6 under the Exchange Act [17 CFR 240.3b-6] and Securities Act Release No. 6084 (June 25, 1979) (44 FR 33810).

8. Registrants are only required to discuss the effects of inflation and other changes in prices when considered material. This discussion may be made in whatever manner appears appropriate under the circumstances. All that is required is a brief textual presentation of management's views. No specific numerical financial data need be presented except as Rule 3-20(c) of Regulation S-X (§ 210.3-20(c) of this chapter) otherwise requires. However, registrants may elect to voluntarily disclose supplemental information on the effects of changing prices as provided for in Statement of Financial Accounting Standards No. 89, "Financial Reporting and Changing Prices" or through other supplemental disclosures. The Commission encourages experimentation with these disclosures in order to provide the most meaningful presentation of the impact of price changes on the registrant's financial statements.

9. Registrants that elect to disclose supplementary information on the effects of changing prices as specified by SFAS No. 89, "Financial Reporting and Changing Prices," may combine such explanations with the discussion and analysis required pursuant to this Item or may supply such information separately with appropriate cross reference.

10. All references to the registrant in the discussion and in this Item shall mean the registrant and its subsidiaries consolidated.

11. Foreign private registrants also shall discuss briefly any pertinent governmental economic, fiscal, monetary, or potential policies or factors that have materially affected or could materially affect, directly or indirectly, their operations or investments by United States nationals.

12. If the registrant is a foreign private issuer, the discussion shall focus on the primary financial statements presented in the registration statement or report. There shall be a reference to the reconciliation to United States generally accepted accounting principles, and a discussion of any aspects of the difference between foreign and United States generally accepted accounting principles, not discussed in the reconciliation, that the registrant believes is necessary for an understanding of the financial statements as a whole.

Instructions to Paragraph 303(a)(4):

1. No obligation to make disclosure under paragraph (a)(4) of this Item shall arise in respect of an off-balance sheet arrangement until a definitive agreement that is unconditionally binding or

subject only to customary closing conditions exists or, if there is no such agreement, when settlement of the transaction occurs.

2. Registrants should aggregate off-balance sheet arrangements in groups or categories that provide material information in an efficient and understandable manner and should avoid repetition and disclosure of immaterial information. Effects that are common or similar with respect to a number of off-balance sheet arrangements must be analyzed in the aggregate to the extent the aggregation increases understanding. Distinctions in arrangements and their effects must be discussed to the extent the information is material, but the discussion should avoid repetition and disclosure of immaterial information.

3. For purposes of paragraph (a)(4) of this Item only, contingent liabilities arising out of litigation, arbitration or regulatory actions are not considered to be off-balance sheet arrangements.

4. Generally, the disclosure required by paragraph (a)(4) shall cover the most recent fiscal year. However, the discussion should address changes from the previous year where such discussion is necessary to an understanding of the disclosure.

5. In satisfying the requirements of paragraph (a)(4) of this Item, the discussion of off-balance sheet arrangements need not repeat information provided in the footnotes to the financial statements, provided that such discussion clearly cross-references to specific information in the relevant footnotes and integrates the substance of the footnotes into such discussion in a manner designed to inform readers of the significance of the information that is not included within the body of such discussion.

(b) *Interim periods.* If interim period financial statements are included or are required to be included by Article 3 of Regulations S-X (17 CFR 210), a management's discussion and analysis of the financial condition and results of operations shall be provided so as to enable the reader to assess material changes in financial condition and results of operations between the periods specified in paragraphs (b)(1) and (2) of this Item. The discussion and analysis shall include a discussion of material changes in those items specifically listed in paragraph (a) of this Item, except that the impact of inflation and changing prices on operations for interim periods need not be addressed.

(1) *Material changes in financial condition.* Discuss any material changes in financial condition from the end of the preceding fiscal year to the date of the most recent interim balance sheet provided. If the interim financial statements include an interim balance sheet as of the corresponding interim date of the preceding fiscal year, any material changes in financial condition from that date to the date of the most recent interim balance sheet provided also shall be discussed. If discussions of changes from both the end and the corresponding interim date of the preceding fiscal year are required, the discussions may be combined at the discretion of the registrant.

(2) *Material changes in results of operations.* Discuss any material changes in the registrant's results of operations with respect to the most recent fiscal year-to-date period for which an income statement is provided and the corresponding year-to-date period of the preceding fiscal year. If the registrant is required to or has elected to provide an income statement for the most recent fiscal quarter, such discussion also shall cover material changes with respect to that fiscal quarter and the corresponding fiscal quarter in the preceding fiscal year. In addition, if the registrant has elected to provide an income statement for the twelve-month period ended as of the date of the most recent interim balance sheet provided, the discussion also shall cover material changes with respect to that twelve-month and the twelve-month period ended as of the corresponding interim balance sheet date of the preceding fiscal year. Notwithstanding the above, if for purposes of a registration statement a registrant subject to paragraph (b) of § 210.3-03 of Regulation S-X provides a statement of income for the twelve-month period ended as of the date of the most recent interim balance sheet provided in lieu of the interim income statements otherwise required, the discussion of material changes in that twelve-month period will be in respect to the preceding fiscal year rather than the corresponding preceding period.

Instructions to Paragraph (b) of Item 303. 1. If interim financial statements are presented together with financial statements for full fiscal years, the discussion of the interim financial information shall be prepared pursuant to this paragraph (b) and the discussion of the full fiscal year's information shall be prepared pursuant to paragraph (a) of this Item. Such discussions may be combined.

2. In preparing the discussion and analysis required by this paragraph (b), the registrant may presume that users of the interim financial information have read or have access to the discussion and analysis required by paragraph (a) for the preceding fiscal year.

3. The discussion and analysis required by this paragraph (b) is required to focus only on material changes. Where the interim financial statements reveal material changes from period to period in one or more significant line items, the causes for the changes shall be described if they have not already been disclosed: *Provided, however,* That if the causes for a change in one line item also relate to other line items, no repetition is required. Registrants need not recite the amounts of changes from period to period which are readily computable from the financial statements. The discussion shall not merely repeat numerical data contained in the financial statements. The information provided shall include that which is available to the registrant without undue effort or expense and which does not clearly appear in the registrant's condensed interim financial statements.

4. The registrant's discussion of material changes in results of operations shall identify any significant elements of the registrant's income or loss from continuing operations which do not arise from or are not necessarily representative of the registrant's ongoing business.

5. The registrant shall discuss any seasonal aspects of its business which have had a material effect upon its financial condition or results of operation.

6. Any forward-looking information supplied is expressly covered by the safe harbor rule for projections. See Rule 175 under the Securities Act (17 CFR 230.175), Rule 3b-6 under the Exchange Act (17 CFR 249.3b-6) and Securities Act Release No. 6084 (June 25, 1979) (44 FR 38810).

7. The registrant is not required to include the table required by paragraph (a)(5) of this Item for interim periods. Instead, the registrant should disclose material changes outside the ordinary course of the registrant's business in the specified contractual obligations during the interim period.

(c) *Safe harbor.* (1) The safe harbor provided in Section 27A of the Securities Act of 1933 (15 U.S.C. 77z-2) and Section 21E of the Securities Exchange Act of 1934 (15 U.S.C. 78u-5) ("statutory safe harbors") shall apply to forward-looking information provided pursuant to paragraphs (a)(4) and (5) of this Item, provided that the disclosure is made by: an issuer; a person acting on behalf of the issuer; an outside reviewer retained by the issuer making a statement on behalf of the issuer; or an underwriter, with respect to information provided by the issuer or information derived from information provided by the issuer.

(2) For purposes of paragraph (c) of this Item only:

(i) All information required by paragraphs (a)(4) and (5) of this Item is deemed to be a *forward looking statement* as that term is defined in the statutory safe harbors, except for historical facts.

(ii) With respect to paragraph (a)(4) of this Item, the meaningful cautionary statements element of the statutory safe harbors will be satisfied if a registrant satisfies all requirements of that same paragraph (a)(4) of this Item.

Item 304. Changes in and Disagreements with Accountants on Accounting and Financial Disclosure

(a)(1) If during the registrant's two most recent fiscal years or any subsequent interim period, an independent accountant who was previously engaged as the principal accountant to audit the registrant's financial statements, or an independent accountant who was previously engaged to audit a significant subsidiary and on whom the principal accountant expressed reliance in its report, has resigned (or indicated it has declined to stand for re-election after the completion of the current audit) or was dismissed, then the registrant shall:

(i) State whether the former accountant resigned, declined to stand for re-election or was dismissed and the date thereof.

(ii) State whether the principal accountant's report on the financial statements for either of the past two years contained an adverse opinion or a disclaimer of opinion, or was qualified or modified as to uncertainty, audit scope, or accounting principles; and also describe the nature of each such adverse opinion, disclaimer of opinion, modification, or qualification.

(iii) State whether the decision to change accountants was recommended or approved by:

(A) any audit or similar committee of the board of directors, if the issuer has such a committee; or

(B) the board of directors, if the issuer has no such committee.

(iv) State whether during the registrant's two most recent fiscal years and any subsequent interim period preceding such resignation, declination or dismissal there were any disagreements with the former accountant on any matter of accounting principles or practices, financial statement disclosure, or auditing scope of procedure, which disagreement(s), if not resolved to the satisfaction of the former accountant, would have caused it to make reference to the subject matter of the disagreement(s) in connection with its report. Also, (A) describe each such disagreement; (B) state whether any audit or similar committee of the board of directors, or the board of directors, discussed the subject matter of each of such disagreements with the former accountant; and (C) state whether the registrant has authorized the former accountant to respond fully to the inquiries of the successor accountant concerning the subject matter of each of such disagreements and, if not, describe the nature of any limitation thereon and the reason therefore. The disagreements required to be reported in response to this Item include both those resolved to the former accountant's satisfaction and those not resolved to the former accountant's satisfaction. Disagreements contemplated by this Item are those that occur at the decision-making level, i.e., between personnel of the registrant responsible for presentation of its financial statements and personnel of the accounting firm responsible for rendering its report.

(v) Provide the information required by paragraphs (a)(1)(iv) of this Item for each of the kinds of events (even though the registrant and the former accountant did not express a difference of opinion regarding the event) listed in paragraphs (A) through (D) below, that occurred within the registrant's two most recent fiscal years and any subsequent interim period preceding the former accountant's resignation, declination to stand for re-election, or dismissal ("reportable events"). If the event led to a disagreement or difference of opinion, then the event should be reported as a disagreement under paragraph (a)(1)(iv) and need not be repeated under this paragraph.

(A) The accountant's having advised the registrant that the internal controls necessary for the registrant to develop reliable financial statements do not exist;

(B) the accountant's having advised the registrant that information has come to the accountant's attention that has led it to no longer be able to rely on management's representations, or that has made it unwilling to be associated with the financial statements prepared by management;

(C) (1) the accountant's having advised the registrant of the need to expand significantly the scope of its audit, or that information has come to the accountant's attention during the time period covered by Item 304(a)(1)(iv), that if further investigated may (i) materially impact the fairness or reliability of either: a previously issued audit report or the underlying financial statements; or the financial statements issued or to be issued covering the fiscal period(s) subsequent to the date of the most recent financial statements covered by an audit report (including information that may prevent it from rendering an unqualified audit report on those financial statements), or (ii) cause it to be unwilling to rely on management's representations or be associated with the registrant's financial statements, and (2) due to the accountant's resignation (due to audit scope limitations or otherwise) or dismissal, or for any other reason, the accountant did not so expand the scope of its audit or conduct such further investigation; or

(D) (1) the accountant's having advised the registrant that information has come to the accountant's attention that it has concluded materially impacts the fairness or reliability of either (i) a previously issued audit report or the underlying financial statements, or (ii) the financial statements issued or to be issued covering the fiscal period(s) subsequent to the date of the most recent financial statements covered by an audit report (including information that, unless resolved to the accountant's satisfaction, would prevent it from rendering an unqualified audit report on those financial statements), and (2) due to the accountant's resignation, dismissal or declination to stand for re-election, or for any other reason, the issue has not been resolved to the accountant's satisfaction prior to its resignation, dismissal or declination to stand for re-election.

(2) If during the registrant's two most recent fiscal years or any subsequent interim period, a new independent accountant has been engaged as either the principal accountant to audit the registrant's financial statements, or as an independent accountant to audit a significant subsidiary and on whom the principal accountant is expected to express reliance in its report, then the registrant shall identify the newly engaged accountant and indicate the date of such accountant's engagement. In addition, if during the registrant's two most recent fiscal years, and any subsequent interim period prior to engaging that accountant, the registrant (or someone on its behalf) consulted the newly engaged accountant regarding (i) either: the application of accounting principles to a specified transaction, either completed or proposed; or the type of audit opinion that might be rendered on the registrant's financial statements, and either a written report was provided to the registrant or oral advice was provided that the new accountant concluded was an important factor considered by the registrant in reaching a decision as to the accounting, auditing or financial reporting issue; or (ii) any matter that was either the subject of a disagreement (as defined in paragraph 304(a)(1)(iv) and the related instructions to this item) or a reportable event (as described in paragraph 304(a)(1)(v)), then the registrant shall:

(A) so state and identify the issues that were the subjects of those consultations;

(B) briefly describe the views of the newly engaged accountant as expressed orally or in writing to the registrant on each such issue and, if written views were received by the registrant, file them as an exhibit to the report or registration statement requiring compliance with this Item 304(a);

(C) state whether the former accountant was consulted by the registrant regarding any such issues, and if so, provide a summary of the former accountant's views; and

(D) request the newly engaged accountant to review the disclosure required by this Item 304(a) before it is filed with the Commission and provide the new accountant the opportunity to furnish the registrant with a letter addressed to the Commission containing any new information, clarification of the registrant's expression of its views, or the respects in which it does not agree with the statements made by the registrant in response to Item 304(a). The registrant shall file any such letter as an exhibit to the report or registration statement containing the disclosure required by this Item.

(3) The registrant shall provide the former accountant with a copy of the disclosures it is making in response to this Item 304(a) that the former accountant shall receive no later than the day that the disclosures are filed with the Commission. The registrant shall request the former accountant to furnish the registrant with a letter addressed to the Commission stating whether it agrees with the statements made by the registrant in response to this Item 304(a) and, if not, stating the respects in which it does not agree. The registrant shall file the former accountant's letter as an exhibit to the report or registration statement containing this disclosure. If the former accountant's letter is unavailable at the time of filing such report or registration statement, then the registrant shall request the former accountant to provide the letter as promptly as possible so that the registrant can file the letter with the Commission within ten business days after the filing of the report or registration statement. Notwithstanding the ten business day period, the registrant shall file the letter by amendment within two business days of receipt; if the letter is received on a Saturday, Sunday or holiday on which the Commission is not open for business, then the two business day period shall begin to run on and shall include the first business day thereafter. The former accountant may provide the registrant with an interim letter highlighting specific areas of concern and indicating that a more detailed letter will be forthcoming within the ten business day period noted above. If not filed with the report or registration statement containing the registrant's disclosure under this Item 304(a), then the interim letter, if any, shall be filed by the registrant by amendment within two business days of receipt.

(b) If, (1) in connection with a change in accountants subject to paragraph (a) of this Item 304, there was any disagreement of the type described in paragraph (a)(1)(iv) or any reportable event as described in paragraph (a)(1)(v) of this Item; (2) during the fiscal year in which the change in accountants took place or during the subsequent fiscal year, there have been any transactions or events similar to those which involved such disagreement or reportable event and (3) such transactions or events were material and were accounted for or disclosed in a manner different from that which the former accountants apparently would have concluded was required, the registrant shall state the existence and nature of the disagreement or reportable event and also state the effect on the financial statements if the method had been followed which the former accountants apparently would have concluded was required. These disclosures need not be made if the method asserted by the former accountants ceases to be generally accepted because of authoritative standards or interpretations subsequently issued.

Instructions to Item 304: 1. The disclosure called for by paragraph (a) of this Item need not be provided if it has been previously reported (as that term is defined in Rule 12b-2 under the Exchange Act (§ 240.12b-2 of this chapter); the disclosure called for by paragraph (a) must be provided, however, notwithstanding prior disclosure, if required pursuant to Item 9 of Schedule 14A (§ 240.14a-101 of this chapter). The disclosure called for by paragraph (b) of this section must be furnished, where required, notwithstanding any prior disclosure about accountant changes or disagreements.

2. When disclosure is required by paragraph (a) of this section in an annual report to security holders pursuant to Rule 14a-3 (§ 240.14a-3 of this chapter) or Rule 14c-3 (§ 240.14c-3 of this chapter), or in a proxy or information statement filed pursuant to the requirements of Schedule 14A or 14C (§ 240.14a-101 or § 240.14c-101 of this chapter), in lieu of a letter pursuant to paragraph (a)(2)(D) or (a)(3), prior to filing such materials with or furnishing such materials to the Commission, the registrant shall furnish the disclosure required by paragraph (a) of this section to any former accountant engaged by the registrant during the period set forth in paragraph (a) of this section and to the newly engaged accountant. If any such accountant believes that the statements made in response to paragraph (a) of this section are incorrect or incomplete, it may present its views in a brief statement, ordinarily expected not to exceed 200 words, to be included in the annual report or proxy or information statement. This statement shall be submitted to the registrant within ten business days of the date the accountant receives the registrant's disclosure. Further, unless the written views of the newly engaged accountant required to be filed as an exhibit by paragraph (a)(2)(B) of this Item 304 have been previously filed with the Commission the registrant shall file a Form 8-K concurrently with the annual report or proxy or information statement for the purpose of filing the written views as exhibits thereto.

3. The information required by Item 304(a) need not be provided for a company being acquired by the registrant that is not subject to the filing requirements of either section 13(a) or 15(d) of the Exchange Act, or, because of section 12(i) of the Exchange Act, has not furnished an annual report to security holders pursuant to Rule 14a-3 Rule 14c-3 for its latest fiscal year.

4. The term 'disagreements' as used in this Item shall be interpreted broadly, to include any difference of opinion concerning any matter of accounting principles or practices, financial statement disclosure, or auditing scope or procedure which (if not resolved to the satisfaction of the former accountant) would have caused it to make reference to the subject matter of the disagreement in connection with its report. It is not necessary for there to have been an argument to have had a disagreement, merely a difference of opinion. For purposes of this Item, however, the term disagreements does not include initial differences of opinion based on incomplete facts or preliminary information that were later resolved to the former accountant's satisfaction by, and providing the registrant and the accountant do not continue to have a difference of opinion upon, obtaining additional relevant facts or information.

5. In determining whether any disagreement or reportable event has occurred, an oral communication from the engagement partner or another person responsible for rendering the accounting firm's opinion (or their designee) will generally suffice as the accountant advising the registrant of a reportable event or as a statement of a disagreement at the "decision-making level" within the accounting firm and require disclosure under this Item.

692

Item 305. Quantitative and Qualitative Disclosures About Market Risk

(a) Quantitative information about market risk.

(1) Registrants shall provide, in their reporting currency, quantitative information about market risk as of the end of the latest fiscal year, in accordance with one of the following three disclosure alternatives. In preparing this quantitative information, registrants shall categorize market risk sensitive instruments into instruments entered into for trading purposes and instruments entered into for purposes other than trading purposes. Within both the trading and other than trading portfolios, separate quantitative information shall be presented, to the extent material, for each market risk exposure category (i.e., interest rate risk, foreign currency exchange rate risk, commodity price risk, and other relevant market risks, such as equity price risk). A registrant may use one of the three alternatives set forth below for all of the required quantitative disclosures about market risk. A registrant also may choose, from among the three alternatives, one disclosure alternative for market risk sensitive instruments entered into for trading purposes and another disclosure alternative for market risk sensitive instruments entered into for other than trading purposes. Alternatively, a registrant may choose any disclosure alternative, from among the three alternatives, for each risk exposure category within the trading and other than trading portfolios. The three disclosure alternatives are:

(i) (A) (1) Tabular presentation of information related to market risk sensitive instruments; such information shall include fair values of the market risk sensitive instruments and contract terms sufficient to determine future cash flows from those instruments, categorized by expected maturity dates.

(2) Tabular information relating to contract terms shall allow readers of the table to determine expected cash flows from the market risk sensitive instruments for each of the next five years. Comparable tabular information for any remaining years shall be displayed as an aggregate amount.

(3) Within each risk exposure category, the market risk sensitive instruments shall be grouped based on common characteristics. Within the foreign currency exchange rate risk category, the market risk sensitive instruments shall be grouped by functional currency and within the commodity price risk category, the market risk sensitive instruments shall be grouped by type of commodity.

(4) See the Appendix to this Item for a suggested format for presentation of this information; and

(B) Registrants shall provide a description of the contents of the table and any related assumptions necessary to understand the disclosures required under paragraph (a) (1) (i) (A) of this Item 305; or

(ii) (A) Sensitivity analysis disclosures that express the potential loss in future earnings, fair values, or cash flows of market risk sensitive instruments resulting from one or more selected hypothetical changes in interest rates, foreign currency exchange rates, commodity prices, and other relevant market rates or prices over a selected period of time. The magnitude of selected hypothetical changes in rates or prices may differ among and within market risk exposure categories; and

(B) Registrants shall provide a description of the model, assumptions, and parameters, which are necessary to understand the disclosures required under paragraph (a) (1) (ii) (A) of this Item 305; or

(iii) (A) Value at risk disclosures that express the potential loss in future earnings, fair values, or cash flows of market risk sensitive instruments over a selected period of time, with a selected likelihood of occurrence, from changes in interest rates, foreign currency exchange rates, commodity prices, and other relevant market rates or prices;

(B) (1) For each category for which value at risk disclosures are required under paragraph (a) (1) (iii) (A) of this Item 305, provide either:

(i) The average, high and low amounts, or the distribution of the value at risk amounts for the reporting period; or

(ii) The average, high and low amounts, or the distribution of actual changes in fair values, earnings, or cash flows from the market risk sensitive instruments occurring during the reporting period; or

(iii) The percentage or number of times the actual changes in fair values, earnings, or cash flows from the market risk sensitive instruments exceeded the value at risk amounts during the reporting period;

(2) Information required under paragraph (a)(1)(iii)(B)(1) of this Item 305 is not required for the first fiscal year end in which a registrant must present Item 305 information; and

(C) Registrants shall provide a description of the model, assumptions, and parameters, which are necessary to understand the disclosures required under paragraphs (a)(1)(iii)(A) and (B) of this Item 305.

(2) Registrants shall discuss material limitations that cause the information required under paragraph (a)(1) of this Item 305 not to reflect fully the net market risk exposures of the entity. This discussion shall include summarized descriptions of instruments, positions, and transactions omitted from the quantitative market risk disclosure information or the features of instruments, positions, and transactions that are included, but not reflected fully in the quantitative market risk disclosure information.

(3) Registrants shall present summarized market risk information for the preceding fiscal year. In addition, registrants shall discuss the reasons for material quantitative changes in market risk exposures between the current and preceding fiscal years. Information required by this paragraph (a)(3), however, is not required if disclosure is not required under paragraph (a)(1) of this Item 305 for the current fiscal year. Information required by this paragraph (a)(3) is not required for the first fiscal year end in which a registrant must present Item 305 information.

(4) If registrants change disclosure alternatives or key model characteristics, assumptions, and parameters used in providing quantitative information about market risk (e.g., changing from tabular presentation to value at risk, changing the scope of instruments included in the model, or changing the definition of loss from fair values to earnings), and if the effects of any such change is material, the registrant shall:

(i) Explain the reasons for the change; and

(ii) Either provide summarized comparable information, under the new disclosure method, for the year preceding the current year or, in addition to providing disclosure for the current year under the new method, provide disclosures for the current year and preceding fiscal year under the method used in the preceding year.

Instructions to Paragraph 305(a).

1. Under paragraph 305(a)(1):

A. For each market risk exposure category within the trading and other than trading portfolios, registrants may report the average, high, and low sensitivity analysis or value at risk amounts for the reporting period, as an alternative to reporting year-end amounts.

B. In determining the average, high, and low amounts for the fiscal year under instruction 1.A. of the Instructions to Paragraph 305(a), registrants should use sensitivity analysis or value at risk amounts relating to at least four equal time periods throughout the reporting period (e.g., four quarter-end amounts, 12 month-end amounts, or 52 week-end amounts).

C. Functional currency means functional currency as defined by generally accepted accounting principles (see, e.g., FASB, Statement of Financial Accounting Standards No. 52, "Foreign Currency Translation", ("FAS 52") paragraph 20 (December 1981)).

D. Registrants using the sensitivity analysis and value at risk disclosure alternatives are encouraged, but not required, to provide quantitative amounts that reflect the aggregate market risk inherent in the trading and other than trading portfolios.

2. Under paragraph 305(a)(1)(i):

A. Examples of contract terms sufficient to determine future cash flows from market risk sensitive instruments include, but are not limited to:

i. Debt instruments—principal amounts and weighted average effective interest rates;

ii. Forwards and futures—contract amounts and weighted average settlement prices;

iii. Options—contract amounts and weighted average strike prices;

iv. Swaps—notional amounts, weighted average pay rates or prices, and weighted average receive rates or prices; and

v. Complex instruments—likely to be a combination of the contract terms presented in 2.A.i. through iv. of this Instruction;

B. When grouping based on common characteristics, instruments should be categorized, at a minimum, by the following characteristics, when material:

i. Fixed rate or variable rate assets or liabilities;

ii. Long or short forwards and futures;

iii. Written or purchased put or call options with similar strike prices;

iv. Receive fixed and pay variable swaps, receive variable and pay fixed swaps, and receive variable and pay variable swaps;

v. The currency in which the instruments' cash flows are denominated;

vi. Financial instruments for which foreign currency transaction gains and losses are reported in the same manner as translation adjustments under generally accepted accounting principles (see, e.g., FAS 52 paragraph 20 (December 1981)); and

vii. Derivatives used to manage risks inherent in anticipated transactions;

C. Registrants may aggregate information regarding functional currencies that are economically related, managed together for internal risk management purposes, and have statistical correlations of greater than 75% over each of the past three years;

D. Market risk sensitive instruments that are exposed to rate or price changes in more than one market risk exposure category should be presented within the tabular information for each of the risk exposure categories to which those instruments are exposed;

E. If a currency swap (see, e.g., FAS 52 Appendix E for a definition of currency swap) eliminates all foreign currency exposures in the cash flows of a foreign currency denominated debt instrument, neither the currency swap nor the foreign currency denominated debt instrument are required to be disclosed in the foreign currency risk exposure category. However, both the currency swap and the foreign currency denominated debt instrument should be disclosed in the interest rate risk exposure category; and

F. The contents of the table and related assumptions that should be described include, but are not limited to:

i. The different amounts reported in the table for various categories of the market risk sensitive instruments (e.g., principal amounts for debt, notional amounts for swaps, and contract amounts for options and futures);

ii. The different types of reported market rates or prices (e.g., contractual rates or prices, spot rates or prices, forward rates or prices); and

iii. Key prepayment or reinvestment assumptions relating to the timing of reported amounts.

3. Under paragraph 305(a)(1)(ii):

A. Registrants should select hypothetical changes in market rates or prices that are expected to reflect reasonably possible near-term changes in those rates and prices. In this regard, absent economic justification for the selection of a different amount, registrants should use changes that are not less than 10 percent of end of period market rates or prices;

B. For purposes of instruction 3.A. of the Instructions to Paragraph 305(a), the term reasonably possible has the same meaning as defined by generally accepted accounting principles (see, e.g., FASB, Statement of Financial Accounting Standards No. 5, "Accounting for Contingencies," ("FAS 5") paragraph 3 (March 1975));

C. For purposes of instruction 3.A. of the Instructions to Paragraph 305(a), the term near term means a period of time going forward up to one year from the date of the financial statements (see generally AICPA, Statement of Position 94-6, "Disclosure of Certain Significant Risks and Uncertainties," ("SOP 94-6") at paragraph 7 (December 30, 1994));

D. Market risk sensitive instruments that are exposed to rate or price changes in more than one market risk exposure category should be included in the sensitivity analysis disclosures for each market risk category to which those instruments are exposed;

E. Registrants with multiple foreign currency exchange rate exposures should prepare foreign currency sensitivity analysis disclosures that measure the aggregate sensitivity to changes in all foreign currency exchange rate exposures, including the effects of changes in both transactional currency/functional currency exchange rate exposures and functional currency/ reporting currency exchange rate exposures. For example, assume a French division of a registrant presenting its financial statements in U.S. dollars ($US) invests in a deutschmark(DM)-denominated debt security. In these circumstances, the $US is the reporting currency and the DM is the transactional currency. In addition, assume this division determines that the French franc (FF) is its functional currency according to FAS 52. In preparing the foreign currency sensitivity analysis disclosures, this registrant should report the aggregate potential loss from hypothetical changes in both the DM/FF exchange rate exposure and the FF/$US exchange rate exposure; and

F. Model, assumptions, and parameters that should be described include, but are not limited to, how loss is defined by the model (e.g., loss in earnings, fair values, or cash flows), a general description of the modeling technique (e.g., duration modeling, modeling that measures the change in net present values arising from selected hypothetical changes in market rates or prices, and a description as to how optionality is addressed by the model), the types of instruments covered by the model (e.g., derivative financial instruments, other financial instruments, derivative commodity instruments, and whether other instruments are included voluntarily, such as certain commodity instruments and positions, cash flows from anticipated transactions, and certain financial instruments excluded under instruction 3.C.ii. of the General Instructions to Paragraphs 305(a) and 305(b)), and other relevant information about the model's assumptions and parameters, (e.g., the magnitude and timing of selected hypothetical changes in market rates or prices used, the method by which discount rates are determined, and key prepayment or reinvestment assumptions).

4. Under paragraph 305(a)(1)(iii):

A. The confidence intervals selected should reflect reasonably possible near-term changes in market rates and prices. In this regard, absent economic justification for the selection of different confidence intervals, registrants should use intervals that are 95 percent or higher;

B. For purposes of instruction 4.A. of the Instructions to Paragraph 305(a), the term reasonably possible has the same meaning as defined by generally accepted accounting principles (see, e.g., FAS 5, paragraph 3 (March 1975));

C. For purposes of instruction 4.A. of the Instructions to Paragraphs 305(a), the term near term means a period of time going forward up to one year from the date of the financial statements (see generally SOP 94-6, at paragraph 7 (December 30, 1994));

D. Registrants with multiple foreign currency exchange rate exposures should prepare foreign currency value at risk analysis disclosures that measure the aggregate sensitivity to changes in all foreign currency exchange rate exposures, including the aggregate effects of changes in both transactional currency/functional currency exchange rate exposures and functional currency/reporting currency exchange rate exposures. For example, assume a French division of a registrant presenting its financial statements in U.S. dollars ($US) invests in a deutschmark(DM)-denominated debt security. In these circumstances, the $US is the reporting currency and the DM is the transactional currency. In addition, assume this division determines that the French franc (FF) is its functional currency according to FAS 52. In preparing the foreign currency value at risk disclosures, this registrant should report the aggregate potential loss from hypothetical changes in both the DM/FF exchange rate exposure and the FF/$US exchange rate exposure; and

E. Model, assumptions, and parameters that should be described include, but are not limited to, how loss is defined by the model (e.g., loss in earnings, fair values, or cash flows), the type of model used (e.g., variance/covariance, historical simulation, or Monte Carlo simulation and a description as to how optionality is addressed by the model), the types of instruments covered by the model (e.g., derivative financial instruments, other financial instruments, derivative commodity instruments, and whether other instruments are included voluntarily, such as certain commodity instruments and positions, cash flows from anticipated transactions, and certain financial instruments excluded under instruction 3.C.ii. of the General Instructions to Paragraphs 305(a) and 305(b)), and other relevant information about the model's assumptions and parameters, (e.g., holding periods, confidence intervals, and, when appropriate, the methods used for aggregating value at risk amounts across market risk exposure categories, such as by assuming perfect positive correlation, independence, or actual observed correlation).

5. Under paragraph 305(a)(2), limitations that should be considered include, but are not limited to:

A. The exclusion of certain market risk sensitive instruments, positions, and transactions from the disclosures required under paragraph 305(a)(1) (e.g., derivative commodity instruments not permitted by contract or business custom to be settled in cash or with another financial instrument, commodity positions, cash flows from anticipated transactions, and certain financial instruments excluded under instruction 3.C.ii. of the General Instructions to Paragraphs 305(a) and 305(b)). Failure to include such instruments, positions, and transactions in preparing the disclosures under paragraph 305(a)(1) may be a limitation because the resulting disclosures may not fully reflect the net market risk of a registrant; and

B. The ability of disclosures required under paragraph 305(a)(1) to reflect fully the market risk that may be inherent in instruments with leverage, option, or prepayment features (e.g., options, including written options, structured notes, collateralized mortgage obligations, leveraged swaps, and options embedded in swaps).

(b) Qualitative information about market risk.

(1) To the extent material, describe:

(i) The registrant's primary market risk exposures;

(ii) How those exposures are managed. Such descriptions shall include, but not be limited to, a discussion of the objectives, general strategies, and instruments, if any, used to manage those exposures; and

(iii) Changes in either the registrant's primary market risk exposures or how those exposures are managed, when compared to what was in effect during the most recently completed fiscal year and what is known or expected to be in effect in future reporting periods.

(2) Qualitative information about market risk shall be presented separately for market risk sensitive instruments entered into for trading purposes and those entered into for purposes other than trading.

Instructions to Paragraph 305(b).

1. For purposes of disclosure under paragraph 305(b), primary market risk exposures means:

A. The following categories of market risk: interest rate risk, foreign currency exchange rate risk, commodity price risk, and other relevant market rate or price risks (e.g., equity price risk); and

B. Within each of these categories, the particular markets that present the primary risk of loss to the registrant. For example, if a registrant has a material exposure to foreign currency exchange rate risk and, within this category of market risk, is most vulnerable to changes in dollar/yen, dollar/pound, and dollar/peso exchange rates, the registrant should disclose those exposures. Similarly, if a registrant has a material exposure to interest rate risk and, within this category of market risk, is most vulnerable to changes in short-term U.S. prime interest rates, it should disclose the existence of that exposure.

2. For purposes of disclosure under paragraph 305(b), registrants should describe primary market risk exposures that exist as of the end of the latest fiscal year, and how those exposures are managed.

General Instructions to Paragraphs 305(a) and 305(b).

1. The disclosures called for by paragraphs 305(a) and 305(b) are intended to clarify the registrant's exposures to market risk associated with activities in derivative financial instruments, other financial instruments, and derivative commodity instruments.

2. In preparing the disclosures under paragraphs 305(a) and 305(b), registrants are required to include derivative financial instruments, other financial instruments, and derivative commodity instruments.

3. For purposes of paragraphs 305(a) and 305(b), derivative financial instruments, other financial instruments, and derivative commodity instruments (collectively referred to as "market risk sensitive instruments") are defined as follows:

A. Derivative financial instruments has the same meaning as defined by generally accepted accounting principles (see, e.g., FASB, Statement of Financial Accounting Standards No. 119, "Disclosure about Derivative Financial Instruments and Fair Value of Financial Instruments," ("FAS 119") paragraphs 5-7 (October 1994)), and includes futures, forwards, swaps, options, and other financial instruments with similar characteristics;

B. Other financial instruments means all financial instruments as defined by generally accepted accounting principles for which fair value disclosures are required (see, e.g., FASB, Statement of Financial Accounting Standards No. 107, "Disclosures about Fair Value of Financial Instruments," ("FAS 107") paragraphs 3 and 8 (December 1991)), except for derivative financial instruments, as defined above;

C.i. Other financial instruments include, but are not limited to, trade accounts receivable, investments, loans, structured notes, mortgage-backed securities, trade accounts payable, indexed debt instruments, interest-only and principal-only obligations, deposits, and other debt obligations;

ii. Other financial instruments exclude employers and plans obligations for pension and other post-retirement benefits, substantively extinguished debt, insurance contracts, lease contracts, warranty obligations and rights, unconditional purchase obligations, investments accounted for under the equity method, minority interests in consolidated enterprises, and equity instruments issued by the registrant and classified in stockholders' equity in the statement of financial position (see, e.g., FAS 107, paragraph 8 (December 1991)). For purposes of this item, trade accounts receivable and trade accounts payable need not be considered other financial instruments when their carrying amounts approximate fair value; and

D. Derivative commodity instruments include, to the extent such instruments are not derivative financial instruments, commodity futures, commodity forwards, commodity swaps, commodity options, and other commodity instruments with similar characteristics that are permitted by contract or business custom to be settled in cash or with another financial instrument. For purposes of this paragraph, settlement in cash includes settlement in cash of the net change in value of the derivative commodity instrument (e.g., net cash settlement based on changes in the price of the underlying commodity).

4.A. In addition to providing required disclosures for the market risk sensitive instruments defined in instruction 2. of the General Instructions to Paragraphs 305(a) and 305(b), registrants are encouraged to include other market risk sensitive instruments, positions, and transactions within the disclosures required under paragraphs 305(a) and 305(b). Such instruments, positions, and transactions might include commodity positions, derivative commodity instruments that are not permitted by contract or business custom to be settled in cash or with another financial instrument, cash flows from anticipated transactions, and certain financial instruments excluded under instruction 3.C.ii. of the General Instructions to Paragraphs 305(a) and 305(b).

B. Registrants that voluntarily include other market risk sensitive instruments, positions and transactions within their quantitative disclosures about market risk under the sensitivity analysis or value at risk disclosure alternatives are not required to provide separate market risk disclosures for any voluntarily selected instruments, positions, or transactions. Instead, registrants selecting the sensitivity analysis and value at risk disclosure alternatives are permitted to present comprehensive market risk disclosures, which reflect the combined market risk exposures inherent in both the required and any voluntarily selected instruments, position, or transactions. Registrants that choose the tabular presentation disclosure alternative should present voluntarily selected instruments, positions, or transactions in a manner consistent with the requirements in Item 305(a) for market risk sensitive instruments.

C. If a registrant elects to include voluntarily a particular type of instrument, position, or transaction in their quantitative disclosures about market risk, that registrant should include all, rather than some, of those instruments, positions, or transactions within those disclosures. For example, if a registrant holds in inventory a particular type of commodity position and elects to include that commodity position within their market risk disclosures, the registrant should include the entire commodity position, rather than only a portion thereof, in their quantitative disclosures about market risk.

5.A. Under paragraphs 305(a) and 305(b), a materiality assessment should be made for each market risk exposure category within the trading and other than trading portfolios.

B. For purposes of making the materiality assessment under instruction 5.A. of the General Instructions to Paragraphs 305(a) and 305(b), registrants should evaluate both:

i. The materiality of the fair values of derivative financial instruments, other financial instruments, and derivative commodity instruments outstanding as of the end of the latest fiscal year; and

ii. The materiality of potential, near-term losses in future earnings, fair values, and/or cash flows from reasonably possible near-term changes in market rates or prices.

iii. If either paragraphs B.i. or B.ii. in this instruction of the General Instructions to Paragraphs 305(a) and 305(b) are material, the registrant should disclose quantitative and qualitative information about market risk, if such market risk for the particular market risk exposure category is material.

C. For purposes of instruction 5.B.i. of the General Instructions to Paragraphs 305(a) and 305(b), registrants generally should not net fair values, except to the extent allowed under generally accepted accounting principles (see, e.g., FASB Interpretation No. 39, "Offsetting of Amounts Related to Certain Contracts" (March 1992)). For example, under this instruction, the fair value of assets generally should not be netted with the fair value of liabilities.

D. For purposes of instruction 5.B.ii. of the General Instructions to Paragraphs 305(a) and 305(b), registrants should consider, among other things, the magnitude of:

i. Past market movements;

ii. Reasonably possible, near-term market movements; and

iii. Potential losses that may arise from leverage, option, and multiplier features.

E. For purposes of instructions 5.B.ii and 5.D.ii of the General Instructions to Paragraphs 305(a) and 305(b), the term near term means a period of time going forward up to one year from the date of the financial statements (see generally SOP 94-6, at paragraph 7 (December 30, 1994)).

F. For the purpose of instructions 5.B.ii. and 5.D.ii. of the General Instructions to Paragraphs 305(a) and 305(b), the term reasonably possible has the same meaning as defined by generally accepted accounting principles (see, e.g., FAS 5, paragraph 3 (March 1975)).

6. For purposes of paragraphs 305(a) and 305(b), registrants should present the information outside of, and not incorporate the information into, the financial statements (including the footnotes to the financial statements). In addition, registrants are encouraged to provide the required information in one location. However, alternative presentation, such as inclusion of all or part of the information in Management's Discussion and Analysis, may be used at the discretion of the registrant. If information is disclosed in more than one location, registrants should provide cross-references to the locations of the related disclosures.

7. For purposes of the instructions to paragraphs 305(a) and 305(b), trading purposes has the same meaning as defined by generally accepted accounting principles (see, e.g., FAS 119, paragraph 9a (October 1994)). In addition, anticipated transactions means transactions (other than transactions involving existing assets or liabilities or transactions necessitated by existing firm commitments) an enterprise expects, but is not obligated, to carry out in the normal course of business (see, e.g., FASB, Statement of Financial Accounting Standards No. 80, "Accounting for Futures Contracts," paragraph 9, (August 1984)).

(c) Interim periods. If interim period financial statements are included or are required to be included by Article 3 of Regulation S-X (17 CFR 210), discussion and analysis shall be provided so as to enable the reader to assess the sources and effects of material changes in information that would be provided under Item 305 of Regulation S-K from the end of the preceding fiscal year to the date of the most recent interim balance sheet.

Instructions to Paragraph 305(c).

1. Information required under paragraph (c) of this Item 305 is not required until after the first fiscal year end in which this Item 305 is applicable.

(d) Safe Harbor.

(1) The safe harbor provided in Section 27A of the Securities Act of 1933 (15 U.S.C. 77z-2) and Section 21E of the Securities Exchange Act of 1934 (15 U.S.C. 78u-5) ("statutory safe harbors") shall apply, with respect to all types of issuers and transactions, to information provided pursuant to paragraphs (a), (b), and (c) of this Item 305, provided that the disclosure is made by: an issuer; a person acting on behalf of the issuer; an outside reviewer retained by the issuer making a statement on behalf of the issuer; or an underwriter, with respect to information provided by the issuer or information derived from information provided by the issuer.

(2) For purposes of paragraph (d) of this Item 305 only:

(i) All information required by paragraphs (a), (b)(1)(i), (b)(1)(iii), and (c) of this Item 305 is considered forward looking statements for purposes of the statutory safe harbors, except for historical facts such as the terms of particular contracts and the number of market risk sensitive instruments held during or at the end of the reporting period; and

(ii) With respect to paragraph (a) of this Item 305, the meaningful cautionary statements prong of the statutory safe harbors will be satisfied if a registrant satisfies all requirements of that same paragraph (a) of this Item 305.

(e) Small business issuers. Small business issuers, as defined in § 230.405 of this chapter and § 230.12b-2 of this chapter, need not provide the information required by this Item 305, whether or not they file on forms specially designated as small business issuer forms.

General Instructions to Paragraphs 305(a), 305(b), 305(c), 305(d), and 305(e).

1. Bank registrants, thrift registrants, and non-bank and non-thrift registrants with market capitalizations on January 28, 1997 in excess of $2.5 billion should provide Item 305 disclosures in filings with the Commission that include annual financial statements for fiscal years ending after June 15, 1997. Non-bank and non-thrift registrants with market capitalizations on January 28, 1997 of $2.5 billion or less should provide Item 305 disclosures in filings with the Commission that include financial statements for fiscal years ending after June 15, 1998.

2.A. For purposes of instruction 1. of the General Instructions to Paragraphs 305(a), 305(b), 305(c), 305(d), and 305(e), bank registrants and thrift registrants include any registrant which has control over a depository institution.

B. For purposes of instruction 2.A. of the General Instructions to Paragraphs 305(a), 305(b), 305(c), 305(d), and 305(e), a registrant has control over a depository institution if:

i. The registrant directly or indirectly or acting through one or more other persons owns, controls, or has power to vote 25% or more of any class of voting securities of the depository institution;

ii. The registrant controls in any manner the election of a majority of the directors or trustees of the depository institution; or

iii. The Federal Reserve Board or Office of Thrift Supervision determines, after notice and opportunity for hearing, that the registrant directly or indirectly exercises a controlling influence over the management or policies of the depository institution.

C. For purposes of instruction 2.B. of the General Instructions to Paragraphs 305(a), 305(b), 305(c), 305(d), and 305(e), a depository institution means any of the following:

i. An insured depository institution as defined in section 3(c)(2) of the Federal Deposit Insurance Act (12 U.S.C.A. Sec. 1813(c));

ii. An institution organized under the laws of the United States, any State of the United States, the District of Columbia, any territory of the United States, Puerto Rico, Guam, American Somoa, or the Virgin Islands, which both accepts demand deposits or deposits that the depositor may withdraw by check or similar means for payment to third parties or others and is engaged in the business of making commercial loans.

D. For purposes of instruction 1. of the General Instructions to Paragraphs 305(a), 305(b), 305(c), 305(d) and 305(e), market capitalization is the aggregate market value of common equity as set forth in General Instruction I.B.1. of Form S-3; provided however, that common equity held by affiliates is included in the calculation of market capitalization; and provided further that instead of using the 60 day period prior to filing referenced in General Instruction I.B.1. of Form S-3, the measurement date is January 28, 1997.

Appendix to Item 305—Tabular Disclosures

The tables set forth below are illustrative of the format that might be used when a registrant elects to present the information required by paragraph (a)(1)(i)(A) of Item 305 regarding terms and information about derivative financial instruments, other financial instruments, and derivative commodity instruments. These examples are for illustrative purposes only. Registrants are not required to display the information in the specific format illustrated below. Alternative methods of display are permissible as long as the disclosure requirements of the section are satisfied. Furthermore, these examples were designed primarily to illustrate possible formats for presentation of the information required by the disclosure item and do not purport to illustrate the broad range of derivative financial instruments, other financial instruments, and derivative commodity instruments utilized by registrants.

Interest Rate Sensitivity

The table below provides information about the Company's derivative financial instruments and other financial instruments that are sensitive to changes in interest rates, including interest rate swaps and debt obligations. For debt obligations, the table presents principal cash flows and related weighted average interest rates by expected maturity dates. For interest rate swaps, the table presents notional amounts and weighted average interest rates by expected (contractual) maturity dates. Notional amounts are used to calculate the contractual payments to be exchanged under the contract. Weighted average variable rates are based on implied forward rates in the yield curve at the reporting date. The information is presented in U.S. dollar equivalents, which is the Company's reporting currency. The instrument's actual cash flows are denominated in both U.S. dollars ($US) and German deutschmarks (DM), as indicated in parentheses.

December 31, 19X1

Liabilities
(7) (US$ Equivalent in millions)

	19X2	19X3	19X4	19X5	19X6	Thereafter	Total	Fair value
					Expected maturity date			
Long-term Debt:								
Fixed Rate ($US)	$XXXX	$XXXX	$XXXX	$XXXX	$XXXX	$XXXX	$XXXX	$X
Average interest rate	XX%	XX%	XX%	XX%	XX%	XX%	XX%	
Fixed Rate (DM)	XXX	XXX	XXX	XXX	XXX	XXX	XXX XXX%	
Average interest rate	XX%	XX%	XX%	XX%	XX%	XX%	XX%	
Variable Rate ($US)	XXX	XXX	XXX	XXX	XXX	XXX	XXX	X
Average interest rate	XX%	XX%	XX%	XX%	XX%	XX%	XX%	

Interest Rate Derivatives

(7) (In millions)

	19X2	19X3	19X4	19X5	19X6	Thereafter	Total	Fair value
Interest Rate Swaps:								
Variable to Fixed ($US)	$XXXX	$XXXX	$XXXX	$XXXX	$XXXX	$XXXX	$XXXX	$X
Average pay rate	XX%	XX%	XX%	XX%	XX%	XX%	XX%	
Average receive rate	XX%	XX%	XX%	XX%	XX%	XX%	XX%	
Fixed to Variable ($US)	XXX	XXX	XXX	XXX	XXX	XXX	XXX	X
Average pay rate	XX%	XX%	XX%	XX%	XX%	XX%	XX%	
Average receive rate	XX%	XX%	XX%	XX%	XX%	XX%	XX%	

Exchange Rate Sensitivity

The table below provides information about the Company's derivative financial instruments, other financial instruments, and firmly committed sales transactions by functional currency and presents such information in U.S. dollar equivalents.[1] The table summarizes information on instruments and transactions that are sensitive to foreign currency exchange rates, including foreign currency forward exchange agreements, deutschmark (DM)-denominated debt obligations, and firmly committed DM sales transactions. For debt obligations, the table presents principal cash flows and related weighted average interest rates by expected maturity dates. For firmly committed DM-sales transactions, sales amounts are presented by the expected transaction date, which are not expected to exceed two years. For foreign currency forward exchange agreements, the table presents the notional amounts and weighted average exchange rates by expected (contractual) maturity dates. These notional amounts generally are used to calculate the contractual payments to be exchanged under the contract.

---

[1] The information is presented in U.S. dollars because that is the registrant's reporting currency.

December 31, 19X1

			Expected maturity date					
	19X2	*19X3*	*19X4*	*19X5*	*19X6*	*Thereafter*	*Total*	*Fair value*

On-Balance Sheet Financial Instruments

(7) (US$ Equivalent in millions)

$US Functional Currency[2]:

Liabilities

Long-Term Debt:

	19X2	19X3	19X4	19X5	19X6	Thereafter	Total	Fair value
Fixed Rate (DM)	$XXX	$XXX	$XXX	$XXX	$XXX	$XXX	$XXX	$X
Average interest rate	X.X	X.X	X.X	X.X	X.X	X.X	X.X	

(7) Expected maturity or transaction date

Anticipated Transactions and Related Derivatives[3]

(7) (US$ Equivalent in millions)

$US Functional Currency:

	19X2	19X3	19X4	19X5	19X6	Thereafter	Total	Fair value
Firmly committed Sales Contracts (DM)	$XXX	$XXX	—	—	—	—	$XXX	$X
Forward Exchange Agreements (Receive $US/Pay DM):								
Contract Amount	XXX	XXX	—	—	—	—	XXX	X
Average Contractual Exchange Rate	X.X	X.X	—	—	—	—	X.X	—

[2] Similar tabular information would be provided for other functional currencies.

[3] Pursuant to General Instruction 4. to Items 305(a) and 305(b) of Regulation S-K, registrants may include cash flows from anticipatedtransactions and operating cash flows resulting from non-financial and non-commodity instruments.

Commodity Price Sensitivity

The table below provides information about the Company's corn inventory and futures contracts that are sensitive to changes in commodity prices, specifically corn prices. For inventory, the table presents the carrying amount and fair value at December 31, 19x1. For the futures contracts the table presents the notional amounts in bushels, the weighted average contract prices, and the total dollar contract amount by expected maturity dates, the latest of which occurs one year from the reporting date. Contract amounts are used to calculate the contractual payments and quantity of corn to be exchanged under the futures contracts.

December 31, 19X1

	Carrying amount	Fair value
(1) (In millions)		
On Balance Sheet Commodity Position and Related Derivatives		
Corn Inventory[4]	$XXX	$XXX

	Expected maturity 1992	Fair value
Related Derivatives		
Futures Contracts (Short):		
Contract Volumes (100,000 bushels)	XXX	—
Weighted Average Price (Per 100,000 bushels)	$X.XX	—
Contract Amount ($US in millions)	$XXX	$XXX

[4] Pursuant to General Instruction 4. to Items 305(a) and 305(b) of Regulation S-K, registrants may include information on commodity positions, such as corn inventory.

Item 306. Audit Committee Report

(a) The audit committe must state whether:

(1) The audit committee has reviewed and discussed the audited financial statements with management;

(2) The audit committee has discussed with the independent auditors the matters required to be discussed by SAS 61 (Codification of Statements on Auditing Standards, AU § 380), as may be modified or supplemented;

(3) The audit committee has received the written disclosures and the letter from the independent accountants required by Independence Standards Board Standard No. 1 (Independence Standards Board Standard No. 1, *Independence Discussions with Audit Committees*), as may be modified or supplemented, and has discussed with the independent accountant the independent accountant's independence; and

(4) Based on the review and discussions referred to in paragraphs (a)(1) through (a)(3) of this Item, the audit committee recommended to the Board of Directors that the audited financial statements be included in the company's Annual Report on Form 10-K (17 CFR 249.310) (or, for closed-end investment companies registered under the Investment Company Act of 1940 (15 U.S.C. 80a-1 *et seq.*), the annual report to shareholders required by Section 30(e) of the Investment Company Act of 1940 (15 U.S.C. 80a-29(e)) and Rule 30d-1 (17 CFR 270.30d-1) thereunder) for the last fiscal year for filing with the Commission.

(b) The name of each member of the company's audit committee (or, in the absence of an audit committee, the board committee performing equivalent functions or the entire board of directors) must appear below the disclosure required by this Item.

(c) The information required by paragraphs (a) and (b) of this Item shall not be deemed to be "soliciting material," or to be "filed" with the Commission or subject to Regulation 14A or 14C (17 CFR 240.14a-1 *et seq.* or 240.14c-1 *et seq.*), other than as provided in this Item, or to the liabilities of section 18 of the Exchange Act (15 U.S.C. 78r), except to the extent that the company specifically requests that the information be treated as soliciting material or specifically incorporates it by reference into a document filed under the Securities Act or the Exchange Act.

(d) The information required by paragraphs (a) and (b) of this Item need not be provided in any filings other than a company proxy or information statement relating to an annual meeting of security holders at which directors are to be elected (or special meeting or written consents in lieu of such meeting). Such information will not be deemed to be incorporated by reference into any filing under the Securities Act or the Exchange Act, except to the extent that the company specifically incorporates it by reference.

Item 307. Disclosure Controls and Procedures

Disclose the conclusions of the registrant's principal executive and principal financial officers, or persons performing similar functions, regarding the effectiveness of the registrant's disclosure controls and procedures (as defined in 240.13a-15(e) or 240.15d-15(e) of this chapter) as of the end of the period covered by the report, based on the evaluation of these controls and procedures required by paragraph (b) of § 240.13a-15 or § 240.15d-15 of this chapter.

Item 308. Internal Control Over Financial Reporting

(a) *Management's annual report on internal control over financial reporting.* Provide a report of management on the registrant's internal control over financial reporting (as defined in § 240.13a-15(f) or 240.15d-15(f) of this chapter) that contains:

(1) A statement of management's responsibility for establishing and maintaining adequate internal control over financial reporting for the registrant;

(2) A statement identifying the framework used by management to evaluate the effectiveness of the registrant's internal control over financial reporting as required by paragraph (c) of § 240.13a-15 or 240.15d-15 of this chapter;

(3) Management's assessment of the effectiveness of the registrant's internal control over financial reporting as of the end of the registrant's most recent fiscal year, including a statement as to whether or not internal control over financial reporting is effective. This discussion must include disclosure of any material weakness in the registrant's internal control over financial reporting identified by management. Management is not permitted to conclude that the registrant's internal control over financial reporting is effective if there are one or more material weaknesses in the registrant's internal control over financial reporting; and

(4) A statement that the registered public accounting firm that audited the financial statements included in the annual report containing the disclosure required by this Item has issued an attestation report on management's assessment of the registrant's internal control over financial reporting.

(b) *Attestation report of the registered public accounting firm.* Provide the registered public accounting firm's attestation report on management's assessment of the registrant's internal control over financial reporting in the registrant's annual report containing the disclosure required by this Item.

(c) *Changes in internal control over financial reporting.* Disclose any change in the registrant's internal control over financial reporting identified in connection with the evaluation required by paragraph (d) of -240.13a-15 or 240.15d-15 of this chapter that occurred during the registrant's last fiscal quarter (the registrant's fourth fiscal quarter in the case of an annual report) that has materially affected, or is reasonably likely to materially affect, the registrant's internal control over financial reporting.

Instructions to Item 308

1. The registrant must maintain evidential matter, including documentation, to provide reasonable support for management's assessment of the effectiveness of the registrant's internal control over financial reporting.

2. A registrant that is an Asset-Backed Issuer (as defined in § 240.13a-14(g) and § 240.15d-14(g) of this chapter) is not required to disclose the information required by this Item.

Item 401. Directors, Executive Officers, Promoters and Control Persons

(a) *Identification of directors.* List the names and ages of all directors of the registrant and all persons nominated or chosen to become directors; indicate all positions and offices with the registrant held by each such person; state his term of office as director and any period(s) during which he has served as such; describe briefly any arrangement or understanding between him and any other person(s) (naming such person(s)) pursuant to which he was or is to be selected as a director or nominee.

Instructions to Paragraph (a) of Item 401. 1. Do not include arrangements or understandings with directors or officers of the registrant acting solely in their capacities as such.

2. No nominee or person chosen to become a director who has not consented to act as such shall be named in response to this Item. In this regard, with respect to proxy statements, see Rule 14a-4(d) under the Exchange Act (§ 240.14a-4(d) of this chapter).

3. If the information called for by this paragraph (a) is being presented in a proxy or information statement, no information need be given respecting any director whose term of office as a director will not continue after the meeting to which the statement relates.

4. With regard to proxy statements in connection with action to be taken concerning the election of directors, if fewer nominees are named than the number fixed by or pursuant to the governing instruments, state the reasons for this procedure and that the proxies cannot be voted for a greater number of persons than the number of nominees named.

5. With regard to proxy statements in connection with action to be taken concerning the election of directors, if the solicitation is made by persons other than management, information shall be given as to nominees of the persons making the solicitation. In all other instances, information shall be given as to directors and persons nominated for election or chosen by management to become directors.

(b) *Identification of executive officers.* List the names and ages of all executive officers of the registrant and all persons chosen to become executive officers; indicate all positions and offices with the registrant held by each such person; state his term of office as officer and the period during which he has served as such and describe briefly any arrangement or understanding between him and any other person(s) (naming such person) pursuant to which he was or is to be selected as an officer.

Instructions to Paragraph (b) of Item 401. 1. Do not include arrangements or understandings with directors or officers of the registrant acting solely in their capacities as such.

2. No person chosen to become an executive officer who has not consented to act as such shall be named in response to this Item.

3. The information regarding executive officers called for by this Item need not be furnished in proxy or information statements prepared in accordance with Schedule 14A under the Exchange Act (§ 240.14a-101 of this chapter) by those registrants relying on General Instruction G of Form 10-K and Form 10-KSB under the Exchange Act (§ 249.310 and § 249.310b of this chapter), *Provided,* That such information is furnished in a separate item captioned "Executive officers of the registrant" and included in Part I of the registrant's annual report on Form 10-K and Form 10-KSB.

(c) *Identification of certain significant employees.* Where the registrant employs persons such as production managers, sales managers, or research scientists who are not executive officers but who make or are expected to make significant contributions to the business of the registrant, such persons shall be identified and their background disclosed to the same extent as in the case of executive officers. Such disclosure need not be made if the registrant was subject to section 13(a) or 15(d) of the Exchange Act or was exempt from section 13(a) by section 12(g)(2)(G) of such Act immediately prior to the filing of the registration statement, report, or statement to which this Item is applicable.

(d) *Family relationships.* State the nature of any family relationship between any director, executive officer, or person nominated or chosen by the registrant to become a director or executive officer.

Instruction to Paragraph 401(d). The term "family relationship" means any relationship by blood, marriage, or adoption, not more remote than first cousin.

(e) *Business experience.* (1) *Background.* Briefly describe the business experience during the past five years of each director, executive officer, person nominated or chosen to become a director or executive officer, and each person named in answer to paragraph (c) of Item 401, including: each person's principal occupations and employment during the past five years; the name and principal business of any corporation or other organization in which such occupations and employment were carried on; and whether such corporation or organization is a parent, subsidiary or other affiliate of the registrant. When an executive officer or person named in response to paragraph (c) of Item 401 has been employed by the registrant or a subsidiary of the registrant for less than five years, a brief explanation shall be included as to the nature of the responsibility undertaken by the individual in prior positions to provide adequate disclosure of his prior business experience. What is required is information relating to the level of his professional competence, which may include, depending upon the circumstances, such specific information as the size of the operation supervised.

(2) *Directorships.* Indicate any other directorships held by each director or person nominated or chosen to become a director in any company with a class of securities registered pursuant to section 12 of the Exchange Act or subject to the requirements of section 15(d) of such Act or any company registered as an investment company under the Investment Company Act of 1940, 15 U.S.C. 80a-1, et seq., as amended, naming such company.

Instruction to Paragraph (e) of Item 401. For purposes of paragraph (e)(2), where the other directorships of each director or person nominated or chosen to become a director include directorships of two or more registered investment companies that are part of a "fund complex" as that term is defined in Item 22(a) of Schedule 14A under the Exchange Act (§ 240.14a-101 of this chapter), the registrant may, rather than listing each such investment company, identify the fund complex and provide the number of investment company directorships held by the director or nominee in such fund complex.

(f) *Involvement in certain legal proceedings.* Describe any of the following events that occurred during the past five years and that are material to an evaluation of the ability or integrity of any director, person nominated to become a director or executive officer of the registrant:

(1) A petition under the Federal bankruptcy laws or any state insolvency law was filed by or against, or a receiver, fiscal agent or similar officer was appointed by a court for the business or property of such person, or any partnership in which he was a general partner at or within two years before the time of such filing, or any corporation or business association of which he was an executive officer at or within two years before the time of such filing;

(2) Such person was convicted in a criminal proceeding or is a named subject of a pending criminal proceeding (excluding traffic violations and other minor offenses);

(3) Such person was the subject of any order, judgment, or decree, not subsequently reversed, suspended or vacated, of any court of competent jurisdiction, permanently or temporarily enjoining him from, or otherwise limiting, the following activities:

(i) Acting as a futures commission merchant, introducing broker, commodity trading advisor, commodity pool operator, floor broker, leverage transaction merchant, any other person regulated by the Commodity Futures Trading Commission, or an associated person of any of the foregoing, or as an investment adviser, underwriter, broker or dealer in securities, or as an affiliated person, director or employee of any investment company, bank, savings and loan association or insurance company, or engaging in or continuing any conduct or practice in connection with such activity;

(ii) Engaging in any type of business practice; or

(iii) Engaging in any activity in connection with the purchase or sale of any security or commodity or in connection with any violation of Federal or State securities laws or Federal commodities laws;

(4) Such person was the subject of any order, judgment or decree, not subsequently reversed, suspended or vacated, of any Federal or State authority barring, suspending or otherwise limiting for more than 60 days the right of such person to engage in any activity described in paragraph (f)(3)(i) of this Item, or to be associated with persons engaged in any such activity; or

(5) Such person was found by a court of competent jurisdiction in a civil action or by the Commission to have violated any Federal or State securities law, and the judgment in such civil action or finding by the Commission has not been subsequently reversed, suspended, or vacated.

(6) Such person was found by a court of competent jurisdiction in a civil action or by the Commodity Futures Trading Commmission to have violated any Federal commodities law, and the judgment in such civil action or finding by the Commodity Futures Trading Commission has not been subsequently reversed, suspended or vacated.

Instructions to Paragraph (f) of Item 401. 1. For purposes of computing the five year period referred to in this paragraph, the date of a reportable event shall be deemed the date on which the final order, judgment or decree was entered, or the date on which any rights of appeal from preliminary orders, judgments, or decrees have lapsed. With respect to bankruptcy petitions, the computation date shall be the date of filing for uncontested petitions or the date upon which approval of a contested petition became final.

2. If any event specified in this paragraph (f) has occurred and information in regard thereto is omitted on the grounds that it is not material, the registrant may furnish to the Commission, at time of filing (or at the time preliminary materials are filed, or ten days before definitive materials are filed if preliminary filing is not required, pursuant to Rule 14a-6 or 14c-5 under the Exchange Act (§§ 240.14a-6 and 240.14c-5 of this chapter)), as supplemental information and not as part of the registration statement, report, or proxy or information statement, materials to which the omission relates, a description of the event and a statement of the reasons for the omission of information in regard thereto.

3. The registrant is permitted to explain any mitigating circumstances associated with events reported pursuant to this paragraph.

4. If the information called for by this paragraph (f) is being presented in a proxy or information statement, no information need be given respecting any director whose term of office as a director will not continue after the meeting to which the statement relates.

(g) *Promoters and control persons.* (1) Registrants, which have not been subject to the reporting requirements of Section 13(a) or 15(d) of the Exchange Act for the twelve months immediately prior to the filing of the registration statement, report, or statement to which this Item is applicable, and which were organized within the last five years, shall describe with respect to any promoter, any of the events enumerated in paragraphs (f)(1) through (f)(6) of this section that occurred during the past five years and that are material to a voting or investment decision.

(2) Registrants, which have not been subject to the reporting requirements of Section 13(a) or 15(d) of the Exchange Act for the twelve months immediately prior to the filing of the registration statement, report, or statement to which this Item is applicable, shall describe with respect to any control person, any of the events enumerated in paragraphs (f)(1) through (f)(6) of this section that occurred during the past five years and that are material to a voting or investment decision.

Instructions to Paragraph (g) of Item 401. 1. Instructions 1. through 3. to paragraph (f) shall apply to this paragraph (g).

2. Paragraph (g) shall not apply to any subsidiary of a registrant which has been reporting pursuant to Section 13(a) or 15(d) of the Exchange Act for the twelve months immediately prior to the filing of the registration statement, report or statement.

(h) *Audit committee financial expert.* (1)(i) Disclose that the registrant's board of directors has determined that the registrant either:

(A) Has at least one audit committee financial expert serving on its audit committee; or

(B) Does not have an audit committee financial expert serving on its audit committee.

(ii) If the registrant provides the disclosure required by paragraph (h)(1)(i)(A) of this Item, it must disclose the name of the audit committee financial expert and whether that person is *independent,* as that term is used in Item 7(d)(3)(iv) of Schedule 14A (240.14a-101 of this chapter) under the Exchange Act.

(iii) If the registrant provides the disclosure required by paragraph (h)(1)(i)(B) of this Item, it must explain why it does not have an audit committee financial expert.

Instruction to paragraph (h)(1) of Item 401

If the registrant's board of directors has determined that the registrant has more than one audit committee financial expert serving on its audit committee, the registrant may, but is not required to, disclose the names of those additional persons. A registrant choosing to identify such persons must indicate whether they are independent pursuant to Item 401(h)(1)(ii).

(2) For purposes of this Item, an *audit committee financial expert* means a person who has the following attributes:

(i) An understanding of generally accepted accounting principles and financial statements;

(ii) The ability to assess the general application of such principles in connection with the accounting for estimates, accruals and reserves;

(iii) Experience preparing, auditing, analyzing or evaluating financial statements that present a breadth and level of complexity of accounting issues that are generally comparable to the breadth and complexity of issues that can reasonably be expected to be raised by the registrant's financial statements, or experience actively supervising one or more persons engaged in such activities;

(iv) An understanding of internal control over financial reporting; and

(v) An understanding of audit committee functions.

(3) A person shall have acquired such attributes through:

(i) Education and experience as a principal financial officer, principal accounting officer, controller, public accountant or auditor or experience in one or more positions that involve the performance of similar functions;

(ii) Experience actively supervising a principal financial officer, principal accounting officer, controller, public accountant, auditor or person performing similar functions;

(iii) Experience overseeing or assessing the performance of companies or public accountants with respect to the preparation, auditing or evaluation of financial statements; or

(iv) Other relevant experience.

(4) *Safe Harbor*

(i) A person who is determined to be an audit committee financial expert will not be deemed an expert for any purpose, including without limitation for purposes of section 11 of the Securities Act of 1933 (15 U.S.C. 77k), as a result of being designated or identified as an audit committee financial expert pursuant to this Item 401.

(ii) The designation or identification of a person as an audit committee financial expert pursuant to this Item 401 does not impose on such person any duties, obligations or liability that are greater than the duties, obligations and liability imposed on such person as a member of the audit committee and board of directors in the absence of such designation or identification.

(iii) The designation or identification of a person as an audit committee financial expert pursuant to this Item 401 does not affect the duties, obligations or liability of any other member of the audit committee or board of directors.

Instructions to Item 401(h)

1. The disclosure under Item 401(h) is required only in a registrant's annual report. The registrant need not provide the disclosure required by this Item 401(h) in a proxy or information statement unless that registrant is electing to incorporate this information by reference from the proxy or information statement into its annual report pursuant to general instruction G(3) to Form 10-K.

2. If a person qualifies as an audit committee financial expert by means of having held a position described in paragraph (h)(3)(iv) of this Item, the registrant shall provide a brief listing of that person's relevant experience. Such disclosure may be made by reference to disclosures required under paragraph (e) of this Item 401 (§ 229.401(e) or this chapter).

3. In the case of a foreign private issuer with a two-tier board of directors, for purposes of this Item 401(h), the term *board of directors* means the supervisory or non-management board. In the case of a foreign private issuer meeting the requirements of § 240.10A-3(c)(3), for purposes of this Item 401(h), the term *board of directors* means the issuer's board of auditors (or similar body) or statutory auditors, as applicable. Also, in the case of a foreign private issuer, the term *generally*

accepted accounting principles in paragraph (h)(2)(i) of this Item means the body of generally accepted accounting principles used by that issuer in its primary financial statements filed with the Commission.

4. A registrant that is an Asset-Backed Issuer (as defined in §240.13a-14(g) and §240.15d-14(g) of this chapter) is not required to disclose the information required by this Item 401(h).

(i) *Identification of the audit committee.* (1) If you meet the following requirements, provide the disclosure in paragraph (i)(2) of this section:

(i) You are a listed issuer, as defined in §240.10A-3 of this chapter;

(ii) You are filing either an annual report on Form 10-K or 10-KSB (17 CFR 249.310 or 17 CFR 249.310b), or a proxy statement or information statement pursuant to the Exchange Act (15 U.S.C. 78a *et seq.*) if action is to be taken with respect to the election of directors; and

(iii) You are neither:

(A) A subsidiary of another listed issuer that is relying on the exemption in §240.10A-3(c)(2) of this chapter; nor

(B) Relying on any of the exemptions in §240.10A-3(c)(4) through (c)(7) of this chapter.

(2)(i) State whether or not the registrant has a separately-designated standing audit committee established in accordance with section 3(a)(58)(A) of the Exchange Act (15 U.S.C. 78c(a)(58)(A)), or a committee performing similar functions. If the registrant has such a committee, however designated, identify each committee member. If the entire board of directors is acting as the registrant's audit committee as specified in section 3(a)(58)(B) of the Exchange Act (15 U.S.C. 78c(a)(58)(B)), so state.

(ii) If applicable, provide the disclosure required by §240.10A-3(d) of this chapter regarding an exemption from the listing standards for audit committees.

(j) Describe any material changes to the procedures by which security holders may recommend nominees to the registrant's board of directors, where those changes were implemented after the registrant last provided disclosure in response to the requirements of Item 7(d)(2)(ii)(G) of Schedule 14A (§240.14a-101), or this Item.

Instructions to paragraph (j) of Item 401:

1. The disclosure required in paragraph (j) need only be provided in a registrant's quarterly or annual reports.

2. For purposes of paragraph (j), adoption of procedures by which security holders may recommend nominees to the registrant's board of directors, where the registrant's most recent disclosure in response to the requirements of Item 7(d)(2)(ii)(G) of Schedule 14A (§240.14a-101), or this Item, indicated that the registrant did not have in place such procedures, will constitute a material change.

Item 402. Executive Compensation

(a) *General.*

(1) *Treatment of Specific Types of Issuers.*

(i) *Small Business Issuers.* A registrant that qualifies as "small business issuer," as defined by Item 10(a)(1) of Regulation S-B [17 CFR 228.10(a)(1)], will be deemed to comply with this item if it provides the information required by paragraph (b) (Summary Compensation Table), paragraphs (c)(1) and (c)(2)(i)-(v) (Option/SAR Grants Table), paragraph (d) (Aggregated Option/SAR Exercise and Fiscal Year-End Option/SAR Value Table), paragraph (e) (Long-Term Incentive Plan Awards Table), paragraph (g) (Compensation of Directors), paragraph (h) (Employment Contracts, Termination of Employment and Change in Control Arrangements) and paragraph (i)(1) and (2) (Report on Repricing of Options/SARs) of this item.

(ii) *Foreign Private Issuers.* A foreign private issuer will be deemed to comply with this item if it provides the information required by Items 6.B. and 6.E.2. of Form 20-F (17 CFR 249.220f) with more detailed information provided if otherwise made publicly available.

(2) *All Compensation Covered.* This item requires clear, concise and understandable disclosure of all plan and non-plan compensation awarded to, earned by, or paid to the named executive

officers designated under paragraph (a)(3) of this item, and directors covered by paragraph (g) of this item by any person for all services rendered in all capacities to the registrant and its subsidiaries, unless otherwise specified in this item. Except as provided by paragraph (a)(5) of this item, all such compensation shall be reported pursuant to this item, even if also called for by another requirement, including transactions between the registrant and a third party where the primary purpose of the transaction is to furnish compensation to any such named executive officer or director. No item reported as compensation for one fiscal year need be reported as compensation for a subsequent fiscal year.

(3) *Persons Covered.* Disclosure shall be provided pursuant to this item for each of the following (the "named executive officers"):

(i) all individuals serving as the registrant's chief executive officer or acting in a similar capacity during the last completed fiscal year ("CEO"), regardless of compensation level;

(ii) the registrant's four most highly compensated executive officers other than the CEO who were serving as executive officers at the end of the last completed fiscal year; and

(iii) up to two additional individuals for whom disclosure would have been provided pursuant to paragraph (a)(3)(ii) of this item but for the fact that the individual was not serving as an executive officer of the registrant at the end of the last completed fiscal year.

Instructions to Item 402(a)(3).

1. *Determination of Most Highly Compensated Executive Officers.* The determination as to which executive officers are most highly compensated shall be made by reference to total annual salary and bonus for the last completed fiscal year (as required to be disclosed pursuant to paragraph (b)(2)(iii)(A) and (B) of this item), but including the dollar value of salary or bonus amounts forgone pursuant to Instruction 3 to paragraph (b)(2)(iii)(A) and (B) of this item, *provided, however,* that no disclosure need be provided for any executive officer, other than the CEO, whose total annual salary and bonus, as so determined, does not exceed $100,000.

2. *Inclusion of Executive Officer of Subsidiary.* It may be appropriate in certain circumstances for a registrant to include an executive officer of a subsidiary in the disclosure required by this item. *See* Rule 3b-7 under the Exchange Act [17 CFR 240.3b-7].

3. *Exclusion of Executive Officer due to Unusual or Overseas Compensation.* It may be appropriate in limited circumstances for a registrant not to include in the disclosure required by this item an individual, other than its CEO, who is one of the registrant's most highly conpensated executive officers. Among the factors that should be considered in determining not to name an individual are: (a) the distribution or accural of an unusually large amount of cash compensation (such as a bonus or commission) that is not part of a recurring arrangement and is unlikely to continue; and (b) the payment of amounts of cash compensation relating to overseas assignments that may be attributed predominantly to such assignments.

(4) *Information for Full Fiscal Year.* If the CEO served in that capacity during part of a fiscal year with respect to which information is required information should be provided as to all of his or her compensation for the full fiscal year. If a named executive officer (other than the CEO) served as an executive officer of the registrant (whether or not in the same position) during any part of a fiscal year with respect to which information is required, information shall be provided as to all compensation of that individual for the full fiscal year.

(5) *Transactions With Third Parties Reported under Item 404.* This item includes transactions between the registrant and a third party where the primary purpose of the transaction is to furnish compensation to a named executive officer. No information need to given in response to any paragraph of this item, other than paragraph (j), as to any such third-party transaction if the transaction has been reported in response to Item 404 of Regulation S-K (§ 229.404).

(6) *Omission of Table or Column.* A table or column may be omitted, if there has been no compensation awarded to, earned by or paid to any of the named executives required to be reported in that table or column in any fiscal year covered by that table.

(7) *Definitions.* For purposes of this item:

(i) The term "stock appreciation rights" ("SARs") refers to SARs payable in cash or stock, including SARs payable in cash or stock at the election of the registrant or a named executive officer.

(ii) The term "plan" includes, but is not limited to, the following: any plan, contract, authorization or arrangement, whether or not set forth in any formal documents, pursuant to which the following may be received: cash, stock, restricted stock or restricted stock units, phantom stock, stock options, SARs, stock options in tandem with SARs, warrants, convertible securities, performance units and performance shares, and similar instruments. A plan may be applicable to one person. Registrants may omit information regarding group life, health, hospitalization, medical reimbursement or relocation plans that do not discriminate in scope, terms or operation, in favor of executive officers or directors of the registrant and that are available generally to all salaried employees.

(iii) The term "long-term incentive plan" means any plan providing compensation intended to serve as incentive for performance to occur over a period longer than one fiscal year, whether such performance is measured by reference to financial performance of the registrant or an affiliate, the registrant's stock price, or any other measure, but excluding restricted stock, stock option and SAR plans.

(8) *Location of Specified Information.* The information required by paragraphs (i), (k) and (*l*) of this item need not provided in any filings other than a registrant proxy or information statement relating to an annual meeting of security holders at which directors are to be elected (or special meeting or written consents in lieu of such meeting). Such information will not be deemed to be incorporated by reference into any filing under the Securities Act or the Exchange Act, except to the extent that the registrant specifically incorporates it by reference.

(9) *Liability for Specified Information.* The information required by paragraphs (k) and (*l*) of this item shall not be deemed to be "soliciting material" or to be "filed" with the Commission or subject to Regulations 14A or 14C [17 CFR 240.14a-1 *et seq.* or 240.14c-1 *et seq.*], other than as provided in this item, or to the liabilities of Section 18 of the Exchange Act [15 U.S.C. 78r], except to the extent that the registrant specifically requests that such information be treated as soliciting material or specifically incorporates it by reference into a filing under the Securities Act or the Exchange Act.

(b) *Summary Compensation Table.* (1) *General.* The information specified in paragraph (b)(2) of this item, concerning the compensation of the named executive officers for each of the registrant's last three completed fiscal years, shall be provided in a Summary Compensation Table, in the tabular format specified below.

SUMMARY COMPENSATION TABLE

		Annual Compensation			Long Term Compensation			
					Awards		Payouts	
(a)	(b)	(c)	(d)	(e)	(f)	(g)	(h)	(i)
Name and Principal Position	Year	Salary ($)	Bonus ($)	Other Annual Compensation ($)	Restricted Stock Award(s) ($)	Securities Underlying Options/ SARs (#)	LTIP Payouts ($)	All Other Compensation ($)
CEO	___							
	___							
	___							
A	___							
	___							
	___							
B	___							
	___							
	___							
C	___							

(a)	(b)	___Annual Compensation___			___Long Term Compensation___			
					Awards		Payouts	
(a)	(b)	(c)	(d)	(e)	(f)	(g)	(h)	(i)
Name and Principal Position	Year	Salary ($)	Bonus ($)	Other Annual Compensation ($)	Restricted Stock Award(s) ($)	Securities Underlying Options/ SARs (#)	LTIP Payouts ($)	All Other Compensation ($)

D

(2) The Table shall include:

(i) The name and principal position of the executive officer (column (a));

(ii) Fiscal year covered (column (b));

(iii) Annual compensation (columns (c), (d) and (e)), including:

(A) The dollar value of base salary (cash and non-cash) earned by the named executive office during the fiscal year covered (column (c));

(B) The dollar value of bonus (cash and non-cash) earned by the named executive officer during the fiscal year covered (column (d)); and

Instructions to Item 402(b)(2)(iii)(A) and (B).

1. Amounts deferred at the election of a named executive officer, whether pursuant to a plan established under Section 401(k) of the Internal Revenue Code [26 U.S.C. 401(k)], or otherwise, shall be included in the salary column (column (c)) or bonus column (column (d)), as appropriate, for the fiscal year in which earned. If the amount of salary or bonus earned in a given fiscal year is not calculable through the latest practicable date, that fact must be disclosed in a footnote and such amount must be disclosed in the subsequent fiscal year in the appropriate column for the fiscal year in which earned.

2. For stock or any other form of non-cash compensation, disclose the fair market value at the time the compensation is awarded, earned or paid.

3. Registrants need not include in the salary column (column (c)) or bonus column (column (d)) any amount of salary or bonus forgone at the election of a named executive officer pursuant to a registrant program under which stock, stock-based or other forms of non-cash compensation may be received by a named executive in lieu of a portion of annual compensation earned in a covered fiscal year. However, the receipt of any such form of non-cash compensation in lieu of salary or bonus earned for a covered fiscal year must be disclosed in the appropriate column of the Table corresponding to that fiscal year (i.e., restricted stock awards (column (f)); options or SARs (column (g)); all other compensation (column (i)), or, if made pursuant to a long-term incentive plan and therefore not reportable at grant in the Summary Compensation Table, a footnote must be added to the salary or bonus column so disclosing and referring to the Long-Term Incentive Plan Table (required by paragraph (e) of this item) where the award is reported.

(C) The dollar value of other annual compensation not properly categorized as salary or bonus, as follows (column (e)):

(*1*) Perquisites and other personal benefits, securities or property, unless the aggregate amount of such compensation is the lesser of either $50,000 or 10% of the total of annual salary and bonus reported for the named executive officer in columns (c) and (d);

(*2*) Above-market or preferential earnings on restricted stock, options, SARs or deferred compensation paid during the fiscal year or payable during that period but deferred at the election of the named executive officer;

(*3*) Earnings on long-term incentive plan compensation paid during the fiscal year or payable during that period but deferred at the election of the named executive officer;

714

(4) Amounts reimbursed during the fiscal year for the payment of taxes; and

(5) The dollar value of the difference between the price paid by a named executive officer for any security of the registrant or its subsidiaries purchased from the registrant or its subsidiaries (through deferral of salary or bonus, or otherwise), and the fair market value of such security at the date of purchase, unless that discount is available generally, either to all security holders or to all salaried employees of the registrant.

Instructions to Item 402(b)(2)(iii)(C).

1. Each perquisite or other personal benefit exceeding 25% of the total perquisites and other personal benefits reported for a named executive officer must be identified by type and amount in a footnote or accompanying narrative discussion to column (e).

2. Perquisities and other personal benefits shall be valued on the basis of the aggregate incremental cost to the registrant and its subsidiaries.

3. Interest on deferred or long-term compensation is above-market only if the rate of interest exceeds 120% of the applicable federal long-term rate, with compounding (as prescribed under Section 1274(d) of the Internal Revenue Code, [26 U.S.C. 1274(d)]) at the rate that corresponds most closely to the rate under the registrant's plan at the time the interest rate or formula is set. In the event of a discretionary reset of the interest rate, the requisite calculation must be made on the basis of the interest rate at the time of such reset, rather than when originally established. Only the above-market portion of the interest must be included. If the applicable interest rates vary depending upon conditions such as a minimum period of continued service, the reported amount should be calculated assuming satisfaction of all conditions to receiving interest at the highest rate.

4. Dividends (and dividend equivalents) on restricted stock, options, SARs or deferred compensation denominated in stock ("deferred stock") are preferential only if earned at a rate higher than dividends on the registrant's common stock. Only the preferential portion of the dividends or equivalents must be included.

(iv) Long-term compensation (columns (f), (g) and (h)), including:

(A) The dollar value (net of any consideration paid by the named executive officer) of any award of restricted stock, including share units (calculated by multiplying th closing market price of the registrant's unrestricted stock on the date of grant by the number of shares awarded) (column (f));

(B) The sum of the number of securities underlying stock options granted (including options that subsequently have been transferred), with or without tandem SARs, and the number of freestanding SARs (column (g)); and

(C) The dollar value of all payouts pursuant to long-term incentive plans ("LTIPs") as defined in paragraph (a)(7)(iii) of this item (column (h)).

Instructions to Item 402(b)(2)(iv).

1. Awards of restricted stock that are subject to performance-based conditions on vesting, in addition to lapse of time and/or continued service with the registrant or a subsidiary, may be reported as LTIP awards pursuant to paragraph (e) of this item instead of in column (f). If this approach is selected, once the restricted stock vests, it must be reported as an LTIP payout in column (h).

2. The registrant shall, in a footnote to the Summary Compensation Table (appended to column (f), if included), disclose:

a. The number and value of the aggregate restricted stock holdings at the end of the last completed fiscal year. The value shall be calculated in the manner specified in paragraph (b)(2)(iv)(A) of this item using the value of the registrant's shares at the end of the last completed fiscal year;

b. For any restricted stock award reported in the Summary Compensation Table that will vest, in whole or in part, in under three years from the date of grant, the total number of shares awarded and the vesting schedule; and

c. Whether dividends will be paid on the restricted stock reported in column (f).

3. If at any time during the last completed fiscal year, the registrant has adjusted or amended the exercise price of stock options or freestanding SARs previously awarded to a named executive

offier, whether through amendment, cancellation or replacement grants, or any other means ("repriced"), the registrant shall include the number of options or freestanding SARs so repriced as Stock Options/SARs granted and required to be reported in column (g).

4. If any specified performance target, goal or condition to payout was waived with respect to any amount included in LTIP payouts reported in column (h), the registrant shall so state in a footnote to column (h).

(v) All other compensation for the covered fiscal year that the registrant could not properly report in any other column of the Summary Compensation Table (column (i)). Any compensation reported in this column for the last completed fiscal year shall be identified and quantified in a footnote. Such compensation shall include, but not be limited to:

(A) The amount paid, payable or accrued to any named executive officer pursuant to a plan or arrangement in connection with:

(1) the resignation, retirement or any other termination of such executive officer's employment with the registrant and its subsidiaries; or

(2) a change in control of the registrant or a change in the executive officer's responsibilities following such a change in control;

(B) The dollar value of above-market or preferential amounts earned on restricted stock, options, SARs or deferred compensation during the fiscal year, or calculated with respect to that period, except that if such amounts are paid during the period, or payable during the period but deferred at the election of a named executive officer, this information shall be reported as Other Annual Compensation in column (e). *See* Instructions 3 and 4 to paragraph 402(b)(2)(iii)(C) of this item;

(C) The dollar value of amounts earned on long-term incentive plan compensation during the fiscal year, or calculated with respect to that period, except that if such amounts are paid during that period, or payable during that period at the election of the named executive officer, this information shall be reported as Other Annual Compensation in column (e);

(D) Annual registrant contributions or other allocations to vested and unvested defined contribution plans; and

(E) The dollar value of any insurance premiums paid by, or on behalf of, the registrant during the covered fiscal year with respect to term life insurance for the benefit of a named executive officer, and, if there is any arrangement or understanding, whether formal or informal, that such executive officer has or will receive or be allocated an interest in any cash surrender value under the insurance policy, either:

(1) The full dollar value of the remainder of the premiums paid by, or on behalf of, the registrant; or

(2) If the premiums will be refunded to the registrant on termination of the policy, the dollar value of the benefit to the executive officer of the remainder of the premium paid by, or on behalf of, the registrant during the fiscal year. The benefit shall be determined for the period, projected on an actuarial basis, between payment of the premium and the refund.

Instructions to Item 402(b)(2)(v).

1. LTIP awards and amounts received on exercise of options and SARs need not be reported as All Other Compensation in column (i).

2. Information relating to defined benefit and actuarial plans should not be reported pursuant to paragraph (b) of this item, but instead should be reported pursuant to paragraph (f) of this item.

3. Where alternative methods of reporting are available under paragraph (b)(2)(v)(E) of this item, the same method should be used for each of the named executive officers. If the registrant chooses to change methods from one year to the next, that fact, and the reason therefor, should be disclosed in a footnote to column (i).

Instruction to Item 402(b).

Information with respect to fiscal years prior to the last completed fiscal year will not be required if the registrant was not a reporting company pursuant to Section 13(a) or 15(d) of the Exchange Act at any time during that year, except that the registrant will be required to provide information for any such year if that information previously was required to be provided in response to a Commission filing requirement.

(c) *Option/SAR Grants Table.*

(1) The information specified in paragraph (c)(2) of this item, concerning individual grants of stock options (whether or not in tandem with SARs), and freestanding SARs (including options and SARs that subsequently have been transferred) made during the last completed fiscal year to each of the named executive officers shall be provided in the tabular format specified below:

Option/SAR Grants in Last Fiscal Year

	Individual Grants				Potential Realized Value at Assumed Annual Rates of Stock Price Appreciation for Option Term		Alternative to (f) and (g): Grant Date Value
(a)	(b)	(c)	(d)	(e)	(f)	(g)	(f)
	Number of Securities Underlying Options/ SARs Granted (#)	% of Total Options/ SARs Granted to Employees in Fiscal Year	Exercise or Base Price ($/Sh)				Grant Date Present Value $
Name				Expiration Date	5% ($)	10% ($)	
CEO							
A							
B							
C							
D							

(2) The Table shall include, with respect to each grant:

(i) The name of the executive officer (column (a));

(ii) The number of securities underlying options and SARs granted column (b));

(iii) The percent the grant represents of total options and SARs granted to employees during the fiscal year (column (c));

(iv) The per-share exercise or base price of the options or SARs granted (column (d)). If such exercise or base price is less than the market price of the underlying security on the date of grant, a separate, adjoining column shall be added showing market price on the date of grant;

(v) The expiration date of the options or SARs (column (e)); and

(vi) Either (A) the potential realizable value of each grant of options or freestanding SARs or (B) the present value of each grant, as follows:

(A) The potential realizable value of each grant of options or freestanding SARs, assuming that the market price of the underlying security appreciates in value from the date of grant to the end of the option or SAR term, at the following annualized rates:

(*1*) 5% (column (f));

(*2*) 10% (column (g)); and

(*3*) If the exercise or base price was below the market price of the underlying security at the date of grant, provide an additional column labeled 0%, to show the value at grant-date market price; or

(B) The present value of the grant at the date of grant, under any option pricing model (alternative column (f)).

Instructions to Item 402(c).

1. If more than one grant of options and/or freestanding SARs was made to a named executive officer during the last completed fiscal year, a separate line should be used to provide disclosure of each such grant. However, multiple grants during a single fiscal year may be aggregated where each grant was made at the same exercise and/or base price and has the same expiration date, and the same performance vesting thresholds, if any. A single grant consisting of options and/or freestanding SARs shall be reported as separate grants with respect to each tranche with a different exercise and/or base price, performance vesting threshold, or expiration date.

2. Options or freestanding SARs granted in connection with an option repricing transaction shall be reported in this table. *See* Instruction 3 to paragraph (b)(2)(iv) of this item.

3. Any material term of the grant, including but not limited to the date of exercisability, the number of SARs, performance units or other instruments granted in tandem with options, a

performance-based condition to exercisability, a reload feature, or a tax-reimbursement feature, shall be footnoted.

4. If the exercise or base price is adjustable over the term of any option or freestanding SAR in accordance with any prescribed standard or formula, including but not limited to an index or premium price provision, describe the following, either by footnote to column (c) or in narrative accompanying the Table: (a) the standard of formula; and (b) any constant assumption made by the registrant regarding any adjustment to the exercise price in calculating the potential option or SAR value.

5. If any provision of a grant (other than an antidilution provision) could cause the exercise price to be lowered, registrants must clearly and fully disclose these provisions and their potential consequences either by a footnote or accompanying textual narrative.

6. In determining the grant-date market or base price of the security underlying options or freestanding SARs, the registrant may use either the closing market price per share of the security, or any other formula prescribed for the security.

7. The potential realizable dollar value of a grant (columns (f) and (g)) shall be the product of: (a) the difference between: (1) the product of the per-share market price at the time of the grant and the sum of 1 plus the adjusted stock price appreciation rate (the assumed rate of appreciation compounded annually over the term of the option or SAR); and (ii) the per-share exercise price of the option or SAR; and (b) the number of securities underlying the grant at fiscal year-end.

8. Registrants may add one or more separate columns using the formula prescribed in Instruction 7 to paragraph (c) of this item, to reflect the following:

a. the registrant's historic rate of appreciation over a period equivalent to the term of such options and/or SARs;

b. 0% appreciation, where the exercise or base price was equal to or greater than the market price of the underlying securities on the date of grant; and

c. N% appreciation, the percentage appreciation by which the exercise or base price exceeded the market price at grant. Where the grant included multiple tranches with exercise or base prices exceeding the market price of the underlying security by varying degrees, include an additional column for each additional tranche.

9. Where the registrant chooses to use the grant-date valuation alternative specified in paragraph (c)(2)(vi)(B) of this item, the valuation shall be footnoted to describe the valuation method used. Where the registrant has used a variation of the Black-Scholes or binomial option pricing model, the description shall identify the use of such pricing model and describe the assumptions used relating to the expected volatility, risk-free rate of return, dividend yield and time of exercise. Any adjustments for non-transferability or risk of forfeiture also shall be disclosed. In the event another valuation method is used, the registrant is required to describe the methodology as well as any material assumptions.

(d) *Aggregated Option/SAR Exercises and Fiscal Year-End Option/SAR Value Table.*

(1) The information specified in paragraph (d)(2) of this item, concerning each exercise of stock options (or tandem SARs) and freestanding SARs during the last completed fiscal year by each of the named executive officers and the fiscal year-end value of unexercised options and SARs, shall be provided on an aggregated basis in the tabular format specified below:

Aggregated Option/SAR Exercises in Last Fiscal Year and FY-End Option/SAR Values

(a)	(b)	(c)	(d)	(e)
			Number of Securities Underlying Unexercised Options/SARs at FY-End (#)	**Value of Unexercised In-the-Money Options/SARs at FY-End ($)**
Name	**Shares Acquired on Exercise (#)**	**Value Realized ($)**	**Exercisable/ Unexercisable**	**Exercisable/ Unexercisable**

CEO

A

B

C

D

(2) The table shall include:

(i) The name of the executive officer (column (a));

(ii) The number of shares received upon exercise, or, if no shares were received, the number of securities with respect to which the options or SARs were exercised (column (b));

(iii) The aggregate dollar value realized upon exercise (column (c));

(iv) The total number of securities underlying unexercised options and SARs held at the end of the last completed fiscal year, separately identifying the exercisable and unexercisable options and SARs (column (d)); and

(v) The aggregate dollar value of in-the-money, unexercised options and SARs held at the end of the fiscal year, separately identifying the exercisable and unexercisable options and SARs (column (e)).

Instructions to Item 402(d)(2).

1. Options or freestanding SARs are in-the-money if the fair market value of the underlying securities exceeds the exercise or base price of the option or SAR. The dollar values in columns (c) and (e) are calculated by determining the difference between the fair market value of the securities underlying the options or SARs and the exercise or base price of the options or SARs at exercise or fiscal year-end, respectively.

2. In calculating the dollar value realized upon exercise (column (c)), the value of any related payment or other consideration provided (or to be provided) by the registrant to or on behalf of a named executive officer, whether in payment of the exercise price or related taxes, shall not be included. Payments by the registrant in reimbursement of tax obligations incurred by a named executive officer are required to be disclosed in accordance with paragraph (b)(2)(iii)(C)(4) of this item.

(e) *Long-Term Incentive Plan ("LTIP") Awards Table.*

(1) The information specified in paragraph (e)(2) of this item, regarding each award made to a named executive officer in the last completed fiscal year under any LTIP, shall be provided in the tabular format specified below:

Long-Term Incentive Plans - Awards in Last Fiscal Year

			Estimated Future Payouts under Non-Stock Price-Based Plans		
(a)	**(b)**	**(c)**	**(d)**	**(e)**	**(f)**
Name	**Number of Shares, Units or Other Rights (#)**	**Performance or Other Period Until Maturation or Payout**	**Threshold ($ or #)**	**Target ($ or #)**	**Maximum ($ or #)**
CEO					
A					
B					
C					
D					

(2) The Table shall include:

(i) The name of the executive officer (column (a));

(ii) The number of shares, units or other rights awarded under any LTIP, and, if applicable, the number of shares underlying any such unit or right (column (b));

(iii) The performance or other time period until payout or maturation of the award (column (c)); and

(iv) For plans not based on stock price, the dollar value of the estimated payout, the number of shares to be awarded as the payout or a range of estimated payouts denominated in dollars or number of shares under the award (threshold, target and maximum amount) (columns (d) through (f)).

Instructions to Item 402(e).

1. For purposes of this paragraph, the term "long-term incentive plan" or "LTIP" shall be defined in accordance with paragraph (a)(7)(iii) of this item.

2. Describe in a footnote or in narrative text accompanying this table the material terms of any award, including a general description of the formula or criteria to be applied in determining the amounts payable. Registrants are not required to disclose any factor, criterion or performance-related or other condition to payout or maturation of a particular award that involves confidential commercial or business information, disclosure of which would adversely affect the registrant's competitive position.

3. Separate disclosure shall be provided in the Table for each award made to a named executive officer, accompanied by the information specified in Instruction 2 to this paragraph. If awards are made to a named executive officer during the fiscal year under more than one plan, identify the particular plan under which each such award was made.

4. For column (d), "threshold" refers to the minimum amount payable for a certain level of performance under the plan. For column (e), "target" refers to the amount payable if the specified performance target(s) are reached. For column (f), "maximum" refers to the maximum payout possible under the plan.

5. In column (e), registrants must provide a representative amount based on the previous fiscal year's performance if the target award is not determinable.

6. A tandem grant of two instruments, only one of which is pursuant to a LTIP, need be reported only in the table applicable to the other instrument. For example, an option granted in tandem with a performance share would be reported only as an option grant, with the tandem feature noted.

(f) *Defined Benefit or Actuarial Plan Disclosure.*

(1) *Pension Plan Table.*

(i) For any defined benefit or actuarial plan under which benefits are determined primarily by final compensation (or average final compensation) and years of service, provide a separate Pension Plan Table showing estimated annual benefits payable upon retirement (including amounts attributable to any defined benefit supplementary or excess pension award plans) in specified compensation and years of service classifications in the format specified below.

PENSION PLAN TABLE

	Years of Service				
Remuneration	15	20	25	30	35
125,000					
150,000					
175,000					
200,000					
225,000					
250,000					
300,000					
400,000					

Remuneration	Years of Service				
	15	**20**	**25**	**30**	**35**
450,000					
500,000					

(ii) Immediately following the Table, the registrant shall disclose:

(A) The compensation covered by the plan(s), including the relationship of such covered compensation to the annual compensation reported in the Summary Compensation Table required by paragraph (b)(2)(iii) of this item, and state the current compensation covered by the plan for any named executive officer whose covered compensation differs substantially (by more than 10%) from that set forth in the annual compensation columns of the Summary Compensation Table;

(B) The estimated credited years of service for each of the named executive officers; and

(C) A statement as to the basis upon which benefits are computed (e.g., straight-life annuity amounts), and whether or not the benefits listed in the Pension Plan Table are subject to any deduction for Social Security or other offset amounts.

(2) *Alternative Pension Plan Disclosure.* For any defined benefit or actuarial plan under which benefits are not determined primarily by final compensation (or average final compensation) and years of service, the registrant shall state in narrative form:

(i) The formula by which benefits are determined; and

(ii) The estimated annual benefits payable upon retirement at normal retirement age for each of the named executive officers.

Instructions to Item 402(f).

1. *Pension Levels.* Compensation set forth in the Pension Plan Table pursuant to paragraph (f)(1)(i) of this item shall allow for reasonable increases in existing compensation levels; alternatively, registrants may present as the highest compensation level in the Pension Plan Table an amount equal to 120% of the amount of covered compensation of the most highly compensated individual named in the Summary Compensation Table required by paragraph (b)(2) of this item.

2. *Normal Retirement Age.* The term "normal retirement age" means normal retirement age as defined in a pension or similar plan or, if not defined therein, the earliest time at which a participant may retire without any benefit reduction due to age.

(g) *Compensation of Directors.*

(1) *Standard Arrangements.* Describe any standard arrangements, stating amounts, pursuant to which directors of the registrant are compensated for any services provided as a director, including any additional amounts payable for committee participation or special assignments.

(2) *Other Arrangements.* Describe any other arrangements pursuant to which any director of the registrant was compensated during the registrant's last completed fiscal year for any service provided as a director, stating the amount paid and the name of the director.

Instruction to Item 402(g)(2).

The information required by paragraph (g)(2) of this item shall include any arrangement, including consulting contracts, entered into in consideration of the director's service on the board. The material terms of any such arrangement shall be included.

(h) *Employment Contracts and Termination of Employment and Change-in-Control Arrangements.* Describe the terms and conditions of each of the following contracts or arrangements:

(1) Any employment contract between the registrant and a named executive officer; and

(2) Any compensatory plan or arrangement, including payments to be received from the registrant, with respect to a named executive officer, if such plan or arrangement results or will result from the resignation, retirement or any other termination of such executive officer's employment with the registrant and its subsidiaries or from a change-in-control of the registrant or a change in the named executive officer's responsibilities following a change-in-control and the amount involved, including all periodic payments or installments, exceeds $100,000.

(i) *Report on Repricing of Options/SARs.* (1) If at any time during the last completed fiscal year, the registrant, while a reporting company pursuant to Section 13(a) or 15(d) of the Exchange Act [15 U.S.C. 78 m(a), 78*o* (d)], has adjusted or amended the exercise price of stock options or

SARs previously awarded to any of the named executive officers, whether through amendment, cancellation or replacement grants, or any other means ("repriced"), the registrant shall provide the information specified in paragraphs (i)(2) and (i)(3) of this item.

(2) The compensation committee (or other board committee performing equivalent functions or, in the absence of any such committee, the entire board of directors) shall explain in reasonable detail any such repricing of options and/or SARs held by a named executive officer in the last completed fiscal year, as well as the basis for each such repricing.

(3)(i) The information specified in paragraph (i)(3)(*ii*) of this item, concerning all such repricings of options and SARs held by *any* executive officer during the last ten completed fiscal years, shall be provided in the tabular format specified below:

Ten-Year Option/SAR Repricings

(a)	(b)	(c)	(d)	(e)	(f)	(g)
Name	Date	Number of Securities Underlying Options/ SARs Repriced or Amended (#)	Market Price of Stock at Time of Repricing or Amendment ($)	Exercise Price at Time of Repricing or Amendment ($)	New Exercise Price ($)	Length of Original Option Term Remaining at Date of Repricing or Amendment

(ii) The Table shall include, with respect to each repricing:

(A) The name and position of the executive officer (column (a));

(B) The date of each repricing (column (b));

(C) The number of securities underlying replacement or amended options or SARs (column (c));

(D) The per-share market price of the underlying security at the time of repricing (column (d));

(E) The original exercise price or base price of the cancelled or amended option or SAR (column (e));

(F) The per-share exercise price of base price of the replacement option or SAR (column (f)); and

(G) The amount of time remaining before the replaced or amended option or SAR would have expired (column (g)).

Instructions to Item 402(i).

1. The required report shall be made over the name of each member of the registrant's compensation committee, or other board committee performing equivalent functions or, in the absence of any such committee, the entire board of directors.

2. A replacement grant is any grant of options or SARs reasonably related to any prior or potential option or SAR cancellation, whether by an exchange or existing options or SARs for options or SARs with new terms; the grant of new options or SARs in tandem with previously granted options or SARs that will operate to cancel the previously granted options or SARs upon exercise; repricing of previously granted options or SARs; or otherwise. If a corresponding original grant was canceled in a prior year, information about such grant nevertheless must be disclosed pursuant to this paragraph.

3. If the replacement grant is not made at the current market price, describe the terms of the grant in a footnote or accompanying textual narrative.

4. This paragraph shall not apply to any repricing occurring through the operation of:

a. a plan formula or mechanism that results in the periodic adjustment of the option or SAR exercise or base price;

b. a plan antidilution provision; or

c. a recapitalization or similar transaction equally affecting all holders of the class of securities underlying the options or SARs.

5. Information required by paragraph (i)(3) of this item shall not be provided for any repricing effected before the registrant became a reporting company pursuant to Section 13(a) or 15(d) of the Exchange Act.

(j) *Additional Information with Respect to Compensation Committee Interlocks and Insider Participation in Compensation Decisions.* Under the caption "Compensation Committee Interlocks and Insider Participation,"

(1) The registrant shall identify each person who served as a member of the compensation committee of the registrant's board of directors (or board committee performing equivalent functions) during the last completed fiscal year, indicating each committee member who:

(i) was, during the fiscal year, an officer or employee of the registrant or any of its subsidiaries;

(ii) was formerly an officer of the registrant or any of its subsidiaries; or

(iii) had any relationship requiring disclosure by the registrant under any paragraph of Item 404 of Regulation S-K (§ 229.404). In this event, the disclosure required by Item 404 shall accompany such identification.

(2) If the registrant has no compensation committee (or other board committee performinig equivalent functions), the registrant shall identify each officer and employee of the registrant or any of its subsidiaries, and any former officer of the registrant or any of its subsidiaries, who, during, the last completed fiscal year, participated in deliberations of the registrant's board of directors concerning executive officer compensation.

(3) The registrant shall describe any of the following relationships that existed during the last completed fiscal year:

(i) an executive officer of the registrant served as a member of the compensation committee (or other board committee performing equivalent functions or, in the absence of any such committee, the entire board of directors) of another entity, one of whose executive officers served on the compensation committee (or other board committee performing equivalent functions or, in the absence of any such committee, the entire board of directors) of the registrant;

(ii) an executive officer of the registrant served as a director of another entity, one of whose executive officers served on the compensation committee (or other board committee performining equivalent functions or, in the absence of any such committee, the entire board of directors) of the registrant; and

(iii) an executive officer of the registrant served as a member of the compensation committee (or other board committee performing equivalent functions or, in the absence of any such committee, the entire board of directors) of another entity, one of whose executive officers served as a director of the registrant.

(4) Disclosure required under paragraph (j)(3) of this item regarding any compensation committee member or other director of the registrant who also served as an executive officer of another entity shall be accompanied by the disclosure called for by Item 404 (§ 229.404) with respect to that person.

Instruction to Item 402(j).

For purposes of this paragraph, the term "entity" shall not include an entity exempt from tax under Section 501(c)(3) of the Internal Revenue Code [26 U.S.C. 501(c)(3)].

(k) *Board Compensation Committee Report on Executive Compensation.*

(1) Disclosure of the compensation committee's compensation policies applicable to the registrant's executive officers (including the named executive officers), including the specific relationship of corporate performance to executive compensation, is required with respect to compensation reported for the last completed fiscal year.

(2) Discussion is required of the compensation committee's bases for the CEO's compensation reported for the last completed fiscal year, including the factors and criteria upon which the CEO's compensation was based. The committee shall include a specific discussion of the relationship of the registrant's performance to the CEO's compensation for the last completed fiscal year,

describing each measure of the registrant's performance, whether qualitative or quantitative, on which the CEO's compensation was based.

(3) The required disclosure shall be made over the name of each member of the registrant's compensation committee (or, in the absence of a compensation committee, the board committee performing equivalent functions or the entire board of directors). If the board of directors modified or rejected in any material way any action or recommendation by such committee with respect to such decision in the last completed fiscal year, the disclosure must so indicate and explain the reasons for the board's actions, and be made over the names of all members of the board.

Instructions to Item 402(k).

1. Boilerplate language should be avoided in describing factors and criteria underlying awards or payments of executive compensation in the statement required.

2. Registrants are not required to disclose target levels with respect to specific quantitative or qualitative performance-related factors considered by the committee (or board), or any factors or criteria involving confidential commercial or business information, the disclosure of which would have an adverse effect on the registrant.

(l) *Performance Graph.*

(1) Provide a line graph comparing the yearly percentage change in the registrant's cumulative total shareholder return on a class of common stock registered under Section 12 of the Exchange Act (as measured by dividing (i) the sum of (A) the cumulative amount of dividends for the measurement period, assuming dividend reinvestment, and (B) the difference between the registrant's share price at the end and the beginning of the measurement period; by (ii) the share price at the beginning of the measurement period) with

(i) the cumulative total return of a board equity market index assuming reinvestment of dividends, that includes companies whose equity securities are traded on the same exchange or NASDAQ market or are of comparable market capitalization; *provided, however,* that if the registrant is a company within the Standard & Poor's 500 Stock Index, the registrant must use that index; and

(ii) the cumulative total return, assuming reinvestment of dividends, of:

(A) a published industry or line-of-business index;

(B) peer issuer(s) selected in good faith. If the registrant does not select its peer issuer(s) on an industry or line-of-business basis, the registrant shall disclose the basis for its selection; or

(C) Issuer(s) with similar market capitalization(s), but only if the registrant does not use a published industry or line-of-business index and does not believe it can reasonably identify a peer group. If the registrant uses this alternative, the graph shall be accompanied by a statement of the reasons for this selection.

(2) For purposes of paragraph (l)(1) of this item, the term "measurement period" shall be the period beginning at the "measurement point" established by the market close on the last trading day before the beginning of the registrant's fifth preceding fiscal year, through and including the end of the registrant's last completed fiscal year. If the class of securities has been registered under section 12 of the Exchange Act for a shorter period of time, the period covered by the comparison may correspond to that time period.

(3) For purposes of paragraph (l)(1)(ii)(A) of this item, the term "published industry or line-of-business index" means any index that is prepared by a party other than the registrant or an affiliate and is accessible to the registrant's security holders; provided, however, that registrants may use an index prepared by the registrant or affiliate if such index is widely recognized and used.

(4) If the registrant selects a different index from an index used for the immediately preceding fiscal year, explain the reason(s) for this change and also compare the registrant's total return with that of both the newly selected index and the index used in the immediately preceding fiscal year.

Instructions to Item 402(l).

1. In preparing the required graphic comparisons, the registrant should:

a. use, to the extent feasible, comparable methods of presentation and assumptions for the total return calculations required by paragraph (*l*) (1) of this item; *provided, however,* that if the registrant constructs its own peer group index under paragraph (*l*) (1) (ii) (B), the same methodology must be used in calculating both the registrant's total return and that on the peer group index; and

b. assume the reinvestment of dividends into additional shares of the same class of equity securities at the frequency with which dividends are paid on such securities during the applicable fiscal year.

2. In constructing the graph:

(a) The closing price at the measurement point must be converted into a fixed investment, stated in dollars, in the registrant's stock (or in the stocks represented by a given index), with cumulative returns for each subsequent fiscal year measured as a change from that investment; and

(b) Each fiscal year should be plotted with points showing the cumulative total return as of that point. The value of the investment as of each point plotted on a given return line is the number of shares held at that point multiplied by the then-prevailing share price.

3. The registrant is required to present information for the registrant's last five fiscal years, and may choose to graph a longer period; but the measurement point, however, shall remain the same.

4. Registrants may include comparisons using performance measures in addition to total return, such as return on average common shareholders' equity, so long as the registrant's compensation committee (or other board committee performing equivalent functions or, in the absence of any such committee, the entire board of directors) describes the link between that measure and the level of executive compensation in the statement required by paragraph (k) of this Item.

5. If the registrant uses a peer issuer(s) comparison or comparison with issuer(s) with similar market capitalizations, the identity of those issuers must be disclosed and the returns of each component issuer of the group must be weighted according to the respective issuer's stock market capitalization at the beginning of each period for which a return is indicated.

Item 403. Security Ownership of Certain Beneficial Owners and Management

(a) *Security ownership of certain beneficial owners.* Furnish the following information, as of the most recent practicable date, in substantially the tabular form indicated, with respect to any person (including any "group" as that term is used in section 13(d) (3) of the Exchange Act) who is known to the registrant to be the beneficial owner of more than five percent of any class of the registrant's voting securities. The address given in column (2) may be a business, mailing or residence address. Show in column (3) the total number of shares beneficially owned and in column (4) the percentage of class so owned. Of the number of shares shown in column (3), indicate by footnote or otherwise the amount known to be shares with respect to which such listed beneficial owner has the right to acquire beneficial ownership, as specified in Rule 13d-3(d) (1) under the Exchange Act (§ 240.13d-3(d) (1) of this chapter).

(1) Title of class	(2) Name and address of beneficial owner	(3) Amount and nature of beneficial ownership	(4) Percent of class

(b) *Security ownership of management.* Furnish the following information, as of the most recent practicable date, in substantially the tabular form indicated, as to each class of equity securities of the registrant or any of its parents or subsidiaries other than directors' qualifying shares, beneficially owned by all directors and nominees, naming them, each of the named executive officers as defined in Item 402(a) (3) (§ 229.402(a) (3)), and directors and executive officers of the registrant as a group, without naming them. Show in column (3) the total number of shares beneficially owned and in column (4) the percent of class so owned. Of the number of shares shown in column (3), indicate, by footnote or otherwise, the amount of shares with respect to which such persons have the right to acquire beneficial ownership as specified in § 240.13d-3(d) (1) of this chapter.

(1) Title of class	(2) Name of beneficial owner	(3) Amount and nature of beneficial ownership	(4) Percent of class

(c) *Changes in control.* Describe any arrangements, known to the registrant, including any pledge by any person of securities of the registrant or any of its parents, the operation of which may at a subsequent date result in a change in control of the registrant.

> *Instructions to Item 403.* 1. The percentages are to be calculated on the basis of the amount of outstanding securities, excluding securities held by or for the account of the registrant or its subsidiaries, plus securities deemed outstanding pursuant to Rule 13d-3(d)(1) under the Exchange Act [17 CFR 240.13d-3(d)(1)]. For purposes of paragraph (b), if the percentage of shares beneficially owned by any director or nominee, or by all directors and officers of the registrant as a group, does not exceed one percent of the class so owned, the registrant may, in lieu of furnishing a precise percentage, indicate this fact by means of an asterisk and explanatory footnote or other similar means.

> 2. For the purposes of this Item, beneficial ownership shall be determined in accordance with Rule 13d-3 under the Exchange Act (§ 240.13d-3 of this chapter). Include such additional subcolumns or other appropriate explanation of column (3) necessary to reflect amounts as to which the beneficial owner has (A) sole voting power, (B) shared voting power, (C) sole investment power, or (D) shared investment power.

> 3. The registrant shall be deemed to know the contents of any statements filed with the Commission pursuant to section 13(d) or 13(g) of the Exchange Act. When applicable, a registrant may rely upon information set forth in such statements unless the registrant knows or has reason to believe that such information is not complete or accurate or that a statement or amendment should have been filed and was not.

> 4. For purposes of furnishing information pursuant to paragraph (a) of this Item, the registrant may indicate the source and date of such information.

> 5. Where more than one beneficial owner is known to be listed for the same securities, appropriate disclosure should be made to avoid confusion. For purposes of paragraph (b), in computing the aggregate number of shares owned by directors and officers of the registrant as a group, the same shares shall not be counted more than once.

> 6. Paragraph (c) of this Item does not require a description of ordinary default provisions contained in the charter, trust indentures or other governing instruments relating to securities of the registrant.

> 7. Where the holder(s) of voting securities reported pursuant to paragraph (a) hold more than five percent of any class of voting securities of the registrant pursuant to any voting trust or similar agreement, state the title of such securities, the amount held or to be held pursuant to the trust or agreement (if not clear from the table) and the duration of the agreement. Give the names and addresses of the voting trustees and outline briefly their voting rights and other powers under the trust or agreement.

Item 404. Certain Relationships and Related Transactions

(a) *Transactions with management and others.* Describe briefly any transaction, or series of similar transactions, since the beginning of the registrant's last fiscal year, or any currently proposed transaction, or series of similar transactions, to which the registrant or any of its subsidiaries was or is to be a party, in which the amount involved exceeds $60,000 and in which any of the following persons had, or will have, a direct or indirect material interest, naming such person and indicating the person's relationship to the registrant, the nature of such person's interest in the transaction(s), the amount of such transaction(s) and, where practicable, the amount of such person's interest in the transaction(s):

(1) Any director or executive officer of the registrant;

(2) Any nominee for election as a director;

(3) Any security holder who is known to the registrant to own of record or beneficially more than five percent of any class of the registrant's voting securities; and

(4) Any member of the immediate family of any of the foregoing persons.

Instructions to Paragraph (a) of Item 404. 1. The materiality of any interest is to be determined on the basis of the significance of the information to investors in light of all the circumstances of the particular case. The importance of the interest to the person having the interest, the relationship of the parties to the transaction with each other and the amount involved in the transactions are among the factors to be considered in determining the significance of the information to investors.

2. For purposes of paragraph (a), a person's immediate family shall include such person's spouse; parents; children; siblings; mothers and fathers-in-law; sons and daughters-in-law; and brothers and sisters-in-law.

3. In computing the amount involved in the transaction or series of similar transactions, include all periodic installments in the case of any lease or other agreement providing for periodic payments or installments.

4. The amount of the interest of any person specified in paragraphs (a)(1) through (4) shall be computed without regard to the amount of the profit or loss involved in the transaction(s).

5. In describing any transaction involving the purchase or sale of assets by or to the registrant or any of its subsidiaries, otherwise than in the ordinary course of business, state the cost of the assets to the purchaser and, if acquired by the seller within two years prior to the transaction, the cost thereof to the seller. Indicate the principle followed in determining the registrant's purchase or sale price and the name of the person making such determination.

6. Information shall be furnished in answer to paragraph (a) with respect to transactions that involve remuneration from the registrant or its subsidiaries, directly or indirectly, to any of the persons specified in paragraphs (a)(1) through (4) for services in any capacity unless the interest of such person arises solely from the ownership individually and in the aggregate of less than ten percent of any class of equity securities of another corporation furnishing the services to the registrant or its subsidiaries.

7. No information need be given in answer to paragraph (a) as to any transactions where:

   A. The rates or charges involved in the transaction are determined by competitive bids, or the transaction involves the rendering of services as a common or contract carrier, or public utility, at rates or charges fixed in conformity with law or governmental authority;

   B. The transaction involves services as a bank depositary of funds, transfer agent, registrar, trustee under a trust indenture, or similar services; or

   C. The interest of the person specified in paragraphs (a)(1) through (4) arises solely from the ownership of securities of the registrant and such person receives no extra or special benefit not shared on a pro rata basis.

8. Paragraph (a) requires disclosure of indirect, as well as direct, material interests in transactions. A person who has a position or relationship with a firm, corporation, or other entity that engages in a transaction with the registrant or its subsidiaries may have an indirect interest in such transaction by reason of such position or relationship. Such an interest, however, shall not be deemed "material" within the meaning of paragraph (a) where:

   A. The interest arises only (i) from such person's position as a director of another corporation or organization which is a party to the transaction; or (ii) from the direct or indirect ownership by such person and all other persons specified in paragraphs (a)(1) through (4), in the aggregate, of less than a ten percent equity interest in another person (other than a partnership) which is a party to the transaction; or (iii) from both such position and ownership;

   B. The interest arises only from such person's position as a limited partner in a partnership in which the person and all other persons specified in paragraphs (a)(1) through (4) have an interest of less than ten percent; or

C. The interest of such person arises solely from the holding of an equity interest (including a limited partnership interest, but excluding a general partnership interest) or a creditor interest in another person that is a party to the transaction with the registrant or any of its subsidiaries, and the transaction is not material to such other person.

9. There may be situations where, although these instructions do not expressly authorize nondisclosure, the interest of a person specified in paragraphs (a)(1) through (4) in a particular transaction or series of transactions is not a direct or indirect material interest. In that case, information regarding such interest and transaction is not required to be disclosed in response to this paragraph.

(b) *Certain business relationships.* Describe any of the following relationships regarding directors or nominees for director that exist, or have existed during the registrant's last fiscal year, indicating the identity of the entity with which the registrant has such a relationship, the name of the nominee or director affiliated with such entity and the nature of such nominee's or director's affiliation, the relationship between such entity and the registrant and the amount of the business done between the registrant and the entity during the registrant's last full fiscal year or proposed to be done during the registrant's current fiscal year:

(1) If the nominee or director is, or during the last fiscal year has been, an executive officer of, or owns, or during the last fiscal year has owned, of record or beneficially in excess of ten percent equity interest in, any business or professional entity that has made during the registrant's last full fiscal year, or proposes to make during the registrant's current fiscal year, payments to the registrant or its subsidiaries for property or services in excess of five percent of (i) the registrant's consolidated gross revenues for its last full fiscal year, or (ii) the other entity's consolidated gross revenues for its last full fiscal year;

(2) If the nominee or director is, or during the last fiscal year has been, an executive officer of, or owns, or during the last fiscal year has owned, of record or beneficially in excess of ten percent equity interest in, any business or professional entity to which the registrant or its subsidiaries has made during the registrant's last full fiscal year, or proposes to make during the registrant's current fiscal year, payments for property or services in excess of five percent of (i) the registrant's consolidated gross revenues for its last full fiscal year, or (ii) the other entity's consolidated gross revenues for its last full fiscal year;

(3) If the nominee or director is, or during the last fiscal year has been, an executive officer of, or owns, or during the last fiscal year has owned, of record or beneficially in excess of ten percent equity interest in, any business or professional entity to which the registrant or its subsidiaries was indebted at the end of the registrant's last full fiscal year in an aggregate amount in excess of five percent of the registrant's total consolidated assets at the end of such fiscal year;

(4) If the nominee or director is, or during the last fiscal year has been, a member of, or of counsel to, a law firm that the issuer has retained during the last fiscal year or proposes to retain during the current fiscal year; *Provided, however,* that the dollar amount of fees paid to a law firm by the registrant need not be disclosed if such amount does not exceed five percent of the law firm's gross revenues for that firm's last full fiscal year;

(5) If the nominee or director is, or during the last fiscal year has been, a partner or executive officer of any investment banking firm that has performed services for the registrant, other than as a participating underwriter in a syndicate, during the last fiscal year or that the registrant proposes to have perform services during the current year; *Provided, however,* that the dollar amount of compensation received by an investment banking firm need not be disclosed if such amount does not exceed five percent of the investment banking firm's consolidated gross revenues for that firm's last full fiscal year; or

(6) Any other relationships that the registrant is aware of between the nominee or director and the registrant that are substantially similar in nature and scope to those relationships listed in paragraphs (b)(1) through (5).

Instructions to Paragraph (b) of Item 404. 1. In order to determine whether payments or indebtedness exceed five percent of the consolidated gross revenues of any entity, other than the registrant, it is appropriate to rely on information provided by the nominee or director.

2. In calculating payments for property and services the following may be excluded:

A. Payments where the rates or charges involved in the transaction are determined by competitive bids, or the transaction involves the rendering of services as a common contract carrier, or public utility, at rates or charges fixed in conformity with law or governmental authority;

B. Payments that arise solely from the ownership of securities of the registrant and no extra or special benefit not shared on a pro rata basis by all holders of the class of securities is received; or

C. Payments made or received by subsidiaries other than significant subsidiaries as defined in Rule 1-02(w) of Regulation S-X [§ 210.1-02(w) of this chapter], provided that all such subsidiaries making or receiving payments, when considered in the aggregate as a single subsidiary, would not constitute a significant subsidiary as defined in Rule 1-02(w).

3. In calculating indebtedness the following may be excluded:

A. Debt securities that have been publicly offered, admitted to trading on a national securities exchange, or quoted on the automated quotation system of a registered securities association;

B. Amounts due for purchases subject to the usual trade terms; or

C. Indebtedness incurred by subsidiaries other than significant subsidiaries as defined in Rule 1-02(w) of Regulation S-X [§ 210.1-02(w) of this chapter], provided that all such subsidiaries incurring indebtedness, when considered in the aggregate as a single subsidiary, would not constitute a significant subsidiary as defined in Rule 1-02(w).

4. No information called for by paragraph (b) need be given respecting any director who is no longer a director at the time of filing the registration statement or report containing such disclosure. If such information is being presented in a proxy or information statement, no information need be given respecting any director whose term of office as a director will not continue after the meeting to which the statement relates.

(c) *Indebtedness of management.* If any of the following persons has been indebted to the registrant or its subsidiaries at any time since the beginning of the registrant's last fiscal year in an amount in excess of $60,000, indicate the name of such person, the nature of the person's relationship by reason of which such person's indebtedness is required to be described, the largest aggregate amount of indebtedness outstanding at any time during such period, the nature of the indebtedness and of the transaction in which it was incurred, the amount thereof outstanding as of the latest practicable date and the rate of interest paid or charged thereon:

(1) Any director or executive officer of the registrant;

(2) Any nominee for election as a director;

(3) Any member of the immediate family of the persons specified in paragraph (c)(1) or (2);

(4) Any corporation or organization (other than the registrant or a majority-owned subsidiary of the registrant) of which any of the persons specified in paragraphs (c)(1) or (2) is an executive officer or partner or is, directly or indirectly, the beneficial owner of ten percent or more of any class of equity securities; and

(5) Any trust or other estate in which any of the persons specified in paragraph (c)(1) or (2) has a substantial beneficial interest or as to which such person serves as a trustee or in a similar capacity.

Instructions to Paragraph (c) of Item 404. 1. For purposes of paragraph (c), the members of a person's immediate family are those persons specified in Instruction 2 to Item 404(a).

2. Exclude from the determination of the amount of indebtedness all amounts due from the particular person for purchases subject to usual trade terms, for ordinary travel and expense payments and for other transactions in the ordinary course of business.

3. If the lender is a bank, savings and loan association, or broker-dealer extending credit under Federal Reserve Regulation T [12 CFR Part 220] and the loans are not disclosed as nonaccrual, past due, restructured or potential problems (see Item III.C.1. and 2. of Industry Guide 3, Statistical Disclosure by Bank Holding Companies), disclosure may consist of a statement, if such is the case, that the loans to such persons (A) were made in the ordinary course of business, (B) were made on substantially the same terms, including interest rates and collateral, as those prevailing at the time for comparable transactions with other persons, and (C) did not involve more than the normal risk of collectibility or present other unfavorable features.

4. If any indebtedness required to be described arose under Section 16(b) of the Exchange Act and has not been discharged by payment, state the amount of any profit realized, that such profit will inure to the benefit of the registrant or its subsidiaries and whether suit will be brought or other steps taken to recover such profit. If, in the opinion of counsel, a question reasonably exists as to the recoverability of such profit, it will suffice to state all facts necessary to describe the transactions, including the prices and number of shares involved.

(d) *Transactions with promoters.* Registrants that have been organized within the past five years and that are filing a registration statement on Form S-1 under the Securities Act (§ 239.11 of this chapter) or on Form 10 and Form 10-SB under the Exchange Act (§ 249.210 and § 249.210b of this chapter) shall:

(1) State the names of the promoters, the nature and amount of anything of value (including money, property, contracts, options or rights of any kind) received or to be received by each promoter, directly or indirectly, from the registrant and the nature and amount of any assets, services or other consideration therefor received or to be received by the registrant; and

(2) As to any assets acquired or to be acquired by the registrant from a promoter, state the amount at which the assets were acquired or are to be acquired and the principle followed or to be followed in determining such amount and identify the persons making the determination and their relationship, if any, with the registrant or any promoter. If the assets were acquired by the promoter within two years prior to their transfer to the registrant, also state the cost thereof to the promoter.

Instructions to Item 404.

1. No information need be given in response to any paragraph of Item 404 as to any compensation or other transaction reported in response to any other paragraph of Item 404 or to Item 402 of Regulation S-K (§ 229.402 of this chapter) or as to any compensation or transaction with respect to which information may be omitted pursuant to Item 402.

2. If the information called for by Item 404 is being presented in a registration statement filed pursuant to the Securities Act or the Exchange Act, information shall be given for the periods specified in this Item and, in addition, for the two fiscal years preceding the registrant's last fiscal year.

3. A foreign private issuer will be deemed to comply with Item 404 if it provides the information required by Item 7.B of Form 20-F (17 CFR 249.220f).

Item 405. Compliance With Section 16(a) of the Exchange Act

Every registrant having a class of equity securities registered pursuant to Section 12 of the Exchange Act (15 U.S.C. 78*l*), every closed-end investment company registered under the Investment Company Act of 1940 (15 U.S.C. § 80a-1 *et seq.*), and every holding company registered pursuant to the Public Utility Holding Company Act of 1935 (15 U.S.C. § 79a *et seq.*) shall:

(a) Based solely upon a review of Forms 3 (§ 249.103) and 4 (§ 249.104) and amendments thereto furnished to the registrant pursuant to § 240.16a-3(e) during its most recent fiscal year and Forms 5 and amendments thereto (§ 249.105) furnished to the registrant with respect to its most recent fiscal year, and any written representation referred to in (b)(2)(i) below:

(1) Under the caption "Section 16(a) Beneficial Ownership Reporting Compliance," identify each person who, at any time during the fiscal year, was a director, officer, beneficial owner of more than ten percent of any class of equity securities of the registrant registered pursuant to section 12 of the Exchange Act, or any other person subject to section 16 of the Exchange Act with respect to the registrant because of the requirements of section 30 of the Investment Company Act or section 17 of the Public Utility Holding Company Act ("reporting person") that failed to file on a timely basis, as disclosed in the above Forms, reports required by section 16(a) of the Exchange Act during the most recent fiscal year or prior fiscal years.

(2) For each such person, set forth the number of late reports, the number of transactions that were not reported on a timely basis, and any known failure to file a required Form. A known failure to file would include, but not be limited to, a failure to file a Form 3, which is required of all reporting persons, and a failure to file a Form 5 in the absence of the written representation referred to in paragraph (b)(2)(i) of this section, unless the registrant otherwise knows that no Form 5 is required.

Note: The disclosure requirement is based on a review of the forms submitted to the registrant during and with respect to its most recent fiscal year, as specified above. Accordingly, a failure to file timely need only be disclosed once. For example, if in the most recently concluded fiscal year a reporting person filed a Form 4 disclosing a transaction that took place in the prior fiscal year, and should have been reported in that year, the registrant should disclose that late filing and transaction pursuant to this Item 405 with respect to the most recently concluded fiscal year, but not in material filed with respect to subsequent years.

(b) With respect to the disclosure required by paragraph (a) of this Item:

(1) A form received by the registrant within three calendar days of the required filing date may be presumed to have been filed with the Commission by the required filing date.

(2) If the registrant (i) receives a written representation from the reporting person that no Form 5 is required; and (ii) maintains the representation for two years, making a copy available to the Commission or its staff upon request, the registrant need not identify such reporting person pursuant to paragraph (a) as having failed to file a Form 5 with respect to that fiscal year.

Item 406. Code of Ethics

(a) Disclose whether the registrant has adopted a code of ethics that applies to the registrant's principal executive officer, principal financial officer, principal accounting officer or controller, or persons performing similar functions. If the registrant has not adopted such a code of ethics, explain why it has not done so.

(b) For purposes of this Item 406, the term *code of ethics* means written standards that are reasonably designed to deter wrongdoing and to promote:

(1) Honest and ethical conduct, including the ethical handling of actual or apparent conflicts of interest between personal and professional relationships;

(2) Full, fair, accurate, timely, and understandable disclosure in reports and documents that a registrant files with, or submits to, the Commission and in other public communications made by the registrant;

(3) Compliance with applicable governmental laws, rules and regulations;

(4) The prompt internal reporting of violations of the code to an appropriate person or persons identified in the code; and

(5) Accountability for adherence to the code.

(c) The registrant must:

(1) File with the Commission a copy of its code of ethics that applies to the registrant's principal executive officer, principal financial officer, principal accounting officer or controller, or persons performing similar functions, as an exhibit to its annual report;

(2) Post the text of such code of ethics on its Internet website and disclose, in its annual report, its Internet address and the fact that it has posted such code of ethics on its Internet website; or

(3) Undertake in its annual report filed with the Commission to provide to any person without charge, upon request, a copy of such code of ethics and explain the manner in which such request may be made.

(d) If the registrant intends to satisfy the disclosure requirement under Item 10 of Form 8-K regarding an amendment to, or a waiver from, a provision of its code of ethics that applies to the registrant's principal executive officer, principal financial officer, principal accounting officer or controller, or persons performing similar functions and that relates to any element of the code of ethics definition enumerated in paragraph (b) of this Item by posting such information on its Internet website, disclose the registrant's Internet address and such intention.

Instructions to Item 406.

1. A registrant may have separate codes of ethics for different types of officers. Furthermore, a *code of ethics* within the meaning of paragraph (b) of this Item may be a portion of a broader document that addresses additional topics or that applies to more persons than those specified in paragraph (a). In satisfying the requirements of paragraph (c), a registrant need only file, post or provide the portions of a broader document that constitutes a *code of ethics* as defined in paragraph (b) and that apply to the persons specified in paragraph (a).

2. If a registrant elects to satisfy paragraph (c) of this Item by posting its code of ethics on its website pursuant to paragraph (c)(2), the code of ethics must remain accessible on its website for as long as the registrant remains subject to the requirements of this Item and chooses to comply with this Item by posting its code on its website pursuant to paragraph (c)(2).

3. A registrant that is an Asset-Backed Issuer (as defined in §240.13a-14(g) and §240.15d-14(g) of this chapter) is not required to disclose the information required by this Item.

Subpart 500—Registration Statement and Prospectus Provisions

Item 501. Forepart of Registration Statement and Outside Front Cover Page of Prospectus

The registrant must furnish the following information in plain English. See §230.421(d) of Regulation C of this chapter.

(a) *Front Cover Page of the Registration Statement.* Where appropriate, include the delaying amendment legend from §230.473 of Regulation C of this chapter.

(b) *Outside Front Cover Page of the Prospectus.* Limit the outside cover page to one page. If the following information applies to your offering, disclose it on the outside cover page of the prospectus.

(1) *Name.* The registrant's name. A foreign registrant must give the English translation of its name.

Instruction to paragraph 501(b)(1).

If your name is the same as that of a company that is well known, include information to eliminate any possible confusion with the other company. If your name indicates a line of business in which you are not engaged or you are engaged only to a limited extent, include information to eliminate any misleading inference as to your business. In some circumstances, disclosure may not be sufficient and you may be required to change your name. You will not be required to change your name if you are an established company, the character of your business has changed, and the investing public is generally aware of the change and the character of your current business.

(2) *Title and amount of securities.* The title and amount of securities offered. Separately state the amount of securities offered by selling security holders, if any. If the underwriter has any arrangement with the issuer, such as an over-allotment option, under which the underwriter may purchase additional shares in connection with the offering, indicate that this arrangement exists and state the amount of additional shares that the underwriter may purchase under the arrangement. Give a brief description of the securities except where the information is clear from the title of the security. For example, you are not required to describe common stock that has full voting, dividend and liquidation rights usually associated with common stock.

(3) *Offering price of the securities.* Where you offer securities for cash, the price to the public of the securities, the underwriter's discounts and commissions, the net proceeds you receive, and any selling shareholder's net proceeds. Show this information on both a per share or unit basis and for the total amount of the offering. If you make the offering on a minimum/maximum basis, show this information based on the total minimum and total maximum amount of the offering. You may present the information in a table, term sheet format, or other clear presentation. You may present the information in any format that fits the design of the cover page so long as the information can be easily read and is not misleading;

Instructions to paragraph 501(b)(3)

1. If a preliminary prospectus is circulated and you are not subject to the reporting requirements of Section 13(a) or 15(d) of the Exchange Act, provide, as applicable:

(A) A bona fide estimate of the range of the maximum offering price and the maximum number of securities offered; or

(B) A bona fide estimate of the principal amount of the debt securities offered.

2. If it is impracticable to state the price to the public, explain the method by which the price is to be determined. If the securities are to be offered at the market price, or if the offering price is to be determined by a formula related to the market price, indicate the market and market price of the securities as of the latest practicable date.

3. If you file a registration statement on Form S-8, you are not required to comply with this paragraph (b)(3).

(4) *Market for the Securities.* Whether any national securities exchange or the Nasdaq Stock Market lists the securities offered, naming the particular market(s), and identifying the trading symbol(s) for those securities;

(5) *Risk Factors.* A cross-reference to the risk factors section, including the page number where it appears in the prospectus. Highlight this cross-reference by prominent type or in another manner;

(6) *State Legend.* Any legend or statement required by the law of any state in which the securities are to be offered. You may combine this with any legend required by the SEC, if appropriate;

(7) *Commission Legend.* A legend that indicates that neither the Securities and Exchange Commission nor any state securities commission has approved or disapproved of the securities or passed upon the accuracy or adequacy of the disclosures in the prospectus and that any contrary representation is a criminal offense. You may use one of the following or other clear, plain language:

Example A: Neither the Securities and Exchange Commission nor any state securities commission has approved or disapproved of these securities or passed upon the adequacy or accuracy of this prospectus. Any representation to the contrary is a criminal offense.

Example B: Neither the Securities and Exchange Commission nor any state securities commission has approved or disapproved of these securities or determined if this prospectus is truthful or complete. Any representation to the contrary is a criminal offense.

(8) *Underwriting.* (i) Name(s) of the lead or managing underwriter(s) and an identification of the nature of the underwriting arrangements;

(ii) If the offering is not made on a firm commitment basis, a brief description of the underwriting arrangements. You may use any clear, concise, and accurate description of the underwriting arrangements. You may use the following descriptions of underwriting arrangements where appropriate:

Example A: Best efforts offering. The underwriters are not required to sell any specific number or dollar amount of securities but will use their best efforts to sell the securities offered.

Example B: Best efforts, minimum-maximum offering. The underwriters must sell the minimum number of securities offered (insert number) if any are sold. The underwriters are required to use only their best efforts to sell the maximum number of securities offered (insert number).

(iii) If you offer the securities on a best efforts or best efforts minimum/maximum basis, the date the offering will end, any minimum purchase requirements, and any arrangements to place the funds in an escrow, trust, or similar account. If you have not made any of these arrangements, state this fact and describe the effect on investors;

(9) *Date of Prospectus.* The date of the prospectus;

(10) *Prospectus "Subject to Completion" Legend.* If you use the prospectus before the effective date of the registration statement, a prominent statement that:

(i) The information in the prospectus will be amended or completed;

(ii) A registration statement relating to these securities has been filed with the Securities and Exchange Commission;

(iii) The securities may not be sold until the registration statement becomes effective; and

(iv) The prospectus is not an offer to sell the securities and it is not soliciting an offer to buy the securities in any state where offers or sales are not permitted. The legend may be in the following or other clear, plain language:

> The information in this prospectus is not complete and may be changed. We may not sell these securities until the registration statement filed with the Securities and Exchange Commission is effective. This prospectus is not an offer to sell these securities and it is not soliciting an offer to buy these securities in any state where the offer or sale is not permitted.

(11) If you use § 230.430A of this chapter to omit pricing information and the prospectus is used before you determine the public offering price, the information and legend in paragraph (b) (10) of this section.

Item 502. Inside Front and Outside Back Cover Pages of Prospectus

The registrant must furnish this information in plain English. See § 230.421(d) of Regulation C of this chapter.

(a) *Table of Contents.* On either the inside front or outside back cover page of the prospectus, provide a reasonably detailed table of contents. It must show the page number of the various sections or subdivisions of the prospectus. Include a specific listing of the risk factors section required by Item 503 of this Regulation S-K (17 CFR 229.503). You must include the table of contents immediately following the cover page in any prospectus you deliver electronically.

(b) *Dealer Prospectus Delivery Obligation.* On the outside back cover page of the prospectus, advise dealers of their prospectus delivery obligation, including the expiration date specified by Section 4(3) of the Securities Act (15 U.S.C. 77d(3)) and § 230.174 of this chapter. If you do not know the expiration date on the effective date of the registration statement, include the expiration date in the copy of the prospectus you file under § 230.424(b) of this chapter. You do not have to include this information if dealers are not required to deliver a prospectus under § 230.174 of this chapter or Section 24(d) of the Investment Company Act (15 U.S.C. 80a-24). You may use the following or other clear, plain language:

> Dealer Prospectus Delivery Obligation
>
> Until (insert date), all dealers that effect transactions in these securities, whether or not participating in this offering, may be required to deliver a prospectus. This is in addition to the dealers' obligation to deliver a prospectus when acting as underwriters and with respect to their unsold allotments or subscriptions.

Item 503. Prospectus Summary, Risk Factors, and Ratio of Earnings to Fixed Charges

The registrant must furnish this information in plain English. See § 230.421(d) of Regulation C of this chapter.

(a) *Prospectus Summary.* Provide a summary of the information in the prospectus where the length or complexity of the prospectus makes a summary useful. The summary should be brief. The summary should not contain, and is not required to contain, all of the detailed information in the prospectus. If you provide summary business or financial information, even if you do not caption it as a summary, you still must provide that information in plain English.

Instruction to paragraph 503(a).

The summary should not merely repeat the text of the prospectus but should provide a brief overview of the key aspects of the offering. Carefully consider and identify those aspects of the offering that are the most significant and determine how best to highlight those points in clear, plain language.

(b) *Address and Telephone Number.* Include, either on the cover page or in the summary section of the prospectus, the complete mailing address and telephone number of your principal executive offices.

(c) *Risk Factors.* Where appropriate, provide under the caption "Risk Factors" a discussion of the most significant factors that make the offering speculative or risky. This discussion must be concise and organized logically. Do not present risks that could apply to any issuer or any offering. Explain how the risk affects the issuer or the securities being offered. Set forth each risk factor under a subcaption that adequately describes the risk. The risk factor discussion must immediately follow the summary section. If you do not include a summary section, the risk factor section must immediately follow the cover page of the prospectus or the pricing information section that immediately follows the cover page. Pricing information means price and price-related information that you may omit from the prospectus in an effective registration statement based on § 230.430A(a) of this chapter. The risk factors may include, among other things, the following:

(1) Your lack of an operating history;

(2) Your lack of profitable operations in recent periods;

(3) Your financial position;

(4) Your business or proposed business; or

(5) The lack of a market for your common equity securities or securities convertible into or exercisable for common equity securities.

(d) *Ratio of Earnings to Fixed Charges.* If you register debt securities, show a ratio of earnings to fixed charges. If you register preference equity securities, show the ratio of combined fixed charges and preference dividends to earnings. Present the ratio for each of the last five fiscal years and the latest interim period for which financial statements are presented in the document. If you will use the proceeds from the sale of debt or preference securities to repay any of your outstanding debt or to retire other securities and the change in the ratio would be ten percent or greater, you must include a ratio showing the application of the proceeds, commonly referred to as the pro forma ratio.

Instructions to paragraph 503(d)

1. *Definitions.* In calculating the ratio of earnings to fixed charges, you must use the following definitions:

(A) *Fixed charges.* The term "fixed charges" means the sum of the following: (a) interest expensed and capitalized, (b) amortized premiums, discounts and capitalized expenses related to indebtedness, (c) an estimate of the interest within rental expense, and (d) preference security dividend requirements of consolidated subsidiaries.

(B) *Preference security dividend.* The term "preference security dividend" is the amount of pre-tax earnings that is required to pay the dividends on outstanding preference securities. The dividend requirement must be computed as the amount of the dividend divided by (1 minus the effective income tax rate applicable to continuing operations).

(C) *Earnings.* The term "earnings" is the amount resulting from adding and subtracting the following items. Add the following: (a) pretax income from continuing operations before adjustment for minority interests in consolidated subsidiaries or income or loss from equity investees, (b) fixed charges, (c) amortization of capitalized interest, (d) distributed income of equity investees, and (e) your share of pre-tax losses of equity investees for which charges arising from guarantees are included in fixed charges. From the total of the added items, subtract the following: (a) interest capitalized, (b) preference security dividend requirements of consolidated subsidiaries, and (c) the minority interest in pre-tax income of subsidiaries that have not incurred fixed charges. Equity investees are investments that you account for using the equity method of accounting. Public utilities following SFAS 71 should not add amortization of capitalized interest in determining earnings, nor reduce fixed charges by any allowance for funds used during construction.

2. *Disclosure.* Disclose the following information when showing the ratio of earnings to fixed charges:

(A) *Deficiency.* If a ratio indicates less than one-to-one coverage, disclose the dollar amount of the deficiency.

(B) *Pro forma ratio.* You may show the pro forma ratio only for the most recent fiscal year and the latest interim period. Use the net change in interest or dividends from the refinancing to calculate the pro forma ratio.

(C) *Foreign private issuers.* A foreign private issuer must show the ratio based on the figures in the primary financial statement. A foreign private issuer must show the ratio based on the figures resulting from the reconciliation to U.S. generally accepted accounting principles if this ratio is materially different.

(D) *Summary Section.* If you provide a summary or similar section in the prospectus, show the ratios in that section.

3. *Exhibit.* File an exhibit to the registration statement to show the figures used to calculate the ratios. See paragraph (b)(12) of Item 601 of Regulation S-K (17 CFR 229.601(b)(12)).

Item 504. Use of Proceeds

State the principal purposes for which the net proceeds to the registrant from the securities to be offered are intended to be used and the approximate amount intended to be used for each such purpose. Where registrant has no current specific plan for the proceeds, or a significant portion thereof, the registrant shall so state and discuss the principal reasons for the offering.

Instructions to Item 504. 1. Where less than all the securities to be offered may be sold and more than one use is listed for the proceeds, indicate the order of priority of such purposes and discuss the registrant's plans if substantially less than the maximum proceeds are obtained. Such discussion need not be included if underwriting arrangements with respect to such securities are such that, if any securities are sold to the public, it reasonably can be expected that the actual proceeds will not be substantially less than the aggregate proceeds to the registrant shown pursuant to Item 501 of Regulation S-K (§ 229.501).

2. Details of proposed expenditures need not be given; for example, there need be furnished only a brief outline of any program of construction or addition of equipment. Consideration should be given as to the need to include a discussion of certain matters addressed in the discussion and analysis of registrant's financial condition and results of operations, such as liquidity and capital expenditures.

3. If any material amounts of other funds are necessary to accomplish the specified purposes for which the proceeds are to be obtained, state the amounts and sources of such other funds needed for each such specified purpose and the sources thereof.

4. If any material part of the proceeds is to be used to discharge indebtedness, set forth the interest rate and maturity of such indebtedness. If the indebtedness to be discharged was incurred within one year, describe the use of the proceeds of such indebtedness other than short-term borrowings used for working capital.

5. If any material amount of the proceeds is to be used to acquire assets, otherwise than in the ordinary course of business, describe briefly and state the cost of the assets and, where such assets are to be acquired from affiliates of the registrant or their associates, give the names of the persons from whom they are to be acquired and set forth the principle followed in determining the cost to the registrant.

6. Where the registrant indicates that the proceeds may, or will, be used to finance acquisitions of other businesses, the identity of such businesses, if known, or, if not known, the nature of the businesses to be sought, the status of any negotiations with respect to the acquisition, and a brief description of such business shall be included. Where, however, pro forma financial statements reflecting such acquisition are not required by Regulation S-X to be included, in the registration statement, the possible

terms of any transaction, the identification of the parties thereto or the nature of the business sought need not be disclosed, to the extent that the registrant reasonably determines that public disclosure of such information would jeopardize the acquisition. Where Regulation S-X [17 CFR 210] would require financial statements of the business to be acquired to be included, the description of the business to be acquired shall be more detailed.

7. The registrant may reserve the right to change the use of proceeds, provided that such reservation is due to certain contingencies that are discussed specifically and the alternatives to such use in that event are indicated.

Item 505. Determination of Offering Price

(a) *Common equity.* Where common equity is being registered for which there is no established public trading market for purposes of paragraph (a) of Item 201 of Regulation S-K (§ 229.201(a)) or where there is a material disparity between the offering price of the common equity being registered and the market price of outstanding shares of the same class, describe the various factors considered in determining such offering price.

(b) *Warrants, rights and convertible securities.* Where warrants, rights or convertible securities exercisable for common equity for which there is no established public trading market for purposes of paragraph (a) of Item 201 of Regulation S-K (§ 229.201(a)) are being registered, describe the various factors considered in determining their exercise or conversion price.

Item 506. Dilution

Where common equity securities are being registered and there is substantial disparity between the public offering price and the effective cash cost to officers, directors, promoters and affiliated persons of common equity acquired by them in transactions during the past five years, or which they have the right to acquire, and the registrant is not subject to the reporting requirements of section 13(a) or 15(d) of the Exchange Act immediately prior to filing of the registration statement, there shall be included a comparison of the public contribution under the proposed public offering and the effective cash contribution of such persons. In such cases, and in other instances where common equity securities are being registered by a registrant that has had losses in each of its last three fiscal years and there is a material dilution of the purchasers' equity interest, the following shall be disclosed:

(a) The net tangible book value per share before and after the distribution;

(b) The amount of the increase in such net tangible book value per share attributable to the cash payments made by purchasers of the shares being offered; and

(c) The amount of the immediate dilution from the public offering price which will be absorbed by such purchasers.

Item 507. Selling Security Holders

If any of the securities to be registered are to be offered for the account of security holders, name each such security holder, indicate the nature of any position, office, or other material relationship which the selling security holder has had within the past three years with the registrant or any of its predecessors or affiliates, and state the amount of securities of the class owned by such security holder prior to the offering, the amount to be offered for the security holder's account, the amount and (if one percent or more) the percentage of the class to be owned by such security holder after completion of the offering.

Item 508. Plan of Distribution

(a) *Underwriters and underwriting obligation.* If the securities are to be offered through underwriters, name the principal underwriters, and state the respective amounts underwritten. Identify each such underwriter having a material relationship with the registrant and state the nature of the relationship. State briefly the nature of the obligation of the underwriter(s) to take the securities.

Instruction to Paragraph 508(a). All that is required as to the nature of the underwriters' obligation is whether the underwriters are or will be committed to take and to pay for all of the securities if any are taken, or whether it is merely an agency or the type of "best efforts" arrangement under which the underwriters are required to take and to pay for only such securities as they may sell to the public. Conditions precedent to the underwriters' taking the securities, including "market-outs," need not be described except in the case of an agency or "best efforts" arrangement.

(b) *New underwriters.* Where securities being registered are those of a registrant that has not previously been required to file reports pursuant to section 13(a) or 15(d) of the Exchange Act, or where a prospectus is required to include reference on its cover page to material risks pursuant to Item 501 of Regulation S-K (§ 229.501), and any one or more of the managing underwriter(s) (or where there are no managing underwriters, a majority of the principal underwriters) has been organized, reactivated, or first registered as a broker-dealer within the past three years, these facts concerning such underwriter(s) shall be disclosed in the prospectus together with, where applicable, the disclosures that the principal business function of such underwriter(s) will be to sell the securities to be registered, or that the promoters of the registrant have a material relationship with such underwriter(s). Sufficient details shall be given to allow full appreciation of such underwriter(s) experience and its relationship with the registrant, promoters and their controlling persons.

(c) *Other distributions.* Outline briefly the plan of distribution of any securities to be registered that are to be offered otherwise than through underwriters.

(1) If any securities are to be offered pursuant to a dividend or interest reinvestment plan the terms of which provide for the purchase of some securities on the market, state whether the registrant or the participant pays fees, commissions, and expenses incurred in connection with the plan. If the participant will pay such fees, commissions and expenses, state the anticipated cost to participants by transaction or other convenient reference.

(2) If the securities are to be offered through the selling efforts of brokers or dealers, describe the plan of distribution and the terms of any agreement, arrangement, or understanding entered into with broker(s) or dealer(s) prior to the effective date of the registration statement, including volume limitations on sales, parties to the agreement and the conditions under which the agreement may be terminated. If known, identify the broker(s) or dealer(s) which will participate in the offering and state the amount to be offered through each.

(3) If any of the securities being registered are to be offered otherwise than for cash, state briefly the general purposes of the distribution, the basis upon which the securities are to be offered, the amount of compensation and other expenses of distribution, and by whom they are to be borne. If the distribution is to be made pursuant to a plan of acquisition, reorganization, readjustment or succession, describe briefly the general effect of the plan and state when it became or is to become operative. As to any material amount of assets to be acquired under the plan, furnish information corresponding to that required by Instruction 5 of Item 504 of Regulation S-K (§ 229.504).

(d) *Offerings on exchange.* If the securities are to be offered on an exchange, indicate the exchange. If the registered securities are to be offered in connection with the writing of exchange-traded call options, describe briefly such transactions.

(e) *Underwriter's compensation.* Provide a table that sets out the nature of the compensation and the amount of discounts and commissions to be paid to the underwriter for each security and in total. The table must show the separate amounts to be paid by the company and the selling shareholders. In addition, include in the table all other items considered by the National Association of Securities Dealers to be underwriting compensation for purposes of that Association's Rules of Fair Practice.

Instructions to paragraph 508(e)

1. The term "commissions" is defined in paragraph (17) of Schedule A of the Securities Act. Show separately in the table the cash commissions paid by the registrant and selling security holders. Also show in the table commissions paid by other persons. Disclose any finder's fee or similar payments in the table.

2. Disclose the offering expenses specified in Item 511 of Regulation S-K (17 CFR 229.511).

3. If the underwriter has any arrangement with the issuer, such as an over-allotment option, under which the underwriter may purchase additional shares in connection with the offering, indicate that this arrangement exists and state the amount of additional shares that the underwriter may purchase under the arrangement. Where the underwriter has such an arrangement, present maximum-minimum information in a separate column to the table, based on the purchase of all or none of the shares subject to the arrangement. Describe the key terms of the arrangement in the narrative.

(f) *Underwriter's representative on board of directors.* Describe any arrangement whereby the underwriter has the right to designate or nominate a member or members of the board of directors of the registrant. The registrant shall disclose the identity of any director so designated or nominated, and indicate whether or not a person so designated or nominated, or allowed to be designated or nominated by the underwriter is or may be a director, officer, partner, employee or affiliate of the underwriter.

(g) *Indemnification of underwriters.* If the underwriting agreement provides for indemnification by the registrant of the underwriters or their controlling persons against any liability arising under the Securities Act, furnish a brief description of such indemnification provisions.

(h) *Dealers' compensation.* State briefly the discounts and commissions to be allowed or paid to dealers, including all cash, securities, contracts or other considerations to be received by any dealer in connection with the sale of the securities. If any dealers are to act in the capacity of sub-underwriters and are to be allowed or paid any additional discounts or commissions for acting in such capacity, a general statement to that effect will suffice without giving the additional amounts to be sold.

(i) *Finders.* Identify any finder and, if applicable, describe the nature of any material relationship between such finder and the registrant, its officers, directors, principal stockholders, finders or promoters or the principal underwriter(s), or if there is a managing underwriter(s), the managing underwriter(s) (including, in each case, affiliates or associates thereof).

(j) *Discretionary accounts.* If the registrant was not, immediately prior to the filing of the registration statement, subject to the requirements of section 13(a) or 15(d) of the Exchange Act, identify any principal underwriter that intends to sell to any accounts over which it exercises discretionary authority and include an estimate of the amount of securities so intended to be sold. The response to this paragraph shall be contained in a pre-effective amendment which shall be circulated if the information is not available when the registration statement is filed.

(k) *Passive market making.* If the underwriters or any selling group members intend to engage in passive market making transactions as permitted by Rule 103 of Regulation M (§ 242.103 of this chapter), indicate such intention and briefly describe passive market making.

(l) *Stabilization and other transactions.* (1) Briefly describe any transaction that the underwriter intends to conduct during the offering that stabilizes, maintains, or otherwise affects the market price of the offered securities. Include information on stabilizing transactions, syndicate short covering transactions, penalty bids, or any other transaction that affects the offered security's price. Describe the nature of the transactions clearly and explain how the transactions affect the offered security's price. Identify the exchange or other market on which these transactions may occur. If true, disclose that the underwriter may discontinue these transactions at any time;

(2) If the stabilizing began before the effective date of the registration statement, disclose the amount of securities bought, the prices at which they were bought and the period within which they were bought. If you use § 230.430A of this chapter, the prospectus you file under § 230.424(b) of this chapter or include in a post-effective amendment must contain information on the stabilizing transactions that took place before the determination of the public offering price; and

(3) If you are making a warrants or rights offering of securities to existing security holders and any securities not purchased by existing security holders are to be reoffered to the public, disclose in a supplement to the prospectus or in the prospectus used in connection with the reoffering:

(i) The amount of securities bought in stabilization activities during the offering period and the price or range of prices at which the securities were bought;

(ii) The amount of the offered securities subscribed for during the offering period;

(iii) The amount of the offered securities subscribed for by the underwriter during the offering period;

(iv) The amount of the offered securities sold during the offering period by the underwriter and the price or price ranges at which the securities were sold; and

(v) The amount of the offered securities that will be reoffered to the public and the public offering price.

Item 509. Interests of Named Experts and Counsel

If (a) any expert named in the registration statement as having prepared or certified any part thereof (or is named as having prepared or certified a report or valuation for use in connection with the registration statement), or (b) counsel for the registrant, underwriters or selling security holders named in the prospectus as having given an opinion upon the validity of the securities being registered or upon other legal matters in connection with the registration or offering of such securities, was employed for such purpose on a contingent basis, or at the time of such preparation, certification or opinion or at any time thereafter through the date of effectiveness of the registration statement or that part of the registration statement to which such preparation, certification or opinion relates, had, or is to receive in connection with the offering, a substantial interest, direct or indirect, in the registrant or any of its parents or subsidiaries or was connected with the registrant or any of its parents or subsidiaries as a promoter, managing underwriter (or any principal underwriter, if there are no managing underwriters), voting trustee, director, officer, or employee, furnish a brief statement of the nature of such contingent basis, interest, or connection.

Instructions to Item 509. 1. The interest of an expert (other than an accountant) or counsel will not be deemed substantial and need not be disclosed if the interest, including the fair market value of all securities of the registrant owned, received and to be received, or subject to options, warrants or rights received or to be received by the expert or counsel does not exceed $50,000. For the purpose of this Instruction, the term "expert" or counsel includes the firm, corporation, partnership or other entity, if any, by which such expert or counsel is employed or of which he is a member or of counsel to and all attorneys in the case of counsel, and all nonclerical personnel in the case of named experts, participating in such matter on behalf of such firm, corporation, partnership or entity.

2. Accountants, providing a report on the financial statements, presented or incorporated by reference in the registration statement, should note § 210.2-01 of Regulation S-X (17 CFR 210) for the Commission's requirements regarding "Qualification of Accountants" which discusses disqualifying interests.

Item 510. Disclosure of Commission Position on Indemnification for Securities Act Liabilities

In addition to the disclosure prescribed by Item 702 of Regulation S-K (§ 229.702), if the undertaking required by paragraph (h) of Item 512 of Regulation S-K (§ 229.512) is not required to be included in the registration statement because acceleration of the effective date of the registration statement is not being requested, and if waivers have not been obtained comparable to those specified in paragraph (h), a brief description of the indemnification provisions relating to directors, officers and controlling persons of the registrant against liability arising under the Securities Act (including any provision of the underwriting agreement which relates to indemnification of the underwriter or its controlling persons by the registrant against such liabilities where a director, officer or controlling person of the registrant is such an underwriter or controlling person thereof or a member of any firm which is such an underwriter) shall be included in the prospectus, together with a statement in substantially the following form:

740

Insofar as indemnification for liabilities arising under the Securities Act of 1933 may be permitted to directors, officers or persons controlling the registrant pursuant to the foregoing provisions, the registrant has been informed that in the opinion of the Securities and Exchange Commission such indemnification is against public policy as expressed in the Act and is therefore unenforceable.

Item 511. Other Expenses of Issuance and Distribution

Furnish a reasonably itemized statement of all expenses in connection with the issuance and distribution of the securities to be registered, other than underwriting discounts and commissions. If any of the securities to be registered are to be offered for the account of security holders, indicate the portion of such expenses to be borne by such security holder.

Instruction to Item 511. Insofar as practicable, registration fees, Federal taxes, States taxes and fees, trustees' and transfer agents' fees, costs of printing and engraving, and legal, accounting, and engineering fees shall be itemized separately. Include as a separate item any premium paid by the registrant or any selling security holder on any policy obtained in connection with the offering and sale of the securities being registered which insures or indemnifies directors or officers against any liabilities they may incur in connection with the registration, offering, or sale of such securities. The information may be given as subject to future contingencies. If the amounts of any items are not known, estimates, identified as such, shall be given.

Item 512. Undertakings

Include each of the following undertakings that is applicable to the offering being registered.

(a) *Rule 415 offering.*[1] Include the following if the securities are registered pursuant to Rule 415 under the Securities Act (§ 230.415 of this chapter):

The undersigned registrant hereby undertakes:

(1) To file, during any period in which offers or sales are being made, a post-effective amendment to this registration statement:

(i) To include any prospectus required by section 10(a)(3) of the Securities Act of 1933;

(ii) To reflect in the prospectus any facts or events arising after the effective date of the registration statement (or the most recent post-effective amendment thereof) which, individually or in the aggregate, represent a fundamental change in the information set forth in the registration statement. Notwithstanding the foregoing, any increase or decrease in volume of securities offered (if the total dollar value of securities offered would not exceed that which was registered) and any deviation from the low or high end of the estimated maximum offering range may be reflected in the form of prospectus filed with the Commission pursuant to Rule 424(b) (§ 230.424(b) of this chapter) if, in the aggregate, the changes in volume and price represent no more than a 20% change in the maximum aggregate offering price set forth in the "Calculation of Registration Fee" table in the effective registration statement;

(iii) To include any material information with respect to the plan of distribution not previously disclosed in the registration statement or any material change to such information in the registration statement;

Provided, however, That paragraphs (a)(1)(i) and (a)(1)(ii) of this section do not apply if the registration statement is on Form S-3 (§ 239.13 of this chapter), Form S-8 (§ 239.16b of this chapter) or Form F-3 (§ 239.33 of this chapter), and the information required to be included in a post-effective amendment by those paragraphs is contained in periodic reports filed with or furnished to the Commission by the registrant pursuant to section 13 or section 15(d) of the Securities Exchange Act of 1934 that are incorporated by reference in the registration statement.

(2) That, for the purpose of determining any liability under the Securities Act of 1933, each such post-effective amendment shall be deemed to be a new registration statement relating to the

---

[1] Paragraph (a) reflects proposals made in Securities Act Release No. 6334 (Aug. 6, 1981).

securities offered therein, and the offering of such securities at that time shall be deemed to be the initial bona fide offering thereof.

(3) To remove from registration by means of a post-effective amendment any of the securities being registered which remain unsold at the termination of the offering.

(4) If the registrant is a foreign private issuer, to file a post-effective amendment to the registration statement to include any financial statements required by Item 8.A of Form 20-F (17 CFR 249.220f) at the start of any delayed offering or throughout a continuous offering. Financial statements and information otherwise required by Section 10(a)(3) of the Act need not be furnished, *provided* that the registrant includes in the prospectus, by means of a post-effective amendment, financial statements required pursuant to this paragraph (a)(4) and other information necessary to ensure that all other information in the prospectus is at least as current as the date of those financial statements. Notwithstanding the foregoing, with respect to registration statements on Form F-3 (§ 239.33 of this chapter), a post-effective amendment need not be filed to include financial statements and information required by Section 10(a)(3) of the Act or § 210.3-19 of this chapter if such financial statements and information are contained in periodic reports filed with or furnished to the Commission by the registrant pursuant to section 13 or section 15(d) of the Securities Exchange Act of 1934 that are incorporated by reference in the Form F-3.

(b) *Filings incorporating subsequent Exchange Act documents by reference.* Include the following if the registration statement incorporates by reference any Exchange Act document filed subsequent to the effective date of the registration statement:

> The undersigned registrant hereby undertakes that, for purposes of determining any liability under the Securities Act of 1933, each filing of the registrant's annual report pursuant to section 13(a) or section 15(d) of the Securities Exchange Act of 1934 (and, where applicable, each filing of an employee benefit plan's annual report pursuant to section 15(d) of the Securities Exchange Act of 1934) that is incorporated by reference in the registration statement shall be deemed to be a new registration statement relating to the securities offered therein, and the offering of such securities at that time shall be deemed to be the initial bona fide offering thereof.

(c) *Warrants and rights offerings.* Include the following, with appropriate modifications to suit the particular case, if the securities to be registered are to be offered to existing security holders pursuant to warrants or rights and any securities not taken by security holders are to be reoffered to the public:

> The undersigned registrant hereby undertakes to supplement the prospectus, after the expiration of the subscription period, to set forth the results of the subscription offer, the transactions by the underwriters during the subscription period, the amount of unsubscribed securities to be purchased by the underwriters, and the terms of any subsequent reoffering thereof. If any public offering by the underwriters is to be made on terms differing from those set forth on the cover page of the prospectus, a post-effective amendment will be filed to set forth the terms of such offering.

(d) *Competitive bids.* Include the following, with appropriate modifications to suit the particular case, if the securities to be registered are to be offered at competitive bidding:

> The undersigned registrant hereby undertakes (1) to use its best efforts to distribute prior to the opening of bids, to prospective bidders, underwriters, and dealers, a reasonable number of copies of a prospectus which at that time meets the requirements of section 10(a) of the Act, and relating to the securities offered at competitive bidding, as contained in the registration statement, together with any supplements thereto, and (2) to file an amendment to the registration statement reflecting the results of bidding, the terms of the reoffering and related matters to the extent required by the applicable form, not later than the first use, authorized by the issuer after the opening of bids, of a prospectus relating to the securities offered at competitive bidding, unless no further public offering of such securities by the issuer and no reoffering of such securities by the purchasers is proposed to be made.

(e) *Incorporated annual and quarterly reports.* Include the following if the registration statement specifically incorporates by reference (other than by indirect incorporation by reference through a Form 10-K and Form 10-KSB (§ 249.310 and § 249.310b of this chapter) report) in the prospectus all or any part of the annual report to security holders meeting the requirements of Rule 14a-3 or Rule 14c-3 under the Exchange Act (§ § 240.14a-3 and 240.14c-3 of this chapter):

> The undersigned registrant hereby undertakes to deliver or cause to be delivered with the prospectus, to each person to whom the prospectus is sent or given, the latest annual report to security holders that is incorporated by reference in the prospectus and furnished pursuant to and meeting the requirements of Rule 14a-3 or Rule 14c-3 under the Securities Exchange Act of 1934; and, where interim financial information required to be presented by Article 3 of Regulation S-X are not set forth in the prospectus, to deliver, or cause to be delivered to each person to whom the prospectus is sent or given, the latest quarterly report that is specifically incorporated by reference in the prospectus to provide such interim financial information.

(f) *Equity offerings of nonreporting registrants.* Include the following if equity securities of a registrant that prior to the offering had no obligation to file reports with the Commission pursuant to section 13(a) or 15(d) of the Exchange Act are being registered for sale in an underwritten offering:

> The undersigned registrant hereby undertakes to provide to the underwriter at the closing specified in the underwriting agreements certificates in such denominations and registered in such names as required by the underwriter to permit prompt delivery to each purchaser.

(g) *Registration on Form S-4 or F-4 of securities offered for resale.* Include the following if the securities are being registered on Form S-4 or F-4 (§ 239.23, 25 or 34 of this chapter) in connection with a transaction specified in paragraph (a) of Rule 145 (§ 230.145 of this chapter).

(1) The undersigned registrant hereby undertakes as follows: that prior to any public reoffering of the securities registered hereunder through use of a prospectus which is a part of this registration statement, by any person or party who is deemed to be an underwriter within the meaning of Rule 145(c), the issuer undertakes that such reoffering prospectus will contain the information called for by the applicable registration form with respect to reofferings by persons who may be deemed underwriters, in addition to the information called for by the other Items of the applicable form.

(2) The registrant undertakes that every prospectus (i) that is filed pursuant to paragraph (1) immediately preceding, or (ii) that purports to meet the requirements of section 10(a)(3) of the Act and is used in connection with an offering of securities subject to Rule 415 (§ 230.415 of this chapter), will be filed as a part of an amendment to the registration statement and will not be used until such amendment is effective, and that, for purposes of determining any liability under the Securities Act of 1933, each such post-effective amendment shall be deemed to be a new registration statement relating to the securities offered therein, and the offering of such securities at that time shall be deemed to be the initial bona fide offering thereof.

(h) *Request for acceleration of effective date or filing of registration statement on Form S-8.* Include the following if acceleration is requested of the effective date of the registration statement pursuant to Rule 461 under the Securities Act (§ 230.461 of this chapter), or if the registration statement is filed on Form S-8, and: (1) any provision or arrangement exists whereby the registrant may indemnify a director, officer or controlling person of the registrant against liabilities arising under the Securities Act, or (2) the underwriting agreement contains a provision whereby the registrant indemnifies the underwriter or controlling persons of the underwriter against such liabilities and a director, officer or controlling person of the registrant is such an underwriter or controlling person thereof or a member of any firm which is such an underwriter, and (3) the benefits of such indemnification are not waived by such persons:

> Insofar as indemnification for liabilities arising under the Securities Act of 1933 may be permitted to directors, officers and controlling persons of the registrant pursuant to the foregoing provisions, or otherwise, the registrant has been advised that in the opinion of the Securities and Exchange Commission such indemnification is against public policy as expressed in the Act and is, therefore, unenforceable. In the event that a claim for indemnification against such liabilities (other than the payment by the registrant of

expenses incurred or paid by a director, officer or controlling person of the registrant in the successful defense of any action, suit or proceeding) is asserted by such director, officer or controlling person in connection with the securities being registered, the registrant will, unless in the opinion of its counsel the matter has been settled by controlling precedent, submit to a court of appropriate jurisdiction the question whether such indemnification by it is against public policy as expressed in the Act and will be governed by the final adjudication of such issue.

(i) Include the following in a registration statement permitted by Rule 430A under the Securities Act of 1933 [§ 230.430A of this chapter]:

The undersigned registrant hereby undertakes that:

(1) For purposes of determining any liability under the Securities Act of 1933, the information omitted from the form of prospectus filed as part of this registration statement in reliance upon Rule 430A and contained in a form of prospectus filed by the registrant pursuant to Rule 424(b)(1) or (4) or 497(h) under the Securities Act shall be deemed to be part of this registration statement as of the time it was declared effective.

(2) For the purpose of determining any liability under the Securities Act of 1933, each post-effective amendment that contains a form of prospectus shall be deemed to be a new registration statement relating to the securities offered therein, and the offering of such securities at that time shall be deemed to be the initial bona fide offering thereof.

(j) *Qualification of trust indentures under the Trust Indenture Act of 1939 for delayed offerings.* Include the following if the registrant intends to rely on Section 305(b)(2) of the Trust Indenture Act of 1939 for determining the eligibility of the trustee under indentures for securities to be issued, offered, or sold on a delayed basis by or on behalf of the registrant:

"The undersigned registrant hereby undertakes to file an application for the purpose of determining the eligibility of the trustee to act under subsection (a) of Section 310 of the Trust Indenture Act ('Act') in accordance with the rules and regulations prescribed by the Commission under Section 305(b)(2) of the Act."

Subpart 600—Exhibits

Item 601. Exhibits

(a) *Exhibits and index required.*

(1) Subject to Rule 411(c) (§ 230.411(c) of this chapter) under the Securities Act and Rule 12b-32 (§ 240.12b-32 of this chapter) under the Exchange Act regarding incorporation of exhibits by reference, the exhibits required in the exhibit table shall be filed as indicated, as part of the registration statement or report.

(2) Each registration statement or report shall contain an exhibit index, which shall precede immediately the exhibits filed with such registration statement. For convenient reference, each exhibit shall be listed in the exhibit index according to the number assigned to it in the exhibit table. The exhibit index shall indicate, by handwritten, typed, printed, or other legible form of notation in the manually signed original registration statement or report, the page number in the sequential numbering system where such exhibit can be found. Where exhibits are incorporated by reference, this fact shall be noted in the exhibit index referred to in the preceding sentence. Further, the first page of the manually signed registration statement shall list the page in the filing where the exhibit index is located. For a description of each of the exhibits included in the exhibit table, see paragraph (b) of this Item.

(3) This Item applies only to the forms specified in the exhibit table. With regard to forms not listed in that table, reference shall be made to the appropriate form for the specific exhibit filing requirements applicable thereto.

(4) If a material contract or plan of acquisition, reorganization, arrangement, liquidation or succession is executed or becomes effective during the reporting period reflected by a Form 10-Q or Form 10-K, it shall be filed as an exhibit to the Form 10-Q or Form 10-K filed for the corresponding period. Any amendment or modification to a previously filed exhibit to a Form 10, 10-K or 10-Q document shall be filed as an exhibit to a Form 10-Q or Form 10-K. Such amendment

or modification need not be filed where such previously filed exhibit would not be currently required.

    Instructions to Item 601. 1. If an exhibit to a registration statement (other than an opinion or consent), filed in preliminary form, has been changed only (A) to insert information as to interest, dividend or conversion rates, redemption or conversion prices, purchase or offering prices, underwriters' or dealers' commissions, names, addresses or participation of underwriters or similar matters, which information appears elsewhere in an amendment to the registration statement or a prospectus filed pursuant to Rule 424(b) under the Securities Act [§ 230.424(b) of this chapter], or (B) to correct typographical errors, insert signatures or make other similar immaterial changes, then, notwithstanding any contrary requirement of any rule or form, the registrant need not refile such exhibit as so amended. Any such incomplete exhibit may not, however, be incorporated by reference in any subsequent filing under any Act administered by the Commission.

    2. In any case where two or more indentures, contracts, franchises, or other documents required to be filed as exhibits are substantially identical in all material respects except as to the parties thereto, the dates of execution, or other details, the registrant need file a copy of only one of such documents, with a schedule identifying the other documents omitted and setting forth the material details in which such documents differ from the document a copy of which is filed. The Commission may at any time in its discretion require filing of copies of any documents so omitted.

    3. Only copies, rather than originals, need be filed of each exhibit required except as otherwise specifically noted.

    4. *Electronic filings.* Whenever an exhibit is filed in paper pursuant to a hardship exemption (§§ 232.201 and 232.202 of this chapter), the letter "P" (paper) shall be placed next to the exhibit in the list of exhibits required by Item 601(a)(2) of this Rule. Whenever an electronic confirming copy of an exhibit is filed pursuant to a hardship exemption (§ 232.201 or § 232.202(d) of this chapter), the exhibit index should specify where the confirming electronic copy can be located; in addition, the designation "CE" (confirming electronic) should be placed next to the listed exhibit in the exhibit index.

Exhibit Table

Instructions to the Exhibit Table. 1. The exhibit table indicates those documents that must be filed as exhibits to the respective forms listed.

    2. The "X" designation indicates the documents which are required to be filed with each form even if filed previously with another document. *Provided, however,* that such previously filed documents may be incorporated by reference to satisfy the filing requirements.

    3. The number used in the far left column of the table refers to the appropriate subsection in paragraph (b) where a description of the exhibit can be found. Whenever necessary, alphabetical or numerical subparts may be used.

EXHIBIT TABLE

	Securities Act Forms										Exchange Act Forms			
	S-1	S-2	S-3	S-4³	S-8	S-11	F-1	F-2	F-3	F-4³	10	8-K⁵	10-Q	10-K
(1) Underwriting agreement	X	X	X	X	—	X	X	X	X	X	—	X	—	—
(2) Plan of acquisition, reorganization, arrangement, liquidation or succession	X	X	X	X	—	X	X	X	X	X	X	X	X	X
(3) (i) Articles of incorporation	X	—	—	X	—		X	—	—	X	X	X	X	X
(ii) Bylaws	X	—	—	X	—	X	X	—	—	X	X	X	X	X
			—			X			—					
						X								
(4) Instruments defining the rights of security holders, including indentures	X	X	X	X	X	X	X	X	X	X	X	X	X	X

EXHIBIT TABLE

	Securities Act Forms										Exchange Act Forms			
	S-1	S-2	S-3	S-4[3]	S-8	S-11	F-1	F-2	F-3	F-4[3]	10	8-K[5]	10-Q	10-K
(5) Opinion re legality	X	X	X	X	X	X	X	X	X	X	—	—	—	—
(6) [Reserved]	N/A	N/A	N/A	N/A	N/A	N/A	N/A	N/A	N/A	N/A	N/A	N/A	N/A	N/A
(7) Correspondence from an independent accountant regarding non-reliance on a previously issued audit report or completed interim review	—	—	—	—	—	—	—	—	—	—	—	X	—	—
(8) Opinion re tax matters	X	X	X	X	—	X	X	X	X	X	—	—	—	—
(9) Voting trust agreement	X	—	—	X	—	X	X	—	—	X	X	—	—	X
(10) Material contracts	X	X	—	X	—	X	X	X	—	X	X	—	X	X
(11) Statement re computation of per share earnings	X	X	—	X	—	X	X	X	—	X	X	—	X	X
(12) Statements re computation of ratios	X	X	X	X	—	X	X	X	—	X	X	—	—	X
(13) Annual report to security holders, Form 10-Q and 10-QSB, or quarterly report to security holders[1]	—	X	—	X	—	—	—	—	—	—	—	—	—	X
(14) Code of Ethics														X
(15) Letter re unaudited interim financial information	X	X	X	X	X	X	X	X	X	X	—	—	X	—
(16) Letter re change in certifying accountant[4]	X	X	—	X	—	X	—	—	—	—	X	X	—	X
(17) Correspondence on departure of director	—	—	—	—	—	—	—	—	—	—	—	X	—	—
(18) Letter re change in accounting principles	—	—	—	—	—	—	—	—	—	—	—	—	X	X
(19) Report furnished to security holders	—	—	—	—	—	—	—	—	—	—	—	—	X	—
(20) Other documents or statements to security holders	—	—	—	—	—	—	—	—	—	—	—	X	—	—
(21) Subsidiaries of the registrant	X	—	—	X	—	X	X	—	—	X	X	—	—	X
(22) Published report regarding matters submitted to vote of security holders	—	—	—	—	—	—	—	—	—	—	—	—	X	X
(23) Consents of experts and counsel	X	X	X	X	X	X	X	X	X	X	—	X[2]	X[2]	X[2]
(24) Power of attorney	X	X	X	X	X	X	X	X	X	X	X	X	X	X
(25) Statement of eligibility of trustee	X	X	X	X	—	X	X	X	X	X	—	—	—	—
(26) Invitations for competitive bids	X	X	X	X	—	—	X	X	X	X	—	—	—	—
(27) through (30) [Reserved]														
(31) Rule 13a-14(a)/15d-14(a) Certifications	—	—	—	—	—	—	—	—	—	—	—	—	X	X

EXHIBIT TABLE

			Securities Act Forms							Exchange Act Forms			
	S-1	S-2	S-3	S-4[3]	S-8	S-11	F-1	F-2	F-3	F-4[3]	10	8-K[5]	10-Q	10-K
(32) Section 1350 Certifications	—	—	—	—	—	—	—	—	—	—	—	—	X	X
(33) through (98) [Reserved]	N/A	N/A	N/A	N/A	N/A	N/A	N/A	N/A	N/A	N/A	N/A	N/A	N/A	N/A
(99) Additional exhibits	X	X	X	X	X	X	X	X	X	X	X	X	X	X

[1] Where incorporated by reference into the text of the prospectus and delivered to security holders along with the prospectus as permitted by the registration statement; or, in the case of the Form 10-K, where the annual report to security holders is incorporated by reference into the text of the Form 10-K.

[2] Where the opinion of the expert or counsel has been incorporated by reference into a previously filed Securities Act registration statement.

[3] An exhibit need not be provided about a company if: (1) With respect to such company an election has been made under Form S-4 or F-4 to provide information about such company at a level prescribed by Forms S-2, S-3, F-2 or F-3 and (2) the form, the level of which has been elected under Forms S-4 or F-4, would not require such company to provide such exhibit if it were registering a primary offering.

[4] If required pursuant to Item 304 of Regulation S-K.

[5] A Form 8-K exhibit is required only if relevant to the subject matter reported on the Form 8-K report. For example, if the Form 8-K pertains to the departure of a director, only the exhibit described in paragraph (b)(17) of this section need be filed. A required exhibit may be incorporated by reference from a previous filing.

(b) *Description of exhibits.* Set forth below is a description of each document listed in the exhibit tables.

(1) *Underwriting agreement*—Each underwriting contract or agreement with a principal underwriter pursuant to which the securities being registered are to be distributed; if the terms of such documents have not been determined, the proposed forms thereof. Such agreement may be filed as an exhibit to a report on Form 8-K (§ 249.308 of this chapter) which is incorporated by reference into a registration statement subsequent to its effectiveness.

(2) *Plan of acquisition, reorganization, arrangement, liquidation or succession*—Any material plan of acquisition, disposition, reorganization, readjustment, succession, liquidation or arrangement and any amendments thereto described in the statement or report. Schedules (or similar attachments) to these exhibits shall not be filed unless such schedules contain information which is material to an investment decision and which is not otherwise disclosed in the agreement or the disclosure document. The plan filed shall contain a list briefly identifying the contents of all omitted schedules, together with an agreement to furnish supplementally a copy of any omitted schedule to the Commission upon request.

(3) (i) *Articles of incorporation.* The articles of incorporation of the registrant or instruments corresponding thereto as currently in effect and any amendments thereto. Whenever the registrant files an amendment to its articles of incorporation, it must file a complete copy of the articles as amended. However, if such amendment is being reported on Form 8-K (§ 249.308 of this chapter), the registrant is required to file only the text of the amendment as a Form 8-K exhibit. In such case, a complete copy of the articles of incorporation as amended must be filed as an exhibit to the next Securities Act registration statement or periodic report filed by the registrant to which this exhibit requirement applies. Where it is impracticable for the registrant to file a charter amendment authorizing new securities with the appropriate state authority prior to the effective date of the registration statement registering such securities, the registrant may file as an exhibit to the registration statement the form of amendment to be filed with the state authority. In such a case, if material changes are made after the copy is filed, the registrant must also file the changed copy.

(ii) *Bylaws.* The bylaws of the registrant or instruments corresponding thereto as currently in effect and any amendments thereto. Whenever the registrant files an amendment to the bylaws, it must file a complete copy of the amended bylaws. However, if such amendment is being reported on Form 8-K (§ 249.308 of this chapter), the registrant is required to file only the text of the amendment as a Form 8-K exhibit. In such case, a complete copy of the bylaws as amended must be filed as an exhibit to the next Securities Act registration statement or periodic report filed by the registrant to which this exhibit requirement applies.

(4) *Instruments defining the rights of security holders, including indentures*—(i) All instruments defining the rights of holders of the equity or debt securities being registered including, where applicable, the relevant portion of the articles of incorporation or by-laws of the registrant.

(ii) Except as set forth in (iii) below, for filings on Forms S-1, S-4, S-11, S-14 and F-4 under the Securities Act (§ § 239.1, 25, 18, 23 and 34 of this chapter) and Forms 10 and 10-K (§ § 249.210 and 310 of this chapter) under the Exchange Act all instruments defining the rights of holders of long-term debt of the registrant and its consolidated subsidiaries and for any of its unconsolidated subsidiaries for which financial statements are required to be filed.

(iii) Where the instrument defines the rights of holders of long-term debt of the registrant and its consolidated subsidiaries and for any of its unconsolidated subsidiaries for which financial statements are required to be filed, there need not be filed (A) any instrument with respect to long-term debt not being registered if the total amount of securities authorized thereunder does not exceed 10 percent of the total assets of the registrant and its subsidiaries on a consolidated basis and if there is filed an agreement to furnish a copy of such agreement to the Commission upon request; (B) any instrument with respect to any class of securities if appropriate steps to assure the redemption or retirement of such class will be taken prior to or upon delivery by the registrant of the securities being registered; or (C) copies of instruments evidencing scrip certificates for fractions of shares.

(iv) If any of the securities being registered are, or will be, issued under an indenture to be qualified under the Trust Indenture Act, the copy of such indenture which is filed as an exhibit shall include or be accompanied by (A) a reasonably itemized and informative table of contents; and (B) a cross-reference sheet showing the location in the indenture of the provisions inserted pursuant to sections 310 through 318(a) inclusive of the Trust Indenture Act of 1939.

(v) With respect to Forms 8-K and 10-Q under the Exchange Act which are filed and which disclose, in the text of the Form 10-Q, the interim financial statements, or the footnotes thereto, the creation of a new class of securities or indebtedness or the modification of existing rights of security holders, file all instruments defining the rights of holders of these securities or indebtedness. However, there need not be filed any instrument with respect to long-term debt not being registered which meets the exclusion set forth above in paragraph (iii) (A).

Instruction 1 to paragraph (b)(4). There need not be filed any instrument which defines the rights of participants (not as security holders) pursuant to an employee benefit plan.

Instruction 2 to paragraph (b)(4) (for electronic filings). If the instrument defining the rights of security holders is in the form of a certificate, the text appearing on the certificate shall be reproduced in an electronic filing together with a description of any other graphic and image material appearing on the certificate, as provided in Rule 304 of Regulation S-T (§ 232.304 of this chapter).

(5) *Opinion re legality*—(i) An opinion of counsel as to the legality of the securities being registered, indicating whether they will, when sold, be legally issued, fully paid and non-assessable, and, if debt securities, whether they will be binding obligations of the registrant.

(ii) If the securities being registered are issued under a plan and the plan is subject to the requirements of ERISA furnish either:

(A) An opinion of counsel which confirms compliance of the provisions of the written documents constituting the plan with the requirements of ERISA pertaining to such provisions; or

(B) A copy of the Internal Revenue Service determination letter that the plan is qualified under section 401 of the Internal Revenue Code; or

(iii) If the securities being registered are issued under a plan which is subject to the requirements of ERISA and the plan has been amended subsequent to the filing of (ii) (A) or (B) above, furnish either:

(A) An opinion of counsel which confirms compliance of the amended provisions of the plan with the requirements of ERISA pertaining to such provisions; or

(B) A copy of the Internal Revenue Service determination letter that the amended plan is qualified under section 401 of the Internal Revenue Code.

Note: Attention is directed to Item 8 of Form S-8 for exemptions to this exhibit requirement applicable to that Form.

(6) [Reserved.]

(7) *Correspondence from an independent accountant regarding non-reliance on a previously issued audit report or completed interim review.* Any written notice from the registrant's current or previously engaged independent accountant that the independent accountant is withdrawing a previously issued audit report or that a previously issued audit report or completed interim review, covering one or more years or interim periods for which the registrant is required to provide financial statements under Regulation S-X (part 210 of this chapter), should no longer be relied upon. In addition, any letter, pursuant to Item 4.02(c) of Form 8-K (§ 249.308 of this chapter), from the independent accountant to the Commission stating whether the independent accountant agrees with the statements made by the registrant describing the events giving rise to the notice.

(8) *Opinion re tax matters*—For filings on Form S-11 under the Securities Act (§ 239.18) or those to which Securities Act Industry Guide 5 applies, an opinion of counsel or of an independent public or certified public accountant or, in lieu thereof, a revenue ruling from the Internal Revenue Service, supporting the tax matters and consequences to the shareholders as described in the filing when such tax matters are material to the transaction for which the registration statement is being filed. This exhibit otherwise need only be filed with the other applicable registration forms where the tax consequences are material to an investor and a representation as to tax consequences is set forth in the filing. If a tax opinion is set forth in full in the filing, an indication that such is the case may be made in lieu of filing the otherwise required exhibit. Such tax opinions may be conditioned or may be qualified, so long as such conditions and qualifications are adequately described in the filing.

(9) *Voting trust agreement* —Any voting trust agreements and amendments thereto.

(10) *Material contracts*—(i) Every contract not made in the ordinary course of business which is material to the registrant and is to be performed in whole or in part at or after the filing of the registration statement or report or was entered into not more than two years before such filing. Only contracts need be filed as to which the registrant or subsidiary of the registrant is a party or has succeeded to a party by assumption or assignment or in which the registrant or such subsidiary has a beneficial interest.

(ii) If the contract is such as ordinarily accompanies the kind of business conducted by the registrant and its subsidiaries, it will be deemed to have been made in the ordinary course of business and need not be filed unless it falls within one or more of the following categories, in which case it shall be filed except where immaterial in amount or significance:

(A) Any contract to which directors, officers, promoters, voting trustees, security holders named in the registration statement or report, or underwriters are parties other than contracts involving only the purchase or sale of current assets having a determinable market price, at such market price;

(B) Any contract upon which the registrant's business is substantially dependent, as in the case of continuing contracts to sell the major part of registrant's products or services or to purchase the major part of registrant's requirements of goods, services or raw materials or any franchise or license or other agreement to use a patent, formula, trade secret, process or trade name upon which registrant's business depends to a material extent;

(C) Any contract calling for the acquisition or sale of any property, plant or equipment for a consideration exceeding 15 percent of such fixed assets of the registrant on a consolidated basis; or

(D) Any material lease under which a part of the property described in the registration statement or report is held by the registrant.

(iii)(A) Any management contract or any compensatory plan, contract or arrangement, including but not limited to plans relating to options, warrants or rights, pension, retirement or deferred compensation or bonus, incentive or profit sharing (or if not set forth in any formal document, a written description thereof) in which any director or any of the named executive officers of the registrant, as defined by Item 402(a)(3) (§ 229.402(a)(31), participates shall be deemed material and shall be filed; and any other management contract or any compensatory plan, contract, or arrangement in which any other executive officer of the registrant participates shall be filed unless immaterial in amount or significance.

(B) Any compensatory plan, contract or arrangement adopted without the approval of security holders pursuant to which equity may be awarded, including, but not limited to, options, warrants or rights (or if not set forth in any formal document, a written description thereof), in which any employee (whether or not an executive officer of the registrant) participates shall be filed unless immaterial in amount or significance. A compensation plan assumed by a registrant in connection with a merger, consolidation or other acquisition transaction pursuant to which the registrant may make further grants or awards of its equity securities shall be considered a compensation plan of the registrant for purposes of the preceding sentence.

(C) Notwithstanding paragraph (iii)(A) above, the following management contracts or compensatory plans, contracts or arrangements need not be filed:

(1) Ordinary purchase and sales agency agreements.

(2) Agreements with managers of stores in a chain organization or similar organization.

(3) Contracts providing for labor or salesmen's bonuses or payments to a class of security holders, as such.

(4) Any compensatory plan, contract or arrangement which pursuant to its terms is available to employees, officers or directors generally and which in operation provides for the same method of allocation of benefits between management and nonmanagement participants.

(5) Any compensatory plan, contract or arrangement if the registrant is a foreign private issuer that furnishes compensatory information on an aggregate basis as permitted by General Instruction 1 to Item 402 (§ 229.402) or by Item 6.B of Form 20-F (§ 249.220f of this chapter).

(6) Any compensatory plan, contract, or arrangement if the registrant is a wholly owned subsidiary of a company that has a class of securities registered pursuant to section 12 or files reports pursuant to section 15(d) of the Exchange Act and is filing a report on Form 10-K and Form 10-KSB or registering debt instruments or preferred stock which are not voting securities on Form S-2.

Instruction 1 to paragraph (b)(10). With the exception of management contracts, in order to comply with paragraph (iii) above, registrants need only file copies of the various remunerative plans and need not file each individual director's or executive officer's personal agreement under the plans unless there are particular provisions in such personal agreements whose disclosure in an exhibit is necessary to an investor's understanding of that individual's compensation under the plan.

Instruction 2 to paragraph (b)(10). If a material contract is executed or becomes effective during the reporting period reflected by a Form 10-Q or Form 10-K, it shall be filed as an exhibit to the Form 10-Q or Form 10-K filed for the corresponding period. *See* paragraph (a)(4) of this Item. With respect to quarterly reports on Form 10-Q, only those contracts executed or becoming effective during the most recent period reflected in the report shall be filed.

(11) *Statement re computation of per share earnings.* A statement setting forth in reasonable detail the computation of per share earnings, unless the computation can be clearly determined from the material contained in the registration statement or report. The information with respect to the computation of per share earnings on both primary and fully diluted bases, presented by exhibit or otherwise, must be furnished even though the amounts of per share earnings on the fully diluted basis are not required to be presented in the income statement under the provisions of Accounting Principles Board Opinion No. 15. That Opinion provides that any reduction of less than 3% need not be considered as dilution (see footnote to paragraph 14 of the Opinion) and that a computation on the fully diluted basis which results in improvement of earnings per share not be taken into account (see paragraph 40 of the Opinion).

(12) *Statements re computation of ratios*—A statement setting forth in reasonable detail the computation of any ratio of earnings to fixed charges, any ratio of earnings to combined fixed charges and preferred stock dividends or any other ratios which appear in the registration statement or report. See Item 503(d) of Regulation S-K (§ 229.503(d)).

(13) *Annual report to security holders, Form 10-Q or 10-QSB, or quarterly report to security holders*—(i) The registrant's annual report to security holders for its last fiscal year, its Form 10-Q and Form 10-QSB (if specifically incorporated by reference in the prospectus) or its quarterly

report to security holders, if all or a portion thereof is incorporated by reference in the filing. Such report, except for those portions thereof which are expressly incorporated by reference in the filing, is to be furnished for the information of the Commission and is not to be deemed "filed" as part of the filing. If the financial statements in the report have been incorporated by reference in the filing, the accountant's certificate shall be manually signed in one copy. See Rule 411(b) (§ 230.411(b) of this chapter).

(ii) *Electronic filings.* If all, or any portion, of the annual or quarterly report to security holders is incorporated by reference into any electronic filing, all, or such portion of the annual or quarterly report to security holders so incorporated, shall be filed in electronic format as an exhibit to the filing.

(14) *Code of ethics.* Any code of ethics, or amendment thereto, that is the subject of the disclosure required by Item 406 of Regulation S-K (-229.406) or Item 10 of Form 8-K (-249.308 of this chapter), to the extent that the registrant intends to satisfy the Item 406 or Item 10 requirements through filing of an exhibit.

(15) *Letter re unaudited interim financial information*—A letter, where applicable, from the independent accountant which acknowledges awareness of the use in a registration statement of a report on unaudited interim financial information which pursuant to Rule 436(c) under the Securities Act (§ 230.436(c) of this chapter) is not considered a part of a registration statement prepared or certified by an accountant or a report prepared or certified by an accountant within the meaning of sections 7 and 11 of that Act. Such letter may be filed with the registration statement, an amendment thereto, or a report on Form 10-Q which is incorporated by reference into the registration statement.

(16) *Letter re change in certifying accountant* —A letter from the registrant's former independent accountant regarding its concurrence or disagreement with the statements made by the registrant in the current report concerning the resignation or dismissal as the registrant's principal accountant.

(17) *Correspondence on departure of director.* Any written correspondence from a former director concerning the circumstances surrounding the former director's retirement, resignation, refusal to stand for re-election or removal, including any letter from the former director to the registrant stating whether the former director agrees with statements made by the registrant describing the former director's departure.

(18) *Letter re change in accounting principles*—Unless previously filed, a letter from the registrant's independent accountant indicating whether any change in accounting principles or practices followed by the registrant, or any change in the method of applying any such accounting principles or practices, which affected the financial statements being filed with the Commission in the report or which is reasonably certain to affect the financial statements of future fiscal years is to an alternative principle which in his judgment is preferable under the circumstances. No such letter need be filed when such change is made in response to a standard adopted by the Financial Accounting Standards Board that creates a new accounting principle, that expresses a preference for an accounting principle, or that rejects a specific accounting principle.

(19) *Report furnished to security holders*—If the registrant makes available to its stockholders or otherwise publishes, within the period prescribed for filing the report, a document or statement containing information meeting some or all of the requirements of Part I of Form 10-Q, the information called for may be incorporated by reference to such published document or statement provided copies thereof are included as an exhibit to the registration statement or to Part I of the Form 10-Q report.

(20) *Other documents or statements to security holders*—If the registrant makes available to its stockholders or otherwise publishes, within the period prescribed for filing the report, a document or statement containing information meeting some or all of the requirements of this form the information called for may be incorporated by reference to such published document or statement provided copies thereof are filed as an exhibit to the report on this form.

(21) *Subsidiaries of the registrant* —(i) List all subsidiaries of the registrant, the state or other jurisdiction of incorporation or organization of each, and the names under which such subsidiaries

do business. This list may be incorporated by reference from a document which includes a complete and accurate list.

(ii) The names of particular subsidiaries may be omitted if the unnamed subsidiaries, considered in the aggregate as a single subsidiary, would not constitute a significant subsidiary as of the end of the year covered by this report. (See the definition of "significant subsidiary" in Rule 1-02(w) (17 CFR 210.1-02(w)) of Regulation S-X.) The names of consolidated wholly-owned multiple subsidiaries carrying on the same line of business, such as chain stores or small loan companies, may be omitted, provided the name of the immediate parent, the line of business, the number of omitted subsidiaries operating in the United States and the number operating in foreign countries are given. This instruction shall not apply, however, to banks, insurance companies, savings and loan associations or to any subsidiary subject to regulation by another Federal agency.

(22) *Published report regarding matters submitted to vote of security holders*— Published reports containing all of the information called for by Item 4 of Part II of Form 10-Q or Item 4 of Part I of Form 10-K which is referred to therein in lieu of providing disclosure in Form 10-Q or 10-K, which are required to be filed as exhibits by Rule 12b-23(a)(3) under the Exchange Act (§ 240.12b-23(a)(3) of this chapter).

(23) *Consents of experts and counsel* —(i) Securities Act filings—All written consents required to be filed shall be dated and manually signed. Where the consent of an expert or counsel is contained in his report or opinion or elsewhere in the registration statement or document filed therewith, a reference shall be made in the index to the report, the part of the registration statement or document or opinion, containing the consent.

(ii) Exchange Act reports—where the filing of a written consent is required with respect to material incorporated by reference in a previously filed registration statement under the Securities Act, such consent may be filed as an exhibit to the material incorporated by reference. Such consents shall be dated and manually signed.

(24) *Power of attorney*—If any name is signed to the registration statement or report pursuant to power of attorney, manually signed copies of such power of attorney shall be filed. Where the power of attorney is contained elsewhere in the registration statement or documents filed therewith a reference shall be made in the index to the part of the registration statement or document containing such power of attorney. In addition, if the name of any officer signing on behalf of the registrant is signed pursuant to a power of attorney, certified copies of a resolution of the registrant's board of directors authorizing such signature shall also be filed. A power of attorney that is filed with the Commission shall relate to a specific filing or an amendment thereto, provided, however, that a power of attorney relating to a registration statement under the Securities Act or an amendment thereto also may relate to any registration statement for the same offering that is to be effective upon filing pursuant to Rule 462(b) under the Securities Act (§ 230.462(b) of this chapter). A power of attorney that is filed with the Commission shall relate to a specific filing or an amendment thereto. A power of attorney that confers general authority shall not be filed with the Commission.

(25) *Statement of eligibility of trustee*—(i) A statement of eligibility and qualification of each person designated to act as trustee under an indenture to be qualified under the Trust Indenture Act of 1939. Such statement of eligibility shall be bound separately from the other exhibits.

(ii) *Electronic filings.* The requirement to bind separately the statement of eligibility and qualification of each person designated to act as a trustee under the Trust Indenture Act of 1939 from other exhibits shall not apply to statements submitted in electronic format. Rather, such statements must be submitted as exhibits in the same electronic submission as the registration statement to which they relate, or in an amendment thereto, except that electronic filers that rely on Trust Indenture Act Section 305(b)(2) for determining the eligibility of the trustee under indentures for securities to be issued, offered or sold on a delayed basis by or on behalf of the registrant shall file such statements separately in the manner prescribed by § 260.5b-1 through § 260.5b-3 of this chapter and by the EDGAR Filer Manual.

(26) *Invitations for competitive bids*—If the registration statement covers securities to be offered at competitive bidding, any form of communication which is an invitation for competitive bid which will be sent or given to any person shall be filed.

(27) through (30) [Reserved]

(31) *Rule 13a-14(a)/15d-14(a) Certifications.* The certifications required by Rule 13a-14(a) (17 CFR 240.13a-14(a)) or Rule 15d-14(a) (17 CFR 240.15d-14(a)) exactly as set forth below:

CERTIFICATIONS

I, [identify the certifying individual], certify that:

I have reviewed this [specify report] of [identify registrant];

Based on my knowledge, this report does not contain any untrue statement of a material fact or omit to state a material fact necessary to make the statements made, in light of the circumstances under which such statements were made, not misleading with respect to the period covered by this report;

Based on my knowledge, the financial statements, and other financial information included in this report, fairly present in all material respects the financial condition, results of operations and cash flows of the registrant as of, and for, the periods presented in this report;

The registrant's other certifying officer(s) and I are responsible for establishing and maintaining disclosure controls and procedures (as defined in Exchange Act Rules 13a-15(e) and 15d-15(e)) and internal control over financial reporting (as defined in Exchange Act Rules 13a-15(f) and 15d-15(f)) for the registrant and have: (a) Designed such disclosure controls and procedures, or caused such disclosure controls and procedures to be designed under our supervision, to ensure that material information relating to the registrant, including its consolidated subsidiaries, is made known to us by others within those entities, particularly during the period in which this report is being prepared;

(b) Designed such internal control over financial reporting, or caused such internal control over financial reporting to be designed under our supervision, to provide reasonable assurance regarding the reliability of financial reporting and the preparation of financial statements for external purposes in accordance with generally accepted accounting principles;

(c) Evaluated the effectiveness of the registrant's disclosure controls and procedures and presented in this report our conclusions about the effectiveness of the disclosure controls and procedures, as of the end of the period covered by this report based on such evaluation; and

(d) Disclosed in this report any change in the registrant's internal control over financial reporting that occurred during the registrant's most recent fiscal quarter (the registrant's fourth fiscal quarter in the case of an annual report) that has materially affected, or is reasonably likely to materially affect, the registrant's internal control over financial reporting; and

The registrant's other certifying officer(s) and I have disclosed, based on our most recent evaluation of internal control over financial reporting, to the registrant's auditors and the audit committee of the registrant's board of directors (or persons performing the equivalent functions): (a) All significant deficiencies and material weaknesses in the design or operation of internal control over financial reporting which are reasonably likely to adversely affect the registrant's ability to record, process, summarize and report financial information; and

(b) Any fraud, whether or not material, that involves management or other employees who have a significant role in the registrant's internal control over financial reporting.

Date: . . . .

[Signature]

[Title]

* Provide a separate certification for each principal executive officer and principal financial officer of the registrant. See Rules 13a-14(a) and 15d-14(a).

(32) Section 1350 Certifications.

(i) The certifications required by Rule 13a-14(b) (17 CFR 240.13a-14(b)) or Rule 15d-14(b) (17 CFR 240.15d-14(b)) and Section 1350 of Chapter 63 of Title 18 of the United States Code (18 U.S.C. 1350).

(ii) A certification furnished pursuant to this item will not be deemed "filed" for purposes of Section 18 of the Exchange Act (15 U.S.C. 78r), or otherwise subject to the liability of that section. Such certification will not be deemed to be incorporated by reference into any filing under the Securities Act or the Exchange Act, except to the extent that the registrant specifically incorporates it by reference.

(33) through (98) [Reserved]

(99) *Additional exhibits*—(i) Any additional exhibits which the registrant may wish to file shall be so marked as to indicate clearly the subject matters to which they refer. (ii) Any document (except for an exhibit) or part thereof which is incorporated by reference in the filing and is not otherwise required to be filed by this Item or is not a Commission filed document incorporated by reference in a Securities Act registration statement.

(iii) If pursuant to Section 11(a) of the Securities Act (15 U.S.C. 77k(a)) an issuer makes generally available to its security holders an earnings statement covering a period of at least 12 months beginning after the effective date of the registration statement, and if such earnings statement is made available by "other methods" than those specified in paragraph (a) or (b) of § 230.158 of this chapter, it must be filed as an exhibit to the Form 10-Q or the Form 10-K, as appropriate, covering the period in which the earnings statement was released.

Subpart 700—Miscellaneous

Item 701. Recent Sales of Unregistered Securities; Use of Proceeds from Registered Securities

Furnish the following information as to all securities of the registrant sold by the registrant within the past three years which were not registered under the Securities Act. Include sales of reacquired securities, as well as new issues, securities issued in exchange for property, services, or other securities, and new securities resulting from the modification of outstanding securities.

(a) *Securities sold.* Give the date of sale and the title and amount of securities sold.

(b) *Underwriters and other purchasers.* Give the names of the principal underwriters, if any. As to any such securities not publicly offered, name the persons or identify the class of persons to whom the securities were sold.

(c) *Consideration.* As to securities sold for cash, state the aggregate offering price and the aggregate underwriting discounts or commissions. As to any securities sold otherwise than for cash, state the nature of the transaction and the nature and aggregate amount of consideration received by the registrant.

(d) *Exemption from registration claimed.* Indicate the section of the Securities Act or the rule of the Commission under which exemption from registration was claimed and state briefly the facts relied upon to make the exemption available.

(e) *Terms of conversion or exercise.* If the information called for by this paragraph (e) is being presented on Form 8-K, Form 10-QSB, Form 10-Q, Form 10-KSB or Form 10-K (§§ 249.308, 249.308b, 249.308a, 249.310b or 249.310) under the Exchange Act, and where the securities sold by the registrant are convertible or exchangeable into equity securities, or are warrants or options representing equity securities, disclose the terms of conversion or exercise of the securities.

(f) *Use of Proceeds.* As required by § 230.463 of this chapter, following the effective date of the first registration statement filed under the Securities Act by an issuer, the issuer or successor issuer shall report the use of proceeds on its first periodic report filed pursuant to sections 13(a) and 15(d) of the Exchange Act (15 U.S.C. 78m(a) and 78o(d)) after effectiveness of its Securities Act registration statement, and thereafter on each of its subsequent periodic reports filed pursuant to sections 13(a) and 15(d) of the Exchange Act through the later of disclosure of the application of all the offering proceeds, or disclosure of the termination of the offering. If a report of the use of proceeds is required with respect to the first effective registration statement of the predecessor issuer, the successor issuer shall provide such a report. The information provided pursuant to paragraphs (f)(2) through (f)(4) of this Item need only be provided with respect to the first periodic report filed pursuant to sections 13(a) and 15(d) of the Exchange Act after effectiveness of the registration statement filed under the Securities Act. Subsequent periodic reports filed pursuant to sections 13(a) and 15(d) of the Exchange Act need only provide the information required in paragraphs (f)(2) through (f)(4) of this Item if any of such required information has changed since the last periodic report filed. In disclosing the use of proceeds in the first periodic report filed pursuant to the Exchange Act, the issuer or successor issuer should include the following information:

(1) The effective date of the Securities Act registration statement for which the use of proceeds information is being disclosed and the Commission file number assigned to the registration statement;

(2) If the offering has commenced, the offering date, and if the offering has not commenced, an explanation why it has not;

(3) If the offering terminated before any securities were sold, an explanation for such termination; and

(4) If the offering did not terminate before any securities were sold, disclose:

(i) Whether the offering has terminated and, if so, whether it terminated before the sale of all securities registered;

(ii) The name(s) of the managing underwriter(s), if any;

(iii) The title of each class of securities registered and, where a class of convertible securities is being registered, the title of any class of securities into which such securities may be converted;

(iv) For each class of securities (other than a class of securities into which a class of convertible securities registered may be converted without additional payment to the issuer) the following information, provided for both the account of the issuer and the account(s) of any selling security holder(s): the amount registered, the aggregate price of the offering amount registered, the amount sold and the aggregate offering price of the amount sold to date;

(v) From the effective date of the Securities Act registration statement to the ending date of the reporting period, the amount of expenses incurred for the issuer's account in connection with the issuance and distribution of the securities registered for underwriting discounts and commissions, finders' fees, expenses paid to or for underwriters, other expenses and total expenses. Indicate if a reasonable estimate for the amount of expenses incurred is provided instead of the actual amount of expense. Indicate whether such payments were:

(A) Direct or indirect payments to directors, officers, general partners of the issuer or their associates; to persons owning ten (10) percent or more of any class of equity securities of the issuer; and to affiliates of the issuer; or

(B) Direct or indirect payments to others;

(vi) The net offering proceeds to the issuer after deducting the total expenses described in paragraph (f)(4)(v) of this Item;

(vii) From the effective date of the Securities Act registration statement to the ending date of the reporting period, the amount of net offering proceeds to the issuer used for construction of plant, building and facilities; purchase and installation of machinery and equipment; purchases of real estate; acquisition of other business(es); repayment of indebtedness; working capital; temporary investments (which should be specified); and any other purposes for which at least five (5) percent of the issuer's total offering proceeds or $100,000 (whichever is less) has been used (which should be specified). Indicate if a reasonable estimate for the amount of net offering proceeds applied is provided instead of the actual amount of net offering proceeds used. Indicate whether such payments were:

(A) Direct or indirect payments to directors, officers, general partners of the issuer or their associates; to persons owning ten (10) percent or more of any class of equity securities of the issuer; and to affiliates of the issuer; or

(B) Direct or indirect payments to others; and

(viii) If the use of proceeds in paragraph (f)(4)(vii) of this Item represents a material change in the use of proceeds described in the prospectus, the issuer should describe briefly the material change.

Instructions. 1. Information required by this Item 701 need not be set forth as to notes, drafts, bills of exchange, or bankers' acceptances which mature not later than one year from the date of issuance.

2. If the sales were made in a series of transactions, the information may be given by such totals and periods as will reasonably convey the information required.

Item 702. Indemnification of Directors and Officers

State the general effect of any statute, charter provisions, by-laws, contract or other arrangements under which any controlling persons, director or officer of the registrant is insured or indemnified in any manner against liability which he may incur in his capacity as such.

Item 703. Purchases of Equity Securities by the Issuer and Affiliated Purchasers

(a) In the following tabular format, provide the information specified in paragraph (b) of this Item with respect to any purchase made by or on behalf of the issuer or any "affiliated purchaser," as defined in § 240.10b-18(a)(3) of this chapter, of shares or other units of any class of the issuer's equity securities that is registered by the issuer pursuant to section 12 of the Exchange Act (15 U.S.C. 78*l*).

Period	(a) Total Number of Shares (or Units) Purchased	(b) Average Price Paid per Share (or Unit)	(c) Total Number of Shares (or Units) Purchased as Part of Publicly Announced Plans or Programs	(d) Maximum Number (or Approximate Dollar Value) of Shares (or Units) that May Yet Be Purchased Under the Plans or Programs
Month #1 (identify beginning and ending dates)				
Month #2 (identify beginning and ending dates)				
Month #3 (identify beginning and ending dates)				
Total				

(b) The table shall include the following information for each class or series of securities for each month included in the period covered by the report:

(1) The total number of shares (or units) purchased (column (a));

Instruction to paragraph (b)(1) of Item 703

Include in this column all issuer repurchases, including those made pursuant to publicly announced plans or programs and those not made pursuant to publicly announced plans or programs. Briefly disclose, by footnote to the table, the number of shares purchased other than through a publicly announced plan or program and the nature of the transaction (*e.g.*, whether the purchases were made in open-market transactions, tender offers, in satisfaction of the company's obligations upon exercise of outstanding put options issued by the company, or other transactions).

(2) The average price paid per share (or unit) (column (b));

(3) The total number of shares (or units) purchased as part of publicly announced repurchase plans or programs (column (c)); and

(4) The maximum number (or approximate dollar value) of shares (or units) that may yet be purchased under the plans or programs (column (d)).

Instructions to paragraphs (b)(3) and (b)(4) of Item 703

1. In the table, disclose this information in the aggregate for all plans or programs publicly announced.

2. By footnote to the table, indicate:

a. The date each plan or program was announced;

b. The dollar amount (or share or unit amount) approved;

c. The expiration date (if any) of each plan or program;

d. Each plan or program that has expired during the period covered by the table; and

e. Each plan or program the issuer has determined to terminate prior to expiration, or under which the issuer does not intend to make further purchases.

Instruction to Item 703

Disclose all purchases covered by this Item, including purchases that do not satisfy the conditions of the safe harbor of § 240.10b-18 of this chapter.

Subpart 800—List of Industry Guides

Item 801. Securities Act Industry Guides

(a) Guide 1. [Removed and reserved in Release No. 33-7300, May 31, 1996, effective July 15, 1996, 61 F.R. 30397.]

(b) Guide 2. Disclosure of oil and gas operations.

(c) Guide 3. Statistical disclosure by bank holding companies.

(d) Guide 4. Prospectuses relating to interests in oil and gas programs.

(e) Guide 5. Preparation of registration statements relating to interests in real estate limited partnerships.

(f) Guide 6. Disclosures concerning unpaid claims and claim adjustment expenses of property-casualty underwriters.

(g) Guide 7. Description of Property by Issuers Engaged or To Be Engaged in Significant Mining Operations.

Item 802. Exchange Act Industry Guides

(a) Guide 1. [Removed and reserved in Release No. 33-7300, May 31, 1996, effective July 15, 1996, 61 F.R. 30397.]

(b) Guide 2. Disclosure of oil and gas operations.

(c) Guide 3. Statistical disclosure by bank holding companies.

(d) Guide 4. Disclosures concerning unpaid claims and claim adjustment expenses of property-casualty underwriters.

(e) [Reserved].

(f) [Reserved].

(g) Guide 7. Description of Property by Issuers Engaged or To Be Engaged in Significant Mining Operations.

REGULATION S-X—SELECTED PROVISIONS

17 C.F.R. §§ 210.2-01-210.2-02; 210.2.07

Item	Subject
2-01	Qualifications of accountants
2-02	Accountants' reports
2-07	Communication with audit committees

Article 2—Qualifications and Reports of Accountants

Item 2-01. Qualifications of Accountants

Preliminary Note

Rule 2-01 is designed to ensure that auditors are qualified and independent of their audit clients both in fact and in appearance. Accordingly, the rule sets forth restrictions on financial, employment, and business relationships between an accountant and an audit client and restrictions on an accountant providing certain non-audit services to an audit client.

Rule 2-01(b) sets forth the general standard of auditor independence. Paragraphs (c)(1) to (c)(5) reflect the application of the general standard to particular circumstances. The rule does not purport to, and the Commission could not, consider all circumstances that raise independence concerns, and these are subject to the general standard in paragraph 2-01(b). In considering this standard, the Commission looks in the first instance to whether a relationship or the provision of a service: (a) creates a mutual or conflicting interest between the accountant and the audit client; (b) places the accountant in the position of auditing his or her own work; (c) results in the accountant acting as management or an employee of the audit client; or (d) places the accountant in a position of being an advocate for the audit client.

These factors are general guidance only and their application may depend on particular facts and circumstances. For that reason, Rule 2-01 provides that, in determining whether an accountant is independent, the Commission will consider all relevant facts and circumstances. For the same reason, registrants and accountants are encouraged to consult with the Commission's Office of the Chief Accountant before entering into relationships, including relationships involving the provision of services, that are not explicitly described in the Rule.

(a) The Commission will not recognize any person as a certified public accountant who is not duly registered and in good standing as such under the laws of the place of his residence or principal office. The Commission will not recognize any person as a public accountant who is not in good standing and entitled to practice as such under the laws of the place of his residence or principal office.

(b) The Commission will not recognize an accountant as independent, with respect to an audit client, if the accountant is not, or a reasonable investor with knowledge of all relevant facts and circumstances would conclude that the accountant is not, capable of exercising objective and impartial judgment on all issues encompassed within the accountant's engagement. In determining whether an accountant is independent, the Commission will consider all relevant circumstances, including all relationships between the accountant and the audit client, and not just those relating to reports filed with the Commission.

(c) This paragraph sets forth a non-exclusive specification of circumstances inconsistent with paragraph (b) of this section.

(1) *Financial relationships.* An accountant is not independent if, at any point during the audit and professional engagement period, the accountant has a direct financial interest or a material indirect financial interest in the accountant's audit client, such as:

(i) *Investments in audit clients.* An accountant is not independent when:

(A) The accounting firm, any covered person in the firm, or any of his or her immediate family members, has any direct investment in an audit client, such as stocks, bonds, notes, options, or other securities. The term *direct investment* includes an investment in an audit client through an intermediary if:

(1) The accounting firm, covered person, or immediate family member, alone or together with other persons, supervises or participates in the intermediary's investment decisions or has control over the intermediary; or

(2) The intermediary is not a diversified management investment company, as defined by Section 5(b)(1) of the Investment Company Act of 1940, 15 U.S.C. 80a-5(b)(1), and has an investment in the audit client that amounts to 20% or more of the value of the intermediary's total investments.

(B) Any partner, principal, shareholder, or professional employee of the accounting firm, any of his or her immediate family members, any close family member of a covered person in the firm, or any group of the above persons has filed a Schedule 13D or 13G (17 CFR 240.13d-101 or 240.13d-102) with the Commission indicating beneficial ownership of more than five percent of an audit client's equity securities or controls an audit client, or a close family member of a partner, principal, or shareholder of the accounting firm controls an audit client.

(C) The accounting firm, any covered person in the firm, or any of his or her immediate family members, serves as voting trustee of a trust, or executor of an estate, containing the securities of an audit client, unless the accounting firm, covered person in the firm, or immediate family member has no authority to make investment decisions for the trust or estate.

(D) The accounting firm, any covered person in the firm, any of his or her immediate family members, or any group of the above persons has any material indirect investment in an audit client. For purposes of this paragraph, the term *material indirect investment* does not include ownership by any covered person in the firm, any of his or her immediate family members, or any group of the above persons of 5% or less of the outstanding shares of a diversified management investment company, as defined by Section 5(b)(1) of the Investment Company Act of 1940, 15 U.S.C. 80a-5(b)(1), that invests in an audit client.

(E) The accounting firm, any covered person in the firm, or any of his or her immediate family members:

(1) Has any direct or material indirect investment in an entity where:

(i) An audit client has an investment in that entity that is material to the audit client and has the ability to exercise significant influence over that entity; or

(ii) The entity has an investment in an audit client that is material to that entity and has the ability to exercise significant influence over that audit client;

(2) Has any material investment in an entity over which an audit client has the ability to exercise significant influence; or

(3) Has the ability to exercise significant influence over an entity that has the ability to exercise significant influence over an audit client.

(ii) *Other financial interests in audit client.* An accountant is not independent when the accounting firm, any covered person in the firm, or any of his or her immediate family members has:

(A) *Loans/debtor-creditor relationship.* Any loan (including any margin loan) to or from an audit client, or an audit client's officers, directors, or record or beneficial owners of more than ten percent of the audit client's equity securities, except for the following loans obtained from a financial institution under its normal lending procedures, terms, and requirements:

(1) Automobile loans and leases collateralized by the automobile;

(2) Loans fully collateralized by the cash surrender value of an insurance policy;

(3) Loans fully collateralized by cash deposits at the same financial institution; and

(*4*) A mortgage loan collateralized by the borrower's primary residence provided the loan was not obtained while the covered person in the firm was a covered person.

(B) *Savings and checking accounts.* Any savings, checking, or similar account at a bank, savings and loan, or similar institution that is an audit client, if the account has a balance that exceeds the amount insured by the Federal Deposit Insurance Corporation or any similar insurer, except that an accounting firm account may have an uninsured balance provided that the likelihood of the bank, savings and loan, or similar institution experiencing financial difficulties is remote.

(C) *Broker-dealer accounts.* Brokerage or similar accounts maintained with a broker-dealer that is an audit client, if:

(*1*) Any such account includes any asset other than cash or securities (within the meaning of "security" provided in the Securities Investor Protection Act of 1970 ("SIPA") (15 U.S.C. 78aaa *et seq.*));

(*2*) The value of assets in the accounts exceeds the amount that is subject to a Securities Investor Protection Corporation advance, for those accounts, under Section 9 of SIPA (15 U.S.C. 78fff-3); or

(*3*) With respect to non-U.S. accounts not subject to SIPA protection, the value of assets in the accounts exceeds the amount insured or protected by a program similar to SIPA.

(D) *Futures commission merchant accounts.* Any futures, commodity, or similar account maintained with a futures commission merchant that is an audit client.

(E) *Credit cards.* Any aggregate outstanding credit card balance owed to a lender that is an audit client that is not reduced to $10,000 or less on a current basis taking into consideration the payment due date and any available grace period.

(F) *Insurance products.* Any individual policy issued by an insurer that is an audit client unless:

(*1*) The policy was obtained at a time when the covered person in the firm was not a covered person in the firm; and

(*2*) The likelihood of the insurer becoming insolvent is remote.

(G) *Investment companies.*Any financial interest in an entity that is part of an investment company complex that includes an audit client.

(iii) *Exceptions.* Notwithstanding paragraphs (c)(1)(i) and (c)(1)(ii) of this section, an accountant will not be deemed not independent if:

(A) *Inheritance and gift.* Any person acquires an unsolicited financial interest, such as through an unsolicited gift or inheritance, that would cause an accountant to be not independent under paragraph (c)(1)(i) or (c)(1)(ii) of this section, and the financial interest is disposed of as soon as practicable, but no later than 30 days after the person has knowledge of and the right to dispose of the financial interest.

(B) *New audit engagement.* Any person has a financial interest that would cause an accountant to be not independent under paragraph (c)(1)(i) or (c)(1)(ii) of this section, and:

(*1*) The accountant did not audit the client's financial statements for the immediately preceding fiscal year; and

(*2*) The accountant is independent under paragraph (c)(1)(i) and (c)(1)(ii) of this section before the earlier of:

(*i*) Signing an initial engagement letter or other agreement to provide audit, review, or attest services to the audit client; or

(*ii*) Commencing any audit, review, or attest procedures (including planning the audit of the client's financial statements).

(C) *Employee compensation and benefit plans.* An immediate family member of a person who is a covered person in the firm only by virtue of paragraphs (f)(11)(iii) or (f)(11)(iv) of this section has a financial interest that would cause an accountant to be not independent under paragraph (c)(1)(i) or (c)(1)(ii) of this section, and the acquisition of the financial interest was an unavoidable consequence of participation in his or her employer's employee compensation or benefits program, provided that the financial interest, other than unexercised employee stock options, is disposed of as soon as practicable, but no later than 30 days after the person has the right to dispose of the financial interest.

(iv) *Audit clients' financial relationships.* An accountant is not independent when:

(A) *Investments by the audit client in the accounting firm.* An audit client has, or has agreed to acquire, any direct investment in the accounting firm, such as stocks, bonds, notes, options, or other securities, or the audit client's officers or directors are record or beneficial owners of more than 5% of the equity securities of the accounting firm.

(B) *Underwriting.* An accounting firm engages an audit client to act as an underwriter, broker-dealer, market-maker, promoter, or analyst with respect to securities issued by the accounting firm.

(2) *Employment relationships.* An accountant is not independent if, at any point during the audit and professional engagement period, the accountant has an employment relationship with an audit client, such as:

(i) *Employment at audit client of accountant.* A current partner, principal, shareholder, or professional employee of the accounting firm is employed by the audit client or serves as a member of the board of directors or similar management or governing body of the audit client.

(ii) *Employment at audit client of certain relatives of accountant.* A close family member of a covered person in the firm is in an accounting role or financial reporting oversight role at an audit client, or was in such a role during any period covered by an audit for which the covered person in the firm is a covered person.

(iii) *Employment at audit client of former employee of accounting firm.*

(A) A former partner, principal, shareholder, or professional employee of an accounting firm is in an accounting role or financial reporting oversight role at an audit client, unless the individual:

(*1*) Does not influence the accounting firm's operations or financial policies;

(*2*) Has no capital balances in the accounting firm; and

(*3*) Has no financial arrangement with the accounting firm other than one providing for regular payment of a fixed dollar amount (which is not dependent on the revenues, profits, or earnings of the accounting firm):

(*i*) Pursuant to a fully funded retirement plan, rabbi trust, or, in jurisdictions in which a rabbi trust does not exist, a similar vehicle; or

(*ii*) In the case of a former professional employee who was not a partner, principal, or shareholder of the accounting firm and who has been disassociated from the accounting firm for more than five years, that is immaterial to the former professional employee; and

(B) A former partner, principal, shareholder, or professional employee of an accounting firm is in a financial reporting oversight role at an issuer (as defined in section 10A(f) of the Securities Exchange Act of 1934 (15 U.S.C. 78j-1(f)), except an issuer that is an investment company registered under section 8 of the Investment Company Act of 1940 (15 U.S.C. 80a-8), unless the individual:

(1) Employed by the issuer was not a member of the audit engagement team of the issuer during the one year period preceding the date that audit procedures commenced for the fiscal period that included the date of initial employment of the audit engagement team member by the issuer;

(2) For purposes of paragraph (c)(2)(iii)(B)(1) of this section, the following individuals are not considered to be members of the audit engagement team:

(i) Persons, other than the lead partner and the concurring partner, who provided ten or fewer hours of audit, review, or attest services during the period covered by paragraph (c)(2)(iii)(B)(1) of this section;

(ii) Individuals employed by the issuer as a result of a business combination between an issuer that is an audit client and the employing entity, provided employment was not in contemplation of the business combination and the audit committee of the successor issuer is aware of the prior employment relationship; and

(iii) Individuals that are employed by the issuer due to an emergency or other unusual situation provided that the audit committee determines that the relationship is in the interest of investors;

(3) For purposes of paragraph (c)(2)(iii)(B)(1) of this section, audit procedures are deemed to have commenced for a fiscal period the day following the filing of the issuer's periodic annual report with the Commission covering the previous fiscal period; or

(C) A former partner, principal, shareholder, or professional employee of an accounting firm is in a financial reporting oversight role with respect to an investment company registered under section 8 of the Investment Company Act of 1940 (15 U.S.C. 80a-8), if

(1) The former partner, principal, shareholder, or professional employee of an accounting firm is employed in a financial reporting oversight role related to the operations and financial reporting of the registered investment company at an entity in the investment company complex, as defined in (f)(14) of this section, that includes the registered investment company; and

(2) The former partner, principal, shareholder, or professional employee of an accounting firm employed by the registered investment company or any entity in the investment company complex was a member of the audit engagement team of the registered investment company or any other registered investment company in the investment company complex during the one year period preceding the date that audit procedures commenced that included the date of initial employment of the audit engagement team member by the registered investment company or any entity in the investment company complex.

(3) For purposes of paragraph (c)(2)(iii)(C)(2) of this section, the following individuals are not considered to be members of the audit engagement team:

(i) Persons, other than the lead partner and concurring partner, who provided ten or fewer hours of audit, review or attest services during the period covered by paragraph (c)(2)(iii)(C)(2) of this section;

(ii) Individuals employed by the registered investment company or any entity in the investment company complex as a result of a business combination between a registered investment company or any entity in the investment company complex that is an audit client and the employing entity, provided employment was not in contemplation of the business combination and the audit committee of the registered investment company is aware of the prior employment relationship; and

(iii) Individuals that are employed by the registered investment company or any entity in the investment company complex due to an emergency or other unusual situation provided that the audit committee determines that the relationship is in the interest of investors.

(4) For purposes of paragraph (c)(2)(iii)(C)(2) of this section, audit procedures are deemed to have commenced the day following the filing of the registered investment company's periodic annual report with the Commission.

(iv) *Employment at accounting firm of former employee of audit client.* A former officer, director, or employee of an audit client becomes a partner, principal, shareholder, or professional employee of the accounting firm, unless the individual does not participate in, and is not in a position to influence, the audit of the financial statements of the audit client covering any period during which he or she was employed by or associated with that audit client.

(3) *Business relationships.* An accountant is not independent if, at any point during the audit and professional engagement period, the accounting firm or any covered person in the firm has any direct or material indirect business relationship with an audit client, or with persons associated with the audit client in a decision-making capacity, such as an audit client's officers, directors, or substantial stockholders. The relationships described in this paragraph do not include a relationship in which the accounting firm or covered person in the firm provides professional services to an audit client or is a consumer in the ordinary course of business.

(4) *Non-audit services.* An accountant is not independent if, at any point during the audit and professional engagement period, the accountant provides the following non-audit services to an audit client:

(i) *Bookkeeping or other services related to the accounting records or financial statements of the audit client.* Any service, unless it is reasonable to conclude that the results of these services will not be subject to audit procedures during an audit of the audit client's financial statements, including:

(A) Maintaining or preparing the audit client's accounting records;

(B) Preparing the audit client's financial statements that are filed with the Commission or that form the basis of financial statements filed with the Commission; or

(C) Preparing or originating source data underlying the audit client's financial statements.

(ii) *Financial information systems design and implementation.* Any service, unless it is reasonable to conclude that the results of these services will not be subject to audit procedures during an audit of the audit client's financial statements, including:

(A) Directly or indirectly operating, or supervising the operation of, the audit client's information system or managing the audit client's local area network; or

(B) Designing or implementing a hardware or software system that aggregates source data underlying the financial statements or generates information that is significant to the audit client's financial statements or other financial information systems taken as a whole.

(iii) *Appraisal or valuation services, fairness opinions, or contribution-in-kind reports.* Any appraisal service, valuation service, or any service involving a fairness opinion or contribution-in-kind report for an audit client, unless it is reasonable to conclude that the results of these services will not be subject to audit procedures during an audit of the audit client's financial statements.

(iv) *Actuarial services.* Any actuarially-oriented advisory service involving the determination of amounts recorded in the financial statements and related accounts for the audit client other than assisting a client in understanding the methods, models, assumptions, and inputs used in computing an amount, unless it is reasonable to conclude that the results of these services will not be subject to audit procedures during an audit of the audit client's financial statements.

(v) *Internal audit outsourcing services.* Any internal audit service that has been outsourced by the audit client that relates to the audit client's internal accounting controls, financial systems, or financial statements, for an audit client unless it is reasonable to conclude that the results of these services will not be subject to audit procedures during an audit of the audit client's financial statements.

(vi) *Management functions.* Acting, temporarily or permanently, as a director, officer, or employee of an audit client, or performing any decision-making, supervisory, or ongoing monitoring function for the audit client.

(vii) *Human resources.* (A) Searching for or seeking out prospective candidates for managerial, executive, or director positions;

(B) Engaging in psychological testing, or other formal testing or evaluation programs;

(C) Undertaking reference checks of prospective candidates for an executive or director position;

(D) Acting as a negotiator on the audit client's behalf, such as determining position, status or title, compensation, fringe benefits, or other conditions of employment; or

(E) Recommending, or advising the audit client to hire, a specific candidate for a specific job (except that an accounting firm may, upon request by the audit client, interview candidates and advise the audit client on the candidate's competence for financial accounting, administrative, or control positions).

(viii) *Broker-dealer, investment adviser, or investment banking services.* Acting as a broker-dealer (registered or unregistered), promoter, or underwriter, on behalf of an audit client, making investment decisions on behalf of the audit client or otherwise having discretionary authority over an audit client's investments, executing a transaction to buy or sell an audit client's investment, or having custody of assets of the audit client, such as taking temporary possession of securities purchased by the audit client.

(ix) *Legal services.* Providing any service to an audit client that, under circumstances in which the service is provided, could be provided only by someone licensed, admitted, or otherwise qualified to practice law in the jurisdiction in which the service is provided.

(x) *Expert services unrelated to the audit.* Providing an expert opinion or other expert service for an audit client, or an audit client's legal representative, for the purpose of advocating an audit client's interests in litigation or in a regulatory or administrative proceeding or investigation. In any litigation or regulatory or administrative proceeding or investigation, an accountant's independence shall not be deemed to be impaired if the accountant provides factual accounts, including in testimony, of work performed or explains the positions taken or conclusions reached during the performance of any service provided by the accountant for the audit client.

(5) *Contingent fees.* An accountant is not independent if, at any point during the audit and professional engagement period, the accountant provides any service or product to an audit client for a contingent fee or a commission, or receives a contingent fee or commission from an audit client.

(6) *Partner rotation.* (i) Except as provided in paragraph (c)(6)(ii) of this section, an accountant is not independent of an audit client when:

(A) Any audit partner as defined in paragraph (f)(7)(ii) of this section performs:

(*1*) The services of a lead partner, as defined in paragraph (f)(7)(ii)(A) of this section, or concurring partner, as defined in paragraph (f)(7)(ii)(B) of this section, for more than five consecutive years; or

(*2*) One or more of the services defined in paragraphs (f)(7)(ii)(C) and (D) of this section for more than seven consecutive years;

(B) Any audit partner:

(*1*) Within the five consecutive year period following the performance of services for the maximum period permitted under paragraph (c)(6)(i)(A)(*1*) of this section, performs for that audit client the services of a lead partner, as defined in paragraph (f)(7)(ii)(A) of this section, or concurring partner, as defined in paragraph (f)(7)(ii)(B) of this section, or a combination of those services, or

(*2*) Within the two consecutive year period following the performance of services for the maximum period permitted under paragraph (c)(6)(i)(A)(*2*) of this section, performs one or more of the services defined in paragraph (f)(7)(ii) of this section.

(ii) Any accounting firm with less than five audit clients that are issuers (as defined in section 10A(f) of the Securities Exchange Act of 1934 (15 U.S.C. 78j-1(f))) and less than ten partners shall be exempt from paragraph (c)(6)(i) of this section *provided* the Public Company Accounting Oversight Board conducts a review at least once every three years of each of the audit client engagements that would result in a lack of auditor independence under this paragraph.

(iii) For purposes of paragraph (c)(6)(i) of this section, an audit client that is an investment company registered under section 8 of the Investment Company Act of 1940 (15 U.S.C. 80a-8), does not include an affiliate of the audit client that is an entity in the same investment company complex, as defined in paragraph (f)(14) of this section, except for another registered investment company in the same investment company complex. For purposes of calculating consecutive years of service under paragraph (c)(6)(i) of this section with respect to investment companies in an investment company complex, audits of registered investment companies with different fiscal year-ends that are performed in a continuous 12-month period count as a single consecutive year.

(7) *Audit committee administration of the engagement.* An accountant is not independent of an issuer (as defined in section 10A(f) of the Securities Exchange Act of 1934 (15 U.S.C. 78j-1(f))), other than an issuer that is an Asset-Backed Issuer as defined in §240.13a-14(g) and §240.15d-14(g) of this chapter, or an investment company registered under section 8 of the Investment Company Act of 1940 (15 U.S.C. 80a-8), other than a unit investment trust as defined by section 4(2) of the Investment Company Act of 1940 (15 U.S.C. 80a-4(2)), unless:

(i) In accordance with Section 10A(i) of the Securities Exchange Act of 1934 (15 U.S.C. 78j-1(i)) either:

(A) Before the accountant is engaged by the issuer or its subsidiaries, or the registered investment company or its subsidiaries, to render audit or non-audit services, the engagement is approved by the issuer's or registered investment company's audit committee; or

(B) The engagement to render the service is entered into pursuant to pre-approval policies and procedures established by the audit committee of the issuer or registered investment company, *provided* the policies and procedures are detailed as to the particular service and the audit committee is informed of each service and such policies and procedures do not include delegation of the audit committees responsibilities under the Securities Exchange Act of 1934 to management; or

(C) With respect to the provision of services other than audit, review or attest services the pre-approval requirement is waived if:

(1) The aggregate amount of all such services provided constitutes no more than five percent of the total amount of revenues paid by the audit client to its accountant during the fiscal year in which the services are provided;

(2) Such services were not recognized by the issuer or registered investment company at the time of the engagement to be non-audit services; and

(3) Such services are promptly brought to the attention of the audit committee of the issuer or registered investment company and approved prior to the completion of the audit by the audit committee or by one or more members of the audit committee who are members of the board of directors to whom authority to grant such approvals has been delegated by the audit committee.

(ii) A registered investment company's audit committee also must pre-approve its account-ant's engagements for non-audit services with the registered investment company's investment adviser (not including a sub-adviser whose role is primarily portfolio management and is sub-contracted or overseen by another investment adviser) and any entity controlling, controlled by, or under common control with the investment adviser that provides ongoing services to the registered investment company in accordance with paragraph (c)(7)(i) of this section, if the engagement relates directly to the operations and financial reporting of the registered investment company, except that with respect to the waiver of the pre-approval requirement under paragraph (c)(7)(i)(C) of this section, the aggregate amount of all services provided constitutes no more than five percent of the total amount of revenues paid to the registered investment company's accountant by the registered investment company, its investment adviser and any entity control-ling, controlled by, or under common control with the investment adviser that provides ongoing services to the registered investment company during the fiscal year in which the services are provided that would have to be pre-approved by the registered investment company's audit committee pursuant to this section.

(8) *Compensation.* An accountant is not independent of an audit client if, at any point during the audit and professional engagement period, any audit partner earns or receives compensation based on the audit partner procuring engagements with that audit client to provide any products or services other than audit, review or attest services. Any accounting firm with fewer than ten partners and fewer than five audit clients that are issuers (as defined in section 10A(f) of the Securities Exchange Act of 1934 (15 U.S.C. 78j-1(f))) shall be exempt from the requirement stated in the previous sentence.

(d) *Quality controls.* An accounting firm's independence will not be impaired solely because a covered person in the firm is not independent of an audit client provided:

(1) The covered person did not know of the circumstances giving rise to the lack of independence;

(2) The covered person's lack of independence was corrected as promptly as possible under the relevant circumstances after the covered person or accounting firm became aware of it; and

(3) The accounting firm has a quality control system in place that provides reasonable assurance, taking into account the size and nature of the accounting firm's practice, that the accounting firm and its employees do not lack independence, and that covers at least all employees and associated entities of the accounting firm participating in the engagement, including employees and associated entities located outside of the United States.

(4) For an accounting firm that annually provides audit, review, or attest services to more than 500 companies with a class of securities registered with the Commission under Section 12 of the Securities Exchange Act of 1934 (15 U.S.C. 78*l*), a quality control system will not provide such reasonable assurance unless it has at least the following features:

(i) Written independence policies and procedures;

(ii) With respect to partners and managerial employees, an automated system to identify their investments in securities that might impair the accountant's independence;

(iii) With respect to all professionals, a system that provides timely information about entities from which the accountant is required to maintain independence;

(iv) An annual or on-going firm-wide training program about auditor independence;

(v) An annual internal inspection and testing program to monitor adherence to independence requirements;

(vi) Notification to all accounting firm members, officers, directors, and employees of the name and title of the member of senior management responsible for compliance with auditor independence requirements;

(vii) Written policies and procedures requiring all partners and covered persons to report promptly to the accounting firm when they are engaged in employment negotiations with an audit client, and requiring the firm to remove immediately any such professional from that audit client's engagement and to review promptly all work the professional performed related to that audit client's engagement; and

(viii) A disciplinary mechanism to ensure compliance with this section.

(e)(1) *Transition and grandfathering.* Provided the following relationships did not impair the accountant's independence under pre-existing requirements of the Commission, the Independence Standards, Board, or the accounting profession in the United States, the existence of the relationship on May 6, 2003, will not be deemed to impair an accountant's independence:

(i) Employment relationships that commenced at the issuer prior to May 6, 2003, as described in paragraph (c)(2)(iii)(B) of this section.

(ii) Compensation earned or received, as described in paragraph (c)(8) of this section during the fiscal year of the accounting firm that includes the effective date of this section.

(iii) Until May 6, 2004, the provision of services described in paragraph (c)(4) of this section provided those services are pursuant to contracts in existence on May 6, 2003.

(iv) The provision of services by the accountant under contracts in existence on May 6, 2003, that have not been pre-approved by the audit committee as described in paragraph (c)(7) of this section.

(v) Until the first day of the issuer's fiscal year beginning after May 6, 2003, by a "lead'" partner and other audit partner (other than the "concurring" partner) providing services in excess of those permitted under paragraph (c)(6) of this section. An accountant's independence will not be deemed to be impaired until the first day of the issuer's fiscal year beginning after May 6, 2004, by a "concurring" partner providing services in excess of those permitted under paragraph (c)(6) of this section. For the purposes of calculating periods of service under paragraph (c)(6) of this section:

(A) For the "lead" and "concurring" partner, the period of service includes time served as the "lead'" or "concurring" partner prior to May 6, 2003,; and

(B) For audit partners other than the "lead" partner or "'concurring" partner, and for audit partners in foreign firms, the period of service does not include time served on the audit engagement team prior to the first day of issuer's fiscal year beginning on or after May 6, 2003.

(2) *Settling financial arrangements with former professionals.* To the extent not required by pre-existing requirements of the Commission, the Independence Standards Board, or the accounting profession in the United States, the requirement in paragraph (c)(2)(iii) of this section to settle financial arrangements with former professionals applies to situations that arise after the effective date of this section.

(f) *Definitions of terms.* For purposes of this section:

(1) *Accountant,* as used in paragraphs (b) through (e) of this section, means a registered public accounting firm, certified public accountant or public accountant performing services in connection with an engagement for which independence is required. References to the accountant include any accounting firm with which the certified public accountant or public accountant is affiliated.

(2) *Accounting firm* means an organization (whether it is a sole proprietorship, incorporated association, partnership, corporation, limited liability company, limited liability partnership, or other legal entity) that is engaged in the practice of public accounting and furnishes reports or other documents filed with the Commission or otherwise prepared under the securities laws, and

all of the organization's departments, divisions, parents, subsidiaries, and associated entities, including those located outside of the United States. Accounting firm also includes the organization's pension, retirement, investment, or similar plans.

(3) (i) *Accounting role* means a role in which a person is in a position to or does exercise more than minimal influence over the contents of the accounting records or anyone who prepares them.

(ii) *Financial reporting oversight role* means a role in which a person is in a position to or does exercise influence over the contents of the financial statements or anyone who prepares them, such as when the person is a member of the board of directors or similar management or governing body, chief executive officer, president, chief financial officer, chief operating officer, general counsel, chief accounting officer, controller, director of internal audit, director of financial reporting, treasurer, or any equivalent position.

(4) *Affiliate of the audit client* means:

(i) An entity that has control over the audit client, or over which the audit client has control, or which is under common control with the audit client, including the audit client's parents and subsidiaries;

(ii) An entity over which the audit client has significant influence, unless the entity is not material to the audit client;

(iii) An entity that has significant influence over the audit client, unless the audit client is not material to the entity; and

(iv) Each entity in the investment company complex when the audit client is an entity that is part of an investment company complex.

(5) *Audit and professional engagement period* includes both:

(i) The period covered by any financial statements being audited or reviewed (the "audit period"); and

(ii) The period of the engagement to audit or review the audit client's financial statements or to prepare a report filed with the Commission (the "professional engagement period"):

(A) The professional engagement period begins when the accountant either signs an initial engagement letter (or other agreement to review or audit a client's financial statements) or begins audit, review, or attest procedures, whichever is earlier; and

(B) The professional engagement period ends when the audit client or the accountant notifies the Commission that the client is no longer that accountant's audit client.

(iii) For audits of the financial statements of foreign private issuers, the "audit and professional engagement period" does not include periods ended prior to the first day of the last fiscal year before the foreign private issuer first filed, or was required to file, a registration statement or report with the Commission, provided there has been full compliance with home country independence standards in all prior periods covered by any registration statement or report filed with the Commission.

(6) *Audit client* means the entity whose financial statements or other information is being audited, reviewed, or attested and any affiliates of the audit client, other than, for purposes of paragraph (c) (1) (i) of this section, entities that are affiliates of the audit client only by virtue of paragraph (f) (4) (ii) or (f) (4) (iii) of this section.

(7) (i) *Audit engagement team* means all partners, principals, shareholders and professional employees participating in an audit, review, or attestation engagement of an audit client, including audit partners and all persons who consult with others on the audit engagement team during the audit, review, or attestation engagement regarding technical or industry-specific issues, transactions, or events.

(ii) *Audit partner* means a partner or persons in an equivalent position, other than a partner who consults with others on the audit engagement team during the audit, review, or attestation engagement regarding technical or industry-specific issues, transactions, or events, who is a member of the audit engagement team who has responsibility for decision-making on significant auditing, accounting, and reporting matters that affect the financial statements, or who maintains regular contact with management and the audit committee and includes the following:

(A) The lead or coordinating audit partner having primary responsibility for the audit or review (the"lead partner");

(B) The partner performing a second level of review to provide additional assurance that the financial statements subject to the audit or review are in conformity with generally accepted accounting principles and the audit or review and any associated report are in accordance with generally accepted auditing standards and rules promulgated by the Commission or the Public Company Accounting Oversight Board (the "concurring or reviewing partner");

(C) Other audit engagement team partners who provide more than ten hours of audit, review, or attest services in connection with the annual or interim consolidated financial statements of the issuer or an investment company registered under section 8 of the Investment Company Act of 1940 (15 U.S.C. 80a-8); and

(D) Other audit engagement team partners who serve as the "lead partner" in connection with any audit or review related to the annual or interim financial statements of a subsidiary of the issuer whose assets or revenues constitute 20% or more of the assets or revenues of the issuer's respective consolidated assets or revenues.

(8) *Chain of command* means all persons who:

(i) Supervise or have direct management responsibility for the audit, including at all successively senior levels through the accounting firm's chief executive;

(ii) Evaluate the performance or recommend the compensation of the audit engagement partner; or

(iii) Provide quality control or other oversight of the audit.

(9) *Close family members* means a person's spouse, spousal equivalent, parent, dependent, nondependent child, and sibling.

(10) *Contingent fee* means, except as stated in the next sentence, any fee established for the sale of a product or the performance of any service pursuant to an arrangement in which no fee will be charged unless a specified finding or result is attained, or in which the amount of the fee is otherwise dependent upon the finding or result of such product or service. Solely for the purposes of this section, a fee is not a "contingent fee" if it is fixed by courts or other public authorities, or, in tax matters, if determined based on the results of judicial proceedings or the findings of governmental agencies. Fees may vary depending, for example, on the complexity of services rendered.

(11) *Covered persons in the firm* means the following partners, principals, shareholders, and employees of an accounting firm:

(i) The "audit engagement team";

(ii) The "chain of command";

(iii) Any other partner, principal, shareholder, or managerial employee of the accounting firm who has provided ten or more hours of non-audit services to the audit client for the period beginning on the date such services are provided and ending on the date the accounting firm signs the report on the financial statements for the fiscal year during which those services are provided, or who expects to provide ten or more hours of non-audit services to the audit client on a recurring basis; and

(iv) Any other partner, principal, or shareholder from an "office" of the accounting firm in which the lead audit engagement partner primarily practices in connection with the audit.

(12) *Group* means two or more persons who act together for the purposes of acquiring, holding, voting, or disposing of securities of a registrant.

(13) *Immediate family members* means a person's spouse, spousal equivalent, and dependents.

(14) *Investment company complex.*

(i) "Investment company complex" includes:

(A) An investment company and its investment adviser or sponsor;

(B) Any entity controlled by or controlling an investment adviser or sponsor in paragraph (f)(14)(i)(A) of this section, or any entity under common control with an investment adviser or sponsor in paragraph (f)(14)(i)(A) of this section if the entity:

(*1*) Is an investment adviser or sponsor; or

(2) Is engaged in the business of providing administrative, custodian, underwriting, or transfer agent services to any investment company, investment adviser, or sponsor; and

(C) Any investment company or entity that would be an investment company but for the exclusions provided by Section 3(c) of the Investment Company Act of 1940 (15 U.S.C. 80a-3(c)) that has an investment adviser or sponsor included in this definition by either paragraph (f)(14)(i)(A) or (f)(14)(i)(B) of this section.

(ii) An investment adviser, for purposes of this definition, does not include a sub-adviser whose role is primarily portfolio management and is subcontracted with or overseen by another investment adviser.

(iii) Sponsor, for purposes of this definition, is an entity that establishes a unit investment trust.

(15) *Office* means a distinct sub-group within an accounting firm, whether distinguished along geographic or practice lines.

(16) *Rabbi trust* means an irrevocable trust whose assets are not accessible to the accounting firm until all benefit obligations have been met, but are subject to the claims of creditors in bankruptcy or insolvency.

(17) *Audit committee* means a committee (or equivalent body) as defined in section 3(a)(58) of the Securities Exchange Act of 1934 (15 U.S.C. 78c(a)(58)).

Item 2-02. Accountants' reports and attestation reports on management's assessment of internal control over financial reporting

(a) *Technical requirements for accountants' reports.* The accountant's report (1) shall be dated; (2) shall be signed manually; (3) shall indicate the city and State where issued; and (4) shall identify without detailed enumeration the financial statements covered by the report.

(b) *Representations as to the audit included in accountants' reports.* The accountant's report (1) shall state whether the audit was made in accordance with generally accepted auditing standards; and (2) shall designate any auditing procedures deemed necessary by the accountant under the circumstances of the particular case, which have been omitted, and the reasons for their omission. Nothing in this rule shall be construed to imply authority for the omission of any procedure which independent accountants would ordinarily employ in the course of an audit made for the purpose of expressing the opinions required by paragraph (c) of this section.

(c) *Opinions to be expressed in accountants' reports.* The accountant's report shall state clearly: (1) The opinion of the accountant in respect of the financial statements covered by the report and the accounting principles and practices reflected therein; and (2) the opinion of the accountant as to the consistency of the application of the accounting principles, or as to any changes in such principles which have a material effect on the financial statements.

(d) *Exceptions identified in accountants' reports.* Any matters to which the accountant takes exception shall be clearly identified, the exception thereto specifically and clearly stated, and, to the extent practicable, the effect of each such exception on the related financial statements given. (See § 101 of the Codification of Financial Reporting Policies.)

(e) Paragraph (e) of this section applies only to registrants that are providing financial statements in a filing for a period with respect to which Arthur Andersen LLP or a foreign affiliate of Arthur Andersen LLP ("Andersen") issued an accountants' report. Notwithstanding any other Commission rule or regulation, a registrant that cannot obtain an accountants' report that meets the technical requirements of paragraph (a) of this section after reasonable efforts may include in the document a copy of the latest signed and dated accountants' report issued by Andersen for such period in satisfaction of that requirement, if prominent disclosure that the report is a copy of the previously issued Andersen accountants' report and that the report has not been reissued by Andersen is set forth on such copy.

(f) *Attestation report on management's assessment of internal control over financial reporting.* Every registered public accounting firm that issues or prepares an accountant's report for a registrant, other than an investment company registered under section 8 of the Investment Company Act of 1940 (15 U.S.C. 80a-8), that is included in an annual report required by section 13(a) or 15(d) of the Securities Exchange Act of 1934 (15 U.S.C. 78a *et seq.*) containing an assessment by management of the effectiveness of the registrant's internal control over financial reporting must attest to, and report on, such assessment. The attestation report on management's assessment of internal control over financial reporting shall be dated, signed manually, identify the period covered by the report and clearly state the opinion of the accountant as to whether management's assessment of the effectiveness of the registrant's internal control over financial reporting is fairly stated in all material respects, or must include an opinion to the effect that an overall opinion cannot be expressed. If an overall opinion cannot be expressed, explain why. The attestation report on management's assessment of internal control over financial reporting may be separate from the accountant's report.

Item 2-07. Communicaton with Audit Committees

(a) Each registered public accounting firm that performs for an audit client that is an issuer (as defined in section 10A(f) of the Securities Exchange Act of 1934 (15 U.S.C. 78j-1(f))), other than an issuer that is an Asset-Backed Issuer as defined in § 240.13a-14(g) and § 240.15d-14(g) of this chapter, or an investment company registered under section 8 of the Investment Company Act of 1940 (15 U.S.C. 80a-8), other than a unit investment trust as defined by section 4(2) of the Investment Company Act of 1940 (15 U.S.C. 80a-4(2)), any audit required under the securities laws shall report, prior to the filing of such audit report with the Commission (or in the case of a registered investment company, annually, and if the annual communication is not within 90 days prior to the filing, provide an update, in the 90 day period prior to the filing, of any changes to the previously reported information), to the audit committee of the issuer or registered investment company:

(1) All critical accounting policies and practices to be used;

(2) All alternative treatments within Generally Accepted Accounting Principles for policies and practices related to material items that have been discussed with management of the issuer or registered investment company, including:

(i) Ramifications of the use of such alternative disclosures and treatments; and

(ii) The treatment preferred by the registered public accounting firm;

(3) Other material written communications between the registered public accounting firm and the management of the issuer or registered investment company, such as any management letter or schedule of unadjusted differences;

(4) If the audit client is an investment company, all non-audit services provided to any entity in an investment company complex, as defined in 210.2-01(f)(14) of this section, that were not pre-approved by the registered investment company's audit committee pursuant to 210.2-01(c)(7) of this section.

(b) [Reserved]

REGULATION M

17 C.F.R. §§ 242.100-242.105

PART 242—REGULATION M

Rule 100. Definitions

(a) Preliminary Note: Any transaction or series of transactions, whether or not effected pursuant to the provisions of Regulation M, remain subject to the antifraud and antimanipulation provisions of the securities laws, including, without limitation, Section 17(a) of the Securities Act of 1933 [15 U.S.C. 77q(a)] and Sections 9, 10(b), and 15(c) of the Securities Exchange Act of 1934 [15 U.S.C. 78i, 78j(b), and 78o(c)].

(b) For purposes of this section, the following definitions shall apply:

ADTV means the worldwide average daily trading volume during the two full calendar months immediately preceding, or any 60 consecutive calendar days ending within the 10 calendar days preceding, the filing of the registration statement; or, if there is no registration statement or if the distribution involves the sale of securities on a delayed basis pursuant to § 230.415 of this chapter, two full calendar months immediately preceding, or any consecutive 60 calendar days ending within the 10 calendar days preceding, the determination of the offering price.

Affiliated purchaser means:

(1) A person acting, directly or indirectly, in concert with a distribution participant, issuer, or selling security holder in connection with the acquisition or distribution of any covered security; or

(2) An affiliate, which may be a separately identifiable department or division of a distribution participant, issuer, or selling security holder, that, directly or indirectly, controls the purchases of any covered security by a distribution participant, issuer, or selling security holder, whose purchases are controlled by any such person, or whose purchases are under common control with any such person; or

(3) An affiliate, which may be a separately identifiable department or division of a distribution participant, issuer, or selling security holder, that regularly purchases securities for its own account or for the account of others, or that recommends or exercises investment discretion with respect to the purchase or sale of securities; *Provided, however,* That this paragraph (3) shall not apply to such affiliate if the following conditions are satisfied:

(i) The distribution participant, issuer, or selling security holder:

(A) Maintains and enforces written policies and procedures reasonably designed to prevent the flow of information to or from the affiliate that might result in a violation of §§ 242.101, 242.102, and 242.104; and

(B) Obtains an annual, independent assessment of the operation of such policies and procedures; and

(ii) The affiliate has no officers (or persons performing similar functions) or employees (other than clerical, ministerial, or support personnel) in common with the distribution participant, issuer, or selling security holder that direct, effect, or recommend transactions in securities; and

(iii) The affiliate does not, during the applicable restricted period, act as a market maker (other than as a specialist in compliance with the rules of a national securities exchange), or engage, as a broker or a dealer, in solicited transactions or proprietary trading, in covered securities.

Agent independent of the issuer means a trustee or other person who is independent of the issuer. The agent shall be deemed to be independent of the issuer only if:

(1) The agent is not an affiliate of the issuer; and

(2) Neither the issuer nor any affiliate of the issuer exercises any direct or indirect control or influence over the prices or amounts of the securities to be purchased, the timing of, or the manner in which, the securities are to be purchased, or the selection of a broker or dealer (other than the independent agent itself) through which purchases may be executed; *Provided, however,* That the issuer or its affiliate will not be deemed to have such control or influence solely because it revises not more than once in any three-month period the source of the shares to fund the plan, the basis for determining the amount of its contributions to a plan, or the basis for determining the frequency of its allocations to a plan, or any formula specified in a plan that determines the amount or timing of securities to be purchased by the agent.

Asset-backed security has the meaning contained in General Instruction I.B.5. to Form S-3 (§ 239.13 of this chapter).

At-the-market offering means an offering of securities at other than a fixed price.

Business day refers to a 24 hour period determined with reference to the principal market for the securities to be distributed, and that includes a complete trading session for that market.

Completion of participation in a distribution. Securities acquired in the distribution for investment by any person participating in a distribution, or any affiliated purchaser of such person, shall be deemed to be distributed. A person shall be deemed to have completed its participation in a distribution as follows:

(1) An issuer or selling security holder, when the distribution is completed;

(2) An underwriter, when such person's participation has been distributed, including all other securities of the same class that are acquired in connection with the distribution, and any stabilization arrangements and trading restrictions in connection with the distribution have been terminated; *Provided, however,* That an underwriter's participation will not be deemed to have been completed if a syndicate overallotment option is exercised in an amount that exceeds the net syndicate short position at the time of such exercise; and

(3) Any other person participating in the distribution, when such person's participation has been distributed.

Covered security means any security that is the subject of a distribution, or any reference security.

Current exchange rate means the current rate of exchange between two currencies, which is obtained from at least one independent entity that provides or disseminates foreign exchange quotations in the ordinary course of its business.

Distribution means an offering of securities, whether or not subject to registration under the Securities Act, that is distinguished from ordinary trading transactions by the magnitude of the offering and the presence of special selling efforts and selling methods.

Distribution participant means an underwriter, prospective underwriter, broker, dealer, or other person who has agreed to participate or is participating in a distribution.

Electronic communications network has the meaning contained in § 240.11Ac1-1(a)(8) of this chapter.

Employee has the meaning contained in Form S-8 (§ 239.16b of this chapter) relating to employee benefit plans.

Exchange Act means the Securities Exchange Act of 1934 (15 U.S.C. 78a et seq.).

Independent bid means a bid by a person who is not a distribution participant, issuer, selling security holder, or affiliated purchaser.

NASD means the National Association of Securities Dealers, Inc. or any of its subsidiaries.

Nasdaq means the Nasdaq system as defined in § 240.11Ac12(a)(3) of this chapter.

Nasdaq security means a security that is authorized for quotation on Nasdaq, and such authorization is not suspended, terminated, or prohibited.

Net purchases means the amount by which a passive market maker's purchases exceed its sales.

Offering price means the price at which the security is to be or is being distributed.

Passive market maker means a market maker that effects bids or purchases in accordance with the provisions of § 242.103.

Penalty bid means an arrangement that permits the managing underwriter to reclaim a selling concession from a syndicate member in connection with an offering when the securities originally sold by the syndicate member are purchased in syndicate covering transactions.

Plan means any bonus, profit-sharing, pension, retirement, thrift, savings, incentive, stock purchase, stock option, stock ownership, stock appreciation, dividend reinvestment, or similar plan; or any dividend or interest reinvestment plan or employee benefit plan as defined in § 230.405 of this chapter.

Principal market means the single securities market with the largest aggregate reported trading volume for the class of securities during the 12 full calendar months immediately preceding the filing of the registration statement; or, if there is no registration statement or if the distribution involves the sale of securities on a delayed basis pursuant to § 230.415 of this chapter, during the 12 full calendar months immediately preceding the determination of the offering price. For the purpose of determining the aggregate trading volume in a security, the trading volume of depositary shares representing such security shall be included, and shall be multiplied by the multiple or fraction of the security represented by the depositary share. For purposes of this paragraph, depositary share means a security, evidenced by a depositary receipt, that represents another security, or a multiple or fraction thereof, deposited with a depositary.

Prospective underwriter means a person:

(1) Who has submitted a bid to the issuer or selling security holder, and who knows or is reasonably certain that such bid will be accepted, whether or not the terms and conditions of the underwriting have been agreed upon; or

(2) Who has reached, or is reasonably certain to reach, an understanding with the issuer or selling security holder, or managing underwriter that such person will become an underwriter, whether or not the terms and conditions of the underwriting have been agreed upon.

Public float value shall be determined in the manner set forth on the front page of Form 10-K (§ 249.310 of this chapter), even if the issuer of such securities is not required to file Form 10-K, relating to the aggregate market value of common equity securities held by non-affiliates of the issuer.

Reference period means the two full calendar months immediately preceding the filing of the registration statement or, if there is no registration statement or if the distribution involves the sale of securities on a delayed basis pursuant to § 230.415 of this chapter, the two full calendar months immediately preceding the determination of the offering price.

Reference security means a security into which a security that is the subject of a distribution ("subject security") may be converted, exchanged, or exercised or which, under the terms of the subject security, may in whole or in significant part determine the value of the subject security.

Restricted period means:

(1) For any security with an ADTV value of $100,000 or more of an issuer whose common equity securities have a public float value of $25 million or more, the period beginning on the later of one business day prior to the determination of the offering price or such time that a person becomes a distribution participant, and ending upon such person's completion of participation in the distribution; and

(2) For all other securities, the period beginning on the later of five business days prior to the determination of the offering price or such time that a person becomes a distribution participant, and ending upon such person's completion of participation in the distribution.

(3) In the case of a distribution involving a merger, acquisition, or exchange offer, the period beginning on the day proxy solicitation or offering materials are first disseminated to security holders, and ending upon the completion of the distribution.

Securities Act means the Securities Act of 1933 (15 U.S.C. 77a et seq.).

Selling security holder means any person on whose behalf a distribution is made, other than an issuer.

Stabilize or stabilizing means the placing of any bid, or the effecting of any purchase, for the purpose of pegging, fixing, or maintaining the price of a security.

Syndicate covering transaction means the placing of any bid or the effecting of any purchase on behalf of the sole distributor or the underwriting syndicate or group to reduce a short position created in connection with the offering.

30% ADTV limitation means 30 percent of the market maker's ADTV in a covered security during the reference period, as obtained from the NASD.

Underwriter means a person who has agreed with an issuer or selling security holder:

(1) To purchase securities for distribution; or

(2) To distribute securities for or on behalf of such issuer or selling security holder; or

(3) To manage or supervise a distribution of securities for or on behalf of such issuer or selling security holder.

Rule 101. Activities by Distribution Participants

(a) *Unlawful Activity.* In connection with a distribution of securities, it shall be unlawful for a distribution participant or an affiliated purchaser of such person, directly or indirectly, to bid for, purchase, or attempt to induce any person to bid for or purchase, a covered security during the applicable restricted period; *Provided, however,* That if a distribution participant or affiliated purchaser is the issuer or selling security holder of the securities subject to the distribution, such person shall be subject to the provisions of § 242.102, rather than this section.

(b) *Excepted Activity.* The following activities shall not be prohibited by paragraph (a) of this section:

(1) *Research.* The publication or dissemination of an information, opinion, or recommendation, if the conditions of § 230.138 or § 230.139 of this chapter are met; or

(2) *Transactions complying with certain other sections.* Transactions complying with § 242.103 or § 242.104; or

(3) *Odd-lot transactions.* Transactions in odd-lots; or transactions to offset odd-lots in connection with an odd-lot tender offer conducted pursuant to § 240.13e-4(h)(5) of this chapter; or

(4) *Exercises of securities.* The exercise of any option, warrant, right, or any conversion privilege set forth in the instrument governing a security; or

(5) *Unsolicited transactions.* Unsolicited brokerage transactions; or unsolicited purchases that are not effected from or through a broker or dealer, on a securities exchange, or through an inter-dealer quotation system or electronic communications network; or

(6) *Basket transactions.* (i) Bids or purchases, in the ordinary course of business, in connection with a basket of 20 or more securities in which a covered security does not comprise more than 5% of the value of the basket purchased; or

(ii) Adjustments to such a basket in the ordinary course of business as a result of a change in the composition of a standardized index; or

(7) *De minimis transactions.* Purchases during the restricted period, other than by a passive market maker, that total less than 2% of the ADTV of the security being purchased, or unaccepted bids; *Provided, however,* That the person making such bid or purchase has maintained and enforces written policies and procedures reasonably designed to achieve compliance with the other provisions of this section; or

(8) *Transactions in connection with a distribution.* Transactions among distribution participants in connection with a distribution, and purchases of securities from an issuer or selling security holder in connection with a distribution, that are not effected on a securities exchange, or through an interdealer quotation system or electronic communications network; or

(9) *Offers to sell or the solicitation of offers to buy.* Offers to sell or the solicitation of offers to buy the securities being distributed (including securities acquired in stabilizing), or securities offered as principal by the person making such offer or solicitation; or

(10) *Transactions in Rule 144A securities.* Transactions in securities eligible for resale under § 230.144A(d)(3) of this chapter, or any reference security, if the Rule 144A securities are offered or sold in the United States solely to:

(i) Qualified institutional buyers, as defined in § 230.144A(a)(1) of this chapter, or to offerees or purchasers that the seller and any person acting on behalf of the seller reasonably believes are qualified institutional buyers, in transactions exempt from registration under section 4(2) of the Securities Act (15 U.S.C. 77d(2)) or § 230.144A or § 230.501 through § 230.508 of this chapter; or

(ii) Persons not deemed to be "U.S. persons" for purposes of § 230.902(o)(2) or § 230.902(o)(7) of this chapter, during distribution qualifying under paragraph (b)(10)(i) of this section.

(c) *Excepted Securities.* The provisions of this section shall not apply to any of the following securities:

(1) *Actively-traded securities.* Securities that have an ADTV value of at least $1 million and are issued by an issuer whose common equity securities have a public float value of at least $150 million; *Provided, however,* That such securities are not issued by the distribution participant or an affiliate of the distribution participant; or

(2) *Investment grade nonconvertible and asset-backed securities.* Nonconvertible debt securities, nonconvertible preferred securities, and asset-backed securities, that are rated by at least one nationally recognized statistical rating organization, as that term is used in § 240.15c3-1 of this chapter, in one of its generic rating categories that signifies investment grade; or

(3) *Exempted securities.* "Exempted securities" as defined in section 3(a)(12) of the Exchange Act (15 U.S.C. 78c(a)(12)); or

(4) *Face-amount certificates or securities issued by an open-end management investment company or unit investment trust.* Face-amount certificates issued by a face-amount certificate company, or redeemable securities issued by an open-end management investment company or a unit investment trust. Any terms used in this paragraph (c)(4) that are defined in the Investment Company Act of 1940 (15 U.S.C. 80a-1 et seq.) shall have the meanings specified in such Act.

(d) *Exemptive Authority.* Upon written application or upon its own motion, the Commission may grant an exemption from the provisions of this section, either unconditionally or on specified terms and conditions, to any transaction or class of transactions, or to any security or class of securities.

Rule 102. Activities by Issuers and Selling Security Holders During a Distribution

(a) *Unlawful Activity.* In connection with a distribution of securities effected by or on behalf of an issuer or selling security holder, it shall be unlawful for such person, or any affiliated purchaser of such person, directly or indirectly, to bid for, purchase, or attempt to induce any person to bid for or purchase, a covered security during the applicable restricted period; *Except That* if an affiliated purchaser is a distribution participant, such affiliated purchaser may comply with § 242.101, rather than this section.

(b) *Excepted Activity.* The following activities shall not be prohibited by paragraph (a) of this section:

(1) *Odd-lot transactions.* Transactions in odd-lots, or transactions to offset odd-lots in connection with an odd-lot tender offer conducted pursuant to § 240.13e-4(h)(5) of this chapter; or

(2) *Transactions by closed-end investment companies.* (i) Transactions complying with § 270.23c-3 of this chapter; or

(ii) Periodic tender offers of securities, at net asset value, conducted pursuant to § 240.13e-4 of this chapter by a closed-end investment company that engages in a continuous offering of its securities pursuant to § 230.415 of this chapter; *provided, however*, That such securities are not traded on a securities exchange or through an inter-dealer quotation system or electronic communications network; or

(3) *Redemptions by commodity pools or limited partnerships.* Redemptions by commodity pools or limited partnerships, at a price based on net asset value, which are effected in accordance with the terms and conditions of the instruments governing the securities; *Provided, however*, That such securities are not traded on a securities exchange, or through an inter-dealer quotation system or electronic communications network; or

(4) *Exercises of securities.* The exercise of any option, warrant, right, or any conversion privilege set forth in the instrument governing a security; or

(5) *Offers to sell or the solicitation of offers to buy.* Offers to sell or the solicitation of offers to buy the securities being distributed; or

(6) *Unsolicited purchases.* Unsolicited purchases that are not effected from or through a broker or dealer, on a securities exchange, or through an inter-dealer quotation system or electronic communications network; or

(7) *Transactions in Rule 144A securities.* Transactions in securities eligible for resale under § 230.144A(d)(3) of this chapter, or any reference security, if the Rule 144A securities are offered or sold in the United States solely to:

(i) Qualified institutional buyers, as defined in § 230.144A(a)(1) of this chapter, or to offerees or purchasers that the seller and any person acting on behalf of the seller reasonably believes are qualified institutional buyers, in transactions exempt from registration under section 4(2) of the Securities Act (15 U.S.C. 77d(2)) or § 230.144A or § 230.501 through § 230.508 of this chapter; or

(ii) Persons not deemed to be "U.S. persons" for purposes of § 230.902(o)(2) or § 230.902(o)(7) of this chapter, during a distribution qualifying under paragraph (b)(7)(i) of this section.

(c) *Plans.*

(1) Paragraph (a) of this section shall not apply to distributions of securities pursuant to a plan, which are made:

(i) Solely to employees or security holders of an issuer or its subsidiaries, or to a trustee or other person acquiring such securities for the accounts of such persons; or

(ii) To persons other than employees or security holders, if bids for or purchases of securities pursuant to the plan are effected solely by an agent independent of the issuer and the securities are from a source other than the issuer or an affiliated purchaser of the issuer.

(2) Bids for or purchases of any security made or effected by or for a plan shall be deemed to be a purchase by the issuer unless the bid is made, or the purchase is effected, by an agent independent of the issuer.

(d) *Excepted Securities.* The provisions of this section shall not apply to any of the following securities:

(1) *Actively-traded reference securities.* Reference securities with an ADTV value of at least $1 million that are issued by an issuer whose common equity securities have a public float value of at least $150 million; *Provided, however*, That such securities are not issued by the issuer, or any affiliate of the issuer, of the security in distribution.

(2) *Investment grade nonconvertible and asset-backed securities.* Nonconvertible debt securities, nonconvertible preferred securities, and asset-backed securities, that are rated by at least one nationally recognized statistical rating organization, as that term is used in § 240.15c3-1 of this chapter, in one of its generic rating categories that signifies investment grade; or

(3) *Exempted securities.* "Exempted securities" as defined in section 3(a)(12) of the Exchange Act (15 U.S.C. 78c(a)(12)); or

(4) *Face-amount certificates or securities issued by an open-end management investment company or unit investment trust.* Face-amount certificates issued by a face-amount certificate company, or redeemable securities issued by an open-end management investment company or a unit investment trust. Any terms used in this paragraph (d)(4) that are defined in the Investment Company Act of 1940 (15 U.S.C. 80a-1 et seq.) shall have the meanings specified in such Act.

(e) *Exemptive Authority.* Upon written application or upon its own motion, the Commission may grant an exemption from the provisions of this section, either unconditionally or on specified terms and conditions, to any transaction or class of transactions, or to any security or class of securities.

Rule 103. Nasdaq Passive Market Making

(a) *Scope of Section.* This section permits broker-dealers to engage in market making transactions in covered securities that are Nasdaq securities without violating the provisions of § 242.101; *Except That* this section shall not apply to any security for which a stabilizing bid subject to § 242.104 is in effect, or during any at-the-market offering or best efforts offering.

(b) *Conditions to be Met.*

(1) *General limitations.* A passive market maker must effect all transactions in the capacity of a registered market maker on Nasdaq. A passive market maker shall not bid for or purchase a covered security at a price that exceeds the highest independent bid for the covered security at the time of the transaction, except as permitted by paragraph (b)(3) of this section or required by a rule promulgated by the Commission or the NASD governing the handling of customer orders.

(2) *Purchase limitation.* On each day of the restricted period, a passive market maker's net purchases shall not exceed the greater of its 30% ADTV limitation or 200 shares (together, "purchase limitation"); *Provided, however,* That a passive market maker may purchase all of the securities that are part of a single order that, when executed, results in its purchase limitation being equalled or exceeded. If a passive market maker's net purchases equal or exceed its purchase limitation, it shall withdraw promptly its quotations from Nasdaq. If a passive market maker withdraws its quotations pursuant to this paragraph, it may not effect any bid or purchase in the covered security for the remainder of that day, irrespective of any later sales during that day, unless otherwise permitted by § 242.101.

(3) *Requirement to lower the bid.* If all independent bids for a covered security are reduced to a price below the passive market maker's bid, the passive market maker must lower its bid promptly to a level not higher than the then highest independent bid; *Provided, however,* That a passive market maker may continue to bid and effect purchases at its bid at a price exceeding the then highest independent bid until the passive market maker purchases an aggregate amount of the covered security that equals or, through the purchase of all securities that are part of a single order, exceeds the lesser of two times the minimum quotation size for the security, as determined by NASD rules, or the passive market maker's remaining purchasing capacity under paragraph (b)(2) of this section.

(4) *Limitation on displayed size.* At all times, the passive market maker's displayed bid size may not exceed the lesser of the minimum quotation size for the covered security, or the passive market maker's remaining purchasing capacity under paragraph (b)(2) of this section; *Provided, however,* That a passive market maker whose purchasing capacity at any time is between one and 99 shares may display a bid size of 100 shares.

(5) *Identification of a passive market making bid.* The bid displayed by a passive market maker shall be designated as such.

(6) *Notification and reporting to the NASD.* A passive market maker shall notify the NASD in advance of its intention to engage in passive market making, and shall submit to the NASD information regarding passive market making purchases, in such form as the NASD shall prescribe.

(7) *Prospectus disclosure.* The prospectus for any registered offering in which any passive market maker intends to effect transactions in any covered security shall contain the information required in §§ 228.502, 228.508, 229.502, and 229.508 of this chapter.

(c) *Transactions at Prices Resulting From Unlawful Activity.* No transaction shall be made at a price that the passive market maker knows or has reason to know is the result of activity that is fraudulent, manipulative, or deceptive under the securities laws, or any rule or regulation thereunder.

Rule 104. Stabilizing and Other Activities in Connection With an Offering

(a) *Unlawful Activity.* It shall be unlawful for any person, directly or indirectly, to stabilize, to effect any syndicate covering transaction, or to impose a penalty bid, in connection with an offering of any security, in contravention of the provisions of this section. No stabilizing shall be effected at a price that the person stabilizing knows or has reason to know is in contravention of this section, or is the result of activity that is fraudulent, manipulative, or deceptive under the securities laws, or any rule or regulation thereunder.

(b) *Purpose.* Stabilizing is prohibited except for the purpose of preventing or retarding a decline in the market price of a security.

(c) *Priority.* To the extent permitted or required by the market where stabilizing occurs, any person stabilizing shall grant priority to any independent bid at the same price irrespective of the size of such independent bid at the time that it is entered.

(d) *Control of Stabilizing.* No sole distributor or syndicate or group stabilizing the price of a security or any member or members of such syndicate or group shall maintain more than one stabilizing bid in any one market at the same price at the same time.

(e) *At-the-Market Offerings.* Stabilizing is prohibited in an at-the-market offering.

(f) *Stabilizing Levels.*

(1) *Maximum stabilizing bid.* Notwithstanding the other provisions of this paragraph (f), no stabilizing shall be made at a price higher than the lower of the offering price or the stabilizing bid for the security in the principal market (or, if the principal market is closed, the stabilizing bid in the principal market at its previous close).

(2) *Initiating stabilizing.*

(i) *Initiating stabilizing when the principal market is open.* After the opening of quotations for the security in the principal market, stabilizing may be initiated in any market at a price no higher than the last independent transaction price for the security in the principal market if the security has traded in the principal market on the day stabilizing is initiated or on the most recent prior day of trading in the principal market and the current asked price in the principal market is equal to or greater than the last independent transaction price. If both conditions of the preceding sentence are not satisfied, stabilizing may be initiated in any market after the opening of quotations in the principal market at a price no higher than the highest current independent bid for the security in the principal market.

(ii) *Initiating stabilizing when the principal market is closed.*

(A) When the principal market for the security is closed, but immediately before the opening of quotations for the security in the market where stabilizing will be initiated, stabilizing may be initiated at a price no higher than the lower of:

(1) The price at which stabilizing could have been initiated in the principal market for the security at its previous close; or

(2) The most recent price at which an independent transaction in the security has been effected in any market since the close of the principal market, if the person stabilizing knows or has reason to know of such transaction.

(B) When the principal market for the security is closed, but after the opening of quotations in the market where stabilizing will be initiated, stabilizing may be initiated at a price no higher than the lower of:

(1) The price at which stabilization could have been initiated in the principal market for the security at its previous close; or

(2) The last independent transaction price for the security in that market if the security has traded in that market on the day stabilizing is initiated or on the last preceding business day and the current asked price in that market is equal to or greater than the last independent transaction price. If both conditions of the preceding sentence are not satisfied, under this paragraph (f)(2)(ii)(B)(2), stabilizing may be initiated at a price no higher than the highest current independent bid for the security in that market.

(iii) *Initiating stabilizing when there is no market for the security or before the offering price is determined.* If no bona fide market for the security being distributed exists at the time stabilizing is initiated, no stabilizing shall be initiated at a price in excess of the offering price. If stabilizing is initiated before the offering price is determined, then stabilizing may be continued after determination of the offering price at the price at which stabilizing then could be initiated.

(3) *Maintaining or carrying over a stabilizing bid.* stabilizing bid initiated pursuant to paragraph (f)(2) of this section, which has not been discontinued, may be maintained, or carried over into another market, irrespective of changes in the independent bids or transaction prices for the security.

(4) *Increasing or reducing a stabilizing bid.* A stabilizing bid may be increased to a price no higher than the highest current independent bid for the security in the principal market if the principal market is open, or, if the principal market is closed, to a price no higher than the highest independent bid in the principal market at the previous close thereof. A stabilizing bid may be reduced, or carried over into another market at a reduced price, irrespective of changes in the independent bids or transaction prices for the security. If stabilizing is discontinued, it shall not be resumed at a price higher than the price at which stabilizing then could be initiated.

(5) *Initiating, maintaining, or adjusting a stabilizing bid to reflect the current exchange rate.* If a stabilizing bid is expressed in a currency other than the currency of the principal market for the security, such bid may be initiated, maintained, or adjusted to reflect the current exchange rate, consistent with the provisions of this section. If, in initiating, maintaining, or adjusting a stabilizing bid pursuant to this paragraph (f)(5), the bid would be at or below the midpoint between two trading differentials, such stabilizing bid shall be adjusted downward to the lower differential.

(6) *Adjustments to stabilizing bid.* If a security goes ex-dividend, ex-rights, or ex-distribution, the stabilizing bid shall be reduced by an amount equal to the value of the dividend, right, or distribution. If, in reducing a stabilizing bid pursuant to this paragraph (f)(6), the bid would be at or below the midpoint between two trading differentials, such stabilizing bid shall be adjusted downward to the lower differential.

(7) *Stabilizing of components.* When two or more securities are being offered as a unit, the component securities shall not be stabilized at prices the sum of which exceeds the then permissible stabilizing price for the unit.

(8) *Special prices.* Any stabilizing price that otherwise meets the requirements of this section need not be adjusted to reflect special prices available to any group or class of persons (including employees or holders of warrants or rights).

(g) *Offerings With no U.S. Stabilizing Activities.*

(1) Stabilizing to facilitate an offering of a security in the United States shall not be deemed to be in violation of this section if all of the following conditions are satisfied:

(i) No stabilizing is made in the United States;

(ii) Stabilizing outside the United States is made in a jurisdiction with statutory or regulatory provisions governing stabilizing that are comparable to the provisions of this section; and

(iii) No stabilizing is made at a price above the offering price in the United States, except as permitted by paragraph (f)(5) of this section.

(2) For purposes of this paragraph (g), the Commission by rule, regulation, or order may determine whether a foreign statute or regulation is comparable to this section considering, among other things, whether such foreign statute or regulation: specifies appropriate purposes for which stabilizing is permitted; provides for disclosure and control of stabilizing activities; places limitations on stabilizing levels; requires appropriate recordkeeping; provides other protections comparable to the provisions of this section; and whether procedures exist to enable the Commission to obtain information concerning any foreign stabilizing transactions.

(h) *Disclosure and Notification.*

(1) Any person displaying or transmitting a bid that such person knows is for the purpose of stabilizing shall provide prior notice to the market on which such stabilizing will be effected, and shall disclose its purpose to the person with whom the bid is entered.

(2) Any person effecting a syndicate covering transaction or imposing a penalty bid shall provide prior notice to the self-regulatory organization with direct authority over the principal market in the United States for the security for which the syndicate covering transaction is effected or the penalty bid is imposed.

(3) Any person subject to this section who sells to, or purchases for the account of, any person any security where the price of such security may be or has been stabilized, shall send to the purchaser at or before the completion of the transaction, a prospectus, offering circular, confirmation, or other document containing a statement similar to that comprising the statement provided for in Item 502(d) of Regulation S-B (§ 228.502(d) of this chapter) or Item 502(d) of Regulation S-K (§ 229.502(d) of this chapter).

(i) *Recordkeeping Requirements.* A person subject to this section shall keep the information and make the notification required by § 240.17a-2 of this chapter.

(j) *Excepted Securities.* The provisions of this section shall not apply to:

(1) *Exempted Securities.* "Exempted securities," as defined in section 3(a)(12) of the Exchange Act (15 U.S.C. 78c(a)(12)); or

(2) *Transactions of Rule 144A securities.* Transactions in securities eligible for resale under § 230.144A(d)(3) of this chapter, if such securities are offered or sold in the United States solely to:

(i) Qualified institutional buyers, as defined in § 230.144A(a)(1) of this chapter, or to offerees or purchasers that the seller and any person acting on behalf of the seller reasonably believes are qualified institutional buyers, in a transaction exempt from registration under section 4(2) of the Securities Act (15 U.S.C. 77d(2)) or § 230.144A or § 230.501 through § 230.508 of this chapter; or

(ii) Persons not deemed to be "U.S. persons" for purposes of § 230.902(o)(2) or § 230.902(o)(7) of this chapter, during a distribution qualifying under paragraph (j)(2)(i) of this section.

(k) *Exemptive Authority.* Upon written application or upon its own motion, the Commission may grant an exemption from the provisions of this section, either unconditionally or on specified terms and conditions, to any transaction or class of transactions, or to any security or class of securities.

Rule 105. Short Selling in Connection With a Public Offering

(a) *Unlawful Activity.* In connection with an offering of securities for cash pursuant to a registration statement or a notification on Form 1-A (§ 239.90 of this chapter) filed under the Securities Act, it shall be unlawful for any person to cover a short sale with offered securities purchased from an underwriter or broker or dealer participating in the offering, if such short sale occurred during the shorter of:

(1) The period beginning five business days before the pricing of the offered securities and ending with such pricing; or

(2) The period beginning with the initial filing of such registration statement or notification on Form 1-A and ending with the pricing.

(b) *Excepted Offerings.* This section shall not apply to offerings that are not conducted on a firm commitment basis.

(c) *Exemptive Authority.* Upon written application or upon its own motion, the Commission may grant an exemption from the provisions of this section, either unconditionally or on specified terms and conditions, to any transaction or class of transactions, or to any security or class of securities.

REGULATION M-A

17 C.F.R. §§ 229.1000 to 229.1016

Subpart 1000—Mergers and Acquisitions (Regulation M-A)

Item 1000. Definitions

The following definitions apply to the terms used in Regulation M-A (§§ 229.1000 through 229.1016), unless specified otherwise:

(a) *Associate* has the same meaning as in § 240.12b-2 of this chapter;

(b) *Instruction C* means General Instruction C to Schedule 13E-3 (§ 240.13e-100 of this chapter) and General Instruction C to Schedule TO (§ 240.14d-100 of this chapter);

(c) *Issuer tender offer* has the same meaning as in § 240.13e-4(a)(2) of this chapter;

(d) *Offeror* means any person who makes a tender offer or on whose behalf a tender offer is made;

(e) *Rule 13e-3 transaction* has the same meaning as in § 240.13e-3(a)(3) of this chapter;

(f) *Subject company* means the company or entity whose securities are sought to be acquired in the transaction (*e.g.*, the target), or that is otherwise the subject of the transaction;

(g) *Subject securities* means the securities or class of securities that are sought to be acquired in the transaction or that are otherwise the subject of the transaction; and

(h) *Third-party tender offer* means a tender offer that is not an issuer tender offer.

Item 1001. Summary Term Sheet

Summary term sheet. Provide security holders with a summary term sheet that is written in plain English. The summary term sheet must briefly describe in bullet point format the most material terms of the proposed transaction. The summary term sheet must provide security holders with sufficient information to understand the essential features and significance of the proposed transaction. The bullet points must cross-reference a more detailed discussion contained in the disclosure document that is disseminated to security holders.

Instructions to Item 1001:

1. The summary term sheet must not recite all information contained in the disclosure document that will be provided to security holders. The summary term sheet is intended to serve as an overview of all material matters that are presented in the accompanying documents provided to security holders.

2. The summary term sheet must begin on the first or second page of the disclosure document provided to security holders.

3. Refer to Rule 421(b) and (d) of Regulation C of the Securities Act (§ 230.421 of this chapter) for a description of plain English disclosure.

Item 1002. Subject Company Information

(a) *Name and address.* State the name of the subject company (or the issuer in the case of an issuer tender offer), and the address and telephone number of its principal executive offices.

(b) *Securities.* State the exact title and number of shares outstanding of the subject class of equity securities as of the most recent practicable date. This may be based upon information in the most recently available filing with the Commission by the subject company unless the filing person has more current information.

(c) *Trading market and price.* Identify the principal market in which the subject securities are traded and state the high and low sales prices for the subject securities in the principal market (or, if there is no principal market, the range of high and low bid quotations and the source of the quotations) for each quarter during the past two years. If there is no established trading market for the securities (except for limited or sporadic quotations), so state.

(d) *Dividends.* State the frequency and amount of any dividends paid during the past two years with respect to the subject securities. Briefly describe any restriction on the subject company's current or future ability to pay dividends. If the filing person is not the subject company, furnish this information to the extent known after making reasonable inquiry.

(e) *Prior public offerings.* If the filing person has made an underwritten public offering of the subject securities for cash during the past three years that was registered under the Securities Act of 1933 or exempt from registration under Regulation A (§ 230.251 through § 230.263 of this chapter), state the date of the offering, the amount of securities offered, the offering price per share (adjusted for stock splits, stock dividends, etc. as appropriate) and the aggregate proceeds received by the filing person.

(f) *Prior stock purchases.* If the filing person purchased any subject securities during the past two years, state the amount of the securities purchased, the range of prices paid and the average purchase price for each quarter during that period. Affiliates need not give information for purchases made before becoming an affiliate.

Item 1003. Identity and Background of Filing Person

(a) *Name and address.* State the name, business address and business telephone number of each filing person. Also state the name and address of each person specified in Instruction C to the schedule (except for Schedule 14D-9 (§ 240.14d-101 of this chapter)). If the filing person is an affiliate of the subject company, state the nature of the affiliation. If the filing person is the subject company, so state.

(b) *Business and background of entities.* If any filing person (other than the subject company) or any person specified in Instruction C to the schedule is not a natural person, state the person's principal business, state or other place of organization, and the information required by paragraphs (c)(3) and (c)(4) of this section for each person.

(c) *Business and background of natural persons.* If any filing person or any person specified in Instruction C to the schedule is a natural person, provide the following information for each person:

(1) Current principal occupation or employment and the name, principal business and address of any corporation or other organization in which the employment or occupation is conducted;

(2) Material occupations, positions, offices or employment during the past five years, giving the starting and ending dates of each and the name, principal business and address of any corporation or other organization in which the occupation, position, office or employment was carried on;

(3) A statement whether or not the person was convicted in a criminal proceeding during the past five years (excluding traffic violations or similar misdemeanors). If the person was convicted, describe the criminal proceeding, including the dates, nature of conviction, name and location of court, and penalty imposed or other disposition of the case;

(4) A statement whether or not the person was a party to any judicial or administrative proceeding during the past five years (except for matters that were dismissed without sanction or settlement) that resulted in a judgment, decree or final order enjoining the person from future violations of, or prohibiting activities subject to, federal or state securities laws, or a finding of any violation of federal or state securities laws. Describe the proceeding, including a summary of the terms of the judgment, decree or final order; and

(5) Country of citizenship.

(d) *Tender offer.* Identify the tender offer and the class of securities to which the offer relates, the name of the offeror and its address (which may be based on the offeror's Schedule TO (§ 240.14d-100 of this chapter) filed with the Commission).

Instruction to Item 1003:

If the filing person is making information relating to the transaction available on the Internet, state the address where the information can be found.

Item 1004. Terms of the Transaction

(a) *Material terms.* State the material terms of the transaction.

(1) *Tender offers.* In the case of a tender offer, the information must include:

(i) The total number and class of securities sought in the offer;

(ii) The type and amount of consideration offered to security holders;

(iii) The scheduled expiration date;

(iv) Whether a subsequent offering period will be available, if the transaction is a third-party tender offer;

(v) Whether the offer may be extended, and if so, how it could be extended;

(vi) The dates before and after which security holders may withdraw securities tendered in the offer;

(vii) The procedures for tendering and withdrawing securities;

(viii) The manner in which securities will be accepted for payment;

(ix) If the offer is for less than all securities of a class, the periods for accepting securities on a pro rata basis and the offeror's present intentions in the event that the offer is oversubscribed;

(x) An explanation of any material differences in the rights of security holders as a result of the transaction, if material;

(xi) A brief statement as to the accounting treatment of the transaction, if material; and

(xii) The federal income tax consequences of the transaction, if material.

(2) *Mergers or Similar Transactions.* In the case of a merger or similar transaction, the information must include:

(i) A brief description of the transaction;

(ii) The consideration offered to security holders;

(iii) The reasons for engaging in the transaction;

(iv) The vote required for approval of the transaction;

(v) An explanation of any material differences in the rights of security holders as a result of the transaction, if material;

(vi) A brief statement as to the accounting treatment of the transaction, if material; and

(vii) The federal income tax consequences of the transaction, if material.

Instruction to Item 1004(a):

If the consideration offered includes securities exempt from registration under the Securities Act of 1933, provide a description of the securities that complies with Item 202 of Regulation S-K (§ 229.202). This description is not required if the issuer of the securities meets the requirements of General Instructions I.A, I.B.1 or I.B.2, as applicable, or I.C. of Form S-3 (§ 239.13 of this chapter) and elects to furnish information by incorporation by reference; only capital stock is to be issued; and securities of the same class are registered under section 12 of the Exchange Act and either are listed for trading or admitted to unlisted trading privileges on a national securities exchange; or are securities for which bid and offer quotations are reported in an automated quotations system operated by a national securities association.

(b) *Purchases.* State whether any securities are to be purchased from any officer, director or affiliate of the subject company and provide the details of each transaction.

(c) *Different terms.* Describe any term or arrangement in the Rule 13e-3 transaction that treats any subject security holders differently from other subject security holders.

(d) *Appraisal rights.* State whether or not dissenting security holders are entitled to any appraisal rights. If so, summarize the appraisal rights. If there are no appraisal rights available under state law for security holders who object to the transaction, briefly outline any other rights that may be available to security holders under the law.

(e) *Provisions for unaffiliated security holders.* Describe any provision made by the filing person in connection with the transaction to grant unaffiliated security holders access to the corporate files of the filing person or to obtain counsel or appraisal services at the expense of the filing person. If none, so state.

(f) *Eligibility for listing or trading.* If the transaction involves the offer of securities of the filing person in exchange for equity securities held by unaffiliated security holders of the subject company, describe whether or not the filing person will take steps to assure that the securities offered are or will be eligible for trading on an automated quotations system operated by a national securities association.

Item 1005. Past Contacts, Transactions, Negotiations and Agreements

(a) *Transactions.* Briefly state the nature and approximate dollar amount of any transaction, other than those described in paragraphs (b) or (c) of this section, that occurred during the past two years, between the filing person (including any person specified in Instruction C of the schedule) and;

(1) The subject company or any of its affiliates that are not natural persons if the aggregate value of the transactions is more than one percent of the subject company's consolidated revenues for:

(i) The fiscal year when the transaction occurred; or

(ii) The past portion of the current fiscal year, if the transaction occurred in the current year; and

Instruction to Item 1005(a)(1):

The information required by this Item may be based on information in the subject company's most recent filing with the Commission, unless the filing person has reason to believe the information is not accurate.

(2) Any executive officer, director or affiliate of the subject company that is a natural person if the aggregate value of the transaction or series of similar transactions with that person exceeds $60,000.

(b) *Significant corporate events.* Describe any negotiations, transactions or material contacts during the past two years between the filing person (including subsidiaries of the filing person and any person specified in Instruction C of the schedule) and the subject company or its affiliates concerning any:

(1) Merger;

(2) Consolidation;

(3) Acquisition;

(4) Tender offer for or other acquisition of any class of the subject company's securities;

(5) Election of the subject company's directors; or

(6) Sale or other transfer of a material amount of assets of the subject company.

(c) *Negotiations or contacts.* Describe any negotiations or material contacts concerning the matters referred to in paragraph (b) of this section during the past two years between:

(1) Any affiliates of the subject company; or

(2) The subject company or any of its affiliates and any person not affiliated with the subject company who would have a direct interest in such matters.

Instruction to paragraphs (b) and (c) of Item 1005:

Identify the person who initiated the contacts or negotiations.

(d) *Conflicts of interest.* If material, describe any agreement, arrangement or understanding and any actual or potential conflict of interest between the filing person or its affiliates and:

(1) The subject company, its executive officers, directors or affiliates; or

(2) The offeror, its executive officers, directors or affiliates.

Instruction to Item 1005(d):

If the filing person is the subject company, no disclosure called for by this paragraph is required in the document disseminated to security holders, so long as substantially the same information was filed with the Commission previously and disclosed in a proxy statement, report or other communication sent to security holders by the subject company in the past year. The document disseminated to security holders, however, must refer specifically to the discussion in the proxy statement, report or other communication that was sent to security holders previously. The information also must be filed as an exhibit to the schedule.

(e) *Agreements involving the subject company's securities.* Describe any agreement, arrangement, or understanding, whether or not legally enforceable, between the filing person (including any person specified in Instruction C of the schedule) and any other person with respect to any securities of the subject company. Name all persons that are a party to the agreements, arrangements, or understandings and describe all material provisions.

Instructions to Item 1005(e):

1. The information required by this Item includes: the transfer or voting of securities, joint ventures, loan or option arrangements, puts or calls, guarantees of loans, guarantees against loss, or the giving or withholding of proxies, consents or authorizations.

2. Include information for any securities that are pledged or otherwise subject to a contingency, the occurrence of which would give another person the power to direct the voting or disposition of the subject securities. No disclosure, however, is required about standard default and similar provisions contained in loan agreements.

Item 1006. Purpose of the Transaction and Plans or Proposals

(a) *Purposes.* State the purposes of the transaction.

(b) *Use of securities acquired.* Indicate whether the securities acquired in the transaction will be retained, retired, held in treasury, or otherwise disposed of.

(c) *Plans.* Describe any plans, proposals or negotiations that relate to or would result in:

(1) Any extraordinary transaction, such as a merger, reorganization or liquidation, involving the subject company or any of its subsidiaries;

(2) Any purchase, sale or transfer of a material amount of assets of the subject company or any of its subsidiaries;

(3) Any material change in the present dividend rate or policy, or indebtedness or capitalization of the subject company;

(4) Any change in the present board of directors or management of the subject company, including, but not limited to, any plans or proposals to change the number or the term of directors or to fill any existing vacancies on the board or to change any material term of the employment contract of any executive officer;

(5) Any other material change in the subject company's corporate structure or business, including, if the subject company is a registered closed-end investment company, any plans or proposals to make any changes in its investment policy for which a vote would be required by Section 13 of the Investment Company Act of 1940 (15 U.S.C. 80a-13);

(6) Any class of equity securities of the subject company to be delisted from a national securities exchange or cease to be authorized to be quoted in an automated quotations system operated by a national securities association;

(7) Any class of equity securities of the subject company becoming eligible for termination of registration under Section 12(g)(4) of the Act (15 U.S.C. 78*l*);

(8) The suspension of the subject company's obligation to file reports under Section 15(d) of the Act (15 U.S.C. 78o);

(9) The acquisition by any person of additional securities of the subject company, or the disposition of securities of the subject company; or

(10) Any changes in the subject company's charter, bylaws or other governing instruments or other actions that could impede the acquisition of control of the subject company.

(d) *Subject company negotiations.* If the filing person is the subject company:

(1) State whether or not that person is undertaking or engaged in any negotiations in response to the tender offer that relate to:

(i) A tender offer or other acquisition of the subject company's securities by the filing person, any of its subsidiaries, or any other person; or

(ii) Any of the matters referred to in paragraphs (c)(1) through (c)(3) of this section; and

(2) Describe any transaction, board resolution, agreement in principle, or signed contract that is entered into in response to the tender offer that relates to one or more of the matters referred to in paragraph (d)(1) of this section.

Instruction to Item 1006(d)(1):

If an agreement in principle has not been reached at the time of filing, no disclosure under paragraph (d)(1) of this section is required of the possible terms of or the parties to the transaction if in the opinion of the board of directors of the subject company disclosure would jeopardize continuation of the negotiations. In that case, disclosure indicating that negotiations are being undertaken or are underway and are in the preliminary stages is sufficient.

Item 1007. Source and Amount of Funds or Other Consideration

(a) *Source of funds.* State the specific sources and total amount of funds or other consideration to be used in the transaction. If the transaction involves a tender offer, disclose the amount of funds or other consideration required to purchase the maximum amount of securities sought in the offer.

(b) *Conditions.* State any material conditions to the financing discussed in response to paragraph (a) of this section. Disclose any alternative financing arrangements or alternative financing plans in the event the primary financing plans fall through. If none, so state.

(c) *Expenses.* Furnish a reasonably itemized statement of all expenses incurred or estimated to be incurred in connection with the transaction including, but not limited to, filing, legal, accounting and appraisal fees, solicitation expenses and printing costs and state whether or not the subject company has paid or will be responsible for paying any or all expenses.

(d) *Borrowed funds.* If all or any part of the funds or other consideration required is, or is expected, to be borrowed, directly or indirectly, for the purpose of the transaction:

(1) Provide a summary of each loan agreement or arrangement containing the identity of the parties, the term, the collateral, the stated and effective interest rates, and any other material terms or conditions of the loan; and

(2) Briefly describe any plans or arrangements to finance or repay the loan, or, if no plans or arrangements have been made, so state.

Instruction to Item 1007(d):

If the transaction is a third-party tender offer and the source of all or any part of the funds used in the transaction is to come from a loan made in the ordinary course of business by a bank as defined by Section 3(a)(6) of the Act (15 U.S.C. 78c), the name of the bank will not be made available to the public if the filing person so requests in writing and files the request, naming the bank, with the Secretary of the Commission.

Item 1008. Interest in Securities of the Subject Company

Item 1009. Persons/Assets, Retained, Employed, Compensated or Used

Item 1010. Financial Statements

Item 1011. Additional information

(a) *Agreements, regulatory requirements and legal proceedings.* If material to a security holder's decision whether to sell, tender or hold the securities sought in the tender offer, furnish the following information:

(1) Any present or proposed material agreement, arrangement, understanding or relationship between the offeror or any of its executive officers, directors, controlling persons or subsidiaries and the subject company or any of its executive officers, directors, controlling persons or subsidiaries (other than any agreement, arrangement or understanding disclosed under any other sections of Regulation M-A (§§ 229.1000 through 229.1016));

Instruction to paragraph (a)(1):

In an issuer tender offer disclose any material agreement, arrangement, understanding or relationship between the offeror and any of its executive officers, directors, controlling persons or subsidiaries.

(2) To the extent known by the offeror after reasonable investigation, the applicable regulatory requirements which must be complied with or approvals which must be obtained in connection with the tender offer;

(3) The applicability of any anti-trust laws;

(4) The applicability of margin requirements under Section 7 of the Act (15 U.S.C. 78g) and the applicable regulations; and

(5) Any material pending legal proceedings relating to the tender offer, including the name and location of the court or agency in which the proceedings are pending, the date instituted, the principal parties, and a brief summary of the proceedings and the relief sought.

Instruction to Item 1011(a)(5):

A copy of any document relating to a major development (such as pleadings, an answer, complaint, temporary restraining order, injunction, opinion, judgment or order) in a material pending legal proceeding must be furnished promptly to the Commission staff on a supplemental basis.

(b) *Other material information.* Furnish such additional material information, if any, as may be necessary to make the required statements, in light of the circumstances under which they are made, not materially misleading.

Item 1012. The Solicitation or Recommendation

Item 1013. Purposes, Alternatives, Reasons and Effects in a Going-Private Transaction

Item 1014. Fairness of the Going-Private Transaction

Item 1015. Reports, Opinions, Appraisals and Negotiations

Item 1016. Exhibits

REGULATION ATS—SELECTED PROVISIONS

17 C.F.R. §§ 242.300-242.301

Rule	Subject
	Preliminary notes
300	Definitions
301	Requirements for alternative trading systems

Reg. § 242.300 through § 242.303—Preliminary Notes

1. An alternative trading system is required to comply with the requirements in this Regulation ATS, unless such alternative trading system:

(a) Is registered as a national securities exchange;

(b) Is exempt from registration as a national securities exchange based on the limited volume of transactions effected on the alternative trading system; or

(c) Trades only government securities and certain other related instruments.

All alternative trading systems must comply with the antifraud, antimanipulation, and other applicable provisions of the federal securities laws.

2. The requirements imposed upon an alternative trading system by Regulation ATS are in addition to any requirements applicable to broker-dealers registered under Section 15 of the Act, (15 U.S.C. 78o).

3. An alternative trading system must comply with any applicable state law relating to the offer or sale of securities or the registration or regulation of persons or entities effecting transactions in securities.

4. The disclosures made pursuant to the provisions of this section are in addition to any other disclosure requirements under the federal securities laws.

Rule 300. Definitions

For purposes of this section, the following definitions shall apply:

(a) *Alternative trading system* means any organization, association, person, group of persons, or system:

(1) That constitutes, maintains, or provides a market place or facilities for bringing together purchasers and sellers of securities or for otherwise performing with respect to securities the functions commonly performed by a stock exchange within the meaning of § 240.3b-16 of this chapter; and

(2) That does not:

(i) Set rules governing the conduct of subscribers other than the conduct of such subscribers' trading on such organization, association, person, group of persons, or system; or

(ii) Discipline subscribers other than by exclusion from trading.

(b) *Subscriber* means any person that has entered into a contractual agreement with an alternative trading system to access such alternative trading system for the purpose of effecting transactions in securities or submitting, disseminating, or displaying orders on such alternative trading system, including a customer, member, user, or participant in an alternative trading system. A subscriber, however, shall not include a national securities exchange or national securities association.

(c) *Affiliate of a subscriber* means any person that, directly or indirectly, controls, is under common control with, or is controlled by, the subscriber, including any employee.

(d) *Debt security* shall mean any security other than an equity security, as defined in § 240.3a11-1 of this chapter, as well as non-participatory preferred stock.

(e) *Order* means any firm indication of a willingness to buy or sell a security, as either principal or agent, including any bid or offer quotation, market order, limit order, or other priced order.

(f) *Control* means the power, directly or indirectly, to direct the management or policies of an alternative trading system, whether through ownership of securities, by contract, or otherwise. A person is presumed to control an alternative trading system, if that person:

(1) Is a director, general partner, or officer exercising executive responsibility (or having similar status or performing similar functions);

(2) Directly or indirectly has the right to vote 25 percent or more of a class of voting security or has the power to sell or direct the sale of 25 percent or more of a class of voting securities of the alternative trading system; or

(3) In the case of a partnership, has contributed, or has the right to receive upon dissolution, 25 percent or more of the capital of the alternative trading system.

(g) *Covered security* shall have the meaning provided in § 240.11Ac1-1(a)(6) of this chapter, provided, however, that a debt or convertible debt security shall not be deemed a covered security for purposes of Regulation ATS.

(h) *Effective transaction reporting plan* shall have the meaning provided in § 240.11Aa3-1(a)(3) of this chapter.

(i) *Exchange market maker* shall have the meaning provided in § 240.11Ac1-1(a)(9) of this chapter.

(j) *OTC market maker* shall have the meaning provided in § 240.11Ac1-1(a)(13) of this chapter.

(k) *Investment grade corporate debt security* shall mean any security that:

(1) Evidences a liability of the issuer of such security;

(2) Has a fixed maturity date that is at least one year following the date of issuance;

(3) Is rated in one of the four highest ratings categories by at least one Nationally Recognized Statistical Ratings Organization; and

(4) Is not an exempted security, as defined in Section 3(a)(12) of the Act (15 U.S.C. 78c(a)(12)).

(l) *Non-investment grade corporate debt security* shall mean any security that:

(1) Evidences a liability of the issuer of such security;

(2) Has a fixed maturity date that is at least one year following the date of issuance;

(3) Is not rated in one of the four highest ratings categories by at least one Nationally Recognized Statistical Ratings Organization; and

(4) Is not an exempted security, as defined in Section 3(a)(12) of the Act (15 U.S.C. 78c(a)(12)).

(m) *Commercial paper* shall mean any note, draft, or bill of exchange which arises out of a current transaction or the proceeds of which have been or are to be used for current transactions, and which has a maturity at the time of issuance of not exceeding nine months, exclusive of days of grace, or any renewal thereof the maturity of which is likewise limited.

Rule 301. Requirements for Alternative Trading Systems

(a) *Scope of section.* An alternative trading system shall comply with the requirements in paragraph (b) of this section, unless such alternative trading system:

(1) Is registered as an exchange under Section 6 of the Act, (15 U.S.C. 78f);

(2) Is exempted by the Commission from registration as an exchange based on the limited volume of transactions effected;

(3) Is operated by a national securities association;

(4) (i) Is registered as a broker-dealer under Sections 15(b) or 15C of the Act (15 U.S.C. 78o(b), and 78o-5), or is a bank, and

(ii) Limits its securities activities to the following instruments:

(A) Government securities, as defined in Section 3(a)(42) of the Act, (15 U.S.C. 78c(a)(42));

(B) Repurchase and reverse repurchase agreements solely involving securities included within paragraph (a)(4)(ii)(A) of this section;

(C) Any put, call, straddle, option, or privilege on a government security, other than a put, call, straddle, option, or privilege that:

(1) Is traded on one or more national securities exchanges; or

(2) For which quotations are disseminated through an automated quotation system operated by a registered securities association; and

(D) Commercial paper.

(5) Is exempted, conditionally or unconditionally, by Commission order, after application by such alternative trading system, from one or more of the requirements of paragraph (b) of this section. The Commission will grant such exemption only after determining that such an order is consistent with the public interest, the protection of investors, and the removal of impediments to, and perfection of the mechanisms of, a national market system.

(b) *Requirements.* Every alternative trading system subject to this Regulation ATS, pursuant to paragraph (a) of this section, shall comply with the requirements in this paragraph (b).

(1) *Broker-dealer registration.* The alternative trading system shall register as a broker-dealer under Section 15 of the Act, (15 U.S.C. 78o).

(2) *Notice.* (i) The alternative trading system shall file an initial operation report on Form ATS, § 249.637 of this chapter, in accordance with the instructions therein, at least 20 days prior to commencing operation as an alternative trading system, or if the alternative trading system is operating as of April 21, 1999, no later than May 11, 1999.

(ii) The alternative trading system shall file an amendment on Form ATS at least 20 calendar days prior to implementing a material change to the operation of the alternative trading system.

(iii) If any information contained in the initial operation report filed under paragraph (b)(2)(i) of this section becomes inaccurate for any reason and has not been previously reported to the Commission as an amendment on Form ATS, the alternative trading system shall file an amendment on Form ATS correcting such information within 30 calendar days after the end of each calendar quarter in which the alternative trading system has operated.

(iv) The alternative trading system shall promptly file an amendment on Form ATS correcting information previously reported on Form ATS after discovery that any information filed under paragraphs (b)(2)(i), (ii) or (iii) of this section was inaccurate when filed.

(v) The alternative trading system shall promptly file a cessation of operations report on Form ATS in accordance with the instructions therein upon ceasing to operate as an alternative trading system.

(vi) Every notice or amendment filed pursuant to this paragraph (b)(2) shall constitute a "report" within the meaning of Sections 11A, 17(a), 18(a), and 32(a), (15 U.S.C. 78k-1, 78q(a), 78r(a), and 78ff(a)), and any other applicable provisions of the Act.

(vii) The reports provided for in paragraph (b)(2) of this section shall be considered filed upon receipt by the Division of Market Regulation, Stop 10-2, at the Commission's principal office in Washington, D.C. Duplicate originals of the reports provided for in paragraphs (b)(2)(i) through (v) of this section must be filed with surveillance personnel designated as such by any self-regulatory organization that is the designated examining authority for the alternative trading system pursuant to § 240.17d-1 of this chapter simultaneously with filing with the Commission. Duplicates of the reports required by paragraph (b)(9) of this section shall be provided to surveillance personnel of such self-regulatory authority upon request. All reports filed pursuant to this paragraph (b)(2) and paragraph (b)(9) of this section shall be deemed confidential when filed.

(3) *Order display and execution access.* (i) An alternative trading system shall comply with the requirements set forth in paragraph (b)(3)(ii) of this section, with respect to any covered security in which the alternative trading system:

(A) Displays subscriber orders to any person (other than alternative trading system employees); and

(B) During at least 4 of the preceding 6 calendar months, had an average daily trading volume of 5 percent or more of the aggregate average daily share volume for such covered security as reported by an effective transaction reporting plan or disseminated through an automated quotation system as described in Section 3(a)(51)(A)(ii) of the Act, (15 U.S.C. 78c(a)(51)(A)(ii)).

(ii) Such alternative trading system shall provide to a national securities exchange or national securities association the prices and sizes of the orders at the highest buy price and the lowest sell price for such covered security, displayed to more than one person in the alternative trading system, for inclusion in the quotation data made available by the exchange or association to quotation vendors pursuant to § 240.11Ac1-1 of this chapter.

(iii) With respect to any order displayed pursuant to paragraph (b)(3)(ii) of this section, an alternative trading system shall provide to any broker-dealer that has access to the national securities exchange or national securities association to which the alternative trading system provides the prices and sizes of displayed orders pursuant to paragraph (b)(3)(ii)(A) of this section, the ability to effect a transaction with such orders that is:

(A) Equivalent to the ability of such broker-dealer to effect a transaction with other orders displayed on the exchange or by the association; and

(B) At the price of the highest priced buy order or lowest priced sell order displayed for the lesser of the cumulative size of such priced orders entered therein at such price, or the size of the execution sought by such broker-dealer.

(4) *Fees.* The alternative trading system shall not charge any fee to broker-dealers that access the alternative trading system through a national securities exchange or national securities association, that is inconsistent with equivalent access to the alternative trading system required by paragraph (b)(3)(iii) of this section. In addition, if the national securities exchange or national securities association to which an alternative trading system provides the prices and sizes of orders under paragraphs (b)(3)(ii) and (b)(3)(iii) of this section establishes rules designed to assure consistency with standards for access to quotations displayed on such national securities exchange, or the market operated by such national securities association, the alternative trading system shall not charge any fee to members that is contrary to, that is not disclosed in the manner required by, or that is inconsistent with any standard of equivalent access established by such rules.

(5) *Fair access.* (i) An alternative trading system shall comply with the requirements in paragraph (b)(5)(ii) of this section, if during at least 4 of the preceding 6 calendar months, such alternative trading system had:

(A) With respect to any covered security, 20 percent or more of the average daily volume in that security reported by an effective transaction reporting plan or disseminated through an automated quotation system as described in Section 3(a)(51)(A)(ii) of the Act (15 U.S.C. 78c(a)(51)(A)(ii));

(B) With respect to an equity security that is not a covered security and for which transactions are reported to a self-regulatory organization, 20 percent or more of the average daily volume in that security as calculated by the self-regulatory organization to which such transactions are reported;

(C) With respect to municipal securities, 20 percent or more of the average daily volume traded in the United States;

(D) With respect to investment grade corporate debt, 20 percent or more of the average daily volume traded in the United States;

(E) With respect to non-investment grade corporate debt, 20 percent or more of the average daily volume traded in the United States.

(ii) An alternative trading system shall:

(A) Establish written standards for granting access to trading on its system;

(B) Not unreasonably prohibit or limit any person in respect to access to services offered by such alternative trading system by applying the standards established under paragraph (b) (5) (ii) (A) of this section in an unfair or discriminatory manner; and

(C) Make and keep records of:

(1) All grants of access including, for all subscribers, the reasons for granting such access;

(2) All denials or limitations of access and reasons, for each applicant, for denying or limiting access.

(D) Report the information required on Form ATS-R, § 249.638 of this chapter, regarding grants, denials, and limitations of access.

(iii) Notwithstanding paragraph (b) (5) (i) of this section, an alternative trading system shall not be required to comply with the requirements in paragraph (b) (5) (ii) of this section, if such alternative trading system:

(A) Matches customer orders for a security with other customer orders;

(B) Such customers' orders are not displayed to any person, other than employees of the alternative trading system; and

(C) Such orders are executed at a price for such security disseminated by an effective transaction reporting plan or through an automated quotation system as described in Section 3(a) (51) (A) (ii) of the Act, (15 U.S.C. 78c(a) (51) (A) (ii)), or derived from such prices.

(6) *Capacity, integrity, and security of automated systems.* (i) The alternative trading system shall comply with the requirements in paragraph (b) (6) (ii) of this section, if during at least 4 of the preceding 6 calendar months, such alternative trading system had:

(A) With respect to any covered security, 20 percent or more of the average daily volume reported by the effective transaction reporting plan or disseminated through an automated quotation system as described in Section 3(a) (51) (A) (ii) of the Act, (15 U.S.C. 78c(a) (51) (A) (ii));

(B) With respect to equity securities that are not covered securities and for which transactions are reported to a self-regulatory organization, 20 percent or more of the average daily volume as calculated by the self-regulatory organization to which such transactions are reported;

(C) With respect to municipal securities, 20 percent or more of the average daily volume traded in the United States;

(D) With respect to investment grade corporate debt, 20 percent or more of the average daily volume traded in the United States;

(E) With respect to non-investment grade corporate debt, 20 percent or more of the average daily volume traded in the United States.

(ii) With respect to those systems that support order entry, order routing, order execution, transaction reporting, and trade comparison, the alternative trading system shall:

(A) Establish reasonable current and future capacity estimates;

(B) Conduct periodic capacity stress tests of critical systems to determine such system's ability to process transactions in an accurate, timely, and efficient manner;

(C) Develop and implement reasonable procedures to review and keep current its system development and testing methodology;

(D) Review the vulnerability of its systems and data center computer operations to internal and external threats, physical hazards, and natural disasters;

(E) Establish adequate contingency and disaster recovery plans;

(F) On an annual basis, perform an independent review, in accordance with established audit procedures and standards, of such alternative trading system's controls for ensuring that paragraphs (b) (6) (ii) (A) through (E) of this section are met, and conduct a review by senior management of a report containing the recommendations and conclusions of the independent review; and

(G) Promptly notify the Commission staff of material systems outages and significant systems changes.

(iii) Notwithstanding paragraph (b) (6) (i) of this section, an alternative trading system shall not be required to comply with the requirements in paragraph (b) (6) (ii) of this section, if such alternative trading system:

(A) Matches customer orders for a security with other customer orders;

(B) Such customers' orders are not displayed to any person, other than employees of the alternative trading system; and

(C) Such orders are executed at a price for such security disseminated by an effective transaction reporting plan or through an automated quotation system as described in Section 3(a)(51)(A)(ii) of the Act, (15 U.S.C. 78c(a)(51)(A)(ii)), or derived from such prices.

(7) *Examinations, inspections, and investigations.* The alternative trading system shall permit the examination and inspection of its premises, systems, and records, and cooperate with the examination, inspection, or investigation of subscribers, whether such examination is being conducted by the Commission or by a self-regulatory organization of which such subscriber is a member.

(8) *Recordkeeping.* The alternative trading system shall:

(i) Make and keep current the records specified in § 242.302; and

(ii) Preserve the records specified in § 242.303.

(9) *Reporting.* The alternative trading system shall:

(i) File the information required by Form ATS-R (§ 249.638 of this chapter) within 30 calendar days after the end of each calendar quarter in which the market has operated after the effective date of this section; and

(ii) File the information required by Form ATS-R within 10 calendar days after an alternative trading system ceases to operate.

(10) *Procedures to ensure the confidential treatment of trading information.*

(i) The alternative trading system shall establish adequate safeguards and procedures to protect subscribers' confidential trading information. Such safeguards and procedures shall include:

(A) Limiting access to the confidential trading information of subscribers to those employees of the alternative trading system who are operating the system or responsible for its compliance with these or any other applicable rules;

(B) Implementing standards controlling employees of the alternative trading system trading for their own accounts; and

(ii) The alternative trading system shall adopt and implement adequate oversight procedures to ensure that the safeguards and procedures established pursuant to paragraph (b)(10)(i) of this section are followed.

(11) *Name.* The alternative trading system shall not use in its name the word "exchange," or derivations of the word "exchange," such as the term "stock market."

REGULATION AC

17 C.F.R. §§ 242.500 to 242.505

Rule	Subject
500	Definitions
501	Certifications in connection with research reports
502	Certifications in connection with public appearances
503	Certain foreign research reports
504	Notification to associated persons
505	Exclusion for news media

Rule 500. Definitions

For purposes of Regulation AC (§§ 242.500 through 242.505 of this chapter) the term:

Covered person of a broker or dealer means an associated person of that broker or dealer but does not include:

(1) An associated person:

(i) If the associated person has no officers (or persons performing similar functions) or employees in common with the broker or dealer who can influence the activities of research analysts or the content of research reports; and

(ii) If the broker or dealer maintains and enforces written policies and procedures reasonably designed to prevent the broker or dealer, any controlling persons, officers (or persons performing similar functions), and employees of the broker or dealer from influencing the activities of research analysts and the content of research reports prepared by the associated person.

(2) An associated person who is an investment adviser:

(i) Not registered with the Commission as an investment adviser because of the prohibition of section 203A of the Investment Advisers Act of 1940 (15 U.S.C. 80b-3a); and

(ii) Not registered or required to be registered with the Commission as a broker or dealer.

Note to definition of covered person : An associated person of a broker or dealer who is not a covered person continues to be subject to the federal securities laws, including the anti-fraud provisions of the federal securities laws.

Foreign person means any person who is not a U.S. person.

Foreign security means a security issued by a foreign issuer for which a U.S. market is not the principal trading market.

Public appearance means any participation by a research analyst in a seminar, forum (including an interactive electronic forum), or radio or television or other interview, in which the research analyst makes a specific recommendation or provides information reasonably sufficient upon which to base an investment decision about a security or an issuer.

Registered broker or dealer means a broker or dealer registered or required to register pursuant to section 15 or section 15B of the Securities Exchange Act of 1934 (15 U.S.C. 78o or 78o-4) or a government securities broker or government securities dealer registered or required to register pursuant to section 15C(a)(1)(A) of the Securities Exchange Act of 1934 (15 U.S.C. 78o-5(a)(1)(A)).

Research analyst means any natural person who is primarily responsible for the preparation of the content of a research report.

Research report means a written communication (including an electronic communication) that includes an analysis of a security or an issuer and provides information reasonably sufficient upon which to base an investment decision.

Third party research analyst means:

(1) With respect to a broker or dealer, any research analyst not employed by that broker or dealer or any associated person of that broker or dealer; and

(2) With respect to a covered person of a broker or dealer, any research analyst not employed by that covered person, by the broker or dealer with whom that covered person is associated, or by any other associated person of the broker or dealer with whom that covered person is associated.

United States has the meaning contained in § 230.902(l) of this chapter.

U.S. person has the meaning contained in § 230.902(k) of this chapter.

Rule 501. Certifications in connection with research reports

(a) A broker or dealer or covered person that publishes, circulates, or provides a research report prepared by a research analyst to a U.S. person in the United States shall include in that research report a clear and prominent certification by the research analyst containing the following:

(1) A statement attesting that all of the views expressed in the research report accurately reflect the research analyst's personal views about any and all of the subject securities or issuers; and

(2) (i) A statement attesting that no part of the research analyst's compensation was, is, or will be, directly or indirectly, related to the specific recommendations or views expressed by the research analyst in the research report; or

(ii) A statement:

(A) Attesting that part or all of the research analyst's compensation was, is, or will be, directly or indirectly, related to the specific recommendations or views expressed by the research analyst in the research report;

(B) Identifying the source, amount, and purpose of such compensation; and

(C) Further disclosing that the compensation could influence the recommendations or views expressed in the research report.

(b) A broker or dealer or covered person that publishes, circulates, or provides a research report prepared by a third party research analyst to a U.S. person in the United States shall be exempt from the requirements of this section with respect to such research report if the following conditions are satisfied:

(1) The employer of the third party research analyst has no officers (or persons performing similar functions) or employees in common with the broker or dealer or covered person; and

(2) The broker or dealer (or, with respect to a covered person, the broker or dealer with whom the covered person is associated) maintains and enforces written policies and procedures reasonably designed to prevent the broker or dealer, any controlling persons, officers (or persons performing similar functions), and employees of the broker or dealer from influencing the activities of the third party research analyst and the content of research reports prepared by the third party research analyst.

Rule 502. Certifications in connection with public appearances

(a) If a broker or dealer publishes, circulates, or provides a research report prepared by a research analyst employed by the broker or dealer or covered person to a U.S. person in the United States, the broker or dealer must make a record within thirty days after any calendar quarter in which the research analyst made a public appearance that contains the following:

(1) A statement by the research analyst attesting that the views expressed by the research analyst in all public appearances during the calendar quarter accurately reflected the research analyst's personal views at that time about any and all of the subject securities or issuers; and

(2) A statement by the research analyst attesting that no part of the research analyst's compensation was, is, or will be, directly or indirectly, related to the specific recommendations or views expressed by the research analyst in such public appearances.

(b) If the broker or dealer does not obtain a statement by the research analyst in accordance with paragraph (a) of this section:

(1) The broker or dealer shall promptly notify in writing its examining authority, designated pursuant to section 17(d) of the Securities Exchange Act of 1934 (15 U.S.C. 78q(d)) and 240.17d-2 of this chapter, that the research analyst did not provide the certifications specified in paragraph (a) of this section; and

(2) For 120 days following notification pursuant to paragraph (b)(1) of this section, the broker or dealer shall disclose in any research report prepared by the research analyst and published, circulated, or provided to a U.S. person in the United States that the research analyst did not provide the certifications specified in paragraph (a) of this section.

(c) In the case of a research analyst who is employed outside the United States by a foreign person located outside the United States, this section shall only apply to a public appearance while the research analyst is physically present in the United States.

(d) A broker or dealer shall preserve the records specified in paragraphs (a) and (b) of this section in accordance with § 240.17a-4 of this chapter and for a period of not less than 3 years, the first 2 years in an accessible place.

Rule 503. Certain foreign research reports

A foreign person, located outside the United States and not associated with a registered broker or dealer, who prepares a research report concerning a foreign security and provides it to a U.S. person in the United States in accordance with the provisions of § 240.15a-6(a)(2) of this chapter shall be exempt from the requirements of this regulation.

Rule 504. Notification to associated persons

A broker or dealer shall notify any person with whom that broker or dealer is associated who publishes, circulates, or provides research reports:

(a) Whether the broker or dealer maintains and enforces written policies and procedures reasonably designed to prevent the broker or dealer, any controlling persons, officers (or persons performing similar functions), or employees of the broker or dealer from influencing the activities of research analysts and the content of research reports prepared by the associated person; and

(b) Whether the associated person has any officers (or persons performing similar functions) or employees in common with the broker or dealer who can influence the activities of research analysts or the content of research reports and, if so, the identity of those persons.

Rule 505. Exclusion for news media

No provision of this Regulation AC shall apply to any person who:

(a) Is the publisher of any bona fide newspaper, news magazine or business or financial publication of general and regular circulation; and

(b) Is not registered or required to be registered with the Commission as a broker or dealer or investment adviser.

REGULATION FD

17 C.F.R. §§ 243.100-243.103

Rule	Subject
100	General rule regarding selective disclosure
101	Definitions
102	No effect on antifraud liability
103	No effect on Exchange Act reporting status

Rule 100. Regulation FD—General Rule Regarding Selective Disclosure

(a) Whenever an issuer, or any person acting on its behalf, discloses any material nonpublic information regarding that issuer or its securities to any person described in paragraph (b)(1) of this section, the issuer shall make public disclosure of that information as provided in § 243.101(e):

(1) Simultaneously, in the case of an intentional disclosure; and

(2) Promptly, in the case of a non-intentional disclosure.

(b)(1) Except as provided in paragraph (b)(2) of this section, paragraph (a) of this section shall apply to a disclosure made to any person outside the issuer:

(i) Who is a broker or dealer, or a person associated with a broker or dealer, as those terms are defined in Section 3(a) of the Securities Exchange Act of 1934 (15 U.S.C. 78c(a));

(ii) Who is an investment adviser, as that term is defined in Section 202(a)(11) of the Investment Advisers Act of 1940 (15 U.S.C. 80b-2(a)(11)); an institutional investment manager, as that term is defined in Section 13(f)(5) of the Securities Exchange Act of 1934 (15 U.S.C. 78m(f)(5)), that filed a report on Form 13F (17 CFR 249.325) with the Commission for the most recent quarter ended prior to the date of the disclosure; or a person associated with either of the foregoing. For purposes of this paragraph, a "person associated with an investment adviser or institutional investment manager" has the meaning set forth in Section 202(a)(17) of the Investment Advisers Act of 1940 (15 U.S.C. 80b-2(a)(17)), assuming for these purposes that an institutional investment manager is an investment adviser;

(iii) Who is an investment company, as defined in Section 3 of the Investment Company Act of 1940 (15 U.S.C. 80a-3), or who would be an investment company but for Section 3(c)(1) (15 U.S.C. 80a-3(c)(1)) or Section 3(c)(7) (15 U.S.C. 80a-3(c)(7)) thereof, or an affiliated person of either of the foregoing. For purposes of this paragraph, "affiliated person" means only those persons described in Section 2(a)(3)(C), (D), (E), and (F) of the Investment Company Act of 1940 (15 U.S.C. 80a-2(a)(3)(C), (D), (E), and (F)), assuming for these purposes that a person who would be an investment company but for Section 3(c)(1) (15 U.S.C. 80a-3(c)(1)) or Section 3(c)(7) (15 U.S.C. 80a-3(c)(7)) of the Investment Company Act of 1940 is an investment company; or

(iv) Who is a holder of the issuer's securities, under circumstances in which it is reasonably foreseeable that the person will purchase or sell the issuer's securities on the basis of the information.

(2) Paragraph (a) of this section shall not apply to a disclosure made:

(i) To a person who owes a duty of trust or confidence to the issuer (such as an attorney, investment banker, or accountant);

(ii) To a person who expressly agrees to maintain the disclosed information in confidence;

(iii) To an entity whose primary business is the issuance of credit ratings, provided the information is disclosed solely for the purpose of developing a credit rating and the entity's ratings are publicly available; or

(iv) In connection with a securities offering registered under the Securities Act, other than an offering of the type described in any of Rule 415(a)(1)(i)-(vi) (§230.415(a)(1)(i)-(vi) of this chapter).

Rule 101. Definitions

This section defines certain terms as used in Regulation FD (§§243.100 -243.103).

(a) Intentional. A selective disclosure of material nonpublic information is "intentional" when the person making the disclosure either knows, or is reckless in not knowing, that the information he or she is communicating is both material and nonpublic.

(b) Issuer. An "issuer" subject to this regulation is one that has a class of securities registered under Section 12 of the Securities Exchange Act of 1934 (15 U.S.C. 78l), or is required to file reports under Section 15(d) of the Securities Exchange Act of 1934 (15 U.S.C. 78o(d)), including any closed-end investment company (as defined in Section 5(a)(2) of the Investment Company Act of 1940) (15 U.S.C. 80a-5(a)(2)), but not including any other investment company or any foreign government or foreign private issuer, as those terms are defined in Rule 405 under the Securities Act (§230.405 of this chapter).

(c) Person acting on behalf of an issuer. "Person acting on behalf of an issuer" means any senior official of the issuer (or, in the case of a closed-end investment company, a senior official of the issuer's investment adviser), or any other officer, employee, or agent of an issuer who regularly communicates with any person described in §243.100(b)(1)(i), (ii), or (iii), or with holders of the issuer's securities. An officer, director, employee, or agent of an issuer who discloses material nonpublic information in breach of a duty of trust or confidence to the issuer shall not be considered to be acting on behalf of the issuer.

(d) Promptly. "Promptly" means as soon as reasonably practicable (but in no event after the later of 24 hours or the commencement of the next day's trading on the New York Stock Exchange) after a senior official of the issuer (or, in the case of a closed-end investment company, a senior official of the issuer's investment adviser) learns that there has been a non-intentional disclosure by the issuer or person acting on behalf of the issuer of information that the senior official knows, or is reckless in not knowing, is both material and nonpublic.

(e) Public disclosure. (1) Except as provided in paragraph (e)(2) of this section, an issuer shall make the "public disclosure" of information required by §243.100(a) by furnishing to or filing with the Commission a Form 8-K (17 CFR 249.308) disclosing that information.

(2) An issuer shall be exempt from the requirement to furnish or file a Form 8-K if it instead disseminates the information through another method (or combination of methods) of disclosure that is reasonably designed to provide broad, non-exclusionary distribution of the information to the public.

(f) Senior official. "Senior official" means any director, executive officer (as defined in §240.3b-7 of this chapter), investor relations or public relations officer, or other person with similar functions.

(g) Securities offering. For purposes of §243.100(b)(2)(iv):

(1) Underwritten offerings. A securities offering that is underwritten commences when the issuer reaches an understanding with the broker-dealer that is to act as managing underwriter and continues until the later of the end of the period during which a dealer must deliver a prospectus or the sale of the securities (unless the offering is sooner terminated);

(2) Non-underwritten offerings. A securities offering that is not underwritten:

(i) If covered by Rule 415(a)(1)(x) (§230.415(a)(1)(x) of this chapter), commences when the issuer makes its first bona fide offer in a takedown of securities and continues until the later of the end of the period during which each dealer must deliver a prospectus or the sale of the securities in that takedown (unless the takedown is sooner terminated);

(ii) If a business combination as defined in Rule 165(f)(1) (§230.165(f)(1) of this chapter), commences when the first public announcement of the transaction is made and continues until the completion of the vote or the expiration of the tender offer, as applicable (unless the transaction is sooner terminated);

(iii) If an offering other than those specified in paragraphs (a) and (b) of this section, commences when the issuer files a registration statement and continues until the later of the end of the period during which each dealer must deliver a prospectus or the sale of the securities (unless the offering is sooner terminated).

Rule 102. No Effect on Antifraud Liability

No failure to make a public disclosure required solely by § 243.100 shall be deemed to be a violation of Rule 10b-5 (17 CFR 240.10b-5) under the Securities Exchange Act.

Rule 103. No Effect on Exchange Act Reporting Status

A failure to make a public disclosure required solely by § 243.100 shall not affect whether:

(a) For purposes of Forms S-2 (17 CFR 239.12), S-3 (17 CFR 239.13) and S-8 (17 CFR 239.16b) under the Securities Act, an issuer is deemed to have filed all the material required to be filed pursuant to Section 13 or 15(d) of the Securities Exchange Act of 1934 (15 U.S.C. 78m or 78o(d)) or, where applicable, has made those filings in a timely manner; or

(b) There is adequate current public information about the issuer for purposes of § 230.144(c) of this chapter (Rule 144(c)).

REGULATION G

17 C.F.R. §§ 244.100-244.102

Rule	Subject
100	General rules regarding disclosure of non-GAAP financial measures
101	Definitions
102	No effect on antifraud liability

Rule 100. General Rules Regarding Disclosure of Non-GAAP Financial Measures

(a) Whenever a registrant, or person acting on its behalf, publicly discloses material information that includes a non-GAAP financial measure, the registrant must accompany that non-GAAP financial measure with:

(1) A presentation of the most directly comparable financial measure calculated and presented in accordance with Generally Accepted Accounting Principles (GAAP); and

(2) A reconciliation (by schedule or other clearly understandable method), which shall be quantitative for historical non-GAAP measures presented, and quantitative, to the extent available without unreasonable efforts, for forward-looking information, of the differences between the non-GAAP financial measure disclosed or released with the most comparable financial measure or measures calculated and presented in accordance with GAAP identified in paragraph (a)(1) of this section.

(b) A registrant, or a person acting on its behalf, shall not make public a non-GAAP financial measure that, taken together with the information accompanying that measure and any other accompanying discussion of that measure, contains an untrue statement of a material fact or omits to state a material fact necessary in order to make the presentation of the non-GAAP financial measure, in light of the circumstances under which it is presented, not misleading.

(c) This section shall not apply to a disclosure of a non-GAAP financial measure that is made by or on behalf of a registrant that is a foreign private issuer if the following conditions are satisfied:

(1) The securities of the registrant are listed or quoted on a securities exchange or inter-dealer quotation system outside the United States;

(2) The non-GAAP financial measure is not derived from or based on a measure calculated and presented in accordance with generally accepted accounting principles in the United States; and

(3) The disclosure is made by or on behalf of the registrant outside the United States, or is included in a written communication that is released by or on behalf of the registrant outside the United States.

(d) This section shall not apply to a non-GAAP financial measure included in disclosure relating to a proposed business combination, the entity resulting therefrom or an entity that is a party thereto, if the disclosure is contained in a communication that is subject to § 230.425 of this chapter, § 240.14a-12 or § 240.14d-2(b)(2) of this chapter or § 229.1015 of this chapter.

Notes to § 244.100:

1. If a non-GAAP financial measure is made public orally, telephonically, by webcast, by broadcast, or by similar means, the requirements of paragraphs (a)(1)(i) and (a)(1)(ii) of this section will be satisfied if:

(i) The required information in those paragraphs is provided on the registrant's web site at the time the non-GAAP financial measure is made public; and

(ii) The location of the web site is made public in the same presentation in which the non-GAAP financial measure is made public.

2. The provisions of paragraph (c) of this section shall apply notwithstanding the existence of one or more of the following circumstances:

(i) A written communication is released in the United States as well as outside the United States, so long as the communication is released in the United States contemporaneously with or after the release outside the United States and is not otherwise targeted at persons located in the United States;

(ii) Foreign journalists, U.S. journalists or other third parties have access to the information;

(iii) The information appears on one or more web sites maintained by the registrant, so long as the web sites, taken together, are not available exclusively to, or targeted at, persons located in the United States; or

(iv) Following the disclosure or release of the information outside the United States, the information is included in a submission by the registrant to the Commission made under cover of a Form 6-K.

Rule 101. Definitions

This section defines certain terms as used in Regulation G (§ § 244.100 through 244.102).

(a) (1) *Non-GAAP financial measure.* A non-GAAP financial measure is a numerical measure of a registrant's historical or future financial performance, financial position or cash flows that:

(i) Excludes amounts, or is subject to adjustments that have the effect of excluding amounts, that are included in the most directly comparable measure calculated and presented in accordance with GAAP in the statement of income, balance sheet or statement of cash flows (or equivalent statements) of the issuer; or

(ii) Includes amounts, or is subject to adjustments that have the effect of including amounts, that are excluded from the most directly comparable measure so calculated and presented.

(2) A non-GAAP financial measure does not include operating and other financial measures and ratios or statistical measures calculated using exclusively one or both of:

(i) Financial measures calculated in accordance with GAAP; and

(ii) Operating measures or other measures that are not non-GAAP financial measures.

(3) A non-GAAP financial measure does not include financial measures required to be disclosed by GAAP, Commission rules, or a system of regulation of a government or governmental authority or self-regulatory organization that is applicable to the registrant.

(b) *GAAP.* GAAP refers to generally accepted accounting principles in the United States, except that (1) in the case of foreign private issuers whose primary financial statements are prepared in accordance with non-U.S. generally accepted accounting principles, GAAP refers to the principles under which those primary financial statements are prepared; and (2) in the case of foreign private issuers that include a non-GAAP financial measure derived from a measure calculated in accordance with U.S. generally accepted accounting principles, GAAP refers to U.S. generally accepted accounting principles for purposes of the application of the requirements of Regulation G to the disclosure of that measure.

(c) *Registrant.* A registrant subject to this regulation is one that has a class of securities registered under Section 12 of the Securities Exchange Act of 1934 (15 U.S.C. 78*l*), or is required to file reports under Section 15(d) of the Securities Exchange Act of 1934 (15 U.S.C. 78o(d)), excluding any investment company registered under Section 8 of the Investment Company Act of 1940 (15 U.S.C. 80a-8).

(d) *United States.* United States means the United States of America, its territories and possessions, any State of the United States, and the District of Columbia.

Rule 102. No Effect on Antifraud Liability

Neither the requirements of this Regulation G (17 CFR § 244.100 through 244.102) nor a person's compliance or non-compliance with the requirements of this Regulation shall in itself affect any person's liability under Section 10(b) (15 U.S.C. 78j(b)) of the Securities Exchange Act of 1934 or § 240.10b-5 of this chapter.

806

RULES OF PRACTICE AND INVESTIGATIONS—SELECTED PROVISIONS

17 C.F.R. §§ 201.100-205.7

SUBPART D—RULES OF PRACTICE
Part 201, Title 17, Code of Federal Regulations, September 7, 1995, 60 F.R. 46498

General Rules

Rule 100. Scope of the Rules of Practice

(a) Unless provided otherwise, these Rules of Practice govern proceedings before the Commission under the statutes that it administers.

(b) These rules do not apply to:

(1) Investigations, except where made specifically applicable by the Rules Relating to Investigations, part 203 of this chapter; or

(2) Actions taken by the duty officer pursuant to delegated authority under 17 CFR 200.43.

(c) The Commission, upon its determination that to do so would serve the interests of justice and not result in prejudice to the parties to the proceeding, may by order direct, in a particular proceeding, that an alternative procedure shall apply or that compliance with an otherwise applicable rule is unnecessary.

Rule 101. Definitions

(a) For purposes of these Rules of Practice, unless explicitly stated to the contrary:

(1) *Commission* means the United States Securities and Exchange Commission, or a panel of Commissioners constituting a quorum of the Commission, or a single Commissioner acting as duty officer pursuant to 17 CFR 200.42;

(2) *Counsel* means any attorney representing a party or any other person representing a party pursuant to § 201.102(b);

807

(3) *Disciplinary proceeding* means an action pursuant to §201.102(e);

(4) *Enforcement proceeding* means an action, initiated by an order instituting proceedings, held for the purpose of determining whether or not a person is about to violate, has violated, has caused a violation of, or has aided or abetted a violation of any statute or rule administered by the Commission, or whether to impose a sanction as defined in Section 551(10) of the Administrative Procedure Act, 5 U.S.C. 551(10);

(5) *Hearing officer* means an administrative law judge, a panel of Commissioners constituting less than a quorum of the Commission, an individual Commissioner, or any other person duly authorized to preside at a hearing;

(6) *Interested division* means a division or an office assigned primary responsibility by the Commission to participate in a particular proceeding;

(7) *Order instituting proceedings* means an order issued by the Commission commencing a proceeding or an order issued by the Commission to hold a hearing;

(8) *Party* means the interested division, any person named as a respondent in an order instituting proceedings, any applicant named in the caption of any order, persons entitled to notice in a stop order proceeding as set forth in §201.200(a)(2) or any person seeking Commission review of a decision;

(9) *Proceeding* means any agency process initiated:

(i) By an order instituting proceedings; or

(ii) By the filing, pursuant to § 201.410, of a petition for review of an initial decision by a hearing officer; or

(iii) By the filing, pursuant to § 201.420, of an application for review of a self-regulatory organization determination; or

(iv) By the filing, pursuant to § 201.430, of a notice of intention to file a petition for review of a determination made pursuant to delegated authority; or

(v) By the filing, pursuant to § 201.440, of an application for review of a determination by the Public Company Accounting Oversight Board; or

(vi) By the filing, pursuant to § 240.11Aa3-1(f) of this chapter, of an application for review of an action or failure to act in connection with the implementation or operation of any effective transaction reporting plan; or

(vii) By the filing, pursuant to § 240.11Aa3-2(e) of this chapter, of an application for review of an action taken or failure to act in connection with the implementation or operation of any effective national market system plan; or

(viii) By the filing, pursuant to Section 11A(b)(5) of the Securities Exchange Act of 1934, of an application for review of a determination of a registered securities information processor;

(10) *Secretary* means the Secretary of the Commission;

(11) *Temporary sanction* means a temporary cease-and-desist order or a temporary suspension of the registration of a broker, dealer, municipal securities dealer, government securities broker, government securities dealer, or transfer agent pending final determination whether the registration shall be revoked; and

(12) *Board* means the Public Company Accounting Oversight Board.

(b) [Reserved]

Rule 102. Appearance and Practice Before the Commission

A person shall not be represented before the Commission or a hearing officer except as stated in paragraphs (a) and (b) of this section or as otherwise permitted by the Commission or a hearing officer.

(a) *Representing oneself.* In any proceeding, an individual may appear on his or her own behalf.

(b) *Representing others.* In any proceeding, a person may be represented by an attorney at law admitted to practice before the Supreme Court of the United States or the highest court of any State (as defined in Section 3(a)(16) of the Exchange Act, 15 U.S.C. 78c(a)(16)); a member of a partnership may represent the partnership; a bona fide officer of a corporation, trust or association may represent the corporation, trust or association; and an officer or employee of a state commission or of a department or political subdivision of a state may represent the state commission or the department or political subdivision of the state.

(c) *Former Commission employees.* Former employees of the Commission must comply with the restrictions on practice contained in the Commission's Conduct Regulation, Subpart M, 17 CFR 200.735.

(d) *Designation of address for service; notice of appearance; power of attorney; withdrawal.*

(1) *Representing oneself.* When an individual first makes any filing or otherwise appears on his or her own behalf before the Commission or a hearing officer in a proceeding as defined in § 201.101(a), he or she shall file with the Commission, or otherwise state on the record, and keep current, an address at which any notice or other written communication required to be served upon him or her or furnished to him or her may be sent and a telephone number where he or she may be reached during business hours.

(2) *Representing others.* When a person first makes any filing or otherwise appears in a representative capacity before the Commission or a hearing officer in a proceeding as defined in § 201.101(a), that person shall file with the Commission, and keep current, a written notice stating the name of the proceeding; the representative's name, business address and telephone number; and the name and address of the person or persons represented.

(3) *Power of attorney.* Any individual appearing or practicing before the Commission in a representative capacity may be required to file a power of attorney with the Commission showing his or her authority to act in such capacity.

(4) *Withdrawal.* Any person seeking to withdraw his or her appearance in a representative capacity shall file a notice of withdrawal with the Commission or the hearing officer. The notice shall state the name, address, and telephone number of the withdrawing representative; the name, address, and telephone number of the person for whom the appearance was made; and the effective date of the withdrawal. If the person seeking to withdraw knows the name, address, and telephone number of the new representative, or knows that the person for whom the appearance was made intends to represent him- or herself, that information shall be included in the notice. The notice must be served on the parties in accordance with § 201.150. The notice shall be filed at least five days before the proposed effective date of the withdrawal.

(e) *Suspension and disbarment.*

(1) *Generally.* The Commission may censure a person or deny, temporarily or permanently, the privilege of appearing or practicing before it in any way to any person who is found by the Commission after notice and opportunity for hearing in the matter:

(i) Not to possess the requisite qualifications to represent others; or

(ii) To be lacking in character or integrity or to have engaged in unethical or improper professional conduct; or

(iii) To have willfully violated, or willfully aided and abetted the violation of any provision of the Federal securities laws or the rules and regulations thereunder.

(iv) With respect to persons licensed to practice as accountants, "improper professional conduct" under § 201.102(e)(1)(ii) means:

(A) Intentional or knowing conduct, including reckless conduct, that results in a violation of applicable professional standards; or

(B) Either of the following two types of negligent conduct:

(1) A single instance of highly unreasonable conduct that results in a violation of applicable professional standards in circumstances in which an accountant knows, or should know, that heightened scrutiny is warranted.

(2) Repeated instances of unreasonable conduct, each resulting in a violation of applicable professional standards, that indicate a lack of competence to practice before the Commission.

(2) *Certain professionals and convicted persons.* Any attorney who has been suspended or disbarred by a court of the United States or of any State; or any person whose license to practice as an accountant, engineer, or other professional or expert has been revoked or suspended in any State; or any person who has been convicted of a felony or a misdemeanor involving moral turpitude shall be forthwith suspended from appearing or practicing before the Commission. A

disbarment, suspension, revocation or conviction within the meaning of this section shall be deemed to have occurred when the disbarring, suspending, revoking or convicting agency or tribunal enters its judgment or order, including a judgment or order on a plea of nolo contendere, regardless of whether an appeal of such judgment or order is pending or could be taken.

(3) *Temporary suspensions.* An order of temporary suspension shall become effective upon service on the respondent. No order of temporary suspension shall be entered by the Commission pursuant to paragraph (e)(3)(i) of this section more than 90 days after the date on which the final judgment or order entered in a judicial or administrative proceeding described in paragraph (e)(3)(i)(A) or (e)(3)(i)(B) of this section has become effective, whether upon completion of review or appeal procedures or because further review or appeal procedures are no longer available.

(i) The Commission, with due regard to the public interest and without preliminary hearing, may, by order, temporarily suspend from appearing or practicing before it any attorney, accountant, engineer, or other professional or expert who has been by name:

(A) Permanently enjoined by any court of competent jurisdiction, by reason of his or her misconduct in an action brought by the Commission, from violating or aiding and abetting the violation of any provision of the Federal securities laws or of the rules and regulations thereunder; or

(B) Found by any court of competent jurisdiction in an action brought by the Commission to which he or she is a party or found by the Commission in any administrative proceeding to which he or she is a party to have violated (unless the violation was found not to have been willful) or aided and abetted the violation of any provision of the Federal securities laws or of the rules and regulations thereunder.

(ii) Any person temporarily suspended from appearing and practicing before the Commission in accordance with paragraph (e)(3)(i) of this section may, within 30 days after service upon him or her of the order of temporary suspension, petition the Commission to lift the temporary suspension. If no petition has been received by the Commission within 30 days after service of the order, the suspension shall become permanent.

(iii) Within 30 days after the filing of a petition in accordance with paragraph (e)(3)(ii) of this section, the Commission shall either lift the temporary suspension, or set the matter down for hearing at a time and place designated by the Commission, or both, and, after opportunity for hearing, may censure the petitioner or disqualify petitioner from appearing or practicing before the Commission for a period of time or permanently. In every case in which the temporary suspension has not been lifted, every hearing held and other action taken pursuant to this paragraph (e)(3) shall be expedited in accordance with § 201.500. If the hearing is held before a hearing officer, the time limits set forth in § 201.531 will govern review of the hearing officer's initial decision.

(iv) In any hearing held on a petition filed in accordance with paragraph (e)(3)(ii) of this section, the staff of the Commission shall show either that the petitioner has been enjoined as described in paragraph (e)(3)(i)(A) of this section or that the petitioner has been found to have committed or aided and abetted violations as described in paragraph (e)(3)(i)(B) of this section and that showing, without more, may be the basis for censure or disqualification. Once that showing has been made, the burden shall be upon the petitioner to show cause why he or she should not be censured or temporarily or permanently disqualified from appearing and practicing before the Commission. In any such hearing, the petitioner may not contest any finding made against him or her or fact admitted by him or her in the judicial or administrative proceeding upon which the proceeding under this paragraph (e)(3) is predicated. A person who has consented to the entry of a permanent injunction as described in paragraph (e)(3)(i)(A) of this section without admitting the facts set forth in the complaint shall be presumed for all purposes under this paragraph (e)(3) to have been enjoined by reason of the misconduct alleged in the complaint.

(4) *Filing of prior orders.* Any person appearing or practicing before the Commission who has been the subject of an order, judgment, decree, or finding as set forth in paragraph (e)(3) of this section shall promptly file with the Secretary a copy thereof (together with any related opinion or

statement of the agency or tribunal involved). Failure to file any such paper, order, judgment, decree or finding shall not impair the operation of any other provision of this section.

(5) *Reinstatement.*

(i) An application for reinstatement of a person permanently suspended or disqualified under paragraph (e)(1) or (e)(3) of this section may be made at any time, and the applicant may, in the Commission's discretion, be afforded a hearing; however, the suspension or disqualification shall continue unless and until the applicant has been reinstated by the Commission for good cause shown.

(ii) Any person suspended under paragraph (e)(2) of this section shall be reinstated by the Commission, upon appropriate application, if all the grounds for application of the provisions of that paragraph are subsequently removed by a reversal of the conviction or termination of the suspension, disbarment, or revocation. An application for reinstatement on any other grounds by any person suspended under paragraph (e)(2) of this section may be filed at any time and the applicant shall be accorded an opportunity for a hearing in the matter; however, such suspension shall continue unless and until the applicant has been reinstated by order of the Commission for good cause shown.

(6) *Other proceedings not precluded.* A proceeding brought under paragraph (e)(1), (e)(2) or (e)(3) of this section shall not preclude another proceeding brought under these same paragraphs.

(7) *Public hearings.* All hearings held under this paragraph (e) shall be public unless otherwise ordered by the Commission on its own motion or after considering the motion of a party.

(f) *Practice defined.* For the purposes of these Rules of Practice, practicing before the Commission shall include, but shall not be limited to:

(1) Transacting any business with the Commission; and

(2) The preparation of any statement, opinion or other paper by any attorney, accountant, engineer or other professional or expert, filed with the Commission in any registration statement, notification, application, report or other document with the consent of such attorney, accountant, engineer or other professional or expert.

PART 205—STANDARDS OF PROFESSIONAL CONDUCT FOR ATTORNEYS APPEARING AND PRACTICING BEFORE THE COMMISSION IN THE REPRESENTATION OF AN ISSUER

Rule 205.1. Purpose and Scope

This part sets forth minimum standards of professional conduct for attorneys appearing and practicing before the Commission in the representation of an issuer. These standards supplement applicable standards of any jurisdiction where an attorney is admitted or practices and are not intended to limit the ability of any jurisdiction to impose additional obligations on an attorney not inconsistent with the application of this part. Where the standards of a state or other United States jurisdiction where an attorney is admitted or practices conflict with this part, this part shall govern.

Rule 205.2. Definitions

For purposes of this part, the following definitions apply:

(a) *Appearing and practicing* before the Commission:

(1) Means:

(i) Transacting any business with the Commission, including communications in any form;

(ii) Representing an issuer in a Commission administrative proceeding or in connection with any Commission investigation, inquiry, information request, or subpoena;

(iii) Providing advice in respect of the United States securities laws or the Commission's rules or regulations thereunder regarding any document that the attorney has notice will be filed with or submitted to, or incorporated into any document that will be filed with or submitted to, the

Commission, including the provision of such advice in the context of preparing, or participating in the preparation of, any such document; or

(iv) Advising an issuer as to whether information or a statement, opinion, or other writing is required under the United States securities laws or the Commission's rules or regulations thereunder to be filed with or submitted to, or incorporated into any document that will be filed with or submitted to, the Commission; but

(2) Does not include an attorney who:

(i) Conducts the activities in paragraphs (a)(1)(i) through (a)(1)(iv) of this section other than in the context of providing legal services to an issuer with whom the attorney has an attorney-client relationship; or

(ii) Is a non-appearing foreign attorney.

(b) *Appropriate response* means a response to an attorney regarding reported evidence of a material violation as a result of which the attorney reasonably believes:

(1) That no material violation, as defined in paragraph (i) of this section, has occurred, is ongoing, or is about to occur;

(2) That the issuer has, as necessary, adopted appropriate remedial measures, including appropriate steps or sanctions to stop any material violations that are ongoing, to prevent any material violation that has yet to occur, and to remedy or otherwise appropriately address any material violation that has already occurred and to minimize the likelihood of its recurrence; or

(3) That the issuer, with the consent of the issuer's board of directors, a committee thereof to whom a report could be made pursuant to 205.3(b)(3), or a qualified legal compliance committee, has retained or directed an attorney to review the reported evidence of a material violation and either:

(i) Has substantially implemented any remedial recommendations made by such attorney after a reasonable investigation and evaluation of the reported evidence; or

(ii) Has been advised that such attorney may, consistent with his or her professional obligations, assert a colorable defense on behalf of the issuer (or the issuer's officer, director, employee, or agent, as the case may be) in any investigation or judicial or administrative proceeding relating to the reported evidence of a material violation.

(c) *Attorney* means any person who is admitted, licensed, or otherwise qualified to practice law in any jurisdiction, domestic or foreign, or who holds himself or herself out as admitted, licensed, or otherwise qualified to practice law.

(d) *Breach of fiduciary duty* refers to any breach of fiduciary or similar duty to the issuer recognized under an applicable federal or state statute or at common law, including but not limited to misfeasance, nonfeasance, abdication of duty, abuse of trust, and approval of unlawful transactions.

(e) *Evidence of a material violation* means credible evidence, based upon which it would be unreasonable, under the circumstances, for a prudent and competent attorney not to conclude that it is reasonably likely that a material violation has occurred, is ongoing, or is about to occur.

(f) *Foreign government issuer* means a foreign issuer as defined in 17 CFR 230.405 eligible to register securities on Schedule B of the Securities Act of 1933 (15 U.S.C. 77a *et seq.*, Schedule B).

(g) *In the representation of an issuer* means providing legal services as an attorney for an issuer, regardless of whether the attorney is employed or retained by the issuer.

(h) *Issuer* means an issuer (as defined in section 3 of the Securities Exchange Act of 1934 (15 U.S.C. 78c)), the securities of which are registered under section 12 of that Act (15 U.S.C. 78*l*), or that is required to file reports under section 15(d) of that Act (15 U.S.C. 78o(d)), or that files or has filed a registration statement that has not yet become effective under the Securities Act of 1933 (15 U.S.C. 77a *et seq.*), and that it has not withdrawn, but does not include a foreign government issuer. For purposes of paragraphs (a) and (g) of this section, the term "issuer" includes any person controlled by an issuer, where an attorney provides legal services to such person on behalf of, or at the behest, or for the benefit of the issuer, regardless of whether the attorney is employed or retained by the issuer.

(i) *Material violation* means a material violation of an applicable United States federal or state securities law, a material breach of fiduciary duty arising under United States federal or state law, or a similar material violation of any United States federal or state law.

(j) *Non-appearing foreign attorney* means an attorney:

(1) Who is admitted to practice law in a jurisdiction outside the United States;

(2) Who does not hold himself or herself out as practicing, and does not give legal advice regarding, United States federal or state securities or other laws (except as provided in paragraph (j)(3)(ii) of this section); and

(3) Who:

(i) Conducts activities that would constitute appearing and practicing before the Commission only incidentally to, and in the ordinary course of, the practice of law in a jurisdiction outside the United States; or

(ii) Is appearing and practicing before the Commission only in consultation with counsel, other than a non-appearing foreign attorney, admitted or licensed to practice in a state or other United States jurisdiction.

(k) *Qualified legal compliance committee* means a committee of an issuer (which also may be an audit or other committee of the issuer) that:

(1) Consists of at least one member of the issuer's audit committee (or, if the issuer has no audit committee, one member from an equivalent committee of independent directors) and two or more members of the issuer's board of directors who are not employed, directly or indirectly, by the issuer and who are not, in the case of a registered investment company, "interested persons" as defined in section 2(a)(19) of the Investment Company Act of 1940 (15 U.S.C. 80a-2(a)(19));

(2) Has adopted written procedures for the confidential receipt, retention, and consideration of any report of evidence of a material violation under § 205.3;

(3) Has been duly established by the issuer's board of directors, with the authority and responsibility:

(i) To inform the issuer's chief legal officer and chief executive officer (or the equivalents thereof) of any report of evidence of a material violation (except in the circumstances described in § 205.3(b)(4));

(ii) To determine whether an investigation is necessary regarding any report of evidence of a material violation by the issuer, its officers, directors, employees or agents and, if it determines an investigation is necessary or appropriate, to:

(A) Notify the audit committee or the full board of directors;

(B) Initiate an investigation, which may be conducted either by the chief legal officer (or the equivalent thereof) or by outside attorneys; and

(C) Retain such additional expert personnel as the committee deems necessary; and

(iii) At the conclusion of any such investigation, to:

(A) Recommend, by majority vote, that the issuer implement an appropriate response to evidence of a material violation; and

(B) Inform the chief legal officer and the chief executive officer (or the equivalents thereof) and the board of directors of the results of any such investigation under this section and the appropriate remedial measures to be adopted; and

(4) Has the authority and responsibility, acting by majority vote, to take all other appropriate action, including the authority to notify the Commission in the event that the issuer fails in any material respect to implement an appropriate response that the qualified legal compliance committee has recommended the issuer to take.

(l) *Reasonable* or *reasonably* denotes, with respect to the actions of an attorney, conduct that would not be unreasonable for a prudent and competent attorney.

(m) *Reasonably believes* means that an attorney believes the matter in question and that the circumstances are such that the belief is not unreasonable.

(n) *Report* means to make known to directly, either in person, by telephone, by e-mail, electronically, or in writing.

Rule 205.3. Issuer as Client

(a) *Representing an issuer.* An attorney appearing and practicing before the Commission in the representation of an issuer owes his or her professional and ethical duties to the issuer as an organization. That the attorney may work with and advise the issuer's officers, directors, or employees in the course of representing the issuer does not make such individuals the attorney's clients.

(b) *Duty to report evidence of a material violation.* (1) If an attorney, appearing and practicing before the Commission in the representation of an issuer, becomes aware of evidence of a material violation by the issuer or by any officer, director, employee, or agent of the issuer, the attorney shall report such evidence to the issuer's chief legal officer (or the equivalent thereof) or to both the issuer's chief legal officer and its chief executive officer (or the equivalents thereof) forthwith. By communicating such information to the issuer's officers or directors, an attorney does not reveal client confidences or secrets or privileged or otherwise protected information related to the attorney's representation of an issuer.

(2) The chief legal officer (or the equivalent thereof) shall cause such inquiry into the evidence of a material violation as he or she reasonably believes is appropriate to determine whether the material violation described in the report has occurred, is ongoing, or is about to occur. If the chief legal officer (or the equivalent thereof) determines no material violation has occurred, is ongoing, or is about to occur, he or she shall notify the reporting attorney and advise the reporting attorney of the basis for such determination. Unless the chief legal officer (or the equivalent thereof) reasonably believes that no material violation has occurred, is ongoing, or is about to occur, he or she shall take all reasonable steps to cause the issuer to adopt an appropriate response, and shall advise the reporting attorney thereof. In lieu of causing an inquiry under this paragraph (b), a chief legal officer (or the equivalent thereof) may refer a report of evidence of a material violation to a qualified legal compliance committee under paragraph (c)(2) of this section if the issuer has duly established a qualified legal compliance committee prior to the report of evidence of a material violation.

(3) Unless an attorney who has made a report under paragraph (b)(1) of this section reasonably believes that the chief legal officer or the chief executive officer of the issuer (or the equivalent thereof) has provided an appropriate response within a reasonable time, the attorney shall report the evidence of a material violation to:

(i) The audit committee of the issuer's board of directors;

(ii) Another committee of the issuer's board of directors consisting solely of directors who are not employed, directly or indirectly, by the issuer and are not, in the case of a registered investment company, "interested persons" as defined in section 2(a)(19) of the Investment Company Act of 1940 (15 U.S.C. 80a-2(a)(19)) (if the issuer's board of directors has no audit committee); or

(iii) The issuer's board of directors (if the issuer's board of directors has no committee consisting solely of directors who are not employed, directly or indirectly, by the issuer and are not, in the case of a registered investment company, "interested persons" as defined in section 2(a)(19) of the Investment Company Act of 1940 (15 U.S.C. 80a-2(a)(19))).

(4) If an attorney reasonably believes that it would be futile to report evidence of a material violation to the issuer's chief legal officer and chief executive officer (or the equivalents thereof) under paragraph (b)(1) of this section, the attorney may report such evidence as provided under paragraph (b)(3) of this section.

(5) An attorney retained or directed by an issuer to investigate evidence of a material violation reported under paragraph (b)(1), (b)(3), or (b)(4) of this section shall be deemed to be appearing and practicing before the Commission. Directing or retaining an attorney to investigate reported evidence of a material violation does not relieve an officer or director of the issuer to whom such evidence has been reported under paragraph (b)(1), (b)(3), or (b)(4) of this section from a duty to respond to the reporting attorney.

(6) An attorney shall not have any obligation to report evidence of a material violation under this paragraph (b) if:

(i) The attorney was retained or directed by the issuer's chief legal officer (or the equivalent thereof) to investigate such evidence of a material violation and:

(A) The attorney reports the results of such investigation to the chief legal officer (or the equivalent thereof); and

(B) Except where the attorney and the chief legal officer (or the equivalent thereof) each reasonably believes that no material violation has occurred, is ongoing, or is about to occur, the chief legal officer (or the equivalent thereof) reports the results of the investigation to the issuer's board of directors, a committee thereof to whom a report could be made pursuant to paragraph (b)(3) of this section, or a qualified legal compliance committee; or

(ii) The attorney was retained or directed by the chief legal officer (or the equivalent thereof) to assert, consistent with his or her professional obligations, a colorable defense on behalf of the issuer (or the issuer's officer, director, employee, or agent, as the case may be) in any investigation or judicial or administrative proceeding relating to such evidence of a material violation, and the chief legal officer (or the equivalent thereof) provides reasonable and timely reports on the progress and outcome of such proceeding to the issuer's board of directors, a committee thereof to whom a report could be made pursuant to paragraph (b)(3) of this section, or a qualified legal compliance committee.

(7) An attorney shall not have any obligation to report evidence of a material violation under this paragraph (b) if such attorney was retained or directed by a qualified legal compliance committee:

(i) To investigate such evidence of a material violation; or

(ii) To assert, consistent with his or her professional obligations, a colorable defense on behalf of the issuer (or the issuer's officer, director, employee, or agent, as the case may be) in any investigation or judicial or administrative proceeding relating to such evidence of a material violation.

(8) An attorney who receives what he or she reasonably believes is an appropriate and timely response to a report he or she has made pursuant to paragraph (b)(1), (b)(3), or (b)(4) of this section need do nothing more under this section with respect to his or her report.

(9) An attorney who does not reasonably believe that the issuer has made an appropriate response within a reasonable time to the report or reports made pursuant to paragraph (b)(1), (b)(3), or (b)(4) of this section shall explain his or her reasons therefor to the chief legal officer (or the equivalent thereof), the chief executive officer (or the equivalent thereof), and directors to whom the attorney reported the evidence of a material violation pursuant to paragraph (b)(1), (b)(3), or (b)(4) of this section.

(10) An attorney formerly employed or retained by an issuer who has reported evidence of a material violation under this part and reasonably believes that he or she has been discharged for so doing may notify the issuer's board of directors or any committee thereof that he or she believes that he or she has been discharged for reporting evidence of a material violation under this section.

(c) *Alternative reporting procedures for attorneys retained or employed by an issuer that has established a qualified legal compliance committee.* (1) If an attorney, appearing and practicing before the Commission in the representation of an issuer, becomes aware of evidence of a material violation by the issuer or by any officer, director, employee, or agent of the issuer, the attorney may, as an alternative to the reporting requirements of paragraph (b) of this section, report such evidence to a qualified legal compliance committee, if the issuer has previously formed such a committee. An attorney who reports evidence of a material violation to such a qualified legal compliance committee has satisfied his or her obligation to report such evidence and is not required to assess the issuer's response to the reported evidence of a material violation.

(2) A chief legal officer (or the equivalent thereof) may refer a report of evidence of a material violation to a previously established qualified legal compliance committee in lieu of causing an inquiry to be conducted under paragraph (b)(2) of this section. The chief legal officer (or the equivalent thereof) shall inform the reporting attorney that the report has been referred to a qualified legal compliance committee. Thereafter, pursuant to the requirements under § 205.2(k),

the qualified legal compliance committee shall be responsible for responding to the evidence of a material violation reported to it under this paragraph (c).

(d) *Issuer confidences.* (1) Any report under this section (or the contemporaneous record thereof) or any response thereto (or the contemporaneous record thereof) may be used by an attorney in connection with any investigation, proceeding, or litigation in which the attorney's compliance with this part is in issue.

(2) An attorney appearing and practicing before the Commission in the representation of an issuer may reveal to the Commission, without the issuer's consent, confidential information related to the representation to the extent the attorney reasonably believes necessary:

(i) To prevent the issuer from committing a material violation that is likely to cause substantial injury to the financial interest or property of the issuer or investors;

(ii) To prevent the issuer, in a Commission investigation or administrative proceeding from committing perjury, proscribed in 18 U.S.C. 1621; suborning perjury, proscribed in 18 U.S.C. 1622; or committing any act proscribed in 18 U.S.C. 1001 that is likely to perpetrate a fraud upon the Commission; or

(iii) To rectify the consequences of a material violation by the issuer that caused, or may cause, substantial injury to the financial interest or property of the issuer or investors in the furtherance of which the attorney's services were used.

Rule 205.4. Responsibilities of Supervisory Attorneys

(a) An attorney supervising or directing another attorney who is appearing and practicing before the Commission in the representation of an issuer is a supervisory attorney. An issuer's chief legal officer (or the equivalent thereof) is a supervisory attorney under this section.

(b) A supervisory attorney shall make reasonable efforts to ensure that a subordinate attorney, as defined in § 205.5(a), that he or she supervises or directs conforms to this part. To the extent a subordinate attorney appears and practices before the Commission in the representation of an issuer, that subordinate attorney's supervisory attorneys also appear and practice before the Commission.

(c) A supervisory attorney is responsible for complying with the reporting requirements in § 205.3 when a subordinate attorney has reported to the supervisory attorney evidence of a material violation.

(d) A supervisory attorney who has received a report of evidence of a material violation from a subordinate attorney under § 205.3 may report such evidence to the issuer's qualified legal compliance committee if the issuer has duly formed such a committee.

Rule 205.5. Responsibilities of a Subordinate Attorney

(a) An attorney who appears and practices before the Commission in the representation of an issuer on a matter under the supervision or direction of another attorney (other than under the direct supervision or direction of the issuer's chief legal officer (or the equivalent thereof)) is a subordinate attorney.

(b) A subordinate attorney shall comply with this part notwithstanding that the subordinate attorney acted at the direction of or under the supervision of another person.

(c) A subordinate attorney complies with § 205.3 if the subordinate attorney reports to his or her supervising attorney under § 205.3(b) evidence of a material violation of which the subordinate attorney has become aware in appearing and practicing before the Commission.

(d) A subordinate attorney may take the steps permitted or required by § 205.3(b) or (c) if the subordinate attorney reasonably believes that a supervisory attorney to whom he or she has reported evidence of a material violation under § 205.3(b) has failed to comply with § 205.3.

Rule 205.6. Sanctions and Discipline

(a) A violation of this part by any attorney appearing and practicing before the Commission in the representation of an issuer shall subject such attorney to the civil penalties and remedies for a violation of the federal securities laws available to the Commission in an action brought by the Commission thereunder.

(b) An attorney appearing and practicing before the Commission who violates any provision of this part is subject to the disciplinary authority of the Commission, regardless of whether the attorney may also be subject to discipline for the same conduct in a jurisdiction where the attorney is admitted or practices. An administrative disciplinary proceeding initiated by the Commission for violation of this part may result in an attorney being censured, or being temporarily or permanently denied the privilege of appearing or practicing before the Commission.

(c) An attorney who complies in good faith with the provisions of this part shall not be subject to discipline or otherwise liable under inconsistent standards imposed by any state or other United States jurisdiction where the attorney is admitted or practices.

(d) An attorney practicing outside the United States shall not be required to comply with the requirements of this part to the extent that such compliance is prohibited by applicable foreign law.

Rule 205.7. No Private Right of Action

(a) Nothing in this part is intended to, or does, create a private right of action against any attorney, law firm, or issuer based upon compliance or noncompliance with its provisions.

(b) Authority to enforce compliance with this part is vested exclusively in the Commission.

STAFF ACCOUNTING BULLETINS—SELECTED RELEASE

Release No.	Subject
99	Materiality

Release No. 99, August 12, 1999

Materiality

ACTION: Publication of Staff Accounting Bulletin

SUMMARY: This staff accounting bulletin expresses the views of the staff that exclusive reliance on certain quantitative benchmarks to assess materiality in preparing financial statements and performing audits of those financial statements is inappropriate; misstatements are not immaterial simply because they fall beneath a numerical threshold.

DATE: August 12, 1999

FOR FURTHER INFORMATION CONTACT: W. Scott Bayless, Associate Chief Accountant, or Robert E. Burns, Chief Counsel, Office of the Chief Accountant (202-942-4400), or David R. Fredrickson, Office of General Counsel (202-942-0900), Securities and Exchange Commission, 450 Fifth Street, N.W., Washington, D.C. 20549-1103; electronic addresses: BaylessWS@sec.gov; BurnsR@sec.gov; FredricksonD@sec.gov.

SUPPLEMENTARY INFORMATION: The statements in the staff accounting bulletins are not rules or interpretations of the Commission, nor are they published as bearing the Commission's official approval. They represent interpretations and practices followed by the Division of Corporation Finance and the Office of the Chief Accountant in administering the disclosure requirements of the Federal securities laws.

Part 211—(AMEND)

Accordingly, Part 211 of Title 17 of the Code of Federal Regulations is amended by adding Staff Accounting Bulletin No. 99 to the table found in Subpart B.

STAFF ACCOUNTING BULLETIN NO. 99

The staff hereby adds Section M to Topic 1 of the Staff Accounting Bulletin Series. Section M, entitled "Materiality," provides guidance in applying materiality thresholds to the preparation of financial statements filed with the Commission and the performance of audits of those financial statements.

Assessing materiality

Facts: During the course of preparing or auditing year-end financial statements, financial management or the registrant's independent auditor becomes aware of misstatements in a registrant's financial statements. When combined, the misstatements result in a 4% overstatement of net income and a $.02 (4%) overstatement of earnings per share. Because no item in the registrant's consolidated financial statements is misstated by more than 5%, management and the independent auditor conclude that the deviation from GAAP is immaterial and that the accounting is permissible.[1]

Question: Each Statement of Financial Accounting Standards adopted by the FASB states, "The provisions of this Statement need not be applied to immaterial items." In the staff's view, may a registrant or the auditor of its financial statements assume the immateriality of items that fall below a percentage threshold set by management or the auditor to determine whether amounts and items are material to the financial statements?

Interpretive Response: No. The staff is aware that certain registrants, over time, have developed quantitative thresholds as "rules of thumb" to assist in the preparation of their financial statements, and that auditors also have used these thresholds in their evaluation of whether items might be considered material to users of a registrant's financial statements. One rule of thumb in particular suggests that the misstatement or omission[2] of an item that falls under a 5% threshold is not material in the absence of particularly egregious circumstances, such as self-dealing or misappropriation by senior management. The staff reminds registrants and the auditors of their financial statements that exclusive reliance on this or any percentage or numerical threshold has no basis in the accounting literature or the law.

The use of a percentage as a numerical threshold, such as 5%, may provide the basis for a preliminary assumption that—without considering all relevant circumstances—a deviation of less than the specified percentage with respect to a particular item on the registrant's financial statements is unlikely to be material. The staff has no objection to such a "rule of thumb" as an initial step in assessing materiality. But quantifying, in percentage terms, the magnitude of a misstatement is only the beginning of an analysis of materiality; it cannot appropriately be used as a substitute for a full analysis of all relevant considerations. Materiality concerns the significance of an item to users of a registrant's financial statements. A matter is "material" if there is a substantial likelihood that a reasonable person would consider it important. In its Concepts Statement 2, the FASB stated the essence of the concept of materiality as follows:

The omission or misstatement of an item in a financial report is material if, in the light of surrounding circumstances, the magnitude of the item is such that it is probable that the judgment of a reasonable person relying upon the report would have been changed or influenced by the inclusion or correction of the item.[3]

This formulation in the accounting literature is in substance identical to the formulation used by the courts in interpreting the federal securities laws. The Supreme Court has held that a fact is material if there is -

a substantial likelihood that the . . . fact would have been viewed by the reasonable investor as having significantly altered the "total mix" of information made available.[4]

Under the governing principles, an assessment of materiality requires that one views the facts in the context of the "surrounding circumstances," as the accounting literature puts it, or the "total mix" of information, in the words of the Supreme Court. In the context of a misstatement of a

---

[1] AU 312 states that the auditor should consider audit risk and materiality both in (a) planning and setting the scope for the audit and (b) evaluating whether financial statements taken as a whole are fairly presented in all material respects in conformity with GAAP. The purpose of this SAB is to provide guidance to financial management and independent auditors with respect to the evaluation of the materiality of misstatements that are identified in the audit process or preparation of the financial statements (i.e., (b) above). This SAB is not intended to provide definitive guidance for assessing "materiality" in other contexts, such as evaluations of auditor independence, as other factors may apply. There may be other rules that address financial

presentation. See, e.g., Rule 2a-4, 17 CFR 270.2a-4, under the Investment Company Act of 1940.

[2] As used in this SAB, "misstatement" or "omission" refers to a financial statement assertion that would not be in conformity with GAAP.

[3] Concepts Statement 2, paragraph 132. See also Concepts Statement 2, Glossary of Terms—Materiality.

[4] TSC Industries v. Northway, Inc., 426 U.S. 438, 449 (1976). See also Basic, Inc. v. Levinson, 485 U.S. 224 (1988). As the Supreme Court has noted, determinations of materiality require "delicate assessments of the inferences a 'reasonable shareholder' would draw from a given set of facts and the significance of those inferences to him . . . ." TSC Industries, 426 U.S. at 450.

financial statement item, while the "total mix" includes the size in numerical or percentage terms of the misstatement, it also includes the factual context in which the user of financial statements would view the financial statement item. The shorthand in the accounting and auditing literature for this analysis is that financial management and the auditor must consider both "quantitative" and "qualitative" factors in assessing an item's materiality.[5] Court decisions, Commission rules and enforcement actions, and accounting and auditing literature[6] have all considered "qualitative" factors in various contexts.

The FASB has long emphasized that materiality cannot be reduced to a numerical formula. In its Concepts Statement 2, the FASB noted that some had urged it to promulgate quantitative materiality guides for use in a variety of situations. The FASB rejected such an approach as representing only a "minority view, stating -

The predominant view is that materiality judgments can properly be made only by those who have all the facts. The Board's present position is that no general standards of materiality could be formulated to take into account all the considerations that enter into an experienced human judgment.[7]

The FASB noted that, in certain limited circumstances, the Commission and other authoritative bodies had issued quantitative materiality guidance, citing as examples guidelines ranging from one to ten percent with respect to a variety of disclosures.[8] And it took account of contradictory studies, one showing a lack of uniformity among auditors on materiality judgments, and another suggesting widespread use of a "rule of thumb" of five to ten percent of net income.[9] The FASB also considered whether an evaluation of materiality could be based solely on anticipating the market's reaction to accounting information.[10]

The FASB rejected a formulaic approach to discharging "the onerous duty of making materiality decisions"[11] in favor of an approach that takes into account all the relevant considerations. In so doing, it made clear that -

[M]agnitude by itself, without regard to the nature of the item and the circumstances in which the judgment has to be made, will not generally be a sufficient basis for a materiality judgment.[12]

Evaluation of materiality requires a registrant and its auditor to consider *all* the relevant circumstances, and the staff believes that there are numerous circumstances in which misstatements below 5% could well be material. Qualitative factors may cause misstatements of quantitatively small amounts to be material; as stated in the auditing literature:

As a result of the interaction of quantitative and qualitative considerations in materiality judgments, misstatements of relatively small amounts that come to the auditor's attention could have a material effect on the financial statements.[13]

Among the considerations that may well render material a quantitatively small misstatement of a financial statement item are -

---

[5] See, e.g., Concepts Statement 2, paragraphs 123-124; AU 312A.10 (materiality judgments are made in light of surrounding circumstances and necessarily involve both quantitative and qualitative considerations); AU 312A.34 ("Qualitative considerations also influence the auditor in reaching a conclusion as to whether misstatements are material."). As used in the accounting literature and in this SAB, "qualitative" materiality refers to the surrounding circumstances that inform an investor's evaluation of financial statement entries. Whether events may be material to investors for non-financial reasons is a matter not addressed by this SAB.

[6] See, e.g., Rule 1-02(o) of Regulation S-X, 17 CFR 210.1-02(o), Rule 405 of Regulation C, 17 CFR 230.405, and Rule 12b-2, 17 CFR 240.12b-2; AU 312A.10 - .11, 317.13, 411.04 n. 1, and 508.36; In re Kidder Peabody Securities Litigation, 10 F. Supp. 2d 398 (S.D.N.Y. 1998);

Parnes v. Gateway 2000, Inc., 122 F.3d 539 (8th Cir. 1997); In re Westinghouse Securities Litigation, 90 F.3d 696 (3d Cir. 1996); In the Matter of W.R. Grace & Co., Accounting and Auditing Enforcement Release ("AAER") 1140 (June 30, 1999); In the Matter of Eugene Gaughan, AAER 1141 (June 30, 1999); In the Matter of Thomas Scanlon, AAER 1142 (June 30, 1999); and In re Sensormatic Electronics Corporation, Sec. Act Rel. No. 7518 (March 25, 1998).

[7] Concepts Statement 2, paragraph 131.

[8] Concepts Statement 2, paragraphs 131 and 166.

[9] Concepts Statement 2, paragraph 167.

[10] Concepts Statement 2, paragraphs 168-169.

[11] Concepts Statement 2, paragraph 170.

[12] Concepts Statement 2, paragraph 125.

[13] AU 312.11.

• whether the misstatement arises from an item capable of precise measurement or whether it arises from an estimate and, if so, the degree of imprecision inherent in the estimate[14]

• whether the misstatement masks a change in earnings or other trends

• whether the misstatement hides a failure to meet analysts' consensus expectations for the enterprise

• whether the misstatement changes a loss into income or vice versa

• whether the misstatement concerns a segment or other portion of the registrant's business that has been identified as playing a significant role in the registrant's operations or profitability

• whether the misstatement affects the registrant's compliance with regulatory requirements

• whether the misstatement affects the registrant's compliance with loan covenants or other contractual requirements

• whether the misstatement has the effect of increasing management's compensation—for example, by satisfying requirements for the award of bonuses or other forms of incentive compensation

• whether the misstatement involves concealment of an unlawful transaction.

This is not an exhaustive list of the circumstances that may affect the materiality of a quantitatively small misstatement.[15] Among other factors, the demonstrated volatility of the price of a registrant's securities in response to certain types of disclosures may provide guidance as to whether investors regard quantitatively small misstatements as material. Consideration of potential market reaction to disclosure of a misstatement is by itself "too blunt an instrument to be depended on" in considering whether a fact is material.[16] When, however, management or the independent auditor expects (based, for example, on a pattern of market performance) that a known misstatement may result in a significant positive or negative market reaction, that expected reaction should be taken into account when considering whether a misstatement is material.[17]

For the reasons noted above, the staff believes that a registrant and the auditors of its financial statements should not assume that even small intentional misstatements in financial statements, for example those pursuant to actions to "manage" earnings, are immaterial.[18] While the intent of management does not render a misstatement material, it may provide significant evidence of materiality. The evidence may be particularly compelling where management has intentionally misstated items in the financial statements to "manage" reported earnings. In that instance, it presumably has done so believing that the resulting amounts and trends would be significant to users of the registrant's financial statements.[19] The staff believes that investors generally would

---

[14] As stated in Concepts Statement 2, paragraph 130:

Another factor in materiality judgments is the degree of precision that is attainable in estimating the judgment item. The amount of deviation that is considered immaterial may increase as the attainable degree of precision decreases. For example, accounts payable usually can be estimated more accurately than can contingent liabilities arising from litigation or threats of it, and a deviation considered to be material in the first case may be quite trivial in the second.

This SAB is not intended to change current law or guidance in the accounting literature regarding accounting estimates. See, e.g., Accounting Principles Board Opinion 20, Accounting Changes 10, 11, 31-33 (July 1971).

[15] The staff understands that the Big Five Audit Materiality Task Force ("Task Force") was convened in March of 1998 and has made recommendations to the Auditing Standards Board including suggestions regarding communications with audit committees about

unadjusted misstatements. See generally Big Five Audit Materiality Task Force. "Materiality in a Financial Statement Audit—Considering Qualitative Factors When Evaluating Audit Findings" (August 1998).

[16] See Concepts Statement 2, paragraph 169.

[17] If management does not expect a significant market reaction, a misstatement still may be material and should be evaluated under the criteria discussed in this SAB.

[18] Intentional management of earnings and intentional misstatements, as used in this SAB, do not include insignificant errors and omissions that may occur in systems and recurring processes in the normal course of business. See notes 37 and 49 infra.

[19] Assessments of materiality should occur not only at year-end, but also during the preparation of each quarterly or interim financial statement. See, e.g., In the Matter of Venator Group, Inc., AAER 1049 (June 29, 1998).

regard as significant a management practice to over- or under-state earnings up to an amount just short of a percentage threshold in order to "manage" earnings. Investors presumably also would regard as significant an accounting practice that, in essence, rendered all earnings figures subject to a management-directed margin of misstatement.

The materiality of a misstatement may turn on where it appears in the financial statements. For example, a misstatement may involve a segment of the registrant's operations. In that instance, in assessing materiality of a misstatement to the financial statements taken as a whole, registrants and their auditors should consider not only the size of the misstatement but also the significance of the segment information to the financial statements taken as a whole.[20] "A misstatement of the revenue and operating profit of a relatively small segment that is represented by management to be important to the future profitability of the entity"[21] is more likely to be material to investors than a misstatement in a segment that management has not identified as especially important. In assessing the materiality of misstatements in segment information—as with materiality generally—situations may arise in practice where the auditor will conclude that a matter relating to segment information is qualitatively material even though, in his or her judgment, it is quantitatively immaterial to the financial statements taken as a whole.[22]

Aggregating and Netting Misstatements

In determining whether multiple misstatements cause the financial statements to be materially misstated, registrants and the auditors of their financial statements should consider each misstatement separately and the aggregate effect of all misstatements.[23] A registrant and its auditor should evaluate misstatements in light of quantitative and qualitative factors and "consider whether, in relation to individual amounts, subtotals, or totals in the financial statements, they materially misstate the financial statements taken as a whole."[24] This requires consideration of—the significance of an item to a particular entity (for example, inventories to a manufacturing company), the pervasiveness of the misstatement (such as whether it affects the presentation of numerous financial statement items), and the effect of the misstatement on the financial statements taken as a whole . . . .[25]

Registrants and their auditors first should consider whether each misstatement is material, irrespective of its effect when combined with other misstatements. The literature notes that the analysis should consider whether the misstatement of "individual amounts" causes a material misstatement of the financial statements taken as a whole. As with materiality generally, this analysis requires consideration of both quantitative and qualitative factors.

If the misstatement of an individual amount causes the financial statements as a whole to be materially misstated, that effect cannot be eliminated by other misstatements whose effect may be to diminish the impact of the misstatement on other financial statement items. To take an obvious example, if a registrant's revenues are a material financial statement item and if they are materially overstated, the financial statements taken as a whole will be materially misleading even if the effect on earnings is completely offset by an equivalent overstatement of expenses.

Even though a misstatement of an individual amount may not cause the financial statements taken as a whole to be materially misstated, it may nonetheless, when aggregated with other

---

[20] See, e.g., In the Matter of W.R. Grace & Co., AAER 1140 (June 30, 1999).

[21] AU 9326.33.

[22] *Id.*

[23] The auditing literature notes that the "concept of materiality recognizes that some matters, either individually or in the aggregate, are important for fair presentation of financial statements in conformity with generally accepted accounting principles." AU 312.03. *See* also AU 312.04.

[24] AU 312.34. Quantitative materiality assessments often are made by comparing adjustments to revenues,

gross profit, pretax and net income, total assets, stockholders' equity, or individual line items in the financial statements. The particular items in the financial statements to be considered as a basis for the materiality determination depend on the proposed adjustment to be made and other factors, such as those identified in this SAB. For example, an adjustment to inventory that is immaterial to pretax income or net income may be material to the financial statements because it may affect a working capital ratio or cause the registrant to be in default of loan covenants.

[25] AU 508.36.

misstatements, render the financial statements taken as a whole to be materially misleading. Registrants and the auditors of their financial statements accordingly should consider the effect of the misstatement on subtotals or totals. The auditor should aggregate all misstatements that affect each subtotal or total and consider whether the misstatements in the aggregate affect the subtotal or total in a way that causes the registrant's financial statements taken as a whole to be materially misleading.[26]

The staff believes that, in considering the aggregate effect of multiple misstatements on a subtotal or total, registrants and the auditors of their financial statements should exercise particular care when considering whether to offset (or the appropriateness of offsetting) a misstatement of an estimated amount with a misstatement of an item capable of precise measurement. As noted above, assessments of materiality should never be purely mechanical; given the imprecision inherent in estimates, there is by definition a corresponding imprecision in the aggregation of misstatements involving estimates with those that do not involve an estimate.

Registrants and auditors also should consider the effect of misstatements from prior periods on the current financial statements. For example, the auditing literature states,

Matters underlying adjustments proposed by the auditor but not recorded by the entity could potentially cause future financial statements to be materially misstated, even though the auditor has concluded that the adjustments are not material to the current financial statements.[27]

This may be particularly the case where immaterial misstatements recur in several years and the cumulative effect becomes material in the current year.

2. Immaterial misstatements that are intentional

Facts: A registrant's management intentionally has made adjustments to various financial statement items in a manner inconsistent with GAAP. In each accounting period in which such actions were taken, none of the individual adjustments is by itself material, nor is the aggregate effect on the financial statements taken as a whole material for the period. The registrant's earnings "management" has been effected at the direction or acquiescence of management in the belief that any deviations from GAAP have been immaterial and that accordingly the accounting is permissible.

Question: In the staff's view, may a registrant make intentional immaterial misstatements in its financial statements?

Interpretive Response: No. In certain circumstances, intentional immaterial misstatements are unlawful.

Considerations of the books and records provisions under the Exchange Act

Even if misstatements are immaterial,[28] registrants must comply with Sections 13(b)(2)—(7) of the Securities Exchange Act of 1934 (the "Exchange Act").[29] Under these provisions, each registrant with securities registered pursuant to Section 12 of the Exchange Act,[30] or required to file reports pursuant to Section 15(d),[31] must make and keep books, records, and accounts, which, in reasonable detail, accurately and fairly reflect the transactions and dispositions of assets of the registrant and must maintain internal accounting controls that are sufficient to provide reasonable assurances that, among other things, transactions are recorded as necessary to permit the preparation of financial statements in conformity with GAAP.[32] In this context, determinations of

---

[26] AU 312.34.

[27] AU 380.09.

[28] FASB Statements generally provide that "[t]he provisions of this Statement need not be applied to immaterial items." This SAB is consistent with that provision of the Statements. In theory, this language is subject to the interpretation that the registrant is free intentionally to set forth immaterial items in financial statements in a manner that plainly would be contrary to GAAP if the

misstatement were material. The staff believes that the FASB did not intend this result.

[29] 15 U.S.C. 78m(b)(2)—(7).

[30] 15 U.S.C. 78l.

[31] 15 U.S.C. 78o(d).

[32] Criminal liability may be imposed if a person knowingly circumvents or knowingly fails to implement a system of internal accounting controls or knowingly falsifies books, records or accounts. 15 U.S.C. 78m(4)

what constitutes "reasonable assurance" and "reasonable detail" are based not on a "materiality" analysis but on the level of detail and degree of assurance that would satisfy prudent officials in the conduct of their own affairs.[33] Accordingly, failure to record accurately immaterial items, in some instances, may result in violations of the securities laws.

The staff recognizes that there is limited authoritative guidance[34] regarding the "reasonableness" standard in Section 13(b)(2) of the Exchange Act. A principal statement of the Commission's policy in this area is set forth in an address given in 1981 by then Chairman Harold M. Williams.[35] In his address, Chairman Williams noted that, like materiality, "reasonableness" is not an "absolute standard of exactitude for corporate records."[36] Unlike materiality, however, "reasonableness" is not solely a measure of the significance of a financial statement item to investors. "Reasonableness," in this context, reflects a judgment as to whether an issuer's failure to correct a known misstatement implicates the purposes underlying the accounting provisions of Sections 13(b)(2)—(7) of the Exchange Act.[37]

In assessing whether a misstatement results in a violation of a registrant's obligation to keep books and records that are accurate "in reasonable detail," registrants and their auditors should consider, in addition to the factors discussed above concerning an evaluation of a misstatement's potential materiality, the factors set forth below.

• The significance of the misstatement. Though the staff does not believe that registrants need to make finely calibrated determinations of significance with respect to immaterial items, plainly it is "reasonable" to treat misstatements whose effects are clearly inconsequential differently than more significant ones.

• How the misstatement arose. It is unlikely that it is ever "reasonable" for registrants to record misstatements or not to correct known misstatements—even immaterial ones—as part of an ongoing effort directed by or known to senior management for the purposes of "managing" earnings. On the other hand, insignificant misstatements that arise from the operation of systems or recurring processes in the normal course of business generally will not cause a registrant's books to be inaccurate "in reasonable detail."[38]

(Footnote Continued)

and (5). See also Rule 13b2-1 under the Exchange Act, 17 CFR 240.13b2-1, which states, "No person shall, directly or indirectly, falsify or cause to be falsified, any book, record or account subject to Section 13(b)(2)(A) of the Securities Exchange Act."

[33] 15 U.S.C. 78m(b)(7). The books and records provisions of section 13(b) of the Exchange Act originally were passed as part of the Foreign Corrupt Practices Act ("FCPA"). In the conference committee report regarding the 1988 amendments to the FCPA, the committee stated:

The conference committee adopted the prudent man qualification in order to clarify that the current standard does not connote an unrealistic degree of exactitude or precision. The concept of reasonableness of necessity contemplates the weighing of a number of relevant factors, including the costs of compliance.

Cong. Rec. H2116 (daily ed. April 20, 1988).

[34] So far as the staff is aware, there is only one judicial decision that discusses Section 13(b)(2) of the Exchange Act in any detail, SEC v. World-Wide Coin Investments, Ltd., 567 F. Supp. 724 (N.D. Ga. 1983), and the courts generally have found that no private right of action exists under the accounting and books and records provisions of the Exchange Act. See e.g., Lamb v. Phillip Morris Inc., 915 F.2d 1024 (6th Cir. 1990) and JS Service Center Corporation v. General Electric Tech-

nical Services Company, 937 F. Supp. 216 (S.D.N.Y. 1996).

[35] The Commission adopted the address as a formal statement of policy in Securities Exchange Act Release No. 17500 (January 29, 1981), 46 FR 11544 (February 9, 1981), 21 SEC Docket 1466 (February 10, 1981).

[36] Id. at 46 FR 11546.

[37] Id.

[38] For example, the conference report regarding the 1988 amendments to the FCPA stated:

The Conferees intend to codify current Securities and Exchange Commission (SEC) enforcement policy that penalties not be imposed for insignificant or technical infractions or inadvertent conduct. The amendment adopted by the Conferees [Section 13(b)(4)] accomplishes this by providing that criminal penalties shall not be imposed for failing to comply with the FCPA's books and records or accounting provisions. This provision [Section 13(b)(5)] is meant to ensure that criminal penalties would be imposed where acts of commission or omission in keeping books or records or administering accounting controls have the purpose of falsifying books, records or accounts, or of circumventing the accounting controls set forth in the Act. This would include the deliberate falsification of books and records and other conduct calculated to evade the internal accounting controls requirement.

- The cost of correcting the misstatement. The books and records provisions of the Exchange Act do not require registrants to make major expenditures to correct small misstatements.[39] Conversely, where there is little cost or delay involved in correcting a misstatement, failing to do so is unlikely to be "reasonable."

- The clarity of authoritative accounting guidance with respect to the misstatement. Where reasonable minds may differ about the appropriate accounting treatment of a financial statement item, a failure to correct it may not render the registrant's financial statements inaccurate "in reasonable detail." Where, however, there is little ground for reasonable disagreement, the case for leaving a misstatement uncorrected is correspondingly weaker.

There may be other indicators of "reasonableness" that registrants and their auditors may ordinarily consider. Because the judgment is not mechanical, the staff will be inclined to continue to defer to judgments that "allow a business, acting in good faith, to comply with the Act's accounting provisions in an innovative and cost-effective way."[40]

The Auditor's Response to Intentional Misstatements

Section 10A(b) of the Exchange Act requires auditors to take certain actions upon discovery of an "illegal act."[41] The statute specifies that these obligations are triggered "whether or not [the illegal acts are] perceived to have a material effect on the financial statements of the issuer . . . ." Among other things, Section 10A(b)(1) requires the auditor to inform the appropriate level of management of an illegal act (unless clearly inconsequential) and assure that the registrant's audit committee is "adequately informed" with respect to the illegal act.

As noted, an intentional misstatement of immaterial items in a registrant's financial statements may violate Section 13(b)(2) of the Exchange Act and thus be an illegal act. When such a violation occurs, an auditor must take steps to see that the registrant's audit committee is "adequately informed" about the illegal act. Because Section 10A(b)(1) is triggered regardless of whether an illegal act has a material effect on the registrant's financial statements, where the illegal act consists of a misstatement in the registrant's financial statements, the auditor will be required to report that illegal act to the audit committee irrespective of any "netting" of the misstatements with other financial statement items.

The requirements of Section 10A echo the auditing literature. See, for example, SAS Nos. 54 and 99. Pursuant to paragraph 77 of SAS 99, if the auditor determines there is evidence that fraud may exist, the auditor must discuss the matter with the appropriate level of management that is at least one level above those involved, and with senior management and the audit committee. The auditor must report directly to the audit committee fraud involving senior management and fraud that causes a material misstatement of the financial statements. Paragraph 6 of SAS 99 states that "misstatements arising from fraudulent financial reporting are intentional misstatements or omissions of amounts or disclosures in financial statements designed to deceive financial statement users . . ."[42] SAS 99 further states that fraudulent financial reporting may involve falsification or alteration of accounting records; misrepresenting or omitting events, transactions or other information in the financial statements; and the intentional misapplication of accounting principles relating to amounts, classifications, the manner of presentation, or disclosures in the financial

---

(Footnote Continued)

Cong. Rec. H2115 (daily ed. April 20, 1988).

[39] As Chairman Williams noted with respect to the internal control provisions of the FCPA, "[t]housands of dollars ordinarily should not be spent conserving hundreds." 46 FR 11546.

[40] *Id.*, at 11547.

[41] Section 10A(f) defines, for purposes of Section 10A, an "illegal act" as "an act or omission that violates any law, or any rule or regulation having the force of law." This is broader than the definition of an "illegal act" in AU 317.02, which states, "Illegal acts by clients do not

include personal misconduct by the entity's personnel unrelated to their business activities."

[42] An unintentional illegal act triggers the same procedures and considerations by the auditor as a fraudulent misstatement if the illegal act has a direct and material effect on the financial statements. See AU 110 n. 1, 317.05 and 317.07. Although distinguishing between intentional and unintentional misstatements is often difficult, the auditor must plan and perform the audit to obtain reasonable assurance that the financial statements are free of material misstatements in either case.

statements.[43] The clear implication of SAS 99 is that immaterial misstatements may be fraudulent financial reporting.[44]

Auditors that learn of intentional misstatements may also be required to (1) re-evaluate the degree of audit risk involved in the audit engagement, (2) determine whether to revise the nature, timing, and extent of audit procedures accordingly, and (3) consider whether to resign.[45]

Intentional misstatements also may signal the existence of reportable conditions or material weaknesses in the registrant's system of internal accounting control designed to detect and deter improper accounting and financial reporting.[46] As stated by the National Commission on Fraudulent Financial Reporting, also known as the Treadway Commission, in its 1987 report,

The tone set by top management—the corporate environment or culture within which financial reporting occurs—is the most important factor contributing to the integrity of the financial reporting process. Notwithstanding an impressive set of written rules and procedures, if the tone set by management is lax, fraudulent financial reporting is more likely to occur.[47]

An auditor is required to report to a registrant's audit committee any reportable conditions or material weaknesses in a registrant's system of internal accounting control that the auditor discovers in the course of the examination of the registrant's financial statements.[48]

GAAP precedence over industry practice

Some have argued to the staff that registrants should be permitted to follow an industry accounting practice even though that practice is inconsistent with authoritative accounting literature. This situation might occur if a practice is developed when there are few transactions and the accounting results are clearly inconsequential, and that practice never changes despite a subsequent growth in the number or materiality of such transactions. The staff disagrees with this argument. Authoritative literature takes precedence over industry practice that is contrary to GAAP.[49]

General comments

This SAB is not intended to change current law or guidance in the accounting or auditing literature.[50] This SAB and the authoritative accounting literature cannot specifically address all of

---

[43] Although the auditor is not required to plan or perform the audit to detect misstatements that are immaterial to the financial statements, SAS 99 requires the auditor to evaluate several fraud "risk factors" that may bring such misstatements to his or her attention. For example, an analysis of fraud risk factors under SAS 99 must include, among other things, consideration of management's interest in maintaining or increasing the registrant's stock price or earnings trend through the use of unusually aggressive accounting practices, whether management has a practice of committing to analysts or others that it will achieve unduly aggressive or clearly unrealistic forecasts, and the existence of assets, liabilities, revenues, or expenses based on significant estimates that involve unusually subjective judgments or uncertainties.

[44] In requiring the auditor to consider whether fraudulent misstatements are material, and in requiring differing responses depending on whether the misstatement is material, SAS 99 makes clear that fraud can involve immaterial misstatements. Indeed, a misstatement can be "inconsequential" and still involve fraud.

Under SAS 99, assessing whether misstatements due to fraud are material to the financial statements is a "cumulative process" that should occur both during and at the completion of the audit. SAS 99 further states that

this accumulation is primarily a "qualitative matter" based on the auditor's judgment. The staff believes that in making these assessments, management and auditors should refer to the discussion in Part 1 of this SAB.

[45] Auditors should document their determinations in accordance with SAS 96, SAS 99, and other appropriate sections of the audit literature.

[46] See, e.g., SAS 99.

[47] Report of the National Commission on Fraudulent Financial Reporting at 32 (October 1987). See also Report and Recommendations of the Blue Ribbon Committee on Improving the Effectiveness of Corporate Audit Committees (February 8, 1999).

[48] AU 325.02. See also AU 380.09, which, in discussing matters to be communicated by the auditor to the audit committee, states:

The auditor should inform the audit committee about adjustments arising from the audit that could, in his judgment, either individually or in the aggregate, have a significant effect on the entity's financial reporting process. For purposes of this section, an audit adjustment, whether or not recorded by the entity, is a proposed correction of the financial statements . . .

[49] See AU 411.05.

[50] The FASB Discussion Memorandum, "Criteria for Determining Materiality," states that the financial ac-

the novel and complex business transactions and events that may occur. Accordingly, registrants may account for, and make disclosures about, these transactions and events based on analogies to similar situations or other factors. The staff may not, however, always be persuaded that a registrant's determination is the most appropriate under the circumstances. When disagreements occur after a transaction or an event has been reported, the consequences may be severe for registrants, auditors, and, most importantly, the users of financial statements who have a right to expect consistent accounting and reporting for, and disclosure of, similar transactions and events. The staff, therefore, encourages registrants and auditors to discuss on a timely basis with the staff proposed accounting treatments for, or disclosures about, transactions or events that are not specifically covered by the existing accounting literature.

(Footnote Continued)

counting and reporting process considers that "a great deal of the time might be spent during the accounting process considering insignificant matters . . . If presentations of financial information are to be prepared economically on a timely basis and presented in a concise intelligible form, the concept of materiality is crucial." This SAB is not intended to require that misstatements arising from insignificant errors and omissions (individually and in the aggregate) arising from the normal recurring accounting close processes, such as a clerical error or an adjustment for a missed accounts payable invoice, always be corrected, even if the error is identified in the audit process and known to management. Management and the auditor would need to consider the various factors described elsewhere in this SAB in assessing whether such misstatements are material, need to be corrected to comply with the FCPA, or trigger procedures under Section 10A of the Exchange Act. Because this SAB does not change current law or guidance in the accounting or auditing literature, adherence to the principles described in this SAB should not raise the costs associated with recordkeeping or with audits of financial statements.

Sarbanes-Oxley Act of 2002

SARBANES-OXLEY ACT OF 2002

H.R. 3763

One Hundred Seventh Congress

of the

United States of America

AT THE SECOND SESSION

Begun and held at the City of Washington on Wednesday,
the twenty-third day of January, two thousand and two

An Act

To protect investors by improving the accuracy and reliability of corporate disclosures made
pursuant to the securities laws, and for other purposes.

*Be it enacted by the Senate and House of Representatives of the United States of America in
Congress assembled,*

SEC. 1. SHORT TITLE; TABLE OF CONTENTS.

(a) SHORT TITLE—This Act may be cited as the 'SarbanesOxley Act of 2002'.

(b) TABLE OF CONTENTS—The table of contents for this Act is as follows:

SEC. 2. DEFINITIONS.

SEC. 3. COMMISSION RULES AND ENFORCEMENT.

(a) REGULATORY ACTION—The Commission shall promulgate such rules and regulations, as may be necessary or appropriate in the public interest or for the protection of investors, and in furtherance of this Act.

(b) ENFORCEMENT

(1) IN GENERAL—A violation by any person of this Act, any rule or regulation of the Commission issued under this Act, or any rule of the Board shall be treated for all purposes in the same manner as a violation of the Securities Exchange Act of 1934 (15 U.S.C. 78a et seq.) or the rules and regulations issued thereunder, consistent with the provisions of this Act, and any such person shall be subject to the same penalties, and to the same extent, as for a violation of that Act or such rules or regulations.

(2) INVESTIGATIONS, INJUNCTIONS, AND PROSECUTION OF OFFENSES—Section 21 of the Securities Exchange Act of 1934 (15 U.S.C. 78u) is amended—

(A) in subsection (a)(1), by inserting 'the rules of the Public Company Accounting Oversight Board, of which such person is a registered public accounting firm or a person associated with such a firm,' after 'is a participant,';

(B) in subsection (d)(1), by inserting 'the rules of the Public Company Accounting Oversight Board, of which such person is a registered public accounting firm or a person associated with such a firm,' after 'is a participant,';

(C) in subsection (e), by inserting 'the rules of the Public Company Accounting Oversight Board, of which such person is a registered public accounting firm or a person associated with such a firm,' after 'is a participant,'; and

(D) in subsection (f), by inserting 'or the Public Company Accounting Oversight Board' after 'self-regulatory organization' each place that term appears.

(3) CEASE-AND-DESIST PROCEEDINGS—Section 21C(c)(2) of the Securities Exchange Act of 1934 (15 U.S.C. 78u-3(c)(2)) is amended by inserting 'registered public accounting firm (as defined in section 2 of the Sarbanes-Oxley Act of 2002),' after 'government securities dealer,'.

(4) ENFORCEMENT BY FEDERAL BANKING AGENCIES. Section 12(i) of the Securities Exchange Act of 1934 (15 U.S.C. 78l(i)) is amended by—

(A) striking 'sections 12,' each place it appears and inserting 'sections 10A(m), 12,'; and

(B) striking 'and 16,' each place it appears and inserting 'and 16 of this Act, and sections 302, 303, 304, 306, 401(b), 404, 406, and 407 of the Sarbanes-Oxley Act of 2002,'.

(c) EFFECT ON COMMISSION AUTHORITY—Nothing in this Act or the rules of the Board shall be construed to impair or limit—

(1) the authority of the Commission to regulate the accounting profession, accounting firms, or persons associated with such firms for purposes of enforcement of the securities laws;

(2) the authority of the Commission to set standards for accounting or auditing practices or auditor independence, derived from other provisions of the securities laws or the rules or regulations thereunder, for purposes of the preparation and issuance of any audit report, or otherwise under applicable law; or

(3) the ability of the Commission to take, on the initiative of the Commission, legal, administrative, or disciplinary action against any registered public accounting firm or any associated person thereof.

TITLE I—PUBLIC COMPANY ACCOUNTING OVERSIGHT BOARD

SEC. 101. ESTABLISHMENT; ADMINISTRATIVE PROVISIONS.

(a) ESTABLISHMENT OF BOARD—There is established the Public Company Accounting Oversight Board, to oversee the audit of public companies that are subject to the securities laws, and related matters, in order to protect the interests of investors and further the public interest in the preparation of informative, accurate, and independent audit reports for companies the securities of which are sold to, and held by and for, public investors. The Board shall be a body corporate, operate as a nonprofit corporation, and have succession until dissolved by an Act of Congress.

(b) STATUS—The Board shall not be an agency or establishment of the United States Government, and, except as otherwise provided in this Act, shall be subject to, and have all the powers conferred upon a nonprofit corporation by, the District of Columbia Nonprofit Corporation Act. No member or person employed by, or agent for, the Board shall be deemed to be an officer or employee of or agent for the Federal Government by reason of such service.

(c) DUTIES OF THE BOARD—The Board shall, subject to action by the Commission under section 107, and once a determination is made by the Commission under subsection (d) of this section—

(1) register public accounting firms that prepare audit reports for issuers, in accordance with section 102;

(2) establish or adopt, or both, by rule, auditing, quality control, ethics, independence, and other standards relating to the preparation of audit reports for issuers, in accordance with section 103;

(3) conduct inspections of registered public accounting firms, in accordance with section 104 and the rules of the Board;

(4) conduct investigations and disciplinary proceedings concerning, and impose appropriate sanctions where justified upon, registered public accounting firms and associated persons of such firms, in accordance with section 105;

(5) perform such other duties or functions as the Board (or the Commission, by rule or order) determines are necessary or appropriate to promote high professional standards among, and improve the quality of audit services offered by, registered public accounting firms and associated persons thereof, or otherwise to carry out this Act, in order to protect investors, or to further the public interest;

(6) enforce compliance with this Act, the rules of the Board, professional standards, and the securities laws relating to the preparation and issuance of audit reports and the obligations and liabilities of accountants with respect thereto, by registered public accounting firms and associated persons thereof; and

(7) set the budget and manage the operations of the Board and the staff of the Board.

(d) COMMISSION DETERMINATION—The members of the Board shall take such action (including hiring of staff, proposal of rules, and adoption of initial and transitional auditing and other professional standards) as may be necessary or appropriate to enable the Commission to determine, not later than 270 days after the date of enactment of this Act, that the Board is so organized and has the capacity to carry out the requirements of this title, and to enforce compliance with this title by registered public accounting firms and associated persons thereof. The Commission shall be responsible, prior to the appointment of the Board, for the planning for the establishment and administrative transition to the Board's operation.

(e) BOARD MEMBERSHIP

(1) COMPOSITION—The Board shall have 5 members, appointed from among prominent individuals of integrity and reputation who have a demonstrated commitment to the interests of investors and the public, and an understanding of the responsibilities for and nature of the financial disclosures required of issuers under the securities laws and the obligations of accountants with respect to the preparation and issuance of audit reports with respect to such disclosures.

(2) LIMITATION—Two members, and only 2 members, of the Board shall be or have been certified public accountants pursuant to the laws of 1 or more States, provided that, if 1 of those 2 members is the chairperson, he or she may not have been a practicing certified public accountant for at least 5 years prior to his or her appointment to the Board.

(3) FULL-TIME INDEPENDENT SERVICE—Each member of the Board shall serve on a full-time basis, and may not, concurrent with service on the Board, be employed by any other person or engage in any other professional or business activity. No member of the Board may share in any of the profits of, or receive payments from, a public accounting firm (or any other person, as determined by rule of the Commission), other than fixed continuing payments, subject to such conditions as the Commission may impose, under standard arrangements for the retirement of members of public accounting firms.

(4) APPOINTMENT OF BOARD MEMBERS

(A) INITIAL BOARD—Not later than 90 days after the date of enactment of this Act, the Commission, after consultation with the Chairman of the Board of Governors of the Federal Reserve System and the Secretary of the Treasury, shall appoint the chairperson and other initial members of the Board, and shall designate a term of service for each.

(B) VACANCIES—A vacancy on the Board shall not affect the powers of the Board, but shall be filled in the same manner as provided for appointments under this section.

(5) TERM OF SERVICE

(A) IN GENERAL—The term of service of each Board member shall be 5 years, and until a successor is appointed, except that—

(i) the terms of office of the initial Board members (other than the chairperson) shall expire in annual increments, 1 on each of the first 4 anniversaries of the initial date of appointment; and

(ii) any Board member appointed to fill a vacancy occurring before the expiration of the term for which the predecessor was appointed shall be appointed only for the remainder of that term.

(B) TERM LIMITATION—No person may serve as a member of the Board, or as chairperson of the Board, for more than 2 terms, whether or not such terms of service are consecutive.

(6) REMOVAL FROM OFFICE—A member of the Board may be removed by the Commission from office, in accordance with section 107(d)(3), for good cause shown before the expiration of the term of that member.

(f) POWERS OF THE BOARD—In addition to any authority granted to the Board otherwise in this Act, the Board shall have the power, subject to section 107—

(1) to sue and be sued, complain and defend, in its corporate name and through its own counsel, with the approval of the Commission, in any Federal, State, or other court;

(2) to conduct its operations and maintain offices, and to exercise all other rights and powers authorized by this Act, in any State, without regard to any qualification, licensing, or other provision of law in effect in such State (or a political subdivision thereof);

(3) to lease, purchase, accept gifts or donations of or otherwise acquire, improve, use, sell, exchange, or convey, all of or an interest in any property, wherever situated;

(4) to appoint such employees, accountants, attorneys, and other agents as may be necessary or appropriate, and to determine their qualifications, define their duties, and fix their salaries or other compensation (at a level that is comparable to private sector self-regulatory, accounting, technical, supervisory, or other staff or management positions);

(5) to allocate, assess, and collect accounting support fees established pursuant to section 109, for the Board, and other fees and charges imposed under this title; and

(6) to enter into contracts, execute instruments, incur liabilities, and do any and all other acts and things necessary, appropriate, or incidental to the conduct of its operations and the exercise of its obligations, rights, and powers imposed or granted by this title.

(g) RULES OF THE BOARD—The rules of the Board shall, subject to the approval of the Commission—

(1) provide for the operation and administration of the Board, the exercise of its authority, and the performance of its responsibilities under this Act;

(2) permit, as the Board determines necessary or appropriate, delegation by the Board of any of its functions to an individual member or employee of the Board, or to a division of the Board, including functions with respect to hearing, determining, ordering, certifying, reporting, or otherwise acting as to any matter, except that—

(A) the Board shall retain a discretionary right to review any action pursuant to any such delegated function, upon its own motion;

(B) a person shall be entitled to a review by the Board with respect to any matter so delegated, and the decision of the Board upon such review shall be deemed to be the action of the Board for all purposes (including appeal or review thereof); and

(C) if the right to exercise a review described in subparagraph (A) is declined, or if no such review is sought within the time stated in the rules of the Board, then the action taken by the holder of such delegation shall for all purposes, including appeal or review thereof, be deemed to be the action of the Board;

(3) establish ethics rules and standards of conduct for Board members and staff, including a bar on practice before the Board (and the Commission, with respect to Board-related matters) of 1 year for former members of the Board, and appropriate periods (not to exceed 1 year) for former staff of the Board; and

(4) provide as otherwise required by this Act.

(h) ANNUAL REPORT TO THE COMMISSION—The Board shall submit an annual report (including its audited financial statements) to the Commission, and the Commission shall transmit a copy of that report to the Committee on Banking, Housing, and Urban Affairs of the Senate, and the Committee on Financial Services of the House of Representatives, not later than 30 days after the date of receipt of that report by the Commission.

SEC. 102. REGISTRATION WITH THE BOARD.

(a) MANDATORY REGISTRATION—Beginning 180 days after the date of the determination of the Commission under section 101(d), it shall be unlawful for any person that is not a registered public accounting firm to prepare or issue, or to participate in the preparation or issuance of, any audit report with respect to any issuer.

(b) APPLICATIONS FOR REGISTRATION

(1) FORM OF APPLICATION—A public accounting firm shall use such form as the Board may prescribe, by rule, to apply for registration under this section.

(2) CONTENTS OF APPLICATIONS—Each public accounting firm shall submit, as part of its application for registration, in such detail as the Board shall specify—

(A) the names of all issuers for which the firm prepared or issued audit reports during the immediately preceding calendar year, and for which the firm expects to prepare or issue audit reports during the current calendar year;

(B) the annual fees received by the firm from each such issuer for audit services, other accounting services, and non-audit services, respectively;

(C) such other current financial information for the most recently completed fiscal year of the firm as the Board may reasonably request;

(D) a statement of the quality control policies of the firm for its accounting and auditing practices;

(E) a list of all accountants associated with the firm who participate in or contribute to the preparation of audit reports, stating the license or certification number of each such person, as well as the State license numbers of the firm itself;

(F) information relating to criminal, civil, or administrative actions or disciplinary proceedings pending against the firm or any associated person of the firm in connection with any audit report;

(G) copies of any periodic or annual disclosure filed by an issuer with the Commission during the immediately preceding calendar year which discloses accounting disagreements between such issuer and the firm in connection with an audit report furnished or prepared by the firm for such issuer; and

(H) such other information as the rules of the Board or the Commission shall specify as necessary or appropriate in the public interest or for the protection of investors.

(3) CONSENTS—Each application for registration under this subsection shall include—

(A) a consent executed by the public accounting firm to cooperation in and compliance with any request for testimony or the production of documents made by the Board in the furtherance of its authority and responsibilities under this title (and an agreement to secure and enforce similar consents from each of the associated persons of the public accounting firm as a condition of their continued employment by or other association with such firm); and

(B) a statement that such firm understands and agrees that cooperation and compliance, as described in the consent required by subparagraph (A), and the securing and enforcement of such consents from its associated persons, in accordance with the rules of the Board, shall be a condition to the continuing effectiveness of the registration of the firm with the Board.

(c) ACTION ON APPLICATIONS

(1) TIMING—The Board shall approve a completed application for registration not later than 45 days after the date of receipt of the application, in accordance with the rules of the Board,

unless the Board, prior to such date, issues a written notice of disapproval to, or requests more information from, the prospective registrant.

(2) TREATMENT—A written notice of disapproval of a completed application under paragraph (1) for registration shall be treated as a disciplinary sanction for purposes of sections 105(d) and 107(c).

(d) PERIODIC REPORTS—Each registered public accounting firm shall submit an annual report to the Board, and may be required to report more frequently, as necessary to update the information contained in its application for registration under this section, and to provide to the Board such additional information as the Board or the Commission may specify, in accordance with subsection (b)(2).

(e) PUBLIC AVAILABILITY—Registration applications and annual reports required by this subsection, or such portions of such applications or reports as may be designated under rules of the Board, shall be made available for public inspection, subject to rules of the Board or the Commission, and to applicable laws relating to the confidentiality of proprietary, personal, or other information contained in such applications or reports, provided that, in all events, the Board shall protect from public disclosure information reasonably identified by the subject accounting firm as proprietary information.

(f) REGISTRATION AND ANNUAL FEES—The Board shall assess and collect a registration fee and an annual fee from each registered public accounting firm, in amounts that are sufficient to recover the costs of processing and reviewing applications and annual reports.

SEC. 103. AUDITING, QUALITY CONTROL, AND INDEPENDENCE STANDARDS AND RULES.

(a) AUDITING, QUALITY CONTROL, AND ETHICS STANDARDS

(1) IN GENERAL—The Board shall, by rule, establish, including, to the extent it determines appropriate, through adoption of standards proposed by 1 or more professional groups of accountants designated pursuant to paragraph (3)(A) or advisory groups convened pursuant to paragraph (4), and amend or otherwise modify or alter, such auditing and related attestation standards, such quality control standards, and such ethics standards to be used by registered public accounting firms in the preparation and issuance of audit reports, as required by this Act or the rules of the Commission, or as may be necessary or appropriate in the public interest or for the protection of investors.

(2) RULE REQUIREMENTS—In carrying out paragraph (1), the Board—

(A) shall include in the auditing standards that it adopts, requirements that each registered public accounting firm shall—

(i) prepare, and maintain for a period of not less than 7 years, audit work papers, and other information related to any audit report, in sufficient detail to support the conclusions reached in such report;

(ii) provide a concurring or second partner review and approval of such audit report (and other related information), and concurring approval in its issuance, by a qualified person (as prescribed by the Board) associated with the public accounting firm, other than the person in charge of the audit, or by an independent reviewer (as prescribed by the Board); and

(iii) describe in each audit report the scope of the auditor's testing of the internal control structure and procedures of the issuer, required by section 404(b), and present (in such report or in a separate report)—

(I) the findings of the auditor from such testing;

(II) an evaluation of whether such internal control structure and procedures—

(aa) include maintenance of records that in reasonable detail accurately and fairly reflect the transactions and dispositions of the assets of the issuer;

(bb) provide reasonable assurance that transactions are recorded as necessary to permit preparation of financial statements in accordance with generally accepted accounting principles, and that receipts and expenditures of the issuer are being made only in accordance with authorizations of management and directors of the issuer; and

(III) a description, at a minimum, of material weaknesses in such internal controls, and of any material noncompliance found on the basis of such testing.

(B) shall include, in the quality control standards that it adopts with respect to the issuance of audit reports, requirements for every registered public accounting firm relating to—

(i) monitoring of professional ethics and independence from issuers on behalf of which the firm issues audit reports;

(ii) consultation within such firm on accounting and auditing questions;

(iii) supervision of audit work;

(iv) hiring, professional development, and advancement of personnel;

(v) the acceptance and continuation of engagements;

(vi) internal inspection; and

(vii) such other requirements as the Board may prescribe, subject to subsection (a)(1).

(3) AUTHORITY TO ADOPT OTHER STANDARDS

(A) IN GENERAL—In carrying out this subsection, the Board—

(i) may adopt as its rules, subject to the terms of section 107, any portion of any statement of auditing standards or other professional standards that the Board determines satisfy the requirements of paragraph (1), and that were proposed by 1 or more professional groups of accountants that shall be designated or recognized by the Board, by rule, for such purpose, pursuant to this paragraph or 1 or more advisory groups convened pursuant to paragraph (4); and

(ii) notwithstanding clause (i), shall retain full authority to modify, supplement, revise, or subsequently amend, modify, or repeal, in whole or in part, any portion of any statement described in clause (i).

(B) INITIAL AND TRANSITIONAL STANDARDS—The Board shall adopt standards described in subparagraph (A)(i) as initial or transitional standards, to the extent the Board determines necessary, prior to a determination of the Commission under section 101(d), and such standards shall be separately approved by the Commission at the time of that determination, without regard to the procedures required by section 107 that otherwise would apply to the approval of rules of the Board.

(4) ADVISORY GROUPS—The Board shall convene, or authorize its staff to convene, such expert advisory groups as may be appropriate, which may include practicing accountants and other experts, as well as representatives of other interested groups, subject to such rules as the Board may prescribe to prevent conflicts of interest, to make recommendations concerning the content (including proposed drafts) of auditing, quality control, ethics, independence, or other standards required to be established under this section.

(b) INDEPENDENCE STANDARDS AND RULES—The Board shall establish such rules as may be necessary or appropriate in the public interest or for the protection of investors, to implement, or as authorized under, title II of this Act.

(c) COOPERATION WITH DESIGNATED PROFESSIONAL GROUPS OF ACCOUNTANTS AND ADVISORY GROUPS

(1) IN GENERAL—The Board shall cooperate on an ongoing basis with professional groups of accountants designated under subsection (a)(3)(A) and advisory groups convened under subsection (a)(4) in the examination of the need for changes in any standards subject to its authority under subsection (a), recommend issues for inclusion on the agendas of such designated professional groups of accountants or advisory groups, and take such other steps as it deems appropriate to increase the effectiveness of the standard setting process.

(2) BOARD RESPONSES—The Board shall respond in a timely fashion to requests from designated professional groups of accountants and advisory groups referred to in paragraph (1) for any changes in standards over which the Board has authority.

(d) EVALUATION OF STANDARD SETTING PROCESS—The Board shall include in the annual report required by section 101(h) the results of its standard setting responsibilities during the period to which the report relates, including a discussion of the work of the Board with any designated professional groups of accountants and advisory groups described in paragraphs (3)(A) and (4) of subsection (a), and its pending issues agenda for future standard setting projects.

SEC. 104. INSPECTIONS OF REGISTERED PUBLIC ACCOUNTING FIRMS.

(a) IN GENERAL—The Board shall conduct a continuing program of inspections to assess the degree of compliance of each registered public accounting firm and associated persons of that firm with this Act, the rules of the Board, the rules of the Commission, or professional standards, in connection with its performance of audits, issuance of audit reports, and related matters involving issuers.

(b) INSPECTION FREQUENCY

(1) IN GENERAL—Subject to paragraph (2), inspections required by this section shall be conducted—

(A) annually with respect to each registered public accounting firm that regularly provides audit reports for more than 100 issuers; and

(B) not less frequently than once every 3 years with respect to each registered public accounting firm that regularly provides audit reports for 100 or fewer issuers.

(2) ADJUSTMENTS TO SCHEDULES—The Board may, by rule, adjust the inspection schedules set under paragraph (1) if the Board finds that different inspection schedules are consistent with the purposes of this Act, the public interest, and the protection of investors. The Board may conduct special inspections at the request of the Commission or upon its own motion.

(c) PROCEDURES—The Board shall, in each inspection under this section, and in accordance with its rules for such inspections—

(1) identify any act or practice or omission to act by the registered public accounting firm, or by any associated person thereof, revealed by such inspection that may be in violation of this Act, the rules of the Board, the rules of the Commission, the firm's own quality control policies, or professional standards;

(2) report any such act, practice, or omission, if appropriate, to the Commission and each appropriate State regulatory authority; and

(3) begin a formal investigation or take disciplinary action, if appropriate, with respect to any such violation, in accordance with this Act and the rules of the Board.

(d) CONDUCT OF INSPECTIONS—In conducting an inspection of a registered public accounting firm under this section, the Board shall—

(1) inspect and review selected audit and review engagements of the firm (which may include audit engagements that are the subject of ongoing litigation or other controversy between the firm and 1 or more third parties), performed at various offices and by various associated persons of the firm, as selected by the Board;

(2) evaluate the sufficiency of the quality control system of the firm, and the manner of the documentation and communication of that system by the firm; and

(3) perform such other testing of the audit, supervisory, and quality control procedures of the firm as are necessary or appropriate in light of the purpose of the inspection and the responsibilities of the Board.

(e) RECORD RETENTION—The rules of the Board may require the retention by registered public accounting firms for inspection purposes of records whose retention is not otherwise required by section 103 or the rules issued thereunder.

(f) PROCEDURES FOR REVIEW—The rules of the Board shall provide a procedure for the review of and response to a draft inspection report by the registered public accounting firm under inspection. The Board shall take such action with respect to such response as it considers appropriate (including revising the draft report or continuing or supplementing its inspection activities before issuing a final report), but the text of any such response, appropriately redacted to protect information reasonably identified by the accounting firm as confidential, shall be attached to and made part of the inspection report.

(g) REPORT—A written report of the findings of the Board for each inspection under this section, subject to subsection (h), shall be—

(1) transmitted, in appropriate detail, to the Commission and each appropriate State regulatory authority, accompanied by any letter or comments by the Board or the inspector, and any letter of response from the registered public accounting firm; and

(2) made available in appropriate detail to the public (subject to section 105(b)(5)(A), and to the protection of such confidential and proprietary information as the Board may determine to be appropriate, or as may be required by law), except that no portions of the inspection report that deal with criticisms of or potential defects in the quality control systems of the firm under inspection shall be made public if those criticisms or defects are addressed by the firm, to the satisfaction of the Board, not later than 12 months after the date of the inspection report.

(h) INTERIM COMMISSION REVIEW

(1) REVIEWABLE MATTERS—A registered public accounting firm may seek review by the Commission, pursuant to such rules as the Commission shall promulgate, if the firm—

(A) has provided the Board with a response, pursuant to rules issued by the Board under subsection (f), to the substance of particular items in a draft inspection report, and disagrees with the assessments contained in any final report prepared by the Board following such response; or

(B) disagrees with the determination of the Board that criticisms or defects identified in an inspection report have not been addressed to the satisfaction of the Board within 12 months of the date of the inspection report, for purposes of subsection (g)(2).

(2) TREATMENT OF REVIEW—Any decision of the Commission with respect to a review under paragraph (1) shall not be reviewable under section 25 of the Securities Exchange Act of 1934 (15 U.S.C. 78y), or deemed to be 'final agency action' for purposes of section 704 of title 5, United States Code.

(3) TIMING—Review under paragraph (1) may be sought during the 30-day period following the date of the event giving rise to the review under subparagraph (A) or (B) of paragraph (1).

SEC. 105. INVESTIGATIONS AND DISCIPLINARY PROCEEDINGS.

(a) IN GENERAL—The Board shall establish, by rule, subject to the requirements of this section, fair procedures for the investigation and disciplining of registered public accounting firms and associated persons of such firms.

(b) INVESTIGATIONS

(1) AUTHORITY—In accordance with the rules of the Board, the Board may conduct an investigation of any act or practice, or omission to act, by a registered public accounting firm, any associated person of such firm, or both, that may violate any provision of this Act, the rules of the Board, the provisions of the securities laws relating to the preparation and issuance of audit reports and the obligations and liabilities of accountants with respect thereto, including the rules of the Commission issued under this Act, or professional standards, regardless of how the act, practice, or omission is brought to the attention of the Board.

(2) TESTIMONY AND DOCUMENT PRODUCTION—In addition to such other actions as the Board determines to be necessary or appropriate, the rules of the Board may—

(A) require the testimony of the firm or of any person associated with a registered public accounting firm, with respect to any matter that the Board considers relevant or material to an investigation;

(B) require the production of audit work papers and any other document or information in the possession of a registered public accounting firm or any associated person thereof, wherever domiciled, that the Board considers relevant or material to the investigation, and may inspect the books and records of such firm or associated person to verify the accuracy of any documents or information supplied;

(C) request the testimony of, and production of any document in the possession of, any other person, including any client of a registered public accounting firm that the Board considers relevant or material to an investigation under this section, with appropriate notice, subject to the needs of the investigation, as permitted under the rules of the Board; and

(D) provide for procedures to seek issuance by the Commission, in a manner established by the Commission, of a subpoena to require the testimony of, and production of any document in the possession of, any person, including any client of a registered public accounting firm, that the Board considers relevant or material to an investigation under this section.

(3) NONCOOPERATION WITH INVESTIGATIONS

(A) IN GENERAL—If a registered public accounting firm or any associated person thereof refuses to testify, produce documents, or otherwise cooperate with the Board in connection with an investigation under this section, the Board may—

(i) suspend or bar such person from being associated with a registered public accounting firm, or require the registered public accounting firm to end such association;

(ii) suspend or revoke the registration of the public accounting firm; and

(iii) invoke such other lesser sanctions as the Board considers appropriate, and as specified by rule of the Board.

(B) PROCEDURE—Any action taken by the Board under this paragraph shall be subject to the terms of section 107(c).

(4) COORDINATION AND REFERRAL OF INVESTIGATIONS

(A) COORDINATION—The Board shall notify the Commission of any pending Board investigation involving a potential violation of the securities laws, and thereafter coordinate its work with the work of the Commission's Division of Enforcement, as necessary to protect an ongoing Commission investigation.

(B) REFERRAL—The Board may refer an investigation under this section—

(i) to the Commission;

(ii) to any other Federal functional regulator (as defined in section 509 of the Gramm-Leach-Bliley Act (15 U.S.C. 6809)), in the case of an investigation that concerns an audit report for an institution that is subject to the jurisdiction of such regulator; and (iii) at the direction of the Commission, to—

(I) the Attorney General of the United States;

(II) the attorney general of 1 or more States; and

(III) the appropriate State regulatory authority.

(5) USE OF DOCUMENTS

(A) CONFIDENTIALITY—Except as provided in subparagraph (B), all documents and information prepared or received by or specifically for the Board, and deliberations of the Board and its employees and agents, in connection with an inspection under section 104 or with an investigation under this section, shall be confidential and privileged as an evidentiary matter (and shall not be subject to civil discovery or other legal process) in any proceeding in any Federal or State court or administrative agency, and shall be exempt from disclosure, in the hands of an agency or establishment of the Federal Government, under the Freedom of Information Act (5 U.S.C. 552a), or otherwise, unless and until presented in connection with a public proceeding or released in accordance with subsection (c).

(B) AVAILABILITY TO GOVERNMENT AGENCIES—Without the loss of its status as confidential and privileged in the hands of the Board, all information referred to in subparagraph (A) may—

(i) be made available to the Commission; and

(ii) in the discretion of the Board, when determined by the Board to be necessary to accomplish the purposes of this Act or to protect investors, be made available to—

(I) the Attorney General of the United States;

(II) the appropriate Federal functional regulator (as defined in section 509 of the Gramm-LeachBliley Act (15 U.S.C. 6809)), other than the Commission, with respect to an audit report for an institution subject to the jurisdiction of such regulator;

(III) State attorneys general in connection with any criminal investigation; and

(IV) any appropriate State regulatory authority, each of which shall maintain such information as confidential and privileged.

(6) IMMUNITY—Any employee of the Board engaged in carrying out an investigation under this Act shall be immune from any civil liability arising out of such investigation in the same manner and to the same extent as an employee of the Federal Government in similar circumstances.

(c) DISCIPLINARY PROCEDURES

(1) NOTIFICATION; RECORDKEEPING—The rules of the Board shall provide that in any proceeding by the Board to determine whether a registered public accounting firm, or an associated person thereof, should be disciplined, the Board shall—

(A) bring specific charges with respect to the firm or associated person;

(B) notify such firm or associated person of, and provide to the firm or associated person an opportunity to defend against, such charges; and

(C) keep a record of the proceedings.

(2) PUBLIC HEARINGS—Hearings under this section shall not be public, unless otherwise ordered by the Board for good cause shown, with the consent of the parties to such hearing.

(3) SUPPORTING STATEMENT—A determination by the Board to impose a sanction under this subsection shall be supported by a statement setting forth—

(A) each act or practice in which the registered public accounting firm, or associated person, has engaged (or omitted to engage), or that forms a basis for all or a part of such sanction;

(B) the specific provision of this Act, the securities laws, the rules of the Board, or professional standards which the Board determines has been violated; and

(C) the sanction imposed, including a justification for that sanction.

(4) SANCTIONS—If the Board finds, based on all of the facts and circumstances, that a registered public accounting firm or associated person thereof has engaged in any act or practice, or omitted to act, in violation of this Act, the rules of the Board, the provisions of the securities laws relating to the preparation and issuance of audit reports and the obligations and liabilities of accountants with respect thereto, including the rules of the Commission issued under this Act, or professional standards, the Board may impose such disciplinary or remedial sanctions as it determines appropriate, subject to applicable limitations under paragraph (5), including—

(A) temporary suspension or permanent revocation of registration under this title;

(B) temporary or permanent suspension or bar of a person from further association with any registered public accounting firm;

(C) temporary or permanent limitation on the activities, functions, or operations of such firm or person (other than in connection with required additional professional education or training);

(D) a civil money penalty for each such violation, in an amount equal to—

(i) not more than $100,000 for a natural person or $2,000,000 for any other person; and

(ii) in any case to which paragraph (5) applies, not more than $750,000 for a natural person or $15,000,000 for any other person;

(E) censure;

(F) required additional professional education or training; or

(G) any other appropriate sanction provided for in the rules of the Board.

(5) INTENTIONAL OR OTHER KNOWING CONDUCT—The sanctions and penalties described in subparagraphs (A) through (C) and (D)(ii) of paragraph (4) shall only apply to—

(A) intentional or knowing conduct, including reckless conduct, that results in violation of the applicable statutory, regulatory, or professional standard; or

(B) repeated instances of negligent conduct, each resulting in a violation of the applicable statutory, regulatory, or professional standard.

(6) FAILURE TO SUPERVISE

(A) IN GENERAL—The Board may impose sanctions under this section on a registered accounting firm or upon the supervisory personnel of such firm, if the Board finds that—

(i) the firm has failed reasonably to supervise an associated person, either as required by the rules of the Board relating to auditing or quality control standards, or otherwise, with a view to preventing violations of this Act, the rules of the Board, the provisions of the securities laws relating to the preparation and issuance of audit reports and the obligations and liabilities of accountants with respect thereto, including the rules of the Commission under this Act, or professional standards; and

(ii) such associated person commits a violation of this Act, or any of such rules, laws, or standards.

(B) RULE OF CONSTRUCTION—No associated person of a registered public accounting firm shall be deemed to have failed reasonably to supervise any other person for purposes of subparagraph (A), if—

(i) there have been established in and for that firm procedures, and a system for applying such procedures, that comply with applicable rules of the Board and that would reasonably be expected to prevent and detect any such violation by such associated person; and

(ii) such person has reasonably discharged the duties and obligations incumbent upon that person by reason of such procedures and system, and had no reasonable cause to believe that such procedures and system were not being complied with.

(7) EFFECT OF SUSPENSION

(A) ASSOCIATION WITH A PUBLIC ACCOUNTING FIRMIt shall be unlawful for any person that is suspended or barred from being associated with a registered public accounting firm under this subsection willfully to become or remain associated with any registered public accounting firm, or for any registered public accounting firm that knew, or, in the exercise of reasonable care should have known, of the suspension or bar, to permit such an association, without the consent of the Board or the Commission.

(B) ASSOCIATION WITH AN ISSUER—It shall be unlawful for any person that is suspended or barred from being associated with an issuer under this subsection willfully to become or remain associated with any issuer in an accountancy or a financial management capacity, and for any issuer that knew, or in the exercise of reasonable care should have known, of such suspension or bar, to permit such an association, without the consent of the Board or the Commission.

(d) REPORTING OF SANCTIONS

(1) RECIPIENTS—If the Board imposes a disciplinary sanction, in accordance with this section, the Board shall report the sanction to—

(A) the Commission;

(B) any appropriate State regulator authority or any foreign accountancy licensing board with which such firm or person is licensed or certified; and

(C) the public (once any stay on the imposition of such sanction has been lifted).

(2) CONTENTS—The information reported under paragraph (1) shall include—

(A) the name of the sanctioned person;

(B) a description of the sanction and the basis for its imposition; and

(C) such other information as the Board deems appropriate.

(e) STAY OF SANCTIONS

(1) IN GENERAL—Application to the Commission for review, or the institution by the Commission of review, of any disciplinary action of the Board shall operate as a stay of any such disciplinary action, unless and until the Commission orders (summarily or after notice and

opportunity for hearing on the question of a stay, which hearing may consist solely of the submission of affidavits or presentation of oral arguments) that no such stay shall continue to operate.

(2) EXPEDITED PROCEDURES—The Commission shall establish for appropriate cases an expedited procedure for consideration and determination of the question of the duration of a stay pending review of any disciplinary action of the Board under this subsection.

SEC. 106. FOREIGN PUBLIC ACCOUNTING FIRMS.

(a) APPLICABILITY TO CERTAIN FOREIGN FIRMS

(1) IN GENERAL—Any foreign public accounting firm that prepares or furnishes an audit report with respect to any issuer, shall be subject to this Act and the rules of the Board and the Commission issued under this Act, in the same manner and to the same extent as a public accounting firm that is organized and operates under the laws of the United States or any State, except that registration pursuant to section 102 shall not by itself provide a basis for subjecting such a foreign public accounting firm to the jurisdiction of the Federal or State courts, other than with respect to controversies between such firms and the Board.

(2) BOARD AUTHORITY—The Board may, by rule, determine that a foreign public accounting firm (or a class of such firms) that does not issue audit reports nonetheless plays such a substantial role in the preparation and furnishing of such reports for particular issuers, that it is necessary or appropriate, in light of the purposes of this Act and in the public interest or for the protection of investors, that such firm (or class of firms) should be treated as a public accounting firm (or firms) for purposes of registration under, and oversight by the Board in accordance with, this title.

(b) PRODUCTION OF AUDIT WORKPAPERS

(1) CONSENT BY FOREIGN FIRMS—If a foreign public accounting firm issues an opinion or otherwise performs material services upon which a registered public accounting firm relies in issuing all or part of any audit report or any opinion contained in an audit report, that foreign public accounting firm shall be deemed to have consented—

(A) to produce its audit workpapers for the Board or the Commission in connection with any investigation by either body with respect to that audit report; and

(B) to be subject to the jurisdiction of the courts of the United States for purposes of enforcement of any request for production of such workpapers.

(2) CONSENT BY DOMESTIC FIRMS—A registered public accounting firm that relies upon the opinion of a foreign public accounting firm, as described in paragraph (1), shall be deemed—

(A) to have consented to supplying the audit workpapers of that foreign public accounting firm in response to a request for production by the Board or the Commission; and

(B) to have secured the agreement of that foreign public accounting firm to such production, as a condition of its reliance on the opinion of that foreign public accounting firm.

(c) EXEMPTION AUTHORITY—The Commission, and the Board, subject to the approval of the Commission, may, by rule, regulation, or order, and as the Commission (or Board) determines necessary or appropriate in the public interest or for the protection of investors, either unconditionally or upon specified terms and conditions exempt any foreign public accounting firm, or any class of such firms, from any provision of this Act or the rules of the Board or the Commission issued under this Act.

(d) DEFINITION—In this section, the term 'foreign public accounting firm' means a public accounting firm that is organized and operates under the laws of a foreign government or political subdivision thereof.

SEC. 107. COMMISSION OVERSIGHT OF THE BOARD.

(a) GENERAL OVERSIGHT RESPONSIBILITY—The Commission shall have oversight and enforcement authority over the Board, as provided in this Act. The provisions of section 17(a)(1) of the Securities Exchange Act of 1934 (15 U.S.C. 78q(a)(1)), and of section 17(b)(1) of the Securities Exchange Act of 1934 (15 U.S.C. 78q(b)(1)) shall apply to the Board as fully as if the Board were a 'registered securities association' for purposes of those sections 17(a)(1) and 17(b)(1).

(b) RULES OF THE BOARD

(1) DEFINITION—In this section, the term 'proposed rule' means any proposed rule of the Board, and any modification of any such rule.

(2) PRIOR APPROVAL REQUIRED—No rule of the Board shall become effective without prior approval of the Commission in accordance with this section, other than as provided in section 103(a)(3)(B) with respect to initial or transitional standards.

(3) APPROVAL CRITERIA—The Commission shall approve a proposed rule, if it finds that the rule is consistent with the requirements of this Act and the securities laws, or is necessary or appropriate in the public interest or for the protection of investors.

(4) PROPOSED RULE PROCEDURES—The provisions of paragraphs (1) through (3) of section 19(b) of the Securities Exchange Act of 1934 (15 U.S.C. 78s(b)) shall govern the proposed rules of the Board, as fully as if the Board were a 'registered securities association' for purposes of that section 19(b), except that, for purposes of this paragraph—

(A) the phrase 'consistent with the requirements of this title and the rules and regulations thereunder applicable to such organization' in section 19(b)(2) of that Act shall be deemed to read 'consistent with the requirements of title I of the Sarbanes-Oxley Act of 2002, and the rules and regulations issued thereunder applicable to such organization, or as necessary or appropriate in the public interest or for the protection of investors'; and

(B) the phrase 'otherwise in furtherance of the purposes of this title' in section 19(b)(3)(C) of that Act shall be deemed to read 'otherwise in furtherance of the purposes of title I of the Sarbanes-Oxley Act of 2002'.

(5) COMMISSION AUTHORITY TO AMEND RULES OF THE BOARD—The provisions of section 19(c) of the Securities Exchange Act of 1934 (15 U.S.C. 78s(c)) shall govern the abrogation, deletion, or addition to portions of the rules of the Board by the Commission as fully as if the Board were a 'registered securities association' for purposes of that section 19(c), except that the phrase 'to conform its rules to the requirements of this title and the rules and regulations thereunder applicable to such organization, or otherwise in furtherance of the purposes of this title' in section 19(c) of that Act shall, for purposes of this paragraph, be deemed to read 'to assure the fair administration of the Public Company Accounting Oversight Board, conform the rules promulgated by that Board to the requirements of title I of the Sarbanes-Oxley Act of 2002, or otherwise further the purposes of that Act, the securities laws, and the rules and regulations thereunder applicable to that Board'.

(c) COMMISSION REVIEW OF DISCIPLINARY ACTION TAKEN BY THE BOARD

(1) NOTICE OF SANCTION—The Board shall promptly file notice with the Commission of any final sanction on any registered public accounting firm or on any associated person thereof, in such form and containing such information as the Commission, by rule, may prescribe.

(2) REVIEW OF SANCTIONS—The provisions of sections 19(d)(2) and 19(e)(1) of the Securities Exchange Act of 1934 (15 U.S.C. 78s (d)(2) and (e)(1)) shall govern the review by the Commission of final disciplinary sanctions imposed by the Board (including sanctions imposed under section 105(b)(3) of this Act for noncooperation in an investigation of the Board), as fully as if the Board were a self-regulatory organization and the Commission were the appropriate regulatory agency for such organization for purposes of those sections 19(d)(2) and 19(e)(1), except that, for purposes of this paragraph—

(A) section 105(e) of this Act (rather than that section 19(d)(2)) shall govern the extent to which application for, or institution by the Commission on its own motion of, review of any disciplinary action of the Board operates as a stay of such action;

(B) references in that section 19(e)(1) to 'members' of such an organization shall be deemed to be references to registered public accounting firms;

(C) the phrase 'consistent with the purposes of this title' in that section 19(e)(1) shall be deemed to read 'consistent with the purposes of this title and title I of the Sarbanes-Oxley Act of 2002';

(D) references to rules of the Municipal Securities Rulemaking Board in that section 19(e)(1) shall not apply; and (E) the reference to section 19(e)(2) of the Securities Exchange Act of 1934 shall refer instead to section 107(c)(3) of this Act.

(3) COMMISSION MODIFICATION AUTHORITY—The Commission may enhance, modify, cancel, reduce, or require the remission of a sanction imposed by the Board upon a registered public accounting firm or associated person thereof, if the Commission, having due regard for the public interest and the protection of investors, finds, after a proceeding in accordance with this subsection, that the sanction—

(A) is not necessary or appropriate in furtherance of this Act or the securities laws; or

(B) is excessive, oppressive, inadequate, or otherwise not appropriate to the finding or the basis on which the sanction was imposed.

(d) CENSURE OF THE BOARD; OTHER SANCTIONS

(1) RESCISSION OF BOARD AUTHORITY—The Commission, by rule, consistent with the public interest, the protection of investors, and the other purposes of this Act and the securities laws, may relieve the Board of any responsibility to enforce compliance with any provision of this Act, the securities laws, the rules of the Board, or professional standards.

(2) CENSURE OF THE BOARD; LIMITATIONS—The Commission may, by order, as it determines necessary or appropriate in the public interest, for the protection of investors, or otherwise in furtherance of the purposes of this Act or the securities laws, censure or impose limitations upon the activities, functions, and operations of the Board, if the Commission finds, on the record, after notice and opportunity for a hearing, that the Board—

(A) has violated or is unable to comply with any provision of this Act, the rules of the Board, or the securities laws; or

(B) without reasonable justification or excuse, has failed to enforce compliance with any such provision or rule, or any professional standard by a registered public accounting firm or an associated person thereof.

(3) CENSURE OF BOARD MEMBERS; REMOVAL FROM OFFICEThe Commission may, as necessary or appropriate in the public interest, for the protection of investors, or otherwise in furtherance of the purposes of this Act or the securities laws, remove from office or censure any member of the Board, if the Commission finds, on the record, after notice and opportunity for a hearing, that such member—

(A) has willfully violated any provision of this Act, the rules of the Board, or the securities laws;

(B) has willfully abused the authority of that member; or

(C) without reasonable justification or excuse, has failed to enforce compliance with any such provision or rule, or any professional standard by any registered public accounting firm or any associated person thereof.

SEC. 108. ACCOUNTING STANDARDS.

(a) AMENDMENT TO SECURITIES ACT OF 1933—Section 19 of the Securities Act of 1933 (15 U.S.C. 77s) is amended—

(1) by redesignating subsections (b) and (c) as subsections (c) and (d), respectively; and

(2) by inserting after subsection (a) the following:

'(b) RECOGNITION OF ACCOUNTING STANDARDS

'(1) IN GENERAL—In carrying out its authority under subsection (a) and under section 13(b) of the Securities Exchange Act of 1934, the Commission may recognize, as 'generally accepted' for purposes of the securities laws, any accounting principles established by a standard setting body—

'(A) that—

'(i) is organized as a private entity;

'(ii) has, for administrative and operational purposes, a board of trustees (or equivalent body) serving in the public interest, the majority of whom are not, concurrent with their service on such board, and have not been during the 2-year period preceding such service, associated persons of any registered public accounting firm;

'(iii) is funded as provided in section 109 of the Sarbanes-Oxley Act of 2002;

'(iv) has adopted procedures to ensure prompt consideration, by majority vote of its members, of changes to accounting principles necessary to reflect emerging accounting issues and changing business practices; and

'(v) considers, in adopting accounting principles, the need to keep standards current in order to reflect changes in the business environment, the extent to which international convergence on high quality accounting standards is necessary or appropriate in the public interest and for the protection of investors; and

'(B) that the Commission determines has the capacity to assist the Commission in fulfilling the requirements of subsection (a) and section 13(b) of the Securities Exchange Act of 1934, because, at a minimum, the standard setting body is capable of improving the accuracy and effectiveness of financial reporting and the protection of investors under the securities laws.

'(2) ANNUAL REPORT—A standard setting body described in paragraph (1) shall submit an annual report to the Commission and the public, containing audited financial statements of that standard setting body.'.

(b) COMMISSION AUTHORITY—The Commission shall promulgate such rules and regulations to carry out section 19(b) of the Securities Act of 1933, as added by this section, as it deems necessary or appropriate in the public interest or for the protection of investors.

(c) NO EFFECT ON COMMISSION POWERS—Nothing in this Act, including this section and the amendment made by this section, shall be construed to impair or limit the authority of the Commission to establish accounting principles or standards for purposes of enforcement of the securities laws.

(d) STUDY AND REPORT ON ADOPTING PRINCIPLES-BASED ACCOUNTING

(1) STUDY

(A) IN GENERAL—The Commission shall conduct a study on the adoption by the United States financial reporting system of a principlesbased accounting system.

SEC. 109. FUNDING.

(a) IN GENERAL—The Board, and the standard setting body designated pursuant to section 19(b) of the Securities Act of 1933, as amended by section 108, shall be funded as provided in this section.

(b) ANNUAL BUDGETS—The Board and the standard setting body referred to in subsection (a) shall each establish a budget for each fiscal year. The budget of the Board shall be subject to approval by the Commission.

(c) SOURCES AND USES OF FUNDS

(1) RECOVERABLE BUDGET EXPENSES—The budget of the Board, for each fiscal year of each of those 2 entities, shall be payable from annual accounting support fees, in accordance with subsections (d) and (e). Accounting support fees and other receipts of the Board and of such standard-setting body shall not be considered public monies of the United States.

(2) FUNDS GENERATED FROM THE COLLECTION OF MONETARY PENALTIES— Subject to the availability in advance in an appropriations Act, and notwithstanding subsection (i), all funds collected by the Board as a result of the assessment of monetary penalties shall be used to fund a merit scholarship program for undergraduate and graduate students enrolled in accredited accounting degree programs, which program is to be administered by the Board or by an entity or agent identified by the Board.

(d) ANNUAL ACCOUNTING SUPPORT FEE FOR THE BOARD

(1) ESTABLISHMENT OF FEE—The Board shall establish, with the approval of the Commission, a reasonable annual accounting support fee (or a formula for the computation thereof), as may be necessary or appropriate to establish and maintain the Board. Such fee may also cover costs incurred in the Board's first fiscal year (which may be a short fiscal year), or may be levied separately with respect to such short fiscal year.

(2) ASSESSMENTS—The rules of the Board under paragraph (1) shall provide for the equitable allocation, assessment, and collection by the Board (or an agent appointed by the Board) of the fee established under paragraph (1), among issuers, in accordance with subsection (g), allowing for differentiation among classes of issuers, as appropriate.

(e) ANNUAL ACCOUNTING SUPPORT FEE FOR STANDARD SETTING BODY—The annual accounting support fee for the standard setting body referred to in subsection (a)—

(1) shall be allocated in accordance with subsection (g), and assessed and collected against each issuer, on behalf of the standard setting body, by 1 or more appropriate designated collection agents, as may be necessary or appropriate to pay for the budget and provide for the expenses of that standard setting body, and to provide for an independent, stable source of funding for such body, subject to review by the Commission; and

(2) may differentiate among different classes of issuers.

(f) LIMITATION ON FEE—The amount of fees collected under this section for a fiscal year on behalf of the Board or the standards setting body, as the case may be, shall not exceed the recoverable budget expenses of the Board or body, respectively (which may include operating, capital, and accrued items), referred to in subsection (c)(1).

(g) ALLOCATION OF ACCOUNTING SUPPORT FEES AMONG ISSUERSAny amount due from issuers (or a particular class of issuers) under this section to fund the budget of the Board or the standard setting body referred to in subsection (a) shall be allocated among and payable by each issuer (or each issuer in a particular class, as applicable) in an amount equal to the total of such amount, multiplied by a fraction—

(1) the numerator of which is the average monthly equity market capitalization of the issuer for the 12-month period immediately preceding the beginning of the fiscal year to which such budget relates; and

(2) the denominator of which is the average monthly equity market capitalization of all such issuers for such 12-month period.

TITLE II—AUDITOR INDEPENDENCE

SEC. 201. SERVICES OUTSIDE THE SCOPE OF PRACTICE OF AUDITORS.

(a) PROHIBITED ACTIVITIES—Section 10A of the Securities Exchange Act of 1934 (15 U.S.C. 78j-1) is amended by adding at the end the following: '(g) PROHIBITED ACTIVITIES—Except as provided in subsection (h), it shall be unlawful for a registered public accounting firm (and any associated person of that firm, to the extent determined appropriate by the Commission) that performs for any issuer any audit required by this title or the rules of the Commission under this title or, beginning 180 days after the date of commencement of the operations of the Public Company Accounting Oversight Board established under section 101 of the Sarbanes-Oxley Act of 2002 (in this section referred to as the 'Board'), the rules of the Board, to provide to that issuer, contemporaneously with the audit, any non-audit service, including—

'(1) bookkeeping or other services related to the accounting records or financial statements of the audit client;

'(2) financial information systems design and implementation;

'(3) appraisal or valuation services, fairness opinions, or contribution-in-kind reports;

'(4) actuarial services;

'(5) internal audit outsourcing services;

'(6) management functions or human resources;

'(7) broker or dealer, investment adviser, or investment banking services;

'(8) legal services and expert services unrelated to the audit; and

'(9) any other service that the Board determines, by regulation, is impermissible.

'(h) PREAPPROVAL REQUIRED FOR NON-AUDIT SERVICES—A registered public accounting firm may engage in any nonaudit service, including tax services, that is not described in any of paragraphs (1) through (9) of subsection (g) for an audit client, only if the activity is approved in advance by the audit committee of the issuer, in accordance with subsection (i).'.

(b) EXEMPTION AUTHORITY—The Board may, on a case by case basis, exempt any person, issuer, public accounting firm, or transaction from the prohibition on the provision of services under section 10A(g) of the Securities Exchange Act of 1934 (as added by this section), to the extent that such exemption is necessary or appropriate in the public interest and is consistent with the protection of investors, and subject to review by the Commission in the same manner as for rules of the Board under section 107.

SEC. 202. PREAPPROVAL REQUIREMENTS.

Section 10A of the Securities Exchange Act of 1934 (15 U.S.C. 78j-1), as amended by this Act, is amended by adding at the end the following:

'(i) PREAPPROVAL REQUIREMENTS

'(1) IN GENERAL

'(A) AUDIT COMMITTEE ACTION—All auditing services (which may entail providing comfort letters in connection with securities underwritings or statutory audits required for insurance companies for purposes of State law) and non-audit services, other than as provided in subparagraph (B), provided to an issuer by the auditor of the issuer shall be preapproved by the audit committee of the issuer.

'(B) DE MINIMUS EXCEPTION—The preapproval requirement under subparagraph (A) is waived with respect to the provision of non-audit services for an issuer, if—

'(i) the aggregate amount of all such non-audit services provided to the issuer constitutes not more than 5 percent of the total amount of revenues paid by the issuer to its auditor during the fiscal year in which the nonaudit services are provided;

'(ii) such services were not recognized by the issuer at the time of the engagement to be non-audit services; and

'(iii) such services are promptly brought to the attention of the audit committee of the issuer and approved prior to the completion of the audit by the audit committee or by 1 or more members of the audit committee who are members of the board of directors to whom authority to grant such approvals has been delegated by the audit committee.

'(2) DISCLOSURE TO INVESTORS—Approval by an audit committee of an issuer under this subsection of a non-audit service to be performed by the auditor of the issuer shall be disclosed to investors in periodic reports required by section 13(a).

'(3) DELEGATION AUTHORITY—The audit committee of an issuer may delegate to 1 or more designated members of the audit committee who are independent directors of the board of directors, the authority to grant preapprovals required by this subsection. The decisions of any member to whom authority is delegated under this paragraph to preapprove an activity under this subsection shall be presented to the full audit committee at each of its scheduled meetings.

'(4) APPROVAL OF AUDIT SERVICES FOR OTHER PURPOSESIn carrying out its duties under subsection (m)(2), if the audit committee of an issuer approves an audit service within the scope of the engagement of the auditor, such audit service shall be deemed to have been preapproved for purposes of this subsection.'.

SEC. 203. AUDIT PARTNER ROTATION.

Section 10A of the Securities Exchange Act of 1934 (15 U.S.C. 78j-1), as amended by this Act, is amended by adding at the end the following:

'(j) AUDIT PARTNER ROTATION—It shall be unlawful for a registered public accounting firm to provide audit services to an issuer if the lead (or coordinating) audit partner (having primary responsibility for the audit), or the audit partner responsible for reviewing the audit, has performed audit services for that issuer in each of the 5 previous fiscal years of that issuer.'.

SEC. 204. AUDITOR REPORTS TO AUDIT COMMITTEES.

Section 10A of the Securities Exchange Act of 1934 (15 U.S.C. 78j-1), as amended by this Act, is amended by adding at the end the following:

'(k) REPORTS TO AUDIT COMMITTEES—Each registered public accounting firm that performs for any issuer any audit required by this title shall timely report to the audit committee of the issuer—

'(1) all critical accounting policies and practices to be used;

'(2) all alternative treatments of financial information within generally accepted accounting principles that have been discussed with management officials of the issuer, ramifications of the use of such alternative disclosures and treatments, and the treatment preferred by the registered public accounting firm; and

'(3) other material written communications between the registered public accounting firm and the management of the issuer, such as any management letter or schedule of unadjusted differences.'.

SEC. 205. CONFORMING AMENDMENTS.

SEC. 206. CONFLICTS OF INTEREST.

Section 10A of the Securities Exchange Act of 1934 (15 U.S.C. 78j-1), as amended by this Act, is amended by adding at the end the following:

'(l) CONFLICTS OF INTEREST—It shall be unlawful for a registered public accounting firm to perform for an issuer any audit service required by this title, if a chief executive officer, controller, chief financial officer, chief accounting officer, or any person serving in an equivalent position for the issuer, was employed by that registered independent public accounting firm and participated in any capacity in the audit of that issuer during the 1-year period preceding the date of the initiation of the audit.'.

SEC. 207. STUDY OF MANDATORY ROTATION OF REGISTERED PUBLIC ACCOUNTING FIRMS.

SEC. 208. COMMISSION AUTHORITY.

(a) COMMISSION REGULATIONS—Not later than 180 days after the date of enactment of this Act, the Commission shall issue final regulations to carry out each of subsections (g) through (l) of section 10A of the Securities Exchange Act of 1934, as added by this title.

(b) AUDITOR INDEPENDENCE—It shall be unlawful for any registered public accounting firm (or an associated person thereof, as applicable) to prepare or issue any audit report with respect to any issuer, if the firm or associated person engages in any activity with respect to that issuer prohibited by any of subsections (g) through (l) of section 10A of the Securities Exchange Act of 1934, as added by this title, or any rule or regulation of the Commission or of the Board issued thereunder.

SEC. 209. CONSIDERATIONS BY APPROPRIATE STATE REGULATORY AUTHORITIES.

In supervising nonregistered public accounting firms and their associated persons, appropriate State regulatory authorities should make an independent determination of the proper standards applicable, particularly taking into consideration the size and nature of the business of the accounting firms they supervise and the size and nature of the business of the clients of those firms. The standards applied by the Board under this Act should not be presumed to be applicable for purposes of this section for small and medium sized nonregistered public accounting firms.

TITLE III—CORPORATE RESPONSIBILITY

SEC. 301. PUBLIC COMPANY AUDIT COMMITTEES.

Section 10A of the Securities Exchange Act of 1934 (15 U.S.C. 78f) is amended by adding at the end the following:

'(m) STANDARDS RELATING TO AUDIT COMMITTEES.

'(1) COMMISSION RULES

'(A) IN GENERAL—Effective not later than 270 days after the date of enactment of this subsection, the Commission shall, by rule, direct the national securities exchanges and national securities associations to prohibit the listing of any security of an issuer that is not in compliance with the requirements of any portion of paragraphs (2) through (6).

'(B) OPPORTUNITY TO CURE DEFECTS—The rules of the Commission under subparagraph (A) shall provide for appropriate procedures for an issuer to have an opportunity to cure any defects that would be the basis for a prohibition under subparagraph (A), before the imposition of such prohibition.

'(2) RESPONSIBILITIES RELATING TO REGISTERED PUBLIC ACCOUNTING FIRMS— The audit committee of each issuer, in its capacity as a committee of the board of directors, shall be directly responsible for the appointment, compensation, and oversight of the work of any registered public accounting firm employed by that issuer (including resolution of disagreements between management and the auditor regarding financial reporting) for the purpose of preparing or issuing an audit report or related work, and each such registered public accounting firm shall report directly to the audit committee.

'(3) INDEPENDENCE

'(A) IN GENERAL—Each member of the audit committee of the issuer shall be a member of the board of directors of the issuer, and shall otherwise be independent.

'(B) CRITERIA—In order to be considered to be independent for purposes of this paragraph, a member of an audit committee of an issuer may not, other than in his or her capacity as a member of the audit committee, the board of directors, or any other board committee—

'(i) accept any consulting, advisory, or other compensatory fee from the issuer; or

'(ii) be an affiliated person of the issuer or any subsidiary thereof.

'(C) EXEMPTION AUTHORITY—The Commission may exempt from the requirements of subparagraph

(B) a particular relationship with respect to audit committee members, as the Commission determines appropriate in light of the circumstances.

'(4) COMPLAINTS—Each audit committee shall establish procedures for—

'(A) the receipt, retention, and treatment of complaints received by the issuer regarding accounting, internal accounting controls, or auditing matters; and

'(B) the confidential, anonymous submission by employees of the issuer of concerns regarding questionable accounting or auditing matters.

'(5) AUTHORITY TO ENGAGE ADVISERS—Each audit committee shall have the authority to engage independent counsel and other advisers, as it determines necessary to carry out its duties.

'(6) FUNDING—Each issuer shall provide for appropriate funding, as determined by the audit committee, in its capacity as a committee of the board of directors, for payment of compensation—

'(A) to the registered public accounting firm employed by the issuer for the purpose of rendering or issuing an audit report; and

'(B) to any advisers employed by the audit committee under paragraph (5).'.

SEC. 302. CORPORATE RESPONSIBILITY FOR FINANCIAL REPORTS.

(a) REGULATIONS REQUIRED—The Commission shall, by rule, require, for each company filing periodic reports under section 13(a) or 15(d) of the Securities Exchange Act of 1934 (15 U.S.C. 78m, 78o(d)), that the principal executive officer or officers and the principal financial officer or officers, or persons performing similar functions, certify in each annual or quarterly report filed or submitted under either such section of such Act that—

(1) the signing officer has reviewed the report;

(2) based on the officer's knowledge, the report does not contain any untrue statement of a material fact or omit to state a material fact necessary in order to make the statements made, in light of the circumstances under which such statements were made, not misleading;

(3) based on such officer's knowledge, the financial statements, and other financial information included in the report, fairly present in all material respects the financial condition and results of operations of the issuer as of, and for, the periods presented in the report;

(4) the signing officers—

(A) are responsible for establishing and maintaining internal controls;

(B) have designed such internal controls to ensure that material information relating to the issuer and its consolidated subsidiaries is made known to such officers by others within those entities, particularly during the period in which the periodic reports are being prepared;

(C) have evaluated the effectiveness of the issuer's internal controls as of a date within 90 days prior to the report; and

(D) have presented in the report their conclusions about the effectiveness of their internal controls based on their evaluation as of that date;

(5) the signing officers have disclosed to the issuer's auditors and the audit committee of the board of directors (or persons fulfilling the equivalent function)—

(A) all significant deficiencies in the design or operation of internal controls which could adversely affect the issuer's ability to record, process, summarize, and report financial data and have identified for the issuer's auditors any material weaknesses in internal controls; and

(B) any fraud, whether or not material, that involves management or other employees who have a significant role in the issuer's internal controls; and

(6) the signing officers have indicated in the report whether or not there were significant changes in internal controls or in other factors that could significantly affect internal controls subsequent to the date of their evaluation, including any corrective actions with regard to significant deficiencies and material weaknesses.

(b) FOREIGN REINCORPORATIONS HAVE NO EFFECT—Nothing in this section 302 shall be interpreted or applied in any way to allow any issuer to lessen the legal force of the statement required under this section 302, by an issuer having reincorporated or having engaged in any other transaction that resulted in the transfer of the corporate domicile or offices of the issuer from inside the United States to outside of the United States.

(c) DEADLINE—The rules required by subsection (a) shall be effective not later than 30 days after the date of enactment of this Act.

SEC. 303. IMPROPER INFLUENCE ON CONDUCT OF AUDITS.

(a) RULES TO PROHIBIT—It shall be unlawful, in contravention of such rules or regulations as the Commission shall prescribe as necessary and appropriate in the public interest or for the protection of investors, for any officer or director of an issuer, or any other person acting under the direction thereof, to take any action to fraudulently influence, coerce, manipulate, or mislead any independent public or certified accountant engaged in the performance of an audit of the financial statements of that issuer for the purpose of rendering such financial statements materially misleading.

(b) ENFORCEMENT—In any civil proceeding, the Commission shall have exclusive authority to enforce this section and any rule or regulation issued under this section.

(c) NO PREEMPTION OF OTHER LAW—The provisions of subsection (a) shall be in addition to, and shall not supersede or preempt, any other provision of law or any rule or regulation issued thereunder.

(d) DEADLINE FOR RULEMAKING—The Commission shall—

(1) propose the rules or regulations required by this section, not later than 90 days after the date of enactment of this Act; and

(2) issue final rules or regulations required by this section, not later than 270 days after that date of enactment.

SEC. 304. FORFEITURE OF CERTAIN BONUSES AND PROFITS.

(a) ADDITIONAL COMPENSATION PRIOR TO NONCOMPLIANCE WITH COMMISSION FINANCIAL REPORTING REQUIREMENTS—If an issuer is required to prepare an accounting restatement due to the material noncompliance of the issuer, as a result of misconduct, with any financial reporting requirement under the securities laws, the chief executive officer and chief financial officer of the issuer shall reimburse the issuer for—

(1) any bonus or other incentive-based or equitybased compensation received by that person from the issuer during the 12-month period following the first public issuance or filing with the Commission (whichever first occurs) of the financial document embodying such financial reporting requirement; and

(2) any profits realized from the sale of securities of the issuer during that 12-month period.

(b) COMMISSION EXEMPTION AUTHORITY—The Commission may exempt any person from the application of subsection (a), as it deems necessary and appropriate.

SEC. 305. OFFICER AND DIRECTOR BARS AND PENALTIES.

(a) UNFITNESS STANDARD

(1) SECURITIES EXCHANGE ACT OF 1934—Section 21(d)(2) of the Securities Exchange Act of 1934 (15 U.S.C. 78u(d)(2)) is amended by striking 'substantial unfitness' and inserting 'unfitness'.

(2) SECURITIES ACT OF 1933—Section 20(e) of the Securities Act of 1933 (15 U.S.C. 77t(e)) is amended by striking 'substantial unfitness' and inserting 'unfitness'.

(b) EQUITABLE RELIEF—Section 21(d) of the Securities Exchange Act of 1934 (15 U.S.C. 78u(d)) is amended by adding at the end the following:

'(5) EQUITABLE RELIEF—In any action or proceeding brought or instituted by the Commission under any provision of the securities laws, the Commission may seek, and any Federal court may grant, any equitable relief that may be appropriate or necessary for the benefit of investors.'.

SEC. 306. INSIDER TRADES DURING PENSION FUND BLACKOUT PERIODS.

(a) PROHIBITION OF INSIDER TRADING DURING PENSION FUND BLACKOUT PERIODS

(1) IN GENERAL—Except to the extent otherwise provided by rule of the Commission pursuant to paragraph (3), it shall be unlawful for any director or executive officer of an issuer of any equity security (other than an exempted security), directly or indirectly, to purchase, sell, or otherwise acquire or transfer any equity security of the issuer (other than an exempted security) during any blackout period with respect to such equity security if such director or officer acquires such equity security in connection with his or her service or employment as a director or executive officer.

(2) REMEDY

(A) IN GENERAL—Any profit realized by a director or executive officer referred to in paragraph (1) from any purchase, sale, or other acquisition or transfer in violation of this subsection shall inure to and be recoverable by the issuer, irrespective of any intention on the part of such director or executive officer in entering into the transaction.

(B) ACTIONS TO RECOVER PROFITS—An action to recover profits in accordance with this subsection may be instituted at law or in equity in any court of competent jurisdiction by the issuer, or by the owner of any security of the issuer in the name and in behalf of the issuer if the issuer fails or refuses to bring such action within 60 days after the date of request, or fails diligently to prosecute the action thereafter, except that no such suit shall be brought more than 2 years after the date on which such profit was realized.

(3) RULEMAKING AUTHORIZED—The Commission shall, in consultation with the Secretary of Labor, issue rules to clarify the application of this subsection and to prevent evasion thereof. Such rules shall provide for the application of the requirements of paragraph (1) with respect to entities treated as a single employer with respect to an issuer under section 414(b), (c), (m), or (o) of the Internal Revenue Code of 1986 to the extent necessary to clarify the application of such requirements and to prevent evasion thereof. Such rules may also provide for appropriate exceptions from the requirements of this subsection, including exceptions for purchases pursuant to an automatic dividend reinvestment program or purchases or sales made pursuant to an advance election.

(4) BLACKOUT PERIOD—For purposes of this subsection, the term 'blackout period', with respect to the equity securities of any issuer—

(A) means any period of more than 3 consecutive business days during which the ability of not fewer than 50 percent of the participants or beneficiaries under all individual account plans maintained by the issuer to purchase, sell, or otherwise acquire or transfer an interest in any equity of such issuer held in such an individual account plan is temporarily suspended by the issuer or by a fiduciary of the plan; and

(B) does not include, under regulations which shall be prescribed by the Commission—

(i) a regularly scheduled period in which the participants and beneficiaries may not purchase, sell, or otherwise acquire or transfer an interest in any equity of such issuer, if such period is—

(I) incorporated into the individual account plan; and

(II) timely disclosed to employees before becoming participants under the individual account plan or as a subsequent amendment to the plan; or

(ii) any suspension described in subparagraph (A) that is imposed solely in connection with persons becoming participants or beneficiaries, or ceasing to be participants or beneficiaries, in an individual account plan by reason of a corporate merger, acquisition, divestiture, or similar transaction involving the plan or plan sponsor.

(5) INDIVIDUAL ACCOUNT PLAN—For purposes of this subsection, the term 'individual account plan' has the meaning provided in section 3(34) of the Employee Retirement Income Security Act of 1974 (29 U.S.C. 1002(34), except that such term shall not include a one-participant retirement plan (within the meaning of section 101(i)(8)(B) of such Act (29 U.S.C. 1021(i)(8)(B))).

(6) NOTICE TO DIRECTORS, EXECUTIVE OFFICERS, AND THE COMMISSION—In any case in which a director or executive officer is subject to the requirements of this subsection in connection with a blackout period (as defined in paragraph (4)) with respect to any equity

securities, the issuer of such equity securities shall timely notify such director or officer and the Securities and Exchange Commission of such blackout period.

(b) NOTICE REQUIREMENTS TO PARTICIPANTS AND BENEFICIARIES UNDER ERISA

(1) IN GENERAL—Section 101 of the Employee Retirement Income Security Act of 1974 (29 U.S.C. 1021) is amended by redesignating the second subsection (h) as subsection (j), and by inserting after the first subsection (h) the following new subsection:

'(i) NOTICE OF BLACKOUT PERIODS TO PARTICIPANT OR BENEFICIARY UNDER INDIVIDUAL ACCOUNT PLAN

'(1) DUTIES OF PLAN ADMINISTRATOR—In advance of the commencement of any blackout period with respect to an individual account plan, the plan administrator shall notify the plan participants and beneficiaries who are affected by such action in accordance with this subsection.

'(2) NOTICE REQUIREMENTS

'(A) IN GENERAL—The notices described in paragraph (1) shall be written in a manner calculated to be understood by the average plan participant and shall include—

'(i) the reasons for the blackout period,

'(ii) an identification of the investments and other rights affected,

'(iii) the expected beginning date and length of the blackout period,

'(iv) in the case of investments affected, a statement that the participant or beneficiary should evaluate the appropriateness of their current investment decisions in light of their inability to direct or diversify assets credited to their accounts during the blackout period, and

'(v) such other matters as the Secretary may require by regulation.

'(B) NOTICE TO PARTICIPANTS AND BENEFICIARIESExcept as otherwise provided in this subsection, notices described in paragraph

(1) shall be furnished to all participants and beneficiaries under the plan to whom the blackout period applies at least 30 days in advance of the blackout period.

'(C) EXCEPTION TO 30-DAY NOTICE REQUIREMENTIn any case in which—

'(i) a deferral of the blackout period would violate the requirements of subparagraph (A) or (B) of section 404(a)(1), and a fiduciary of the plan reasonably so determines in writing, or

'(ii) the inability to provide the 30day advance notice is due to events that were unforeseeable or circumstances beyond the reasonable control of the plan administrator, and a fiduciary of the plan reasonably so determines in writing,

subparagraph (B) shall not apply, and the notice shall be furnished to all participants and beneficiaries under the plan to whom the blackout period applies as soon as reasonably possible under the circumstances unless such a notice in advance of the termination of the blackout period is impracticable.

'(D) WRITTEN NOTICE—The notice required to be provided under this subsection shall be in writing, except that such notice may be in electronic or other form to the extent that such form is reasonably accessible to the recipient.

'(E) NOTICE TO ISSUERS OF EMPLOYER SECURITIES SUBJECT TO BLACKOUT PERIOD—In the case of any blackout period in connection with an individual account plan, the plan administrator shall provide timely notice of such blackout period to the issuer of any employer securities subject to such blackout period.

'(3) EXCEPTION FOR BLACKOUT PERIODS WITH LIMITED APPLICABILITY—In any case in which the blackout period applies only to 1 or more participants or beneficiaries in connection with a merger, acquisition, divestiture, or similar transaction involving the plan or plan sponsor and occurs solely in connection with becoming or ceasing to be a participant or beneficiary under the plan by reason of such merger, acquisition, divestiture, or transaction, the requirement of this subsection that the notice be provided to all participants and beneficiaries shall be treated as met if the notice required under paragraph (1) is provided to such participants or beneficiaries to whom the blackout period applies as soon as reasonably practicable.

'(4) CHANGES IN LENGTH OF BLACKOUT PERIOD—If, following the furnishing of the notice pursuant to this subsection, there is a change in the beginning date or length of the blackout period (specified in such notice pursuant to paragraph (2)(A)(iii)), the administrator shall provide affected participants and beneficiaries notice of the change as soon as reasonably practicable. In relation to the extended blackout period, such notice shall meet the requirements of paragraph (2)(D) and shall specify any material change in the matters referred to in clauses (i) through (v) of paragraph (2)(A).

'(5) REGULATORY EXCEPTIONS—The Secretary may provide by regulation for additional exceptions to the requirements of this subsection which the Secretary determines are in the interests of participants and beneficiaries.

'(6) GUIDANCE AND MODEL NOTICES—The Secretary shall issue guidance and model notices which meet the requirements of this subsection.

'(7) BLACKOUT PERIOD—For purposes of this subsection—

'(A) IN GENERAL—The term 'blackout period' means, in connection with an individual account plan, any period for which any ability of participants or beneficiaries under the plan, which is otherwise available under the terms of such plan, to direct or diversify assets credited to their accounts, to obtain loans from the plan, or to obtain distributions from the plan is temporarily suspended, limited, or restricted, if such suspension, limitation, or restriction is for any period of more than 3 consecutive business days.

'(B) EXCLUSIONS—The term 'blackout period' does not include a suspension, limitation, or restriction—

'(i) which occurs by reason of the application of the securities laws (as defined in section 3(a)(47) of the Securities Exchange Act of 1934),

'(ii) which is a change to the plan which provides for a regularly scheduled suspension, limitation, or restriction which is disclosed to participants or beneficiaries through any summary of material modifications, any materials describing specific investment alternatives under the plan, or any changes thereto, or

'(iii) which applies only to 1 or more individuals, each of whom is the participant, an alternate payee (as defined in section 206(d)(3)(K)), or any other beneficiary pursuant to a qualified domestic relations order (as defined in section 206(d)(3)(B)(i)).

'(8) INDIVIDUAL ACCOUNT PLAN

'(A) IN GENERAL—For purposes of this subsection, the term 'individual account plan' shall have the meaning provided such term in section 3(34), except that such term shall not include a one-participant retirement plan.

'(B) ONE-PARTICIPANT RETIREMENT PLAN—For purposes of subparagraph (A), the term 'oneparticipant retirement plan' means a retirement plan that—

'(i) on the first day of the plan year—

'(I) covered only the employer (and the employer's spouse) and the employer owned the entire business (whether or not incorporated), or

'(II) covered only one or more partners (and their spouses) in a business partnership (including partners in an S or C corporation (as defined in section 1361(a) of the Internal Revenue Code of 1986)),

'(ii) meets the minimum coverage requirements of section 410(b) of the Internal Revenue Code of 1986 (as in effect on the date of the enactment of this paragraph) without being combined with any other plan of the business that covers the employees of the business,

'(iii) does not provide benefits to anyone except the employer (and the employer's spouse) or the partners (and their spouses),

'(iv) does not cover a business that is a member of an affiliated service group, a controlled group of corporations, or a group of businesses under common control, and

'(v) does not cover a business that leases employees.'.

(2) ISSUANCE OF INITIAL GUIDANCE AND MODEL NOTICEThe Secretary of Labor shall issue initial guidance and a model notice pursuant to section 101(i)(6) of the Employee Retirement Income Security Act of 1974 (as added by this subsection) not later than January 1, 2003. Not later than 75 days after the date of the enactment of this Act, the Secretary shall promulgate interim final rules necessary to carry out the amendments made by this subsection.

(3) CIVIL PENALTIES FOR FAILURE TO PROVIDE NOTICESection 502 of such Act (29 U.S.C. 1132) is amended—

(A) in subsection (a)(6), by striking '(5), or (6)' and inserting '(5), (6), or (7)';

(B) by redesignating paragraph (7) of subsection (c) as paragraph (8); and

(C) by inserting after paragraph (6) of subsection (c) the following new paragraph:

'(7) The Secretary may assess a civil penalty against a plan administrator of up to $100 a day from the date of the plan administrator's failure or refusal to provide notice to participants and beneficiaries in accordance with section 101(i). For purposes of this paragraph, each violation with respect to any single participant or beneficiary shall be treated as a separate violation.'.

(3) PLAN AMENDMENTS—If any amendment made by this subsection requires an amendment to any plan, such plan amendment shall not be required to be made before the first plan year beginning on or after the effective date of this section, if—

(A) during the period after such amendment made by this subsection takes effect and before such first plan year, the plan is operated in good faith compliance with the requirements of such amendment made by this subsection, and

(B) such plan amendment applies retroactively to the period after such amendment made by this subsection takes effect and before such first plan year.

(c) EFFECTIVE DATE—The provisions of this section (including the amendments made thereby) shall take effect 180 days after the date of the enactment of this Act. Good faith compliance with the requirements of such provisions in advance of the issuance of applicable regulations thereunder shall be treated as compliance with such provisions.

SEC. 307. RULES OF PROFESSIONAL RESPONSIBILITY FOR ATTORNEYS.

Not later than 180 days after the date of enactment of this Act, the Commission shall issue rules, in the public interest and for the protection of investors, setting forth minimum standards of professional conduct for attorneys appearing and practicing before the Commission in any way in the representation of issuers, including a rule—

(1) requiring an attorney to report evidence of a material violation of securities law or breach of fiduciary duty or similar violation by the company or any agent thereof, to the chief legal counsel or the chief executive officer of the company (or the equivalent thereof); and

(2) if the counsel or officer does not appropriately respond to the evidence (adopting, as necessary, appropriate remedial measures or sanctions with respect to the violation), requiring the attorney to report the evidence to the audit committee of the board of directors of the issuer or to another committee of the board of directors comprised solely of directors not employed directly or indirectly by the issuer, or to the board of directors.

SEC. 308. FAIR FUNDS FOR INVESTORS.

(a) CIVIL PENALTIES ADDED TO DISGORGEMENT FUNDS FOR THE RELIEF OF VICTIMS—If in any judicial or administrative action brought by the Commission under the securities laws (as such term is defined in section 3(a)(47) of the Securities Exchange Act of 1934 (15 U.S.C. 78c(a)(47)) the Commission obtains an order requiring disgorgement against any person for a violation of such laws or the rules or regulations thereunder, or such person agrees in settlement of any such action to such disgorgement, and the Commission also obtains pursuant to such laws a civil penalty against such person, the amount of such civil penalty shall, on the motion or at the direction of the Commission, be added to and become part of the disgorgement fund for the benefit of the victims of such violation.

(b) ACCEPTANCE OF ADDITIONAL DONATIONS—The Commission is authorized to accept, hold, administer, and utilize gifts, bequests and devises of property, both real and personal, to the United States for a disgorgement fund described in subsection (a). Such gifts, bequests, and devises of money and proceeds from sales of other property received as gifts, bequests, or devises shall be deposited in the disgorgement fund and shall be available for allocation in accordance with subsection (a).

(c) STUDY REQUIRED

(1) SUBJECT OF STUDY—The Commission shall review and analyze—

(A) enforcement actions by the Commission over the five years preceding the date of the enactment of this Act that have included proceedings to obtain civil penalties or disgorgements to identify areas where such proceedings may be utilized to efficiently, effectively, and fairly provide restitution for injured investors; and

(B) other methods to more efficiently, effectively, and fairly provide restitution to injured investors, including methods to improve the collection rates for civil penalties and disgorgements.

(d) CONFORMING AMENDMENTS—Each of the following provisions is amended by inserting ', except as otherwise provided in section 308 of the Sarbanes-Oxley Act of 2002' after 'Treasury of the United States':

(1) Section 21(d)(3)(C)(i) of the Securities Exchange Act of 1934 (15 U.S.C. 78u(d)(3)(C)(i)).

(2) Section 21A(d)(1) of such Act (15 U.S.C. 78u1(d)(1)).

(3) Section 20(d)(3)(A) of the Securities Act of 1933 (15 U.S.C. 77t(d)(3)(A)).

(4) Section 42(e)(3)(A) of the Investment Company Act of 1940 (15 U.S.C. 80a-41(e)(3)(A)).

(5) Section 209(e)(3)(A) of the Investment Advisers Act of 1940 (15 U.S.C. 80b-9(e)(3)(A)).

(e) DEFINITION—As used in this section, the term 'disgorgement fund' means a fund established in any administrative or judicial proceeding described in subsection (a).

TITLE IV—ENHANCED FINANCIAL DISCLOSURES

SEC. 401. DISCLOSURES IN PERIODIC REPORTS.

(a) DISCLOSURES REQUIRED—Section 13 of the Securities Exchange Act of 1934 (15 U.S.C. 78m) is amended by adding at the end the following:

'(i) ACCURACY OF FINANCIAL REPORTS—Each financial report that contains financial statements, and that is required to be prepared in accordance with (or reconciled to) generally accepted accounting principles under this title and filed with the Commission shall reflect all material correcting adjustments that have been identified by a registered public accounting firm in accordance with generally accepted accounting principles and the rules and regulations of the Commission.

'(j) OFF-BALANCE SHEET TRANSACTIONS—Not later than 180 days after the date of enactment of the Sarbanes-Oxley Act of 2002, the Commission shall issue final rules providing that each annual and quarterly financial report required to be filed with the Commission shall disclose all material off-balance sheet transactions, arrangements, obligations (including contingent obligations), and other relationships of the issuer with unconsolidated entities or other persons, that may have a material current or future effect on financial condition, changes in financial condition, results of operations, liquidity, capital expenditures, capital resources, or significant components of revenues or expenses.'.

(b) COMMISSION RULES ON PRO FORMA FIGURES—Not later than 180 days after the date of enactment of the Sarbanes-Oxley Act fo 2002, the Commission shall issue final rules providing that pro forma financial information included in any periodic or other report filed with the Commission pursuant to the securities laws, or in any public disclosure or press or other release, shall be presented in a manner that—

(1) does not contain an untrue statement of a material fact or omit to state a material fact necessary in order to make the pro forma financial information, in light of the circumstances under which it is presented, not misleading; and

(2) reconciles it with the financial condition and results of operations of the issuer under generally accepted accounting principles.

(c) STUDY AND REPORT ON SPECIAL PURPOSE ENTITIES

(1) STUDY REQUIRED—The Commission shall, not later than 1 year after the effective date of adoption of off-balance sheet disclosure rules required by section 13(j) of the Securities Exchange Act of 1934, as added by this section, complete a study of filings by issuers and their disclosures to determine—

(A) the extent of off-balance sheet transactions, including assets, liabilities, leases, losses, and the use of special purpose entities; and

(B) whether generally accepted accounting rules result in financial statements of issuers reflecting the economics of such offbalance sheet transactions to investors in a transparent fashion.

(2) REPORT AND RECOMMENDATIONS—Not later than 6 months after the date of completion of the study required by paragraph (1), the Commission shall submit a report to the President, the Committee on Banking, Housing, and Urban Affairs of the Senate, and the Committee on Financial Services of the House of Representatives, setting forth—

(A) the amount or an estimate of the amount of off-balance sheet transactions, including assets, liabilities, leases, and losses of, and the use of special purpose entities by, issuers filing periodic reports pursuant to section 13 or 15 of the Securities Exchange Act of 1934;

(B) the extent to which special purpose entities are used to facilitate off-balance sheet transactions;

(C) whether generally accepted accounting principles or the rules of the Commission result in financial statements of issuers reflecting the economics of such transactions to investors in a transparent fashion;

(D) whether generally accepted accounting principles specifically result in the consolidation of special purpose entities sponsored by an issuer in cases in which the issuer has the majority of the risks and rewards of the special purpose entity; and

(E) any recommendations of the Commission for improving the transparency and quality of reporting off-balance sheet transactions in the financial statements and disclosures required to be filed by an issuer with the Commission.

SEC. 402. ENHANCED CONFLICT OF INTEREST PROVISIONS.

(a) PROHIBITION ON PERSONAL LOANS TO EXECUTIVES

Section 13 of the Securities Exchange Act of 1934 (15 U.S.C. 78m), as amended by this Act, is amended by adding at the end the following:

'(k) PROHIBITION ON PERSONAL LOANS TO EXECUTIVES

'(1) IN GENERAL—It shall be unlawful for any issuer (as defined in section 2 of the SarbanesOxley Act of 2002), directly or indirectly, including through any subsidiary, to extend or maintain credit, to arrange for the extension of credit, or to renew an extension of credit, in the form of a personal loan to or for any director or executive officer (or equivalent thereof) of that issuer. An extension of credit maintained by the issuer on the date of enactment of this subsection shall not be subject to the provisions of this subsection, provided that there is no material modification to any term of any such extension of credit or any renewal of any such extension of credit on or after that date of enactment.

'(2) LIMITATION—Paragraph (1) does not preclude any home improvement and manufactured home loans (as that term is defined in section 5 of the Home Owners' Loan Act (12 U.S.C. 1464)), consumer credit (as defined in section 103 of the Truth in Lending Act (15 U.S.C. 1602)), or any extension of credit under an open end credit plan (as defined in section 103 of the Truth in Lending Act (15 U.S.C. 1602)), or a charge card (as defined in section 127(c)(4)(e) of the Truth in Lending Act (15 U.S.C. 1637(c)(4)(e)), or any extension of credit by a broker or dealer registered under section 15 of this title to an employee of that broker or dealer to buy, trade, or carry securities, that is permitted under rules or regulations of the Board of Governors of the Federal

Reserve System pursuant to section 7 of this title (other than an extension of credit that would be used to purchase the stock of that issuer), that is—

'(A) made or provided in the ordinary course of the consumer credit business of such issuer;

'(B) of a type that is generally made available by such issuer to the public; and

'(C) made by such issuer on market terms, or terms that are no more favorable than those offered by the issuer to the general public for such extensions of credit.

'(3) RULE OF CONSTRUCTION FOR CERTAIN LOANSParagraph (1) does not apply to any loan made or maintained by an insured depository institution (as defined in section 3 of the Federal Deposit Insurance Act (12 U.S.C. 1813)), if the loan is subject to the insider lending restrictions of section 22(h) of the Federal Reserve Act (12 U.S.C. 375b).'.

SEC. 403. DISCLOSURES OF TRANSACTIONS INVOLVING MANAGEMENT AND PRINCIPAL STOCKHOLDERS.

(a) AMENDMENT—Section 16 of the Securities Exchange Act of 1934 (15 U.S.C. 78p) is amended by striking the heading of such section and subsection (a) and inserting the following:

'SEC. 16. DIRECTORS, OFFICERS, AND PRINCIPAL STOCKHOLDERS.

'(a) DISCLOSURES REQUIRED

'(1) DIRECTORS, OFFICERS, AND PRINCIPAL STOCKHOLDERS REQUIRED TO FILE— Every person who is directly or indirectly the beneficial owner of more than 10 percent of any class of any equity security (other than an exempted security) which is registered pursuant to section 12, or who is a director or an officer of the issuer of such security, shall file the statements required by this subsection with the Commission (and, if such security is registered on a national securities exchange, also with the exchange).

'(2) TIME OF FILING—The statements required by this subsection shall be filed—

'(A) at the time of the registration of such security on a national securities exchange or by the effective date of a registration statement filed pursuant to section 12(g);

'(B) within 10 days after he or she becomes such beneficial owner, director, or officer;

'(C) if there has been a change in such ownership, or if such person shall have purchased or sold a security-based swap agreement (as defined in section 206(b) of the Gramm-Leach-Bliley Act (15 U.S.C. 78c note)) involving such equity security, before the end of the second business day following the day on which the subject transaction has been executed, or at such other time as the Commission shall establish, by rule, in any case in which the Commission determines that such 2-day period is not feasible.

'(3) CONTENTS OF STATEMENTS—A statement filed—

'(A) under subparagraph (A) or (B) of paragraph (2) shall contain a statement of the amount of all equity securities of such issuer of which the filing person is the beneficial owner; and

'(B) under subparagraph (C) of such paragraph shall indicate ownership by the filing person at the date of filing, any such changes in such ownership, and such purchases and sales of the security-based swap agreements as have occurred since the most recent such filing under such subparagraph.

'(4) ELECTRONIC FILING AND AVAILABILITY—Beginning not later than 1 year after the date of enactment of the Sarbanes-Oxley Act of 2002—

'(A) a statement filed under subparagraph (C) of paragraph (2) shall be filed electronically;

'(B) the Commission shall provide each such statement on a publicly accessible Internet site not later than the end of the business day following that filing; and

'(C) the issuer (if the issuer maintains a corporate website) shall provide that statement on that corporate website, not later than the end of the business day following that filing.'.

(b) EFFECTIVE DATE—The amendment made by this section shall be effective 30 days after the date of the enactment of this Act.

SEC. 404. MANAGEMENT ASSESSMENT OF INTERNAL CONTROLS.

(a) RULES REQUIRED—The Commission shall prescribe rules requiring each annual report required by section 13(a) or 15(d) of the Securities Exchange Act of 1934 (15 U.S.C. 78m or 78o(d)) to contain an internal control report, which shall—

(1) state the responsibility of management for establishing and maintaining an adequate internal control structure and procedures for financial reporting; and

(2) contain an assessment, as of the end of the most recent fiscal year of the issuer, of the effectiveness of the internal control structure and procedures of the issuer for financial reporting.

(b) INTERNAL CONTROL EVALUATION AND REPORTING—With respect to the internal control assessment required by subsection (a), each registered public accounting firm that prepares or issues the audit report for the issuer shall attest to, and report on, the assessment made by the management of the issuer. An attestation made under this subsection shall be made in accordance with standards for attestation engagements issued or adopted by the Board. Any such attestation shall not be the subject of a separate engagement.

SEC. 405. EXEMPTION.

Nothing in section 401, 402, or 404, the amendments made by those sections, or the rules of the Commission under those sections shall apply to any investment company registered under section 8 of the Investment Company Act of 1940 (15 U.S.C. 80a-8).

SEC. 406. CODE OF ETHICS FOR SENIOR FINANCIAL OFFICERS.

(a) CODE OF ETHICS DISCLOSURE—The Commission shall issue rules to require each issuer, together with periodic reports required pursuant to section 13(a) or 15(d) of the Securities Exchange Act of 1934, to disclose whether or not, and if not, the reason therefor, such issuer has adopted a code of ethics for senior financial officers, applicable to its principal financial officer and comptroller or principal accounting officer, or persons performing similar functions.

(b) CHANGES IN CODES OF ETHICS—The Commission shall revise its regulations concerning matters requiring prompt disclosure on Form 8-K (or any successor thereto) to require the immediate disclosure, by means of the filing of such form, dissemination by the Internet or by other electronic means, by any issuer of any change in or waiver of the code of ethics for senior financial officers.

(c) DEFINITION—In this section, the term 'code of ethics' means such standards as are reasonably necessary to promote—

(1) honest and ethical conduct, including the ethical handling of actual or apparent conflicts of interest between personal and professional relationships;

(2) full, fair, accurate, timely, and understandable disclosure in the periodic reports required to be filed by the issuer; and

(3) compliance with applicable governmental rules and regulations.

(d) DEADLINE FOR RULEMAKING—The Commission shall—

(1) propose rules to implement this section, not later than 90 days after the date of enactment of this Act; and

(2) issue final rules to implement this section, not later than 180 days after that date of enactment.

SEC. 407. DISCLOSURE OF AUDIT COMMITTEE FINANCIAL EXPERT.

(a) RULES DEFINING 'FINANCIAL EXPERT'—The Commission shall issue rules, as necessary or appropriate in the public interest and consistent with the protection of investors, to require each issuer, together with periodic reports required pursuant to sections 13(a) and 15(d) of the Securities Exchange Act of 1934, to disclose whether or not, and if not, the reasons therefor, the audit committee of that issuer is comprised of at least 1 member who is a financial expert, as such term is defined by the Commission.

(b) CONSIDERATIONS—In defining the term 'financial expert' for purposes of subsection (a), the Commission shall consider whether a person has, through education and experience as a public accountant or auditor or a principal financial officer, comptroller, or principal accounting officer of an issuer, or from a position involving the performance of similar functions—

(1) an understanding of generally accepted accounting principles and financial statements;

(2) experience in—

(A) the preparation or auditing of financial statements of generally comparable issuers; and

(B) the application of such principles in connection with the accounting for estimates, accruals, and reserves;

(3) experience with internal accounting controls; and

(4) an understanding of audit committee functions.

(c) DEADLINE FOR RULEMAKING—The Commission shall—

(1) propose rules to implement this section, not later than 90 days after the date of enactment of this Act; and

(2) issue final rules to implement this section, not later than 180 days after that date of enactment.

SEC. 408. ENHANCED REVIEW OF PERIODIC DISCLOSURES BY ISSUERS.

(a) REGULAR AND SYSTEMATIC REVIEW—The Commission shall review disclosures made by issuers reporting under section 13(a) of the Securities Exchange Act of 1934 (including reports filed on Form 10-K), and which have a class of securities listed on a national securities exchange or traded on an automated quotation facility of a national securities association, on a regular and systematic basis for the protection of investors. Such review shall include a review of an issuer's financial statement.

(b) REVIEW CRITERIA—For purposes of scheduling the reviews required by subsection (a), the Commission shall consider, among other factors—

(1) issuers that have issued material restatements of financial results;

(2) issuers that experience significant volatility in their stock price as compared to other issuers;

(3) issuers with the largest market capitalization;

(4) emerging companies with disparities in price to earning ratios;

(5) issuers whose operations significantly affect any material sector of the economy; and

(6) any other factors that the Commission may consider relevant.

(c) MINIMUM REVIEW PERIOD—In no event shall an issuer required to file reports under section 13(a) or 15(d) of the Securities Exchange Act of 1934 be reviewed under this section less frequently than once every 3 years.

SEC. 409. REAL TIME ISSUER DISCLOSURES.

Section 13 of the Securities Exchange Act of 1934 (15 U.S.C. 78m), as amended by this Act, is amended by adding at the end the following:

'(l) REAL TIME ISSUER DISCLOSURES—Each issuer reporting under section 13(a) or 15(d) shall disclose to the public on a rapid and current basis such additional information concerning material changes in the financial condition or operations of the issuer, in plain English, which may include trend and qualitative information and graphic presentations, as the Commission determines, by rule, is necessary or useful for the protection of investors and in the public interest.'.

TITLE V—ANALYST CONFLICTS OF INTEREST

SEC. 501. TREATMENT OF SECURITIES ANALYSTS BY REGISTERED SECURITIES ASSOCIATIONS AND NATIONAL SECURITIES EXCHANGES.

(a) RULES REGARDING SECURITIES ANALYSTS—The Securities Exchange Act of 1934 (15 U.S.C. 78a et seq.) is amended by inserting after section 15C the following new section:

'SEC. 15D. SECURITIES ANALYSTS AND RESEARCH REPORTS.

'(a) ANALYST PROTECTIONS—The Commission, or upon the authorization and direction of the Commission, a registered securities association or national securities exchange, shall have adopted, not later than 1 year after the date of enactment of this section, rules reasonably designed to address conflicts of interest that can arise when securities analysts recommend equity securities in research reports and public appearances, in order to improve the objectivity of research and provide investors with more useful and reliable information, including rules designed—

'(1) to foster greater public confidence in securities research, and to protect the objectivity and independence of securities analysts, by—

'(A) restricting the prepublication clearance or approval of research reports by persons employed by the broker or dealer who are engaged in investment banking activities, or persons not directly responsible for investment research, other than legal or compliance staff;

'(B) limiting the supervision and compensatory evaluation of securities analysts to officials employed by the broker or dealer who are not engaged in investment banking activities; and

'(C) requiring that a broker or dealer and persons employed by a broker or dealer who are involved with investment banking activities may not, directly or indirectly, retaliate against or threaten to retaliate against any securities analyst employed by that broker or dealer or its affiliates as a result of an adverse, negative, or otherwise unfavorable research report that may adversely affect the present or prospective investment banking relationship of the broker or dealer with the issuer that is the subject of the research report, except that such rules may not limit the authority of a broker or dealer to discipline a securities analyst for causes other than such research report in accordance with the policies and procedures of the firm;

'(2) to define periods during which brokers or dealers who have participated, or are to participate, in a public offering of securities as underwriters or dealers should not publish or otherwise distribute research reports relating to such securities or to the issuer of such securities;

'(3) to establish structural and institutional safeguards within registered brokers or dealers to assure that securities analysts are separated by appropriate informational partitions within the firm from the review, pressure, or oversight of those whose involvement in investment banking activities might potentially bias their judgment or supervision; and

'(4) to address such other issues as the Commission, or such association or exchange, determines appropriate.

'(b) DISCLOSURE—The Commission, or upon the authorization and direction of the Commission, a registered securities association or national securities exchange, shall have adopted, not later than 1 year after the date of enactment of this section, rules reasonably designed to require each securities analyst to disclose in public appearances, and each registered broker or dealer to disclose in each research report, as applicable, conflicts of interest that are known or should have been known by the securities analyst or the broker or dealer, to exist at the time of the appearance or the date of distribution of the report, including—

'(1) the extent to which the securities analyst has debt or equity investments in the issuer that is the subject of the appearance or research report;

'(2) whether any compensation has been received by the registered broker or dealer, or any affiliate thereof, including the securities analyst, from the issuer that is the subject of the appearance or research report, subject to such exemptions as the Commission may determine appropriate and necessary to prevent disclosure by virtue of this paragraph of material non-public information regarding specific potential future investment banking transactions of such issuer, as is appropriate in the public interest and consistent with the protection of investors;

'(3) whether an issuer, the securities of which are recommended in the appearance or research report, currently is, or during the 1-year period preceding the date of the appearance or date of distribution of the report has been, a client of the registered broker or dealer, and if so, stating the types of services provided to the issuer;

'(4) whether the securities analyst received compensation with respect to a research report, based upon (among any other factors) the investment banking revenues (either generally or specifically earned from the issuer being analyzed) of the registered broker or dealer; and

'(5) such other disclosures of conflicts of interest that are material to investors, research analysts, or the broker or dealer as the Commission, or such association or exchange, determines appropriate.

'(c) DEFINITIONS—In this section—

'(1) the term 'securities analyst' means any associated person of a registered broker or dealer that is principally responsible for, and any associated person who reports directly or indirectly to a securities analyst in connection with, the preparation of the substance of a research report, whether or not any such person has the job title of 'securities analyst'; and

'(2) the term 'research report' means a written or electronic communication that includes an analysis of equity securities of individual companies or industries, and that provides information reasonably sufficient upon which to base an investment decision.'.

(b) ENFORCEMENT—Section 21B(a) of the Securities Exchange Act of 1934 (15 U.S.C. 78u-2(a)) is amended by inserting '15D,' before '15B'.

(c) COMMISSION AUTHORITY—The Commission may promulgate and amend its regulations, or direct a registered securities association or national securities exchange to promulgate and amend its rules, to carry out section 15D of the Securities Exchange Act of 1934, as added by this section, as is necessary for the protection of investors and in the public interest.

TITLE VI—COMMISSION RESOURCES AND AUTHORITY

SEC. 601. AUTHORIZATION OF APPROPRIATIONS.

Section 35 of the Securities Exchange Act of 1934 (15 U.S.C. 78kk) is amended to read as follows:

'SEC. 35. AUTHORIZATION OF APPROPRIATIONS.

'In addition to any other funds authorized to be appropriated to the Commission, there are authorized to be appropriated to carry out the functions, powers, and duties of the Commission, $776,000,000 for fiscal year 2003, of which—

'(1) $102,700,000 shall be available to fund additional compensation, including salaries and benefits, as authorized in the Investor and Capital Markets Fee Relief Act (Public Law 107123; 115 Stat. 2390 et seq.);

'(2) $108,400,000 shall be available for information technology, security enhancements, and recovery and mitigation activities in light of the terrorist attacks of September 11, 2001; and

'(3) $98,000,000 shall be available to add not fewer than an additional 200 qualified professionals to provide enhanced oversight of auditors and audit services required by the Federal securities laws, and to improve Commission investigative and disciplinary efforts with respect to such auditors and services, as well as for additional professional support staff necessary to strengthen the programs of the Commission involving Full Disclosure and Prevention and Suppression of Fraud, risk management, industry technology review, compliance, inspections, examinations, market regulation, and investment management.'.

SEC. 602. APPEARANCE AND PRACTICE BEFORE THE COMMISSION.

The Securities Exchange Act of 1934 (15 U.S.C. 78a et seq.) is amended by inserting after section 4B the following:

'SEC. 4C. APPEARANCE AND PRACTICE BEFORE THE COMMISSION.

'(a) AUTHORITY TO CENSURE—The Commission may censure any person, or deny, temporarily or permanently, to any person the privilege of appearing or practicing before the Commission in any way, if that person is found by the Commission, after notice and opportunity for hearing in the matter—

'(1) not to possess the requisite qualifications to represent others;

'(2) to be lacking in character or integrity, or to have engaged in unethical or improper professional conduct; or

'(3) to have willfully violated, or willfully aided and abetted the violation of, any provision of the securities laws or the rules and regulations issued thereunder.

'(b) DEFINITION—With respect to any registered public accounting firm or associated person, for purposes of this section, the term 'improper professional conduct' means—

'(1) intentional or knowing conduct, including reckless conduct, that results in a violation of applicable professional standards; and

'(2) negligent conduct in the form of—

'(A) a single instance of highly unreasonable conduct that results in a violation of applicable professional standards in circumstances in which the registered public accounting firm or associated person knows, or should know, that heightened scrutiny is warranted; or

'(B) repeated instances of unreasonable conduct, each resulting in a violation of applicable professional standards, that indicate a lack of competence to practice before the Commission.'.

SEC. 603. FEDERAL COURT AUTHORITY TO IMPOSE PENNY STOCK BARS.

(a) Securities Exchange Act of 1934—Section 21(d) of the Securities Exchange Act of 1934 (15 U.S.C. 78u(d)), as amended by this Act, is amended by adding at the end the following:

'(6) AUTHORITY OF A COURT TO PROHIBIT PERSONS FROM PARTICIPATING IN AN OFFERING OF PENNY STOCK

'(A) IN GENERAL—In any proceeding under paragraph (1) against any person participating in, or, at the time of the alleged misconduct who was participating in, an offering of penny stock, the court may prohibit that person from participating in an offering of penny stock, conditionally or unconditionally, and permanently or for such period of time as the court shall determine.

'(B) DEFINITION—For purposes of this paragraph, the term 'person participating in an offering of penny stock' includes any person engaging in activities with a broker, dealer, or issuer for purposes of issuing, trading, or inducing or attempting to induce the purchase or sale of, any penny stock. The Commission may, by rule or regulation, define such term to include other activities, and may, by rule, regulation, or order, exempt any person or class of persons, in whole or in part, conditionally or unconditionally, from inclusion in such term.'.

(b) Securities Act of 1933—Section 20 of the Securities Act of 1933 (15 U.S.C. 77t) is amended by adding at the end the following:

'(g) AUTHORITY OF A COURT TO PROHIBIT PERSONS FROM PARTICIPATING IN AN OFFERING OF PENNY STOCK

'(1) IN GENERAL—In any proceeding under subsection (a) against any person participating in, or, at the time of the alleged misconduct, who was participating in, an offering of penny stock, the court may prohibit that person from participating in an offering of penny stock, conditionally or unconditionally, and permanently or for such period of time as the court shall determine.

'(2) DEFINITION—For purposes of this subsection, the term 'person participating in an offering of penny stock' includes any person engaging in activities with a broker, dealer, or issuer for purposes of issuing, trading, or inducing or attempting to induce the purchase or sale of, any penny stock. The Commission may, by rule or regulation, define such term to include other activities, and may, by rule, regulation, or order, exempt any person or class of persons, in whole or in part, conditionally or unconditionally, from inclusion in such term.'.

SEC. 604. QUALIFICATIONS OF ASSOCIATED PERSONS OF BROKERS AND DEALERS.

TITLE VII—STUDIES AND REPORTS

SEC. 701. GAO STUDY AND REPORT REGARDING CONSOLIDATION OF PUBLIC ACCOUNTING FIRMS.

SEC. 702. COMMISSION STUDY AND REPORT REGARDING CREDIT RATING AGENCIES.

SEC. 703. STUDY AND REPORT ON VIOLATORS AND VIOLATIONS.

SEC. 704. STUDY OF ENFORCEMENT ACTIONS.

SEC. 705. STUDY OF INVESTMENT BANKS.

TITLE VIII—CORPORATE AND CRIMINAL FRAUD ACCOUNTABILITY

SEC. 801. SHORT TITLE.

This title may be cited as the 'Corporate and Criminal Fraud Accountability Act of 2002'.

SEC. 802. CRIMINAL PENALTIES FOR ALTERING DOCUMENTS.

(a) IN GENERAL—Chapter 73 of title 18, United States Code, is amended by adding at the end the following:

'Sec. 1519. Destruction, alteration, or falsification of records in Federal investigations and bankruptcy

'Whoever knowingly alters, destroys, mutilates, conceals, covers up, falsifies, or makes a false entry in any record, document, or tangible object with the intent to impede, obstruct, or influence the investigation or proper administration of any matter within the jurisdiction of any department or agency of the United States or any case filed under title 11, or in relation to or contemplation of any such matter or case, shall be fined under this title, imprisoned not more than 20 years, or both.

'Sec. 1520. Destruction of corporate audit records

'(a)(1) Any accountant who conducts an audit of an issuer of securities to which section 10A(a) of the Securities Exchange Act of 1934 (15 U.S.C. 78j-1(a)) applies, shall maintain all audit or review workpapers for a period of 5 years from the end of the fiscal period in which the audit or review was concluded.

'(2) The Securities and Exchange Commission shall promulgate, within 180 days, after adequate notice and an opportunity for comment, such rules and regulations, as are reasonably necessary, relating to the retention of relevant records such as workpapers, documents that form the basis of an audit or review, memoranda, correspondence, communications, other documents, and records (including electronic records) which are created, sent, or received in connection with an audit or review and contain conclusions, opinions, analyses, or financial data relating to such an audit or review, which is conducted by any accountant who conducts an audit of an issuer of securities to which section 10A(a) of the Securities Exchange Act of 1934 (15 U.S.C. 78j-1(a)) applies. The Commission may, from time to time, amend or supplement the rules and regulations that it is required to promulgate under this section, after adequate notice and an opportunity for comment, in order to ensure that such rules and regulations adequately comport with the purposes of this section.

'(b) Whoever knowingly and willfully violates subsection (a)(1), or any rule or regulation promulgated by the Securities and Exchange Commission under subsection (a)(2), shall be fined under this title, imprisoned not more than 10 years, or both.

'(c) Nothing in this section shall be deemed to diminish or relieve any person of any other duty or obligation imposed by Federal or State law or regulation to maintain, or refrain from destroying, any document.'.

(b) CLERICAL AMENDMENT—The table of sections at the beginning of chapter 73 of title 18, United States Code, is amended by adding at the end the following new items:

'1519. Destruction, alteration, or falsification of records in Federal investigations and bankruptcy.

'1520. Destruction of corporate audit records.'.

SEC. 803. DEBTS NONDISCHARGEABLE IF INCURRED IN VIOLATION OF SECURITIES FRAUD LAWS.

SEC. 804. STATUTE OF LIMITATIONS FOR SECURITIES FRAUD.

(a) IN GENERAL—Section 1658 of title 28, United States Code, is amended—

(1) by inserting '(a)' before 'Except'; and

(2) by adding at the end the following:

'(b) Notwithstanding subsection (a), a private right of action that involves a claim of fraud, deceit, manipulation, or contrivance in contravention of a regulatory requirement concerning the securities laws, as defined in section 3(a)(47) of the Securities Exchange Act of 1934 (15 U.S.C. 78c(a)(47)), may be brought not later than the earlier of—

'(1) 2 years after the discovery of the facts constituting the violation; or

'(2) 5 years after such violation.'.

(b) EFFECTIVE DATE—The limitations period provided by section 1658(b) of title 28, United States Code, as added by this section, shall apply to all proceedings addressed by this section that are commenced on or after the date of enactment of this Act.

(c) NO CREATION OF ACTIONS—Nothing in this section shall create a new, private right of action.

SEC. 805. REVIEW OF FEDERAL SENTENCING GUIDELINES FOR OBSTRUCTION OF JUSTICE AND EXTENSIVE CRIMINAL FRAUD.

SEC. 806. PROTECTION FOR EMPLOYEES OF PUBLICLY TRADED COMPANIES WHO PROVIDE EVIDENCE OF FRAUD.

(a) IN GENERAL—Chapter 73 of title 18, United States Code, is amended by inserting after section 1514 the following:

'Sec. 1514A. Civil action to protect against retaliation in fraud cases

'(a) WHISTLEBLOWER PROTECTION FOR EMPLOYEES OF PUBLICLY TRADED COMPANIES—No company with a class of securities registered under section 12 of the Securities Exchange Act of 1934 (15 U.S.C. 78l), or that is required to file reports under section 15(d) of the Securities Exchange Act of 1934 (15 U.S.C. 78o(d)), or any officer, employee, contractor, subcontractor, or agent of such company, may discharge, demote, suspend, threaten, harass, or in any other manner discriminate against an employee in the terms and conditions of employment because of any lawful act done by the employee—

'(1) to provide information, cause information to be provided, or otherwise assist in an investigation regarding any conduct which the employee reasonably believes constitutes a violation of section 1341, 1343, 1344, or 1348, any rule or regulation of the Securities and Exchange Commission, or any provision of Federal law relating to fraud against shareholders, when the information or assistance is provided to or the investigation is conducted by—

'(A) a Federal regulatory or law enforcement agency;

'(B) any Member of Congress or any committee of Congress; or

'(C) a person with supervisory authority over the employee (or such other person working for the employer who has the authority to investigate, discover, or terminate misconduct); or

'(2) to file, cause to be filed, testify, participate in, or otherwise assist in a proceeding filed or about to be filed (with any knowledge of the employer) relating to an alleged violation of section 1341, 1343, 1344, or 1348, any rule or regulation of the Securities and Exchange Commission, or any provision of Federal law relating to fraud against shareholders.

'(b) ENFORCEMENT ACTION

'(1) IN GENERAL—A person who alleges discharge or other discrimination by any person in violation of subsection (a) may seek relief under subsection (c), by—

'(A) filing a complaint with the Secretary of Labor; or

'(B) if the Secretary has not issued a final decision within 180 days of the filing of the complaint and there is no showing that such delay is due to the bad faith of the claimant, bringing an action at law or equity for de novo review in the appropriate district court of the United States, which shall have jurisdiction over such an action without regard to the amount in controversy.

'(2) PROCEDURE

'(A) IN GENERAL—An action under paragraph (1)(A) shall be governed under the rules and procedures set forth in section 42121(b) of title 49, United States Code.

'(B) EXCEPTION—Notification made under section 42121(b)(1) of title 49, United States Code, shall be made to the person named in the complaint and to the employer.

'(C) BURDENS OF PROOF—An action brought under paragraph (1)(B) shall be governed by the legal burdens of proof set forth in section 42121(b) of title 49, United States Code.

'(D) STATUTE OF LIMITATIONS—An action under paragraph (1) shall be commenced not later than 90 days after the date on which the violation occurs.

'(c) REMEDIES

'(1) IN GENERAL—An employee prevailing in any action under subsection (b)(1) shall be entitled to all relief necessary to make the employee whole.

'(2) COMPENSATORY DAMAGES—Relief for any action under paragraph (1) shall include—

'(A) reinstatement with the same seniority status that the employee would have had, but for the discrimination;

'(B) the amount of back pay, with interest; and

'(C) compensation for any special damages sustained as a result of the discrimination, including litigation costs, expert witness fees, and reasonable attorney fees.

'(d) RIGHTS RETAINED BY EMPLOYEE—Nothing in this section shall be deemed to diminish the rights, privileges, or remedies of any employee under any Federal or State law, or under any collective bargaining agreement.'.

(b) CLERICAL AMENDMENT—The table of sections at the beginning of chapter 73 of title 18, United States Code, is amended by inserting after the item relating to section 1514 the following new item:

'1514A. Civil action to protect against retaliation in fraud cases.'.

SEC. 807. CRIMINAL PENALTIES FOR DEFRAUDING SHAREHOLDERS OF PUBLICLY TRADED COMPANIES.

(a) IN GENERAL—Chapter 63 of title 18, United States Code, is amended by adding at the end the following:

'Sec. 1348. Securities fraud

'Whoever knowingly executes, or attempts to execute, a scheme or artifice—

'(1) to defraud any person in connection with any security of an issuer with a class of securities registered under section 12 of the Securities Exchange Act of 1934 (15 U.S.C. 78l) or that is required to file reports under section 15(d) of the Securities Exchange Act of 1934 (15 U.S.C. 78o(d)); or

'(2) to obtain, by means of false or fraudulent pretenses, representations, or promises, any money or property in connection with the purchase or sale of any security of an issuer with a class of securities registered under section 12 of the Securities Exchange Act of 1934 (15 U.S.C. 78l) or that is required to file reports under section 15(d) of the Securities Exchange Act of 1934 (15 U.S.C. 78o(d));

shall be fined under this title, or imprisoned not more than 25 years, or both.'.

(b) CLERICAL AMENDMENT—The table of sections at the beginning of chapter 63 of title 18, United States Code, is amended by adding at the end the following new item:

'1348. Securities fraud.'.

TITLE IX—WHITE-COLLAR CRIME PENALTY ENHANCEMENTS

SEC. 901. SHORT TITLE.

This title may be cited as the 'White-Collar Crime Penalty Enhancement Act of 2002'.

SEC. 902. ATTEMPTS AND CONSPIRACIES TO COMMIT CRIMINAL FRAUD OFFENSES.

(a) IN GENERAL—Chapter 63 of title 18, United States Code, is amended by inserting after section 1348 as added by this Act the following:

'Sec. 1349. Attempt and conspiracy

'Any person who attempts or conspires to commit any offense under this chapter shall be subject to the same penalties as those prescribed for the offense, the commission of which was the object of the attempt or conspiracy.

(b) CLERICAL AMENDMENT—The table of sections at the beginning of chapter 63 of title 18, United States Code, is amended by adding at the end the following new item:

'1349. Attempt and conspiracy.'.

SEC. 903. CRIMINAL PENALTIES FOR MAIL AND WIRE FRAUD.

(a) MAIL FRAUD—Section 1341 of title 18, United States Code, is amended by striking 'five' and inserting '20'.

(b) WIRE FRAUD—Section 1343 of title 18, United States Code, is amended by striking 'five' and inserting '20'.

SEC. 904. CRIMINAL PENALTIES FOR VIOLATIONS OF THE EMPLOYEE RETIREMENT INCOME SECURITY ACT OF 1974.

Section 501 of the Employee Retirement Income Security Act of 1974 (29 U.S.C. 1131) is amended—

(1) by striking '$5,000' and inserting '$100,000';

(2) by striking 'one year' and inserting '10 years'; and

(3) by striking '$100,000' and inserting '$500,000'.

SEC. 905. AMENDMENT TO SENTENCING GUIDELINES RELATING TO CERTAIN WHITE-COLLAR OFFENSES.

SEC. 906. CORPORATE RESPONSIBILITY FOR FINANCIAL REPORTS.

(a) IN GENERAL—Chapter 63 of title 18, United States Code, is amended by inserting after section 1349, as created by this Act, the following:

'Sec. 1350. Failure of corporate officers to certify financial reports

(a) CERTIFICATION OF PERIODIC FINANCIAL REPORTS—Each periodic report containing financial statements filed by an issuer with the Securities Exchange Commission pursuant to section 13(a) or 15(d) of the Securities Exchange Act of 1934 (15 U.S.C. 78m(a) or 78o(d)) shall be accompanied by a written statement by the chief executive officer and chief financial officer (or equivalent thereof) of the issuer.

'(b) CONTENT—The statement required under subsection (a) shall certify that the periodic report containing the financial statements fully complies with the requirements of section 13(a) or 15(d) of the Securities Exchange Act pf 1934 (15 U.S.C. 78m or 78o(d)) and that information contained in the periodic report fairly presents, in all material respects, the financial condition and results of operations of the issuer.

'(c) CRIMINAL PENALTIES—Whoever—

'(1) certifies any statement as set forth in subsections (a) and (b) of this section knowing that the periodic report accompanying the statement does not comport with all the requirements set forth in this section shall be fined not more than $1,000,000 or imprisoned not more than 10 years, or both; or

'(2) willfully certifies any statement as set forth in subsections (a) and (b) of this section knowing that the periodic report accompanying the statement does not comport with all the requirements set forth in this section shall be fined not more than $5,000,000, or imprisoned not more than 20 years, or both.'.

(b) CLERICAL AMENDMENT—The table of sections at the beginning of chapter 63 of title 18, United States Code, is amended by adding at the end the following:

'1350. Failure of corporate officers to certify financial reports.'.

TITLE X—CORPORATE TAX RETURNS

SEC. 1001. SENSE OF THE SENATE REGARDING THE SIGNING OF CORPORATE TAX RETURNS BY CHIEF EXECUTIVE OFFICERS.

It is the sense of the Senate that the Federal income tax return of a corporation should be signed by the chief executive officer of such corporation.

TITLE XI—CORPORATE FRAUD ACCOUNTABILITY

SEC. 1101. SHORT TITLE.

This title may be cited as the 'Corporate Fraud Accountability Act of 2002'.

SEC. 1102. TAMPERING WITH A RECORD OR OTHERWISE IMPEDING AN OFFICIAL PROCEEDING.

Section 1512 of title 18, United States Code, is amended—

(1) by redesignating subsections (c) through (i) as subsections (d) through (j), respectively; and

(2) by inserting after subsection (b) the following new subsection:

'(c) Whoever corruptly—

'(1) alters, destroys, mutilates, or conceals a record, document, or other object, or attempts to do so, with the intent to impair the object's integrity or availability for use in an official proceeding; or

'(2) otherwise obstructs, influences, or impedes any official proceeding, or attempts to do so, shall be fined under this title or imprisoned not more than 20 years, or both.'.

SEC. 1103. TEMPORARY FREEZE AUTHORITY FOR THE SECURITIES AND EXCHANGE COMMISSION.

(a) IN GENERAL—Section 21C(c) of the Securities Exchange Act of 1934 (15 U.S.C. 78u-3(c)) is amended by adding at the end the following:

'(3) TEMPORARY FREEZE

'(A) IN GENERAL

'(i) ISSUANCE OF TEMPORARY ORDERWhenever, during the course of a lawful investigation involving possible violations of the Federal securities laws by an issuer of publicly traded securities or any of its directors, officers, partners, controlling persons, agents, or employees, it shall appear to the Commission that it is likely that the issuer will make extraordinary payments (whether compensation or otherwise) to any of the foregoing persons, the Commission may petition a Federal district court for a temporary order requiring the issuer to escrow, subject to court supervision, those payments in an interest-bearing account for 45 days.

'(ii) STANDARD—A temporary order shall be entered under clause (i), only after notice and opportunity for a hearing, unless the court determines that notice and hearing prior to entry of the order would be impracticable or contrary to the public interest.

'(iii) EFFECTIVE PERIOD—A temporary order issued under clause (i) shall—

'(I) become effective immediately;

'(II) be served upon the parties subject to it; and

'(III) unless set aside, limited or suspended by a court of competent jurisdiction, shall remain effective and enforceable for 45 days.

'(iv) EXTENSIONS AUTHORIZED—The effective period of an order under this subparagraph may be extended by the court upon good cause shown for not longer than 45 additional days, provided that the combined period of the order shall not exceed 90 days.

'(B) PROCESS ON DETERMINATION OF VIOLATIONS

'(i) VIOLATIONS CHARGED—If the issuer or other person described in subparagraph (A) is charged with any violation of the Federal securities laws before the expiration of the effective period of a temporary order under subparagraph (A) (including any applicable extension period), the order shall remain in effect, subject to court approval, until the conclusion of any legal proceedings related thereto, and the affected issuer or other person, shall have the right to petition the court for review of the order.

'(ii) VIOLATIONS NOT CHARGED—If the issuer or other person described in subparagraph (A) is not charged with any violation of the Federal securities laws before the expiration of the effective period of a temporary order under subparagraph (A) (including any applicable extension period), the escrow shall terminate at the expiration of the 45-day effective period (or the expiration of any extension period, as applicable), and the disputed payments (with accrued interest) shall be returned to the issuer or other affected person.'.

(b) TECHNICAL AMENDMENT—Section 21C(c)(2) of the Securities Exchange Act of 1934 (15 U.S.C. 78u-3(c)(2)) is amended by striking 'This' and inserting 'paragraph (1)'.

SEC. 1104. AMENDMENT TO THE FEDERAL SENTENCING GUIDELINES.

(a) REQUEST FOR IMMEDIATE CONSIDERATION BY THE UNITED STATES SENTENCING COMMISSION—Pursuant to its authority under section 994(p) of title 28, United

States Code, and in accordance with this section, the United States Sentencing Commission is requested to—

(1) promptly review the sentencing guidelines applicable to securities and accounting fraud and related offenses;

(2) expeditiously consider the promulgation of new sentencing guidelines or amendments to existing sentencing guidelines to provide an enhancement for officers or directors of publicly traded corporations who commit fraud and related offenses; and

(3) submit to Congress an explanation of actions taken by the Sentencing Commission pursuant to paragraph (2) and any additional policy recommendations the Sentencing Commission may have for combating offenses described in paragraph (1).

(b) CONSIDERATIONS IN REVIEW—In carrying out this section, the Sentencing Commission is requested to—

(1) ensure that the sentencing guidelines and policy statements reflect the serious nature of securities, pension, and accounting fraud and the need for aggressive and appropriate law enforcement action to prevent such offenses;

(2) assure reasonable consistency with other relevant directives and with other guidelines;

(3) account for any aggravating or mitigating circumstances that might justify exceptions, including circumstances for which the sentencing guidelines currently provide sentencing enhancements;

(4) ensure that guideline offense levels and enhancements for an obstruction of justice offense are adequate in cases where documents or other physical evidence are actually destroyed or fabricated;

(5) ensure that the guideline offense levels and enhancements under United States Sentencing Guideline 2B1.1 (as in effect on the date of enactment of this Act) are sufficient for a fraud offense when the number of victims adversely involved is significantly greater than 50;

(6) make any necessary conforming changes to the sentencing guidelines; and

(7) assure that the guidelines adequately meet the purposes of sentencing as set forth in section 3553(a)(2) of title 18, United States Code.

(c) EMERGENCY AUTHORITY AND DEADLINE FOR COMMISSION ACTION—The United States Sentencing Commission is requested to promulgate the guidelines or amendments provided for under this section as soon as practicable, and in any event not later than the 180 days after the date of enactment of this Act, in accordance with the procedures sent forth in section 21(a) of the Sentencing Reform Act of 1987, as though the authority under that Act had not expired.

SEC. 1105. AUTHORITY OF THE COMMISSION TO PROHIBIT PERSONS FROM SERVING AS OFFICERS OR DIRECTORS.

(a) SECURITIES EXCHANGE ACT OF 1934—Section 21C of the Securities Exchange Act of 1934 (15 U.S.C. 78u-3) is amended by adding at the end the following:

'(f) AUTHORITY OF THE COMMISSION TO PROHIBIT PERSONS FROM SERVING AS OFFICERS OR DIRECTORS—In any cease-anddesist proceeding under subsection (a), the Commission may issue an order to prohibit, conditionally or unconditionally, and permanently or for such period of time as it shall determine, any person who has violated section 10(b) or the rules or regulations thereunder, from acting as an officer or director of any issuer that has a class of securities registered pursuant to section 12, or that is required to file reports pursuant to section 15(d), if the conduct of that person demonstrates unfitness to serve as an officer or director of any such issuer.'.

(b) SECURITIES ACT OF 1933—Section 8A of the Securities Act of 1933 (15 U.S.C. 77h-1) is amended by adding at the end of the following:

'(f) AUTHORITY OF THE COMMISSION TO PROHIBIT PERSONS FROM SERVING AS OFFICERS OR DIRECTORS—In any cease-anddesist proceeding under subsection (a), the

Commission may issue an order to prohibit, conditionally or unconditionally, and permanently or for such period of time as it shall determine, any person who has violated section 17(a)(1) or the rules or regulations thereunder, from acting as an officer or director of any issuer that has a class of securities registered pursuant to section 12 of the Securities Exchange Act of 1934, or that is required to file reports pursuant to section 15(d) of that Act, if the conduct of that person demonstrates unfitness to serve as an officer or director of any such issuer.'.

SEC. 1106. INCREASED CRIMINAL PENALTIES UNDER SECURITIES EXCHANGE ACT OF 1934.

Section 32(a) of the Securities Exchange Act of 1934 (15 U.S.C. 78ff(a)) is amended—

(1) by striking '$1,000,000, or imprisoned not more than 10 years' and inserting '$5,000,000, or imprisoned not more than 20 years'; and

(2) by striking '$2,500,000' and inserting '$25,000,000'.

SEC. 1107. RETALIATION AGAINST INFORMANTS.

(a) IN GENERAL—Section 1513 of title 18, United States Code, is amended by adding at the end the following:

'(e) Whoever knowingly, with the intent to retaliate, takes any action harmful to any person, including interference with the lawful employment or livelihood of any person, for providing to a law enforcement officer any truthful information relating to the commission or possible commission of any Federal offense, shall be fined under this title or imprisoned not more than 10 years, or both.'.

Speaker of the House of Representatives.

Vice President of the United States and

President of the Senate.

END

INVESTMENT ADVISERS ACT OF 1940—SELECTED PROVISIONS

15 U.S.C. §§80b-1 et seq.

Act	15 U.S.C. Section	Subject
201	80b-1	Findings
202(a)	80b-2(a)	Definitions
		(11) Investment adviser
203	80b-3	Registration of investment advisers
203A	80b-3a	State and federal responsibilities
204A	80b-4a	Prevention of misuse of nonpublic information
205	80b-5	Investment advisory contracts
206	80b-6	Prohibited transactions by investment advisers

Sec. 201. FINDINGS

Upon the basis of facts disclosed by the record and report of the Securities and Exchange Commission made pursuant to section 30 of the Public Utility Holding Company Act of 1935, and facts otherwise disclosed and ascertained, it is hereby found that investment advisers are of national concern, in that among other things—

(1) their advice, counsel, publications, writings, analyses, and reports are furnished and distributed, and their contracts, subscription agreements, and other arrangements with clients are negotiated and performed, by the use of the mails and means and instrumentalities of interstate commerce;

(2) their advice, counsel, publications, writings, analyses, and reports customarily relate to the purchase and sale of securities traded on national securities exchanges and in interstate over-the-counter markets, securities issued by companies engaged in business in interstate commerce, and securities issued by national banks and member banks of the Federal Reserve System; and

(3) the foregoing transactions occur in such volume as substantially to affect interstate commerce, national securities exchanges, and other securities markets, the national banking system and the national economy.

Sec. 202. DEFINITIONS

(a) When used in this title, unless the context otherwise requires, the following definitions shall apply:

(11) [Investment Adviser]

"Investment adviser" means any person who, for compensation, engages in the business of advising others, either directly or through publications or writings, as to the value of securities or as to the advisability of investing in, purchasing, or selling securities, or who, for compensation and as part of a regular business, issues or promulgates analyses or reports concerning securities; but does not include (A) a bank, or any bank holding company as defined in the Bank Holding Company Act of 1956, which is not an investment company, except that the term 'investment adviser' includes any bank or bank holding company to the extent that such bank or bank holding company serves or acts as an investment adviser to a registered investment company, but if, in the case of a bank, such services or actions are performed through a separately identifiable department or division, the department or division, and not the bank itself, shall be deemed to be the investment adviser; (B) any lawyer, accountant, engineer, or teacher whose performance of such services is solely incidental to the practice of his profession; (C) any broker or dealer whose performance of such services is solely incidental to the conduct of his business as a broker or dealer and who receives no special compensation therefor; (D) the publisher of any bona fide newspaper, news magazine or business or financial publication of general and regular circulation; (E) any person whose advice, analyses, or reports relate to no securities other than securities which are direct obligations of or obligations guaranteed as to principal or interest by the United States, or securities issued or guaranteed by corporations in which the United States has a direct or indirect interest which shall have been designated by the Secretary of the Treasury, pursuant to section 3(a)(12) of the Securities Exchange Act of 1934, as exempted securities for the purposes of that Act; or (F) s uch other persons not within the intent of this paragraph, as the Commission may designate by rules and regulations or order.

Sec. 203. REGISTRATION OF INVESTMENT ADVISERS

(a) Except as provided in subsection (b) and section 203A, it shall be unlawful for any investment adviser, unless registered under this section, to make use of the mails or any means or instrumentality of interstate commerce in connection with his or its business as an investment adviser.

(b) The provisions of subsection (a) shall not apply to—

(1) Any investment adviser all of whose clients are residents of the State within which such investment adviser maintains his or its principal office and place of business, and who does not furnish advice or issue analyses or reports with respect to securities listed or admitted to unlisted trading privileges on any national securities exchange;

(2) any investment adviser whose only clients are insurance companies;

(3) any investment adviser who during the course of the preceding twelve months has had fewer than fifteen clients and who neither holds himself out generally to the public as an investment adviser nor acts as an investment adviser to any investment company registered under title I of this Act, or a company which has elected to be a business development company pursuant to section 54 of title I of this Act and has not withdrawn its election. For purposes of determining the number of clients of an investment adviser under this paragraph, no shareholder, partner, or beneficial owner of a business development company, as defined in this title, shall be deemed to be a client of such investment adviser unless such person is a client of such investment adviser separate and apart from his status as a shareholder, partner, or beneficial owner;

(4) any investment adviser that is a charitable organization as defined in section 3(c)(10(B) of the Investment Company Act of 1940, or is a trustee, director, officer, employee, or volunteer of such a charitable organization acting within the scope of such person's employment or duties with such organization, whose advice, analyses, or reports are provided only to one or more of the following:

(A) any such charitable organization;

(B) a fund that is excluded from the definition of an investment company under section 3(c)(10(B) of the Investment Company Act of 1940; or

(C) a trust or other donative instrument described in section 3(c)(10(B) of the Investment Company Act of 1940, or the trustees, administrators, settlors (or potential settlors), or beneficiaries of any such trust or other instrument;

(5) any plan described in section 414(e) of the Internal Revenue Code of 1986, any person or entity eligible to establish and maintain such a plan under the Internal Revenue Code of 1986, or any trustee, director, officer, or employee of or volunteer for any such plan or person, if such person or entity, acting in such capacity, provides investment advice exclusively to, or with respect to, any plan, person, or entity or any company, account, or fund that is excluded from the definition of an investment company under section 3(c)(14) of the Investment Company Act of 1940; or

(6) any investment adviser that is registered with the Commodity Futures Trading Commission as a commodity trading advisor whose business does not consist primarily of acting as an investment adviser, as defined in section 202(a)(11) of this title, and that does not act as an investment adviser to—

(A) an investment company registered under title I of this Act; or

(B) a company which has elected to be a business development company pursuant to section 54 of title I of this Act and has not withdrawn its election.

(c)(1) An investment adviser, or any person who presently contemplates becoming an investment adviser, may be registered by filing with the Commission an application for registration in such form and containing such of the following information and documents as the Commission, by rule, may prescribe as necessary or appropriate in the public interest or for the protection of investors:

(A) the name and form of organization under which the investment adviser engages or intends to engage in business; the name of the State or other sovereign power under which such investment adviser is organized; the location of his or its principal business office and branch offices, if any; the names and addresses of his or its partners, officers, directors, and persons performing similar functions or, if such an investment adviser be an individual, of such individual; and the number of his or its employees;

(B) the education, the business affiliations for the past ten years, and the present business affiliations of such investment adviser and of his or its partners, officers, directors, and persons performing similar functions and of any controlling person thereof;

(C) the nature of the business of such investment adviser, including the manner of giving advice and rendering analyses or reports;

(D) a balance sheet certified by an independent public accountant and other financial statements (which shall, as the Commission specifies, be certified);

(E) the nature and scope of the authority of such investment adviser with respect to clients' funds and accounts;

(F) the basis or bases upon which such investment adviser is compensated;

(G) whether such investment adviser, or any person associated with such investment adviser, is subject to any disqualification which would be a basis for denial, suspension, or revocation of registration of such investment adviser under the provisions of subsection (e) of this section; and

(H) a statement as to whether the principal business of such investment adviser consists or is to consist of acting as investment adviser and a statement as to whether a substantial part of the business of such investment adviser, consists or is to consist of rendering investment supervisory services.

(2) Within forty-five days of the date of the filing of such application (or within such longer period as to which the applicant consents) the Commission shall—

(A) by order grant such registration; or

(B) institute proceedings to determine whether registration should be denied. Such proceedings shall include notice of the grounds for denial under consideration and opportunity for hearing and shall be concluded within one hundred twenty days of the date of the filing of the application for registration. At the conclusion of such proceedings the Commission, by order, shall grant or deny such registration. The Commission may extend the time for conclusion of such proceedings for up to ninety days if it finds good cause for such extension and publishes its reasons for so finding or for such longer period as to which the applicant consents.

The Commission shall grant such registration if the Commission finds that the requirements of this section are satisfied and that the applicant is not prohibited from registering as an investment adviser under section 203A. The Commission shall deny such registration if it does not make such a finding or if it finds that if the applicant were so registered, its registration would be subject to suspension or revocation under subsection (e) of this section.

(d) Any provision of this title (other than subsection (a) of this section) which prohibits any act, practice, or course of business if the mails or any means or instrumentality of interstate commerce are used in connection therewith, shall also prohibit any such act, practice, or course of business by any investment adviser registered pursuant to this section or any person acting on behalf of such an investment adviser, irrespective of any use of the mails or any means or instrumentality of interstate commerce in connection therewith.

(e) The Commission, by order, shall censure, place limitations on the activities, functions, or operations of, suspend for a period not exceeding twelve months, or revoke the registration of any investment adviser if it finds, on the record after notice and opportunity for hearing, that such censure, placing of limitations, suspension, or revocation is in the public interest and that such investment adviser, or any person associated with such investment adviser, whether prior to or subsequent to becoming so associated—

(1) has willfully made or caused to be made in any application for registration or report required to be filed with the Commission under this title, or in any proceeding before the Commission with respect to registration, any statement which was at the time and in the light of the circumstances under which it was made false or misleading with respect to any material fact, or has omitted to state in any such application or report any material fact which is required to be stated therein.

(2) has been convicted within ten years preceding the filing of any application for registration or at any time thereafter of any felony or misdemeanor or of a substantially equivalent crime by a foreign court of competent jurisdiction which the Commission finds—

(A) involves the purchase or sale of any security, the taking of a false oath, the making of a false report, bribery, perjury, burglary, any substantially equivalent activity however denominated by laws of the relevant foreign government, or conspiracy to commit any such offense;

(B) arises out of the conduct of the business of a broker, dealer, municipal securities dealer, investment adviser, bank, insurance company, government securities broker, government securities dealer, fiduciary, transfer agent foreign person performing a function substantially equivalent to any of the above, or entity or person required to be registered under the Commodity Exchange Act or any substantially equivalent statute or regulation;

(C) involves the larceny, theft, robbery, extortion, forgery, counterfeiting, fraudulent concealment, embezzlement, fraudulent conversion, or misappropriation of funds or securities; or substantially equivalent activity however denominated by the laws of the relevant foreign government or

(D) involves the violation of sections 152, 1341, 1342, or 1343 or chapter 25 or 47 of title 18, United States Code, or a violation of substantially equivalent foreign statute.

(3) has been convicted during the 10-year period preceding the date of filing of any application for registration, or at any time thereafter, of—

(A) any crime that is punishable by imprisonment for 1 or more years, and that is not described in paragraph (2); or

(B) a substantially equivalent crime by a foreign court of competent jurisdiction.

(4) is permanently or temporarily enjoined by order, judgment, or decree of any court of competent jurisdiction, including any foreign court of competent jurisdiction, from acting as an investment adviser, underwriter, broker, dealer, municipal securities dealer, government securities broker, government securities dealer, transfer agent foreign person performing a function substantially equivalent to any of the above, or entity or person required to be registered under the Commodity Exchange Act or any substantially equivalent statute or regulation, or as an affiliated person or employee of any investment company, bank, insurance company foreign entity substantially equivalent to any of the above, or entity or person required to be registered under

the Commodity Exchange Act or any substantially equivalent statute or regulation, or from engaging in or continuing any conduct or practice in connection with any such activity, or in connection with the purchase or sale of any security.

(5) has willfully violated any provision of the Securities Act of 1933, the Securities Exchange Act of 1934, the Investment Company Act of 1940, this title, the Commodity Exchange Act, or the rules, or regulations under any such statutes or any rule of the Municipal Securities Rulemaking Board, or is unable to comply with any such provision.

(6) has willfully aided, abetted, counseled, commanded, induced, or procured the violation by any other person of any provision of the Securities Act of 1933, the Securities Exchange Act of 1934, the Investment Company Act of 1940, this title, the Commodity Exchange Act, the rules or regulations under any of such statutes, or the rules of the Municipal Securities Rulemaking Board, or has failed reasonably to supervise, with a view to preventing violations of the provisions of such statutes, rules, and regulations, another person who commits such a violation, if such other person is subject to his supervision. For the purposes of this paragraph no person shall be deemed to have failed reasonably to supervise any person, if—

(A) there have been established procedures, and a system for applying such procedures, which would reasonably be expected to prevent and detect, insofar as practicable, any such violation by such other person, and

(B) such person has reasonably discharged the duties and obligations incumbent upon him by reason of such procedures and system without reasonable cause to believe that such procedures and system were not being complied with.

(7) is subject to any order of the Commission barring or suspending the right of the person to be associated with an investment adviser;

(8) has been found by a foreign financial regulatory authority to have—

(A) made or caused to be made in any application for registration or report required to be filed with a foreign securities authority, or in any proceeding before a foreign securities authority with respect to registration, any statement that was at the time and in light of the circumstances under which it was made false or misleading with respect to any material fact, or has omitted to state in any application or report to a foreign securities authority any material fact that is required to be stated therein;

(B) violated any foreign statute or regulation regarding transactions in securities or contracts of sale of a commodity for future delivery traded on or subject to the rules of a contract market or any board of trade; or

(C) aided, abetted, counseled, commanded, induced, or procured the violation by any other person of any foreign statute or regulation regarding transactions in securities or contracts of sale of a commodity for future delivery traded on or subject to the rules of a contract market or any board of trade, or has been found, by the foreign financial regulatory authority, to have failed reasonably to supervise, with a view to preventing violations of statutory provisions, and rules and regulations promulgated thereunder, another person who commits such a violation, if such other person is subject to his supervision; or

(9) is subject to any final order of a State securities commission (or any agency or officer performing like functions), State authority that supervises or examines banks, savings associations, or credit unions, State insurance commission (or any agency or office performing like functions), an appropriate Federal banking agency (as defined in section 3 of the Federal Deposit Insurance Act (12 U.S.C. 1813(q))), or the National Credit Union Administration, that—

(A) bars such person from association with an entity regulated by such commission, authority, agency, or officer, or from engaging in the business of securities, insurance, banking, savings association activities, or credit union activities; or

(B) constitutes a final order based on violations of any laws or regulations that prohibit fraudulent, manipulative, or deceptive conduct.

(f) The Commission, by order, shall censure or place limitations on the activities of any person associated, seeking to become associated, or, at the time of the alleged misconduct, associated or seeking to become associated with, or, at the time of the alleged misconduct, associated or seeking to become associated an investment adviser, or suspend for a period not exceeding twelve months or bar any such person from being associated with an investment adviser, if the Commission finds, on the record after notice and opportunity for hearing, that such censure, placing of limitations, suspension, or bar is in the public interest and that such person has committed or omitted any act or omission enumerated in paragraph (1), (5), (6), (8), or (9) of subsection (e) or has been convicted of any offense specified in paragraph (2) or (3) of subsection (e) within ten years of the commencement of the proceedings under this subsection, or is enjoined from any action, conduct, or practice specified in paragraph (4) of subsection (e). It shall be unlawful for any person as to whom such an order suspending or barring him from being associated with an investment adviser is in effect willfully to become, or to be, associated with an investment adviser without the consent of the Commission, and it shall be unlawful for any investment adviser to permit such a person to become, or remain, a person associated with him without the consent of the Commission, if such investment adviser knew, or in the exercise of reasonable care, should have known, of such order.

(g) Any successor to the business of an investment adviser registered under this section shall be deemed likewise registered hereunder, if within thirty days from its succession to such business it shall file an application for registration under this section, unless and until the Commission, pursuant to subsection (c) or subsection (e) of this section, shall deny registration to or revoke or suspend the registration of such successor.

(h) Any person registered under this section may, upon such terms and conditions as the Commission finds necessary in the public interest or for the protection of investors, withdraw from registration by filing a written notice of withdrawal with the Commission. If the Commission finds that any person registered under this section, or who has pending an application for registration filed under this section, is no longer in existence, is not engaged in business as an investment adviser, or is prohibited from registering as an investment adviser under section 203A, the Commission shall by order cancel the registration of such person.

[Money Penalties in Administrative Proceedings]

(i) MONEY PENALTIES IN ADMINISTRATIVE PROCEEDINGS.—

(1) AUTHORITY OF COMMISSION.—In any proceeding instituted pursuant to subsection (e) or (f) against any person, the Commission may impose a civil penalty if it finds, on the record after notice and opportunity for hearing, that such person—

(A) has willfully violated any provision of the Securities Act of 1933, the Securities Exchange Act of 1934, the Investment Company Act of 1940, or this title, or the rules or regulations thereunder;

(B) has willfully aided, abetted, counseled, commanded, induced, or procured such a violation by any other person;

(C) has willfully made or caused to be made in any application for registration or report required to be filed with the Commission under this title, or in any proceeding before the Commission with respect to registration, any statement which was, at the time and in the light of the circumstances under which it was made, false or misleading with respect to any material fact, or has omitted to state in any such application or report any material fact which was required to be stated therein; or

(D) has failed reasonably to supervise, within the meaning of subsection (e)(6) of this title, with a view to preventing violations of the provisions of this title and the rules and regulations thereunder, another person who commits such a violation, if such other person is subject to his supervision;

and that such penalty is in the public interest.

[Maximum Amount of Penalty]

(2) MAXIMUM AMOUNT OF PENALTY.—

(A) FIRST TIER.—The maximum amount of penalty for each act or omission described in paragraph (1) shall be $5,000 for a natural person or $50,000 for any other person.

(B) SECOND TIER.—Notwithstanding subparagraph (A), the maximum amount of penalty for each such act or omission shall be $50,000 for a natural person or $250,000 for any other person if the act or omission described in paragraph (1) involved fraud, deceit, manipulation, or deliberate or reckless disregard of a regulatory requirement.

(C) THIRD TIER.—Notwithstanding subparagraphs (A) and (B), the maximum amount of penalty fr each such act or omission shall be $100,000 for a natural person or $500,000 for any other person if—

(i) the act or omission described in paragraph (1) involved fraud, deceit, manipulation, or deliberate or reckless disregard of a regulatory requirement; and

(ii) such act or omission directly or indirectly resulted in substantial losses or created a significant risk of substantial losses to other persons or resulted in substantial pecuniary gain to the person who committed the act or omission.

[Public Interest]

(3) DETERMINATION OF PUBLIC INTEREST.—In considering under this section whether a penalty is in the public interest, the Commission may consider—

(A) whether the act or omission for which such penalty is assessed involved fraud, deceit, manipulation, or deliberate or reckless disregard of a regulatory requirement;

(B) the harm to other persons resulting either directly or indirectly from such act or omission;

(C) the extent to which any person was unjustly enriched, taking into account any restitution made to persons injured by such behavior;

(D) whether such person previously has been found by the Commission, another appropriate regulatory agency, or a self-regulatory organization to have violated the Federal securities laws, State securities laws, or the rules of a self-regulatory organization, has been enjoined by a court of competent jurisdiction from violations of such laws or rules, or has been convicted by a court of competent jurisdiction of violations of such laws or of any felony or misdemeanor described in section 203(e)(2) of this title;

(E) the need to deter such person and other persons from committing such acts or omissions; and

(F) such other matters as justice may require.

[Ability to Pay]

(4) EVIDENCE CONCERNING ABILITY TO PAY.—In any proceeding in which the Commission may impose a penalty under this section, a respondent may present evidence of the respondent's ability to pay such penalty. The Commission may, in its discretion, consider such evidence in determining whether such penalty is in the public interest. Such evidence may relate to the extent of such person's ability to continue in business and the collectability of a penalty, taking into account any other claims of the United States or third parties upon such person's assests and the amount of such person's assets.

[Accounting and Disgorgement.]

(j) AUTHORITY TO ENTER AN ORDER REQUIRING AN ACCOUNTING AND DISGORGEMENT.—In any proceeding in which the Commission may impose a penalty under this section, the Commission may enter an order requiring accounting and disgorgement, including reasonable interest. The Commission is authorized to adopt rules, regulations, and orders concerning payments to investors, rates of interest, periods of accrual, and such other matters as it deems appropriate to implement this subsection.

[Cease-and-Desist Proceedings]

(k) CEASE.—AND—DESIST PROCEEDINGS.—

(1) AUTHORITY OF THE COMMISSION.—If the Commission finds, after notice and opportunity for hearing, that any person is violating, has violated, or is about to violate any provision of this title, or any rule or regulation thereunder, the Commission may publish its findings and enter an order requiring such person, and any other person that is, was, or would be a cause of the violation, due

to an act or omission the person knew or should have known would contribute to such violation, to cease and desist from committing or causing such violation and any future violation of the same provision, rule, or regulation. Such order may, in addition to requiring a person to cease and desist from committing or causing a violation, require such person to comply, or to take steps to effect compliance, with such provision, rule, or regulation, upon such terms and conditions and within such time as the Commission may specify in such order. Any such order may, as the Commission deems appropriate, require future compliance or steps to effect future compliance, either permanently or for such period of time as the Commission may specify, with such provision rule, or regulation with respect to any security, any issuer, or any other person.

[Hearing]

(2) HEARING.—The notice instituting proceedings pursuant to paragraph (1) shall fix a hearing date not earlier than 30 days nor later than 60 days after service of the notice unless an earlier or a later date is set by the Commission with the consent of any respondent so served.

[Temporary Order]

(3) TEMPORARY ORDER.—

(A) IN GENERAL.—Whenever the Commission determines that the alleged violation or threatened violation specified in the notice instituting proceedings pursuant to paragraph (1), or the continuation thereof, is likely to result in significant dissipation or conversion of assets, significant harm to investors, or substantial harm to the public interest, including, but not limited to, losses to the Securities Investor Protection Corporation, prior to the completion of the proceedings, the Commission may enter a temporary order requiring the respondent to cease and desist from the violation or threatened violation and to take such action to prevent the violation or threatened violation and to prevent dissipation or conversion of assets, significant harm to investors, or substantial harm to the public interest as the Commission deems appropriate pending completion of such proceedings. Such an order shall be entered only after notice and opportunity for a hearing, unless the Commission, notwithstanding section 211(c) of this title, determines that notice and hearing prior to entry would be impracticable to contrary to the public interest. A temporary order shall become effective upon service upon the respondent and, unless set aside, limited, or suspended by the Commission or a court of competent jurisdiction, shall remain effective and enforceable pending the completion of the proceedings.

(B) APPLICABILITY.—This paragraph shall apply only to a respondent that acts, or, at the time of the alleged misconduct acted, as a broker, dealer, investment adviser, investment company, municipal securities dealer, government securities broker, government securities dealer, or transfer agent, or is, or was at the time of the alleged misconduct, an associated person of, or a person seeking to become associated with, any of the foregoing.

(4) REVIEW OF TEMPORARY ORDERS.—

(A) COMMISSION REVIEW.—At any time after the respondent has been served with a temporary cease-and-desist order pursuant to paragraph (3), the respondent may apply to the Commission to have the order set aside, limited or suspended. If the respondent has been served with a temporary cease-and-desist order entered without a prior Commission hearing, the respondent may, within 10 days after the date on which the order was served, request a hearing on such application and the Commission shall hold a hearing and render a decision on such application at the earliest possible time.

(B) JUDICIAL REVIEW.—Within—

(i) 10 days after the date the respondent was served with a temporary cease-and-desist order entered with a prior Commission hearing, or

(ii) 10 days after the Commission renders a decision on an application and hearing under subparagraph (A), with respect to any temporary cease-and-desist order entered without a prior Commission hearing,

the respondent may apply to the United States district court for the district in which the respondent resides or has its principal place of business, or for the District of Columbia, for an order setting aside, limiting, or suspending the effectiveness or enforcement of the order, and the court shall have jurisdiction to enter such an order. A respondent served with a temporary cease-

and-desist order entered without a prior Commission hearing may not apply to the court except after hearing and decision by the Commission on the respondent's application under subparagraph (A) of this paragraph.

(C) No AUTOMATIC STAY OF TEMPORARY ORDER.—The commencement of proceedings under subparagraph (B) of this paragraph shall not, unless specifically ordered by the court, operate as a stay of the Commission's order.

(D) EXCLUSIVE REVIEW.—Section 213 of this title shall not apply to a temporary order entered pursuant to this section.

(5) AUTHORITY TO ENTER AN ORDER REQUIRING AN ACCOUNTING AND DISGORGEMENT.—In any cease-and-desist proceeding under paragraph (1), the Commission may enter an order requiring accounting and disgorgement, including reasonable interest. The Commission is authorized to adopt rules, regulations, and orders concerning payments to investors, rates of interest, periods of accrual, and such other matters as it deems appropriate to implement this subsection.

Sec. 203A. STATE AND FEDERAL RESPONSIBILITIES

(a) Advisers Subject to State Authorities.—

(1) In general.—No investment adviser that is regulated or required to be regulated as an investment adviser in the State in which it maintains its principal office and place of business shall register under section 203, unless the investment adviser—

(A) has assets under management of not less than $25,000,000, or such higher amount as the Commission may, by rule, deem appropriate in accordance with the purposes of this title; or

(B) is an adviser to an investment company registered under title I of this Act.

(2) Definition.—For purposes of this subsection, the term "assets under management" means the securities portfolios with respect to which an investment adviser provides continuous and regular supervisory or management services.

(b) Advisers Subject to Commission Authority.—

(1) In general.—No law of any State or political subdivision thereof requiring the registration, licensing, or qualification as an investment adviser or supervised person of an investment adviser shall apply to any person—

(A) that is registered under section 203 as an investment adviser, or that is a supervised person of such person, except that a State may license, register, or otherwise qualify any investment adviser representative who has a place of business located within that State; or

(B) that is not registered under section 203 because that person is excepted from the definition of an investment adviser under section 202(a)(11).

(2) Limitation.—Nothing in this subsection shall prohibit the securities commission (or any agency or office performing like functions) of any State from investigating and bringing enforcement actions with respect to fraud or deceit against an investment adviser or person associated with an investment adviser.

(c) Exemptions.—Notwithstanding subsection (a), the Commission, by rule or regulation upon its own motion, or by order upon application, may permit the registration with the Commission of any person or class of persons to which the application of subsection (a) would be unfair, a burden on interstate commerce, or otherwise inconsistent with the purposes of this section.

(d) Filing Depositories.—The Commission may, by rule, require an investment adviser—

(1) to file with the Commission any fee, application, report, or notice required by this title or by the rules issued under this title through any entity designated by the Commission for that purpose; and

(2) to pay the reasonable costs associated with such filing.

(e) State Assistance.—Upon request of the securities commissioner (or any agency or officer performing like functions) of any State, the Commission may provide such training, technical assistance, or other reasonable assistance in connection with the regulation of investment advisers by the State.

Sec. 204A. PREVENTION OF MISUSE OF NONPUBLIC INFORMATION

Every investment adviser subject to section 204 of this title shall establish, maintain, and enforce written policies and procedures reasonably designed, taking into consideration the nature of such investment adviser's business, to prevent the misuse in violation of this Act or the Securities Exchange Act of 1934, or the rules or regulations thereunder, of material, nonpublic information by such investment adviser or any person associated with such investment adviser. The Commission, as it deems necessary or appropriate in the public interest or for the protection of investors, shall adopt rules or regulations to require specific policies or procedures reasonably designed to prevent misuse in violation of this Act or the Securities Exchange Act of 1934 (or the rules or regulations thereunder) of material, nonpublic information.

Sec. 205. INVESTMENT ADVISORY CONTRACTS

(a) No investment adviser, unless exempt from registration pursuant to section 203(b), shall make use of the mails or any means or instrumentality of interstate commerce, directly or indirectly, to enter into, extend, or renew any investment advisory contract, or in any way to perform any investment advisory contract entered into, extended, or renewed on or after the effective date of this title, if such contract—

(1) provides for compensation to the investment adviser on the basis of a share of capital gains upon or capital appreciation of the funds or any portion of the funds of the client;

(2) fails to provide, in substance, that no assignment of such contract shall be made by the investment adviser without the consent of the other party to the contract; or

(3) fails to provide, in substance, that the investment adviser, if a partnership, will notify the other party to the contract of any change in the membership of such partnership within a reasonable time after such change.

(b) Paragraph (1) of this section shall not

(1) be construed to prohibit an investment advisory contract which provides for compensation based upon the total value of a fund averaged over a definite period, or as of definite dates, or taken as of a definite date;

(2) apply to an investment advisory contract with—

(A) an investment company registered under title I of this Act, or

(B) any other person (except a trust, governmental plan, collective trust fund, or separate account referred to in section 3(c)(11) of title I of this Act), provided that the contract relates to the investment of assets in excess of $1 million,

if the contract provides for compensation based on the asset value of the company or fund under management averaged over a specified period and increasing and decreasing proportionately with the investment performance of the company or fund over a specified period in relation to the investment record of an appropriate index of securities prices or such other measure of investment performance as the Commission by rule, regulation, or order may specify;

(3) apply with respect to any investment advisory contract between an investment adviser and a business development company, as defined in this title, if (A) the compensation provided for in such contract does not exceed 20 per centum of the realized capital gains upon the funds of the business development company over a specified period or as of definite dates, computed net of all realized capital losses and unrealized capital depreciation, and the condition of section 61(a)(3)(B)(iii) of title I of this Act is satisfied, and (B) the business development company does not have outstanding any option, warrant, or right issued pursuant to section 61(a)(3)(B) of title I of this Act and does not have a profit-sharing plan described in section 57(n) of title I of this Act;

(4) apply to an investment advisory contract with a company excepted from the definition of an investment company under section 3(c)(7) of title I of this Act; or

(5) apply to an investment advisory contract with a person who is not a resident of the United States.

(c) For purposes of paragraph (2) of subsection (b), the point from which increases and decreases in compensation are measured shall be the fee which is paid or earned when the investment performance of such company or fund is equivalent to that of the index or other measure of performance, and an index of securities prices shall be deemed appropriate unless the Commission by order shall determine otherwise.

(d) As used in paragraphs (2) and (3) of this subsection (a), 'investment advisory contract' means any contract or agreement whereby a person agrees to act as investment adviser or to manage any investment or trading account of another person other than an investment company registered under title I of this Act.

(e) The Commission, by rule or regulation, upon its own motion, or by order upon application, may conditionally or unconditionally exempt any person or transaction, or any class or classes of persons or transactions, from subsection (a)(1), if and to the extent that the exemption relates to an investment advisory contract with any person that the Commission determines does not need the protections of subsection (a)(1), on the basis of such factors as financial sophistication, net worth, knowledge of and experience in financial matters, amount of assets under management, relationship with a registered investment adviser, and such other factors as the Commission determines are consistent with this section.

Sec. 206. PROHIBITED TRANSACTIONS BY INVESTMENT ADVISERS

It shall be unlawful for any investment adviser, by use of the mails or any means or instrumentality of interstate commerce, directly or indirectly—

(1) to employ any device, scheme, or artifice to defraud any client or prospective client;

(2) to engage in any transaction, practice, or course of business which operates as a fraud or deceit upon any client or prospective client;

(3) acting as principal for his own account, knowingly to sell any security to or purchase any security from a client, or acting as broker for a person other than such client, knowingly to effect any sale or purchase of any security for the account of such client, without disclosing to such client in writing before the completion of such transaction the capacity in which he is acting and obtaining the consent of the client to such transaction. The prohibitions of this paragraph (3) shall not apply to any transaction with a customer of a broker or dealer if such broker or dealer is not acting as an investment adviser in relation to such transaction;

(4) to engage in any act, practice, or course of business which is fraudulent, deceptive, or manipulative. The Commission shall, for the purposes of this paragraph (4) by rules and regulations define, and prescribe means reasonably designed to prevent, such acts, practices, and courses of business as are fraudulent, deceptive, or manipulative.

Sec. 206A. EXEMPTIONS

The Commission, by rules and regulations, upon its own motion, or by order upon application, may conditionally or unconditionally exempt any person or transaction or any class or classes or persons, or transactions, from any provision or provisions of this title or of any rule or regulation thereunder, if and to the extent that such exemption is necessary or appropriate in the public interest and consistent with the protection of investors and the purposes fairly intended by the policy and provisions of this title.

ADVISERS ACT RULES—SELECTED PROVISIONS

17 C.F.R. §§ 275.204-3— 275.206(4)-7

Rule 204-3. Written Disclosure Statements

(a) *General Requirement.*—Unless otherwise provided in this rule, an investment adviser, registered or required to be registered pursuant to Section 203 of the Act shall, in accordance with the provisions of this section, furnish each advisory client and prospective advisory client with a written disclosure statement which may be either a copy of Part II of its Form ADV which complies with §275.204-1(b) under the Act or a written document containing at least the information then so required by Part II of Form ADV.

(b) *Delivery.*—(1) An investment adviser, except as provided in paragraph (2), shall deliver the statement required by this section to an advisory client or prospective advisory client (i) not less than 48 hours prior to entering into any written or oral investment advisory contract with such client or prospective client, or (ii) at the time of entering into any such contract, if the advisory client has a right to terminate the contract without penalty within five business days after entering into the contract.

(2) Delivery of the statement required by paragraph (1) need not be made in connection with entering into (i) an investment company contract or (ii) a contract for impersonal advisory services.

(c) *Offer to Deliver.*—(1) An investment adviser, except as provided in paragraph (2), annually shall, without charge, deliver or offer in writing to deliver upon written request to each of its advisory clients the statement required by this section.

(2) The delivery or offer required by paragraph (1) need not be made to advisory clients receiving advisory services solely pursuant to (i) an investment company contract or (ii) a contract for impersonal advisory services requiring a payment of less than $200;

(3) With respect to an advisory client entering into a contract or receiving advisory services pursuant to a contract for impersonal advisory services which requires a payment of $200 or more, an offer of the type specified in paragraph (1) shall also be made at the time of entering into an advisory contract.

Any statement requested in writing by an advisory client pursuant to an offer required by this paragraph must be mailed or delivered within seven days of the receipt of the request.

(d) *Omission of Inapplicable Information.*—If an investment adviser renders substantially different types of investment advisory services to different advisory clients, any information required by Part II of Form ADV may be omitted from the statement furnished to an advisory client or prospective advisory client if such information is applicable only to a type of investment advisory service or fee which is not rendered or charged, or proposed to be rendered or charged, to that client or prospective client.

(e) *Other disclosures.*—Nothing in this rule shall relieve any investment advisor from any obligation pursuant to any provision of the Act or the rules and regulations thereunder or other federal or state law to disclose any information to its advisory clients or prospective advisory clients not specifically required by this rule.

(f) *Sponsors of Wrap Fee Programs.*—(1) An investment adviser, registered or required to be registered pursuant to Section 203 of the Act, that is compensated under a wrap fee program for sponsoring, organizing, or administering the program, or for selecting, or providing advice to clients regarding the selection of, other investment advisers in the program, shall, in lieu of the written disclosure statement required by paragraph (a) of this section and in accordance with the other provisions of this section, furnish each client and prospective client of the wrap fee program with a written disclosure statement containing at least the information required by Schedule H of Form ADV (§ 279.1 of this Chapter). Any additional information included in such disclosure should be limited to information concerning wrap fee programs sponsored by the investment adviser.

(2) If the investment adviser is required under this paragraph (f) to furnish disclosure statements to clients or prospective clients of more than one wrap fee program, the investment adviser may omit from the disclosure statement furnished to clients and prospective clients of a wrap fee program or programs any information required by Schedule H that is not applicable to clients or prospective clients of that wrap fee program or programs.

(3) An investment adviser need not furnish the written disclosure statement required by paragraph (f)(1) of this section to clients and prospective clients of a wrap fee program if another investment adviser is required to furnish and does furnish the written disclosure statement to all clients and prospective clients of the wrap fee program.

(4) An investment adviser that is required under this paragraph (f) to furnish a disclosure statement to clients of a wrap fee program shall furnish the disclosure statement to each client of the wrap fee program (including clients that have previously been furnished the brochure required under paragraph (a) of this section) no later than October 1, 1994.

(g) *Definitions.*—For the purpose of this rule: (1) "contract for impersonal advisory services" means any contract relating solely to the provision of investment advisory services (i) by means of written material or oral statements which do not purport to meet the objectives or needs of specific individuals or accounts; (ii) through the issuance of statistical information containing no expression of opinion as to the investment merits of a particular security; or (iii) any combination of the foregoing services.

(2) "entering into," in reference to an investment advisory contract, does not include an extension or renewal without material change of any such contract which is in effect immediately prior to such extension or renewal.

(3) "investment company contract" means a contract with an investment company registered under the Investment Company Act of 1940 which meets the requirements of Section 15(c) of that Act.

(4) *Wrap fee program* means a program under which any client is charged a specified fee or fees not based directly upon transactions in a client's account for investment advisory services (which may include portfolio management or advice concerning the selection of other investment advisers) and execution of client transactions.

Rule 205-3. Exemption from the Compensation Prohibition of Section 205(a)(1) for Investment Advisers

(a) *General.* The provisions of section 205(a)(1) of the Act (15 U.S.C. 80b-5(a)(1)) will not be deemed to prohibit an investment adviser from entering into, performing, renewing or extending an investment advisory contract that provides for compensation to the investment adviser on the basis of a share of the capital gains upon, or the capital appreciation of, the funds, or any portion of the funds, of a client, *Provided,* That the client entering into the contract subject to this section is a qualified client, as defined in paragraph (d)(1) of this section.

(b) *Identification of the client.* In the case of a private investment company, as defined in paragraph (d)(3) of this section, an investment company registered under the Investment Company Act of 1940, or a business development company, as defined in section 202(a)(22) of the Act (15 U.S.C. 80b-2(a)(22)), each equity owner of any such company (except for the investment adviser entering into the contract and any other equity owners not charged a fee on the basis of a share of capital gains or capital appreciation) will be considered a client for purposes of paragraph (a) of this section.

(c) *Transition rule.* An investment adviser that entered into a contract before August 20, 1998 and satisfied the conditions of this section as in effect on the date that the contract was entered into will be considered to satisfy the conditions of this section; *Provided, however,* that this section will apply with respect to any natural person or company who is not a party to the contract prior to and becomes a party to the contract after August 20, 1998.

(d) *Definitions.* For the purposes of this section:

(1) The term "qualified client" means:

(i) A natural person who or a company that immediately after entering into the contract has at least $750,000 under the management of the investment adviser;

(ii) A natural person who or a company that the investment adviser entering into the contract (and any person acting on his behalf) reasonably believes, immediately prior to entering into the contract, either:

(A) Has a net worth (together, in the case of a natural person, with assets held jointly with a spouse) of more than $1,500,000 at the time the contract is entered into; or

(B) Is a qualified purchaser as defined in section 2(a)(51)(A) of the Investment Company Act of 1940 (15 U.S.C. 80a-2(a)(51)(A)) at the time the contract is entered into; or

(iii) A natural person who immediately prior to entering into the contract is:

(A) An executive officer, director, trustee, general partner, or person serving in a similar capacity, of the investment adviser; or

(B) An employee of the investment adviser (other than an employee performing solely clerical, secretarial or administrative functions with regard to the investment adviser) who, in connection with his or her regular functions or duties, participates in the investment activities of such investment adviser, provided that such employee has been performing such functions and duties for or on behalf of the investment adviser, or substantially similar functions or duties for or on behalf of another company for at least 12 months.

(2) The term "company" has the same meaning as in section 202(a)(5) of the Act (15 U.S.C. 80b-2(a)(5)), but does not include a company that is required to be registered under the Investment Company Act of 1940 but is not registered.

(3) The term "private investment company" means a company that would be defined as an investment company under section 3(a) of the Investment Company Act of 1940 (15 U.S.C. 80a-3(a)) but for the exception provided from that definition by section 3(c)(1) of such Act (15 U.S.C. 80a-3(c)(1)).

(4) The term "executive officer" means the president, any vice president in charge of a principal business unit, division or function (such as sales, administration or finance), any other officer who performs a policy-making function, or any other person who performs similar policy-making functions, for the investment adviser.

Rule 206(4)-1. Advertisements by Investment Advisers

(a) It shall constitute a fraudulent, deceptive, or manipulative act, practice, or course of business within the meaning of section 206(4) of the Act [15 U.S.C. 80b-6(4)] for any investment adviser registered or required to be registered under section 203 of the Act [15 U.S.C. 80b-3], directly or indirectly, to publish, circulate, or distribute any advertisement:

(1) Which refers, directly or indirectly, to any testimonial of any kind concerning the investment adviser or concerning any advice, analysis, report or other service rendered by such investment adviser; or

(2) Which refers, directly or indirectly, to past specific recommendations of such investment adviser which were or would have been profitable to any person; *provided, however,* that this shall not prohibit an advertisement which sets out or offers to furnish a list of all recommendations made by such investment adviser within the immediately preceding period of not less than one

year if such advertisement, and such list if it is furnished separately: (A) state the name of each such security recommended, the date and nature of each such recommendation (e.g., whether to buy, sell or hold), the market price at that time, the price at which the recommendation was to be acted upon, and the market price of each such security as of the most recent practicable date, and (B) contain the following cautionary legend on the first page thereof in print or type as large as the largest print or type used in the body or text thereof: "it should not be assumed that recommendations made in the future will be profitable or will equal the performance of the securities in this list"; or

(3) Which represents, directly or indirectly, that any graph, chart, formula or other device being offered can in and of itself be used to determine which securities to buy or sell, or when to buy or sell them; or which represents, directly or indirectly, that any graph, chart, formula or other device being offered will assist any person in making his own decisions as to which securities to buy or sell, or when to buy or sell them, without prominently disclosing in such advertisement the limitations thereof and the difficulties with respect to its use; or

(4) which contains any statement to the effect that any report, analysis, or other service will be furnished free or without charge, unless such report, analysis or other service actually is or will be furnished entirely free and without any condition or obligation, directly or indirectly; or

(5) which contains any untrue statement of a material fact, or which is otherwise false or misleading.

(b) For the purposes of this rule the term "advertisement" shall include any notice, circular, letter or other written communication addressed to more than one person, or any notice or other announcement in any publication or by radio or television, which offers (1) any analysis, report, or publication concerning securities, or which is to be used in making any determination as to when to buy or sell any security, or which security to buy or sell, or (2) any graph, chart, formula or other device to be used in making any determination as to when to buy or sell any security, or which security to buy or sell, or (3) any other investment advisory service with regard to securities.

Rule 206(4)-4. Financial and Disciplinary Information that Investment Advisers Must Disclose to Clients

(a) It shall constitute a fraudulent, deceptive, or manipulative act, practice, or course of business within the meaning of section 206(4) of the Act [15 U.S.C. 80b-6(4)] for any investment adviser registered or required to be registered under section 203 of the Act [15 U.S.C. 80b-3] to fail to disclose to any client or prospective client all material facts with respect to:

(1) A financial condition of the adviser that is reasonably likely to impair the ability of the adviser to meet contractual commitments to clients, if the adviser has discretionary authority (express or implied) or custody over such client's funds or securities, or requires prepayment of advisory fees of more than $500 from such client, 6 months or more in advance; or

(2) A legal or disciplinary event that is material to an evaluation of the adviser's integrity or ability to meet contractual commitments to clients.

(b) It shall constitute a rebuttable presumption that the following legal or disciplinary events involving the adviser or a management person of the adviser (any of the foregoing being referred to hereafter as "person") that were not resolved in the person's favor or subsequently reversed, suspended, or vacated are material within the meaning of paragraph (a)(2) of the rule for a period of 10 years from the time of the event:

(1) A criminal or civil action in a court of competent jurisdiction in which the person—

(i) Was convicted, pleaded guilty or nolo contendere ("no contest") to a felony or misdemeanor, or is the named subject of a pending criminal proceeding (any of the foregoing referred to hereafter as "action"), and such action involved: an investment-related business; fraud, false statements, or omissions; wrongful taking of property; or bribery, forgery, counterfeiting, or extortion;

(ii) Was found to have been involved in a violation of an investment-related statute or regulation; or

(iii) Was the subject of any order, judgment, or decree permanently or temporarily enjoining the person from, or otherwise limiting the person from, engaging in any investment-related activity.

(2) Administrative proceedings before the Securities and Exchange Commission, any other federal regulatory agency or any state agency (any of the foregoing being referred to hereafter as "agency") in which the person—

(i) Was found to have caused an investment-related business to lose its authorization to do business; or

(ii) Was found to have been involved in a violation of an investment-related statute or regulation and was the subject of an order by the agency denying, suspending, or revoking the authorization of the person to act in, or barring or suspending the person's association with, an investment-related business; or otherwise significantly limiting the person's investment-related activities.

(3) Self-Regulatory Organization (SRO) proceedings in which the person—

(i) Was found to have caused an investment-related business to lose its authorization to do business; or

(ii) Was found to have been involved in a violation of the SRO's rules and was the subject of an order by the SRO barring or suspending the person from membership or from association with other members, or expelling the person from membership; fining the person more than $2,500; or otherwise significantly limiting the person's investment-related activities.

(c) The information required to be disclosed by paragraphs (a) shall be disclosed to clients promptly, and to prospective clients not less than 48 hours prior to entering into any written or oral investment advisory contract, or no later than the time of entering into such contract if the client has the right to terminate the contract without penalty within five business days after entering into the contract.

(d) For purposes of this rule:

(1) "Management person" means a person with power to exercise, directly or indirectly, a controlling influence over the management or policies of an adviser which is a company or to determine the general investment advice given to clients.

(2) "Found" means determined or ascertained by adjudication or consent in a final SRO proceeding, administrative proceeding, or court action.

(3) "Investment-related" means pertaining to securities, commodities, banking, insurance, or real estate (including, but not limited to, acting as or being associated with a broker-dealer, investment company, investment adviser, government securities broker or dealer, municipal securities dealer, bank, savings and loan association, entity or person required to be registered under the Commodity Exchange Act [7 U.S.C. 1 *et seq.*], or fiduciary).

(4) "Involved" means acting or aiding, abetting, causing, counseling, commanding, inducing, conspiring with or failing reasonably to supervise another in doing an act.

(5) "Self-Regulatory Organization" or "SRO" means any national securities or commodities exchange, registered association, or registered clearing agency.

(e) For purposes of calculating the 10-year period during which events are presumed to be material under paragraph (b), the date of a reportable event shall be the date on which the final order, judgment, or decree was entered, or the date on which any rights of appeal from preliminary orders, judgments, or decrees lapsed.

(f) Compliance with paragraph (b) of this rule shall not relieve any investment adviser from the disclosure obligations of paragraph (a) of the rule; compliance with paragraph (a) of the rule shall not relieve any investment adviser from any other disclosure requirement under the Act, the rules and regulations thereunder, or under any other federal or state law.

Note: Registered investment advisers may disclose this information to clients and prospective clients in their "brochure," the written disclosure statement to clients under Rule 204-3 [17 CFR 275.204-3]; *provided*, that the delivery of the brochure satisfies the timing of disclosure requirements described in paragraph (c) of this rule.

Rule 206(4)-6. Proxy Voting

If you are an investment adviser registered or required to be registered under section 203 of the Act (15 U.S.C. 80b-3), it is a fraudulent, deceptive, or manipulative act, practice or course of business within the meaning of section 206(4) of the Act (15 U.S.C. 80b-6(4)), for you to exercise voting authority with respect to client securities, unless you:

(a) Adopt and implement written policies and procedures that are reasonably designed to ensure that you vote client securities in the best interest of clients, which procedures must include how you address material conflicts that may arise between your interests and those of your clients;

(b) Disclose to clients how they may obtain information from you about how you voted with respect to their securities; and

(c) Describe to clients your proxy voting policies and procedures and, upon request, furnish a copy of the policies and procedures to the requesting client.

Rule 206(4)-7. Compliance procedures and practices

If you are an investment adviser registered or required to be registered under section 203 of the Investment Advisers Act of 1940 (15 U.S.C. 80b-3), it shall be unlawful within the meaning of section 206 of the Act (15 U.S.C. 80b-6) for you to provide investment advice to clients unless you:

(a) *Policies and procedures.*Adopt and implement written policies and procedures reasonably designed to prevent violation, by you and your supervised persons, of the Act and the rules that the Commission has adopted under the Act;

(b) *Annual review.*Review, no less frequently than annually, the adequacy of the policies and procedures established pursuant to this section and the effectiveness of their implementation; and

(c) *Chief compliance officer.* Designate an individual (who is a supervised person) responsible for administering the policies and procedures that you adopt under paragraph (a) of this section.

INVESTMENT COMPANY ACT OF 1940—SELECTED PROVISIONS

15 U.S.C. §§80a-1 et seq.

Act	15 U.S.C. Section	Subject
1	80a-1	Findings and declaration of policy
2(a)	80a-2	General definitions
		(3) Affiliated person
		(9) Control
		(19) Interested person
		(35) Sales load
		(36) Security
3	80a-3	Definition of investment company
8	80a-8	Registration of investment companies
9	80a-9	Ineligibility of certain affiliated persons and underwriters
10	80a-10	Affiliations of directors
12	80a-12	Functions and activities of investment companies
13	80a-13	Changes in investment policy
15	80a-15	Investment advisory and underwriting contracts
17	80a-17	Transactions of certain affiliated persons and underwriters
18	80a-18	Capital structure
22	80a-22	Distribution, redemption,and repurchase of redeemable securities
36	80a-35	Breach of fiduciary duty
42	80a-41	Enforcement of title
47	80a-46	Validity of contracts

Sec. 1. FINDINGS AND DECLARATION OF POLICY

(a) Upon the basis of facts disclosed by the record and reports of the Securities and Exchange Commission made pursuant to section 30 of the Public Utility Holding Company Act of 1935, and facts otherwise disclosed and ascertained, it is hereby found that investment companies are affected with a national public interest in that, among other things—

(1) the securities issued by such companies, which constitute a substantial part of all securities publicly offered, are distributed, purchased, paid for, exchanged, transferred, redeemed, and repurchased by use of the mails and means and instrumentalities of interstate

commerce, and in the case of the numerous companies which issue redeemable securities this process of distribution and redemption is continuous;

(2) the principal activities of such companies—investing, reinvesting, and trading in securities—are conducted by use of the mails and means and instrumentalities of interstate commerce, including the facilities of national securities exchanges, and constitute a substantial part of all transactions effected in the securities markets of the Nation;

(3) such companies customarily invest and trade in securities issued by, and may dominate and control or otherwise affect the policies and management of, companies engaged in business in interstate commerce;

(4) such companies are media for the investment in the national economy of a substantial part of the national savings and may have a vital effect upon the flow of such savings into the capital markets; and

(5) the activities of such companies, extending over many States, their use of the instrumentalities of interstate commerce and the wide geographic distribution of their security holders, make difficult, if not impossible, effective State regulation of such companies in the interest of investors.

(b) Upon the basis of facts disclosed by the record and reports of the Securities and Exchange Commission made pursuant to section 30 of the Public Utility Holding Company Act of 1935, and facts otherwise disclosed and ascertained, it is hereby declared that the national public interest and the interest of investors are adversely affected—

(1) when investors purchase, pay for, exchange, receive dividends upon, vote, refrain from voting, sell, or surrender securities issued by investment companies without adequate, accurate, and explicit information, fairly presented, concerning the character of such securities and the circumstances, policies, and financial responsibility of such companies and their management;

(2) when investment companies are organized, operated, managed, or their portfolio securities are selected, in the interest of directors, officers, investment advisers, depositors, or other affiliated persons thereof, in the interest of underwriters, brokers, or dealers, in the interest of special classes of their security holders, or in the interest of other investment companies or persons engaged in other lines of business, rather than in the interest of all classes of such companies' security holders;

(3) when investment companies issue securities containing inequitable or discriminatory provisions, or fail to protect the preferences and privileges of the holders of their outstanding securities;

(4) when the control of investment companies is unduly concentrated through pyramiding or inequitable methods of control, or is inequitably distributed, or when investment companies are managed by irresponsible persons;

(5) when investment companies, in keeping their accounts, in maintaining reserves, and in computing their earnings and the asset value of their outstanding securities, employ unsound or misleading methods, or are not subjected to adequate independent scrutiny;

(6) when investment companies are reorganized, become inactive, or change the character of their business, or when the control or management thereof is transferred, without the consent of their security holders;

(7) when investment companies by excessive borrowing and the issuance of excessive amounts of senior securities increase unduly the speculative character of their junior securities; or

(8) when investment companies operate without adequate assets or reserves.

It is hereby declared that the policy and purposes of this title, in accordance with which the provisions of this title shall be interpreted, are to mitigate and, so far as is feasible, to eliminate the conditions enumerated in this section which adversely affect the national public interest and the interest of investors.

Sec. 2. GENERAL DEFINITIONS

(a) When used in this title, unless the context otherwise requires—

(3) [Affiliated Person]

"Affiliated person" of another person means (A) any person directly or indirectly owning, controlling, or holding with power to vote, 5 per centum or more of the outstanding voting securities of such other person; (B) any person 5 per centum or more of whose outstanding voting securities are directly or indirectly owned, controlled, or held with power to vote, by such other person; (C) any person directly or indirectly controlling, controlled by, or under common control with, such other person; (D) any officer, director, partner, copartner, or employee of such other person; (E) if such other person is an investment company, any investment adviser thereof or any member of an advisory board thereof; and (F) if such other person is an unincorporated investment company not having a board of directors, the depositor thereof.

(9) Control

"Control" means the power to exercise a controlling influence over the management or policies of a company, unless such power is solely the result of an official position with such company.

Any person who owns beneficially, either directly or through one or more controlled companies, more than 25 per centum of the voting securities of a company shall be presumed to control such company. Any person who does not so own more than 25 per centum of the voting securities of any company shall be presumed not to control such company. A natural person shall be presumed not to be a controlled person within the meaning of this title. Any such presumption may be rebutted by evidence, but except as hereinafter provided, shall continue until a determination to the contrary made by the Commission by order either on its own motion or on application by an interested person. If an application filed hereunder is not granted or denied by the Commission within sixty days after filing thereof, the determination sought by the application shall be deemed to have been temporarily granted pending final determination of the Commission thereon. The Commission, upon its own motion or upon application, may by order revoke or modify any order issued under this paragraph whenever it shall find that the determination embraced in such original order is no longer consistent with the facts.

(19) [Interested Person]

"Interested person" of another person means—

(A) when used with respect to an investment company—

(i) any affiliated person of such company,

(ii) any member of the immediate family of any natural person who is an affiliated person of such company,

(iii) any interested person of any investment adviser of or principal underwriter for such company,

(iv) any person or partner or employee of any person who at any time since the beginning of the last two completed fiscal years of such company has acted as legal counsel for such company,

(v) any person or any affiliated person of a person (other than a registered investment company) that, at any time during the 6-month period preceding the date of the determination of whether that person or affiliated person is an interested person, has executed any portfolio transactions for, engaged in any principal transactions with, or distributed shares for—

(I) the investment company;

(II) any other investment company having the same investment adviser as such investment company or holding itself out to investors as a related company for purposes of investment or investor services; or

(III) any account over which the investment company's investment adviser has brokerage placement discretion,

(vi) any person or any affiliated person of a person (other than a registered investment company) that, at any time during the 6-month period preceding the date of the determination of whether that person or affiliated person is an interested person, has loaned money or other property to—

(I) the investment company;

(II) any other investment company having the same investment adviser as such investment company or holding itself out to investors as a related company for purposes of investment or investor services; or

(III) any account for which the investment company's investment adviser has borrowing authority,

(vii) any natural person whom the Commission by order shall have determined to be an interested person by reason of having had, at any time since the beginning of the last two completed fiscal years of such company, a material business or professional relationship with such company or with the principal executive officer of such company or with any other investment company having the same investment adviser or principal underwriter or with the principal executive officer of such other investment company:

Provided, That no person shall be deemed to be an interested person of an investment company solely by reason of (aa) his being a member of its board of directors or advisory board or an owner of its securities, or (bb) his membership in the immediate family of any person specified in clause (aa) of this proviso; and

(B) when used with respect to an investment adviser of or principal underwriter for any investment company—

(i) any affiliated person of such investment adviser or principal underwriter,

(ii) any member of the immediate family of any natural person who is an affiliated person of such investment adviser or principal underwriter,

(iii) any person who knowingly has any direct or indirect beneficial interest in, or who is designated as trustee, executor, or guardian of any legal interest in, any security issued either by such investment adviser or principal underwriter or by a controlling person of such investment adviser or principal underwriter,

(iv) any person or partner or employee of any person who at any time since the beginning of the last two completed fiscal years of such investment company has acted as legal counsel for such investment adviser or principal underwriter,

(v) any person or any affiliated person of a person (other than a registered investment company) that, at any time during the 6-month period preceding the date of the determination of whether that person or affiliated person is an interested person, has executed any portfolio transactions for, engaged in any principal transactions with, or distributed shares for—

(I) any investment company for which the investment adviser or principal underwriter serves as such;

(II) any investment company holding itself out to investors, for purposes of investment or investor services, as a company related to any investment company for which the investment adviser or principal underwriter serves as such; or

(III) any account over which the investment adviser has brokerage placement discretion,

(vi) any person or any affiliated person of a person (other than a registered investment company) that, at any time during the 6-month period preceding the date of the determination of whether that person or affiliated person is an interested person, has loaned money or other property to—

(I) any investment company for which the investment adviser or principal underwriter serves as such;

(II) any investment company holding itself out to investors, for purposes of investment or investor services, as a company related to any investment company for which the investment adviser or principal underwriter serves as such; or

(III) any account for which the investment adviser has borrowing authority,

(vii) any natural person whom the Commission by order shall have determined to be an interested person by reason of having had at any time since the beginning of the last two completed fiscal years of such investment company a material business or professional relationship with such investment adviser or principal underwriter or with the principal executive officer or any controlling person of such investment adviser or principal underwriter.

For the purposes of this paragraph (19), "member of the immediate family" means any parent, spouse of a parent, child, spouse of a child, spouse, brother or sister, and includes step and adoptive relationships. The Commission may modify or revoke any order issued under clause (vi) of subparagraph (A) or (B) of this paragraph whenever it finds that such order is no longer consistent with the facts. No order issued pursuant to clause (vi) of subparagraph (A) or (B) of this paragraph shall become effective until at least sixty days after the entry thereof, and no such order shall affect the status of any person for the purposes of this title or for any other purpose for any period prior to the effective date of such order.

(35) [Sales Load]

"Sales load" means the difference between the price of a security to the public and that portion of the proceeds from its sale which is received and invested or held for investment by the issuer (or in the case of a unit investment trust, by the depositor or trustee), less any portion of such difference deducted for trustee's or custodian's fees, insurance premiums, issue taxes, or administrative expenses or fees which are not properly chargeable to sales or promotional activities. In the case of a periodic payment plan certificate, "sales load" includes the sales load on any investment company securities in which the payments made on such certificate are invested, as well as the sales load on the certificate itself.

(36) [Security]

"Security" means any note, stock, treasury stock, security future, bond, debenture, evidence of indebtedness, certificate of interest or participation in any profit-sharing agreement, collateral-trust certificate, preorganization certificate or subscription, transferable share, investment contract, voting-trust certificate, certificate of deposit for a security, fractional undivided interest in oil, gas, or other mineral rights, any put, call, straddle, option, or privilege on any security (including a certificate of deposit) or on any group or index of securities (including any interest therein or based on the value thereof), or any put, call, straddle, option, or privilege entered into on a national securities exchange relating to foreign currency, or, in general, any interest or instrument commonly known as a "security," or any certificate of interest or participation in, temporary or interim certificate for, receipt for, guarantee of, or warrant or right to subscribe to or purchase, any of the foregoing.

Sec. 3. DEFINITION OF INVESTMENT COMPANY

(a) (1) When used in this title, "investment company" means any issuer which—

(A) is or holds itself out as being engaged primarily, or proposes to engage primarily, in the business of investing, reinvesting, or trading in securities;

(B) is engaged or proposes to engage in the business of issuing face-amount certificates of the installment type, or has been engaged in such business and has any such certificate outstanding; or

(C) is engaged or proposes to engage in the business of investing, reinvesting, owning, holding, or trading in securities, and owns or proposes to acquire investment securities having a value exceeding 40 per centum of the value of such issuer's total assets (exclusive of Government securities and cash items) on an unconsolidated basis.

(2) As used in this section, "investment securities" includes all securities except (A) Government securities, (B) securities issued by employees' securities companies, and (C) securities issued by majority-owned subsidiaries of the owner which (i) are not investment companies, and (ii) are not relying on the exception from the definition of investment company in paragraph (1) or (7) of subsection (c).

(b) Notwithstanding paragraph (1)(C) of subsection (a), none of the following persons is an investment company within the meaning of this title:

(1) Any issuer primarily engaged, directly or through a wholly-owned subsidiary or subsidiaries, in a business or businesses other than that of investing, reinvesting, owning, holding, or trading in securities.

(2) Any issuer which the Commission, upon application by such issuer, finds and by order declares to be primarily engaged in a business or businesses other than that of investing, reinvesting, owning, holding, or trading in securities either directly or (A) through majority-owned subsidiaries or (B) through controlled companies conducting similar types of businesses. The filing of an application under this paragraph in good faith by an issuer other than a registered investment company shall exempt the applicant for a period of sixty days from all provisions of this title applicable to investment companies as such. For cause shown, the Commission by order may extend such period of exemption for an additional period or periods. Whenever the Commission, upon its own motion or upon application, finds that the circumstances which gave rise to the issuance of an order granting an application under this paragraph no longer exist, the Commission shall by order revoke such order.

(3) Any issuer all the outstanding securities of which (other than short-term paper and directors' qualifying shares) are directly or indirectly owned by a company excepted from the definition of investment company by paragraph (1) or (2) of this subsection.

(c) Notwithstanding subsection (a), none of the following persons is an investment company within the meaning of this title:

(1) Any issuer whose outstanding securities (other than short-term paper) are beneficially owned by not more than one hundred persons and which is not making and does not presently propose to make a public offering of its securities. Such issuer shall be deemed to be an investment company for purposes of the limitations set forth in subparagraphs (A)(i) and (B)(i) of section 12(d)(1) governing the purchase or other acquisition by such issuer of any security issued by any registered investment company and the sale of any security issued by any registered open-end investment company to any such issuer. For the purposes of this paragraph:

(A) Beneficial ownership by a company shall be deemed to be beneficial ownership by one person, except that, if such company owns 10 per centum or more of the outstanding voting securities of the issuer, and is or, but for the exception provided for in this paragraph or paragraph (7), would be an investment company, the beneficial ownership shall be deemed to be that of the holders of such company's outstanding securities (other than short-term paper).

(B) Beneficial ownership by any person who acquires securities or interests in securities of an issuer described in the first sentence of this paragraph shall be deemed to be beneficial ownership by the person from whom such transfer was made, pursuant to such rules and regulations as the Commission shall prescribe as necessary or appropriate in the public interest and consistent with the protection of investors and the purposes fairly intended by the policy and provisions of this title, where the transfer was caused by legal separation, divorce, death, or other involuntary event.

(2)(A) Any person primarily engaged in the business of underwriting and distributing securities issued by other persons, selling securities to customers, acting as broker, and acting as market intermediary, or any one or more of such activities, whose gross income normally is derived principally from such business and related activities.

(B) For purposes of this paragraph—

(i) the term "market intermediary" means any person that regularly holds itself out as being willing contemporaneously to engage in, and that is regularly engaged in, the business of entering into transactions on both sides of the market for a financial contract or one or more such financial contracts; and

(ii) the term "financial contract" means any arrangement that—

(I) takes the form of an individually negotiated contract, agreement, or option to buy, sell, lend, swap, or repurchase, or other similar individually negotiated transaction commonly entered into by participants in the financial markets;

(II) is in respect of securities, commodities, currencies, interest or other rates, other measures of value, or any other financial or economic interest similar in purpose or function to any of the foregoing; and

(III) is entered into in response to a request from a counter party for a quotation, or is otherwise entered into and structured to accommodate the objectives of the counter party to such arrangement.

(3) Any bank or insurance company; any savings and loan association, building and loan association, cooperative bank, homestead association, or similar institution, or any receiver, conservator, liquidator, liquidating agent, or similar official or person thereof or therefor; or any common trust fund or similar fund maintained by a bank exclusively for the collective investment and reinvestment of moneys contributed thereto by the bank in its capacity as a trustee, executor, administrator, or guardian, if—

(A) such fund is employed by the bank solely as an aid to the administration of trusts, estates, or other accounts created and maintained for a fiduciary purpose;

(B) except in connection with the ordinary advertising of the bank's fiduciary services, interests in such fund are not—

(i) advertised; or

(ii) offered for sale to the general public; and

(C) fees and expenses charged by such fund are not in contravention of fiduciary principles established under applicable Federal or State law.

(4) Any person substantially all of whose business is confined to making small loans, industrial banking, or similar businesses.

(5) Any person who is not engaged in the business of issuing redeemable securities, face-amount certificates of the installment type or periodic payment plan certificates, and who is primarily engaged in one or more of the following businesses: (A) Purchasing or otherwise acquiring notes, drafts, acceptances, open accounts receivable, and other obligations representing part or all of the sales price of merchandise, insurance, and services; (B) making loans to manufacturers, wholesalers, and retailers of, and to prospective purchasers of, specified merchandise, insurance, and services; and (C) purchasing or otherwise acquiring mortgages and other liens on and interests in real estate.

(6) Any company primarily engaged, directly or through majority-owned subsidiaries, in one or more of the businesses described in paragraphs (3), (4), and (5), or in one or more of such businesses (from which not less than 25 per centum of such company's gross income during its last fiscal year was derived) together with an additional business or businesses other than investing, reinvesting, owning, holding, or trading in securities.

(7) (A) Any issuer, the outstanding securities of which are owned exclusively by persons who, at the time of acquisition of such securities, are qualified purchasers, and which is not making and does not at that time propose to make a public offering of such securities. Securities that are owned by persons who received the securities from a qualified purchaser as a gift or bequest, or in a case in which the transfer was caused by legal separation, divorce, death, or other involuntary event, shall be deemed to be owned by a qualified purchaser, subject to such rules, regulations, and orders as the Commission may prescribe as necessary or appropriate in the public interest or for the protection of investors.

(B) Notwithstanding subparagraph (A), an issuer is within the exception provided by this paragraph if—

(i) in addition to qualified purchasers, outstanding securities of that issuer are beneficially owned by not more than 100 persons who are not qualified purchasers, if—

(I) such persons acquired any portion of the securities of such issuer on or before September 1, 1996; and

(II) at the time at which such persons initially acquired the securities of such issuer, the issuer was excepted by paragraph (1); and

(ii) prior to availing itself of the exception provided by this paragraph—

(I) such issuer has disclosed to each beneficial owner, as determined under paragraph (1), that future investors will be limited to qualified purchasers, and that ownership in such issuer is no longer limited to not more than 100 persons; and

(II) concurrently with or after such disclosure, such issuer has provided each beneficial owner, as determined under paragraph (1), with a reasonable opportunity to redeem any part or all of their interests in the issuer, notwithstanding any agreement to the contrary between the issuer and such persons, for that person's proportionate share of the issuer's net assets.

(C) Each person that elects to redeem under subparagraph (B)(ii)(II) shall receive an amount in cash equal to that person's proportionate share of the issuer's net assets, unless the issuer elects to provide such person with the option of receiving, and such person agrees to receive, all or a portion of such person's share in assets of the issuer. If the issuer elects to provide such persons with such an opportunity, disclosure concerning such opportunity shall be made in the disclosure required by subparagraph (B)(ii)(I).

(D) An issuer that is excepted under this paragraph shall nonetheless be deemed to be an investment company for purposes of the limitations set forth in subparagraphs (A)(i) and (B)(i) of section 12(d)(1) relating to the purchase or other acquisition by such issuer of any security issued by any registered investment company and the sale of any security issued by any registered open-end investment company to any such issuer.

(E) For purposes of determining compliance with this paragraph and paragraph (1), an issuer that is otherwise excepted under this paragraph and an issuer that is otherwise excepted under paragraph (1) shall not be treated by the Commission as being a single issuer for purposes of determining whether the outstanding securities of the issuer excepted under paragraph (1) are beneficially owned by not more than 100 persons or whether the outstanding securities of the issuer excepted under this paragraph are owned by persons that are not qualified purchasers. Nothing in this subparagraph shall be construed to establish that a person is a bona fide qualified purchaser for purposes of this paragraph or a bona fide beneficial owner for purposes of paragraph (1).

(8) Any company subject to regulation under the Public Utility Holding Company Act of 1935.

(9) Any person substantially all of whose business consists of owning or holding oil, gas, or other mineral royalties or leases, or fractional interests therein, or certificates of interest or participation in or investment contracts relative to such royalties, leases, or fractional interests.

(10)(A) Any company organized and operated exclusively for religious, educational, benevolent, fraternal, charitable, or reformatory purposes—

(i) no part of the net earnings of which inures to the benefit of any private shareholder or individual; or

(ii) which is or maintains a fund described in subparagraph (B).

(B) For the purposes of subparagraph (A)(ii), a fund is described in this subparagraph if such fund is a pooled income fund, collective trust fund, collective investment fund, or similar fund maintained by a charitable organization exclusively for the collective investment and reinvestment of one or more of the following:

(i) assets of the general endowment fund or other funds of one or more charitable organizations;

(ii) assets of a pooled income fund;

(iii) assets contributed to a charitable organization in exchange for the issuance of charitable gift annuities;

(iv) assets of a charitable remainder trust or of any other trust, the remainder interests of which are irrevocably dedicated to any charitable organization;

(v) assets of a charitable lead trust;

(vi) assets of a trust, the remainder interests of which are revocably dedicated to or for the benefit of 1 or more charitable organizations, if the ability to revoke the dedication is limited to circumstances involving—

(I) an adverse change in the financial circumstances of a settlor or an income beneficiary of the trust;

(II) a change in the identity of the charitable organization or organizations having the remainder interest, provided that the new beneficiary is also a charitable organization; or

(III) both the changes described in subclauses (I) and (II);

(vii) assets of a trust not described in clauses (i) through (v), the remainder interests of which are revocably dedicated to a charitable organization, subject to subparagraph (C); or

(viii) such assets as the Commission may prescribe by rule, regulation, or order in accordance with section 6(c).

(C) A fund that contains assets described in clause (vii) of subparagraph (B) shall be excluded from the definition of an investment company for a period of 3 years after the date of enactment of this subparagraph, but only if—

(i) such assets were contributed before the date which is 60 days after the date of enactment of this subparagraph; and

(ii) such assets are commingled in the fund with assets described in one or more of clauses (i) through (vi) and (viii) of subparagraph (B).

(D) For purposes of this paragraph—

(i) a trust or fund is "maintained" by a charitable organization if the organization serves as a trustee or administrator of the trust or fund or has the power to remove the trustees or administrators of the trust or fund and to designate new trustees or administrators;

(ii) the term "pooled income fund" has the same meaning as in section 642(c)(5) of the Internal Revenue Code of 1986;

(iii) the term "charitable organization" means an organization described in paragraphs (1) through (5) of section 170(c) or section 501(c)(3) of the Internal Revenue Code of 1986;

(iv) the term "charitable lead trust" means a trust described in section 170(f)(2)(B), 2055(e)(2)(B), or 2522(c)(2)(B) of the Internal Revenue Code of 1986;

(v) the term "charitable remainder trust" means a charitable remainder annuity trust or a charitable remainder unitrust, as those terms are defined in section 664(d) of the Internal Revenue Code of 1986; and

(vi) the term "charitable gift annuity" means an annuity issued by a charitable organization that is described in section 501(m)(5) of the Internal Revenue Code of 1986.

(11) Any employee's stock bonus, pension, or profit-sharing trust which meets the requirements for qualification under section 401 of the Internal Revenue Code of 1986 or; any governmental plan described in section 3(a)(2)(C) of the Securities Act of 1933; or any collective trust fund maintained by a bank consisting solely of assets of such trusts or governmental plans, or both; or any separate account the assets of which are derived solely from (A) contributions under pension or profit-sharing plans which meet the requirements of section 401 of the Internal Revenue Code of 1986 or the requirements for deduction of the employer's contribution under section 404(a)(2) of such Code, (B) contributions under governmental plans in connection with which interests, participations, or securities are exempted from the registration provisions of section 5 of the Securities Act of 1933 by section 3(a)(2)(C) of such Act, and (C) advances made by an insurance company in connection with the operation of such separate account.

(12) Any voting trust the assets of which consist exclusively of securities of a single issuer which is not an investment company.

(13) Any security holders' protective committee or similar issuer having outstanding and issuing no securities other than certificates of deposit and short-term paper.

[Church Plans]

(14) Any church plan described in section 414(e) of the Internal Revenue Code of 1986, if, under any such plan, no part of the assets may be used for, or diverted to, purposes other than the exclusive benefit of plan participants or beneficiaries, or any company or account that is—

(A) established by a person that is eligible to establish and maintain such a plan under section 414(e) of the Internal Revenue Code of 1986; and

(B) substantially all of the activities of which consist of—

(i) managing or holding assets contributed to such church plans or other assets which are permitted to be commingled with the assets of church plans under the Internal Revenue Code of 1986; or

(ii) administering or providing benefits pursuant to church plans.

Sec. 8. REGISTRATION OF INVESTMENT COMPANIES

(a) Any investment company organized or otherwise created under the laws of the United States or of a State may register for the purposes of this title by filing with the Commission a notification of registration, in such form as the Commission shall by rules and regulations prescribe as necessary or appropriate in the public interest or for the protection of investors. An investment company shall be deemed to be registered upon receipt by the Commission of such notification of registration.

(b) Every registered investment company shall file with the Commission, within such reasonable time after registration as the Commission shall fix by rules and regulations, an original and such copies of a registration statement, in such form and containing such of the following information and documents as the Commission shall by rules and regulations prescribe as necessary or appropriate in the public interest or for the protection of investors:

(1) a recital of the policy of the registrant in respect of each of the following types of activities, such recital consisting in each case of a statement whether the registrant reserves freedom of action to engage in activities of such type, and if such freedom of action is reserved, a statement briefly indicating, insofar as is practicable, the extent to which the registrant intends to engage therein: (A) the classification and subclassifications, as defined in sections 4 and 5, within which the registrant proposes to operate; (B) borrowing money; (C) the issuance of senior securities; (D) engaging in the business of underwriting securities issued by other persons; (E) concentrating investments in a particular industry or group of industries; (F) the purchase and sale of real estate and commodities, or either of them; (G) making loans to other persons; and (H) portfolio turnover (including a statement showing the aggregate dollar of purchases and sales of portfolio securities, other than Government securities, in each of the last three full fiscal years preceding the filing of such registration statement);

(2) a recital of all investment policies of the registrant, not enumerated in paragraph (1), which are changeable only if authorized by shareholder vote;

(3) a recital of all policies of the registrant, not enumerated in paragraphs (1) and (2), in respect of matters which the registrant deems matters of fundamental policy;

(4) the name and address of each affiliated person of the registrant; the name and principal address of every company, other than the registrant, of which each such person is an officer, director, or partner; a brief statement of the business experience for the preceding five years of each officer and director of the registrant; and

(5) the information and documents which would be required to be filed in order to register under the Securities Act of 1933 and the Securities Exchange Act of 1934 all securities (other than short-term paper) which the registrant has outstanding or proposes to issue.

(c) The Commission shall make provision, by permissive rules and regulations or order, for the filing of the following, or so much of the following as the Commission may designate, in lieu of the information and documents required pursuant to subsection (b):

(1) copies of the most recent registration statement filed by the registrant under the Securities Act of 1933 and currently effective under such Act, or if the registrant has not filed such a statement, copies of a registration statement filed by the registrant under the Securities Exchange Act of 1934 and currently effective under such Act;

(2) copies of any reports filed by the registrant pursuant to section 13 or 15(d) of the Securities Exchange Act of 1934; and

(3) a report containing reasonably current information regarding the matters included in copies filed pursuant to paragraphs (1) and (2), and such further information regarding matters not included in such copies as the Commission is authorized to require under subsection (b).

(d) If the registrant is a unit investment trust substantially all of the assets of which are securities issued by another registered investment company, the Commission is authorized to prescribe for the registrant, by rules and regulations or order, a registration statement which eliminates inappropriate duplication of information contained in the registration statement filed under this section by such other investment company.

(e) If it appears to the Commission that a registered investment company has failed to file the registration statement required by this section or a report required pursuant to section 30(a) or (b), or has filed such a registration statement or report but omitted therefrom material facts required to be stated therein, or has filed such a registration statement or report in violation of section 34(b), the Commission shall notify such company by registered mail or by certified mail of the failure to file such registration statement or report, or of the respects in which such registration statement or report appears to be materially incomplete or misleading, as the case may be, and shall fix a date (in no event earlier than thirty days after the mailing of such notice) prior to which such company may file such registration statement or report or correct the same. If such registration statement or report is not filed or corrected within the time so fixed by the Commission or any extension thereof, the Commission, after appropriate notice and opportunity for hearing, and upon such conditions and with such exemptions as it deems appropriate for the protection of investors, may by order suspend the registration of such company until such statement or report is filed or corrected, or may by order revoke such registration, if the evidence establishes—

(1) that such company has failed to file a registration statement required by this section or a report required pursuant to section 30(a) or (b), or has filed such a registration statement or report but omitted therefrom material facts required to be stated therein, or has filed such a registration statement or report in violation of section 34(b); and

(2) that such suspension or revocation is in the public interest.

(f) Whenever the Commission, on its own motion or upon application, finds that a registered investment company has ceased to be an investment company, it shall so declare by order and upon the taking effect of such order the registration of such company shall cease to be in effect. If necessary for the protection of investors, an order under this subsection may be made upon appropriate conditions. The Commission's denial of any application under this subsection shall be by order.

Sec. 9. INELIGIBILITY OF CERTAIN AFFILIATED PERSONS AND UNDERWRITERS

(a) It shall be unlawful for any of the following persons to serve or act in the capacity of employee, officer, director, member of an advisory board, investment adviser, or depositor of any registered investment company, or principal underwriter for any registered open-end company, registered unit investment trust, or registered face amount certificate company.

(1) any person who within 10 years has been convicted of any felony or misdemeanor involving the purchase or sale of any security or arising out of such person's conduct as an underwriter, broker, dealer, investment adviser, municipal securities dealer, government securities broker, government securities dealer, bank, transfer agent, or entity or person required to be registered under the Commodity Exchange Act, or as an affiliated person, salesman, or employee of any investment company, bank, insurance company, or entity or person required to be registered under the Commodity Exchange Act;

(2) any person who, by reason of any misconduct, is permanently or temporarily enjoined by order, judgment, or decree of any court of competent jurisdiction from acting as an underwriter, broker, dealer, investment adviser, municipal securities dealer, government securities broker, government securities dealer, bank, transfer agent, or entity or person required to be registered under the Commodity Exchange Act, or as an affiliated person, salesman, or employee of any investment company, bank, insurance company, or entity or person required to be registered

under the Commodity Exchange Act, or from engaging in or continuing any conduct or practice in connection with any such activity or in connection with the purchase or sale of any security; or

(3) a company any affiliated person of which is ineligible, by reason of paragraph (1) or (2), to serve or act in the foregoing capacities.

For the purposes of paragraphs (1), (2), and (3) of this subsection, the term "investment adviser" shall include an investment adviser as defined in title II of this Act.

(b) The Commission may, after notice and opportunity for hearing, by order prohibit, conditionally or unconditionally, either permanently or for such period of time as it in its discretion shall deem appropriate in the public interest, any person from serving or acting as an employee, officer, director, member of an advisory board, investment adviser or depositor of, or principal underwriter for, a registered investment company or affiliated person of such investment adviser, depositor, or principal underwriter, if such person—

(1) has willfully made or caused to be made in any registration statement, application or report filed with the Commission under this title any statement which was at the time and in the light of the circumstances under which it was made false or misleading with respect to any material fact, or has omitted to state in any such registration statement, application, or report any material fact which was required to be stated therein;

(2) has willfully violated any provision of the Securities Act of 1933, or of the Securities Exchange Act of 1934, or of title II of this Act, or of this title, or of the Commodity Exchange Act, or of any rule or regulation under any of such statutes;

(3) has willfully aided, abetted, counseled, commanded, induced, or procured the violation by any other person of the Securities Act of 1933, or of the Securities Exchange Act of 1934, or of title II of this Act, or of this title, or of the Commodity Exchange Act, or of any rule of regulation under any of such statutes;

(4) has been found by a foreign financial regulatory authority to have—

(A) made or caused to be made in any application for registration or report required to be filed with a foreign securities authority, or in any proceeding before a foreign securities authority with respect to registration, any statement that was at the time and in light of the circumstances under which it was made false or misleading with respect to any material fact, or has omitted to state in any application or report to a foreign securities authority any material fact that is required to be stated therein;

(B) violated any foreign statute or regulation regarding transactions in securities or contracts of sale of a commodity for future delivery traded on or subject to the rules of a contract market or any board of trade;

(C) aided, abetted, counseled, commanded, induced, or procured the violation by any other person of any foreign statute or regulation regarding transactions in securities or contracts of sale of a commodity for future delivery traded on or subject to the rules of a contract market or any board of trade;

(5) within 10 years has been convicted by a foreign court of competent jurisdiction of a crime, however denominated by the laws of the relevant foreign government, that is substantially equivalent to an offense set forth in paragraph (1) of subsection (a); or

(6) by reason of any misconduct, is temporarily or permanently enjoined by any foreign court of competent jurisdiction from acting in any of the capacities, set forth in paragraph (2) of subsection (a), or a substantially equivalent foreign capacity, or from engaging in or continuing any conduct or practice in connection with any such activity or in connection with the purchase or sale of any security.

(c) Any person who is ineligible, by reason of subsection (a), to serve or act in the capacities enumerated in that subsection, may file with the Commission an application for an exemption from the provisions of that subsection. The Commission shall by order grant such application, either unconditionally or on an appropriate temporary or other conditional basis, if it is established that the prohibitions of subsection (a), as applied to such person, are unduly or disproportionately severe or that the conduct of such person has been such as not to make it against the public interest or protection of investors to grant such application.

(d) MONEY PENALTIES IN ADMINISTRATIVE PROCEEDINGS.—

(1) AUTHORITY OF COMMISSION.—In any proceeding instituted pursuant to subsection (b) against any person, the Commission may impose a civil penalty if it finds, on the record after notice and opportunity for hearing, that such person—

(A) has willfully violated any provision of the Securities Act of 1933, the Securities Exchange Act of 1934, the Investment Advisers Act of 1940, or this title, or the rules or regulations thereunder;

(B) has willfully aided, abetted, counseled, commanded, induced, or procured such a violation by any other person; or

(C) has willfully made or caused to be made in any registration statement, application, or report required to be filed with the Commission under this title, any statement which was, at the time and in the light of the circumstances under which it was made false or misleading with respect to any material fact, or has omitted to state in any such registration statement, application, or report any material fact which was required to be stated therein;

and that such penalty is in the public interest.

(2) MAXIMUM AMOUNT OF PENALTY.—

(A) FIRST TIER.—The maximum amount of penalty for each act or omission described in paragraph (1) shall be $5,000 for a natural person or $50,000 for any other person.

(B) SECOND TIER.—Notwithstanding subparagraph (A), the maximum amount of penalty for each such act or omission shall be $50,000 for a natural person or $250,000 for any other person if the act or omission described in paragraph (1) involved fraud, deceit, manipulation, or deliberate or reckless disregard of a regulatory requirement.

(C) THIRD TIER.—Notwithstanding subparagraphs (A) and (B), the maximum amount of penalty for each such act or omission shall be $100,000 for a natural person or $500,000 for any other person if—

(i) the act or omission described in paragraph (1) involved fraud, deceit, manipulation, or deliberate or reckless disregard of a regulatory requirement; and

(ii) such act or omission directly or indirectly resulted in substantial losses or created a significant risk of substantial losses to other persons or resulted in substantial pecuniary gain to the person who committed the act or omission.

(3) DETERMINATION OF PUBLIC INTEREST.—In considering under this section whether a penalty is in the public interest, the Commission may consider—

(A) whether the act or omission for which such penalty is assessed involved fraud, deceit, manipulation, or deliberate or reckless disregard of a regulatory requirement;

(B) the harm to other persons resulting either directly or indirectly from such act or omission;

(C) the extent to which any person was unjustly enriched, taking into account any restitution made to persons injured by such behavior;

(D) whether such person previously has been found by the Commission, another appropriate regulatory agency, or a self-regulatory organization to have violated the Federal securities laws, State securities laws, or the rules of a self-regulatory organization, has been enjoined by a court of competent jurisdiction from violations of such laws or rules, or has been convicted by a court of competent jurisdiction of violations of such laws or of any felony or misdemeanor described in section 203(e)(2) of the Investment Advisers Act of 1940;

(E) the need to deter such person and other persons from committing such acts or omissions; and

(F) such other matters as justice may require.

(4) EVIDENCE CONCERNING ABILITY TO PAY.—In any proceeding in which the Commission may impose a penalty under this section, a respondent may present evidence of the respondent's ability to pay such penalty. The Commission may, in its discretion, consider such evidence in determining whether such penalty is in the public interest. Such evidence may relate to the extent of such

person's ability to continue in business and the collectability of a penalty, taking into account any other claims of the United States or third parties upon such person's assets and the amount of such person's assets.

(e) AUTHORITY TO ENTER AN ORDER REQUIRING AN ACCOUNTING AND DISGORGEMENT.—In any proceeding in which the Commission may impose a penalty under this section, the Commission may enter an order requiring accounting and disgorgement, including reasonable interest. The Commission is authorized to adopt rules, regulations, and orders concerning payments to investors, rates of interest, periods of accrual, and such other matters as it deems appropriate to implement this subsection.

(f) CEASE-AND-DESIST PROCEEDINGS.—

(1) AUTHORITY OF THE COMMISSION.—If the Commission finds, after notice and opportunity for hearing, that any person is violating, has violated, or is about to violate any provision of this title, or any rule or regulation thereunder, the Commission may publish its findings and enter an order requiring such person, and any other person that is, was, or would be a cause of the violation, due to an act or omission the person knew or should have known would contribute to such violation, to cease and desist from committing or causing such violation and any future violation of the same provision, rule, or regulation. Such order may, in addition to requiring a person to cease and desist from committing or causing a violation, require such person to comply, or to take steps to effect compliance, with such provision, rule, or regulation, upon such terms and conditions and within such time as the Commission may specify in such order. Any such order may, as the Commission deems appropriate, require future compliance or steps to effect future compliance, either permanently or for such period of time as the Commission may specify, with such provision, rule, or regulation with respect to any security, any issuer, or any other person.

(2) HEARING.—The notice instituting proceedings pursuant to paragraph (1) shall fix a hearing date not earlier than 30 days nor later than 60 days after service of the notice unless an earlier or a later date is set by the Commission with the consent of any respondent so served.

(3) TEMPORARY ORDER.—

(A) IN GENERAL.—Whenever the Commission determines that the alleged violation or threatened violation specified in the notice instituting proceedings pursuant to paragraph (1), or the continuation thereof, is likely to result in significant dissipation or conversion of assets, significant harm to investors, or substantial harm to the public interest, including, but not limited to, losses to the Securities Investor Protection Corporation, prior to the completion of the proceeding, the Commission may enter a temporary order requiring the respondent to cease and desist from the violation or threatened violation and to take such action to prevent the violation or threatened violation and to prevent dissipation or conversion of assets, significant harm to investors, or substantial harm to the public interest as the Commission deems appropriate pending completion of such proceedings. Such an order shall be entered only after notice and opportunity for a hearing, unless the Commission, notwithstanding section 40(a) of this title, determines that notice and hearing prior to entry would be impracticable or contrary to the public interest. A temporary order shall become effective upon service upon the respondent and, unless set aside, limited, or suspended by the Commission or a court of competent jurisdiction, shall remain effective and enforceable pending the completion of the proceedings.

(B) APPLICABILITY.—This paragraph shall apply only to a respondent that acts, or, at the time of the alleged misconduct acted, as a broker, dealer, investment adviser, investment company, municipal securities dealer, government securities broker, government securities dealer, or transfer agent, or is, or was at the time of the alleged misconduct, an associated person of, or a person seeking to become associated with, any of the foregoing.

(4) REVIEW OF TEMPORARY ORDERS.—

(A) COMMISSION REVIEW.—At any time after the respondent has been served with a temporary cease-and-desist order pursuant to paragraph (3), the respondent may apply to the Commission to have the order set aside, limited, or suspended. If the respondent has been served with a temporary cease-and-desist order entered without a prior Commission hearing, the respondent may, within 10 days after the date on which the order was served, request a hearing on such application and the Commission shall hold a hearing and render a decision on such application at the earliest possible time.

(B) JUDICIAL REVIEW.—Within—

(i) 10 days after the date the respondent was served with a temporary cease-and-desist order entered with a prior Commission hearing, or

(ii) 10 days after the Commission renders a decision on an application and hearing under subparagraph (A), with respect to any temporary cease-and-desist order entered without a prior Commission hearing.

the respondent may apply to the United States district court for the district in which the respondent resides or has its principal place of business, or for the District of Columbia, for an order setting aside, limiting, or suspending the effectiveness or enforcement of the order, and the court shall have jurisdiction to enter such an order. A respondent served with a temporary cease-and-desist order entered without a prior Commission hearing may not apply to the court except after hearing and decision by the Commission on the respondent's application under subparagraph (A) of this paragraph.

(C) NO AUTOMATIC STAY OF TEMPORARY ORDER.—The commencement of proceedings under subparagraph (B) of this paragraph shall not, unless specifically ordered by the court, operate as a stay of the Commission's order.

(D) EXCLUSIVE REVIEW.—Section 43 of this title shall not apply to a temporary order entered pursuant to this section.

(5) AUTHORITY TO ENTER AN ORDER REQUIRING AN ACCOUNTING AND DISGORGEMENT.—In any cease-and-desist proceeding under subsection (f)(1), the Commission may enter an order requiring accounting and disgorgement, including reasonable interest. The Commission is authorized to adopt rules, regulations, and orders concerning payments to investors, rates of interest, periods of accrual, and such other matters as it deems appropriate to implement this subsection.

(g) For the purposes of this section, the term "investment adviser" includes a corporate or other trustee performing the functions of an investment adviser.

Sec. 10. AFFILIATIONS OR INTEREST OF DIRECTORS, OFFICERS, AND EMPLOYEES

(a) No registered investment company shall have a board of directors more than 60 per centum of the members of which are persons who are interested persons of such registered company.

(b) No registered investment company shall—

(1) employ as regular broker any director, officer, or employee of such registered company, or any person of which any such director, officer, or employee is an affiliated person, unless a majority of the board of directors of such registered company shall be persons who are not such brokers or affiliated persons of any of such brokers;

(2) use as a principal underwriter of securities issued by it any director, officer, or employee of such registered company or any person of which any such director, officer, or employee is an interested person, unless a majority of the board of directors of such registered company shall be persons who are not such principal underwriters or interested persons of any of such principal underwriters; or

(3) have as director, officer, or employee any investment banker, or any affiliated person of an investment banker, unless a majority of the board of directors of such registered company shall be persons who are not investment bankers or affiliated persons of any investment banker. For the purposes of this paragraph, a person shall not be deemed an affiliated person of an investment banker solely by reason of the fact that he is an affiliated person of a company of the character described in section 12(d)(3)(A) and (B).

(c) No registered investment company shall have a majority of its board of directors consisting of persons who are officers, directors, or employees of any one bank (together with its affiliates and subsidiaries) or any one bank holding company (together with its affiliates and subsidiaries) (as such terms are defined in section 2 of the Bank Holding Company Act of 1956), except that, if on March 15, 1940, any registered investment company had a majority of its directors consisting of persons who are directors, officers, or employees of any one bank, such company may continue to have the same percentage of its board of directors consisting of persons who are directors, officers, or employees of such bank.

(d) Notwithstanding subsections (a) and (b)(2) of this section, a registered investment company may have a board of directors all the members of which, except one, are interested persons of the investment adviser of such company, or are officers or employees of such company, if—

(1) such investment company is an open-end company;

(2) such investment adviser is registered under title II of this Act and is engaged principally in the business of rendering investment supervisory services as defined in title II;

(3) no sales load is charged on securities issued by such investment company;

(4) any premium over net asset value charged by such company upon the issuance of any such security, plus any discount from net asset value charged on redemption thereof, shall not in the aggregate exceed 2 per centum;

(5) no sales or promotion expenses are incurred by such registered company; but expenses incurred in complying with laws regulating the issue or sale of securities shall not be deemed sales or promotion expenses;

(6) such investment adviser is the only investment adviser to such investment company, and such investment adviser does not receive a management fee exceeding 1 per centum per annum of the value of such company's net assets averaged over the year or taken as of a definite date or dates within the year;

(7) all executive salaries and executive expenses and office rent of such investment company are paid by such investment adviser; and

(8) such investment company has only one class of securities outstanding, each unit of which has equal voting rights with every other unit.

(e) If by reason of the death, disqualification, or bona fide resignation of any director or directors, the requirements of the foregoing provisions of this section or of section 15(f)(1) in respect of directors shall not be met by a registered investment company, the operation of such provision shall be suspended as to such registered company—

(1) for a period of thirty days if the vacancy or vacancies may be filled by action of the board of directors;

(2) for a period of sixty days if a vote of stockholders is required to fill the vacancy or vacancies; or

(3) for such longer period as the Commission may prescribe, by rules and regulations upon its own motion or by order upon application, as not inconsistent with the protection of investors.

(f) No registered investment company shall knowingly purchase or otherwise acquire, during the existence of any underwriting or selling syndicate, any security (except a security of which such company is the issuer) a principal underwriter of which is an officer, director, member of an advisory board, investment adviser, or employee of such registered company, or is a person (other than a company of the character described in section 12(d)(3)(A) and (B)) of which any such officer, director, member of an advisory board, investment adviser, or employee is an affiliated person, unless in acquiring such security such registered company is itself acting as a principal underwriter for the issuer. The Commission, by rules and regulations upon its own motion or by order upon application, may conditionally or unconditionally exempt any transaction or classes of transactions from any of the provisions of this subsection, if and to the extent that such exemption is consistent with the protection of investors.

(g) In the case of a registered investment company which has an advisory board, such board, as a distinct entity, shall be subject to the same restrictions as to its membership as are imposed upon a board of directors by this section.

(h) In the case of a registered management company which is an unincorporated company not having a board of directors, the provisions of this section shall apply as follows:

(1) the provisions of subsection (a), as modified by subsection (e), shall apply to the board of directors of the depositor of such company;

(2) the provisions of subsections (b) and (c), as modified by subsection (e), shall apply to the board of directors of the depositor and of every investment adviser of such company; and

(3) the provisions of subsection (f) shall apply to purchases and other acquisitions for the account of such company of securities a principal underwriter of which is the depositor or an investment adviser of such company, or an affiliated person of such depositor or investment adviser.

Sec. 12. FUNCTIONS AND ACTIVITIES OF INVESTMENT COMPANIES

(a) It shall be unlawful for any registered investment company, in contravention of such rules and regulations or orders as the Commission may prescribe as necessary or appropriate in the public interest or for the protection of investors—

(1) to purchase any security on margin, except such short-term credits as are necessary for the clearance of transactions;

(2) to participate on a joint or a joint and several basis in any trading account in securities, except in connection with an underwriting in which such registered company is a participant; or

(3) to effect a short sale of any security, except in connection with an underwriting in which such registered company is a participant.

(b) It shall be unlawful for any registered open-end company (other than a company complying with the provisions of section 10(d)) to act as a distributor of securities of which it is the issuer, except through an underwriter, in contravention of such rules and regulations as the Commission may prescribe as necessary or appropriate in the public interest or for the protection of investors.

(c) It shall be unlawful for any registered diversified company to make any commitment as underwriter, if immediately thereafter the amount of its outstanding underwriting commitments, plus the value of its investments in securities of issuers (other than investment companies) of which it owns more than 10 per centum of the outstanding voting securities, exceeds 25 per centum of the value of its total assets.

[Ownership of Stock of Other Investment Companies]

(d) (1) (A) It shall be unlawful for any registered investment company (the "acquiring company") and any company or companies controlled by such acquiring company to purchase or otherwise acquire any security issued by any other investment company (the "acquired company"), and for any investment company (the "acquiring company") and any company or companies controlled by such acquiring company to purchase or otherwise acquire any security issued by any registered investment company (the "acquired company"), if the acquiring company and any company or companies controlled by it immediately after such purchase or acquisition own in the aggregate—

(i) more than 3 per centum of the total outstanding voting stock of the acquired company;

(ii) securities issued by the acquired company having an aggregate value in excess of 5 per centum of the value of the total assets of the acquiring company; or

(iii) securities issued by the acquired company and all other investment companies (other than Treasury stock of the acquiring company) having an aggregate value in excess of 10 per centum of the value of the total assets of the acquiring company.

(B) It shall be unlawful for any registered open-end investment company (the "acquired company"), any principal underwriter therefor, or any broker or dealer registered under the Securities Exchange Act of 1934, knowingly to sell or otherwise dispose of any security issued by the acquired company to any other investment company (the "acquiring company") or any company or companies controlled by the acquiring company, if immediately after such sale or disposition—

(i) more than 3 per centum of the total outstanding voting stock of the acquired company is owned by the acquiring company and any company or companies controlled by it; or

(ii) more than 10 per centum of the total outstanding voting stock of the acquired company is owned by the acquiring company and other investment companies and companies controlled by them.

(C) It shall be unlawful for any investment company (the "acquiring company") and any company or companies controlled by the acquiring company to purchase or otherwise acquire any security issued by a registered closed-end investment company, if immediately after such purchase or acquisition the acquiring company, other investment companies having the same investment adviser, and companies controlled by such investment companies, own more than 10 per centum of the total outstanding voting stock of such close-end company.

(D) The provisions of this paragraph shall not apply to a security received as a dividend or as a result of an offer of exchange approved pursuant to section 11 or of a plan of reorganization of any company (other than a plan devised for the purpose of evading the foregoing provisions).

(E) The provisions of this paragraph shall not apply to a security (or securities) purchased or acquired by an investment company if—

(i) the depositor of, or principal underwriter for, such investment company is a broker or dealer registered under the Securities Exchange Act of 1934, or a person controlled by such a broker or dealer;

(ii) such security is the only investment security held by such investment company (or such securities are the only investment securities held by such investment company, if such investment company is a registered unit investment trust that issues two or more classes or series of securities, each of which provides for the accumulation of shares of a different investment company); and

(iii) the purchase or acquisition is made pursuant to an arrangement with the issuer of, or principal underwriter for, the issuer of the security whereby such investment company is obligated—

(aa) either to seek instructions from its security holders with regard to the voting of all proxies with respect to such security and to vote such proxies only in accordance with such instructions, or to vote the shares held by it in the same proportion as the vote of all other holders of such security, and

(bb) in the event that such investment company is not a registered investment company, to refrain from substituting such security unless the Commission shall have approved such substitution in the manner provided in section 26 of this Act.

(F) The provisions of this paragraph shall not apply to securities purchased or otherwise acquired by a registered investment company if—

(i) immediately after such purchase or acquisition not more than 3 per centum of the total outstanding stock of such issuer is owned by such registered investment company and all affiliated persons of such registered investment company; and

(ii) such registered investment company has not offered or sold after January 1, 1971, and is not proposing to offer or sell any security issued by it through a principal underwriter or otherwise at a public offering price which includes a sales load of more than $1\frac{1}{2}$ per centum.

No issuer of any security purchased or acquired by a registered investment company pursuant to this subparagraph shall be obligated to redeem such security in an amount exceeding 1 per centum of such issuer's total outstanding securities during any period of less than thirty days. Such investment company shall exercise voting rights by proxy or otherwise with respect to any security purchased or acquired pursuant to this subparagraph in the manner prescibed by subparagraph (E) of this subsection.

(G)(i) This paragraph does not apply to securities of a registered open-end investment company or a registered unit investment trust (hereafter in this subparagraph referred to as the "acquired company") purchased or otherwise acquired by a registered open-end investment company or a registered unit investment trust (hereafter in this subparagraph referred to as the "acquiring company") if—

(I) the acquired company and the acquiring company are part of the same group of investment companies;

(II) the securities of the acquired company, securities of other registered open-end investment companies and registered unit investment trusts that are part of the same group of investment companies, Government securities, and short-term paper are the only investments held by the acquiring company;

(III) with respect to—

(aa) securities of the acquired company, the acquiring company does not pay and is not assessed any charges or fees for distribution-related activities, unless the acquiring company does not charge a sales load or other fees or charges for distribution-related activities; or

(bb) securities of the acquiring company, any sales loads and other distribution-related fees charged, when aggregated with any sales load and distribution-related fees paid by the acquiring company with respect to securities of the acquired company, are not excessive under rules adopted pursuant to section 22(b) or section 22(c) by a securities association registered under section 15A of the Securities Exchange Act of 1934, or the Commission;

(IV) the acquired company has a policy that prohibits it from acquiring any securities of registered open-end investment companies or registered unit investment trusts in reliance on this subparagraph or subparagraph (F); and

(V) such acquisition is not in contravention of such rules and regulations as the Commission may from time to time prescribe with respect to acquisitions in accordance with this subparagraph, as necessary and appropriate for the protection of investors.

(ii) For purposes of this subparagraph, the term "group of investment companies" means any 2 or more registered investment companies that hold themselves out to investors as related companies for purposes of investment and investor services.

(H) For the purposes of this paragraph, the value of an investment company's total assets shall be computed as of the time of a purchase or acquisition or as closely thereto as is reasonably possible.

(I) In any action brought to enforce the provisions of this paragraph, the Commission may join as a party the issuer of any security purchased or otherwise acquired in violation of this paragraph (1), and the court may issue any order with respect to such issuer as may be necessary or appropriate for the enforcement of the provisions of this paragraph.

(J) The Commission, by rule or regulation, upon its own motion or by order upon application, may conditionally or unconditionally exempt any person, security, or transaction, or any class or classes of persons, securities, or transactions from any provision of this paragraph, if and to the extent that such exemption is consistent with the public interest and the protection of investors.

[Ownership of Outstanding Voting Stock of Insurance Companies]

(2) It shall be unlawful for any registered investment company and any company or companies controlled by such registered investment company to purchase or otherwise acquire any security (except a security received as a dividend or as a result of a plan of reorganization of any company, other than a plan devised for the purpose of evading the provisions of this paragraph) issued by any insurance company of which such registered investment company and any company or companies controlled by such registered company do not, at the time of such purchase or acquisition, own in the aggregate at least 25 per centum of the total outstanding voting stock, if such registered company and any company or companies controlled by it own in the aggregate, or as a result of such purchase or acquisition will own in the aggregate, more than 10 per centum of the total outstanding voting stock of such insurance company.

[Brokers, Dealers, Underwriters or Investment Advisers]

(3) It shall be unlawful for any registered investment company and any company or companies controlled by such registered investment company to purchase or otherwise acquire any security issued by or any other interest in the business of any person who is a broker, a dealer, is

engaged in the business of underwriting, or is either an investment adviser of an investment company or an investment adviser registered under title II of this Act, unless (A) such person is a corporation all the outstanding securities of which (other than short-term paper, securities representing bank loans, and directors' qualifying shares) are, or after such acquisition will be, owned by one or more registered investment companies; and (B) such person is primarily engaged in the business of underwriting and distributing securities issued by other persons, selling securities to customers, or any one or more of such or related activities, and the gross income of such person normally is derived principally from such business or related activities.

(e) Notwithstanding any provisions of this title, any registered investment company may hereafter purchase or otherwise acquire any security issued by any one corporation engaged or proposing to engage in the business of underwriting, furnishing capital to industry, financing promotional enterprises, purchasing securities of issuers for which no ready market is in existence, and reorganizing companies or similar activities; provided—

(1) That the securities issued by such corporation (other than short-term paper and securities representing bank loans) shall consist solely of one class of common stock and shall have been originally issued or sold for investment to registered investment companies only;

(2) That the aggregate cost of the securities of such corporation purchased by such registered investment company does not exceed 5 per centum of the value of the total assets of such registered company at the time of any purchase or acquisition of such securities; and

(3) That the aggregate paid-in capital and surplus of such corporation does not exceed $100,000,000.

For the purpose of paragraph (1) of section 5(b) any investment in any such corporation shall be deemed to be an investment in an investment company.

(f) Notwithstanding any provisions of this Act, any registered face-amount certificate company may organize not more than two face-amount certificate companies and acquire and own all or any part of the capital stock thereof only if such stock is acquired and held for investment: *Provided,* That the aggregate cost to such registered company of all such stock so acquired shall not exceed six times the amount of the minimum capital stock requirement provided in subdivision (1) of subsection (a) of section 28 for a face-amount company organized on or after March 15, 1940: *And provided further,* That the aggregate cost to such registered company of all such capital stock issued by face-amount certificate companies organized or otherwise created under laws other than the laws of the United States or any State thereof shall not exceed twice the amount of the minimum capital stock requirement provided in subdivision (1) of subsection (a) of section 28 for a company organized on or after March 15, 1940. Nothing contained in this subsection shall be deemed to prevent the sale of any such stock to any other person if the original purchase was made by such registered face-amount certificate company in good faith for investment and not for resale.

(g) Notwithstanding the provisions of this section any registered investment company and any company or companies controlled by such registered company may purchase or otherwise acquire from another investment company or any company or companies controlled by such registered company more than 10 per centum of the total outstanding voting stock of any insurance company owned by any such company or companies, or may acquire the securities of any insurance company if the Commission by order determines that such acquisition is in the public interest because the financial condition of such insurance company will be improved as a result of such acquisition or any plan contemplated as a result thereof. This section shall not be deemed to prohibit the promotion of a new insurance company or the acquisition of the securities of any newly created insurance company by a registered investment company, alone or with other persons. Nothing contained in this section shall in any way affect or derogate from the powers of any insurance commissioner or similar official or agency of the United States or any State, or to affect the right under State law of any insurance company to acquire securities of any other insurance company or insurance companies.

Sec. 13. CHANGES IN INVESTMENT POLICY

(a) No registered investment company shall, unless authorized by the vote of a majority of its outstanding voting securities—

(1) change its subclassification as defined in section 5(a)(1) and (2) of this title or its subclassification from a diversified to a nondiversified company;

(2) borrow money, issue senior securities, underwrite securities issued by other persons, purchase or sell real estate or commodities or make loans to other persons, except in each case in accordance with the recitals of policy contained in its registration statement in respect thereto;

(3) deviate from its policy in respect of concentration of investments in any particular industry or group of industries as recited in its registration statement, deviate from any investment policy which is changeable only if authorized by shareholder vote, or deviate from any policy recited in its registration statement pursuant to section 8(b)(3);

(4) change the nature of its business so as to cease to be an investment company.

(b) In the case of a common-law trust of the character described in section 16(c), either written approval by holders of a majority of the outstanding shares of beneficial interest or the vote of a majority of such outstanding shares cast in person or by proxy at a meeting called for the purpose shall for the purposes of subsection (a) be deemed the equivalent of the vote of a majority of the outstanding voting securities, and the provisions of paragraph (42) of section 2(a) as to a majority shall be applicable to the votes cast at such a meeting.

Sec. 15. INVESTMENT ADVISORY AND UNDERWRITING CONTRACTS

(a) It shall be unlawful for any person to serve or act as investment advisor of a registered investment company, except pursuant to a written contract, which contract, whether with such registered company or with an investment adviser of such registered company, has been approved by the vote of a majority of the outstanding voting securities of such registered company, and—

(1) precisely describes all compensation to be paid thereunder;

(2) shall continue in effect for a period more than two years from the date of its execution, only so long as such continuance is specifically approved at least annually by the board of directors or by vote of a majority of the outstanding voting securities of such company;

(3) provides, in substance, that it may be terminated at any time, without the payment of any penalty, by the board of directors of such registered company or by vote of a majority of the outstanding voting securities of such company on not more than sixty days' written notice to the investment adviser; and

(4) provides, in substance, for its automatic termination in the event of its assignment.

(b) It shall be unlawful for any principal underwriter for a registered open-end company to offer for sale, sell, or deliver after sale any security of which such company is the issuer, except pursuant to a written contract with such company, which contract—

(1) shall continue in effect for a period, more than two years from the date of its execution, only so long as such continuance is specifically approved at least annually by the board of directors or by vote of a majority of the outstanding voting securities of such company; and

(2) provides, in substance, for its automatic termination in the event of its assignment.

(c) In addition to the requirements of subsection (a) and (b) of this section, it shall be unlawful for any registered investment company having a board of directors to enter into, renew, or perform any contract or agreement, written or oral, whereby a person undertakes regularly to serve or act as investment adviser of or principal underwriter for such company unless the terms of such contract or agreement and any renewal thereof have been approved by the vote of a majority of directors, who are not parties to such contract or agreement or interested persons of any such party, cast in person at a meeting called for the purpose of voting on such approval. It shall be the duty of the directors of a registered investment company to request and evaluate, and the duty of an investment adviser to such company to furnish, such information as may reasonably be necessary to evaluate the terms of any contract whereby a person undertakes regularly to serve or act as investment adviser of such company. It shall be unlawful for the directors of a registered investment company, in connection with their evaluation of the terms of any contract whereby a person undertakes regularly to serve or act as investment adviser of such company, to take into account the purchase price or other consideration any person may have paid in connection with a transaction of the type referred to in paragraph (1), (3), or (4) of subsection (f).

(d) In the case of a common-law trust of the character described in section 16(c), either written approval by holders of a majority of the outstanding shares of beneficial interest or the vote of a majority of such outstanding shares cast in person or by proxy at a meeting called for the purpose shall for the purposes of this section be deemed the equivalent of the vote of a majority of the outstanding voting securities, and the provisions of paragraph (42) of section 2(a) as to a majority shall be applicable to the vote cast at such a meeting.

(e) Nothing contained in this section shall be deemed to require or contemplate any action by an advisory board of any registered company or by any of the members of such a board.

(f)(1) An investment adviser, or a corporate trustee performing the functions of an investment adviser, of a registered investment company or an affiliated person of such investment adviser or corporate trustee may receive any amount or benefit in connection with a sale of securities of, or a sale of any other interest in, such investment adviser or corporate trustee which results in an assignment of an investment advisory contract with such company or the change in control of or identity of such corporate trustee, if—

(A) for a period of three years after the time of such action, at least 75 per centum of the members of the board of directors of such registered company or such corporate trustee (or successor thereto, by reorganization or otherwise) are not (i) interested persons of the investment adviser of such company or such corporate trustee, or (ii) interested persons of the predecessor investment adviser or such corporate trustee; and

(B) there is not imposed an unfair burden on such company as a result of such transactions or any express or implied terms, conditions, or understandings applicable thereto.

(2)(A) For the purpose of paragraph (1)(A) of this subsection, interested persons of a corporate trustee shall be determined in accordance with section 2(a)(19)(B): Provided, That no person shall be deemed to be an interested person of a corporate trustee solely by reason of (i) his being a member of its board of directors or advisory board or (ii) his membership in the immediate family of any person specified in clause (i) of this subparagraph.

(B) For the purpose of paragraph (1)(B) of this subsection, an unfair burden on a registered investment company includes any arrangement, during the two-year period after the date on which any such transaction occurs, whereby the investment adviser or corporate trustee or predecessor or successor investment advisers or corporate trustee or any interested person of any such adviser or any such corporate trustee receives or is entitled to receive any compensation directly or indirectly (i) from any person in connection with the purchase or sale of securities or other property to, from, or on behalf of such company, other than bona fide ordinary compensation as principal underwriter for such company, or (ii) from such company or its security holders for other than bona fide investment advisory or other services.

(3) If—

(A) an assignment of an investment advisory contract with a registered investment company results in a successor investment adviser to such company, or if there is a change in control of or identity of a corporate trustee of a registered investment company, and such adviser or trustee is then an investment adviser or corporate trustee with respect to other assets substantially greater in amount than the amount of assets of such company, or

(B) as a result of a merger of, or a sale of substantially all the assets by, a registered investment company with or to another registered investment company with assets substantially greater in amount, a transaction occurs which would be subject to paragraph (1)(A) of this subsection,

such discrepancy in size of assets shall be considered by the Commission in determining whether or to what extent an application under section 6(c) for exemption from the provisions of paragraph (1)(A) should be granted.

(4) Paragraph (1)(A) of this section shall not apply to a transaction in which a controlling block of outstanding voting securities of an investment adviser to a registered investment company or of a corporate trustee performing the functions of an investment adviser to a registered investment company is—

(A) distributed to the public and in which there is, in fact, no change in the identity of the persons who control such investment adviser or corporate trustee, or

(B) transferred to the investment adviser or the corporate trustee, or an affiliated person or persons of such investment adviser or corporate trustee, or is transferred from the investment adviser or corporate trustee to an affiliated person or persons of the investment adviser or corporate trustee: Provided, That (i) each transferee (other than such adviser or trustee) is a natural person and (ii) the transferees (other than such adviser or trustee) owned in the aggregate more than 25 per centum of such voting securities for a period of at least six months prior to such transfer.

Sec. 17. TRANSACTIONS OF CERTAIN AFFILIATED PERSONS AND UNDERWRITERS

(a) It shall be unlawful for any affiliated person or promoter of or principal underwriter for a registered investment company (other than a company of the character described in section 12(d)(3)(A) and (B), or any affiliated person of such a person, promoter, or principal underwriter, acting as principal—

(1) knowingly to sell any security or other property to such registered company or to any company controlled by such registered company, unless such sale involves solely (A) securities of which the buyer is the issuer, (B) securities of which the seller is the issuer and which are part of a general offering to the holders of a class of its securities, or (C) securities deposited with the trustee of a unit investment trust or periodic payment plan by the depositor thereof;

(2) knowingly to purchase from such registered company, or from any company controlled by such registered company, any security or other property (except securities of which the seller is the issuer);

(3) to borrow money or other property from such registered company or from any company controlled by such registered company (unless the borrower is controlled by the lender) except as permitted in section 21(b); or

(4) to loan money or other property to such registered company, or to any company controlled by such registered company, in contravention of such rules, regulations, or orders as the Commission may, after consultation with and taking into consideration the views of the Federal banking agencies (as defined in section 3 of the Federal Deposit Insurance Act), prescribe or issue consistent with the protection of investors.

(b) Notwithstanding subsection (a), any person may file with the Commission an application for an order exempting a proposed transaction of the applicant from one or more provisions of that subsection. The Commission shall grant such application and issue such order of exemption if evidence establishes that—

(1) the terms of the proposed transaction, including the consideration to be paid or received, are reasonable and fair and do not involve overreaching on the part of any person concerned;

(2) the proposed transaction is consistent with the policy of each registered investment company concerned, as recited in its registration statement and reports filed under this title; and

(3) the proposed transaction is consistent with the general purposes of this title.

(c) Notwithstanding subsection (a), a person may, in the ordinary course of business, sell to or purchase from any company merchandise or may enter into a lessor-lessee relationship with any person and furnish the services incident thereto.

(d) It shall be unlawful for any affiliated person of or principal underwriter for a registered investment company (other than a company of the character described in section 12(d)(3)(A) and (B)), or any affiliated person of such a person or principal underwriter, acting as principal to effect any transaction in which such registered company, or a company controlled by such registered company, is a joint or a joint and several participant with such person, principal underwriter, or affiliated person, in contravention of such rules and regulations as the Commission may prescribe for the purpose of limiting or preventing participation by such registered or controlled company on a basis different from or less advantageous than that of such other participant. Nothing contained in this subsection shall be deemed to preclude any affiliated person from acting as manager of any underwriting syndicate or other group in which such registered or controlled company is a participant and receiving compensation therefor.

(e) It shall be unlawful for any affiliated person of a registered investment company, or any affiliated person of such person—

(1) acting as agent, to accept from any source any compensation (other than a regular salary or wages from such registered company) for the purchase or sale of any property to or for such registered company or any controlled company thereof, except in the course of such person's business as an underwriter or broker; or

(2) acting as broker, in connection with the sale of securities to or by such registered company or any controlled company thereof, to receive from any source a commission, fee, or other remuneration for effecting such transaction which exceeds (A) the usual and customary broker's commission if the sale is effected on a securities exchange, or (B) 2 per centum of the sales price if the sale is effected in connection with a secondary distribution of such securities, or (C) 1 per centum of the purchase or sale price of such securities if the sale is otherwise effected unless the Commission shall, by rules and regulations or order in the public interest and consistent with the protection of investors, permit a larger commission.

(f) CUSTODY OF SECURITIES.—

(1) Every registered management company shall place and maintain its securities and similar investments in the custody of (A) a bank or banks having the qualification prescribed in paragraph (1) of section 26(a) of this title for the trustees of unit investment trusts; or (B) a company which is a member of a national securities exchange as defined in the Securities Exchange Act of 1934, subject to such rules and regulations as the Commission may from time to time prescribe for the protection of investors; or (C) such registered company, but only in accordance with such rules and regulations or orders as the Commission may from time to time prescribe for the protection of investors.

(2) Subject to such rules, regulations, and orders as the Commission may adopt as necessary or appropriate for the protection of investors, a registered management company or any such custodian, with the consent of the registered management company for which it acts as custodian, may deposit all or any part of the securities owned by such registered management company in a system for the central handling of securities established by a national securities exchange or national securities association registered with the Commission under the Securities Exchange Act of 1934, or such other person as may be permitted by the Commission, pursuant to which system all securities of any particular class or series of any issuer deposited within the system are treated as fungible and may be transferred or pledged by bookkeeping entry without physical delivery of such securities.

(3) Rules, regulations, and orders of the Commission under this subsection, among other things, may make appropriate provision with respect to such matters as the earmarking, segregation, and hypothecation of such securities and investments, and may provide for or require periodic or other inspections by any or all of the following: Independent public accountants, employees and agents of the Commission, and such other persons as the Commission may designate.

(4) No such member of a national securities exchange which trades in securities for its own account may act as custodian except in accordance with rules and regulations prescribed by the Commission for the protection of investors.

(5) If a registered company maintains its securities and similar investments in the custody of a qualified bank or banks, the cash proceeds from the sale of such securities and similar investments and other cash assets of the company shall likewise be kept in the custody of such a bank or banks, or in accordance with such rules and regulations or orders as the Commission may from time to time prescribe for the protection of investors, except that such a registered company

may maintain a checking account in a bank or banks having the qualifications prescribed in paragraph (1) of section 26(a) of this title for the trustees of unit investment trusts with the balance of such account or the aggregate balances of such accounts at no time in excess of the amount of the fidelity bond, maintained pursuant to section 17(g) of this title, covering the officers or employees authorized to draw on such account or accounts.

(6) The Commission may, after consultation with and taking into consideration the views of the Federal banking agencies (as defined in section 3 of the Federal Deposit Insurance Act), adopt rules and regulations, and issue orders, consistent with the protection of investors, prescribing the conditions under which a bank, or an affiliated person of a bank, either of which is an affiliated person, promoter, organizer, or sponsor of, or principal underwriter for, a registered management company, may serve as custodian of that registered management company.

(g) The Commission is authorized to require by rules and regulations or orders for the protection of investors that any officer or employee of a registered management investment company who may singly, or jointly with others, have access to securities or funds of any registered company, either directly or through authority to draw upon such funds or to direct generally the disposition of such securities (unless the officer or employee has such access solely through his position as an officer or employee of a bank) be bonded by a reputable fidelity insurance company against larceny and embezzlement in such reasonable minimum amounts as the Commission may prescribe.

(h) After one year from the effective date of this title, neither the charter, certificate of incorporation, articles of association, indenture of trust, nor the by-laws of any registered investment company, nor any other instrument pursuant to which such a company is organized or administered, shall contain any provision which protects or purports to protect any director or officer of such company against any liability to the company or to its security holders to which he would otherwise be subject by reason of willful misfeasance, bad faith, gross negligence or reckless disregard of the duties involved in the conduct of his office.

(i) After one year from the effective date of this title no contract or agreement under which any person undertakes to act as investment adviser of, or principal underwriter for, a registered investment company shall contain any provision which protects or purports to protect such person against any liability to such company or its security holders to which he would otherwise be subject by reason of willful misfeasance, bad faith, or gross negligence, in the performance of his duties, or by reason of his reckless disregard of his obligations and duties under such contract or agreement.

(j) It shall be unlawful for any affiliated person of or principal underwriter for a registered investment company or any affiliated person of an investment adviser of or principal underwriter for a registered investment company, to engage in any act, practice, or course of business in connection with the purchase or sale, directly or indirectly, by such person of any security held or to be acquired by such registered investment company in contravention of such rules and regulations as the Commission may adopt to define, and prescribe means reasonably necessary to prevent, such acts, practices, or courses of business as are fraudulent, deceptive or manipulative. Such rules and regulations may include requirements for the adoption of codes of ethics by registered investment companies and investment advisers of, and principal underwriters for, such investment companies establishing such standards as are reasonably necessary to prevent such acts, practices, or courses of business.

Sec. 18. CAPITAL STRUCTURE

(a) It shall be unlawful for any registered closed-end company to issue any class of senior security, or to sell any such security of which it is the issuer, unless—

(1) if such class of senior security represents an indebtedness—

(A) immediately after such issuance or sale, it will have an asset coverage of at least 300 per centum;

(B) provision is made to prohibit the declaration of any dividend (except a dividend payable in stock of the issuer), or the declaration of any other distribution, upon any class of the capital stock of such investment company, or the purchase of any such capital stock, unless, in every such case, such class of senior securities has at the time of the declaration of any such dividend or distribution or at the time of any such purchase an asset coverage of at least 300 per centum after deducting the amount of such dividend, distribution, or purchase price, as the case may be, except that dividends may be declared upon any preferred stock if such senior security representing indebtedness has an asset coverage of at least 200 per centum at the time of declaration thereof after deducting the amount of such dividend; and

(C) provision is made either—

(i) that, if on the last business day of each of twelve consecutive calendar months such class of senior securities shall have an asset coverage of less than 100 per centum, the holders of such securities voting as a class shall be entitled to elect at least a majority of the members of the board of directors of such registered company, such voting right to continue until such class of senior security shall have an asset coverage of 110 per centum or more on the last business day of each of three consecutive calendar months, or

(ii) that, if on the last business day of each of twenty-four consecutive calendar months such class of senior securities shall have an asset coverage of less than 100 per centum, an event of default shall be deemed to have occurred;

(2) if such class of senior security is a stock—

(A) immediately after such issuance or sale it will have an asset coverage of at least 200 per centum;

(B) provision is made to prohibit the declaration of any dividend (except a dividend payable in common stock of the issuer), or the declaration of any other distribution, upon the common stock of such investment company, or the purchase of any such common stock, unless in every such case such class of senior security has at the time of the declaration of any such dividend or distribution or at the time of any such purchase an asset coverage of at least 200 per centum after deducting the amount of such dividend, distribution or purchase price, as the case may be;

(C) provision is made to entitle the holders of such senior securities, voting as a class, to elect at least two directors at all times, and, subject to the prior rights, if any, of the holders of any other class of senior securities outstanding, to elect a majority of the directors if at any time dividends on such class of securities shall be unpaid in an amount equal to two full years' dividends on such securities, and to continue to be so represented until all dividends in arrears shall have been paid or otherwise provided for;

(D) provision is made requiring approval by the vote of a majority of such securities, voting as a class, of any plan of reorganization adversely affecting such securities or of any action requiring a vote of security holders as in section 13(a) provided; and

(E) such class of stock shall have complete priority over any other class as to distribution of assets and payment of dividends, which dividends shall be cumulative.

(b) The asset coverage in respect of a senior security provided for in subsection (a) may be determined on the basis of values calculated as of a time within forty-eight hours (not including Sundays or holidays) next preceding the time of such determination. The time of issue or sale shall, in the case of an offering of such securities to existing stockholders of the issuer, be deemed to be the first date on which such offering is made, and in all other cases shall be deemed to be the time, as of which a firm commitment to issue or sell and to take or purchase such securities shall be made.

(c) Notwithstanding the provisions of subsection (a) it shall be unlawful for any registered closed-end investment company to issue or sell any senior security representing indebtedness if immediately thereafter such company will have outstanding more than one class of senior security representing indebtedness, or to issue or sell any senior security which is a stock if immediately thereafter such company will have outstanding more than one class of senior security which is a stock, except that (1) any such class of indebtedness or stock may be issued in one or more series: *Provided,* That no such series shall have a preference or priority over any other series upon the distribution of the assets of such registered closed-end company or in respect of the payment of interest or dividends, and (2) promissory notes or other evidences of indebtedness issued in consideration of any loan, extension, or renewal thereof, made by a bank or other person and privately arranged, and not intended to be publicly distributed, shall not be deemed to be a separate class of senior securities representing indebtedness within the meaning of this subsection (c).

(d) It shall be unlawful for any registered management company to issue any warrant or right to subscribe to or purchase a security of which such company is the issuer, except in the form of warrants or rights to subscribe expiring not later than one hundred and twenty days after their issuance and issued exclusively and ratably to a class or classes of such company's security holders; except that any warrant may be issued in exchange for outstanding warrants in connection with a plan of reorganization.

(e) The provisions of this section 18 shall not apply to any senior securities issued or sold by any registered closed-end company—

(1) for the purpose of refunding through payment, purchase, redemption, retirement, or exchange, any senior security of such registered investment company except that no senior security representing indebtedness shall be so issued or sold for the purpose of refunding any senior security which is a stock; or

(2) pursuant to any plan of reorganization (other than for refunding as referred to in paragraph (1) of this subsection), provided—

(A) that such senior securities are issued or sold for the purpose of substituting or exchanging such senior securities for outstanding senior securities, and if such senior securities represent indebtedness they are issued or sold for the purpose of substituting or exchanging such senior securities for outstanding senior securities representing indebtedness, of any registered investment company which is a party to such plan of reorganization; or

(B) that the total amount of such senior securities so issued or sold pursuant to such plan does not exceed the total amount of senior securities of all the companies which are parties to such plan, and the total amount of senior securities representing indebtedness so issued or sold pursuant to such plan does not exceed the total amount of senior securities representing indebtedness of all such companies, or, alternatively, the total amount of such senior securities so issued or sold pursuant to such plan does not have the effect of increasing the ratio of senior securities representing indebtedness to the securities representing stock or the ratio of senior securities representing stock to securities junior thereto when compared with such ratios as they existed before such reorganization.

(f) (1) It shall be unlawful for any registered open-end company to issue any class of senior security or to sell any senior security of which it is the issuer, except that any such registered company shall be permitted to borrow from any bank: *Provided,* that immediately after any such borrowing there is an asset coverage of at least 300 per centum for all borrowings of such registered company: *And provided further,* that in the event that such asset coverage shall at any time fall below 300 per centum such registered company shall, within three days thereafter (not including Sundays and holidays) or such longer period as the Commission may prescribe by rules and regulations, reduce the amount of its borrowings to an extent that the asset coverage of such borrowings shall be at least 300 per centum.

(2) "Senior security" shall not, in the case of a registered open-end company, include a class or classes or a number of series of preferred or special stock each of which is preferred over all other classes or series in respect of assets specifically allocated to that class or series: *Provided,* That (A) such company has outstanding no class or series of stock which is not so preferred over all other classes or series, or (B) the only other outstanding class of the issuer's stock consists of a common stock upon which no dividend (other than a liquidating dividend) is permitted to be paid and which in the aggregate represents not more than one-half of 1 per centum of the issuer's outstanding voting securities. For the purpose of insuring fair and equitable treatment of the holders of the outstanding voting securities of each class or series of stock of such company, the Commission may by rule, regulation, or order direct that any matter required to be submitted to the holders of the outstanding voting securities of such company shall not be deemed to have been effectively acted upon unless approved by the holders of such percentage (not exceeding a

majority) of the outstanding voting securities of each class or series of stock affected by such matter as shall be prescribed in such rule, regulation, or order.

(g) Unless otherwise provided: "Senior security" means any bond, debenture, note, or similar obligation or instrument constituting a security and evidencing indebtedness, and any stock of a class having priority over any other class as to distribution of assets or payment of dividends; and "senior security representing indebtedness" means any senior security other than stock.

The term "senior security" when used in subparagraphs (B) and (C) of paragraph (1) of subsection (a), shall not include any promissory note or other evidence of indebtedness issued in consideration of any loan, extension, or renewal thereof, made by a bank or other person and privately arranged, and not intended to be publicly distributed; nor shall such term, when used in this section 18, include any such promissory note or other evidence of indebtedness in any case where such a loan is for temporary purposes only and in an amount not exceeding 5 per centum of the value of the total assets of the issuer at the time when the loan is made. A loan shall be presumed to be for temporary purposes if it is repaid within sixty days and is not extended or renewed; otherwise it shall be presumed not to be for temporary purposes. Any such presumption may be rebutted by evidence.

(h) "Asset coverage" of a class of senior security representing an indebtedness of an issuer means the ratio which the value of the total assets of such issuer, less all liabilities and indebtedness not represented by senior securities, bears to the aggregate amount of senior securities representing indebtedness of such issuer. "Asset coverage" of a class of senior security of an issuer which is a stock means the ratio which the value of the total assets of such issuer, less all liabilities and indebtedness not represented by senior securities, bears to the aggregate amount of senior securities representing indebtedness of such issuer plus the aggregate of the involuntary liquidation preference of such class of senior security which is a stock. The involuntary liquidation preference of a class of senior security which is a stock shall be deemed to mean the amount to which such class of senior security would be entitled on involuntary liquidation of the issuer in preference to a security junior to it.

(i) Except as provided in subsection (a) of this section, or as otherwise required by law, every share of stock hereafter issued by a registered management company (except a common-law trust of the character described in section 16(c)) shall be a voting stock and have equal voting rights with every other outstanding voting stock: *Provided,* That this subsection shall not apply to shares issued pursuant to the terms of any warrant or subscription right outstanding on March 15, 1940, or any firm contract entered into before March 15, 1940, to purchase such securities from such company nor to shares issued in accordance with any rules, regulations, or orders which the Commission may make permitting such issue.

(j) Notwithstanding any provision of this title, it shall be unlawful, after the date of enactment of this title, for any registered face-amount certificate company—

(1) to issue, except in accordance with such rules, regulations, or orders as the Commission may prescribe in the public interest or as necessary or appropriate for the protection of investors, any security other than (A) a face-amount certificate; (B) a common stock having a par value and being without preference as to dividends or distributions and having at least equal voting rights with any outstanding security of such company; or (C) short-term payment or promissory notes or other indebtedness issued in consideration of any loan, extension, or renewal thereof, made by a bank or other person and privately arranged and not intended to be publicly offered;

(2) if such company has outstanding any security, other than such face-amount certificates, common stock, promissory notes, or other evidence of indebtedness, to make any distribution or declare or pay any dividend on any capital security in contravention of such rules and regulations or orders as the Commission may prescribe in the public interest or as necessary or appropriate for the protection of investors or to insure the financial integrity of such company, to prevent the impairment of the company's ability to meet its obligations upon its face-amount certificates; or

(3) to issue any of its securities except for cash or securities including securities of which such company is the issuer.

(k) The provisions of subparagraphs (A) and (B) of paragraph (1) of subsection (a) of this section shall not apply to investment companies operating under the Small Business Investment Act of 1958, and the provisions of paragraph (2) of said subsection shall not apply to such companies so long as such class of senior security shall be held or guaranteed by the Small Business Administration.

Sec. 22. DISTRIBUTION, REDEMPTION, AND REPURCHASE OF REDEEMABLE SECURITIES

(a) A securities association registered under section 15A of the Securities Exchange Act of 1934 may prescribe, by rules adopted and in effect in accordance with said section and subject to all provisions of said section applicable to the rules of such an association—

(1) a method or methods for computing the minimum price at which a member thereof may purchase from any investment company any redeemable security issued by such company and the maximum price at which a member may sell to such company any redeemable security issued by it or which he may receive for such security upon redemption, so that the price in each case will bear such relation to the current net asset value of such security computed as of such time as the rules may prescribe; and

(2) a minimum period of time which must elapse after the sale or issue of such security before any resale to such company by a member or its redemption upon surrender by a member;

[(a) continued] in each case for the purpose of eliminating or reducing so far as reasonably practicable any dilution of the value of other outstanding securities of such company or any other result of such purchase, redemption, or sale which is unfair to holders of such other outstanding securities; and said rules may prohibit the members of the association from purchasing, selling, or surrendering for redemption any such redeemable securities in contravention of said rules.

(b) (1) Such a securities association may also, by rules adopted and in effect in accordance with said section 15A, and notwithstanding the provisions of subsection (b) (6) thereof but subject to all other provisions of said section applicable to the rules of such an association, prohibit its members from purchasing, in connection with a primary distribution of redeemable securities of which any registered investment company is the issuer, any such security from the issuer or from any principal underwriter except at a price equal to the price at which such security is then offered to the public less a commission, discount, or spread which is computed in conformity with a method or methods, and within such limitations as to the relation thereof to said public offering price, as such rules may prescribe in order that the price at which such security is offered or sold to the public shall not include an excessive sales load but shall allow for reasonable compensation for sales personnel, broker-dealers, and underwriters, and for reasonable sales loads to investors. The Commission shall on application or otherwise, if it appears that smaller companies are subject to relatively higher operating costs, make due allowance therefor by granting any such company or class of companies appropriate qualified exemptions from the provisions of this section.

(2) At any time after the expiration of eighteen months from the date of enactment of the Investment Company Amendments Act of 1970, the Commission may alter or supplement the rules of any securities association as may be necessary to effectuate the purposes of this subsection in the manner provided by section 19(c) of the Securities Exchange Act of 1934.

(3) If any provision of this subsection is in conflict with any provision of any law of the United States in effect on the date this subsection takes effect, the provisions of this subsection shall prevail.

(c) The Commission may make rules and regulations applicable to registered investment companies and to principal underwriters of, and dealers in, the redeemable securities of any registered investment company, whether or not members of any securities association, to the same extent, covering the same subject matter, and for the accomplishment of the same ends as are prescribed in subsection (a) of this section in respect of the rules which may be made by a registered securities association governing its members. Any rules and regulations so made by the Commission, to the extent that they may be inconsistent with the rules of any such association, shall so long as they remain in force supersede the rules of the association and be binding upon its members as well as all other underwriters and dealers to whom they may be applicable.

(d) No registered investment company shall sell any redeemable security issued by it to any person except either to or through a principal underwriter for distribution or at a current public offering price described in the prospectus, and, if such class of security is being currently offered to the public by or through an underwriter, no principal underwriter of such security and no dealer shall sell any such security to any person except a dealer, a principal underwriter, or the issuer, except at a current public offering price described in the prospectus. Nothing in this subsection shall prevent a sale made (i) pursuant to an offer of exchange permitted by section 11 including any offer made pursuant to section 11(b); (ii) pursuant to an offer made solely to all registered holders of the securities, or of a particular class or series of securities issued by the company proportionate to their holdings or proportionate to any cash distribution made to them by the company (subject to appropriate qualifications designed solely to avoid issuance of fractional securities); or (iii) in accordance with rules and regulations of the Commission made pursuant to subsection (b) of section 12.

(e) No registered investment company shall suspend the right of redemption, or postpone the date of payment or satisfaction upon redemption of any redeemable security in accordance with its terms for more than seven days after the tender of such security to the company or its agent designated for that purpose for redemption, except—

(1) for any period (A) during which the New York Stock Exchange is closed other than customary week-end and holiday closings or (B) during which trading on the New York Stock Exchange is restricted;

(2) for any period during which an emergency exists as a result of which (A) disposal by the company of securities owned by it is not reasonably practicable or (B) it is not reasonably practicable for such company fairly to determine the value of its net assets; or

(3) for such other periods as the Commission may by order permit for the protection of security holders of the company.

The Commission shall by rules and regulations determine the conditions under which (i) trading shall be deemed to be restricted and (ii) an emergency shall be deemed to exist within the meaning of this subsection.

(f) No registered open-end company shall restrict the transferability or negotiability of any security of which it is the issuer except in conformity with the statements with respect thereto contained in its registration statement nor in contravention of such rules and regulations as the Commission may prescribe in the interest of the holders of all of the outstanding securities of such investment company.

(g) No registered open-end company shall issue any of its securities (1) for services; or (2) for property other than cash or securities (including securities of which such registered company is the issuer), except as a dividend or distribution to its security holders or in connection with a reorganization.

Sec. 36. BREACH OF FIDUCIARY DUTY

(a) The Commission is authorized to bring an action in the proper district court of the United States, or in the Unites States court of any territory or other place subject to the jurisdiction of the United States, alleging that a person serving or acting in one or more of the following capacities has engaged within five years of the commencement of the action or is about to engage in any act or practice constituting a breach of fiduciary duty involving personal misconduct in respect of any registered investment company for which such person so serves or acts—

(1) as officer, director, member of any advisory board, investment adviser, or depositor; or

(2) as principal underwriter, if such registered company is an open-end company, unit investment trust, or face-amount certificate company.

If such allegations are established, the court may enjoin such person from acting in any or all such capacities either permanently or temporarily and award such injunctive or other relief against such person as may be reasonable and appropriate in the circumstances, having due regard to the protection of investors and to the effectuation of the policies declared in section 1(b) of this title.

(b) For the purposes of this subsection, the investment adviser of a registered investment company shall be deemed to have a fiduciary duty with respect to the receipt of compensation for services, or of payments of a material nature, paid by such registered investment company, or by the security holders therof, to such investment adviser or any affiliated person of such investment adviser. An action may be brought under this subsection by the Commission, or by a security holder of such registered investment company on behalf of such company, against such investment adviser, or any affiliated person of such investment adviser, or any other person enumerated in subsection (a) of this section who has a fiduciary duty concerning such compensation or payments, for breach of fiduciary duty in respect of such compensation or payments paid by such registered investment company or by the security holders thereof to such investment adviser or person. With respect to any such action the following provisions shall apply:

(1) It shall not be necessary to allege or prove that any defendant engaged in personal misconduct, and the plaintiff shall have the burden of proving a breach of fiduciary duty.

(2) In any such action approval by the board of directors of such investment company of such compensation or payments, or of contracts or other arrangements providing for such compensation or payments, and ratification or approval of such compensation or payments, or of contracts or other arrangements providing for such compensation or payments, by the shareholders of such investment company, shall be given such consideration by the court as is deemed appropriate under all the circumstances.

(3) No such action shall be brought or maintained against any person other than the recipient of such compensation or payments, and no damages or other relief shall be granted against any person other than the recipient of such compensation or payments. No award of damages shall be recoverable for any period prior to one year before the action was instituted. Any award of damages against such recipient shall be limited to the actual damages resulting from the breach of fiduciary duty and shall in no event exceed the amount of compensation or payments received from such investment company, or the security holders therof, by such recipient.

(4) This subsection shall not apply to compensation or payments made in connection with transactions subject to section 17 of this title, or rules, regulations, or orders thereunder, or to sales loads for the acquisition of any security issued by a registered investment company.

(5) Any action pursuant to this subsection may be brought only in an appropriate district court of the United States.

(6) No finding by a court with respect to a breach of fiduciary duty under this subsection shall be made a basis (A) for a finding of a violation of this title for the purposes of sections 9 and 49 of this title, section 15 of the Securities Exchange Act of 1934, or section 203 of title II of this Act, or (B) for an injunction to prohibit any person from serving in any of the capacities enumerated in subsection (a) of this section.

(c) For the purposes of subsections (a) and (b) the term "investment adviser" includes a corporate or other trustee performing the functions of an investment adviser.

Sec. 42. ENFORCEMENT OF TITLE

(a) The Commission may make such investigations as it deems necessary to determine whether any person has violated or is about to violate any provision of this title or of any rule, regulation, or order hereunder, or to determine whether any action in any court or any proceeding before the Commission shall be instituted under this title against a particular person or persons, or with respect to a particular transaction or transactions. The Commission shall permit any person to file with it a statement in writing, under oath or otherwise as the Commission shall determine, as to all the facts and circumstances concerning the matter to be investigated.

(b) For the purpose of any investigation or any other proceeding under this title, any member of the Commission, or any officer thereof designated by it, is empowered to administer oaths and affirmations, subpena witnesses, compel their attendance, take evidence, and require the production of any books, papers, correspondence, memoranda, contracts, agreements, or other records which are relevant or material to the inquiry. Such attendance of witnesses and the production of any such records may be required from any place in any State or in any Territory or other place subject to the jurisdiction of the United States at any designated place of hearing.

(c) In case of contumacy by, or refusal to obey a subpena issued to, any person, the Commission may invoke the aid of any court of the United States within the jurisdiction of which such investigation or proceeding is carried on, or where such person resides or carries on business, in requiring the attendance and testimony of witnesses and the production of books, papers, correspondence, memoranda, contracts, agreements, and other records. And such court may issue an order requiring such person to appear before the Commission or member or officer designated by the Commission, there to produce records, if so ordered, or to give testimony touching the matter under investigation or in question; any failure to obey such order of the court may be punished by such court as a contempt thereof. All process in any such case may be served in the judicial district whereof such person is an inhabitant or wherever he may be found. Any person who without just cause shall fail or refuse to attend and testify or to answer any lawful inquiry or to produce books, papers, correspondence, memoranda, contracts, agreements, or other records, if in his or its power so to do, in obedience to the subpena of the Commission, shall be guilty of a misdemeanor, and upon conviction shall be subject to a fine of not more than $1,000 or to imprisonment for a term of not more than one year, or both.

[Violations Enjoined]

(d) Whenever it shall appear to the Commission that any person has engaged or is about to engage in any act or practice constituting a violation of any provision of this title, or of any rule, regulation, or order hereunder, it may in its discretion bring an action in the proper district court of the United States, or the proper United States court of any Territory or other place subject to the jurisdiction of the United States, to enjoin such acts or practices and to enforce compliance with this title or any rule, regulation, or order hereunder. Upon a showing that such person has engaged or is about to engage in any such act or practice, a permanent or temporary injunction or decree or restraining order shall be granted without bond. In any proceeding under this subsection to enforce compliance with section 7, the court as a court of equity may, to the extent it deems necessary or appropriate, take exclusive jurisdiction and possession of the investment company or companies involved and the books, records, and assets thereof, wherever located; and the court shall have jurisdiction to appoint a trustee, who with the approval of the court shall have power to dispose of any or all of such assets, subject to such terms and conditions as the court may prescribe. The Commission may transmit such evidence as may be available concerning any violation of the provisions of this title, or of any rule, regulation, or order thereunder, the Attorney General, who, in his discretion, may institute the appropriate criminal proceedings under this title.

(e) MONEY PENALTIES IN CIVIL ACTIONS.—

(1) AUTHORITY OF COMMISSION.—Whenever it shall appear to the Commission that any person has violated any provision of this title, the rules or regulations thereunder, or a cease-and-desist order entered by the Commission pursuant to section 9(f) of this title, the Commission may bring an action in a United States district court to seek, and the court shall have jurisdiction to impose, upon a proper showing, a civil penalty to be paid by the person who committed such violation.

(2) AMOUNT OF PENALTY.—

(A) FIRST TIER.—The amount of the penalty shall be determined by the court in light of the facts and circumstances. For each violation, the amount of the penalty shall not exceed the greater of (i) $5,000 for a natural person or $50,000 for any other person, or (ii) the gross amount of pecuniary gain to such defendant as a result of the violation.

(B) SECOND TIER.—Notwithstanding subparagraph (A), the amount of penalty for each such violation shall not exceed the greater of (i) $50,000 for a natural person or $250,000 for any other person, or (ii) the gross amount of pecuniary gain to such defendant as a result of the violation, if the violation described in paragraph (1) involved fraud, deceit, manipulation, or deliberate or reckless disregard of a regulatory requirement.

(C) THIRD TIER.—Notwithstanding subparagraphs (A) and (B), the amount of penalty for each such violation shall not exceed the greater of (i) $100,000 for a natural person or $500,000 for any other person, or (ii) the gross amount of pecuniary gain to such defendant as a result of the violation, if—

(I) the violation described in paragraph (1) involved fraud, deceit, manipulation, or deliberate or reckless disregard of a regulatory requirement; and

(II) such violation directly or indirectly resulted in substantial losses or created a significant risk of substantial losses to other persons.

(3) PROCEDURES FOR COLLECTION.—

(A) PAYMENT OF PENALTY TO TREASURY.—A penalty imposed under this section shall be payable into the Treasury of the United States, except as otherwise provided in section 308 of the Sarbanes-Oxley Act of 2002.

(B) COLLECTION OF PENALTIES.—If a person upon whom such a penalty is imposed shall fail to pay such penalty within the time prescribed in the court's order, the Commission may refer the matter to the Attorney General who shall recover such penalty by action in the appropriate United States district court.

(C) REMEDY NOT EXCLUSIVE.—The actions authorized by this subsection may be brought in addition to any other action that the Commission or the Attorney General is entitled to bring.

(D) JURISDICTION AND VENUE.—For purposes of section 44 of this title, actions under this paragraph shall be actions to enforce a liability or a duty created by this title.

(4) SPECIAL PROVISIONS RELATING TO A VIOLATION OF A CEASE-AND-DESIST ORDER.—In an action to enforce a cease-and-desist order entered by the Commission pursuant to section 9(f), each separate violation of such order shall be a separate offense, except that in the case of a violation through a continuing failure to comply with the order, each day of the failure to comply shall be deemed a separate offense.

INVESTMENT COMPANY ACT RULES—SELECTED PROVISIONS

17 C.F.R. §§270.2a-4—270.38a-1

Rule	Subject
2a-4	Definition of "current net asset value" for use in computing periodically the current price of redeemable security
3a-1	Certain *prima facie* investment companies
12b-1	Distribution of shares by registered open-end management investment company
17a-6	Exemption for transactions with portfolio affiliates
17a-7	Exemption of certain purchase or sale transactions between an investment company and certain affiliated persons thereof
17d-1	Applications regarding joint enterprises or arrangements and certain profit-sharing plans
17j-1	Personal investment activity of investment company personnel
22c-1	Pricing of redeemable securities for distribution, redemption and repurchase
30a-3	Disclosure controls and procedureds related to preparation of required filings
30b1-4	Report of proxy voting record
34b-1	Sales literature deemed to be misleading
38a-1	Compliance procedures and practices of certain investment companies

Rule 2a-4. Definition of "Current Net Asset Value" for use in Computing Periodically the Current Price of Redeemable Security

(a) The current net asset value of any redeemable security issued by a registered investment company used in computing periodically the current price for the purpose of distribution, redemption, and repurchase means an amount which reflects calculations, whether or not recorded in the books of account, made substantially in accordance with the following, with estimates used where necessary or appropriate:

(1) Portfolio securities with respect to which market quotations are readily available shall be valued at current market value, and other securities and assets shall be valued at fair value as determined in good faith by the board of directors of the registered company.

(2) Changes in holdings of portfolio securities shall be reflected no later than in the first calculation on the first business day following the trade date.

(3) Changes in the number of outstanding shares of the registered company resulting from distributions, redemptions, and repurchases shall be reflected no later than in the first calculation on the first business day following such change.

(4) Expenses, including any investment advisory fees, shall be included to date of calculation. Appropriate provision shall be made for Federal income taxes if required. Investment companies which retain realized capital gains designated as a distribution to shareholders shall comply with paragraph (h) of §210.6-03 of Regulation S-X.

(5) Dividends receivable shall be included to date of calculation either at ex-dividend dates or record dates, as appropriate.

(6) Interest income and other income shall be included to date of calculation.

(b) The items which would otherwise be required to be reflected by subparagraphs (4) and (6) above need not be so reflected if cumulatively, when netted, they do not amount to as much as 1 cent per outstanding share.

(c) Notwithstanding the requirements of paragraph (a) above, any interim determination of current net asset value between calculations made as of the close of the New York Stock Exchange on the preceding business day and the current business day may be estimated so as to reflect any change in current net asset value since the closing calculation on the preceding business day.

Rule 3a-1. Certain Prima Facie Investment Companies

Notwithstanding section 3(a)(1)(C) of the Act (15 U.S.C. 80a-3(a)(1)(c)), an issuer will be deemed not to be an investment company under the Act; *Provided*, That:

(a) No more than 45 percent of the value (as defined in section 2(a)(41) of the Act) of such issuer's total assets (exclusive of Government securities and cash items) consists of, and no more than 45 percent of such issuer's net income after taxes (for the last four fiscal quarters combined) is derived from, securities other than:

(1) Government securities;

(2) Securities issued by employees' securities companies;

(3) Securities issued by majority-owned subsidiaries of the issuer (other than subsidiaries relying on the exclusion from the definition of investment companies in section 3(b)(3) or section 3(c)(1) of the Act) which are not investment companies; and

(4) Securities issued by companies:

(i) Which are controlled primarily by such issuer;

(ii) Through which such issuer engages in a business other than that of investing, reinvesting, owning, holding or trading in securities; and

(iii) Which are not investment companies;

(b) The issuer is not an investment company as defined in section 3(a)(1)(A) or 3(a)(1)(B) of the Act (15 U.S.C. 80a-3(a)(1)(A) or 80a-3(a)(1)(B)) and is not a special situation investment company; and

(c) The percentages described in paragraph (a) of this section are determined on an unconsolidated basis, except that the issuer shall consolidate its financial statements with the financial statements of any wholly-owned subsidiaries.

Rule 12b-1. Distribution of Shares by Registered Open-End Management Investment Company

(a)(1) Except as provided in this section, it shall be unlawful for any registered open-end management investment company (other than a company complying with the provisions of section 10(d) of the Act [15 U.S.C. 80a-10(d)]) to act as a distributor of securities of which it is the issuer, except through an underwriter.

(2) For purposes of this section, such a company will be deemed to be acting as a distributor of securities of which it is the issuer, other than through an underwriter, if it engages directly or indirectly in financing any activity which is primarily intended to result in the sale of shares issued by such company, including, but not necessarily limited to, advertising, compensation of underwriters, dealers, and sales personnel, the printing and mailing of prospectuses to other than current shareholders, and the printing and mailing of sales literature.

(b) A registered, open-end management investment company ("company") may act as a distributor of securities of which it is the issuer, *Provided* That any payments made by such company in connection with such distribution are made pursuant to a written plan describing all material aspects of the proposed financing of distribution and that all agreements with any person relating to implementation of the plan are in writing, *and further provided* That:

(1) Such plan has been approved by a vote of at least a majority of the outstanding voting securities of such company, if adopted after any public offering of the company's voting securities

or the sale of such securities to persons who are not affiliated persons of the company, affiliated persons of such persons, promoters of the company, or affiliated persons of such promoters;

(2) Such plan, together with any related agreements, has been approved by a vote of the board of directors of such company, and of the directors who are not interested persons of the company and have no direct or indirect financial interest in the operation of the plan or in any agreements related to the plan, cast in person at a meeting called for the purpose of voting on such plan or agreements; and

(3) Such plan or agreement provides, in substance:

(i) That it shall continue in effect for a period of more than one year from the date of its execution or adoption only so long as such continuance is specifically approved at least annually in the manner described in paragraph (b)(2);

(ii) That any person authorized to direct the disposition of monies paid or payable by such company pursuant to the plan or any related agreement shall provide to the company's board of directors, and the directors shall review, at least quarterly, a written report of the amounts so expended and the purposes for which such expenditures were made; and

(iii) In the case of a plan, that it may be terminated at any time by vote of a majority of the members of the board of directors of the company who are not interested persons of the company and have no direct or indirect financial interest in the operation of the plan or in any agreements related to the plan or by vote of a majority of the outstanding voting securities of such company; and

(iv) In the case of an agreement related to a plan,

(A) That it may be terminated at any time, without the payment of any penalty, by vote of a majority of the members of the board of directors of such company who are not interested persons of the company and have no direct or indirect financial interest in the operation of the plan or in any agreements related to the plan or by vote of a majority of the outstanding voting securities of such company on not more than sixty days' written notice to any other party to the agreement, and

(B) For its automatic termination in the event of its assignment; and

(4) Such plan provides that it may not be amended to increase materially the amount to be spent for distribution without shareholder approval and that all material amendments of the plan must be approved in the manner described in paragraph (b)(2);

(5) Such plan is implemented and continued in a manner consistent with the provisions of paragraphs (c), (d), and (e) of this section;

(c) A registered open-end management investment company may rely on the provisions of paragraph (b) of this section only if:

(1) A majority of the directors of the company are not interested persons of the company, and those directors select and nominate any other disinterested directors of the company; and

(2) Any person who acts as legal counsel for the disinterested directors of the company is an independent legal counsel;

(c) A registered open-end management investment company may rely on the provisions of paragraph (b) of this section only if its board of directors satisfies the fund governance standards as defined in § 270.0-1(a)(7);

(d) In considering whether a registered open-end management investment company should implement or continue a plan in reliance on paragraph (b) of this section, the directors of such company shall have a duty to request and evaluate, and any person who is a party to any agreement with such company relating to such plan shall have a duty to furnish, such information as may reasonably be necessary to an informed determination of whether such plan should be implemented or continued; in fulfilling their duties under this paragraph the directors should consider and give appropriate weight to all pertinent factors, and minutes describing the factors considered and the basis for the decision to use company assets for distribution must be made and preserved in accordance with paragraph (f) of this section;

Note: For a discussion of factors which may be relevant to a decision to use company assets for distribution, see Investment Company Act Releases Nos. 10862, September 7, 1979, and 11414, October 28, 1980.

(e) A registered open-end management investment company may implement or continue a plan pursuant to paragraph (b) of this section only if the directors who vote to approve such implementation or continuation conclude, in the exercise of reasonable business judgment and in light of their fiduciary duties under state law and under sections 36(a) and (b) [15 U.S.C. 80a-35(a) and (b)] of the Act, that there is a reasonable likelihood that the plan will benefit the company and its shareholders; and

(f) A registered open-end management investment company must preserve copies of any plan, agreement or report made pursuant to this section for a period of not less than six years from the date of such plan, agreement or report, the first two years in an easily accessible place.

(g) If a plan covers more than one series or class of shares, the provisions of the plan must be severable for each series or class, and whenever this section provides for any action to be taken with respect to a plan, that action must be taken separately for each series or class affected by the matter. Nothing in this paragraph (g) shall affect the rights of any purchase class under § 270.18f-3(e)(2)(iii).

Rule 17a-6. Exemption for Transactions with Portfolio Affiliates.

(a) A transaction to which a Fund, or a company controlled by a Fund, and a Portfolio Affiliate of the Fund are parties is exempt from the provisions of section 17(a) of the Act (15 U.S.C. 80a-17(a)), provided that none of the following persons is a party to the transaction, or has a direct or indirect Financial Interest in a party to the transaction other than the Fund:

(1) An officer, director, employee, investment adviser, member of an advisory board, depositor, promoter of or principal underwriter for the Fund;

(2) A person directly or indirectly controlling the Fund;

(3) A person directly or indirectly owning, controlling or holding with power to vote five percent or more of the outstanding voting securities of the Fund;

(4) A person directly or indirectly under common control with the Fund, other than:

(i) A Portfolio Affiliate of the Fund; or

(ii) A Fund whose sole interest in the transaction or a party to the transaction is an interest in the Portfolio Affiliate; or

(5) An affiliated person of any of the persons mentioned in paragraphs (a)(1) - (4) of this section, other than the Fund or a Portfolio Affiliate of the Fund.

(b) *Definitions.*

(1) *Financial Interest.*

(i) The term *Financial Interest* as used in this section does not include:

(A) Any interest through ownership of securities issued by the Fund;

(B) Any interest of a wholly-owned subsidiary of a Fund;

(C) Usual and ordinary fees for services as a director;

(D) An interest of a non-executive employee;

(E) An interest of an insurance company arising from a loan or policy made or issued by it in the ordinary course of business to a natural person;

(F) An interest of a bank arising from a loan or account made or maintained by it in the ordinary course of business to or with a natural person, unless it arises from a loan to a person who is an officer, director or executive of a company which is a party to the transaction, or from a loan to a person who directly or indirectly owns, controls, or holds with power to vote, five percent or more of the outstanding voting securities of a company which is a party to the transaction;

(G) An interest acquired in a transaction described in paragraph (d)(3) of -270.17d-1; or

(H) Any other interest that the board of directors of the Fund, including a majority of the directors who are not interested persons of the Fund, finds to be not material, provided that the directors record the basis for that finding in the minutes of their meeting.

(ii) A person has a Financial Interest in any party in which it has a Financial Interest, in which it had a Financial Interest within six months prior to the transaction, or in which it will acquire a Financial Interest pursuant to an arrangement in existence at the time of the transaction.

(2) *Fund* means a registered investment company or separate series of a registered investment company.

(3) *Portfolio Affiliate of a Fund* means a person that is an affiliated person (or an affiliated person of an affiliated person) of a Fund solely because the Fund, a Fund under common control with the Fund, or both:

(i) Controls such person (or an affiliated person of such person); or

(ii) Owns, controls, or holds with power to vote five percent or more of the outstanding voting securities of such person (or an affiliated person of such person).

Rule 17a-7. Exemption of Certain Purchase or Sale Transactions Between an Investment Company and Certain Affiliated Persons Thereof

A purchase or sale transaction between registered investment companies or separate series of registered investment companies, which are affiliated persons, or affiliated persons of affiliated persons, of each other, between separate series of a registered investment company, or between a registered investment company or a separate series of a registered investment company and a person which is an affiliated person of such registered investment company (or affiliated person of such person) solely by reason of having a common investment adviser or investment advisers which are affiliated persons of each other, common directors, and/or common officers, is exempt from section 17(a) of the Act; *Provided,* That:

(a) The transaction is a purchase or sale, for no consideration other than cash payment against prompt delivery of a security for which market quotations are readily available;

(b) The transaction is effected at the independent current market price of the security. For purposes of this paragraph the "current market price" shall be:

(1) If the security is a "reported security" as that term is defined in rule 11Aa3-1 under the Securities Exchange Act of 1934 [17 CFR 240.-11Aa3-1], the last sale price with respect to such security reported in the consolidated transaction reporting system ("consolidated system") or the average of the highest current independent bid and lowest current independent offer for such security (reported pursuant to rule 11Ac1-1 under the Securities Exchange Act of 1934 [17 CFR 240.11Ac1-1]) if there are no reported transactions in the consolidated system that day; or

(2) If the security is not a reported security, and the principal market for such security is an exchange, then the last sale on such exchange or the average of the highest current independent bid and lowest current independent offer on such exchange if there are no reported transactions on such exchange that day; or

(3) If the security is not a reported security and is quoted in the NASDAQ System, then the average of the highest current independent bid and lowest current independent offer reported on Level 1 of NASDAQ; or

(4) For all other securities, the average of the highest current independent bid and lowest current independent offer determined on the basis of reasonable inquiry;

(c) The transaction is consistent with the policy of each registered investment company and separate series of a registered investment company participating in the transaction, as recited in its registration statement and reports filed under the Act;

(d) No brokerage commission, fee (except for customary transfer fees), or other remuneration is paid in connection with the transaction;

(e) The board of directors of the investment company, including a majority of the directors who are not interested persons of such investment company, (1) adopts procedures pursuant to which such purchase or sale transactions may be effected for the company, which are reasonably designed to provide that all the conditions of this section in paragraphs (a) through (d) have been complied with, (2) makes and approves such changes as the board deems necessary, and (3) determines no less frequently than quarterly that all such purchases or sales made during the preceding quarter were effected in compliance with such procedures;

(f) (1) A majority of the directors of the investment company are not interested persons of the company, and those directors select and nominate any other disinterested directors of the company; and

(2) Any person who acts as legal counsel for the disinterested directors of the company is an independent legal counsel; and

(f) The board of directors of the investment company satisfies the fund governance standards defined in § 270.0-1(a)(7).

(g) The investment company (1) maintains and preserves permanently in an easily accessible place a written copy of the procedures (and any modifications thereto) described in paragraph (e) of this section, and (2) maintains and preserves for a period not less than six years from the end of the fiscal year in which any transactions occurred, the first two years in an easily accessible place, a written record of each such transaction setting forth a description of the security purchased or sold, the identity of the person on the other side of the transaction, the terms of the purchase or sale transaction, and the information or materials upon which the determinations described in paragraph (e)(3) of this section were made.

Rule 17d-1. Applications Regarding Joint Enterprises or Arrangements and Certain Profit-Sharing Plans

(a) No affiliated person of or principal underwriter for any registered investment company (other than a company of the character described in Section 12(d)(3)(A) and (B) of the Act) and no affiliated person of such a person or principal underwriter, acting as principal, shall participate in, or effect any transaction in connection with, any joint enterprise or other joint arrangement or profit-sharing plan in which any such registered company, or a company controlled by such registered company, is a participant, and which is entered into, adopted or modified subsequent to the effective date of this rule, unless an application regarding such joint enterprise, arrangement or profit-sharing plan has been filed with the Commission and has been granted by an order entered prior to the submission of such plan or modification to security holders for approval, or prior to such adoption or modification if not so submitted, except that the provisions of this rule shall not preclude any affiliated person from acting as manager of any underwriting syndicate or other group in which such registered or controlled company is a participant and receiving compensation therefor.

(b) In passing upon such applications, the Commission will consider whether the participation of such registered or controlled company in such joint enterprise, joint arrangement or profit-sharing plan on the basis proposed is consistent with the provisions, policies and purposes of the Act and the extent to which such participation is on a basis different from or less advantageous than that of other participants.

(c) "Joint enterprise or other joint arrangement or profit-sharing plan" as used in this rule shall mean any written or oral plan, contract, authorization or arrangement, or any practice or understanding concerning an enterprise or undertaking whereby a registered investment company or a controlled company thereof and any affiliated person of or a principal underwriter for such registered investment company, or any affiliated person of such a person or principal underwriter, have a joint or a joint and several participation, or share in the profits of such enterprise or undertaking, including, but not limited to, any stock option or stock purchase plan, but shall not include an investment advisory contract subject to Section 15 of the Act.

(d) Notwithstanding the requirements of paragraph (a) of this section, no application need be filed pursuant to this section with respect to any of the following:

(1) Any profit-sharing, stock option or stock purchase plan provided by any controlled company which is not an investment company for its officers, directors or employees, or the purchase of stock or the granting, modification or exercise of options pursuant to such a plan, provided:

(a) no individual participates therein who is either; (i) an affiliated person of any investment company which is an affiliated person of such controlled company; or (ii) an affiliated person of the investment adviser or principal underwriter of such investment company; and

(b) no participant has been an affiliated person of such investment company, its investment adviser or principal underwriter during the life of the plan and for six months prior to, as the case may be: (i) institution of the profit-sharing plan; (ii) the purchase of stock pursuant to a stock purchase plan; or (iii) the granting of any options pursuant to a stock option plan.

(2) Any plan provided by any registered investment company or any controlled company for its officers or employees if such plan has been qualified under Section 401 of the Internal Revenue Code of 1954 and all contributions paid under said plan by the employer qualify as deductible under Section 404 of said Code.

(3) Any loan or advance of credit to, or acquisition of securities or other property of, a small business concern, or any agreement to do any of the foregoing, ("Investments") made by a bank and a small business investment company (SBIC) licensed under the Small Business Investment Act of 1958, whether such transactions are contemporaneous or separated in time, where the bank is an affiliated person of either (i) the SBIC or (ii) an affiliated person of the SBIC; but reports containing pertinent details as to investments and transactions relating thereto shall be made at such time, on such forms and by such persons as the Commission may from time to time prescribe.

(4) The issuance by a registered investment company which is licensed by the Small Business Administration ("SBA") pursuant to the Small Business Investment Company Act of 1958 of stock options which qualify under Section 422 of the Internal Revenue Code, as amended, and which conform to § 107.805(b) of Chapter I of Title 13 of the Code of Federal Regulations.

(5) Any joint enterprise or other joint arrangement or profit-sharing plan ("joint enterprise") in which a registered investment company or a company controlled by such a company, is a participant, and in which a Portfolio Affiliate (as defined in 270.17a-6(b)(3)) of such registered investment company is also a participant, provided that:

(i) None of the persons identified in -270.17a-6(a) is a participant in the joint enterprise, or has a direct or indirect Financial Interest in a participant in the joint enterprise (other than the registered investment company);

(ii) *Financial Interest.*

(A) The term *Financial Interest* as used in this section does not include:

(*1*) Any interest through ownership of securities issued by the registered investment company;

(*2*) Any interest of a wholly-owned subsidiary of the registered investment company;

(*3*) Usual and ordinary fees for services as a director;

(*4*) An interest of a non-executive employee;

(*5*) An interest of an insurance company arising from a loan or policy made or issued by it in the ordinary course of business to a natural person;

(*6*) An interest of a bank arising from a loan to a person who is an officer, director, or executive of a company which is a participant in the joint transaction or from a loan to a person who directly or indirectly owns, controls, or holds with power to vote, five percent or more of the outstanding voting securities of a company which is a participant in the joint transaction;

(*7*) An interest acquired in a transaction described in paragraph (d)(3) of this section; or

(*8*) Any other interest that the board of directors of the investment company, including a majority of the directors who are not interested persons of the investment company, finds to be not material, provided that the directors record the basis for that finding in the minutes of their meeting.

(B) A person has a Financial Interest in any party in which it has a Financial Interest, in which it had a Financial Interest within six months prior to the investment company's participation in the enterprise, or in which it will acquire a Financial Interest pursuant to an arrangement in existence at the time of the investment company's participation in the enterprise.

(6) The receipt of securities and/or cash by an investment company or a controlled company thereof and an affiliated person of such investment company or an affiliated person of such person pursuant to a plan of reorganization: *Provided,* That no person identified in -270.17a-6(a)(1) or any company in which such a person has a direct or indirect Financial Interest (as defined in paragraph (d)(5)(iii) of this section):

(i) has a direct or indirect financial interest in the corporation under reorganization, except owning securities of the class or classes owned by such investment company or controlled company;

(ii) receives pursuant to such plan any securities or other property, except securities of the same class and subject to the same terms as the securities received by such investment company or controlled company, and/or cash in the same proportion as is received by the investment company or controlled company based on securities of the company under reorganization owned by such persons; and

(iii) is, or has a direct or indirect financial interest in any person (other than such investment company or controlled company) who is, (A) purchasing assets from the company under reorganization or (B) exchanging shares with such person in a transaction not in compliance with the standards described in this paragraph (d)(6).

(7) Any arrangement regarding liability insurance policies (other than a bond required pursuant to rule 17g-1 (§ 270.17g-1) under the Act); *Provided,* That:

(i) the investment company's participation in the joint liability insurance policy is in the best interests of the investment company;

(ii) the proposed premium for the joint liability insurance policy to be allocated to the investment company, based upon its proportionate share of the sum of the premiums that would have been paid if such insurance coverage were purchased separately by the insured parties, is fair and reasonable to the investment company;

(iii) The joint liability insurance policy does not exclude coverage for bona fide claims made against any director who is not an interested person of the investment company, or against the investment company if it is a co-defendant in the claim with the disinterested director, by another person insured under the joint liability insurance policy;

(iv) the board of directors of the investment company, including a majority of the directors who are not interested persons with respect thereto, determine no less frequently than annually that the standards described in paragraphs (i) and (ii) have been satisfied; and

(v) The board of directors of the investment company satisfies the fund governance standards defined in § 270.0-1(a)(7).

(8) An investment adviser's bearing expenses in connection with a merger, consolidation or purchase or sale of substantially all of the assets of a company which involves a registered investment company of which it is an affiliated person.

Rule 17j-1. Personal Investment Activity of Investment Company Personnel

(a) *Definitions.* For purposes of this section:

(1) *Access Person* means:

(i) Any Advisory Person of a Fund or of a Fund's investment adviser. If an investment adviser's primary business is advising Funds or other advisory clients, all of the investment adviser's directors, officers, and general partners are presumed to be Access Persons of any Fund advised by the investment adviser. All of a Fund's directors, officers, and general partners are presumed to be Access Persons of the Fund.

(ii) Any director, officer or general partner of a principal underwriter who, in the ordinary course of business, makes, participates in or obtains information regarding, the purchase or sale of Covered Securities by the Fund for which the principal underwriter acts, or whose functions or duties in the ordinary course of business relate to the making of any recommendation to the Fund regarding the purchase or sale of Covered Securities.

(2) *Advisory Person* of a Fund or of a Fund's investment adviser means:

(i) Any director, officer, general partner or employee of the Fund or investment adviser (or of any company in a control relationship to the Fund or investment adviser) who, in connection with his or her regular functions or duties, makes, participates in, or obtains information regarding, the purchase or sale of Covered Securities by a Fund, or whose functions relate to the making of any recommendations with respect to such purchases or sales; and

(ii) Any natural person in a control relationship to the Fund or investment adviser who obtains information concerning recommendations made to the Fund with regard to the purchase or sale of Covered Securities by the Fund.

(3) *Control* has the same meaning as in section 2(a)(9) of the Act [15 U.S.C. 80a-2(a)(9)].

(4) *Covered Security* means a security as defined in section 2(a)(36) of the Act [15 U.S.C. 80a-2(a)(36)], except that it does not include:

(i) Direct obligations of the Government of the United States;

(ii) Bankers' acceptances, bank certificates of deposit, commercial paper and high quality short-term debt instruments, including repurchase agreements; and

(iii) Shares issued by open-end Funds.

(5) *Fund* means an investment company registered under the Investment Company Act.

(6) An *Initial Public Offering* means an offering of securities registered under the Securities Act of 1933 [15 U.S.C. 77a], the issuer of which, immediately before the registration, was not subject to the reporting requirements of sections 13 or 15(d) of the Securities Exchange Act of 1934 [15 U.S.C. 78m or 78o(d)].

(7) *Investment Personnel* of a Fund or of a Fund's investment adviser means:

(i) Any employee of the Fund or investment adviser (or of any company in a control relationship to the Fund or investment adviser) who, in connection with his or her regular functions or duties, makes or participates in making recommendations regarding the purchase or sale of securities by the Fund.

(ii) Any natural person who controls the Fund or investment adviser and who obtains information concerning recommendations made to the Fund regarding the purchase or sale of securities by the Fund.

(8) A *Limited Offering* means an offering that is exempt from registration under the Securities Act of 1933 pursuant to section 4(2) or section 4(6) [15 U.S.C. 77d(2) or 77d(6)] or pursuant to rule 504, rule 505, or rule 506 [17 CFR 230.504, 230.505, or 230.506] under the Securities Act of 1933.

(9) *Purchase or sale of a Covered Security* includes, among other things, the writing of an option to purchase or sell a Covered Security.

(10) *Security Held or to be Acquired* by a Fund means:

(i) Any Covered Security which, within the most recent 15 days:

(A) Is or has been held by the Fund; or

(B) Is being or has been considered by the Fund or its investment adviser for purchase by the Fund; and

(ii) Any option to purchase or sell, and any security convertible into or exchangeable for, a Covered Security described in paragraph (a)(10)(i) of this section.

(11) *Automatic Investment Plan* means a program in which regular periodic purchases (or withdrawals) are made automatically in (or from) investment accounts in accordance with a predetermined schedule and allocation. An Automatic Investment Plan includes a dividend reinvestment plan.

(b) *Unlawful Actions.* It is unlawful for any affiliated person of or principal underwriter for a Fund, or any affiliated person of an investment adviser of or principal underwriter for a Fund, in connection with the purchase or sale, directly or indirectly, by the person of a Security Held or to be Acquired by the Fund:

(1) To employ any device, scheme or artifice to defraud the Fund;

(2) To make any untrue statement of a material fact to the Fund or omit to state a material fact necessary in order to make the statements made to the Fund, in light of the circumstances under which they are made, not misleading;

(3) To engage in any act, practice or course of business that operates or would operate as a fraud or deceit on the Fund; or

(4) To engage in any manipulative practice with respect to the Fund.

(c) *Code of Ethics.*

(1) *Adoption and Approval of Code of Ethics.*

(i) Every Fund (other than a money market fund or a Fund that does not invest in Covered Securities) and each investment adviser of and principal underwriter for the Fund, must adopt a written code of ethics containing provisions reasonably necessary to prevent its Access Persons from engaging in any conduct prohibited by paragraph (b) of this section.

(ii) The board of directors of a Fund, including a majority of directors who are not interested persons, must approve the code of ethics of the Fund, the code of ethics of each investment adviser and principal underwriter of the Fund, and any material changes to these codes. The board must base its approval of a code and any material changes to the code on a determination that the code contains provisions reasonably necessary to prevent Access Persons from engaging in any conduct prohibited by paragraph (b) of this section. Before approving a code of a Fund, investment adviser or principal underwriter or any amendment to the code, the board of directors must receive a certification from the Fund, investment adviser or principal underwriter that it has adopted procedures reasonably necessary to prevent Access Persons from violating the Fund's, investment adviser's, or principal underwriter's code of ethics. The Fund's board must approve the code of an investment adviser or principal underwriter before initially retaining the services of the investment adviser or principal underwriter. The Fund's board must approve a material change to a code no later than six months after adoption of the material change.

(iii) If a Fund is a unit investment trust, the Fund's principal underwriter or depositor must approve the Fund's code of ethics, as required by paragraph (c)(1)(ii) of this section. If the Fund has more than one principal underwriter or depositor, the principal underwriters and depositors may designate, in writing, which principal underwriter or depositor must conduct the approval required by paragraph (c)(1)(ii) of this section, if they obtain written consent from the designated principal underwriter or depositor.

(2) *Administration of Code of Ethics.*

(i) The Fund, investment adviser and principal underwriter must use reasonable diligence and institute procedures reasonably necessary to prevent violations of its code of ethics.

(ii) No less frequently than annually, every Fund (other than a unit investment trust) and its investment advisers and principal underwriters must furnish to the Fund's board of directors, and the board of directors must consider, a written report that:

(A) Describes any issues arising under the code of ethics or procedures since the last report to the board of directors, including, but not limited to, information about material violations of the code or procedures and sanctions imposed in response to the material violations; and

(B) Certifies that the Fund, investment adviser or principal underwriter, as applicable, has adopted procedures reasonably necessary to prevent Access Persons from violating the code.

(3) *Exception for Principal Underwriters.* The requirements of paragraphs (c)(1) and (c)(2) of this section do not apply to any principal underwriter unless:

(i) The principal underwriter is an affiliated person of the Fund or of the Fund's investment adviser; or

(ii) An officer, director or general partner of the principal underwriter serves as an officer, director or general partner of the Fund or of the Fund's investment adviser.

(d) *Reporting Requirements of Access Persons.*

(1) *Reports Required.* Unless excepted by paragraph (d)(2) of this section, every Access Person of a Fund (other than a money market fund or a Fund that does not invest in Covered Securities) and every Access Person of an investment adviser of or principal underwriter for the Fund, must report to that Fund, investment adviser or principal underwriter:

(i) *Initial Holdings Reports.* No later than 10 days after the person becomes an Access Person (which information must be current as of a date no more than 45 days prior to the date the person becomes an Access Person):

(A) The title, number of shares and principal amount of each Covered Security in which the Access Person had any direct or indirect beneficial ownership when the person became an Access Person;

(B) The name of any broker, dealer or bank with whom the Access Person maintained an account in which any securities were held for the direct or indirect benefit of the Access Person as of the date the person became an Access Person; and

(C) The date that the report is submitted by the Access Person.

(ii) *Quarterly Transaction Reports.* No later than 30 days after the end of a calendar quarter, the following information:

(A) With respect to any transaction during the quarter in a Covered Security in which the Access Person had any direct or indirect beneficial ownership:

(1) The date of the transaction, the title, the interest rate and maturity date (if applicable), the number of shares and the principal amount of each Covered Security involved;

(2) The nature of the transaction (*i.e.*, purchase, sale or any other type of acquisition or disposition);

(3) The price of the Covered Security at which the transaction was effected;

(4) The name of the broker, dealer or bank with or through which the transaction was effected; and

(5) The date that the report is submitted by the Access Person.

(B) With respect to any account established by the Access Person in which any securities were held during the quarter for the direct or indirect benefit of the Access Person:

(1) The name of the broker, dealer or bank with whom the Access Person established the account;

(2) The date the account was established; and

(3) The date that the report is submitted by the Access Person.

(iii) *Annual Holdings Reports.* Annually, the following information (which information must be current as of a date no more than 45 days before the report is submitted):

(A) The title, number of shares and principal amount of each Covered Security in which the Access Person had any direct or indirect beneficial ownership;

(B) The name of any broker, dealer or bank with whom the Access Person maintains an account in which any securities are held for the direct or indirect benefit of the Access Person; and

(C) The date that the report is submitted by the Access Person.

(2) *Exceptions from Reporting Requirements.*

(i) A person need not make a report under paragraph (d)(1) of this section with respect to transactions effected for, and Covered Securities held in, any account over which the person has no direct or indirect influence or control.

(ii) A director of a Fund who is not an "interested person" of the Fund within the meaning of section 2(a)(19) of the Act [15 U.S.C. 80a-2(a)(19)], and who would be required to make a report solely by reason of being a Fund director, need not make:

(A) An initial holdings report under paragraph (d)(1)(i) of this section and an annual holdings report under paragraph (d)(1)(iii) of this section; and

(B) A quarterly transaction report under paragraph (d)(1)(ii) of this section, unless the director knew or, in the ordinary course of fulfilling his or her official duties as a Fund director, should have known that during the 15-day period immediately before or after the director's transaction in a Covered Security, the Fund purchased or sold the Covered Security, or the Fund or its investment adviser considered purchasing or selling the Covered Security.

(iii) An Access Person to a Fund's principal underwriter need not make a report to the principal underwriter under paragraph (d)(1) of this section if:

(A) The principal underwriter is not an affiliated person of the Fund (unless the Fund is a unit investment trust) or any investment adviser of the Fund; and

(B) The principal underwriter has no officer, director or general partner who serves as an officer, director or general partner of the Fund or of any investment adviser of the Fund.

(iv) An Access Person to an investment adviser need not make a separate report to the investment adviser under paragraph (d)(1) of this section to the extent the information in the report would duplicate information required to be recorded under § 275.204-2(a)(13) of this chapter.

(v) An Access Person need not make a quarterly transaction report under paragraph (d)(1)(ii) of this section if the report would duplicate information contained in broker trade confirmations or account statements received by the Fund, investment adviser or principal underwriter with respect to the Access Person in the time period required by paragraph (d)(1)(ii), if all of the information required by that paragraph is contained in the broker trade confirmations or account statements, or in the records of the Fund, investment adviser or principal underwriter.

(vi) An Access Person need not make a quarterly transaction report under paragraph (d)(1)(ii) of this section with respect to transactions effected pursuant to an Automatic Investment Plan.

(3) *Review of Reports.* Each Fund, investment adviser and principal underwriter to which reports are required to be made by paragraph (d)(1) of this section must institute procedures by which appropriate management or compliance personnel review these reports.

(4) *Notification of Reporting Obligation.* Each Fund, investment adviser and principal underwriter to which reports are required to be made by paragraph (d)(1) of this section must identify all Access Persons who are required to make these reports and must inform those Access Persons of their reporting obligation.

(5) *Beneficial Ownership.* For purposes of this section, beneficial ownership is interpreted in the same manner as it would be under §240.16a-1(a)(2) of this chapter in determining whether a person is the beneficial owner of a security for purposes of section 16 of the Securities Exchange Act of 1934 [15 U.S.C. 78p] and the rules and regulations thereunder. Any report required by paragraph (d) of this section may contain a statement that the report will not be construed as an admission that the person making the report has any direct or indirect beneficial ownership in the Covered Security to which the report relates.

(e) *Pre-approval of Investments in IPOs and Limited Offerings.* Investment Personnel of a Fund or its investment adviser must obtain approval from the Fund or the Fund's investment adviser before directly or indirectly acquiring beneficial ownership in any securities in an Initial Public Offering or in a Limited Offering.

(f) *Recordkeeping Requirements.*

(1) Each Fund, investment adviser and principal underwriter that is required to adopt a code of ethics or to which reports are required to be made by Access Persons must, at its principal place of business, maintain records in the manner and to the extent set out in this paragraph (f), and must make these records available to the Commission or any representative of the Commission at any time and from time to time for reasonable periodic, special or other examination:

(A) A copy of each code of ethics for the organization that is in effect, or at any time within the past five years was in effect, must be maintained in an easily accessible place;

(B) A record of any violation of the code of ethics, and of any action taken as a result of the violation, must be maintained in an easily accessible place for at least five years after the end of the fiscal year in which the violation occurs;

(C) A copy of each report made by an Access Person as required by this section, including any information provided in lieu of the reports under paragraph (d)(2)(v) of this section, must be maintained for at least five years after the end of the fiscal year in which the report is made or the information is provided, the first two years in an easily accessible place;

(D) A record of all persons, currently or within the past five years, who are or were required to make reports under paragraph (d) of this section, or who are or were responsible for reviewing these reports, must be maintained in an easily accessible place; and

(E) A copy of each report required by paragraph (c)(2)(ii) of this section must be maintained for at least five years after the end of the fiscal year in which it is made, the first two years in an easily accessible place.

(2) A Fund or investment adviser must maintain a record of any decision, and the reasons supporting the decision, to approve the acquisition by investment personnel of securities under paragraph (e), for at least five years after the end of the fiscal year in which the approval is granted.

Rule 22c-1. Pricing of Redeemable Securities for Distribution, Redemption and Repurchase

(a) No registered investment company issuing any redeemable security, no person designated in such issuer's prospectus as authorized to consummate transactions in any such security, and no principal underwriter of, or dealer in, any such security shall sell, redeem, or repurchase any such security except at a price based on the current net asset value of such security which is next computed after receipt of a tender of such security for redemption or of an order to purchase or sell such security; *Provided,* That:

(1) This paragraph shall not prevent a sponsor of a unit investment trust (hereinafter referred to as the "Trust") engaged exclusively in the business of investing in eligible trust securities (as defined in Rule 14a-3(b) [17 CFR 270.14a-3(b)]) from selling or repurchasing Trust units in a secondary market at a price based on the offering side evaluation of the eligible trust securities in the Trust's portfolio, determined at any time on the last business day of each week, effective for all sales made during the following week, if on the days that such sales or repurchases are made the sponsor receives a letter from a qualified evaluator stating, in its opinion, that:

(i) in the case of repurchases, the current bid price is not higher than the offering side evaluation, computed on the last business day of the previous week; and

(ii) in the case of resales, the offering side evaluation, computed as of the last business day of the previous week, is not more than one-half of one percent ($5.00 on a unit representing $1,000 principal amount of eligible trust securities) greater than the current offering price.

(2) This paragraph shall not prevent any registered investment company from adjusting the price of its redeemable securities sold pursuant to a merger, consolidation or purchase of substantially all of the assets of a company which meets the conditions specified in § 270.17a-8.

(b) For the purposes of this section, (1) the current net asset value of any such security shall be computed no less frequently than once daily, Monday through Friday, at the specific time or times during the day that the board of directors of the investment company sets, in accordance with paragraph (e) of this section, except on:

(i) days on which changes in the value of the investment company's portfolio securities will not materially affect the current net asset value of the investment company's redeemable securities;

(ii) days during which no security is tendered for redemption and no order to purchase or sell such security is received by the investment company; or

(iii) customary national business holidays described or listed in the prospectus and local and regional business holidays listed in the prospectus; and

(2) a "qualified evaluator" shall mean any evaluator which represents it is in a position to determine, on the basis of an informal evaluation of the eligible trust securities held in the Trust's portfolio, whether—

(i) the current bid price is higher than the offering side evalution, computed on the last business day of the previous week, and

(ii) the offering side evaluation, computed as of the last business day of the previous week, is more than one-half of one percent ($5.00 on a unit representing $1,000 principal amount of eligible trust securities) greater than the current offering price.

(c) Notwithstanding the provisions above, any registered separate account offering variable annuity contracts, any person designated in such account's prospectus as authorized to consummate transactions in such contracts, and any principal underwriter of or dealer in such contracts shall be permitted to apply the initial purchase payment for any such contract at a price based on the current net asset value of such contract which is next computed:

(1) Not later than two business days after receipt of the order to purchase by the insurance company sponsoring the separate account ("insurer"), if the contract application and other information necessary for processing the order to purchase (collectively, "application") are complete upon receipt; or

(2) Not later than two business days after an application which is incomplete upon receipt by the insurer is made complete, *Provided,* That, if an incomplete application is not made complete within five business days after receipt,

(i) The prospective purchaser shall be informed of the reasons for the delay, and

(ii) The initial purchase payment shall be returned immediately and in full, unless the prospective purchaser specifically consents to the insurer retaining the purchase payment until the application is made complete.

(3) As used in this section:

(i) "Prospective Purchaser" shall mean either an individual contract-owner or an individual participant in a group contract.

(ii) "Initial Purchase Payment" shall refer to the first purchase payment submitted to the insurer by, or on behalf of, a prospective purchaser.

(d) The board of directors shall initially set the time or times during the day that the current net asset value shall be computed, and shall make and approve such changes as the board deems necessary.

Rule 30a-3. Controls and Procedures

(a) Every registered management investment company, other than a small business investment company registered on Form N-5 (§§ 239.24 and 274.5 of this chapter), must maintain disclosure controls and procedures (as defined in paragraph (c) of this section) and internal control over financial reporting (as defined in paragraph (d) of this section).

(b) Each such registered management investment company's management must evaluate, with the participation of the company's principal executive and principal financial officers, or persons performing similar functions, the effectiveness of the company's disclosure controls and procedures, within the 90-day period prior to the filing date of each report on Form N-CSR (§§ 249.331 and 274.128 of this chapter) and Form N-Q (§§ 249.332 and 274.130 of this chapter).

(c) For purposes of this section, the term *disclosure controls and procedures* means controls and other procedures of a registered management investment company that are designed to ensure that information required to be disclosed by the investment company on Form N-CSR (§§ 249.331 and 274.128 of this chapter) and Form N-Q (§§ 249.332 and 274.130 of this chapter) is recorded, processed, summarized, and reported within the time periods specified in the Commission's rules and forms. Disclosure controls and procedures include, without limitation, controls and procedures designed to ensure that information required to be disclosed by an investment company in the reports that it files or submits on Form N-CSR and Form N-Q is accumulated and communicated to the investment company's management, including its principal executive and principal financial officers, or persons performing similar functions, as appropriate to allow timely decisions regarding required disclosure.

(d) The term *internal control over financial reporting* is defined as a process designed by, or under the supervision of, the registered management investment company's principal executive and principal financial officers, or persons performing similar functions, and effected by the company's board of directors, management, and other personnel, to provide reasonable assurance regarding the reliability of financial reporting and the preparation of financial statements for external purposes in accordance with generally accepted accounting principles and includes those policies and procedures that:

(1) Pertain to the maintenance of records that in reasonable detail accurately and fairly reflect the transactions and dispositions of the assets of the investment company;

(2) Provide reasonable assurance that transactions are recorded as necessary to permit preparation of financial statements in accordance with generally accepted accounting principles, and that receipts and expenditures of the investment company are being made only in accordance with authorizations of management and directors of the investment company; and

(3) Provide reasonable assurance regarding prevention or timely detection of unauthorized acquisition, use, or disposition of the investment company's assets that could have a material effect on the financial statements.

Rule 30b1-4. Report of proxy voting record

Every registered management investment company, other than a small business investment company registered on Form N-5 (§§ 239.24 and 274.5 of this chapter), shall file an annual report on Form N-PX (-274.129 of this chapter) not later than August 31 of each year, containing the registrant's proxy voting record for the most recent twelve-month period ended June 30.

Rule 34b-1. Sales Literature Deemed to Be Misleading

Any advertisement, pamphlet, circular, form letter, or other sales literature addressed to or intended for distribution to prospective investors that is required to he filed with the Commission by Section 24(b) of the Act [15 U.S.C. 80a-24(b)] ("sales literature") shall have omitted to state a fact necessary in order to make the statements made therein not materially misleading unless the sales literature includes the information specified in paragraphs (a) and (b) of this section.

Note to introductory text of §270.34b-1: The fact that the sales literature includes the information specified in paragraphs (a) and (b) of this section does not relieve the investment company, underwriter, or dealer of any obligations with respect to the sales literature under the antifraud provisions of the federal securities laws. For guidance about factors to be weighed in determining whether statements, representations, illustrations, and descriptions contained in investment company sales literature are misleading, *see* §230.156 of this chapter.

(a) Sales literature for a money market fund shall contain the information required by paragraph (b)(4) of §230.482 of this chapter, presented in the manner required by paragraph (b)(5) of §230.482 of this chapter.

(b)(1) Except as provided in paragraph (b)(3) of this section:

(i) In any sales literature that contains performance data for an investment company, include the disclosure required by paragraph (b)(3) of §230.482 of this chapter, presented in the manner required by paragraph (b)(5) of §230.482 of this chapter.

(ii) In any sales literature for a money market fund:

(A) Accompany any quotation of yield or similar quotation purporting to demonstrate the income earned or distributions made by the money market fund with a quotation of current yield specified by paragraph (e)(1)(i) of §230.482 of this chapter;

(B) Accompany any quotation of the money market fund's tax equivalent yield or tax equivalent effective yield with a quotation of current yield as specified in paragraph (e)(1)(iii) of §230.482 of this chapter; and

(C) Accompany any quotation of the money market fund's total return with a quotation of the money market fund's current yield specified in paragraph (e)(1)(i) of §230.482 of this chapter. Place the quotations of total return and current yield next to each other, in the same size print, and if there is a material difference between the quoted total return and the quoted current yield, include a statement that the yield quotation more closely reflects the current earnings of the money market fund than the total return quotation.

(iii) In any sales literature for an investment company other than a money market fund that contains performance data:

(A) Include the total return information required by paragraph (d)(3) of §230.482 of this chapter;

(B) Accompany any quotation of performance adjusted to reflect the effect of taxes (not including a quotation of tax equivalent yield or other similar quotation purporting to demonstrate the tax equivalent yield earned or distributions made by the company) with the quotations of total return specified by paragraph (d)(4) of §230.482 of this chapter;

(C) If the sales literature (other than sales literature for a company that is permitted under §270.35d-1(a)(4) to use a name suggesting that the company's distributions are exempt from federal income tax or from both federal and state income tax) represents or implies that the company is managed to limit or control the effect of taxes on company performance, include the quotations of total return specified by paragraph (d)(4) of §230.482 of this chapter;

(D) Accompany any quotation of yield or similar quotation purporting to demonstrate the income earned or distributions made by the company with a quotation of current yield specified by paragraph (d)(1) of §230.482 of this chapter; and

(E) Accompany any quotation of tax equivalent yield or other similar quotation purporting to demonstrate the tax equivalent yield earned or distributions made by the company with a quotation of tax equivalent yield specified in paragraph (d)(2) and current yield specified by paragraph (d)(1) of §230.482 of this chapter.

(2) Any performance data included in sales literature under paragraphs (b)(1)(ii) or (iii) of this section must meet the currentness requirements of paragraph (g) of §230.482 of this chapter.

(3) The requirements specified in paragraph (b)(1) of this section shall not apply to any quarterly, semi-annual, or annual report to shareholders under Section 30 of the Act (15 U.S.C. 80a-29) containing performance data for a period commencing no earlier than the first day of the period covered by the report; nor shall the requirements of paragraphs (d)(3)(ii), (d)(4)(ii), and (g) of § 230.482 of this chapter apply to any such periodic report containing any other performance data.

NOTE: Sales literature (except that of a money market fund) containing a quotation of yield or tax equivalent yield must also contain the total return information. In the case of sales literature, the currentness provisions apply from the date of distribution and not the date of submission for publication.

Rule 38a-1. Compliance procedures and practices of certain investment companies

(a) Each registered investment company and business development company ("fund") must:

(1) *Policies and procedures.* Adopt and implement written policies and procedures reasonably designed to prevent violation of the Federal Securities Laws by the fund, including policies and procedures that provide for the oversight of compliance by each investment adviser, principal underwriter, administrator, and transfer agent of the fund;

(2) *Board approval.* Obtain the approval of the fund's board of directors, including a majority of directors who are not interested persons of the fund, of the fund's policies and procedures and those of each investment adviser, principal underwriter, administrator, and transfer agent of the fund, which approval must be based on a finding by the board that the policies and procedures are reasonably designed to prevent violation of the Federal Securities Laws by the fund, and by each investment adviser, principal underwriter, administrator, and transfer agent of the fund;

(3) *Annual review.* Review, no less frequently than annually, the adequacy of the policies and procedures of the fund and of each investment adviser, principal underwriter, administrator, and transfer agent and the effectiveness of their implementation;

(4) *Chief compliance officer.* Designate one individual responsible for administering the fund's policies and procedures adopted under paragraph (a)(1):

(i) Whose designation and compensation must be approved by the fund's board of directors, including a majority of the directors who are not interested persons of the fund;

(ii) Who may be removed from his or her responsibilities by action of (and only with the approval of) the fund's board of directors, including a majority of the directors who are not interested persons of the fund;

(iii) Who must, no less frequently than annually, provide a written report to the board that, at a minimum, addresses:

(A) The operation of the policies and procedures of the fund and each investment adviser, principal underwriter, administrator, and transfer agent of the fund, any material changes made to those policies and procedures since the date of the last report, and any material changes to the policies and procedures recommended as a result of the annual review conducted pursuant to paragraph (a)(3) of this section; and

(B) Each Material Compliance Matter that occurred since the date of the last report; and

(iv) Who must, no less frequently than annually, meet separately with the fund's independent directors.

(b) *Unit investment trusts.* If the fund is a unit investment trust, the fund's principal under-writer or depositor must approve the fund's policies and procedures and chief compliance officer, must receive all annual reports, and must approve the removal of the chief compliance officer from his or her responsibilities.

(c) *Undue influence prohibited.* No officer, director, or employee of the fund, its investment adviser, or principal underwriter, or any person acting under such person's direction may directly or indirectly take any action to coerce, manipulate, mislead, or fraudulently influence the fund's chief compliance officer in the performance of his or her duties under this section.

(d) *Recordkeeping.* The fund must maintain:

(1) A copy of the policies and procedures adopted by the fund under paragraph (a)(1) that are in effect, or at any time within the past five years were in effect, in an easily accessible place; and

(2) Copies of materials provided to the board of directors in connection with their approval under paragraph (a)(2) of this section, and written reports provided to the board of directors pursuant to paragraph (a)(4)(iii) of this section (or, if the fund is a unit investment trust, to the fund's principal underwriter or depositor, pursuant to paragraph (b) of this section) for at least five years after the end of the fiscal year in which the documents were provided, the first two years in an easily accessible place; and

(3) Any records documenting the fund's annual review pursuant to paragraph (a)(3) of this section for at least five years after the end of the fiscal year in which the annual review was conducted, the first two years in an easily accessible place.

(e) *Definitions.* For purposes of this section:

(1) *Federal Securities Laws* means the Securities Act of 1933 (15 U.S.C. 77a-aa), the Securities Exchange Act of 1934 (15 U.S.C. 78a-mm), the Sarbanes-Oxley Act of 2002 (Pub. L. 107-204, 116 Stat. 745 (2002)), the Investment Company Act of 1940 (15 U.S.C. 80a), the Investment Advisers Act of 1940 (15 U.S.C. 80b), Title V of the Gramm-Leach-Bliley Act (Pub. L. No. 106-102, 113 Stat. 1338 (1999), any rules adopted by the Commission under any of these statutes, the Bank Secrecy Act (31 U.S.C. 5311-5314; 5316-5332) as it applies to funds, and any rules adopted thereunder by the Commission or the Department of the Treasury.

(2) A *Material Compliance Matter* means any compliance matter about which the fund's board of directors would reasonably need to know to oversee fund compliance, and that involves, without limitation:

(i) A violation of the Federal Securities Laws by the fund, its investment adviser, principal underwriter, administrator or transfer agent (or officers, directors, employees or agents thereof),

(ii) A violation of the policies and procedures of the fund, its investment adviser, principal underwriter, administrator or transfer agent, or

(iii) A weakness in the design or implementation of the policies and procedures of the fund, its investment adviser, principal underwriter, administrator or transfer agent.